# Ordnance Survey

# STREET ATLAS
# Hertfordshire

## Contents

| | |
|---|---|
| III | *Key to map symbols* |
| IV-V | *Key to map pages* |
| VI | *Administrative and post code boundaries* |
| 1 | *Street maps* |
| 177 | *Explanation of street index reference system* |
| 177 | *Key to town, village and rural locality abbreviations in index* |
| 178 | *Index of hospitals, railway stations, schools, shopping centres, street names and universities* |

PHILIP'S

D1512889

First edition published 1993
Second edition published 1994
First colour edition published 1996
and reprinted in 1997 by

Ordnance Survey®
Romsey Road, Maybush,
Southampton SO16 4GU

and

George Philip Ltd.
an imprint of Reed Books
Michelin House, 81 Fulham Road,
London SW3 6RB
and Auckland, Melbourne, Singapore
and Toronto

ISBN 0-540-06176-X  (pocket edition)

© Crown copyright 1996

© Reed International Books Ltd 1996

Printed and bound in Spain by Cayfosa

**The mapping between pages 1 and 176 (inclusive)
in this atlas is derived from Ordnance Survey®
OSCAR® and Land-Line® data, and Landranger®
mapping.**

Ordnance Survey, OSCAR, Land-Line and
Landranger are registered trade marks of Ordnance
Survey, the National Mapping Agency of Great Britain.

## Also available in various formats

◆ **Berkshire**

◆ **Bristol and Avon**

◆ **Buckinghamshire**

◆ **Cardiff, Swansea and Glamorgan**

◆ **Cheshire**

◆ **Derbyshire**

◆ **Durham**

◆ **Edinburgh & East Central Scotland**

◆ **East Essex**

◆ **West Essex**

◆ **Glasgow & West Central Scotland**

◆ **Greater Manchester**

◆ **North Hampshire**

◆ **South Hampshire**

◆ **East Kent**

◆ **West Kent**

◆ **Lancashire**

◆ **Merseyside**

◆ **Nottinghamshire**

◆ **Oxfordshire**

◆ **Staffordshire**

◆ **Surrey**

◆ **East Sussex**

◆ **West Sussex**

◆ **Tyne and Wear**

◆ **Warwickshire**

◆ **South Yorkshire**

◆ **West Yorkshire**

◆ Colour editions (Hardback, Spiral, Pocket)   ◆ Black and white editions (Hardback, Softback, Pocket)

# Key to map symbols

| Symbol | Description |
|---|---|
| | Motorway |
| | Primary Routes (Dual carriageway and single) |
| | A Roads (Dual carriageway and single) |
| | B Roads (Dual carriageway and single) |
| | C Roads (Dual carriageway and single) |
| | Minor Roads |
| – – – | Roads under construction |
| .–..–..– | County boundaries |
| | All Railways |
| | Track or private road |
| | Gate or obstruction to traffic (restrictions may not apply at all times or to all vehicles) |
| – – – | All paths, bridleways, BOAT's, RUPP's, dismantled railways, etc. |

The representation in this atlas of a road, track or path is no evidence of the existence of a right of way

| **174** | Adjoining page indicator |

| | | | |
|---|---|---|---|
| Acad | Academy | Mon | Monument |
| Cemy | Cemetery | Mus | Museum |
| C Ctr | Civic Centre | Obsy | Observatory |
| CH | Club House | Pal | Royal Palace |
| Coll | College | PH | Public House |
| Ex H | Exhibition Hall | Resr | Reservoir |
| Ind Est | Industrial Estate | Ret Pk | Retail Park |
| Inst | Institute | Sch | School |
| Ct | Law Court | Sh Ctr | Shopping Centre |
| L Ctr | Leisure Centre | Sta | Station |
| LC | Level Crossing | TH | Town Hall/House |
| Liby | Library | Trad Est | Trading Estate |
| Mkt | Market | Univ | University |
| Meml | Memorial | YH | Youth Hostel |

| Symbol | Description |
|---|---|
| | British Rail station |
| | Private railway station |
| | Bus, coach station |
| | Ambulance station |
| | Coastguard station |
| | Fire station |
| | Police station |
| + | Casualty entrance to hospital |
| + | Churches, Place of worship |
| **H** | Hospital |
| **i** | Information Centre |
| **P** | Parking |
| ▢ | Post Office |
| ● | Public Convenience |
| | Important buildings, schools, colleges, universities and hospitals |
| River Soar | Water Name |
| | Stream |
| | River or canal (minor and major) |
| | Water Fill |
| | Tidal Water |
| | Woods |
| | Houses |

| 0 | ¼ | ½ | ¾ | 1 mile |
|---|---|---|---|---|
| 0 | 250m | 500m | 750m | 1 Kilometre |

**The scale of the maps is 3.92 cm to 1 km (2½ inches to 1 mile)**

The small numbers around the edges of the maps identify the 1 kilometre National Grid lines

# Key to map pages

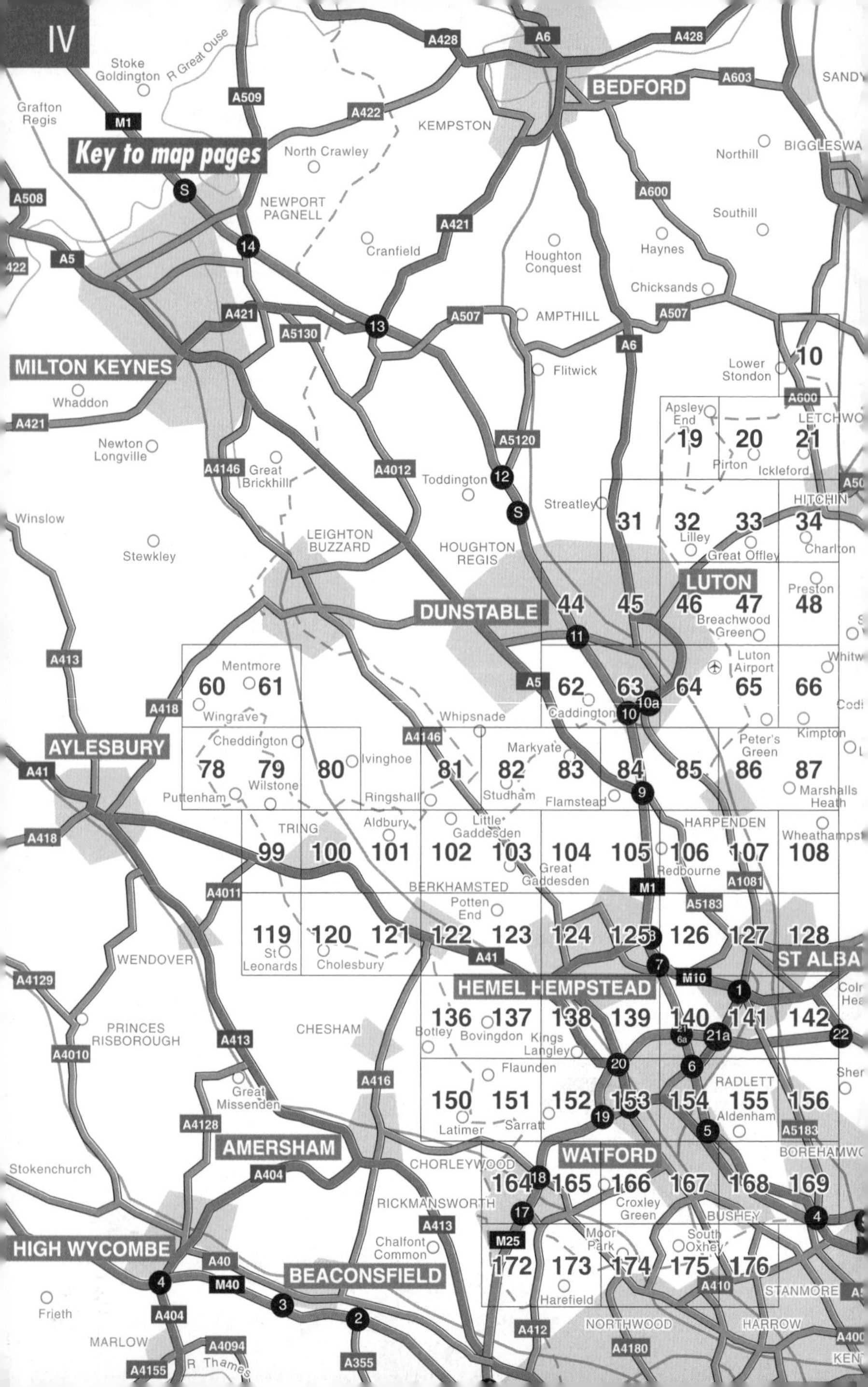

BEDFORD
MILTON KEYNES
AYLESBURY
DUNSTABLE
LUTON
HEMEL HEMPSTEAD
ST ALBA
WATFORD
AMERSHAM
HIGH WYCOMBE
BEACONSFIELD
Stoke Goldington
R Great Ouse
Grafton Regis
KEMPSTON
North Crawley
NEWPORT PAGNELL
Cranfield
Houghton Conquest
Haynes
Northill
Southill
BIGGLESWA
SANDY
Chicksands
AMPTHILL
Flitwick
Lower Stondon
Whaddon
Newton Longville
Great Brickhill
Toddington
Streatley
Winslow
Stewkley
LEIGHTON BUZZARD
HOUGHTON REGIS
Apsley End
Pirton
Ickleford
LETCHWO
HITCHIN
Lilley
Great Offley
Charlton
Preston
Breachwood Green
Luton Airport
Mentmore
Wingrave
Caddington
Whipsnade
Cheddington
Ivinghoe
Markyate
Peter's Green
Kimpton
Puttenham
Wilstone
Ringshall
Studham
Flamstead
Marshalls Heath
TRING
Aldbury
Little Gaddesden
HARPENDEN
Wheathampst
Redbourne
Great Gaddesden
BERKHAMSTED
Potten End
St Leonards
Cholesbury
WENDOVER
PRINCES RISBOROUGH
CHESHAM
Botley
Bovingdon
Kings Langley
Flaunden
RADLETT
Aldenham
Great Missenden
Latimer
Sarratt
BOREHAMWO
CHORLEYWOOD
RICKMANSWORTH
Croxley Green
BUSHEY
Stokenchurch
Chalfont Common
Moor Park
South Oxhey
Harefield
STANMORE
NORTHWOOD
HARROW
Frieth
MARLOW
R Thames
10 19 20 21 31 32 33 34 44 45 46 47 48
60 61 62 63 64 65 66
78 79 80 81 82 83 84 85 86 87
99 100 101 102 103 104 105 106 107 108
119 120 121 122 123 124 125 126 127 128
136 137 138 139 140 141 142
150 151 152 153 154 155 156
164 165 166 167 168 169
172 173 174 175 176
M1 M10 M25 M40
A428 A6 A603 A509 A422 A508 A5 A421 A600 A507 A5130 A5120 A4146 A4012 A413 A418 A41 A4011 A1081 A5183 A4129 A4010 A416 A4128 A404 A40 A412 A4180 A410 A4155 A4094 A355 A404

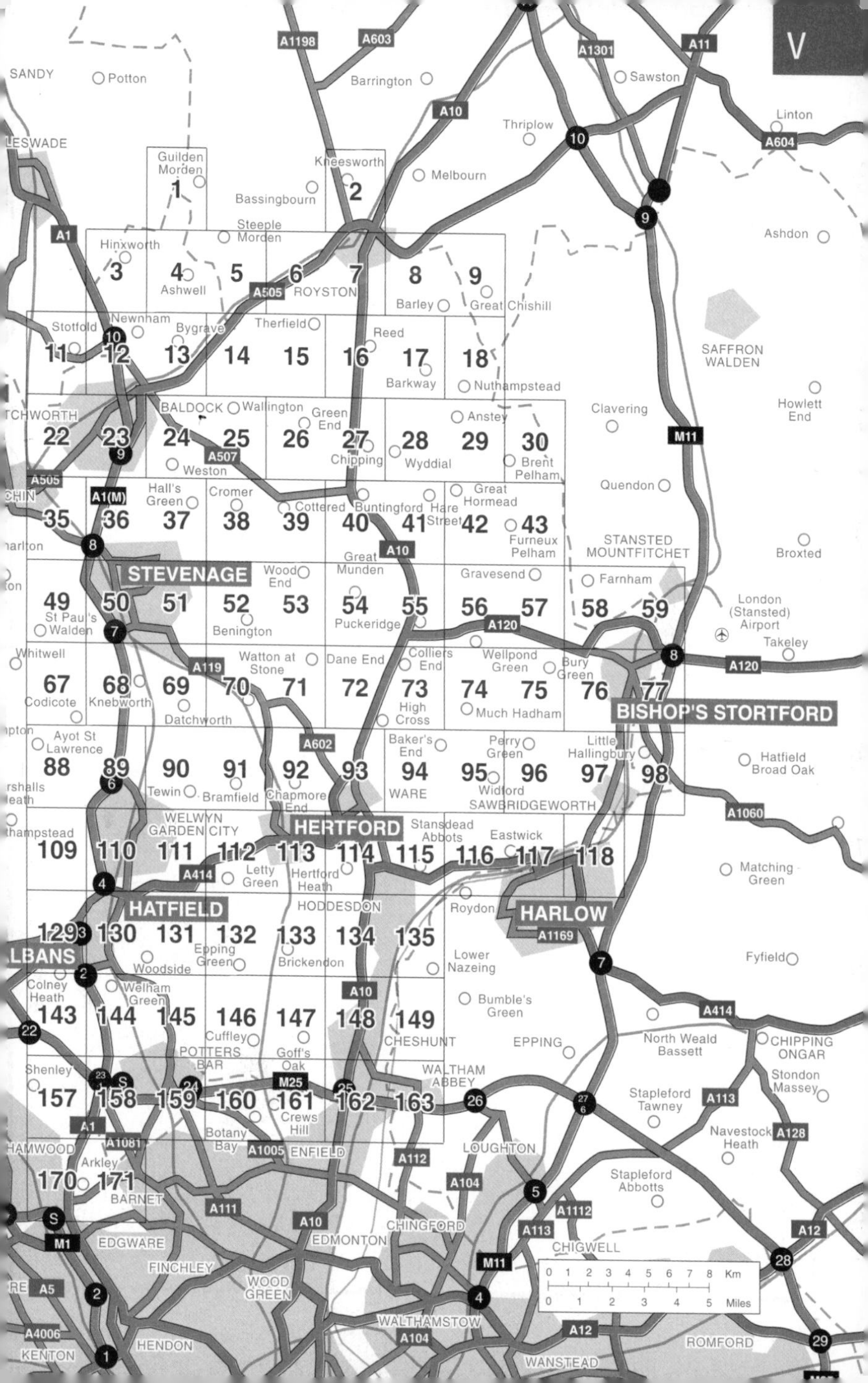

A1198
A603
A1301
A11
SANDY
Potton
Barrington
Sawston
A10
Linton
Thriplow
10
A604
BIGGLESWADE
Guilden Morden
1
Kneesworth
2
Melbourn
Bassingbourn
9
A1
Steeple Morden
Ashdon
Hinxworth
3
4
5
6
7
8
9
Ashwell
A505
ROYSTON
Barley
Great Chishill
Stotfold
Newnham
Bygrave
Therfield
Reed
SAFFRON WALDEN
11
12
13
14
15
16
17
18
Barkway
Nuthampstead
Howlett End
Linton
LETCHWORTH
BALDOCK
Wallington
Green End
Anstey
Clavering
22
23
24
25
26
27
28
29
30
M11
Weston
A507
Chipping
Wyddial
Brent Pelham
A505
HITCHIN
A1(M)
Hall's Green
Cromer
Cottered
Buntingford
Hare Street
Great Hormead
Quendon
35
36
37
38
39
40
41
42
43
Furneux Pelham
STANSTED MOUNTFITCHET
Broxted
Charlton
A10
Great Munden
STEVENAGE
Wood End
Gravesend
Farnham
London (Stansted) Airport
49
50
51
52
53
54
55
56
57
58
59
St Paul's Walden
Benington
Puckeridge
A120
Takeley
8
A120
Whitwell
Watton at Stone
Dane End
Colliers End
Wellpond Green
Bury Green
A119
67
68
69
70
71
72
73
74
75
76
77
Codicote
Knebworth
Datchworth
High Cross
Much Hadham
BISHOP'S STORTFORD
Ayot St Lawrence
A602
Baker's End
Perry Green
Little Hallingbury
Hatfield Broad Oak
88
89
90
91
92
93
94
95
96
97
98
Tewin
Bramfield
Chapmore End
WARE
Widford
SAWBRIDGEWORTH
A1060
WELWYN GARDEN CITY
HERTFORD
Stansdead Abbots
Eastwick
Wheathampstead
109
110
111
112
113
114
115
116
117
118
A414
Letty Green
Hertford Heath
Matching Green
HATFIELD
HODDESDON
Roydon
HARLOW
129
130
131
132
133
134
135
A1169
ST ALBANS
Epping Green
Brickendon
Lower Nazeing
Fyfield
Woodside
Colney Heath
Welham Green
A10
Bumble's Green
143
144
145
146
147
148
149
A414
Cuffley
Goff's Oak
CHESHUNT
EPPING
North Weald Bassett
CHIPPING ONGAR
POTTERS BAR
Shenley
WALTHAM ABBEY
Stondon Massey
M25
157
158
159
160
161
162
163
Stapleford Tawney
A113
Crews Hill
A1
A1081
Botany Bay
A1005
ENFIELD
A112
LOUGHTON
Navestock Heath
A128
BOREHAMWOOD
Arkley
Stapleford Abbotts
170
171
BARNET
A104
A111
A10
A1112
M1
EDGWARE
EDMONTON
CHINGFORD
A113
A12
CHIGWELL
FINCHLEY
M11
0 1 2 3 4 5 6 7 8 Km
0 1 2 3 4 5 Miles
A5
WOOD GREEN
A4006
WALTHAMSTOW
A12
KENTON
HENDON
A104
ROMFORD
WANSTEAD

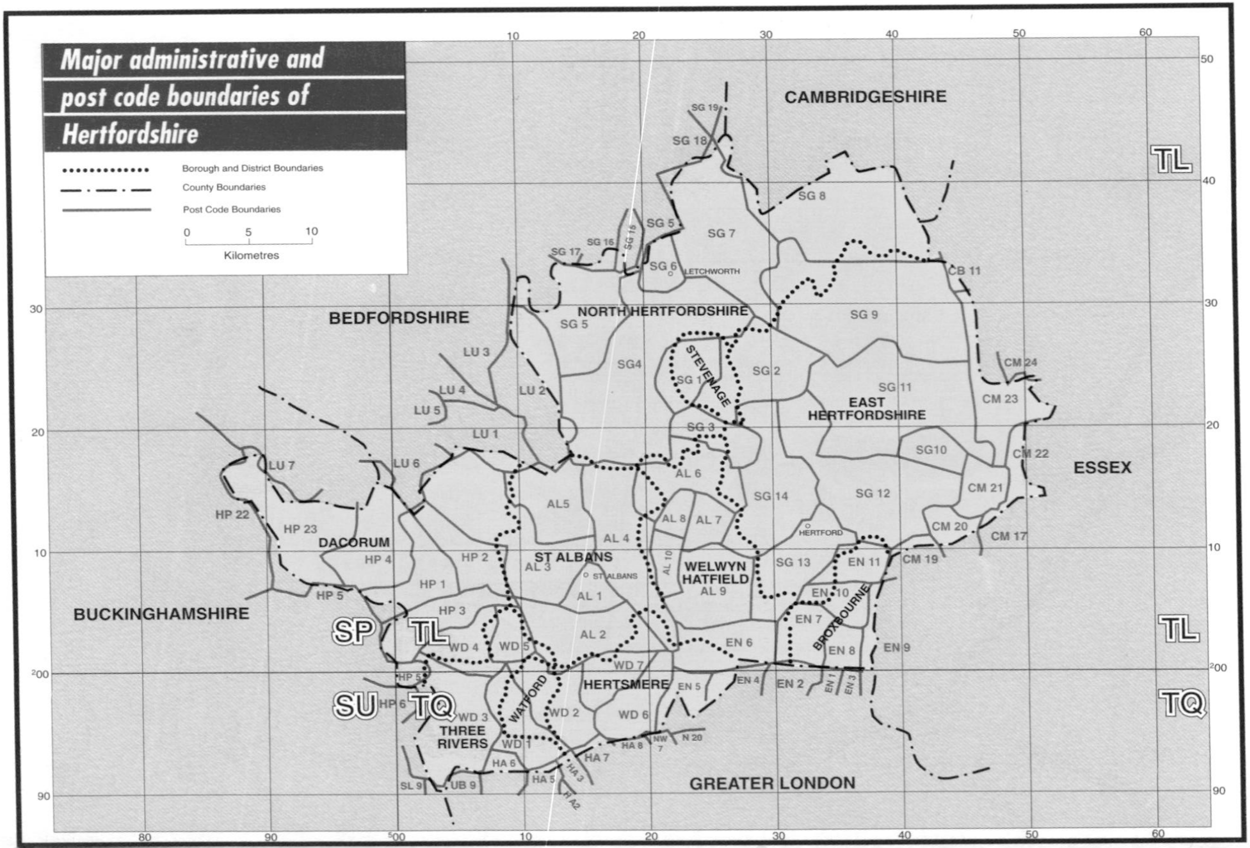

# Major administrative and post code boundaries of Hertfordshire

Borough and District Boundaries
County Boundaries
Post Code Boundaries

0 5 10
Kilometres

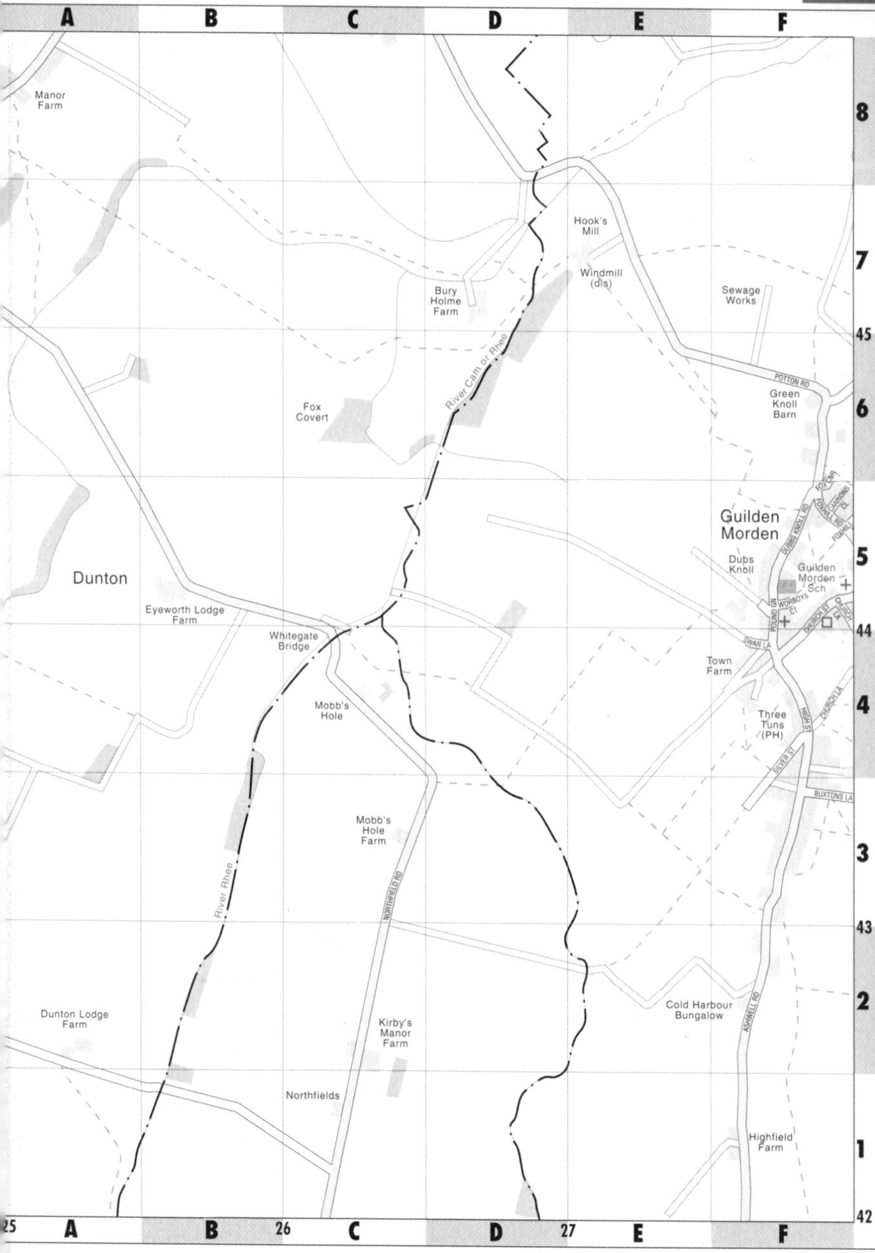

A    B    C    D    E    F

8

Manor
Farm

7

Hook's
Mill

45

Windmill
(dis)

Bury
Holme
Farm

Sewage
Works

River Cam or Rhee

POTTON RD

Green
Knoll
Barn

6

Fox
Covert

Guilden
Morden

Dunton

Dubs
Knoll

Guilden
Morden
Sch

5

Eyeworth Lodge
Farm

Whitegate
Bridge

SWAN LA

Town
Farm

44

Mobb's
Hole

Three
Tuns
(PH)

SILVER ST

4

River Rhee

BUXTONS LA

Mobb's
Hole
Farm

NORTHFIELD RD

3

43

Cold Harbour
Bungalow

ASHWELL RD

2

Dunton Lodge
Farm

Kirby's
Manor
Farm

Northfields

Highfield
Farm

1

25    A    B    26    C    D    27    E    F    42

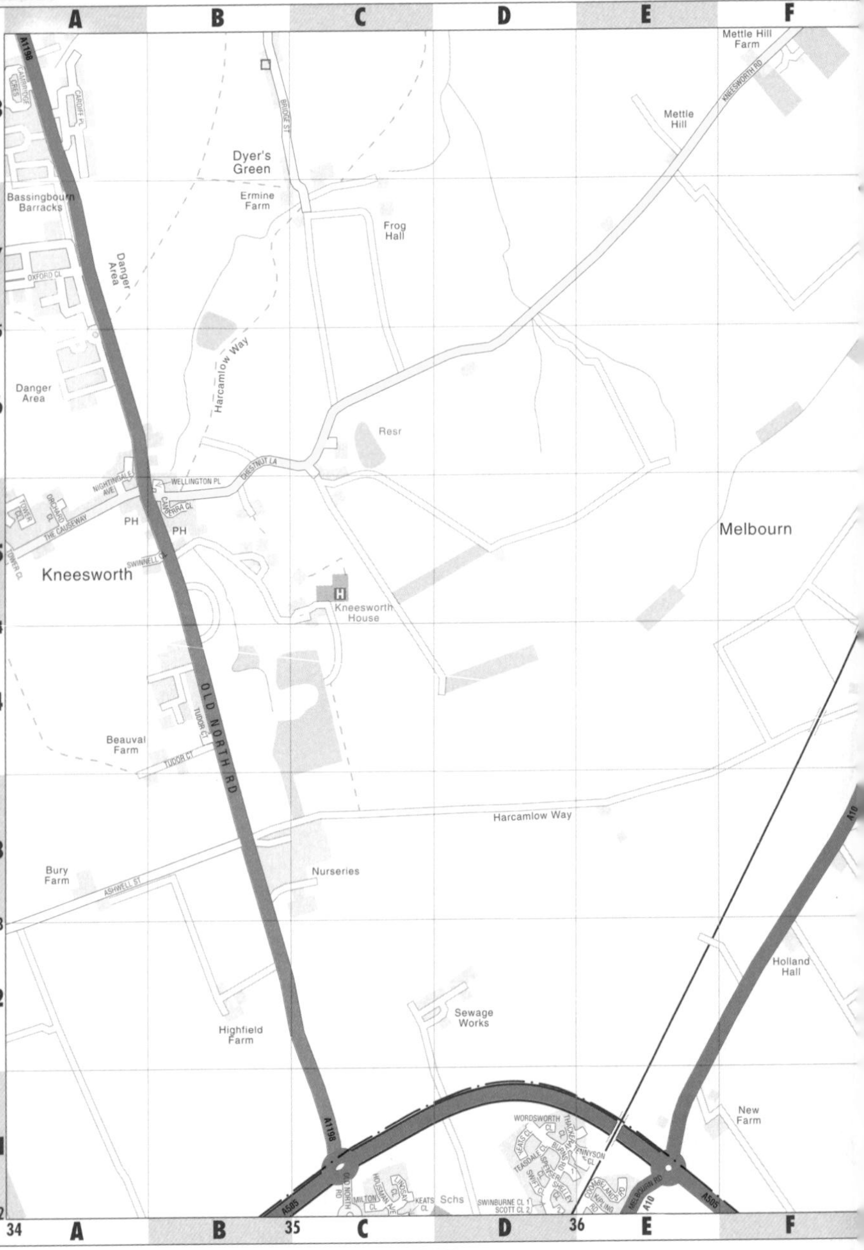
A
B
C
D
E
F
8
7
45
6
5
44
4
3
43
2
1
42
34
35
36
A1198
Mettle Hill Farm
KNEESWORTH RD
Mettle Hill
Dyer's Green
BRIDGE ST
CARDIFF PL
Bassingbourn Barracks
Ermine Farm
Frog Hall
OXFORD CL
Danger Area
Harcamlow Way
Danger Area
Resr
CHESTNUT LA
WELLINGTON PL
NIGHTINGALE AVE
CANBERRA CL
ORCHARD CL
TOWER CL
THE CAUSEWAY
PH
PH
SWINNELL CL
Melbourn
Kneesworth
Kneesworth House
OLD NORTH RD
TUDOR CT
Beauval Farm
TUDOR CT
Harcamlow Way
Bury Farm
ASHWELL ST
Nurseries
A10
Holland Hall
Sewage Works
Highfield Farm
New Farm
WORDSWORTH CL
THACKERAY CL
TENNYSON CL
KEATS CL
TEASDALE CL
BURNS RD
SPENSER CL
SWIFT CL
SHELLEY
A505
OLD NORTH RD
MILTON CL
HOUSMAN AVE
LINDSAY CL
KEATS CL
Schs
SWINBURNE CL
SCOTT CL
COOMBELANDS RD
KIPLING RD
MELBOURN RD
A10
A505

7

4

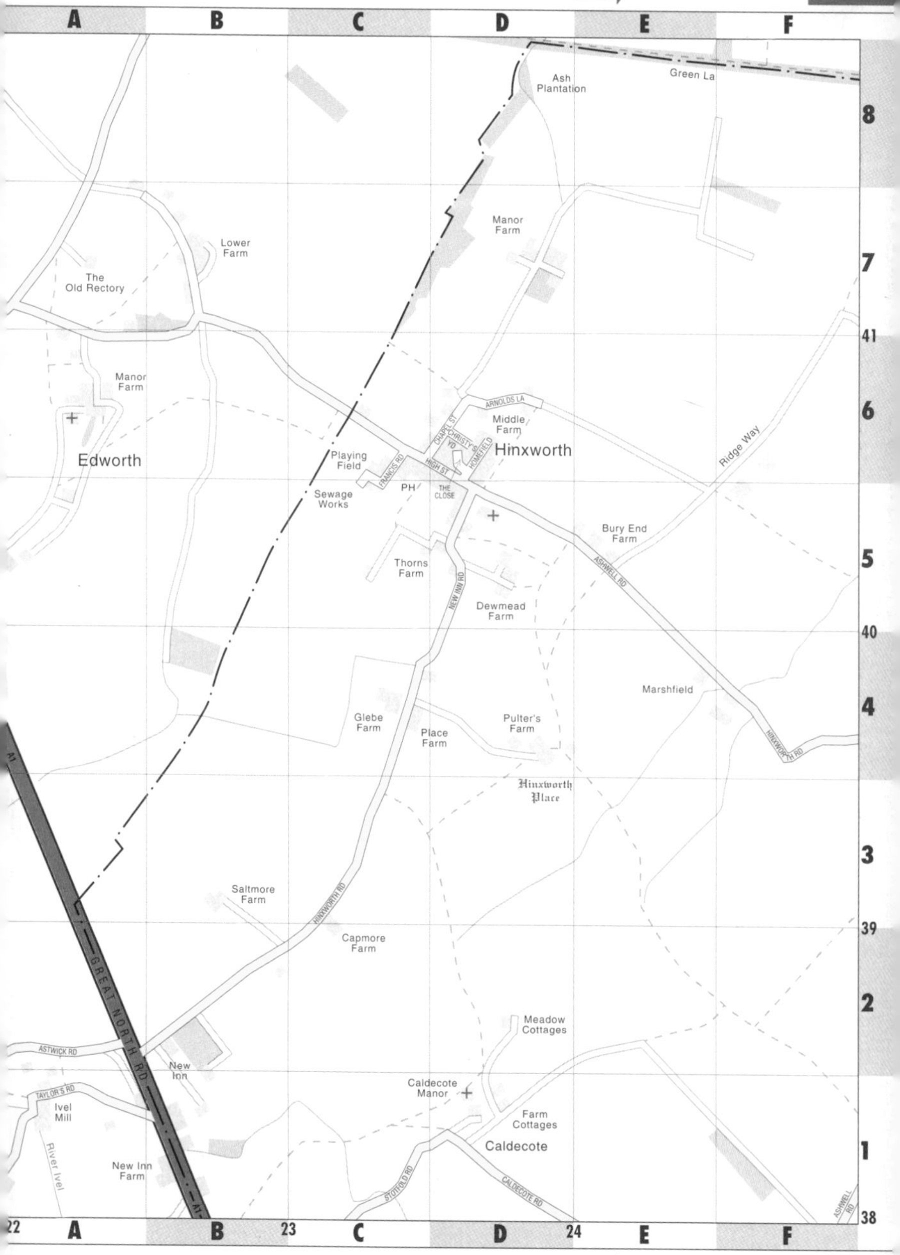
A
B
C
D
E
F
8
7
41
6
5
40
4
3
39
2
1
38
22
23
24
Ash Plantation
Green La
Manor Farm
Lower Farm
The Old Rectory
Manor Farm
Edworth
ARNOLDS LA
Middle Farm
CHAPEL ST
CHRISTY'S YD
HOMEFIELD
Hinxworth
Playing Field
FRANCIS RD
HIGH ST
PH
THE CLOSE
Sewage Works
Ridge Way
Bury End Farm
Thorns Farm
ASHWELL RD
NEW INN RD
Dewmead Farm
Marshfield
Glebe Farm
Place Farm
Pulter's Farm
HINXWORTH RD
A1
Hinxworth Place
Saltmore Farm
HINXWORTH RD
Capmore Farm
GREAT NORTH RD
Meadow Cottages
ASTWICK RD
New Inn
TAYLOR'S RD
Ivel Mill
Caldecote Manor
Farm Cottages
Caldecote
River Ivel
New Inn Farm
STOTFOLD RD
CALDECOTE RD
ASHWELL RD

12
4

3
1

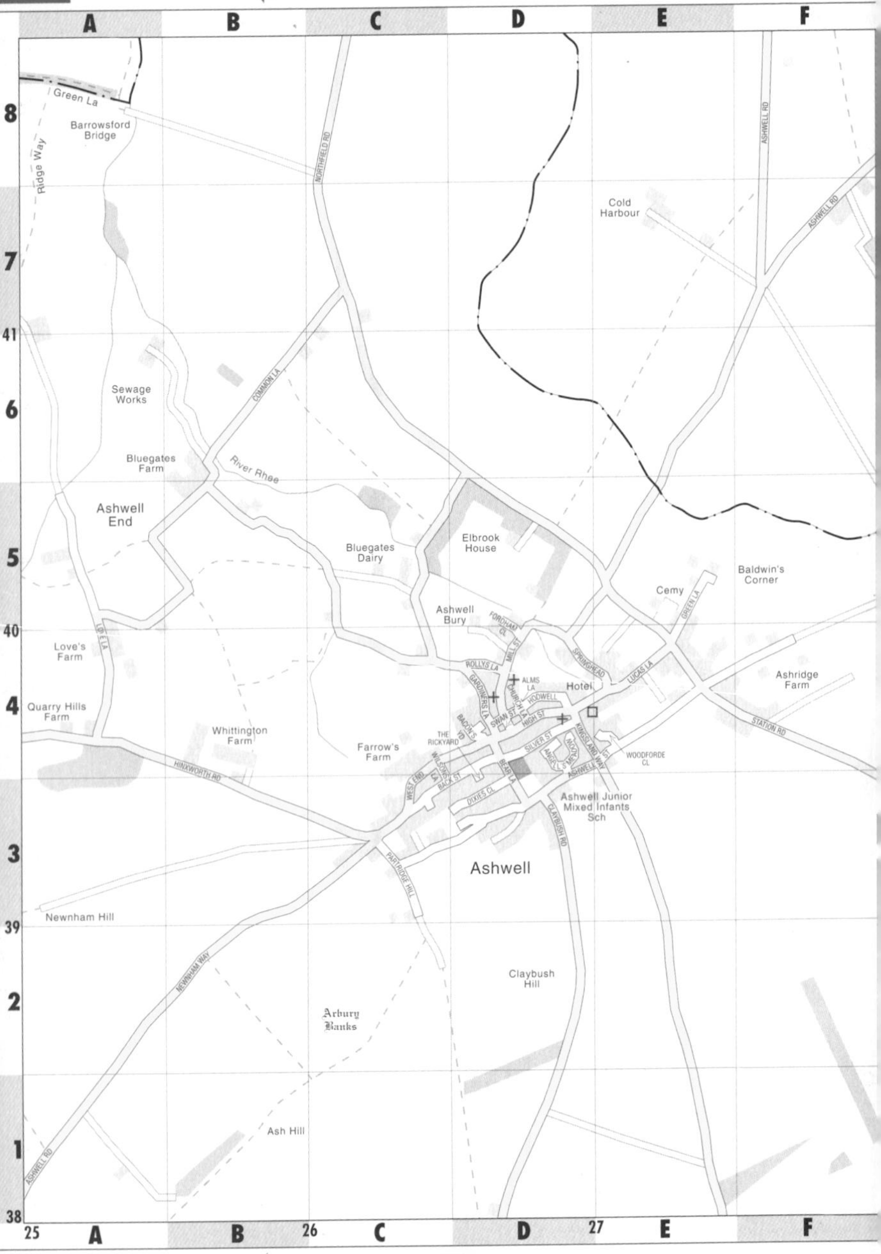
A
B
C
D
E
F
8
7
41
6
5
40
4
3
39
2
38
1
25
26
27
Green La
Barrowsford Bridge
Ridge Way
Northfield Rd
Ashwell Rd
Cold Harbour
Sewage Works
Common La
Bluegates Farm
River Rhee
Ashwell End
Bluegates Dairy
Elbrook House
Ashwell Bury
Fordham Cl
Mill St
Rollys La
Gardiners La
Alms La
Church La
Hodwell
Swan St
High St
Bacon's Yd
The Rickyard
Silver St
Angell's Meadow
Kingsland Way
Woodforde Cl
Springhead
Lucas La
Hotel
Cemy
Green La
Baldwin's Corner
Ashridge Farm
Station Rd
Love's Farm
Lodge La
Quarry Hills Farm
Whittington Farm
Hinxworth Rd
Farrow's Farm
West End
Wilson's La
Back St
Bear La
Dixies Cl
Ashwell St
Ashwell Junior Mixed Infants Sch
Claybush Rd
Partridge Hill
Ashwell
Newnham Hill
Newnham Way
Claybush Hill
Arbury Banks
Ash Hill
Ashwell Rd

3
13

A B C D E F

8

7

41

6

5

40

4

3

39

2

1

38

Steeple
Morden

Wyndmere
Farm

ASHWELL RD

WESTBROOK?

Gatley
End

Upper
Gatley End

High
Farm

Ashwell St

STATION RD

Chalk
Pit

Morden
Grange
Farm

Morden
Grange
Plantation

New
Part

Shire Balk

STATION RD

Next
Odsey

Cheyneys
Lodge

Redlands
Farm

Chain Walk

A505

...shwell
Fields

PH

Ashwell &
Morden Sta

Highley
Hill

Odsey

Gallows
Hill

Heath
Barn

A505

A B C D E F
29 30

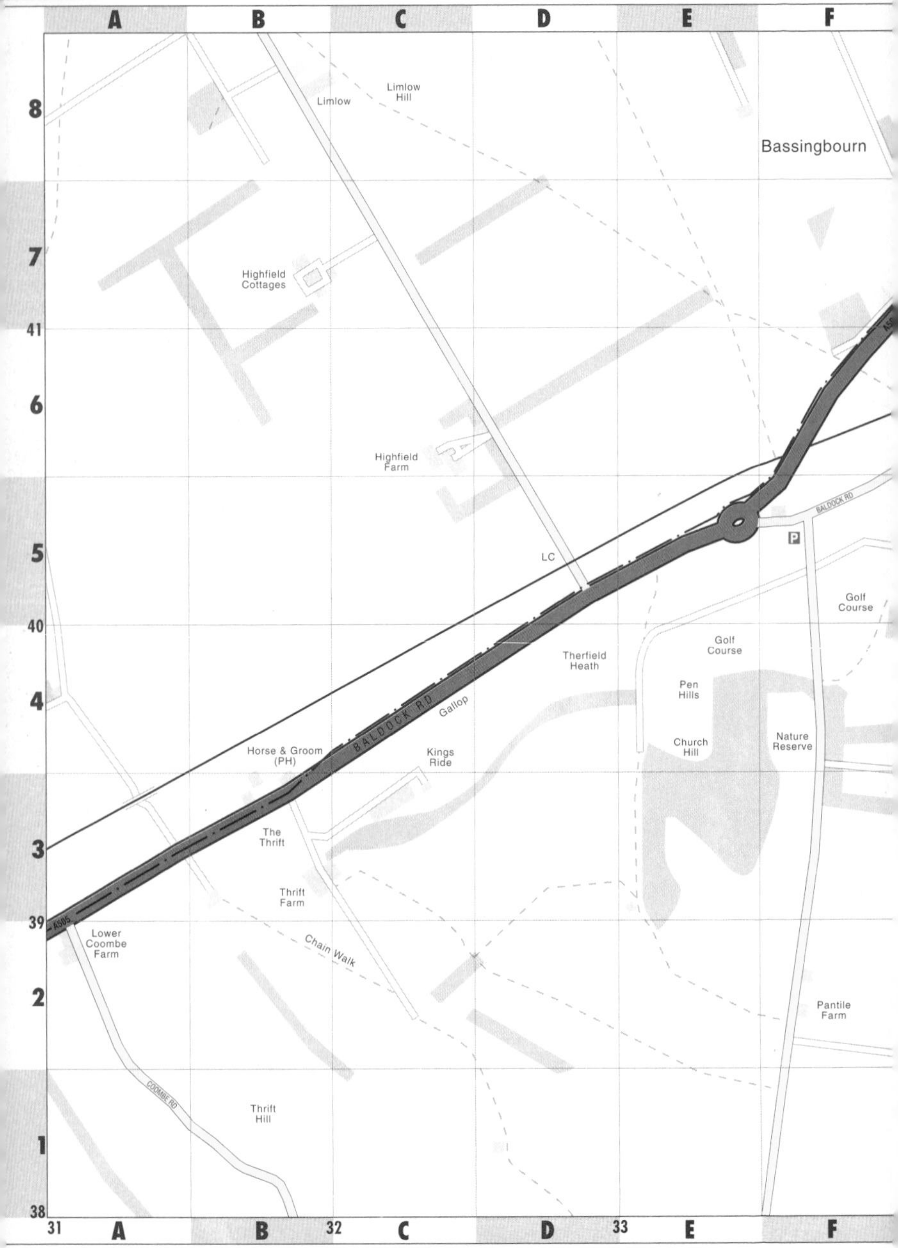

A B C D E F

8

Limlow

Limlow
Hill

Bassingbourn

7

Highfield
Cottages

41

6

Highfield
Farm

5

LC

BALDOCK RD

P

Golf
Course

40

Therfield
Heath

Golf
Course

4

BALDOCK RD

Gallop

Horse & Groom
(PH)

Kings
Ride

Pen
Hills

Church
Hill

Nature
Reserve

3

The
Thrift

39

Thrift
Farm

Chain Walk

Lower
Coombe
Farm

2

Pantile
Farm

COOMBE RD

Thrift
Hill

1

38

2
8

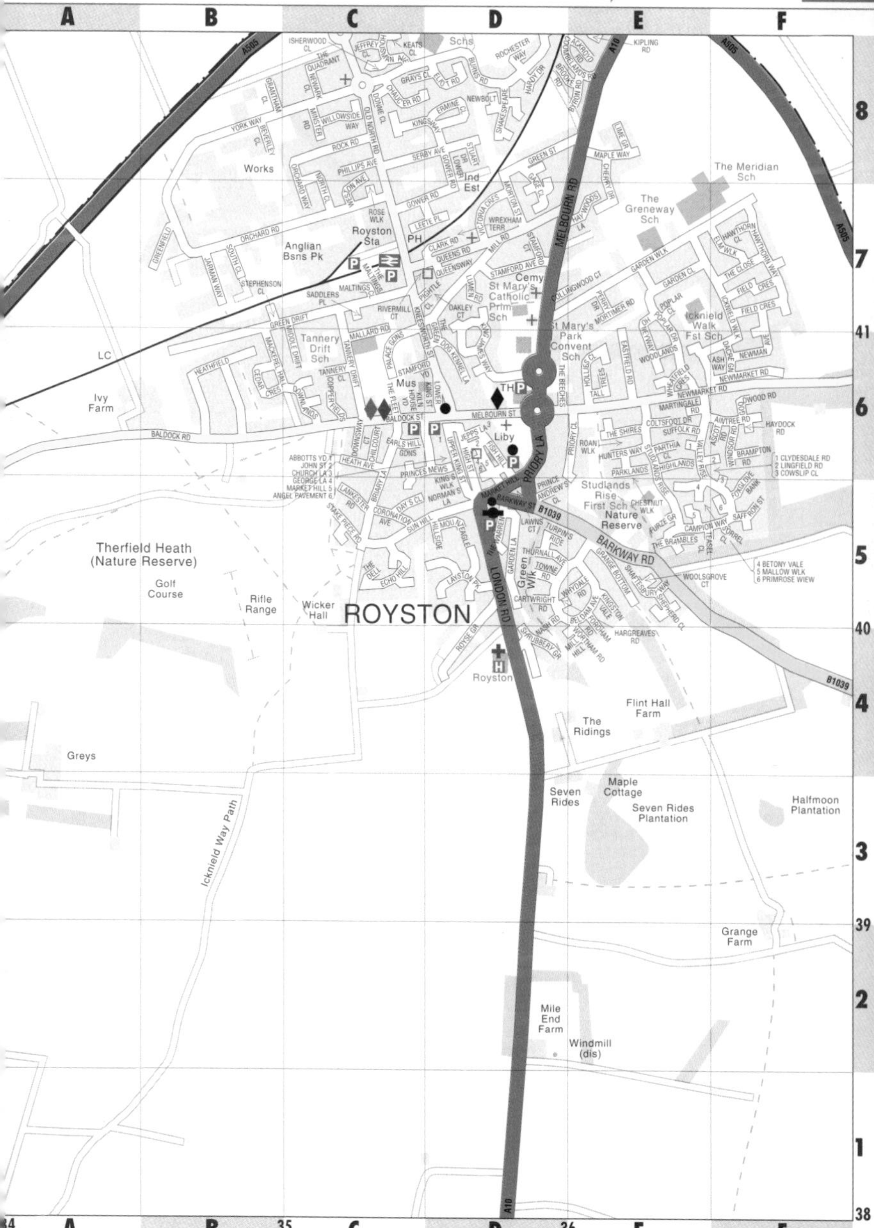
A
B
C
D
E
F
8
7
41
6
5
40
4
3
39
2
1
38
34
35
36
ROYSTON
Works
Anglian
Bsns Pk
Royston
Sta
PH
Ind
Est
Schs
LC
Ivy
Farm
Tannery
Drift
Sch
Mus
TH
Liby
Cemy
St Mary's
Catholic
Prim
Sch
St Mary's
Park
Convent
Sch
The Meridian
Sch
The
Greneway
Sch
Icknield
Walk
Fst Sch
Studlands
Rise
First Sch
Nature
Reserve
Therfield Heath
(Nature Reserve)
Golf
Course
Rifle
Range
Wicker
Hall
Royston
Flint Hall
Farm
The
Ridings
Greys
Seven
Rides
Maple
Cottage
Seven Rides
Plantation
Halfmoon
Plantation
Icknield Way Path
Grange
Farm
Mile
End
Farm
Windmill
(dis)
A505
A10
B1039
MELBOURN RD
LONDON RD
BARKWAY RD
PRIORY LA
BALDOCK RD
BALDOCK ST
MELBOURN ST
NEWMARKET RD
ORCHARD RD
YORK WAY
ROCK RD
GREEN ST
MAPLE WAY
GARDEN WALK
1 CLYDESDALE RD
2 LINGFIELD RD
3 COWSLIP CL
ABBOTTS YD 1
JOHN ST 2
CHURCH LA 3
GEORGE LA 4
MARKET HILL 5
ANGEL PAVEMENT 6
4 BETONY VALE
5 MALLOW WLK
6 PRIMROSE WIEW

16
8

7

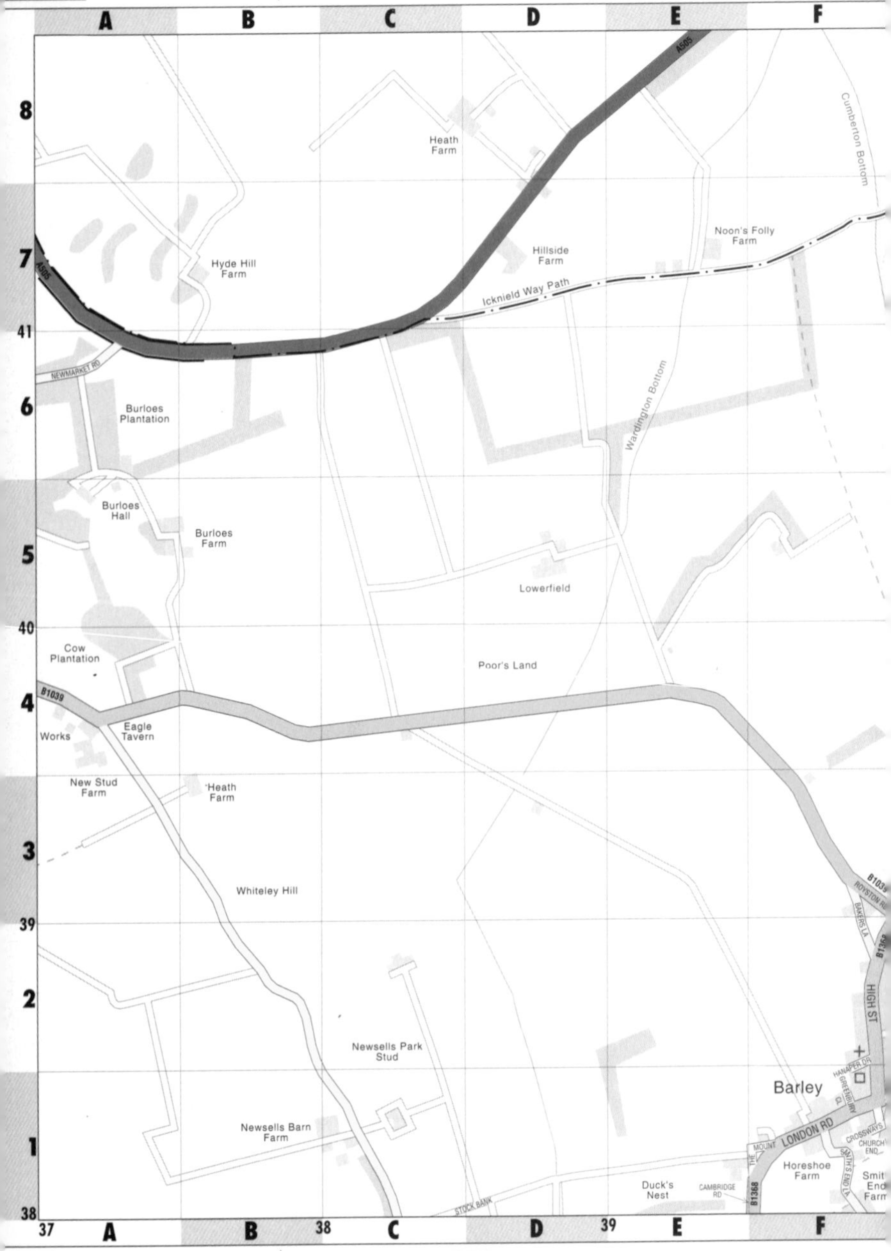

A B C D E F

8

Heath
Farm

Cumberton Bottom

Noon's Folly
Farm

7

Hyde Hill
Farm

Hillside
Farm

Icknield Way Path

41

NEWMARKET RD

Wardington Bottom

6

Burloes
Plantation

Burloes
Hall

Burloes
Farm

5

Lowerfield

40

Cow
Plantation

Poor's Land

B1039

4

Works

Eagle
Tavern

New Stud
Farm

Heath
Farm

3

Whiteley Hill

B1039

ROYSTON RD

SHAFTS LA

POND LA

39

HIGH ST

2

Newsells Park
Stud

Barley

HANAFER ST
THE GREENWAY
CL
HARRIET CL

1

Newsells Barn
Farm

LONDON RD

Horeshoe
Farm

MOUNT PL
CROSSWAYS
CHURCH END L
SMITH END L

Smit
End
Farm

CAMBRIDGE
RD

B1368

Duck's
Nest

STOCK BANK

38

37 A B 38 C D 39 E F

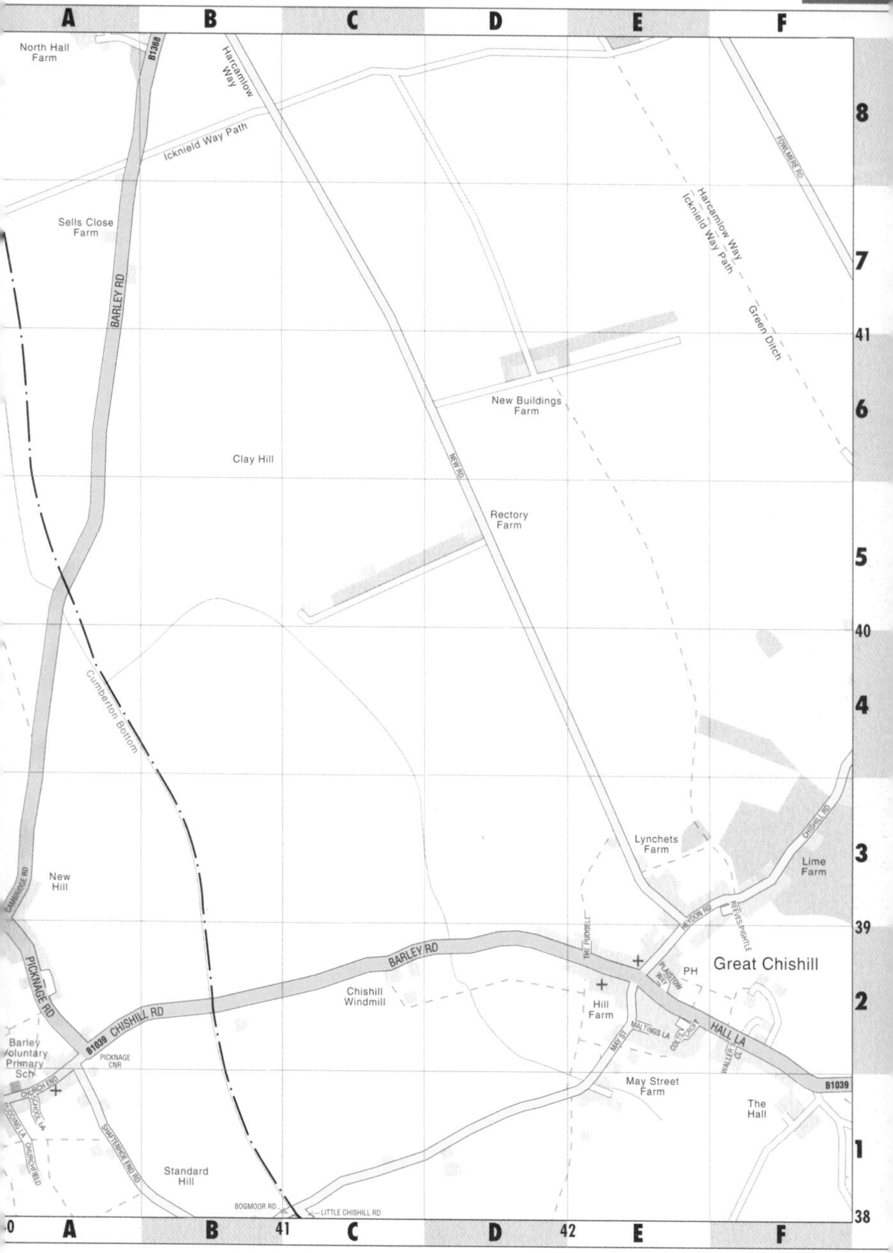

North Hall Farm

Sells Close Farm

BARLEY RD

B1368

Harcamlow Way

Icknield Way Path

Clay Hill

Cumberton Bottom

New Buildings Farm

Rectory Farm

MER RD

Harcamlow Way

Icknield Way Path

Green Ditch

TRUE LINE RD

New Hill

Lynchets Farm

Lime Farm

Great Chishill

DROVE RD

REEVES HALL

BARLEY RD

Chishill Windmill

THE THORNDELL

BACKDOWN RD

Hill Farm

PH

HALL LA

PICKNAGE RD

CHISHILL RD

B1039

PICKNAGE CNR

Barley Voluntary Primary Sch

CHURCH END

SCHOOL LA

Standard Hill

MAY ST

MALTINGS LA

COOL COURT

May Street Farm

B1039

The Hall

BOGMOOR RD

LITTLE CHISHILL RD

A   B   C   D   E   F

8   41   7   6   5   40   4   39   3   2   38   1

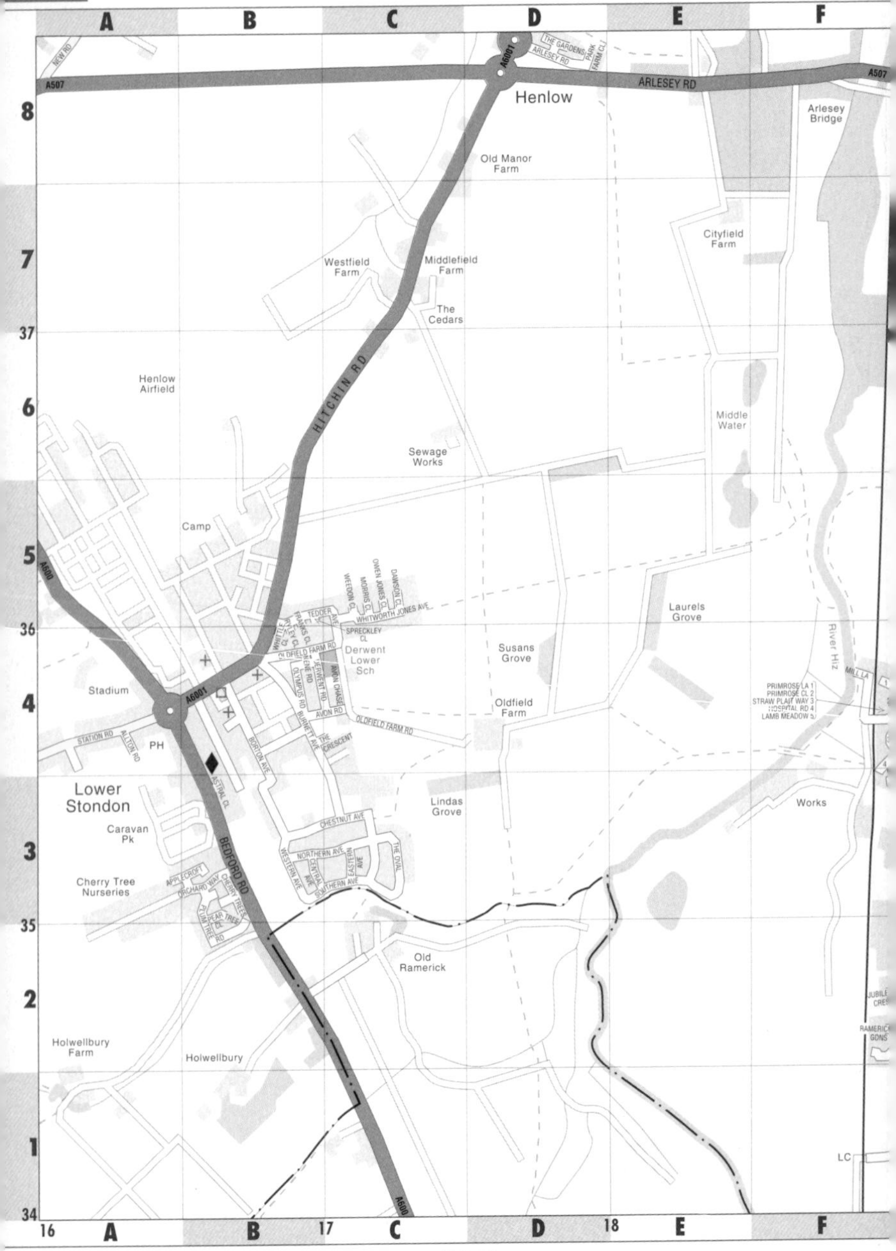

Henlow

Arlesey
Bridge

Old Manor
Farm

Cityfield
Farm

Westfield
Farm

Middlefield
Farm

The
Cedars

Henlow
Airfield

Middle
Water

Sewage
Works

Camp

Laurels
Grove

TEDDER

SPRECKLEY

WHITWORTH  JONES AVE.

Derwent
Lower
Sch

Susans
Grove

PRIMROSE LA 1
PRIMROSE CL 2
STRAW PLAIT WAY 3
HOSPITAL RD 4
LAMB MEADOW 5

Stadium

Oldfield
Farm

STATION RD

PH

Lower
Stondon

Works

Caravan
Pk

Lindas
Grove

Cherry Tree
Nurseries

CHESTNUT AVE

THE OVAL

NORTHERN RD.

Old
Ramerick

Holwellbury
Farm

Holwellbury

LC

A   B   C   D   E   F

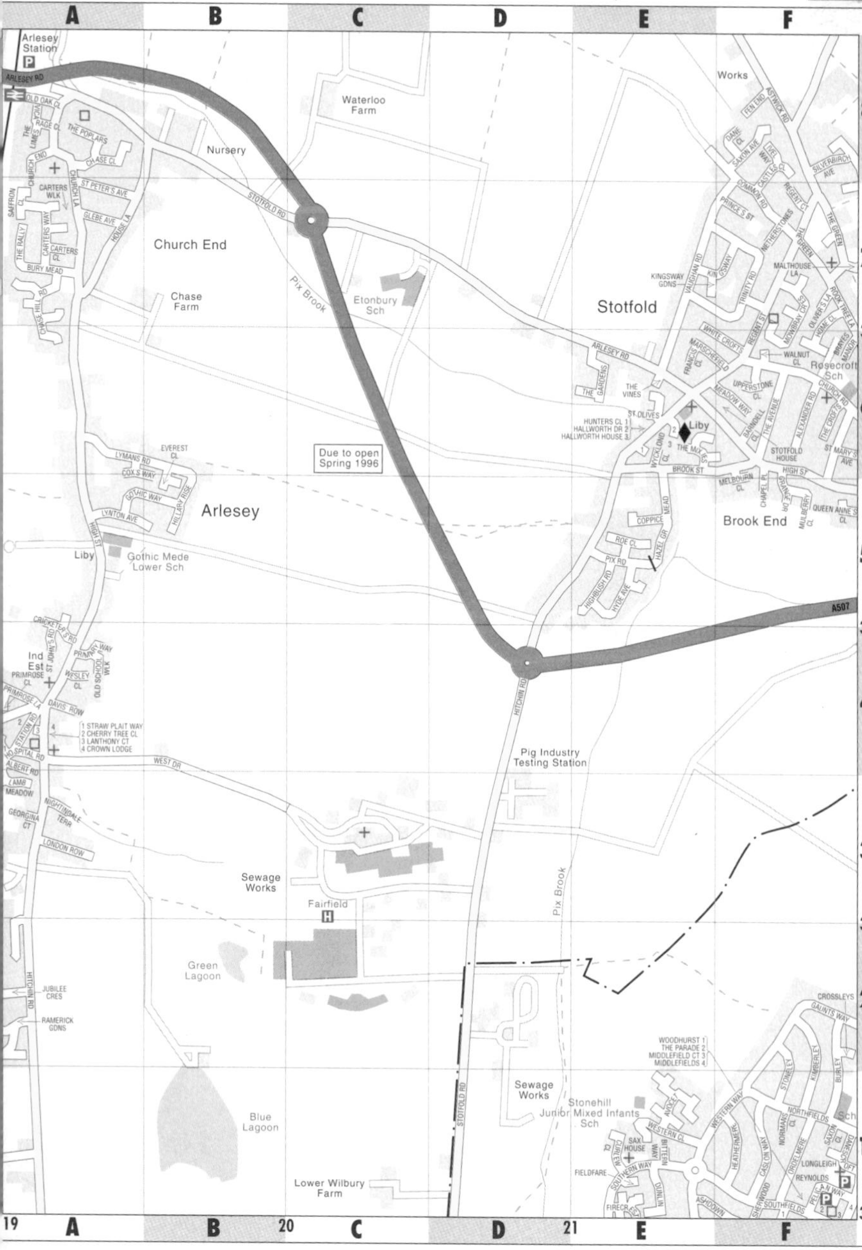
A
B
C
D
E
F
Arlesey Station
ARLESEY RD
OLD OAK CL
THE LIMES
YORK RD
RAGE CL
THE POPLARS
CHASE CL
Nursery
Waterloo Farm
Works
FEN END
ASTWICK RD
DANE CL
SAXON AVE
IVEL WAY
CASTLES CL
COMMON RD
SILVERBIRCH AVE
REGENT CT
PRINCE'S ST
NETHERSTONES
THE GREEN
8
SAFFRON CL
CHURCH END
CARTERS WLK
CHURCH LA
ST PETER'S AVE
STOTFOLD RD
GLEBE AVE
HOUSE LA
THE RALLY
CARTERS WAY
CARTERS CL
BURY MEAD
Church End
CHASE HILL RD
Chase Farm
Pix Brook
Etonbury Sch
Stotfold
KINGSWAY GDNS
VAUGHAN RD
KINGSWAY
TRINITY RD
MALTHOUSE LA
7
37
WHITE CROFT
REGENT ST
MOWBRAY CRES
OLIVER'S LA
HOME CL
ROOK TREE LA
BRAYES MANOR
ARLESEY RD
MARSCHEFIELD
FRANCIS CL
WALNUT CL
Rosecroft Sch
THE GARDENS
THE VINES
ST OLIVES
MEADOW WAY
UPPERSTONE CL
CHURCH RD
THE CROFTS
ALEXANDER RD
THE AVENUE
BARNDELL CL
HUNTERS CL 1
HALLWORTH DR 2
HALLWORTH HOUSE 3
Liby
THE MIXIES
WYCKLOND CL
STOTFOLD HOUSE
ST MARY'S AVE
6
EVEREST CL
LYMANS RD
COX'S WAY
GOTHIC WAY
HILLARY RISE
LYNTON AVE
Due to open Spring 1996
BROOK ST
HIGH ST
MELBOURN CL
CHAPEL PL
GRANGE DR
MULBERRY CL
QUEEN ANNE'S CL
Arlesey
COPPICE MEAD
Brook End
HIGH ST
Liby
Gothic Mede Lower Sch
ROE CL
HAZEL GR
PIX RD
5
HIGHBUSH RD
HYDE AVE
A507
36
CRICKETER'S RD
PRIMARY WAY
OLD SCHOOL WLK
Ind Est
ST JOHN'S RD
WESLEY CL
PRIMROSE CL
PRIMROSE LA
DAVIS ROW
HITCHIN RD
4
STATION RD
1 STRAW PLAIT WAY
2 CHERRY TREE CL
3 LANTHONY CT
4 CROWN LODGE
HOSPITAL RD
ALBERT RD
WEST DR
Pig Industry Testing Station
LAMB MEADOW
GEORGINA CT
NIGHTINGALE TERR
LONDON ROW
3
Sewage Works
Fairfield
Pix Brook
35
Green Lagoon
HITCHIN RD
JUBILEE CRES
RAMERICK GDNS
2
CROSSLEYS
GAUNTS WAY
WOODHURST 1
THE PARADE 2
MIDDLEFIELD CT 3
MIDDLEFIELDS 4
STONELEY
KIMBERLEY
BURLEY
Sewage Works
STOTFOLD RD
Stonehill Junior Mixed Infants Sch
AVOCET
WESTERN WAY
NORTHFIELDS
Sch
Blue Lagoon
WESTERN CL
HEATHERMERE
NORMANS CL
SAXON CL
DANECROFT
1
SAX HOUSE
CURLEW CL
BITTERN WAY
CASLON WAY
CROSSMERE
LONGLEIGH
FIELDFARE
SOUTHERN WAY
REYNOLDS
Lower Wilbury Farm
DUNLIN
ASHDOWN
SHERWOOD
SOUTHFIELDS
PELICAN WAY
FIRECREST
34
19
20
21

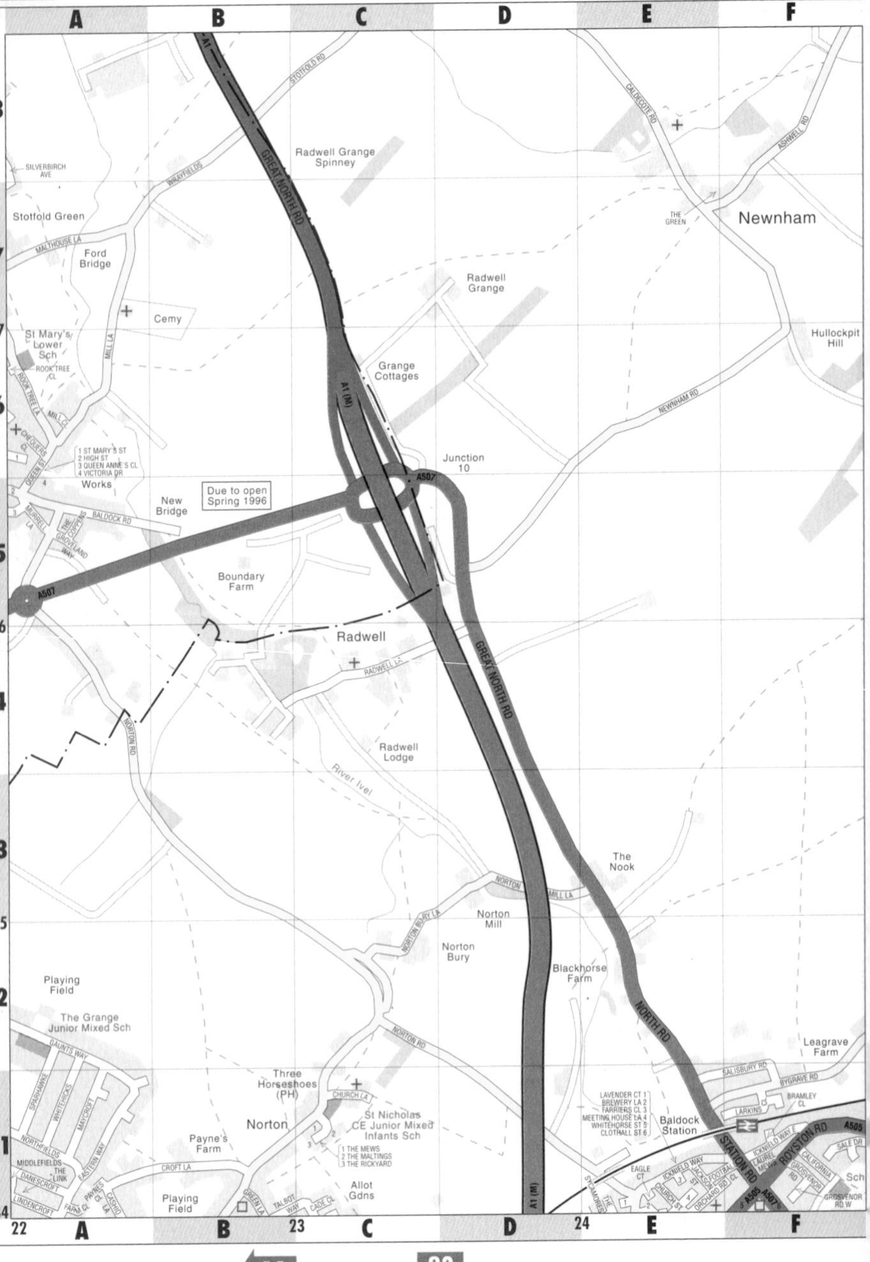
A B C D E F
8 7 37 6 5 36 4 3 35 2 1 34
22 23 24
A1
GREAT NORTH RD
STOTFOLD RD
Radwell Grange Spinney
SILVERBIRCH AVE
WRAYFIELDS
Stotfold Green
MALTHOUSE LA
Ford Bridge
Cemy
MILL LA
St Mary's Lower Sch
ROOK TREE CL
ROOK TREE LA
MILL CL
CHEQUERS CL
QUEEN ST
1 ST MARY'S ST
2 HIGH ST
3 QUEEN ANNE'S CL
4 VICTORIA DR
Works
New Bridge
Due to open Spring 1996
BALDOCK RD
MURRELL LA
THE COPPINS
GROVELAND WAY
A507
Boundary Farm
Radwell
RADWELL LA
Radwell Grange
Grange Cottages
A1 (M)
Junction 10
A507
CALDECOTE RD
ASHWELL RD
THE GREEN
Newnham
Hullockpit Hill
NEWNHAM RD
NORTON RD
Radwell Lodge
River Ivel
The Nook
NORTON MILL LA
Norton Mill
NORTON BURY LA
Norton Bury
Blackhorse Farm
NORTH RD
Playing Field
The Grange Junior Mixed Sch
GAUNTS WAY
SPARHAWKE
WHITEHICKS
MAYCROFT
NORTHFIELDS
EASTERN WAY
MIDDLEFIELDS
THE LINK
DANESCROFT
LINDENCROFT
FARM CL
PAYNES CL
CASHIO LA
Three Horseshoes (PH)
CHURCH LA
Norton
St Nicholas CE Junior Mixed Infants Sch
1 THE MEWS
2 THE MALTINGS
3 THE RICKYARD
Payne's Farm
CROFT LA
Playing Field
GREEN LA
TALBOT WAY
CADE CL
Allot Gdns
Leagrave Farm
SALISBURY RD
BYGRAVE RD
BRAMLEY CL
LARKINS
LAVENDER CT 1
BREWERY LA 2
FARRIERS CL 3
MEETING HOUSE LA 4
WHITEHORSE ST 5
CLOTHALL ST 6
Baldock Station
STATION RD
ROYSTON RD
A505
ICKNIELD WAY E
LAUREL MEWS
CALIFORNIA
GROSVENOR RD
GROSVENOR RD W
Sch
THE SYCAMORES
EAGLE CT
ICKNIELD WAY
JACKSON ST
CHURCH ST
FOOTBALL CL
ORCHARD RD
A505
A507

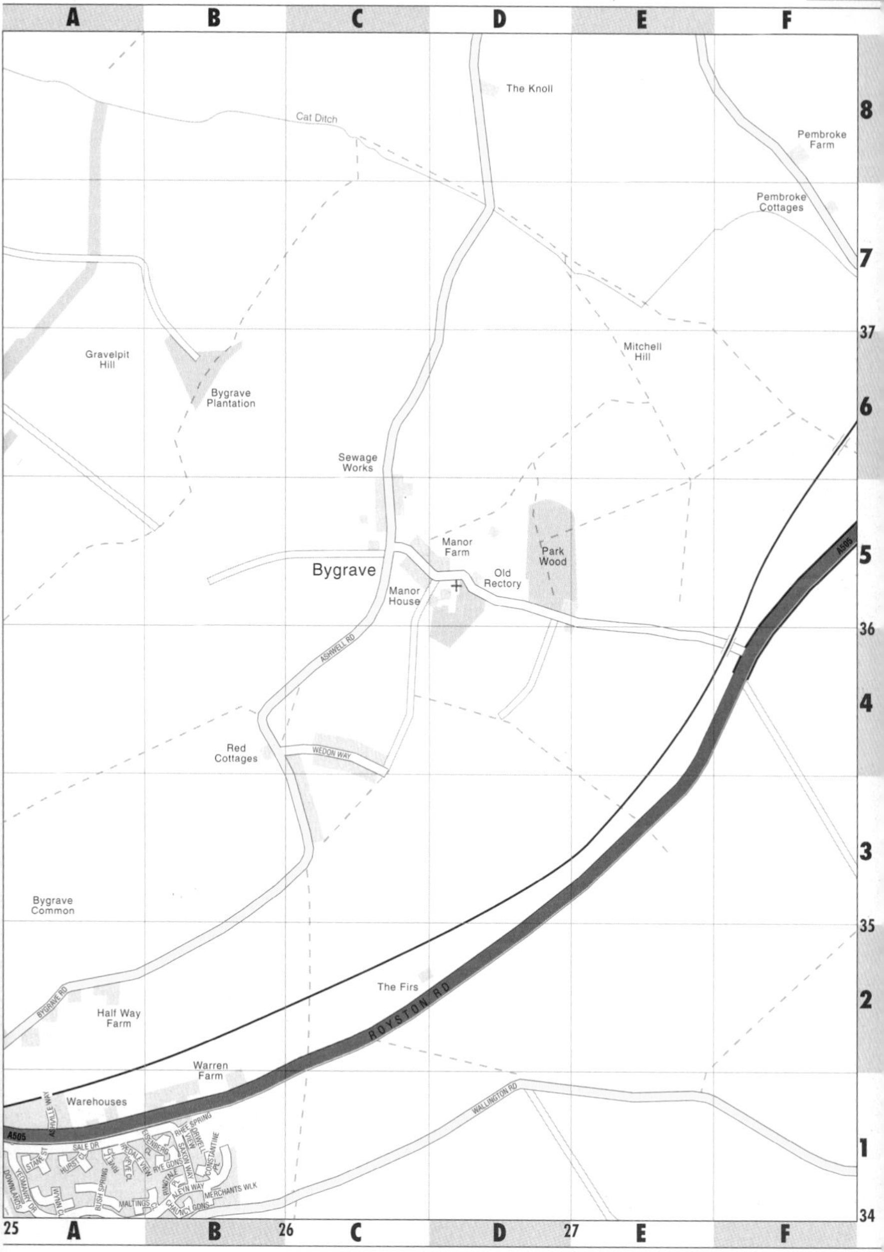

A | B | C | D | E | F

**8**

The Knoll

Pembroke
Farm

Pembroke
Cottages

**7**

Cat Ditch

**37**

Gravelpit
Hill

Mitchell
Hill

Bygrave
Plantation

**6**

Sewage
Works

Manor
Farm

Park
Wood

**5**

Bygrave

Manor
House

Old
Rectory

ASHWELL RD

**36**

**4**

Red
Cottages

WEDON WAY

A505

**3**

Bygrave
Common

**35**

The Firs

ROYSTON RD

**2**

Half Way
Farm

Warren
Farm

Warehouses

**1**

SALE DR

WALLINGTON RD

A505

MERCHANTS WLK

MALTING

**34**

25 | A | B | 26 | C | D | 27 | E | F

13
5

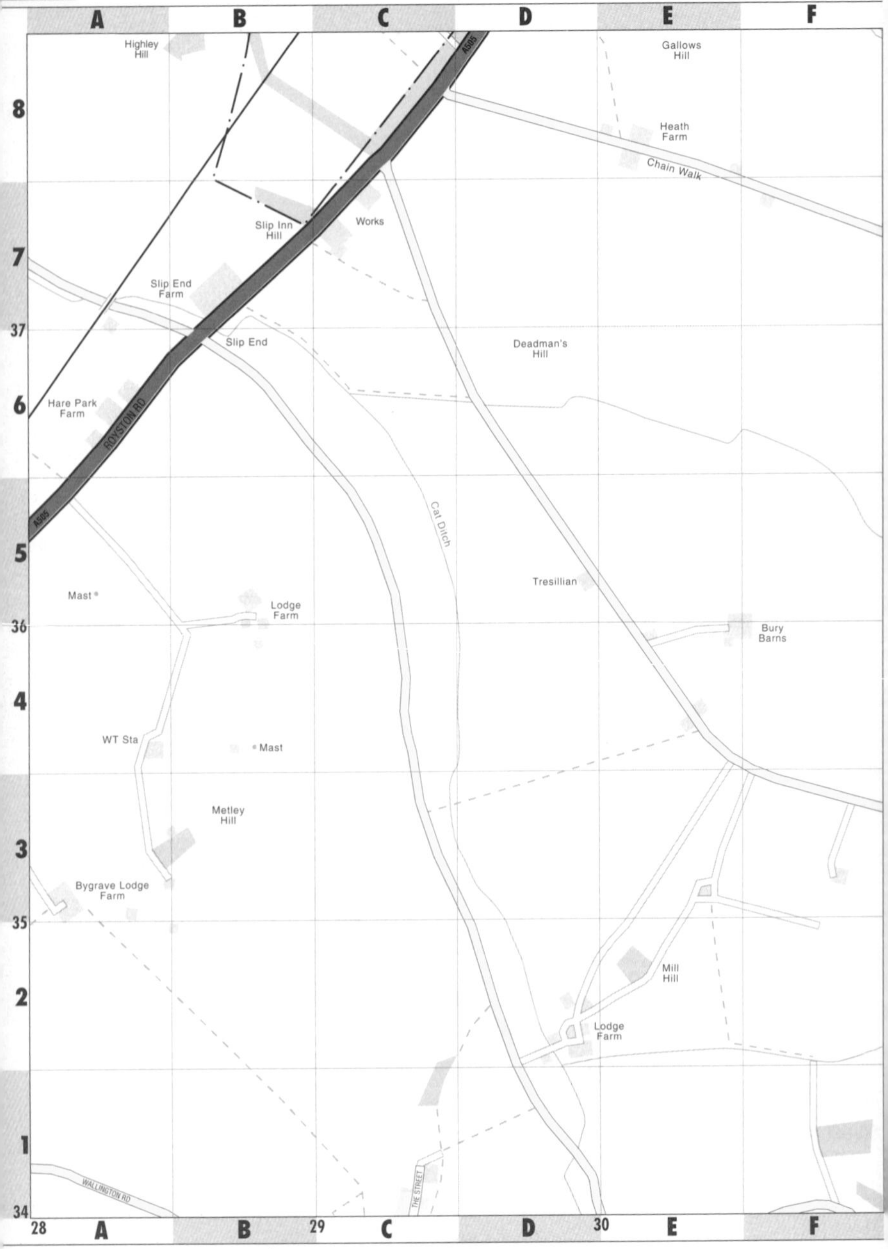
A
B
C
D
E
F
8
7
37
6
5
36
4
3
35
2
1
34
28
29
30
Highley Hill
Gallows Hill
A505
Heath Farm
Chain Walk
Slip Inn Hill
Works
Slip End Farm
Slip End
Deadman's Hill
Hare Park Farm
ROYSTON RD
A505
Cat Ditch
Mast
Lodge Farm
Tresillian
Bury Barns
WT Sta
Mast
Metley Hill
Bygrave Lodge Farm
Mill Hill
Lodge Farm
WALLINGTON RD
THE STREET

13
25

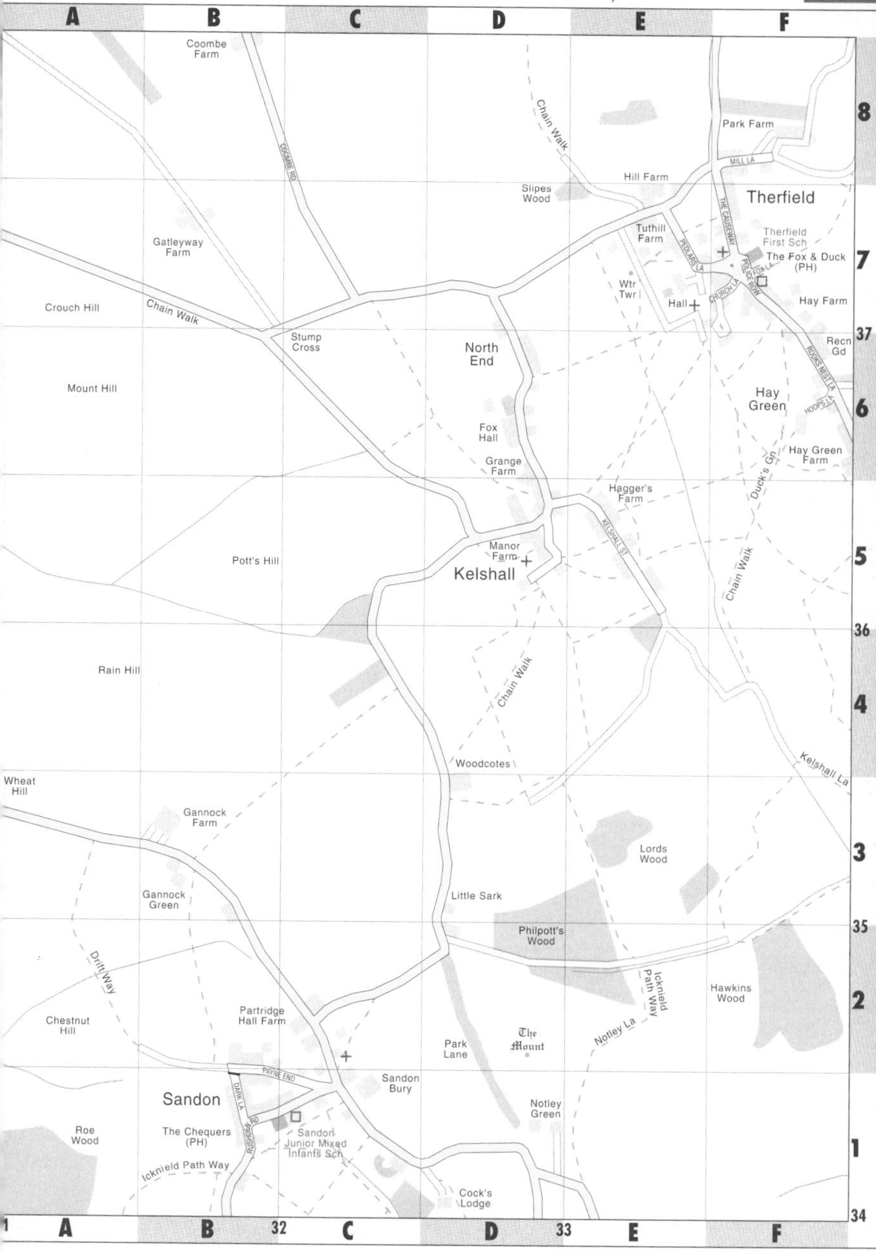

A B C D E F

8
Coombe Farm
Chain Walk
Park Farm
Hill Farm
MILL LA
Slipes Wood
Therfield
Tuthill Farm
Therfield First Sch
7
Gatleyway Farm
Wtr Twr
The Fox & Duck (PH)
Crouch Hill
Chain Walk
Hall
Hay Farm
37
Stump Cross
North End
Recn Gd
Mount Hill
Fox Hall
Hay Green
6
Grange Farm
Hay Green Farm
Hagger's Farm
Duck's Gn
Pott's Hill
Manor Farm
Chain Walk
5
Kelshall
36
Rain Hill
Chain Walk
4
Woodcotes
Kelshall La
Wheat Hill
Gannock Farm
Lords Wood
3
Gannock Green
Little Sark
Philpott's Wood
35
Drift Way
Hawkins Wood
Icknield Path Way
2
Chestnut Hill
Partridge Hall Farm
Park Lane
The Mount
Notley La
PATH END
Sandon Bury
DUCK LA
Sandon
Roe Wood
The Chequers (PH)
Sandon Junior Mixed Infants Sch
Notley Green
1
Icknield Path Way
Cock's Lodge
34

A B C D E F

15
7

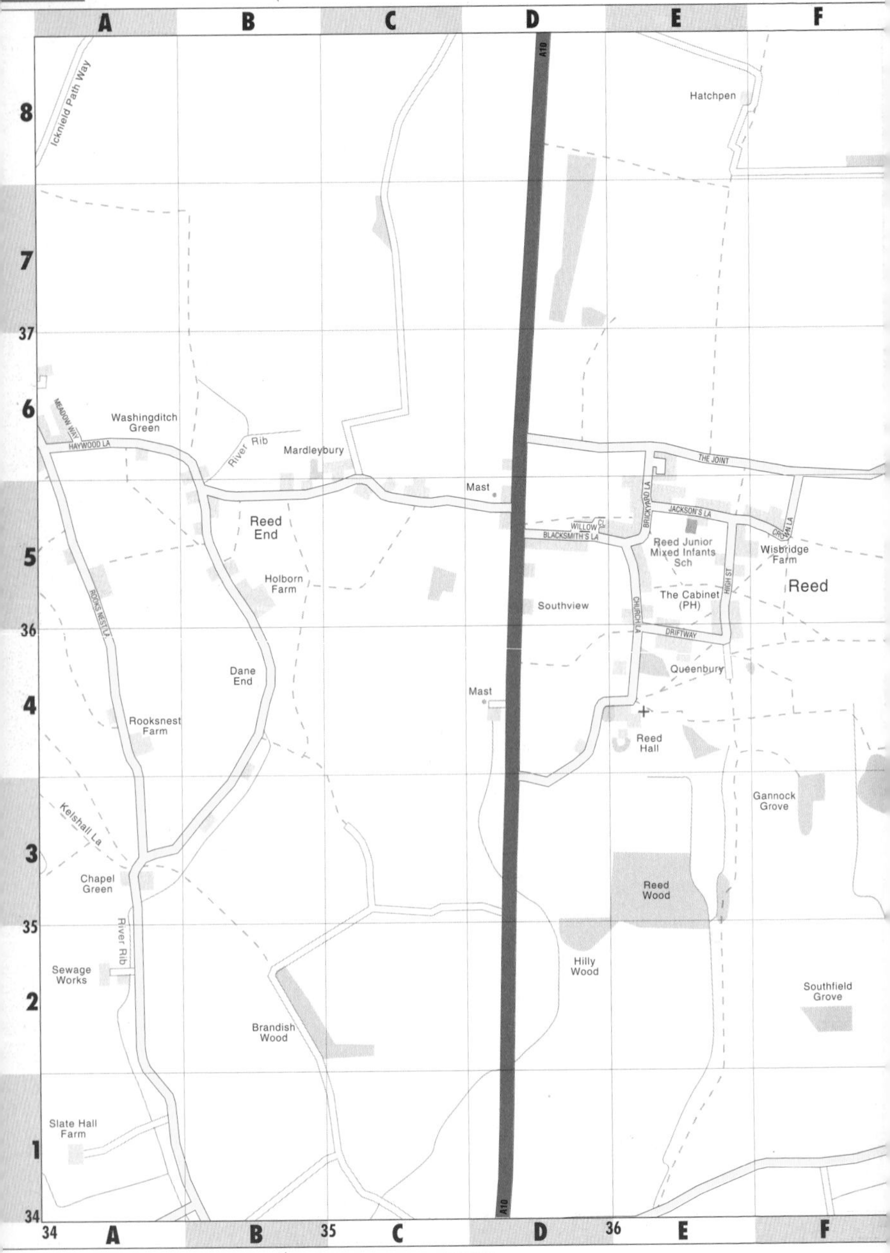
A
B
C
D
E
F
8
7
37
6
5
36
4
3
35
2
1
34
Icknield Path Way
A10
Hatchpen
Washingditch
Green
MEADOW WAY
HAYWOOD LA
River Rib
Mardleybury
Mast
THE JOINT
BRICKYARD LA
JACKSON'S LA
WILLOW CL
BLACKSMITH'S LA
CROWN LA
Reed
End
Reed Junior
Mixed Infants
Sch
Wisbridge
Farm
Holborn
Farm
ROOKS NEST LA
HIGH ST
Reed
The Cabinet
(PH)
Southview
CHURCH LA
DRIFTWAY
Queenbury
Dane
End
Mast
Rooksnest
Farm
Reed
Hall
Gannock
Grove
Kelshall La
Chapel
Green
Reed
Wood
River Rib
Hilly
Wood
Sewage
Works
Southfield
Grove
Brandish
Wood
Slate Hall
Farm
34
35
36

15
27

8
18

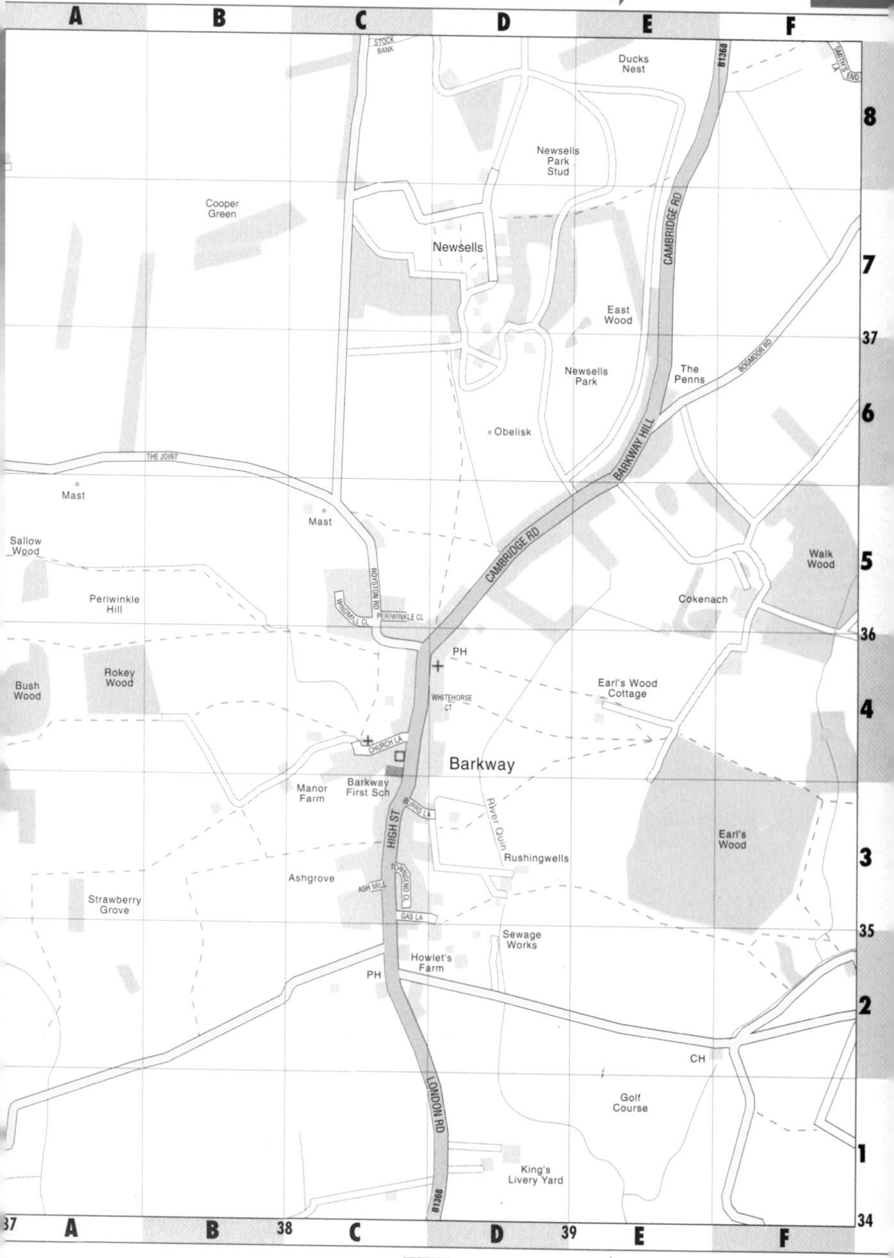
A
B
C
D
E
F
8
7
37
6
5
36
4
3
35
2
1
34
37
38
39
STOCK BANK
Ducks Nest
B1368
SMITH'S END LA
Newsells Park Stud
Cooper Green
Newsells
CAMBRIDGE RD
East Wood
Newsells Park
The Penns
BOGMOOR RD
Obelisk
THE JOINT
BARKWAY HILL
Mast
Mast
Sallow Wood
CAMBRIDGE RD
Walk Wood
ROYSTON RD
Periwinkle Hill
WINDMILL CL
PERIWINKLE CL
Cokenach
PH
Bush Wood
Rokey Wood
WHITEHORSE CT
Earl's Wood Cottage
CHURCH LA
Barkway
Manor Farm
Barkway First Sch
BURRS LA
River Quin
HIGH ST
Earl's Wood
Rushingwells
Ashgrove
TOWNSEND CL
ASH MILL
Strawberry Grove
GAS LA
Sewage Works
Howlet's Farm
PH
CH
LONDON RD
Golf Course
King's Livery Yard
B1368

28
18

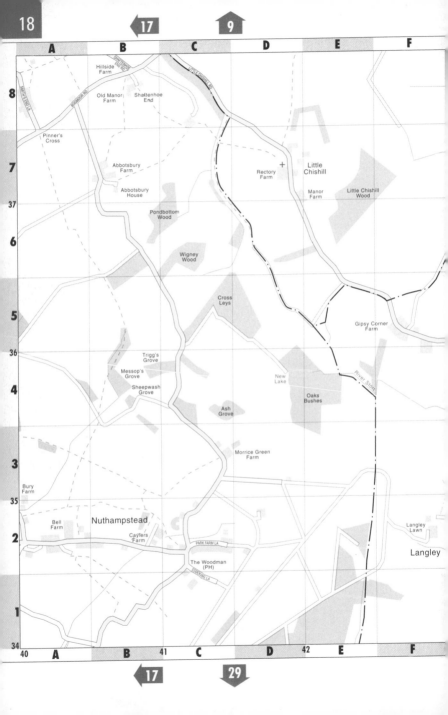

A    B    C    D    E    F

8

Hillside Farm

Old Manor Farm    Shattenhoe End

Pinner's Cross

7

Abbotsbury Farm

37

Abbotsbury House

Pondbottom Wood

Rectory Farm

Little Chishill

Manor Farm

Little Chishill Wood

6

Wigney Wood

Cross Leys

5

Gipsy Corner Farm

36

Trigg's Grove

Messop's Grove

Sheepwash Grove

New Lake

River Stort

4

Ash Grove

Oaks Bushes

Morrice Green Farm

3

Bury Farm

35

Bell Farm

Nuthampstead

Cayters Farm

PARK FARM LA

Langley Lawn

Langley

2

The Woodman (PH)

STOCKING LA

1

34

40    A    B    41    C    D    42    E    F

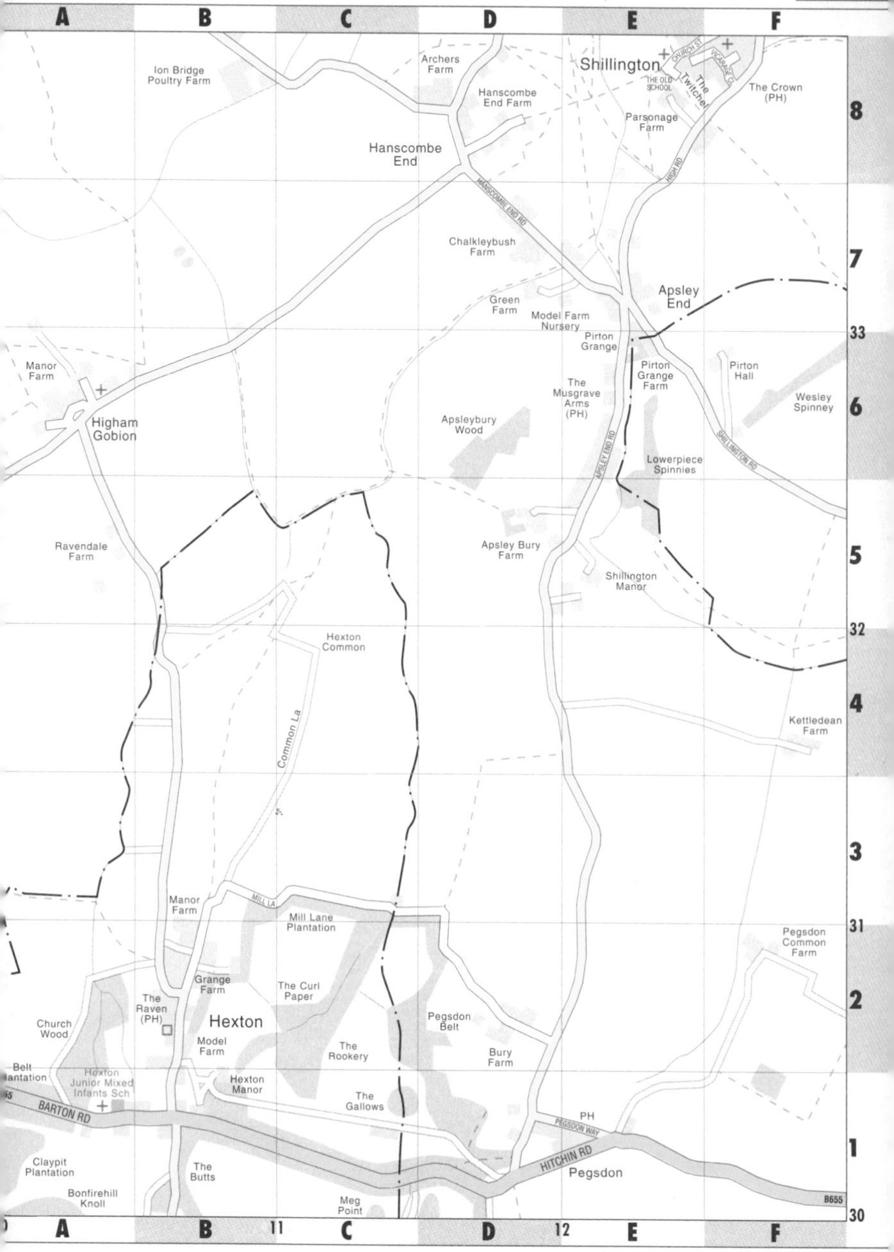
A
B
C
D
E
F
Ion Bridge Poultry Farm
Archers Farm
Hanscombe End Farm
Shillington
CHURCH ST
VICARAGE CL
THE OLD SCHOOL
The Twitchel
The Crown (PH)
Parsonage Farm
Hanscombe End
HIGH RD
HANSCOMBE END RD
8
Chalkleybush Farm
7
Apsley End
Green Farm
Model Farm Nursery
Pirton Grange
33
Manor Farm
Pirton Grange Farm
Pirton Hall
The Musgrave Arms (PH)
Wesley Spinney
Higham Gobion
Apsleybury Wood
6
APSLEY END RD
SHILLINGTON RD
Lowerpiece Spinnies
Ravendale Farm
Apsley Bury Farm
5
Shillington Manor
32
Hexton Common
4
Kettledean Farm
Common La
3
Manor Farm
MILL LA
Mill Lane Plantation
31
Pegsdon Common Farm
Grange Farm
The Curl Paper
The Raven (PH)
2
Church Wood
Hexton
Pegsdon Belt
Model Farm
The Rookery
Bury Farm
Belt Plantation
Hexton Junior Mixed Infants Sch
Hexton Manor
The Gallows
BARTON RD
PH
PEGSDON WAY
1
HITCHIN RD
Claypit Plantation
The Butts
Pegsdon
Bonfirehill Knoll
Meg Point
B655
30
A
B
11
C
D
12
E
F

A B C D E F

8

Rosehill
Farm

7

33

6

New Wrights
Farm

WALBELL RD

SHILLINGTON RD

Hammonds
Farm

Burge End

West Lane
Farm

5

Wrights
Farm

WEST LA

BURGE END LA

32

Rectory
Farm

Pirton Junior
Mixed
Infants Sch

PH

Pirton

Hambridge Way

4

Water
Tower

The Cat
& Fiddle
(PH)

Toot
Hill

Icknield Way Path

Playing
Field

3

Walnut Tree
Farm

Icknield Way Path

31

Wood La

2

Highdown
Farm

Lower
Plantation

HEGHRD

Tingley
Wood

High Down
House

Highdown
Plantation

Punch's
Cross

1

Tingley
Field
Plantation

Hanginghill
Plantation

30

B655

B655

13 A B 14 C D 15 E F

10
22

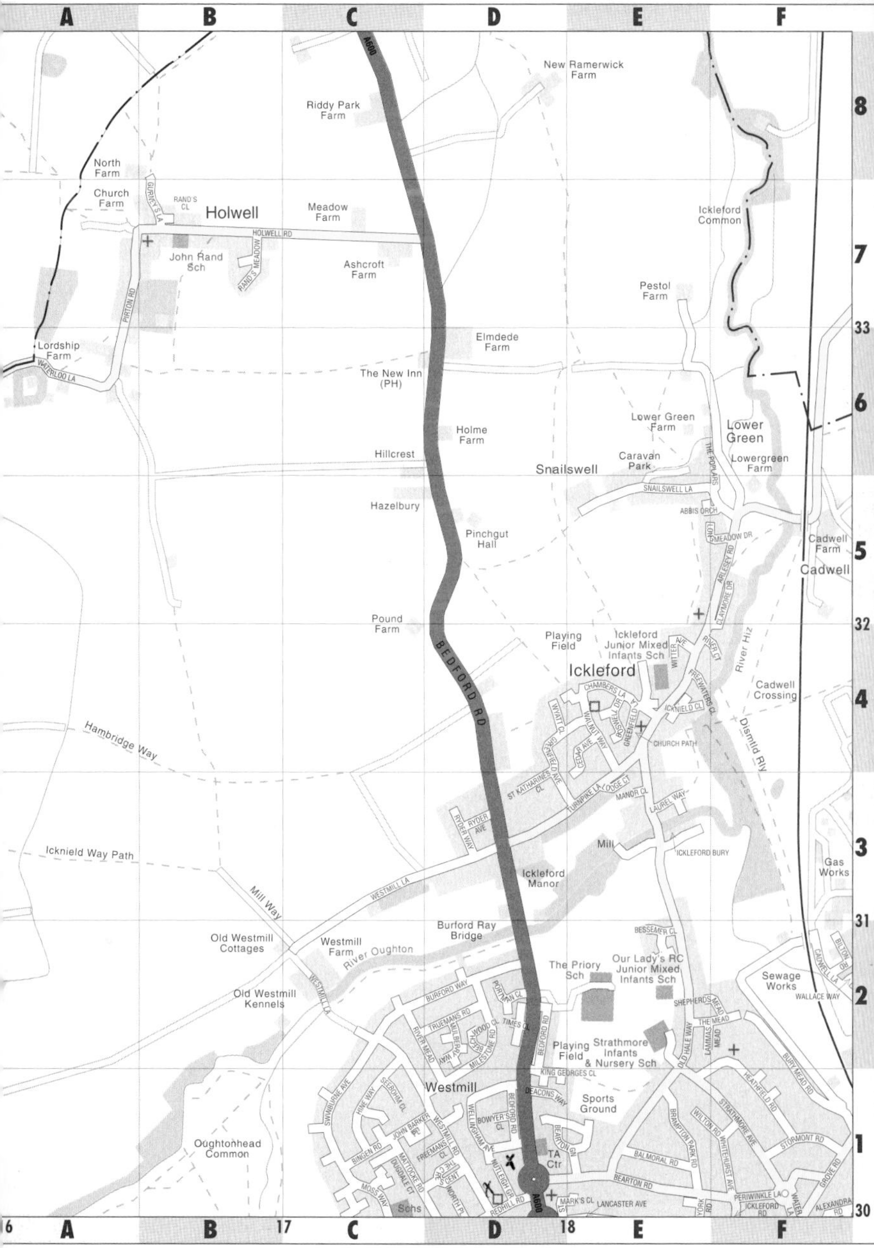
A
B
C
D
E
F
8
7
33
6
5
32
4
3
31
2
1
30
6
17
18
A600
New Ramerwick Farm
Riddy Park Farm
North Farm
Church Farm
RAND'S CL
GURNEY'S LA
Holwell
HOLWELL RD
Meadow Farm
John Rand Sch
RAND'S MEADOW
Ashcroft Farm
PIRTON RD
Ickleford Common
Pestol Farm
Lordship Farm
WATERLOO LA
Elmdede Farm
The New Inn (PH)
Holme Farm
Lower Green Farm
Lower Green
Hillcrest
Caravan Park
Snailswell
THE POPLARS
Lowergreen Farm
SNAILSWELL LA
Hazelbury
ABBIS ORCH
Pinchgut Hall
MEADOW DR
ARLESEY RD
Cadwell Farm
Cadwell
CLAYMORE DR
Pound Farm
Playing Field
Ickleford Junior Mixed Infants Sch
BEDFORD RD
RIVER CT
River Hiz
Ickleford
CHAMBERS LA
FREWATERS CL
Cadwell Crossing
ICKNIELD CL
WYATT CL
WALNUT WAY
Dismtld Rly
Hambridge Way
CHURCH PATH
CEDAR AVE
GREENFIELD AVE
ST KATHARINES CL
TURNPIKE LA
LODGE CT
MANOR CL
LAUREL WAY
RYDER AVE
RYDER WAY
Mill
ICKLEFORD BURY
Icknield Way Path
Gas Works
Ickleford Manor
Mill Way
WESTMILL LA
Burford Ray Bridge
Old Westmill Cottages
Westmill Farm
River Oughton
BESSEMER CL
The Priory Sch
Our Lady's RC Junior Mixed Infants Sch
Sewage Works
CADWELL LA
BILTON WAY
WALLACE WAY
Old Westmill Kennels
WESTMILL LA
BURFORD WAY
SHEPHERDS MEAD
TRUEMANS RD
TIMES CL
THE MEAD
RIVER MEAD
MILBERRY WAY
MILESTONE RD
OLD HALE WAY
LAMMAS MEAD
Playing Field
Strathmore Infants & Nursery Sch
BURY MEAD RD
KING GEORGES CL
Westmill
DEACONS WAY
Sports Ground
HEATHFIELD RD
SWINBURNE AVE
HINE WAY
SEEBOHM CL
WELLINGHAM AVE
BOWYER'S CL
BEDFORD RD
BEARTON GN
STRATHMORE AVE
WILTON RD
BRAMPTON PARK RD
JOHN BARKER PL
WESTMILL RD
WHITEHURST AVE
STORMONT RD
Oughtonhead Common
BINGEN RD
FREEMANS CL
TA Ctr
BALMORAL RD
MATTOCKE RD
THE CRESCENT
NUTLEIGH GR
BEARTON RD
GROVE RD
DUGDALE CT
MOSS WAY
NORTH PL
REDHILL RD
MARK'S CL
LANCASTER AVE
YORK RD
PERIWINKLE LA
ICKLEFORD RD
WATER LA
ALEXANDRA RD
Schs

34
22

21
11

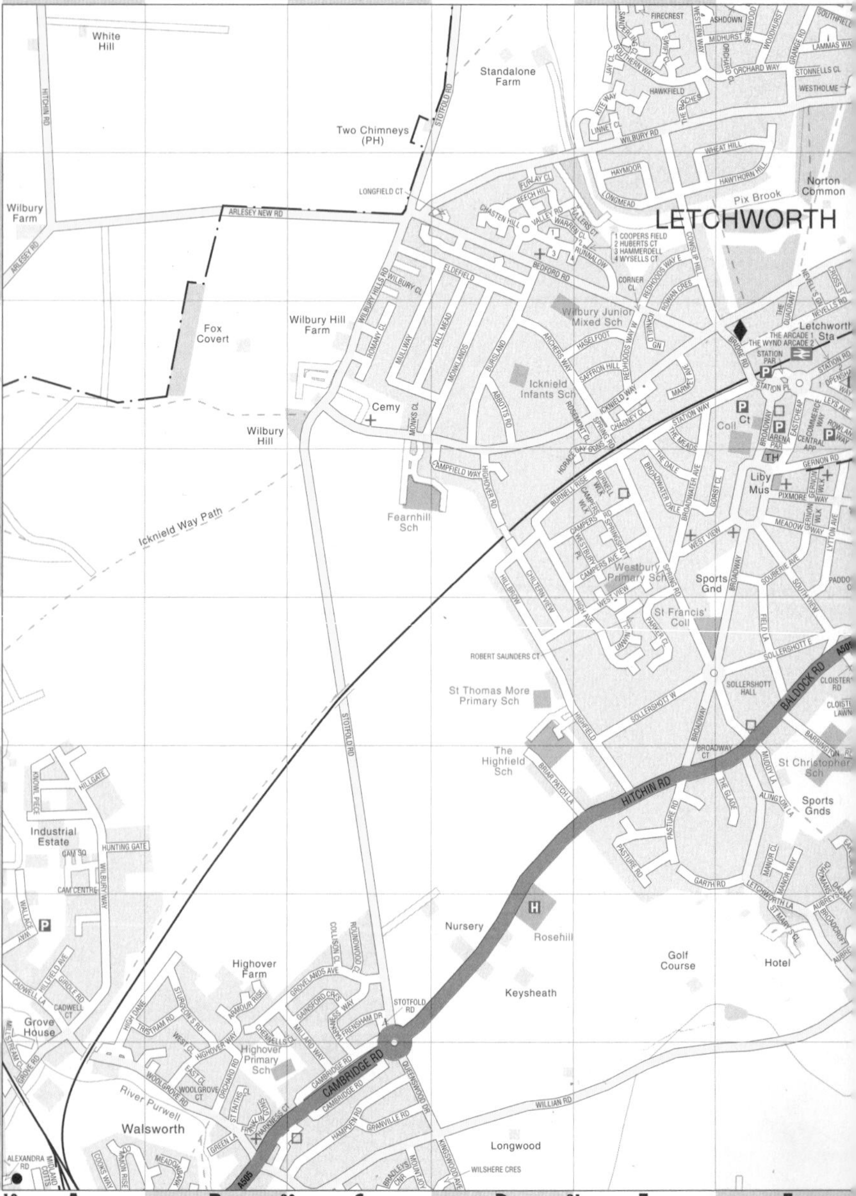
A
B
C
D
E
F
White Hill
Standalone Farm
Two Chimneys (PH)
Wilbury Farm
LETCHWORTH
Norton Common
Pix Brook
Fox Covert
Wilbury Hill Farm
Wilbury Junior Mixed Sch
Icknield Infants Sch
Cemy
Wilbury Hill
Fearnhill Sch
Icknield Way Path
Letchworth Sta
Coll
Liby
Mus
Westbury Primary Sch
Sports Gnd
St Francis' Coll
St Thomas More Primary Sch
The Highfield Sch
Sollershott Hall
St Christopher Sch
Sports Gnds
Industrial Estate
Nursery
Rosehill
Golf Course
Hotel
Keysheath
Highover Farm
Highover Primary Sch
Grove House
River Purwell
Walsworth
Longwood
STOTFOLD RD
HITCHIN RD
ARLESEY NEW RD
ARLESEY RD
WILBURY RD
BEDFORD RD
CAMBRIDGE RD
BALDOCK RD
WILLIAN RD
LONGFIELD CT
1 COOPERS FIELD
2 HUBERTS CT
3 HAMMERDELL
4 WYSELLS CT
ROBERT SAUNDERS CT
WILSHERE CRES
A505
8
7
33
6
5
32
4
3
31
2
1
30
19
20
21

21
35

12
24

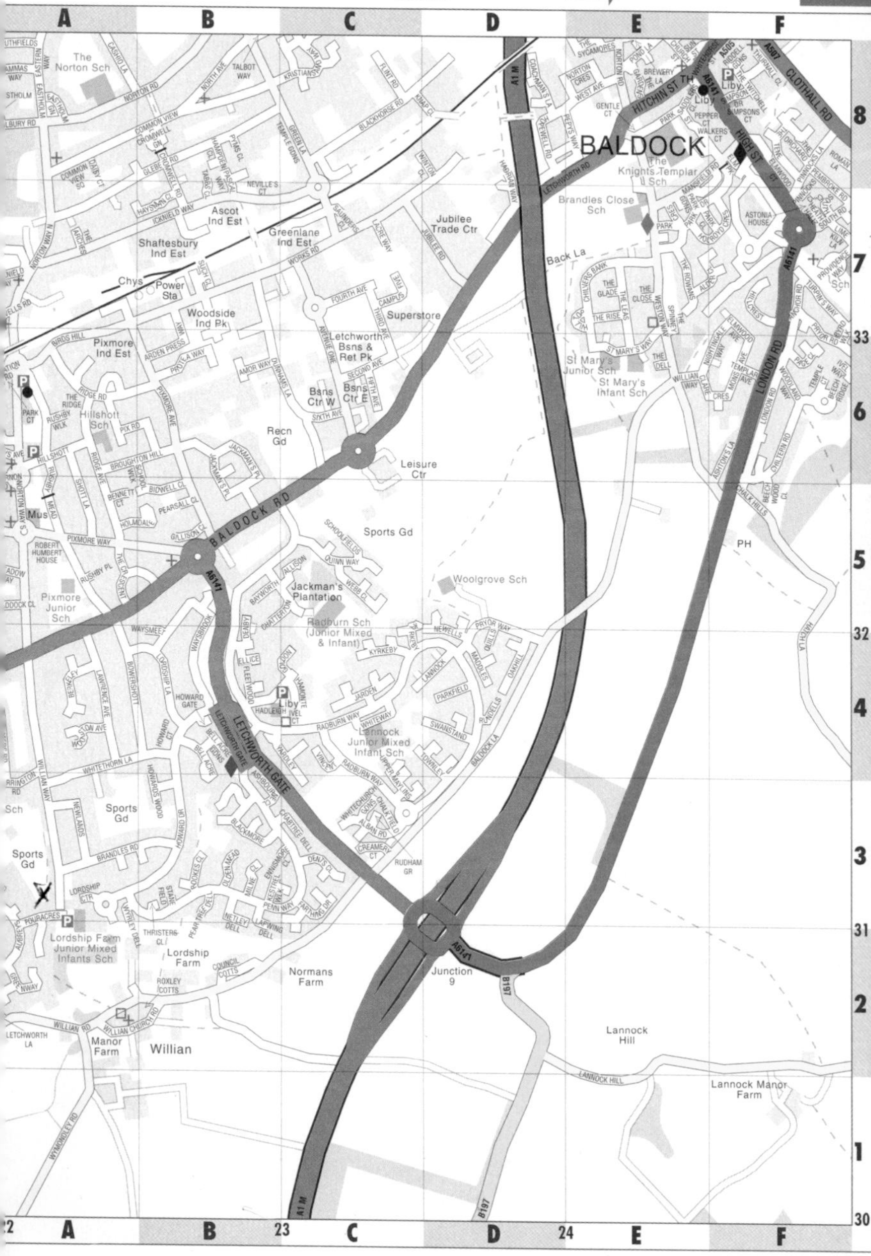
A
B
C
D
E
F
8
7
33
6
5
32
4
3
31
2
1
30
22
23
24
BALDOCK
The Norton Sch
NORTON RD
TALBOT WAY
NORTH AVE
COMMON VIEW
CROMWELL GN
GLEBE RD
COMMON VIEW SQ
ICKNIELD WAY
Ascot Ind Est
Shaftesbury Ind Est
Greenlane Ind Est
Jubilee Trade Ctr
WORKS RD
Chys
Power Sta
Woodside Ind Pk
Pixmore Ind Est
Superstore
Letchworth Bsns & Ret Pk
Bsns Ctr W
Bsns Ctr E
Recn Gd
Leisure Ctr
Hillshott Sch
BALDOCK RD
A6141
Mus
ROBERT HUMBERT HOUSE
Pixmore Junior Sch
Sports Gd
Jackman's Plantation
Radburn Sch (Junior Mixed & Infant)
Woolgrove Sch
Lannock Junior Mixed Infant Sch
LETCHWORTH GATE
Liby
Sports Gd
Lordship Farm Junior Mixed Infants Sch
Lordship Farm
Normans Farm
Junction 9
B197
A1 M
Manor Farm
Willian
WILLIAN RD
WILLIAN CHURCH RD
WYMONDLEY RD
LETCHWORTH LA
Lannock Hill
LANNOCK HILL
Lannock Manor Farm
PH
The Knights Templar Sch
Brandles Close Sch
Back La
St Mary's Junior Sch
St Mary's Infant Sch
HITCHIN ST
HIGH ST
CLOTHALL RD
LONDON RD
A505
A507
LETCHWORTH RD
ASTONIA HOUSE
Sch

36
24

A B C D E F

8 | Nursery | Clothall Common
Home Land

7 | Cambrai Farm
The Homestead | WARREN LA
Caravan Park

33 | Cockpit
Quickswood

6 | Icknield Way Path | CLOTHALL RD | Bird Hill | Icknield Way Path
Windmill Hill
Welbury Farm

5 | Weston Hills | Clothall Bury

32 | Newfield Hill
Ashanger Hill

4 | Green Grove | Clothall
Hickman's Hill

3 | Bush Wood | The Barley Mow (PH)

31

2 | Green End
Darnall's Hall Farm
Mill Farm | Weston Windmill (dis)
Old Farm | PH

1 | POST OFFICE ROW | Weston | Weston Bury
Weston Junior Mixed Infant Sch | Oakley's Farm

30 | Town Farm | Works | Recn Gd | Church End
Manor House

25 A B 26 C D 27 E F

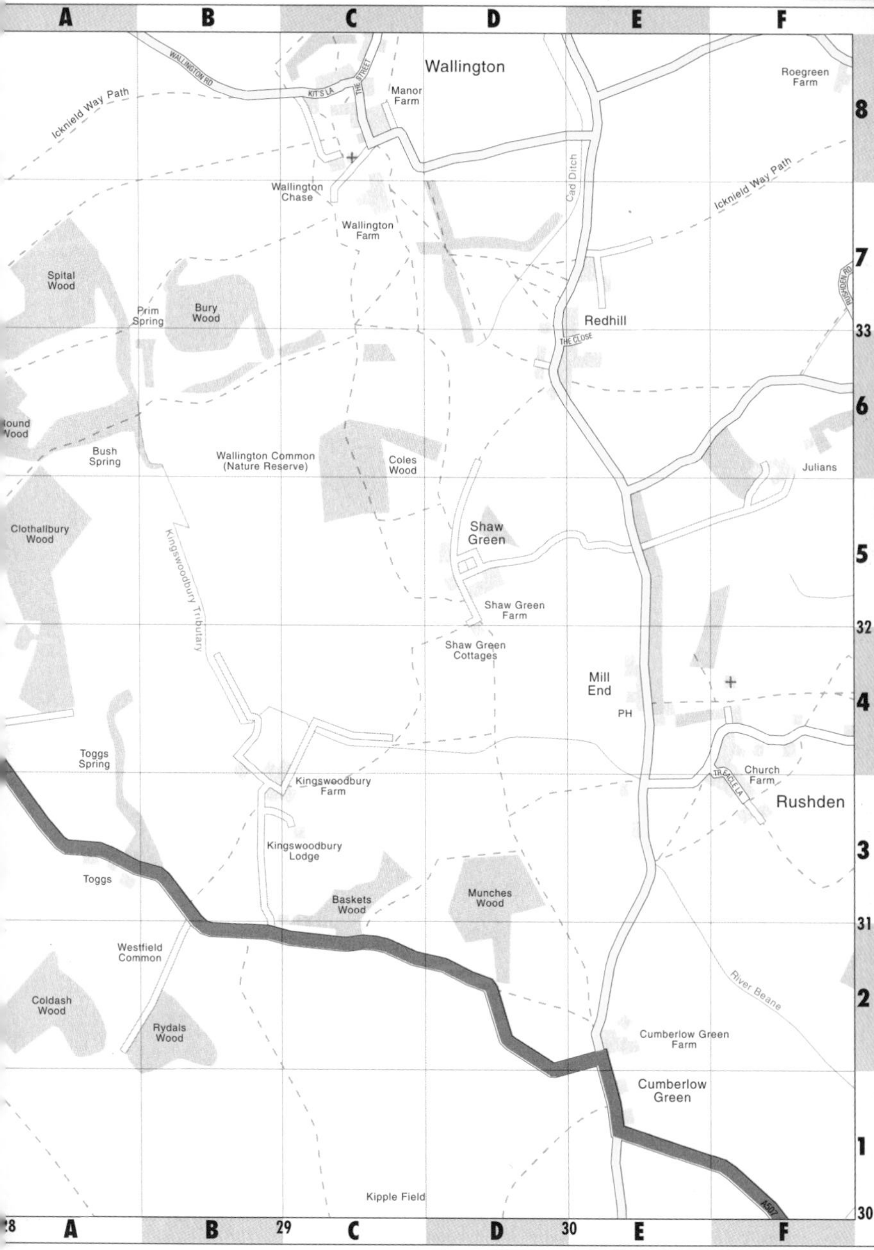

A    B    C    D    E    F

Wallington

Roegreen
Farm

Icknield Way Path

Manor
Farm

8

Wallington
Chase

Icknield Way Path

Wallington
Farm

7

Spital
Wood

Prim
Spring

Bury
Wood

Redhill

Cad Ditch

THE CLOSE

33

Round
Wood

Bush
Spring

Wallington Common
(Nature Reserve)

Coles
Wood

6

Julians

Clothallbury
Wood

Shaw
Green

5

Kingswoodbury Tributary

Shaw Green
Farm

32

Shaw Green
Cottages

Mill
End

PH

4

Toggs
Spring

Kingswoodbury
Farm

Church
Farm

TRACKLEY

Rushden

Toggs

Kingswoodbury
Lodge

3

Baskets
Wood

Munches
Wood

31

Westfield
Common

River Beane

2

Coldash
Wood

Rydals
Wood

Cumberlow Green
Farm

Cumberlow
Green

1

Kipple Field

A    B    C    D    E    F

28    29    30    30

A507

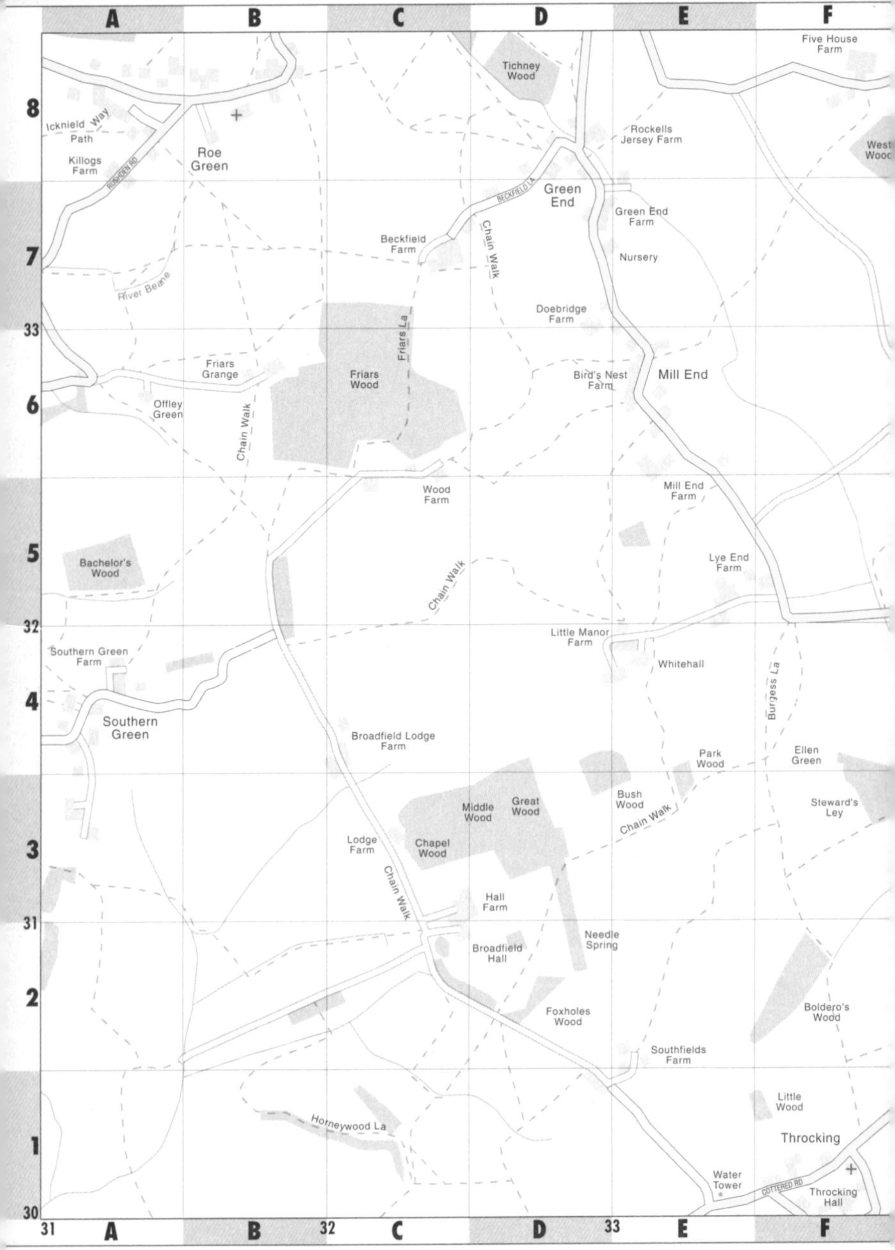

**A**    **B**    **C**    **D**    **E**    **F**

Five House Farm

Tichney Wood

**8**

Icknield Way Path

Killogs Farm

Roe Green

Rockells Jersey Farm

West Wood

Green End

Green End Farm

**7**

Beckfield Farm

Chain Walk

Nursery

River Beane

Doebridge Farm

**33**

Friars Grange

Friars Wood

Friars La

Bird's Nest Farm

Mill End

**6**

Offley Green

Chain Walk

Wood Farm

Mill End Farm

**5**

Bachelor's Wood

Chain Walk

Lye End Farm

**32**

Southern Green Farm

Little Manor Farm

Whitehall

Burgess La

**4**

Southern Green

Broadfield Lodge Farm

Park Wood

Ellen Green

Middle Wood

Great Wood

Bush Wood

Chain Walk

Steward's Ley

**3**

Lodge Farm

Chapel Wood

Chain Walk

Hall Farm

**31**

Broadfield Hall

Needle Spring

**2**

Foxholes Wood

Southfields Farm

Boldero's Wood

Little Wood

**1**

Horneywood La

Throcking

Water Tower

Throcking Hall

COTTERED RD

**30**

**31**   **A**    **B**   **32**   **C**    **D**   **33**   **E**    **F**

16
28

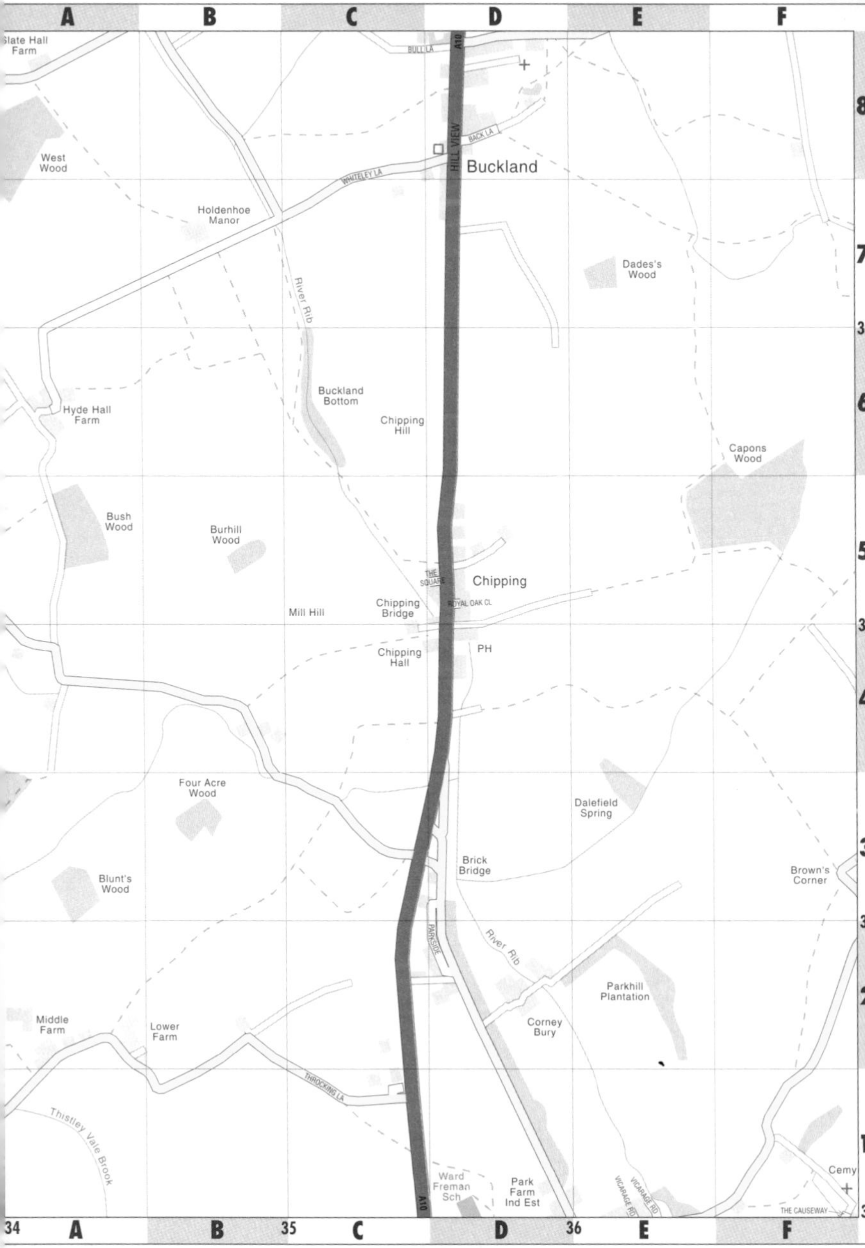
A
B
C
D
E
F
Slate Hall Farm
BULL LA
A10
HILL VIEW
BACK LA
West Wood
WHITELEY LA
Buckland
Holdenhoe Manor
Dades's Wood
River Rib
Buckland Bottom
Chipping Hill
Hyde Hall Farm
Capons Wood
Bush Wood
Burhill Wood
THE SQUARE
Chipping
ROYAL OAK CL
Chipping Bridge
Mill Hill
Chipping Hall
PH
Four Acre Wood
Dalefield Spring
Brick Bridge
Blunt's Wood
Brown's Corner
PARKSIDE
River Rib
Parkhill Plantation
Corney Bury
Middle Farm
Lower Farm
THROCKING LA
Thistley Vale Brook
Ward Freman Sch
Park Farm Ind Est
VICARAGE RD
VICARAGE RD
Cemy
THE CAUSEWAY
8
7
33
6
5
32
4
3
31
2
1
30
34
35
36

40
28

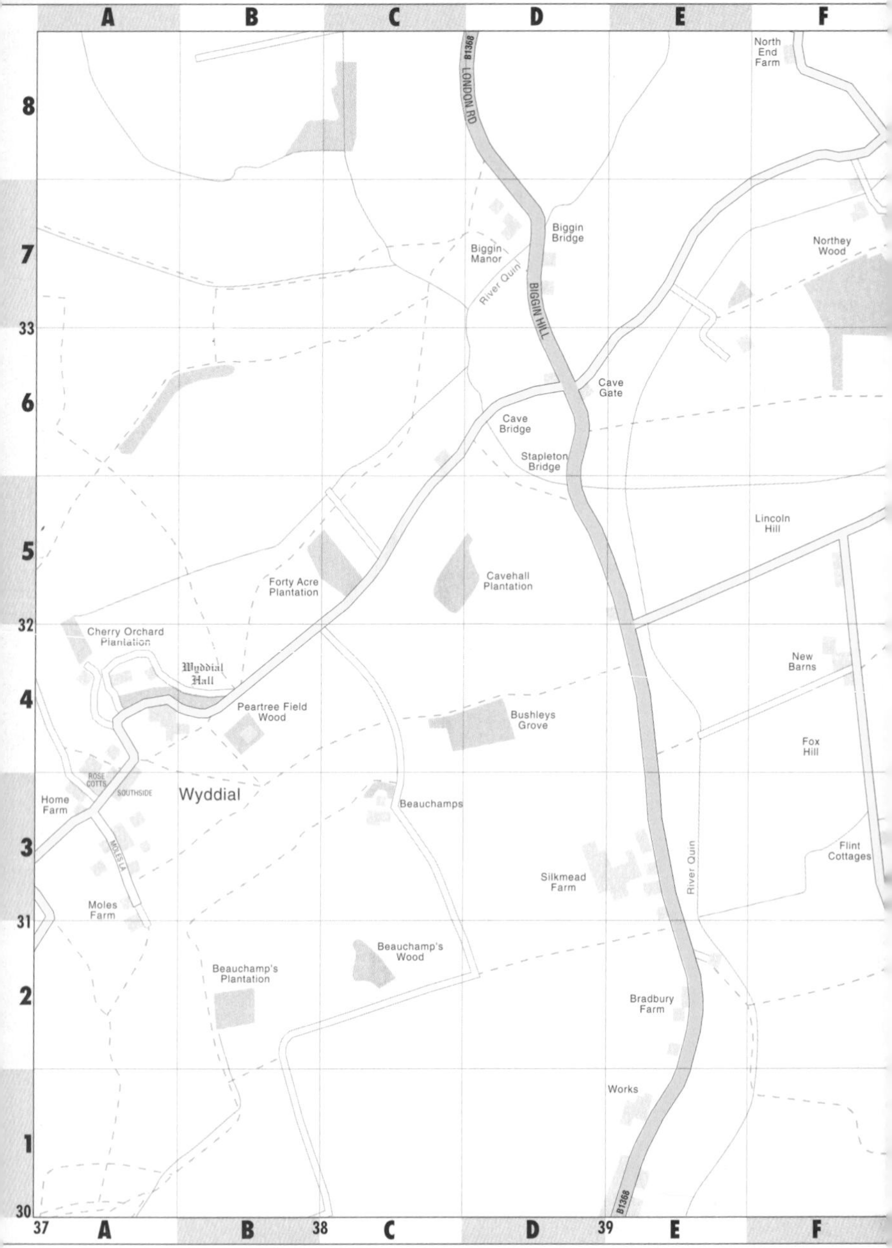

8

7

33

6

5

32

4

3

31

2

1

30

A B C D E F

North End Farm

Biggin Bridge

Northey Wood

Biggin Manor

River Quin

BIGGIN HILL

A1060 LONDON RD

Cave Gate

Cave Bridge

Stapleton Bridge

Lincoln Hill

Forty Acre Plantation

Cavehall Plantation

Cherry Orchard Plantation

New Barns

Wyddial Hall

Peartree Field Wood

Bushleys Grove

Fox Hill

ROSE COTTS

Home Farm

SOUTHSIDE

Wyddial

Beauchamps

Flint Cottages

Moles Farm

Silkmead Farm

River Quin

Beauchamp's Wood

Beauchamp's Plantation

Bradbury Farm

Works

B1368

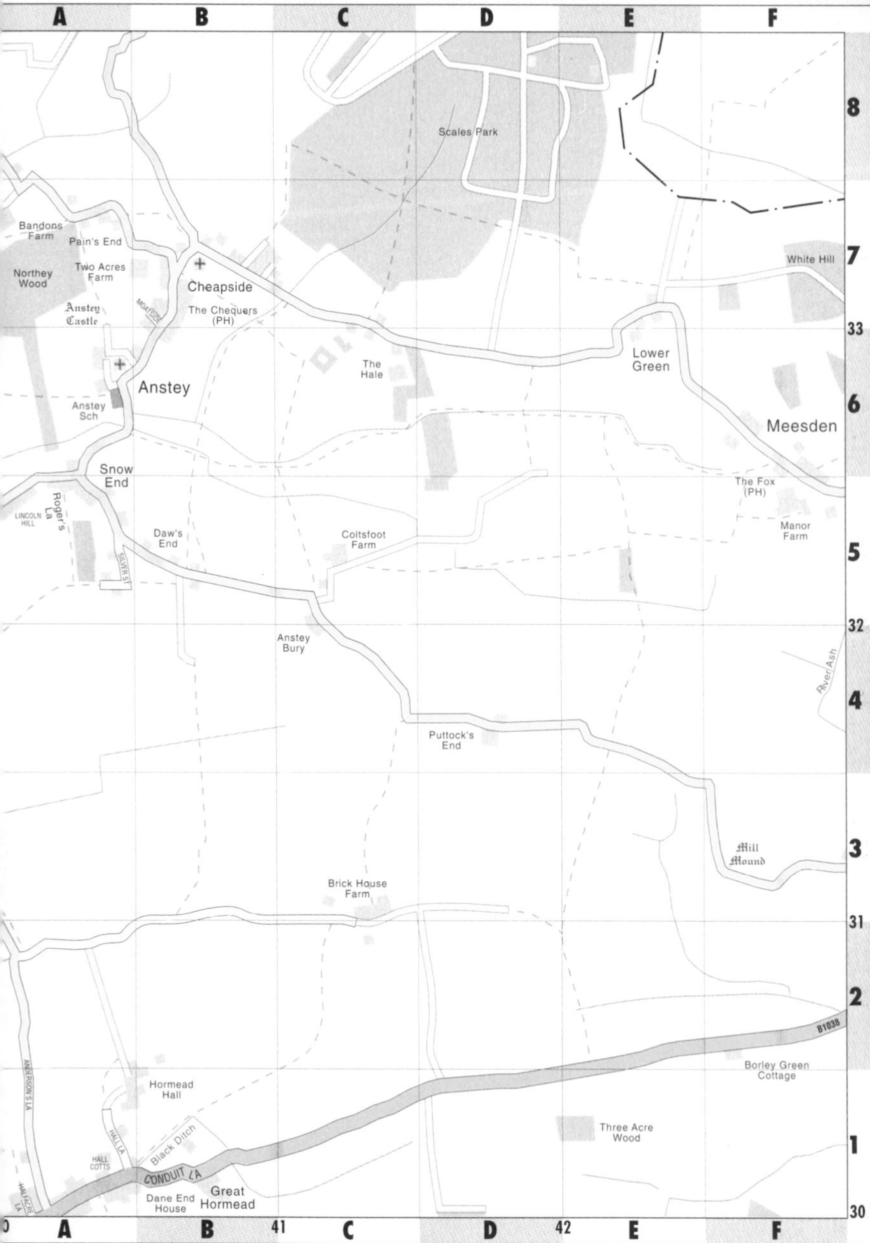
A
B
C
D
E
F
8
7
33
6
5
32
4
3
31
2
1
30
41
42
Scales Park
Bandons Farm
Pain's End
Northey Wood
Two Acres Farm
Cheapside
The Chequers (PH)
Anstey Castle
MOATSIDE
White Hill
Anstey
Anstey Sch
The Hale
Lower Green
Meesden
Snow End
The Fox (PH)
LINCOLN HILL
Roger's La
Daw's End
Coltsfoot Farm
Manor Farm
SILVER ST
Anstey Bury
River Ash
Puttock's End
Mill Mound
Brick House Farm
B1038
ANDERSON'S LA
Hormead Hall
Borley Green Cottage
Three Acre Wood
Black Ditch
HALL LA
HALL COTTS
CONDUIT LA
HALFACRE LA
Dane End House
Great Hormead

29

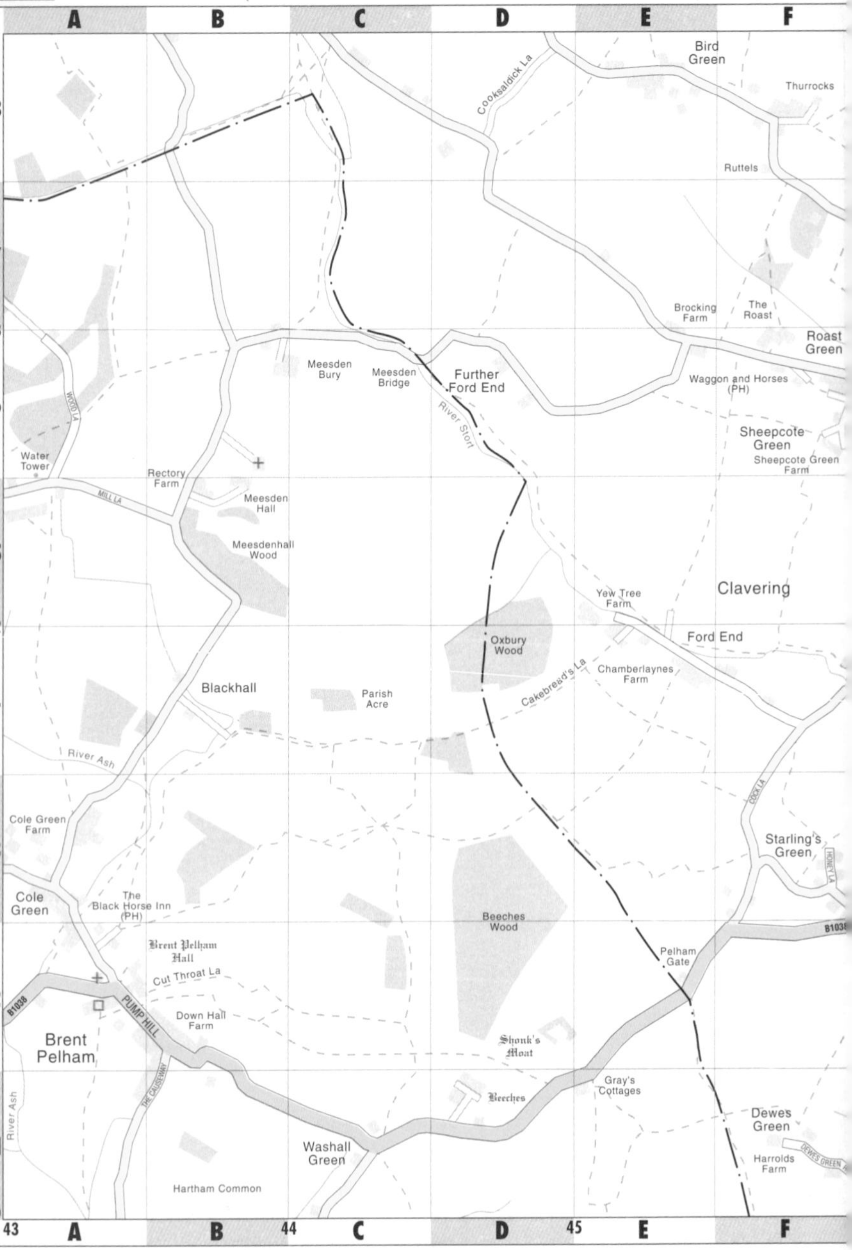

| | A | B | C | D | E | F |
|---|---|---|---|---|---|---|

**8**

Cooksaldock La

Bird Green

Thurrocks

Ruttels

**7**

Brocking Farm

The Roast

**33**

Meesden Bury

Meesden Bridge

Further Ford End

Roast Green

Waggon and Horses (PH)

**6**

River Stort

Sheepcote Green

Sheepcote Green Farm

Water Tower

WOOD LA

Rectory Farm

MILL LA

Meesden Hall

Meesdenhall Wood

**5**

Clavering

**32**

Yew Tree Farm

Oxbury Wood

Ford End

Cakebread's La

Chamberlaynes Farm

**4**

Blackhall

Parish Acre

River Ash

Cole Green Farm

**3**

Starling's Green

**31**

Cole Green

The Black Horse Inn (PH)

Brent Pelham Hall

Cut Throat La

Beeches Wood

Pelham Gate

B1038

**2**

B1038

PUMP HILL

Down Hall Farm

Brent Pelham

THE CAUSEWAY

Shonk's Moat

Beeches

Gray's Cottages

Dewes Green

**1**

River Ash

Washall Green

Harrolds Farm

**30**

Hartham Common

| 43 | A | | B | 44 | C | | D | 45 | E | | F |
|---|---|---|---|---|---|---|---|---|---|---|---|

29
43

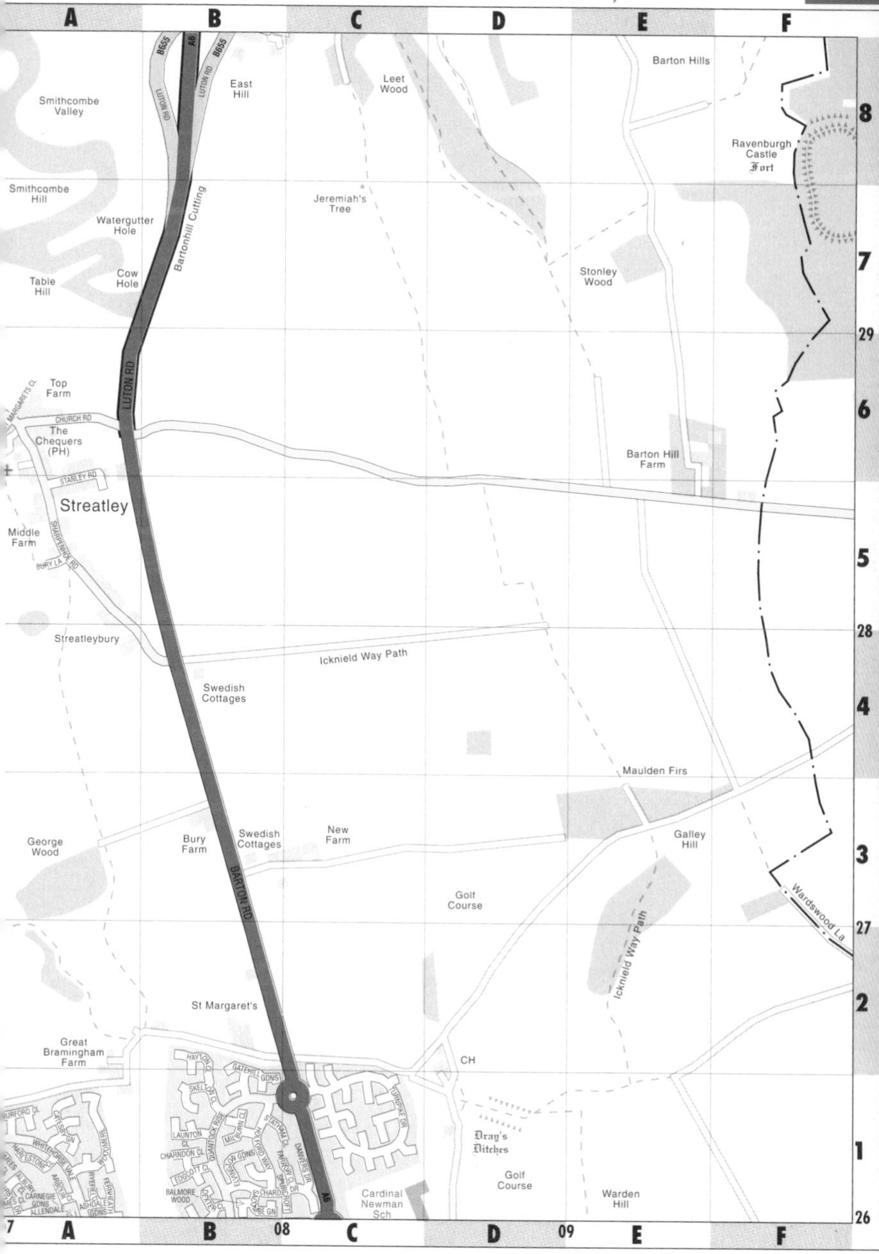

| A | B | C | D | E | F |

Barton Hills

Smithcombe
Valley

East Hill

Leet
Wood

Ravenburgh
Castle
Fort

**8**

Smithcombe
Hill

Watergutter
Hole

Jeremiah's
Tree

Stonley
Wood

**7**

Table
Hill

Cow
Hole

Bartonhill Cutting

**29**

Top
Farm

LUTON RD

CHURCH RD

Barton Hill
Farm

**6**

The
Chequers
(PH)

STANLEY RD

Streatley

Middle
Farm

BURY LA

**5**

Streatleybury

Icknield Way Path

**28**

Swedish
Cottages

**4**

Maulden Firs

George
Wood

Bury
Farm

Swedish
Cottages

New
Farm

Galley
Hill

**3**

Wardswood La

Golf
Course

Icknield Way Path

**27**

St Margaret's

**2**

Great
Bramingham
Farm

CH

Drag's
Ditches

Cardinal
Newman
Sch

Golf
Course

Warden
Hill

**1**

BALMORE
WOOD

**26**

| A | | B | 08 | C | | D | 09 | E | | F |

**7**

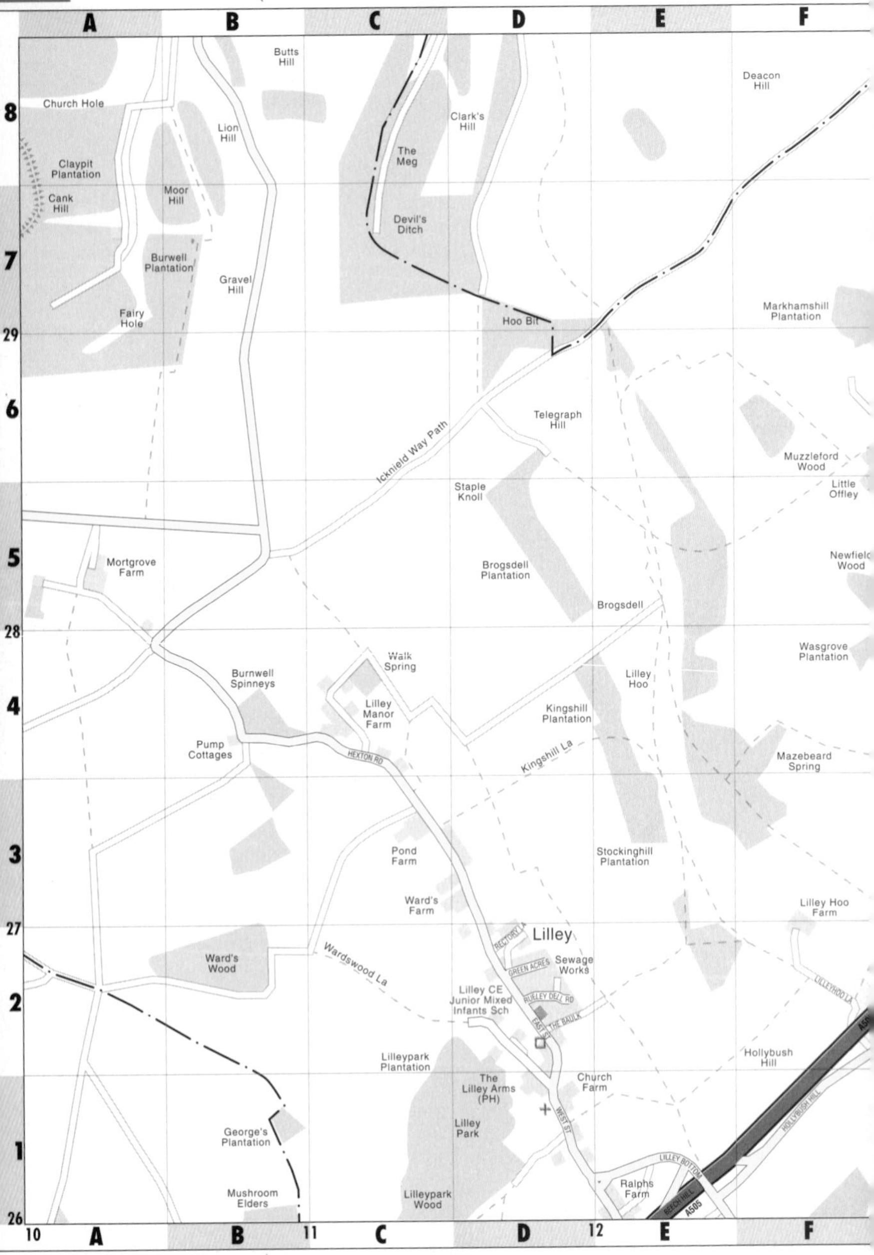
A
B
C
D
E
F
8
7
29
6
5
28
4
3
27
2
1
26
10
11
12
Church Hole
Claypit Plantation
Cank Hill
Butts Hill
Lion Hill
Moor Hill
Burwell Plantation
Gravel Hill
Fairy Hole
The Meg
Devil's Ditch
Clark's Hill
Deacon Hill
Hoo Bit
Markhamshill Plantation
Telegraph Hill
Icknield Way Path
Muzzleford Wood
Little Offley
Staple Knoll
Newfield Wood
Mortgrove Farm
Brogsdell Plantation
Brogsdell
Wasgrove Plantation
Walk Spring
Burnwell Spinneys
Lilley Hoo
Lilley Manor Farm
Kingshill Plantation
Pump Cottages
HEXTON RD
Kingshill La
Mazebeard Spring
Pond Farm
Stockinghill Plantation
Ward's Farm
Lilley Hoo Farm
Lilley
RECTORY LA
Ward's Wood
Wardswood La
GREEN ACRES
Sewage Works
Lilley CE Junior Mixed Infants Sch
RUELEY DELL RD
THE BAULK
EAST ST
LILLEYHOO LA
Hollybush Hill
Lilleypark Plantation
The Lilley Arms (PH)
Church Farm
HOLLYBUSH HILL
WEST ST
George's Plantation
Lilley Park
LILLEY BOTTOM
Ralphs Farm
Mushroom Elders
Lilleypark Wood
BEECH HILL
A505

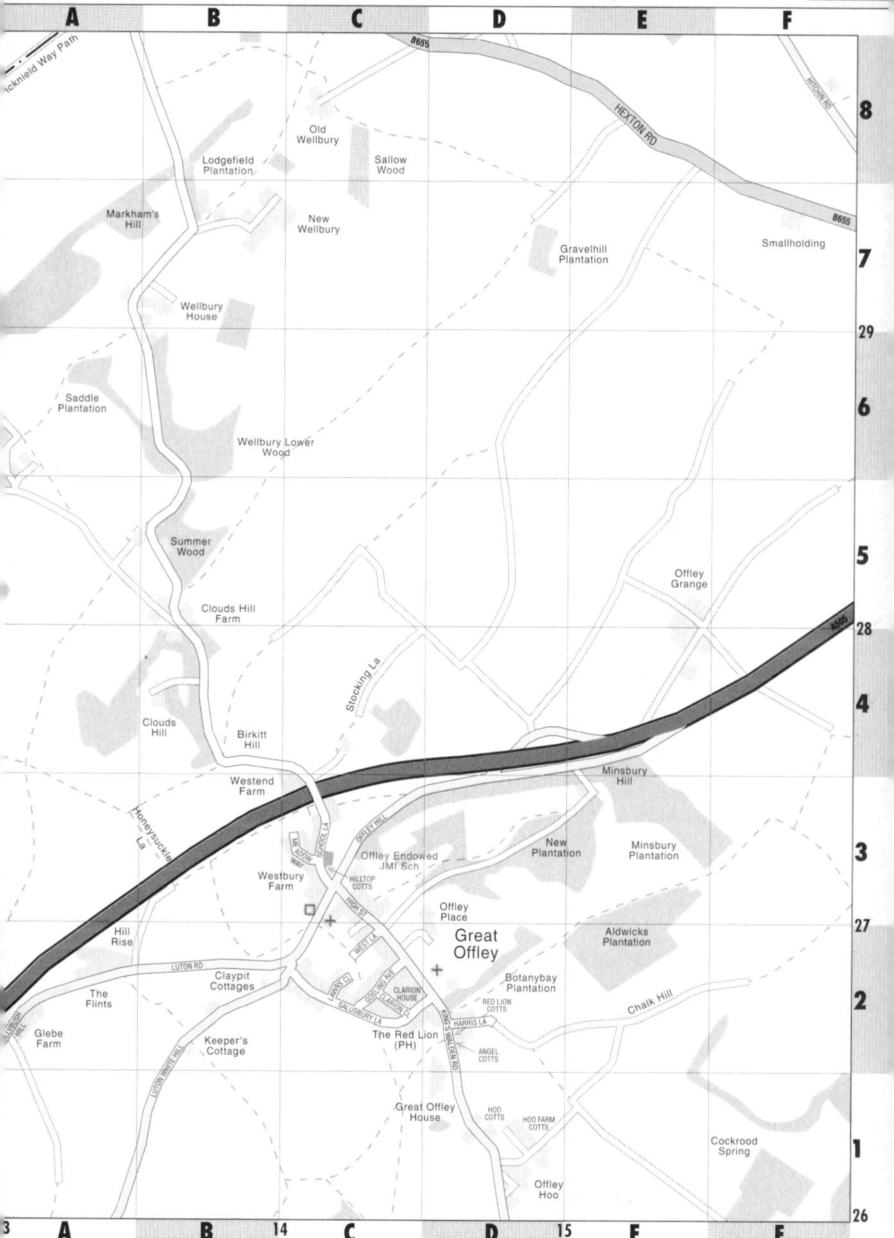

A B C D E F

8

Icknield Way Path

B655

Old Wellbury

Lodgefield Plantation

Sallow Wood

HEXTON RD

B655

Markham's Hill

New Wellbury

Gravelhill Plantation

Smallholding

7

Wellbury House

29

Saddle Plantation

Wellbury Lower Wood

6

Summer Wood

Offley Grange

5

Clouds Hill Farm

A505

28

Stocking La

4

Clouds Hill

Birkitt Hill

Westend Farm

Minsbury Hill

Honeysuckle La

Offley Endowed JMI Sch

New Plantation

Minsbury Plantation

3

Westbury Farm

HILLTOP COTTS

Hill Rise

Offley Place

Great Offley

Aldwicks Plantation

27

LUTON RD

Claypit Cottages

SALISBURY LA

CLARION HOUSE

Botanybay Plantation

RED LION COTTS

Chalk Hill

The Flints

Glebe Farm

Keeper's Cottage

The Red Lion (PH)

HARRIS LA

ANGEL COTTS

2

Great Offley House

HOO COTTS

HOO FARM COTTS

Cockrood Spring

1

Offley Hoo

26

A B 14 C D 15 E F

33
21

D8
1 MATTOCK RD
2 NORTH PL
3 BEAUMONT CL
4 CHESTNUT CT
5 SPELLBROOKE
6 BERKELEY CL
7 FOSMAN CL
8 CHALKDELL PATH

E7
1 MAPLES CT
2 BRAHAM CT
3 WEST ALLEY
4 ARCADE WLK
5 ARCADE
6 CHURCHYARD WLK
7 CHURCHGATE

F5
1 DOWER CT
2 TRAHERNE CL
3 WHITEHILL RD
4 PULTER'S WAY
5 KENDALE RD
6 WALTHAM RD

F6
1 CANNON HOUSE
2 ST ANDREW'S PL

F7
1 WOODCOTE HOUSE
2 GARRISON CT

F8
1 ST AUGUSTINE CL
2 WATER LA
3 ANDERSON'S HOUSE
4 REGAL CT
5 FORGE CL
6 GARDEN ROW

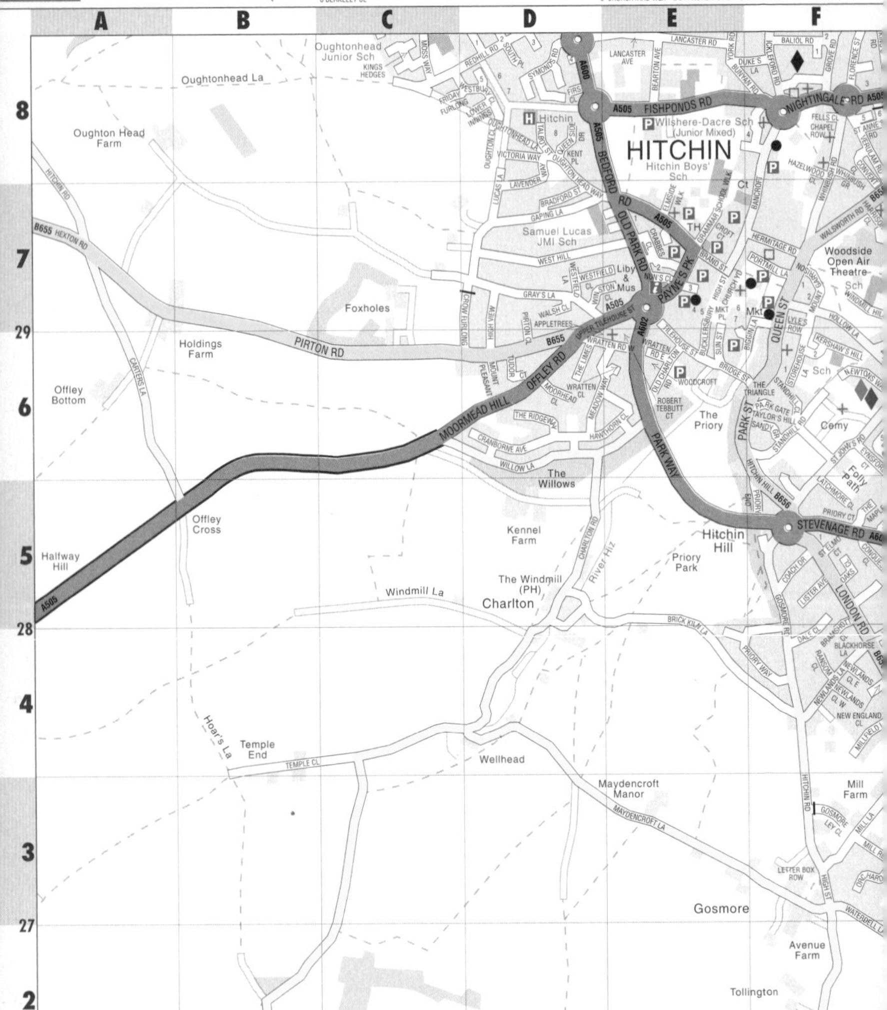


33
48

22
36

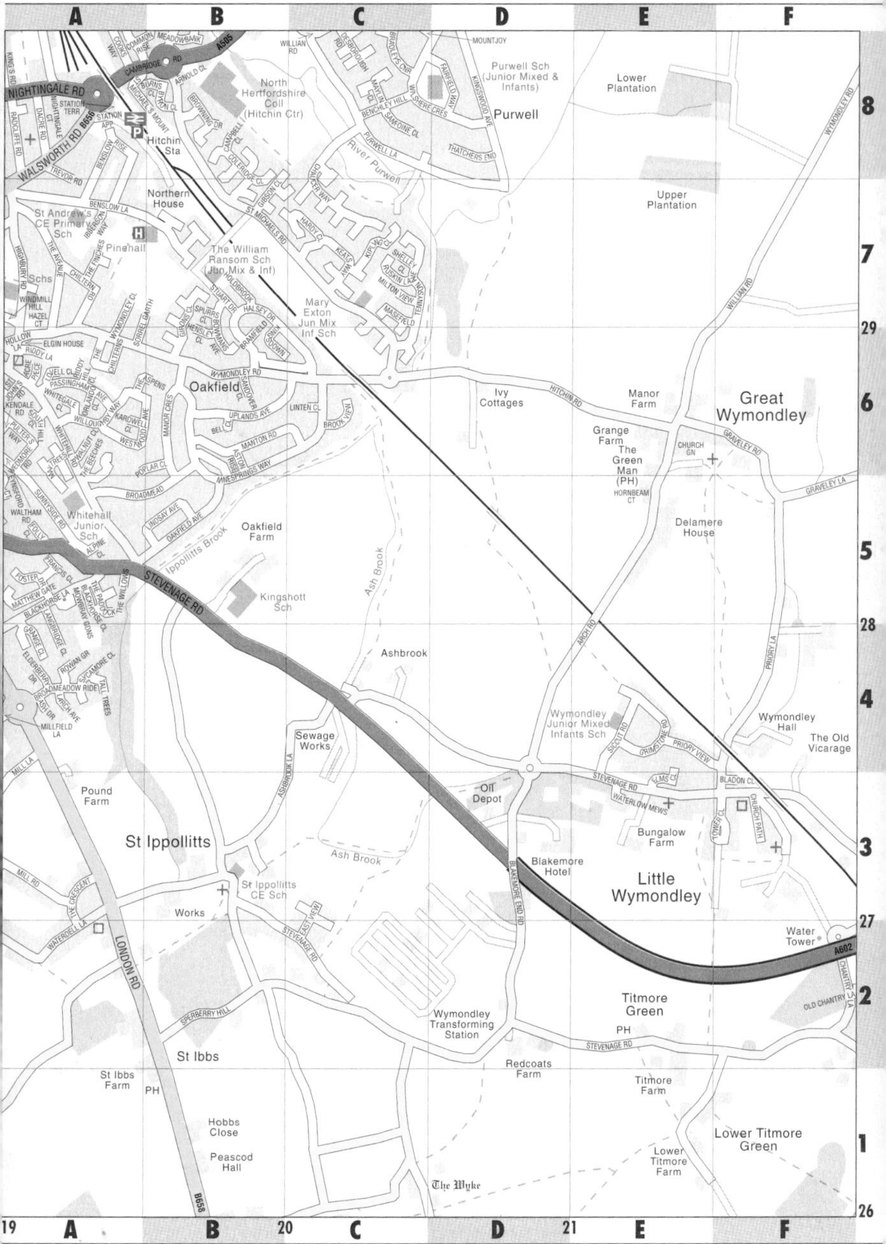
A B C D E F
8 7 6 5 4 3 2 1
29 28 27 26
19 20 21
North Hertfordshire Coll (Hitchin Ctr)
Purwell Sch (Junior Mixed & Infants)
Purwell
Lower Plantation
Upper Plantation
Hitchin Sta
Northern House
St Andrew's CE Primary Sch
Pinehall
The William Ransom Sch (Jun Mix & Inf)
Mary Exton Jun Mix Inf Sch
River Purwell
Oakfield
Ivy Cottages
Manor Farm
Great Wymondley
Grange Farm
The Green Man (PH)
Delamere House
Whitehall Junior Sch
Oakfield Farm
Ippollitts Brook
Kingshott Sch
Ash Brook
Ashbrook
Wymondley Junior Mixed Infants Sch
Wymondley Hall
The Old Vicarage
Sewage Works
Oil Depot
Pound Farm
St Ippollitts
Blakemore Hotel
Little Wymondley
Bungalow Farm
St Ippollitts CE Sch
Works
Water Tower
Titmore Green
PH
Wymondley Transforming Station
St Ibbs
St Ibbs Farm
Redcoats Farm
Titmore Farm
Hobbs Close
Peascod Hall
Lower Titmore Green
Lower Titmore Farm
The Wyke
NIGHTINGALE RD
WALSWORTH RD
CAMBRIDGE RD
A505
B656
STEVENAGE RD
LONDON RD
B658
HITCHIN RD
WYMONDLEY RD
WILLIAN RD
ARCH RD
PRIORY LA
GRAVELEY RD
GRAVELEY LA
BLAKEMORE END RD
ASHBROOK LA
SPERBERRY HILL
A602
CHANTRY LA
OLD CHANTRY

49
36

35
23

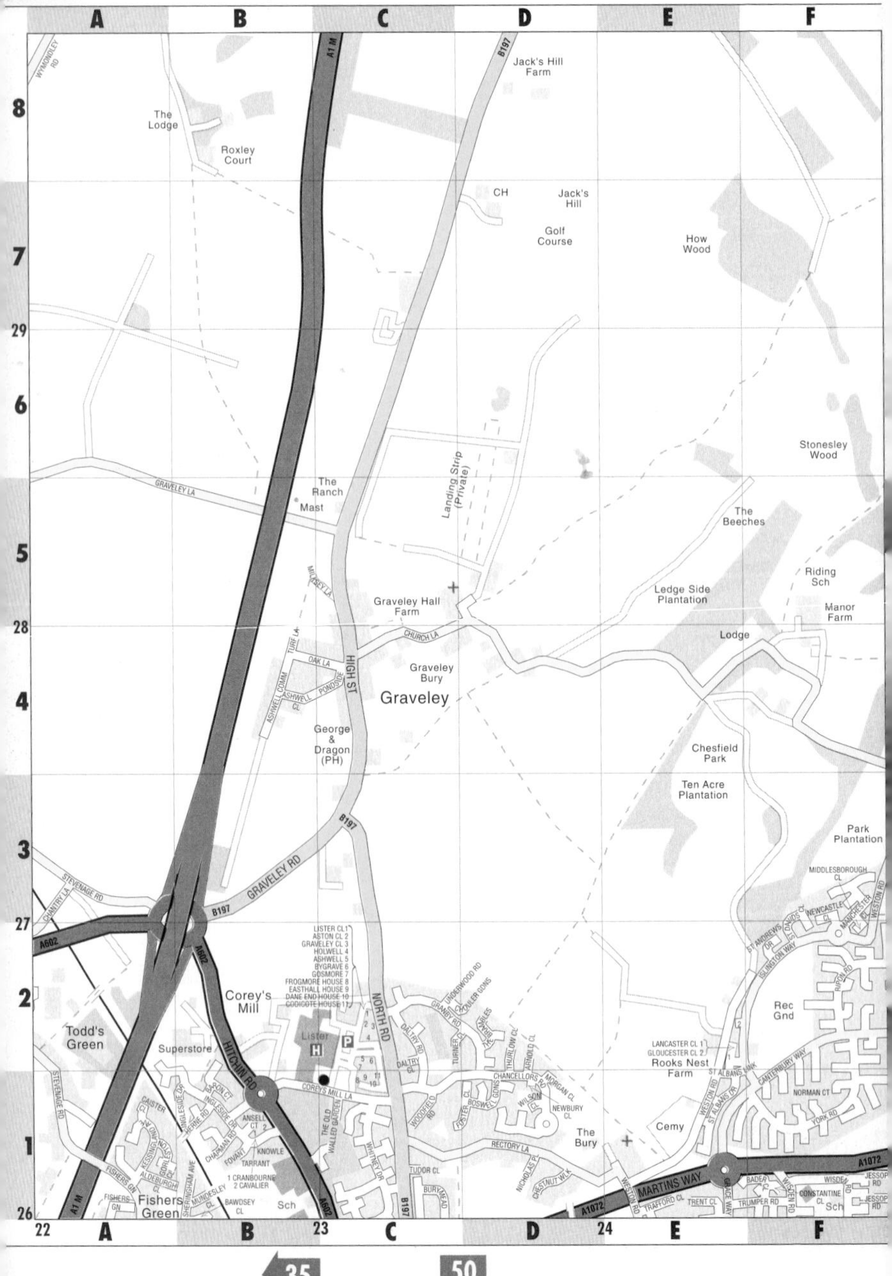
A
B
C
D
E
F
8
7
29
6
5
28
4
3
27
2
1
26
22
23
24
WYMONDLEY RD
A1 M
B197
Jack's Hill Farm
The Lodge
Roxley Court
CH
Jack's Hill
Golf Course
How Wood
Stonesley Wood
GRAVELEY LA
The Ranch
Mast
Landing Strip (Private)
The Beeches
Riding Sch
Ledge Side Plantation
Manor Farm
MILKSEY LA
Graveley Hall Farm
CHURCH LA
Lodge
TURF LA
OAK LA
HIGH ST
Graveley Bury
Graveley
ASHWELL COMM
ASHWELL CL
PONDSIDE
George & Dragon (PH)
Chesfield Park
Ten Acre Plantation
Park Plantation
B197
GRAVELEY RD
STEVENAGE RD
CHANTRY LA
B197
A602
A602
MIDDLESBOROUGH CL
NEWCASTLE CL
MANCHESTER CL
WESTON RD
ST ANDREWS DR
ST DAVIDS CL
SLINGTON WAY
RIPON RD
LISTER CL 1
ASTON CL 2
GRAVELEY CL 3
HOLWELL 4
ASHWELL 5
BYGRAVE 6
GOSMORE 7
FROGMORE HOUSE 8
EASTHALL HOUSE 9
DANE END HOUSE 10
CODICOTE HOUSE 11
NORTH RD
UNDERWOOD RD
GRANBY RD
FOWLER GDNS
BRAMBLES
Corey's Mill
Todd's Green
Superstore
Lister
H
P
HITCHIN RD
DALTRY RD
DALTRY CL
TURNER CL
THURLOW CL
ARNOLD CL
CHANCELLORS RD
MORGAN CL
Rec Gnd
LANCASTER CL 1
GLOUCESTER CL 2
Rooks Nest Farm
ST ALBANS LINK
CANTERBURY WAY
NORMAN CT
STEVENAGE RD
CAISTER
INGLESIDE DR
BARON CT
HERNE RD
COREYS MILL LA
WOODFIELD RD
FOSTER CL
BOSWELL GDNS
WILSON CL
NEWBURY CL
ST ALBANS DR
WESTON RD
YORK RD
ANSELL CT
CHAPMAN RD
KESSINGWORTH
GORLESTON
ALDEBURGH CL
FOVANT
KNOWLE
TARRANT
1 CRANBOURNE
2 CAVALIER
THE OLD WALLED GARDEN
WHITNEY DR
RECTORY LA
The Bury
Cemy
FISHERS GN
SHERINGHAM AVE
MUNDESLEY CL
BAWDSEY CL
Fishers Green
Sch
TUDOR CL
BURYMEAD
NICHOLAS PL
CHESTNUT WLK
MARTINS WAY
A1072
WESTON RD
TRAFFORD CL
TRENT CL
GRACE WAY
BADER CL
TRUMPER RD
WISDEN RD
CONSTANTINE CL
JESSOP RD
Sch
A1072

35
50

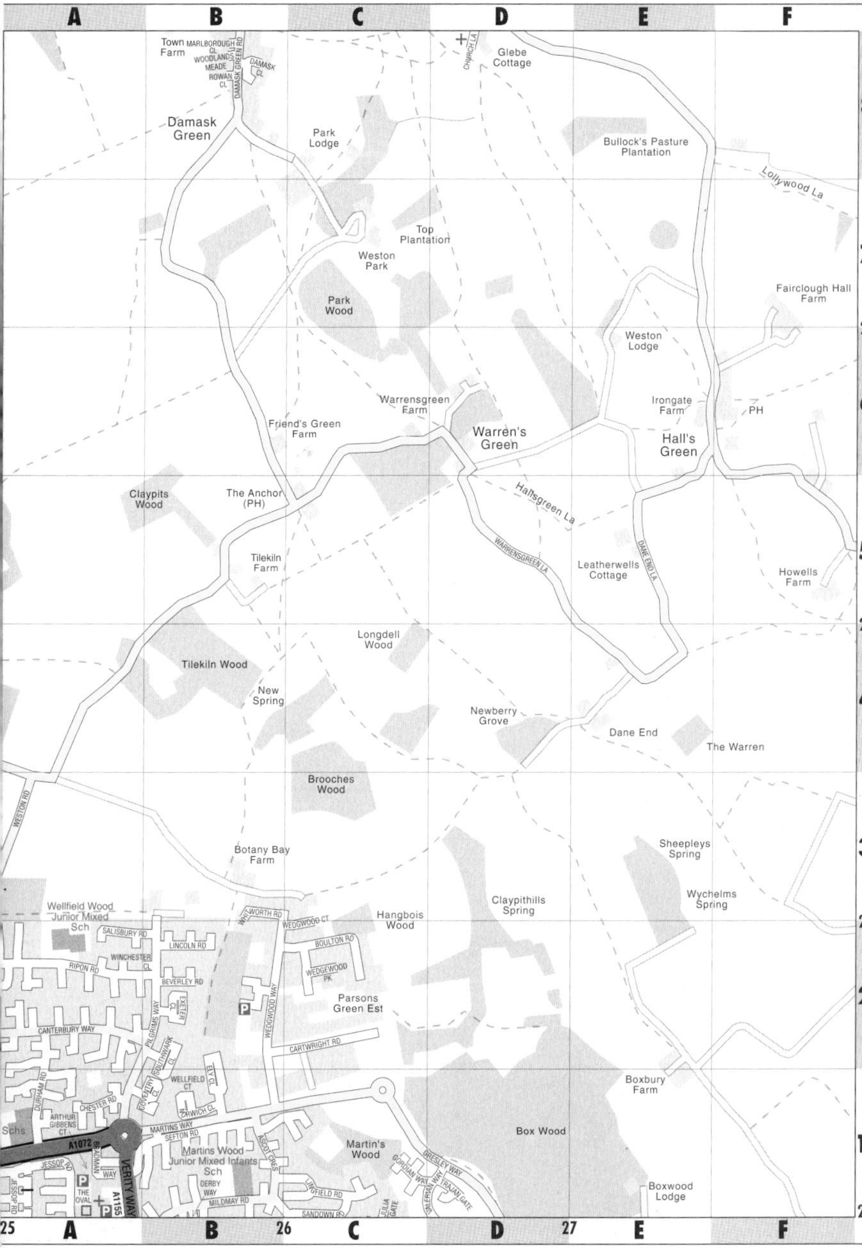
A
B
C
D
E
F
Town Farm
MARLBOROUGH CL
WOODLANDS
MEADE
ROWAN CL
DAMASK GREEN RD
DAMASK CL
CHURCH LA
Glebe Cottage
Damask Green
Park Lodge
Bullock's Pasture Plantation
Lollywood La
Top Plantation
Weston Park
Park Wood
Fairclough Hall Farm
Weston Lodge
Warrensgreen Farm
Irongate Farm
PH
Friend's Green Farm
Warren's Green
Hall's Green
Claypits Wood
The Anchor (PH)
Hallsgreen La
DANE END LA
WARRENSGREEN LA
Tilekiln Farm
Leatherwells Cottage
Howells Farm
Longdell Wood
Tilekiln Wood
New Spring
Newberry Grove
Dane End
The Warren
Brooches Wood
WESTON RD
Botany Bay Farm
Sheepleys Spring
Wellfield Wood
Junior Mixed Sch
Claypithills Spring
Wychelms Spring
Hangbois Wood
WHITWORTH RD
WEDGWOOD CT
SALISBURY RD
LINCOLN RD
BOULTON RD
WINCHESTER CL
RIPON RD
WEDGEWOOD PK
BEVERLEY RD
EXETER CL
PILGRIMS WAY
WEDGWOOD WAY
Parsons Green Est
CANTERBURY WAY
SOUTHWARK CL
CARTWRIGHT RD
WELLFIELD CT
ELY CL
DURHAM RD
COVENTRY CL
Boxbury Farm
CHESTER RD
NORWICH CL
ARTHUR GIBBENS CT
MARTINS WAY
Box Wood
Schs
SEFTON RD
A1072
BRADMAN WAY
Martin's Wood
Martins Wood Junior Mixed Infants Sch
ASCOT CRES
GRESLEY WAY
GORDIAN WAY
JESSOP RD
VERITY WAY
THE OVAL
A1155
DERBY WAY
LINGFIELD RD
VALERIAN WAY
TRAJAN GATE
Boxwood Lodge
MILDMAY RD
SANDOWN RD
JULIA GATE
8
7
29
6
5
28
4
3
27
2
1
26
25
26
27

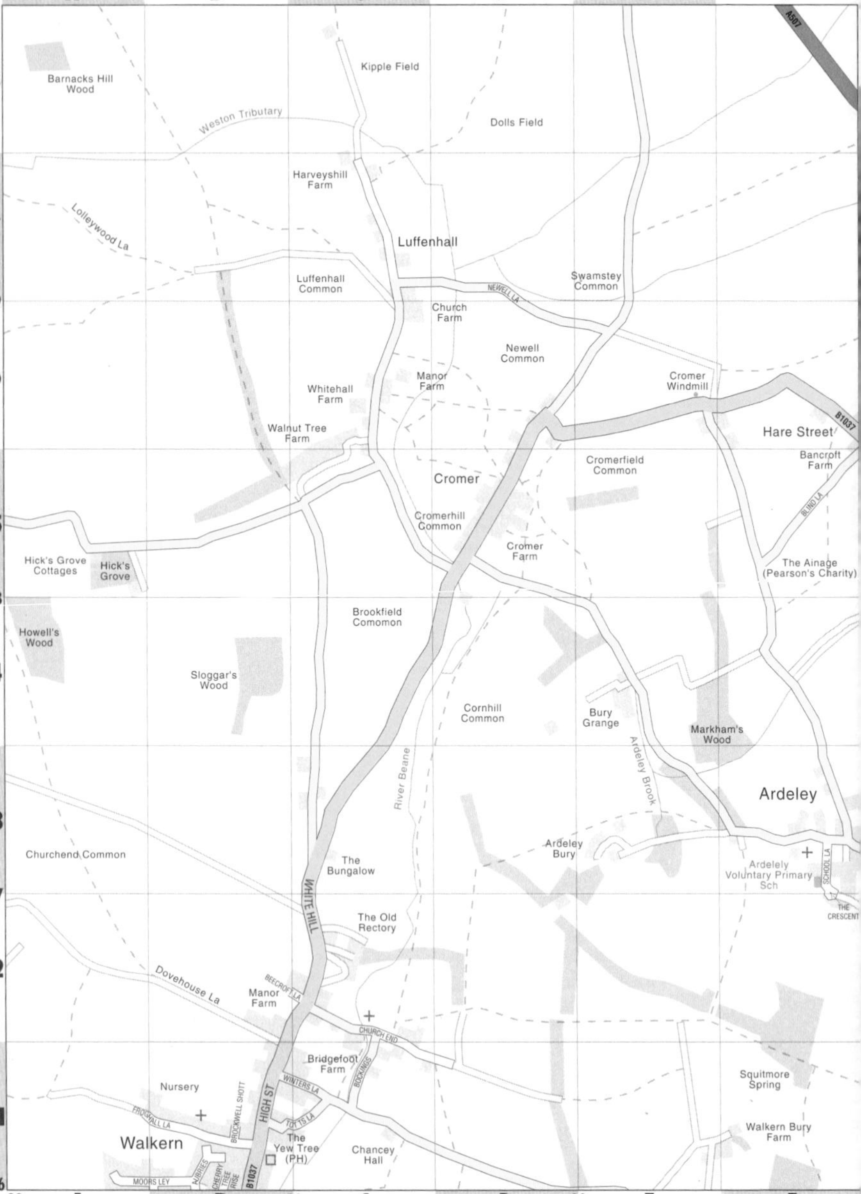
A
B
C
D
E
F
8
7
29
6
5
28
4
3
27
2
1
26
28
29
30
A507
Barnacks Hill Wood
Kipple Field
Weston Tributary
Dolls Field
Harveyshill Farm
Lolleywood La
Luffenhall
Luffenhall Common
Swamstey Common
NEWELL LA
Church Farm
Newell Common
Manor Farm
Cromer Windmill
Whitehall Farm
B1037
Walnut Tree Farm
Hare Street
Cromerfield Common
Bancroft Farm
Cromer
BLIND LA
Cromerhill Common
Hick's Grove Cottages
Hick's Grove
Cromer Farm
The Ainage (Pearson's Charity)
Brookfield Comomon
Howell's Wood
Sloggar's Wood
Cornhill Common
Bury Grange
Markham's Wood
Ardeley Brook
River Beane
Ardeley
Churchend Common
The Bungalow
Ardeley Bury
Ardeley Voluntary Primary Sch
SCHOOL LA
WHITE HILL
THE CRESCENT
The Old Rectory
Dovehouse La
BEECROFT LA
Manor Farm
CHURCH END
Bridgefoot Farm
BOCKINGS
Squitmore Spring
Nursery
BROCKWELL SHOTT
WINTERS LA
HIGH ST
FROGHALL LA
TOTTS LA
Walkern Bury Farm
Walkern
The Yew Tree (PH)
Chancey Hall
MOORS LEY
AUBRIES
CHERRY TREE RISE
B1037

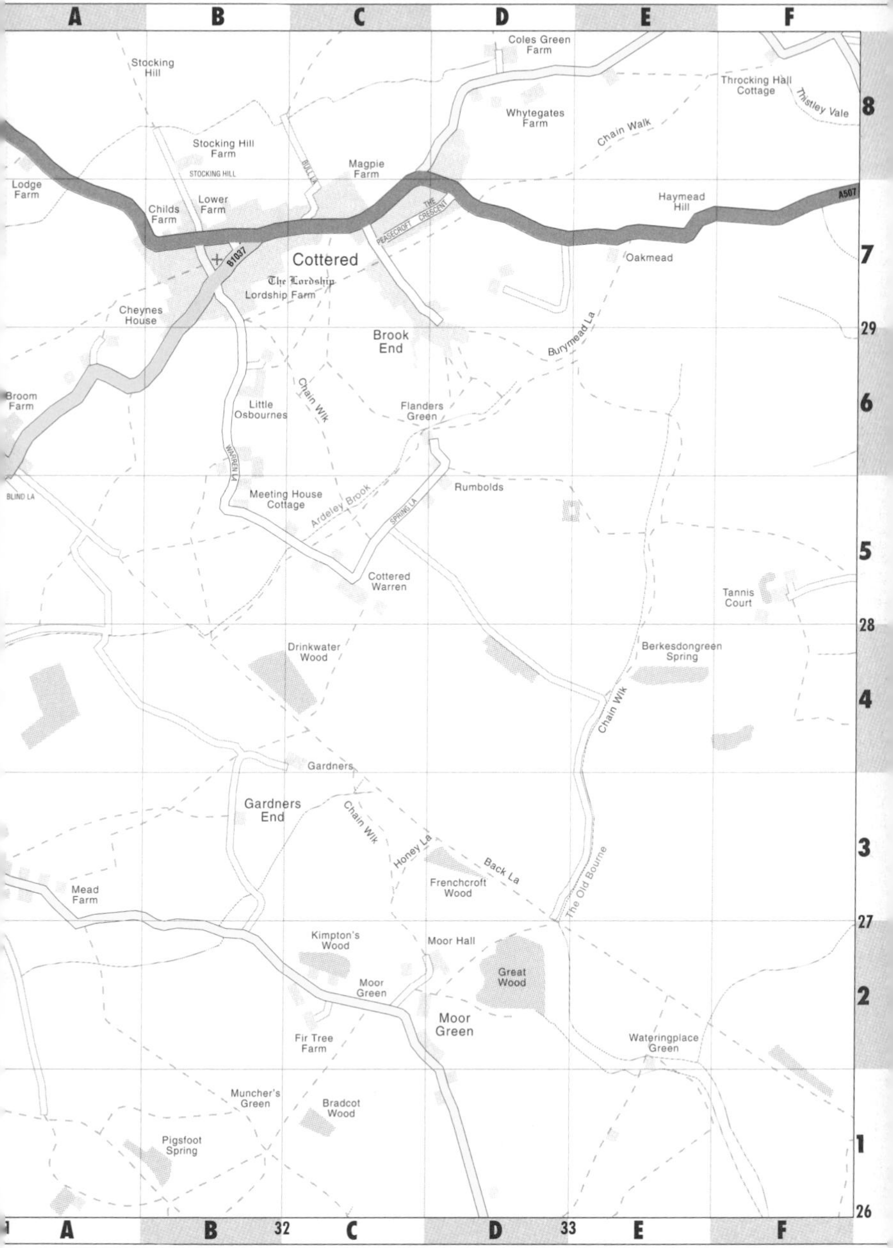
A
B
C
D
E
F
Coles Green Farm
Stocking Hill
Throcking Hall Cottage
Thistley Vale
8
Whytegates Farm
Chain Walk
Stocking Hill Farm
STOCKING HILL
BULL LA
Magpie Farm
Lodge Farm
Lower Farm
Childs Farm
Haymead Hill
A507
THE CRESCENT
PEASECROFT
B1037
Cottered
Oakmead
7
The Lordship
Lordship Farm
Cheynes House
Brook End
29
Burymead La
Broom Farm
Chain Wlk
Little Osbournes
Flanders Green
6
WARREN LA
BLIND LA
Meeting House Cottage
Rumbolds
Ardeley Brook
SPRING LA
5
Cottered Warren
Tannis Court
28
Drinkwater Wood
Berkesdongreen Spring
4
Chain Wlk
Gardners
Gardners End
Chain Wlk
3
Honey La
Back La
The Old Bourne
Frenchcroft Wood
Mead Farm
27
Kimpton's Wood
Moor Hall
Great Wood
Moor Green
2
Moor Green
Fir Tree Farm
Wateringplace Green
Muncher's Green
Bradcot Wood
1
Pigsfoot Spring
26
A
B
32
C
D
33
E
F

39
27

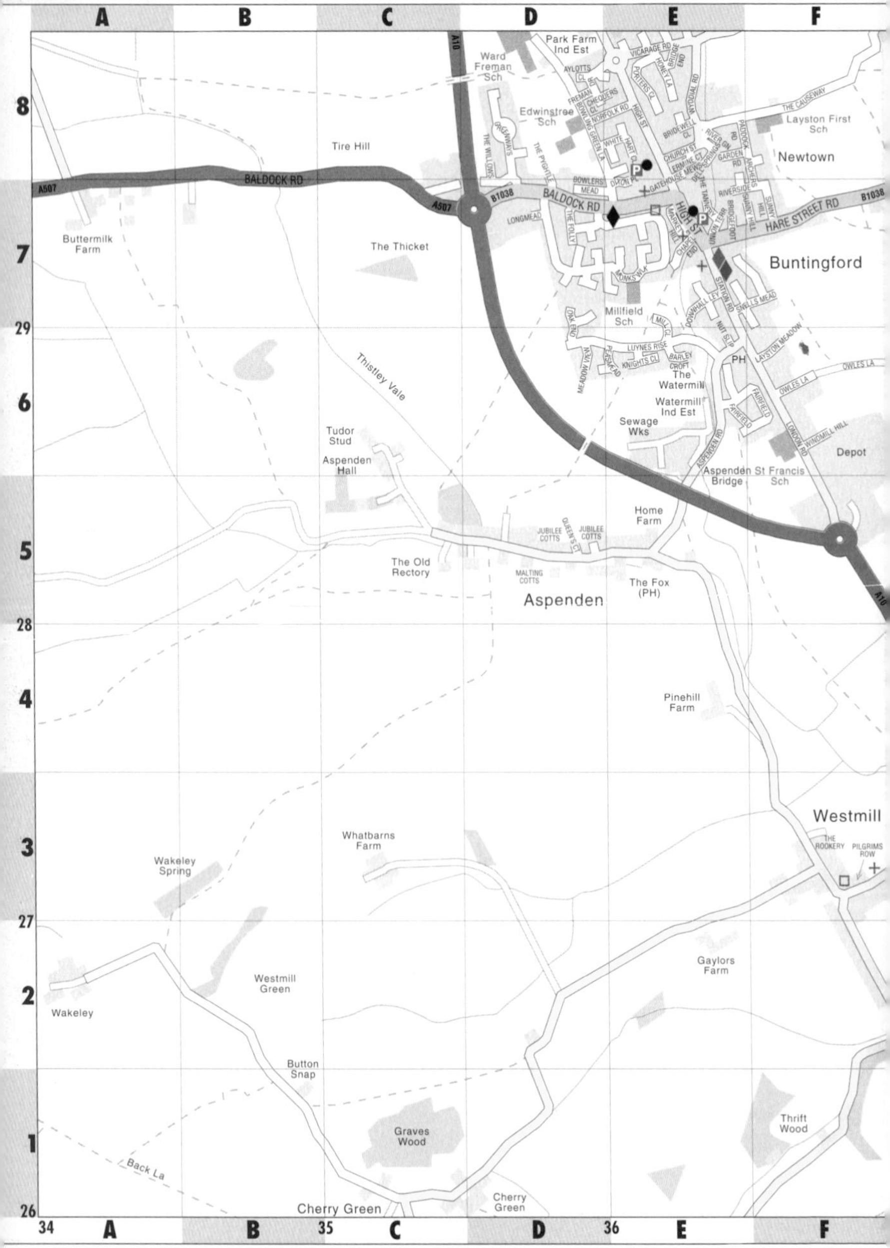
A
B
C
D
E
F
8
7
29
6
5
28
4
3
27
2
1
26
34
35
36
Park Farm
Ind Est
Ward
Freman
Sch
Edwinstree
Sch
Layston First
Sch
Newtown
Tire Hill
BALDOCK RD
A507
A10
B1038
HARE STREET RD
THE CAUSEWAY
HIGH ST
Buttermilk
Farm
The Thicket
Buntingford
Millfield
Sch
Thistley Vale
The
Watermill
Watermill
Ind Est
Sewage
Wks
PH
Depot
Tudor
Stud
Aspenden
Hall
Aspenden
Bridge
St Francis
Sch
Home
Farm
JUBILEE
COTTS
The Old
Rectory
MALTING
COTTS
The Fox
(PH)
Aspenden
Pinehill
Farm
Westmill
THE
ROOKERY
PILGRIMS
ROW
Whatbarns
Farm
Wakeley
Spring
Gaylors
Farm
Westmill
Green
Wakeley
Button
Snap
Thrift
Wood
Graves
Wood
Back La
Cherry Green
Cherry
Green

39
54

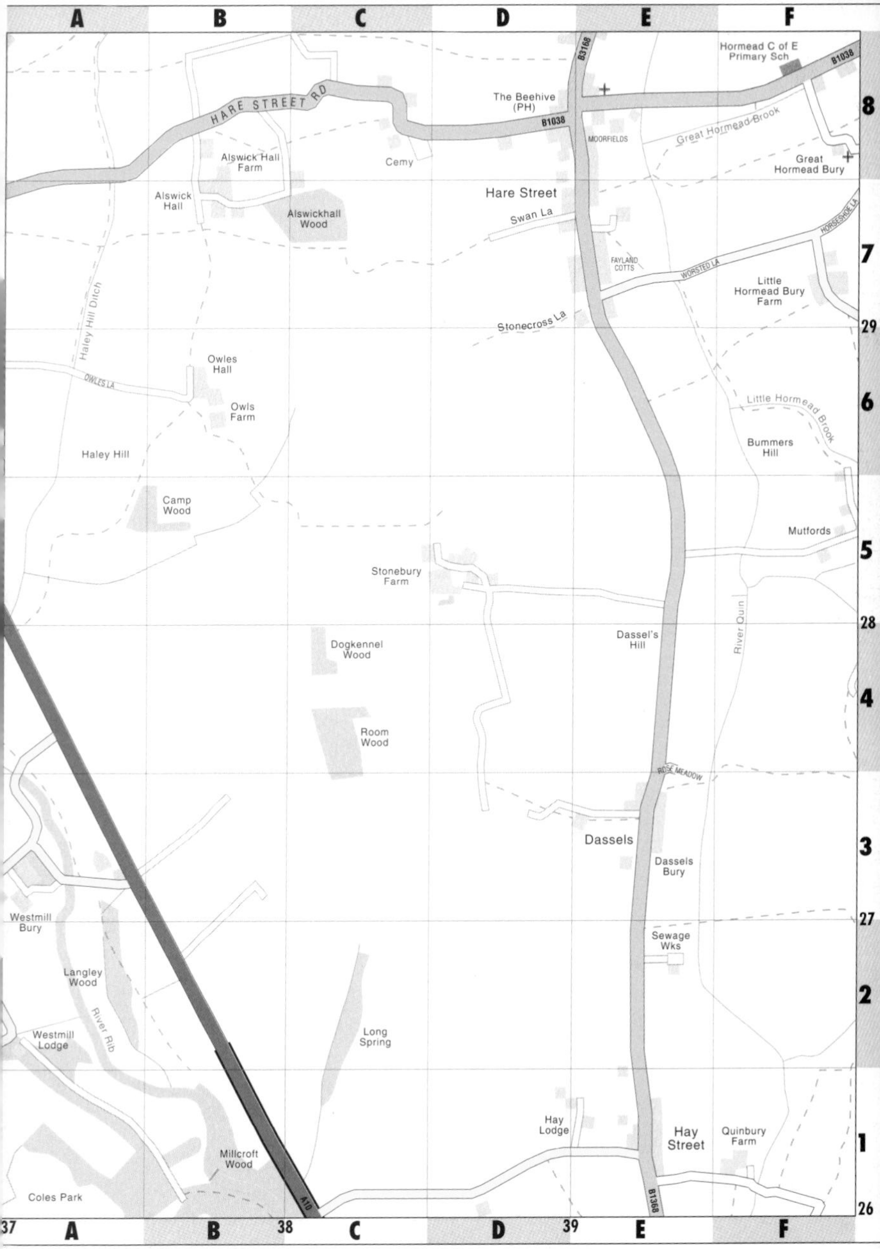

**A** **B** **C** **D** **E** **F**

HARE STREET RD

B1038

Hormead C of E
Primary Sch

B1038

The Beehive
(PH)

B1038

+

MOORFIELDS

Great Hormead Brook

8

Alswick Hall
Farm

Cemy

Great
Hormead Bury

+

Alswick
Hall

Alswickhall
Wood

Hare Street

Swan La

FAYLAND
COTTS

WORSTED LA

HORMEAD LA

Little
Hormead Bury
Farm

7

Haley Hill Ditch

Stonecross La

29

OWLES LA

Owles
Hall

Little Hormead Brook

6

Owls
Farm

Bummers
Hill

Haley Hill

Camp
Wood

Mutfords

5

Stonebury
Farm

River Quin

28

Dogkennel
Wood

Dassel's
Hill

4

Room
Wood

BECK MEADOW

Dassels

3

Westmill
Bury

Dassels
Bury

27

River Rib

Langley
Wood

Sewage
Wks

2

Westmill
Lodge

Long
Spring

A10

Hay
Lodge

Hay
Street

Quinbury
Farm

1

Millcroft
Wood

Coles Park

A10

26

37
**A** 38 **B** **C** 39 **D** **E** **F**

41
29
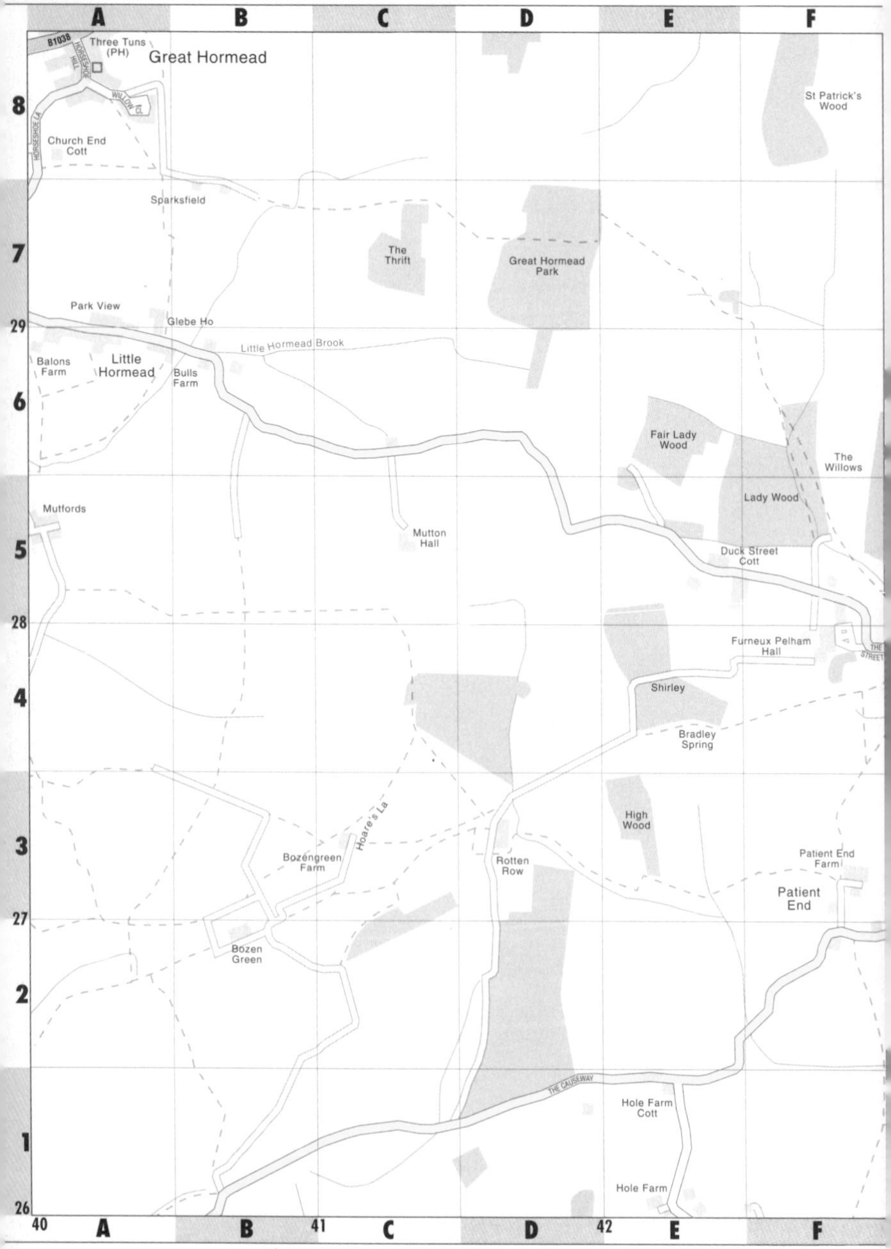
A
B
C
D
E
F
B1038
Three Tuns (PH)
Great Hormead
HORSESHOE HILL
WILLOW CL
HORSESHOE LA
Church End Cott
St Patrick's Wood
Sparksfield
The Thrift
Great Hormead Park
Park View
Glebe Ho
Little Hormead Brook
Balons Farm
Little Hormead
Bulls Farm
Fair Lady Wood
The Willows
Lady Wood
Mutfords
Mutton Hall
Duck Street Cott
Furneux Pelham Hall
THE STREET
Shirley
Bradley Spring
High Wood
Hoare's La
Bozengreen Farm
Rotten Row
Patient End Farm
Patient End
Bozen Green
THE CAUSEWAY
Hole Farm Cott
Hole Farm
8
7
29
6
5
28
4
3
27
2
1
26
40
41
42
41
56

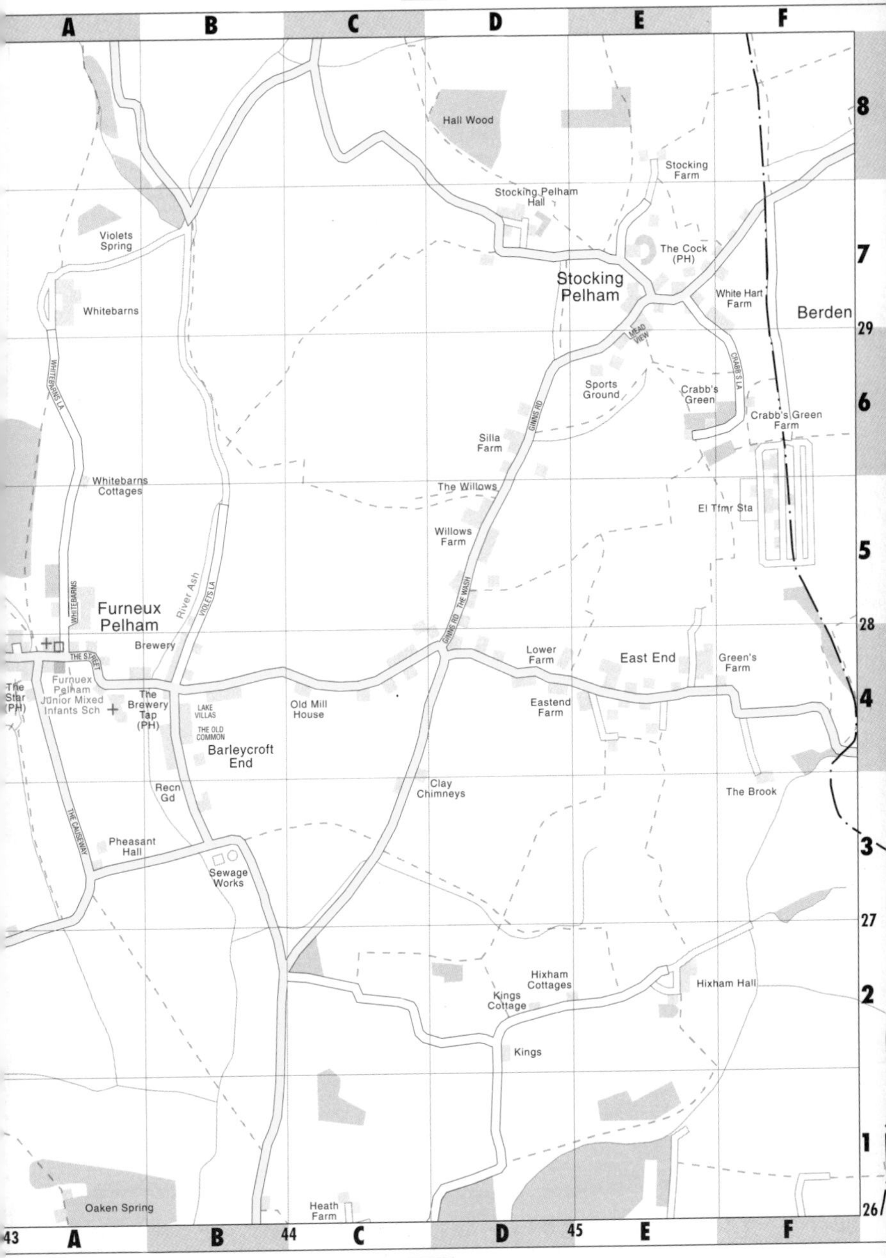

A B C D E F

8

Hall Wood

Stocking
Farm

Stocking Pelham
Hall

7

Violets
Spring

The Cock
(PH)

Stocking
Pelham

White Hart
Farm

Whitebarns

Berden

29

Sports
Ground

Crabb's
Green

6

Silla
Farm

Crabb's Green
Farm

Whitebarns
Cottages

The Willows

El Tfmr Sta

Willows
Farm

5

River Ash

Furneux
Pelham

Lower
Farm

East End

Green's
Farm

28

Brewery

THE STR...

Old Mill
House

Eastend
Farm

4

The Star
(PH)

Furneux
Pelham
Junior Mixed
Infants Sch

The Brewery
Tap
(PH)

LAKE
VILLAS

THE OLD
COMMON

The Brook

Barleycroft
End

Recn
Gd

Clay
Chimneys

3

Pheasant
Hall

27

THE CAUSEWAY

Sewage
Works

Hixham
Cottages

Hixham Hall

2

Kings
Cottage

Kings

1

Oaken Spring

Heath
Farm

26

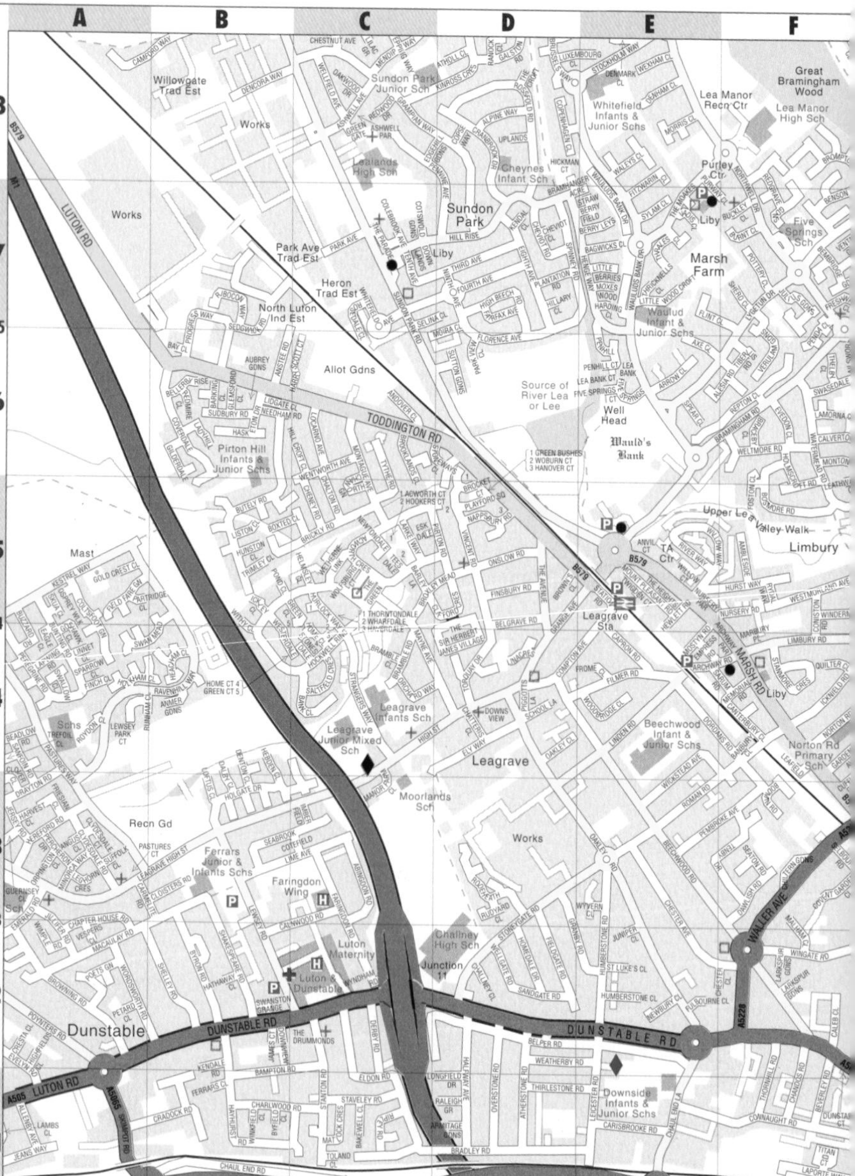
A
B
C
D
E
F
8
7
25
6
5
24
4
3
23
2
1
22
04
05
06
Willowgate Trad Est
Works
Sundon Park Junior Sch
Lealands High Sch
Cheynes Infant Sch
Sundon Park
Whitefield Infants & Junior Schs
Lea Manor Recn Ctr
Lea Manor High Sch
Great Bramingham Wood
Purley Ctr
Liby
Marsh Farm
Five Springs Sch
Park Ave Trad Est
Heron Trad Est
North Luton Ind Est
Allot Gdns
Waulud Infant & Junior Schs
Source of River Lea or Lee
Well Head
Wauld's Bank
Pirton Hill Infants & Junior Schs
TODDINGTON RD
LUTON RD
Upper Lea Valley Walk
Limbury
TA Ctr
Leagrave Sta
MARSH RD
Mast
Leagrave Infants Sch
Leagrave Junior Mixed Sch
Leagrave
Beechwood Infant & Junior Schs
Norton Rd Primary Sch
Moorlands Sch
Recn Gd
Ferrars Junior & Infants Schs
Faringdon Wing
Luton Maternity
Luton & Dunstable
Challney High Sch
Junction 11
Dunstable
DUNSTABLE RD
WALLER AVE
Downside Infants & Junior Schs
HATTERS WAY
Icknield Way Path
B579
A505
A5065
A5228
M1
CHAUL END RD

62

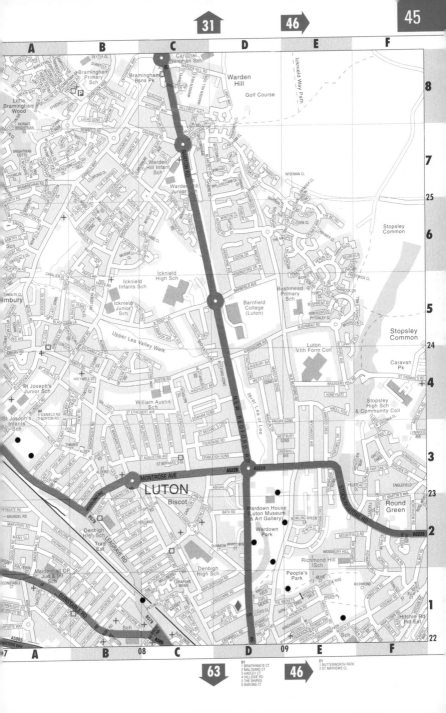

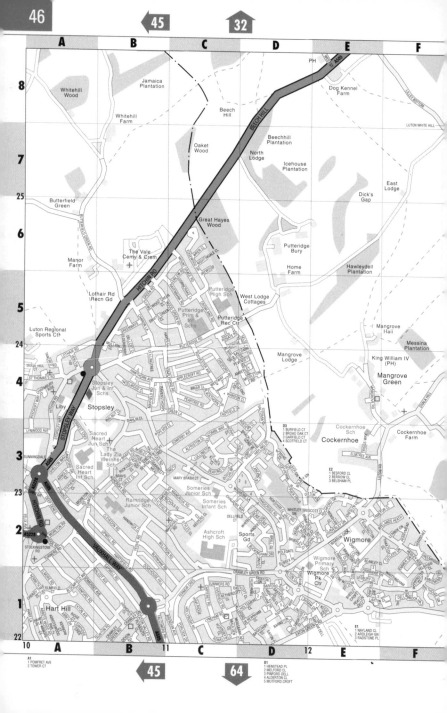

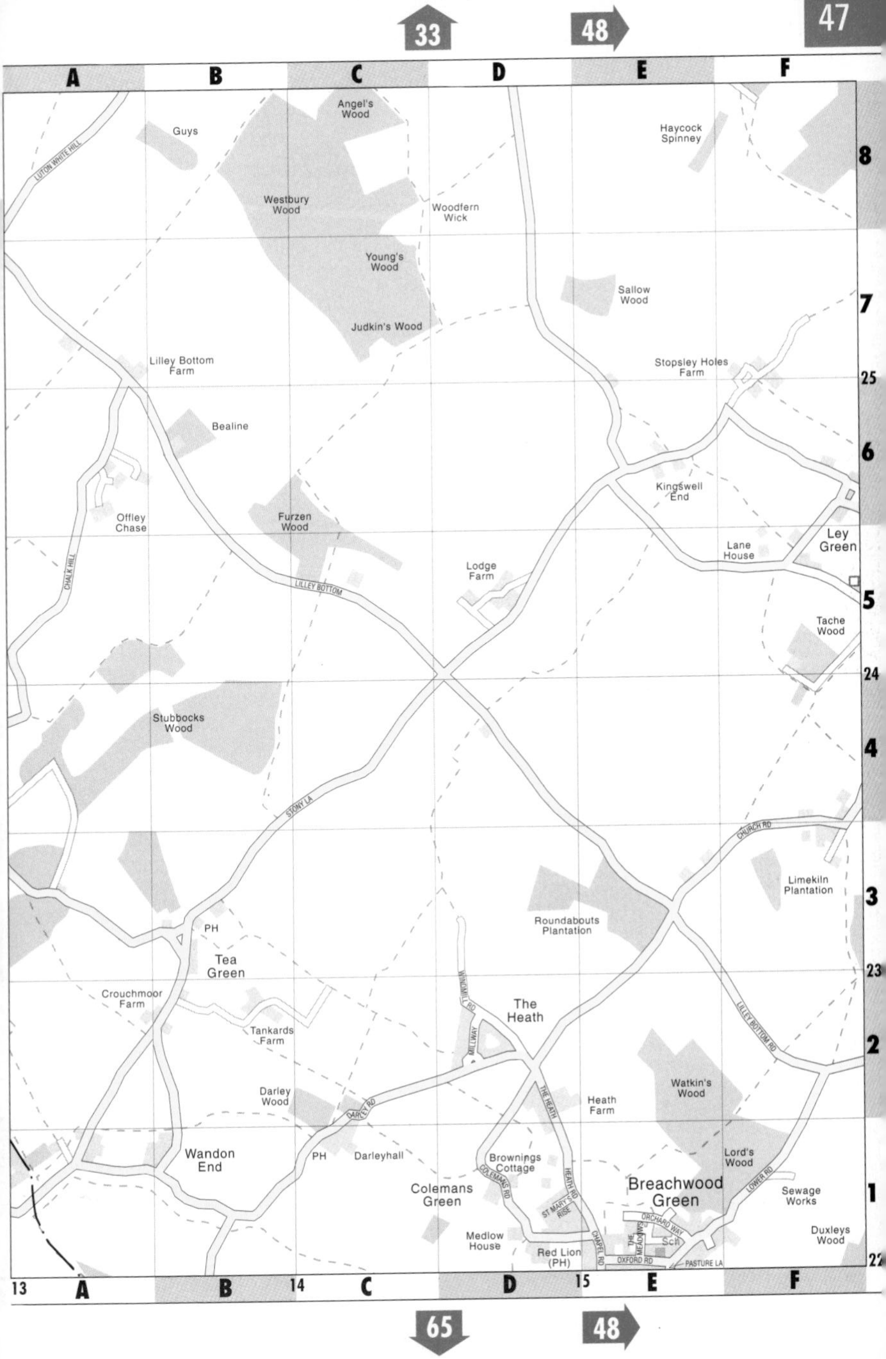

A B C D E F

8

Guys
Angel's
Wood

Haycock
Spinney

Westbury
Wood

Woodfern
Wick

Young's
Wood

Sallow
Wood

7

Judkin's Wood

Lilley Bottom
Farm

Stopsley Holes
Farm

25

Bealine

6

Kingswell
End

Offley
Chase

Furzen
Wood

Lane
House

Ley
Green

Lilley Bottom

Lodge
Farm

5

Tache
Wood

24

Stubbocks
Wood

4

STORT LA

3

Limekiln
Plantation

Roundabouts
Plantation

PH

23

Tea
Green

The
Heath

Crouchmoor
Farm

Tankards
Farm

2

Watkin's
Wood

Darley
Wood

Lord's
Wood

Wandon
End

PH

Darleyhall

The Heath

Browning's
Cottage

Heath
Farm

Breachwood
Green

Sewage
Works

1

Colemans
Green

Medlow
House

Red Lion
(PH)

Duxleys
Wood

PASTURE LA

22

13 A B 14 C D 15 E F

47
34

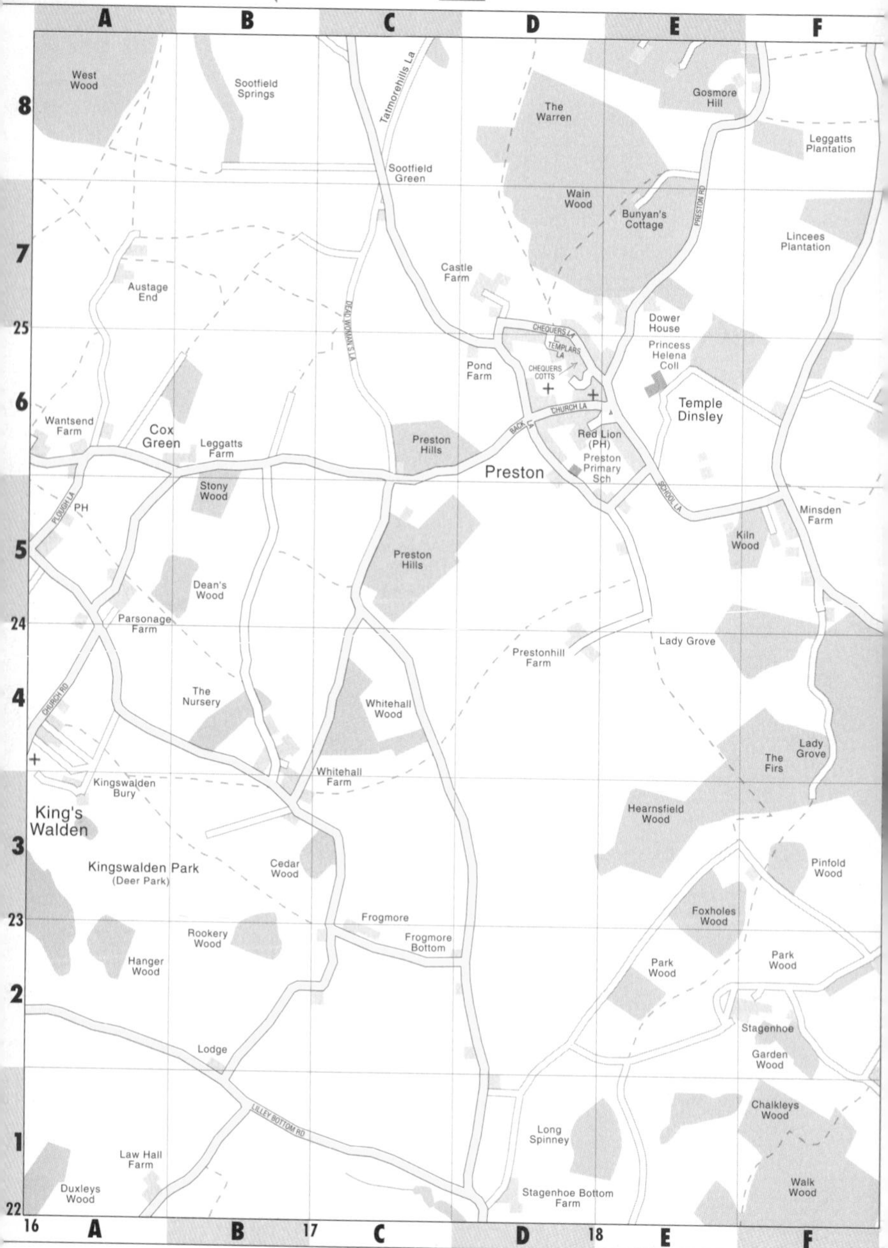
A
B
C
D
E
F
8
7
25
6
5
24
4
3
23
2
1
22
16
17
18
West Wood
Sootfield Springs
Tatmorehills La
The Warren
Gosmore Hill
Leggatts Plantation
Sootfield Green
Wain Wood
Bunyan's Cottage
PRESTON RD
Lincees Plantation
Austage End
Castle Farm
DEAD WOMAN'S LA
CHEQUERS LA
TEMPLARS LA
CHEQUERS COTTS
Dower House
Princess Helena Coll
Pond Farm
Temple Dinsley
CHURCH LA
BACK LA
Wantsend Farm
Cox Green
Leggatts Farm
Preston Hills
Red Lion (PH)
Preston Primary Sch
Preston
SCHOOL LA
Stony Wood
PLOUGH LA
PH
Minsden Farm
Kiln Wood
Preston Hills
Dean's Wood
Parsonage Farm
Lady Grove
Prestonhill Farm
CHURCH RD
The Nursery
Whitehall Wood
Lady Grove
The Firs
Kingswalden Bury
Whitehall Farm
King's Walden
Hearnsfield Wood
Kingswalden Park (Deer Park)
Cedar Wood
Pinfold Wood
Foxholes Wood
Frogmore
Rookery Wood
Frogmore Bottom
Hanger Wood
Park Wood
Park Wood
Stagenhoe
Garden Wood
Lodge
LILLEY BOTTOM RD
Chalkleys Wood
Long Spinney
Law Hall Farm
Duxleys Wood
Stagenhoe Bottom Farm
Walk Wood

47
66

35
50

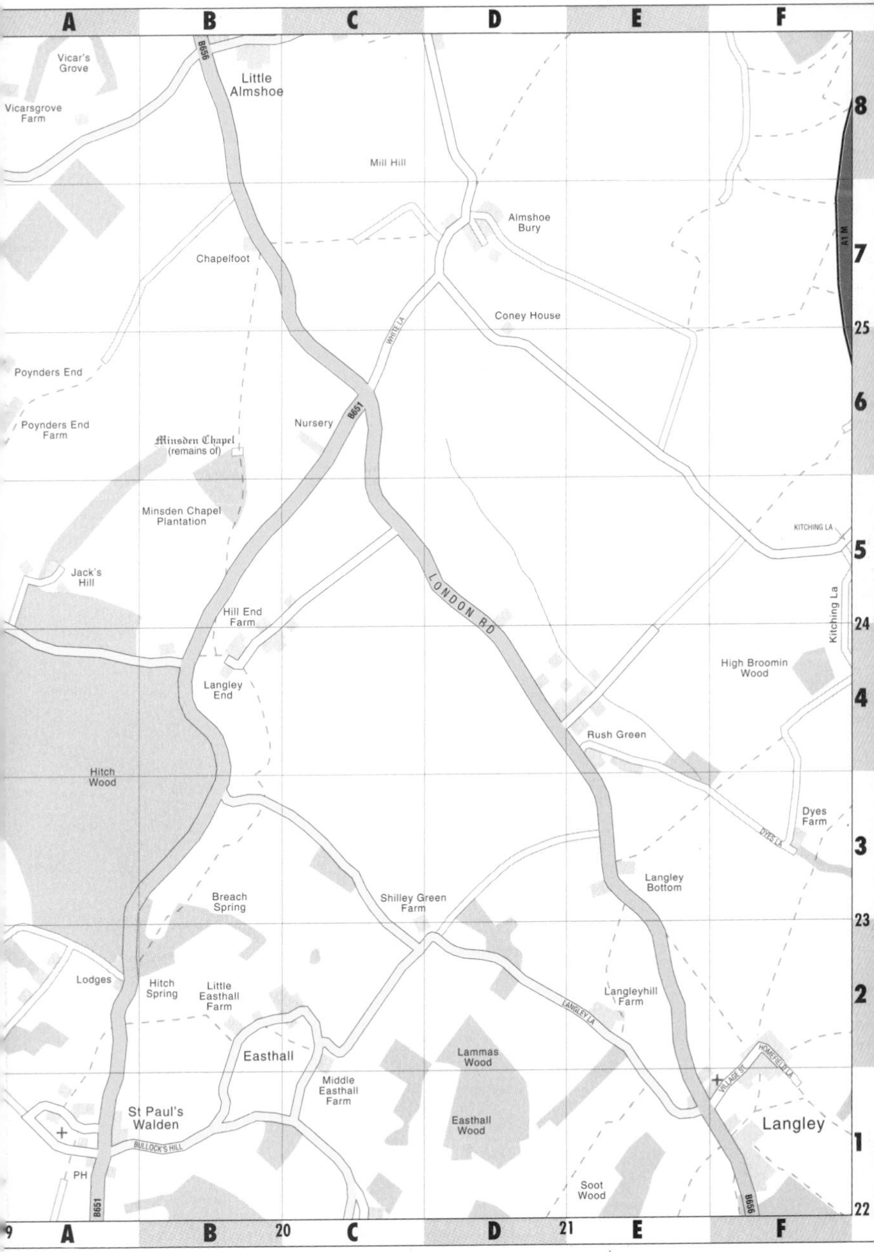
A
B
C
D
E
F
Vicar's Grove
Little Almshoe
Vicarsgrove Farm
Mill Hill
Almshoe Bury
Chapelfoot
Coney House
A1 M
Poynders End
Poynders End Farm
Nursery
Minsden Chapel (remains of)
Minsden Chapel Plantation
Jack's Hill
Hill End Farm
LONDON RD
KITCHING LA
Kitching La
High Broomin Wood
Langley End
Rush Green
Hitch Wood
Dyes Farm
DYES LA
Breach Spring
Shilley Green Farm
Langley Bottom
Lodges
Hitch Spring
Little Easthall Farm
LANGLEY LA
Langleyhill Farm
Easthall
Lammas Wood
Middle Easthall Farm
VILLAGE ST
HOMEFIELD LA
St Paul's Walden
Easthall Wood
Langley
BULLOCK'S HILL
PH
Soot Wood
B656
B651
WHITE LA
8
7
25
6
5
24
4
3
23
2
1
22
9
20
21

67
50

49
36

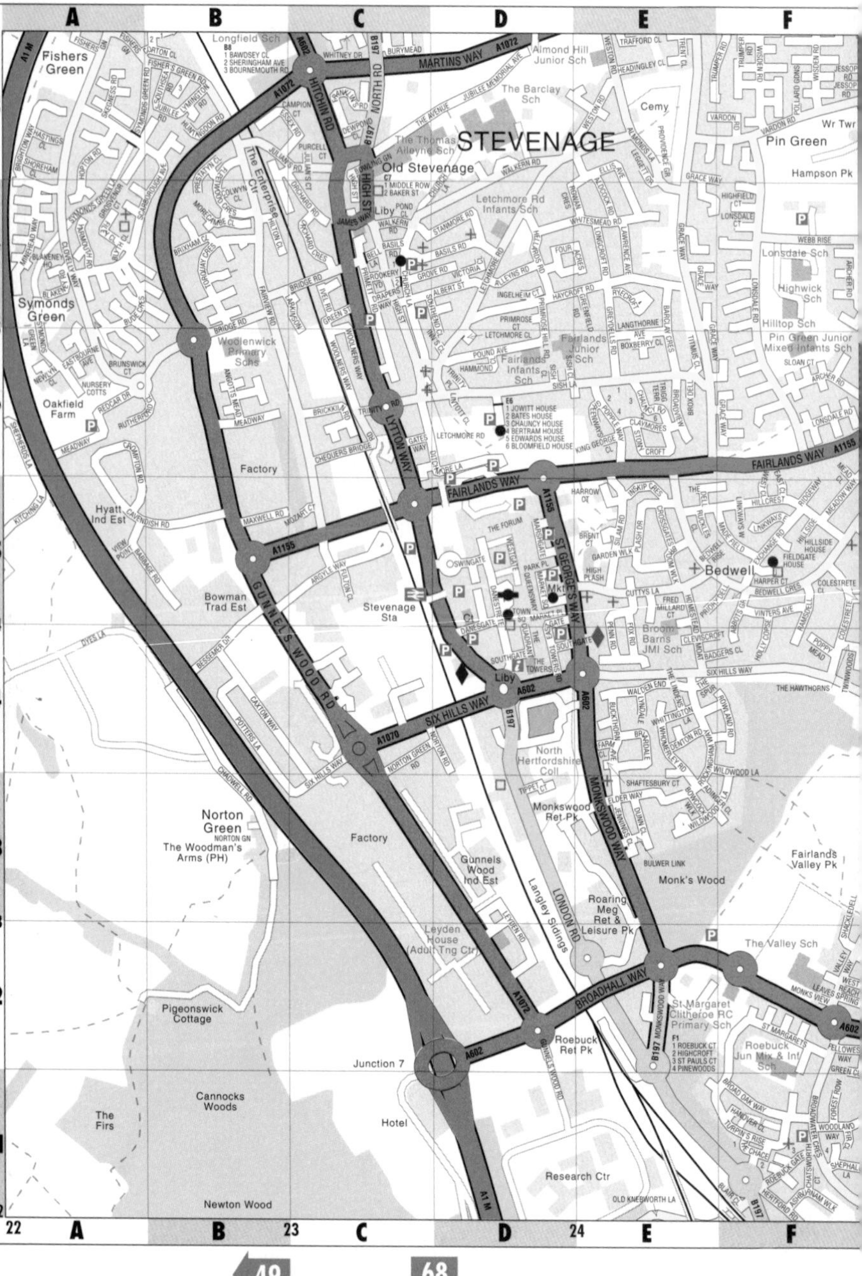
A
B
C
D
E
F
Fishers Green
Longfield Sch
B8
1 BAWDSEY CL
2 SHERINGHAM AVE
3 BOURNEMOUTH RD
MARTINS WAY
A1072
Almond Hill Junior Sch
The Barclay Sch
Cemy
STEVENAGE
The Thomas Alleyne Sch
Old Stevenage
Pin Green
Wr Twr
Hampson Pk
HITCHIN RD
NORTH RD
HIGH ST
Liby
C7
1 MIDDLE ROW
2 BAKER ST
The Enterprise Ctr
Letchmore Rd Infants Sch
Lonsdale Sch
Highwick Sch
Hilltop Sch
Pin Green Junior Mixed Infants Sch
Symonds Green
Woolenwick Primary Schs
Fairlands Junior Sch
Fairlands Infants Sch
Oakfield Farm
E6
1 JOWITT HOUSE
2 BATES HOUSE
3 CHAUNCY HOUSE
4 BERTRAM HOUSE
5 EDWARDS HOUSE
6 BLOOMFIELD HOUSE
LYTTON WAY
FAIRLANDS WAY
A1155
Factory
Hyatt Ind Est
THE FORUM
Bedwell
Bowman Trad Est
Stevenage Sta
Mkt
ST GEORGE'S WAY
Broom Barns JMI Sch
GUNNELS WOOD RD
SIX HILLS WAY
A602
A1070
B197
North Hertfordshire Coll
MONKSWOOD WAY
Monkswood Ret Pk
Norton Green
The Woodman's Arms (PH)
Factory
Gunnels Wood Ind Est
Langley Sidings
LONDON RD
Monk's Wood
Fairlands Valley Pk
Roaring Meg Ret & Leisure Pk
Leyden House (Adult Tng Ctr)
The Valley Sch
BROADHALL WAY
Pigeonswick Cottage
St Margaret Clitheroe RC Primary Sch
F1
1 ROEBUCK CT
2 HIGHCROFT
3 ST PAULS CT
4 PINEWOODS
Roebuck Ret Pk
Roebuck Jun Mix & Inf Sch
Junction 7
Cannocks Woods
The Firs
Hotel
Research Ctr
Newton Wood
OLD KNEBWORTH LA
A1 M
8
7
25
6
5
24
4
3
23
2
1
22
22
23
24

49
68

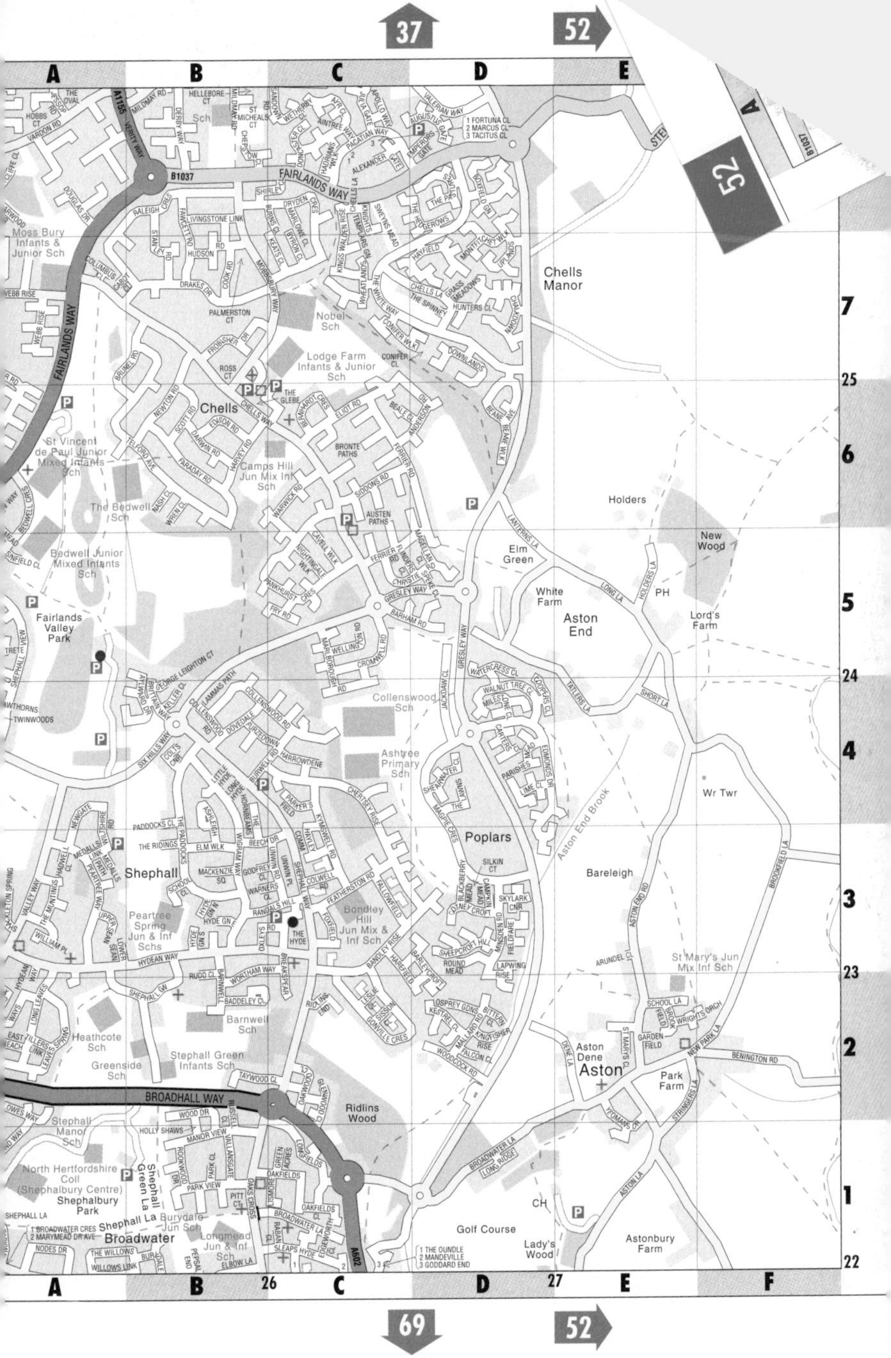

37
52
52
69
52
A
B
C
D
E
F
7
25
6
5
24
4
3
23
2
1
22
26
27
A1155
B1037
A602
FAIRLANDS WAY
BROADHALL WAY
VERITY WAY
GRESLEY WAY
HELLEBORE CT
MILDMAY RD
DERBY WAY
ST MICHAELS CT
SANDOWN RD
WETHERBY
AYR CL
JULIA GATE
APOLLO WAY
AINTREE WAY
PACATIAN WAY
AUGUSTUS GATE
EMPERORS GATE
VALERIAN WAY
1 FORTUNA CL
2 MARCUS CL
3 TACITUS CL
ALEXANDER GATE
HADRIANS WLK
CHEPSTOW CL
HOBBS CT
VARDON RD
THE OVAL
DOUGLAS DR
RALEIGH CRES
LIVINGSTONE LINK
SHIRLEY
DRYDEN CRES
MARLOWE CL
BYRON CL
KEATS CL
BURNS CL
KINGS WALDEN RISE
TEMPLARS GN
KNIGHTS
SWEYNS MEAD
CHELLS LA
HUDSON RD
STANLEY RD
FAWCETT RD
COOK RD
MOBBSBURY WAY
DRAKES DR
COLUMBUS CL
CABOT CL
Moss Bury Infants & Junior Sch
WEBB RISE
PALMERSTON CT
FROBISHER DR
ROSS CT
Nobel Sch
Lodge Farm Infants & Junior Sch
CONIFER CL
CONIFER WLK
DOWNLANDS
HUNTERS CL
CHALKDOWN
THE SPINNEY
GRASS MEADOWS
CHELLS LA
THE WHITE WAY
WHEATLANDS
HAYFIELD
MONTFICHET WLK
UPLANDS
THE HEDGEROWS
THE PASTURES
BOXFIELD GN
Chells Manor
Chells
CHELLS WAY
THE GLEBE
BRUNEL RD
NEWTON RD
SCOTT RD
EDISON RD
DARWIN RD
HARVEY RD
FARADAY RD
TELFORD AVE
NASH CL
WREN CL
BRONTE PATHS
ELIOT RD
BEALE CL
ANDERSON RD
FERRIER RD
BEANE AVE
BEANE WLK
SIDDONS RD
AUSTEN PATHS
WARWICK RD
CAVELL WLK
NIGHTINGALE WLK
PANKHURST CRES
FRY RD
FERRIER RD
FLINDERS CL
MAGELLAN CL
CHRISTIE RD
SPIKE CL
GRESLEY WAY
BARHAM RD
St Vincent de Paul Junior Mixed Infants Sch
Camps Hill Jun Mix Inf Sch
The Bedwell Sch
Bedwell Junior Mixed Infants Sch
BEDWELL CRES
SINFIELD CL
Fairlands Valley Park
SHEPHALL VIEW
HAWTHORNS
TWINWOODS
Holders
New Wood
Elm Green
LANTERNS LA
White Farm
LONG LA
HOLDERS LA
PH
Aston End
Lord's Farm
WELLING RD
MARLBOROUGH RD
CROMWELL RD
GEORGE LEIGHTON CT
AYLWARD DR
BRITTAIN WAY
KELLER CL
LAMMAS PATH
COLLENSWOOD RD
DOVEDALE
FURZEDOWN
HARROWDENE
Collenswood Sch
Ashtree Primary Sch
JACKDAW CL
WATERCRESS CL
WALNUT TREE CL
MILESTONE CL
COOPERS CL
TATLERS LA
SHORT LA
CARTERS CL
PARISHES MEAD
EDMONDS DR
LIME CL
SIX HILLS WAY
COLTS CNR
LITTLE HYDE
LONG HYDE
BURWELL RD
PARKER'S FIELD
CHERTSEY RISE
KYMSWELL RD
HAYLEY COMM
SHEEPWATER CL
THE LAWNS
MAGPIE CRES
Poplars
SILKIN CT
Aston End Brook
Wr Twr
Bareleigh
BROOKFIELD LA
NEWGATE
MEDALLS LINK
MEDALLS PATH
PEARTREE WAY
PADDOCKS CL
THE PADDOCKS
THE RIDINGS
ELM WLK
ASHLEIGH
HORNBEAMS
WIGRAM WAY
BEECH DR
UNWIN RD
UNWIN PL
SHEPHALL WAY
COLWELL RD
FEATHERSTON RD
FALLOWFIELD
Shephall
MACKENZIE SQ
GODFREY CL
WARNERS CL
RANDALS HILL
BLACKBERRY MEAD
CAMPKIN MEAD
SKYLARK CNR
GATNEY CROFT
MINSDEN RD
FIELDFARE
HADWELL CL
THE MUNTINGS
VALLEY WAY
SHACKLETON SPRING
WILLIAM PL
UPPER SEAN
LOWER SEAN
Peartree Spring Jun & Inf Schs
HYDE GN
HYDE GN S
HYDE GN N
OXLEYS RD
THE HYDE
Bondley Hill Jun Mix & Inf Sch
FOXFIELD
BANDLEY RISE
HAREFIELD
BARLEYCROFT
SHEEPCROFT HILL
ROUND MEAD
LAPWING RISE
ASTON END RD
ARUNDEL CL
St Mary's Jun Mix Inf Sch
HYDEAN WAY
RUDD CL
BARNWELL
WORTHAM WAY
BREAKSPEAR
SHEPHALL GN
BADDELEY CL
RIDLINS END
LESLIE CL
GISSON CL
GONVILLE CRES
OSPREY GDNS
KESTREL CL
BITTERN CL
KINGFISHER RISE
MALLARD RD
FALCON CL
WOODCOCK RD
SCHOOL LA
FIELD
BROOK
WRIGHTS ORCH
GARDEN FIELD
ST MARY'S CL
DENE LA
NEW PARK LA
BENINGTON RD
LONG LEAVES
EAST REACH
TILLERS LINK
LEAVES SPRING
Heathcote Sch
Barnwell Sch
Stephall Green Infants Sch
Greenside Sch
Aston Dene
Aston
Park Farm
STRINGERS LA
TAYWOOD CL
OAKWOOD
GLENWOOD CL
Ridlins Wood
YEOMANS DR
Stephall Manor Sch
WOOD DR
HOLLY SHAWS
MANOR VIEW
RUSSELL CL
ROOKWOOD DR
PARK CL
VALLANSGATE
GREEN ACRES
LONGFIELDS
OAKFIELDS
BROADWATER LA
LONG RIDGE
North Hertfordshire Coll (Shephalbury Centre)
Shephalbury Park
Shephall Green La
PARK VIEW
PITT CT
OAKS CROSS
ASTON LA
CH
SHEPHALL LA
1 BROADWATER CRES
2 MARYMEAD DR AVE
Shephall La
Burydale Jun Sch
Broadwater
Longmead Jun & Inf Sch
RABAN CT
BROADWATER LA
OAKFIELDS CL
EDGEWORTH CL
SLEAPS HYDE
Golf Course
Lady's Wood
Astonbury Farm
NODES DR
THE WILLOWS
WILLOWS LINK
BURYDALE
PEPSAL END
ELBOW LA
1 THE DUNDLE
2 MANDEVILLE
3 GODDARD END

51
38

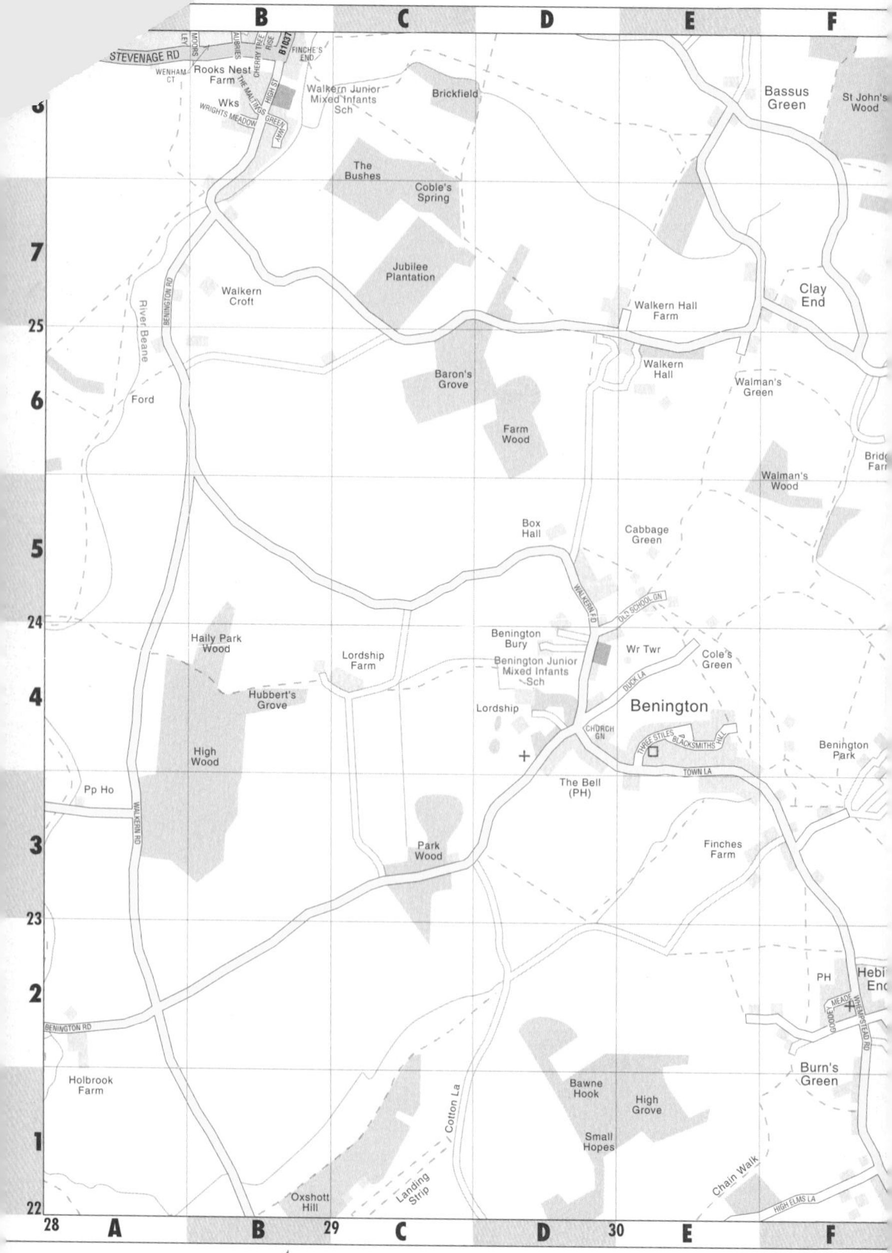
B
C
D
E
F
STEVENAGE RD
LEY
MOORS
AUBRIES
CHERRY TREE
RISE
B1037
FINCHE'S END
WENHAM CT
Rooks Nest Farm
THE MALTINGS
HIGH ST
Wks
WRIGHTS MEADOW
GREEN WAY
Walkern Junior Mixed Infants Sch
Brickfield
Bassus Green
St John's Wood
The Bushes
Coble's Spring
7
Jubilee Plantation
Walkern Croft
BENINGTON RD
River Beane
Walkern Hall Farm
Clay End
25
Walkern Hall
Baron's Grove
Walman's Green
6
Ford
Farm Wood
Walman's Wood
Box Hall
Cabbage Green
5
WALKERN RD
OLD SCHOOL GN
24
Haily Park Wood
Benington Bury
Wr Twr
Lordship Farm
Cole's Green
Benington Junior Mixed Infants Sch
DUCK LA
4
Hubbert's Grove
Lordship
Benington
CHURCH GN
THREE STILES
BLACKSMITHS HILL
High Wood
Benington Park
TOWN LA
The Bell (PH)
Pp Ho
WALKERN RD
3
Park Wood
Finches Farm
23
2
PH
MEADE
GOODE
WHEMPSTEAD RD
BENINGTON RD
Holbrook Farm
Burn's Green
Bawne Hook
High Grove
Cotton La
1
Small Hopes
Chain Walk
Landing Strip
Oxshott Hill
HIGH ELMS LA
22
28
A
B
29
C
D
30
E
F

51
70

39
54

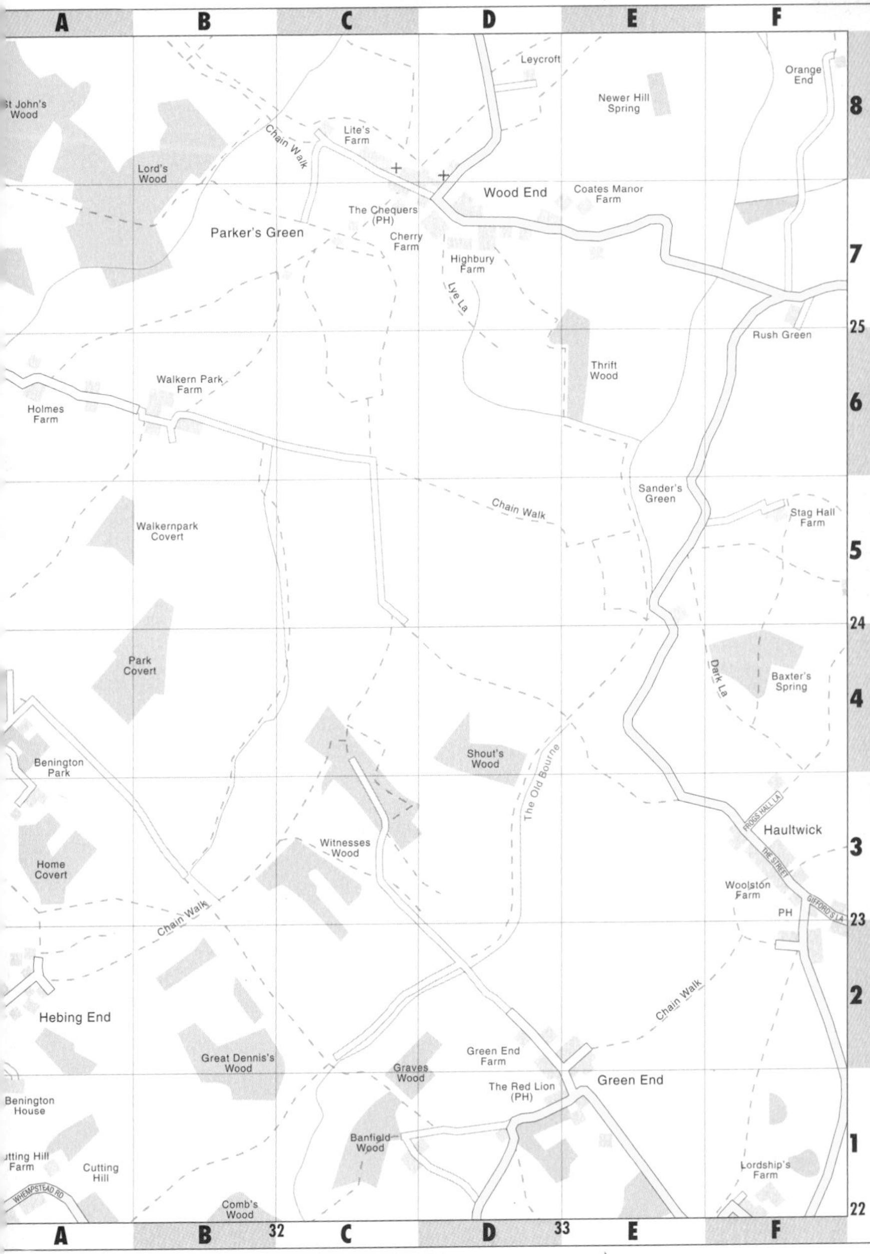
A
B
C
D
E
F
St John's Wood
Lord's Wood
Chain Walk
Lite's Farm
Leycroft
Newer Hill Spring
Orange End
8
Wood End
Coates Manor Farm
The Chequers (PH)
Parker's Green
Cherry Farm
Highbury Farm
Lye La
7
25
Rush Green
Thrift Wood
Walkern Park Farm
Holmes Farm
6
Sander's Green
Chain Walk
Stag Hall Farm
Walkernpark Covert
5
24
Park Covert
Dark La
Baxter's Spring
4
Shout's Wood
Benington Park
The Old Bourne
FROGS HALL LA
Haultwick
Witnesses Wood
THE STREET
3
Home Covert
Woolston Farm
Chain Walk
GIFFORD'S LA
PH
23
Chain Walk
2
Hebing End
Green End Farm
Great Dennis's Wood
Graves Wood
Green End
The Red Lion (PH)
Benington House
Banfield Wood
1
Cutting Hill Farm
Cutting Hill
Lordship's Farm
WHEMPSTEAD RD
Comb's Wood
22
32
33

71
54

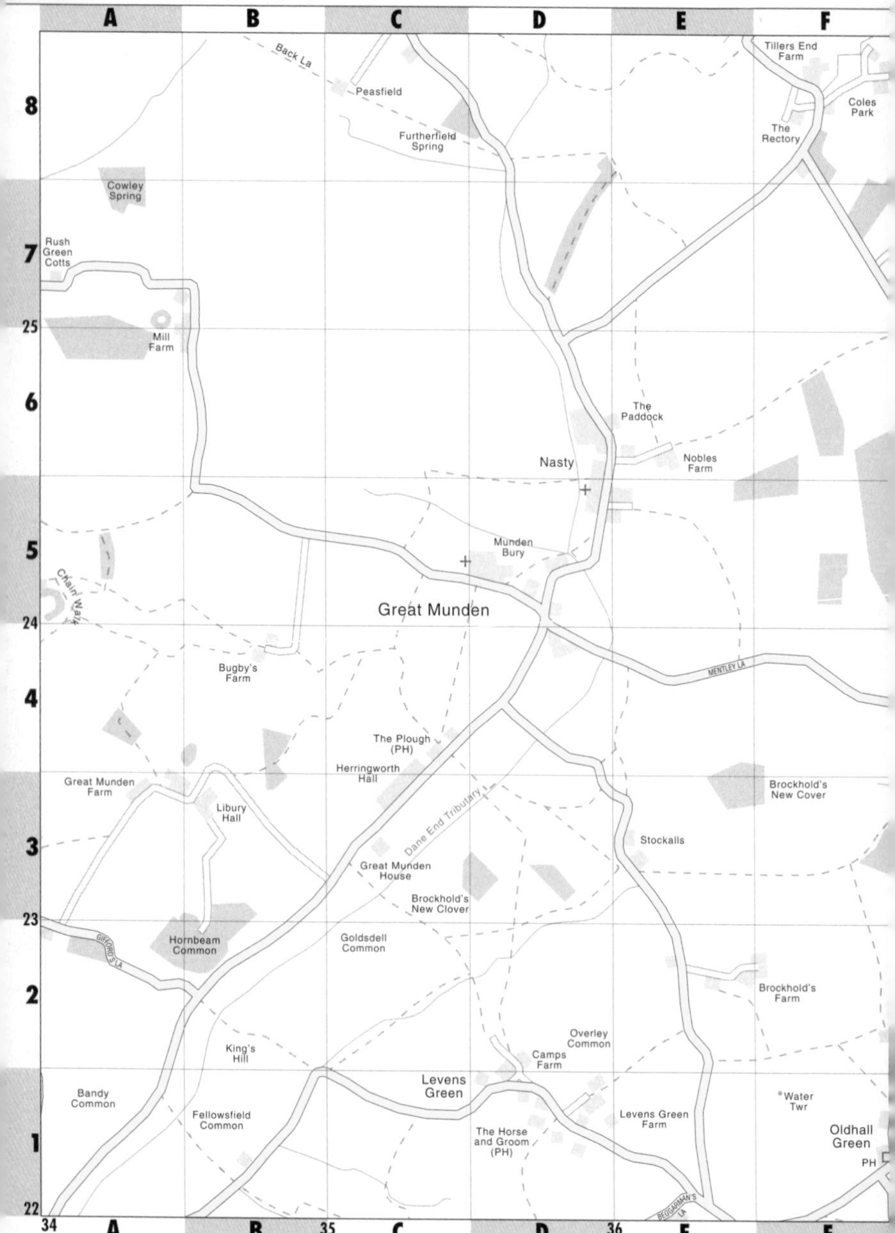

A   B   C   D   E   F

8

Tillers End
Farm

Back La

Peasfield

Furtherfield
Spring

Coles
Park

The
Rectory

Cowley
Spring

7
Rush
Green
Cotts

25
Mill
Farm

6

The
Paddock

Nasty

Nobles
Farm

5
Chalk Walk

Munden
Bury

24
Great Munden

Bugby's
Farm

MENTLEY LA

4

The Plough
(PH)

Brockhold's
New Cover

Great Munden
Farm

Herringworth
Hall

Libury
Hall

3
Dane End Tributary

Stockalls

Great Munden
House

Brockhold's
New Clover

23
Hornbeam
Common

Goldsdell
Common

Brockhold's
Farm

2

King's
Hill

Overley
Common

Camps
Farm

Bandy
Common

Levens
Green

Levens Green
Farm

*Water
Twr

Oldhall
Green

1
Fellowsfield
Common

The Horse
and Groom
(PH)

PH

22
34   A   B   35   C   D   36   E   F

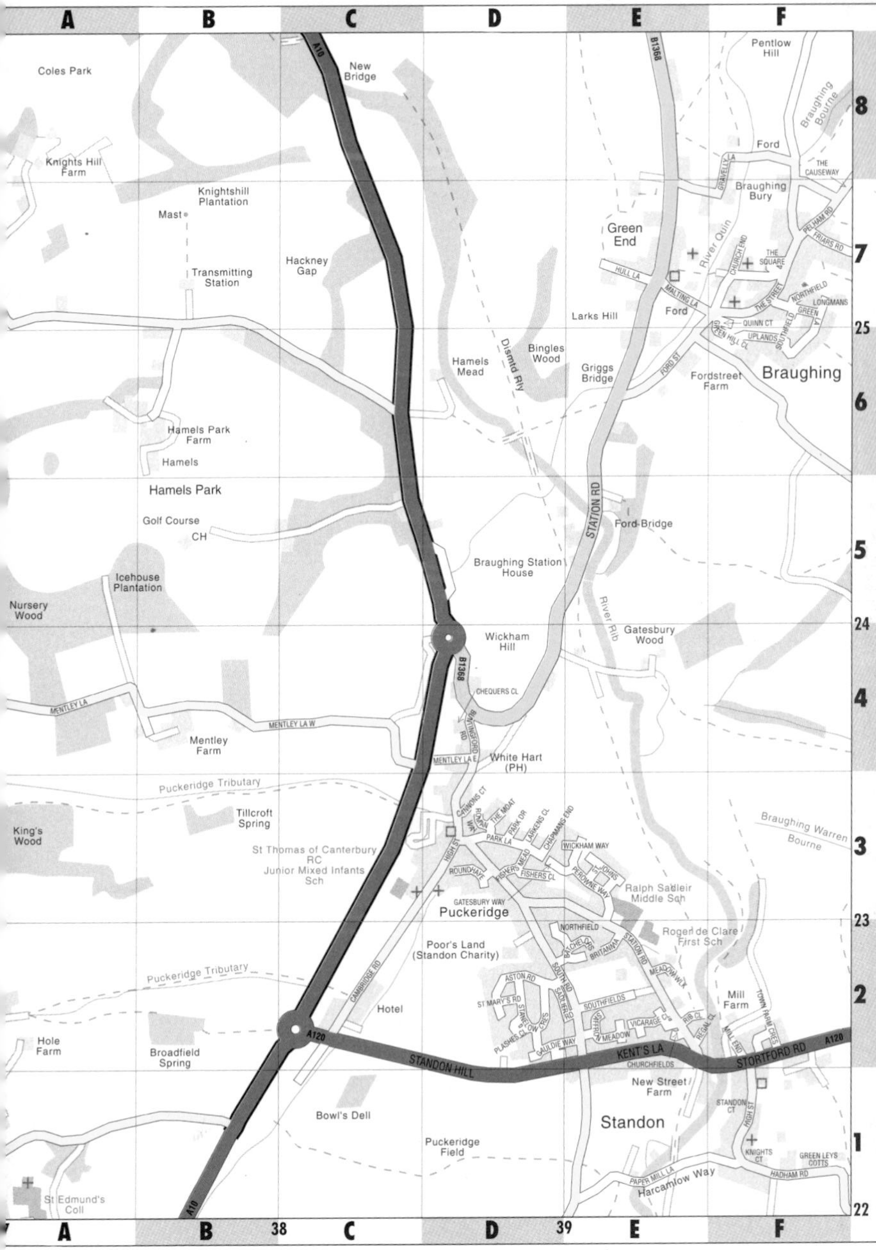

Coles Park

Knights Hill Farm

Knightshill Plantation

Mast

Transmitting Station

Hackney Gap

New Bridge

A10

Pentlow Hill

Braughing Bourne

Ford

THE CAUSEWAY

Braughing Bury

Green End

River Quin

THE SQUARE

THE STREET

NORTHFIELD

LONGMANS GREEN

Larks Hill

Ford

QUINN CT

UPLANDS

Hamels Mead

Bingles Wood

Disemd Rly

Griggs Bridge

Fordstreet Farm

Braughing

Hamels Park Farm

Hamels

Hamels Park

Golf Course

CH

STATION RD

Ford-Bridge

Braughing Station House

Icehouse Plantation

Nursery Wood

River Rib

Gatesbury Wood

Wickham Hill

B1368

CHEQUERS CL

MENTLEY LA

MENTLEY LA W

Mentley Farm

MENTLEY LA E

White Hart (PH)

Puckeridge Tributary

Tillcroft Spring

King's Wood

St Thomas of Canterbury RC Junior Mixed Infants Sch

Braughing Warren Bourne

PARK LA

WICKHAM WAY

Ralph Sadleir Middle Sch

GATESBURY WAY

Puckeridge

ROUNDAH

FISHERS CL

NORTHFIELD

BRITANNIA

Roger de Clare First Sch

Poor's Land (Standon Charity)

Puckeridge Tributary

Hotel

CAMBRIDGE RD

ASTON RD

ST MARY'S RD

SOUTHFIELDS

MEADOW

Mill Farm

STORTFORD RD

A120

Hole Farm

Broadfield Spring

A120

STANDON HILL

KENT'S LA

CHURCHFIELDS

New Street Farm

STANDON CT

Bowl's Dell

Puckeridge Field

Standon

KNIGHTS CT

GREEN LEYS COTTS

HADHAM RD

PUPIN MILL LA

Harcamlow Way

St Edmund's Coll

A10

55
42

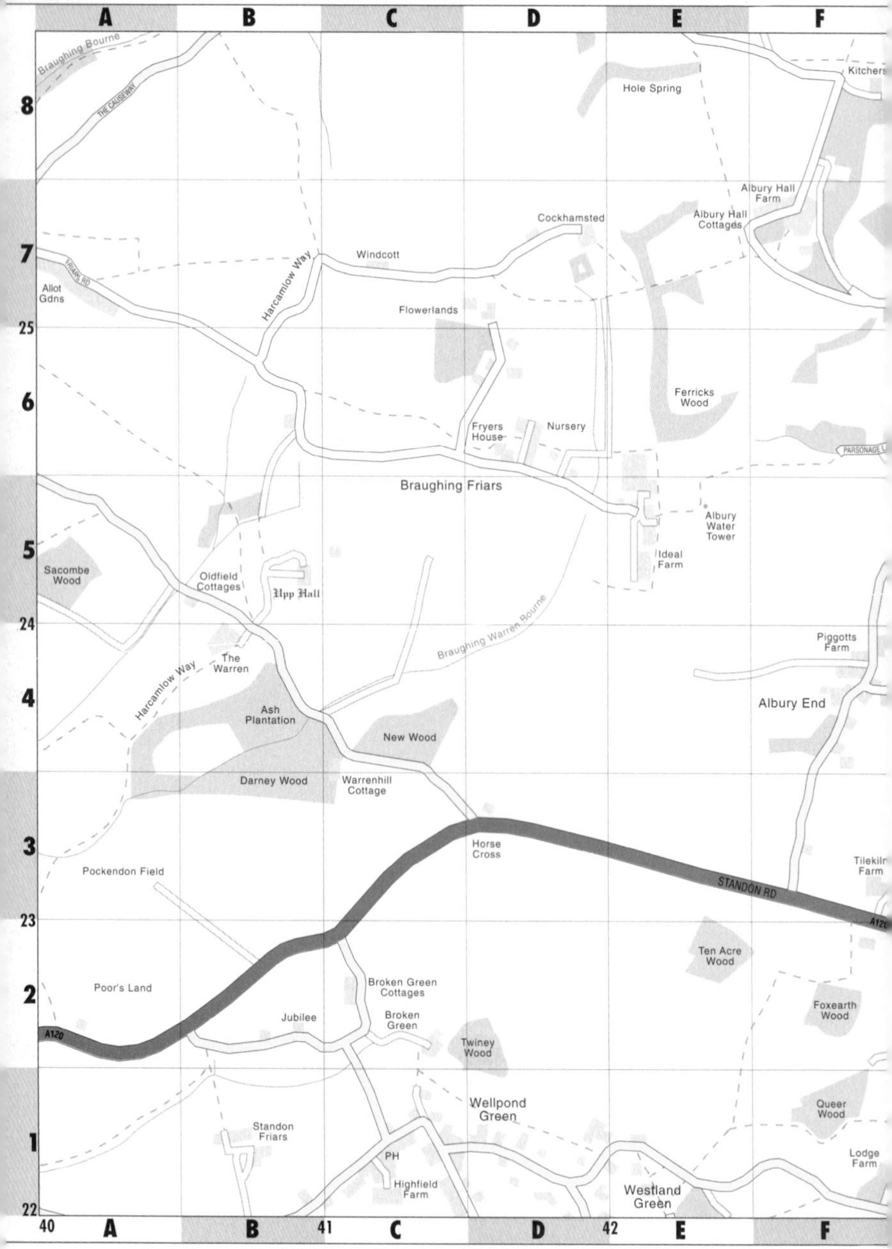
A
B
C
D
E
F
8
7
25
6
5
24
4
3
23
2
1
22
40
41
42
Braughing Bourne
THE CAUSEWAY
Hole Spring
Kitchers
Albury Hall
Farm
Albury Hall
Cottages
Cockhamsted
Windcott
Harcamlow Way
FRIARS RD
Allot
Gdns
Flowerlands
Ferricks
Wood
Fryers
House
Nursery
PARSONAGE L
Braughing Friars
Albury
Water
Tower
Ideal
Farm
Sacombe
Wood
Oldfield
Cottages
Upp Hall
Braughing Warren Bourne
Piggotts
Farm
The
Warren
Harcamlow Way
Ash
Plantation
Albury End
New Wood
Darney Wood
Warrenhill
Cottage
Horse
Cross
Tilekiln
Farm
Pockendon Field
STANDON RD
A120
Ten Acre
Wood
Poor's Land
Broken Green
Cottages
Foxearth
Wood
Jubilee
Broken
Green
A120
Twiney
Wood
Wellpond
Green
Queer
Wood
Standon
Friars
Lodge
Farm
PH
Highfield
Farm
Westland
Green

55
74

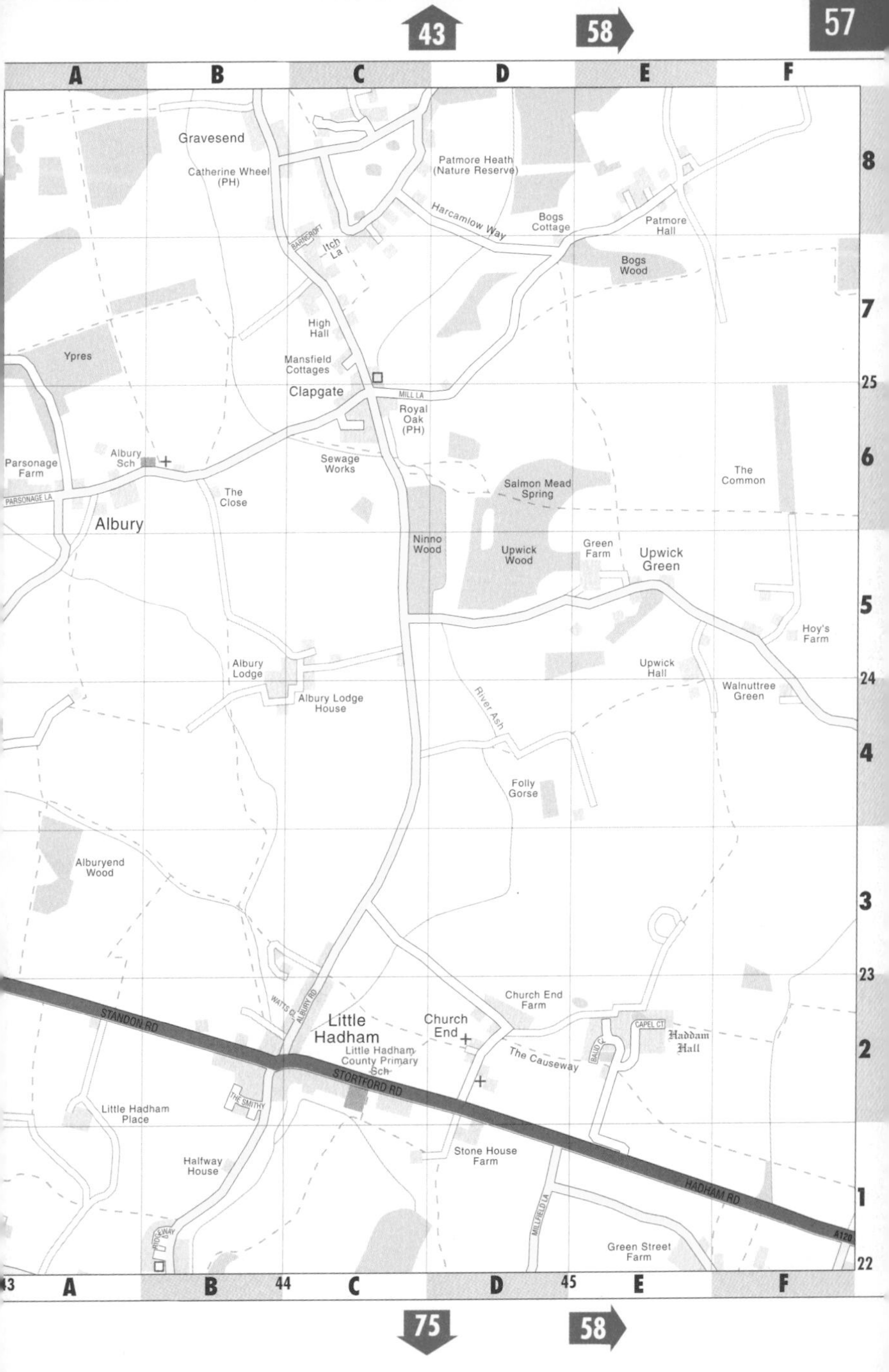
43
58
A
B
C
D
E
F
Gravesend
Catherine Wheel (PH)
Patmore Heath (Nature Reserve)
Harcamlow Way
Bogs Cottage
Patmore Hall
Bogs Wood
Barncroft
Itch La
High Hall
Ypres
Mansfield Cottages
Clapgate
Mill La
Royal Oak (PH)
Parsonage Farm
Parsonage La
Albury Sch
Sewage Works
Salmon Mead Spring
The Common
The Close
Albury
Ninno Wood
Upwick Wood
Green Farm
Upwick Green
Hoy's Farm
Albury Lodge
Upwick Hall
Walnuttree Green
Albury Lodge House
River Ash
Folly Gorse
Alburyend Wood
Church End Farm
Standon Rd
Watts Cl
Albury Rd
Little Hadham
Church End
Capel Ct
Haddam Hall
Baud Ct
Little Hadham County Primary Sch
The Causeway
Stortford Rd
The Smithy
Little Hadham Place
Stone House Farm
Halfway House
Hadham Rd
Millfield La
Green Street Farm
A120
Ridgeway
8
7
25
6
5
24
4
3
23
2
1
22
43
44
45
75
58

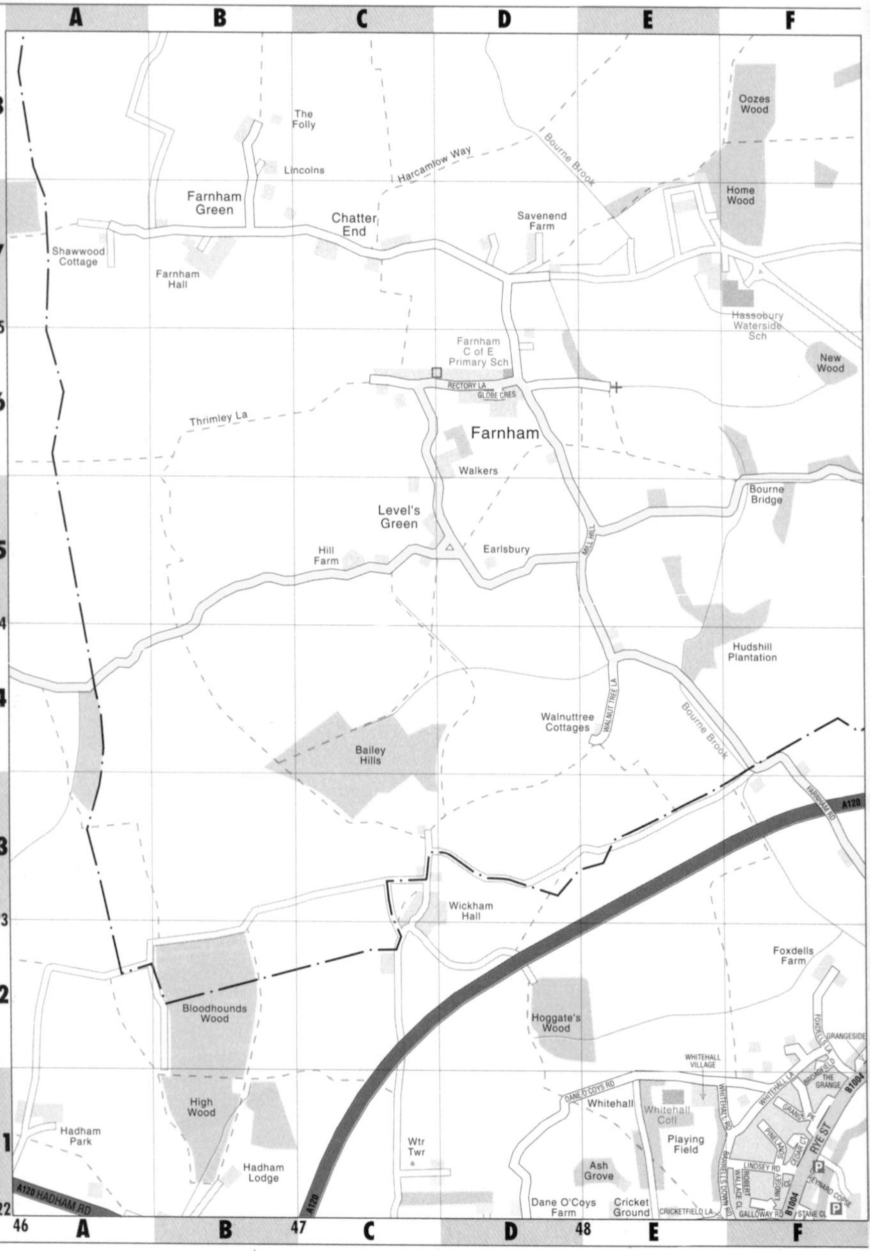

8

The Folly

Lincolns

Harcamlow Way

Bourne Brook

Oozes Wood

Home Wood

Farnham Green

Chatter End

Savenend Farm

7

Shawwood Cottage

Farnham Hall

Hassobury Waterside Sch

25

New Wood

Farnham C of E Primary Sch

RECTORY LA
GLOBE CRES

6

Thrimley La

Farnham

Walkers

Bourne Bridge

Level's Green

Earlsbury

5

Hill Farm

Hudshill Plantation

24

Walnuttree Cottages

4

Bailey Hills

WALNUT TREE LA

Bourne Brook

A120

3

Wickham Hall

23

Foxdells Farm

2

Bloodhounds Wood

Hoggate's Wood

WHITEHALL VILLAGE

GRANGESIDE

THE GRANGE

High Wood

Whitehall

Whitehall Coll

Playing Field

1

Hadham Park

Hadham Lodge

Wtr Twr

DANE O'COYS RD

Ash Grove

Cricket Ground

RYE ST

P

A120 HADHAM RD

A120

Dane O'Coys Farm

CRICKETFIELD LA

22

46 A B 47 C D 48 E F

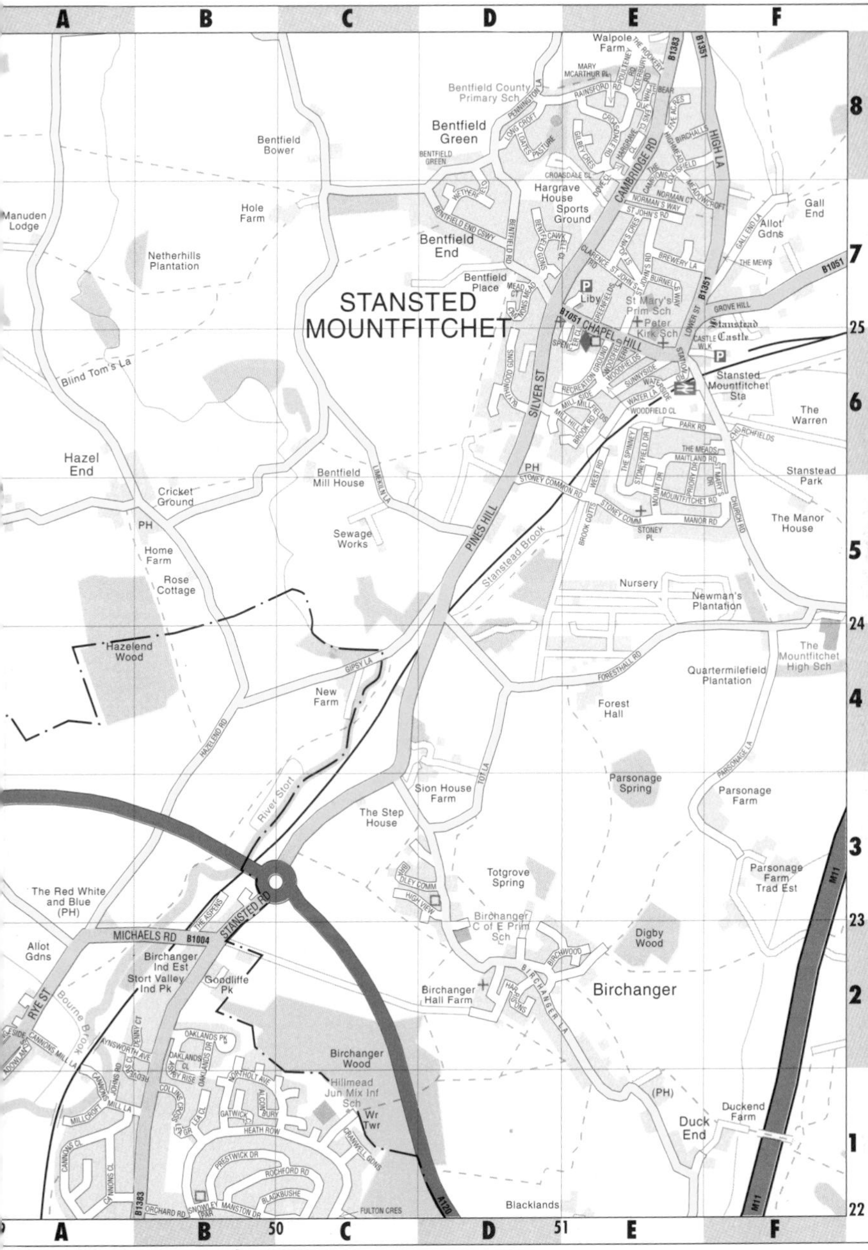
A
B
C
D
E
F
8
7
25
6
5
24
4
3
23
2
1
22
50
51
Walpole Farm
Bentfield County Primary Sch
Bentfield Green
Bentfield Bower
Hole Farm
Manuden Lodge
Netherhills Plantation
Hargrave House
Sports Ground
Bentfield End
Bentfield Place
STANSTED MOUNTFITCHET
Liby
St Mary's Prim Sch
Peter Kirk Sch
Stansted Castle
Stansted Mountfitchet Sta
Gall End
Allot Gdns
The Warren
Stanstead Park
The Manor House
Blind Tom's La
Hazel End
Cricket Ground
Bentfield Mill House
Sewage Works
PH
Home Farm
Rose Cottage
Hazelend Wood
Nursery
Newman's Plantation
The Mountfitchet High Sch
Quartermilefield Plantation
Forest Hall
New Farm
Parsonage Spring
Parsonage Farm
Sion House Farm
The Step House
River Stort
Stanstead Brook
Totgrove Spring
Parsonage Farm Trad Est
The Red White and Blue (PH)
Allot Gdns
Birchanger Ind Est
Stort Valley Ind Pk
Goodliffe Pk
Birchanger C of E Prim Sch
Digby Wood
Birchanger Hall Farm
Birchanger
Birchanger Wood
Hillmead Jun Mix Inf Sch
Wr Twr
(PH)
Duckend Farm
Duck End
Blacklands
Bourne Brook
B1383
B1351
B1051
B1004
B1383
A120
M11
CAMBRIDGE RD
HIGH LA
SILVER ST
PINES HILL
CHAPEL HILL
STATION RD
LOWER ST
GROVE HILL
THE MEWS
GALL END LA
CHURCH RD
STONEY COMMON RD
WEST RD
BROOK COTTS
LIMEKILN LA
GIPSY LA
HAZELEND RD
FORESTHALL RD
PARSONAGE LA
TOT LA
BIRCHANGER LA
STANSTED RD
MICHAELS RD
RYE ST
CANNONS MILL LA
OAKLANDS DR
NORTHOLT AVE
HEATH ROW
PRESTWICK DR
ROCHFORD RD
BLACKBUSHE
MANSTON DR
SNOWLEY PAR
ORCHARD RD
FULTON CRES
CRANWELL GDNS
GATWICK CL
MILLCROFT
JOHNS RD
COLLINS CROSS
ASHBY RISE
LEA CL
THE ASPENS
HIGH VIEW
BIRCHWOOD
BENTFIELD RD
BENTFIELD END CSWY
BENTFIELD GDNS
WETHERFIELD
PENNINGTON LA
LONG CROFT
OATES PASTURE
RAINSFORD RD
GILBEY CRES
CROASDALE CL
NORMAN'S WAY
ST JOHN'S RD
BREWERY LA
BIRCHALLS
MEADOWCROFT
RECREATION GROUND
SUNNYSIDE
WATERSIDE
WATER LA
WOODFIELD CL
PARK RD
CHURCHFIELDS
THE MEADS
MAITLAND RD
MOUNTFITCHET RD
MANOR RD
STONEY PL
THE SPINNEY
STONEYFIELD DR
PRIORY DR
MOUNT DR
MILL HILL
MILL SIDE
BROOK RD

77

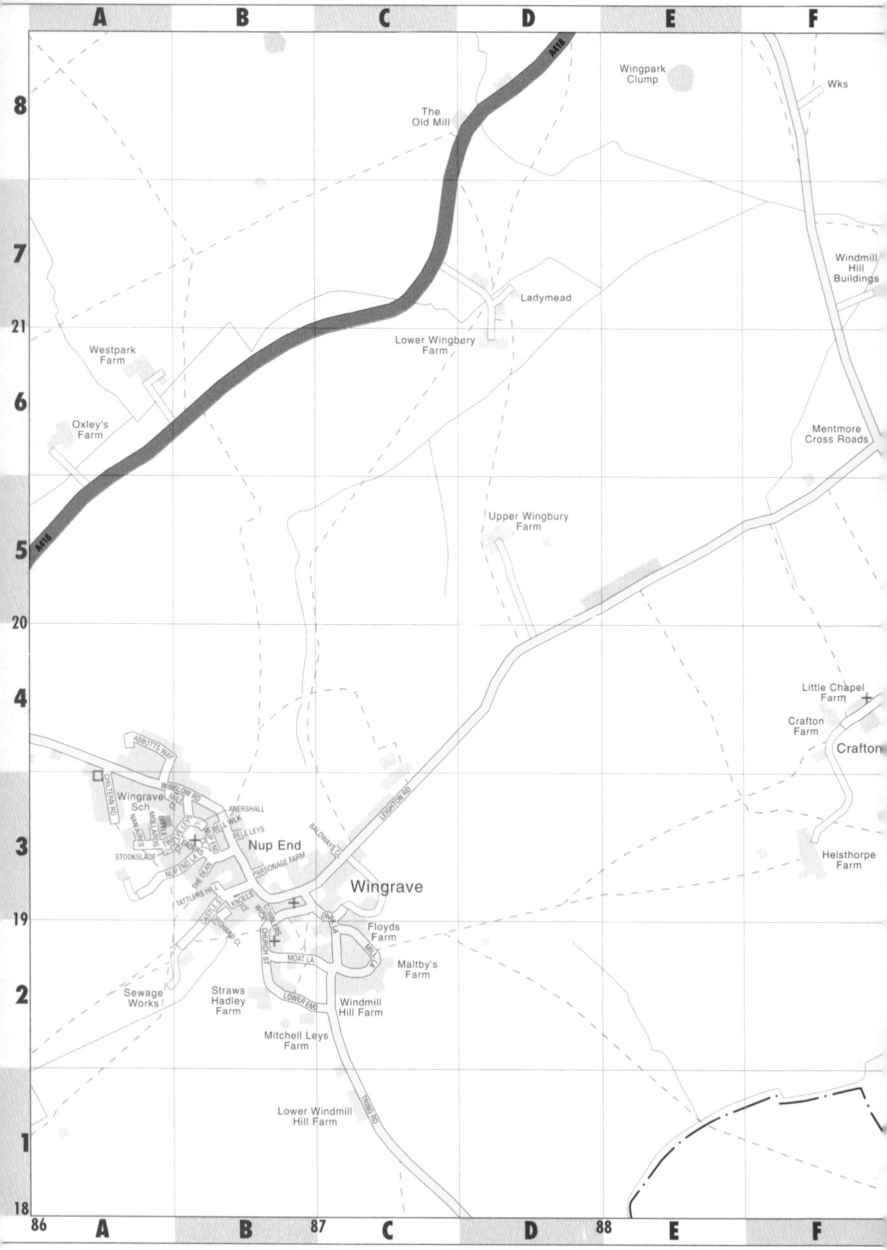

A   B   C   D   E   F

8

Wingpark
Clump

Wks

The
Old Mill

7

Windmill
Hill
Buildings

21

Westpark
Farm

Ladymead

Lower Wingbury
Farm

6

Oxley's
Farm

Mentmore
Cross Roads

5

Upper Wingbury
Farm

20

4

Little Chapel
Farm

Crafton
Farm

Crafton

ABBOTTS MED

Winglow RD

Wingrave
Sch.

AMERSHALL

BELLE LEYS

Nup End

BALDWAY CL

LEIGHTON RD

Helsthorpe
Farm

3

STOOKSLADE

NUP END LA

PARSONAGE FARM

Wingrave

19

TATTLERS HILL

MOCKES

Floyds
Farm

2

Sewage
Works

Straws
Hadley
Farm

MOAT LA

LOWER END

Maltby's
Farm

Windmill
Hill Farm

Mitchell Leys
Farm

PAGE RD

1

Lower Windmill
Hill Farm

18

86   A   B   87   C   D   88   E   F

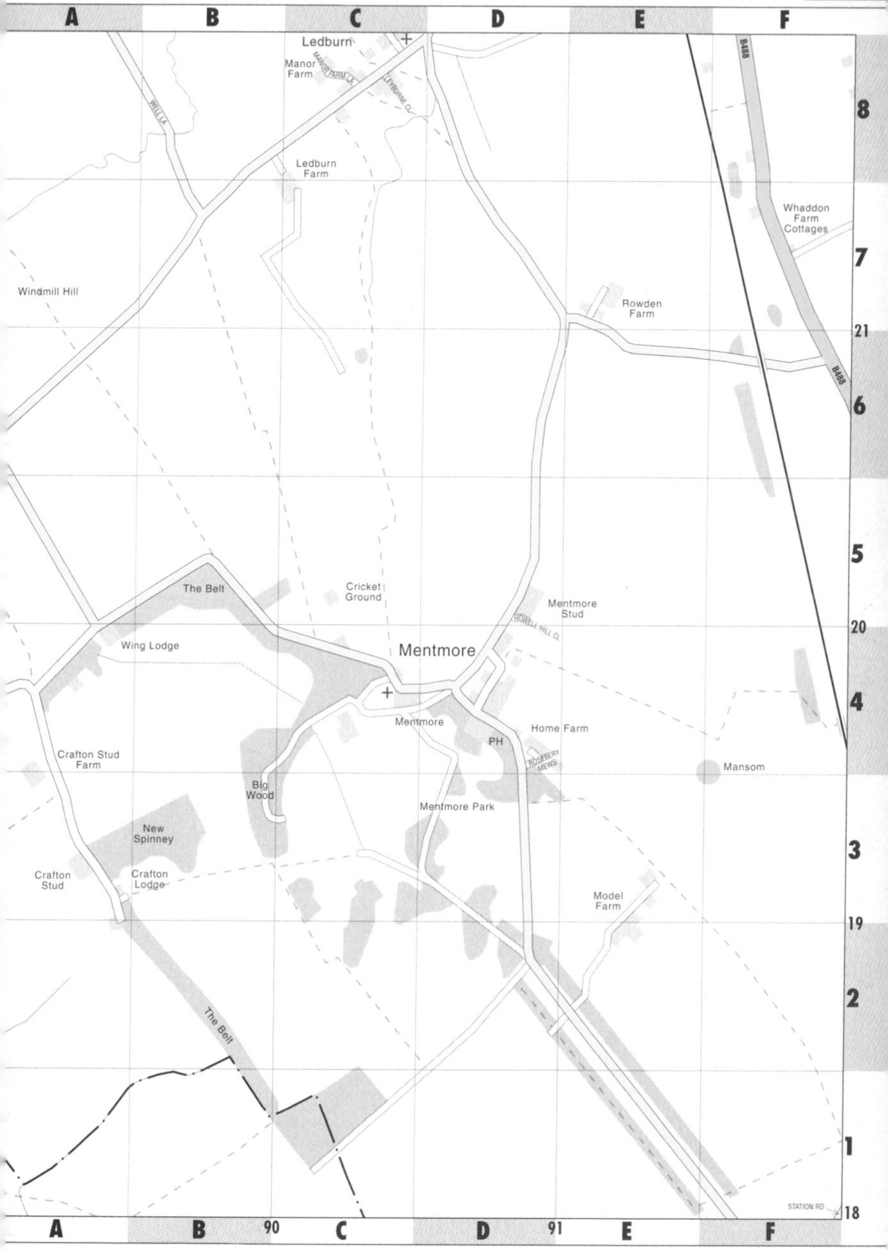

A B C D E F

8

Ledburn
Manor
Farm
Ledburn
Farm

Whaddon
Farm
Cottages

7

Windmill Hill

Rowden
Farm

21

6

5

The Belt

Cricket
Ground

Mentmore
Stud

20

Wing Lodge

Mentmore

4

Crafton Stud
Farm

Mentmore

PH

Home Farm

Mansom

Big
Wood

New
Spinney

Mentmore Park

3

Crafton
Stud

Crafton
Lodge

Model
Farm

19

2

The Belt

1

STATION RD

18

A B 90 C D 91 E F

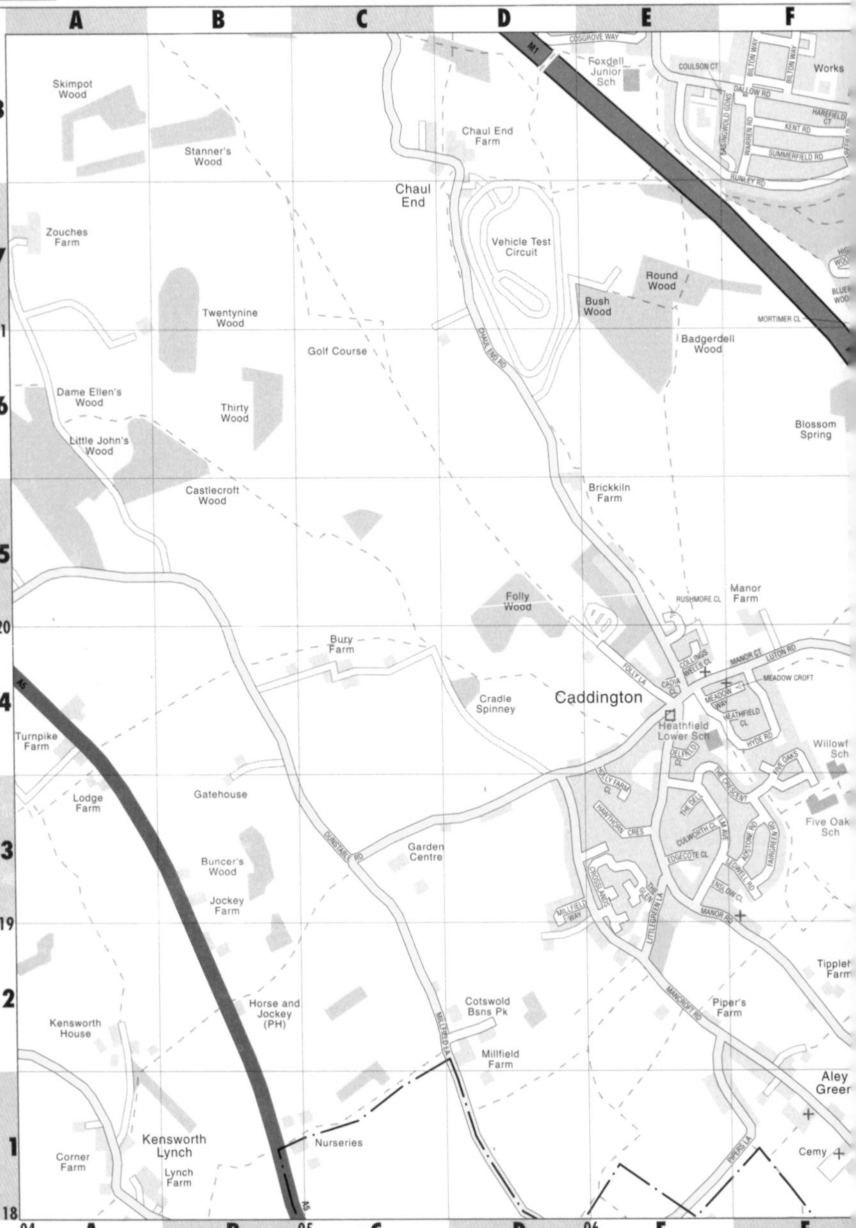

44

| | A | B | C | D | E | F |

**8**
Skimpot Wood
Stanner's Wood
Chaul End Farm
Foxdell Junior Sch
COSGROVE WAY
M1
COULSON CT
Works
BILTON WAY
DALLOW RD
HAREFIELD CT
KENT RD
SUMMERFIELD RD
DUNFLY RD

Chaul End

**7**
Zouches Farm
Vehicle Test Circuit
Round Wood
Bush Wood
MORTIMER CL
HIGH WOOD
BLUE
WOOD

**21**
Twentynine Wood
Golf Course
Badgerdell Wood

**6**
Dame Ellen's Wood
Thirty Wood
Blossom Spring
Little John's Wood

Castlecroft Wood
Brickkiln Farm

**5**
RUSHMORE CL
Manor Farm

**20**
Folly Wood
LUTON RD
MANOR CT
MEADOW CROFT
MEADOW

Bury Farm

**4**
Turnpike Farm
Caddington
Heathfield Lower Sch
Willowf Sch
Cradle Spinney
THE OAKS
HYDE RD

Lodge Farm
Gatehouse
Five Oak Sch

**3**
Buncer's Wood
Garden Centre
LADBROOKE CRES

Jockey Farm
MANOR RD

**19**
Tipplet Farm
MILLFIELD WAY
Piper's Farm

**2**
Kensworth House
Horse and Jockey (PH)
Cotswold Bsns Pk
Millfield Farm
Aley Greer

**1**
Corner Farm
Kensworth Lynch
Nurseries
Cemy
Lynch Farm

| 04 | A | B | 05 | C | D | 06 | E | F |

83

D8
1 HILLSIDE RD
2 THE BARLEYCORN
3 DOWNTON CT
4 THE MOUNT
5 BEDFORD GDNS
6 VILLA CT
7 ST NINIAN'S CT
8 DEACONS CT

E6
1 ROBERT ALLEN CT
2 ROCHDALE CT
3 KIRKDALE CT
4 ESSEX CT
5 CHOBHAM WLK
6 FLOWERS IND EST
7 HOLLY ST TRAD EST
8 LONGLEY TERR IND PK
9 JAMES CT
10 TRACEY CT
11 TELMERE IND EST

E8
1 ELGAR PATH
2 BUTTERWORTH PATH
3 BERKELEY PATH
4 HAVELOCK RD
5 ALBION CT

45
64


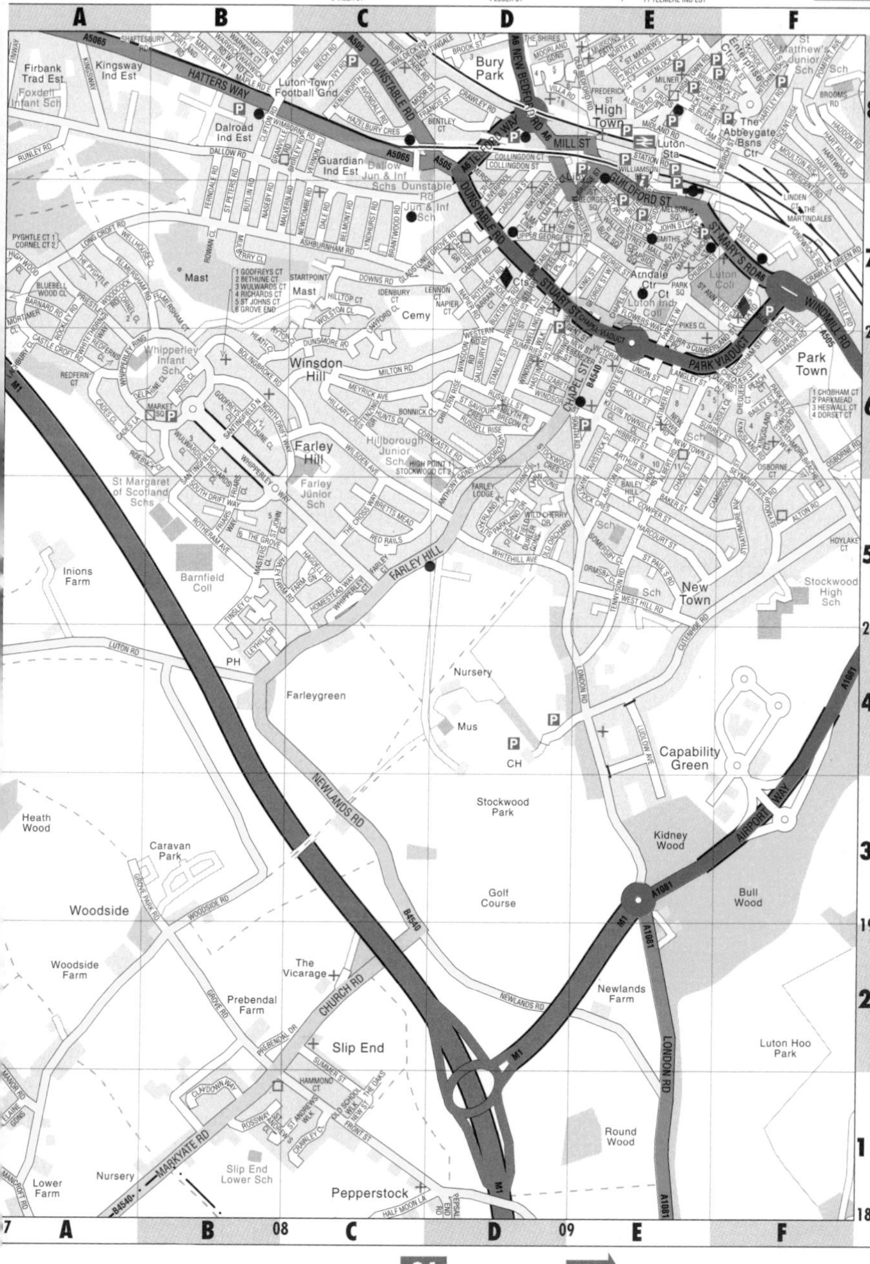


84
64

63
46

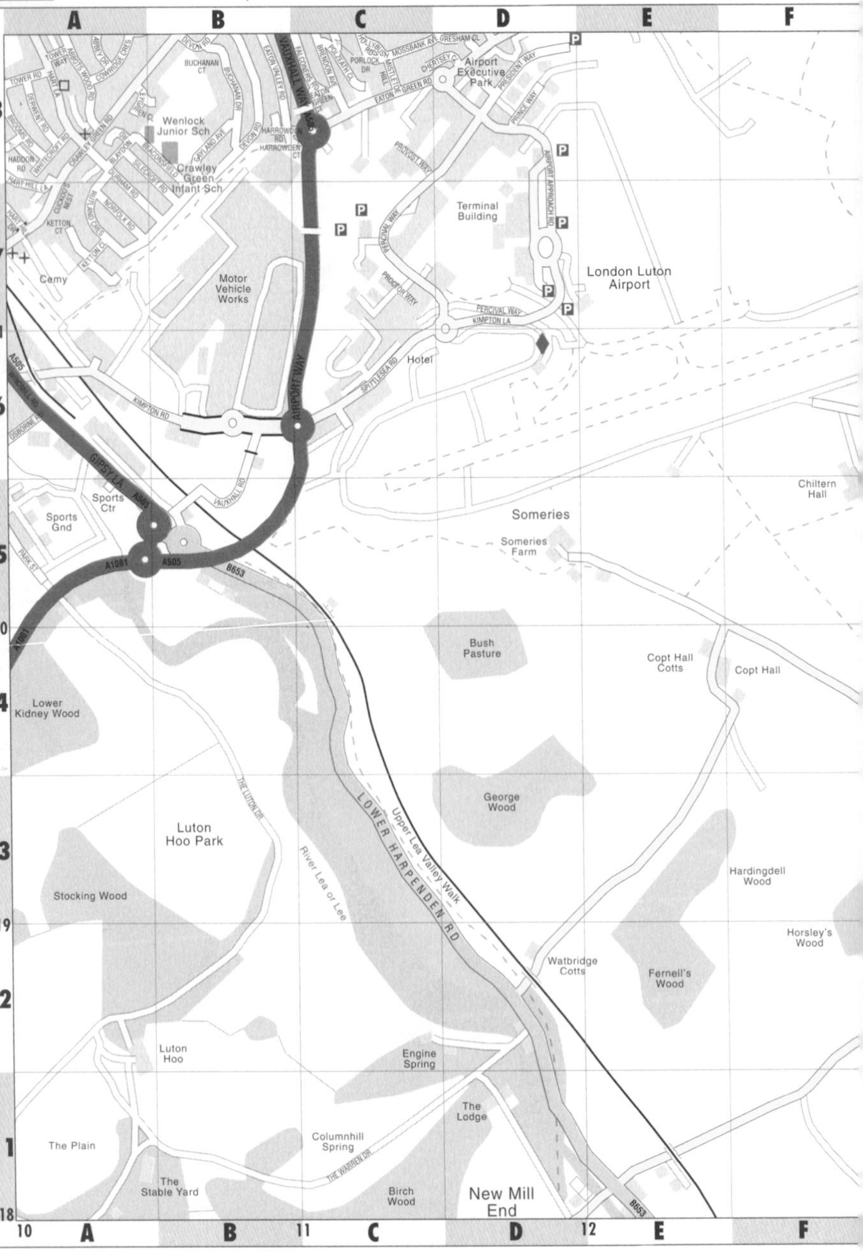

A B C D E F

8

7

21

6

5

20

4

3

19

2

1

18

LOWER RD
Wenlock Junior Sch
Crawley Green Infant Sch
HADDON RD
KETTON CT
BUCHANAN CT
Cemy
Motor Vehicle Works
Sports Ctr
Sports Gnd
A505
A1081
B653
Lower Kidney Wood
Luton Hoo Park
Stocking Wood
The Luton Dri
Luton Hoo
The Plain
The Stable Yard
Columnhill Spring
THE WARREN DRI
Birch Wood
New Mill End
The Lodge
Engine Spring
Airport Executive Park
Terminal Building
London Luton Airport
Hotel
KIMPTON RD
KIMPTON LA
PERCIVAL WAY
Someries
Somaries Farm
Bush Pasture
George Wood
Watbridge Cotts
Chiltern Hall
Copt Hall Cotts
Copt Hall
Hardingdell Wood
Horsley's Wood
Fernell's Wood
River Lea or Lee
Upper Lea Valley Walk
LOWER HARPENDEN RD
B653

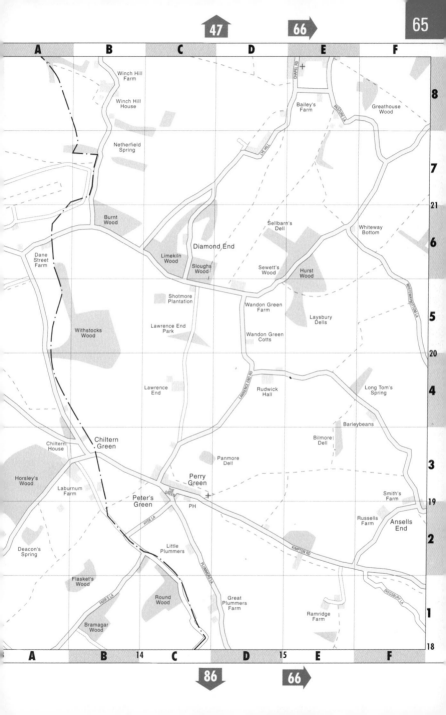

A  B  C  D  E  F

8

Winch Hill Farm

Winch Hill House

Bailey's Farm

Greathouse Wood

Netherfield Spring

7

21

Burnt Wood

Sellbarn's Dell

Whiteway Bottom

6

Dane Street Farm

Limekiln Wood

Diamond End

Sloughs Wood

Sewett's Wood

Hurst Wood

Shotmore Plantation

Wandon Green Farm

5

Withstocks Wood

Lawrence End Park

Wandon Green Cotts

Laysbury Dells

20

Lawrence End

Rudwick Hall

Long Tom's Spring

4

Barleybeans

Chiltern Green

Bilmore Dell

Chiltern House

Panmore Dell

Perry Green

Smith's Farm

3

Horsley's Wood

Laburnum Farm

Peter's Green

PH

19

Russells Farm

Ansells End

Deacon's Spring

Little Plummers

KIMPTON RD

2

Flasket's Wood

Round Wood

Great Plummers Farm

Ramridge Farm

Bramagar Wood

1

18

A  B  14  C  D  15  E  F

65
48

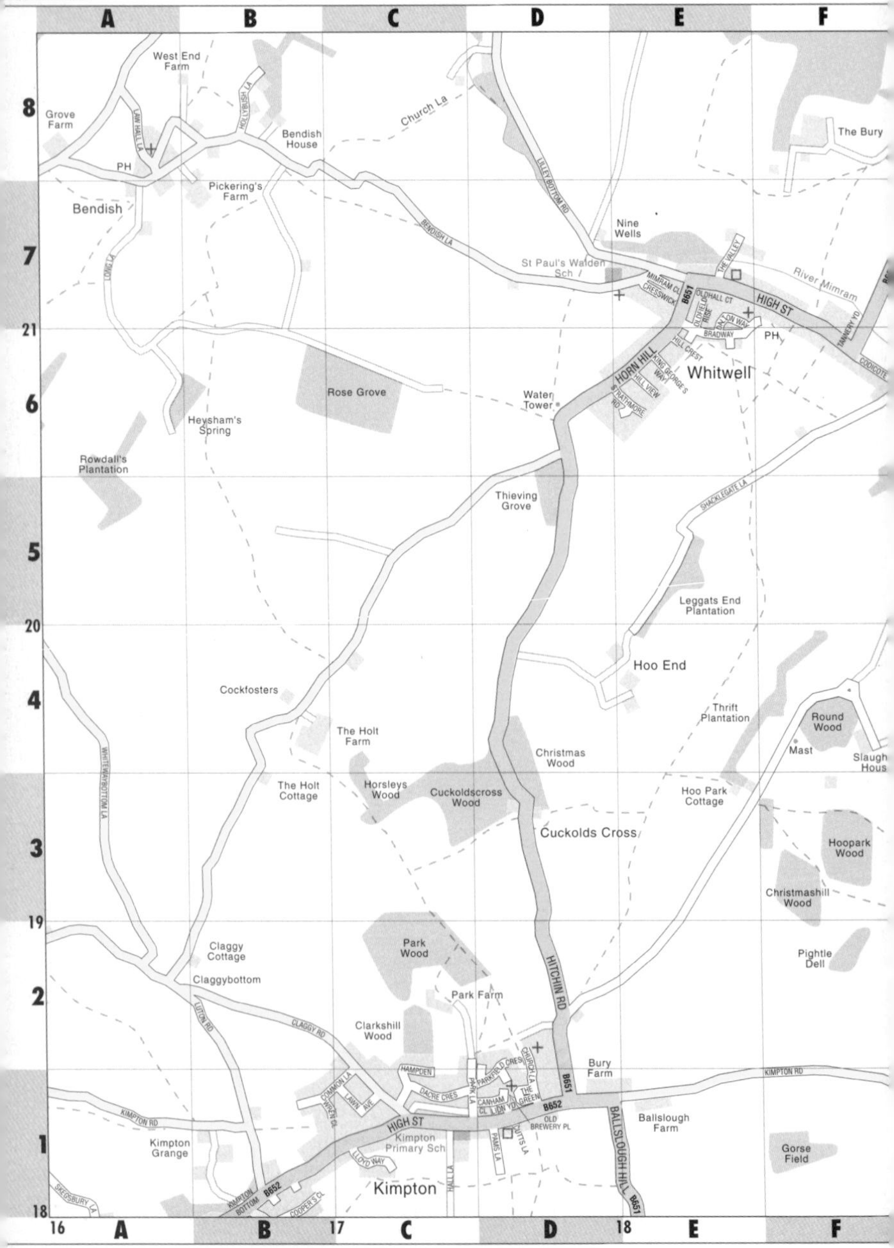
A
B
C
D
E
F
8
7
21
6
5
20
4
3
19
2
1
18
16
17
18
West End Farm
Grove Farm
LAW HALL LA
HOLLYBUSH LA
Church La
Bendish House
PH
Pickering's Farm
Bendish
LONG LA
BENDISH LA
LILLEY BOTTOM RD
The Bury
Nine Wells
St Paul's Walden Sch
THE VALLEY
River Mimram
MIMRAM CL
CRESSWICK
B651
OLDHALL CT
OLDFIELD RISE
DALTON WAY
HIGH ST
TANNERY YD
BRADWAY
PH
HILL CREST
HORN HILL
KING GEORGE'S WAY
HILL VIEW
STRATHMORE RD
Whitwell
CODICOTE
Rose Grove
Water Tower
Heysham's Spring
Rowdall's Plantation
Thieving Grove
SHACKLEGATE LA
Leggats End Plantation
Hoo End
Cockfosters
Thrift Plantation
Round Wood
Mast
Slaugh Hous
The Holt Farm
Christmas Wood
WHITEWAYBOTTOM LA
The Holt Cottage
Horsleys Wood
Cuckoldscross Wood
Hoo Park Cottage
Cuckolds Cross
Hoopark Wood
Christmashill Wood
Pightle Dell
Claggy Cottage
Park Wood
HITCHIN RD
Claggybottom
Park Farm
LUTON RD
CLAGGY RD
Clarkshill Wood
HAMPDEN
PARKFIELD CRES
CHURCH LA
Bury Farm
KIMPTON RD
COMMON LA
DACRE CRES
PARK LA
THE GREEN
B651
LAWN AVE
WREN CL
CANHAM CL
LIDN YD
B652
KIMPTON RD
HIGH ST
OLD BREWERY PL
BALLSLOUGH HILL
Ballslough Farm
Kimpton Grange
Kimpton Primary Sch
PAMS LA
CUTTS LA
Gorse Field
LLOYD WAY
HALL LA
SKEGSBURY LA
KIMPTON BOTTOM
B652
COOPER'S CL
Kimpton
B651

65
87

49
68

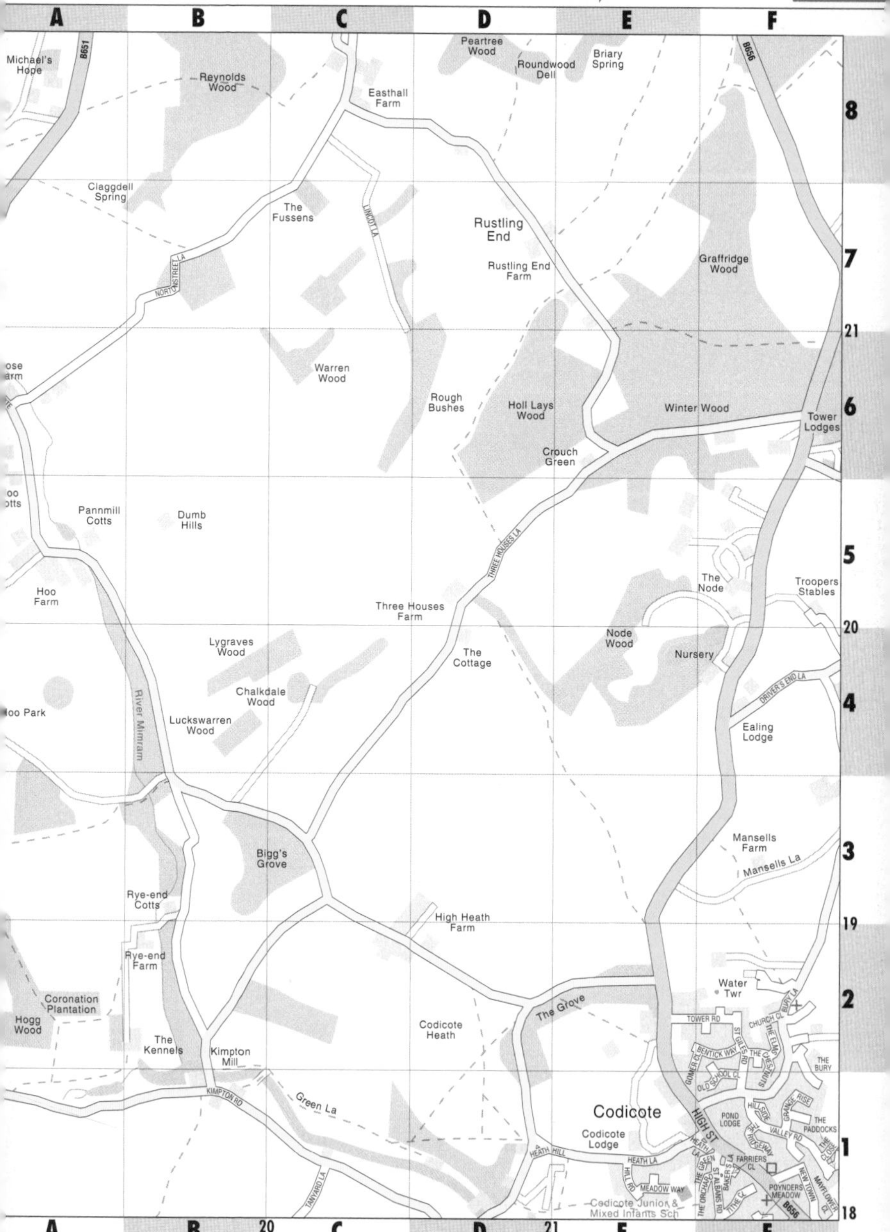
A
B
C
D
E
F
Michael's Hope
B651
Reynolds Wood
Peartree Wood
Roundwood Dell
Briary Spring
B656
Easthall Farm
Claggdell Spring
The Fussens
LINCOTT LA
Rustling End
Rustling End Farm
Graffridge Wood
NORTON STREET LA
Warren Wood
Rough Bushes
Holl Lays Wood
Winter Wood
Tower Lodges
Crouch Green
Pannmill Cotts
Dumb Hills
THREE HOUSES LA
Hoo Farm
Three Houses Farm
The Node
Troopers Stables
Lygraves Wood
The Cottage
Node Wood
Nursery
DRIVER'S END LA
River Mimram
Chalkdale Wood
Hoo Park
Luckswarren Wood
Ealing Lodge
Bigg's Grove
Mansells Farm
Mansells La
Rye-end Cotts
High Heath Farm
Rye-end Farm
Water Twr
Coronation Plantation
The Grove
BURY LA
Hogg Wood
Codicote Heath
TOWER RD
CHURCH CL
The Kennels
Kimpton Mill
BENTICK WAY
ST GILES RD
THE ELMS
THE CHESTNUTS
THE BURY
GOMER CL
OLD SCHOOL CL
KIMPTON RD
Green La
Codicote
HIGH ST
POND LODGE
HILLSIDE
GRANGE RISE
THE PADDOCKS
Codicote Lodge
THE RIDGEWAY
VALLEY RD
HEATH HILL
HEATH LA
FARRIERS CL
HILL RD
MEADOW WAY
THE GREEN
ST ALBANS RD
BAKER'S LA
NEW TOWN
MAYFLOWER CL
TANYARD LA
THE ORCHARD
TITHE CL
POYNDERS MEADOW
Codicote Junior & Mixed Infants Sch
8
7
21
6
5
20
4
3
19
2
1
18
20
21

88
68

67
50

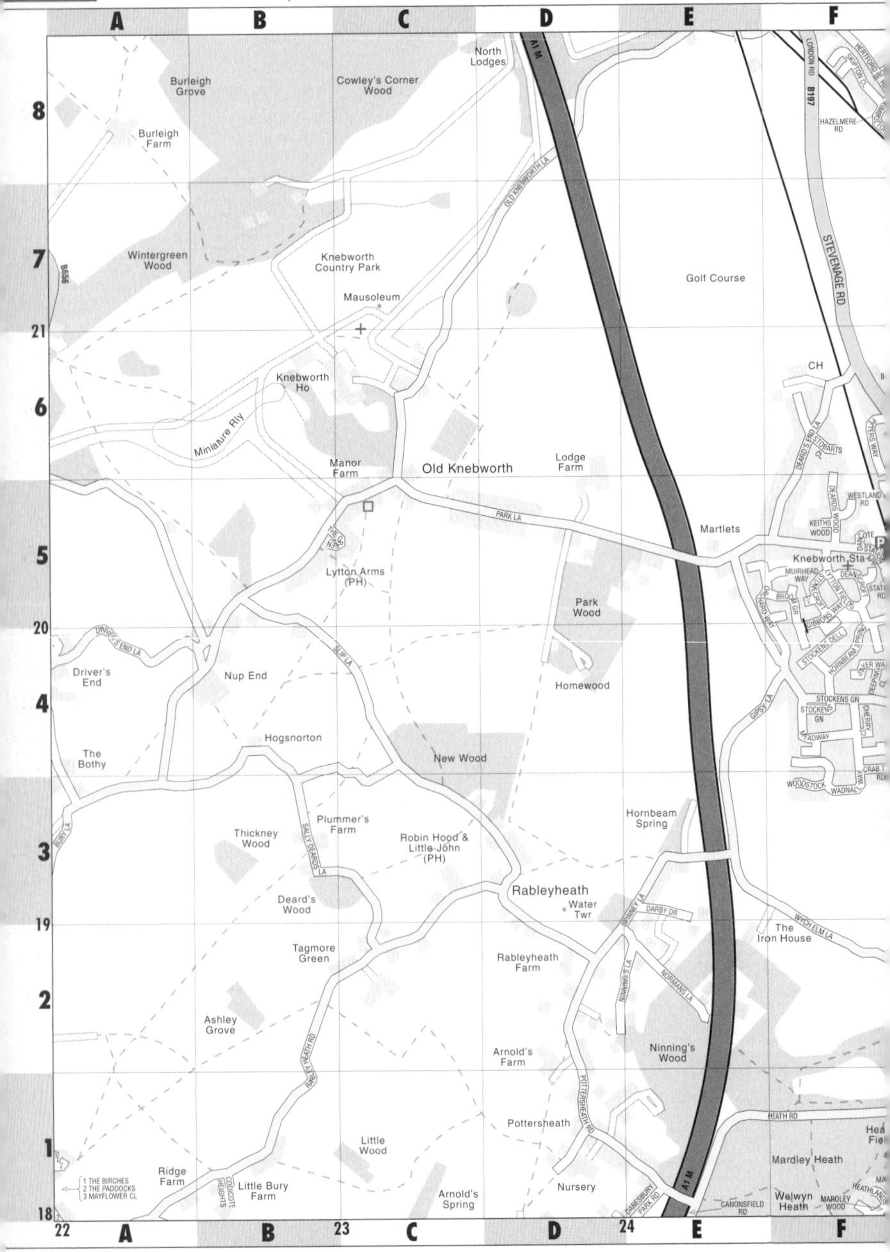
A
B
C
D
E
F
8
7
21
6
5
20
4
3
19
2
1
18
22
23
24
North Lodges
A1 M
Burleigh Grove
Cowley's Corner Wood
LONDON RD
B197
HERTFORD RD
SKIPTON CL
HAZELMERE RD
Burleigh Farm
OLD KNEBWORTH LA
STEVENAGE RD
Wintergreen Wood
B656
Knebworth Country Park
Golf Course
Mausoleum
CH
Knebworth Ho
Miniature Rly
DEARD'S END LA
STOBARTS CL
PYERS WAY
Manor Farm
Old Knebworth
Lodge Farm
DEARDS WOOD
WESTLAND RD
PARK LA
Martlets
KEITHS WOOD
THE GREEN
Knebworth Sta
MUIRHEAD WAY
DEANSCROFT
LYTTON FIELDS
STATION RD
Lytton Arms (PH)
Park Wood
ORCHARD WAY
BROOM GR
GIBBONS WAY
DRIVER'S END LA
SLIP LA
STOCKENS DELL
HORNBEAM SPRING
Driver's End
Nup End
Homewood
STOCKENS GN
STOCKENS GN
CHERRY CL
GIPSY LA
MEADWAY
Hogsnorton
The Bothy
New Wood
CRAB TREE RD
WOODSTOCK
WADNAL WAY
BURY LA
Plummer's Farm
Hornbeam Spring
Thickney Wood
SALLY DEARDS LA
Robin Hood & Little John (PH)
Rableyheath
Water Twr
Deard's Wood
SPINNEY LA
DARBY DR
The Iron House
WYCH ELM LA
Tagmore Green
Rableyheath Farm
NINNINGS LA
NORMANS LA
Ashley Grove
RABLEY HEATH RD
Arnold's Farm
Ninning's Wood
POTTERSHEATH RD
HEATH RD
Pottersheath
Little Wood
Mardley Heath
Ridge Farm
1 THE BIRCHES
2 THE PADDOCKS
3 MAYFLOWER CL
CODICOTE HEIGHTS
Little Bury Farm
Arnold's Spring
Nursery
DANESBURY PARK RD
CANONSFIELD RD
Welwyn Heath
MARDLEY WOOD
HEATHLANDS

67
89

51
70

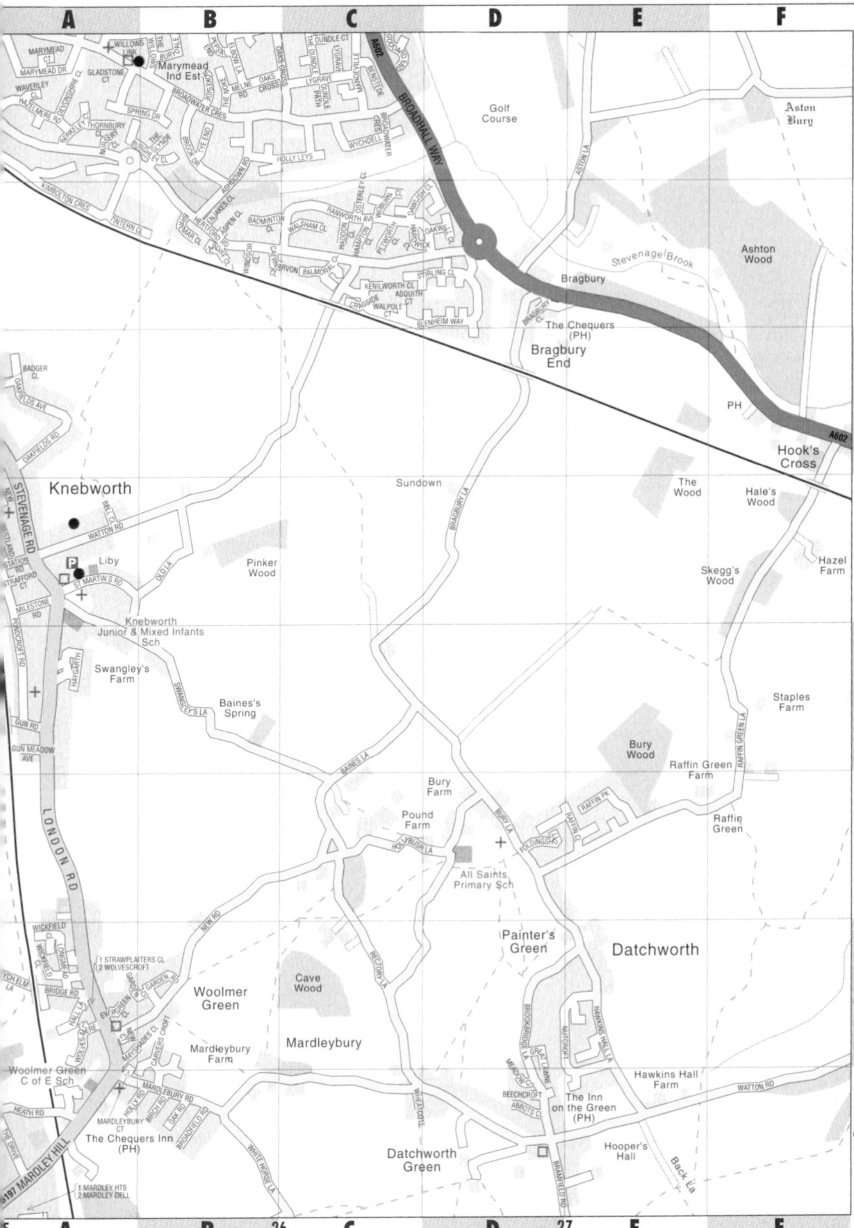
A
B
C
D
E
F
Marymead Ind Est
BROADHALL WAY
A602
Golf Course
Aston Bury
ASTON LA
Ashton Wood
Stevenage Brook
Bragbury
The Chequers (PH)
Bragbury End
PH
Hook's Cross
The Wood
Hale's Wood
Sundown
BRAGBURY LA
Knebworth
STEVENAGE RD
WATTON RD
Liby
ST MARTIN'S RD
OLD LA
Pinker Wood
Skegg's Wood
Hazel Farm
Knebworth Junior & Mixed Infants Sch
Swangley's Farm
SWANGLEY'S LA
Baines's Spring
Staples Farm
Bury Wood
Raffin Green Farm
RAFFIN GREEN LA
LONDON RD
BAINES LA
Bury Farm
Pound Farm
HOLLYBUSH LA
BURY LA
Raffin Green
All Saints Primary Sch
NEW RD
Painter's Green
Datchworth
Woolmer Green
Cave Wood
RECTORY LA
Mardleybury Farm
Mardleybury
Woolmer Green C of E Sch
The Chequers Inn (PH)
MARDLEY HILL
WHITE HORSE LA
WHEATCOTE
Datchworth Green
The Inn on the Green (PH)
HAWKINS HALL LA
Hawkins Hall Farm
WATTON RD
Hooper's Hall
Back La
BRAMFIELD RD
8
7
21
6
5
20
4
3
19
2
1
18
26
27

90
70

69
52

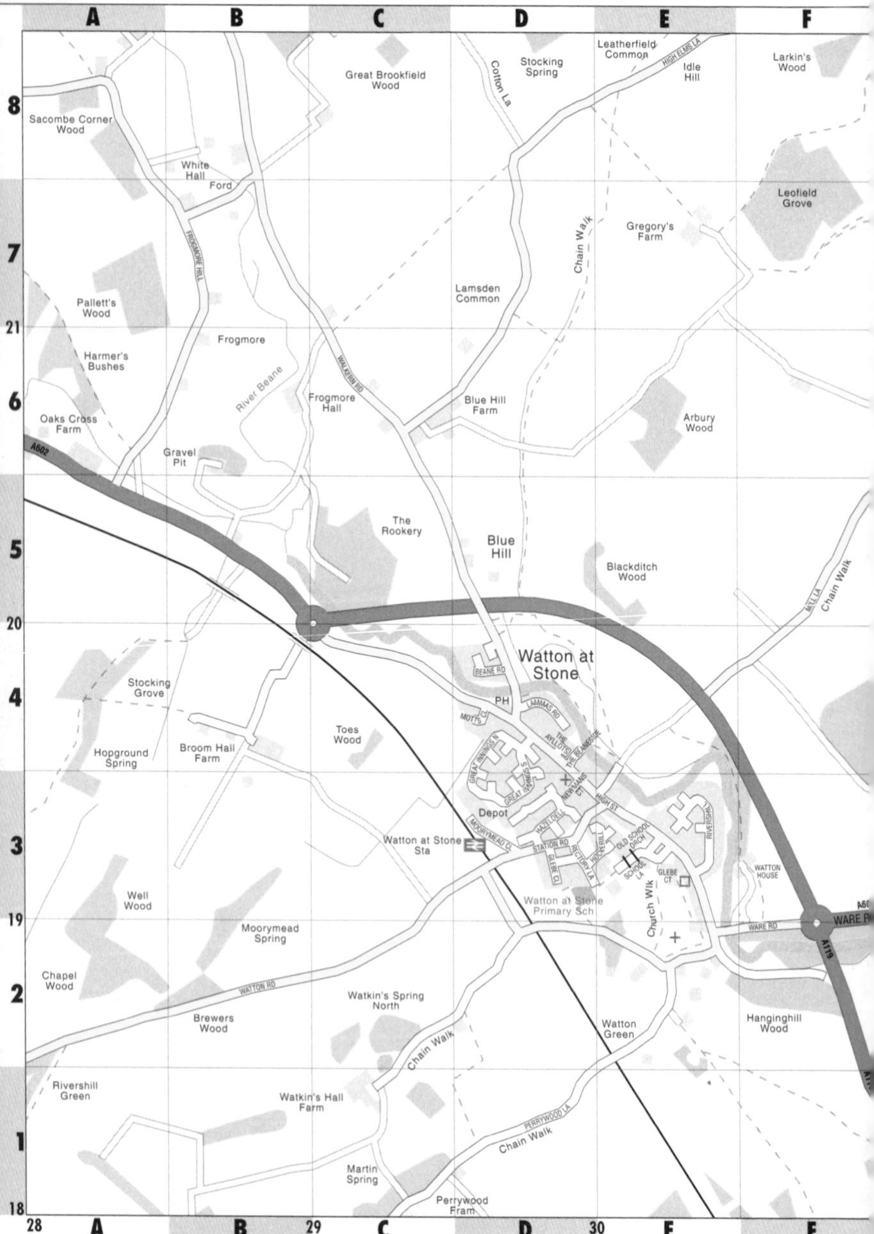
A
B
C
D
E
F
8
7
21
6
5
20
4
3
19
2
1
18
28
29
30
Great Brookfield Wood
Cotton La
Stocking Spring
Leatherfield Common
HIGH ELMS LA
Idle Hill
Larkin's Wood
Sacombe Corner Wood
White Hall
Ford
Leofield Grove
FROGMORE HILL
Gregory's Farm
Chain Walk
Lamsden Common
Pallett's Wood
Frogmore
Harmer's Bushes
WALKERN RD
River Beane
Frogmore Hall
Blue Hill Farm
Arbury Wood
Oaks Cross Farm
A602
Gravel Pit
The Rookery
Blue Hill
Blackditch Wood
MILL LA
Chain Walk
Watton at Stone
BEANE RD
Stocking Grove
PH
LAMMAS RD
MOTTS CL
Toes Wood
THE AYLLOTS
THE BEANESIDE
Hopground Spring
Broom Hall Farm
GREAT INNINGS N
GREAT INNINGS S
NEWMANS CT
HIGH ST
Depot
HAZELDELL
RIVERSHILL
MOORYMEAD CL
OLD SCHOOL ORCH
Watton at Stone Sta
STATION RD
RECTORY LA
GLEBE CL
SCHOOL LA
GLEBE CT
WATTON HOUSE
Watton at Stone Primary Sch
Church Wlk
Well Wood
WARE RD
WARE R
A602
Moorymead Spring
A119
Chapel Wood
WATTON RD
Watkin's Spring North
Brewers Wood
Watton Green
Hanginghill Wood
Chain Walk
Rivershill Green
Watkin's Hall Farm
PERRYWOOD LA
Chain Walk
Martin Spring
Perrywood Fram

69
91

53
72

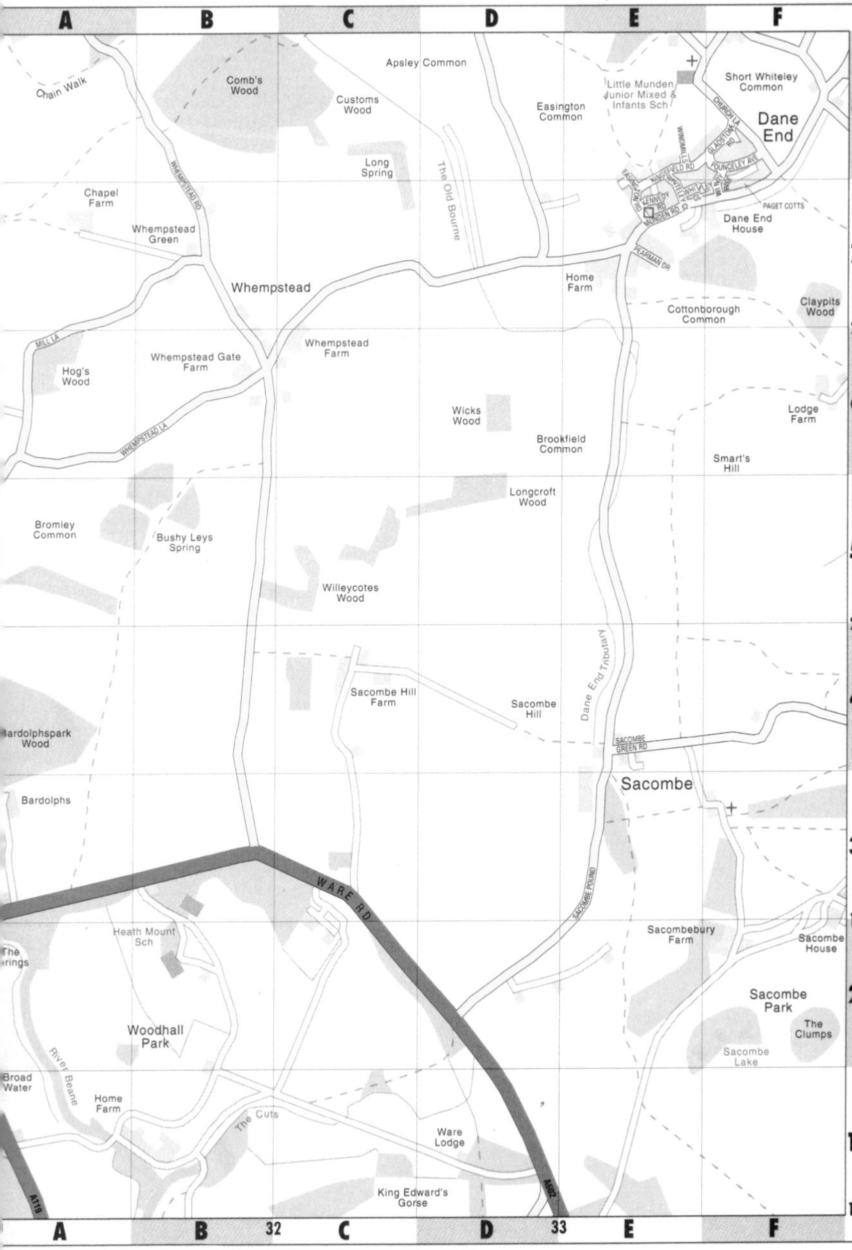
A
B
C
D
E
F
8
7
21
6
5
20
4
3
19
2
1
18
32
33
Chain Walk
Comb's Wood
Customs Wood
Apsley Common
Easington Common
Little Munden Junior Mixed & Infants Sch
Short Whiteley Common
Dane End
CHURCH LA
GLADSTONE RD
FOUNCELEY AVE
WINDMILLS
KINGSFIELD RD
KENNEDY RD
WHITELEY CL
MUNDEN RD
EASINGTON RD
PAGET COTTS
Dane End House
PEARMAN DR
Long Spring
The Old Bourne
Chapel Farm
WHEMPSTEAD RD
Whempstead Green
Whempstead
Home Farm
Cottonborough Common
Claypits Wood
MILL LA
Hog's Wood
Whempstead Gate Farm
Whempstead Farm
WHEMPSTEAD LA
Wicks Wood
Brookfield Common
Lodge Farm
Smart's Hill
Longcroft Wood
Bromley Common
Bushy Leys Spring
Willeycotes Wood
Dane End Tributary
Sacombe Hill Farm
Sacombe Hill
Bardolphspark Wood
SACOMBE GREEN RD
Sacombe
Bardolphs
WARE RD
SACOMBE POUND
Heath Mount Sch
Sacombebury Farm
Sacombe House
Sacombe Park
The Clumps
Sacombe Lake
Woodhall Park
River Beane
Broad Water
Home Farm
The Cuts
Ware Lodge
King Edward's Gorse
A119
A602

92
72

71
54

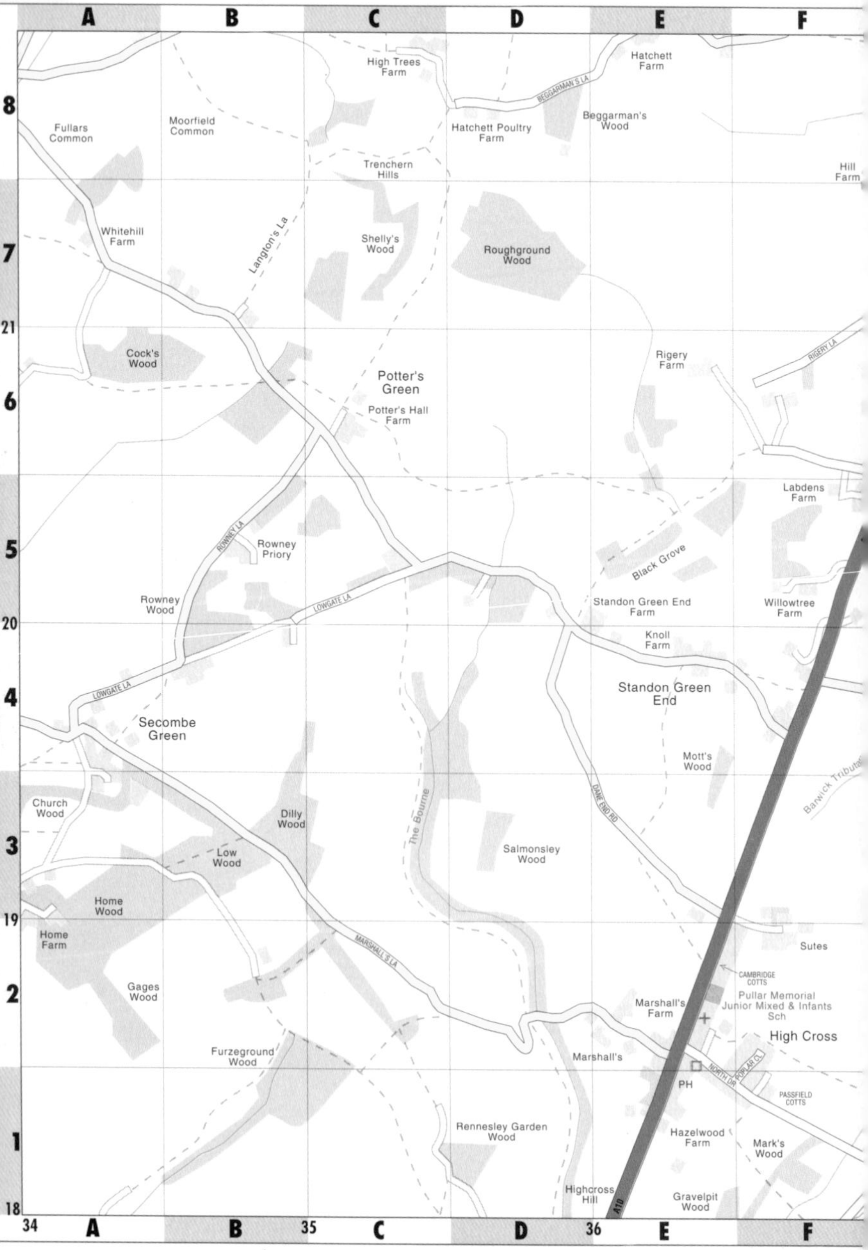
A
B
C
D
E
F
8
7
21
6
5
20
4
3
19
2
1
18
34
35
36
High Trees Farm
Hatchett Farm
BEGGARMAN'S LA
Beggarman's Wood
Fullars Common
Moorfield Common
Hatchett Poultry Farm
Trenchern Hills
Hill Farm
Whitehill Farm
Langton's La
Shelly's Wood
Roughground Wood
Cock's Wood
Rigery Farm
RIGERY LA
Potter's Green
Potter's Hall Farm
Labdens Farm
ROWNEY LA
Rowney Priory
Black Grove
Rowney Wood
LOWGATE LA
Standon Green End Farm
Willowtree Farm
Knoll Farm
Standon Green End
Secombe Green
Mott's Wood
Barwick Tributa
Church Wood
Dilly Wood
DANE END RD
The Bourne
Low Wood
Salmonsley Wood
Home Wood
Home Farm
Sutes
MARSHALL'S LA
CAMBRIDGE COTTS
Gages Wood
Marshall's Farm
Pullar Memorial Junior Mixed & Infants Sch
High Cross
Furzeground Wood
Marshall's
NORTH DR
POPLAR CL
PH
PASSFIELD COTTS
Rennesley Garden Wood
Hazelwood Farm
Mark's Wood
Highcross Hill
Gravelpit Wood
A10

71
93

55
74

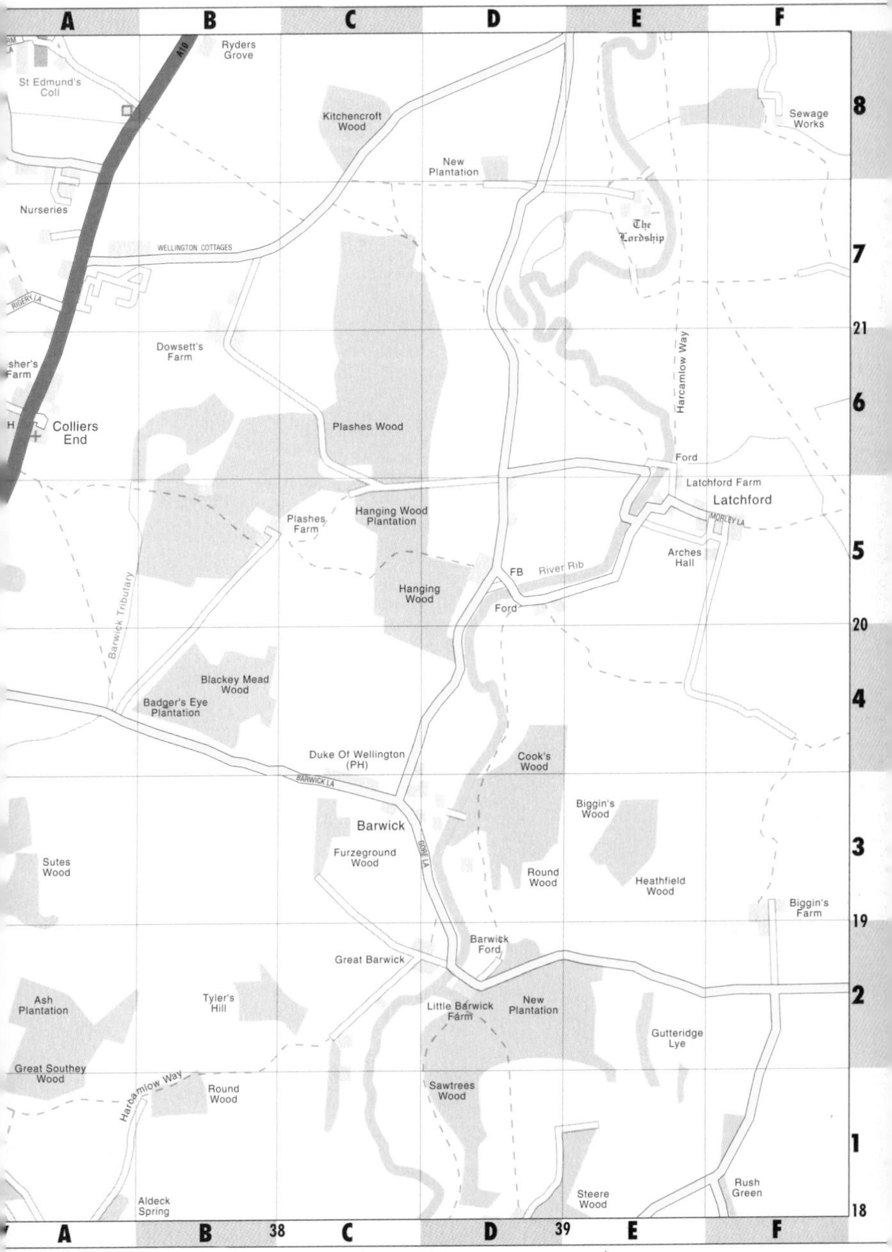
A
B
C
D
E
F
Ryders Grove
St Edmund's Coll
A10
Kitchencroft Wood
New Plantation
Sewage Works
Nurseries
The Lordship
WELLINGTON COTTAGES
RIGERY LA
Dowsett's Farm
sher's Farm
Harcamlow Way
Colliers End
Plashes Wood
Ford
Latchford Farm
Latchford
MORLEY LA
Plashes Farm
Hanging Wood Plantation
Arches Hall
FB
River Rib
Hanging Wood
Ford
Barwick Tributary
Blackey Mead Wood
Badger's Eye Plantation
Duke Of Wellington (PH)
BARWICK LA
Cook's Wood
Biggin's Wood
Barwick
Furzeground Wood
GORE LA
Sutes Wood
Round Wood
Heathfield Wood
Biggin's Farm
Barwick Ford
Great Barwick
Ash Plantation
Tyler's Hill
Little Barwick Farm
New Plantation
Gutteridge Lye
Great Southey Wood
Harcamlow Way
Round Wood
Sawtrees Wood
Aldeck Spring
Steere Wood
Rush Green
8
7
21
6
5
20
4
3
19
2
1
18
38
39

94
74

73
56

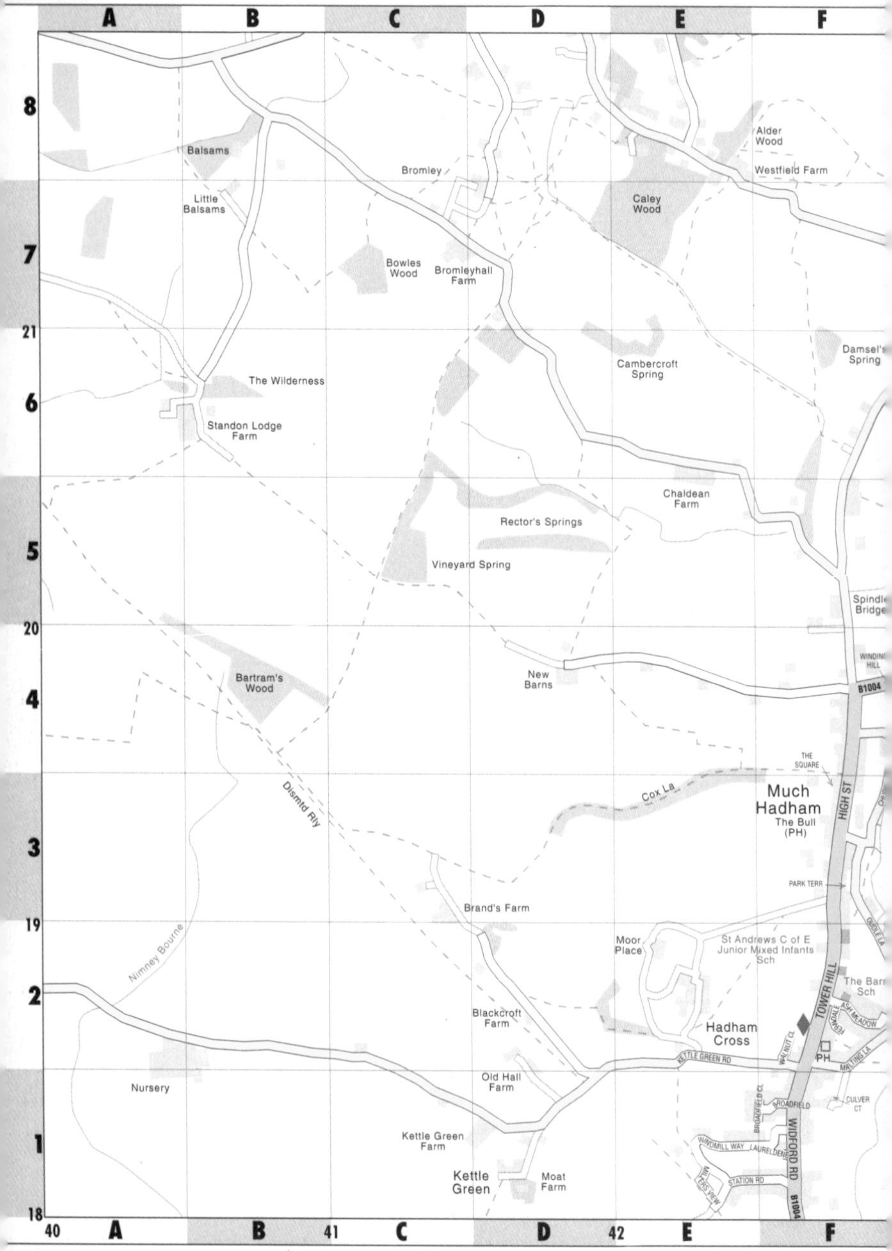
A
B
C
D
E
F
8
7
21
6
5
20
4
3
19
2
1
18
40
41
42
Balsams
Little Balsams
Bromley
Alder Wood
Westfield Farm
Caley Wood
Bowles Wood
Bromleyhall Farm
The Wilderness
Standon Lodge Farm
Cambercroft Spring
Damsel's Spring
Chaldean Farm
Rector's Springs
Vineyard Spring
Spindle Bridge
WINDING HILL
B1004
New Barns
Bartram's Wood
Dismtd Rly
THE SQUARE
Cox La
Much Hadham
The Bull (PH)
HIGH ST
PARK TERR
Brand's Farm
Moor Place
St Andrews C of E Junior Mixed Infants Sch
Nimney Bourne
The Barn Sch
TOWER HILL
Blackcroft Farm
Hadham Cross
ASH MEADOW
FERNDALE
WALNUT CL
KETTLE GREEN RD
PH
MALTING LA
Old Hall Farm
Nursery
BROADFIELD CL
ROADFIELD
CULVER CT
WINDMILL WAY
LAURELDENE
WIDFORD RD
Kettle Green Farm
Kettle Green
Moat Farm
MILLERS VIEW
STATION RD
B1004

73
95

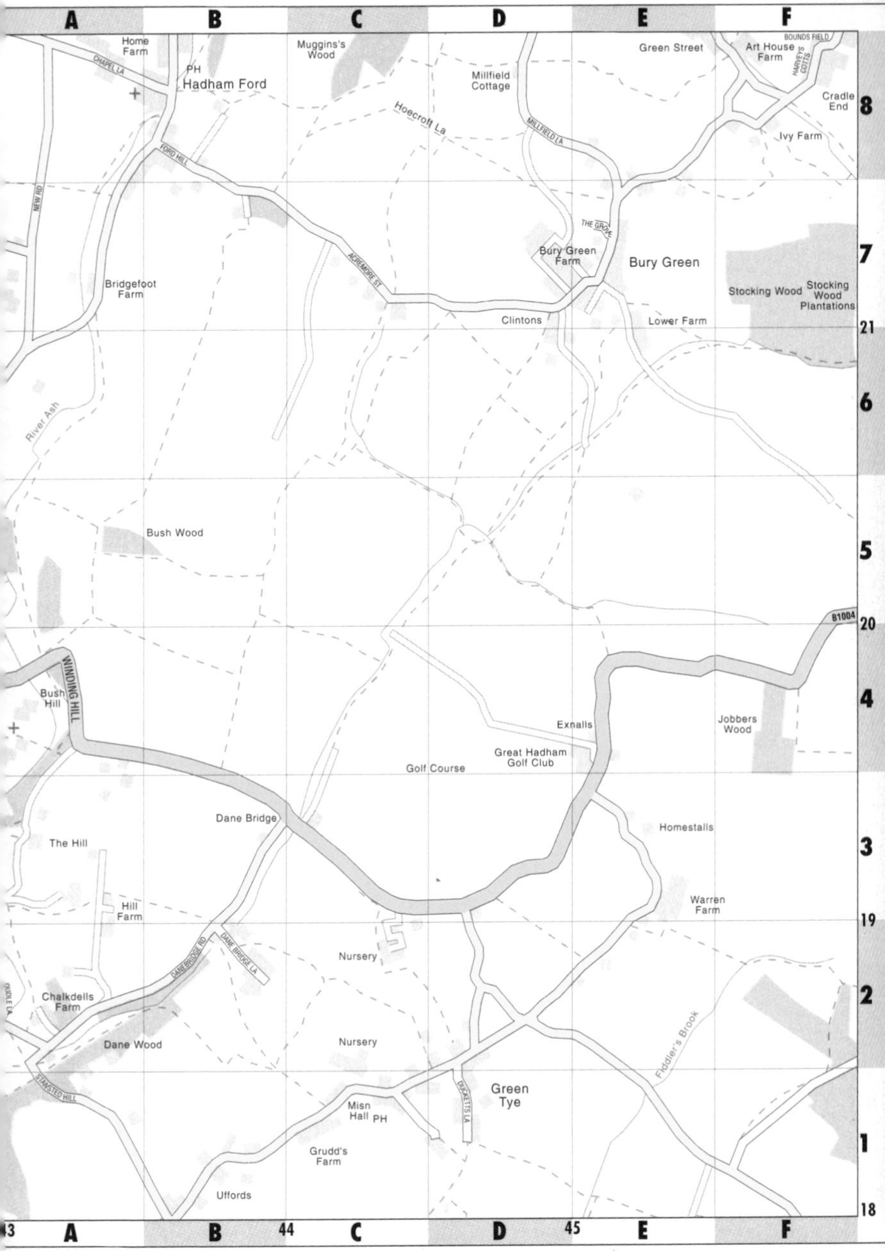

A B C D E F

Home Farm
CHAPEL LA
PH
Hadham Ford
Muggins's Wood
Millfield Cottage
Green Street
Art House Farm
BOUNDS FIELD
HARRIETTS COTTS

8

Hoecroft La
MILLFIELD LA
Cradle End
Ivy Farm

FORD HILL

THE GROVE

Bridgefoot Farm

ACREMORE ST

Bury Green Farm
Bury Green

7

Stocking Wood
Stocking Wood Plantations

River Ash

Clintons
Lower Farm

21

6

Bush Wood

5

B1004

20

WINDING HILL
Bush Hill

Exnalls
Jobbers Wood

4

Golf Course
Great Hadham Golf Club

Dane Bridge
Homestalls

The Hill

3

Hill Farm

Warren Farm

19

DANE BRIDGE RD
DANE BRIDGE LA

Nursery

Chalkdells Farm

Fiddler's Brook

2

Dane Wood

Nursery

STREETS HILL

Misn Hall PH
Green Tye

BARTLES LA

Grudd's Farm

1

Uffords

18

43 A B 44 C D 45 E F

75
58

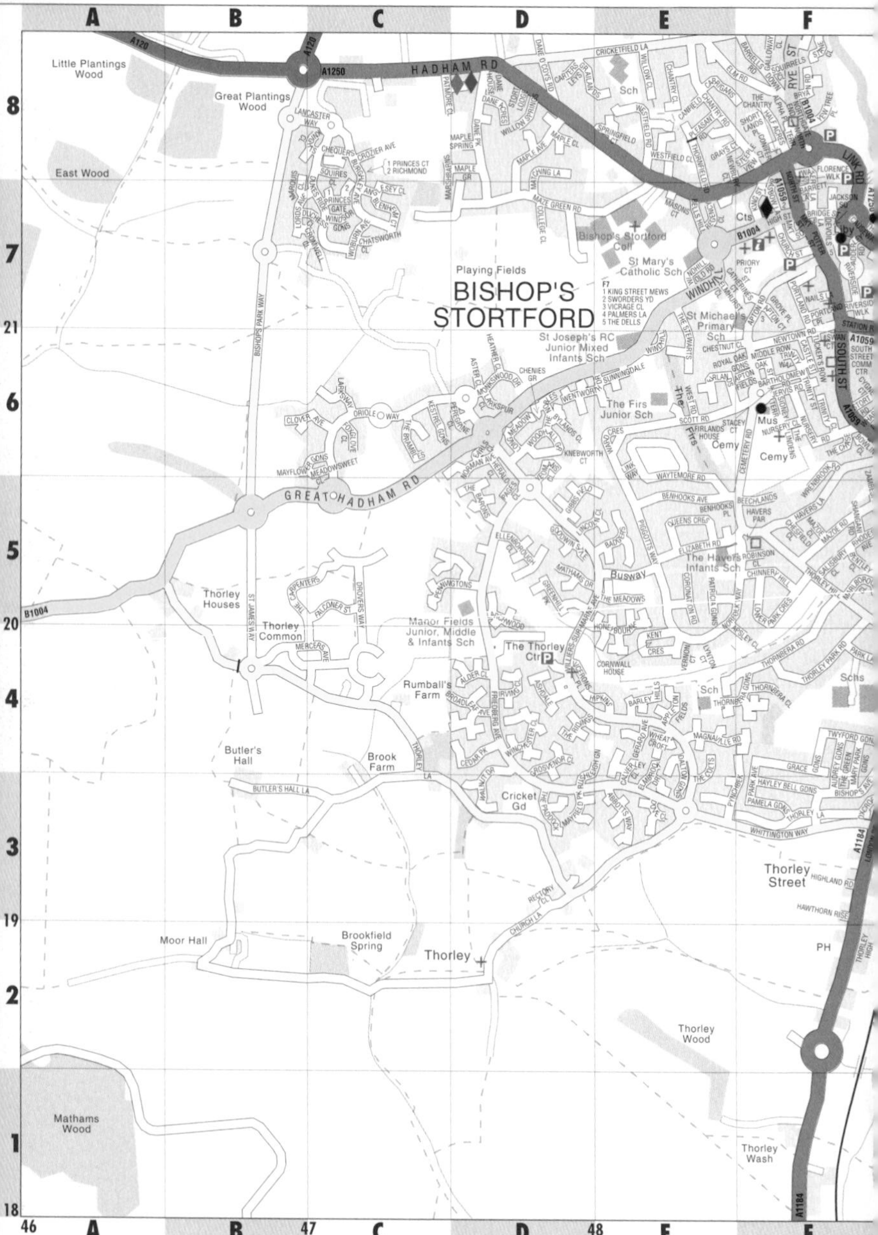
A
B
C
D
E
F
8
7
21
6
5
20
4
3
19
2
1
18
46
47
48
Little Plantings Wood
Great Plantings Wood
East Wood
A120
A1250
HADHAM RD
BISHOP'S STORTFORD
Playing Fields
Bishop's Stortford Coll
St Mary's Catholic Sch
F7
1 KING STREET MEWS
2 SWORDERS YD
3 VICRAGE CL
4 PALMERS LA
5 THE DELLS
St Michael's Primary Sch
St Joseph's RC Junior Mixed Infants Sch
The Firs Junior Sch
1 PRINCES CT
2 RICHMOND
BISHOPS PARK WAY
GREAT HADHAM RD
B1004
B1004
A1059
A1184
LINK RD
SOUTH ST
STATION RD
WINDHILL
Sch
Cts
Mus
Cemy
Busway
The Havers Infants Sch
Thorley Houses
Thorley Common
Manor Fields Junior, Middle & Infants Sch
The Thorley Ctr
Rumball's Farm
Butler's Hall
Brook Farm
BUTLER'S HALL LA
THORLEY LA
Cricket Gd
Schs
Sch
WHITTINGTON WAY
Thorley Street
HIGHLAND RD
HAWTHORN RISE
PH
Moor Hall
Brookfield Spring
Thorley
CHURCH LA
RECTORY CL
Thorley Wood
Mathams Wood
Thorley Wash

75
97

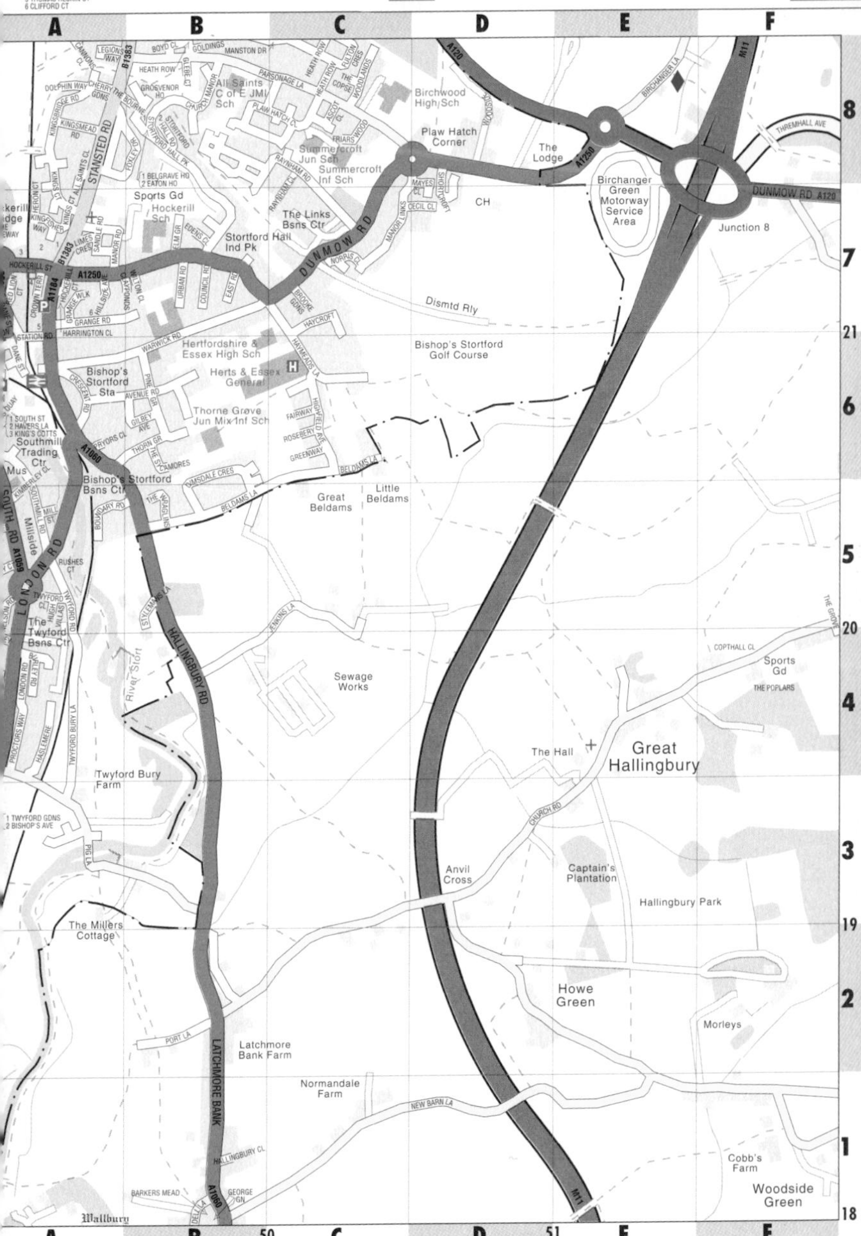

A7
1 FULLER CT
2 THE OLD MALTINGS
3 CASTLE VIEW
4 BAKERS CT
5 THOMAS HESKIN CT
6 CLIFFORD CT

A | B | C | D | E | F

8

THRESHALL AVE

M11

A120

Birchwood
High Sch

Plaw Hatch
Corner

The
Lodge

A1250

Birchanger
Green
Motorway
Service
Area

DUNMOW RD  A120

Junction 8

7

21

Bishop's Stortford
Golf Course

Dismtd Rly

6

THE GRANGE

5

20

Sewage
Works

COPTHALL CL
Sports
Gd
THE POPLARS

4

The Hall
Great
Hallingbury

Twyford Bury
Farm

3

19

Anvil
Cross

Captain's
Plantation

Hallingbury Park

The Millers
Cottage

Howe
Green

2

Morleys

1 TWYFORD GDNS
2 BISHOP'S AVE

Latchmore
Bank Farm

Normandale
Farm

NEW BARN LA

Cobb's
Farm

1

18

Woodside
Green

Wallbury

BARKERS MEAD

GEORGE GN

M11

A | B | C | D | E | F

50

51

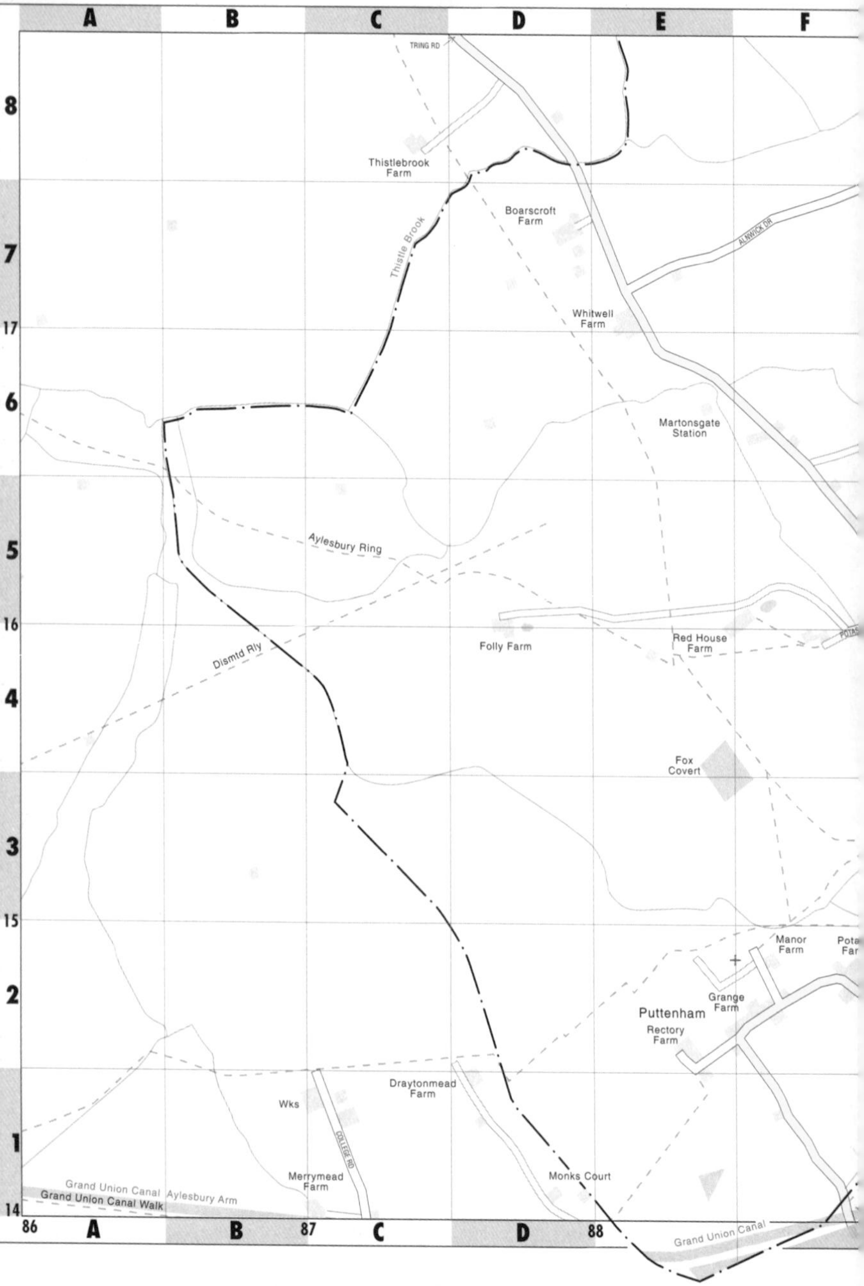

60

A    B    C    D    E    F

TRING RD

8

Thistlebrook
Farm

Boarscroft
Farm

7

ALDWICK DR

17

Whitwell
Farm

Thistle Brook

6

Martonsgate
Station

Aylesbury Ring

5

16

Dismtd Rly

Folly Farm

Red House
Farm

POTAS

4

Fox
Covert

3

15

Manor
Farm

Potas
Far

2

Grange
Farm

Puttenham

Rectory
Farm

Draytonmead
Farm

1

Wks

COLLEGE RD

Merrymead
Farm

Monks Court

Grand Union Canal  Aylesbury Arm
Grand Union Canal Walk

14

86    A    B    87    C    D    88    F

Grand Union Canal

61
80

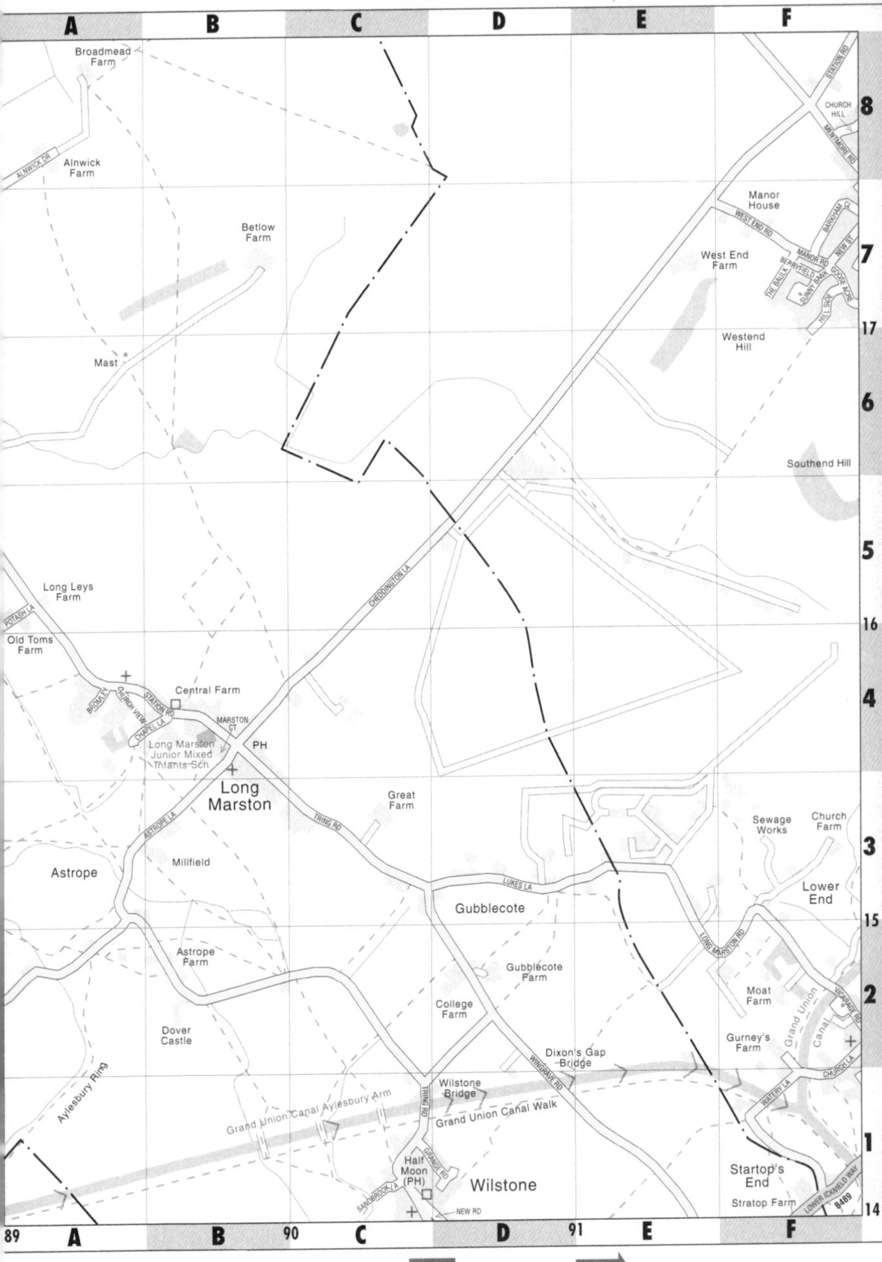
A
B
C
D
E
F
Broadmead Farm
Alnwick Farm
ALNWICK DR
STATION RD
CHURCH HILL
MENTMORE RD
8
Betlow Farm
Manor House
WEST END RD
BARKHAM CL
MANOR RD
NEW ST
West End Farm
BERRYFIELD
SUNNY BANK
GOOSE ACRE
THE BAULK
HILL SIDE
7
17
Mast
Westend Hill
6
Southend Hill
5
Long Leys Farm
POTASH LA
CHEDDINGTON LA
16
Old Toms Farm
Central Farm
BROMLEY
CHURCH VIEW
STATION RD
CHAPEL LA
MARSTON CT
PH
4
Long Marston Junior Mixed Infants Sch
Long Marston
Great Farm
ASTROPE LA
TRING RD
Sewage Works
Church Farm
3
Astrope
Millfield
LUKES LA
Lower End
Gubblecote
15
LONG MARSTON RD
Astrope Farm
Gubblecote Farm
Moat Farm
Grand Union Canal
VICARAGE RD
2
College Farm
Dover Castle
Gurney's Farm
Dixon's Gap Bridge
WINGRAVE RD
Aylesbury Ring
Wilstone Bridge
TRING RD
WATERY LA
CHURCH LA
Grand Union Canal Aylesbury Arm
Grand Union Canal Walk
1
Half Moon (PH)
GRANGE RD
Wilstone
Startop's End
SANDBROOK LA
NEW RD
Stratop Farm
LOWER ICKNIELD WAY
B489
14
89
A
B
90
C
D
91
E
F

99
80

79

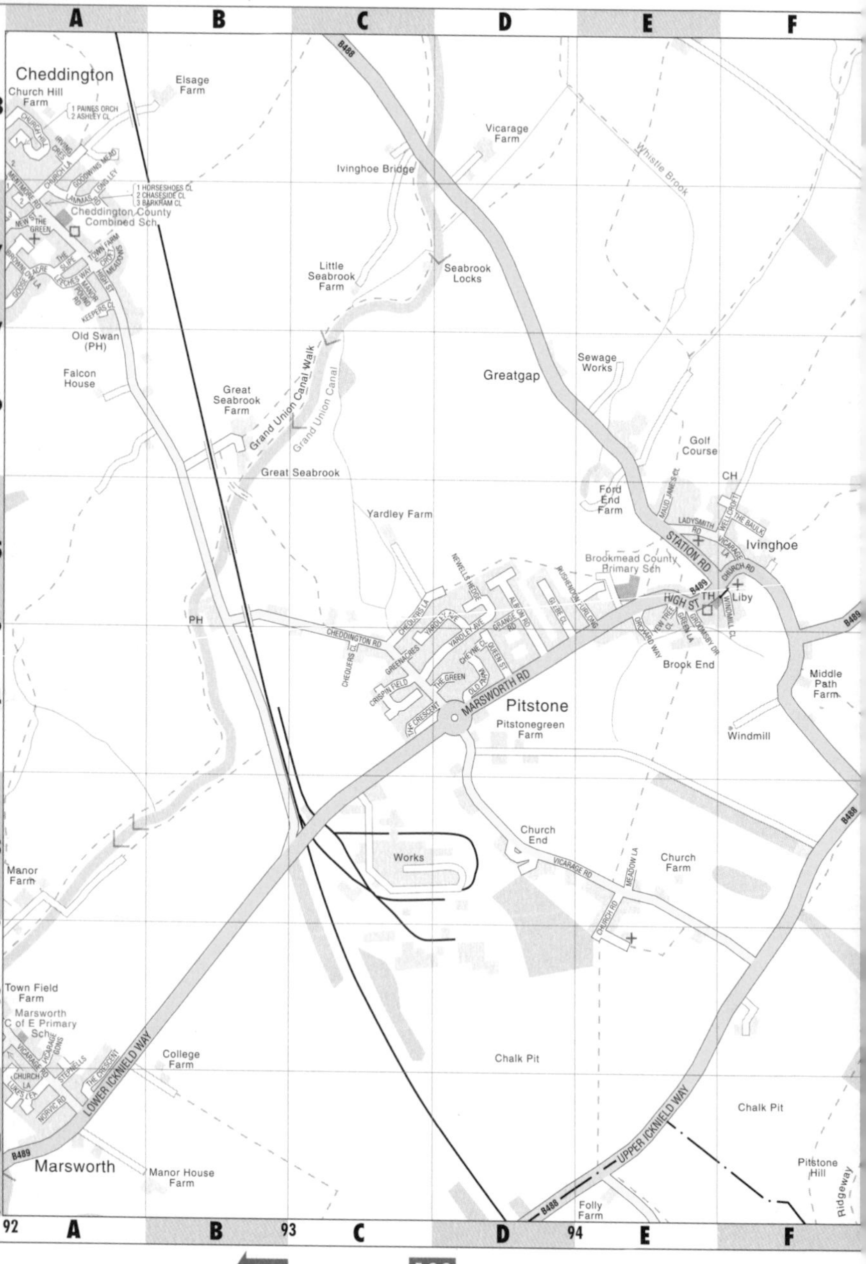
A
B
C
D
E
F
Cheddington
Church Hill Farm
1 PAINES ORCH
2 ASHLEY CL
Elsage Farm
B488
Vicarage Farm
Ivinghoe Bridge
Whistle Brook
1 HORSESHOES CL
2 CHASESIDE CL
3 BARKHAM CL
Cheddington County Combined Sch
Little Seabrook Farm
Seabrook Locks
Old Swan (PH)
Falcon House
Grand Union Canal Walk
Grand Union Canal
Great Seabrook Farm
Greatgap
Sewage Works
Golf Course
Great Seabrook
CH
Ford End Farm
Yardley Farm
Ivinghoe
Brookmead County Primary Sch
STATION RD
HIGH ST
TH
Liby
PH
CHEDDINGTON RD
MARSWORTH RD
Brook End
Pitstone
Pitstonegreen Farm
Middle Path Farm
Windmill
Church End
Works
VICARAGE RD
MEADOW LA
Church Farm
CHURCH RD
Manor Farm
Town Field Farm
Marsworth C of E Primary Sch
College Farm
Chalk Pit
LOWER ICKNIELD WAY
UPPER ICKNIELD WAY
Chalk Pit
Marsworth
Manor House Farm
Folly Farm
Pitstone Hill
Ridgeway
B489
92
93
94
8
7
17
6
5
16
4
3
15
2
1
14

79
100

82

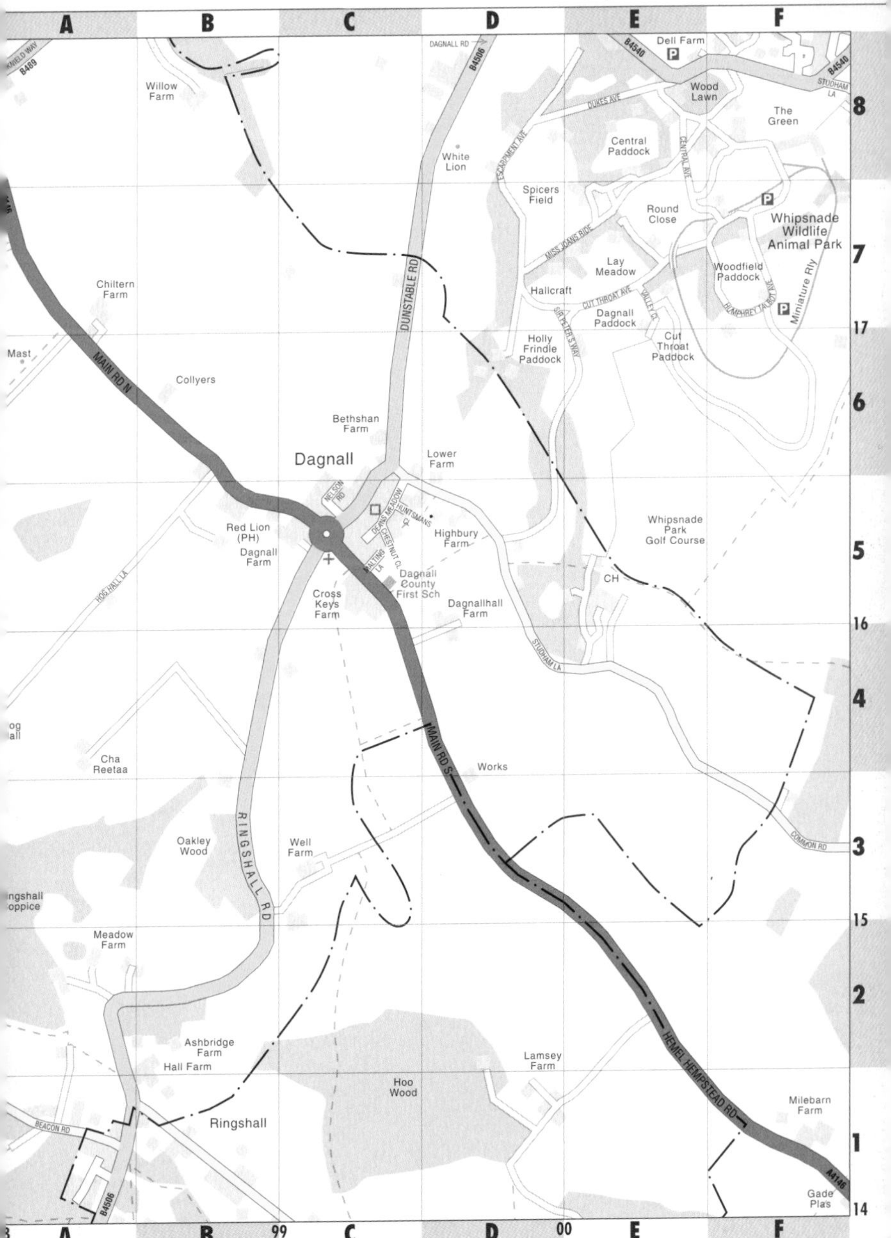
A
B
C
D
E
F
ICKNIELD WAY
B489
Willow Farm
DAGNALL RD
B4506
B4540
Dell Farm
P
Wood Lawn
STUDHAM LA
The Green
DUKES AVE
Central Paddock
CENTRAL AVE
ESCARPMENT AVE
White Lion
Spicers Field
Round Close
P
Whipsnade Wildlife Animal Park
MISS JOANS RIDE
Lay Meadow
Woodfield Paddock
Chiltern Farm
DUNSTABLE RD
Hallcraft
CUT THROAT AVE
VALLEY CL
HUMPHREY TALBOT AVE
P
Miniature Rly
SIR PETER'S WAY
Dagnall Paddock
Cut Throat Paddock
Holly Frindle Paddock
Mast
MAIN RD N
Collyers
Bethshan Farm
Dagnall
Lower Farm
NELSON RD
DEANS MEADOW
HUNTSMANS CL
CHESTNUT CL
Highbury Farm
Whipsnade Park Golf Course
Red Lion (PH)
Dagnall Farm
MALTING LA
Dagnall County First Sch
CH
HOG HALL LA
Cross Keys Farm
Dagnallhall Farm
STUDHAM LA
og
all
Cha Reetaa
MAIN RD S
Works
RINGSHALL RD
Oakley Wood
Well Farm
COMMON RD
ingshall
oppice
Meadow Farm
Ashbridge Farm
Hall Farm
Lamsey Farm
Hoo Wood
HEMEL HEMPSTEAD RD
Milebarn Farm
BEACON RD
Ringshall
B4506
A4146
Gade Plas
8
7
17
6
5
16
4
3
15
2
1
14
99
00

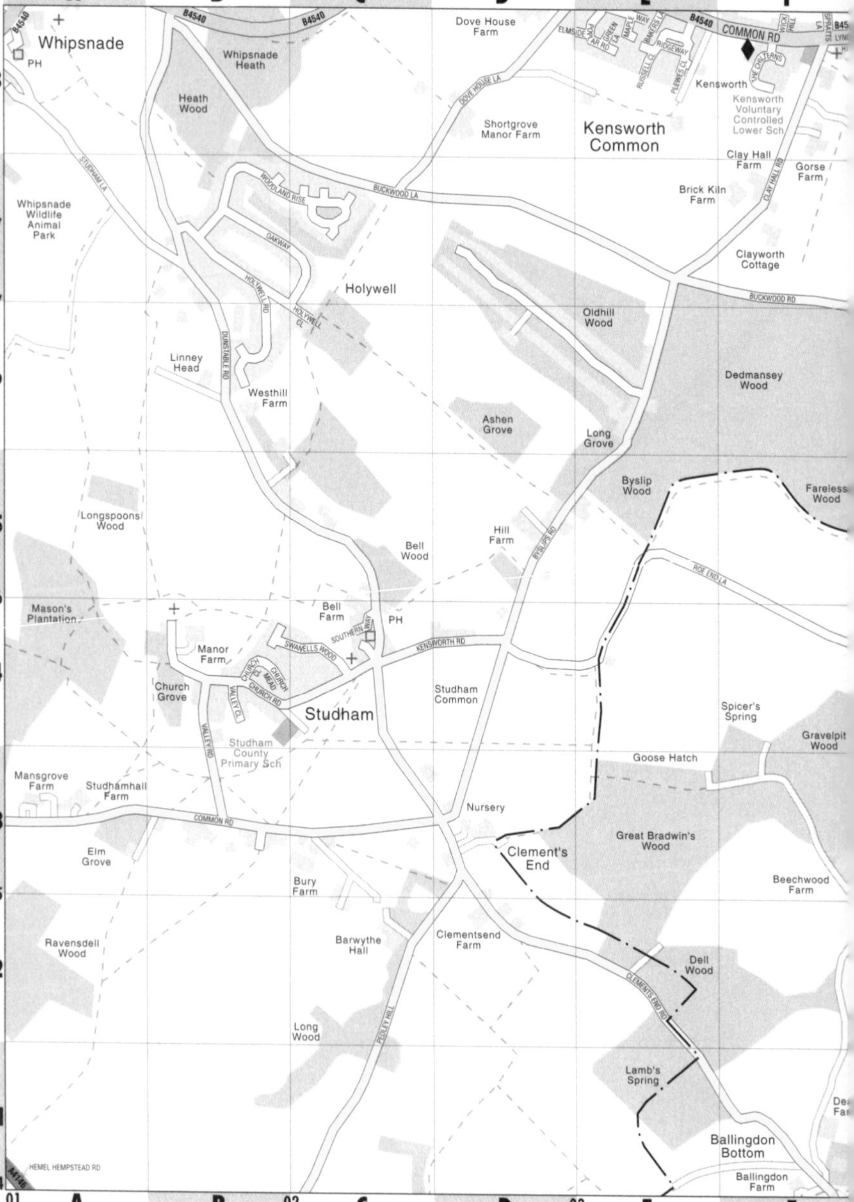

**A**    **B**    **C**    **D**    **E**    **F**

Whipsnade
PH

Whipsnade Heath

Heath Wood

Dove House Farm

Shortgrove Manor Farm

Kensworth Common

Kensworth

Kensworth Voluntary Controlled Lower Sch

COMMON RD

Clay Hall Farm

Gorse Farm

**8**

Whipsnade Wildlife Animal Park

Brick Kiln Farm

Clayworth Cottage

BUCKWOOD LA

Holywell

BUCKWOOD RD

**7**

WOODLAND RISE

OAKWAY

**17**

Oidhill Wood

Dedmansey Wood

Linney Head

Westhill Farm

**6**

Ashen Grove

Long Grove

Longspoons Wood

Byslip Wood

Fareless Wood

**5**

Bell Wood

Hill Farm

**16**

Mason's Plantation

Bell Farm

PH

KENSWORTH RD

Studham Common

Spicer's Spring

Gravelpit Wood

**4**

Manor Farm

SWANELLS WOOD

SOUTH RISE

Church Grove

Studham

Goose Hatch

**3**

Mansgrove Farm

Studhamhall Farm

COMMON RD

Studham County Primary Sch

Nursery

Great Bradwin's Wood

Beechwood Farm

**15**

Elm Grove

Bury Farm

Clement's End

Clementsend Farm

Dell Wood

**2**

Ravensdell Wood

Barwythe Hall

CLEMENTS END RD

FOLLY HILL

Long Wood

Lamb's Spring

**1**

HEMEL HEMPSTEAD RD

Ballingdon Bottom

Ballingdon Farm

**14**

**01**   **A**    **B**   **02**   **C**    **D**   **03**   **E**    **F**

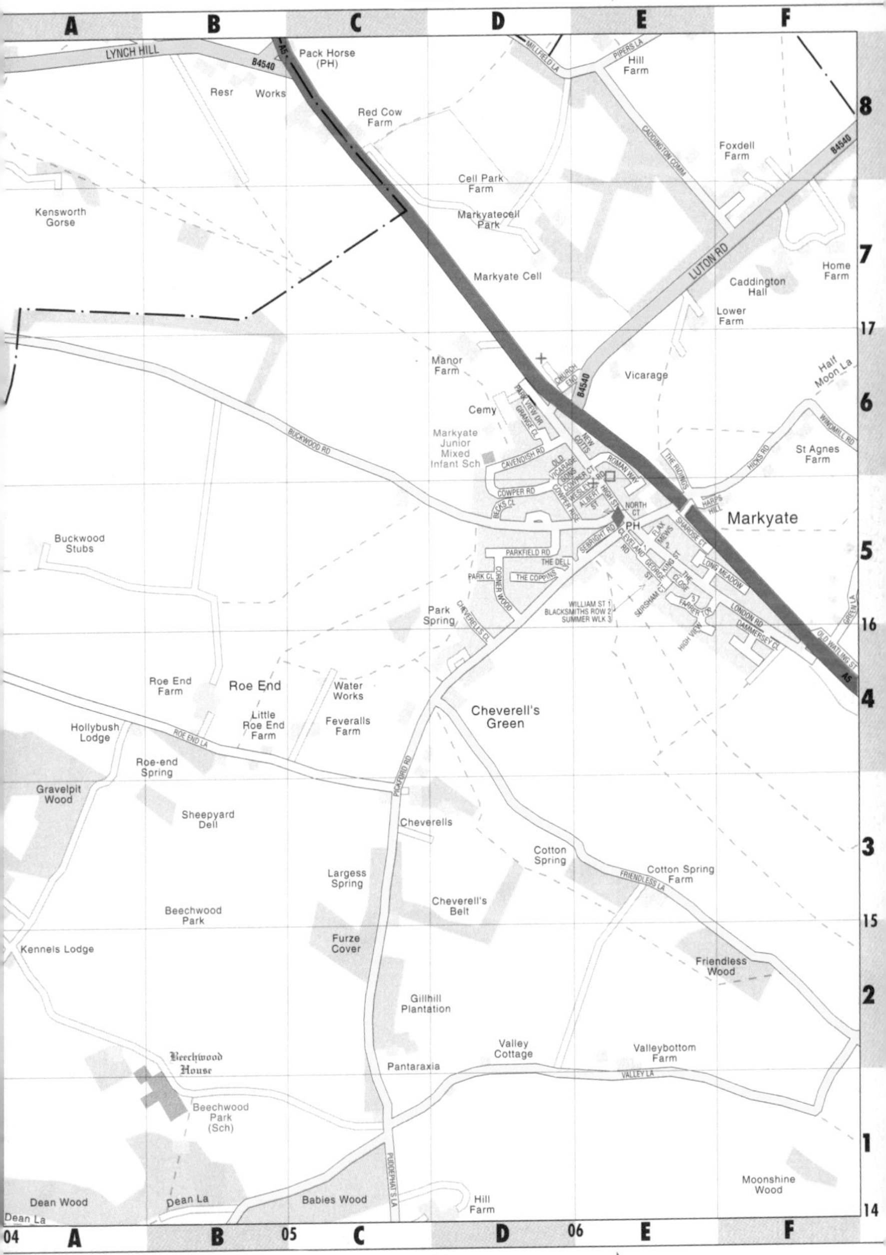
A
B
C
D
E
F
LYNCH HILL
B4540
A5
Pack Horse
(PH)
MILLFIELD LA
PIPERS LA
Hill
Farm
Resr
Works
Red Cow
Farm
8
CADDINGTON COMM
Foxdell
Farm
B4540
Cell Park
Farm
Kensworth
Gorse
Markyatecell
Park
LUTON RD
7
Home
Farm
Caddington
Hall
Markyate Cell
Lower
Farm
17
Manor
Farm
CHURCH END
B4540
Vicarage
Half
Moon La
Cemy
6
GRANGE CL
WINDMILL RD
BUCKWOOD RD
Markyate
Junior
Mixed
Infant Sch
ROMAN WAY
THE RIDINGS
HICKS RD
St Agnes
Farm
CAVENDISH RD
COWPER RD
BECKS CL
HIGH ST
NORTH CT
HARPS HILL
Markyate
PH
Buckwood
Stubs
PARKFIELD RD
SEBRIGHT RD
CLEVELAND RD
FLAX MEWS
SHARDSE CT
KING ST
5
THE DELL
LONG MEADOW
PARK CL
THE COPPINS
CORNER WOOD
GEORGE ST
THE CLOSE
WILLIAM ST 1
BLACKSMITHS ROW 2
SUMMER WLK 3
SURSHAM CL
FARRER TOP
LONDON RD
GREEN LA
Park
Spring
CHEVERELLS CL
HIGH VIEW
DAMMERSEY CL
16
OLD WATLING ST
A5
Roe End
Farm
Roe End
Water
Works
4
Cheverell's
Green
Little
Roe End
Farm
Feveralls
Farm
Hollybush
Lodge
ROE END LA
Roe-end
Spring
PICKFORD RD
Gravelpit
Wood
Sheepyard
Dell
Cheverells
3
Cotton
Spring
Largess
Spring
Cotton Spring
Farm
FRIENDLESS LA
Beechwood
Park
Cheverell's
Belt
15
Kennels Lodge
Furze
Cover
Friendless
Wood
2
Gillhill
Plantation
Valley
Cottage
Valleybottom
Farm
Beechwood
House
Pantaraxia
VALLEY LA
Beechwood
Park
(Sch)
1
Moonshine
Wood
PUDDEPHAT'S LA
Dean Wood
Dean La
Babies Wood
Hill
Farm
Dean La
14
04
A
B
05
C
D
06
E
F

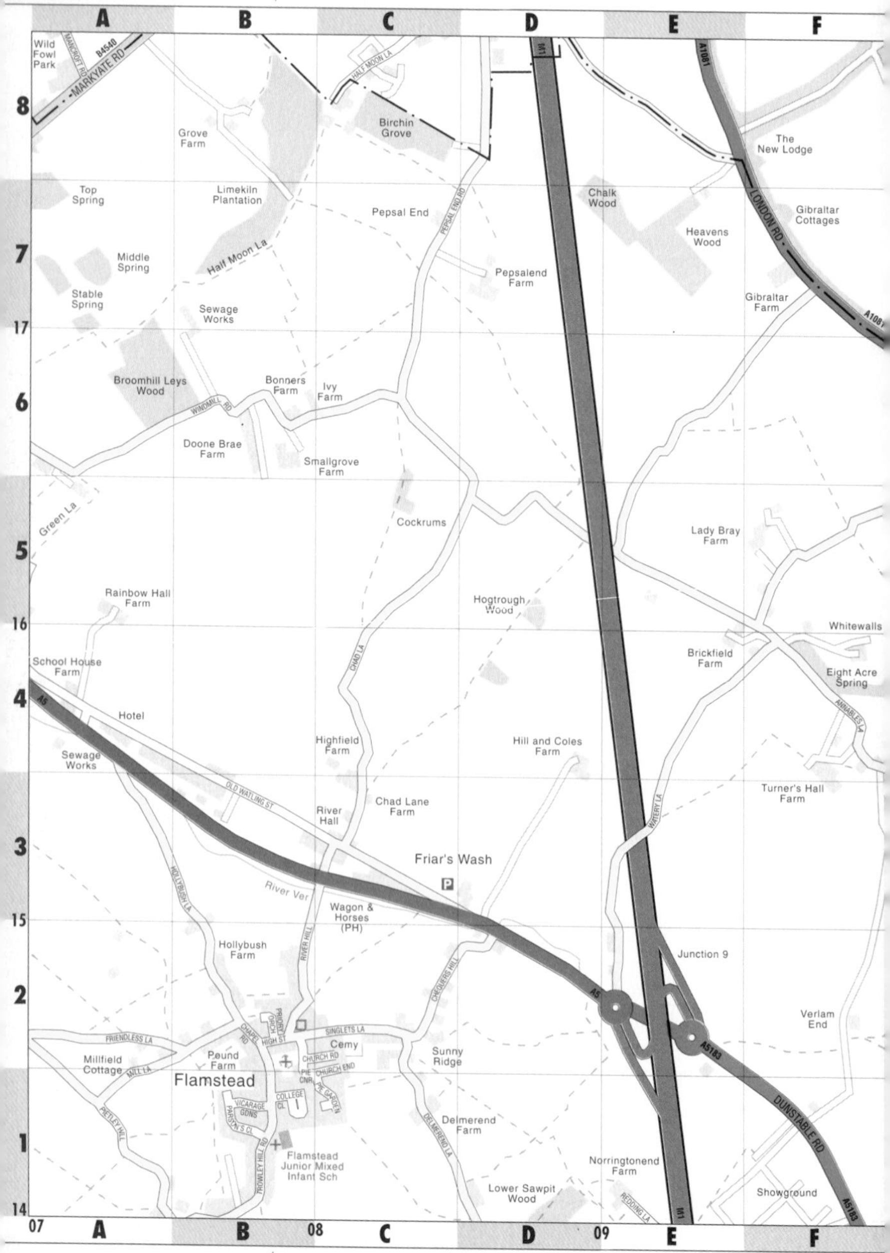
A
B
C
D
E
F
8
7
17
6
5
16
4
3
15
2
1
14
07
08
09
Wild Fowl Park
MANCROFT RD
B4540
MARKYATE RD
Grove Farm
HALF MOON LA
Birchin Grove
M1
A1081
The New Lodge
Top Spring
Limekiln Plantation
Pepsal End
PEPSAL END RD
Chalk Wood
LONDON RD
Gibraltar Cottages
Heavens Wood
Middle Spring
Half Moon La
Stable Spring
Pepsalend Farm
Gibraltar Farm
Sewage Works
A1081
Broomhill Leys Wood
Bonners Farm
Ivy Farm
WINDMILL RD
Doone Brae Farm
Smallgrove Farm
Green La
Cockrums
Lady Bray Farm
Rainbow Hall Farm
Hogtrough Wood
Whitewalls
School House Farm
CHAD LA
Brickfield Farm
Eight Acre Spring
A5
Hotel
ANNABLES LA
Sewage Works
Highfield Farm
Hill and Coles Farm
OLD WATLING ST
Turner's Hall Farm
River Hall
Chad Lane Farm
WATERY LA
Friar's Wash
P
HOLLYBUSH LA
River Ver
Wagon & Horses (PH)
Hollybush Farm
RIVER HILL
Junction 9
CHEQUERS HILL
A5
PRIORY ORCH
SINGLETS LA
Verlam End
FRIENDLESS LA
CHAPEL RD
HIGH ST
Cemy
A5183
Millfield Cottage
MILL LA
Pound Farm
CHURCH RD
Sunny Ridge
Flamstead
PIE CNR
CHURCH END
PIE GARDEN
COLLEGE CL
VICARAGE GDNS
DUNSTABLE RD
PIETLEY HILL
PARSON'S CL
Delmerend Farm
DELMEREND LA
TROWLEY HILL RD
Flamstead Junior Mixed Infant Sch
Norringtonend Farm
Lower Sawpit Wood
REDDING LA
Showground
M1
A5183

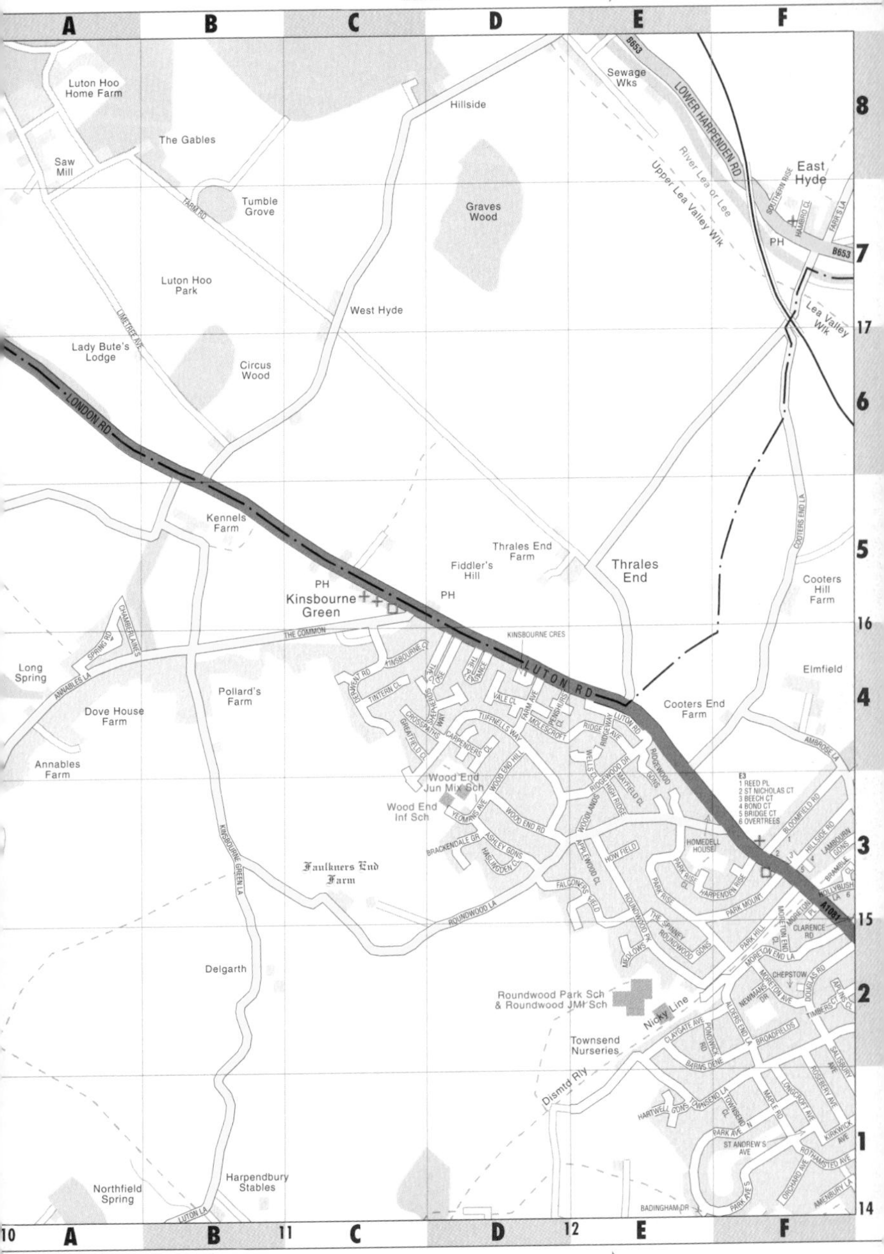
A
B
C
D
E
F
8
7
17
6
5
16
4
3
15
2
1
14
10
11
12
Luton Hoo
Home Farm
Saw
Mill
The Gables
Tumble
Grove
FARM RD
Hillside
Sewage
Wks
B653
LOWER HARPENDEN RD
River Lea or Lee
Upper Lea Valley Wlk
East
Hyde
SOUTHERN RISE
HAMBRO CL
FARR'S LA
PH
Graves
Wood
Luton Hoo
Park
LIMETREE AVE
West Hyde
Lea Valley
Wlk
Lady Bute's
Lodge
Circus
Wood
LONDON RD
COOTERS END LA
Kennels
Farm
Thrales End
Farm
Fiddler's
Hill
Thrales
End
Cooters
Hill
Farm
PH
Kinsbourne
Green
PH
THE COMMON
KINSBOURNE CRES
CHAMBERLAINS
SPRING RD
Long
Spring
ANNABLES LA
Elmfield
LUTON RD
Pollard's
Farm
Dove House
Farm
Cooters End
Farm
DERWENT RD
KINSBOURNE CL
TINTERN CL
VALE CL
FARM AVE
PENSHURST CL
CROSSPATHS
SHEPHERDS WAY
CARPENDERS CL
TUFFNELLS WAY
MOLESCROFT
RIDGEWAY
RIDGE AVE
LUTON RD
GREATFIELD CL
AMBROSE LA
Annables
Farm
RIDGEWOOD GDNS
WELLS CL
RIDGEWOOD DR
MAYFIELD CL
HIGH RIDGE
WOODLANDS
E3
1 REED PL
2 ST NICHOLAS CT
3 BEECH CT
4 BOND CT
5 BRIDGE CT
6 OVERTREES
BLOOMFIELD RD
HILLSIDE RD
LAMBOURN GDNS
Wood End
Jun Mix Sch
Wood End
Inf Sch
WOOD END HILL
YEOMANS AVE
WOOD END RD
BRACKENDALE GR
ASHLEY GDNS
HASLINGDEN CL
HOW FIELD
APPLEWOOD CL
HOMEDELL HOUSE
PARK RISE CL
HARPENDEN RISE
PARK RISE
KINSBOURNE GREEN LA
Faulkners End
Farm
FALCONERS FIELD
ROUNDWOOD PK
PARK MOUNT
HOLLYBUSH LA
BRAMBLE
A1081
ROUNDWOOD LA
THE SPINNEY
ROUNDWOOD GDNS
PARK HILL
MORETON END CL
MORETON PL
CLARENCE RD
MORETON END LA
MEDLOWS
Delgarth
CHEPSTOW
DOUGLAS RD
NEWMANS DR
MORETON AVE
APPLINS CL
TIMBERS CL
Roundwood Park Sch
& Roundwood JMI Sch
Nicky Line
CLAYGATE AVE
POMOWICK RD
ALDERS END LA
BROADFIELDS
Townsend
Nurseries
BARNS DENE
SALISBURY AVE
ROSEBERY AVE
Dismtd Rly
HARTWELL GDNS
TOWNSEND LA
TOWNSEND CL
MAPLE RD
LONGCROFT AVE
KIRKWICK AVE
PARK AVE
ST ANDREW'S AVE
ROTHAMSTED AVE
ORCHARD AVE
Northfield
Spring
Harpendbury
Stables
LUTON LA
PARK AVE S
BADINGHAM DR
AMENBURY LA

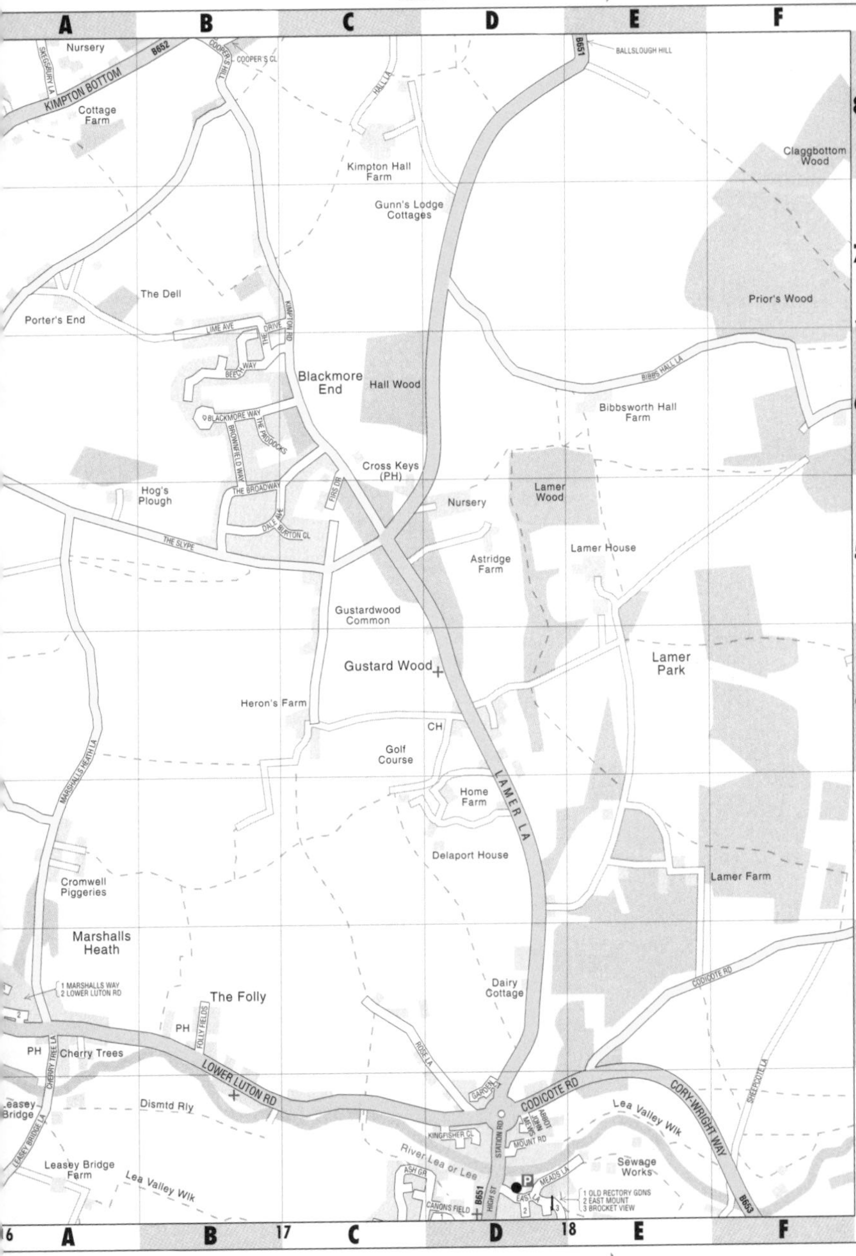
A
B
C
D
E
F
Nursery
SKEGSBURY LA
B652
KIMPTON BOTTOM
COOPER'S HILL
COOPER'S CL
HALL LA
B651
BALLSLOUGH HILL
8
Cottage Farm
Kimpton Hall Farm
Claggbottom Wood
Gunn's Lodge Cottages
7
The Dell
Prior's Wood
Porter's End
LIME AVE
THE DRIVE
KIMPTON RD
17
BEECH WAY
Blackmore End
Hall Wood
BIBBS HALL LA
BLACKMORE WAY
THE PADDOCKS
BROWNFIELD WAY
Bibbsworth Hall Farm
6
Cross Keys (PH)
FIRS DR
THE BROADWAY
Hog's Plough
Lamer Wood
Nursery
DALE AVE
BURTON CL
THE SLYPE
Astridge Farm
Lamer House
5
Gustardwood Common
16
Gustard Wood
Lamer Park
Heron's Farm
4
CH
Golf Course
MARSHALLS HEATH LA
Home Farm
LAMER LA
3
Delaport House
Cromwell Piggeries
Lamer Farm
15
Marshalls Heath
Dairy Cottage
CODICOTE RD
1 MARSHALLS WAY
2 LOWER LUTON RD
The Folly
2
PH
FOLLY FIELDS
PH
Cherry Trees
CHERRY TREE LA
ROSE LA
LOWER LUTON RD
GARDEN CT
CODICOTE RD
SHEEPCOTE LA
CORY-WRIGHT WAY
Leasey Bridge
Dismtd Rly
Lea Valley Wlk
ABBOT
JOHN
MEWS
KINGFISHER CL
STATION RD
MOUNT RD
1
River Lea or Lee
Sewage Works
LEASEY BRIDGE LA
Leasey Bridge Farm
ASH GR
MEADS LA
Lea Valley Wlk
B651
HIGH ST
EAST LA
1 OLD RECTORY GDNS
2 EAST MOUNT
3 BROCKET VIEW
B653
CANONS FIELD
14
16
A
B
17
C
D
18
E
F

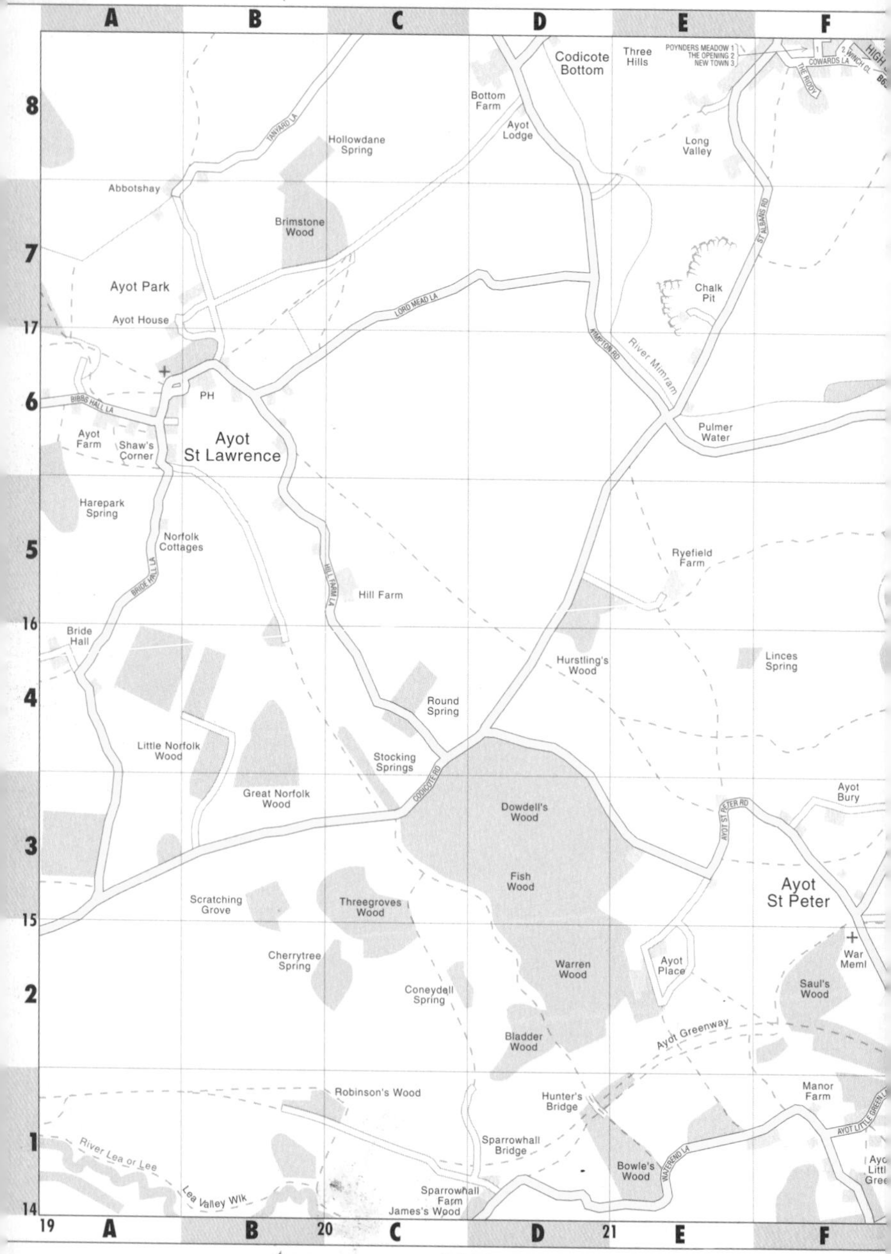

87

67

A    B    C    D    E    F

8

**Codicote Bottom**    Three Hills

POYNDERS MEADOW 1
THE OPENING 2
NEW TOWN 3

COWARDS LA

HIGH

THE BURY RD

Bottom Farm

Ayot Lodge

Long Valley

Hollowdane Spring

7

Abbotshay

Brimstone Wood

LORD MEAD LA

KIMPTON RD

River Mimram

Chalk Pit

17

Ayot Park

Ayot House

+

BIBBS HALL LA

PH

Ayot St Lawrence

Shaw's Corner

Ayot Farm

Pulmer Water

6

Harepark Spring

Norfolk Cottages

Ryefield Farm

5

BRIDE HALL LA

HILL FARM LA

Hill Farm

Linces Spring

16

Bride Hall

Hurstling's Wood

4

Round Spring

Little Norfolk Wood

CODICOTE RD

Stocking Springs

Dowdell's Wood

Ayot Bury

AYOT ST PETER RD

Great Norfolk Wood

Fish Wood

Ayot St Peter

3

Scratching Grove

Threegroves Wood

+
War Meml

15

Cherrytree Spring

Warren Wood

Ayot Place

Saul's Wood

2

Coneydell Spring

Bladder Wood

Ayot Greenway

Robinson's Wood

Hunter's Bridge

Manor Farm

AYOT LITTLE GREEN

Ayo
Littl
Gree

1

River Lea or Lee

Lea Valley Wlk

Sparrowhall Bridge

Bowle's Wood

WATEREND LA

Sparrowhall Farm
James's Wood

14

19    A    B    20    C    D    21    E    F

87

109

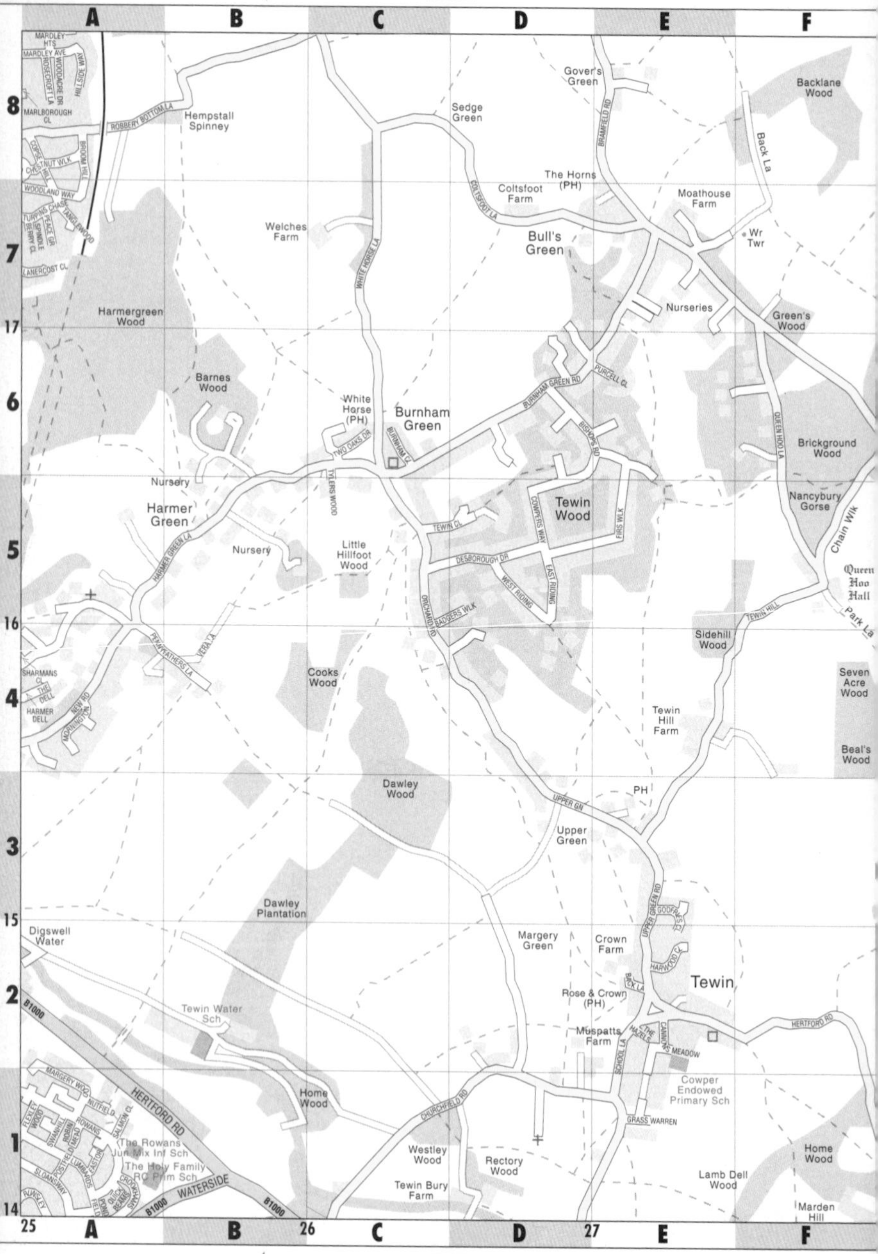

**A**    **B**    **C**    **D**    **E**    **F**

MARDLEY
HTS
MARDLEY AVE
BRIDGROVE LA
SUTTONS CROFT LA
MARLBOROUGH
HOB KNOTT LA

8

CHESTNUT WALK

Hempstall
Spinney

WOODLAND WAY

7
TURPINS RIDE
PEACE WALK
LANNOCK CL

ROBBERY BOTTOM LA

Gover's
Green

Sedge
Green

Coltsfoot
Farm

The Horns
(PH)

Bull's
Green

Welches
Farm

Backlane
Wood

Back La

Moathouse
Farm

Wr
Twr

17

Harmergreen
Wood

WHITE HORSE LA

BRAMBLE RD

BULL'S GREEN RD

Nurseries

Green's
Wood

6

Barnes
Wood

White
Horse
(PH)

Burnham
Green

BURNHAM GREEN RD

FULLERS CL

Brickground
Wood

QUEEN HOO LA

Nancybury
Gorse

Chalk Wlk

5

Harmer
Green

Nursery

Nursery

HARMER GREEN LA

YEWLANDS

TWO OAKS LN

Little
Hillfoot
Wood

TEWIN LA

DESBOROUGH DR

Tewin
Wood

ORCHARD RD

BASTERS WLK

WEST RIDING

EAST RIDING

THIS WLK

COPPER BEECH

Sidehill
Wood

Queen
Hoo
Hall

TEWIN HILL

PARK LA

16

SHARMANS
DELL
HARMER DELL LA

BEAN LA

TWELVE ACRES LA

Cooks
Wood

Tewin
Hill
Farm

Seven
Acre
Wood

Beal's
Wood

4

Dawley
Wood

PH

3

Dawley
Plantation

Upper
Green

UPPER GREEN RD

UPPER GREEN RD

15

Digswell
Water

Margery
Green

Crown
Farm

HARPS FIELD

Tewin

2

B1000

Tewin Water
Sch

CHURCHFIELD RD

Rose & Crown
(PH)

Muspatts
Farm

HIGH MEADOW

Cowper
Endowed
Primary Sch

HERTFORD RD

SCHOOL LA

HERTFORD RD

1

MARGERY WOOD

NUTFIELD

HERTFORD RD

WATERSIDE

B1000

B1000

The Rowans
Jun Mix Inf Sch
The Holy Family
RC Prim Sch

Home
Wood

Westley
Wood

Tewin Bury
Farm

Rectory
Wood

GRASS WARREN

Lamb Dell
Wood

Home
Wood

Marden
Hill

14

25    **A**    **B**    26    **C**    **D**    27    **E**    **F**

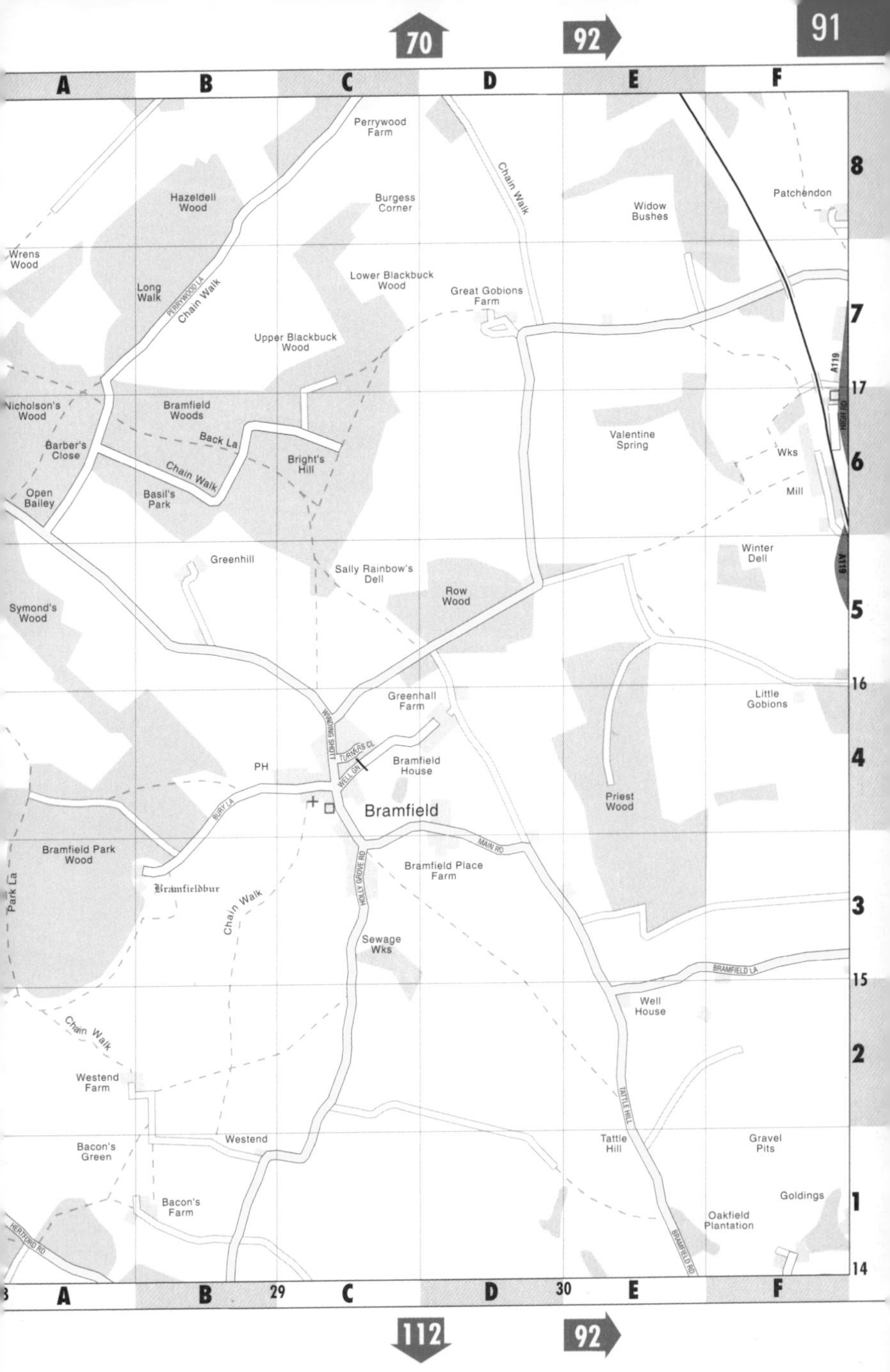
70
92
A
B
C
D
E
F
8
7
17
6
5
16
4
3
15
2
1
14
29
30
112
Perrywood Farm
Hazeldell Wood
Burgess Corner
Chain Walk
Widow Bushes
Patchendon
Wrens Wood
Lower Blackbuck Wood
Long Walk
PERRYWOOD LA
Great Gobions Farm
Upper Blackbuck Wood
A119
Nicholson's Wood
Bramfield Woods
HIGH RD
Barber's Close
Back La
Valentine Spring
Wks
Bright's Hill
Open Bailey
Basil's Park
Mill
Greenhill
Winter Dell
Sally Rainbow's Dell
Row Wood
Symond's Wood
Greenhall Farm
Little Gobions
WINDING SHOTT
TURNERS CL
Bramfield House
WELL GN
PH
Bramfield
Priest Wood
BURY LA
Bramfield Park Wood
MAIN RD
Bramfield Place Farm
HOLLY GROVE RD
Bramfieldbur
Park La
Sewage Wks
BRAMFIELD LA
Well House
Westend Farm
TATTLE HILL
Bacon's Green
Westend
Tattle Hill
Gravel Pits
Goldings
Bacon's Farm
Oakfield Plantation
HERTFORD RD
BRAMFIELD RD

91
71

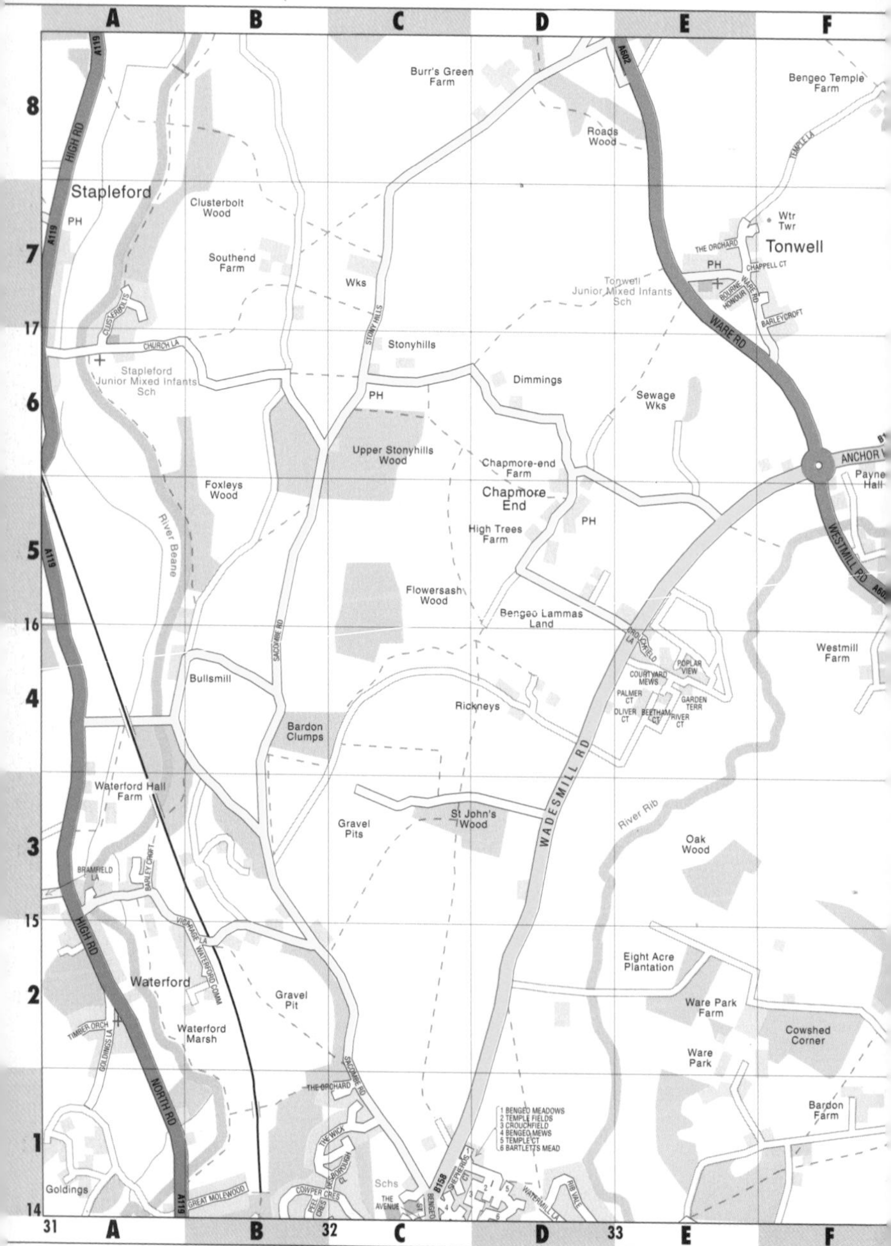
A
B
C
D
E
F
8
7
17
6
5
16
4
3
15
2
1
14
31
32
33
A119
HIGH RD
Stapleford
PH
CLUSTERBOLTS
CHURCH LA
Stapleford
Junior Mixed Infants
Sch
Clusterbolt
Wood
Southend
Farm
Wks
Burr's Green
Farm
STONY HILLS
Stonyhills
PH
Dimmings
Roads
Wood
A602
Bengeo Temple
Farm
TEMPLE LA
Wtr
Twr
Tonwell
THE ORCHARD
PH
CHAPPELL CT
BOURNE HONOUR
WARE RD
BARLEYCROFT
Tonwell
Junior Mixed Infants
Sch
WARE RD
Sewage
Wks
ANCHOR
Payne
Hall
WESTMILL RD
Upper Stonyhills
Wood
Chapmore-end
Farm
Chapmore
End
PH
High Trees
Farm
Foxleys
Wood
River Beane
Flowersash
Wood
Bengeo Lammas
Land
SACOMBE RD
CROUCHFIELD LA
POPLAR VIEW
COURTYARD MEWS
PALMER CT
GARDEN TERR
OLIVER CT
BEETHAM CT
RIVER CT
Westmill
Farm
Bullsmill
Rickneys
Bardon
Clumps
Waterford Hall
Farm
WADESMILL RD
St John's
Wood
Gravel
Pits
River Rib
Oak
Wood
BRAMFIELD LA
BARLEY CROFT
VICARAGE LA
WATERFORD COMM
Eight Acre
Plantation
Waterford
Gravel
Pit
Ware Park
Farm
Cowshed
Corner
TIMBER ORCH
GOLDINGS LA
Waterford
Marsh
Ware
Park
NORTH RD
THE ORCHARD
SACOMBE RD
Bardon
Farm
1 BENGEO MEADOWS
2 TEMPLE FIELDS
3 CROUCHFIELD
4 BENGEO MEWS
5 TEMPLE CT
6 BARTLETTS MEAD
THE WICK
FAIRBOROUGH CL
SHEPHERDS CT
B158
Schs
Goldings
GREAT MOLEWOOD
COWPER CRES
PEEL CRES
THE AVENUE
BENGEO ST
WATERMILL LA
RIB VALE

91
113

72
94

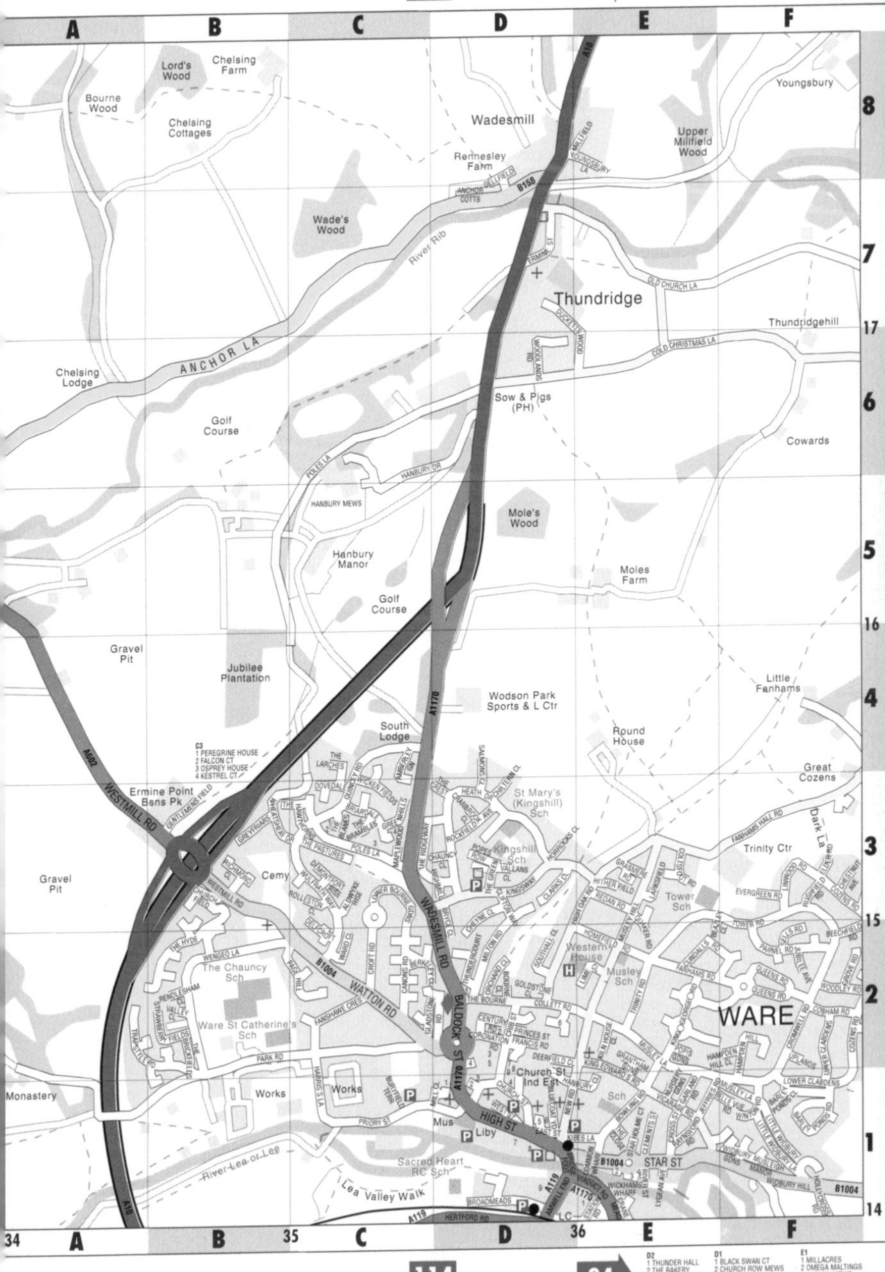


114
94

D2
1 THUNDER HALL
2 THE BAKERY
3 ROKEWOOD MEWS
4 WAGGONERS YD
5 ST EVROUL CT
6 HARTFIELD CT
7 MONKS ROW
8 CAMERON CT
9 THE ALBION

D1
1 BLACK SWAN CT
2 CHURCH ROW MEWS
3 ST MARY'S CTYD
4 OMEGA CT
5 LEASIDE WLK
6 DOLPHIN YD
7 RIVERSIDE MEWS
8 WELLS YD
9 BECKETS WLK

E1
1 MILLACRES
2 OMEGA MALTINGS
3 ALBANY MEWS

93
73

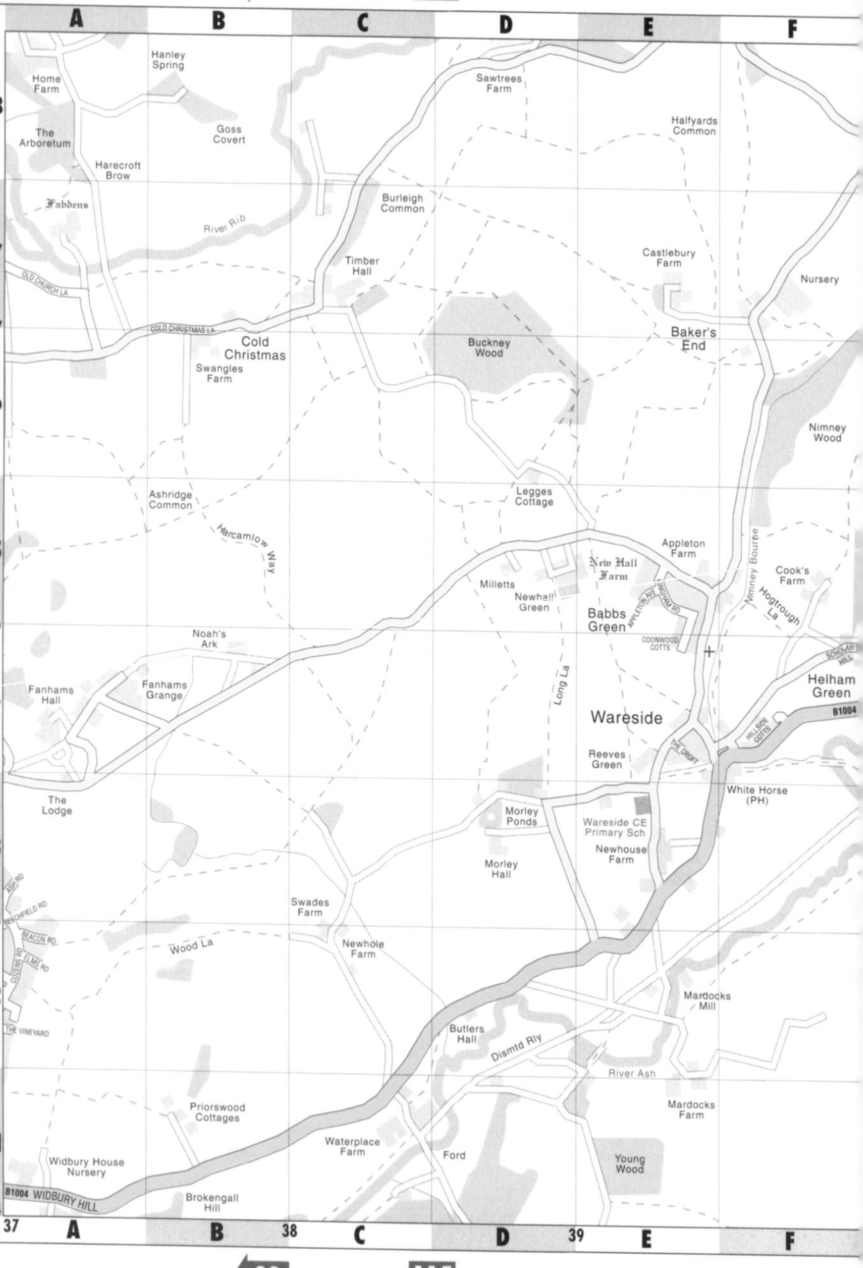
A
B
C
D
E
F
8
7
17
6
5
16
4
3
15
2
1
14
37
38
39
Home Farm
Hanley Spring
Goss Covert
The Arboretum
Harecroft Brow
Fabdens
River Rib
Old Church La
Cold Christmas La
Sawtrees Farm
Halfyards Common
Burleigh Common
Timber Hall
Castlebury Farm
Nursery
Cold Christmas
Swangles Farm
Buckney Wood
Baker's End
Nimney Wood
Ashridge Common
Harcamlow Way
Legges Cottage
Appleton Farm
New Hall Farm
Milletts
Newhall Green
Babbs Green
Appleton Ave
Coonwood Cotts
Nimney Bourne
Cook's Farm
Hogtrough La
Scholar's Hill
Helham Green
Noah's Ark
Fanhams Hall
Fanhams Grange
Long La
Wareside
B1004
Hillside Cotts
Reeves Green
The Croft
The Lodge
Morley Ponds
Wareside CE Primary Sch
White Horse (PH)
Newhouse Farm
Morley Hall
Ash Rd
Beechfield Rd
Beacon Rd
Elms Rd
Cozens Rd
Swades Farm
Wood La
Newhole Farm
The Vineyard
Mardocks Mill
Butlers Hall
Dismtd Rly
River Ash
Priorswood Cottages
Mardocks Farm
Waterplace Farm
Ford
Young Wood
Widbury House Nursery
B1004 Widbury Hill
Brokengall Hill

93
115

74
96

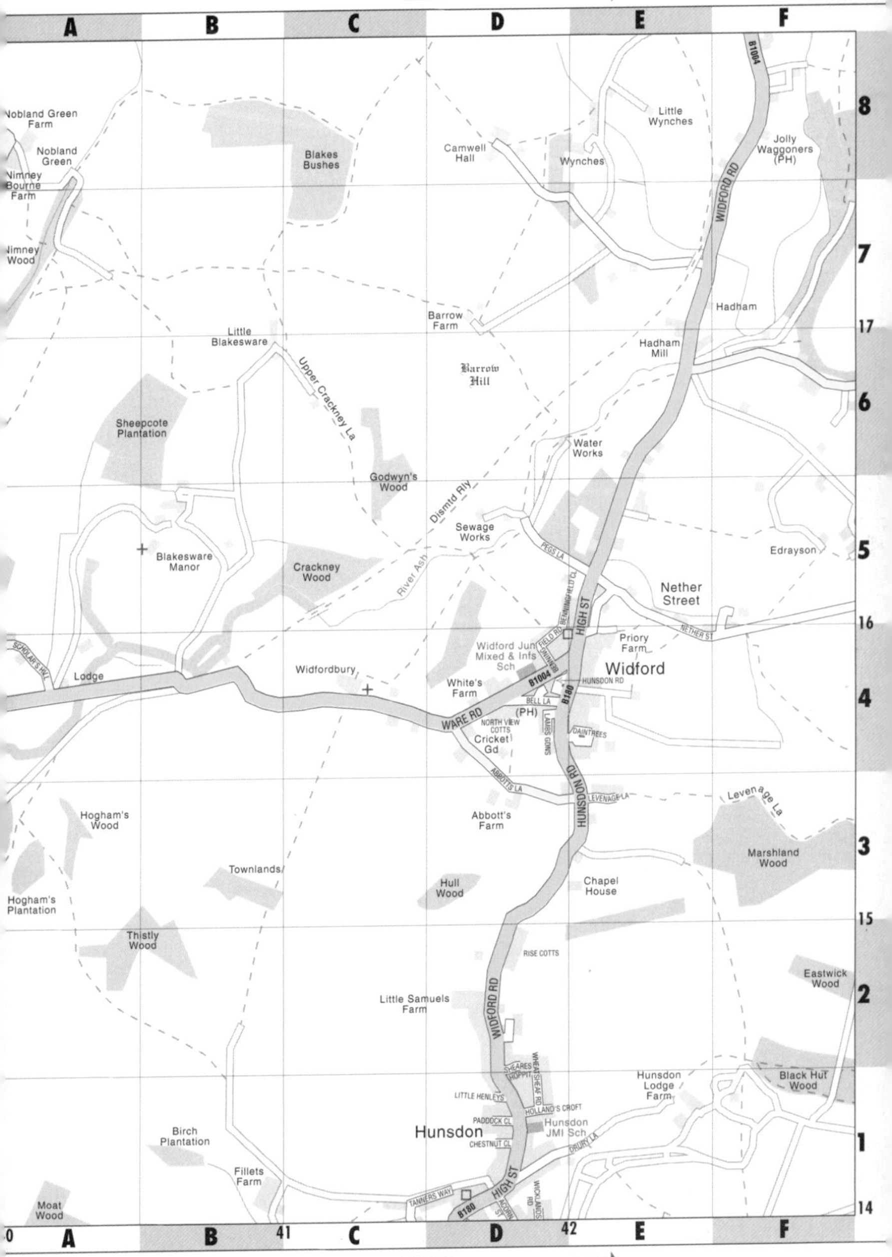
A
B
C
D
E
F
8
7
17
6
5
16
4
3
15
2
1
14
Nobland Green Farm
Nobland Green
Nimney Bourne Farm
Nimney Wood
Blakes Bushes
Camwell Hall
Wynches
Little Wynches
Jolly Waggoners (PH)
WIDFORD RD
B1004
Hadham
Barrow Farm
Little Blakesware
Upper Crackney La
Barrow Hill
Hadham Mill
Sheepcote Plantation
Water Works
Godwyn's Wood
Dismtd Rly
Sewage Works
Blakesware Manor
Crackney Wood
River Ash
PEGS LA
Edrayson
Nether Street
HIGH ST
NETHER ST
Priory Farm
Widford Jun Mixed & Infs Sch
Widford
SCHOLAR'S HILL
Lodge
Widfordbury
White's Farm
B1004
B180
HUNSDON RD
BELL LA
(PH)
WARE RD
NORTH VIEW COTTS
Cricket Gd
LAMBS GDNS
DAINTREES
ABBOTTS LA
HUNSDON RD
LEVENAGE LA
Levenage La
Hogham's Wood
Abbott's Farm
Marshland Wood
Townlands
Hull Wood
Chapel House
Hogham's Plantation
Thistly Wood
RISE COTTS
Eastwick Wood
Little Samuels Farm
WIDFORD RD
SHEARES HOPPIT
WHEATSHEAF RD
Hunsdon Lodge Farm
Black Hut Wood
LITTLE HENLEYS
HOLLAND'S CROFT
PADDOCK CL
Hunsdon JMI Sch
Hunsdon
Birch Plantation
CHESTNUT CL
DRURY LA
Fillets Farm
HIGH ST
TANNERS WAY
B180
ACORN ST
WICKLANDS RD
Moat Wood
40
41
42

116
96

8

7

17

6

5

16

4

3

15

2

1

14

A    B    C    D    E    F

Bucklers Hall Farm

Perry Green

The Chase Farm

Brook La

Blount's Farm

Sacombs Ash

SACOMBS ASH LA

The Hoops Inn (PH)

The Bourne

Hylands Nursery

Warrens

The Queens Head (PH)

South-end

Old Park

Allen's Green

Minges

St Elizabeth's Sch & Home

Dukes Farm

Allensgreen Wood

Turtle Farm

Covey's La

Fiddlers Brook

Chandlers

Chandlers La

NETHER ST

The Rick

Hardings

Levenage Spring

Gangies

GANGIES LA

Carters

Stonards

Hoskins Farm

Mole Wood

Fryars

Golf Course

Lawns Wood

Actons Farm

High Trees

Maplecroft Wood

The Manor of Groves

Cl

Queen's Wood

Battles Wood

Jeffs

Great Pennys Farm

Mabletts

Keeper's

Sayes Coppice

Golden Grove

43   A    B   44   C    D   45   E    F

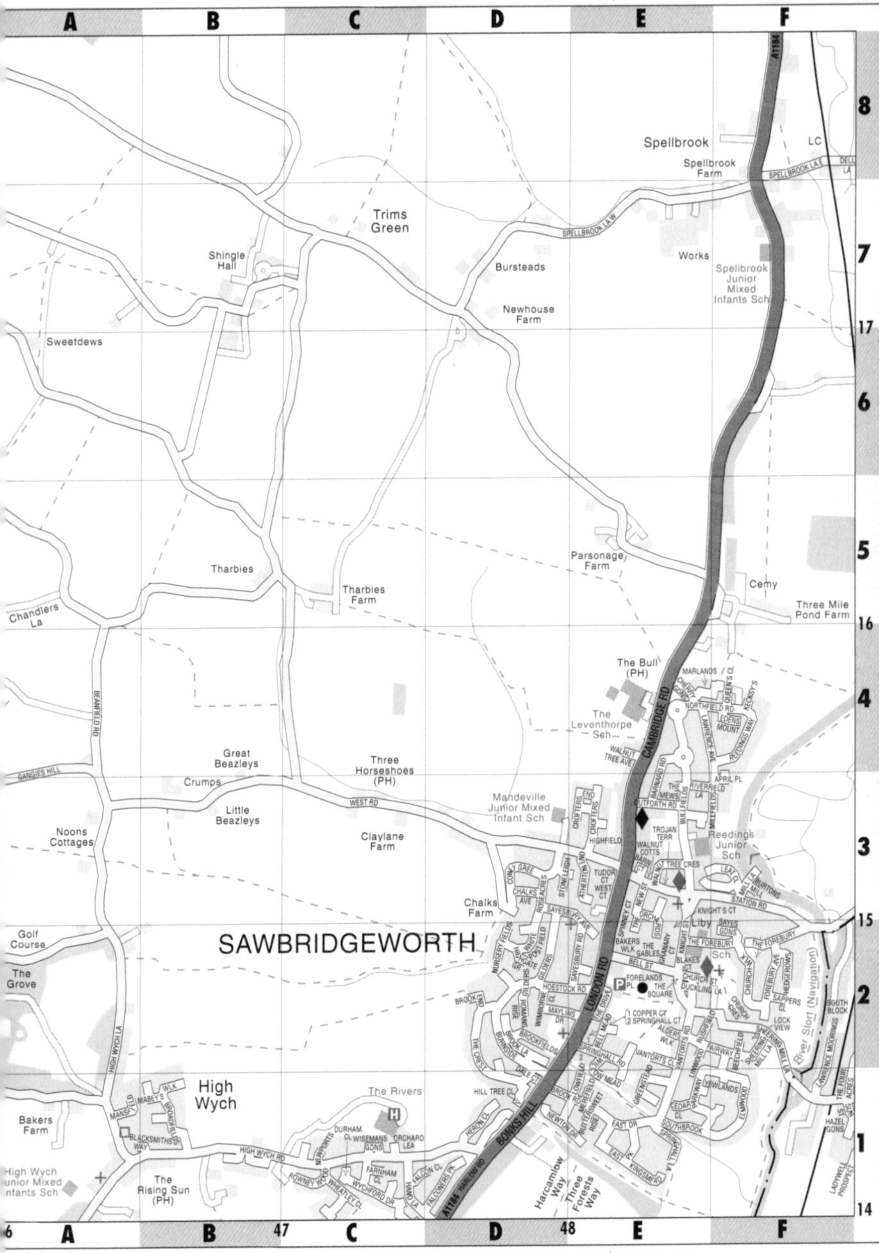
A
B
C
D
E
F
8
7
17
6
5
16
4
3
15
2
1
14
47
48
Spellbrook
LC
Spellbrook Farm
SPELLBROOK LA E
DELL LA
A1184
Trims Green
SPELLBROOK LA W
Shingle Hall
Bursteads
Works
Spellbrook Junior Mixed Infants Sch
Newhouse Farm
Sweetdews
Parsonage Farm
Tharbies
Tharbies Farm
Cemy
Three Mile Pond Farm
Chandlers La
The Bull (PH)
BEANFIELD RD
The Leventhorpe Sch
CAMBRIDGE RD
MARLANDS
QUEEN'S CL
NORTHFIELD RD
EDENS MOUNT
LAWRENCE AVE
REDDINGS WAY
KECKSY'S
WALNUT TREE AVE
GANGIES HILL
Great Beazleys
Crumps
Three Horseshoes (PH)
APRIL PL
RIVERS LA
THE MEWS
BARNARD RD
BULLFIELDS
MILLFIELDS
WEST RD
Mandeville Junior Mixed Infant Sch
CROFTERS
CROFTERS END
OUTFORTH RD
Little Beazleys
Noons Cottages
Claylane Farm
TROJAN TERR
WALNUT COTTS
HIGHFIELD
Reedings Junior Sch
WALNUT TREE CRES
LEAT CL
BURTONS MILL
STATION RD
KNIGHT'S CT
Chalks Farm
TUDOR CT
WEST CT
ATHERTON END
STONELEIGH
CHALKS AVE
SAYESBURY AVE
SPINNEY CT
NEW ST
Liby
SAYES GDNS
THE FOREBURY
Golf Course
SAWBRIDGEWORTH
BAKERS WLK
THE GABLES
GRANARY CT
KNIGHT ST
BLAKES CT
Sch
CHURCH ST
DUCKLING LA
NURSERY FIELDS
HIGHGATE GR
WHITE POST FIELD
GILDERS
SAYESBURY RD
LONDON RD
BELL ST
FORELANDS PL
THE SQUARE
The Grove
HOESTOCK RD
MAYLINS DR
BROOK END
RISE
ROMANS
WIMBORNE CL
THE DRIVE
1 COPPER CT
2 SPRINGHALL CT
ALDERS WLK
CHURCH GRS
FOREBURY AVE
HEDGEROWS
SAPPERS CL
LOCK VIEW
River Stort (Navigation)
SOUTH BLOCK
THE CREST
BURNSIDE
BROOK LA
BROOKFIELDS
BELL MEAD
SPRINGHALL RD
VANTORTS CL
VANTORTS RD
RUSHFIELD
FAIRWAY
BEECHFIELD
SHEERING MILL LA
LAWRENCE MOORINGS
HIGH WYCH LA
High Wych
DALE CT
HILL TREE CL
TOWN MEAD
GREENSTEAD
LINWOOD
PARKWAY
YEWLANDS
ELMWOOD
THE FOUR ACRES
The Rivers
BROOK RD
LOWFIELD
MOREFIELD
BUTTERSWEET RISE
CEDARS
MABEY'S
WLK
BROADFIELD
MANSFIELD
Bakers Farm
BLACKSMITHS WAY
DURHAM CL
WISEMANS GDNS
ORCHARD LEA
HERON CL
BONKS HILL
NEWTON DR
EAST DR
SOUTHBROOK
SPRINGHALL LA
HAZEL GDNS
HIGH WYCH RD
NEWPORTS
FARNHAM CL
FALCON CL
EAST PK
KINGSMEAD
High Wych Junior Mixed Infants Sch
The Rising Sun (PH)
ROWNEY WOOD
WHEATLEY CL
WYCHFORD DR
HAND LA
FALCONERS PK
A1184 HARLOW RD
Harcamlow Way
Three Forests Way
LADYWELL PROSPECT

97
77

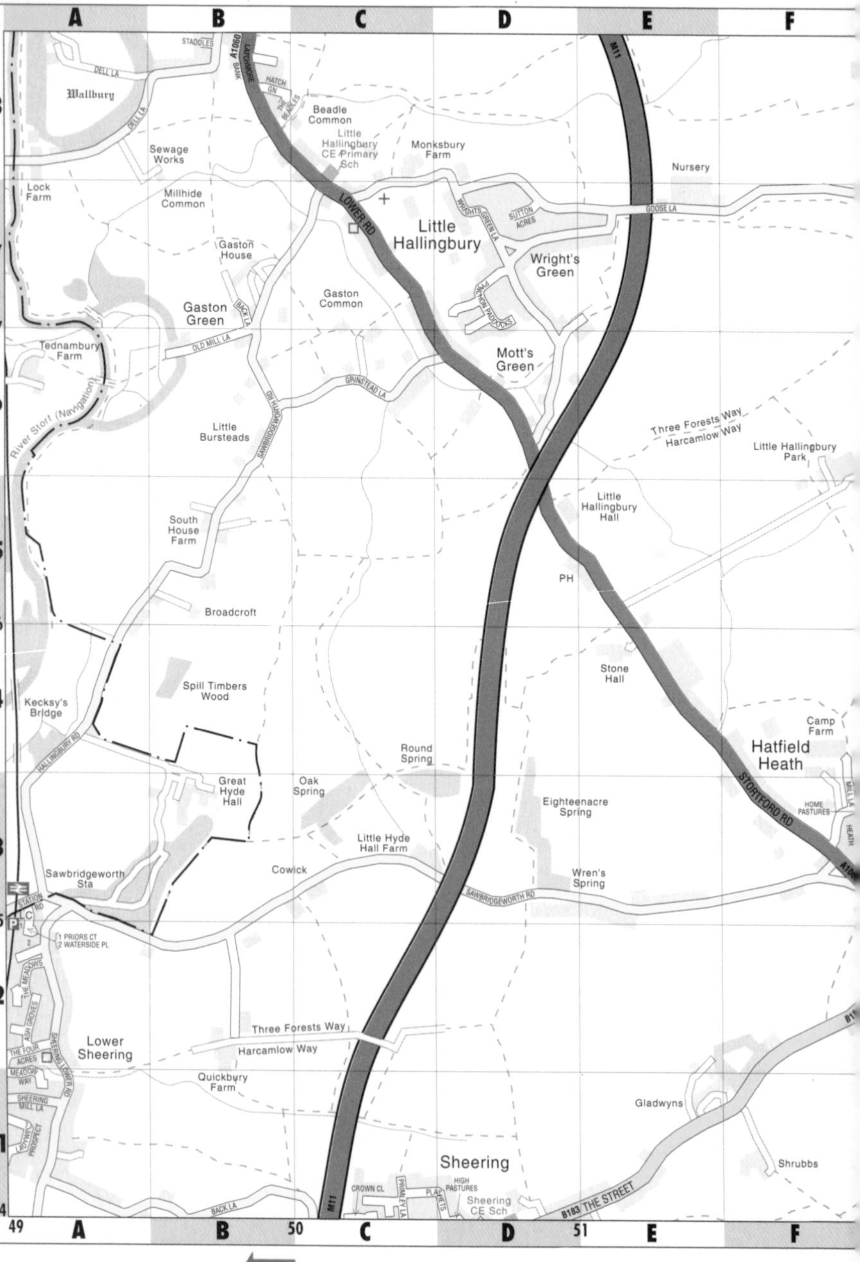
A
B
C
D
E
F
8
7
17
6
5
16
4
3
15
2
1
14
49
50
51
Wallbury
Dell La
Staddles
A1060
Latchmore Bank
Hatch Gn
The Beadles
Beadle Common
Little Hallingbury CE Primary Sch
Monksbury Farm
M11
Sewage Works
Nursery
Lock Farm
Millhide Common
Lower Rd
Wrights Green La
Sutton Acres
Goose La
Little Hallingbury
Gaston House
Wright's Green
Gaston Common
Gaston Green
Back La
Pynchon Paddocks
Tednambury Farm
Old Mill La
Mott's Green
Grinstead La
Sawbridgeworth Rd
River Stort (Navigation)
Little Bursteads
Three Forests Way
Harcamlow Way
Little Hallingbury Park
South House Farm
Little Hallingbury Hall
PH
Broadcroft
Stone Hall
Spill Timbers Wood
Kecksy's Bridge
Camp Farm
Hallingbury Rd
Round Spring
Hatfield Heath
Great Hyde Hall
Oak Spring
Eighteenacre Spring
Stortford Rd
Home Pastures
Mill La
Heath
Little Hyde Hall Farm
Sawbridgeworth Sta
Cowick
Wren's Spring
Station Rd
Sawbridgeworth Rd
1 Priors Ct
2 Waterside Pl
The Meadows
Ash Groves
Lower Sheering
Three Forests Way
Harcamlow Way
The Four Acres
Meadow Way
Sheering Lower Rd
Quickbury Farm
Sheering Mill La
Gladwyns
Roywel Prospect
Shrubbs
Sheering
Crown Cl
Primley La
High Pastures
Sheering CE Sch
B183 The Street
Back La

97

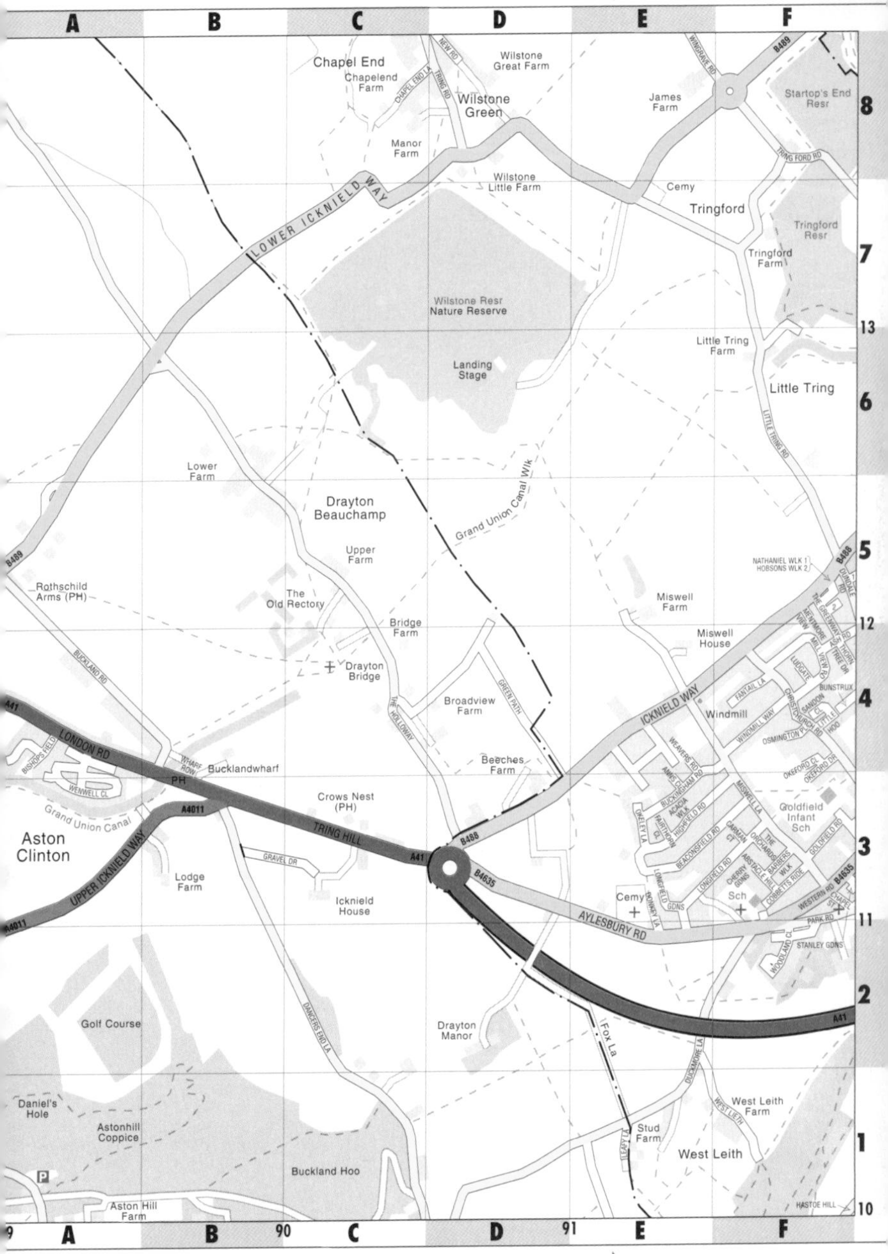

**8**

Chapel End
Chapelend Farm
Wilstone Great Farm
James Farm
Startop's End Resr

Wilstone Green
Manor Farm
Wilstone Little Farm
Cemy
Tringford

LOWER ICKNIELD WAY
B489
Tringford Resr

**7**

Tringford Farm

Wilstone Resr Nature Reserve
Little Tring Farm

**13**

Landing Stage
Little Tring

**6**

Lower Farm
Drayton Beauchamp
Grand Union Canal Wlk
NATHANIEL WLK 1
HOBSONS WLK 2

**5**

Rothschild Arms (PH)
Upper Farm
Miswell Farm
Miswell House

**12**

The Old Rectory
Bridge Farm
Windmill
ICKNIELD WAY

**4**

Drayton Bridge
Broadview Farm
Beeches Farm

Bucklandwharf
London Rd
A41
Grand Union Canal
Crows Nest (PH)
Goldfield Infant Sch

**3**

Aston Clinton
A4011
Tring Hill
A41
B488
B4635
Sch
Cemy
Aylesbury Rd

**11**

Lodge Farm
Icknield House
GRAVEL DR
STANLEY GDNS

**2**

Golf Course
Drayton Manor
Fox Ln
A41
West Leith Farm

Daniel's Hole
Astonhill Coppice
Stud Farm
West Leith

**1**

P
Buckland Hoo
HASTOE HILL

**10**

Aston Hill Farm

99
80

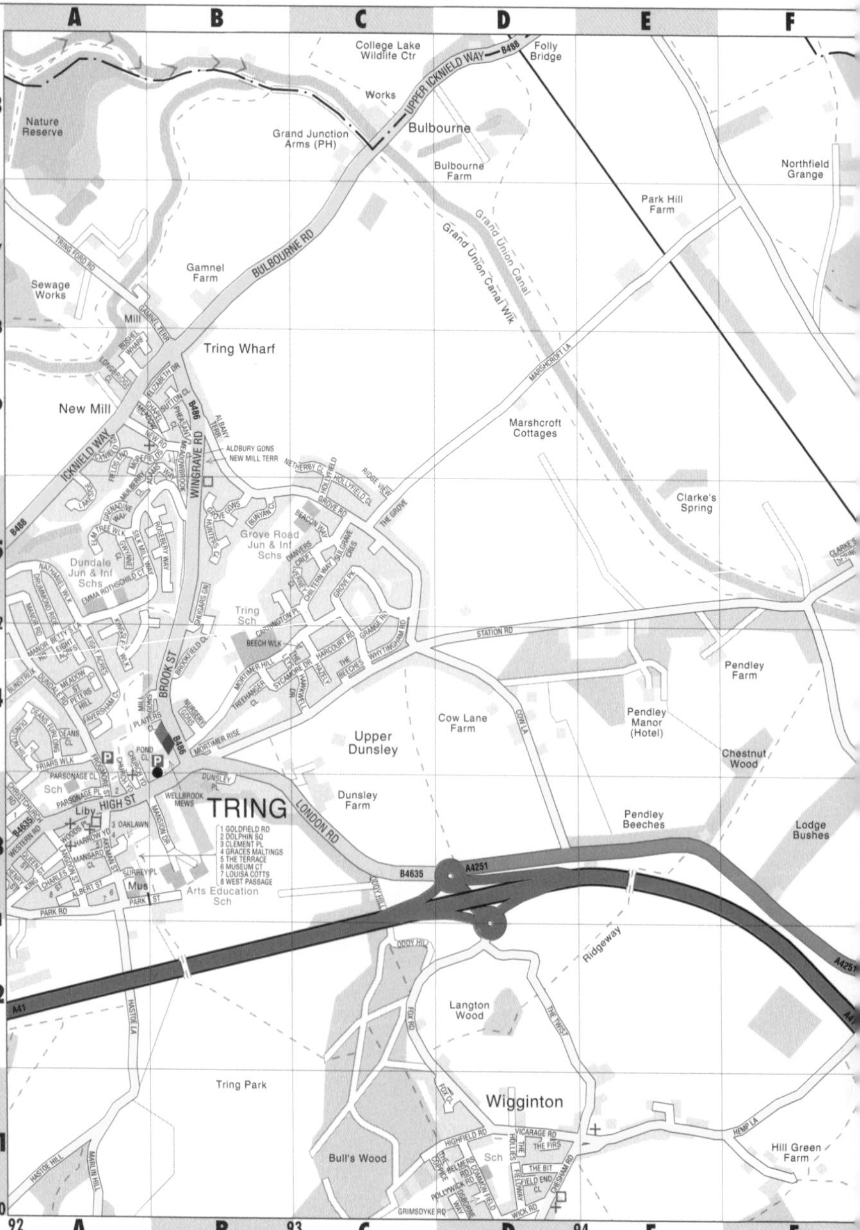
A
B
C
D
E
F
8
7
13
6
5
12
4
3
11
2
1
10
92
93
94
College Lake
Wildlife Ctr
Folly
Bridge
UPPER ICKNIELD WAY
B488
Works
Nature
Reserve
Grand Junction
Arms (PH)
Bulbourne
Bulbourne
Farm
Northfield
Grange
Park Hill
Farm
Grand Union Canal
Grand Union Canal Wlk
BULBOURNE RD
TRING FORD RD
Sewage
Works
Gamnel
Farm
Mill
GAMNEL TERR
BUSHEL WHARF
LONGBRIDGE CL
Tring Wharf
ELIZABETH DR
SUTTON CL
CHAPEL MEADOW
PHEASANT CL
B486
New Mill
ICKNIELD WAY
NEW RD
WINGRAVE RD
ALBANY TERR
ALDBURY GDNS
NEW MILL TERR
MARSHCROFT LA
Marshcroft
Cottages
NETHERBY CL
HOLLYFIELD
HOLLYFIELD CL
RIDGE VIEW
THE GROVE
GROVE RD
Clarke's
Spring
LAKES CT
MULBERRY CL
GRENADINE WAY
ELM TREE WLK
GROVE GDNS
BUNYAN CL
HUNTERS CL
BEACON WAY
Grove Road
Jun & Inf
Schs
DANVERS CROFT
SULGRAVE CRES
ROSEBERY WAY
SILK MILL WAY
B488
Dundale
Jun & Inf
Schs
EMMA ROTHSCHILD CT
NATHANIEL WLK
DRUMMOND RIDE
MANOR RD
BETTY'S LA
EIGHT ACRES
KINGSLEY WLK
CHILTERN WAY
GROVE PK
Tring
Sch
CARRINGTON PL
BEECH WLK
HARCOURT RD
GRANGE RD
WHYTINGHAM RD
STATION RD
Pendley
Farm
MORTIMER HILL
SYCAMORE DR
THE BEECHES
HAZELY
HAWWELL DR
TREEHANGER CL
BROOKFIELD CL
BROOK ST
DUNDALE RD
MEADOW ST
ST PETERS HILL
FAVERSHAM CL
DEANS FURLONG
DEANS CL
BUNSTRUX
NURSERY GDNS
MORTIMER RISE
Cow Lane
Farm
COW LA
Upper
Dunsley
Pendley
Manor
(Hotel)
Chestnut
Wood
FRIARS WLK
PARSONAGE CL
POND CL
P
DUNSLEY PL
WELLBROOK MEWS
Sch
PARSONAGE PL
HIGH ST
Liby
TRING
LONDON RD
Dunsley
Farm
Pendley
Beeches
Lodge
Bushes
B4635
WESTERN RD
WOODS PL
HARROW YD
3 OAKLAWN
MANSION DR
1 GOLDFIELD RD
2 DOLPHIN SQ
3 CLEMENT PL
4 GRACES MALTINGS
5 THE TERRACE
6 MUSEUM CT
7 LOUISA COTTS
8 WEST PASSAGE
MANSARD CL
CHARLES ST
ALBERT ST
SURREY PL
Mus
Arts Education
Sch
PARK RD
PARK ST
B4635
A4251
ODDY HILL
Ridgeway
A4251
A41
HASTOE LA
Langton
Wood
FOX RD
THE TWIST
A41
Tring Park
FOX CL
Wigginton
HEMP LA
HIGHFIELD RD
VICARAGE RD
THE FIRS
Hill Green
Farm
Bull's Wood
Sch
BELMERS RD
THE BIT
FIELD END CL
CHESHAM RD
POLLYWICK RD
WICK RD
GRIMSDYKE RD
HASTOE HILL
MARLIN HILL

99
120

102

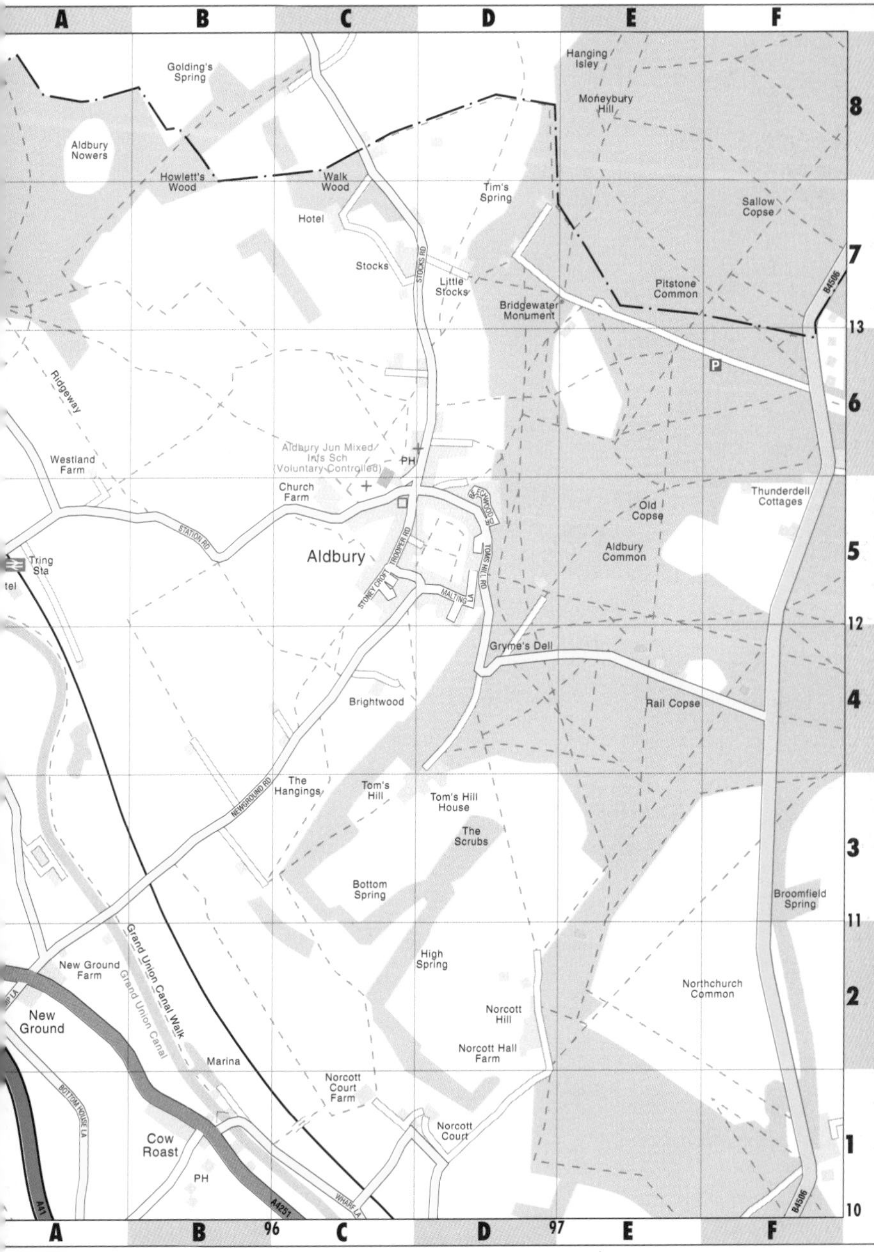
A
B
C
D
E
F
8
7
13
6
5
12
4
3
11
2
1
10
96
97
Hanging Isley
Moneybury Hill
Golding's Spring
Aldbury Nowers
Howlett's Wood
Walk Wood
Tim's Spring
Sallow Copse
Hotel
Stocks
STOCKS RD
Little Stocks
Bridgewater Monument
Pitstone Common
B4506
P
Ridgeway
Westland Farm
Aldbury Jun Mixed Infs Sch (Voluntary Controlled)
PH
Church Farm
STATION RD
TROOPER RD
TOMS HILL RD
Thunderdell Cottages
Old Copse
Aldbury Common
Aldbury
Tring Sta
tel
STONEY CROFT
MALTING LA
Gryme's Dell
Brightwood
Rail Copse
NEWGROUND RD
The Hangings
Tom's Hill
Tom's Hill House
The Scrubs
Bottom Spring
Broomfield Spring
Grand Union Canal Walk
Grand Union Canal
New Ground Farm
High Spring
Norcott Hill
Northchurch Common
New Ground
Norcott Hall Farm
Marina
Norcott Court Farm
BOTTOM HOUSE LA
Cow Roast
Norcott Court
PH
A41
A4251
WHARF LA
B4506

121
102

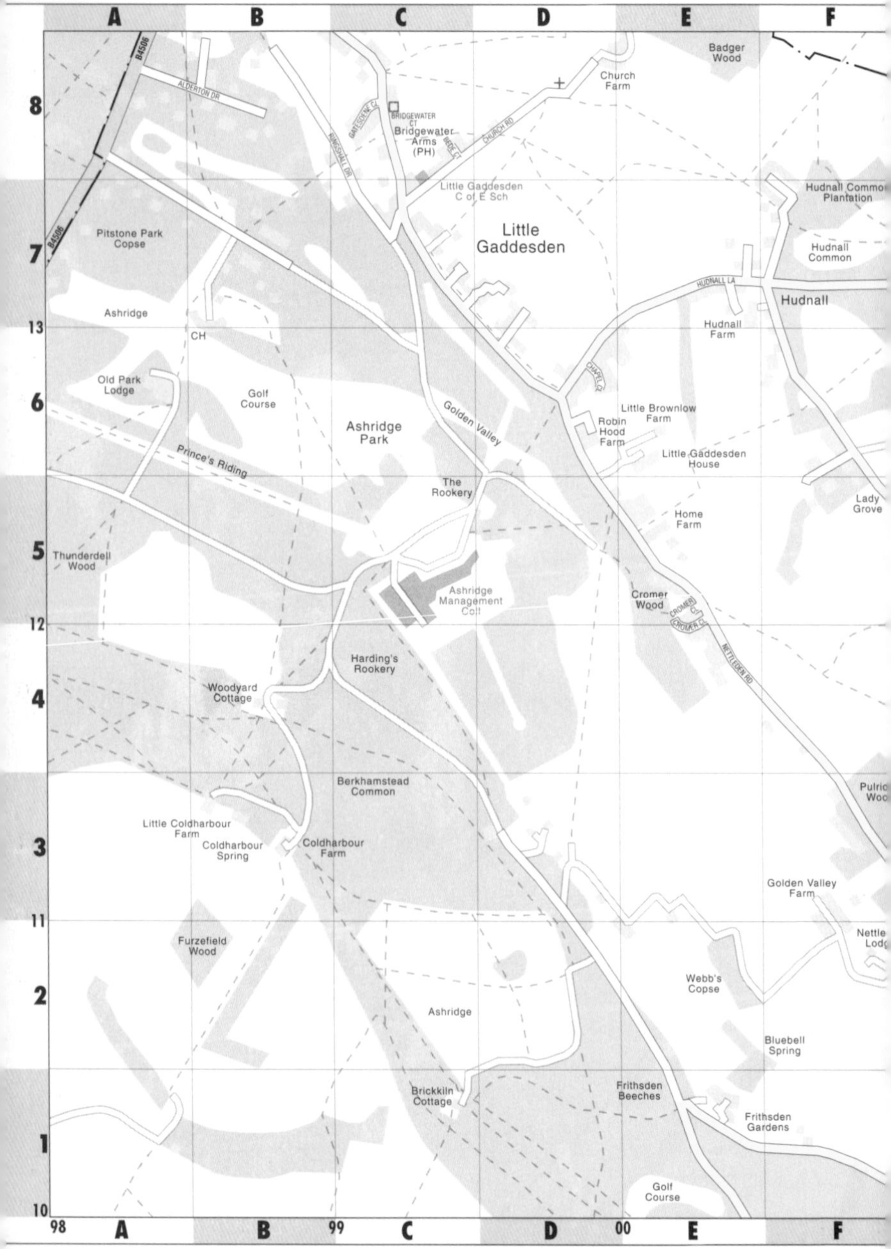

## Map Labels

**Column markers (top):** A B C D E F

**Column markers (bottom):** A B C D E F

**Row markers (left):** 8, 7, 13, 6, 5, 12, 4, 3, 11, 2, 1, 10

**Grid coordinates (bottom):** 98 A B 99 C D 00 E F

Badger Wood

Church Farm

ALDBURY DR

BRIDGEWATER DR

NORTH RD

CHURCH RD

Bridgewater Arms (PH)

BRIDGEWATER

Little Gaddesden C of E Sch

Little Gaddesden

Hudnall Common Plantation

Pitstone Park Copse

Hudnall Common

HUDNALL LA

Hudnall

Ashridge

CH

Hudnall Farm

Old Park Lodge

Golf Course

Ashridge Park

Golden Valley

DRIFT RD

Little Brownlow Farm

Robin Hood Farm

Little Gaddesden House

Prince's Riding

The Rookery

Home Farm

Lady Grove

Thunderdell Wood

Ashridge Management Coll

Cromer Wood

CROMER RD

BEECHER RD

Harding's Rookery

Woodyard Cottage

Berkhamstead Common

Pulric Wool

Little Coldharbour Farm

Coldharbour Spring

Coldharbour Farm

Golden Valley Farm

Furzefield Wood

Nettle Lodg

Webb's Copse

Ashridge

Bluebell Spring

Brickkiln Cottage

Frithsden Beeches

Frithsden Gardens

Golf Course

82
104

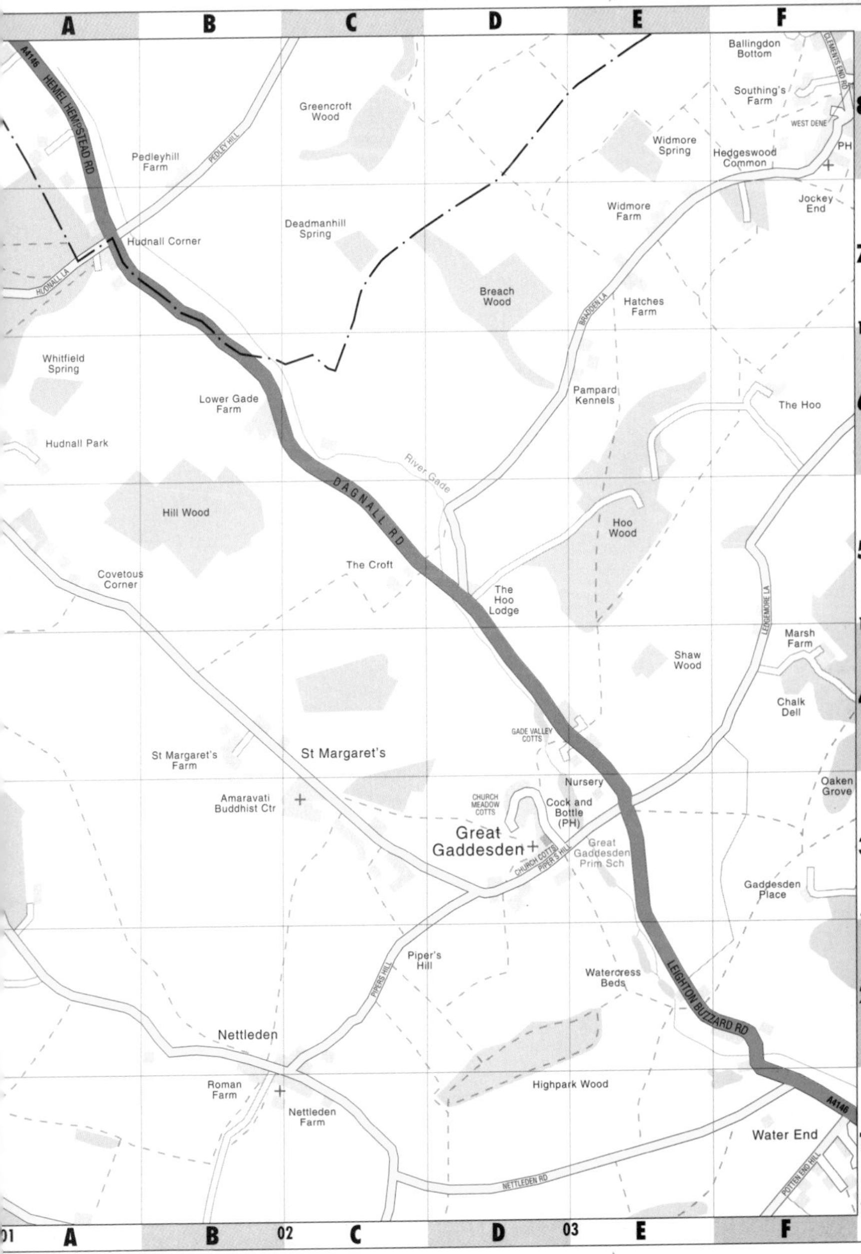
A
B
C
D
E
F
Ballingdon Bottom
CLEMENTS END RD
Southing's Farm
8
WEST DENE
Greencroft Wood
A4146
HEMEL HEMPSTEAD RD
PEDLEY HILL
Pedleyhill Farm
Widmore Spring
Hedgeswood Common
PH
Jockey End
Widmore Farm
Deadmanhill Spring
Hudnall Corner
7
HUDNALL LA
Breach Wood
BRADDEN LA
Hatches Farm
13
Whitfield Spring
Pampard Kennels
Lower Gade Farm
The Hoo
6
Hudnall Park
River Gade
DAGNALL RD
Hill Wood
Hoo Wood
5
Covetous Corner
The Croft
The Hoo Lodge
LEDGEMORE LA
12
Marsh Farm
Shaw Wood
Chalk Dell
4
GADE VALLEY COTTS
St Margaret's Farm
St Margaret's
Nursery
Oaken Grove
Amaravati Buddhist Ctr
CHURCH MEADOW COTTS
Cock and Bottle (PH)
Great Gaddesden
CHURCH COTTS
PIPER'S HILL
Great Gaddesden Prim Sch
3
Gaddesden Place
11
Piper's Hill
PIPERS HILL
Watercress Beds
LEIGHTON BUZZARD RD
2
Nettleden
Roman Farm
Highpark Wood
A4146
Nettleden Farm
Water End
1
POTTEN END HILL
NETTLEDEN RD
10
01
A
B
02
C
D
03
E
F

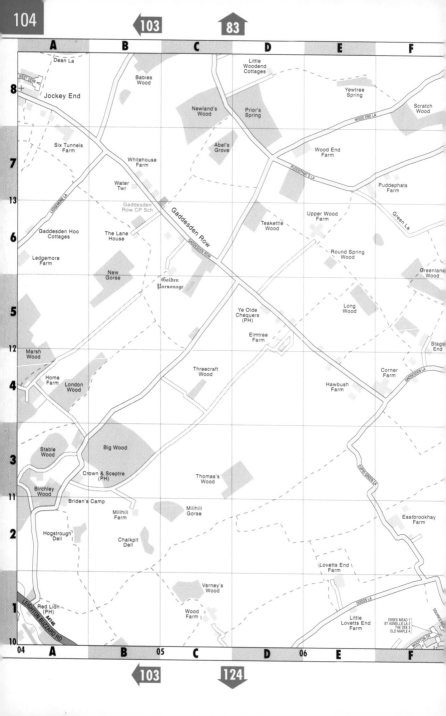

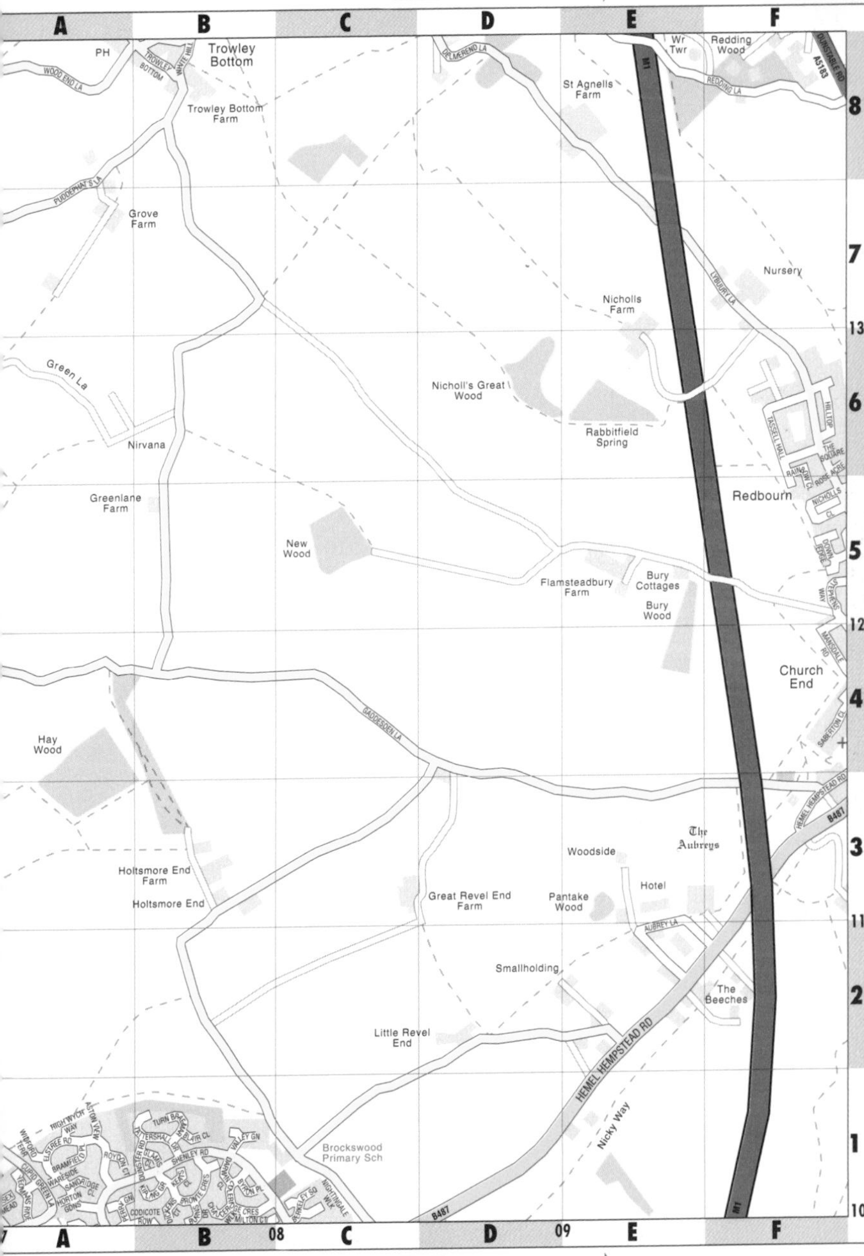

A B C D E F

8

7

13

6

5

12

4

3

11

2

1

10

Trowley Bottom

PH

Trowley Bottom Farm

WOOD END LA

PUDDENHAM LA

Grove Farm

Green La

Nirvana

Greenlane Farm

New Wood

Hay Wood

Holtsmore End Farm

Holtsmore End

SADDERS LA

Great Revel End Farm

Woodside

Pantake Wood

Smallholding

Little Revel End

Brockswood Primary Sch

HIGH WYCH

ASTER RD

TURIN BOL

B487

PLEASEND LA

St Agnells Farm

Nicholls Farm

Nicholl's Great Wood

Rabbitfield Spring

Flamsteadbury Farm

Bury Cottages

Bury Wood

The Aubreys

Hotel

AUBREY LA

The Beeches

HEMEL HEMPSTEAD RD

Nicky Way

Wr Twr

Redding Wood

A5183

REDDING LA

Nursery

Redbourn

Church End

HEMEL HEMPSTEAD RD

B487

A B C D E F

08 09

105
85

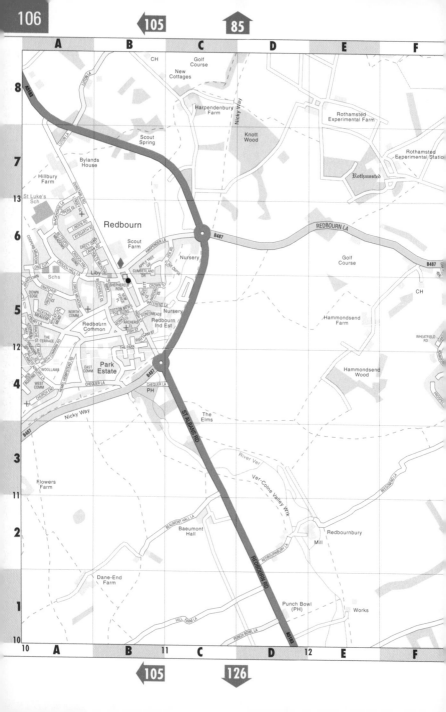
A
B
C
D
E
F
8
7
13
6
5
12
4
3
11
2
1
10
10
11
12
A5183
LUTON LA
CH
Golf Course
New Cottages
Harpendenbury Farm
Nicky Way
Rothamsted Experimental Farm
Knott Wood
Scout Spring
Bylands House
Rothamsted Experimental Station
Rothamsted
Hillbury Farm
St Luke's Sch
DUNSTABLE RD
Redbourn
LINDEN RD
AYSGARTH RD
REDBOURN LA
B487
Scout Farm
HARPENDEN LA
COOPERS MEADOW
CRECY GDNS
CAVAN RD
CROUCH HALL LA
Nursery
LONG CUFT
Golf Course
Liby
APPLE TREE GR
CUMBERLAND DR
FLINT COPSE
Schs
SHEPHERD'S ROW
CROWN ST
CH
DOWN EDGE
NEW FORGE PL
WATEREND LA
Nursery
NORTH COMM
TOTTON MEWS
THE RUINS
POND MEADE
Redbourn Common
Redbourn Ind Est
Hammondsend Farm
ARCHERS CL
FISH ST
FISH FARM ST
THE TERRACE
THE PARK
WHEATFIELD RD
Park Estate
EAST COMM
Hammondsend Wood
WOOLLAMS
WEST COMM
CHEQUER LA
CHEQUER LA
PH
HEMEL HEMPSTEAD RD
CHURCH END
Nicky Way
The Elms
ST ALBANS RD
River Ver
Ver-Colne Valley Wlk
Flowers Farm
BEESONEND LA
BEAUMONT HALL LA
Baeumont Hall
Redbournbury
Mill
REDBOURNBURY LA
REDBOURN RD
Dane-End Farm
Punch Bowl (PH)
Works
HILL FARM LA
PUNCH BOWL LA
A5183

105
126

86
108

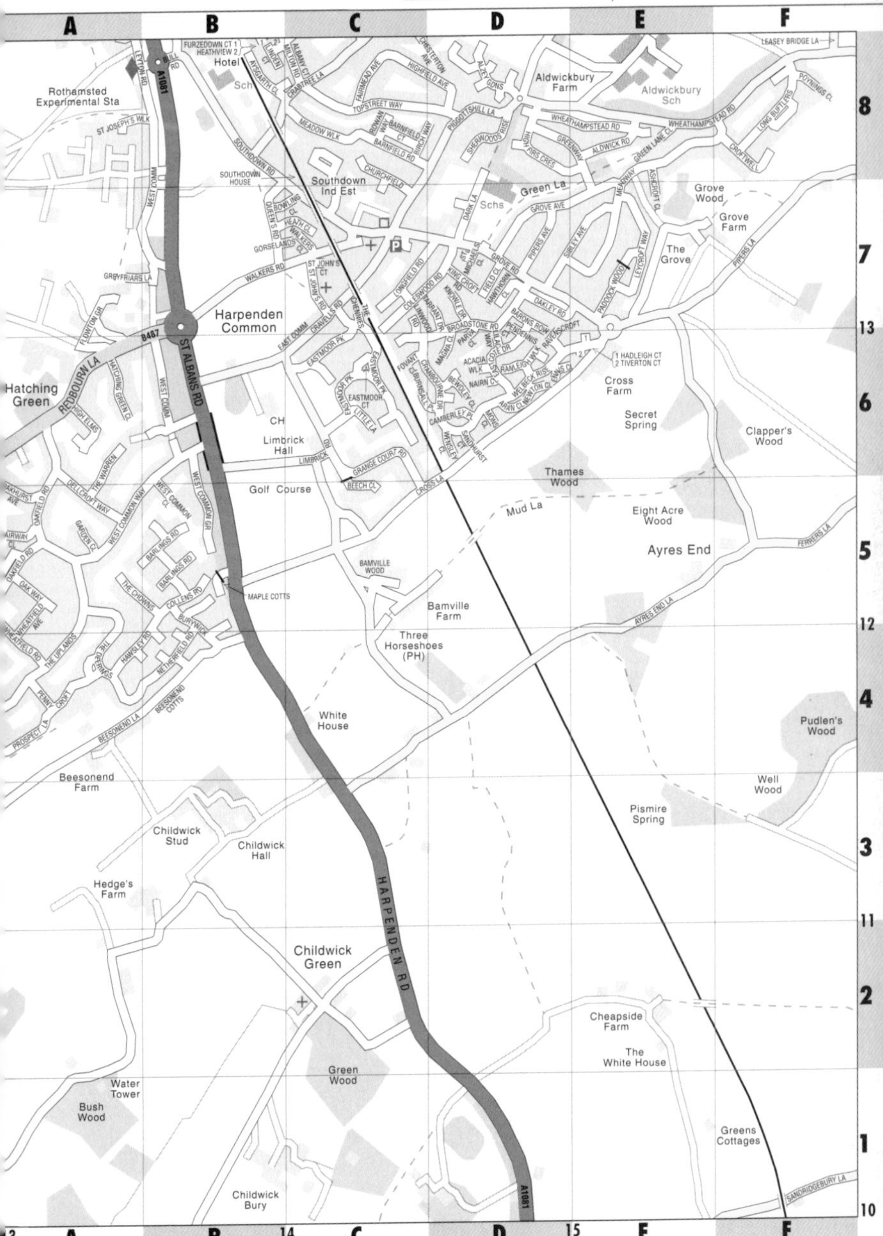
A
B
C
D
E
F
8
7
13
6
5
12
4
3
11
2
1
10
13
14
15
Rothamsted Experimental Sta
Hotel
Sch
Aldwickbury Farm
Aldwickbury Sch
LEASEY BRIDGE LA
FURZEDOWN CT 1
HEATHVIEW 2
A1081
ST ALBANS RD
HARPENDEN RD
B487
REDBOURN LA
Southdown Ind Est
SOUTHDOWN HOUSE
SOUTHDOWN RD
WHEATHAMPSTEAD RD
ALDWICK RD
GREEN LANE CL
Green La
Schs
Grove Wood
Grove Farm
The Grove
PIPERS LA
GROVE AVE
DARK LA
WALKERS RD
GREYFRIARS LA
Harpenden Common
Hatching Green
ST JOSEPH'S WLK
WEST COMM
EAST COMM
1 HADLEIGH CT
2 TIVERTON CT
Cross Farm
Secret Spring
Clapper's Wood
CH
Limbrick Hall
Golf Course
BEECH CL
CROSS LA
Thames Wood
Mud La
Eight Acre Wood
Ayres End
FERRERS LA
BAMVILLE WOOD
MAPLE COTTS
Bamville Farm
Three Horseshoes (PH)
AYRES END LA
White House
Pudlen's Wood
Well Wood
Pismire Spring
BEESONEND LA
BEESONEND COTTS
PROSPECT LA
Beesonend Farm
Childwick Stud
Childwick Hall
Hedge's Farm
Childwick Green
Cheapside Farm
The White House
Green Wood
Water Tower
Bush Wood
Greens Cottages
SANDRIDGEBURY LA
Childwick Bury

127
108

107
87

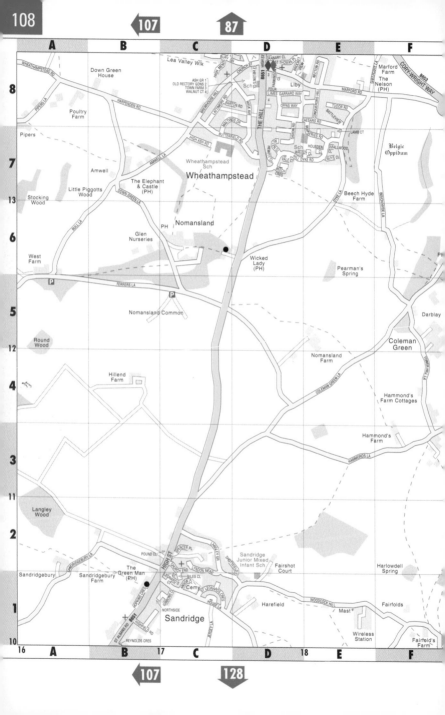
A
B
C
D
E
F
8
7
13
6
5
12
4
3
11
2
1
10
16
17
18
Lea Valley Wlk
Wheathampstead Rd
Down Green House
Bury Gn
High Meads
Church St
St Helen's Cl
High St
B651
Granary Cl
St Thomas Pl
Brocket View
Necton Rd
Sheepcote La
Marford Farm
The Nelson (PH)
Cory-Wright Way
B653
Ash Gr 1
Old Rectory Gdns 2
Town Farm 3
Walnut Ct 4
Sch
Liby
Four Limes
Garrard Way
Marford Rd
Pipers La
Harpenden Rd
Poultry Farm
Brewhouse Hill
Lattimore Rd
Barton Rd
Wick Ave
The Hill
Parkinson Cl
Offas Way
Conquerors Hill
Tudor Rd
Battleview
Caesars Rd
Lamb Ct
Maltings Dr
Butterfield Rd
Saxon Rd
Nurseries Rd
Pipers
High Ash Rd
Hewitt Cl
Helen Cl
Sch
Housden Cl
Smallwood Cl
Wright Cl
Hill Dyke Rd
Davys Cl
Vale Ct
Beech Cres
Belgic Oppidum
Amwell La
Wheathampstead Sch
Wheathampstead
Amwell
The Elephant & Castle (PH)
Little Piggotts Wood
Down Green La
Stocking Wood
Dyke La
Beech Hyde Farm
Beech Hyde La
Bull La
PH
Nomansland
Glen Nurseries
West Farm
Wicked Lady (PH)
Pearman's Spring
P
Ferrers La
P
Nomansland Common
Darblay
Round Wood
Coleman Green
Nomansland Farm
Tower Hill La
Hillend Farm
Coleman Green La
Hammond's Farm Cottages
Hammond's Farm
Hammonds La
Langley Wood
Pound Cl
Spencer Pl
Langley Gr
High St
Shottfield Cl
Sandridge Junior Mixed Infant Sch
Fairshot Court
Harlowdell Spring
Sandridgebury La
The Green Man (PH)
Church End
Lyndon Mead
Sandridgebury
Sandridgebury Farm
St Leonard's Ct
Giles Cl
Anson Cl
Cemy
St Leonards Cres
Hopkins Cres
Gibbons Cl
House La
Harefield
Woodcock Hill
Fairfolds
Northside
Mast
Sandridge
St Albans Rd
B651
Highfield Rd
Jersey La
Wireless Station
Reynolds Cres
Fairfold's Farm

107
128

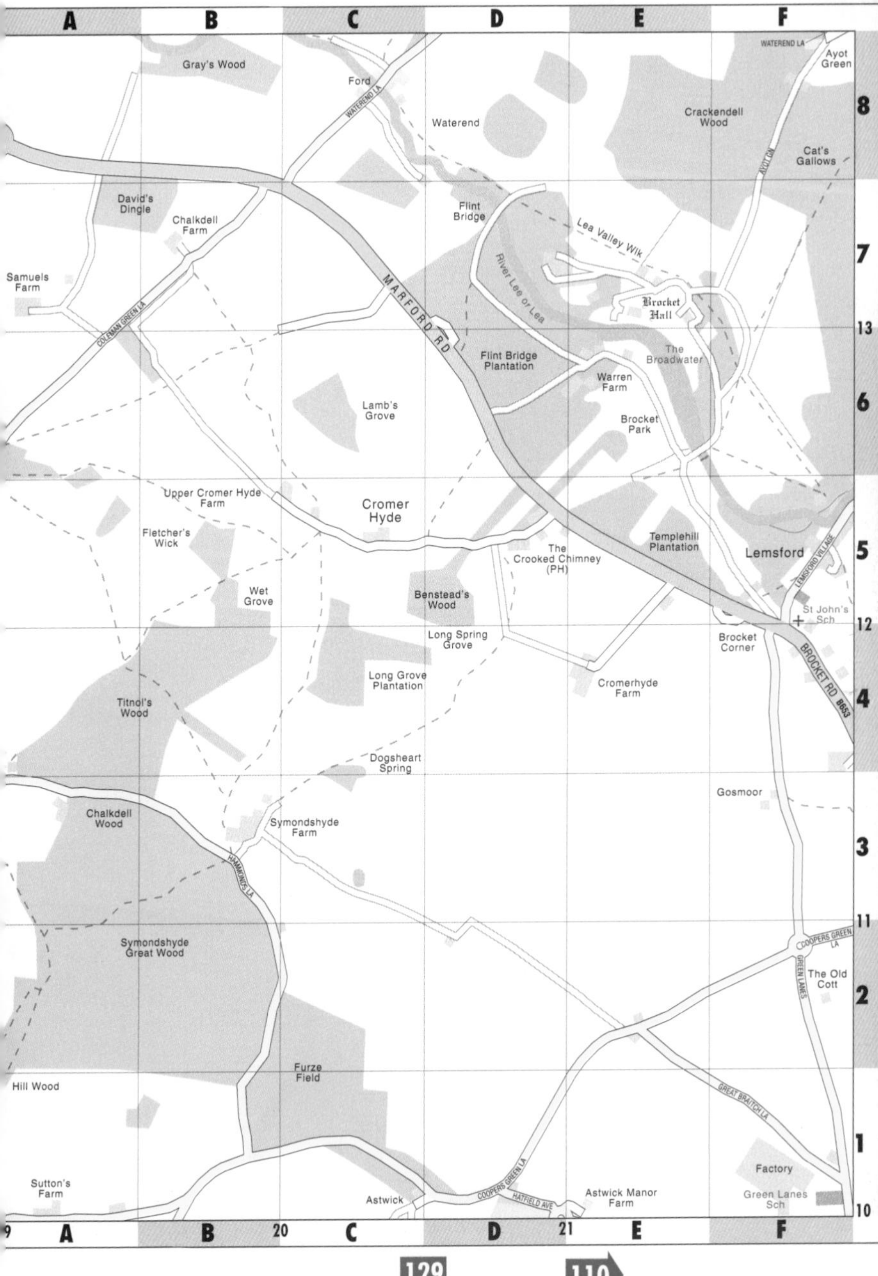
Gray's Wood
Ford
WATEREND LA
Waterend
Crackendell Wood
Ayot Green
WATEREND LA
AYOT GN
Cat's Gallows
David's Dingle
Chalkdell Farm
Flint Bridge
Lea Valley Wlk
River Lee or Lea
Samuels Farm
COLEMAN GREEN LA
MARFORD RD
Brocket Hall
Flint Bridge Plantation
The Broadwater
Warren Farm
Lamb's Grove
Brocket Park
Upper Cromer Hyde Farm
Cromer Hyde
Fletcher's Wick
The Crooked Chimney (PH)
Templehill Plantation
Lemsford
LEMSFORD VILLAGE
Wet Grove
Benstead's Wood
St John's Sch
Brocket Corner
Long Spring Grove
BROCKET RD B653
Long Grove Plantation
Cromerhyde Farm
Titnol's Wood
Dogsheart Spring
Gosmoor
Chalkdell Wood
Symondshyde Farm
HAMMONDS LA
Symondshyde Great Wood
COOPERS GREEN LA
GREEN LANES
The Old Cott
Hill Wood
Furze Field
GREAT BRAITCH LA
Factory
Sutton's Farm
Astwick
COOPERS GREEN LA
HATFIELD AVE
Astwick Manor Farm
Green Lanes Sch

109
89

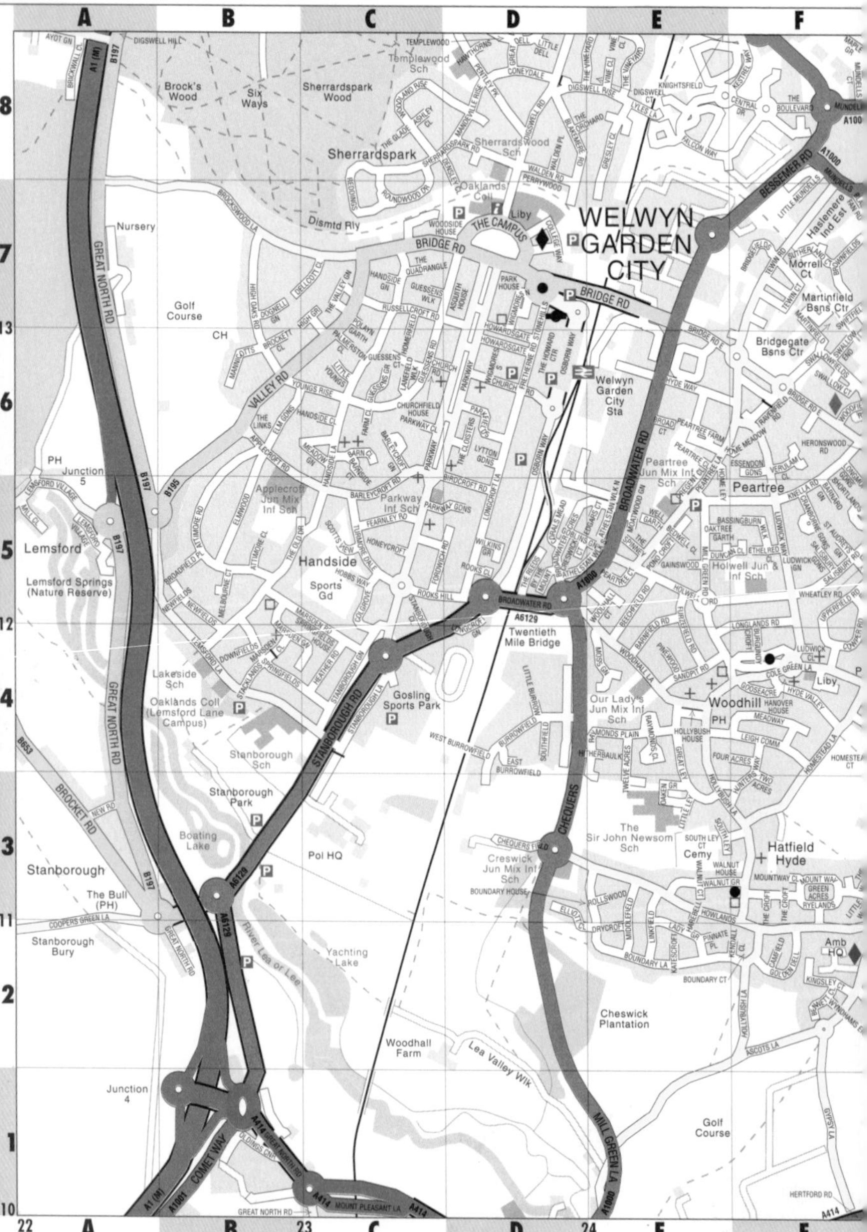
A
B
C
D
E
F
8
7
13
6
5
12
4
3
11
2
1
10
22
23
24
WELWYN GARDEN CITY
Brock's Wood
Six Ways
Sherrardspark Wood
Sherrardspark
Templewood Sch
Sherrardswood Sch
Oaklands Coll
Liby
Dismtd Rly
Nursery
GREAT NORTH RD
Golf Course
CH
BRIDGE RD
THE CAMPUS
VALLEY RD
Welwyn Garden City Sta
BROADWATER RD
BESSEMER RD
A1000
Haslemere Ind Est
Morrell Ct
Martinfield Bsns Ctr
Bridgegate Bsns Ctr
Peartree
Peartree Jun Mix Inf Sch
PH
Junction 5
Lemsford
Lemsford Springs (Nature Reserve)
Applecroft Jun Mix Inf Sch
Parkway Inf Sch
Handside
Sports Gd
Holwell Jun & Inf Sch
Twentieth Mile Bridge
A6129
Lakeside Sch
Oaklands Coll (Lemsford Lane Campus)
Gosling Sports Park
STANBOROUGH RD
Our Lady's Jun Mix Inf Sch
Woodhill
Stanborough Sch
Stanborough Park
Boating Lake
Pol HQ
Stanborough
The Bull (PH)
Stanborough Bury
BROCKET RD
B653
B197
B195
The Sir John Newsom Sch
Cemy
Hatfield Hyde
Creswick Jun Mix Inf Sch
CHEQUERS
River Lea or Lee
Yachting Lake
Amb HQ
Cheswick Plantation
Woodhall Farm
Lea Valley Wlk
Junction 4
COMET WAY
A1(M)
A1001
A414
MOUNT PLEASANT LA
GREAT NORTH RD
MILL GREEN LA
Golf Course
HERTFORD RD

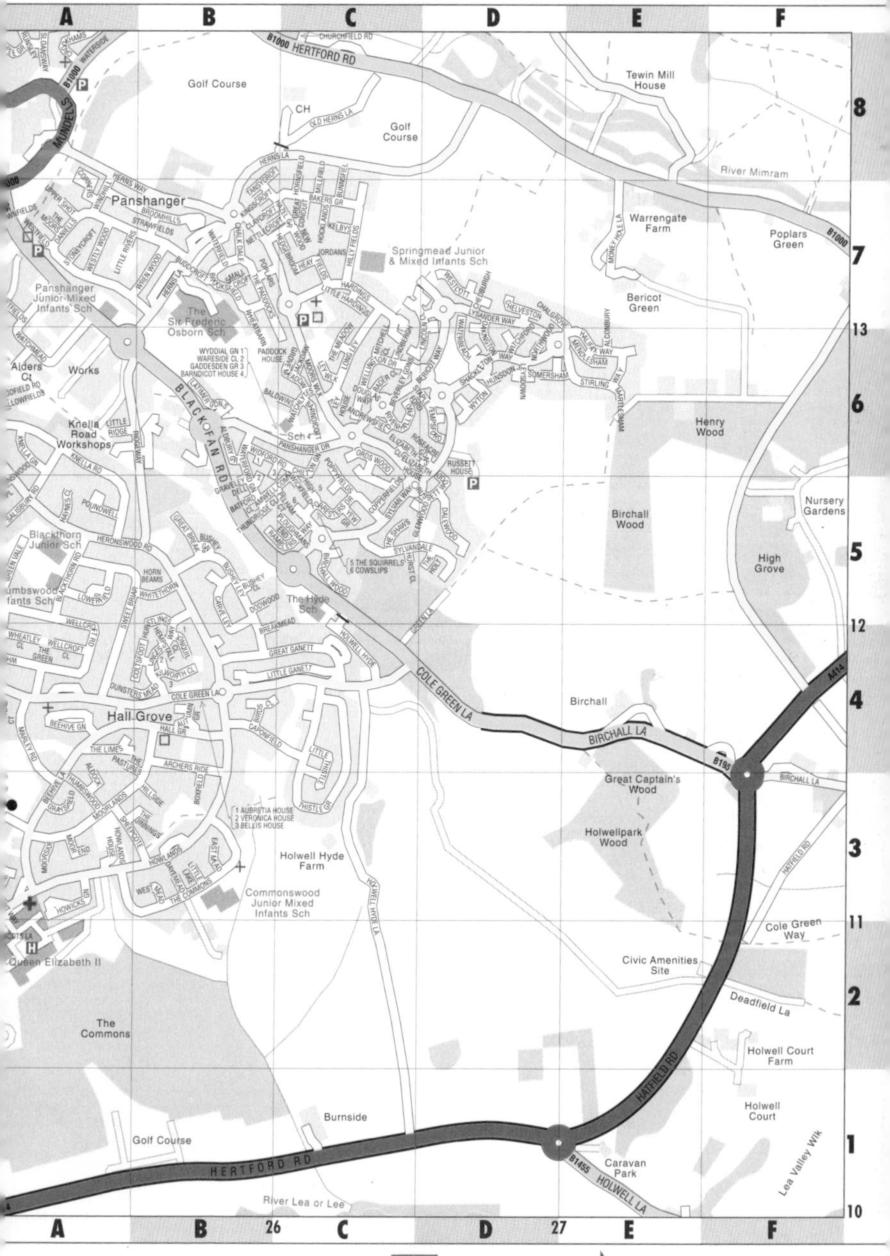
A
B
C
D
E
F
8
7
13
6
5
12
4
3
11
2
1
10
26
27
B1000 HERTFORD RD
CHURCHFIELD RD
Golf Course
CH
OLD HERNS LA
Golf Course
Tewin Mill House
River Mimram
MUNDELLS
Panshanger
Warrengate Farm
Poplars Green
B1000
Springmead Junior & Mixed Infants Sch
Bericot Green
Panshanger Junior Mixed Infants Sch
The Sir Frederic Osborn Sch
WYDDIAL GN 1
WARESIDE CL 2
GADDESDEN GR 3
BARNDICOT HOUSE 4
PADDOCK HOUSE
Alders Ct
Works
BLACKFAN RD
Knella Road Workshops
Henry Wood
RUSSETT HOUSE
PANSHANGER DR
Birchall Wood
Nursery Gardens
Blackthorn Junior Sch
HERONSWOOD RD
5 THE SQUIRRELS
6 COWSLIPS
High Grove
The Hyde Sch
GREEN LA
COLE GREEN LA
Birchall
BIRCHALL LA
A414
B195
Hall Grove
Great Captain's Wood
Holwellpark Wood
1 AUBRETIA HOUSE
2 VERONICA HOUSE
3 BELLIS HOUSE
Holwell Hyde Farm
HOLWELL HYDE LA
HATFIELD RD
Commonswood Junior Mixed Infants Sch
Cole Green Way
Queen Elizabeth II
Civic Amenities Site
Deadfield La
The Commons
Holwell Court Farm
HATFIELD RD
Holwell Court
Burnside
Golf Course
HERTFORD RD
Caravan Park
B1455 HOLWELL LA
Lea Valley Wlk
River Lea or Lee

111
91

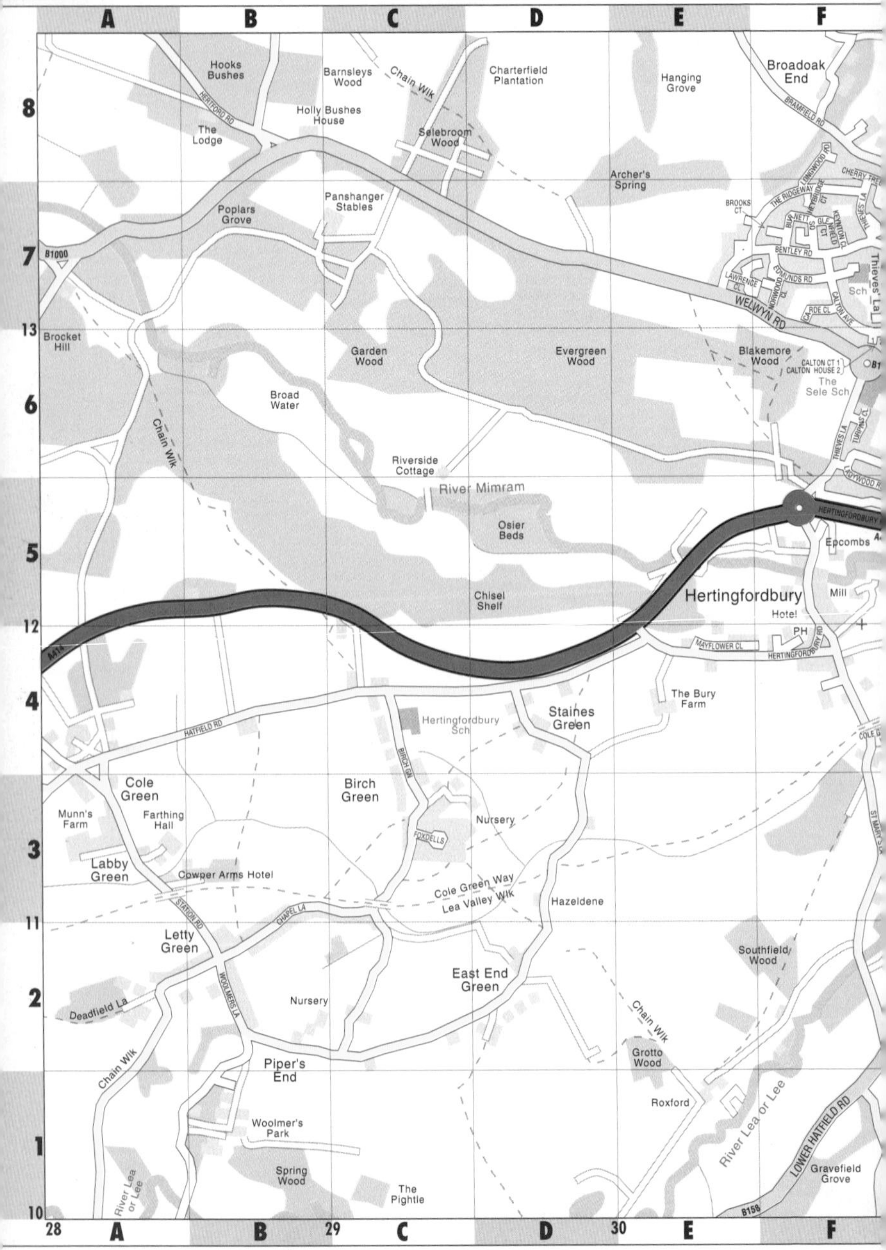
A
B
C
D
E
F
8
7
13
6
5
12
4
3
11
2
1
10
28
29
30
Hooks Bushes
Barnsleys Wood
Chain Wlk
Charterfield Plantation
Hanging Grove
Broadoak End
HERTFORD RD
BRAMFIELD RD
Holly Bushes House
The Lodge
Selebroom Wood
Archer's Spring
CHERRY TREE
LONGWOOD RD
THE RIDGEWAY
BROOKS CT
Panshanger Stables
Poplars Grove
BENTLEY RD
EDMUNDS RD
LAWRENCE CL
Thieves' La
Sch
B1000
WELWYN RD
RDE CL
CALTON AVE
Brocket Hill
Garden Wood
Evergreen Wood
Blakemore Wood
CALTON CT 1
CALTON HOUSE 2
The Sele Sch
Broad Water
Chain Wlk
THIEVES LA
Riverside Cottage
River Mimram
LADYWOOD RD
HERTINGFORDBURY
Osier Beds
Epcombs
Chisel Shelf
Hertingfordbury
Mill
Hotel
PH
A414
MAYFLOWER CL
HERTINGFORDBURY RD
The Bury Farm
Staines Green
Hertingfordbury Sch
HATFIELD RD
BIRCH GN
COLE GN
Cole Green
Birch Green
Munn's Farm
Farthing Hall
Nursery
FOXDELLS
ST MARY'S
Labby Green
Cowper Arms Hotel
Cole Green Way
Lea Valley Wlk
Hazeldene
STATION RD
CHAPEL LA
Letty Green
Southfield Wood
East End Green
WOOLMERS LA
Deadfield La
Nursery
Chain Wlk
Chain Wlk
Grotto Wood
Piper's End
Roxford
River Lea or Lee
LOWER HATFIELD RD
Woolmer's Park
Spring Wood
The Pightle
River Lea or Lee
Gravefield Grove
B158

111
132

92
114

6
ST ANDREW MEWS
MILLBRIDGE MEWS
5
ADAM'S YD
DOLPHIN YD

3 MAIDENHEAD ST
4 EVRON PL
5 HONEY LA
6 MARKET PL
7 SALISBURY SQ
8 THE BIRCHERLEY GREEN CTR
9 SHAFTESBURY QUAY
10 PRIORY WHARF
11 PRIORY CT
12 BIRCHERLEY CT
13 THE MALTHOUSE
14 WARREN PL
15 BLUECOATS CT
16 CHAUNCY CT
17 MITRE CT
18 ST JOHN'S CT

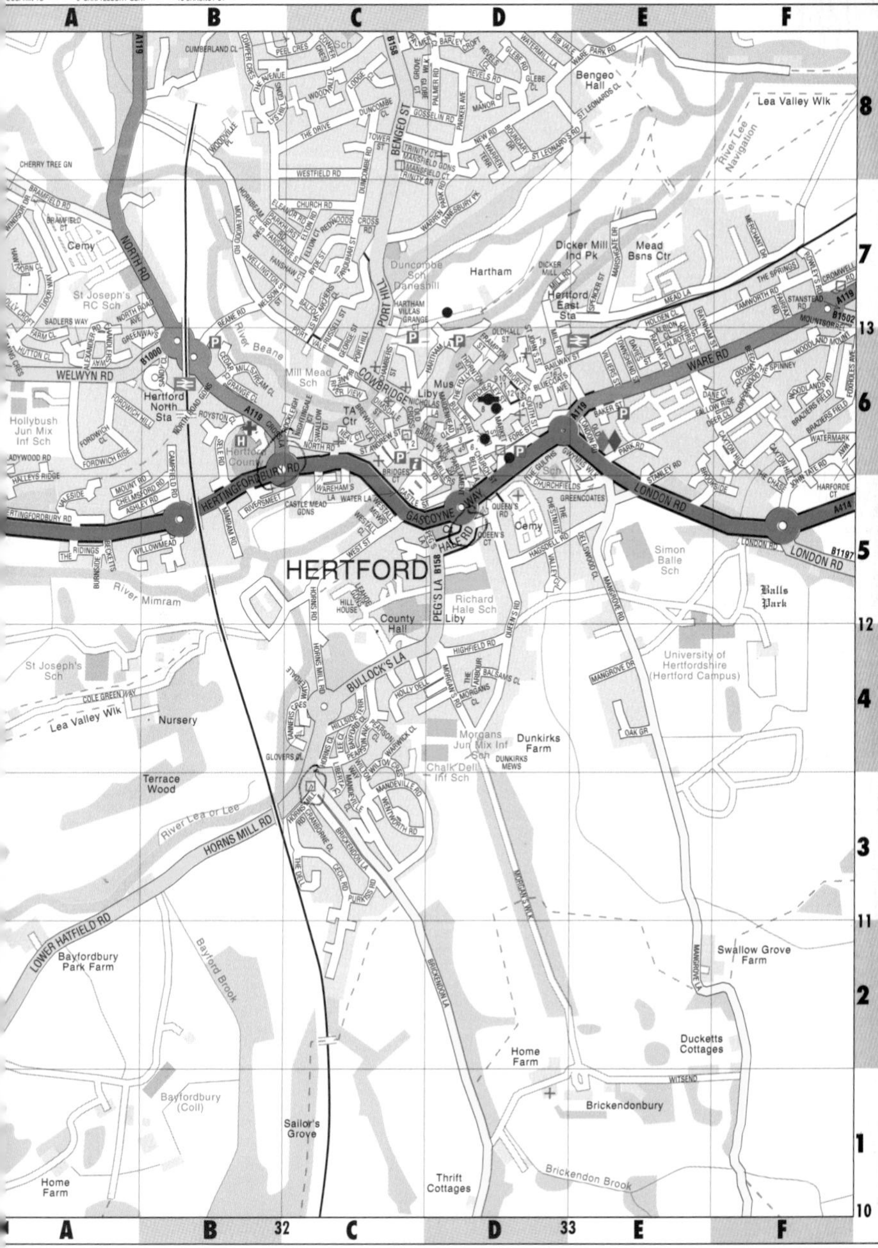


133
114

113
93

A B C D E F

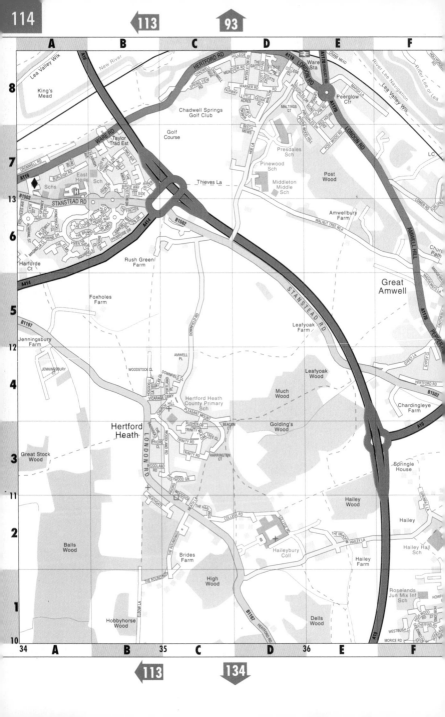
Lea Valley Wlk
New River
King's Mead
A10
HERTFORD RD
Chadwell Springs Golf Club
Golf Course
WARE RD
Taylor Trad Est
CROMWELL RD
A119
East Herts Sch
Schs
STANSTEAD RD
B1502
Thieves La
A414
Harforde Ct
Rush Green Farm
Foxholes Farm
B1197
Jenningsbury Farm
JENNINGSBURY CT
WOODSTOCK CL
AMWELL PL
DOWNFIELD RD
DOWNFIELD CL
VICARAGE CSWY
CHURCH HILL
PLEASANT MOUNT
Hertford Heath County Primary Sch
Hertford Heath
LONDON RD
RUSHEN DR
TRINITY RD
BEACON CT
HARRINGTON CT
WOODLAND RD
POSTWOOD GN
Great Stock Wood
HEATHGATE
WOODSIDE
HEATH LA
THE HARLOWS
COLLEGE RD
THE ROUNDINGS
Brides Farm
Balls Wood
High Wood
ELBOW LA
Hobbyhorse Wood
B1197
HERTFORD RD
Haileybury Coll
Dells Wood
Hailey Farm
THE MEADOW
HAILEY LA
Hailey Wood
Hailey
Hailey Hall Sch
Roselands Jun Mix Inf Sch
WESTBUSH CL
MORICE RD
Springle House
SPRINGLE LA
Chardingleye Farm
A10
B1502
HERTFORD RD
GYPSY LA
Golding's Wood
Much Wood
Leafyoak Wood
Leafyoak Farm
STANSTEAD RD
Great Amwell
AMWELL HILL
A1170
Amwellbury Farm
WALNUT TREE WLK
Middleton Middle Sch
Pinewood Sch
Presdales Sch
Post Wood
LONDON RD
POST WOOD RD
HOE LA
BEECH MEWS
MALTINGS CT
Peerglow Ctr
MARSH LA
Lea Valley Wlk
River Lee Navigation
River Lee or Lea
Ware Sta
Ware Coll
A119
LONDON RD
A1170
VIADUCT RD
CRANE MEAD
MEADVIEW RD
MYDDLETON RD
WARNER RD
FAIRWAY
LITTLE ACRES
CEDAR CL
WALTON RD
COLLEGE CL
HILLSIDE
SPRING VIEW RD
LC
Church Path

34 A B 35 C D 36 E F

113
134

94
116

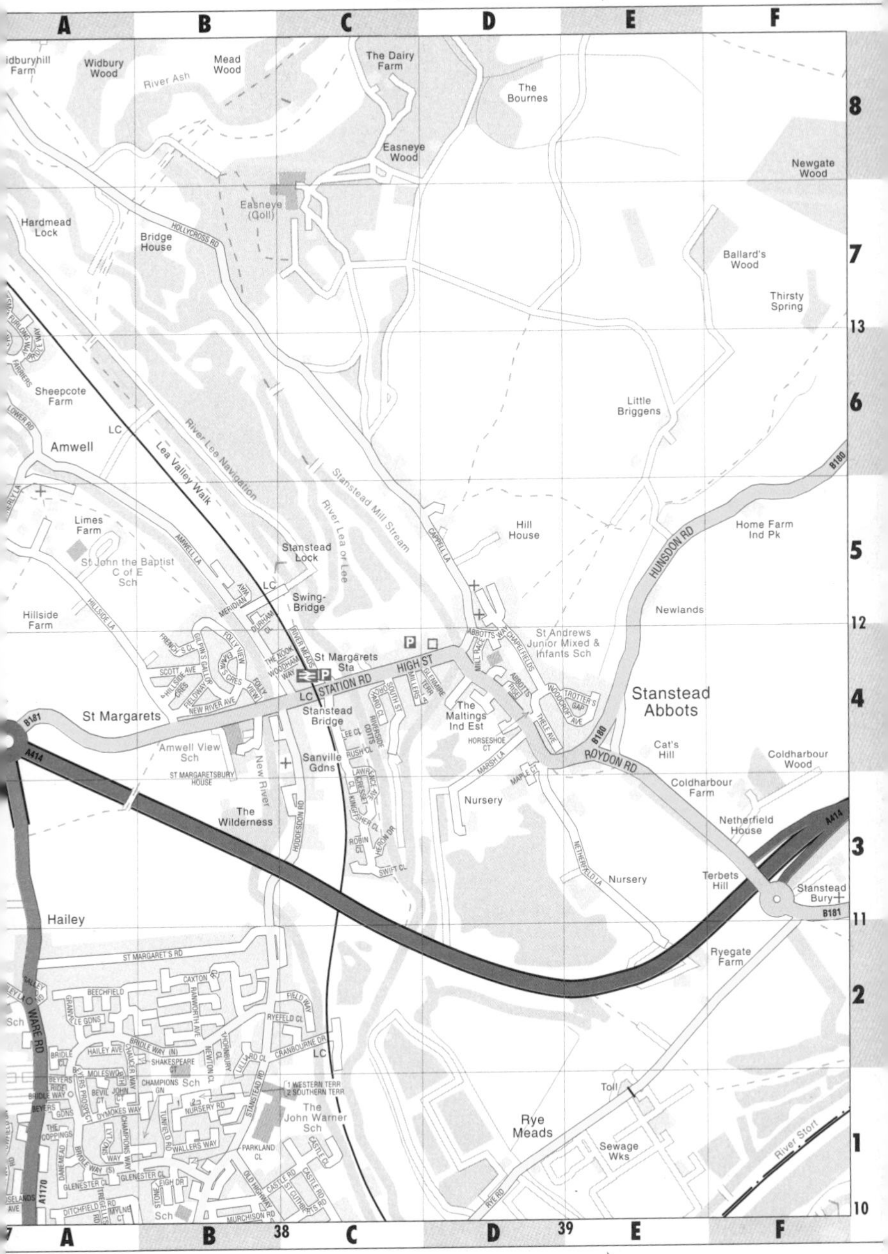
A
B
C
D
E
F
8
7
13
6
5
12
4
3
11
2
1
10
38
39
idburyhill Farm
Widbury Wood
Mead Wood
River Ash
The Dairy Farm
The Bournes
Easneye Wood
Newgate Wood
Easneye (Coll)
Hardmead Lock
Bridge House
HOLLYCROSS RD
Ballard's Wood
Thirsty Spring
Sheepcote Farm
Little Briggens
LC
Amwell
Lea Valley Walk
River Lee Navigation
Stanstead Mill Stream
River Lea or Lee
B180
Limes Farm
AMWELL LA
Stanstead Lock
CAPPELL LA
Hill House
HUNSDON RD
Home Farm Ind Pk
St John the Baptist C of E Sch
Swing-Bridge
Hillside Farm
HILLSIDE LA
MERIDIAN WAY
DURHAM CL
Newlands
St Andrews Junior Mixed & Infants Sch
St Margarets Sta
HIGH ST
STATION RD
ABBOTTS WAY
CHAPELFIELDS
MILL RACE
ABBOTTS RISE
Stanstead Abbots
SCOTT AVE
FOLLY VIEW
NEW RIVER AVE
FIELDWAY
B181
St Margarets
Stanstead Bridge
SOUTH ST
MILLERS
GLENMIRE TERR
The Maltings Ind Est
HORSESHOE CT
TROTTER'S GAP
WOODCROFT AVE
THELE AVE
ROYDON RD
Cat's Hill
Coldharbour Wood
A414
Amwell View Sch
New River
Sanville Gdns
ST MARGARETSBURY HOUSE
MARSH LA
MAPLE CT
Coldharbour Farm
Nursery
The Wilderness
HODDESDON RD
ROBIN CL
HERON DR
SWIFT CL
Netherfield House
NETHERFIELD LA
Terbets Hill
Stanstead Bury
Hailey
Ryegate Farm
ST MARGARET'S RD
CAXTON
BEECHFIELD
RANWORTH AVE
FIELD WAY
RYEFIELD CL
WARE RD
Sch
HAILEY AVE
BRIDLE WAY (N)
SHAKESPEARE CT
CRANBOURNE DR
CHAMPIONS GN
1 WESTERN TERR
2 SOUTHERN TERR
Toll
The John Warner Sch
STANSTEAD RD
NURSERY RD
Rye Meads
DYMOKES WAY
WALLERS WAY
PARKLAND CL
Sewage Wks
River Stort
A1170
GLENESTER CL
OLD HIGHWAY
CASTLE RD
ST CUTHBERTS RD
RYE RD
DITCHFIELD RD
MURCHISON RD

135
116

115
95

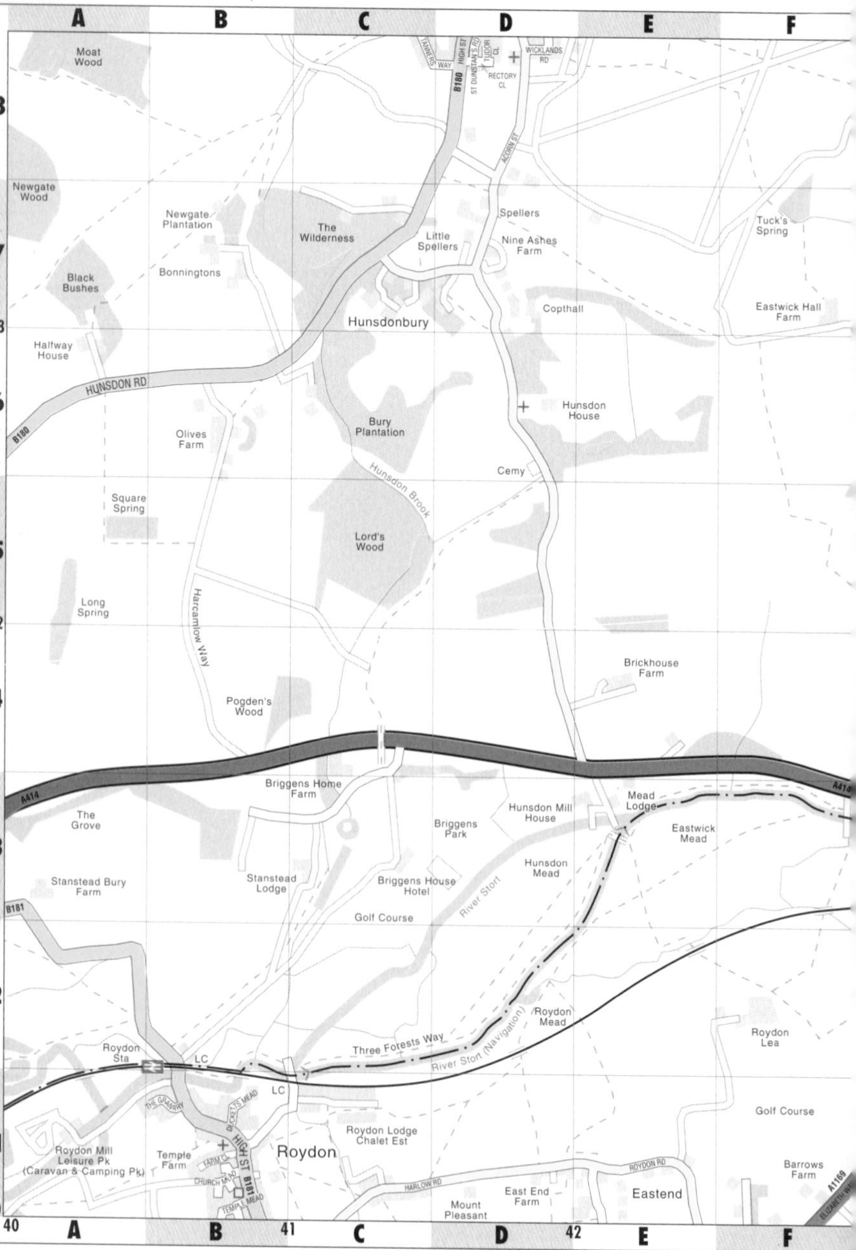
A
B
C
D
E
F
8
7
13
6
5
12
4
3
11
2
1
10
40
41
42
Moat Wood
Newgate Wood
Newgate Plantation
The Wilderness
Little Spellers
Spellers
Nine Ashes Farm
Tuck's Spring
Black Bushes
Bonningtons
Hunsdonbury
Copthall
Eastwick Hall Farm
Halfway House
HUNSDON RD
B180
TANNERS WAY
HIGH ST
ST DUNSTAN'S RD
TUDOR CL
RECTORY CL
WICKLANDS RD
ACORN ST
Olives Farm
Bury Plantation
Hunsdon House
Cemy
Hunsdon Brook
Square Spring
Lord's Wood
Long Spring
Harcamlow Way
Brickhouse Farm
Pogden's Wood
A414
Briggens Home Farm
Mead Lodge
Hunsdon Mill House
The Grove
Briggens Park
Eastwick Mead
Hunsdon Mead
Stanstead Bury Farm
Stanstead Lodge
Briggens House Hotel
River Stort
Golf Course
B181
Roydon Mead
Roydon Lea
Roydon Sta
LC
Three Forests Way
River Stort (Navigation)
THE GRANARY
DICKETTS MEAD
HIGH ST
Golf Course
Roydon Lodge Chalet Est
Roydon Mill Leisure Pk (Caravan & Camping Pk)
Temple Farm
FARM CL
CHURCH MEAD
TEMPLE MEAD
Roydon
ROYDON RD
HARLOW RD
East End Farm
Eastend
Barrows Farm
A1169
Mount Pleasant

115

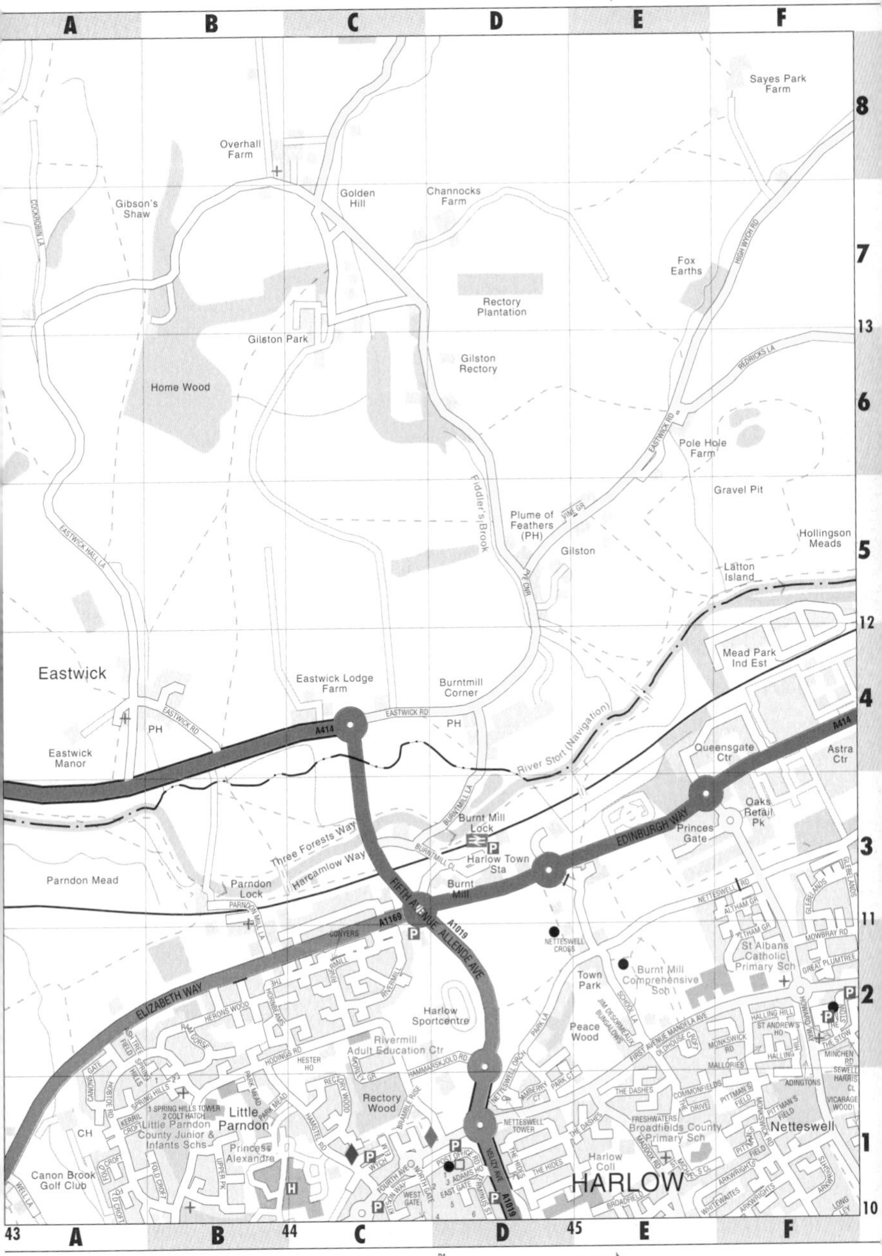
Sayes Park Farm
Overhall Farm
Golden Hill
Channocks Farm
Gibson's Shaw
Fox Earths
Rectory Plantation
Gilston Park
Gilston Rectory
Home Wood
Pole Hole Farm
Gravel Pit
Plume of Feathers (PH)
Gilston
Hollingson Meads
Latton Island
Fiddler's Brook
Mead Park Ind Est
Eastwick
Eastwick Lodge Farm
Burntmill Corner
PH
Eastwick Manor
River Stort (Navigation)
Queensgate Ctr
Astra Ctr
Oaks Retail Pk
Princes Gate
Burnt Mill Lock
Harlow Town Sta
Three Forests Way
Harcamlow Way
Parndon Mead
Parndon Lock
Burnt Mill
EDINBURGH WAY
FIFTH AVENUE
ALLENDE AVE
ELIZABETH WAY
NETTESWELL CROSS
St Albans Catholic Primary Sch
Burnt Mill Comprehensive Sch
Town Park
Harlow Sportcentre
Peace Wood
Rivermill Adult Education Ctr
Rectory Wood
Little Parndon
Little Parndon County Junior & Infants Schs
1 SPRING HILLS TOWER
2 COLT HATCH
Princess Alexandra
CH
Canon Brook Golf Club
Broadfields County Primary Sch
Netteswell
Harlow Coll
HARLOW
A414
A1169
A1019
EASTWICK RD
HIGH WYCH RD
PEDRICKS LA
EASTWICK HALL LA
COCKROBIN LA
FIRST AVENUE
MANDELA AVE
HOWARD WAY
NETTESWELL RD
A B C D E F
8 7 6 5 4 3 2 1
13 12 11 10
43 44 45

117
97

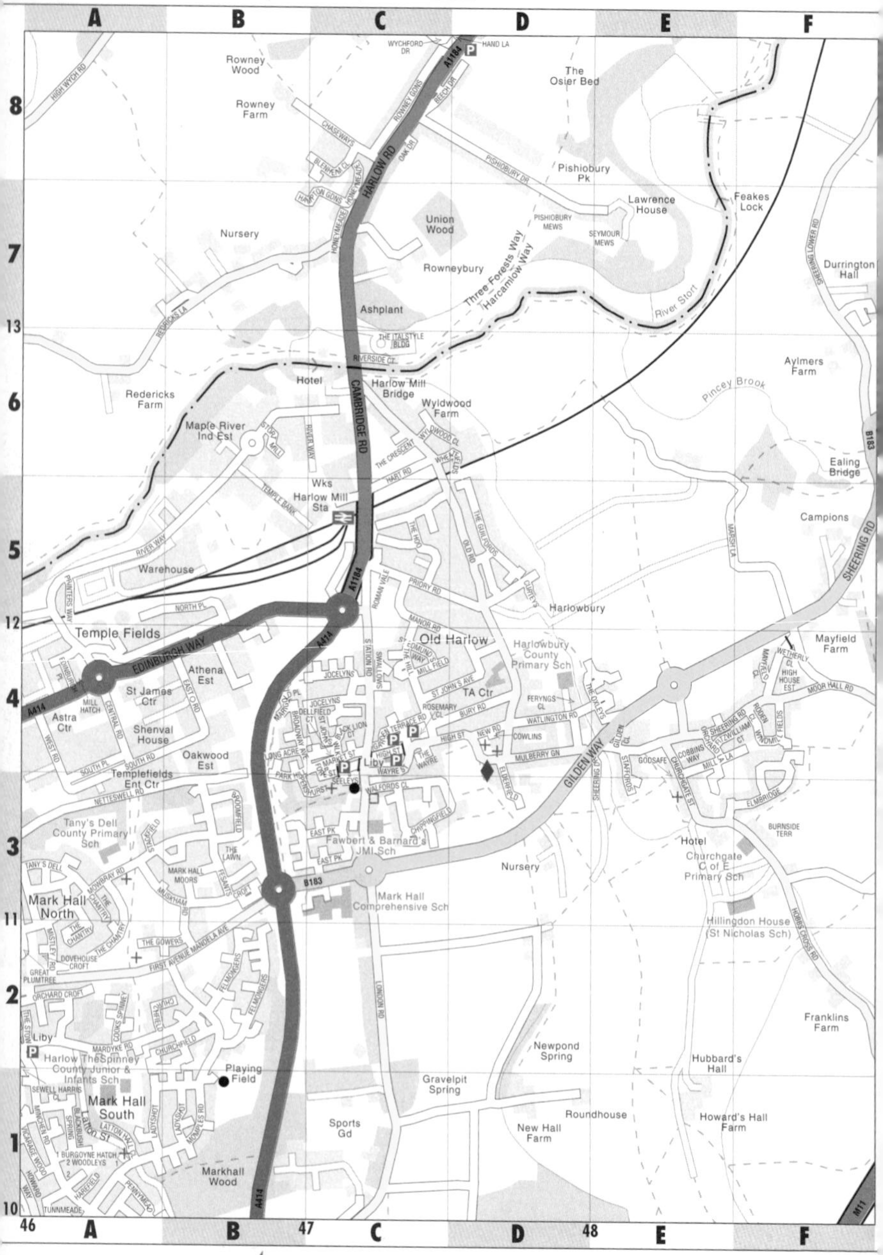
A
B
C
D
E
F
8
7
13
6
5
12
4
3
11
2
1
10
46
47
48
Rowney Wood
Rowney Farm
The Osier Bed
Pishiobury Pk
Lawrence House
Feakes Lock
Union Wood
Nursery
Rowneybury
Durrington Hall
Ashplant
Three Forests Way
Harcamlow Way
River Stort
Aylmers Farm
Redericks Farm
Hotel
Harlow Mill Bridge
Wyldwood Farm
Pincey Brook
Maple River Ind Est
Ealing Bridge
Wks
Harlow Mill Sta
Campions
Warehouse
Harlowbury
Temple Fields
Old Harlow
Mayfield Farm
Harlowbury County Primary Sch
Athena Est
St James Ctr
TA Ctr
Astra Ctr
Shenval House
Oakwood Est
Liby
Templefields Ent Ctr
Tany's Dell County Primary Sch
Fawbert & Barnard's JMI Sch
Hotel
Churchgate C of E Primary Sch
Nursery
Mark Hall North
Mark Hall Comprehensive Sch
Hillingdon House (St Nicholas Sch)
Franklins Farm
Liby
Harlow The Spinney County Junior & Infants Sch
Playing Field
Newpond Spring
Hubbard's Hall
Gravelpit Spring
Mark Hall South
Sports Gd
New Hall Farm
Roundhouse
Howard's Hall Farm
Markhall Wood
HARLOW RD
CAMBRIDGE RD
EDINBURGH WAY
GILDEN WAY
SHEERING RD
A1184
A414
B183
M11

117

99
120

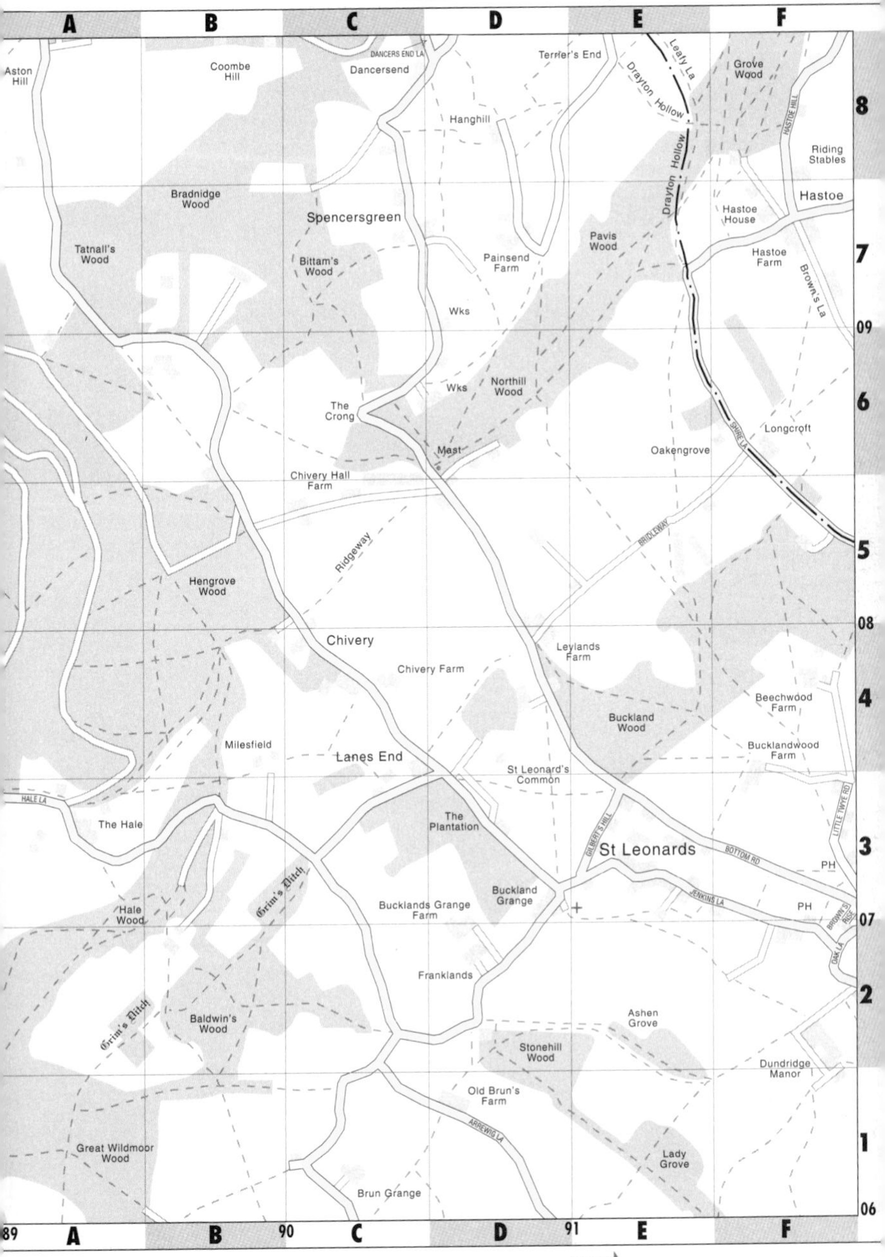
A
B
C
D
E
F
Aston Hill
Coombe Hill
DANCERS END LA
Dancersend
Terrier's End
Leafy La
Drayton Hollow
Grove Wood
HASTOE HILL
Riding Stables
Hanghill
Bradnidge Wood
Spencersgreen
Drayton Hollow
Hastoe
Hastoe House
Tatnall's Wood
Bittam's Wood
Painsend Farm
Pavis Wood
Hastoe Farm
Brown's La
Wks
Northill Wood
The Crong
Longcroft
Mast
Oakengrove
SHIRE LA
Chivery Hall Farm
Ridgeway
BRIDLEWAY
Hengrove Wood
Chivery
Leylands Farm
Chivery Farm
Beechwood Farm
Buckland Wood
Milesfield
Lanes End
Bucklandwood Farm
St Leonard's Common
HALE LA
The Hale
The Plantation
GILBERT'S HILL
St Leonards
BOTTOM RD
LITTLE TWYE RD
PH
Grim's Ditch
Hale Wood
Buckland Grange
Bucklands Grange Farm
JENKINS LA
PH
BROWN'S RISE
OAK LA
Franklands
Grim's Ditch
Ashen Grove
Baldwin's Wood
Stonehill Wood
Dundridge Manor
Old Brun's Farm
ARREWIG LA
Great Wildmoor Wood
Lady Grove
Brun Grange
8
7
09
6
5
08
4
3
07
2
1
06
89
90
91

120

119
100

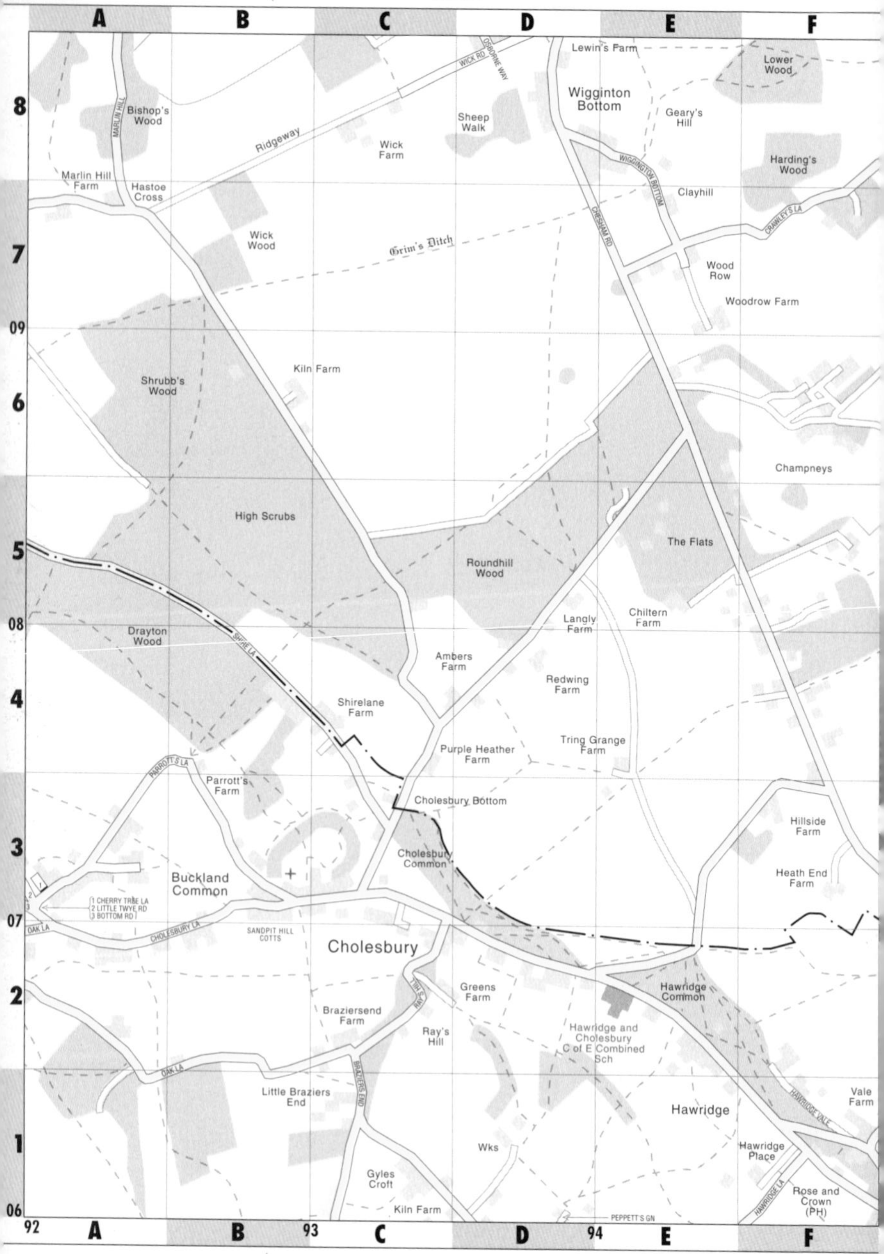
A
B
C
D
E
F
8
7
09
6
5
08
4
3
07
2
1
06
92
93
94
Lewin's Farm
Lower Wood
Wigginton Bottom
Geary's Hill
Bishop's Wood
MARLIN HILL
WICK RD
OSBORNE WAY
Sheep Walk
Ridgeway
Wick Farm
Harding's Wood
Marlin Hill Farm
Hastoe Cross
WIGGINTON BOTTOM
Clayhill
Wick Wood
Grim's Ditch
CHESHAM RD
CRAWLEY'S LA
Wood Row
Woodrow Farm
Kiln Farm
Shrubb's Wood
Champneys
High Scrubs
The Flats
Roundhill Wood
Langly Farm
Chiltern Farm
Drayton Wood
SHIRE LA
Ambers Farm
Redwing Farm
Shirelane Farm
Tring Grange Farm
Purple Heather Farm
PARROTT'S LA
Parrott's Farm
Cholesbury Bottom
Hillside Farm
Cholesbury Common
Heath End Farm
Buckland Common
1 CHERRY TREE LA
2 LITTLE TWYE RD
3 BOTTOM RD
OAK LA
CHOLESBURY LA
SANDPIT HILL COTTS
Cholesbury
RAY'S HILL
Greens Farm
Hawridge Common
Braziersend Farm
Ray's Hill
Hawridge and Cholesbury C of E Combined Sch
OAK LA
Little Braziers End
BRAZIERS END
HAWRIDGE VALE
Vale Farm
Hawridge
Wks
Hawridge Place
Gyles Croft
HAWRIDGE LA
Rose and Crown (PH)
Kiln Farm
PEPPETT'S GN

119

101
122

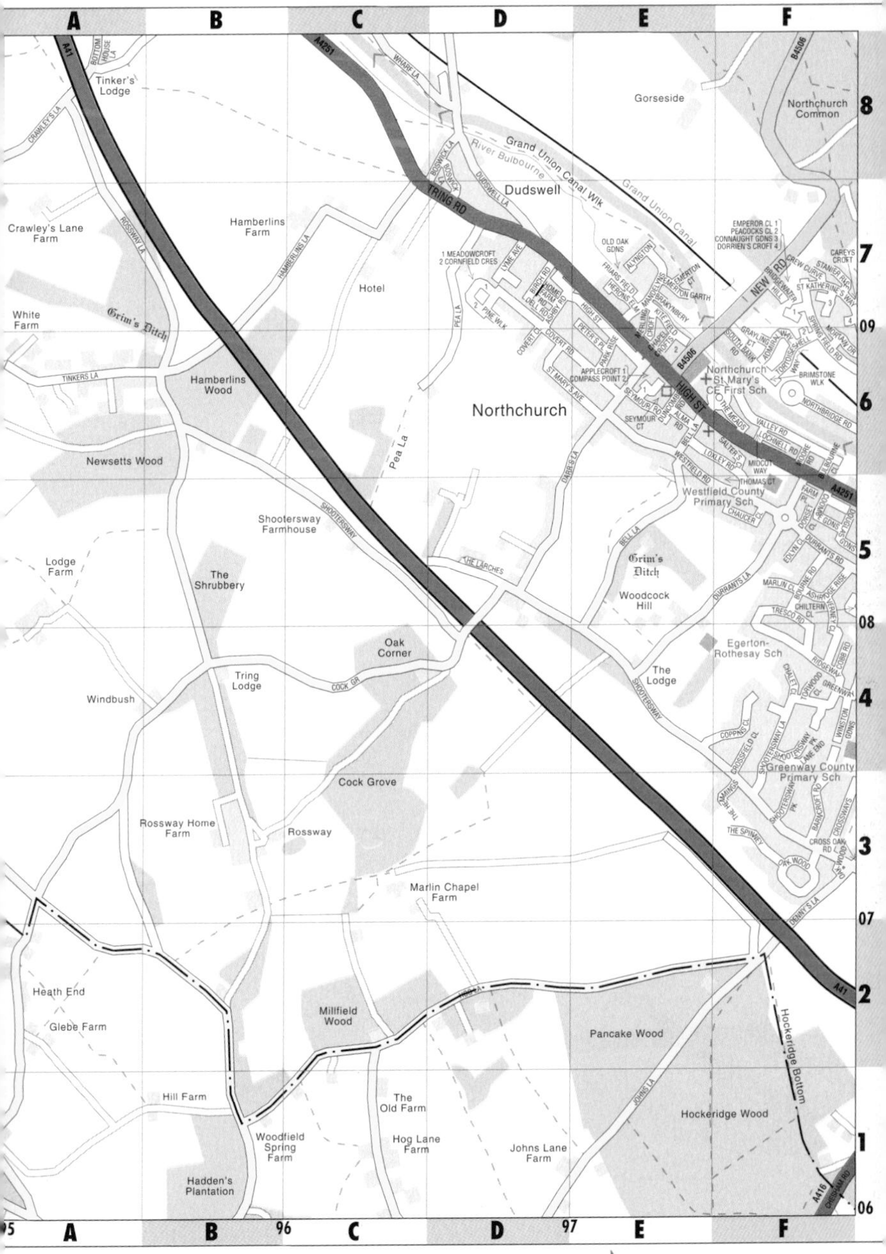
A
B
C
D
E
F
8
7
09
6
5
08
4
3
07
2
1
06
95
96
97
A41
A4251
B4506
A416
Tinker's Lodge
BOTTOM HOUSE LA
CRAWLEY'S LA
WHARF LA
Gorseside
Northchurch Common
Grand Union Canal Wlk
Grand Union Canal
River Bulbourne
Dudswell
BOSWICK LA
DUDSWELL LA
TRING RD
Crawley's Lane Farm
ROSSWAY LA
Hamberlins Farm
HAMBERLINS LA
Hotel
1 MEADOWCROFT
2 CORNFIELD CRES
LYME AVE
OLD OAK GDNS
ALYNGTON
FRIARS FIELD
HERONS ELM
EMERTON CT
EMERTON GARTH
BRAKYNBERY
EMPEROR CL 1
PEACOCKS CL 2
CONNAUGHT GDNS 3
DORRIEN'S CROFT 4
CAREYS CROFT
NEW RD
CREW CURVE
STANIER RISE
ST KATHERINE'S WAY
White Farm
Grim's Ditch
PEA LA
PINE WLK
DELL RD
ASHBY RD
HIGH ST
PETER'S PL
PARK RISE
COVERT CL
COVERT RD
GRAYLING CT
SOUTH BANK RD
ADMIRAL WAY
TORTOISESHELL WAY
SPRING FIELD RD
MORLAND DR
BRIMSTONE WLK
TINKERS LA
Hamberlins Wood
APPLECROFT 1
COMPASS POINT 2
ST MARY'S AVE
Northchurch St Mary's CE First Sch
Northchurch
SEYMOUR RD
SEYMOUR CT
ALMA RD
BELL LA
THE MEADS
VALLEY RD
LOCHNELL RD
NORTHBRIDGE RD
Newsetts Wood
Pea La
DARR'S LA
SALTER'S
OXLEY RD
MIDCOT WAY
THOMAS CT
WESTFIELD RD
Westfield County Primary Sch
CHAUCER
BULBOURNE CL
Shootersway Farmhouse
SHOOTERSWAY
DORSET CL
DURRANTS RD
Lodge Farm
The Shrubbery
THE LARCHES
BELL LA
Grim's Ditch
Woodcock Hill
DURRANTS LA
MARLIN CL
ASHRIDGE RISE
TRESCO RD
CHILTERN CL
Oak Corner
Egerton-Rothesay Sch
COBB RD
RIDGEWAY
GREENWAY
Tring Lodge
COCK GR
The Lodge
CHALET CL
Windbush
SHOOTERSWAY
COPPINS CL
CROSSFIELD CL
SHOOTERSWAY LA
WINSTON GDNS
Greenway County Primary Sch
Cock Grove
THE HEMMINGS
BARNCROFT RD
CROSSWAYS
Rossway Home Farm
Rossway
THE SPINNEY
CROSS OAK RD
OAK WOOD
Marlin Chapel Farm
DENNY'S LA
Heath End
Glebe Farm
Millfield Wood
HOG LA
Pancake Wood
Hockeridge Bottom
Hill Farm
The Old Farm
JOHNS LA
Hockeridge Wood
Woodfield Spring Farm
Hog Lane Farm
Johns Lane Farm
Hadden's Plantation
CHESHAM RD

122

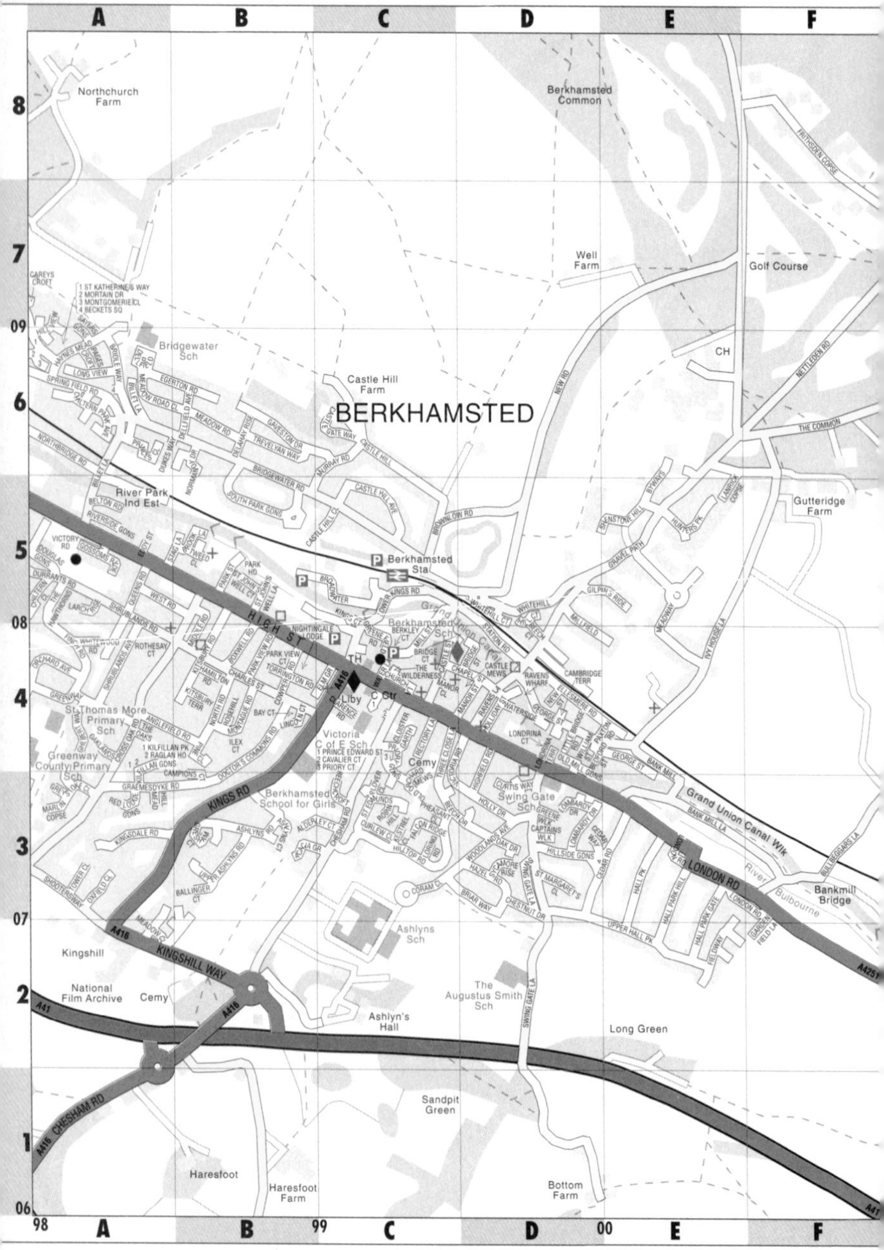
A
B
C
D
E
F
8
7
6
5
4
3
2
1
09
08
07
06
98
99
00
BERKHAMSTED
Northchurch Farm
Berkhamsted Common
Well Farm
Golf Course
CH
Bridgewater Sch
Castle Hill Farm
River Park Ind Est
Berkhamsted Sta
Gutteridge Farm
St Thomas More Primary Sch
Greenway County Primary Sch
Victoria C of E Sch
Cemy
Berkhamsted School for Girls
Swing Gate Sch
Ashlyns Sch
The Augustus Smith Sch
Ashlyn's Hall
Kingshill
National Film Archive
Long Green
Sandpit Green
Haresfoot
Haresfoot Farm
Bottom Farm
Bankmill Bridge
Grand Union Canal Wlk
River Bulbourne
HIGH ST
LONDON RD
KINGS RD
KINGSHILL WAY
CHESHAM RD
A416
A41
A4251
NEW RD
NETTLEDEN RD
THE COMMON
FRITHSDEN COPSE
BULBEGGARS LA
SWING GATE LA
CASTLE HILL AVE
CASTLE HILL
BROWNLOW RD
STATION RD
NORTHBRIDGE RD
BRIDGEWATER RD
SOUTH PARK GDNS
MURRAY RD
GRAVEL PATH
IVY HOUSE LA
SHRUBLANDS RD
SHRUBLANDS AVE
ELLESMERE RD
GEORGE ST
BANK MILL
BANK MILL LA
CEDAR RD
HALL PK
HALL PARK HILL
HALL PARK GATE
UPPER HALL PK
CHESTNUT DR
BRIAR WAY
CORAM CL
ASHLYNS RD
KINGSDALE RD
SHOOTERSWAY
MEADOW RD
DELLFIELD AVE
EGERTON RD
GAVESTON DR
TREVELYAN WAY
DELAHAY RISE
CHILTERN PARK AVE
SPRING FIELD RD
LONG VIEW
BILLET LA
BRIDLE WAY
BELTON RD
RIVERSIDE GDNS
GOSSOMS END
DURRANTS RD
WEST RD
QUEENS RD
ROTHESAY CT
KITSBURY RD
CHARLES ST
PARK VIEW RD
TORRINGTON RD
BAY CT
ANGLEFIELD RD
DOCTOR'S COMMONS RD
GRAEMESDYKE RD
CAMPIONS CT
MARLIN COPSE
TOWER CL
OXFIELD CL
BALLINGER CT
CHESHAM RD
HILLTOP RD
FALCON RIDGE
WOODLANDS AVE
OAK DR
HOLLY DR
HIGHFIELD RD
THREE CLOSE LA
CURTIS WAY
LOMBARDY DR
HILLSIDE GDNS
ST MARGARET'S CL
RECTORY LA
CLOISTER GARTH
MANOR ST
CHAPEL ST
CASTLE ST
MILL ST
GRAND UNION CANAL
WATERSIDE
RAVENS WHARF
CASTLE MEWS
CAMBRIDGE TERR
LONDRINA CT
GILPIN'S RIDE
MILLFIELD
WHITEHILL
SHENSTONE HILL
BYWAYS
HUNTERS PK
MEADWAY
1 ST KATHERINE'S WAY
2 MORTAIN DR
3 MONTGOMERIE CL
4 BECKETS SQ
1 KILFILLAN PK
2 RAGLAN HO
1 PRINCE EDWARD ST
2 CAVALIER CT
3 PRIORY CT
CAREYS CROFT
TH
Liby
C Ctr

103
124

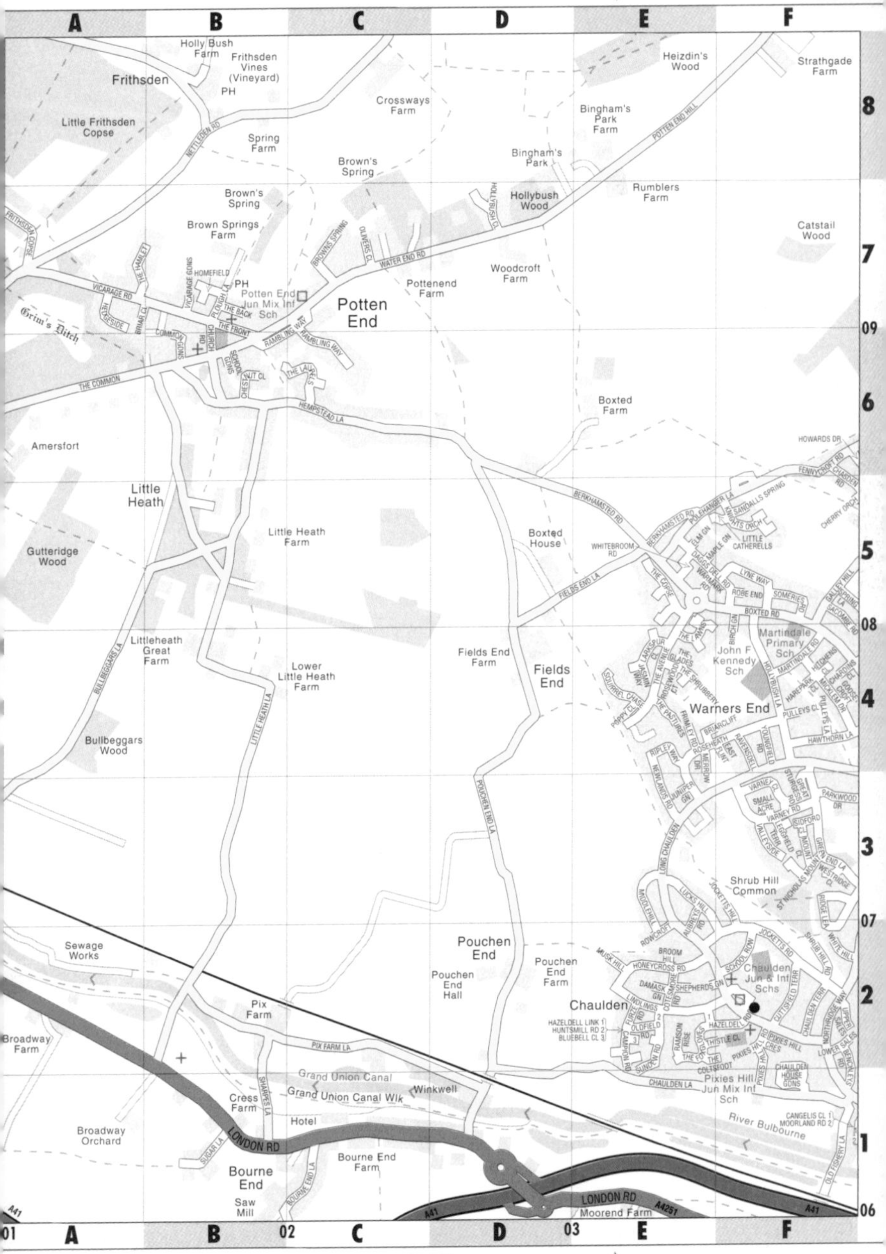
A
B
C
D
E
F
Holly Bush Farm
Frithsden Vines (Vineyard)
Frithsden
PH
Little Frithsden Copse
Crossways Farm
Heizdin's Wood
Strathgade Farm
Bingham's Park Farm
Spring Farm
Brown's Spring
Bingham's Park
Brown's Spring
Hollybush Wood
Rumblers Farm
Brown Springs Farm
Catstail Wood
Woodcroft Farm
Pottenend Farm
PH
Potten End Jun Mix Inf Sch
Potten End
Grim's Ditch
Amersfort
Boxted Farm
Little Heath
Little Heath Farm
Boxted House
Gutteridge Wood
Littleheath Great Farm
Lower Little Heath Farm
Fields End Farm
Fields End
Martindale Primary Sch
John F Kennedy Sch
Warners End
Bullbeggars Wood
Shrub Hill Common
Sewage Works
Pouchen End
Pouchen End Hall
Pouchen End Farm
Chaulden
Chaulden Jun & Inf Schs
Pix Farm
Broadway Farm
Grand Union Canal
Grand Union Canal Wlk
Winkwell
Cress Farm
Hotel
Broadway Orchard
Bourne End Farm
Bourne End
Saw Mill
Moorend Farm
Pixies Hill Jun Mix Inf Sch
River Bulbourne
LONDON RD
A41
A4251
POTTEN END HILL
WATER END RD
THE COMMON
HEMPSTEAD LA
BERKHAMSTED RD
FIELDS END LA
LITTLE HEATH LA
BULLBEGGARS LA
POUCHEN END LA
PIX FARM LA
SHARPES LA
SUGAR LA
BOURNE END LA
NETTLEDEN RD
FRITHSDEN COPSE
CHAULDEN LA
LONG CHAULDEN
HAZELDELL LINK 1
HUNTSMILL RD 2
BLUEBELL CL 3
CANGELIS CL 1
MOORLAND RD 2
8
7
09
6
5
08
4
3
07
2
1
06
01
02
03

137
124

123
104

D5
1 SHARPCROFT
2 BROADCROFT
3 BOXHILL
4 PHYLLIS COURTNAGE HOUSE
5 HELENA PL
6 BOWYERS

E6
1 WATLING CL
2 LANGDALE CT
3 ESKDALE CT
4 BORROWDALE CT

F5
1 TANNSFIELD DR
2 TANNSMORE CL
3 WIDMORE DR

F6
1 MERCURY WLK
F7
1 SHERWOOD PL
2 PETERLEE CT

F8
1 TRESLIAN SQ
2 TORRIDGE WLK
3 THE DART
4 MARION WLK

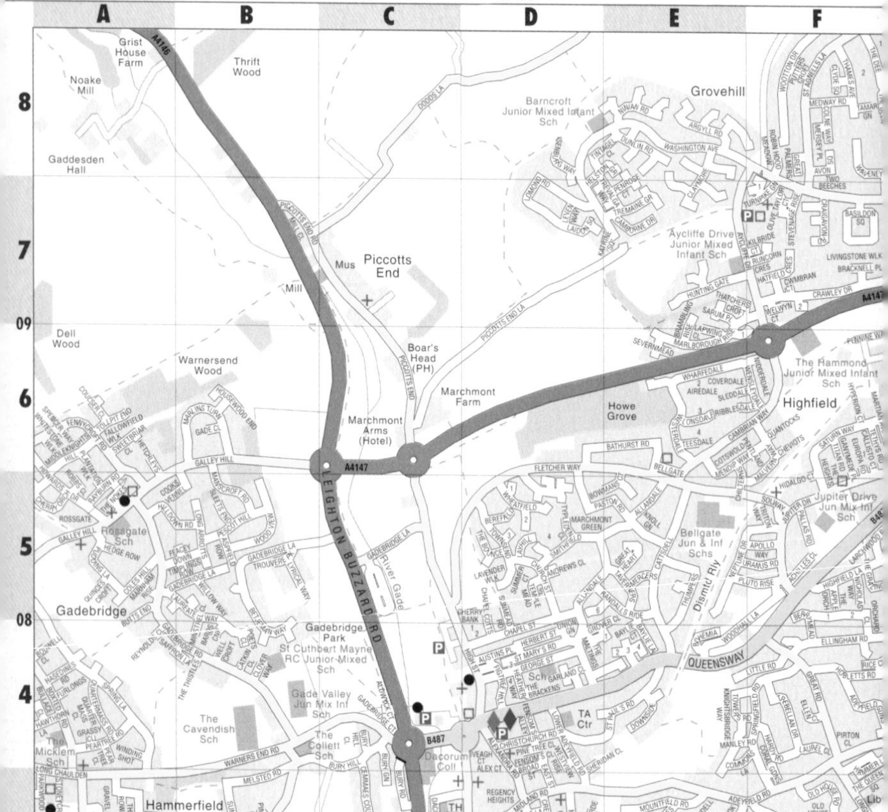


123
138

D1
1 PANXWORTH RD
2 RANWORTH CL
3 STUARTS CL
4 CHARLESWORTH CL
5 FOREST AVE
D4
1 ARMSTRONG PL
2 SUN SQ
3 KING'S MEWS
4 ST MARY'S CT

E1
1 CRABTREE CT
2 WOODMAN RD
3 DOWLING CT
4 RISEDALE HILL
E2
1 FURTHERGROUND

E4
1 CLARENDON CL
2 LITTLE MIMMS
3 LONG MIMMS
4 EAST MIMMS

F1
1 GATECROFT
F2
1 WADLEY CL
2 BENNETTS END RD

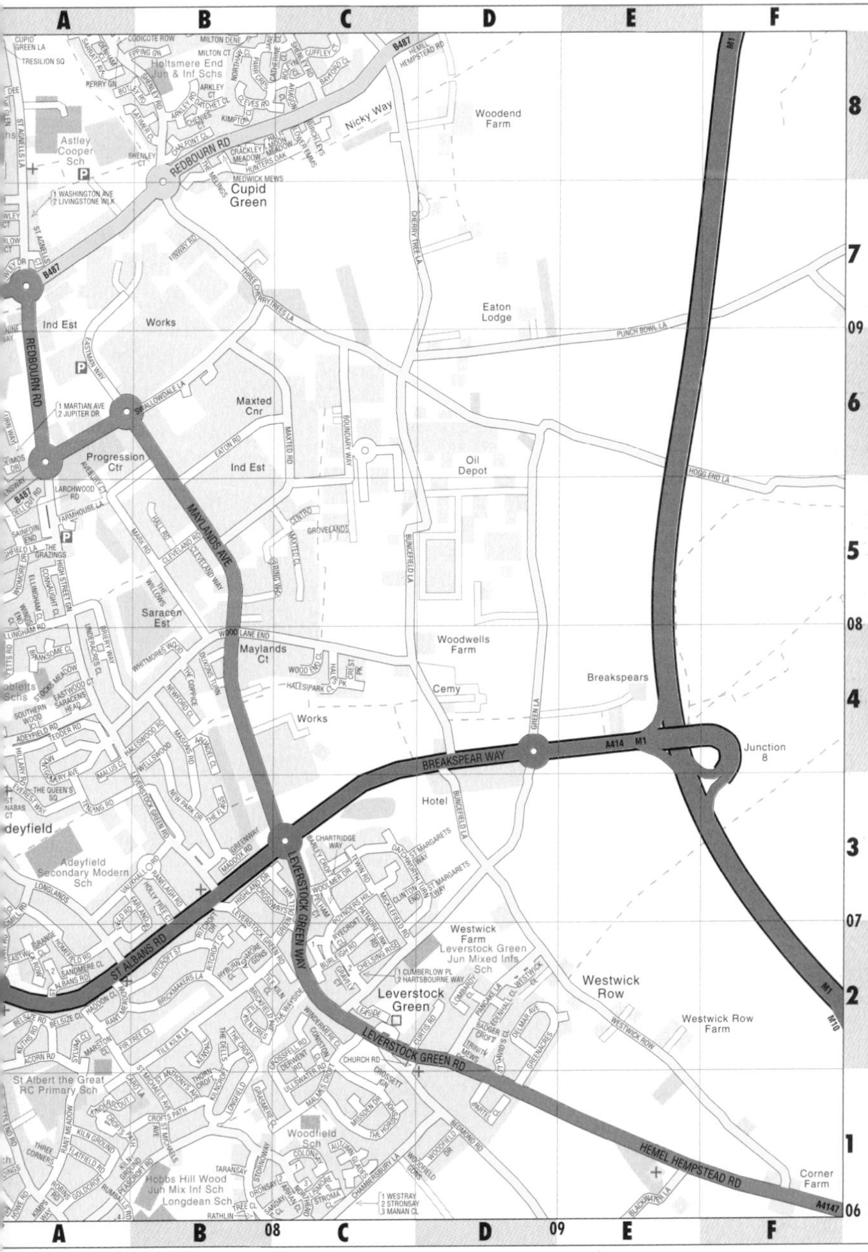

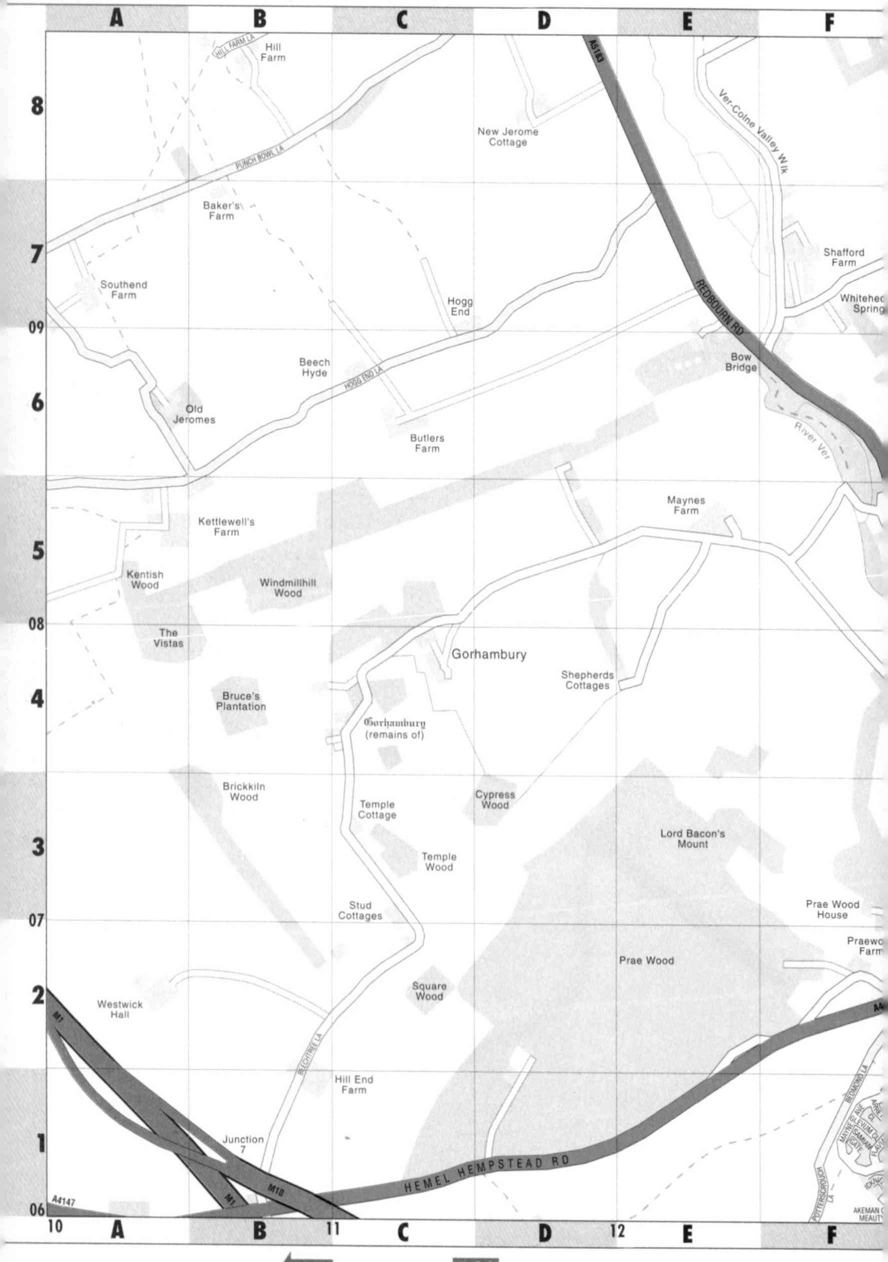
A
B
C
D
E
F
8
7
09
6
5
08
4
3
07
2
1
06
10
11
12
HILL FARM LA
Hill Farm
A5183
New Jerome Cottage
Ver-Colne Valley Wlk
PUNCH BOWL LA
Baker's Farm
Shafford Farm
Southend Farm
Hogg End
Whitehed Spring
REDBOURN RD
Beech Hyde
HOGG END LA
Bow Bridge
Old Jeromes
Butlers Farm
River Ver
Maynes Farm
Kettlewell's Farm
Kentish Wood
Windmillhill Wood
The Vistas
Gorhambury
Shepherds Cottages
Bruce's Plantation
Gorhambury (remains of)
Brickkiln Wood
Cypress Wood
Temple Cottage
Lord Bacon's Mount
Temple Wood
Stud Cottages
Prae Wood House
Praewo Farm
Prae Wood
Square Wood
Westwick Hall
M1
BEECHTREE LA
Hill End Farm
BEDMOND LA
Junction 7
HEMEL HEMPSTEAD RD
A4147
M10
POTTERSCROUCH LA
AKEMAN

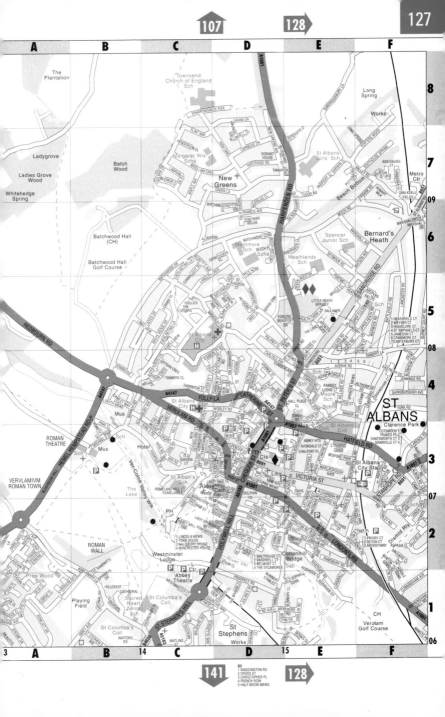

127
108

A B C D E F

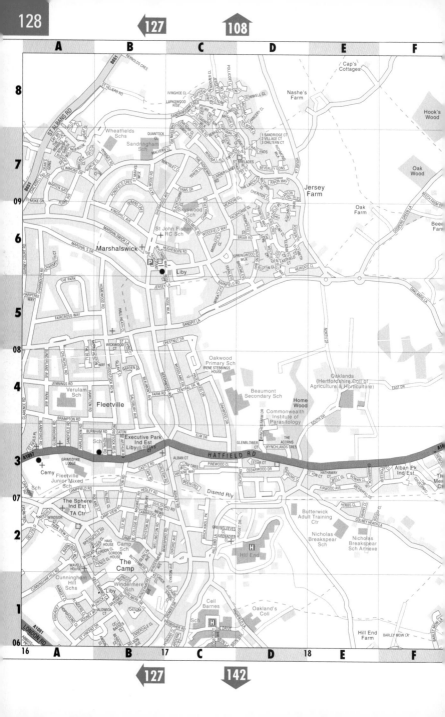
B651
ST ALBANS RD
REYNOLDS CRES
ST HELIERS RD
Wheatfields Schs
Sandringham Sch
QUANTOCK CL
MALVERN CL
IVINGHOE CL
LARKSWOOD RISE
SANDRINGHAM CRES
POLLICOTT CL
PIRTON CL
CROMWELL CL
CHILTERN RD
COTSWOLD CL
MENDIP CL
TILSWORTH WLK
BERKLEY CL
PORTMAN CL
REGENT CL
BELGRAVE CL
CHANCERY CL
HOLBORN CL
1 SANDRIDGE CT
2 VILLAGE CT
3 CHILTERN CT
CRAIGLANDS
RICHMOND WLK
ST BRELADES PL
BEVERLEY GDNS
HOUSE LA
Cap's Cottages
Nashe's Farm
Hook's Wood
Oak Wood
Jersey Farm
Oak Farm
BEECH FARM DR
COOPERS GREEN LA
DOWNES RD
BRECKEN FIELD CL
RUNCIE CL
BIRTON CL
SLIMMONS DR
CHALKDELL FIELDS
DEAN'S GDNS
MARTEN GATE
FURSE AVE
DYMOKE GN
BENTSLEY CL
THE RIDGEWAY
WINDMILL AVE
SUMMERSLAND RD
TEWIN CL
EVANS GR
PONDFIELD CRES
ST MARYS WLK
QUEENS CRES
KINGSHILL AVE
SHERWOOD AVE
BLACKTHORN CL
Skyswood Sch
CHANDLERS RD
HAZELMERE RD
THE LARCHES
MILFORD CL
RIPON WAY
CHERITON CL
STANTON CL
HARLEY CT
MEADOW CL
PACKHORSE CL
THORPEFIELD CL
HARNESS WAY
VILLIERS CRES
KINGSMEAD
HUNT CL
GLADESIDE
ELIZABETH CT
MARSHALSWICK LA
MARSHAL'S DR
St John Fisher RC Sch
WOODFIELD WAY
MIDDLEFIELD AVE
BRIAR RD
Marshalswick
HUGHENDEN RD
WYCOMBE WAY
THE QUADRANT
SPRINGWOOD WLK
ARDENS WAY
WESTFIELD CL
SOUTHFIELD WAY
EASTFIELD CT
NEWGATE CL
BUXTON CL
Liby
ROSE CT
JERSEY LA
FERNLEYS
BROOMLEYS
BARNFIELD RD
WHEATLEYS
GURNEY COURT RD
CHARMOUTH RD
CHARMOUTH CT
THE PARK
HARPTREE WAY
HOMEWOOD RD
HALL HEATH CL
ROSE WLK
FAIRCROSS WAY
SANDPIT LA
OAKLANDS LA
NORTH DR
CHESTNUT DR
WICKWOOD CT
ST JOHNS CT
THE DELL
MONKS HORTON WAY
SUNDERLAND AVE
CHURCHILL RD
GLEAVE CL
GARDEN CL
WOODSTOCK RD N
BEAUMONT AVE
BEECHWOOD AVE
WOODLAND DR
HAZELWOOD DR
Oakwood Primary Sch
IRENE STEBBINGS HOUSE
JENNINGS RD
Verulam Sch
HAMILTON RD
SALISBURY AVE
FARM RD
CENTRAL DR
Beaumont Secondary Sch
Oaklands (Hertfordshire Coll of Agriculture & Horticulture)
EAST DR
Home Wood
PARK AVE
Fleetville
CLARENCE RD
OAKWOOD DR
WINCHES FARM DR
Commonwealth Institute of Parasitology
SOUTH DR
BRAMPTON RD
BLANDFORD RD
GLENFERRIE RD
SANDFIELD RD
HARLESDEN RD
BURNHAM RD
EATON RD
ROYAL RD
WOODSTOCK RD S
ARTHUR RD
Sch
Executive Park Ind Est
Liby
QUEEN'S CT
ELM DR
GLENBLOWER CT
THE ACORNS
WYNCHLANDS CRES
ST PAULS PL
A1057
HATFIELD RD
ALBAN CT
PINEWOOD CL
CEDAR CT
CEDARWOOD DR
GRESFORD CL
ST YON CT
HATHAWAY CT
SEWELL CL
ROWAN CL
CRANBROOK DR
RYECROFT CT
Alban Pk Ind Est
GRIMSDYKE LODGE
Cemy
Fleetville Junior Mixed Sch
Sch
CASTLE RD
CAPE RD
BURLEIGH RD
LOW CRES
OAKDENE WAY
LINDEN CRES
LONGACRES
FIRWOOD AVE
MERRYFIELDS
CAMPFIELD RD
SUTTON RD
VALERIE CL
HEDLEY RD
Dismtd Rly
The Sphere Ind Est
TA Ctr
ROLAND ST
CAMP VIEW RD
MAXWELL RD
SALISBURY CL
GUILDFORD RD
THE MEWS
CAMBRIDGE RD
ASHLEY RD
HOBBS CL
SWANS CL
BOISSY CL
Butterwick Adult Training Ctr
COLNEY HEATH LA
HANKSHILL
WINDSOR CT
PARK VIEW CL
BELLFIELD
SPRINGFIELD RD
ELY RD
COLLEGE RD
ROYSTON RD
WELLINGTON RD
BERESFORD RD
OXFORD AVE
BRICK KNOLL PK
GREENSLEEVES CL
GRENADIER CL
RUSSET DR
HILL END LA
Nicholas Breakspear Sch
Nicholas Breakspear Sch Annexe
HAIG HOUSE
HAIG CL
GORDON CL
GORDON HOUSE
Camp Sch
CAMP RD
GLENLYN AVE
BARNCROFT WAY
WINGATE
KITCHENER CL
BUTTERMERE CL
WINDERMERE AVE
LYNTON AVE
H
Hill End
WAVELL HOUSE
The Camp
Cunningham Hill Schs
CUNNINGHAM HILL RD
CELL BARNES LA
BURNSIDE
Windermere Sch
KESWICK CL
RICHARDS CL
RAMSEY CL
FLINDERS CL
ALDWICK CL
ALDWICK CT
GRASMERE RD
THIRLMERE DR
CATHAM CL
DRAKES DR
Cell Barnes
Oakland's Coll
HIGHFIELD LA
FOXCROFT
HOPGROUND CL
RODNEY AVE
CELL BARNES CL
ENNERDALE CL
FROBISHER RD
Sch
THE DRIVE
A1081
LONDON RD
ABBOTS
ST VINCENT DR
ANSON CL
BENBOW
NELSON AVE
HOWARD CL
ARDERN CL
ROSECROFT AVE
BRYN WAY
Hill End Farm
BARLEY MOW LA
8
7
09
6
5
08
4
3
07
2
1
06
16
17
18

A B C D E F

127
142

109
130

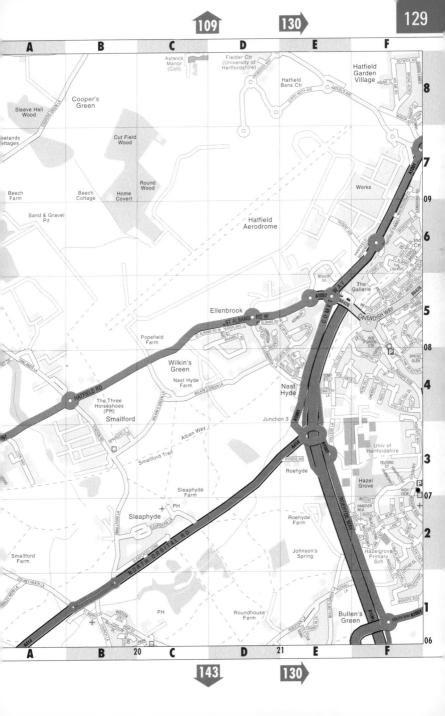
A
B
C
D
E
F
8
7
09
6
5
08
4
3
07
2
1
06
20
21
Astwick Manor (Coll)
Fielder Ctr (University of Hertfordshire)
FROBISHER WAY
Hatfield Bsns Ctr
GYPSY MOTH AVE
HATFIELD AVE
Hatfield Garden Village
ASTWICK AVE
HOLME CL
HOLME RD
BROAD ACRES
GREEN LANES
MANOR RD
MANOR CL
Sleeve Hall Wood
Cooper's Green
COOPERS GREEN LA
Cut Field Wood
Round Wood
Works
Beech Farm
Beech Cottage
Home Covert
Sand & Gravel Pit
Hatfield Aerodrome
TRIDENT AVE
HATFIELD TUNNEL
WORCESTER RD
ELY CL
Ind Ctr
HARPSFIELD BROADWAY
BISHOP SQ
The Galleria
COMET WAY
A1057
B6426
A1001
CAVENDISH WAY
Ellenbrook
ST ALBANS RD W
POPLARS CL
POPLAR AVE
BRAMBLE RD
ELLENBROOK CRES
BROOKSIDE
SELWYN DR
SELWYN CRES
SELWYN AVE
ASHBURY CL
ELLENBROOK LA
HALTSIDE
THE SIDINGS
CROSSBROOK
Popefield Farm
Wilkin's Green
Nast Hyde Farm
WILKIN'S GREEN LA
Nast Hyde
OAKLANDS LA
HATFIELD RD
The Three Horseshoes (PH)
Smallford
STATION RD
SPRINGFIELD RD
LYON WAY
Alban Way
Smallford Trail
Junction 3
A414
ROE GREEN CTR
BISHOPS CL
COLLEGE LA
CHANTRY LA
ROE GREEN CL
TOMS FIELD
WATERY LA
FERN DELLS
HIGH DELLS
CHENNELLS
INDELLS
HILL LEY
MARYLANDS
SPRING GLEN
HILBURY
BISHOPS RISE
ROE HILL CL
HIGH DELLS
ROBERTS WAY
RYDERS AVE
Roehyde
Univ of Hertfordshire
TELFORD CT
Hazel Grove
HIGH VIEW
Sleaphyde Farm
PH
Sleaphyde
SLEAPSHYDE LA
SMALLFORD LA
ROEHYDE WAY
Roehyde Farm
BROOM CL
HANOVER WLK
GORSE CL
TUDOR CL
HAZEL GR
BLACKTHORNE CL
WOODPECKER CL
Smallford Farm
NORTH ORBITAL RD
SLEAPCROSS GDNS
Johnson's Spring
Hazelgrove Primary Sch
REDHALL CL
REDHALL DR
COPPICE CL
BISHOPS RISE
COLNEY HEATH LA
REDHALL LA
BULLEN'S GREEN LA
Bullen's Green
A1(M)
SOUTH WAY A1001
PH
Roundhouse Farm
ST MARKS CL
WISTLEA CRES
RICHARDSON PL
HIGH ST
CHURCH LA
PARK LA
ROESTOCK LA
ROESTOCK GDNS
FRANKLIN CL

143
130

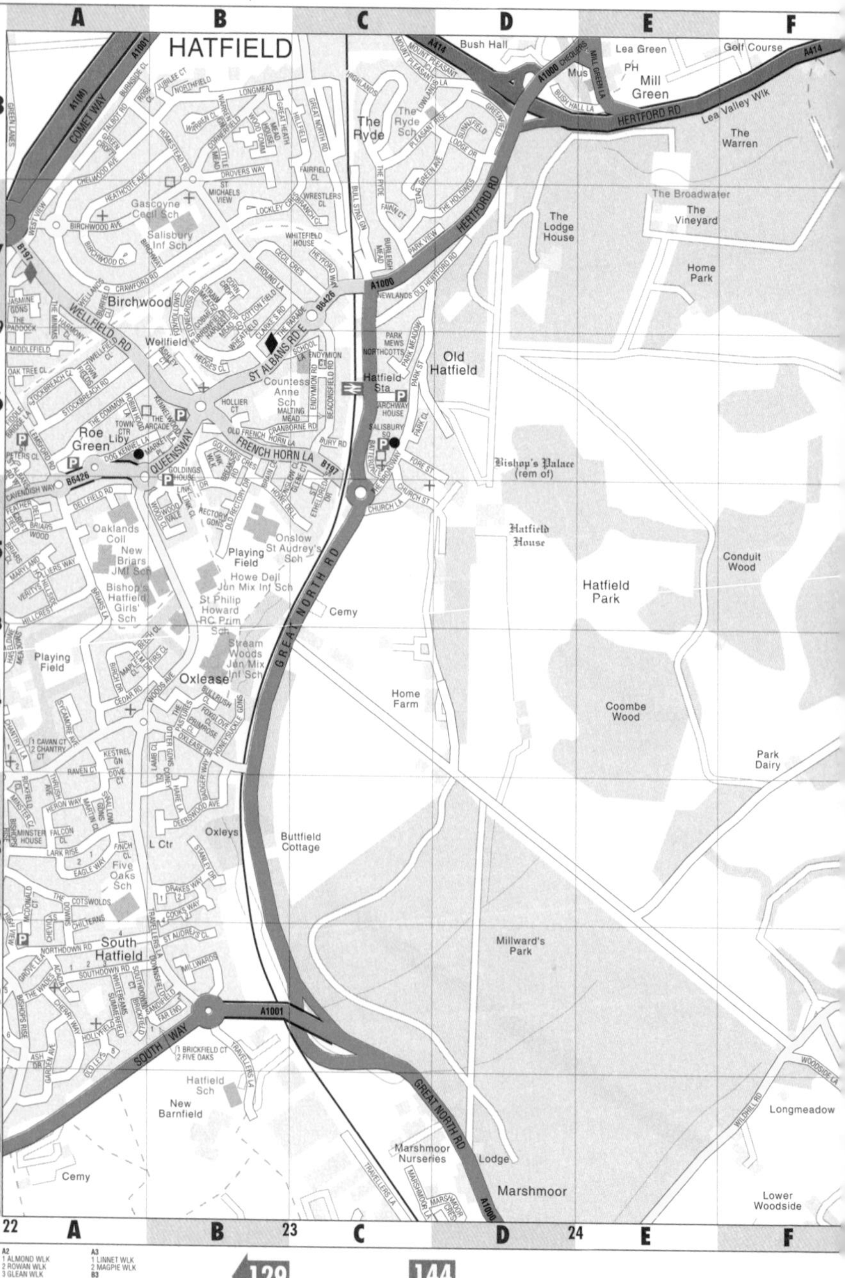

111
132

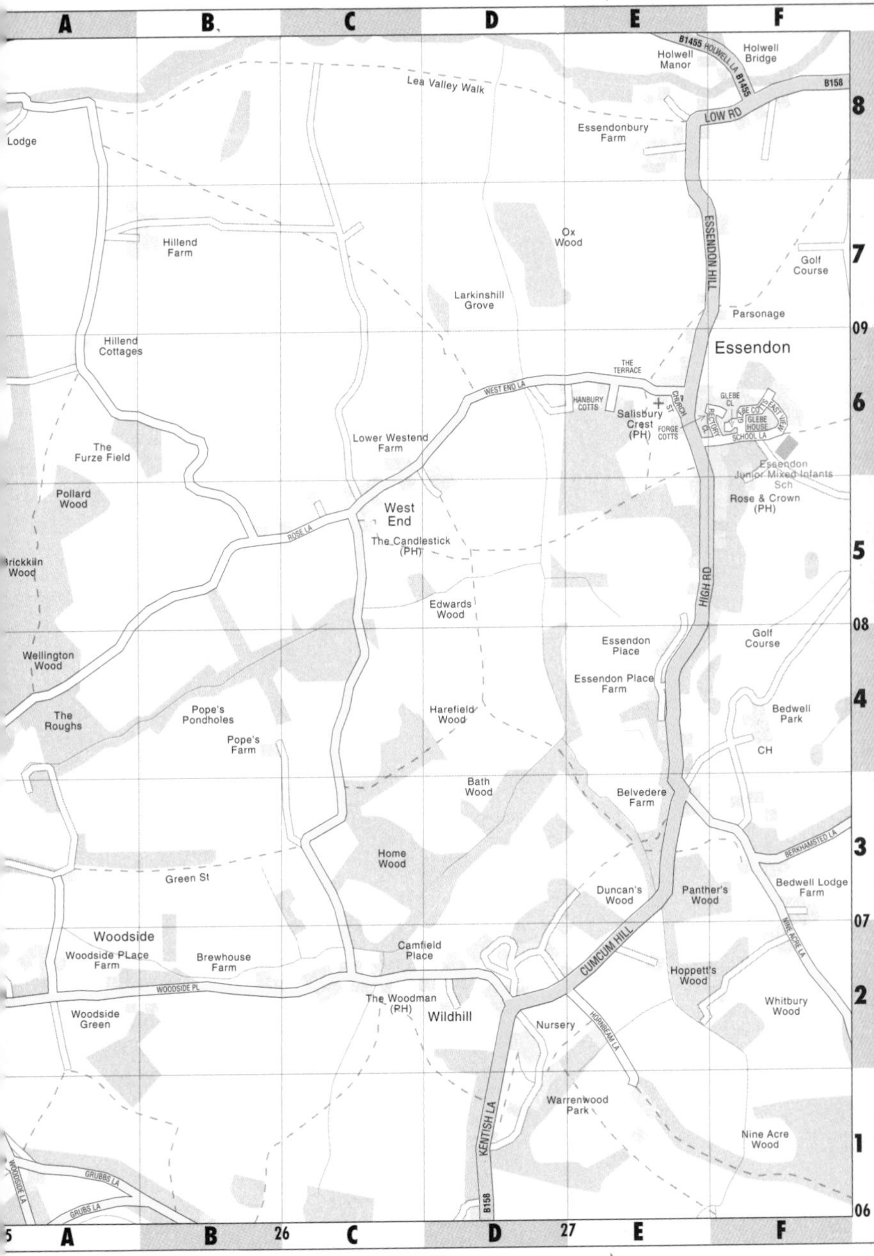
A
B
C
D
E
F
B1455
HOLWELL LA
Holwell Manor
Holwell Bridge
B158
Lea Valley Walk
LOW RD
Lodge
Essendonbury Farm
8
Hillend Farm
Ox Wood
ESSENDON HILL
7
Golf Course
Larkinshill Grove
Parsonage
09
Hillend Cottages
Essendon
THE TERRACE
WEST END LA
HANBURY COTTS
CHURCH ST
GLEBE CL
GLEBE CT
EAST VIEW
RECTORY CL
GLEBE HOUSE
SCHOOL LA
6
Salisbury Crest (PH)
FORGE COTTS
Lower Westend Farm
The Furze Field
Essendon Junior Mixed Infants Sch
Pollard Wood
Rose & Crown (PH)
West End
ROSE LA
The Candlestick (PH)
5
Brickkiln Wood
HIGH RD
Edwards Wood
08
Golf Course
Wellington Wood
Essendon Place
Essendon Place Farm
4
Harefield Wood
Bedwell Park
The Roughs
Pope's Pondholes
Pope's Farm
CH
Bath Wood
Belvedere Farm
BERKHAMSTED LA
3
Home Wood
Green St
Duncan's Wood
Panther's Wood
Bedwell Lodge Farm
NINE ACRE LA
07
Woodside
Camfield Place
CUMCUM HILL
Woodside PLace Farm
Brewhouse Farm
Hoppett's Wood
WOODSIDE PL
2
Whitbury Wood
The Woodman (PH)
Wildhill
Woodside Green
Nursery
HORNBEAM LA
Warrenwood Park
KENTISH LA
1
Nine Acre Wood
WOODSIDE LA
GRUBBS LA
GRUBS LA
B158
06
5
26
27

145
132

131
112

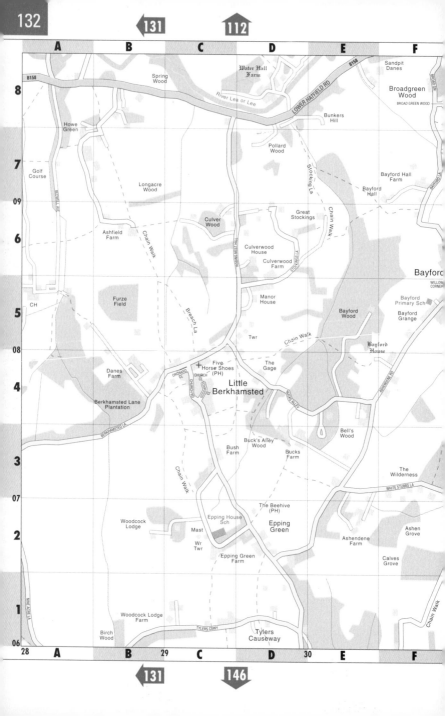
A
B
C
D
E
F
8
7
09
6
5
08
4
3
07
2
1
06
28
29
30
B158
Spring Wood
Water Hall Farm
B158
Sandpit Danes
Broadgreen Wood
BROAD GN
BROAD GREEN WOOD
River Lea or Lee
LOWER HATFIELD RD
Bunkers Hill
Howe Green
Pollard Wood
Golf Course
BEDWELL AVE
Longacre Wood
Stocking La
Bayford Hall Farm
Bayford Hall
BAYFORD LA
Culver Wood
Great Stockings
Chain Walk
Ashfield Farm
Chain Walk
ROBINS NEST HILL
Culverwood House
Culverwood Farm
STOCKINGS LA
Bayford
WILLOW CORNER
Furze Field
Manor House
Bayford Primary Sch
CH
Breach La
Bayford Wood
Bayford Grange
Twr
Chain Walk
Bayford House
Five Horse Shoes (PH)
The Gage
Danes Farm
ORCHARD CL
CHURCH CL
CHURCH RD
GODDARDS CL
Little Berkhamsted
ASHENDENE RD
Berkhamsted Lane Plantation
BUCKS ALLEY
BERKHAMSTED LA
Bell's Wood
Buck's Alley Wood
Bush Farm
Bucks Farm
The Wilderness
Chain Walk
WHITE STUBBS LA
The Beehive (PH)
Woodcock Lodge
Epping House Sch
Epping Green
Mast
Ashen Grove
Ashendene Farm
Wr Twr
Epping Green Farm
Calves Grove
NINE ACRE LA
Woodcock Lodge Farm
Chain Walk
TYLERS CSWY
Birch Wood
Tylers Causeway

131
146

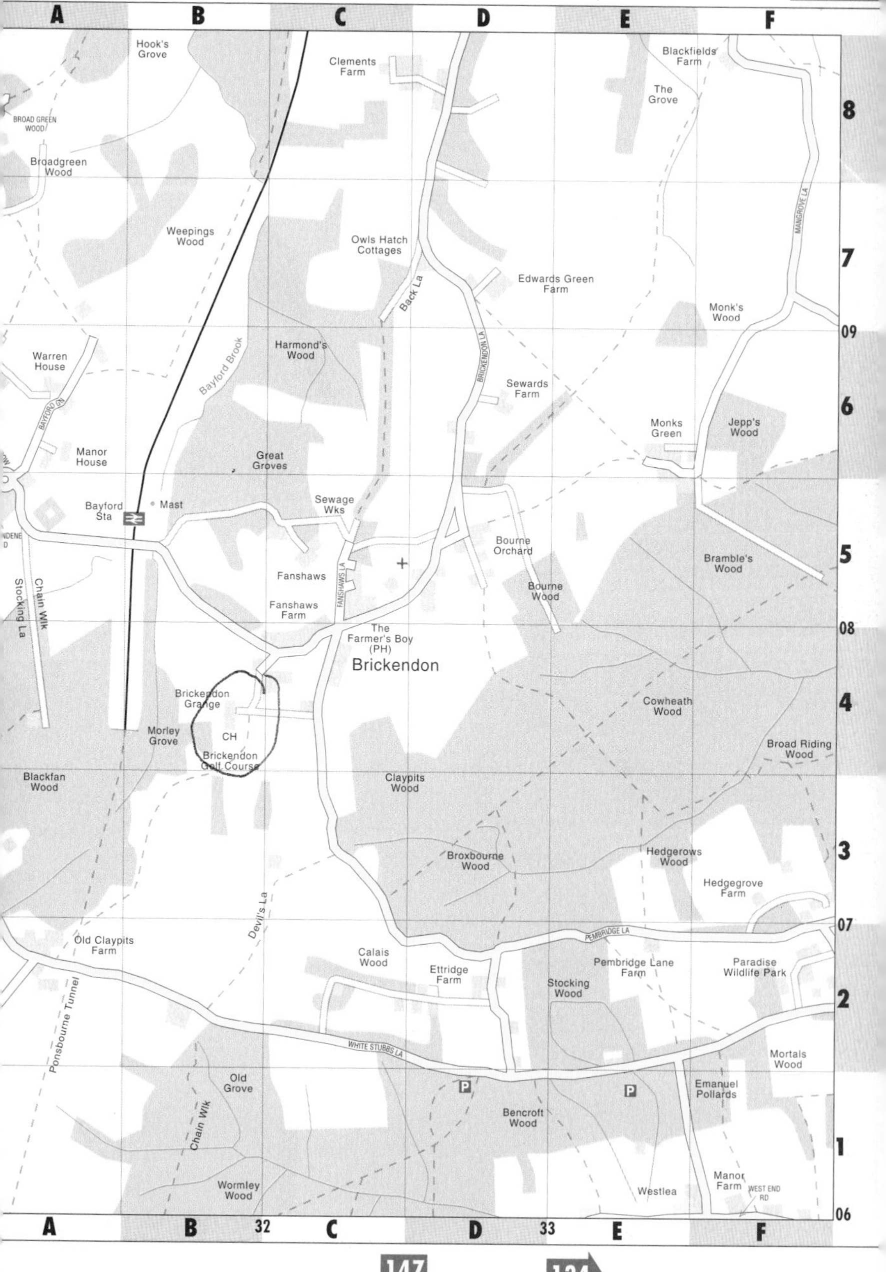
A
B
C
D
E
F
Hook's Grove
Clements Farm
Blackfields Farm
The Grove
BROAD GREEN WOOD
Broadgreen Wood
8
Weepings Wood
Owls Hatch Cottages
Edwards Green Farm
7
MANGROVE LA
Monk's Wood
Warren House
Harmond's Wood
Back La
BRICKENDON LA
Bayford Brook
Sewards Farm
09
BAYFORD GN
6
Monks Green
Jepp's Wood
Manor House
Great Groves
Bayford Sta
Mast
Sewage Wks
Bourne Orchard
5
Bramble's Wood
Fanshaws
FANSHAWS LA
Fanshaws Farm
Bourne Wood
Chain Wlk
Stocking La
The Farmer's Boy (PH)
08
Brickendon
Brickendon Grange
Cowheath Wood
4
Morley Grove
CH
Brickendon Golf Course
Broad Riding Wood
Blackfan Wood
Claypits Wood
3
Broxbourne Wood
Hedgerows Wood
Hedgegrove Farm
Devil's La
07
Old Claypits Farm
PEMBRIDGE LA
Calais Wood
Ettridge Farm
Pembridge Lane Farm
Paradise Wildlife Park
Stocking Wood
2
Ponsbourne Tunnel
WHITE STUBBS LA
Mortals Wood
Old Grove
P
P
Emanuel Pollards
Bencroft Wood
Chain Wlk
1
Wormley Wood
Westlea
Manor Farm
WEST END RD
06
A
B
32
C
D
33
E
F

133
114

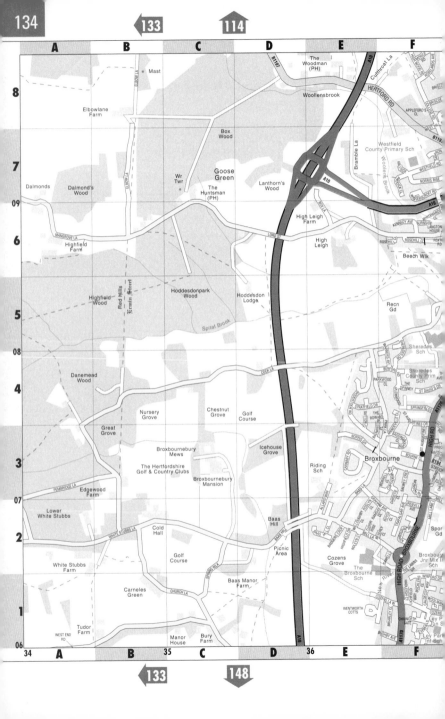
A
B
C
D
E
F
8
7
09
6
5
08
4
3
07
2
1
06
34
35
36
Mast
Elbow La
B1197
The Woodman (PH)
A10
Cutthroat La
Hertford Rd
Woollensbrook
Elbowlane Farm
Box Wood
Bramble La
Westfield County Primary Sch
Woolens Brook
Westfield Rd
Norris Rise
Goose Green
Wr Twr
The Huntsman (PH)
Lanthorn's Wood
Dalmonds
Dalmond's Wood
Box La
High Leigh Farm
Kennedy Ave
Burnside
Mangrove La
Lord St
High Leigh
Rosehill Cl
Highfield Farm
Beech Wlk
Highfield Wood
Red Hills
Ermin Street
Hoddesdonpark Wood
Hoddesdon Lodge
Recn Gd
Spital Brook
Sheredes Sch
Danemead Wood
Cock La
Sheredes County Prim Sch
Parkwood Cl
The Spinney
St David's Dr
Nursery Grove
Chestnut Grove
Golf Course
Stratfield Dr
The Rowans
Springfields
Great Grove
High Rd
Norris Gr
Broxbournebury Mews
Icehouse Grove
The Hertfordshire Golf & Country Clubs
Broxbourne
Riding Sch
Broxbournebury Mansion
Pembridge La
Edgewood Farm
Lower White Stubbs
Baas Hill
Allard Way
Baas La
Cold Hall
White Stubbs La
Baas Hill Cl
Picnic Area
Golf Course
Cozens Grove
The Broxbourne Sch
New River
White Stubbs Farm
High Road Broxbourne
Spring Wlk
Baas Manor Farm
Carneles Green
Church La
Cozens La W
Wentworth Cotts
Tudor Farm
West End Rd
Manor House
Bury Farm
Bushby Ave
A1170

133
148

115

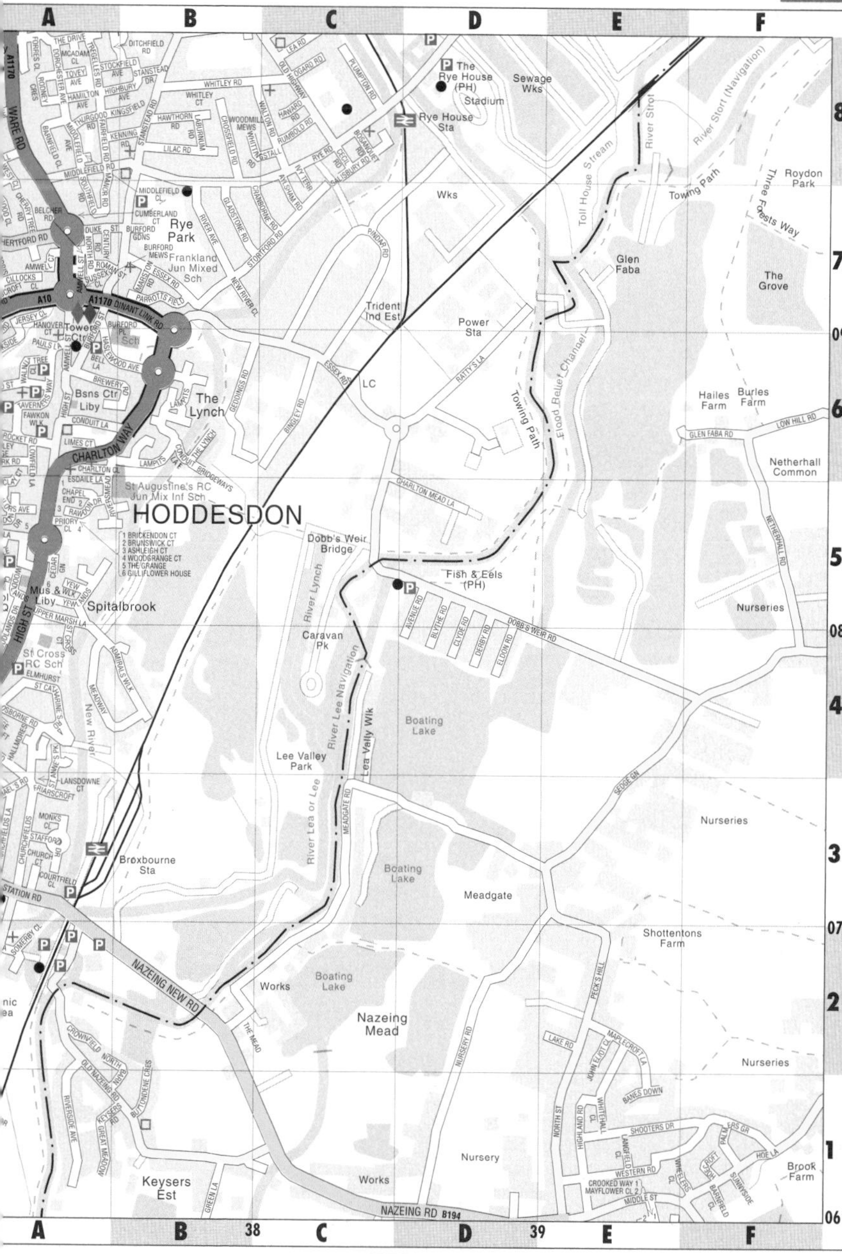

A
B
C
D
E
F
8
7
09
6
5
08
4
3
07
2
1
06
38
39
HODDESDON
Rye Park
Frankland Jun Mixed Sch
The Rye House (PH)
Stadium
Sewage Wks
Rye House Sta
Wks
Trident Ind Est
Power Sta
LC
Toll House Stream
River Stort
River Stort (Navigation)
Towing Path
Roydon Park
Three Forests Way
Glen Faba
The Grove
Flood Relief Channel
Hailes Farm
Burles Farm
GLEN FABA RD
LOW HILL RD
Netherhall Common
NETHERHALL RD
Nurseries
Towers Ctr
Bsns Ctr
Liby
The Lynch
St Augustine's RC Jun Mix Inf Sch
1 BRICKENDON CT
2 BRUNSWICK CT
3 ASHLEIGH CT
4 WOODGRANGE CT
5 THE GRANGE
6 GILLIFLOWER HOUSE
Mus & Liby
Spitalbrook
St Cross RC Sch
Dobb's Weir Bridge
Fish & Eels (PH)
DOBB'S WEIR RD
River Lynch
Caravan Pk
River Lee Navigation
Lea Valley Wlk
Boating Lake
Lee Valley Park
River Lea or Lee
New River
Broxbourne Sta
MEADGATE RD
SEDGE GN
Meadgate
Shottentons Farm
Works
Nazeing Mead
NAZEING NEW RD
NAZEING RD B194
Keysers Est
Nursery
PECK'S HILL
NURSERY RD
NORTH ST
SHOOTERS DR
WESTERN RD
CROOKED WAY
MAYFLOWER CL
MIDDLE ST
Brook Farm
WARE RD
A1170
A10
CHARLTON WAY
HIGH ST
STATION RD
DINANT LINK RD
CROWNFIELD
OLD NAZEING RD
RIVERSIDE AVE
GREAT MEADOW
BUTTONDENE CRES
GREEN LA
THE MEAD
LAKE RD
BANES DOWN


149

122

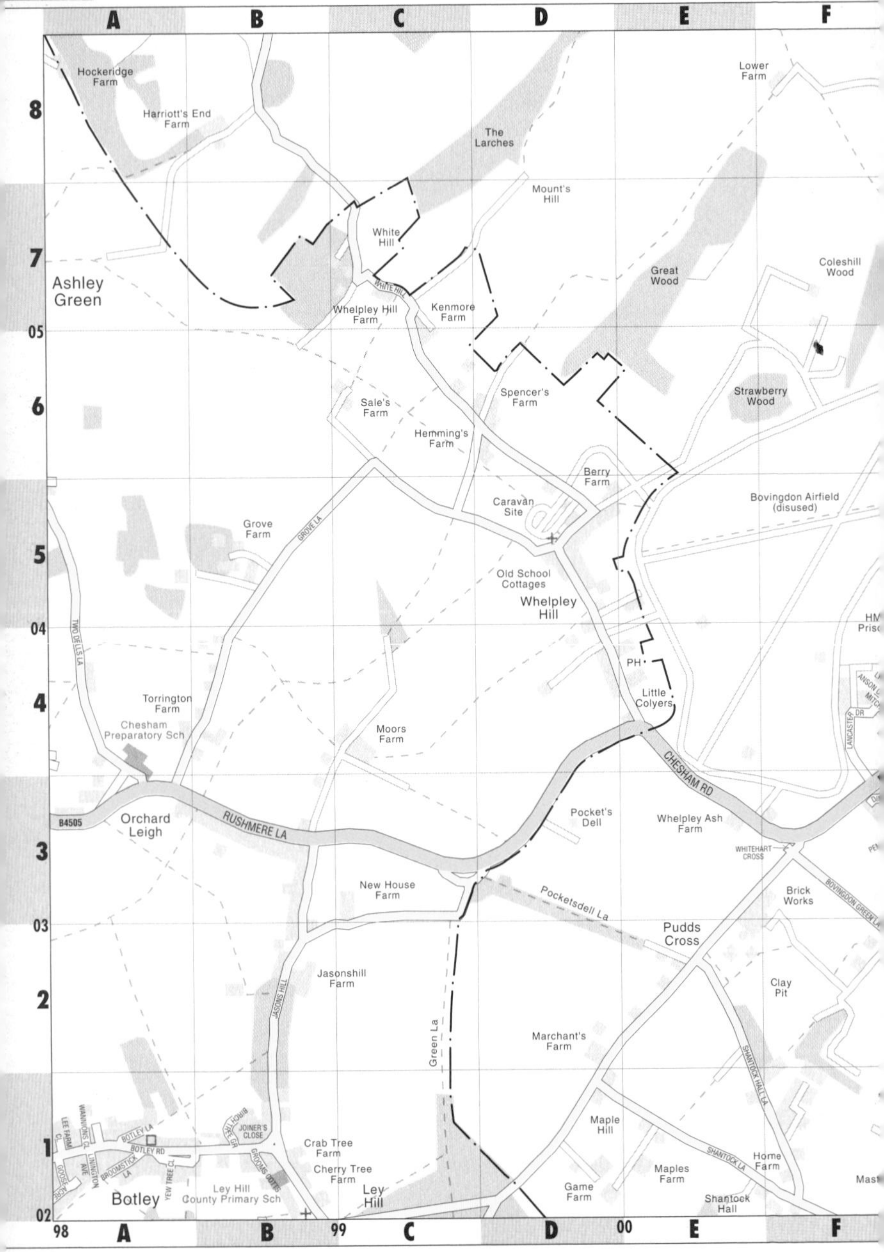

A
B
C
D
E
F
8
7
05
6
5
04
4
3
03
2
1
02
98
99
00
Hockeridge Farm
Harriott's End Farm
The Larches
Lower Farm
Mount's Hill
White Hill
Ashley Green
WHITE HILL
Whelpley Hill Farm
Kenmore Farm
Great Wood
Coleshill Wood
Strawberry Wood
Spencer's Farm
Sale's Farm
Hemming's Farm
Berry Farm
Caravan Site
Bovingdon Airfield (disused)
Grove Farm
GROVE LA
Old School Cottages
Whelpley Hill
TWO DELLS LA
PH
Little Colyers
Torrington Farm
Chesham Preparatory Sch
Moors Farm
CHESHAM RD
LANCASTER DR
ANSON
B4505
Orchard Leigh
RUSHMERE LA
Pocket's Dell
Whelpley Ash Farm
WHITEHART CROSS
New House Farm
Pocketsdell La
Brick Works
BOVINGDON GREEN LA
Pudds Cross
Jasonshill Farm
JASONS HILL
Clay Pit
Green La
Marchant's Farm
SHANTOCK HALL LA
LEE FARM CL
WANNIONS CL
BOTLEY LA
BIRCH TREE GR
JOINER'S CLOSE
BOTLEY RD
LININGTON AVE
BROOMSTICK LA
GOOSE ACRE
YEW TREE CL
GROOMS COTTS
Crab Tree Farm
Cherry Tree Farm
Maple Hill
Maples Farm
SHANTOCK LA
Home Farm
Game Farm
Shantock Hall
Botley
Ley Hill County Primary Sch
Ley Hill


150

123
138

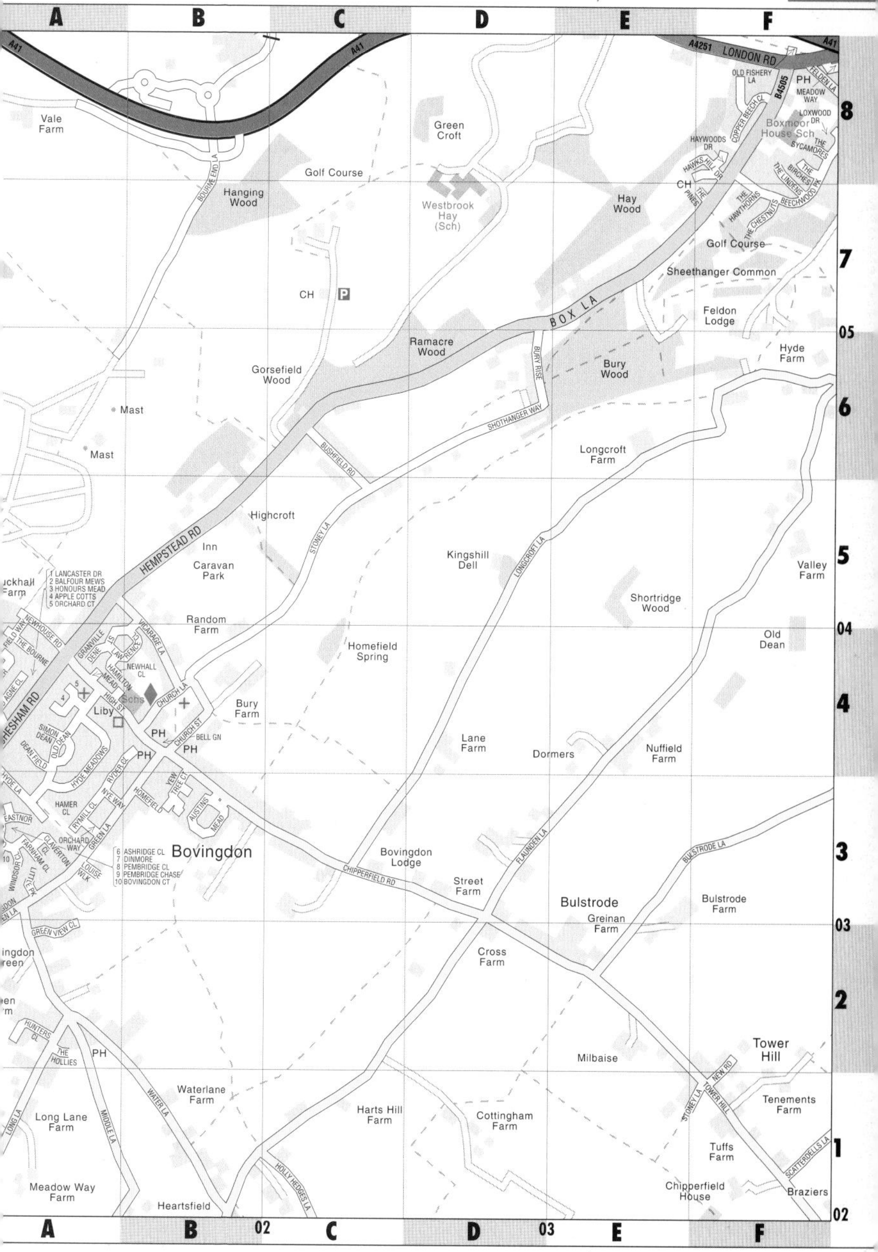
A
B
C
D
E
F
A41
A4251
LONDON RD
B4505
OLD FISHERY LA
FELDEN LA
PH
MEADOW WAY
LOXWOOD DR
Boxmoor House Sch
THE SYCAMORES
COPPER BEECH CL
HAYWOODS DR
HAWKS HILL DR
THE BIRCHES
THE LINDENS
BEECHWOOD PK
THE PINES
THE HAWTHORNS
THE CHESTNUTS
CH
Vale Farm
Green Croft
Golf Course
Hanging Wood
BOURNE END LA
Westbrook Hay (Sch)
Hay Wood
Golf Course
Sheethanger Common
Feldon Lodge
CH
Ramacre Wood
BOX LA
BURY RISE
Bury Wood
Hyde Farm
Gorsefield Wood
Mast
Mast
SHOTHANGER WAY
BUSHFIELD RD
Longcroft Farm
Highcroft
HEMPSTEAD RD
STONEY LA
Inn
Caravan Park
Kingshill Dell
LONGCROFT LA
Valley Farm
Shortridge Wood
Old Dean
1 LANCASTER DR
2 BALFOUR MEWS
3 HONOURS MEAD
4 APPLE COTTS
5 ORCHARD CT
Random Farm
Homefield Spring
NEWHOUSE RD
THE BOURNE
GRANVILLE DENE
ST LAWRENCE CL
VICARAGE LA
NEWHALL CL
HAMILTON MEAD
HIGH ST
Schs
CHURCH LA
Liby
Bury Farm
CHESHAM RD
SIMON DEAN
OLD DEAN
DEAN FIELD
HYDE MEADOWS
PH
CHURCH ST
BELL GN
PH
PH
Lane Farm
Dormers
Nuffield Farm
HYDE LA
RYDER CL
NYE WAY
HOMEFIELD
YEW TREE CT
AUSTINS MEAD
HAMER CL
RYMILL CL
GREEN LA
EASTNOR
CLAVERTON CL
ORCHARD WAY
FARNHAM CL
LOUISE WLK
LITTLE PK
WINDSOR CL
6 ASHRIDGE CL
7 DINMORE
8 PEMBRIDGE CL
9 PEMBRIDGE CHASE
10 BOVINGDON CT
Bovingdon
Bovingdon Lodge
CHIPPERFIELD RD
FLAUNDEN LA
BULSTRODE LA
Street Farm
Bulstrode
Bulstrode Farm
Greinan Farm
GREEN VIEW CL
Cross Farm
HUNTERS CL
THE HOLLIES
PH
Tower Hill
Milbaise
NEW RD
TOWER HILL
STONEY LA
Waterlane Farm
WATER LA
Harts Hill Farm
Cottingham Farm
Tenements Farm
Long Lane Farm
LONG LA
MIDDLE LA
Tuffs Farm
SCATTERDELLS LA
HOLLY HEDGES LA
Meadow Way Farm
Chipperfield House
Braziers
Heartsfield
8
7
05
6
5
04
4
3
03
2
1
02
02
03

151
138

137
124

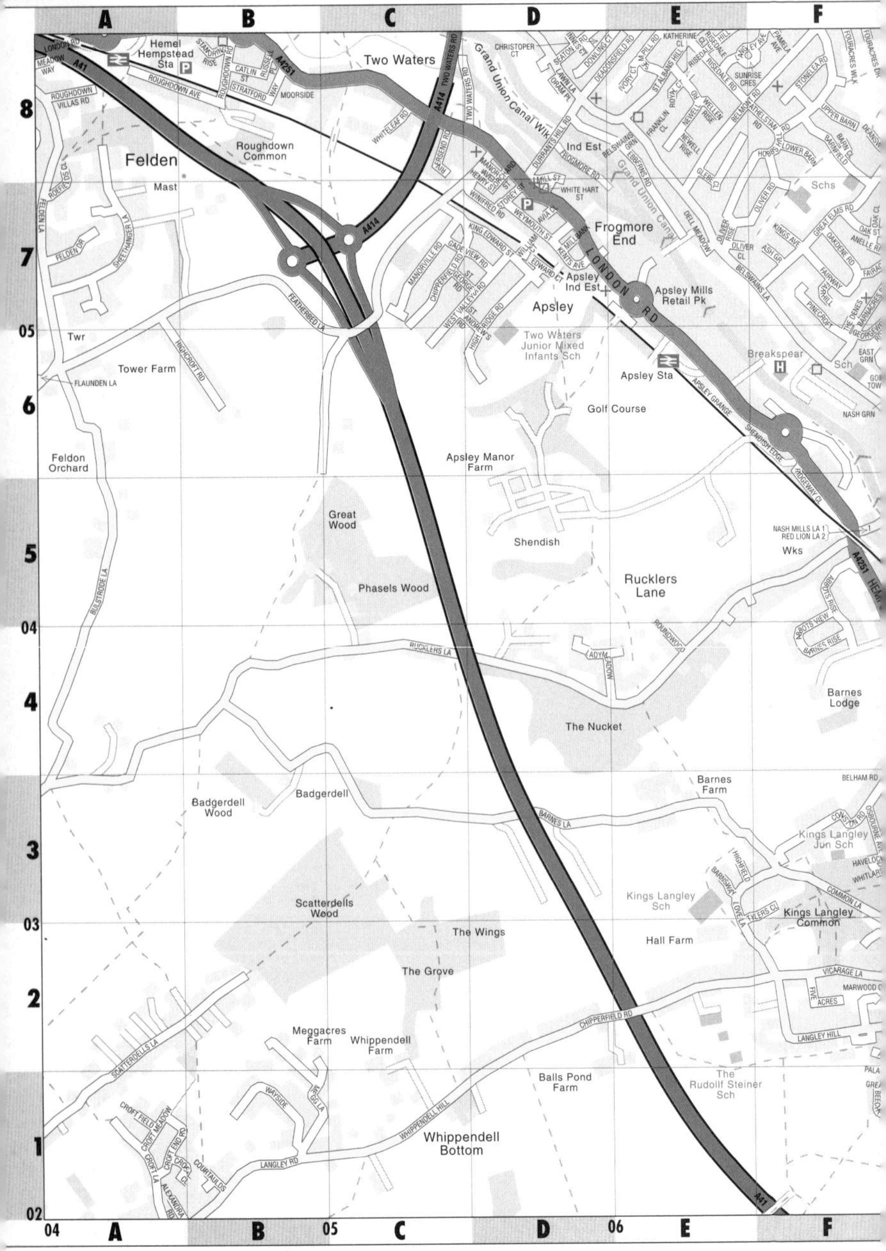
A
B
C
D
E
F
8
7
05
6
5
04
4
3
03
2
1
02
04
05
06
Hemel Hempstead Sta
Two Waters
Grand Union Canal Wlk
Felden
Roughdown Common
Mast
Ind Est
Frogmore End
Apsley Ind Est
Apsley Mills Retail Pk
Apsley
Two Waters Junior Mixed Infants Sch
Apsley Sta
Twr
Tower Farm
FLAUNDEN LA
Golf Course
Breakspear
Schs
Sch
Feldon Orchard
Apsley Manor Farm
Great Wood
Shendish
Phasels Wood
Rucklers Lane
Wks
NASH MILLS LA 1
RED LION LA 2
RUCKLERS LA
The Nucket
Barnes Lodge
Barnes Farm
Badgerdell
Badgerdell Wood
BARNES LA
Kings Langley Jun Sch
Kings Langley Sch
Kings Langley Common
Scatterdells Wood
The Wings
Hall Farm
The Grove
CHIPPERFIELD RD
Meggacres Farm
Whippendell Farm
Balls Pond Farm
The Rudolf Steiner Sch
WHIPPENDELL HILL
Whippendell Bottom
LANGLEY RD
SCATTERDELLS LA
BULSTRODE LA
FEATHERBED LA
HIGHCROFT RD
LONDON RD
A41
A414
A4251

137
152

125
140

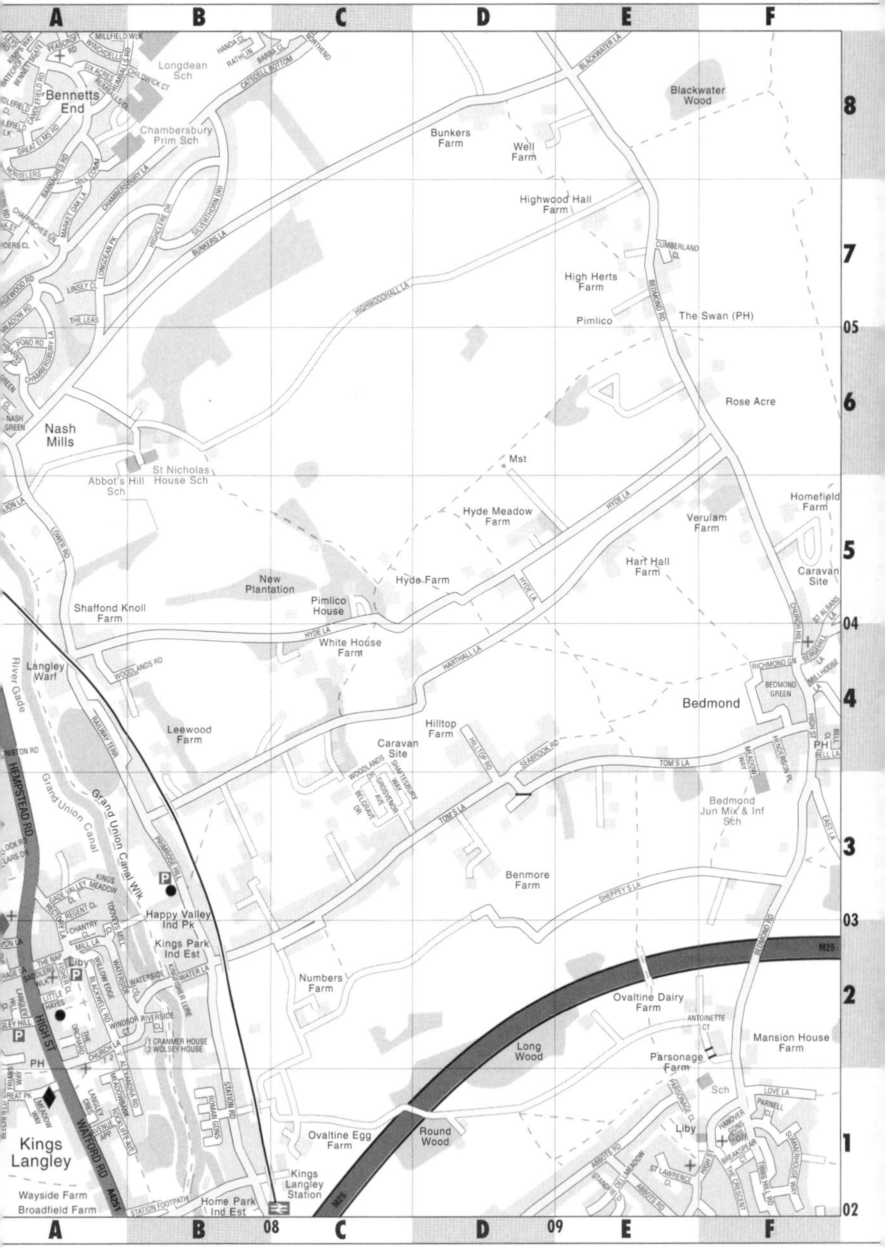
A
B
C
D
E
F
8
7
05
6
5
04
4
3
03
2
1
02
08
09
Bennetts End
Longdean Sch
Chambersbury Prim Sch
Nash Mills
Abbot's Hill Sch
St Nicholas House Sch
Bunkers Farm
Well Farm
Highwood Hall Farm
High Herts Farm
Pimlico
The Swan (PH)
Blackwater Wood
Rose Acre
Mst
Hyde Meadow Farm
Verulam Farm
Homefield Farm
Caravan Site
Hart Hall Farm
Hyde Farm
New Plantation
Pimlico House
Shaffond Knoll Farm
White House Farm
Langley Warf
River Gade
Leewood Farm
Hilltop Farm
Caravan Site
Bedmond
Bedmond Jun Mix & Inf Sch
Benmore Farm
Grand Union Canal
Grand Union Canal Wlk
Happy Valley Ind Pk
Kings Park Ind Est
Numbers Farm
Ovaltine Dairy Farm
Long Wood
Mansion House Farm
Parsonage Farm
Sch
Liby
Coll
Round Wood
Ovaltine Egg Farm
Kings Langley Station
Home Park Ind Est
Kings Langley
Wayside Farm
Broadfield Farm
PH
HEMPSTEAD RD
HIGH ST
WATFORD RD
A4251
M25
BUNKERS LA
HIGHWOODHALL LA
HYDE LA
HARTHALL LA
TOM'S LA
SHEPPEY'S LA
BEDMOND RD
BLACKWATER LA
CUMBERLAND CL
CHURCH HILL
ST ALBANS LA
SERGEHILL LA
MILLHOUSE LA
RICHMOND GN
BEDMOND GREEN
HIGH ST
BELL CL
BELL LA
HENDERSON PL
MEADOW WAY
EAST LA
SEABROOK RD
HILLTOP RD
WOODLANDS DR
SHAFTESBURY WAY
GROSVENOR AVE
BELGRAVE DR
WOODLANDS RD
LOWER RD
RAILWAY TERR
PRIMROSE HILL
STATION RD
ROMAN GDNS
STATION FOOTPATH
LOVE LA
PARNELL CL
HANOVER GDNS
BREAKSPEAR CT
THE CRESCENT
TIBBS HILL RD
SUMMERHOUSE WAY
PARSONAGE CL
ANTOINETTE CT
ABBOTS RD
DELLMEADOW
STANDFIELD
ST LAWRENCE CL
CATSDELL BOTTOM
NORTHEND
HANDA CL
RATHLIN
BARRA CL
MILLFIELD WLK
PEASCROFT RD
WINCHDELLS
SIX ACRES
RUMBALLS CL
CHILDWICK CT
CANDLEFIELD RD
GREAT ELMS RD
BARNACRES RD
HILL COMM
MARKET OAK LA
CHAFFINCHES GN
CHAMBERSBURY LA
LONGDEAN PK
HIGHCLERE DR
SILVERTHORN DR
LINSEY CL
THE LEAS
POND RD
NASH GREEN
KINGS MEADOW
GADE VALLEY CL
REGENT CL
CHANTRY CL
TOOVEYS MILL
MILL LA
WILLOW EDGE
WATERSIDE
BLACKWELL RD
WATERSIDE CT
WATER LA
KINGFISHER LURE
WINDSOR CT
RIVERSIDE CL
1 CRANMER HOUSE
2 WOLSEY HOUSE
CHURCH LA
THE ORCHARD
LITTLE HAYES
FISHER CL
SADDLERS WLK
THE NAP
ALEXANDRA RD
MEADOWBANK
ROCKLIFFE AVE
AVENUE APP
LANGLEY CRES
MEADOW WAY
GREAT PK
FRIARS WAY
LANGLEY HILL

153
140

139
126

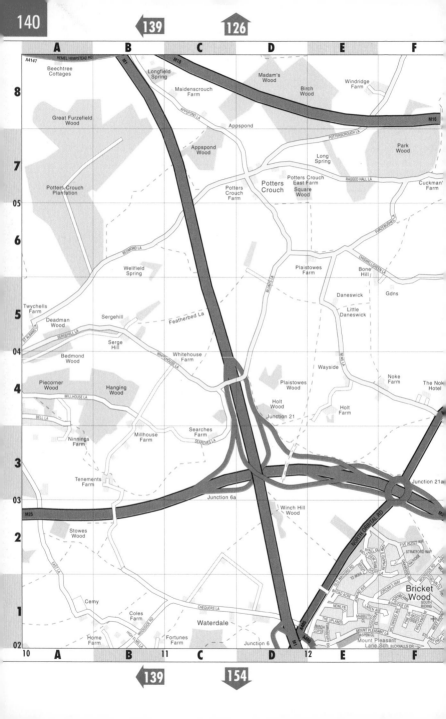
A
B
C
D
E
F
8
7
05
6
5
04
4
3
03
2
1
02
10
11
12
A4147
HEMEL HEMPSTEAD RD
M1
M10
Beechtree Cottages
Longfield Spring
Madam's Wood
Windridge Farm
Maidenscrouch Farm
Birch Wood
Great Furzefield Wood
APPSPOND LA
Appspond
POTTERSCROUCH LA
Appspond Wood
Park Wood
Long Spring
Potters Crouch Plantation
Potters Crouch Farm
Potters Crouch
Potters Crouch East Farm
Square Wood
RAGGED HALL LA
Cuckman's Farm
FURZEBUSHES LA
BEDMOND LA
Wellfield Spring
Plaistowes Farm
Bone Hill
CHISWELLGREEN LA
BLUNTS LA
Gdns
Daneswick
Twychells Farm
Little Daneswick
Deadman Wood
Sergehill
Featherbed La
ST ALBANS LA
SERGEHILL LA
Serge Hill
Bedmond Wood
Whitehouse Farm
WHITEHOUSE LA
NOKE LA
Wayside
Piecorner Wood
Hanging Wood
Plaistowes Wood
Noke Farm
The Noke Hotel
MILLHOUSE LA
Holt Wood
Holt Farm
BELL LA
Junction 21
Searches Farm
Ninnings Farm
Millhouse Farm
SEARCHES LA
Tenements Farm
Junction 21a
Junction 6a
M25
Winch Hill Wood
NORTH ORBITAL RD
Stowes Wood
FIVE ACRES AVE
RYALL CL
STRATFORD WAY
FIELD VIEW RISE
REYNARD'S WAY
OAKRIDGE
EAST LA
OAKWOOD RD
WOODSIDE RD
SHORT LA
OLD WATFORD RD
JORDAN'S WAY
Bricket Wood
BROAD ACRE
JENKINS AVE
HORNBEAMS
SOUTH RIDING
ASHRIDGE DR
Cemy
CHEQUERS LA
NEWLYN CL
LARCH AVE
Coles Farm
THE UPLANDS
MABBUTT CL
ROSEDALE CL
WILDWOOD AVE
PINE GR
MOSS SIDE
BRACKNOWE
WEST RIDING
Waterdale
WOODSIDE RD
A405
BIRCH COPSE
TURNBERRY DR
MOUNT PLEASANT LA
ASPEN CL
Home Farm
HIGH ELMS LA
Fortunes Farm
Junction 6
Mount Pleasant Lane Sch
BUCKNALLS DR

139
154

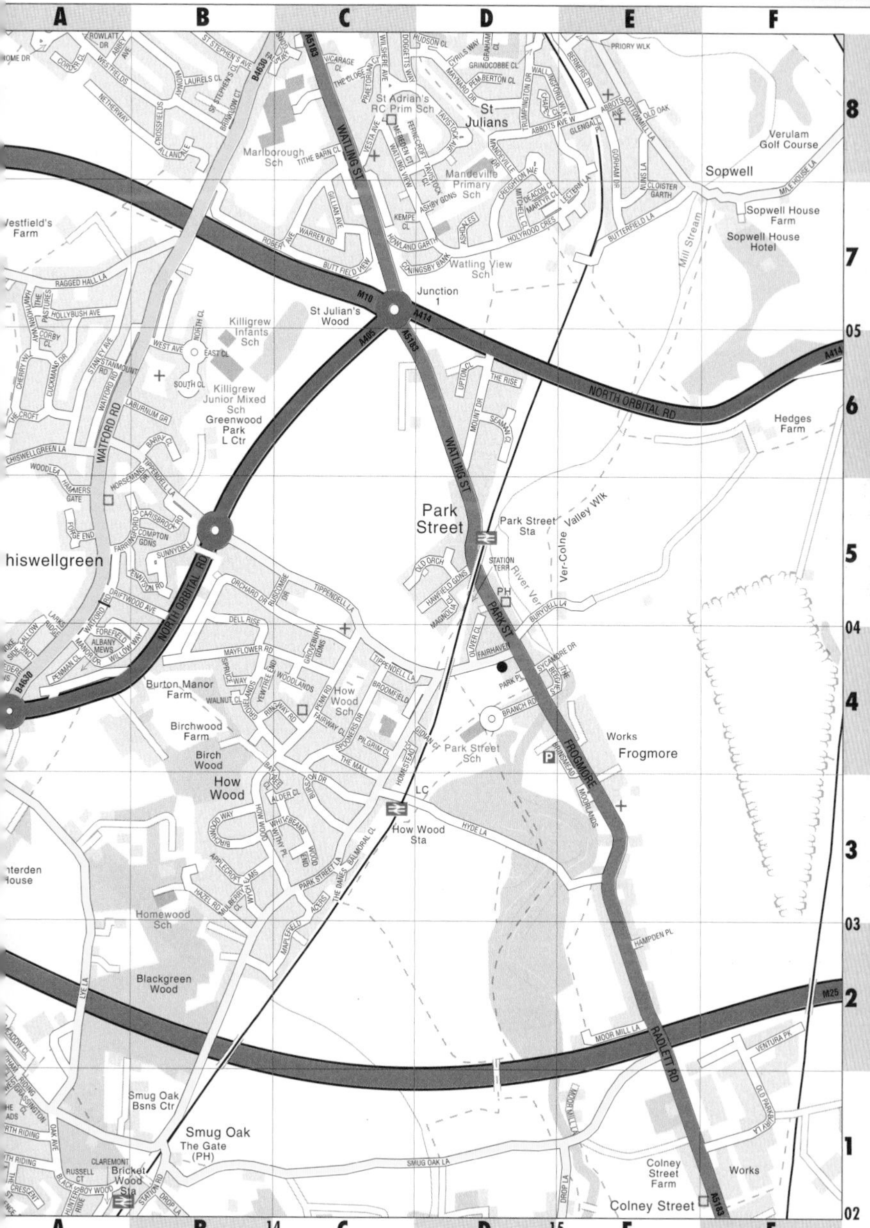
A
B
C
D
E
F
8
7
05
6
5
04
4
3
03
2
1
02
14
15
St Julians
St Adrian's RC Prim Sch
Marlborough Sch
Mandeville Primary Sch
Watling View Sch
Verulam Golf Course
Sopwell
Sopwell House Farm
Sopwell House Hotel
Mill Stream
Junction 1
St Julian's Wood
Killigrew Infants Sch
Killigrew Junior Mixed Sch
Greenwood Park L Ctr
Westfield's Farm
Hedges Farm
Park Street
Park Street Sta
Ver-Colne Valley Wlk
River Ver
Chiswellgreen
Burton Manor Farm
Birchwood Farm
Birch Wood
How Wood
How Wood Sch
Park Street Sch
Works
Frogmore
How Wood Sta
Homewood Sch
Blackgreen Wood
Smug Oak Bsns Ctr
Smug Oak
The Gate (PH)
Bricket Wood Sta
Colney Street Farm
Colney Street
WATLING ST
NORTH ORBITAL RD
WATFORD RD
PARK ST
FROGMORE
RADLETT RD
HYDE LA
SMUG OAK LA
MOOR MILL LA
M10
M25
A414
A405
A5183
B4630

141
128

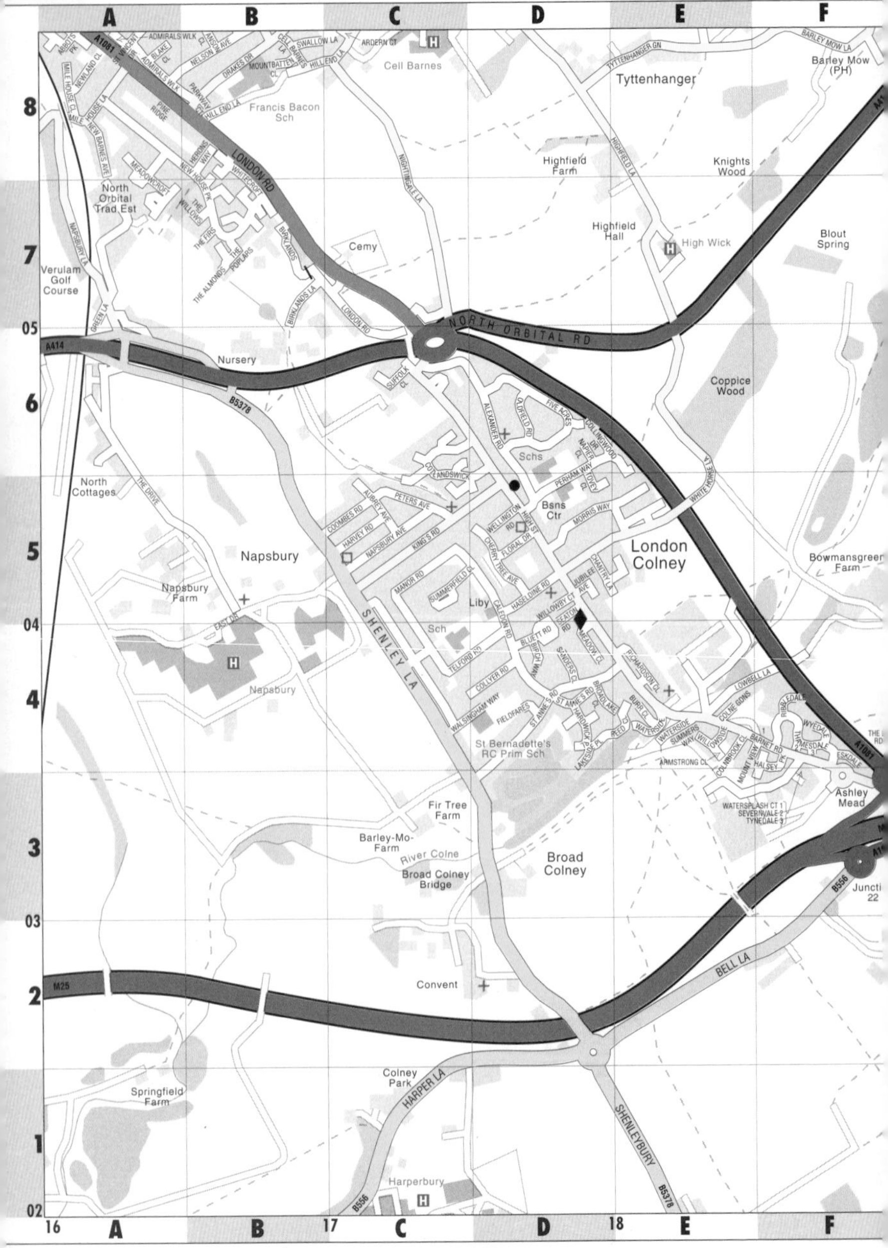
A
B
C
D
E
F
8
7
05
6
5
04
4
3
03
2
1
02
16
17
18
A1081
ADMIRALS WLK
ABBOTS PK
MILE HOUSE CL
NEWLAND CL
ST VINCENT DR
BLAKE CL
NELSON AVE
ANSON CL
DRAKES DR
MOUNTBATTEN CL
CELL BARNES LA
SWALLOW LA
HILL END LA
ARDERN CT
Cell Barnes
PARKWAY
PINE RIDGE
MILE HOUSE LA
NEW BARNES AVE
Francis Bacon Sch
LONDON RD
HERONS WAY
NEW HOUSE PK
WHITECROFT
MEADOWCROFT
North Orbital Trad Est
THE WILLOWS
THE FIRS
THE POPLARS
THE ALMONDS
BIRKLANDS
BIRKLANDS LA
NAPSBURY LA
Verulam Golf Course
GREEN LA
Cemy
NIGHTINGALE LA
TYTTENHANGER GN
Tyttenhanger
BARLEY MOW LA
Barley Mow (PH)
Highfield Farm
HIGHFIELD LA
Knights Wood
Highfield Hall
High Wick
Blout Spring
A414
NORTH ORBITAL RD
Nursery
SUFFOLK CL
B5378
Coppice Wood
ALEXANDER RD
OLDFIELD RD
FIVE ACRES
COLLINGWOOD DR
NAPIER CL
Schs
PERHAM WAY
TOVEY CL
COTLANDSWICK
WHITE HORSE LA
North Cottages
THE DRIVE
PETERS AVE
AUBREY AVE
COOMBES RD
HARVEY RD
NAPSBURY AVE
KING'S RD
WELLINGTON RD
HIGH ST
Bsns Ctr
MORRIS WAY
FLORAL DR
CHERRY TREE AVE
London Colney
Napsbury
MANOR RD
SUMMERFIELD CL
JUBILEE AVE
CHANTRY LA
Bowmansgreen Farm
Napsbury Farm
HASELDINE RD
Liby
WILLOWBY CT
SEATON RD
CALEDON RD
EAST DR
SHENLEY LA
Sch
BLUETT RD
MEADOW CL
TELFORD RD
BIRCH WAY
SANDERS CL
RICHARDSON CL
Napsbury
COLLYER RD
ST ANNE'S RD
BROADLAKE CL
BURR CL
LOWBELL LA
WALSINGHAM WAY
FIELDFARES
HARDWICK PL
REED CL
WATERSIDE
COLNE GDNS
RIBBLEDALE
WYEDALE
THAMESDALE
SUMMERS WAY
WILLOWSIDE
BARNET RD
LAKESIDE PL
St Bernadette's RC Prim Sch
ARMSTRONG CL
COLNBROOK CL
MOUNT VIEW
HALSEY PK
ESKDALE
A1081
Ashley Mead
Fir Tree Farm
WATERSPLASH CT 1
SEVERNVALE 2
TYNEDALE 3
Barley-Mo-Farm
River Colne
Broad Colney
Broad Colney Bridge
B556
Junction 22
BELL LA
M25
Convent
Colney Park
HARPER LA
Springfield Farm
SHENLEYBURY
B5378
Harperbury
B556

141
156

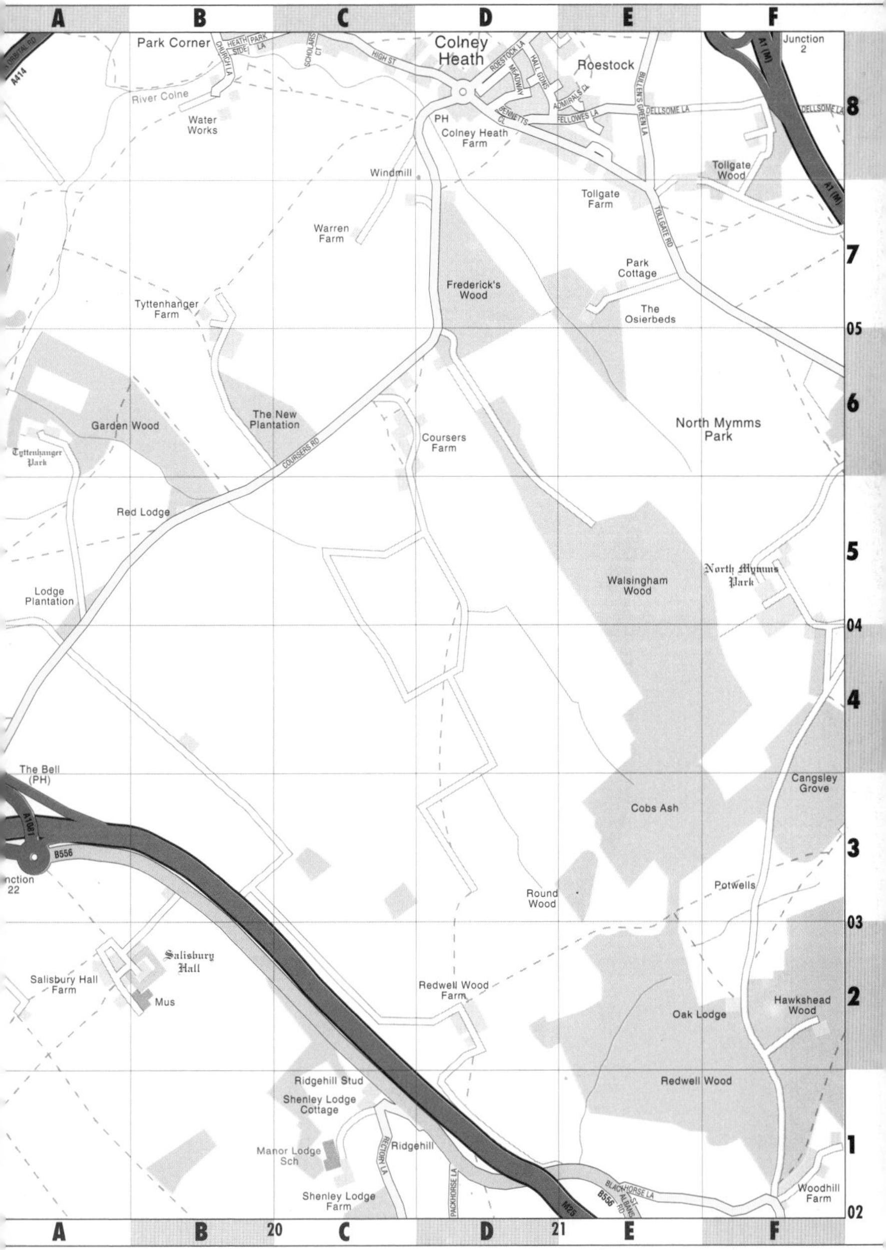
A
B
C
D
E
F
Park Corner
Colney Heath
Roestock
Junction 2
A414
HEATH SIDE
PARK LA
CHURCH LA
SCHOLARS CT
HIGH ST
ROESTOCK LA
MEADWAY
HALL GDNS
ADMIRALS CL
BULLEN'S GREEN LA
DELLSOME LA
A1 (M)
River Colne
Water Works
PH
BENNETTS CL
FELLOWES LA
Colney Heath Farm
Windmill
Tollgate Wood
Tollgate Farm
TOLLGATE RD
Warren Farm
Park Cottage
Frederick's Wood
The Osierbeds
Tyttenhanger Farm
Garden Wood
The New Plantation
North Mymms Park
Coursers Farm
COURSERS RD
Tyttenhanger Park
Red Lodge
Walsingham Wood
Lodge Plantation
The Bell (PH)
Cangsley Grove
Cobs Ash
A1081
B556
Junction 22
Potwells
Round Wood
Salisbury Hall
Salisbury Hall Farm
Mus
Redwell Wood Farm
Hawkshead Wood
Oak Lodge
Ridgehill Stud
Redwell Wood
Shenley Lodge Cottage
Manor Lodge Sch
RECTORY LA
Ridgehill
PACKHORSE LA
Shenley Lodge Farm
M25
BLACKHORSE LA
ST ALBANS RD
Woodhill Farm
8
7
05
6
5
04
4
3
03
2
1
02
20
21

143
130

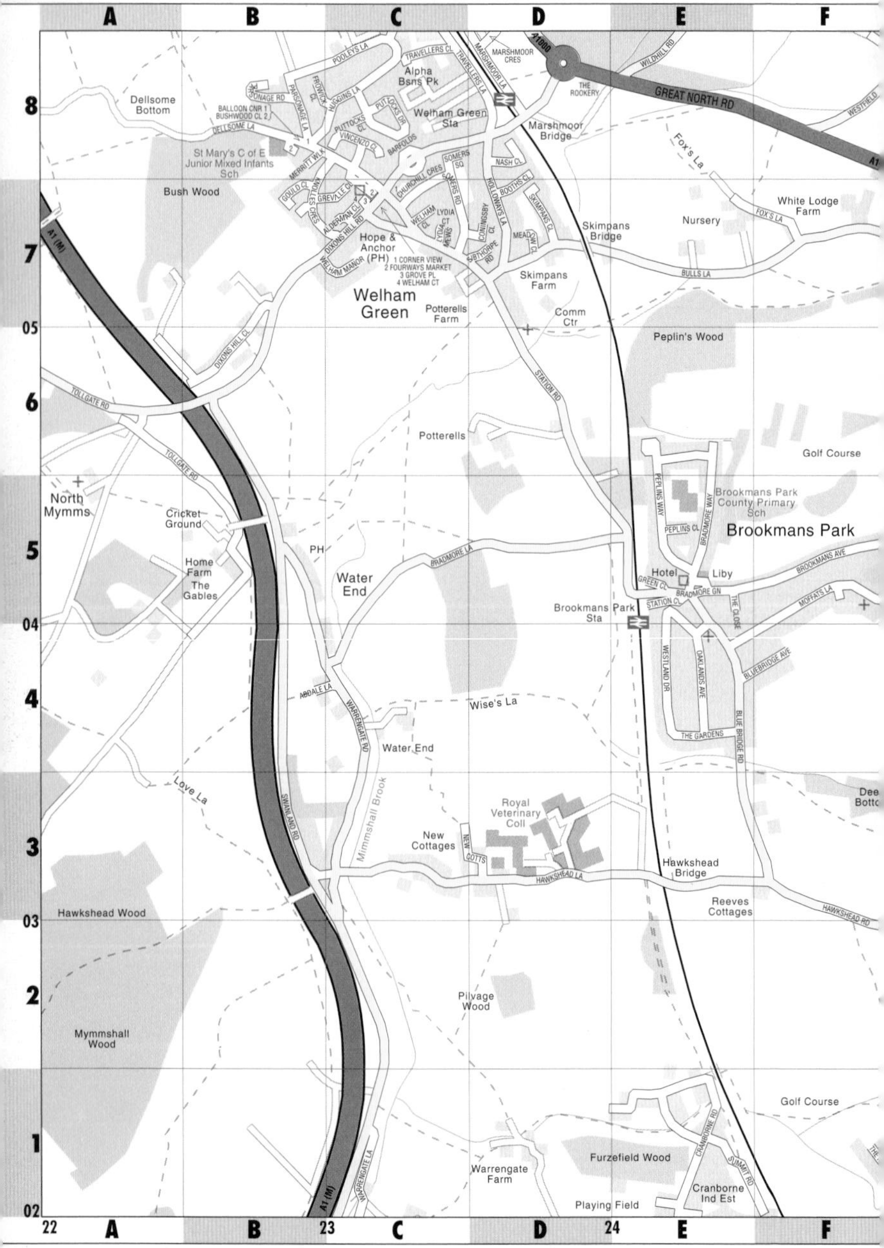
A
B
C
D
E
F
8
7
05
6
5
04
4
3
03
2
1
02
22
23
24
POOLEYS LA
TRAVELLERS CL
MARSHMOOR LA
MARSHMOOR CRES
A1000
WILDHILL RD
Alpha Bsns Pk
PARSONAGE RD
FROWICK CL
HUGGINS LA
PARSONAGE LA
PUTTOCKS CL
PUTTOCKS DR
Welham Green Sta
THE ROOKERY
GREAT NORTH RD
WESTFIELD
Dellsome Bottom
BALLOON CNR 1
BUSHWOOD CL 2
DELLSOME LA
Marshmoor Bridge
VINCENZO CL
BARFOLDS
Fox's La
St Mary's C of E Junior Mixed Infants Sch
MERRITT WLK
SOMERS SQ
NASH CL
A1
CHURCHILL CRES
SOMERS RD
BOOTHS CL
HOLLOWAYS LA
Bush Wood
GOULD CL
GREVALLE CL
LYDIA
SKIMPANS CL
White Lodge Farm
WELHAM CL
Skimpans Bridge
Nursery
FOX'S LA
ALDERMAN CL
DIXONS HILL RD
Hope & Anchor (PH)
CONINGSBY CL
MEAD
A1 (M)
SIBTHORPE RD
BULLS LA
WELHAM MANOR
1 CORNER VIEW
2 FOURWAYS MARKET
3 GROVE PL
4 WELHAM CT
Skimpans Farm
Welham Green
Potterells Farm
Comm Ctr
Peplin's Wood
DIXONS HILL CL
STATION RD
TOLLGATE RD
Potterells
Golf Course
North Mymms
PEPLINS WAY
BRADMORE WAY
Brookmans Park County Primary Sch
Cricket Ground
PEPLINS CL
Brookmans Park
PH
BRADMORE LA
Home Farm
Hotel
Liby
BROOKMANS AVE
Water End
The Gables
GREEN CL
BRADMORE GN
STATION CL
THE CLOSE
MOFFATS LA
Brookmans Park Sta
WESTLAND DR
OAKLANDS AVE
BLUEBRIDGE AVE
ABDALE LA
WARRENGATE RD
Wise's La
THE GARDENS
Water End
BLUE BRIDGE RD
Love La
SWANLAND RD
Mimmshall Brook
Royal Veterinary Coll
New Cottages
NEW COTTS
Hawkshead Bridge
HAWKSHEAD LA
Reeves Cottages
HAWKSHEAD RD
Hawkshead Wood
Pilvage Wood
Mymmshall Wood
Golf Course
CRANBORNE RD
Furzefield Wood
SUMMIT RD
WARRENGATE LA
Warrengate Farm
Cranborne Ind Est
Playing Field
A1 (M)

143
158

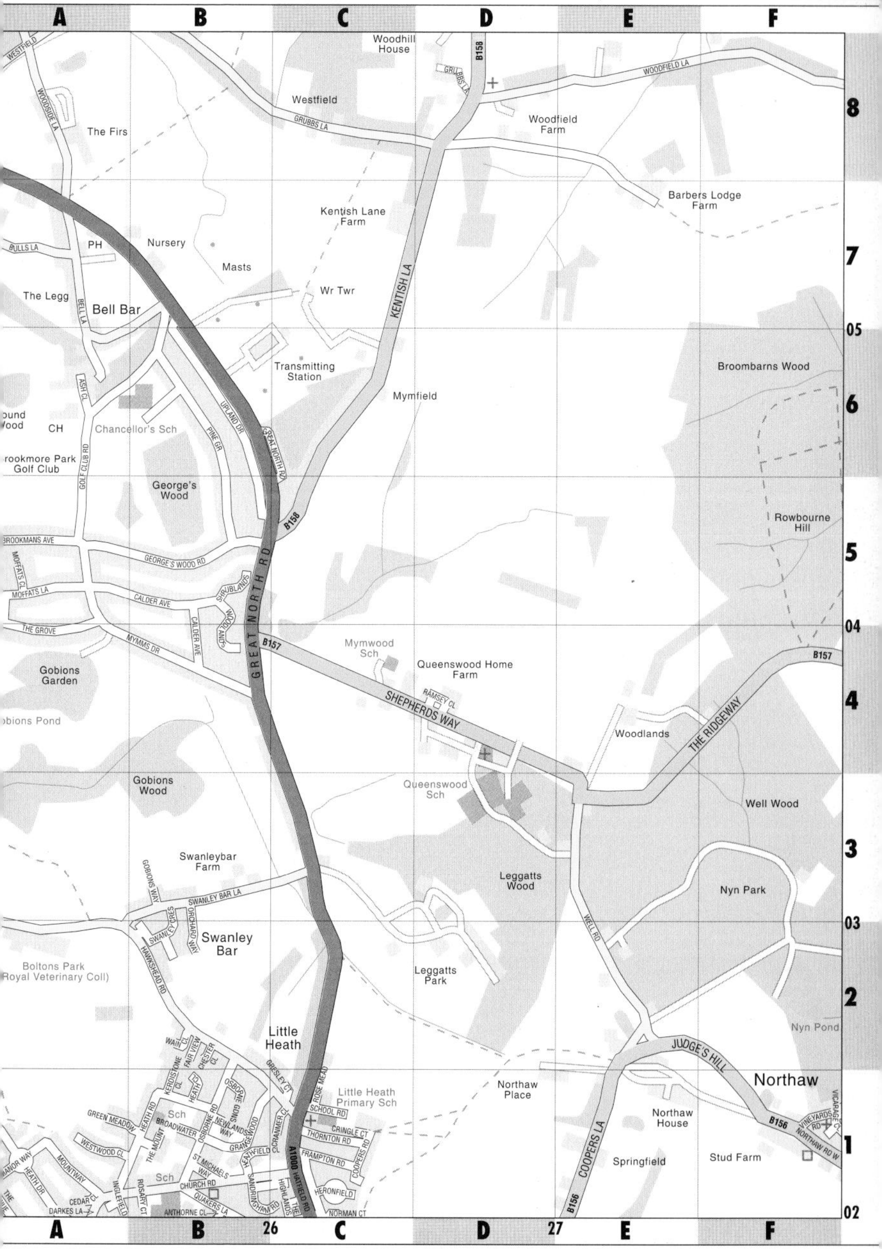
A
B
C
D
E
F
Woodhill House
B158
GRUBBS LA
WOODFIELD LA
WESTFIELD
WOODSIDE LA
Westfield
The Firs
Woodfield Farm
Barbers Lodge Farm
Kentish Lane Farm
BULLS LA
PH
Nursery
Masts
Wr Twr
KENTISH LA
The Legg
BELL LA
Bell Bar
Transmitting Station
Mymfield
Broombarns Wood
ASH CL
UPLAND DR
PINE GR
GREAT NORTH RD
Chancellor's Sch
CH
GOLF CLUB RD
George's Wood
Rowbourne Hill
BROOKMANS AVE
GEORGE'S WOOD RD
MOFFATS CL
MOFFATS LA
CALDER AVE
SHRUBLANDS
WOODLAND
THE GROVE
MYMMS DR
B157
Mymwood Sch
Queenswood Home Farm
Gobions Garden
RAMSEY CL
SHEPHERDS WAY
THE RIDGEWAY
Woodlands
Gobions Wood
Queenswood Sch
Well Wood
Swanleybar Farm
GOBIONS WAY
Leggatts Wood
Nyn Park
SWANLEY BAR LA
SWANLEY CRES
ORCHARD WAY
Swanley Bar
WELL RD
Boltons Park
Royal Veterinary Coll)
HAWKSHEAD RD
Leggatts Park
Little Heath
Nyn Pond
JUDGE'S HILL
Northaw
Northaw Place
GRESLEY CT
ROSE MEAD
Little Heath Primary Sch
Northaw House
COOPERS LA
VICARAGE CL
VINEYARDS RD
B156
NORTHAW RD W
Springfield
Stud Farm
A1000 HATFIELD RD
SCHOOL RD
CRINGLE CT
THORNTON RD
FRAMPTON RD
COOPERS RD
HERONFIELD
NORMAN CT
GREEN MEADOW
HEATH RD
Sch
BROADWATER
OSBORNE RD
NEWLANDS WAY
GRANGEWOOD
CRANMER CL
WESTWOOD CL
THE MOUNT
ST MICHAELS WAY
MOUNTWAY
HEATH DR
CEDAR CL
DARKES LA
INGLEFIELD
ROSARY CT
CHURCH RD
QUAKERS LA
ANTHORNE CL
SANDRINGHAM RD
HIGHLANDS
26
27
8
7
05
6
5
04
4
3
03
2
1
02

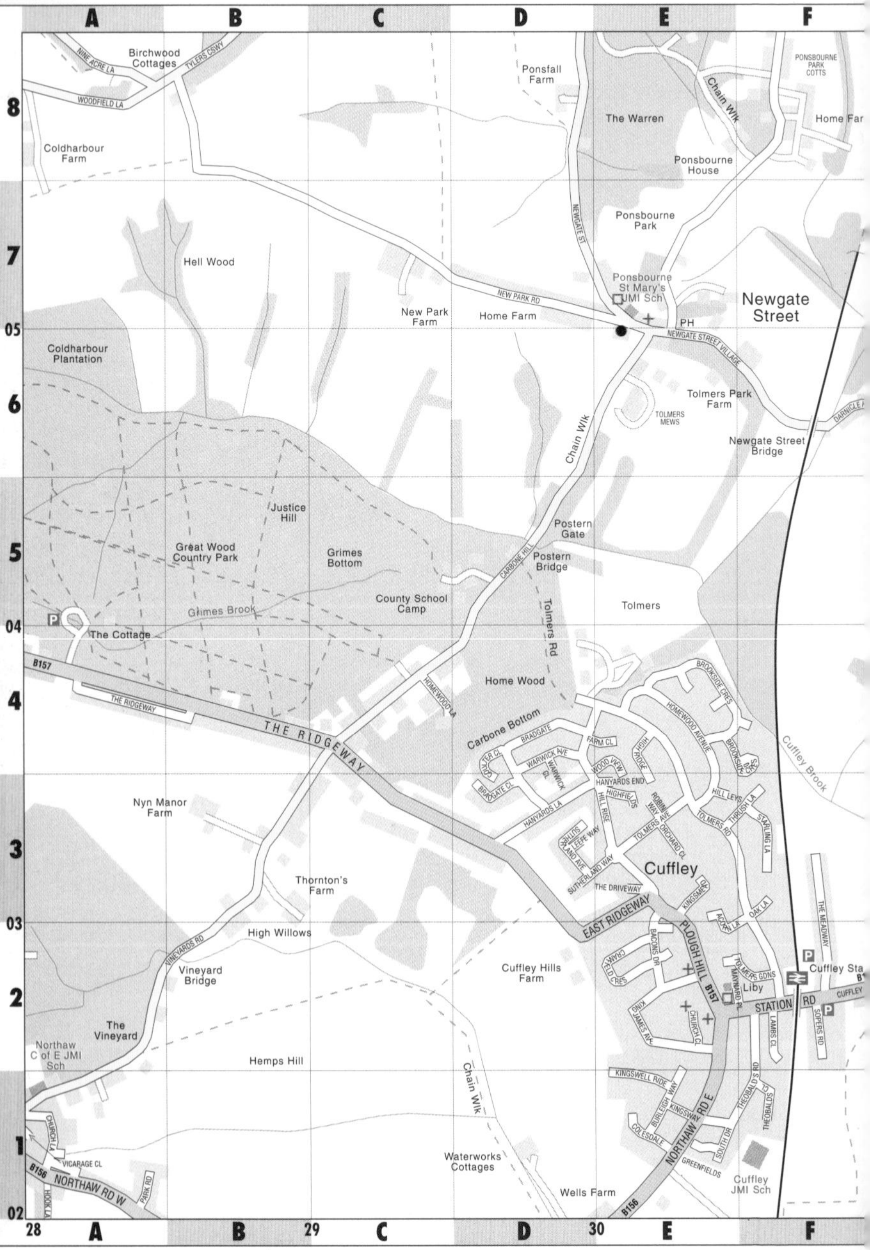
A
B
C
D
E
F
8
7
05
6
5
04
4
3
03
2
1
02
28
29
30
Birchwood Cottages
NINE ACRE LA
TYLERS CSWY
WOODFIELD LA
Coldharbour Farm
Ponsfall Farm
The Warren
Chain Wlk
PONSBOURNE PARK COTTS
Home Far
Ponsbourne House
NEWGATE ST
Ponsbourne Park
Hell Wood
Ponsbourne St Mary's JMI Sch
Newgate Street
New Park Farm
NEW PARK RD
Home Farm
PH
NEWGATE STREET VILLAGE
Coldharbour Plantation
Tolmers Park Farm
TOLMERS MEWS
DARNICLE H
Chain Wlk
Newgate Street Bridge
Justice Hill
Postern Gate
Great Wood Country Park
Grimes Bottom
Postern Bridge
CARBONE HILL
County School Camp
Tolmers
Grimes Brook
P
The Cottage
Tolmers Rd
B157
BROOKSIDE CRES
HOMEWOOD LA
Home Wood
THE RIDGEWAY
HOMEWOOD AVENUE
Carbone Bottom
BRADGATE
FARM CL
HIGH RIDGE
BROOKSIDE CRES
Cuffley Brook
WARWICK AVE
WARWICK CL
WOOD VIEW
BRADGATE CL
HANYARDS END
HIGHFIELDS
ROBIN WAY
HILL LEYS
Nyn Manor Farm
HANYARDS LA
HILL RISE
TOLMERS AVE
TOLMERS RD
THRUSH LA
STARLING LA
LEEFE WAY
ORCHARD CL
SUTHERLAND AVE
SUTHERLAND WAY
Cuffley
Thornton's Farm
THE DRIVEWAY
KINGSMEAD
THE MEADWAY
EAST RIDGEWAY
OAK LA
ACORN LA
High Willows
PLOUGH HILL
VINEYARDS RD
BACONS DR
CRANFIELD CRES
Vineyard Bridge
Cuffley Hills Farm
TOLMERS GDNS
MAYNARD PL
Cuffley Sta
Liby
STATION RD
CUFFLEY
LAMBS CL
SOPERS RD
KING JAMES AVE
CHURCH CL
The Vineyard
Northaw C of E JMI Sch
Hemps Hill
Chain Wlk
KINGSWELL RIDE
THEOBALDS RD
BURLEIGH WAY
KINGSWAY
THEOBALDS CL
CHURCH LA
COLESDALE
NORTHAW RD E
SOUTH DR
VICARAGE CL
Waterworks Cottages
GREENFIELDS
Cuffley JMI Sch
B156
NORTHAW RD W
PARK RD
HOOK LA
Wells Farm

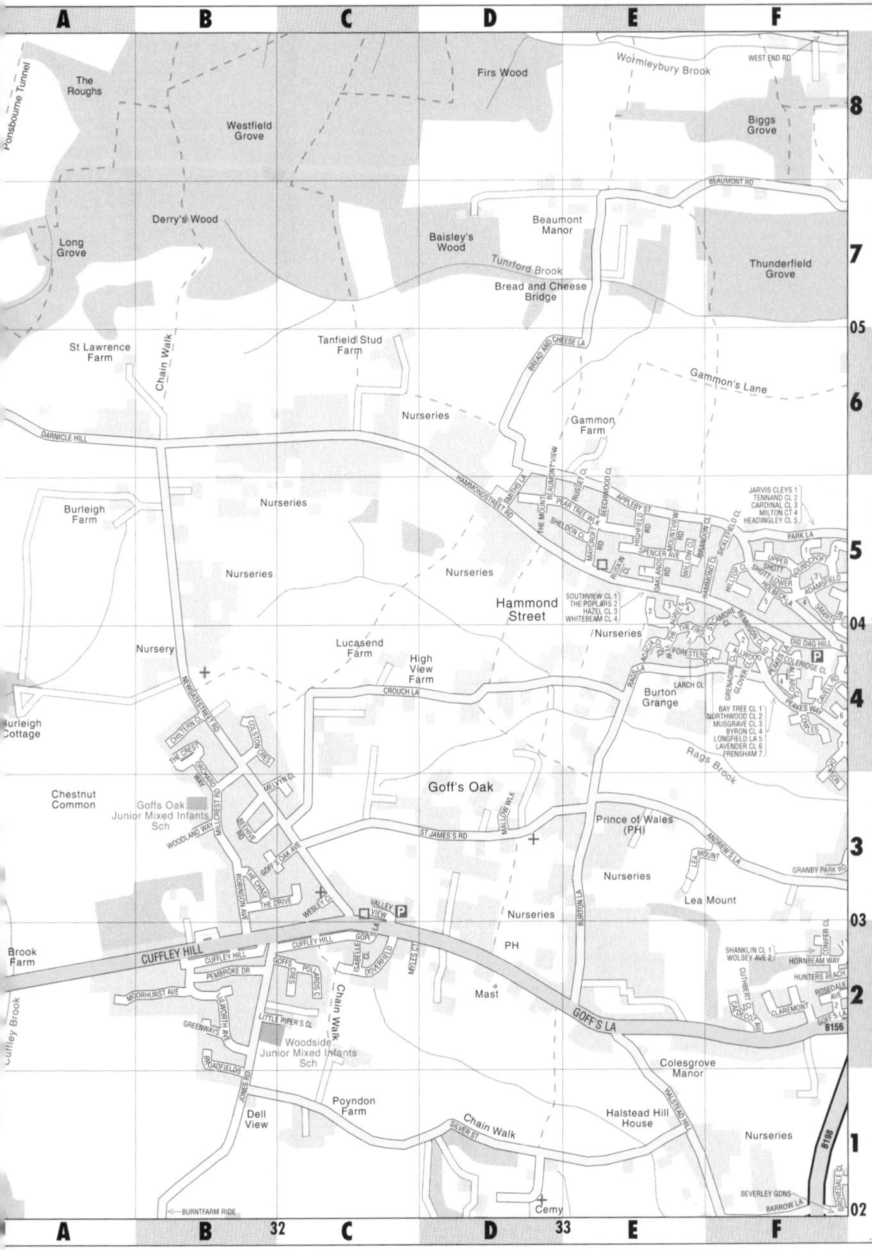

| A | B | C | D | E | F |
|---|---|---|---|---|---|

The Roughs

Pronsbourne Tunnel

Firs Wood

Wormleybury Brook

WEST END RD

Westfield Grove

Biggs Grove

**8**

BEAUMONT RD

Long Grove

Derry's Wood

Baisley's Wood

Beaumont Manor

Thunderfield Grove

**7**

Turnford Brook

BREAD AND CHEESE LA

St Lawrence Farm

Chain Walk

CARNICLE HILL

Tanfield Stud Farm

Bread and Cheese Bridge

Gammon's Lane

**05**

**6**

Nurseries

Gammon Farm

Burleigh Farm

Nurseries

HAMMONDSTREET RD

JARVIS CLEYS 1
TENNAND CL 2
CARDINAL CL 3
MILTON CT 4
HEADINGLEY CL 5

PARK LA

**5**

Nurseries

Nurseries

SHELDON CL

SPENCER AVE

Nurseries

Hammond Street

SOUTHVIEW CL 1
THE POPLARS 2
HAZEL CL 3
WHITEBEAM CL 4

BAY TREE CL 1

**04**

Nursery

Lucasend Farm

High View Farm

'Nurseries'

FORESTERS

Burton Grange

LARCH CL

BAY TREE CL 1
NORTHWOOD CL 2
MUSGRAVE CL 3
BYRON CL 4
LONGFIELD LA 5
LAVENDER CL 6
FRENSHAM 7.

**4**

Burleigh Cottage

CROUCH LA

Rags Brook

Chestnut Common

Goffs Oak Junior Mixed Infants Sch

Goff's Oak

Prince of Wales (PH)

GRANBY PARK RD

ST JAMES'S RD

ANDREWS LA

**3**

Nurseries

LEA MOUNT

Lea Mount

WOODLAND WAY

GOFFS OAK AVE

MILLCREST RD

BURTON RD

Brook Farm

Cuffley Brook

CUFFLEY HILL

CUFFLEY HILL

VALLEY

P

GOFF'S LA

SHANKLIN CL 1
WOLSEY AVE 2

HORNBEAM WAY

HUNTERS REACH

ROSEDALE AVE

**03**

PEMBROKE DR

MOORHURST AVE

Chain Walk

PH

Mast

CLAREMONT

B156

**2**

GREENWAYS

LITTLE PIPER'S CL

Woodside Junior Mixed Infants Sch

GOFFS LA

Colesgrove Manor

BEVERLEY GDNS

Dell View

BROADFIELD

Poyndon Farm

SILVER ST

Chain Walk

Halstead Hill House

HALSTEAD HILL

Nurseries

B198

**1**

BURNTFARM RIDE

Cemy

BARROW LA

**02**

| A | B | 32 | C | D | 33 | E | F |
|---|---|---|---|---|---|---|---|

147
134

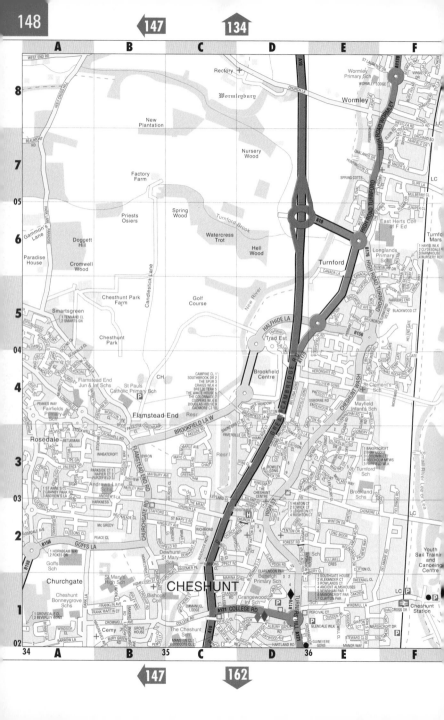
A
B
C
D
E
F
8
7
05
6
5
04
4
3
03
2
1
02
34
35
36
WEST END RD
HOLY CROSS HILL
Rectory
Wormleybury
A10
CHURCH LA
Wormley Primary Sch
Wormley
ST LAURENCE DR
A1170
WORMLEY LODGE CL
HIGH ROAD WORMLEY
New Plantation
BEAUMONT RD
Nursery Wood
Factory Farm
WESTLEA RD
ORCHARD SQ
FAIRFIELD DR
OAKLANDS GR
HUNTINGDON CL
MACER'S LA
SPRING COTTS
SLIPE LA
MULBERRY CL
JUNIPER CL
HIGH ROAD TURNFORD
PARK LANE PARADISE
Gammon's Lane
Priests Osiers
Spring Wood
Turnford Brook
Watercress Trot
Hell Wood
East Herts Coll of F Ed
Doggett Hill
Paradise House
Cromwell Wood
Turnford
CANADA LA
Longlands Primary Sch
NUNSBURY DR
1 HAYES WLK
2 CLYDESDALE
3 FARMHOUSE
4 NURSERY RD
Candlestick Lane
Chesthunt Park Farm
Golf Course
New River
Smartsgreen
1 TENNAND CL
2 SMARTS GN
FARRIERS END
BLACKWOOD CT
HALFHIDE LA
Trad Est
B156
BRICKCROFT
Chesthunt Park
Brookfield Centre
GREAT CAMBRIDGE RD
HERONGATE RD
HILLVIEW GDNS
PRESCOTT RD
OSBORNE RD
ENDEAVOUR RD
CHESHUNT WASH
St Clement's Sch
Mayfield Infant's Sch
Flamstead End Jun & Inf Schs
St Pauls Catholic Primary Sch
CH
CAMPINE CL 1
SOUTHBROOK DR 2
THE SPUR 3
CRAIGS WLK 4
BREEZE TERR 5
THE WHITE HOUSE 6
THE COLONNADE 7
COOPERS WLK 8
DOUGLAS HOUSE 9
CADMORE CT 10
PEAKES WAY
Fairfields Primary Sch
Flamstead End
Resr
BROOKFIELD LA W
Rosedale
STOCKWELL LA
CROMWELL RD
FLAMSTEAD END RD
WHEATCROFT
BYRON CT
MAYBURY AVE
Resr
1 BAKERSCROFT
2 BRAY LODGE
3 GOODWIN CT
4 BEECHOLM MEWS
5 FAIRFIELD WLK
Turnford Sch
Small River Lee or Lea
Andrews Lane Schs
1 ST ANNE'S CL
2 GRANBY PARK RD
3 ANDREW'S LA
THE CHESHUNT CENTRE
HIGH ST
1 HEATON CT
2 EDWICK CT
3 LEIGHTON CT
4 RUSHTON CT
Brookland Schs
CADMORE LA
LC
CHURCHGATE RD
CHURCH LA
Cheshunt
KINGSLEY AVE
RICHMOND CT
WINTON DR
LONG MOOR
ROSEDALE AVE
CUSSONS CL
PEACE CL
B156
GOFFS LA
1 HORNBEAM WAY
2 FOXES DR
Dewhurst St Mary Sch
FOREST RD
Youth Sail Training and Canoeing Centre
B198
Goffs Sch
ROBSONS CT
CLARENDON RD
BULLWELL CRES
Churchgate
St Mary's High Sch
CHESHUNT
Burleigh Primary Sch
1 SOUTHGATE HOUSE
2 ALEXANDER CT
3 ROWLANDS CT
4 ANCIENT ALMSHOUSES
5 NEWNHAM PAR
6 MANORCROFT PAR
7 CLAYTON PAR
Cheshunt Bonneygrove Schs
Bishops' Coll
Grangewood Inf Sch
TURNERS HILL
B176
Sch
WINDMILL LA
Cheshunt Station
FRANKLIN AVE
FRANK MARTIN CT
EMMANUEL LODGE
A121 COLLEGE RD
PERCIVAL CT
SHALCROSS DR
1 GROVEDALE CL
2 BEVERLEY GDNS
CROMWELL AVE
COLLEGE RD
Cemy
GROVE HOUSE
The Cheshunt Sch
ALBURY GROVE RD
GLENDALE WLK
MARSHCROFT DR
WINDSOR CL
BARROW LA
BURY GREEN RD
MANSTON CL 1
WOODCOTE CL 2
HARTLAND RD
GUINEVERE GDNS
STEWARD CL
MANOR WAY
A10
A121

147
162

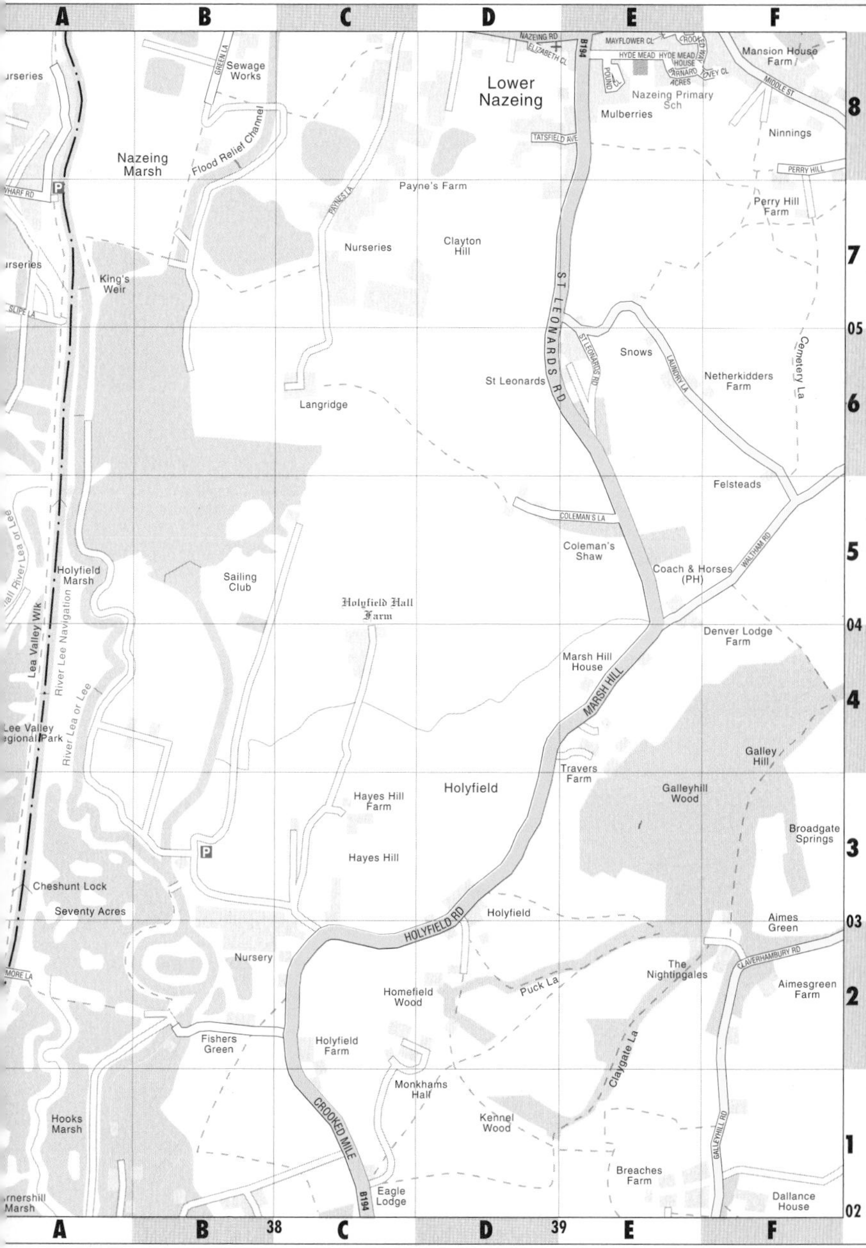

Lower Nazeing

**A** **B** **C** **D** **E** **F**

8
7
05
6
5
04
4
3
03
2
1
02

Nurseries
Nazeing Marsh
King's Weir
Nurseries
SLIPE LA
WHARF RD
GREEN LA
PRINGLE LA
Flood Relief Channel
Sewage Works

Payne's Farm
Clayton Hill
Nurseries
Langridge

St Leonards

NAZEING RD
ELIZABETH CL
MAYFLOWER CL
HYDE MEAD
POUND
Nazeing Primary Sch
Mulberries
CROOKS...
HYDE MEAD HOUSE
ORCHARD ACRES
CONEY CL
TATSFIELD AVE
Mansion House Farm
MIDDLE ST
Ninnings
PERRY HILL
Perry Hill Farm
Cemetery La

B194
ST LEONARDS RD
ST LEONARDS RD
Snows
Netherkidders Farm
FELSTEADS LA

Coleman's Shaw
Coach & Horses (PH)
Felsteads
Denver Lodge Farm
WALTHAM RD
COLEMAN'S LA

Lea Valley Wlk
River Lee Navigation
River Lea or Lee
Bill River Lea or Lee
Lee Valley Regional Park
Holyfield Marsh
Sailing Club
Holyfield Hall Farm
Marsh Hill House
MARSH HILL
Galley Hill
Broadgate Springs

Hayes Hill Farm
Holyfield
Travers Farm
Galleyhill Wood

Cheshunt Lock
Seventy Acres
Hayes Hill
MORE LA

Nursery
Homefield Wood
Holyfield
Puck La
The Nightingales
Aimes Green
Aimesgreen Farm
CLAVERHAMBURY RD
CLAYGATE LA

Fishers Green
Holyfield Farm
HOLYFIELD RD

Hooks Marsh
Monkhams Hall
Kennel Wood
Breaches Farm
GALLEY HILL RD
Dallance House

CROOKED MILE
B194
Eagle Lodge

...mershill Marsh

**A** **B** 38 **C** **D** 39 **E** **F**

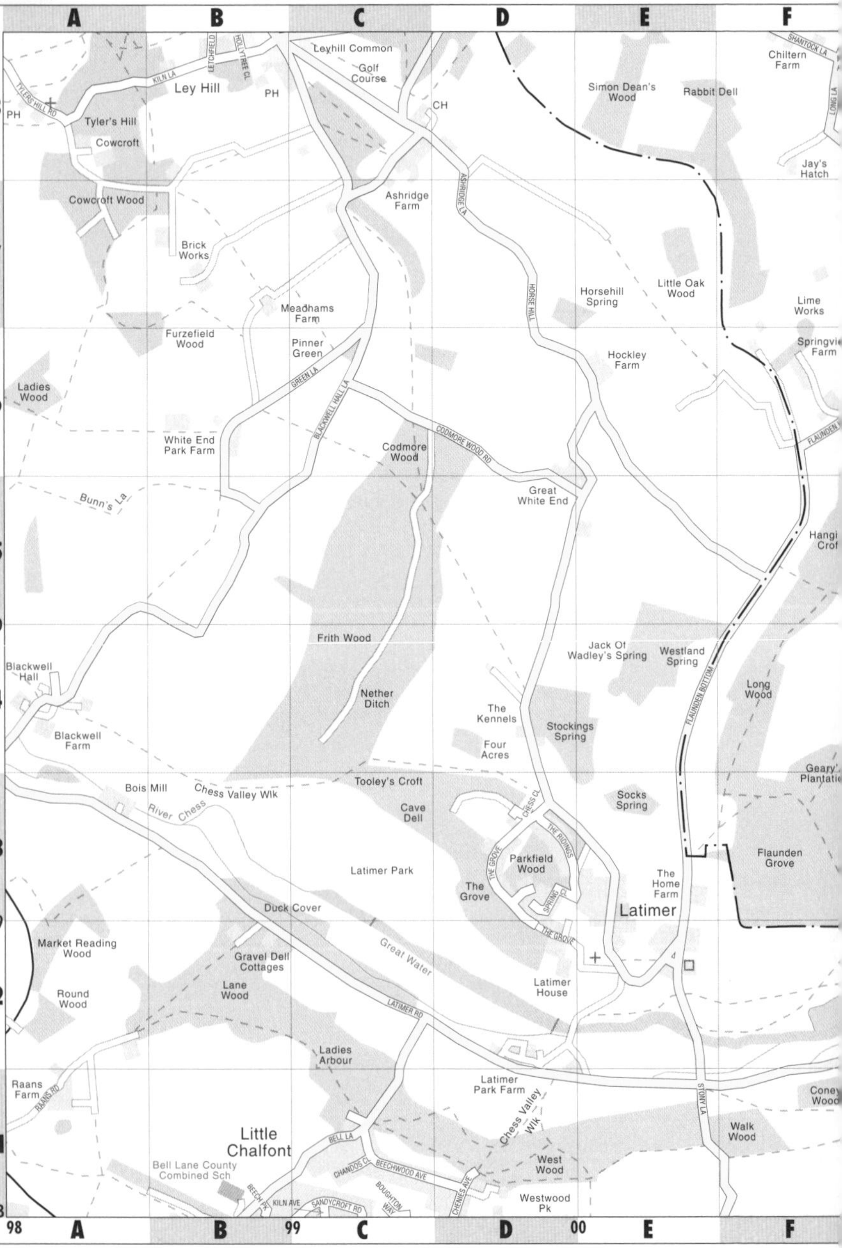

136

**A** **B** **C** **D** **E** **F**

**8**

Leyhill Common
Golf Course
Ley Hill
PH
CH
Chiltern Farm
Simon Dean's Wood
Rabbit Dell
Tyler's Hill
PH
Cowcroft
Jay's Hatch

**7**

Cowcroft Wood
Brick Works
Ashridge Farm
Horsehill Spring
Little Oak Wood
Lime Works
Springvie Farm

**01**

Meadhams Farm
Pinner Green
Furzefield Wood
Hockley Farm

**6**

Ladies Wood
White End Park Farm
GREEN LA
BLACKWELL HALL LA
Codmore Wood
CODMORE WOOD RD
Great White End
HORSE HILL
FLAUNDEN BOTTOM

**5**

Bunn's La
Hangi Crof

**00**

Frith Wood
Jack Of Wadley's Spring
Westland Spring
Long Wood

**4**

Blackwell Hall
Blackwell Farm
Nether Ditch
The Kennels
Stockings Spring
Four Acres
Geary' Plantatio

**3**

Bois Mill
River Chess
Chess Valley Wlk
Tooley's Croft
Cave Dell
Latimer Park
Socks Spring
THE GROVE
Parkfield Wood
The Grove
THE GROVE
The Home Farm
Flaunden Grove
Latimer
STONY LA

**99**

Duck Cover
Market Reading Wood
Great Water

**2**

Round Wood
Gravel Dell Cottages
Lane Wood
LATIMER RD
Latimer House

**1**

Raans Farm
RAANS RD
Ladies Arbour
BELL LA
Little Chalfont
Bell Lane County Combined Sch
CHARTRIDGE LA
BELL LA
BEECHWOOD AVE
BURTONS WY
CHENIES RD
Chess Valley Wlk
West Wood
Westwood Pk
Latimer Park Farm
Walk Wood
Coney Wood

**98**

KILN AVE
SANDYCROFT RD

**A** **B** **99** **C** **D** **00** **E** **F**

137
152

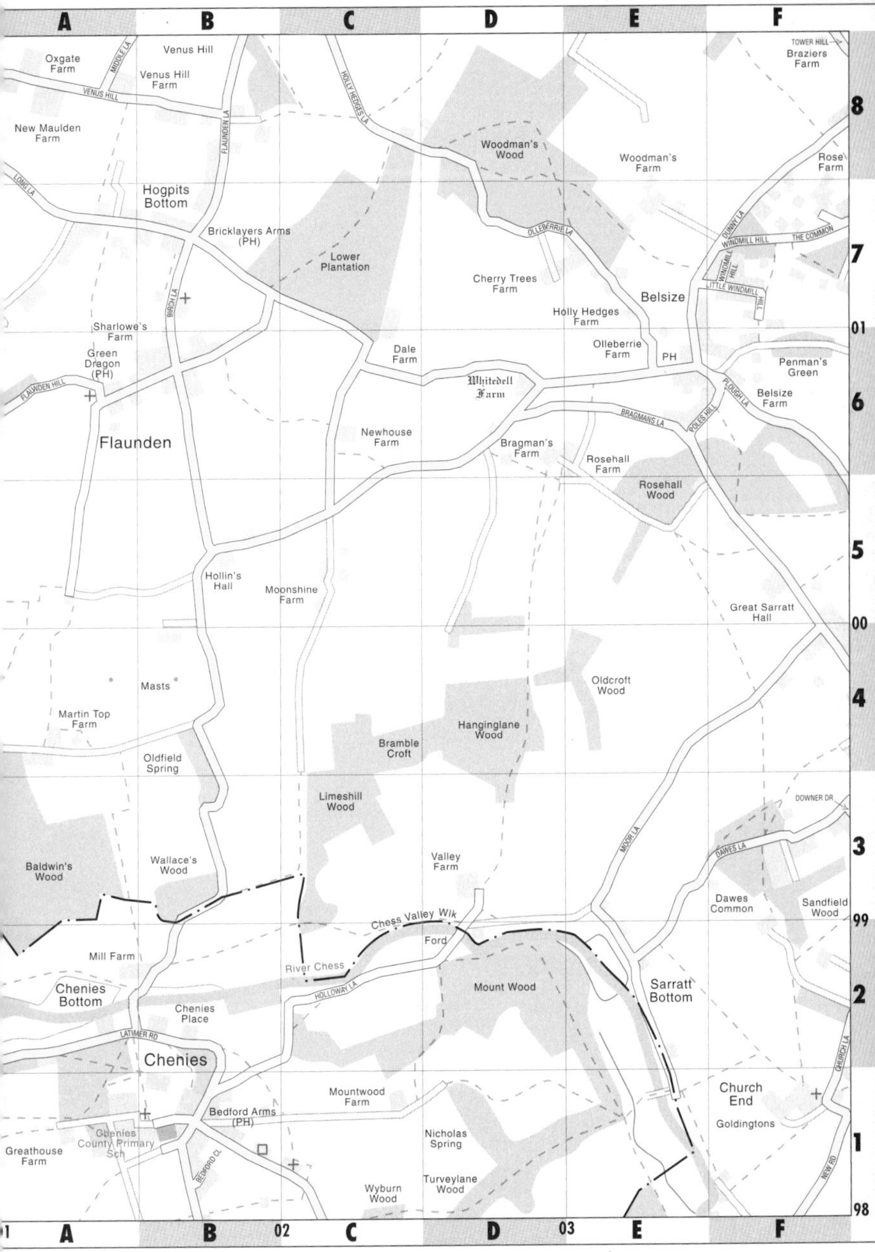
A
B
C
D
E
F
Oxgate Farm
Venus Hill
Venus Hill Farm
MIDDLE LA
VENUS HILL
New Maulden Farm
FLAUNDEN LA
HOLLY HEDGES LA
Woodman's Wood
Woodman's Farm
TOWER HILL
Braziers Farm
Rose Farm
LONG LA
Hogpits Bottom
Bricklayers Arms (PH)
Lower Plantation
OLLEBERRIE LA
Cherry Trees Farm
DUNNY LA
WINDMILL HILL
THE COMMON
WINDMILL HILL
LITTLE WINDMILL HILL
Belsize
Holly Hedges Farm
BIRCH LA
Sharlowe's Farm
Green Dragon (PH)
FLAUNDEN HILL
Dale Farm
Olleberrie Farm
PH
Penman's Green
Whitedell Farm
PLOUGH LA
Belsize Farm
POLES HILL
BRAGMANS LA
Flaunden
Newhouse Farm
Bragman's Farm
Rosehall Farm
Rosehall Wood
Hollin's Hall
Moonshine Farm
Great Sarratt Hall
Masts
Oldcroft Wood
Martin Top Farm
Hanginglane Wood
Bramble Croft
Oldfield Spring
Limeshill Wood
DOWNER DR
MOOR LA
DAWES LA
Baldwin's Wood
Wallace's Wood
Valley Farm
Dawes Common
Sandfield Wood
Chess Valley Wlk
Ford
Mill Farm
River Chess
Chenies Bottom
HOLLOWAY LA
Mount Wood
Sarratt Bottom
Chenies Place
LATIMER RD
Chenies
CHURCH LA
Church End
Mountwood Farm
Bedford Arms (PH)
Goldingtons
Chenies County Primary Sch
Nicholas Spring
Greathouse Farm
BEDFORD CL
NEW RD
Turveylane Wood
Wyburn Wood
8
7
01
6
5
00
4
3
99
2
1
98
1
02
03

164
152

151
138

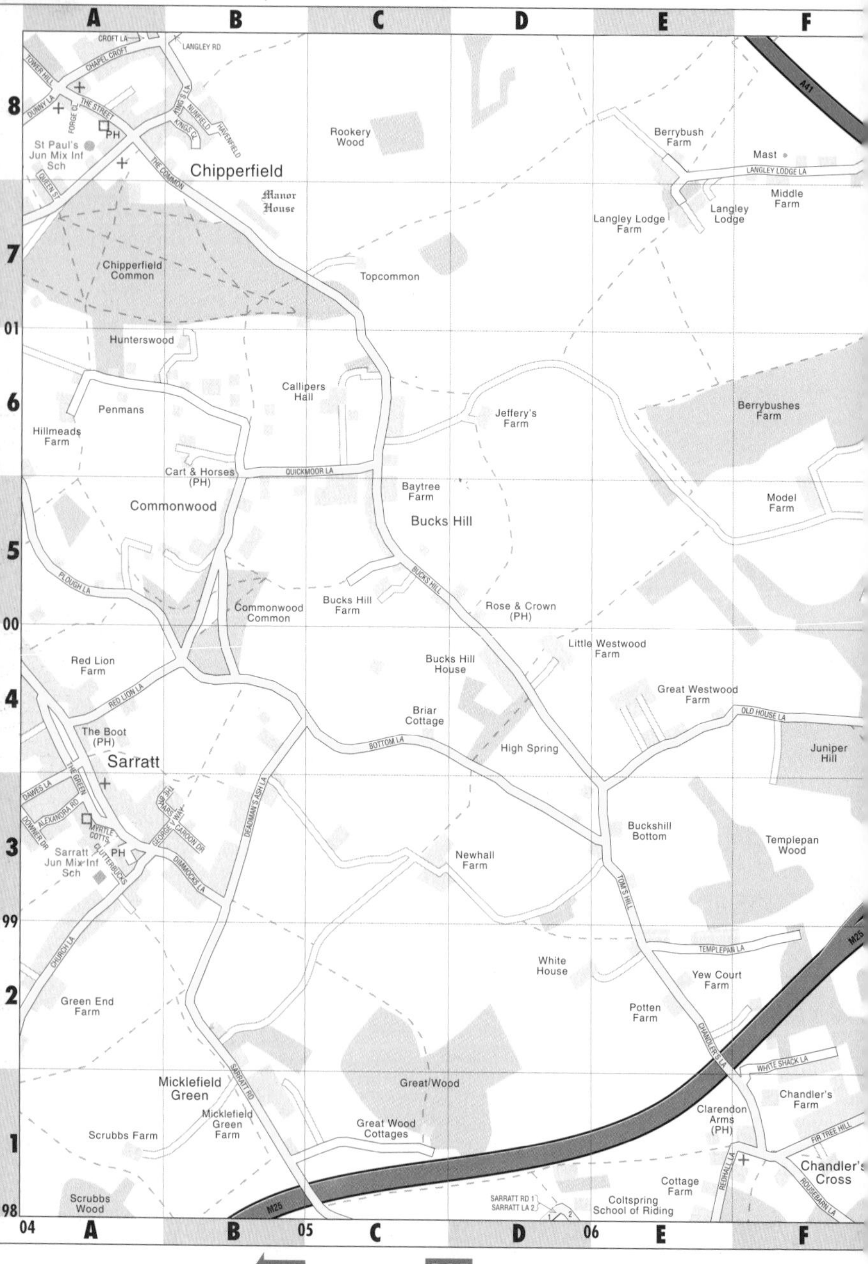
A
B
C
D
E
F
8
7
01
6
5
00
4
3
99
2
1
98
04
05
06
CROFT LA
LANGLEY RD
TOWER HILL
CHAPEL CROFT
DUNNY LA
FORGE CL
THE STREET
KING'S LA
NUNFIELD
HAVENFIELD
KINGS CL
PH
St Paul's
Jun Mix Inf
Sch
QUEEN ST
THE COMMON
Chipperfield
Manor
House
Rookery
Wood
Berrybush
Farm
Mast
LANGLEY LODGE LA
Middle
Farm
Langley
Lodge
Langley Lodge
Farm
A41
Chipperfield
Common
Topcommon
Hunterswood
Callipers
Hall
Penmans
Hillmeads
Farm
Jeffery's
Farm
Berrybushes
Farm
Cart & Horses
(PH)
QUICKMOOR LA
Baytree
Farm
Commonwood
Bucks Hill
Model
Farm
PLOUGH LA
BUCKS HILL
Bucks Hill
Farm
Commonwood
Common
Rose & Crown
(PH)
Little Westwood
Farm
Red Lion
Farm
Bucks Hill
House
Great Westwood
Farm
RED LION LA
Briar
Cottage
OLD HOUSE LA
The Boot
(PH)
BOTTOM LA
High Spring
Juniper
Hill
Sarratt
THE GREEN
DAWES LA
ALEXANDRA RD
DOWNER DR
THE BRIARS
GEORGE V WAY
CAROON DR
DEADMAN'S ASH LA
MYRTLE COTTS
Buckshill
Bottom
Templepan
Wood
Sarratt
Jun Mix Inf
Sch
PH
CLUTTERBUCKS
DIMMOCKS LA
Newhall
Farm
TOM'S HILL
CHURCH LA
TEMPLEPAN LA
M25
White
House
Yew Court
Farm
Green End
Farm
Potten
Farm
CHANDLER'S LA
WHITE SHACK LA
Micklefield
Green
SARRATT RD
Great Wood
Chandler's
Farm
Micklefield
Green
Farm
Clarendon
Arms
(PH)
Scrubbs Farm
Great Wood
Cottages
FIR TREE HILL
REDHALL LA
Chandler's
Cross
Cottage
Farm
ROUSEBARN LA
Scrubbs
Wood
M25
SARRATT RD 1
SARRATT LA 2
Coltspring
School of Riding

151
165

139
154

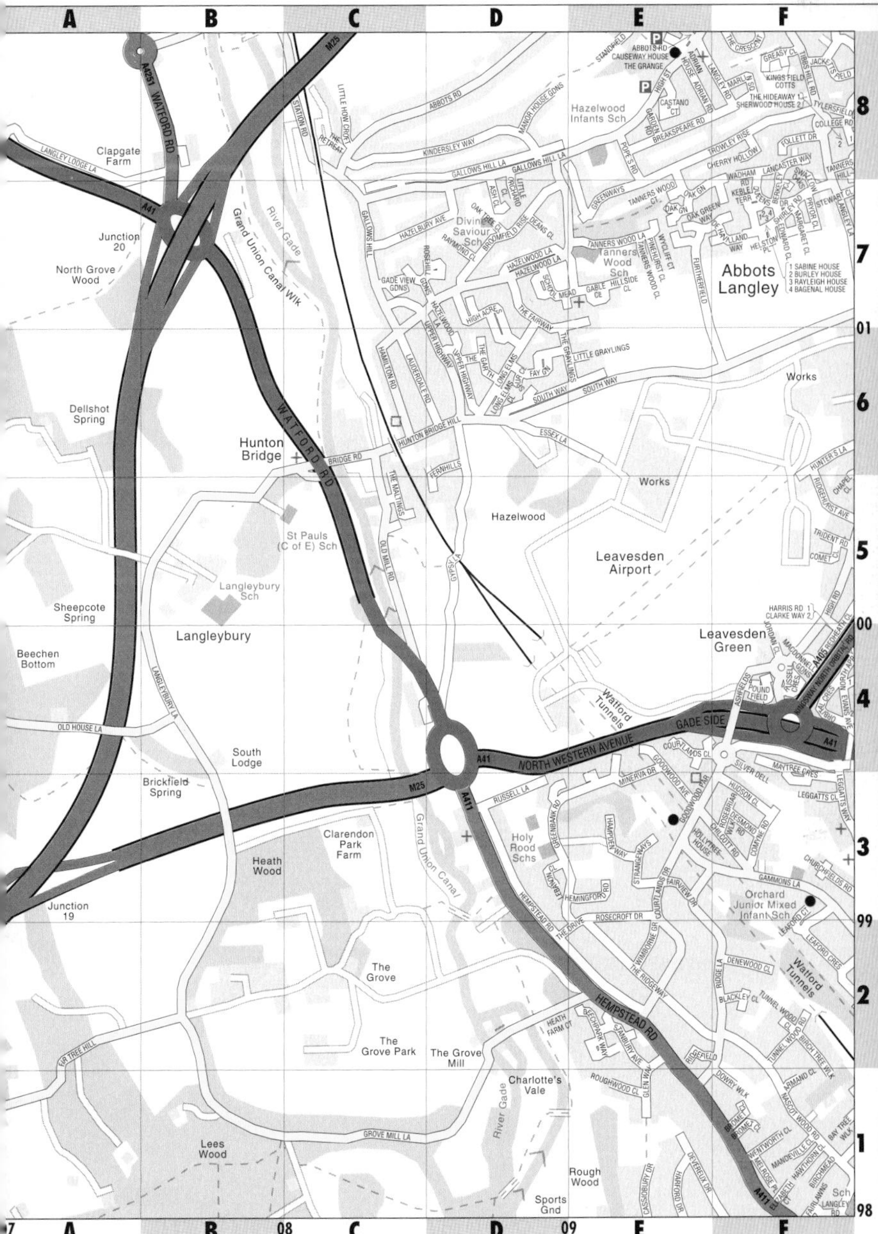
A
B
C
D
E
F
8
7
01
6
5
00
4
3
99
2
1
98
7
08
09
Clapgate Farm
Junction 20
North Grove Wood
Dellshot Spring
Hunton Bridge
St Pauls (C of E) Sch
Langleybury Sch
Sheepcote Spring
Langleybury
Beechen Bottom
South Lodge
Brickfield Spring
Clarendon Park Farm
Heath Wood
Junction 19
The Grove
The Grove Park
The Grove Mill
Charlotte's Vale
Lees Wood
Rough Wood
Sports Gnd
River Gade
Grand Union Canal Wlk
Grand Union Canal
WATFORD RD
A41
A4251
M25
A411
NORTH WESTERN AVENUE
GADE SIDE
HEMPSTEAD RD
Hazelwood Infants Sch
Divine Saviour Sch
Tanners Wood Sch
Abbots Langley
1 SABINE HOUSE
2 BURLEY HOUSE
3 RAYLEIGH HOUSE
4 BAGENAL HOUSE
Works
Hazelwood
Leavesden Airport
Leavesden Green
Watford Tunnels
Holy Rood Schs
Orchard Junior Mixed Infant Sch
Sch
LANGLEY LODGE LA
OLD HOUSE LA
LANGLEYBURY LA
FIR TREE HILL
GROVE MILL LA
BRIDGE RD
HUNTON BRIDGE HILL
ESSEX LA
SOUTH WAY
GALLOWS HILL LA
GALLOWS HILL
KINDERSLEY WAY
ABBOTS RD
STATION RD
LITTLE HOW CROFT
THE RETREAT
MANOR HOUSE GDNS
HAZELBURY AVE
HAMILTON RD
LAUDERDALE RD
UPPER HIGHWAY
THE MALTINGS
OLD MILL RD
FERNHILLS
GYPSY LA
HIGH ACRE
THE FAIRWAY
THE GARTH
LONG ELMS
LITTLE GRAYLINGS
THE GRAYLINGS
HAZELWOOD LA
TANNERS WOOD LA
TANNERS WOOD CL
FURTHERFIELD
BREAKSPEARE RD
TROWLEY RISE
CHERRY HOLLOW
LANCASTER WAY
HIGH ST
RUSSELL LA
MINERVA DR
GOODWOOD AVE
COURTLANDS DR
FAIRVIEW DR
ROSECROFT DR
THE DRIVE
THE RIDGEWAY
RIDGE LA
DENEWOOD CL
BLACKLEY CL
TUNNEL WOOD RD
TUNNEL WOOD CL
GAMMONS LA
LEAFORD CRES
SILVER DELL
MAYTREE CRES
LEGGATTS CL
LEGGATTS WAY
ROUGHWOOD CL
GLEN WAY
CASSIOBURY DR
HARFORD DR
DEVEREUX DR
DOWRY WLK
BROMET CL
WENTWORTH CL
MELROSE PL
MANDEVILLE CL
HAWTHORN CL
BIRCHMEAD
NASCOT WOOD RD
ARMAND CL
BIRCH TREE WLK
BAY TREE WLK
FAIRLAWNS
RIDGEHURST AVE
TRIDENT RD
COMET
HARRIS RD 1
CLARKE WAY 2
A405
NORTH ORBITAL RD

166
154

153
140

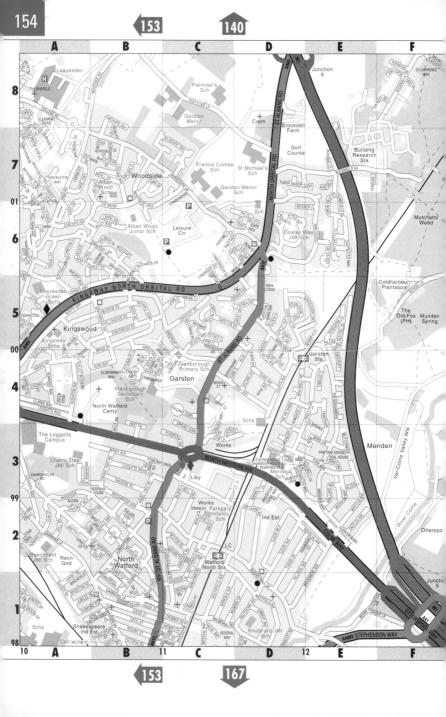
A
B
C
D
E
F
8
7
01
6
5
00
4
3
99
2
1
98
10
11
12
Leavesden
Parmiter's Sch
Garston Manor
Crem
Brookdell Farm
Golf Course
Junction 6
Building Research Sta
Francis Combe Sch
St Michael's Sch
Garston Manor Sch
Woodside
Alban Wood Sch
Alban Wood Junior Sch
Leisure Ctr
Coates Way JMI Sch
Mutchetts Wood
Coldharbour Plantation
The Old Fox (PH)
Munden Spring
Leavesden Green Schs
Kingswood
Kingsway Schs
KINGSWAY NORTH ORBITAL RD
NORTH ORBITAL RD
ST ALBANS RD
Garston Sta
Stanborough Primary Sch
Garston
Stanborough Secondary Sch
North Watford Cemy
The Leggatts Campus
Cherry Tree JMI Sch
NORTH WESTERN AVE
Liby
Works
Meriden
Meriden Sch
Ver-Colne Valley Wlk
Parkgate Infants Sch
Ind Est
River Colne
Otterspo
COLNE WAY
Beechfield JMI Sch
Recn Gnd
North Watford
Watford North Sta
Knutsford JMI Sch
Junctic 5
Shakespeare Ind Est
Schs
Coll
A4008 STEPHENSON WAY
OTTERSPOOL WAY
A405
A412
A41
M1

153
167

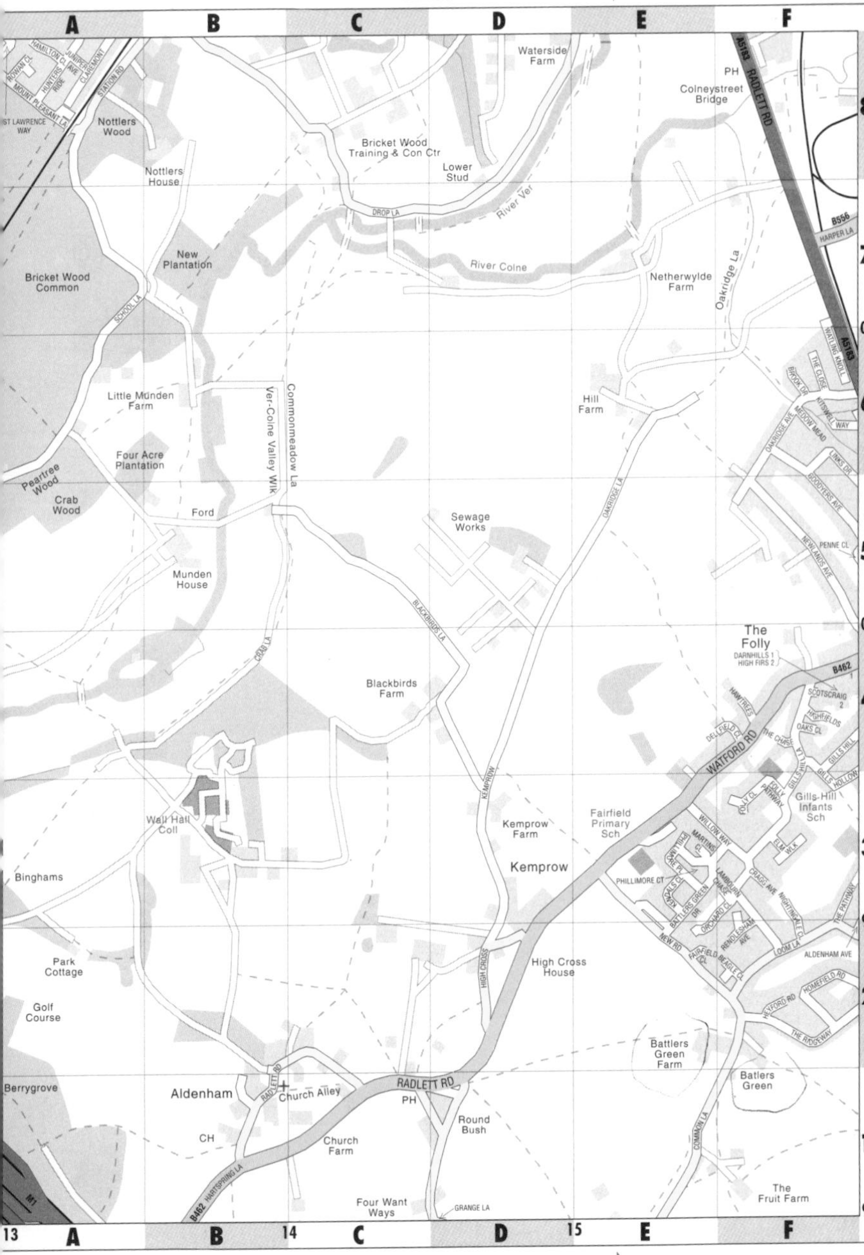
A
B
C
D
E
F
8
7
01
6
5
00
4
3
99
2
1
98
13
14
15
Waterside Farm
PH
Colneystreet Bridge
RADLETT RD
A5183
Nottlers Wood
Bricket Wood Training & Con Ctr
Lower Stud
Nottlers House
DROP LA
River Ver
B556
HARPER LA
New Plantation
River Colne
Bricket Wood Common
Netherwylde Farm
Oakridge La
SCHOOL LA
Little Munden Farm
Commonmeadow La
Ver-Colne Valley Wlk
Hill Farm
Four Acre Plantation
Peartree Wood
Crab Wood
Ford
OAKRIDGE LA
Sewage Works
Munden House
BLACKBIRDS LA
The Folly
CRAG LA
Blackbirds Farm
WATFORD RD
B462
KEMPROW
Wall Hall Coll
Fairfield Primary Sch
Gills Hill Infants Sch
Kemprow Farm
Kemprow
Binghams
PHILLIMORE CT
HIGH CROSS
High Cross House
Park Cottage
Golf Course
Battlers Green Farm
RADLETT RD
Batlers Green
Berrygrove
Aldenham
Church Alley
PH
Round Bush
CH
Church Farm
HARTSPRING LA
COMMON LA
M1
Four Want Ways
GRANGE LA
The Fruit Farm

155
142

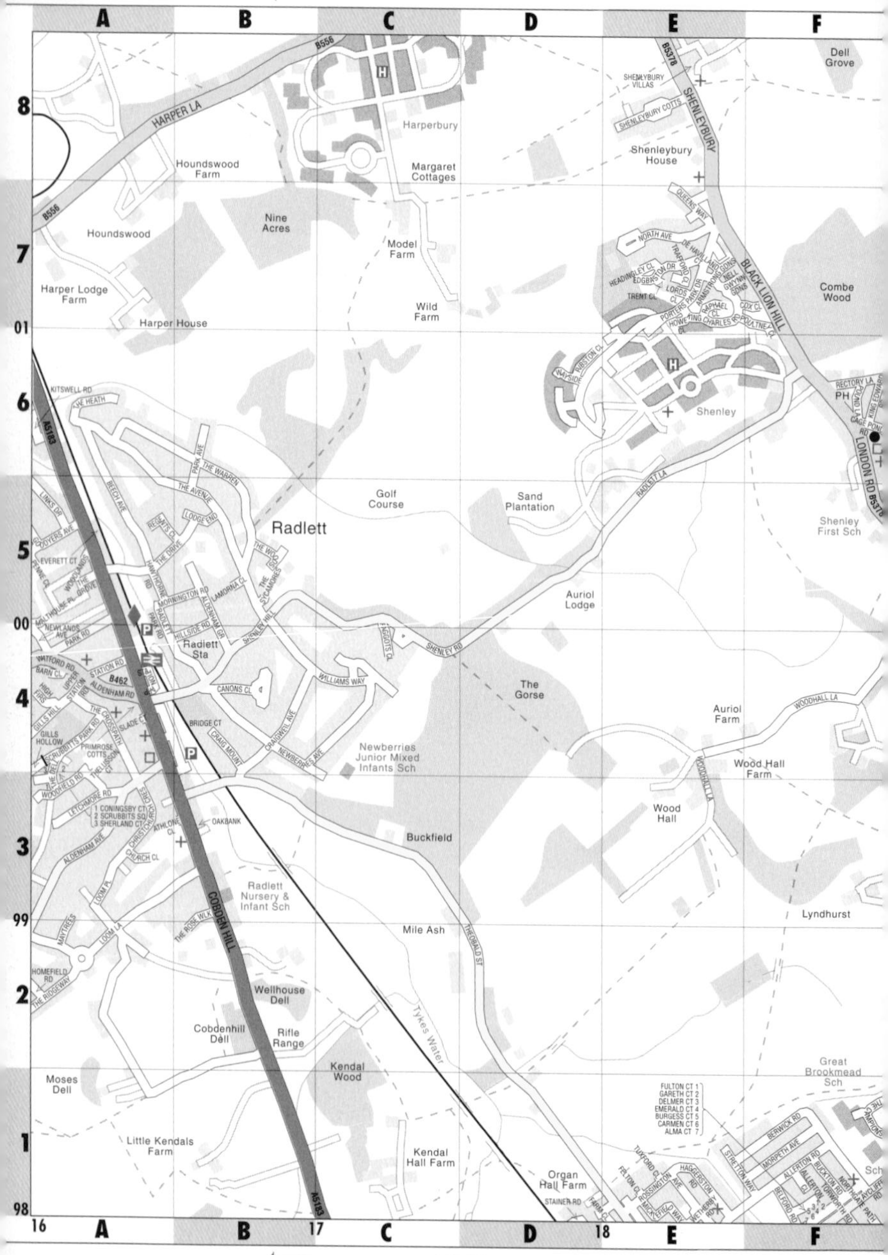
A
B
C
D
E
F
8
7
01
6
5
00
4
3
99
2
1
98
16
17
18
B556
HARPER LA
H
Harperbury
Houndswood Farm
Margaret Cottages
Nine Acres
Houndswood
Model Farm
Harper Lodge Farm
Wild Farm
Harper House
B5378
SHENLEYBURY VILLAS
SHENLEYBURY COTTS
SHENLEYBURY
Shenleybury House
Dell Grove
QUEENS WAY
NORTH AVE
BLACK LION HILL
Combe Wood
HEADINGLEY CL
EDGBASTON DR
TRENT CL
LORDS CL
PORTERS PARK DR
ARMSTRONG GDNS
RAPHAEL CL
HOWE CL
CHARLES RD
COX CL
RIBSTON CL
WAYSIDE
Shenley
PH
RECTORY LA
POUND LA
CAGE POND RD
LONDON RD
KITSWELL RD
HEATH
A5183
PARK AVE
THE WARREN
THE AVENUE
BEECH AVE
LODGE END
LINKS DR
Golf Course
Sand Plantation
RADLETT LA
Shenley First Sch
Radlett
DOYERS AVE
EVERETT CT
THE DRIVE
THE SYCAMORES
MORNINGTON RD
LAMORNA CL
ALDENHAM GR
HAWTHORNE RD
Auriol Lodge
MALTHOUSE PL
NEWLANDS AVE
PARK RD
HILLSIDE RD
SHENLEY HILL
FAGGOTS CL
SHENLEY RD
Radlett Sta
WATFORD RD
BARN CL
STATION RD
B462
ALDENHAM RD
CANONS CL
WILLIAMS WAY
The Gorse
HIGH FIRS
GILLS HILL
GILLS HOLLOW
THE CROSSPATH
SLADE CT
BRIDGE CT
CRAIG MOUNT
CRAIGWEIL AVE
NEWBERRIES AVE
Auriol Farm
WOODHALL LA
SCRUBBITTS PARK RD
PRIMROSE COTTS
Newberries Junior Mixed Infants Sch
Wood Hall Farm
WOODFIELD RD
LETCHMORE RD
1 CONINGSBY CT
2 SCRUBBITS SQ
3 SHERLAND CT
OAKBANK
Wood Hall
ALDENHAM AVE
CHRISTCHURCH CRES
ATHLONE CL
CHURCH CL
Buckfield
Radlett Nursery & Infant Sch
COBDEN HILL
LOOM PL
MAYTREES
LOOM LA
THE ROSE WLK
Mile Ash
THEOBALD ST
Lyndhurst
HOMEFIELD RD
THE RIDGEWAY
Wellhouse Dell
Tykes Water
Cobdenhill Dell
Rifle Range
Moses Dell
Kendal Wood
Great Brookmead Sch
FULTON CT 1
GARETH CT 2
DELMER CT 3
EMERALD CT 4
BURGESS CT 5
CARMEN CT 6
ALMA CT 7
BERWICK RD
MORPETH AVE
Little Kendals Farm
Kendal Hall Farm
TUXFORD CL
FELTON CL
HAGGERSTON RD
ROSSINGTON AVE
STRETTON WAY
ALLERTON RD
BUCKTON RD
Organ Hall Farm
STAINER RD
WETHERBY RD
BELFORD RD
Sch

155
169

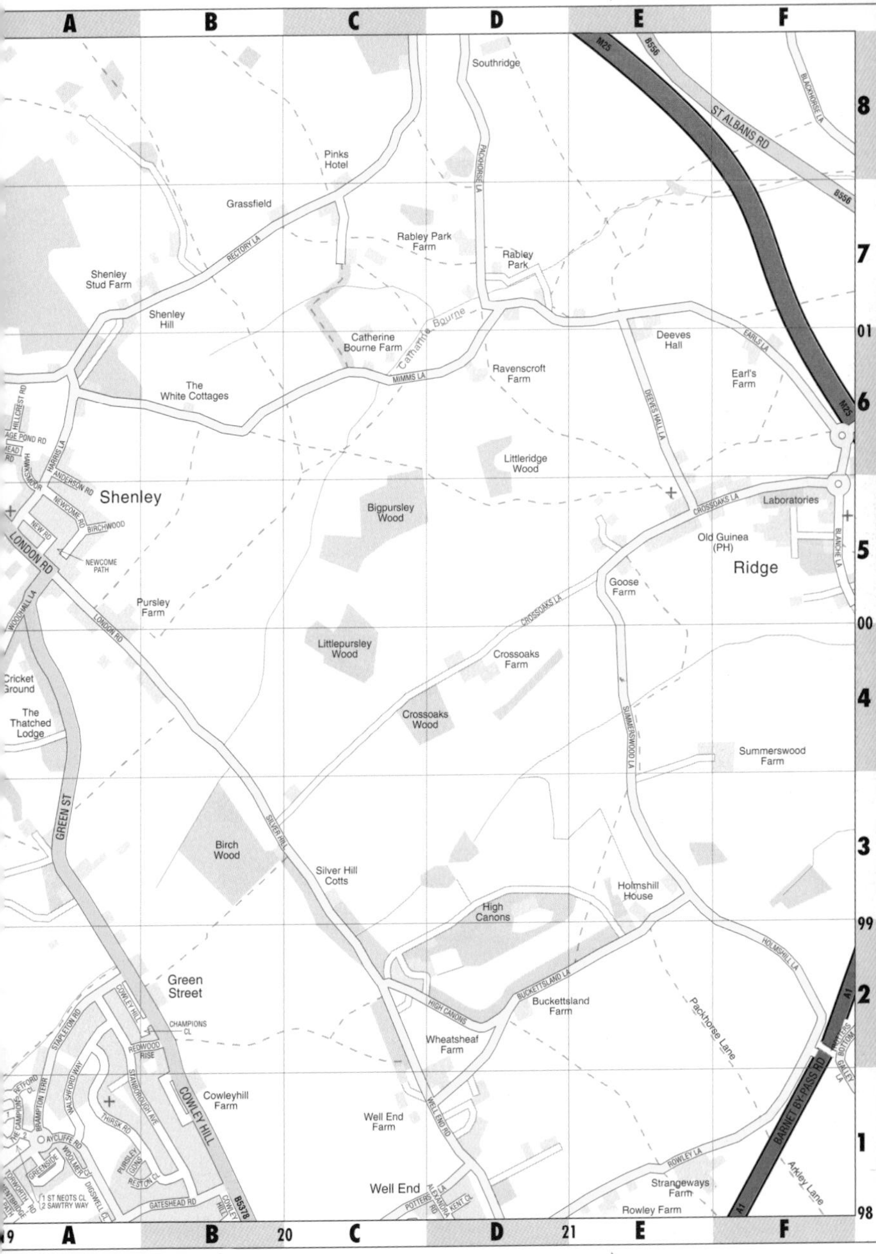
A
B
C
D
E
F
Southridge
M25
B556
ST ALBANS RD
BLACKHORSE LA
Pinks Hotel
Grassfield
RECTORY LA
PACKHORSE LA
Rabley Park Farm
Rabley Park
Shenley Stud Farm
Shenley Hill
Catherine Bourne Farm
Catharine Bourne
Deeves Hall
EARLS LA
Earl's Farm
MIMMS LA
Ravenscroft Farm
The White Cottages
HILLCREST RD
DEEVES HALL LA
POND RD
HARRIS LA
Littleridge Wood
ANDERSON RD
Shenley
NEWCOME RD
Bigpursley Wood
CROSSOAKS LA
Laboratories
BIRCHWOOD
NEW RD
Old Guinea (PH)
LONDON RD
BLANCHE LA
NEWCOME PATH
Ridge
Goose Farm
WOODHALL LA
Pursley Farm
LONDON RD
Littlepursley Wood
Crossoaks Farm
Cricket Ground
The Thatched Lodge
Crossoaks Wood
SUMMERSWOOD LA
Summerswood Farm
GREEN ST
SILVER HILL
Birch Wood
Silver Hill Cotts
Holmshill House
High Canons
HOLMSHILL LA
BUCKETTSLAND LA
A1
Green Street
COWLEY HILL
Buckettsland Farm
HIGH CANONS
CHAMPIONS CL
STAPLETON RD
Packhorse Lane
Wheatsheaf Farm
REDWOOD RISE
BARNET BY-PASS RD
GALLEY LA
WALSHFORD WAY
STANBOROUGH AVE
COWLEY HILL
Cowleyhill Farm
BRAMPTON TERR
THIRSK RD
Well End Farm
WELL END RD
AYCLIFFE RD
WOOLMER
GREENSIDE
PURSLEY GDNS
RESTON CL
ROWLEY LA
Arkley Lane
DIGSWELL CL
Strangeways Farm
1 ST NEOTS CL
2 SAWTRY WAY
GATESHEAD RD
B5378
Well End
POTTERS LA
ALEXANDRA RD
KENT CL
Rowley Farm
8
7
01
6
5
00
4
3
99
2
1
98
19
20
21

157
144

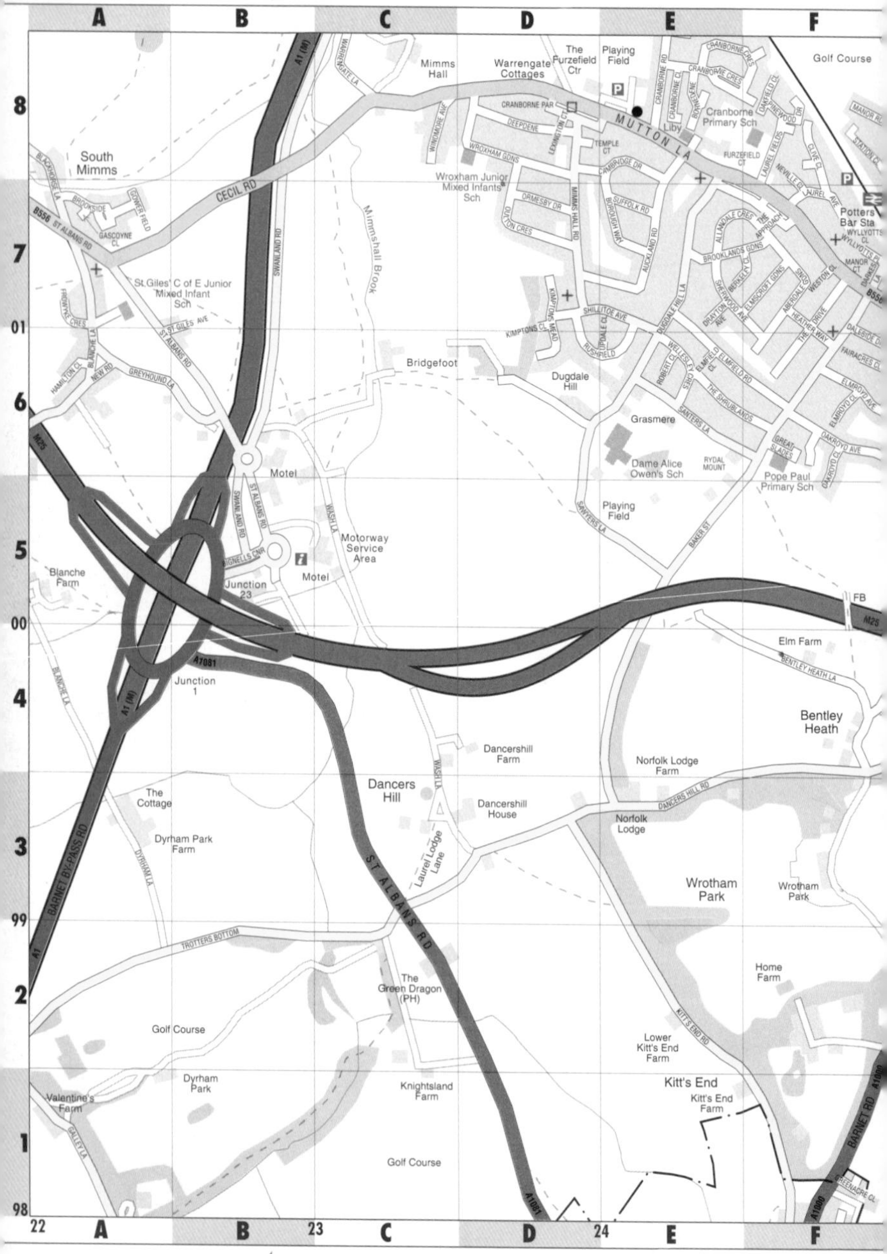
A
B
C
D
E
F
8
7
01
6
5
00
4
3
99
2
1
98
22
23
24
South Mimms
A1(M)
CECIL RD
B556 ST ALBANS RD
BLACKHORSE LA
BROOKSIDE
GOWER FIELD
GASCOYNE CL
St.Giles' C of E Junior Mixed Infant Sch
ST GILES' AVE
ST ALBANS RD
FROWYKE CRES
BLANCHE LA
HAMILTON CL
NEW RD
GREYHOUND LA
SWANLAND RD
WARRENGATE LA
Mimms Hall
Warrengate Cottages
The Furzefield Ctr
Playing Field
MUTTON LA
CRANBORNE PAR
DEEPDENE
WINDMORE AVE
WROXHAM GDNS
LEXINGTON CT
TEMPLE CT
Wroxham Junior Mixed Infants Sch
ORMESBY DR
OULTON CRES
MIMMS HALL RD
CAMBRIDGE DR
SUFFOLK RD
BOROUGH WAY
AUCKLAND RD
CRANBORNE RD
CRANBORNE CRES
CRANBORNE CL
BORWEZENE
Liby
Cranborne Primary Sch
FURZEFIELD CT
LAUREL FIELDS
OAKFIELD CL
PINEWOOD DR
NEVILLE CL
CLIVE CL
LAUREL AVE
MANOR RD
STATION CL
Golf Course
Potters Bar Sta
WYLLYOTTS CL
WYLLYOTTS PL
MANOR CT
DARKES LA
B556
ALLANDALE CRES
THE APPROACH
BROOKLANDS GDNS
SHERWOOD AVE
BERKELEY CL
ELMSCROFT GDNS
DRAYTON AVE
ABERDALE GDNS
WESTON CL
HEATHER WAY
THE DRIVE
DALESIDE DR
FAIRACRES CL
ELMROYD AVE
ELMROYD CL
OAKROYD AVE
OAKROYD CL
Mimmshall Brook
KIMPTONS MEAD
KIMPTONS CL
SHILLITOE AVE
DUGDALE CL
RUSHFIELD
DUGDALE HILL LA
Bridgefoot
Dugdale Hill
ROBERT CL
WELLESLEY CRES
ELMFIELD CL
ELMFIELD RD
THE SHRUBLANDS
SANTERS LA
Grasmere
GREAT SLADES
Dame Alice Owen's Sch
RYDAL MOUNT
Pope Paul Primary Sch
M25
Motel
ST ALBANS RD
SWANLAND RD
WASH LA
Motorway Service Area
SAWYERS LA
Playing Field
BAKER ST
BIGNELLS CNR
Junction 23
Blanche Farm
FB
Elm Farm
BENTLEY HEATH LA
A1081
Junction 1
BLANCHE LA
Bentley Heath
Dancershill Farm
Norfolk Lodge Farm
Dancers Hill
DANCERS HILL RD
Dancershill House
Norfolk Lodge
The Cottage
Dyrham Park Farm
DYRHAM LA
Laurel Lodge Lane
Wrotham Park
Wrotham Park
BARNET BY-PASS RD
TROTTERS BOTTOM
Home Farm
The Green Dragon (PH)
Golf Course
KITT'S END RD
Lower Kitt's End Farm
Dyrham Park
Knightsland Farm
Kitt's End
Kitt's End Farm
Valentine's Farm
GALLEY LA
Golf Course
BARNET RD A1000
GREENACRE CL
A1000

157
171

145
160

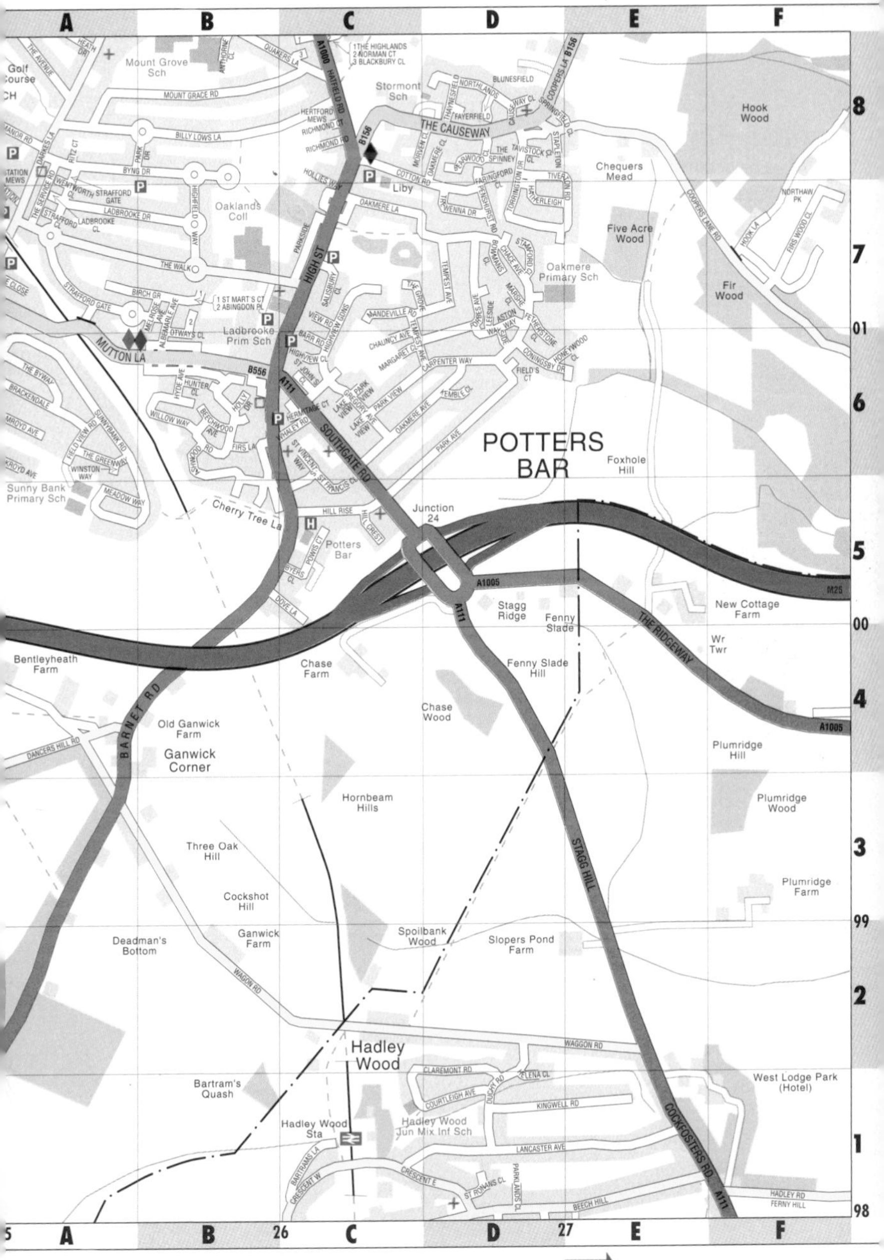
A
B
C
D
E
F
Golf Course
Mount Grove Sch
Stormont Sch
Hook Wood
Chequers Mead
Liby
Oaklands Coll
Five Acre Wood
Oakmere Primary Sch
Fir Wood
Ladbrooke Prim Sch
POTTERS BAR
Foxhole Hill
Sunny Bank Primary Sch
Junction 24
Potters Bar
Cherry Tree La
Stagg Ridge
Fenny Slade
New Cottage Farm
Wr Twr
Bentleyheath Farm
Chase Farm
Fenny Slade Hill
Chase Wood
Old Ganwick Farm
Ganwick Corner
Plumridge Hill
Hornbeam Hills
Plumridge Wood
Three Oak Hill
Cockshot Hill
Plumridge Farm
Deadman's Bottom
Ganwick Farm
Spoilbank Wood
Slopers Pond Farm
Hadley Wood
Bartram's Quash
West Lodge Park (Hotel)
Hadley Wood Sta
Hadley Wood Jun Mix Inf Sch
HIGH ST
HATFIELD RD
A1000
B156
THE CAUSEWAY
COOPERS LA
MUTTON LA
B556
A111
SOUTHGATE RD
M25
A1005
THE RIDGEWAY
BARNET RD
DANCERS HILL RD
WAGON RD
WAGGON RD
STAGG HILL
COCKFOSTERS RD
HADLEY RD
FERNY HILL
CLAREMONT RD
COURTLEIGH AVE
KINGWELL RD
LANCASTER AVE
CRESCENT E
CRESCENT W
BEECH HILL
PARKLANDS CL
ST RONANS CL
DUCHY RD
ELENA CL
BARTRAMS LA
MOUNT GRACE RD
BILLY LOWS LA
BYNG DR
LADBROOKE DR
THE WALK
BIRCH GR
STRAFFORD GATE
MELROSE AVE
ALBEMARLE AVE
OTWAYS CL
1 ST MART'S CT
2 ABINGDON PL
1 THE HIGHLANDS
2 NORMAN CT
3 BLACKBURY CL
QUAKERS LA
ANTHORNE CL
HERTFORD MEWS
RICHMOND CT
RICHMOND RD
HOLLIES WAY
COTTON RD
OAKMERE LA
BLUNESFIELD
NORTHLANDS
FAYERFIELD
TAVISTOCK CL
TIVERTON RD
HATHERLEIGH
TORRINGTON DR
PENSHURST RD
FARINGFORD CL
TREWENNA DR
TEMPEST AVE
THE GROVE
MANDEVILLE RD
CHAUNCY AVE
MARGARET CL
CARPENTER WAY
ASTON WAY
FETHERSTONE CL
CONINGSBY DR
HONEYWOOD CL
FIELD'S CT
STAMFORD CL
CHACE AVE
MARSHE CL
LEESIDE
FORRES AVE
BOWMANS CL
SALISBURY CL
VIEW RD
HIGHVIEW GDNS
BARR RD
HIGHVIEW CL
ST JOHN'S CT
HERMITAGE CT
WHALEY RD
LAKE VIEW
PARK VIEW
GREGORY VIEW
OAKMERE AVE
PARK AVE
EMBLE CL
ST VINCENT WAY
ST FRANCIS CL
HILL RISE
HILL CREST
POWIS CT
BYERS CL
DOVE LA
HYDE AVE
HUNTER CL
HOLLY DR
WILLOW WAY
BEECHWOOD AVE
FIRS LA
ASHWOOD RD
THE BYWAY
BRACKENDALE
SUNNYBANK RD
FIELD VIEW RD
THE GREENWAY
WINSTON WAY
MEADOW WAY
PARKSIDE
COOPERS LANE RD
NORTHAW PK
HOOK LA
FIRS WOOD CL
SPRINGFIELD CL
STAPLETON CL
CAUSEWAY CL
THE SPINNEY
BARWOOD CL
MORVEN CL
OAKMERE CL
THAYNESFIELD
HEATH DR
THE AVENUE
PARK DR
HIGHFIELD WAY
RITZ CT
DARKES LA
THE SERVICE RD
WENTWORTH CL
STRAFFORD CL
LADBROOKE CL
STATION MEWS
8
7
01
6
5
00
4
3
99
2
1
98
26
27

160

159
146

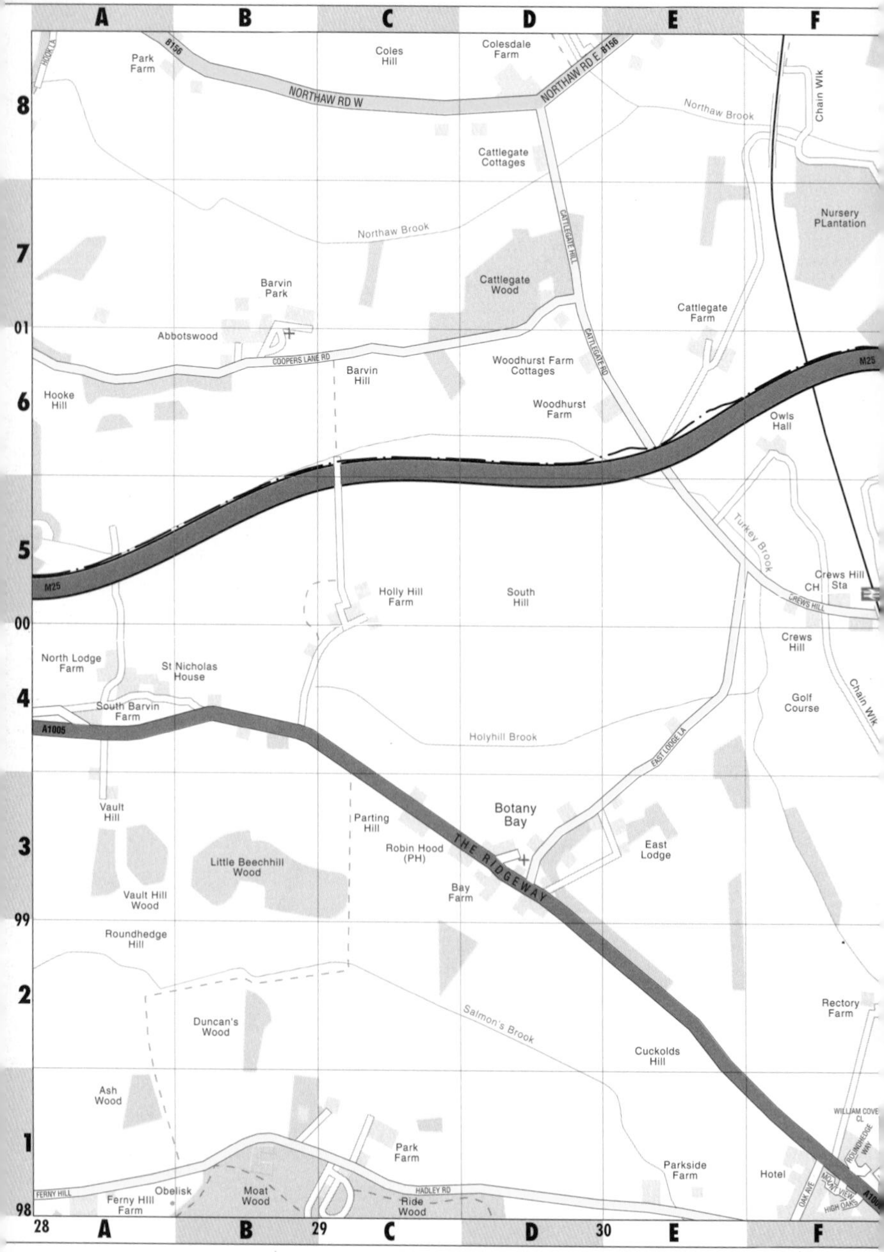
A
B
C
D
E
F
8
7
01
6
5
00
4
3
99
2
1
98
28
29
30
HOOK LA
Park Farm
B156
NORTHAW RD W
Coles Hill
Colesdale Farm
NORTHAW RD E
B156
Chain Wlk
Northaw Brook
Cattlegate Cottages
Northaw Brook
CATTLEGATE HILL
Nursery PLantation
Barvin Park
Cattlegate Wood
Cattlegate Farm
Abbotswood
COOPERS LANE RD
Barvin Hill
Woodhurst Farm Cottages
CATTLEGATE RD
M25
Hooke Hill
Woodhurst Farm
Owls Hall
Turkey Brook
M25
Holly Hill Farm
South Hill
Crews Hill Sta
CH
CREWS HILL
North Lodge Farm
St Nicholas House
Crews Hill
South Barvin Farm
Chain Wlk
Golf Course
A1005
Holyhill Brook
EAST LODGE LA
Vault Hill
Botany Bay
Parting Hill
Robin Hood (PH)
THE RIDGEWAY
East Lodge
Little Beechhill Wood
Bay Farm
Vault Hill Wood
Roundhedge Hill
Rectory Farm
Duncan's Wood
Salmon's Brook
Cuckolds Hill
Ash Wood
WILLIAM COVE CL
ROUNDHEDGE WAY
Park Farm
Parkside Farm
Hotel
FERNY HILL
Obelisk
Ferny HIll Farm
Moat Wood
HADLEY RD
Ride Wood
OAK AVE
MOUNT VIEW
HIGH OAKS

159

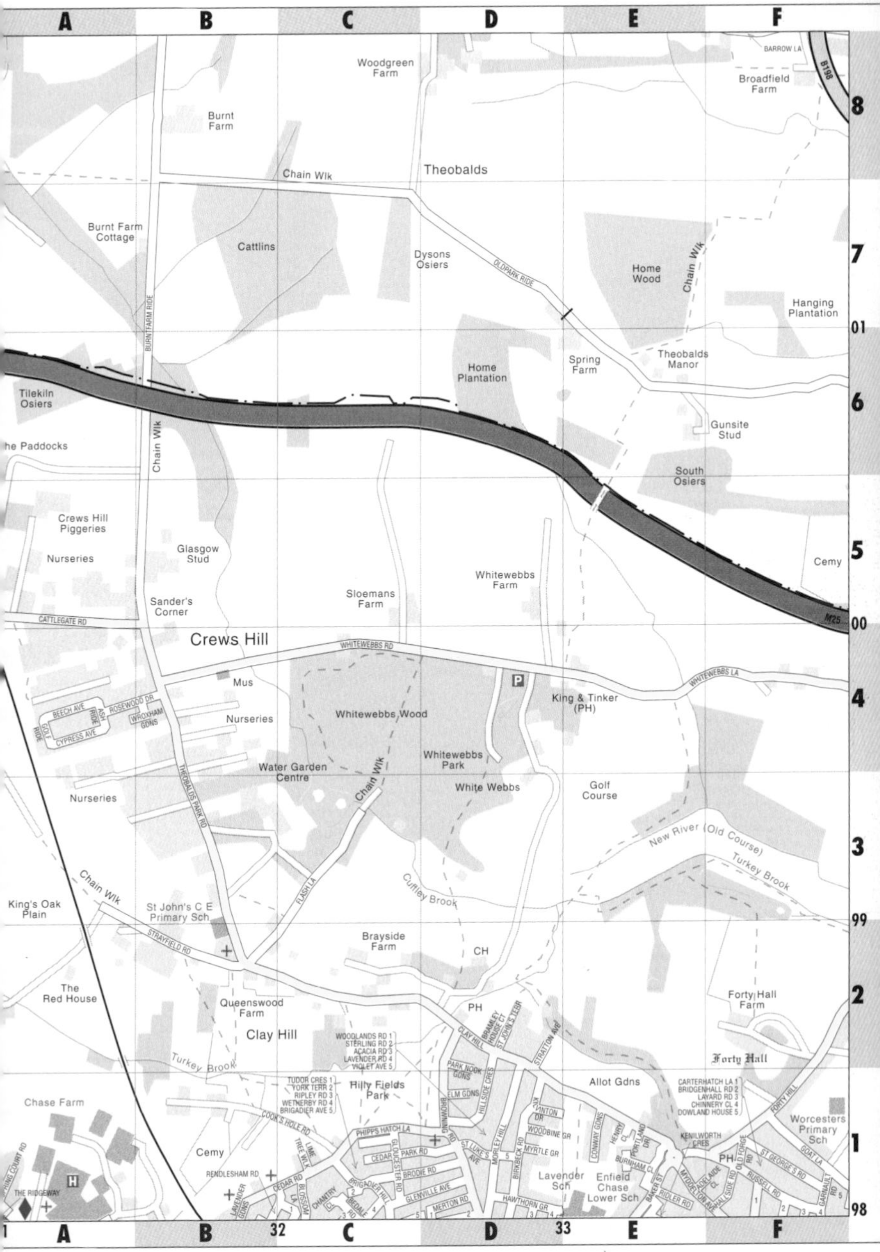

A    B    C    D    E    F

BARROW LA
B198

Woodgreen
Farm

Broadfield
Farm

8

Burnt
Farm

Theobalds

Chain Wlk

7

Burnt Farm
Cottage

Cattlins

Dysons
Osiers

OLD PARK RIDE

Home
Wood

Chain Wlk

Hanging
Plantation

01

Spring
Farm

Theobalds
Manor

Home
Plantation

Tilekiln
Osiers

6

Gunsite
Stud

he Paddocks

Chain Wlk

South
Osiers

M25

Crews Hill
Piggeries

Glasgow
Stud

Whitewebbs
Farm

Cemy

5

Nurseries

Sloemans
Farm

Sander's
Corner

CATTLEGATE RD

00

Crews Hill

WHITEWEBBS RD

4

Mus

Nurseries

Whitewebbs Wood

P

King & Tinker
(PH)

WHITEWEBBS LA

BEECH AVE
CYPRESS AVE
ROSEWOOD DR
BIRCHAM GDNS

Water Garden
Centre

Chain Wlk

Whitewebbs
Park

White Webbs

Golf
Course

Nurseries

New River (Old Course)

Turkey Brook

3

THEOBALDS PARK RD

FLASH LA

Culley Brook

King's Oak
Plain

Chain Wlk

St John's C E
Primary Sch

Brayside
Farm

CH

99

STRAYFIELD RD

The
Red House

Queenswood
Farm

PH

Forty Hall
Farm

2

Clay Hill

Turkey Brook

WOODLANDS RD 1
STERLING RD 2
ACACIA RD 3
LAVENDER RD 4
VIOLET AVE 5

Hilly Fields
Park

CLAY HILL

PARK AVE
STRETTON AVE

Allot Gdns

Forty Hall

CARTERHATCH LA 1
BRIDGENHALL RD 2
LAYARD RD 3
CHINNERY CL 4
DOWLAND HOUSE 5

Worcesters
Primary
Sch

Chase Farm

TUDOR CRES 1
YORK TERR 2
RIPLEY RD 3
WETHERBY RD 4
BRIGADIER AVE 5

ELM GDNS

FENTON AVE

Enfield
Chase
Lower Sch

KENILWORTH
CRES

PH

1

RINGWOOD RD

THE RIDGEWAY

H

Cemy

PHIPPS HATCH LA

RENDLESHAM RD

CEDAR RD

PARK RD

BROOKE AVE

SLEVILLE AVE

MERTON RD

HAWTHORN RD

MYRTLE GR

WOODBINE GR

Lavender
Sch

CONWAY GDNS

ST GEORGE'S RD

FORTY RD

98

A    B    32    C    D    33    E    F

161
148

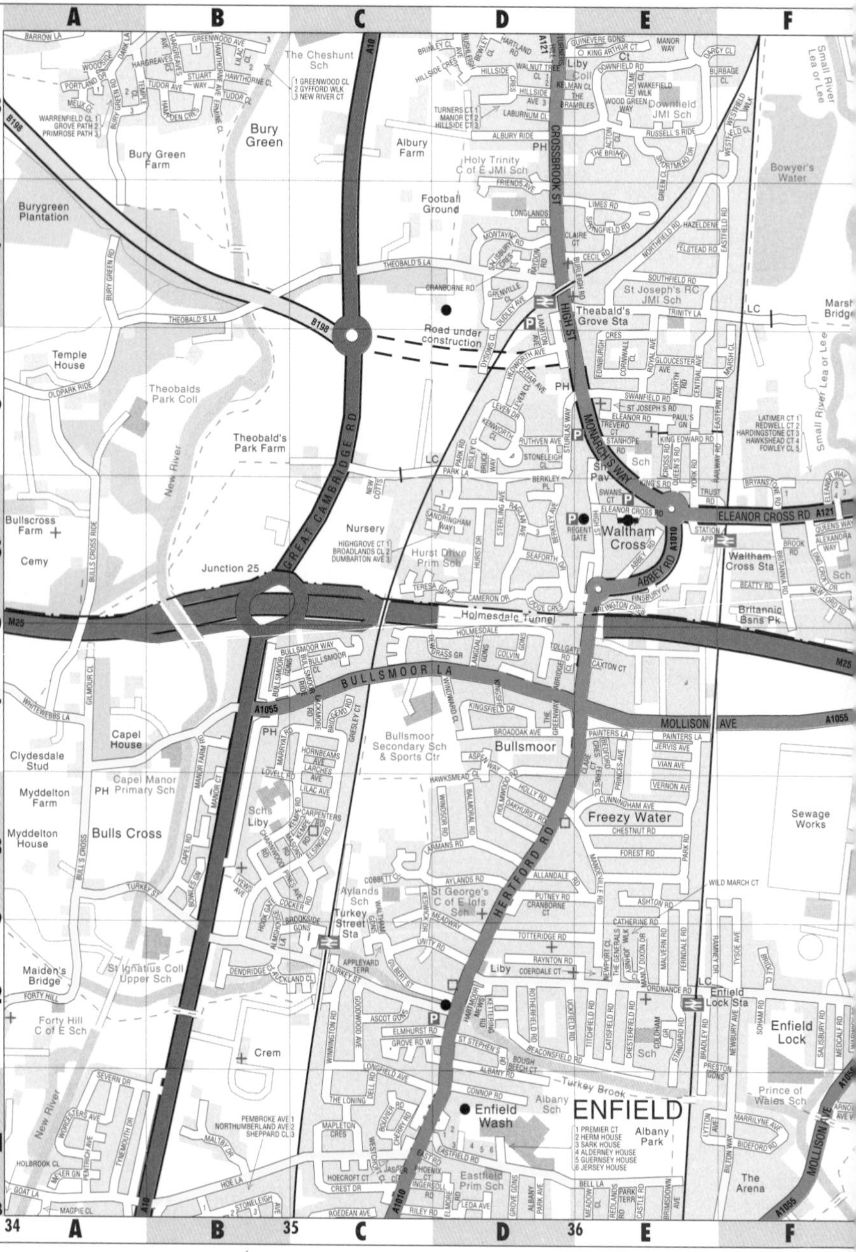
A
B
C
D
E
F
8
7
01
6
5
00
4
3
99
2
1
98
34
35
36
BARROW LA
GREENWOOD AVE
HARGREAVES AVE
HARGREAVES CL
STUART WAY
HAWTHORNE CL
TUDOR AVE
TUDOR CL
PORTLAND DR
WOODSIDE
OAK LA
MEUX CL
WARRENFIELD CL 1
GROVE PATH 2
PRIMROSE PATH 3
BURY GREEN RD
HAYDEN CRES
The Cheshunt Sch
1 GREENWOOD CL
2 GYFFORD WLK
3 NEW RIVER CT
Bury Green
Bury Green Farm
Burygreen Plantation
B198
BRINLEY CL
HARTLAND RD
HILLSIDE CRES
HILLSIDE
WALNUT TREE CL
HILLSIDE AVE
THE BRAMBLES
TURNERS CT 1
MANOR CT 2
HILLSIDE CT 3
LABURNUM CL
ALBURY RIDE
Albury Farm
Holy Trinity C of E JMI Sch
FRIENDS AVE
Football Ground
LONGLANDS CL
MONTAYNE RD
SALISBURY CRES
CLAIRE CT
CECIL RD
THEOBALD'S LA
CRANBORNE RD
GRENVILLE CL
DUDLEY AVE
Road under construction
DYSONS CL
HEDWORTH AVE
CEDAR AVE
LEVEN CL
KENWORTH CL
RUTHVEN AVE
STONELEIGH CL
PARK LA
BERKLEY PL
A121
GUINEVERE GDNS
KING ARTHUR CT
MANOR WAY
DARCY CL
Liby
Coll
KELMAN CL
DOWNFIELD RD
WAKEFIELD WLK
WOOD GREEN WAY
Downfield JMI Sch
RUSSELL'S RIDE
BURBAGE CL
THE BRIARS
PH
CROSSBROOK ST
LIMES RD
SPRINGFIELD RD
NORTHFIELD RD
HAZELDENE
FELSTEAD RD
SOUTHFIELD RD
St Joseph's RC JMI Sch
Theobald's Grove Sta
HIGH ST
TRINITY LA
LC
GLOUCESTER RD
SWANFIELD RD
ST JOSEPH'S RD
ELEANOR RD
TREVERO CT
STANHOPE RD
KING EDWARD RD
MONARCH'S WAY
Sch
Pav
KING'S RD
TRUST RD
ELEANOR CROSS RD
REGENT GATE
Waltham Cross
ABBEY RD
A1010
STATION APP
Waltham Cross Sta
FINSBURY CT
ARLINGTON CRES
Small River Lea or Lee
Bowyer's Water
Marsh Bridge
LATIMER CT 1
REDWELL CT 2
HARDINGSTONE CT 3
HAWKSHEAD CT 4
FOWLEY CL 5
BRYANSTONE RD
QUEENS WAY
ALEXANDRA WAY
BROOK RD
BRITANNIA RD
BEATTY RD
NEW FORD RD
Britannic Bsns Pk
Temple House
OLDPARK RIDE
Theobalds Park Coll
Theobald's Park Farm
New River
GREAT CAMBRIDGE RD
A10
LC
NEW COTTS
Nursery
SANDRINGHAM WAY
HIGHGROVE CT 1
BROADLANDS CL 2
DUMBARTON AVE 3
Hurst Drive Prim Sch
HURST DR
STERLING AVE
RAGLAN AVE
SEAFORTH DR
TERESA GDNS
CAMERON DR
LODGE CRES
Junction 25
Bullscross Farm
Cemy
BULLS CROSS RIDE
M25
Holmesdale Tunnel
HOLMESDALE
DEWGRASS GR
LANGDALE GDNS
COLVIN GDNS
TOLLGATE RD
CAXTON CT
BULLSMOOR WAY
BULLSMOOR GDNS
BULLSMOOR RIDE
BULLSMOOR LA
A1055
LOCKMORE RD
BRIDGENO RD
GRESLEY CT
WINDWARD CL
KINGSFIELD DR
THE GREENWAY
MOLLISON AVE
WHITEWEBBS LA
GILMOUR CL
Capel House
Clydesdale Stud
Myddelton Farm
Myddelton House
Capel Manor Primary Sch
Bulls Cross
MANOR FARM RD
MANOR CT
PH
MARRIYAT RD
HORNBEAMS AVE
LARCHES AVE
LOVELL RD
LILAC AVE
Schs
Liby
CARPENTERS CT
ELSINGE RD
CAPEL RD
BOWLES GN
TURKEY ST
YEWS AVE
PINES AVE
COCKER RD
BROOKSIDE GDNS
HOOK GATE
ALMSHOUSE LA
Bullsmoor Secondary Sch & Sports Ctr
Bullsmoor
BROADOAK AVE
ASPEN WAY
HAWKSMEAD CL
WINDSOR RD
BALMORAL RD
HOLLY RD
OAKHURST RD
HOLMWOOD RD
PAINTERS LA
JERVIS AVE
VIAN AVE
VERNON AVE
BEDFORD RD
PRINCES AVE
CUNNINGHAM AVE
Freezy Water
CHESTNUT RD
FOREST RD
PARK RD
Sewage Works
ARMANS RD
AYLANDS RD
ALLANDALE RD
PUTNEY RD
CRANBORNE CT
ASHTON RD
WILD MARCH CT
COBBETT CL
Aylands Sch
St George's C of E Jnfs Sch
Turkey Street Sta
WALTHAM GDNS
KESWICK DR
MEADWAY
UNITY RD
HERTFORD RD
CATHERINE RD
TOTTERIDGE RD
RAYNTON RD
COERDALE CT
Liby
APPLEYARD TERR
TURKEY ST
DENDRIDGE CL
AUCKLAND CL
St Ignatius Coll Upper Sch
Maiden's Bridge
FORTY HILL
Forty Hill C of E Sch
Crem
GILBERT ST
ASCOT GDNS
ELMHURST RD
GROVE RD W
ST STEPHEN'S RD
BOUGH BEECH CT
ALBANY RD
CONNOP RD
WINNINGTON RD
GOODWOOD AVE
LONGFIELD AVE
THE LONING
DELL RD
BOUVIER RD
CHERRY RD
MAPLETON CRES
WESTCROFT CT
ROTHERFIELD RD
UCKFIELD RD
TITCHFIELD RD
CATSFIELD RD
BEACONSFIELD RD
CHESTERFIELD RD
COLDHAM GR
STANDARD RD
ORDNANCE RD
LC
Enfield Lock Sta
BRADLEY RD
NEWBURY AVE
PRESTON GDNS
SOHAM RD
SALISBURY RD
MEDCALF RD
Enfield Lock
Sch
Turkey Brook
Albany Sch
Enfield Wash
ENFIELD
Albany Park
1 PREMIER CT
2 HERM HOUSE
3 SARK HOUSE
4 ALDERNEY HOUSE
5 GUERNSEY HOUSE
6 JERSEY HOUSE
Prince of Wales Sch
LYTTON AVE
MARRILYNE AVE
BIDEFORD RD
BILTON WAY
The Arena
MOLLISON AVE
PEMBROKE AVE 1
NORTHUMBERLAND AVE 2
SHEPPARD CL 3
MALTBY DR
SEVERN DR
WORCESTERS AVE
PENTRICH AVE
TYNEMOUTH DR
HOLBROOK CL
MEYER GN
GOAT LA
MAGPIE CL
HOE LA
STONELEIGH AVE
HOECROFT CT
CREST DR
RODEAN AVE
JASPER CL
PHOENIX CT
INGERSOLL RD
EASTFIELD RD
Eastfield Prim Sch
LEDA AVE
RILEY RD
ELMORE RD
GROVE GDNS
ALBANY PARK AVE
BELL LA
MEADOW CL
REDLANDS RD
PARK TERR
CASTLE RD
BRIMSDOWN AVE

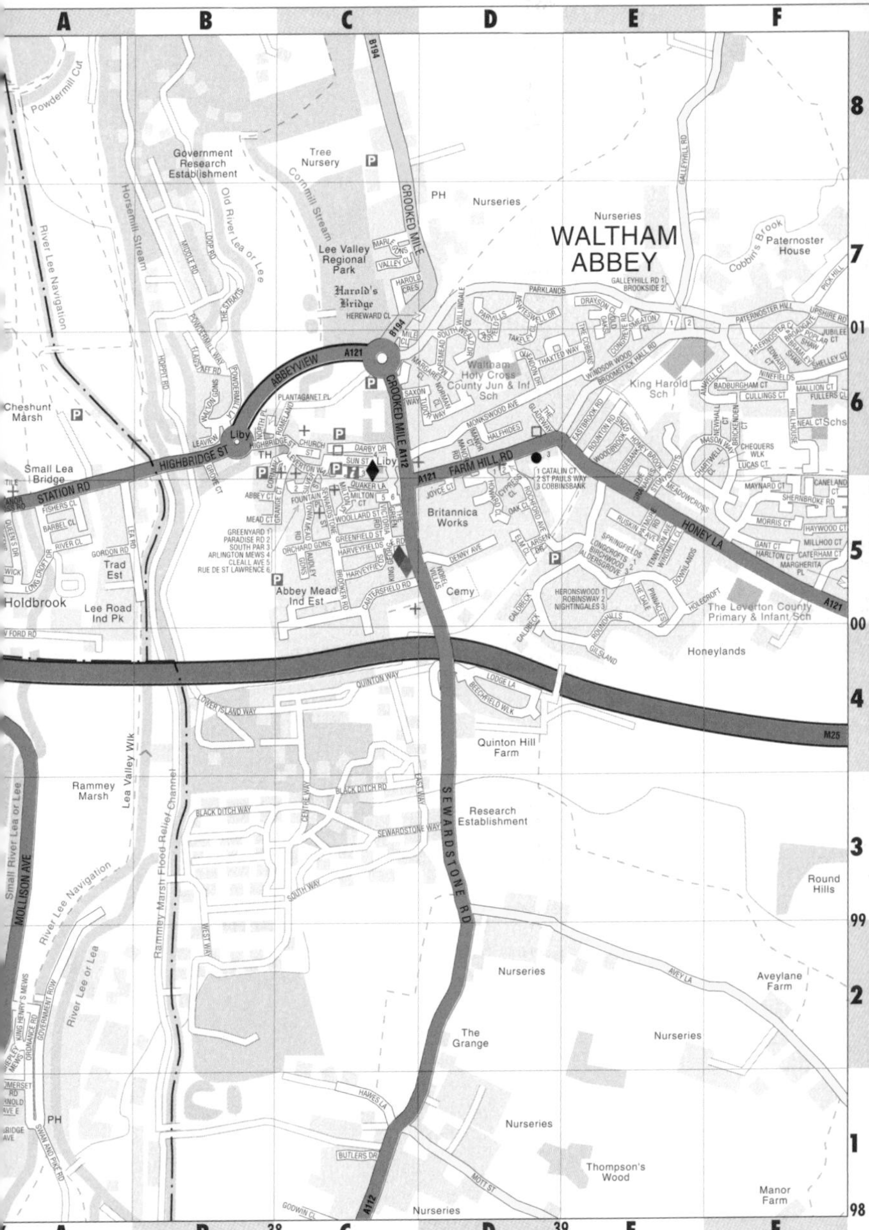
A
B
C
D
E
F
8
7
01
6
5
00
4
3
99
2
1
98
38
39
Government Research Establishment
Tree Nursery
Nurseries
WALTHAM ABBEY
Paternoster House
Lee Valley Regional Park
Harold's Bridge
Waltham Holy Cross County Jun & Inf Sch
King Harold Sch
Cheshunt Marsh
Small Lea Bridge
Britannica Works
Trad Est
Holdbrook
Lee Road Ind Pk
Abbey Mead Ind Est
Cemy
The Leverton County Primary & Infant Sch
Honeylands
Quinton Hill Farm
Rammey Marsh
Research Establishment
Round Hills
Aveylane Farm
The Grange
Thompson's Wood
Manor Farm
HIGHBRIDGE ST
STATION RD
ABBEYVIEW
CROOKED MILE
CROOKED MILE A112
FARM HILL RD
HONEY LA
SEWARDSTONE RD
M25
MOLLISON AVE
River Lee Navigation
Horsemill Stream
Old River Lea or Lee
Cornmill Stream
Powdermill Cut
Lea Valley Wlk
Rammey Marsh Flood Relief Channel
Small River Lea or Lee
River Lee or Lea
GREENYARD 1
PARADISE RD 2
SOUTH PAR 3
ARLINGTON MEWS 4
CLEALL AVE 5
RUE DE ST LAWRENCE 6
1 CATALIN CT
2 ST PAULS WAY
3 COBBINSBANK
HERONSWOOD 1
ROBINSWAY 2
NIGHTINGALES 3
GALLEYHILL RD 1
BROOKSIDE 2
QUINTON WAY
LOWER ISLAND WAY
BLACK DITCH RD
BLACK DITCH WAY
SEWARDSTONE WAY
SOUTH WAY
CENTRE WAY
EAST WAY
WEST WAY
LODGE LA
BEECHFIELD WLK
AVEY LA
HAWES LA
BUTLERS DR
MOTT ST
GODWIN CL
PARKLANDS
PATERNOSTER HILL
UPSHIRE RD
PICK HILL
GALLEYHILL RD
Nurseries

151

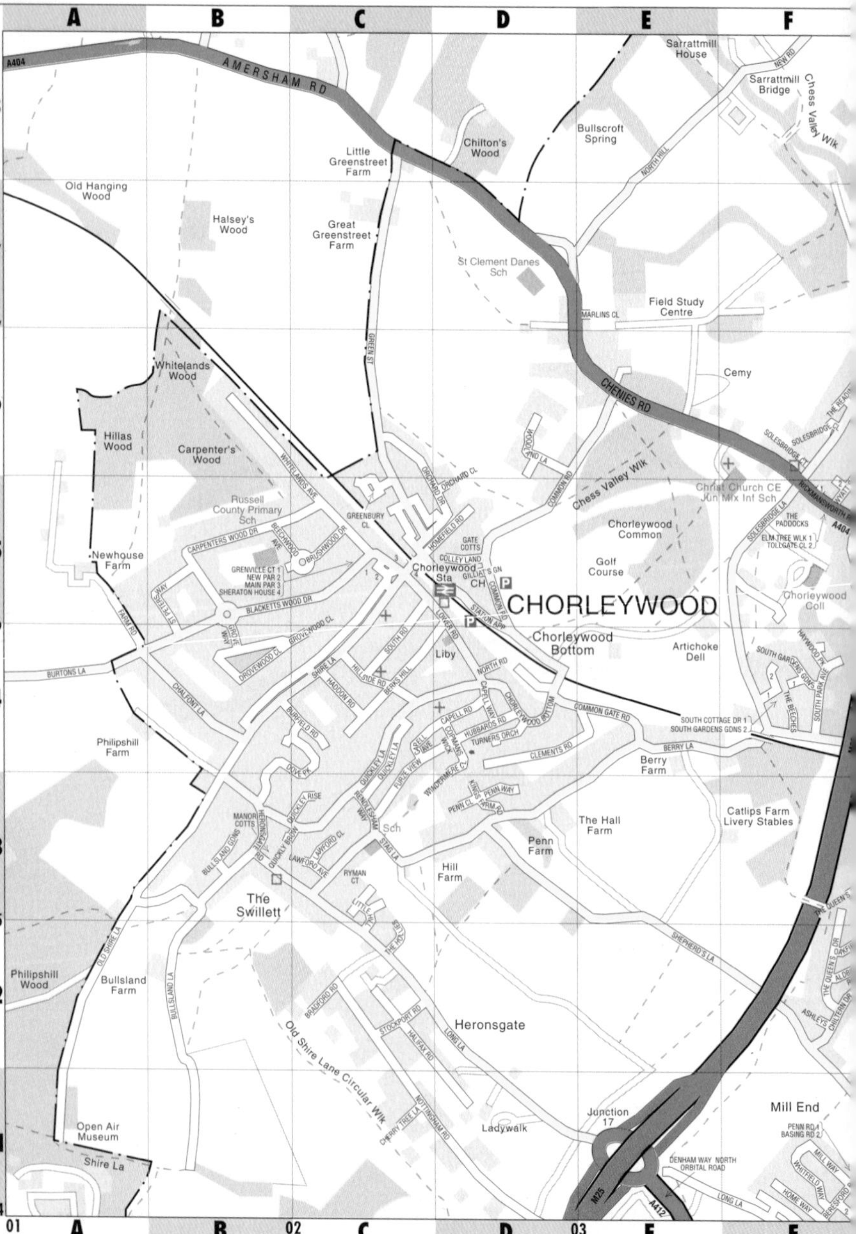
A
B
C
D
E
F
8
7
97
6
5
96
4
3
95
2
1
94
01
02
03
A404
AMERSHAM RD
Sarrattmill House
Sarrattmill Bridge
Chess Valley Wlk
NEW RD
NORTH HILL
Little Greenstreet Farm
Chilton's Wood
Bullscroft Spring
Old Hanging Wood
Halsey's Wood
Great Greenstreet Farm
St Clement Danes Sch
Field Study Centre
MARLINS CL
GREEN ST
Whitelands Wood
CHENIES RD
Cemy
Hillas Wood
Carpenter's Wood
WHITELANDS AVE
WOODLAND LA
ORCHARD DR
ORCHARD CL
COMMON RD
Chess Valley Wlk
SOLESBRIDGE LA
Christ Church CE Jun Mix Inf Sch
RICKMANSWORTH RD
Russell County Primary Sch
GREENBURY CL
HOMEFIELD RD
Chorleywood Common
THE PADDOCKS
ELM TREE WLK 1
TOLLGATE CL 2
A404
CARPENTERS WOOD DR
BEECHWOOD AVE
BRUSHWOOD DR
GATE COTTS
Newhouse Farm
GRENVILLE CT 1
NEW PAR 2
MAIN PAR 3
SHERATON HOUSE 4
COLLEY LAND
Chorleywood Sta
GILLIAT'S GN
CH
Golf Course
Chorleywood Coll
ST PETERS WAY
BLACKETTS WOOD DR
CHORLEYWOOD
STATION APP
COMMON FLD
GROVE WAY
GROVEWOOD CL
SOUTH RD
LOWER RD
Liby
Chorleywood Bottom
Artichoke Dell
FARM RD
DROVEWOOD CL
HAYWOOD PK
SOUTH GARDENS GDNS
BURTONS LA
SHIRE LA
HILLSIDE RD
BERKS HILL
NORTH RD
SOUTH PARK AVE
THE BEECHES
CHALFONT LA
HADDON RD
CAPELL WAY
CHORLEYWOOD BOTTOM
COMMON GATE RD
SOUTH COTTAGE DR 1
SOUTH GARDENS GDNS 2
BURFIELD RD
CAPELL RD
HUBBARDS RD
Philipshill Farm
TURNERS ORCH
COPMANS WICK
CAPELL AVE
BERRY LA
QUICKLEY LA
FURZE VIEW
CLEMENTS RD
Berry Farm
DOVE PK
WINDERMERE CL
KINGS FARM RD
PENN WAY
PENN CL
QUICKLEY RISE
RENDLESHAM WAY
The Hall Farm
Catlips Farm Livery Stables
MANOR COTTS
Sch
HERONSGATE RD
QUICKLY BROW
Penn Farm
BULLSLAND GDNS
LAWFORD CL
LAWFORD AVE
STAG LA
RYMAN CT
Hill Farm
The Swillett
LITTLE WAY
THE HOLLIES
THE QUEEN'S DR
OLD SHIRE LA
SHEPHERD'S LA
Philipshill Wood
Bullsland Farm
BULLSLAND LA
BRADFORD RD
ASHLEYS
CHILTERN DR
Heronsgate
STOCKPORT RD
Old Shire Lane Circular Wlk
HALIFAX RD
LONG LA
Mill End
Junction 17
Open Air Museum
CHERRY TREE LA
NOTTINGHAM RD
Ladywalk
PENN RD 1
BASING RD 2
Shire La
DENHAM WAY NORTH ORBITAL ROAD
MILL WAY
WHITFIELD WAY
M25
A412
LONG LA
HOME WAY

152
166

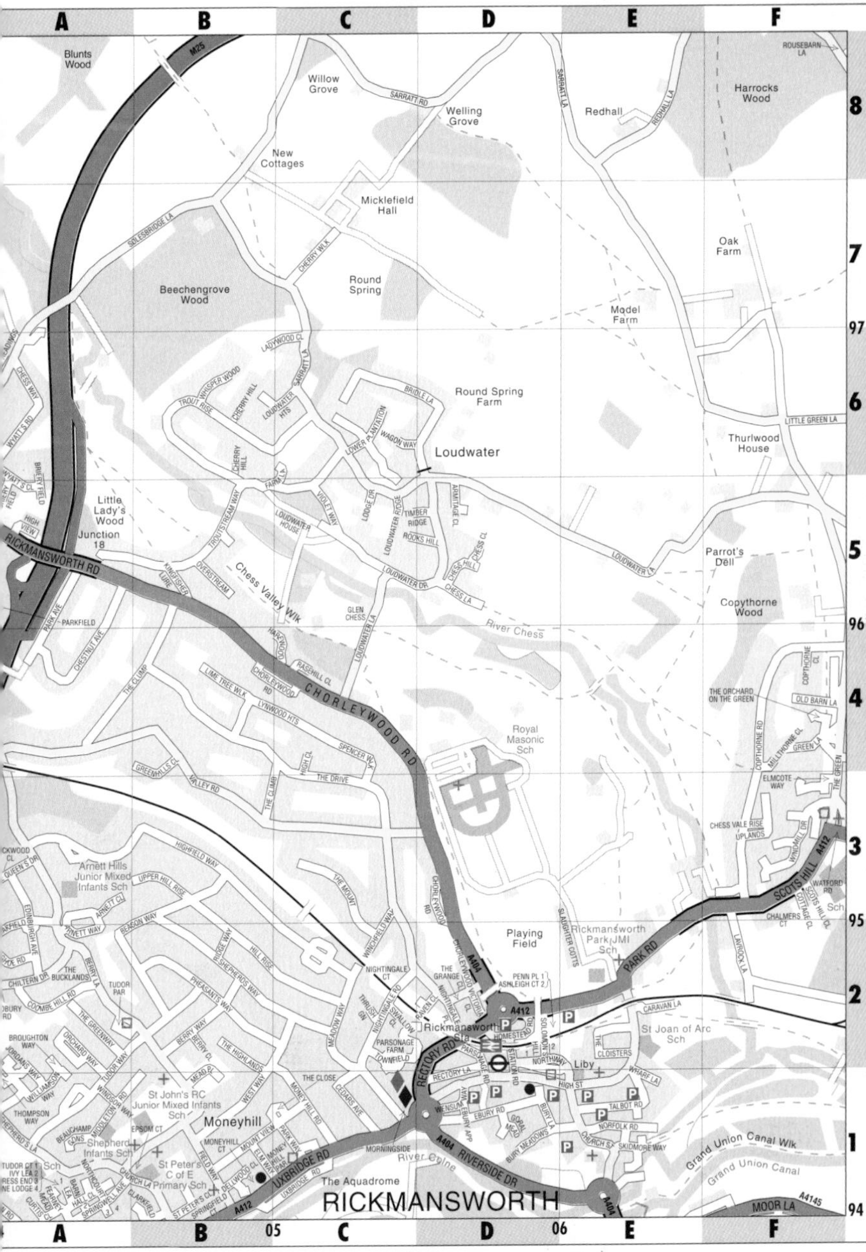
A
B
C
D
E
F
Blunts Wood
M25
Willow Grove
SARRATT RD
Welling Grove
SARRATT LA
Redhall
REDHALL LA
Harrocks Wood
ROUSEBARN LA
New Cottages
Micklefield Hall
SOLESBRIDGE LA
CHERRY WLK
Beechengrove Wood
Round Spring
Oak Farm
Model Farm
LADYWOOD CL
SARRATT LA
WHISPER WOOD
CHERRY HILL
TROUT RISE
LOUDWATER HTS
BRIDLE LA
Round Spring Farm
LOWER PLANTATION
WAGON WAY
Loudwater
LITTLE GREEN LA
Thurlwood House
CHESS WAY
WYATT'S RD
BRIERY FIELD
FARM LA
VIOLET WAY
LODGE DR
LOUDWATER RIDGE
TIMBER RIDGE
ARMITAGE CL
ROOKS HILL
CHESS CL
CHESS HILL
LOUDWATER HOUSE
Little Lady's Wood
Junction 18
TROUTSTREAM WAY
HIGH VIEW
RICKMANSWORTH RD
KINGFISHER LURE
OVERSTREAM
Chess Valley Wlk
LOUDWATER DR
CHESS LA
LOUDWATER LA
Parrot's Dell
Copythorne Wood
PARK AVE
PARKFIELD
CHESTNUT AVE
GLEN CHESS
River Chess
HAREWOOD
RASHILL CL
CHORLEYWOOD RD
LIME TREE WLK
LYNWOOD HTS
THE CLIMB
COPTHORNE CL
THE ORCHARD ON THE GREEN
OLD BARN LA
SPENCER WLK
Royal Masonic Sch
COPTHORNE RD
MILLTHORNE CL
GREEN LA
GREENHILLS CL
HIGH CL
THE DRIVE
VALLEY RD
ELMCOTE WAY
THE GREEN
CHESS VALE RISE
UPLANDS
WINDMILL DR
HIGHFIELD WAY
THE MOUNT
Arnett Hills Junior Mixed Infants Sch
UPPER HILL RISE
ARNETT CL
SCOTS HILL
A412
WATFORD RD
SCOTS HILL CL
COTTAGE CL
CHALMERS CT
Sch
QUEEN'S DR
EDINBURGH AVE
ARNETT WAY
BEACON WAY
RIDGE WAY
HILL RISE
WINCHFIELD WAY
CHORLEYWOOD RD
Playing Field
Rickmansworth Park JMI Sch
SLAUGHTER COTTS
PARK RD
LAVROCK LA
CHILTERN DR
THE BUCKLANDS
BERRY LA
TUDOR PAR
SHEPHERDS WAY
PHEASANTS WAY
NIGHTINGALE CT
THE GRANGE
A404
PENN PL
ASHLEIGH CT
A412
CARAVAN LA
COOMBE HILL RD
THE GREENWAY
ORCHARD WAY
BERRY WAY
BERRY CL
THE HIGHLANDS
MEADOW WAY
THRUSH GN
NIGHTINGALE RD
SWALLOW
RAVEN CL
Rickmansworth Sta
HOMESTEAD RD
SOLOMON'S HILL
St Joan of Arc Sch
BROUGHTON WAY
TUDOR WAY
PARSONAGE FARM
TOWNFIELD
RECTORY RD
PARSONAGE RD
STATION RD
NORTHWAY
THE CLOISTERS
Liby
WHARF LA
JORDANS WAY
WILLIAMSON WAY
WINDSOR WAY
MEAD PL
WEST WAY
THE CLOSE
MONEY HILL RD
CEDARS AVE
RECTORY LA
HIGH ST
TALBOT RD
NORFOLK RD
THOMPSON WAY
St John's RC Junior Mixed Infants Sch
Moneyhill
WENSUM
EBURY APP
EBURY RD
GOAL MEAD
BURY LA
BURY MEADOWS
CHURCH ST
SKIDMORE WAY
BEAUCHAMP GDNS
MIDDLETON RD
EPSOM CT
MONEYHILL CT
MOUNT VIEW
ELM WAY
MONEY HILL PAR
PARK WAY
MORNINGSIDE
A404
RIVERSIDE DR
Grand Union Canal Wlk
Grand Union Canal
Shepherd Infants Sch
St Peter's C of E Primary Sch
FIELD WAY
River Colne
SHEPHERD'S LA
NORTHCOURT
CHURCH LA
DELLWOOD CL
UXBRIDGE RD
The Aquadrome
RICKMANSWORTH
TUDOR CT
IVY LEA
CRESS END
PINE LODGE
Sch
BARN LEA
HALL CL
SPRINGWELL AVE
CLARKFIELD
ST PETER'S CL
SPRINGFIELD
CURTIS FEARNY MEAD
A412
A404
MOOR LA
A4145
8
7
97
6
5
96
4
3
95
2
1
94
05
06

173
166

165
153

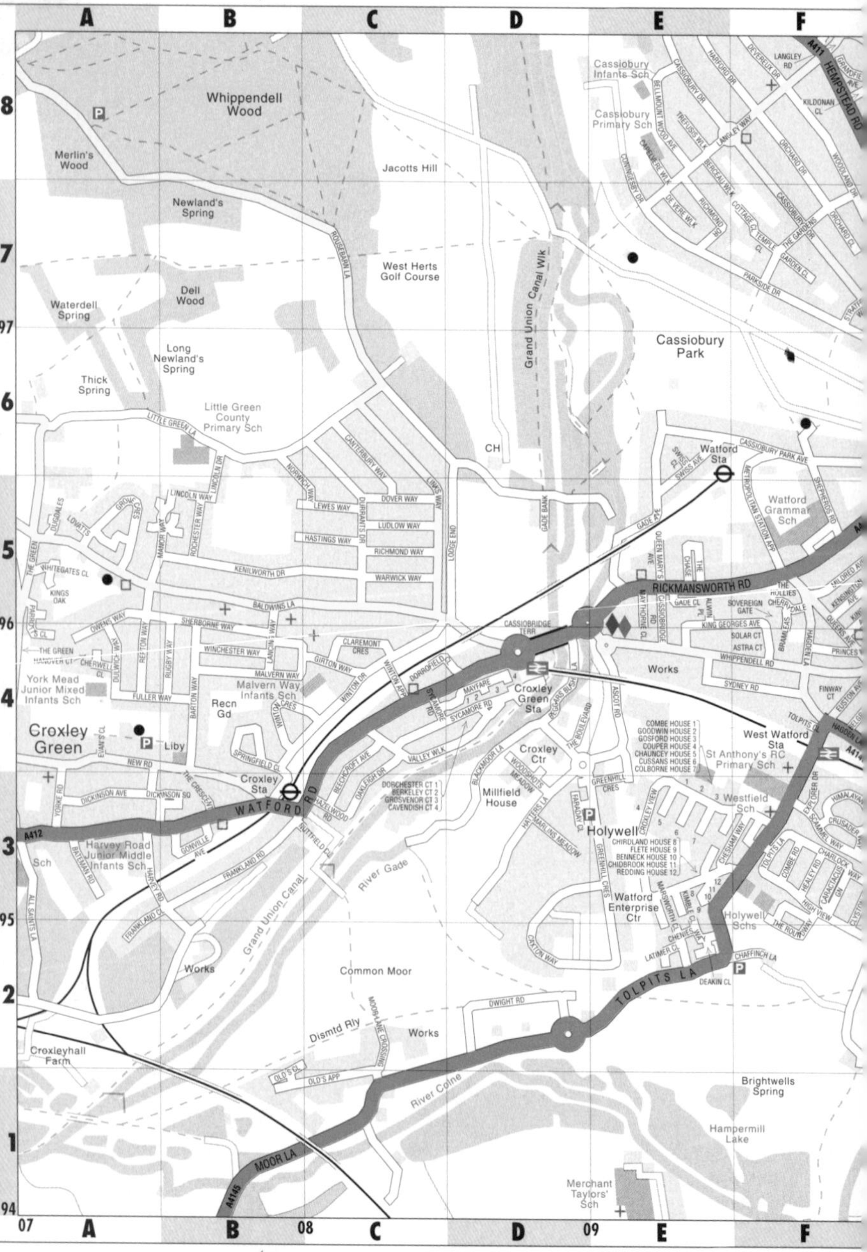
Whippendell Wood
Merlin's Wood
Newland's Spring
Jacotts Hill
ROUSEBARN LA
West Herts Golf Course
Waterdell Spring
Dell Wood
Long Newland's Spring
Thick Spring
Little Green County Primary Sch
LITTLE GREEN LA
Grand Union Canal Wlk
Cassiobury Infants Sch
Cassiobury Primary Sch
Cassiobury Park
HEMPSTEAD RD
A411
CH
Watford Sta
CASSIOBURY PARK AVE
Watford Grammar Sch
METROPOLITAN STATION APP
RICKMANSWORTH RD
GADE AVE
GADE BANK
LODGE END
CANTERBURY WAY
NORWICH WAY
LEWES WAY
DOVER WAY
LUDLOW WAY
HASTINGS WAY
RICHMOND WAY
WARWICK WAY
KENILWORTH DR
BALDWINS LA
SHERBORNE WAY
WINCHESTER WAY
MALVERN WAY
GIRTON WAY
CLAREMONT CRES
LINCOLN WAY
LINCOLN DR
ROCHESTER WAY
MANOR WAY
WHITEGATES CL
KINGS OAK
OWENS WAY
THE GREEN
HANOVER CT
CHERWELL CL
York Mead Junior Mixed Infants Sch
FULLER WAY
BARTON WAY
Malvern Way Infants Sch
Recn Gd
Croxley Green
Liby
NEW RD
DICKINSON AVE
DICKINSON SQ
THE CRESCENT
Croxley Sta
WATFORD RD
A412
Harvey Road Junior Middle Infants Sch
Sch
GONVILLE AVE
FRANKLAND RD
HARVEY RD
ALL SAINTS LA
Works
Grand Union Canal
River Gade
Common Moor
Dismtd Rly
MOORS LANE CROSSING
Croxleyhall Farm
OLD'S APP
River Colne
MOOR LA
A4145
DWIGHT RD
TOLPITS LA
CASSIOBRIDGE TERR
Croxley Green Sta
MAYFARE
SYCAMORE RD
VALLEY WLK
BEECHCROFT AVE
DORCHESTER CT 1
BERKELEY CT 2
GROSVENOR CT 3
CAVENDISH CT 4
Millfield House
Croxley Ctr
THE BOULEVARD
ASCOT RD
Works
WHIPPENDELL RD
SYDNEY RD
KING GEORGES AVE
SOLAR CT
ASTRA CT
SOVEREIGN GATE
COMBE HOUSE 1
GOODWIN HOUSE 2
GOSFORD HOUSE 3
COUPER HOUSE 4
CHAUNCEY HOUSE 5
CUSSANS HOUSE 6
COLBORNE HOUSE 7
West Watford Sta
St Anthony's RC Primary Sch
Westfield Sch
Holywell
CHIRDLAND HOUSE 8
FLETE HOUSE 9
BENNECK HOUSE 10
CHIDBROOK HOUSE 11
REDDING HOUSE 12
Watford Enterprise Ctr
GREENHILL CRES
MARLINS MEADOW
Holywell Schs
CHAFFINCH LA
DEAKIN CL
LATIMER CL
Brightwells Spring
Hampermill Lake
Merchant Taylors' Sch

165
174

154
168

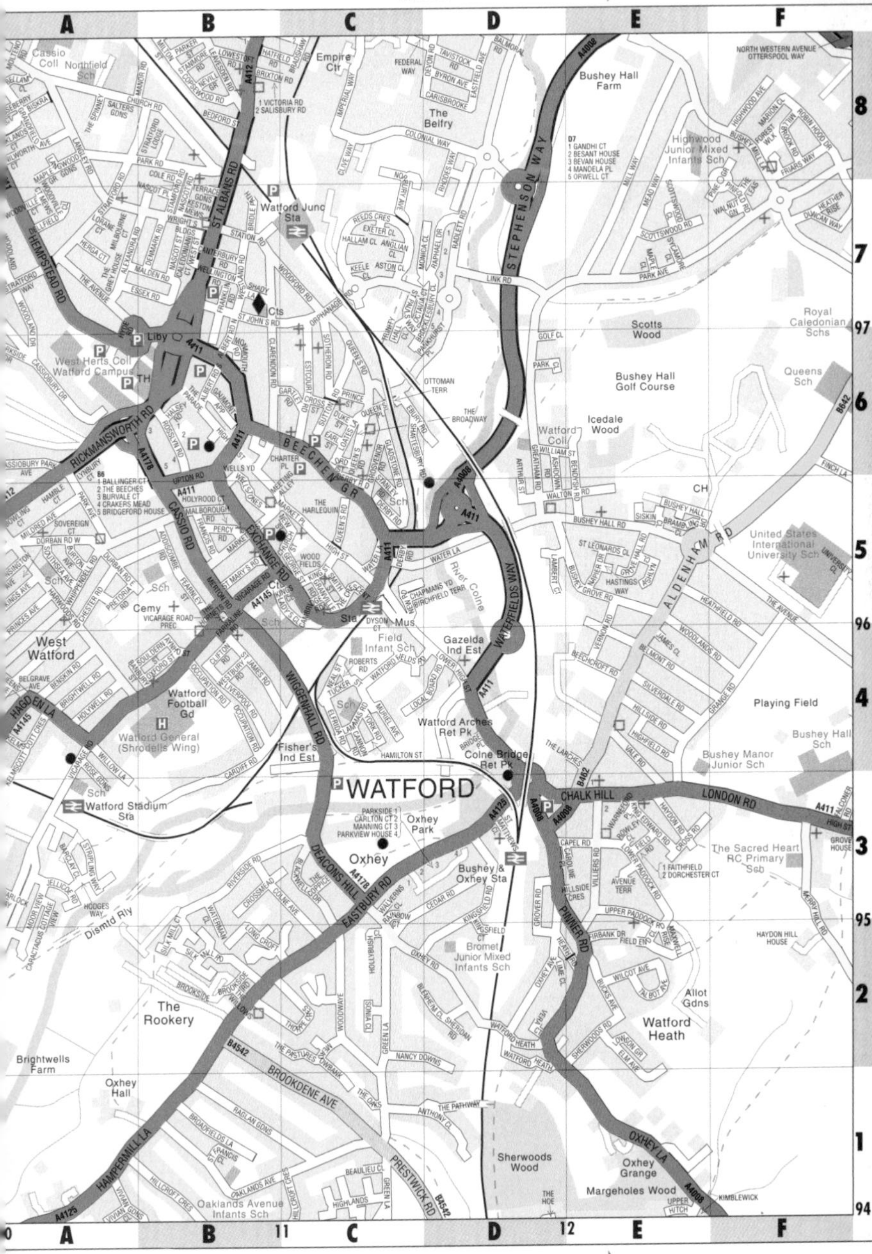
A
B
C
D
E
F
8
7
97
6
5
96
4
3
95
2
1
94
0
11
12
Cassio Coll
Northfield Sch
Empire Ctr
The Belfry
Bushey Hall Farm
Highwood Junior Mixed Infants Sch
D7
1 GANDHI CT
2 BESANT HOUSE
3 BEVAN HOUSE
4 MANDELA PL
5 ORWELL CT
NORTH WESTERN AVENUE OTTERSPOOL WAY
HEMPSTEAD RD
ST ALBANS RD
STEPHENSON WAY
Watford Junc Sta
1 VICTORIA RD
2 SALISBURY RD
COLONIAL WAY
LINK RD
Cts
Liby
Royal Caledonian Schs
Scotts Wood
Bushey Hall Golf Course
Queens Sch
West Herts Coll Watford Campus
TH
RICKMANSWORTH RD
BEECHEN GR
Icedale Wood
Watford Coll
WILLIAM ST
WALTON RD
B6
1 BALLINGER CT
2 THE BEECHES
3 BURVALE CT
4 CRAKERS MEAD
5 BRIDGEFORD HOUSE
THE HARLEQUIN
CH
BUSHEY HALL RD
United States International University Sch
CASSIO RD
EXCHANGE RD
WATER LA
River Colne
WATERFIELDS WAY
ALDENHAM RD
Cemy
Sch
West Watford
Sta
Mus
Field Infant Sch
Gazelda Ind Est
Watford Football Gd
Watford General (Shrodells Wing)
WIGGENHALL RD
Watford Arches Ret Pk
Playing Field
Bushey Hall Sch
HAGDEN LA
Fisher's Ind Est
Colne Bridge Ret Pk
Bushey Manor Junior Sch
WATFORD
CHALK HILL
LONDON RD
Watford Stadium Sta
PARKSIDE 1
CARLTON CT 2
MANNING CT 3
PARKVIEW HOUSE 4
Oxhey Park
Oxhey
The Sacred Heart RC Primary Sch
1 FAITHFIELD
2 DORCHESTER CT
DEACONS HILL
EASTBURY RD
Bushey & Oxhey Sta
Dismtd Rly
Bromet Junior Mixed Infants Sch
PINNER RD
HAYDON HILL HOUSE
Allot Gdns
The Rookery
Watford Heath
Brightwells Farm
BROOKDENE AVE
Oxhey Hall
HAMPERMILL LA
PRESTWICK RD
Sherwoods Wood
OXHEY LA
Oxhey Grange
Margeholes Wood
Oaklands Avenue Infants Sch
THE HOE
KIMBLEWICK

175
168

167
155

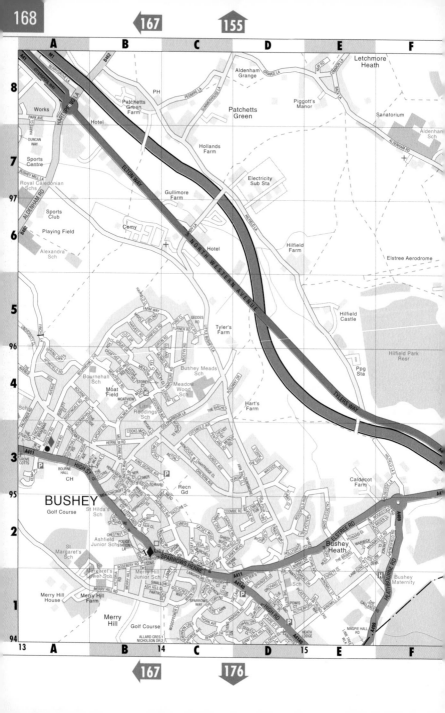
A
B
C
D
E
F
8
7
97
6
5
96
4
3
95
2
1
94
13
14
15
Letchmore Heath
Aldenham Grange
GRANGE LA
NEW RD
COMMON LA
BACK LA
M1
A41
B462
BERRYGROVE LA
OTTERSPOOL WAY
HARTSPRING LA
PH
Patchetts Green Farm
PEGMIRE LA
SUMMERHOUSE LA
Patchetts Green
Piggott's Manor
Sanatorium
Aldenham Sch
ALDENHAM RD
Works
PARK AVE
HARTS CL
DUNCAN WAY
Hotel
Hollands Farm
Sports Centre
BUSHEY MILL LA
ELTON WAY
Electricity Sub Sta
Royal Caledonian Schs
Gullimore Farm
ALDENHAM RD
Sports Club
Playing Field
Cemy
SANDY LA
HILFIELD LA
NORTH WESTERN AVENUE
Hotel
Hilfield Farm
Alexandra Sch
Elstree Aerodrome
HAYFIELD CL
FARM WAY
MIDDLE FURLONG
HARVEST RD
CORNFIELD RD
FORD CL
GEDDES RD
SUTCLIFFE CL
TURNER RD
LITTLE BUSHEY LA
Tyler's Farm
Hilfield Castle
UNIVERSITY CL
FINCH LA
SPRING CRES
HOMEFIELD RD
GIRTIN RD
GULLAND CL
MUNRO RD
MOSTYN RD
Hilfield Park Resr
THE AVENUE
RISE
AVENUE
BOURNEHALL AVE
Bournehall Sch
CRABTREE CL
PURLINGS RD
LITTLE MARTINS
MEADOW RD
LEA CL
BARLEY CL
HARCOURT RD
Bushey Meads Sch
Meadow Wood Sch
ROSSWAY DR
Ppg Sta
Moat Field
MOATFIELD RD
STOREY CT
MOAT CL
EDRIDGE CL
TYLERS WAY
Sch
FALCONER RD
GLENCOE RD
BRAEMAR CT
GOSLETT CT
NIGHTINGALE RD
BOURNE RD
MOATVIEW CT
PALMER AVE
Little Reddings Sch
REDDINGS AVE
RYDER CL
COLDHARBOUR LA
THE BIRCHES
Hart's Farm
THE STUDIOS
RUDOLPH RD
PARK RD
HERKOMER RD
BOURNEHALL LA
THE CLOSE
CLAYGATE RD
COOKS MEAD
MELBOURNE RD
HERNE RD
COTSWOLD AVE
CHEVIOT CL
PENTLAND RD
MENDIP RD
A411
GROVE COTTS
BOURNE HALL
CH
HIGH ST
CHURCH WLK
CASTLE CL
THE CLOISTERS
KING GEORGE AVE
WENDOVER WAY
CHARTRIDGE CL
OUNDLE AVE
CHILTERN AVE
DUNSMORE WAY
THE SQUIRRELS
WAYSIDE AVE
HILFIELD LA S
Caldecot Farm
CALDECOTE LA
Recn Gd
BUSHEY
Golf Course
St Hilda's Sch
MEADOWCROFT
NORMANSFIELD CL
ASHFIELD AVE
PASTURE CL
COOMBE RD
LOWER TUB
THE FOUR TUBS
WOODFIELD RISE
CALDECOTE GDNS
A41
A409
WOODSTOCK RD
ARDEN CL
MONTACUTE RD
ELSTREE RD
LITTLE POTTERS
SOMERS
CATSEY WOOD
CATSEY LA
VEGA RD
BURCHELL CT
SHADY BUSH CL
RICHFIELD RD
CLARKS MEAD
HOLLYGROVE
Bushey Heath
HOWARD CL
WARWICK CL
MAGNAVILLE RD
CLARENCE CL
HAYNESFIELD RD
CHESTNUT RISE
Ashfield Junior Sch
POLICE STATION LA
Liby
St Margaret's Sch
SCHOOL LA
PRIMROSE GDNS
SPARROWS HERNE
ROSEBERY RD
St Margaret's Lower Sch
VICTORIA RD
MERRY HILL RD
Merry Hill Junior Sch
SWALLOW CL
ASH HILL CL
PARTRIDGE CL
GOLDCREST WAY
LANGHOLME
A4140
PRIORY CT
THE LAKE
ST PETER'S CL
SPRINGFIELD
ORCHARD CL
THE PANTILES
NIMMO DR
TITIAN AVE
WINDMILL ST
EVERETT CL
THE BRIARS
LANE GDNS
CLAY LA
WILLOW DENE
Bushey Maternity
HEATHBOURNE RD
Merry Hill House
Merry Hill Farm
SPARROWS WAY
THE COMYNS
ROSE LAWN
WARREN RD
HIGH RD
THE RUTTS
POWIS CT
RUTHERFORD WAY
WINDMILL LA
THE CALLANDERS
Merry Hill
Golf Course
WOODPECKER CL
ROBINSON CRES
PROWSE AVE
THORN AVE
BENMISH DR
STEVENS GN
CLAIRE CT
CALIFORNIA LA
FLORIDA CL
GIANT TREE HILL
SEQUOIA CL
HEATH LODGE
MAGPIE HALL RD
LIME TREE WLK
ALLARD CRES 1
NICHOLSON DR 2

167
176

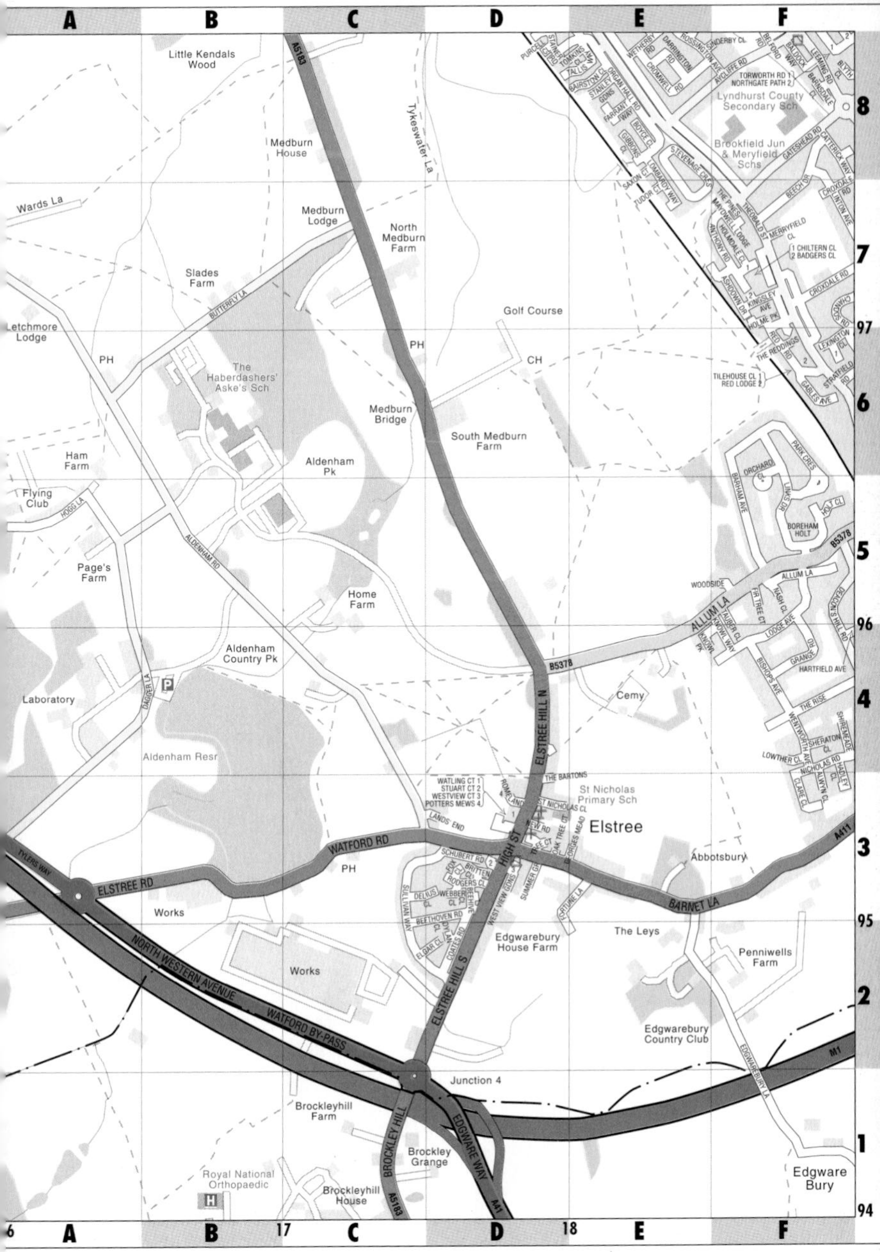
A
B
C
D
E
F
Little Kendals Wood
A5183
Tykeswater La
Medburn House
Wards La
Medburn Lodge
North Medburn Farm
Slades Farm
BUTTERFLY LA
Golf Course
Letchmore Lodge
PH
The Haberdashers' Aske's Sch
CH
Medburn Bridge
South Medburn Farm
Ham Farm
Aldenham Pk
Flying Club
HOGG LA
ALDENHAM RD
Page's Farm
Home Farm
Aldenham Country Pk
B5378
Laboratory
DAGGER LA
Cemy
ELSTREE HILL N
Aldenham Resr
THE BARTONS
St Nicholas Primary Sch
WATLING CT 1
STUART CT 2
WESTVIEW CT 3
POTTERS MEWS 4
LANDS' END
Elstree
WATFORD RD
HIGH ST
ELSTREE RD
Abbotsbury
BARNET LA
A411
Works
The Leys
Edgwarebury House Farm
Penniwells Farm
NORTH WESTERN AVENUE
WATFORD BY-PASS
ELSTREE HILL S
Edgwarebury Country Club
M1
Junction 4
EDGWAREBURY LA
Brockleyhill Farm
BROCKLEY HILL
EDGWARE WAY
Brockley Grange
Royal National Orthopaedic
Brockleyhill House
A41
Edgware Bury
Lyndhurst County Secondary Sch
Brookfield Jun & Meryfield Schs
ALLUM LA
BOREHAM HOLT
HARTFIELD AVE
TYLERS WAY
8
7
97
6
5
96
4
3
95
2
1
94
17
18

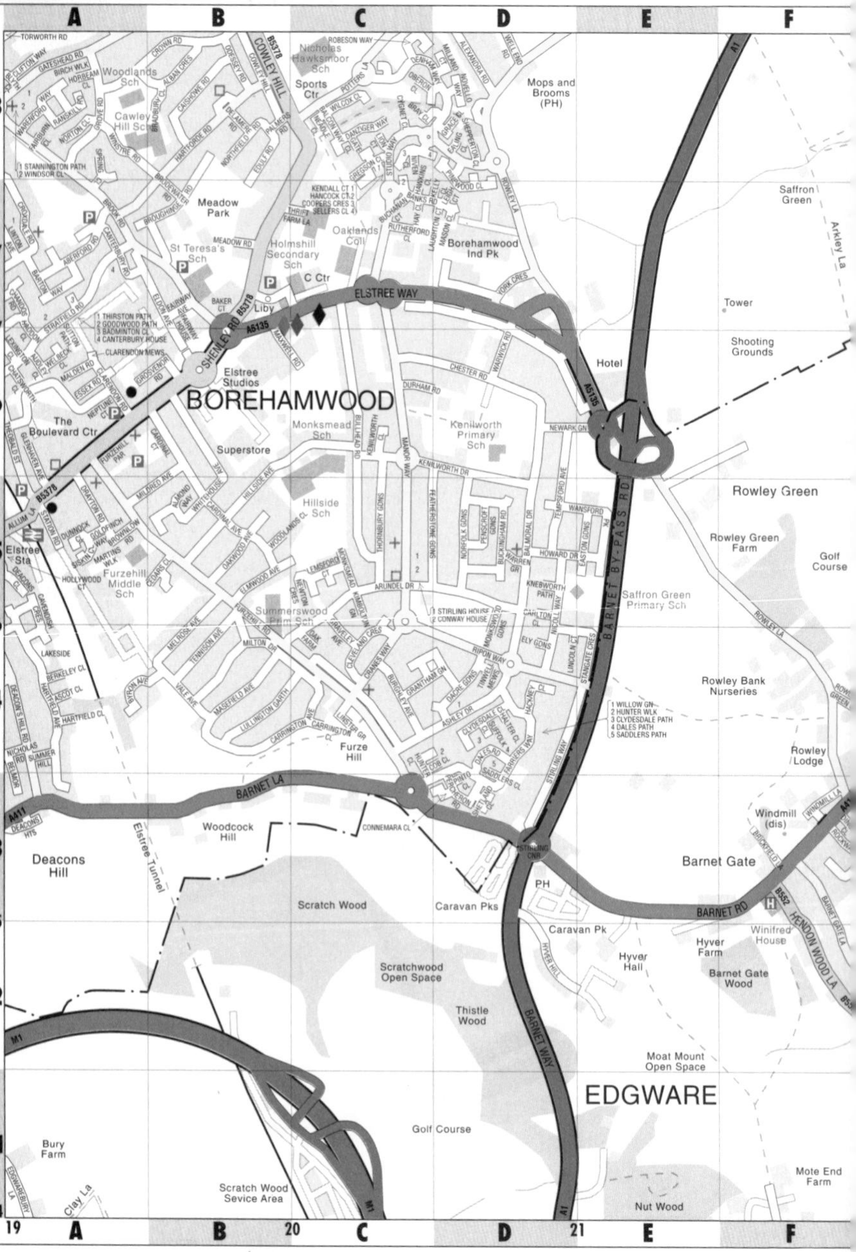

A B C D E F

8

7

97

6 **BOREHAMWOOD**

5

96

4

3

95

2

1

94

19 A B 20 C D 21 E F

TORWORTH RD

Woodlands

Cawley
Hill Sch

Meadow
Park

St Teresa's
Sch

Holmshill
Secondary
Sch

C Ctr

Elstree
Studios

The
Boulevard Ctr

Elstree
Sta

Furzehill
Middle
Sch

Hollywood

Summerswood
Sch

Superstore

Monksmead
Sch

Hillside
Sch

LAKESIDE

Deacons
Hill

Woodcock
Hill

Scratch Wood

Scratchwood
Open Space

Thistle
Wood

Golf Course

Bury
Farm

Scratch Wood
Sevice Area

Nicholas
Hawksmoor
Sch

Sports
Ctr

ROBESON WAY

Oaklands
Cgll

Borehamwood
Ind Pk

ELSTREE WAY

Kenilworth
Primary
Sch

Mops and
Brooms
(PH)

Hotel

BARNET BY-PASS RD

Saffron Green
Primary Sch

Saffron
Green

Tower

Shooting
Grounds

Rowley Green

Rowley Green
Farm

Golf
Course

Rowley Bank
Nurseries

Rowley
Lodge

Windmill
(dis)

Barnet Gate

BARNET RD

Caravan Pks

Caravan Pk

Hyver
Hall

Hyver
Farm

Barnet Gate
Wood

Winifred
House

Moat Mount
Open Space

**EDGWARE**

Nut Wood

Mote End
Farm

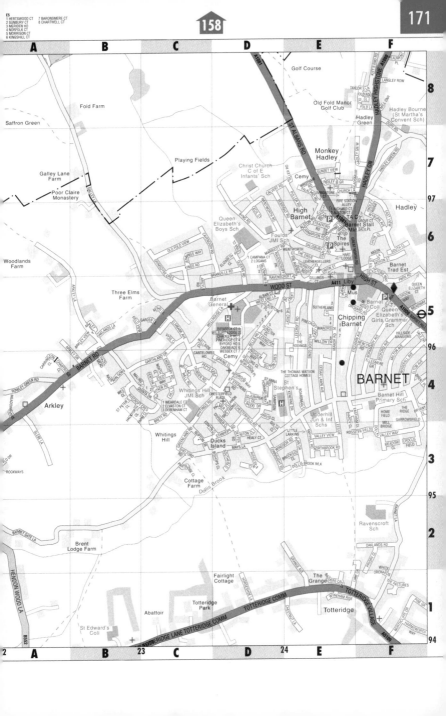

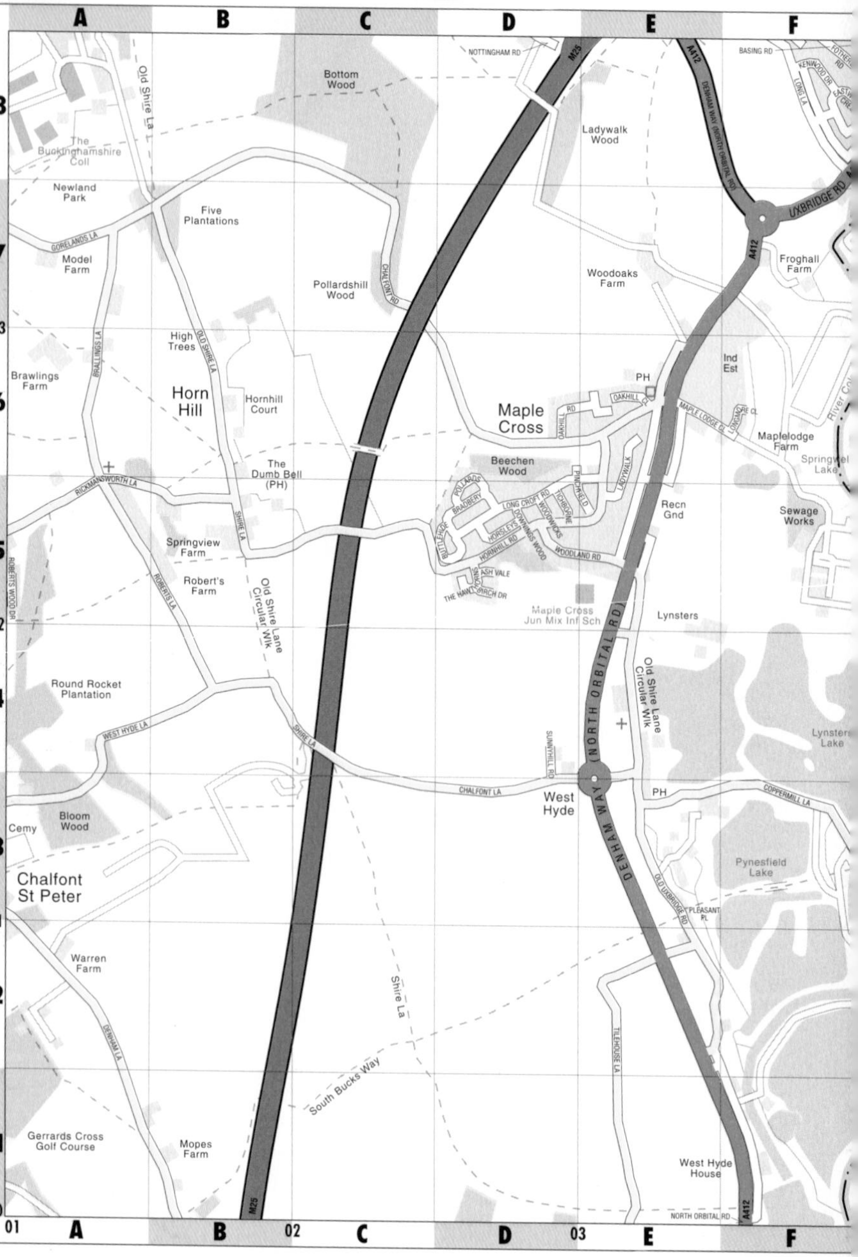

**A** **B** **C** **D** **E** **F**

BASING RD

NOTTINGHAM RD

M25

UXBRIDGE RD

A412

Bottom
Wood

Ladywalk
Wood

Froghall
Farm

The
Buckinghamshire
Coll

Newland
Park

Five
Plantations

Woodoaks
Farm

Model
Farm

GOWLANDS LA

Pollardshill
Wood

PH

Ind
Est

High
Trees

Brawlings
Farm

Horn
Hill

Hornhill
Court

Maple
Cross

OAKHILL

Maplelodge
Farm

Springw
Lake

RICKMANSWORTH LA

The
Dumb Bell
(PH)

Beechen
Wood

Recn
Gnd

Sewage
Works

Springview
Farm

Long Croft Rd

Maple Cross
Jun Mix Inf Sch

WOODLAND RD

Robert's
Farm

ROBERTS LA

The Hawl

Lynsters

Old Shire Lane Circular Wlk

SHIRE LA

Round Rocket
Plantation

WEST HYDE LA

SUNNYHILL RD

Old Shire Lane Circular Wlk

Lynsters
Lake

CHALFONT LA

West
Hyde

PH

COPPERMILL LA

Cemy

Bloom
Wood

Pynesfield
Lake

Chalfont
St Peter

DENHAM WAY (NORTH ORBITAL RD)

OLD UXBRIDGE RD

PLEASANT
PL

Warren
Farm

Shire La

South Bucks Way

TILEHOUSE LA

Gerrards Cross
Golf Course

Mopes
Farm

West Hyde
House

M25

NORTH ORBITAL RD

A412

**A** **B** 02 **C** **D** 03 **E** **F**

01    91    92    93

8  7  6  5  4  3  2  1

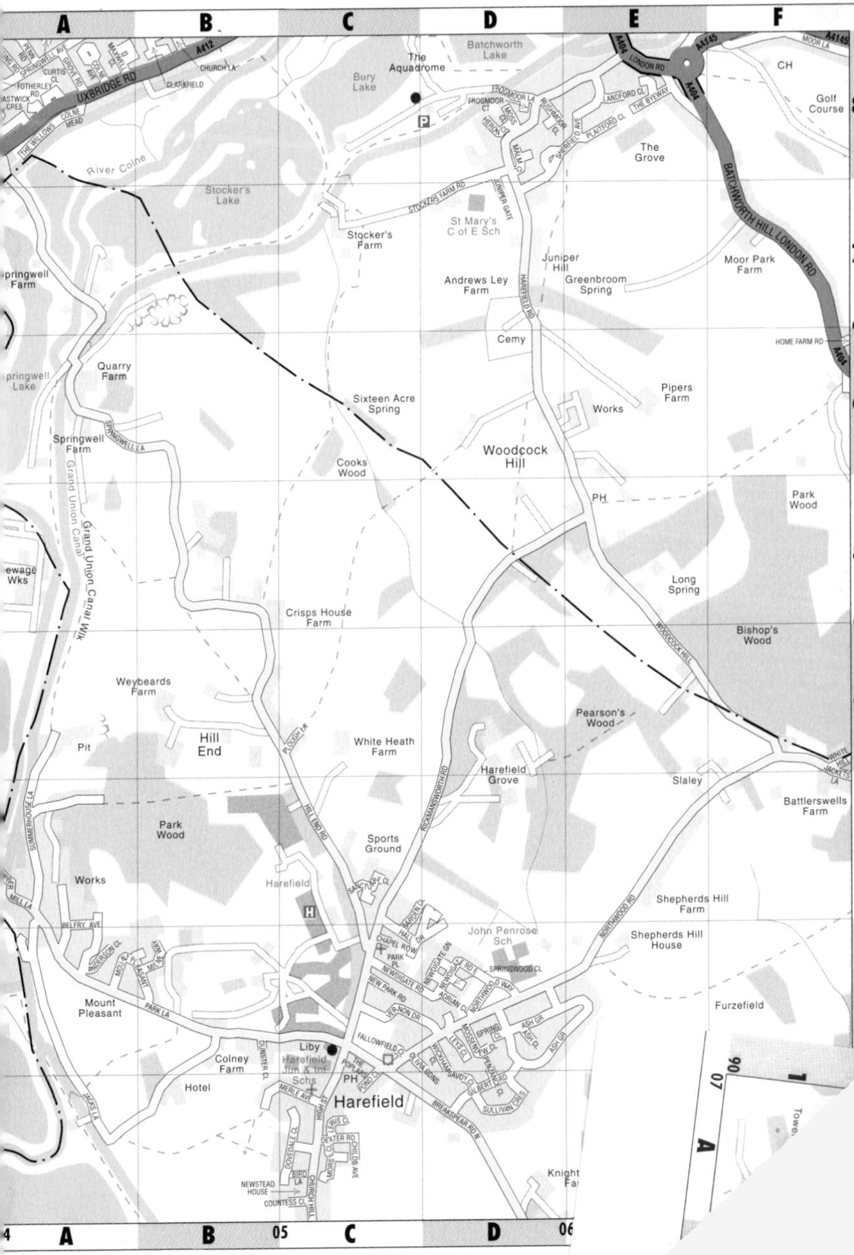

A B C D E F

8 7 93 6 5 92 4 91 3 2 90 07 06

UXBRIDGE RD A412
CHURCH LA
GLASSFIELD
FOTHERLEY RD
CURTIS
EASTWICK CRES
RICKERLEY AVE
RICKMANSWORTH RD

River Colne

The Aquadrome
Batchworth Lake
CH
Golf Course
BATCHWORTH HILL LONDON RD
A404 LONDON RD
A4145
A4145 MOOR LA

Bury Lake

P

Stocker's Lake

Stocker's Farm

St Mary's C of E Sch

The Grove

STOCKERS FARM RD
PROGMOOR LA
FROGMOOR LA
MOOR LA
SHEPHERDS LA
PLATFORD CL
THE BYWAY
LANDFORD CL

Springwell Farm

Quarry Farm

Springwell Lake

Springwell Farm

Juniper Hill
Greenbroom Spring

Andrews Ley Farm

Cemy

Moor Park Farm

HOME FARM RD

Sixteen Acre Spring

Cooks Wood

Woodcock Hill

Works

Pipers Farm

Park Wood

Grand Union Canal

Grand Union Canal Wlk

ewage Wks

PH

Long Spring

Crisps House Farm

Bishop's Wood

Weybeards Farm

Pearson's Wood

Hill End

White Heath Farm

Harefield Grove

Slaley

Battlerswells Farm

Pit

Park Wood

Sports Ground

Shepherds Hill Farm

Works

Harefield

H

John Penrose Sch

Shepherds Hill House

BELFRY AVE

CHAPEL ROW
PARK PL
NEWGATE RD

Mount Pleasant

PARK LA

Liby

Colney Farm

Harefield Jun & Inf Schs

PH

Harefield

Hotel

Furzefield

NEWSTEAD HOUSE
COUNTESS CL
CHURCH HILL

Knight Fa

Tow

A

173
166

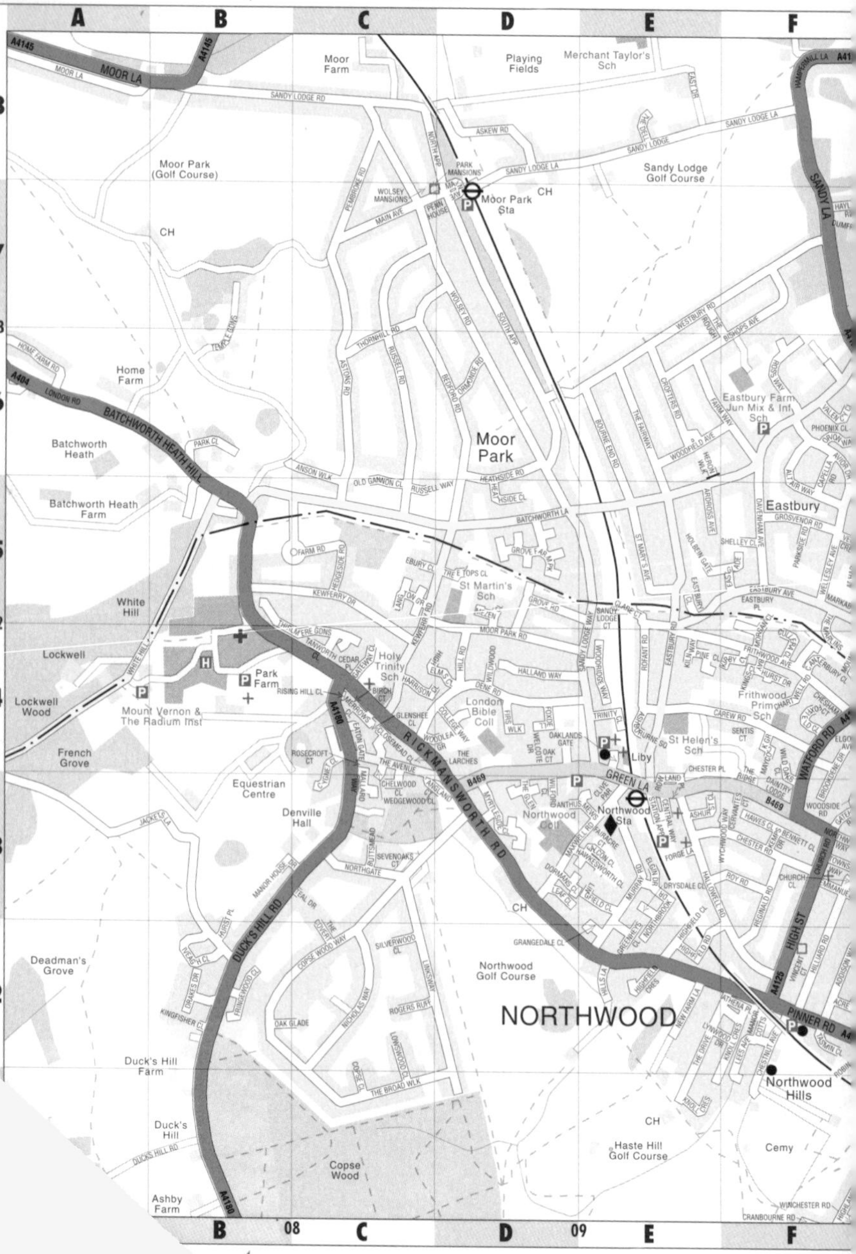
A
B
C
D
E
F
8
7
93
6
5
92
4
3
91
2
08
09
MOOR LA
A4145
SANDY LODGE RD
Moor Farm
Playing Fields
Merchant Taylor's Sch
EAST DR
SANDY LODGE LA
SANDY LODGE
ASKEW RD
PARK MANSIONS
Moor Park (Golf Course)
Moor Park Sta
CH
Sandy Lodge Golf Course
SANDY LA
WOLSEY MANSIONS
MAIN AVE
PENN HOUSE
NORTH APP
PEMBROKE RD
TEMPLE GDNS
THORNHILL RD
WOLSEY RD
SOUTH APP
ASTONS RD
RUSSELL RD
BEDFORD RD
ORMONDE RD
WESTBURY RD
THE BISHOPS AVE
ROSS WAY
Home Farm
HOME FARM RD
A404
LONDON RD
BATCHWORTH HEATH HILL
Batchworth Heath
PARK CL
Moor Park
CROFTERS RD
FARM WAY
THE FAIRWAY
BOURNE END RD
Eastbury Farm Jun Mix & Inf Sch
WOODFIELD AVE
HERON WLK
VALEN CL
PHOENIX CL
ANSON WLK
OLD GANNON CL
RUSSELL WAY
HEATHSIDE RD
HEATHSIDE CL
ARDROSS AVE
Eastbury
Batchworth Heath Farm
BATCHWORTH LA
GROSVENOR RD
DAVENHAM AVE
FARM RD
HEDGESIDE RD
GROVE FARM PK
ST MARY'S AVE
HOLBEIN GATE
SHELLEY CL
PARKSIDE RD
WELLESLEY AVE
EBURY CL
TREETOPS CL
White Hill
KEWFERRY DR
LANGTON GR
KEWFERRY RD
St Martin's Sch
GROVE RD
EASTBURY RD
EASTBURY AVE
EASTBURY PL
CLARE CT
SANDY LODGE CT
92
Lockwell
WHITE HILL
HINDMERE GDNS
TANWORTH CL
CEDAR PL
GATEWAY CL
Holy Trinity Sch
MOOR PARK RD
HILL RD
WILDWOOD
SANDY LODGE WAY
WOODRIDGE WAY
ROFANT RD
KILN WAY
PINE CL
FRITHWOOD AVE
Park Farm
RISING HILL CL
BIRCH CT
HARRISON
ELMS CL
HALLAND WAY
DENE RD
Frithwood Prim Sch
Lockwell Wood
Mount Vernon & The Radium Inst
GLENSHEE CL
COLLEGE WAY
London Bible Coll
FIRS WLK
FOXDELL
TRINITY CL
ASHBOURNE SQ
CAREW RD
SENTIS CT
St Helen's Sch
A4180
RICKMANSWORTH RD
WOODLEA GR
OAKLANDS GATE
WELCOTE DR
OAK CT
Liby
WATFORD RD
French Grove
ROSECROFT CT
THE AVENUE
THE LARCHES
CHESTER PL
THE RIPSE
DAINTRY LODGE
Equestrian Centre
CHELWOOD CL
WEDGEWOOD CL
B469
GREEN LA
Northwood Sta
STATION APP
ASHURST
HAWES CL
BENNETT CL
CHESTER RD
JACKETS LA
Denville Hall
MYRTLESIDE CL
THE GLEN
Northwood Coll
FAIRACRE CT
CLOVE PAR
3
PUTTSMEAD
SEVENOAKS CT
NORTHGATE
HAWKESWORTH CL
DORMANS CL
LEAF CL
MURRAY RD
ELGIN DR
DRYSDALE CL
FORGE LA
WYCHWOOD WAY
ROY RD
REGINALD RD
CHURCH CL
MANOR HOUSE DR
TEAL DR
DUCK'S HILL RD
CH
GRANGEDALE CL
NORTHBROOK
HIGHFIELD CL
HALLOWELL RD
HIGH ST
THE COVERT
COPSE WOOD WAY
SILVERWOOD CL
Deadman's Grove
HURST PL
NEAGH CL
DRAKES DR
FRINGEWOOD CL
Northwood Golf Course
GREENHEYS CL
HIGHFIELD CRES
A4125
VINCENT CT
HILLIARD RD
LINKSWAY
NICHOLAS WAY
ROGERS RUFF
KINGFISHER CL
OAK GLADE
NORTHWOOD
NEW FARM LA
ATHENA PL
PINNER RD
LOWSWOOD CL
LYNWOOD DR
KNOLL CRES
LEES AVE
MANOR COTTS
CHESTNUT AVE
TASMIN CL
Duck's Hill Farm
COPSE
THE BROAD WLK
THE DRIVE
Northwood Hills
Duck's Hill
DUCKS HILL RD
Copse Wood
Haste Hill Golf Course
Cemy
Ashby Farm
WINCHESTER RD
CRANBOURNE RD

173

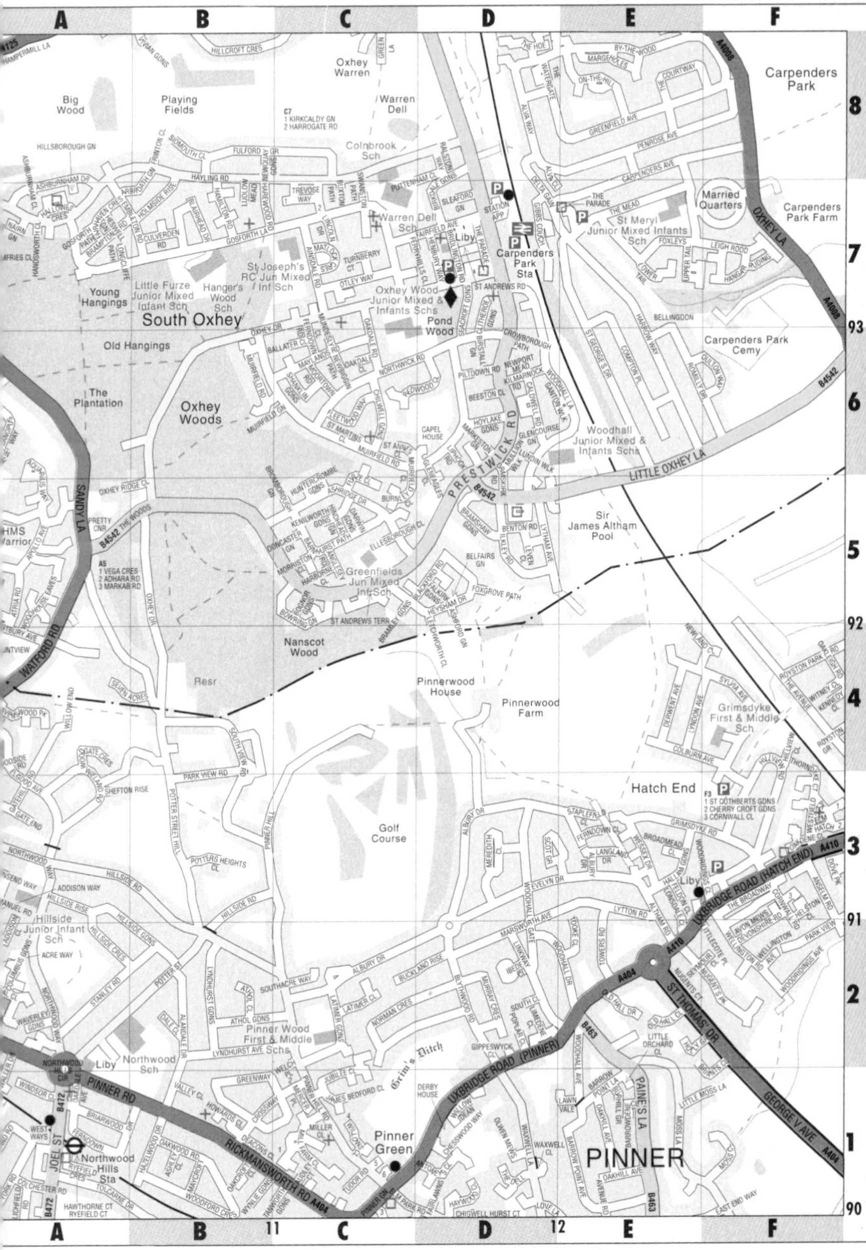

175
168

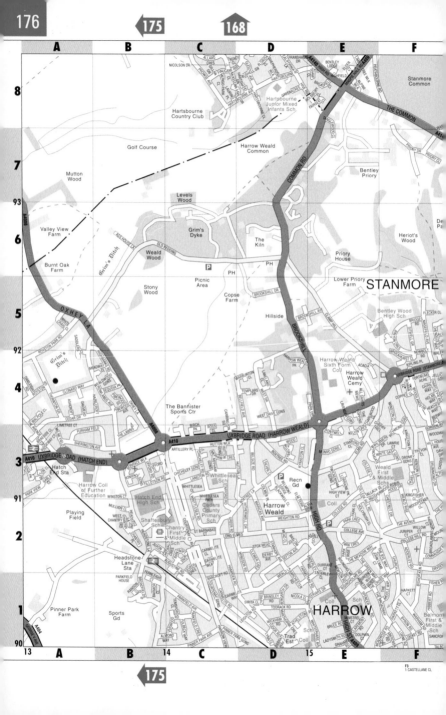
A
B
C
D
E
F
8
7
93
6
5
92
4
3
91
2
1
90
13
14
15
Stanmore Common
THE COMMON
Hartsbourne Country Club
Hartsbourne Junior Mixed Infants Sch
Golf Course
Harrow Weald Common
COMMON RD
Bentley Priory
Mutton Wood
Levels Wood
Grim's Dyke
Valley View Farm
The Kiln
Heriot's Wood
Weald Wood
OLD REDDING
Grim's Ditch
Burnt Oak Farm
Priory House
PH
Picnic Area
Lower Priory Farm
STANMORE
Stony Wood
Copse Farm
BROOKSHILL DR
OXHEY LA
Hillside
BROOKSHILL
Bentley Wood High Sch
Harrow Weald Sixth Form Coll
Harrow Weald Cemy
The Bannister Sports Ctr
UXBRIDGE ROAD (HARROW WEALD)
UXBRIDGE ROAD (HATCH END)
UXBRIDGE ROAD (STANMORE)
A410
A4008
A4140
A409
A404
Hatch End Sta
Harrow Coll of Further Education
Whittlesea Sch
Recn Gd
Weald First & Middle Schs
Hatch End High Sch
Cedars County Primary Sch
Harrow Weald
Playing Field
Shaftesbury Sch
Chantry First & Middle Sch
HIGH RD
Headstone Lane Sta
Pinner Park Farm
Sports Gd
HARROW
HIGH ST A409
Belmont First & Middle Sch
Trad Est
Coll
Sch

175

F3
1 CASTELLANE CL

# EXPLANATION OF THE STREET INDEX REFERENCE SYSTEM

Street names are listed alphabetically and show the locality, the Post Office Postcode District, the page number and a reference to the square in which the name falls on the map page.

Example:     Peterlee Ct. Heml H HP2.....................................124 F7 2

| | |
|---|---|
| Peterlee Ct | This is the full street name, which may have been abbreviated on the map. |
| Heml H | This is the abbreviation for the town, village or locality in which the street falls. |
| HP2 | This is the Post Office Postcode District for the street name. |
| 124 | This is the page number of the map on which the street name appears. |
| F7 | The letter and figure indicate the square on the map in which the centre of the street falls. The square can be found at the junction of the vertical column carrying the appropriate letter and the horizontal row carrying the appropriate figure. |
| 2 | In congested areas numbers may have been used to indicate the location of a street. In certain circumstances, the number used to represent a street will follow the reference in the gazetteer entry. |

## ABBREVIATIONS USED IN THE INDEX
### Road Names

| | | | | | | | |
|---|---|---|---|---|---|---|---|
| Approach | App | Corner | Cnr | Grove | Gr | Promenade | Prom |
| Arcade | Arc | Cottages | Cotts | Heights | Hts | Retail Park | Ret Pk |
| Avenue | Ave | Court | Ct | Industrial Estate | Ind Est | Road | Rd |
| Boulevard | Bvd | Courtyard | Ctyd | Interchange | Intc | Roundabout | Rdbt |
| Buildings | Bldgs | Crescent | Cres | Junction | Junc | South | S |
| Business Park | Bsns Pk | Drive | Dr | Lane | La | Square | Sq |
| Business Centre | Bsns Ctr | Drove | Dro | North | N | Stairs | Strs |
| Bungalows | Bglws | East | E | Orchard | Orch | Steps | Stps |
| Causeway | Cswy | Embankment | Emb | Parade | Par | Street,Saint | St |
| Centre | Ctr | Esplanade | Espl | Park | Pk | Terrace | Terr |
| Circle | Circ | Estate | Est | Passage | Pas | Trading Estate | Trad Est |
| Circus | Cir | Gardens | Gdns | Place | Pl | Walk | Wlk |
| Close | Cl | Green | Gn | Precinct | Prec | West | W |
| Common | Comm | | | | | Yard | Yd |

## Key to abbreviations of Town, Village and Rural locality names used in the index of street names.

| | | | | | | | | | | | |
|---|---|---|---|---|---|---|---|---|---|---|---|
| Abbots Langley | Abb L | 153 | F7 | Crews Hill | Cre H | 161 | B4 | Kensworth Common | Ken Co | 82 | E8 | Rushden | Rus | 25 | F3 |
| Albury | Alb | 57 | A6 | Croxley Green | Cro Gr | 166 | A4 | Kimpton | Kim | 66 | C1 | Sacombe | Sac | 71 | E3 |
| Aldbury | Ald | 101 | C5 | Cuffley | Cuf | 146 | E3 | Kings Langley | Kin L | 139 | A1 | Sandon | San | 15 | B1 |
| Anstey | Ans | 29 | B6 | Dagnall | Dagn | 81 | C6 | Kings Walden | Kin Wd | 48 | A3 | Sandridge | Sand | 108 | C1 |
| Ardeley | Ard | 38 | F3 | Dane End | Dan En | 71 | F8 | Knebworth | Kneb | 69 | A5 | Sarratt | Sar | 152 | A4 |
| Arlesey | Arl | 11 | B5 | Datchworth | Dat | 69 | E2 | Kneesworth | Knee | 2 | A5 | Sawbridgeworth | Saw | 97 | C2 |
| Ashley Green | Ash Gr | 136 | A7 | Dunstable | Dun | 44 | A2 | Langley | Lan | 49 | F1 | Sheering | Sheer | 98 | D1 |
| Ashwell | Ashw | 4 | D3 | Dunton | Dunt | 1 | A5 | Langley (Essex) | Lang | 18 | F2 | Shenley | Shen | 157 | A5 |
| Aspenden | Asp | 40 | D5 | Eastwick | East | 117 | A4 | Latimer | Lat | 150 | E3 | Shillington | Shill | 19 | E8 |
| Aston | Ast | 51 | E2 | Edgware | Edg | 170 | E1 | Letchworth | Letw | 22 | F7 | South Oxhey | Sth Ox | 175 | B7 |
| Aston Clinton | Ast Cl | 99 | A3 | Edworth | Edw | 3 | A6 | Lilley | Lily | 32 | D2 | St Albans | St Alb | 127 | F4 |
| Ayot St Lawrence | A St L | 88 | B6 | Elstree | Elst | 169 | E3 | Little Berkhamsted | L Berk | 132 | C4 | St Ippolitts | St Ipp | 35 | B3 |
| Ayot St Peter | A St P | 88 | F3 | Enfield | Enf | 162 | E1 | Little Chalfont | L Chal | 150 | B1 | St Leonards | St Le | 119 | E3 |
| Baldock | Bal | 23 | E8 | Essendon | Ess | 131 | F6 | Little Gaddesden | L Gad | 102 | D7 | Standon | Stand | 55 | E1 |
| Barkway | Bark | 17 | D4 | Farnham | Far | 58 | D6 | Little Hadham | L Had | 57 | C2 | Stanmore | Stan | 176 | F5 |
| Barley | Bar | 8 | F1 | Felden | Fel | 138 | A8 | Little Hallingbury | L Hal | 98 | D7 | Stansted Abbotts | Sta Ab | 115 | F4 |
| Barnet | Barn | 171 | F4 | Flamstead | Fla | 84 | B1 | Little Hormead | L Hor | 42 | B8 | Stansted Mountfitchet | Sta M | 59 | C7 |
| Bassingbourn | Bas | 6 | F8 | Flaunden | Flau | 151 | A6 | Little Wymondley | L Wym | 35 | E3 | Stapleford | Stap | 92 | A7 |
| Bayford | Bay | 132 | F6 | Furneux Pelham | Fur P | 43 | A5 | London Colney | Lon C | 142 | E5 | Steeple Morden | Ste Mo | 5 | B8 |
| Benington | Ben | 52 | E4 | Goff's Oak | Gofs O | 147 | D3 | Long Marston | Lo M | 79 | B3 | Stevenage | Stev | 50 | D8 |
| Berden | Berd | 43 | F7 | Graveley | Gra | 36 | C4 | Lower Nazeing | Lo Naz | 149 | D8 | Stocking Pelham | Sto P | 43 | E7 |
| Berkhamsted | Berk | 122 | C6 | Great Amwell | Gt Am | 114 | F5 | Lower Stondon | L Ston | 10 | A3 | Stotfold | Stot | 11 | E7 |
| Birchanger | Birhr | 59 | E2 | Great Chishill | Gt Ch | 9 | F2 | Luton | Luton | 45 | C3 | Streatley | Str | 31 | A5 |
| Bishop's Stortford | Bis St | 76 | D7 | Great Gaddesden | Gt Gd | 103 | D3 | Maple Cross | Map Cr | 172 | D6 | Studham | Stu | 82 | C4 |
| Borehamwood | Bor | 170 | B6 | Great Hallingbury | Gt Ha | 77 | E4 | Markyate | Mark | 83 | F5 | Tewin | Tewin | 90 | E2 |
| Botley | Bot | 136 | A1 | Great Hormead | Gt Ho | 42 | B8 | Marsworth | Mars | 80 | A1 | Therfield | Ther | 15 | F7 |
| Bovingdon | Bov | 137 | B3 | Great Munden | Gt Mu | 54 | C5 | Meesden | Mee | 29 | F6 | Thundridge | Thun | 93 | E7 |
| Bramfield | Bram | 91 | C4 | Great Offley | Gt Of | 33 | D2 | Melbourn | Melb | 2 | A5 | Tonwell | Ton | 92 | F7 |
| Braughing | Brag | 55 | F6 | Great Wymondley | Gt Wy | 35 | F6 | Mentmore | Men | 61 | D4 | Tring | Tri | 100 | B3 |
| Breachwood Green | Bre Gr | 47 | E1 | Guilden Morden | Gu M | 1 | F5 | Moor Park | Mo Pk | 174 | D6 | Walkern | Walk | 38 | B1 |
| Brent Pelham | Bre P | 30 | A2 | Hadley Wood | Had W | 159 | C2 | Much Hadham | Muc H | 74 | F3 | Wallington | Wal | 25 | D8 |
| Brickendon | Bric | 133 | C4 | Hammond Street | Ham St | 147 | D5 | New Mill End | Nwml E | 64 | D1 | Waltham Abbey | Wa Aby | 163 | E7 |
| Bricket Wood | Bri Wd | 140 | F1 | Harefield | Hare | 173 | C1 | Newgate Street | New St | 146 | C7 | Ware | Ware | 93 | F2 |
| Brookmans Park | Bro Pk | 144 | F5 | Harlow | Harl | 117 | E1 | Newnham | Newn | 12 | F7 | Wareside | Wars | 94 | E4 |
| Buckland | Buck | 27 | D8 | Harpenden | Harp | 86 | B2 | Northaw | Nort | 145 | F1 | Watford | Watf | 167 | C3 |
| Buntingford | Bun | 40 | F7 | Harrow | Har | 176 | E1 | Northchurch | Nthch | 121 | D6 | Watton at Stone | Wat St | 70 | D4 |
| Bushey | Bus | 168 | A2 | Hatfield | Hat | 130 | B8 | Northwood | Norwd | 174 | E4 | Welham Green | Wel Gr | 144 | C7 |
| Bygrave | Byg | 13 | C5 | Hatfield Heath | Hat H | 98 | F4 | Nuthampstead | Nut | 18 | B2 | Welwyn | Welw | 89 | B4 |
| Caddington | Cad | 62 | E4 | Hemel Hempstead | Heml H | 124 | E1 | Odsey | Odsey | 5 | C1 | Welwyn Garden City | Wel G C | 110 | E7 |
| Chalfont St Peter | C St P | 172 | A3 | Henlow | Henlw | 10 | D8 | Park Street | Pk St | 141 | D5 | Westmill | West | 40 | F3 |
| Cheddington | Ched | 80 | A8 | Hertford | Hert | 113 | C5 | Pinner | Pnr | 175 | E1 | Weston | Wes | 24 | C1 |
| Chenies | Chen | 151 | B2 | Hertford Heath | Hert H | 114 | B3 | Pirton | Pirt | 20 | C4 | Wheathampstead | Whea | 108 | C7 |
| Cheshunt | Ches | 148 | C1 | Hertingfordbury | Hertng | 112 | F5 | Pitstone | Pit | 80 | D4 | Whipsnade | Whip | 82 | A8 |
| Chipperfield | Chipf | 152 | B8 | Hexton | Hex | 19 | B2 | Potten End | Pot En | 123 | C7 | Whitwell | Whit | 66 | E6 |
| Chiswellgreen | Chis | 141 | A5 | High Wych | H Wych | 97 | B1 | Potters Bar | Pot B | 159 | D6 | Widford | Widf | 95 | E4 |
| Cholesbury | Chol | 120 | C2 | Hinxworth | Hin | 3 | D6 | Preston | Pres | 48 | D6 | Wigginton | Wigg | 100 | D1 |
| Chorleywood | Chor | 164 | E5 | Hitchin | Hit | 34 | E8 | Radlett | Radl | 156 | B5 | Wilstone | Wils | 79 | D1 |
| Clavering | Clav | 30 | F5 | Hoddesdon | Hod | 135 | B5 | Redbourn | Red | 106 | B6 | Wingrave | Wing | 60 | C3 |
| Clothall | Clo | 24 | E4 | Holwell | Hol | 21 | B7 | Reed | Reed | 16 | F5 | Wyddial | Wyd | 28 | B3 |
| Codicote | Cod | 67 | E1 | Hunsdon | Hun | 95 | D1 | Rickmansworth | Ric | 165 | D1 | | | | |
| Colney Heath | Coln H | 143 | D8 | Ickleford | Ick | 21 | E4 | Ridge | Ridge | 157 | F5 | | | | |
| Cottered | Cotrd | 39 | C7 | Kelshall | Kel | 15 | D5 | Royston | Royst | 7 | C5 | | | | |

Abbey Ave. St Alb AL3 .... 127 B1
Abbey Ct. Wa Aby EN9 .... 163 B5
Abbey Dr. Abb L WD5 .... 154 A7
Abbey Dr. Luton LU2 .... 46 A1
Abbey Hts. St Alb AL1 .... 127 E3
Abbey Mead Ind Est.
Wa Aby .... 163 C5
Abbey Mill End. St Alb AL3 127 C2
Abbey Mill La. St Alb AL3 . 127 C2
Abbey Rd. Ches EN8 .... 162 E5
Abbey Sch The. St Alb .... 127 D2
Abbey Sta. St Alb .... 127 D1
Abbey Theatre. St Alb .... 127 C1
Abbey View Rd. St Alb AL3 127 C3
Abbey View. St Alb AL1 .... 127 D1
Abbey View. Watf WD2 .... 154 D3
Abbeygate Bsns Ctr The.
Luton .... 63 F8
Abbeyview. Wa Aby EN9 .. 163 C6
Abbis Orch. Ick SG5 .... 21 E5
Abbot John Mews.
Whea AL4 .... 87 D1
Abbots Ave. St Alb AL1 .... 141 E8
Abbots Ave W. St Alb AL1 141 D8
Abbots Cl. Dat SG3 .... 69 D1
Abbots Ct. Luton LU2 .... 46 A1
Abbots Gr. Stev SG1 .... 50 F5
Abbots Langley Sch.
Abb L .... 139 F1
Abbots Pk. St Alb AL1 .... 128 A1
Abbots Rd. Abb L WD5 .... 139 E1
Abbots Rise. Kin L WD4 .... 138 F5
Abbots View. Kin L WD4 .. 138 F4
Abbots Wood Rd.
Luton LU2 .... 46 A1
Abbotswood Par.
Luton LU2 .... 46 A1
Abbotts La. Widf SG12 .... 95 D3
Abbotts Rd. Letw SG6 .... 22 D6
Abbotts Rise.
Sta Ab SG12 .... 115 D4
Abbotts Way. Bis St CM23 . 76 E3
Abbotts Way.
Sta Ab SG12 .... 115 D4
Abbotts Way. Wing HP22 .. 60 A4
Abbotts Yd. Royst SG8 .... 7 D6
Abdale La. Wel G AL9 .... 144 C4
Abel Cl. Heml H HP2 .... 125 A3
Abel Smith Jun Mix Inf Sch.
Hert .... 113 C6
Aberdale Gdns. Pot B EN6 158 F7
Aberdeen Rd. Har HA3 .... 176 F1
Aberford Rd. Bor WD6 .... 170 A7
Abigail Cl. Luton LU3 .... 45 D3
Abingdon Pl. Pot B EN6 .... 159 B7
Abingdon Rd. Dun LU4 .... 44 C3
Aboyne Lodge Prim Sch.
St Alb .... 127 D4
Abridge Cl. Enf EN8 .... 162 D4
Abstacle Hill. Tri HP23 .... 99 F3
Acacia Cl. Ham St EN7 .... 147 E4
Acacia Cl. Stan HA7 .... 176 E4
Acacia Gr. Berk HP4 .... 122 B3
Acacia Rd. Enf EN2 .... 161 D1
Acacia St. Hat AL10 .... 130 A2
Acacia Wlk. Harp AL5 .... 107 D6
Acacia Wlk. Tri HP23 .... 99 E3
Acers. Chis AL2 .... 141 C3
Achilles Cl. Heml H HP2 .... 124 F5
Ackroyd Rd. Royst SG8 .... 7 E8
Acme Rd. Watf WD2 .... 154 B1
Acorn La. Cuf EN6 .... 146 E2
Acorn Pl. Watf WD2 .... 154 A2
Acorn Rd. Heml H HP3 .... 125 A2
Acorn St. Hun SG12 .... 116 D8
Acorns The. St Alb AL4 .... 128 D3
Acre Piece. Hit SG4 .... 35 A6
Acre Way. Norwd HA6 .... 174 F2
Acre Wood. Heml H HP2 .. 124 E2
Acremore St. L Had SG11 .. 75 C7
Acrewood Way.
Coln H AL4 .... 128 F3
Acton Cl. Ches EN8 .... 162 E8
Acworth Cres. Luton LU4 ... 44 C5
Acworth Ct. Luton LU4 .... 44 C5
Adam's Yd. Hert SG14 .... 113 D6 1
Adams House. Harl CM20 117 D1
Adams Way. Tri HP23 .... 100 B6
Adamsfield. Ham St EN7 .. 148 A5
Adderley Rd. Bis St CM23 .. 76 F7
Adderley Rd. Har HA3 .... 176 F2
Addiscombe Rd.
Watf WD1 .... 167 B5
Addiscombe Road Jun Sch.
Watf .... 167 B5
Addison Cl. Norwd HA6 .... 175 A2
Addison Way. Norwd HA6 174 F2
Adelaide Cl. Enf EN1 .... 161 F1
Adelaide St. Luton LU1 .... 63 D7
Adelaide St. St Alb AL3 .... 127 D4
Adele Ave. Welw AL6 .... 89 F3
Adeyfield Gdns.
Heml H HP2 .... 124 F4
Adeyfield Rd. Heml H HP2 124 F3
Adeyfield Sec Mod Sch.
Heml H .... 125 A3
Adhara Rd. Mo Pk HA6 .... 175 A5 2
Adinger Cl. Stev SG1 .... 50 E3
Adingtons. Harl CM20 .... 117 F2
Admiral St. Hert SG13 .... 114 A6
Admiral Way. Nthch HP4 . 121 F6
Admirals Cl. Col H AL4 .... 143 E8
Admirals Wlk. Hod EN11 . 135 B4
Admirals Wlk. St Alb AL1 . 142 A8
Adrian Cl. Hare UB9 .... 173 D2
Adrian House. Abb L WD5 153 E8
Adrian Rd. Abb L WD5 .... 153 E8
Adstone Rd. Cad LU1 .... 62 F3
Ailsworth Rd. Luton LU3 .... 45 A7
Ainsdale Rd. Sth Ox WD1 175 C7
Aintree Rd. Royst SG8 .... 7 F6
Aintree Way. Stev SG1 .... 51 C8
Airedale. Heml H HP2 .... 124 E6
Airport Approach Rd.
Luton LU2 .... 64 D8
Airport Executive Pk. Luton 64 D8
Airport Way.
Luton LU1,LU2 .... 64 C6
Aitken Rd. Barn EN5 .... 171 C4
Akeman Cl. St Alb AL3 .... 126 F1
Akeman St. Tri HP23 .... 100 A3
Alan Dr. Barn EN5 .... 171 E3
Alandale Dr. Pnr HA5 .... 175 B2
Alban Ave. St Alb AL3 .... 127 D5
Alban Cres. Bor WD6 .... 170 B8
Alban Ct. Barn EN5 .... 171 D5
Alban Ct. St Alb AL1 .... 128 C3
Alban Pk Ind Est. Coln H .. 128 F3
Alban Rd. Letw SG6 .... 23 C3
Alban Wood Inf Sch. Watf 154 B7
Alban Wood Jun Sch.
Watf .... 154 B6
Albans View. Watf WD2 .. 154 B6
Albany Cl. Bus WD2 .... 168 D3
Albany Ct. Harp AL5 .... 107 C8
Albany Mews. Chis AL2 .... 141 A4
Albany Mews. Ware SG12 . 93 E1 3
Albany Park Ave. Enf EN3 162 D1
Albany Rd. Enf EN3 .... 162 D1
Albany Terr. Tri HP23 .... 100 B6
Albemarle Ave. Ches EN8 148 C3
Albemarle Ave. Pot B EN6 159 B7
Albeny Gate. St Alb AL1 .... 127 D2
Albert Rd. Arl SG15 .... 11 A4
Albert Rd. Luton LU1 .... 63 E6
Albert Rd N. Watf WD1 .... 167 B6
Albert Rd S. Watf WD1 .... 167 B6
Albert St. Mark AL3 .... 83 E5
Albert St. St Alb AL1 .... 127 D2
Albert St. Stev SG1 .... 50 D7
Albert St. Tri HP23 .... 100 A3
Albion Cl. Hert SG13 .... 113 E7
Albion Ct. Luton LU2 .... 63 E8 5
Albion Hill. Heml H HP2 .... 124 D2
Albion Rd. Luton LU2 .... 63 E8
Albion Rd. Pit LU7 .... 80 D5
Albion Rd. St Alb AL1 .... 127 F3
Albion The. Ware SG12 .... 93 D2 9
Albury Cl. Luton LU3 .... 31 A1
Albury Dr. Pnr HA5 .... 175 D3
Albury Dr. Pnr HA5 .... 175 E3
Albury Grove Rd.
Ches EN8 .... 148 D1
Albury Rd. L Had SG11 .... 57 C2
Albury Ride. Ches EN8 .... 162 D8
Albury Sch. Alb .... 57 A6
Albury Wlk. Ches EN8 .... 148 C1
Alconbury. Bis St CM23 .... 59 B1
Alconbury. Wel G C AL7 ... 111 E6
Aldbury Cl. St Alb AL4 .... 128 C8
Aldbury Cl. Watf WD2 .... 154 D3
Aldbury Gdns. Tri HP23 .... 100 B6
Aldbury Gr. Wel G C AL7 .. 111 B6
Aldbury Jun Mix Inf Sch
(Vol Con). Ald .... 101 C6
Aldbury Rd. Ric WD3 .... 164 F2
Aldcock Rd. Stev SG1 .... 50 E7
Aldeburgh Cl. Stev SG1 .... 36 A1
Aldenham Ave. Radl WD7 156 A3
Aldenham Country Pk.
Elst .... 169 B4
Aldenham Gr. Radl WD7 .. 156 B5
Aldenham Rd. Bus WD2 ... 168 A6
Aldenham Rd. Elst WD6 ... 169 B5
Aldenham Rd. Radl WD7 .. 156 A4
Aldenham Rd. Radl WD7 .. 169 B5
Aldenham Rd. Watf WD2 . 167 E5
Aldenham Sch. Radl .... 168 F7
Alder Cl. Bal SG7 .... 23 F7
Alder Cl. Bis St CM23 .... 76 D4
Alder Cl. Chis AL2 .... 141 C3
Alder Cres. Luton LU3 .... 45 A3
Alder Ct. Luton LU3 .... 45 B3
Alder Wlk. Watf WD2 .... 154 B4
Alderbury Rd. Sta M CM24 59 E8
Alderley Ct. Berk HP4 .... 122 C3
Alderman Cl. Wel G AL9 ... 144 C7
Alderney House. Enf EN3 . 162 D1
Alders Cl. Wel G C .... 111 A6
Alders End La. Harp AL5 .... 85 F2
Alders Wlk. Saw CM21 .... 97 E2
Aldersgrove. Wa Aby EN9 163 E5
Alderton Cl. Luton LU2 .... 46 D1 4
Alderton Dr. L Gad HP4 .... 102 B8
Aldhous Cl. Luton LU3 .... 45 B5
Aldock. Wel G C AL7 .... 111 A3
Aldridge Ave. Enf EN3 .... 163 A1
Aldwick Ct. St Alb AL1 .... 128 B1
Aldwick Rd. Harp AL5 .... 107 E8
Aldwick. St Alb AL1 .... 128 B1
Aldwickbury Cres.
Harp AL5 .... 86 D1
Aldwickbury Sch. Harp .... 107 E8
Aldwyck Ct. Heml H HP1 .. 124 C4
Aldwyke Rise. Ware SG12 . 93 C3
Aldykes. Hat AL10 .... 129 F5
Alesia Rd. Luton LU3 .... 44 F6
Alex Ct. Heml H HP2 .... 124 D4
Alexander Ct. Ches EN8 .... 148 D1
Alexander Gate. Stev SG1 . 51 C8
Alexander Rd. Hert SG14 . 113 A6
Alexander Rd. Lon C AL2 .. 142 D6
Alexander Rd. Stot SG5 .... 11 F6
Alexandra Ave. Luton LU3 .. 45 C2
Alexandra Rd. Bor WD6 .... 170 D8
Alexandra Rd. Chipf WD4 138 A1
Alexandra Rd.
Heml H HP2 .... 124 D4
Alexandra Rd. Hit SG5 .... 21 F1
Alexandra Rd. Sar WD3 .... 152 A3
Alexandra Rd. St Alb AL1 . 127 E3
Alexandra Rd. Watf WD1 . 167 A7
Alexandra Sch. Bus .... 168 A6
Alexandra Way. Ches EN8 162 F5
Aleyn Way. Bal SG7 .... 13 B1
Alfriston Cl. Luton LU2 .... 46 C3
Algar Cl. Stan HA7 .... 176 F5
Alington La. Letw SG6 .... 22 F3
All Saints C of E Jun Mix
Inf Sch. Bis St .... 77 B8
All Saints Cl. Bis St CM23 .. 77 A8
All Saints La. Cro Gr WD3 166 A3
All Saints Mews.
Stan HA3 .... 176 E4
All Saints Prim Sch. Dat .... 69 D3
Allandale Cres. Pot B EN6 158 E7
Allandale. Heml H HP2 .... 124 D5
Allandale Rd. Enf EN3 .... 162 D3
Allandale. St Alb AL3 .... 141 B8
Allard Cl. Ham St EN7 .... 147 F4
Allard Cres. Bus WD2 .... 168 C1
Allard Way. Hod EN10 .... 134 E2
Alldicks Rd. Heml H HP3 .. 124 F1
Allen Cl. Whea AL4 .... 108 D7
Allen Ct. Hat AL10 .... 130 B3 2
Allenby Ave. Dun LU5 .... 44 A1
Allende Ave. Harl CM20 .... 117 D2
Allendale. Luton LU3 .... 31 A1
Allerton Cl. Bor WD6 .... 156 F1
Allerton Rd. Bor WD6 .... 156 F1
Alleyns Rd. Stev SG1 .... 50 D7
Allied Bsns Ctr. Harp .... 86 C3
Allison. Letw SG6 .... 23 C5
Allsaints Cres. Watf WD2 154 D6
Allton Rd. L Ston SG16 .... 10 A4
Allum La. Radl WD6 .... 169 E5
Allwood Rd. Ham St EN7 .. 147 F4
Alma Ct. Bor HA2 .... 156 F1
Alma Cut. St Alb AL1 .... 127 E2
Alma Link. Luton LU1 .... 63 D7
Alma Rd. Nthch HP4 .... 121 E6
Alma Rd. St Alb AL1 .... 127 E2
Alma Row. Har HA3 .... 176 D2
Alma St. Luton LU1 .... 63 D7
Almond Hill Jun Sch. Stev .. 50 E8
Almond Way. Bor WD6 .... 170 B5
Almond Way. Har HA2 .... 176 C1
Almond Wlk. Hat AL10 .... 130 A2 1
Almonds La. Stev SG1 .... 50 E8
Almonds The. St Alb AL1 .. 142 B7
Alms La. Ashw SG7 .... 4 D4
Almshouse La. Enf EN1 .... 162 B2
Alnwick Dr. Lon M HP3 .... 78 F7
Alpha Bsns Pk. Wel G .... 144 C8
Alpha Pl. Bis St CM23 .... 76 F8
Alpine Cl. Hit SG4 .... 35 A5
Alpine Way. Luton LU3 .... 44 D8
Alpine Wlk. Stan HA7 .... 176 E8
Alston Ct. Barn EN5 .... 171 E6
Alston Rd. Barn EN5 .... 171 E6
Alston Rd. Heml H HP1 .... 124 A2
Altair Way. Mo Pk HA6 .... 174 F5
Altham Gr. Harl CM20 .... 117 F2
Altham Rd. Pnr HA5 .... 175 E3
Althorp Rd. Luton LU3 .... 45 C1
Althorp Rd. St Alb AL1 .... 127 F4
Alton Ave. Har HA7 .... 176 F3
Alton Rd. Luton LU1 .... 63 F5
Altwood. Harp AL5 .... 86 D1
Alva Cl. Sth Ox WD1 .... 175 D8
Alva Way. Sth Ox WD1 .... 175 D8
Alverton. St Alb AL3 .... 127 C6
Alwin Pl. Watf WD1 .... 166 E5
Alwyn Cl. Bor WD6 .... 169 F3
Alwyn Cl. Luton LU2 .... 45 E2
Alyngton. Nthch HP4 .... 121 E7
Alzey Gdns. Harp AL5 .... 107 D8
Amberley Cl. Harp AL5 .... 86 B2
Amberley Cl. Luton LU2 .... 46 D4
Amberley Gn. Ware SG12 .. 93 C4
Amberry Ct. Harl CM20 .... 117 D1
Ambleside. Luton LU3 .... 44 F5
Ambrose La. Harp AL5 .... 85 F4
Amenbury La. Harp AL5 .... 86 A1
Amersham Rd.
Chen HP6,WD3 .... 164 B8
Ames Cl. Luton LU3 .... 44 F8
Amor Way. Letw SG6 .... 23 B6
Amwell Comm.
Wel G C AL7 .... 111 C5
Amwell Cl. Hod EN9 .... 135 A7
Amwell Ct. Wa Aby EN9 .... 163 E6
Amwell End. Ware SG12 .... 93 D1
Amwell Hill. Gt Am SG12 . 114 F6
Amwell La. Gt Am SG12 .... 115 B5
Amwell La. Whea AL4 .... 108 B7
Amwell Pl. Hert H SG13 .... 114 C4
Amwell St. Hod EN11 .... 135 A6
Amwell View Sch. Gt Am .. 115 B4
Anchor Cl. Ches EN8 .... 148 D3
Anchor Cotts. Thun SG12 ... 93 D7
Anchor La. Heml H HP1 .... 124 B1
Anchor La. Heml H HP1 .... 124 C2
Anchor La. Ton SG12 .... 93 B6
Anchor Rd. Bal SG7 .... 23 F7
Anchor St. Bis St CM23 .... 77 A6
Ancient Almshouses.
Ches EN8 .... 148 D1
Anderson Cl. Hare UB9 .... 173 A2
Anderson Rd. Shen WD7 . 157 A6
Anderson Rd. Stev SG2 .... 51 D6
Anderson's House.
Hit SG5 .... 34 F8 3
Anderson's La. Gt Ho SG9 . 29 A1
Andover Cl. Luton LU4 .... 44 C6
Andrew's La. Ches EN8 .... 148 B3
Andrew's La. Gofs O EN7 . 147 F3
Andrews Cl. Heml H HP2 . 124 D5
Andrews Lane Jun & Inf
Sch. Ches .... 148 B3
Andrewsfield.
Wel G C AL7 .... 111 C6
Anelle Rise. Heml H HP3 . 138 F7
Anershall. Wing HP22 .... 60 B3
Angel Cotts. Gt Of SG5 .... 33 D2
Angel Pavement. Royst SG8 7 D6
Angell's Meadow.
Ashw SG7 .... 4 D4
Angle Ways. Stev SG2 .... 51 B2
Anglefield Rd. Berk HP4 .. 122 A4
Anglesey Cl. Bis St CM23 ... 76 C7
Anglesey Rd. Sth Ox WD1 175 C5
Anglian Bsns Pk. Royst .... 7 B7
Anglian Cl. Watf WD1 .... 167 C7
Angotts Mead. Stev SG1 .... 50 B6
Angus Cl. Dun LU4 .... 44 A3
Anmer Gdns. Dun LU4 .... 44 B4
Annables La. Harp AL5 .... 85 A4
Annette Cl. Har HA3 .... 176 E1
Anns Cl. Tri HP23 .... 99 E3
Ansell Ct. Stev SG1 .... 36 B1
Anselm Rd. Pnr HA5 .... 175 F3
Anson Cl. Bov HP3 .... 136 F4
Anson Cl. Sand AL4 .... 108 C1
Anson Cl. St Alb AL1 .... 128 B1
Anson Wlk. Mo Pk HA6 .... 174 C6
Anstee Rd. Luton LU4 .... 44 B6
Anstey Sch. Ans .... 29 A6
Anthony Cl. Watf WD1 .... 167 D1
Anthony Gdns. Luton LU1 .. 63 D6
Anthony Rd. Bor WD6 .... 169 F7
Anthorne Cl. Pot B EN6 .... 159 B8
Anthus Mews. Norwd HA6 174 E3
Antoinette Ct. Abb L WD5 139 F2
Antoneys Cl. Pnr HA5 .... 175 D1
Antonine Gate. St Alb AL3 127 A2
Anvil Ct. Luton LU3 .... 44 E5
Anvil House. Harp AL5 .... 86 A2
Aplins Cl. Harp AL5 .... 85 F2
Apollo Ave. Mo Pk HA6 .... 175 A5
Apollo Way. Heml H HP2 . 124 F5
Apollo Way. Stev SG2 .... 51 C8
Apple Cotts. Bov HP3 .... 137 A4
Apple Orch The.
Heml H HP2 .... 124 F5
Apple Tree Gr. Red AL3 .... 106 B6
Appleby St. Ham St EN7 ... 147 E5
Applecroft. Chis AL2 .... 141 B3
Applecroft Jun Mix Inf Sch.
Wel G C .... 110 B5
Applecroft. L Ston SG16 .... 10 B3
Applecroft. Nthch HP4 .... 121 E6
Applecroft Rd. Luton LU2 ... 46 C4
Applecroft Rd.
Wel G C AL8 .... 110 B6
Appleford's Cl. Hod EN11 134 F8
Appleton Ave. Wars SG12 . 94 E5
Appleton Fields.
Bis St CM23 .... 76 E4
Appletree Wlk. Watf WD2 154 B4
Appletrees. Hit SG5 .... 34 D6
Applewood Cl. Harp AL5 ... 85 E3
Appleyard Terr. Enf EN3 .. 162 C2
Approach Rd. St Alb AL1 .. 127 E2
Approach The. Pot B EN6 158 F7
Appspond La. St Alb AL2 .. 140 C8
April Pl. Saw CM21 .... 97 F3
Apsley Cl. Bis St CM23 .... 76 F4
Apsley End Rd. Shil SG5 .... 19 E6
Apsley Grange.
Heml H HP3 .... 138 E6
Apsley Ind Est. Heml H .... 138 D7
Apsley Mills Ret Pk.
Heml H .... 138 E7
Apsley Sta. Heml H .... 138 E6
Apton Ct. Bis St CM23 .... 76 F7
Apton Fields. Bis St CM23 . 76 F6
Apton Rd. Bis St CM23 .... 76 F7
Aquadrome The. Ric .... 173 C8
Aquarius Way. Mo Pk HA6 175 A6
Aragon Cl. Heml H HP2 .... 125 C8
Aran Cl. Harp AL5 .... 107 D6
Arbour Cl. Luton LU3 .... 31 A1
Arbour The. Hert SG13 .... 113 D4
Arbroath Gn. Sth Ox WD1 175 B7
Arcade. Hit SG5 .... 34 E7 5
Arcade The. Hat AL10 .... 130 B6
Arcade The. Letw SG6 .... 22 F6
Arcade Wlk. Hit SG5 .... 34 E7 4
Arch Rd. L Wym SG4 .... 35 E4
Archer Cl. Kin L WD4 .... 138 F2
Archer Rd. Stev SG1 .... 51 A7
Archers. Bun SG9 .... 40 F7
Archers Cl. Hert SG14 .... 113 C7
Archers Cl. Red AL3 .... 106 B5
Archers Fields. St Alb AL1 127 F5
Archers Ride.
Wel G C AL7 .... 111 B4
Archers Way. Letw SG6 .... 22 D6
Arches The. Letw SG6 .... 23 A7
Archfield. Wel G C AL7 .... 89 E1
Archway House. Hat AL9 . 130 C6
Archway Par. Luton LU3 .... 44 F4
Archway Rd. Luton LU3 .... 44 E4
Ardeley Vol Prim Sch. Ard . 38 F3
Arden Cl. Bov HP3 .... 137 A3
Arden Cl. Bus WD2 .... 168 F2
Arden Gr. Harp AL5 .... 86 B1
Arden Pl. Luton LU2 .... 45 E1
Arden Press Way.
Letw SG6 .... 23 B6
Ardens Way. St Alb AL4 ... 128 D6
Ardentinny. St Alb AL1 .... 127 E2
Ardern Ct. St Alb AL1 .... 128 C1
Ardleigh Gn. Luton LU2 .... 46 E1 2
Ardross Ave. Mo Pk HA6 . 174 E5
Arena Par. Letw SG6 .... 22 F6
Arena The. Enf .... 162 F1
Argyle Rd. Barn EN5 .... 171 C5
Argyle Way. Stev SG1 .... 50 C5
Argyll Ave. Luton LU3 .... 45 C2
Argyll Rd. Heml H HP2 .... 124 E8
Arkley Ct. Heml H HP2 .... 125 B8
Arkley Dr. Barn EN5 .... 171 B4
Arkley La. Barn EN5 .... 171 B5
Arkley Pk. Bor NW7 .... 170 D3
Arkley Rd. Heml H HP2 .... 125 B8
Arkley View. Barn EN5 .... 171 B5
Arkwrights. Harl CM20 .... 117 F1
Arlesey New Rd. Arl SG15 . 22 B7
Arlesey Rd. Arl SG15 .... 22 A7
Arlesey Rd. Arl SG16 .... 11 A8
Arlesey Rd. Henlw SG16 .... 10 D8
Arlesey Rd. Henlw SG16 .... 10 E8
Arlesey Rd. Ick SG5 .... 21 F5
Arlesey Rd. Stot SG5 .... 11 E6
Arlesey Sta. Arl .... 11 A8
Arlington Cres. Ches EN8 162 E5
Arlington Mews.
Wa Aby EN9 .... 163 C6
Armand Cl. Watf WD1 .... 153 F1
Armitage Cl. Ric WD3 .... 165 D5

Armitage Gdns. Luton LU4 . 44 D1
Armour Rise. Hit SG4 ......... 22 B2
Armstrong Cl. Lon C AL2 .. 142 E4
Armstrong Gdns. Shen WD7 .................... 156 E7
Armstrong Pl. Heml H HP1 ................ 124 D4 1
Arncliffe Cres. Luton LU2 ... 45 E1
Arndale Ctr. Luton .............. 63 E7
Arnett Cl. Ric WD3 ........... 165 A3
Arnett Hills Jun Mix Inf Sch. Ric ................................ 165 A3
Arnett Way. Ric WD3 ....... 165 A2
Arnold Ave E. Enf EN3 ...... 163 A1
Arnold Ave W. Enf EN3 .... 162 F1
Arnold Cl. Hit SG4 ............ 35 B8
Arnold Cl. Luton LU2 ......... 46 A3
Arnold Cl. Stev SG1 ........... 36 D2
Arnolds La. Hin SG7 ............ 3 D6
Arran Cl. Heml H HP3 ...... 125 C1
Arran Ct. Luton LU1 .......... 63 D7
Arretine Cl. St Alb AL3 ...... 126 F1
Arrewig La. St Le HP5 ...... 119 D1
Arrow Cl. Luton LU3 .......... 44 E6
Arthur Gibbens Ct. Stev SG1 ........................ 37 A1
Arthur Rd. St Alb AL1 ....... 128 B3
Arthur St. Luton LU1 .......... 63 E6
Arthur St. Watf WD2 ....... 167 D5
Artillery Pl. Har HA3 ........ 176 C3
Artisan Cres. St Alb AL3 .. 127 C4
Arts Education Sch. Tri .... 100 B3
Arundel Cl. Ast SG2 ............ 51 E3
Arundel Cl. Ches EN8 ....... 148 C3
Arundel Cl. Heml H HP2 ... 125 B4
Arundel Dr. Bor WD6 ......... 170 C5
Arundel Gr. St Alb AL3 ..... 127 D7
Arundel Rd. Luton LU4 ....... 44 F2
Ascot Cl. Bis St CM23 ........ 77 C8
Ascot Cl. Bor WD6 ........... 170 A4
Ascot Cres. Stev SG1 .......... 37 B1
Ascot Gdns. Enf EN3 ........ 162 C2
Ascot Ind Est. Letw ............ 23 B7
Ascot Rd. Luton LU3 .......... 45 B2
Ascot Rd. Royst SG8 ............ 7 F6
Ascot Rd. Watf WD1 ......... 166 E4
Ascots La. Wel G C AL7 ... 110 F2
Ash Cl. Abb L WD5 ........... 153 D7
Ash Cl. Bro Pk AL9 ........... 145 A6
Ash Cl. Hare UB9 ............. 173 D2
Ash Cl. Watf WD2 ............ 154 B4
Ash Copse. Bri Wd AL2 ...... 154 F8
Ash Dr. Hat AL10 ............. 130 A2
Ash Dr. Hit SG4 .................. 35 A4
Ash Gr. Hare UB9 ............ 173 D2
Ash Gr. Heml H HP3 ......... 138 F7
Ash Gr. Whea AL4 .............. 87 C1
Ash Groves. Sheer CM21 .... 98 A2
Ash Hill Cl. Bus WD2 ....... 168 B1
Ash Meadow. Muc H SG10 74 F2
Ash Mill. Bark SG8 ............. 17 C3
Ash Rd. Luton LU4 ............. 63 B8
Ash Rd. Tri HP23 ................ 99 F4
Ash Rd. Ware SG12 ............ 94 A3
Ash Ride. Cre H EN2 ........ 161 A4
Ash Tree Field. Harl CM20 117 A2
Ash Tree Rd. Watf WD2 ... 154 B3
Ash Vale. Map Cr WD3 .... 172 D5
Ash Way. Royst SG8 ............ 7 F6
Ashanger La. Clo SG7 ........ 24 D4
Ashborurne Sq. Norwd HA6 ................ 174 E4
Ashbourne Cl. Letw SG6 ..... 23 B3
Ashbourne Rd. Hod EN10 134 F2
Ashbrook La. St Ipp SG4 .... 35 C3
Ashburnam Wlk. Stev SG2 . 50 F1
Ashburnham Cl. Sth Ox WD1 ................ 175 A7
Ashburnham Dr. Sth Ox WD1 ................ 175 A7
Ashburnham Rd. Luton LU1 63 C7
Ashbury Cl. Hat AL10 ....... 129 E5
Ashby Gdns. St Alb AL1 .... 141 D7
Ashby Rd. Nthch HP4 ....... 121 D7
Ashby Rd. Watf WD2 ....... 154 A1
Ashby Rise. Bis St CM23 .... 59 B1
Ashcombe. Wel G C AL8 .... 89 E2
Ashcroft Cl. Harp AL5 ...... 107 E8
Ashcroft High Sch. Luton ... 46 C2
Ashcroft. Pnr HA5 ........... 176 A4
Ashcroft Rd. Luton LU2 ...... 46 B3
Ashdale. Bis St CM23 ......... 76 D4
Ashdale Gdns. Luton LU3 ... 31 A1
Ashdale Gr. Har HA7 ........ 176 F4
Ashdales. St Alb AL1 ....... 141 D7
Ashdown Cres. Ches EN8 148 E3
Ashdown Dr. Bor WD6 ..... 169 F7
Ashdown. Letw SG6 ........... 11 F1
Ashdown Rd. Stev SG2 ....... 69 B8
Ashdown Rd. Watf WD2 .. 167 D6
Ashendene Rd. Bay SG13 132 F4
Ashfield Ave. Bus WD2 .... 168 C2
Ashfield Jun Sch. Bus ...... 168 B2
Ashfield Way. Luton LU3 .... 45 A6
Ashfields. Watf WD2 ........ 153 F4
Ashford Gn. Sth Ox WD1 . 175 D5
Ashleigh Ct. Hod EN9 ....... 135 A5
Ashleigh Ct. Ric WD3 ....... 165 D2
Ashleigh. Stev SG2 ............. 51 B4
Ashley Cl. Ched LU7 ........... 80 A8
Ashley Cl. Heml H HP3 ..... 124 F1
Ashley Cl. Pnr HA5 ........... 175 B1
Ashley Cl. Wel G C AL8 .... 110 C8
Ashley Ct. Hat AL10 ......... 130 B6
Ashley Dr. Bor WD6 .......... 170 D4
Ashley Gdns. Harp AL5 ....... 85 D3
Ashley Rd. Hert SG14 ....... 113 B5
Ashley Rd. St Alb AL1 ....... 128 C2
Ashleys. Ric WD3 ............. 164 F2
Ashlyn Cl. Watf WD2 ........ 167 E5
Ashlyns Ct. Berk HP4 ....... 122 B3
Ashlyns Rd. Berk HP4 ...... 122 B3
Ashlyns Sch. Berk ............ 122 C2
Ashmore Gdns. Heml H HP3 ................ 125 B2
Ashridge Cl. Bov HP3 ....... 137 A3
Ashridge Dr. Bri Wd AL2 .. 140 F1
Ashridge Dr. Sth Ox WD1 175 C5
Ashridge La. Bot HP3 ....... 150 D7
Ashridge Management Coll. L Gad .......................... 102 C5
Ashridge Rise. Berk HP4 . 121 F5
Ashton Rd. Enf EN3 ......... 162 E3
Ashton Rd. Luton LU1 ........ 63 E5
Ashton's La. Bal SG7 .......... 23 F6
Ashtree Ct. St Alb AL1 ...... 127 F3
Ashtree Prim Sch. Stev ...... 51 C4
Ashtree Way. Heml H HP1 ................ 124 A2
Ashurst Cl. Norwd HA6 .... 174 E3
Ashville Way. Bal SG7 ........ 13 A1
Ashwell Ave. Luton LU3 ..... 44 C8
Ashwell Cl. Gra SG4 .......... 36 B4
Ashwell Comm. Gra SG4 .... 36 B4
Ashwell Jun Mix Inf Sch. Ashw ................................ 4 D4
Ashwell & Morden Sta. Odsey .............................. 5 D2
Ashwell Par. Luton LU3 ..... 44 C8
Ashwell Pk. Harp AL5 ........ 86 D1
Ashwell Rd. Byg SG7 .......... 13 C4
Ashwell Rd. Gu M SG8 ......... 1 F2
Ashwell Rd. Hin SG7 ............ 3 E5
Ashwell Rd. Newn SG7 ....... 12 F8
Ashwell Rd. Ste Mo SG8 ...... 5 A8
Ashwell St. Ashw SG7 .......... 4 E4
Ashwell St. Knee SG8 .......... 2 A3
Ashwell St. St Alb AL3 ...... 127 D4
Ashwell. Stev SG1 .............. 36 C2
Ashwood Rd. Pot B EN6 .... 159 B6
Askew Rd. Mo Pk HA6 ..... 174 D8
Aspasia Cl. St Alb AL1 ...... 127 F2
Aspen Cl. Bri Wd AL2 ....... 140 E1
Aspen Cl. Stev SG2 ............ 69 B7
Aspen Park Dr. Watf WD2 154 B4
Aspen Way. Enf EN3 ........ 162 D4
Aspenden Rd. Bun SG9 ...... 40 E6
Aspens The. Bis St CM23 ... 59 B3
Aspens The. Hit SG4 .......... 35 A6
Aspfield Row. Heml H HP1 ................ 124 B5
Asquith Ct. Stev SG2 ......... 69 C7
Asquith House. Wel G C AL8 ................ 110 D7
Ass House La. Stan HA3 .. 176 B6
Astall Cl. Har HA3 ............ 176 E2
Aster Cl. Bis St CM23 ........ 76 D6
Astley Cooper Sch. Heml H ........................... 125 A8
Astley Gn. Luton LU2 .......... 46 D2
Astley Rd. Heml H HP1 .... 124 C3
Aston Cl. Bus WD2 ........... 168 C3
Aston Cl. Stev SG1 ............. 36 C2
Aston Cl. Watf WD1 ......... 167 C7
Aston End Rd. Ast SG2 ...... 51 E3
Aston La. Ast SG2 .............. 69 E8
Aston Rd. Stand SG11 ........ 55 D2
Aston Rise. Hit SG4 ........... 35 B6
Aston View. Heml H HP2 . 105 A1
Aston Way. Pot B EN6 ..... 159 D7
Astonia House. Bal ............ 23 F7
Astons Rd. Mo Pk HA6 ..... 174 C6
Astra Ct. Luton LU2 ........... 45 F2
Astra Ct. Watf WD1 .......... 166 F4
Astra Ctr. Harl ................. 117 F4
Astral Cl. Henlw SG16 ....... 10 B3
Astrope La. Lon M HP23 ..... 79 B3
Astwick Ave. Hat AL10 ..... 129 F8
Astwick Rd. Stot SG5 ........... 3 A2
Astwick Rd. Stot SG5 ......... 11 F8
Athelstan Rd. Heml H HP3 ................ 138 F8
Athelstan Wlk N. Wel G C AL7 ................ 110 E5
Athelstan Wlk S. Wel G C AL7 ................ 110 D5
Athelstone Rd. Har HA3 ... 176 D1
Athena Est. Harl .............. 118 B4
Athena Pl. Norwd HA6 ..... 174 F2
Atherstone Rd. Luton LU4 .. 44 D1
Atherton End. Saw CM21 ... 97 E3
Athlone Cl. Radl WD7 ...... 156 B3
Athol Cl. Pnr HA5 ............ 175 B2
Athol Gdns. Pnr HA5 ........ 175 B2
Atholl Cl. Luton LU3 ........... 44 D8
Atria Rd. Mo Pk HA6 ........ 175 A5
Attimore Cl. Wel G C AL8 . 110 B5
Attimore Rd. Wel G C AL8 110 B5
Aubretia House. Wel G C AL7 ................ 111 B4
Aubrey Ave. Lon C AL2 ..... 142 C5
Aubrey Gdns. Luton LU4 .... 44 B6
Aubrey La. Red AL3 .......... 105 E2
Aubreys. Letw SG6 ............ 23 A2
Aubreys Rd. Heml H HP1 . 123 E3
Aubries. Walk SG2 ............. 38 B1
Auckland Cl. Enf EN1 ....... 162 B2
Auckland Rd. Pot B EN6 ... 158 E7
Audley Cl. Bor WD6 ......... 170 A6
Audley Ct. Pnr HA5 .......... 175 C1
Audley Gdns. Wa Aby EN9 163 C5
Audrey Gdns. Bis St CM23 . 76 F4
Audwick Cl. Ches EN8 ...... 148 E3
Augustine Rd. Har HA3 .... 176 C2
Augustus Cl. St Alb AL3 .... 127 A1
Augustus Gate. Stev SG2 ... 51 D8
Augustus Smith Sch The. Berk ............................... 122 D2
Austen Paths. Stev SG2 ..... 51 C6
Austin Rd. Luton LU3 ......... 45 C4
Austins Mead. Bov HP3 ... 137 B3
Austins Pl. Heml H HP2 ... 124 D4
Autumn Glades. Heml H HP3 ................ 125 C1
Autumn Gr. Wel G C AL7 .. 111 B4
Avalon Cl. Watf WD2 ....... 154 E7
Avebury Ave. Luton LU2 ..... 45 D4
Avebury Ct. Heml H HP2 .. 125 A5
Avenue App. Kin L WD4 ... 139 A1
Avenue One. Letw SG6 ...... 23 C6
Avenue Rd. Bis St CM23 .... 77 B6
Avenue Rd. Lo Naz EN11 .. 135 D5
Avenue Rd. Pnr HA5 ........ 175 E1
Avenue Rd. St Alb AL1 ..... 127 E4
Avenue Rise. Bus WD2 ..... 168 A4
Avenue Terr. Watf WD1 .. 167 E3
Avenue The. Barn EN5 ..... 171 E6
Avenue The. Bus WD2 ..... 167 F5
Avenue The. Heml H HP1 . 123 E4
Avenue The. Hert SG14 .... 113 B8
Avenue The. Hit SG4 .......... 35 A7
Avenue The. Hod EN11 .... 135 A4
Avenue The. Luton LU4 ...... 44 D5
Avenue The. Norwd HA6 .. 174 C4
Avenue The. Pot B EN 6 ... 145 A1
Avenue The. Radl WD7 .... 156 B5
Avenue The. Stev SG1 ........ 50 D8
Avenue The. Stot SG5 ........ 11 F6
Avenue The. Watf WD1 .... 167 A7
Avenue The. Watf WD2 .... 167 F5
Avenue The. Welw AL6 ...... 89 D7
Avey La. Wa Aby EN9 ....... 163 E2
Avia Cl. Heml H HP3 ........ 138 D7
Avior Dr. Mo Pk HA6 ....... 174 F6
Avocet. Letw SG6 ............... 11 E1
Avon Chase. Henlw SG16 .. 10 C4
Avon Cl. Watf WD2 .......... 154 C5
Avon Ct. Harp AL5 .............. 86 B1 9
Avon Mews. Pnr HA5 ....... 175 F2
Avon Rd. Henlw SG16 ........ 10 C4
Avon Sq. Heml H HP2 ...... 124 F8
Avondale Ct. St Alb AL1 ... 127 E3
Avondale Rd. Luton LU1 ..... 63 C8
Axe Cl. Luton LU3 ............... 44 E6
Aycliffe Dr. Heml H HP2 ... 124 E7
Aycliffe Drive Jun Mix Inf Sch. Heml H ................ 124 E7
Aycliffe Rd. Bor WD6 ....... 156 F1
Aydon Rd. Luton LU3 ......... 45 B6
Aylands Rd. Enf EN3 ........ 162 D3
Aylands Sch. Enf .............. 162 C3
Aylesbury Rd. Tri HP23 ...... 99 E3
Ayllots The. Wat St SG14 ... 70 D4
Aylotts Cl. Bun SG9 ............ 40 D8
Aylsham Rd. Hod EN11 .... 135 C7
Aylward Dr. Stev SG2 ........ 51 B4
Aynho St. Watf WD1 ........ 167 B4
Aynsworth Ave. Bis St CM23 ..................... 59 B2
Ayot Gn. A St P AL6 ........... 89 A1
Ayot Gn. Hat AL6 ............. 109 F8
Ayot Little Green La. A St P AL6 ...................... 88 F1
Ayot St Peter Rd. A St P AL6 ...................... 88 E3
Ayr Cl. Stev SG1 ................ 51 C8
Ayres End La. Whea AL3,AL5 ............ 107 E5
Aysgarth Cl. Harp AL5 ..... 107 B8
Aysgarth Rd. Red AL3 ...... 106 A6

Baas Hill Cl. Hod EN10 ..... 134 E2
Baas Hill. Hod EN10 ........ 134 D2
Baas La. Hod EN10 .......... 134 E3
Babbage Rd. Stev SG1 ....... 50 B5
Back La. Buck SG9 ............. 27 D8
Back La. L Hal CM22 .......... 98 B7
Back La. Pres SG4 .............. 48 D6
Back La. Radl WD2 .......... 168 E8
Back La. Sheer CM22 ......... 98 B1
Back La. Tewin AL6 ............ 90 E2
Back St. Ashw SG7 ............... 4 C3
Back St. Luton LU2 ............. 63 E8
Back The. Pot En HP4 ...... 123 B7
Bacon's Yd. Ashw SG7 ......... 4 D4
Bacons Dr. Cuf EN6 .......... 146 E2
Badburgham Ct. Wa Aby EN9 ................ 163 F6
Baddeley Cl. Stev SG2 ........ 51 B2
Bader Cl. Stev SG1 ............. 36 F1
Bader Cl. Wel G C AL7 ..... 111 C6
Badger Cl. Kneb SG3 ......... 69 A6
Badger Croft. Heml H HP2 ................ 125 D2
Badger Way. Hat AL10 .... 130 B3
Badgers. Bis St CM23 ........ 76 E5
Badgers Cl. Bor WD6 ....... 169 F7
Badgers Cl. Hert SG13 ..... 114 B6
Badgers Cl. Stev SG1 ......... 50 E4
Badgers Croft. Barn HP2 . 171 E1
Badgers Croft. Hod EN10 134 E2
Badgers Wlk. Tewin AL6 .... 90 C5
Badingham Dr. Harp AL5 ... 85 E1
Badminton Cl. Bor WD6 ... 170 A7
Badminton Cl. Stev SG2 .... 69 B7
Badminton Pl. Hod EN10 .. 134 E3
Bagenal House. Abb L WD5 ................... 153 F7
Bagwicks Cl. Luton LU3 ..... 44 E7
Bailey Hill Ct. Luton LU1 .... 63 E5
Bailey St. Luton LU1 ........... 63 F6
Baines La. Dat SG3 ............ 69 C4
Baird Cl. Bus WD2 ........... 168 B3
Bairstow Cl. Bor WD6 ...... 169 E8
Baker Ct. Bor WD6 .......... 170 B7
Baker St. Enf EN1 ............ 161 E1
Baker St. Hert SG13 ......... 113 E6
Baker St. Luton LU1 ........... 63 E5
Baker St. Pot B EN6 ......... 158 E5
Baker St. Stev SG1 ............. 50 C7 2
Baker's La. Cod SG4 .......... 67 F1
Bakers Ct. Bis St CM23 ...... 77 A7 4
Bakers Gr. Wel G C AL7 ... 111 C7
Bakers La. Bar SG8 .............. 8 F2
Bakers La. Ken Co LU6 ....... 82 E8
Bakers Rd. Ches EN7 ....... 148 B1
Bakers Wlk. Saw CM21 ..... 97 E2
Bakerscroft. Ches EN8 ..... 148 E3
Bakery The. Ware SG12 .... 93 D2 2
Bakewell Cl. Dun LU4 ........ 44 C1
Balcombe Cl. Luton LU2 .... 46 D4
Balcon Way. Bor WD6 ..... 170 C8
Baldock La. Letw SG6 ........ 23 D4
Baldock Rd. Asp SG9 ......... 40 B8
Baldock Rd. Letw SG6 ........ 23 B5
Baldock Rd. Stot SG5 ......... 12 A5
Baldock Rd. Ther SG8 .......... 6 C4
Baldock St. Royst SG8 .......... 7 C6
Baldock St. Ware SG12 ...... 93 D2
Baldock Sta. Bal ................ 12 F1
Baldock Way. Bor WD6 ... 169 F8
Baldways Cl. Wing HP22 .... 60 C3
Baldwins La. Cro Gr WD3 166 B5
Baldwins. Wel G C AL7 .... 111 C6
Balfour Ct. Harp AL5 ......... 86 C3
Balfour Mews. Bov HP3 ... 137 A4
Balfour St. Hert SG14 ...... 113 C7
Baliol Rd. Hit SG5 .............. 34 F8
Ballater Cl. Sth Ox WD1 ... 175 C6
Ballinger Ct. Berk HP4 ..... 122 B3
Ballinger Ct. Watf WD1 ... 167 B6 1
Balloon Cnr. Wel G AL9 ... 144 B8
Ballslough Hill. Kim SG4 .... 66 D1
Balmoral Cl. Chis AL2 ...... 141 C3
Balmoral Cl. Stev SG2 ....... 69 C7
Balmoral Dr. Bor WD6 ..... 170 D5
Balmoral Rd. Abb L WD5 . 154 A7
Balmoral Rd. Enf EN3 ...... 162 D3
Balmoral Rd. Hit SG5 ......... 21 E1
Balmoral Rd. Watf WD2 .. 154 C1
Balmore Wood. Luton LU3 . 31 B1
Balsams Cl. Hert SG13 .... 113 D4
Bampton Rd. Dun LU4 ....... 44 B2
Bamville Wood. Harp AL5 107 C5
Banbury Cl. Luton LU4 ....... 44 F4
Banbury St. Watf WD1 .... 167 B4
Bancroft Gdns. Har HA3 .. 176 C2
Bancroft. Hit SG5 ............... 34 F7
Bancroft Rd. Har HA3 ...... 176 C1
Bancroft Rd. Luton LU3 ..... 45 B5
Bandley Rise. Stev SG2 ...... 51 C3
Banes Down. Lo Naz EN9 . 135 E1
Bank Cl. Luton LU4 ............ 44 C4
Bank Ct. Heml H HP1 ....... 124 C2
Bank Mill. Berk HP4 ......... 122 E4
Bank Mill La. Berk HP4 .... 122 E3
Banks Rd. Bor WD6 ......... 170 C7
Bannister Sports Ctr The. Stan ............................. 176 C4
Barbel Cl. Ches EN8 ........ 163 A5
Barberry Rd. Heml H HP1 124 A3
Barbers Wlk. Tri HP23 ....... 99 F3
Barchester Rd. Har HA3 .. 176 D1
Barclay Cl. Hert H SG13 ... 114 B4
Barclay Cl. Watf WD1 ...... 167 A3
Barclay Cres. Stev SG1 ...... 50 E7
Barclay Ct. Hod EN11 ...... 135 A5
Barclay Sch The. Stev ........ 50 D8
Barden Cl. Hare UB9 ........ 173 C3
Bards Cnr. Heml H HP1 ... 124 B4
Bardwell Ct. St Alb AL1 ... 127 D2
Bardwell Rd. St Alb AL1 ... 127 D2
Barfolds. Wel G AL9 ........ 144 C8
Barford Rise. Luton LU2 .... 46 D1
Bargrove Ave. Heml H HP1 ................ 124 A2
Barham Ave. Bor WD6 ..... 169 F5
Barham Rd. Stev SG2 ........ 51 C5
Barkers Mead. L Hal CM22 77 B1
Barkham Cl. Ched LU7 ....... 79 F7
Barking Cl. Luton LU4 ....... 44 B6
Barkway Fst Sch. Bark ....... 17 C4
Barkway Hill. Bark SG8 ...... 17 E6
Barkway Rd. Royst SG8 ....... 7 E5
Barkway St. Royst SG8 ........ 7 D5
Barley Cl. Bus WD2 .......... 168 B4
Barley Croft. Heml H HP2 125 C3
Barley Croft. Hert SG14 ... 113 D8
Barley Croft. Stap SG14 ..... 92 A3
Barley Hills. Bis St CM23 .... 76 E4
Barley La. Luton LU4 .......... 44 C5
Barley Mow La. Coln H AL4 .................... 142 F8
Barley Ponds Cl. Ware SG12 ...................... 93 F1
Barley Ponds Rd. Ware SG12 ...................... 93 F1
Barley Rd. Gt Ch SG8 .......... 9 A7
Barley Rd. Gt Ch SG8 .......... 9 C2
Barley Rd. Melb SG8 ............ 9 A7
Barley Rise. Bal SG7 .......... 24 B8
Barley Rise. Harp AL5 ....... 86 C4
Barley Vol Prim Sch. Bar ..... 9 A1
Barleycorn The. Luton LU3 63 D8 2
Barleycroft. Bun SG9 ......... 40 E6
Barleycroft Gn. Wel G C AL8 ................ 110 C6
Barleycroft Rd. Wel G C AL8 ................ 110 C5
Barleycroft. Stev SG2 ........ 51 D3
Barleycroft. Ton SG12 ........ 92 F7
Barleyvale. Luton LU3 ........ 45 A8
Barlings Rd. Harp AL5 ..... 107 B5
Barmor Cl. Har HA2 ......... 176 B1
Barn Cl. Heml H HP3 ........ 138 F8
Barn Cl. Radl WD7 ........... 156 A4
Barn Cl. Wel G C AL8 ...... 110 C6
Barn Ct. Saw CM21 ............ 97 E3
Barn Lea. Ric WD3 ........... 165 A1
Barn Sch The. Muc H ......... 74 F2
Barnacres Rd. Heml H HP3 ................ 139 A8
Barnard Acres. Lo Naz EN9 ................... 149 E8
Barnard Gn. Wel G C AL7 110 F5
Barnard Rd. Luton LU1 ...... 63 A7
Barnard Rd. Saw CM21 ...... 97 E3
Barnard Way. Heml H HP3 ................ 124 E1
Barncroft. Alb SG11 ........... 57 C7
Barncroft Jun Mix Inf Sch. Heml H ......................... 124 D8
Barncroft Rd. Berk HP4 ... 121 F3
Barncroft Way. St Alb AL1 128 A2
Barndell Cl. Stot SG5 ........ 11 F6
Barndicot House. Wel G C AL7 ................ 111 C6
Barndicott. Wel G C AL7 .. 111 C6
Barnes La. Kin L WD4 ...... 138 D3
Barnes Rise. Kin L WD4 ... 138 F4
Barnet By-Pass Rd. Bor EN5 ........................ 170 E5

Barnet By-Pass Rd. Pot B EN5 158 A3
Barnet Coll of F Ed. Barn 171 F5
Barnet Gate La. Edg EN5 170 F3
Barnet General Hospl. Barn 171 D5
Barnet Hill. Barn EN5 171 F5
Barnet Hill Prim Sch. Barn 171 F4
Barnet La. Barn EN5,N20 171 F2
Barnet La. Bor WD6 170 B3
Barnet Mus. Barn 171 E5
Barnet Rd. Barn EN5 171 B4
Barnet Rd. Edg EN5 170 E3
Barnet Rd. Lon C AL2 142 F4
Barnet Rd. Pot B EN6,EN5 159 A4
Barnet Stall Mkt. Barn 171 E6
Barnet Trad Est. Barn 171 F6
Barnet Way. Edg EN5 170 D2
Barnfield Ave. Luton LU2 45 D5
Barnfield Cl. Hod EN11 135 A8
Barnfield Cl. Lo Naz EN9 135 F1
Barnfield Coll. Luton 63 B5
Barnfield Coll (Luton). Luton 45 D5
Barnfield Ct. Harp AL5 107 C8
Barnfield. Heml H HP3 138 F8
Barnfield Rd. Harp AL5 107 C8
Barnfield Rd. St Alb AL4 128 C5
Barnfield Rd. Wel G C AL7 110 E4
Barnhurst Path. Sth Ox WD1 175 C5
Barns Dene. Harp AL5 85 E2
Barnsdale Cl. Bor WD6 169 F8
Barnside Ct. Wel G C AL8 110 C6
Barnston Cl. Luton LU2 46 D1
Barnsway. Kin L WD4 138 E3
Barnwell Sch. Stev 51 B2
Barnwell. Stev SG2 51 B2
Baron Ct. Stev SG1 36 B1
Barons Ct. Luton LU2 45 D1 6
Barons Row. Harp AL5 107 D7
Barons The. Bis St CM23 76 D5
Baronsmere Ct. Barn EN5 171 E5 7
Barr Rd. Pot B EN6 159 C6
Barra Cl. Heml H HP3 139 C8
Barratt Way. Har HA3 176 D1
Barrells Down Rd. Bis St CM23 58 E1
Barrett La. Bis St CM23 76 F7
Barrington Rd. Letw SG6 22 F4
Barrow La. Ches EN7 147 F1
Barrow Point Ave. Pnr HA5 175 E1
Barrow Point La. Pnr HA5 175 E1
Barrowby Cl. Luton LU2 46 D1
Barrowdene Cl. Pnr HA5 175 E1
Barry Cl. Chis AL2 141 B6
Bartel Cl. Heml H HP3 125 D1
Bartholomew Court Sch Pavilion. Ches 162 E6
Bartholomew Rd. Bis St CM23 76 F6
Bartletts Mead. Hert SG14 92 D1
Barton Cl. Harp AL5 86 C3
Barton Rd. Hex SG5 19 A1
Barton Rd. Luton LU3 45 C7
Barton Rd. Str LU3 31 B3
Barton Rd. Whea AL4 108 C8
Barton Way. Bor WD6 170 A7
Barton Way. Cro Gr WD3 166 B4
Bartons The. Elst WD6 169 D3
Bartrams La. Had W EN4 159 C1
Barwick La. Stand SG11 73 C3
Basbow La. Bis St CM23 76 F7
Basildon Sq. Heml H HP2 124 F7
Basils Rd. Stev SG1 50 D7
Baslow Cl. Har HA3 176 D2
Bassett Cl. Red AL3 106 B5
Bassil Rd. Heml H HP2 124 D2
Bassingbourne Cl. Hod EN10 134 F3
Bassingburn Wlk. Wel G C AL7 110 F5
Batchelors. Stand SG11 55 E2
Batchwood Dr. St Alb AL3 127 C6
Batchwood Gdns. St Alb AL3 127 D6
Batchwood Hall Golf Course. St Alb 127 B6
Batchwood View. St Alb AL3 127 D5
Batchworth Heath Hill. Ric WD3 174 A6
Batchworth Hill London Rd. Ric WD3 173 F7
Batchworth La. Mo Pk HA6 174 D5
Bateman Rd. Cro Gr WD3 166 A3
Bates House. Stev SG1 50 E6 2
Batford Cl. Wel G C AL7 111 B5
Batford Cty Prim Sch. Harp 86 D4
Batford Rd. Harp AL5 86 D3
Bath Pl. Barn EN5 171 F6
Bath Rd. Luton LU3 45 D2
Bathurst Rd. Heml H HP2 124 E6
Batterdale. Hat AL9 130 C6
Battlefield Rd. St Alb AL1 127 F5
Battlers Green Dr. Radl WD7 155 E3
Battleview. Whea 108 E8
Baud Cl. Alb SG11 57 E2
Baulk The. Ched LU7 79 F7
Baulk The. Lily LU2 32 D2
Baulk The. Pit LU7 80 F5
Bay Cl. Luton LU4 44 B6
Bay Ct. Berk HP4 122 B4
Bay Tree Cl. Chis AL2 141 C3
Bay Tree Cl. Ham St EN7 147 F4
Bay Tree Wlk. Watf WD1 154 A1
Bayford Cl. Heml H HP2 125 C8
Bayford Cl. Hert SG13 113 C4
Bayford Gn. Bay SG13 133 A6
Bayford La. Bay SG13 132 F7
Bayford Prim Sch. Bay 132 F5
Bayford Sta. Bay 133 A5
Bayhurst Dr. Norwd HA6 174 F4
Baylam Dell. Luton LU2 46 E1
Baylie Ct. Heml H HP2 124 E4
Baylie La. Heml H HP2 124 E4
Bayworth. Letw SG6 23 B5
Beacon Ct. Hert H SG13 114 C3
Beacon Rd. Dagn HP4 81 A1
Beacon Rd. Ware SG12 94 A2
Beacon Way. Ric WD3 165 A2
Beacon Way. Tri HP23 100 C5
Beaconsfield. Luton LU2 64 B8
Beaconsfield Rd. Enf EN3 162 D2
Beaconsfield Rd. Hat AL10 130 C6
Beaconsfield Rd. St Alb AL1 127 E3
Beaconsfield Rd. Tri HP23 99 E3
Beadles The. L Hal CM22 98 B8
Beadlow Rd. Dun LU4 44 A4
Beagle Cl. Radl WD7 155 F2
Beale Cl. Stev SG2 51 C6
Beamish Dr. Bus WD2 168 C1
Beane Ave. Stev SG2 51 D6
Beane Rd. Hert SG14 113 B7
Beane Rd. Wat St SG14 70 D4
Beane River View. Hert SG14 113 C6
Beane Wlk. Stev SG2 51 D6
Beaneside The. Wat St SG14 70 D4
Beanfield Rd. H Wy CM21 97 A4
Beanley Cl. Luton LU2 46 E2
Bear La. Ashw SG7 4 D4
Bearton Ave. Hit SG5 34 E8
Bearton Gn. Hit SG5 21 D1
Bearton Rd. Hit SG5 21 E1
Bearwood Cl. Pot B EN6 159 D8
Beatty Rd. Ches EN8 162 F5
Beauchamp Gdns. Ric WD3 165 A1
Beaulieu Cl. Watf WD1 167 C1
Beaumayes Cl. Heml H HP1 124 B2
Beaumont Ave. St Alb AL1 128 B4
Beaumont Cl. Hit SG5 34 D8 3
Beaumont Ct. Harp AL5 86 B1 5
Beaumont Hall La. Red AL3 106 C2
Beaumont Pl. Barn EN5 171 F8
Beaumont Rd. Ham St EN7 147 F7
Beaumont Rd. Luton LU3 45 B2
Beaumont Sec Sch. St Alb 128 C4
Beaumont View. Ham St EN7 147 D5
Beazley Cl. Ware SG12 93 E2
Becket Gdns. Welw AL6 89 C4
Beckets Sq. Berk HP4 122 A6
Beckets Wlk. Ware SG12 93 D1 9
Beckett's Ave. St Alb AL3 127 C6
Becketts. Hert SG14 113 A5
Beckfield La. San SG9 26 D7
Beckham Cl. Luton LU2 45 D7
Becks Cl. Mark AL3 83 D5
Bedale Rd. Enf EN2 161 C1
Bede Cl. Pnr HA5 175 D2
Bede Ct. L Gad HP4 102 C8
Bedford Ave. Barn EN5 171 F4
Bedford Cl. Chen WD3 151 B1
Bedford Cres. Enf EN3 162 E4
Bedford Gdns. Luton LU3 63 D8 5
Bedford Park Rd. St Alb AL1 127 E3
Bedford Rd. Henlw SG16 10 B3
Bedford Rd. Hit SG5 34 E7
Bedford Rd. Ick SG5 21 D4
Bedford Rd. Letw SG6 22 D7
Bedford Rd. Mo Pk HA6 174 D6
Bedford Rd. St Alb AL1 127 E2
Bedford St. Berk HP4 122 D4
Bedford St. Watf WD2 167 B8
Bedmond Gn. Abb L WD5 139 F4
Bedmond Jun Mix & Inf Sch. Abb L 139 F3
Bedmond La. Bri Wd AL3 140 B6
Bedmond La. St Alb AL3 126 F1
Bedmond Rd. Abb L WD5 139 E7
Bedmond Rd. Abb L WD5 139 F2
Bedmond Rd. Heml H HP3 125 D1
Bedwell Ave. L Berk AL9 132 A7
Bedwell Cl. Wel G C AL7 110 E5
Bedwell Cres. Stev SG1 50 F5
Bedwell Jun Mix Inf Sch. Stev 51 A5
Bedwell Rise. Stev SG1 50 E5
Bedwell Sch The. Stev 51 A6
Beech Ave. Cre H EN2 161 A4
Beech Ave. Radl WD7 156 A5
Beech Bottom. St Alb AL3 127 D6
Beech Cl. Harp AL5 107 C5
Beech Cl. Hat AL10 130 A4
Beech Cres. Whea AL4 108 D7
Beech Ct. Berk HP4 122 D4
Beech Ct. Harp AL5 85 F3 3
Beech Dr. Berk HP4 122 C3
Beech Dr. Bor WD6 169 F7
Beech Dr. Saw CM21 118 C8
Beech Dr. Stev SG2 51 B3
Beech Farm Dr. Hat AL4 128 F7
Beech Hill. Had W EN4 159 E1
Beech Hill High Sch. Luton 45 B1
Beech Hill. Letw SG6 22 D7
Beech Hill. Lily LU2 46 D8
Beech Hyde Jun Mix Inf Sch. Whea 108 D7
Beech Hyde La. Whea AL4 108 F6
Beech Mews. Ware SG12 114 D7
Beech Pk. L Chal HP6 150 B1
Beech Pl. St Alb AL3 127 D6
Beech Rd. Luton LU1 63 C8
Beech Rd. St Alb AL3 127 E6
Beech Rd. Watf WD2 154 B2
Beech Ridge. Bal AL5 23 F6
Beech Way. Kim AL4 87 B6
Beech Wlk. Tri HP23 100 C4
Beechcroft Ave. Cro Gr WD3 166 C4
Beechcroft. Berk HP4 122 C3
Beechcroft. Dat SG3 69 D1
Beechcroft Rd. Watf WD2 167 E4
Beechen Gr. Watf HA5 167 C6
Beeches The. Chor WD3 164 F4
Beeches The. Hit SG4 35 A6
Beeches The. Pk St AL2 141 D4
Beeches The. Royst SG8 7 D6
Beeches The. Tri HP23 100 C4
Beeches The. Watf WD1 167 B6 2
Beeches The. Welw AL6 89 C4
Beechfield Cl. Red AL3 106 B5
Beechfield. Hod EN11 115 A2
Beechfield Jun Mix Inf Sch. Watf 154 A2
Beechfield. Kin L WD4 138 F1
Beechfield Rd. Heml H HP1 124 B2
Beechfield Rd. Ware SG12 93 F2
Beechfield Rd. Wel G C AL7 110 E5
Beechfield. Saw CM21 97 F2
Beechfield Wlk. Wa Aby EN9 163 D4
Beeching Cl. Harp AL5 86 B4
Beechlands. Bis St CM23 76 F5
Beecholm Mews. Ches EN8 148 E3
Beechpark Way. Watf WD1 153 E2
Beechtree La. St Alb AL3 126 B2
Beechwood Ave. Chor WD3 164 B5
Beechwood Ave. L Chal HP6 150 C1
Beechwood Ave. Pot B EN6 159 B6
Beechwood Ave. St Alb AL1 128 C4
Beechwood Cl. Bal SG7 23 F5
Beechwood Cl. Ham St EN7 147 E5
Beechwood Cl. Hert SG13 113 F6
Beechwood Cl. Hit SG5 21 D2
Beechwood Dr. Ald HP23 101 D5
Beechwood Inf Sch. Luton 44 E4
Beechwood Jun Sch. Luton 44 E4
Beechwood Park (Sch). Fla 83 B1
Beechwood Pk. Heml H HP3 137 F7
Beechwood Rd. Luton LU4 44 E3
Beechwood Rise. Watf WD2 154 B2
Beecroft La. Walk SG2 38 C2
Beehive Cl. Elst WD6 169 D3
Beehive Gn. Wel G C AL7 111 A4
Beehive La. Wel G C AL7 111 A3
Beehive Rd. Gofs O EN7 147 B3
Beesonend Cotts. Harp AL5 107 B4
Beesonend La. Harp AL5 106 E3
Beeston Cl. Sth Ox WD1 175 D6
Beeston Dr. Ches EN8 148 D4
Beetham Ct. Sac SG14 92 E4
Beethoven Rd. Elst WD6 169 D3
Beeton Cl. Pnr HA5 176 A3
Beggarman's La. Dan En SG11 72 D8
Beggars Bush La. Watf WD1 166 D4
Beken Ct. Watf WD2 154 C4
Belcher Rd. Hod EN11 135 A7
Beldam Ave. Royst SG8 7 E5
Beldams La. Bis St CM23 77 B5
Belfairs. Sth Ox WD1 175 D5
Belford Rd. Bor WD6 156 F1
Belfry Ave. Hare UB9 173 A2
Belfry The. Luton LU2 45 E6
Belfry The. Watf 167 D8
Belgrave Ave. Watf WD1 166 F4
Belgrave Cl. St Alb AL4 128 C7
Belgrave Dr. Abb L WD4 139 C3
Belgrave Rd. Luton LU4 44 D5
Belham Rd. Kin L WD4 139 A3
Bell Acre Gdns. Letw SG6 23 B4
Bell Acre. Letw SG6 23 B4
Bell Cl. Abb L WD5 139 F4
Bell Cl. Hit SG4 35 B6
Bell Cl. Kneb SG3 69 A5
Bell Cl. Pnr HA5 175 C1 3
Bell Gn. Bov HP3 137 B4
Bell La. Abb L WD5 140 A4
Bell La. Bro Pk AL9 145 A7
Bell La. Enf EN3 162 E1
Bell La. Hert SG14 113 D6
Bell La. Hod EN11 134 E2
Bell La. Hod EN11 135 A6
Bell La. L Chal HP6 150 C1
Bell La. Nthch HP4 121 E5
Bell La. Shen AL2 142 E2
Bell La. Stev SG1 50 C7
Bell La. Widf SG12 95 D4
Bell Lane Cty Combd Sch. L Chal 150 B1
Bell Leys. Wing HP22 60 B3
Bell Mead. Saw CM21 97 E2
Bell Rdbt The. Lon C AL2 142 F4
Bell St. Saw CM21 97 E2
Bell Wlk. Wing HP22 60 B3
Bellamy Cl. Watf WD1 167 A8
Bellamy Rd. Ches EN8 148 E2
Belle Vue La. Bus WD2 168 D1
Belle Vue Rd. Ware SG12 93 F1
Bellerby Rise. Luton LU4 44 B6
Bellfield Ave. Stan HA3 176 D4
Bellgate. Heml H HP2 124 E6
Bellgate Inf Sch. Heml H 124 E5
Bellgate Jun Sch. Heml H 124 E5
Bellingdon. Sth Ox WD1 175 E7
Bellis House. Wel G C AL7 111 B4
Bellmount Wood Ave. Watf WD1 166 E8
Bells Hill. Barn EN5 171 D5
Bells Hill. Bis St CM23 76 E7
Belmers Rd. Wigg HP23 100 D1
Belmont Ct. St Alb AL1 127 D2
Belmont Fst & Mid Sch. Har 176 F1
Belmont Hill. St Alb AL1 127 D2
Belmont Lodge. Har HA3 176 D3
Belmont Rd. Heml H HP3 138 E8
Belmont Rd. Luton LU1 63 C7
Belmont Rd. Watf WD2 167 E4
Belmor. Bor WD6 170 A3
Belper Rd. Luton LU4 44 D2
Belsham Pl. Luton LU2 46 E2 3
Belsize Cl. Heml H HP3 125 A2
Belsize Cl. St Alb AL4 128 C8
Belsize Rd. Har HA3 176 D3
Belsize Rd. Heml H HP3 125 A2
Belswains Gn. Heml H HP3 138 E8
Belswains Jun Sch. Heml H 138 F7
Belswains La. Heml H HP3 138 F7
Belswains Prim Sch. Heml H 138 F7
Belton Rd. Berk HP4 122 A5
Beltona Gdns. Ches EN8 148 D4
Belvedere Gdns. Chis AL2 141 A4
Belvedere Rd. Luton LU3 45 B5
Bembridge Gdns. Luton LU3 44 F7
Ben Austins. Red AL3 106 A4
Benbow Cl. St Alb AL1 128 B1
Benchley Hill. Hit SG4 35 C8
Benchleys Rd. Heml H HP1 123 F2
Bencroft. Ham St EN7 148 A5
Bencroft Rd. Heml H HP2 124 E3
Bendish La. Whit SG4 66 C7
Bendysh Rd. Watf WD2 167 E5
Benedictine Gate. Ches EN8 148 E4
Benford Rd. Hod EN11 134 F4
Bengarth Dr. Har HA3 176 D1
Bengeo Inf Sch. Hert 92 C1
Bengeo Jun Sch. Hert 92 C1
Bengeo Meadows. Hert SG14 92 C1
Bengeo Mews. Hert SG14 92 C1
Bengeo St. Hert SG14 113 C8
Benhooks Ave. Bis St CM23 76 E5
Benhooks Pl. Bis St CM23 76 E5
Benington Cl. Luton LU2 45 E5
Benington Jun Mix Inf Sch. Ben 52 D4
Benington Rd. Ast SG2 51 F2
Benington Rd. Ben SG2 52 A7
Bennett Cl. Norwd HA6 174 F3
Bennett Cl. Wel G C AL7 110 F2
Bennett Ct. Letw 23 A5
Bennetts Cl. Col H AL4 143 D8
Bennetts End Cl. Heml H HP3 124 F1
Bennetts End Hospl. Heml H 124 F1
Bennetts End Rd. Heml H HP3 125 A1
Bennettsgate. Heml H HP3 139 A8
Bennick House. Watf WD1 166 E3
Benningfield Rd. Widf SG12 95 D4
Benningfield. Widf SG12 95 D5
Benskin Rd. Watf WD1 167 A4
Benslow La. Hit SG4 35 A7
Benslow Rise. Hit SG4 35 A8
Benson Cl. Luton LU3 44 F7
Benstede. Stev SG2 69 C8
Bentfield Cty Prim Sch. Sta M 59 D8
Bentfield End Cswy. Sta M CM24 59 D7
Bentfield Gdns. Sta M CM24 59 D7
Bentfield Green. Sta M CM24 59 D8
Bentfield Rd. Sta M CM24 59 D7
Bentick Way. Cod SG4 67 F2
Bentley Cl. Bis St CM23 76 F5
Bentley Ct. Luton LU4 63 C8
Bentley Heath La. Pot B EN5 158 F4
Bentley Lodge. Bus WD2 176 E8
Bentley Rd. Hert SG14 112 F7
Bentley Wood High Sch. Stan 176 F5
Benton Rd. Sth Ox WD1 175 D5
Bentsley Cl. St Alb AL4 128 C7
Berceau Wlk. Watf WD1 166 E8
Berefield. Heml H HP2 124 D5
Beresford Rd. Luton LU4 45 A1
Beresford Rd. Ric WD3 164 F1
Beresford Rd. St Alb AL1 128 C2
Bericot Way. Wel G C AL7 111 D6
Berkeley Cl. Abb L WD5 153 F8
Berkeley Cl. Bor WD6 170 A4
Berkeley Cl. Hit SG5 34 D8 6
Berkeley Cl. Pot B EN6 158 F7
Berkeley Cl. Stev SG2 69 A8
Berkeley Cl. Ware SG12 93 C2
Berkeley Ct. Cro Gr WD3 166 D4
Berkeley Ct. Harp AL5 86 A2
Berkeley. Letw SG6 23 A4
Berkeley Path. Luton LU2 63 E8 3
Berkeley Sq. Heml H HP2 105 C1
Berkhamsted La. L Berk AL9 132 B3
Berkhamsted Rd. Heml H HP1 123 E5
Berkhamsted Sch. Berk 122 C4
Berkhamsted Sch for Girls. Berk 122 B3
Berkhamsted Sta. Berk 122 C5
Berkley Ave. Ches EN8 162 D5
Berkley Cl. St Alb AL4 128 C7
Berkley Ct. Berk HP4 122 C4
Berkley Pl. Ches EN8 162 D5

Berks Hill. Chor WD3 ....... 164 C4
Bernard St. St Alb AL3 ..... 127 D4
Bernard's Heath Inf Sch. St Alb ..................... 127 F5
Berners Dr. St Alb AL1 ..... 141 E8
Berners Way. Hod EN10 .. 148 F8
Bernhardt Cres. Stev SG2 .. 51 C6
Berries The. St Alb AL4 .... 128 A7
Berrow Cl. Luton LU2 ........ 46 E2 2
Berry Ave. Watf WD2 ...... 154 B3
Berry Cl. Ric WD3 ............ 165 B2
Berry Grove La. Bus WD2 154 E1
Berry La. Ric WD3 ........... 165 A2
Berry Leys. Luton LU3 ........ 44 E7
Berry Way. Ric WD3 ......... 165 B2
Berryfield. Ched LU7 .......... 79 F7
Berrygrove La. Bus WD2 . 168 A8
Berrymead. Heml H HP2 .. 124 F5
Bertram House. Stev SG1 .. 50 E6 4
Berwick Cl. Ches EN8 ...... 163 A5
Berwick Cl. Har HA7 ....... 176 F4
Berwick Rd. Bor WD6 ...... 156 F1
Besant House. Watf WD2 167 D7
Besford Cl. Luton LU2 ....... 46 E2
Bessemer Cl. Hit SG5 ........ 21 E2
Bessemer Dr. Stev SG1 ..... 50 B4
Bessemer Rd. Wel G C AL7,AL8 ............ 89 E2
Bethune Cl. Luton LU1 ....... 63 B6
Bethune Ct. Luton LU1 ....... 63 B6
Betjeman Cl. Ches EN7 .... 148 A3
Betjeman Way. Heml H HP1 ................. 124 B4
Betony Vale. Royst SG8 ....... 7 E5
Bettespol Meadows. Red AL3 ........................ 106 A6
Betty's La. Tri HP23 ......... 100 A4
Bevan Cl. Heml H HP3 ...... 124 E1
Bevan House. Watf WD2 . 167 D7 3
Beverley Cl. Royst SG8 ....... 7 B8
Beverley Gdns. Ches EN7 148 A1
Beverley Gdns. St Alb AL4 128 D7
Beverley Gdns. Wel G C AL7 ................. 111 C6
Beverley Rd. Luton LU4 ...... 44 F1
Beverley Rd. Luton LU4 ...... 45 A1
Beverley Rd. Stev SG1 ....... 37 B2
Beverly Cl. Hod EN10 ...... 134 E2
Bevil Ct. Hod EN11 .......... 115 A1
Bewdley Cl. Harp AL5 ...... 107 D6
Bewley Cl. Ches EN8 ....... 162 D8
Bexhill Rd. Luton LU2 ......... 46 D2
Beyers Gdns. Hod EN11 ... 115 A1
Beyers Prospect. Hod EN11 .................... 115 A1
Beyers Ride. Hod EN11 .... 115 A1
Bibbs Hall La. Kim SG4 ...... 87 E6
Biddenham Turn. Watf WD2 .................... 154 C4
Bideford Gdns. Luton LU3 .. 45 D4
Bideford Rd. Enf EN3 ....... 162 F1
Bidwell Cl. Letw SG6 .......... 23 B5
Biggin Hill. Wyd SG9 .......... 28 D7
Biggin La. Hit SG5 .............. 34 F7
Bignells Cnr. Pot B EN6 ..... 158 B5
Billet La. Berk HP4 .......... 122 A6
Billy Lows La. Pot B EN6 .. 159 B8
Bilton Rd. Hit SG4 ............. 21 F2
Bilton Way. Enf EN3 ......... 162 F1
Bingen Rd. Hit SG5 ............ 21 C1
Bingley Rd. Hod EN11 ...... 135 C6
Binham Cl. Luton LU2 ........ 45 D7
Binyon Cres. Stan HA7 ..... 176 F5
Birch Copse. Bri Wd AL2 .. 140 E1
Birch Ct. Norwd HA6 ........ 174 C4
Birch Dr. Hat AL10 ........... 130 A4
Birch Dr. Map Cr WD3 ...... 172 D5
Birch Gn. Heml H HP1 ...... 123 F5
Birch Gn. Hertng SG14 ..... 112 C4
Birch Gr. Pot B EN6 .......... 159 B7
Birch Gr. Welw AL6 ............ 89 E8
Birch La. Flau HP3 ........... 151 B7
Birch Leys. Heml H HP2 ... 125 C8
Birch Link. Luton LU4 ......... 45 C1
Birch Pk. Stan HA3 ........... 176 C3
Birch Rd. Nthch HP4 ......... 121 D7
Birch Rd. Welw SG3 ........... 69 B1
Birch Tree Gr. Bot HP5 .... 136 B1
Birch Tree Wlk. Watf WD1 .................... 153 F2
Birch Way. Harp AL5 ........ 107 C8
Birch Way. Lon C AL2 ....... 142 D4
Birch Wlk. Bor WD6 ......... 170 A8
Birchall La. Hertng SG14 . 111 E4
Birchall Wood. Wel G C AL7 ................. 111 C5
Birchalls. Sta M CM24 ....... 59 E8
Birchanger C of E Prim Sch. Birhr ............................... 59 D2
Birchanger Green Motorway Service Area. Gt Ha ....... 77 E7
Birchanger Ind Est. Bis St . 59 B2
Birchanger La. Birhr CM23 59 D2
Birchen Gr. Luton LU2 ........ 45 F3
Bircherley Ct. Hert SG14 .. 113 D6 12
Bircherley Green Ctr The. Hert ............................. 113 C6 8
Bircherley St. Hert SG14 .. 113 D6
Birches The. Bus WD2 ...... 168 C4
Birches The. Cod SG4 ........ 89 A8
Birches The. Heml H HP3 137 F8
Birches The. Letw SG6 ....... 22 E8
Birchfield Rd. Ches EN8 ... 148 C2
Birchfield Terr. Watf WD1 167 C5
Birchfield. Watf WD1 ....... 154 A1
Birchmead Cl. St Alb AL3 . 127 D6
Birchmead. Watf WD1 ...... 153 F1
Birchway. Hat AL10 ......... 130 B7
Birchwood Ave. Hat AL10 130 A7
Birchwood. Birhr CM23 ..... 59 E2
Birchwood Cl. Hat AL10 ..... 130 A7
Birchwood High Sch. Bis St 77 C8
Birchwood. Shen WD7 ...... 157 A5
Birchwood. Wa Aby EN9 .. 163 E5
Birchwood Way. Chis AL2 141 B3
Bird La. Hare UB9 ............ 173 C1
Birdcroft Rd. Wel G C AL8 110 D5
Birdie Way. Hert SG13 ..... 114 B7
Birds Cl. Wel G C AL7 ...... 111 B4
Birds Hill. Letw SG6 .......... 23 A6
Birdsfoot La. Luton LU3 ..... 45 B6
Birkbeck Rd. Enf EN2 ....... 161 D1
Birkdale Gdns. Sth Ox WD1 ................... 175 D7
Birklands La. St Alb AL1 ... 142 B7
Birklands. St Alb AL1 ....... 142 B7
Birling Dr. Luton LU2 ......... 46 C4
Birnbeck Ct. Barn EN5 ..... 171 D5
Birstall Gn. Sth Ox WD1 ... 175 D6
Birtley Ct. Luton LU2 ......... 46 E1
Biscot Rd. Luton LU3 .......... 45 C2
Bishop Ken Rd. Har HA3 .. 176 F2
Bishop Sq. Hat AL10 ........ 129 E5
Bishop Wood Jun Sch. Tri 100 A3
Bishop's Ave. Bis St CM23 . 76 F3
Bishop's Cl. St Alb AL4 ..... 128 A7
Bishop's Garth. St Alb AL4 128 A7
Bishop's Hatfield Girls' Sch. Hat .............................. 130 A5
Bishop's Stortford Bsns Ctr. Bis St ............................. 77 A6
Bishop's Stortford Coll. Bis St ............................. 76 E7
Bishop's Stortford Golf Course. Bis St ............................. 77 D6
Bishop's Stortford High Sch The. Bis St .............. 76 F4
Bishop's Stortford Sta. Bis St ............................. 77 A6
Bishops Ave. Bor WD6 ...... 169 F4
Bishops Ave. Mo Pk HA6 .. 174 F7
Bishops Cl. Barn EN5 ....... 171 D3
Bishops Cl. Hat AL10 ....... 129 F5
Bishops' Coll. Ches .......... 148 B1
Bishops Field. Ast Cl HP22 99 A4
Bishops Mead. Heml H HP1 ................. 124 B1
Bishops Park Way. Bis St CM23 .................. 76 B7
Bishops Rd. Tewin AL6 ...... 90 E6
Bishops Rise. Hat AL10 .... 129 F1
Bishops Rise. Hat AL10 .... 129 F4
Bishopscote Rd. Luton LU3 45 B3
Biskra. Watf WD1 ............ 167 A8
Bisley Cl. Ches EN8 .......... 162 D6
Bit The. Wigg HP23 .......... 100 D1
Bittern Cl. Stev SG2 ........... 51 D2
Bittern Way. Letw SG6 ...... 11 E1
Black Boy Wood. Bri Wd AL2 ................... 141 A1
Black Cut. St Alb AL1 ....... 127 E2
Black Ditch Rd. Wa Aby EN9 .................. 163 C3
Black Ditch Way. Wa Aby EN9 ................. 163 B3
Black Fan Rd. Wel G C AL7 ................. 110 F7
Black Fan Rd. Wel G C AL7 ................. 111 B6
Black Lion Ct. Harl CM17 . 118 C4
Black Lion Hill. Shen WD7 156 F7
Black Swan Ct. Ware SG12 93 D1 1
Black Swan La. Luton LU3 .. 45 A5
Blackberry Mead. Stev SG2 51 D3
Blackbirds La. Radl WD2 . 155 C5
Blackbury Cl. Pot B EN6 ... 159 C8
Blackbush Spring. Harl CM20 ..................... 118 A1
Blackbushe. Bis St CM23 ... 59 C1
Blackdale. Ham St EN7 .... 148 A4
Blacketts Wood Dr. Chor WD3 .................... 164 B5
Blackford Rd. Sth Ox WD1 175 D5
Blackhorse Cl. Hit SG4 ....... 35 A5
Blackhorse La. Hit SG4 ....... 35 A5
Blackhorse La. Red AL3 ... 106 A6
Blackhorse La. Ridge AL2 157 F8
Blackhorse Rd. Letw SG6 ... 23 C8
Blackley Cl. Watf WD1 ..... 153 F2
Blackmoor La. Watf WD1 166 D4
Blackmore. Letw SG6 ......... 23 B3
Blackmore Way. Kim AL4 ... 87 B6
Blacksmith's La. Reed SG8 16 D5
Blacksmith's La. St Alb AL3 .................... 127 B3
Blacksmiths Cl. Gt Am SG12 ................. 115 A7
Blacksmiths Hill. Ben SG2 .. 52 E4
Blacksmiths Row. Mark AL3 ........................ 83 E5
Blacksmiths Way. H Wy CM21 ..................... 97 B1
Blackthorn Cl. St Alb AL4 . 128 C6
Blackthorn Cl. Watf WD2 . 154 B7
Blackthorn Dr. Luton LU2 ... 46 C4
Blackthorn Jun Sch. Wel G C ........................ 111 A5
Blackthorn Rd. Wel G C AL7 ................... 111 A5
Blackthorne Cl. Hat AL10 . 129 F2
Blackwater La. Heml H HP3 ................. 125 E1
Blackwell Cl. Har HA3 ...... 176 D3
Blackwell Dr. Watf WD1 .. 167 C3
Blackwell Hall La. Lat HP5 150 C6
Blackwell Rd. Kin L WD4 .. 139 A2
Blackwood Ct. Ham St ..... 148 A4
Bladon Cl. L Wym SG4 ....... 35 F3
Blair Cl. Heml H HP2 ....... 105 B1
Blair Cl. Stev SG2 ............. 50 F1
Blairhead Dr. Sth Ox WD1 175 B7
Blake Cl. St Alb AL1 .......... 142 A8
Blakemere Rd. Wel G C AL8 ................. 110 D8
Blakemore End Rd. L Wym SG4 .................... 35 D3
Blakeney Dr. Luton LU2 ..... 45 C7
Blakeney Ho. Stev SG1 ...... 50 A7
Blakeney Rd. Stev SG1 ....... 50 A7
Blakes Ct. Saw CM21 ......... 97 E2
Blakes Way. Welw AL6 ....... 89 C6
Blanche La. Ridge WD6 .... 157 F5
Blandford Ave. Luton LU2 ... 45 D6
Blandford Rd. St Alb AL1 .. 128 A3
Blanes The. Ware SG12 ..... 93 C3
Blaydon Rd. Luton LU2 ....... 64 A8
Blenheim Cl. Saw CM21 .... 118 C8
Blenheim Cl. Watf WD1 ... 167 D2
Blenheim Cres. Luton LU3 . 45 C2
Blenheim Ct. Bis St CM23 ... 76 C7
Blenheim Rd. Barn EN5 .... 171 D5
Blenheim Rd. St Alb AL1 .. 127 F4
Blenheim Way. Stev SG2 ... 69 D7
Blenhiem Rd. Abb L WD5 . 154 A7
Blenkin Cl. St Alb AL3 ....... 127 C7
Blind La. Ard SG2 .............. 38 F5
Blindman's La. Ches EN8 .. 148 D2
Bloomfield Ave. Luton LU2 . 46 A1
Bloomfield House. Stev SG1 ........................ 50 E6 6
Bloomfield Rd. Harp AL5 .... 85 F3
Blossom La. Enf EN2 ........ 161 C1
Blue Bridge Rd. Bro Pk AL9 ................... 144 E4
Bluebell Cl. Heml H HP1 .. 123 E2
Bluebell Cl. Hert SG13 ..... 114 A6
Bluebells. Welw AL6 .......... 89 D7
Blueberry Cl. St Alb AL3 .. 127 D7
Bluebridge Ave. Bro Pk AL9 ................... 144 F4
Bluecoat Yd. Ware SG12 ... 93 D1
Bluecoats Ave. Hert SG14 113 D6
Bluecoats Ct. Hert SG14 .. 113 D6 15
Bluehouse Hill. St Alb AL3 127 A3
Bluett Rd. Lon C AL2 ....... 142 D4
Blundell Cl. St Alb AL3 ..... 127 D7
Blundell Rd. Luton LU3 ....... 45 A4
Blunesfield. Pot B EN6 ..... 159 D8
Blunts La. Bri Wd AL2 ...... 140 D5
Blyth Cl. Bor WD6 ............ 170 A8
Blyth Cl. Stev SG1 ............. 50 A7
Blyth Pl. Luton LU1 ............ 63 D6
Blythe Rd. Lo Naz EN11 ... 135 D5
Blythway House. Wel G C AL7 ................... 89 F1
Blythway. Wel G C AL7 ...... 89 F1
Blythwood Gdns. Sta M CM24 ................... 59 D6
Blythwood Rd. Pnr HA5 ... 175 D2
Boardman Cl. Barn EN5 ... 171 E4
Bockings. Walk SG2 ........... 38 C1
Bodmin Rd. Luton LU4 ........ 44 F3
Bodwell Cl. Heml H HP1 .. 124 A4
Bogmoor Rd. Bar SG8 ........ 18 A8
Bognor Gdns. Sth Ox WD1 ................ 175 C5
Bohemia. Heml H HP2 ..... 124 E4
Boissy Cl. Coln H AL4 ....... 128 E2
Boleyn Cl. Heml H HP2 ..... 125 C8
Boleyn Dr. St Alb AL1 ....... 127 D1
Bolingbroke Rd. Luton LU1 63 B6
Bolingbrook. St Alb AL4 ... 128 A7
Bolney Gn. Luton LU2 ......... 46 D3
Bolton Rd. Luton LU1 ......... 63 F7
Boltons Park (Royal Veterinary Coll). Pot B ............................ 145 A2
Bond Ct. Harp AL5 ............. 85 F3 4
Bondley Hill Jun Mix & Inf Sch. Stev ............................... 51 C3
Boniface Gdns. Har HA3 .. 176 B3
Boniface Wlk. Har HA3 .... 176 B3
Bonks Hill. Saw CM21 ........ 97 D1
Bonney Gr. Ches EN7 ....... 148 A1
Bonnick Cl. Luton LU1 ........ 63 C6
Booths Cl. Wel G AL9 ....... 144 D7
Boreham Holt. Bor WD6 ... 169 F5
Borehamwood Ind Pk. Bor 170 D7
Bornedene. Pot B EN6 ..... 158 E8
Borodale. Harp AL5 ........... 86 A1
Borough Way. Pot B EN6 . 158 E7
Borrell Cl. Hod EN10 ........ 134 F3
Borrowdale Ct. Heml H HP2 ................. 124 E6 4
Borton Ave. Henlw SG16 .... 10 B4
Bosanquet Rd. Hod EN11 . 135 C8
Bosmore Rd. Luton LU3 ..... 44 F5
Boswell Dr. Ick SG5 ........... 21 E4
Boswell Gdns. Stev SG1 ..... 36 D1
Boswick La. Nthch HP4 .... 121 D8
Botley La. Bot HP5 ........... 136 A1
Botley Rd. Bot HP5 ........... 136 A1
Botley Rd. Heml H HP2 .... 125 B8
Bottom House La. Wigg HP23 .................. 101 A1
Bottom La. Sar WD3 ........ 152 C4
Bottom Rd. St Le HP23 ..... 119 F3
Bough Beech Ct. Enf EN3 . 162 D2
Boughton Way. L Chal HP6 ................... 150 C1
Boulevard Ctr The. Bor .... 170 A6
Boulevard The. Watf WD1 166 D4
Boulevard The. Wel G C AL7 ................. 110 F8
Boulton Rd. Stev SG1 ......... 37 C2
Bounce The. Heml H HP2 . 124 D5
Boundary Ct. Wel G C AL7 110 F2
Boundary Dr. Hert SG14 .. 113 D8
Boundary House. Wel G C AL7 ................. 110 D3
Boundary La. Wel G C AL7 110 E2
Boundary Rd. Bis St CM23 . 77 A5
Boundary Rd. St Alb AL1 .. 127 E5
Boundary Way. Heml H HP2 ................. 125 C6
Boundary Way. Watf WD2 154 C7
Bounds Field. L Had SG11 .. 75 F8
Bourne Cl. Hod EN10 ....... 134 F3
Bourne Cl. Ware SG12 ....... 93 D2
Bourne End La. Heml H HP1 ................. 123 C1
Bourne End Rd. Mo Pk HA6 .................. 174 E6
Bourne Hall. Bus WD2 ..... 168 A3
Bourne Honour. Ton SG12 . 92 E7
Bourne Rd. Berk HP4 ....... 121 F5
Bourne Rd. Bus WD2 ....... 168 A4
Bourne The. Bis St CM23 ... 77 A8
Bourne The. Bov HP3 ....... 137 A4
Bourne The. Ware SG12 .... 93 D2
Bournehall Ave. Bus WD2 168 A4
Bournehall La. Bus WD2 .. 168 A4
Bournehall Rd. Bus WD2 . 168 A3
Bournehall Sch. Bus ......... 168 B4
Bournemouth Rd. Stev SG1 50 B8 3
Bouvier Rd. Enf EN3 ........ 162 C1
Bovingdon Cres. Watf WD2 .................... 154 D5
Bovingdon Ct. Bov HP3 .... 137 A3
Bovingdon Green La. Bov HP3 ...................... 136 F3
Bovingdon Inf Sch. Bov .... 137 B4
Bovingdon Jun Mix Sch. Bov ................................ 137 B4
Bowbrook Vale. Luton LU2 46 F1
Bowcock Wlk. Stev SG1 ..... 50 E3
Bower Heath La. Whea AL5 86 C6
Bower's Par. Harp AL5 ...... 86 A1
Bowers Way. Harp AL5 ...... 86 A1
Bowershott. Letw SG6 ........ 23 A4
Bowes Lyon Mews. St Alb AL3 .................... 127 D3
Bowgate. St Alb AL1 ........ 127 E4
Bowlers Mead. Bun SG9 .... 40 D7
Bowles Gn. Enf EN1 ......... 162 B3
Bowling Cl. Bis St CM23 ..... 76 F6
Bowling Cl. Harp AL5 ....... 107 C7
Bowling Ct. Watf WD1 ..... 167 A5
Bowling Gn. Stev SG1 ........ 50 C8
Bowling Green La. Bun SG9 40 D8
Bowling Green La. Luton LU2 ...................... 45 E2
Bowling Rd. Ware SG12 ..... 93 E1
Bowman Trad Est. Stev ..... 50 B5
Bowmans Ave. Hit SG4 ...... 35 B6
Bowmans Cl. Pot B EN6 ... 159 D7
Bowmans Cl. Welw AL6 ..... 89 C6
Bowmans Ct. Heml H HP2 124 E5
Bowmans Gn. Watf WD2 . 154 E3
Bowmansgreen Prim Sch (Jun Mix & Inf). Lon C .. 142 C4
Bowring Gn. Sth Ox WD1 . 175 C5
Bowyer's Cl. Hit SG5 .......... 21 D1
Bowyers. Heml H HP2 ..... 124 D5 6
Box La. Heml H HP3 ......... 137 E7
Box La. Hod EN11 ............ 134 E6
Boxberry Cl. Stev SG1 ........ 50 E6
Boxfield Gn. Stev SG2 ........ 51 D8
Boxfield. Wel G C AL7 ...... 111 B3
Boxgrove Cl. Luton LU2 ...... 46 C5
Boxhill. Heml H HP2 ....... 124 D5 3
Boxmoor House Sch. Heml H ......................... 137 F8
Boxmoor Jun Mix Inf Sch. Heml H .......................... 124 A2
Boxted Cl. Luton LU4 .......... 44 C5
Boxted Rd. Heml H HP1 ... 123 F5
Boxtree La. Har HA3 ........ 176 D3
Boxtree Rd. Har HA3 ....... 176 D3
Boxwell Rd. Berk HP4 ...... 122 B4
Boyce Cl. Bor WD6 ........... 169 E8
Boyd Cl. Bis St CM23 ......... 77 B8
Boyle Cl. Luton LU2 ............ 63 E8
Braceby Cl. Luton LU3 ........ 44 F6
Brache Cl. Red AL3 .......... 106 A5
Brache Ct. Luton LU1 ......... 63 F6
Bracken La. Welw AL6 ....... 89 F7
Brackendale Gr. Harp AL5 . 85 D3
Brackendale Gr. Luton LU3 45 B5
Brackendale. Pot B EN6 ... 159 A6
Brackens The. Heml H HP2 ................. 124 D4
Bracklesham Gdns. Luton LU2 ....................... 46 D3
Brackndene. Bri Wd AL2 .. 140 F1
Bracknell Pl. Heml H HP2 124 F7
Bradbery. Map Cr WD3 ... 172 D5
Bradbury Cl. Bor WD6 ..... 170 B8
Bradden La. Gt Gd HP2 ... 103 E7
Bradford Rd. Chor WD3 ... 164 C2
Bradford St. Hit SG5 .......... 34 D7
Bradgate Cl. Cuf EN6 ...... 146 D3
Bradgate. Cuf EN6 ........... 146 D4
Bradgers Hill Rd. Luton LU2 ...................... 45 E4
Bradley Comm. Birhr CM23 59 C3
Bradley Rd. Enf EN3 ........ 162 E2
Bradley Rd. Luton LU4 ....... 44 D1
Bradleys Cnr. Hit SG4 ........ 35 C8
Bradman Way. Stev SG1 .... 37 A1
Bradmore Gn. Bro Pk AL9 144 E5
Bradmore La. Bro Pk AL9 144 C5
Bradmore La. Wel G AL9 . 144 C5
Bradmore Way. Bro Pk AL9 .................. 144 E5
Bradshaw Rd. Watf WD2 . 154 C1
Bradshaws. Hat AL10 ....... 129 F1
Bradway. Whit SG4 ........... 66 E6
Braemar Cl. Stev SG2 ........ 69 B7
Braemar Ct. Bus WD2 ...... 168 A3
Braeside Cl. Pnr HA5 ....... 176 A3
Bragbury Cl. Stev SG2 ....... 69 D7
Bragbury La. Dat SG3 ........ 69 D5
Bragmans La. Sar HP5 ..... 151 E6
Braham Ct. Hit SG5 ........... 34 E7 2
Brain Cl. Hat AL10 ........... 130 B6
Braithwaite Ct. Luton LU3 .. 45 D1 1
Brakynbery. Nthch HP4 .... 121 E7
Brallings La. C St P SL9 .... 172 A6
Bramble Cl. Harp AL5 ........ 85 F3
Bramble Cl. Luton LU4 ........ 44 C4
Bramble Cl. Watf WD2 .... 154 A5
Bramble Rd. Hat AL10 ...... 129 D5
Bramble Rd. Luton LU4 ...... 44 C4
Bramble Rise. Harl CM20 . 117 C1
Brambles The. Bis St CM23 76 C6
Brambles The. Ches EN8 . 162 D8
Brambles The. Royst SG8 .... 7 E5
Brambles The. St Alb AL1 127 D1
Brambles The. Stev SG1 .... 36 D2
Brambles The. Ware SG12 93 C3
Brambles The. Welw AL6 .. 89 E8
Brambling Cl. Watf WD2 .. 167 E5

Brambling Rise. Heml H HP2 ... 124 E6
Bramfield Ct. Hert SG14 .. 113 A7
Bramfield. Hit SG4 ... 35 B6
Bramfield La. Stap SG14 ... 91 F3
Bramfield Pl. Heml H HP2 105 A1
Bramfield Rd. Dat SG3 ... 90 E8
Bramfield Rd. Hert SG14 . 112 F8
Bramfield. Watf WD2 ... 154 E5
Bramhanger Acre. Luton LU3 ... 44 D7
Bramingham Bsns Pk. Luton ... 45 B8
Bramingham Prim Sch. Luton ... 45 B8
Bramingham Rd. Luton LU3 44 E5
Bramleas. Watf WD1 ... 166 F5
Bramley Cl. Bal SG7 ... 12 F1
Bramley Ct. Watf WD2 ... 154 B8
Bramley Gdns. Sth Ox WD1 ... 175 C5
Bramley House Ct. Enf EN2 ... 161 D2
Bramley Shaw. Wa Aby EN9 ... 163 F6
Brampton Cl. Ches EN7 ... 148 A3
Brampton Cl. Harp AL5 ... 86 D1
Brampton Park Rd. Hit SG5 21 E1
Brampton Rd. Royst SG8 ... 7 F6
Brampton Rd. St Alb AL1 . 128 A4
Brampton Rd. Sth Ox WD1 175 A7
Brampton Terr. Bor WD6 157 A1
Bramshaw Gdns. Sth Ox WD1 ... 175 D5
Bramshott Cl. Hit SG4 ... 34 F5
Branch Cl. Hat AL10 ... 130 C7
Branch Rd. Pk St AL2 ... 141 D4
Branch Rd. St Alb AL3 ... 127 B4
Brand St. Hit SG5 ... 34 F7
Brandles Close Sch. Bal ... 23 E7
Brandles Rd. Letw SG6 ... 23 A3
Brandon Cl. Ham St EN7 .. 147 F5
Branksome Cl. Heml H HP2 ... 125 A4
Branton Cl. Luton LU2 ... 46 E2
Brantwood Rd. Luton LU1 .. 63 C7
Bray Cl. Bor WD6 ... 170 C8
Bray Lodge. Ches EN8 ... 148 E3
Brayes Manor. Stot SG5 ... 11 F6
Brays Ct. Luton LU2 ... 46 B3
Brays Rd. Luton LU2 ... 46 B3
Braziers End. Chol HP5 ... 120 C1
Braziers Field. Hert SG13 113 F6
Braziers Quay. Bis St CM23 77 A6
Breachwood Green Cty Prim Sch. Bre Gr ... 47 E1
Bread & Cheese La. Ham St EN7 ... 147 E6
Breadcroft La. Harp AL5 ... 86 B1
Breakmead. Wel G C AL7 . 111 B4
Breaks Rd. Hat AL10 ... 130 B6
Breakspear Ave. St Alb AL1 ... 127 F2
Breakspear Coll. Abb L ... 139 F1
Breakspear Ct. Abb L WD5 ... 139 F1
Breakspear Hospl. Heml H ... 138 F6
Breakspear Rd N. Hare UB9 ... 173 D1
Breakspear. Stev SG2 ... 51 C3
Breakspear Way. Heml H HP2 ... 125 D4
Breakspeare Cl. Watf WD2 ... 154 B1
Breakspeare Rd. Abb L WD5 ... 153 E8
Brecken Cl. St Alb AL4 ... 128 A7
Brecon Cl. Luton LU1 ... 63 D6
Breeze Terr. Ches EN8 ... 148 D3
Brent Ct. Stev SG1 ... 50 E5
Brent Pl. Barn EN5 ... 171 F4
Brett Pl. Watf WD2 ... 154 A2
Brett Rd. Barn EN5 ... 171 C4
Bretts Mead. Luton LU1 ... 63 C5
Brewery La. Bal SG7 ... 23 E8
Brewery La. Sta M CM24 ... 59 E7
Brewery Rd. Hod EN11 ... 135 A6
Brewhouse Hill. Whea AL4 ... 108 C8
Brewhouse La. Hert SG14 113 C6
Briants Cl. Pnr HA5 ... 175 F1
Briar Cl. Ches EN8 ... 148 C2
Briar Cl. Luton LU2 ... 46 C4
Briar Cl. Pot En HP4 ... 123 A7
Briar Patch La. Letw SG6 ... 22 D3
Briar Rd. St Alb AL4 ... 128 D6
Briar Rd. Watf WD2 ... 154 B4
Briar Way. Berk HP4 ... 122 D3
Briarcliff. Heml H HP1 ... 123 E4
Briardale. Stev SG1 ... 50 E4
Briardale. Ware SG12 ... 93 C3
Briarley Cl. Hod EN10 ... 134 F1
Briars Cl. Hat AL10 ... 130 A5
Briars La. Hat AL10 ... 130 A5
Briars The. Bus WD2 ... 168 E2
Briars The. Ches EN8 ... 162 E8
Briars The. Hert SG13 ... 114 A6
Briars The. Sar WD3 ... 152 A3
Briars Wood. Hat AL10 ... 130 A5
Briarwood Dr. Pnr HA6 ... 175 A1
Briary La. Royst SG8 ... 7 C5
Briary Wood End. Welw AL6 ... 89 F8
Briary Wood La. Welw AL6 89 F8
Brick Kiln La. Hit SG4 ... 34 E5
Brick Knoll Pk. St Alb AL1 128 C2
Brickcroft. Ches EN10 ... 148 E5
Brickenden Ct. Wa Aby EN9 ... 163 F6
Brickendon Ct. Hod EN11 135 A5
Brickendon Golf Course. Bric ... 133 B4
Brickendon La. Bric SG13 133 D6
Bricket Rd. St Alb AL1 ... 127 E3
Bricket Wood Sta. Bri Wd 141 A1
Brickfield Ave. Heml H HP3 ... 125 B2
Brickfield Ct. Hat AL10 ... 130 B2
Brickfield. Hat AL10 ... 130 A2
Brickfield La. Edg EN5 ... 170 F3
Brickfields The. Ware SG12 ... 93 B2
Brickkiln Rd. Stev SG1 ... 50 C6
Brickly Rd. Luton LU4 ... 44 C5
Brickmakers La. Heml H HP3 ... 125 B2
Brickwall Cl. A St P AL6 ... 110 A8
Brickyard La. Reed SG8 ... 16 E5
Bride Hall La. A St L AL6 ... 88 A5
Bridewell Cl. Bun SG9 ... 40 E8
Bridge Ct. Berk HP4 ... 122 D4
Bridge Ct. Harp AL5 ... 85 F3 5
Bridge Ct. Radl WD7 ... 156 B4
Bridge End. Bun SG9 ... 40 E8
Bridge Foot. Ware SG12 ... 93 D1
Bridge Pl. Watf WD1 ... 167 D4
Bridge Rd. Abb L WD4 ... 153 C6
Bridge Rd E. Wel G C AL7 110 F6
Bridge Rd. Letw SG6 ... 22 F6
Bridge Rd. Stev SG1 ... 50 C7
Bridge Rd. Wel G C AL8 ... 110 C7
Bridge Rd. Welw SG3 ... 69 A2
Bridge St. Berk HP4 ... 122 D4
Bridge St. Bis St CM23 ... 76 F7
Bridge St. Heml H HP1 ... 124 C2
Bridge St. Hit SG5 ... 34 E6
Bridge St. Knee SG8 ... 2 B8
Bridge St. Luton LU1 ... 63 E8
Bridgefields. Wel G C AL7 110 F7
Bridgefoot. Bun SG9 ... 40 E7
Bridgeford House. Watf WD1 ... 167 B6 5
Bridgegate Bsns Ctr. Wel G C ... 110 F7
Bridgend Rd. Enf EN1 ... 162 C4
Bridgenhall Rd. Enf EN1 ... 161 F1
Bridger Cl. Watf WD2 ... 154 E6
Bridges Ct. Hert SG14 ... 113 C6
Bridges Rd. Stan HA7 ... 176 F5
Bridgewater Ct. L Gad HP4 ... 102 C8
Bridgewater Hill. Nthch HP4 ... 121 F7
Bridgewater Rd. Berk HP4 122 B5
Bridgewater Sch. Berk ... 122 A6
Bridgewater Way. Bus WD2 ... 168 B3
Bridgeways. Hod EN11 ... 135 B6
Bridle Cl. Enf EN3 ... 162 F2
Bridle Cl. Hod EN11 ... 115 A2
Bridle Cl. St Alb AL3 ... 127 E5
Bridle La. Ric WD3 ... 165 D6
Bridle Path. Watf WD2 ... 167 B7
Bridle Way. Berk HP4 ... 122 A6
Bridle Way. Gt Am SG12 .. 115 A6
Bridle Way. Hod EN11 ... 115 A1
Bridle Way (N). Hod EN11 115 B2
Bridle Way (S). Hod EN11 115 A1
Bridleway. St Le HP23 ... 119 E5
Bridlington Rd. Sth Ox WD1 ... 175 D7
Brierley Cl. Luton LU2 ... 46 D2
Briery Field. Chor WD3 ... 165 A5
Briery Way. Heml H HP2 . 125 A4
Brigadier Ave. Enf EN2 ... 161 C1
Brigadier Hill. Enf EN2 ... 161 C1
Brightman Cotts. Luton LU3 45 A7
Brighton Rd. Watf WD2 ... 154 A1
Brighton Way. Stev SG1 ... 50 A8
Brightview Cl. Bri Wd AL2 140 E2
Brightwell Rd. Watf WD1 167 A4
Brill Cl. Luton LU2 ... 46 D2
Brimfield Cl. Luton LU2 ... 46 D2
Brimsdown Ave. Enf EN3 . 162 E1
Brimstone Wlk. Berk HP4 121 F6
Brinklow Ct. St Alb AL3 ... 141 B8
Brinley Cl. Ches EN8 ... 162 D8
Brinsley Rd. Har HA3 ... 176 D1
Brinsmead. Pk St AL2 ... 141 E4
Briscoe Cl. Hod EN11 ... 134 F8
Briscoe Rd. Hod EN11 ... 134 F8
Bristol Rd. Luton LU3 ... 45 B4
Britannia Ave. Luton LU3 ... 45 B4
Britannia Rd. Ches EN8 ... 162 F5
Britannia. Stand SG11 ... 55 E2
Britannic Bsns Pk. Ches ... 162 F5
Britannica Works. Wa Aby 163 D5
Brittain Way. Stev SG2 ... 51 B4
Britten Cl. Elst WD6 ... 169 D3
Britton Ave. St Alb AL3 ... 127 D3
Brixham Cl. Stev SG1 ... 50 B7
Brixton Rd. Watf WD2 ... 167 B8
Broad Acre. Bri Wd AL2 ... 140 E1
Broad Acres. Hat AL10 ... 129 F8
Broad Ct. Wel G C AL7 ... 110 E6
Broad Gn. Bay SG13 ... 132 F8
Broad Green Wood. Bay SG13 ... 133 A8
Broad Mead. Luton LU3 ... 45 A3
Broad Oak Ct. Luton LU2 ... 46 D3 2
Broad Oak Way. Stev SG2 . 50 F1
Broad St. Heml H HP2 ... 124 D4
Broad Wlk. Harl CM20 ... 117 D1
Broad Wlk The. Norwd HA6 ... 174 C1
Broadacres. Luton LU2 ... 45 D6
Broadcroft. Heml H HP2 .. 124 D5 2
Broadcroft. Letw SG6 ... 22 F2
Broadfield. Bis St CM23 ... 58 F2
Broadfield Cl. Muc H SG10 74 E1
Broadfield Ct. Bus WD2 ... 176 E8
Broadfield. Harl CM20 ... 117 E1
Broadfield Inf Sch. Heml H ... 124 F3
Broadfield Jun Sch. Heml H ... 124 F3
Broadfield Pl. Wel G C AL8 ... 110 B5
Broadfield Rd. Heml H HP2 ... 124 F3
Broadfield Rd. Welw SG3 .. 69 B1
Broadfield Way. Muc H SG10 ... 74 F1
Broadfields Cty Prim Sch. Harl ... 117 E1
Broadfields. Gofs O EN7 .. 147 B2
Broadfields. H Wy CM21 ... 97 B1
Broadfields. Har HA2 ... 176 B1
Broadfields. Harp AL5 ... 85 F2
Broadfields La. Watf WD1 167 B1
Broadgate. Wa Aby EN9 .. 163 F7
Broadhall Way. Stev SG2 ... 51 B2
Broadlake Cl. Lon C AL2 ... 142 D4
Broadlands Cl. Ches EN8 . 162 D5
Broadlawns Ct. Har HA3 .. 176 F2
Broadleaf Ave. Bis St CM23 ... 76 D4
Broadmead Cl. Pnr HA5 ... 175 E3
Broadmead. Hit SG4 ... 35 B5
Broadmead Ind Sch. Luton 63 E5
Broadmeadow Ride. Hit SG4 ... 35 A4
Broadmeads. Ware SG12 .. 93 D1
Broadoak Ave. Enf EN3 ... 162 D4
Broadstone Rd. Harp AL5 107 D7
Broadview. Stev SG1 ... 50 E6
Broadwater Ave. Letw SG6 22 E5
Broadwater. Berk HP4 ... 122 C5
Broadwater Cres. Stev SG2 69 C8
Broadwater Cres. Wel G C AL7 ... 110 D5
Broadwater Dale. Letw SG6 ... 22 E5
Broadwater La. Ast SG2 ... 51 D1
Broadwater. Pot B EN6 ... 145 B1
Broadwater Rd. Wel G C AL7 ... 110 E6
Broadway Ave. Harl CM17 118 B4
Broadway Ct. Letw SG6 ... 22 E3
Broadway. Letw SG6 ... 22 F5
Broadway The. Har HA3 .. 176 F1
Broadway The. Hat AL9 ... 130 C6
Broadway The. Kim AL4 ... 87 B5
Broadway The. Pnr HA5 .. 175 F3
Broadway The. Watf WD1 167 C6
Brocket Ct. Luton LU4 ... 44 D5
Brocket Rd. Hat AL8 ... 110 A3
Brocket Rd. Hod EN11 ... 135 A6
Brocket View. Whea AL4 . 108 D8
Brockett Cl. Wel G C AL8 . 110 B6
Brockhurst Cl. Stan HA7 .. 176 F4
Brocklesbury Cl. Watf WD2 ... 167 D7
Brockley Hill. Stan HA7 ... 169 C1
Brockswood La. Wel G C AL8 ... 110 B7
Brockswood Prim Sch. Heml H ... 105 C1
Brockwell Shott. Walk SG2 38 B1
Brodewater Rd. Bor WD6 170 B7
Brodie Rd. Enf EN2 ... 161 C1
Bromborough Gn. Sth Ox WD1 ... 175 C5
Bromet Cl. Watf WD1 ... 153 F1
Bromet Jun Mix Inf Sch. Watf ... 167 D2
Bromleigh Cl. Ches EN8 ... 148 E3
Bromley. Lon M HP23 ... 79 A4
Brompton Cl. Luton LU3 ... 44 F8
Bronte Cres. Heml H HP2 105 B1
Bronte Paths. Stev SG2 ... 51 C6
Brook Cotts. Sta M CM24 .. 59 E5
Brook Dr. Radl WD7 ... 155 F6
Brook Dr. Stev SG2 ... 69 B8
Brook End. Saw CM21 ... 97 D2
Brook Field. Ast SG2 ... 51 E2
Brook La. Berk HP4 ... 122 B5
Brook La. Saw CM21 ... 97 D2
Brook Rd. Bor WD6 ... 170 A7
Brook Rd. Saw CM21 ... 97 D1
Brook Rd. Sta M CM24 ... 59 E6
Brook St. Luton LU3 ... 63 D8
Brook St. Stot SG5 ... 11 E6
Brook St. Tri HP23 ... 100 B4
Brook View. Hit SG4 ... 35 C6
Brookbridge La. Dat SG3 ... 69 D2
Brookdene Ave. Watf WD1 ... 167 C1
Brookdene Dr. Norwd HA6 ... 174 F4
Brooke Cl. Bus WD2 ... 168 C2
Brooke Gdns. Bis St CM23 . 77 C7
Brooke Rd. Royst SG8 ... 7 D8
Brooke Way. Bus WD2 ... 168 C2
Brooker Rd. Wa Aby EN9 . 163 C5
Brookfield Ctr. Ches ... 148 D4
Brookfield Cl. Tri HP23 ... 100 B4
Brookfield Gdns. Ches EN8 ... 148 D4
Brookfield Jun Sch. Bor ... 169 F8
Brookfield La. Ast SG2 ... 51 F3
Brookfield La. Ches EN8 ... 148 B3
Brookfield La E. Ches EN8 148 D3
Brookfield La W. Ches EN8148 C4
Brookfields. Saw CM21 ... 97 D2
Brookhill. Stev SG2 ... 68 F8
Brookland Inf Sch. Ches .. 148 E3
Brookland Jun Sch. Ches . 148 E3
Brooklands Cl. Luton LU4 ... 44 C6
Brooklands Gdns. Pot B EN6 ... 158 E7
Brookmans Ave. Bro Pk AL9 ... 144 F5
Brookmans Park Cty Prim Sch. Bro Pk ... 144 E5
Brookmans Park Sta. Bro Pk ... 144 E5
Brookmead Cty Prim Sch. Pit ... 80 E5
Brookmore Park Golf Club. Bro Pk ... 145 A6
Brooks Ct. Hert SG14 ... 112 F7
Brooksfield. Wel G C AL7 . 111 B7
Brookshill Ave. Stan HA3 . 176 E5
Brookshill Dr. Stan HA3 ... 176 D5
Brookshill. Stan HA3 ... 176 D5
Brookside Cl. Barn EN5 ... 171 E3
Brookside Cres. Cuf EN6 . 146 E4
Brookside Gdns. Enf EN1 . 162 C2
Brookside. Hat AL10 ... 129 D5
Brookside. Hert SG13 ... 113 E5
Brookside. Hod EN11 ... 135 A6
Brookside. Letw SG6 ... 22 F5
Brookside. Pot B EN6 ... 158 A7
Brookside Rd. Watf WD1 . 167 B2
Brookside. Wa Aby EN9 ... 163 E7
Brookside. Watf WD2 ... 154 D3
Brookside. Watf WD2 ... 167 B2
Broom Barns Jun Mix Inf Sch. Stev ... 50 E5
Broom Cl. Ham St EN7 ... 148 A4
Broom Cl. Hat AL10 ... 129 F2
Broom Gr. Kneb SG3 ... 68 F5
Broom Gr. Watf WD1 ... 154 A1
Broom Hill. Heml H HP1 .. 123 E2
Broom Hill. Welw AL6 ... 90 A8
Broom Wlk. Stev SG1 ... 50 E5
Broomer Pl. Ches EN8 ... 148 C2
Broomfield Ave. Ches EN10 ... 148 E5
Broomfield. Chis AL2 ... 141 C4
Broomfield Cl. Welw AL6 ... 89 C4
Broomfield. Harl CM20 ... 118 B3
Broomfield Rd. Welw AL6 .. 89 C4
Broomfield Rise. Abb L WD5 ... 153 D7
Broomhills. Wel G C AL7 .. 111 B7
Broomleys. St Alb AL4 ... 128 D6
Brooms Cl. Wel G C AL8 ... 89 D1
Brooms Rd. Luton LU2 ... 63 F8
Broomstick Hall Rd. Wa Aby EN9 ... 163 E6
Broomstick La. Bot HP5 ... 136 A1
Broughinge Rd. Bor WD6 . 170 B7
Broughton Ave. Luton LU3 . 45 C5
Broughton Hill. Letw SG6 ... 23 B6
Broughton Way. Ric WD3 165 A2
Brow The. Watf WD2 ... 154 B6
Brown's Cl. Luton LU4 ... 44 D5
Brown's Rise. St Le HP23 119 F3
Brownfield Way. Kim AL4 .. 87 B6
Brownfields. Wel G C AL7 110 F7
Browning Dr. Hit SG4 ... 35 B8
Browning Rd. Dun LU4 ... 44 A2
Browning Rd. Enf EN2 ... 161 D1
Browning Rd. Harp AL5 ... 86 C2
Brownlow La. Ched LU7 ... 80 A7
Brownlow Rd. Berk HP4 .. 122 C5
Brownlow Rd. Bor WD6 ... 170 A5
Browns Spring. Pot En HP4 ... 123 C7
Brox Dell. Stev SG1 ... 50 E6
Broxbourne Jun Mix Inf Sch. Hod ... 134 F2
Broxbourne Sch The. Hod 134 E1
Broxbourne Sta. Hod ... 135 A3
Broxbournebury Sch. Hod 134 E3
Broxley Mead. Luton LU4 ... 44 D5
Bruce Gr. Watf WD2 ... 154 C1
Bruce Rd. Barn EN5 ... 171 E6
Bruce Rd. Har HA3 ... 176 E1
Bruce Way. Ches EN8 ... 162 D6
Brunel Rd. Stev SG2 ... 51 B7
Brunswick Ct. Hod EN11 .. 135 A5
Brunswick Ct. Stev SG1 ... 50 A7
Brunswick St. Luton LU2 ... 63 E8
Brushrise. Watf WD2 ... 154 A3
Brushwood Dr. Chor WD3 164 C5
Brussels Way. Luton LU3 ... 44 D8
Bryan Rd. Bis St CM23 ... 76 F8
Bryanstone Rd. Ches EN8 162 F5
Bryant Cl. Barn EN5 ... 171 F4
Bryant Ct. Harp AL5 ... 86 A3
Bryce Cl. Ware SG12 ... 93 D3
Bryn La. St Alb AL4 ... 128 C1
Bryn Way. St Alb AL4 ... 128 C1
Bsns Ctr E. Letw ... 23 C6
Bsns Ctr W. Letw ... 23 C6
Buchanan Ct. Bor WD6 ... 170 C7
Buchanan Ct. Luton LU2 ... 64 B8
Buchanan Dr. Luton LU2 ... 64 B8
Buckettsland La. Shen WD6 ... 157 D2
Buckingham Dr. Luton LU2 46 D2
Buckingham Rd. Bor WD6 170 D5
Buckingham Rd. Tri HP23 .. 99 E3
Buckingham Rd. Watf WD2 ... 154 C2
Buckinghamshire Coll The. L Chal ... 172 A8
Buckland Rd. Ast Cl HP22 .. 99 A4
Buckland Rise. Pnr HA5 ... 175 D2
Bucklands The. Ric WD3 .. 165 A2
Bucklers Cl. Hod EN10 ... 134 F1
Bucklersbury. Hit SG5 ... 34 E6
Buckley Cl. Luton LU3 ... 44 F7
Bucknalls Cl. Watf WD2 ... 154 E7
Bucknalls Dr. Bri Wd AL2 . 154 F8
Bucknalls La. Bri Wd WD2 154 E7
Bucknalls La. Watf WD2 ... 154 E7
Bucks Alley. L Berk SG13 . 132 D4
Bucks Ave. Watf WD1 ... 167 E2
Bucks Hill. Sar WD4 ... 152 C5
Buckthorn Ave. Stev SG1 ... 50 E4
Buckton Rd. Bor WD6 ... 156 F1
Buckwood La. Whip LU6 ... 82 C7
Buckwood Rd. Mark AL3 ... 83 C6
Buddcroft. Wel G C AL7 ... 111 B7
Bude Cres. Stev SG1 ... 50 A7
Bulbourne Cl. Berk HP4 ... 121 F6
Bulbourne Ct. Heml H HP1 124 A2
Bulbourne Rd. Tri HP23 ... 100 B7
Bull La. Buck SG8 ... 27 C8
Bull La. Cotrd SG9 ... 39 C8
Bull La. Whea ... 108 A6
Bull Plain. Hert SG14 ... 113 D6
Bull Rd. Harp AL5 ... 107 B8
Bull Stag Gn. Hat AL9 ... 130 C7
Bull's Cross. Enf EN2 ... 162 A3
Bullace Cl. Heml H HP1 ... 124 A4
Bullbeggars La. Berk HP4 123 A4

Bullbeggars La. Pot En HP4 .................. 123 A4
Bullen's Green La. Coln H AL4 .................. 143 E8
Bullfields. Saw CM21 ......... 97 E3
Bullhead Rd. Bor WD6 ..... 170 C6
Bullock's Hill. Whit SG4 ...... 49 B1
Bullock's La. Hert SG13 ... 113 C4
Bullrush Cl. Hat AL10 ....... 130 B4
Bulls Cross Ride. Gofs O EN7 .................. 162 A5
Bulls La. Bro Pk AL9 ......... 144 E7
Bulls La. Wel G AL9 .......... 144 E7
Bullsland Gdns. Chor WD3 .................. 164 B3
Bullsland La. Chor WD3 ... 164 B2
Bullsmoor Cl. Enf EN8 ...... 162 C4
Bullsmoor Gdns. Enf EN8 . 162 B4
Bullsmoor La. Enf EN1,EN3 ................ 162 C4
Bullsmoor Ride. Enf EN8 .. 162 C4
Bullsmoor Sec Sch & Sports Ctr. Enf .................................. 162 C4
Bullsmoor Way. Enf EN8 .. 162 C4
Bullwell Cres. Ches EN8 ... 148 E2
Bulstrode La. Chipf HP3 ... 137 F3
Bulstrode La. Heml H HP3 138 A5
Bulwer Link. Stev SG1 ........ 50 E3
Buncefield La. Heml H HP2 ................. 125 C5
Bungalows The. Harp AL5 . 86 C3
Bunkers La. Heml H HP3 . 139 B7
Bunnsfield. Wel G C AL7 .. 111 C7
Bunstrux. Tri HP23 .......... 100 A4
Bunting Rd. Dun LU4 .......... 44 A4
Buntingford Rd. Stand SG11 .................... 55 D4
Bunyan Cl. Pirt SG5 ............ 20 D4
Bunyan Cl. Tri HP23 ......... 100 B5
Bunyan Rd. Hit SG5 ............ 34 F8
Bunyans Cl. Luton LU3 ....... 45 A5
Burbage Cl. Ches EN8 ...... 162 F8
Burchell Ct. Bus WD2 ....... 168 C2
Burfield Cl. Hat AL10 ....... 130 A7
Burfield Ct. Luton LU2 ........ 46 D3 1
Burfield Rd. Chor WD3 .... 164 C4
Burford Cl. Luton LU3 ........ 31 A1
Burford Gdns. Hod EN11 . 135 B7
Burford Mews. Hod EN11 135 A7
Burford Pl. Hod EN11 ....... 135 A7
Burford St. Hod EN11 ...... 135 A7
Burford Way. Hit SG5 ........ 21 D2
Burge End La. Pirt SG5 ...... 20 C5
Burgess Ct. Bor WD6 ....... 156 F1
Burghley Ave. Bis St CM23 76 C7
Burghley Ave. Bor WD6 ... 170 C4
Burghley Cl. Stev SG2 ........ 69 A8
Burgoyne Hatch. Harl CM20 .................... 118 A1
Burgundy Croft. Wel G C AL7 ................. 110 F4
Burhill Gr. Pnr HA5 .......... 175 E1
Burleigh Mead. Hat AL9 ... 130 C7
Burleigh Prim Sch. Ches .. 148 D1
Burleigh Rd. Ches EN8 ..... 162 E7
Burleigh Rd. Heml H HP2 . 125 C2
Burleigh Rd. Hert SG13 .... 114 A7
Burleigh Rd. St Alb AL1 ..... 128 B3
Burleigh Way. Cuf EN6 ..... 146 E1
Burley House. Abb L WD5 153 F7
Burley. Letw SG6 ............... 11 F2
Burley Rd. Bis St CM23 ...... 77 A4
Burnell Rise. Letw SG6 ...... 22 D5
Burnell Wlk. Letw SG6 ....... 22 E5
Burnells Way. Sta M CM24 59 E7
Burnet Cl. Heml H HP3 .... 124 E2
Burnett Ave. Henlw SG16 ... 10 B4
Burnett Sq. Hert SG14 ..... 112 F7
Burnham Cl. Dat AL6 .......... 90 C6
Burnham Cl. Enf EN1 ....... 161 E1
Burnham Green Rd. Dat AL6,SG3 .................. 90 D6
Burnham Rd. Luton LU2 ..... 46 B2
Burnham Rd. St Alb AL1 ... 128 B3
Burnley Cl. Sth Ox WD1 ... 175 C5
Burns Cl. Hit SG4 ............... 35 B8
Burns Cl. Stev SG2 ............. 51 C8
Burns Dr. Heml H HP2 ..... 105 B1
Burns Rd. Royst SG8 ........... 7 D8
Burnsall Pl. Harp AL5 ....... 107 C6
Burnside Cl. Hat AL10 ...... 130 A8
Burnside. Hert SG14 ........ 113 A5
Burnside. Hod EN11 ......... 134 F6
Burnside. Saw CM21 ......... 97 D2
Burnside. St Alb AL1 ......... 128 B1
Burnside Terr. Harl CM17 118 F3
Burnt Cl. Luton LU3 ........... 44 F7
Burnt Mill Comp Sch. Harl 117 E2
Burntfarm Ride. Gofs O EN2,EN7 .......... 161 B7
Burntmill Cl. Harl CM20 ... 117 C3
Burntmill La. Harl CM20 .. 117 D3
Burr Cl. Lon C AL2 ............ 142 E4
Burr St. Luton LU2 ............. 63 E8
Burr's Pl. Luton LU1 ........... 63 E6
Burrowfield. Wel G C AL7 110 D4
Burrs La. Bark SG8 ............ 17 C3
Bursland. Letw SG6 ........... 22 D6
Burston Dr. Chis AL2 ....... 141 C3
Burton Ave. Watf WD1 .... 167 A5
Burton Cl. Kim AL4 ............. 87 C5
Burton La. Gofs O EN7 ..... 147 E3
Burtons La. L Chal WD3 ... 164 A4
Burtons Mill. Saw CM21 .... 97 F3
Burvale Ct. Watf WD1 ..... 167 B6 3
Burwell Rd. Stev SG2 ......... 51 C4
Bury Cotts. Fla AL3 .......... 105 E5
Bury End. Pirt SG5 ............ 20 D4
Bury Gn. Heml H HP1 ....... 124 C4
Bury Gn. Whea AL4 .......... 108 C8
Bury Green Rd. Ches EN7 162 A7
Bury Green Rd. Ches EN7 162 A8
Bury Hill Cl. Heml H HP1 .. 124 C4
Bury Hill. Heml H HP1 ...... 124 C4
Bury Holme. Hod EN10 .... 148 F8
Bury La. Bram SG14 ........... 91 B4
Bury La. Cod SG4 ............... 67 F2
Bury La. Dat SG3 ................ 69 D3
Bury La. Ric WD3 ............. 165 D1
Bury La. Str LU3 ................. 31 A5
Bury Mead. Arl SG15 ......... 11 A7
Bury Mead Rd. Hit SG5 ...... 21 F1
Bury Meadows. Ric WD3 . 165 D1
Bury Park Rd. Luton LU1 .... 63 C8
Bury Rd. Harl CM17 ......... 118 D4
Bury Rd. Hat AL10 ............ 130 C6
Bury Rd. Heml H HP1 ....... 124 C3
Bury Rise. Heml H HP3 .... 137 D6
Bury The. Cod SG4 ............ 67 F2
Burycroft. Wel G C AL8 ....... 89 E1
Burydale Jun Sch. Stev ...... 51 B1
Burydell La. Pk St AL2 ...... 141 D5
Buryfield Terr. Ware SG12 93 C1
Burymead. Stev SG1 .......... 36 C1
Burywick. Harp AL5 .......... 107 B5
Bush Hall La. Hat AL9 ...... 130 D8
Bush Spring. Bal SG7 ......... 13 A1
Bushbarns. Ches EN7 ....... 148 A2
Bushby Ave. Hod EN10 .... 134 F1
Bushel Wharf. Tri HP23 ... 100 A6
Bushell Gn. Bus WD2 ....... 176 D8
Bushey Cl. Wel G C AL7 ... 111 B5
Bushey Gn. Wel G C AL7 .. 111 B5
Bushey Grove Rd. Watf WD2 .................... 167 E5
Bushey Hall Dr. Watf WD2 167 E5
Bushey Hall Golf Course. Bus .............................. 167 E6
Bushey Hall Rd. Watf WD2 .................... 167 E5
Bushey Hall Sch. Bus ....... 167 F4
Bushey Heath Jun Mix Inf Prim Sch. Bus ............. 168 D1
Bushey Manor Jun Sch. Watf .............................. 167 E4
Bushey Maternity Hospl. Stan ............................ 168 F1
Bushey Meads Sch. Bus ... 168 C4
Bushey Mill Cres. Watf WD2 .................... 154 C3
Bushey Mill La. Bus WD2 . 167 E8
Bushey Mill La. Watf WD2 154 D1
Bushey & Oxhey Sta. Watf 167 D3
Bushfield Rd. Bov HP3 ..... 137 C6
Bushmead Prim Sch. Luton 45 E5
Bushmead Rd. Luton LU2 ... 45 E5
Bushwood Cl. Wel G AL9 . 144 B8
Bute Sq. Luton LU1 ............ 63 E7
Bute St. Luton LU1 ............. 63 E7
Butely Rd. Luton LU4 .......... 44 B5
Butler's Hall La. H Wy CM23 .................... 76 A3
Butlers Dr. Wa Aby EN9 .. 163 C1
Butlin Rd. Luton LU1 .......... 63 B7
Butt Field View. St Alb AL1 141 C7
Butterfield Green Rd. Str LU2 ............................ 46 A6
Butterfield La. St Alb AL1 . 141 E7
Butterfield Rd. Whea AL4 108 C7
Butterfly La. Radl WD6 ..... 169 B7
Buttermere Cl. St Alb AL1 128 B2
Buttersweet Rise. Saw CM21 ...................... 97 E1
Butterwick Adult Training Ctr. St Alb .......................... 128 D2
Butterwick. Watf WD2 ...... 154 E3
Butterworth Path. Luton LU2 ...................... 63 E8 2
Buttlehide. Map Cr WD3 .. 172 D5
Buttondene Cres. Lo Naz EN10 ................. 135 B1
Butts End. Heml H HP1 .... 124 A5
Butts The. Ches EN10 ...... 148 E7
Buttsmead. Norwd HA6 .. 174 C3
Buxton Cl. St Alb AL4 ....... 128 D6
Buxton Path. Sth Ox WD1 175 C7
Buxton Rd. Luton LU1 ........ 63 D7
Buxtons La. Gu M SG8 ......... 1 F3
Buzzard Rd. Dun LU4 ......... 44 A4
By The Mount. Wel G C AL7 ................. 110 D5
By-The-Wood. Sth Ox WD1 ................. 175 E8
Byde St. Hert SG14 .......... 113 C7
Bye Way The. Har HA3 .... 176 F2
Byers Cl. Pot B EN6 .......... 159 C5
Byeway The. Ric WD3 ...... 173 E8
Byfield Cl. Dun LU4 ........... 44 B1
Byfield. Wel G C AL8 .......... 89 E1
Byford House. Barn EN5 .. 171 D5
Bygrave Rd. Bal SG7 .......... 12 F1
Bygrave. Stev SG1 ............. 36 C2
Bylands Cl. Bis St CM23 ..... 76 D6
Byng Dr. Pot B EN6 .......... 159 A8
Byng Rd. Barn EN5 .......... 171 D6
Byrd Wlk. Bal SG7 ............. 23 F7
Byron Ave. Bor WD6 ........ 170 A4
Byron Ave. Watf WD2 ...... 167 D8
Byron Cl. Ham St EN7 ...... 147 F4
Byron Cl. Hit SG4 ............... 35 B8
Byron Cl. Stev SG2 ............. 51 C7
Byron Ct. Ches EN2 .......... 148 B3
Byron Pl. Heml H HP2 ...... 105 B1
Byron Rd. Dun LU4 ............ 44 B2
Byron Rd. Har HA3 ........... 176 F1
Byron Rd. Harp AL5 ........... 86 A2
Byron Rd. Royst SG8 ............ 7 E8
Byslips Rd. Stu LU6 ............ 82 D5
Byslips Rd. Whip LU6 ........ 82 D5
Byway The. Pot B EN6 ...... 159 A6
Byways. Berk HP4 ............ 122 E5

Cabot Cl. Stev SG2 ............ 51 A7
Caddington Comm. Mark AL3 ........................ 83 E8
Caddis Cl. Har HA7 .......... 176 F3
Cade Cl. Letw SG6 .............. 12 C1
Cades Cl. Luton LU1 ........... 63 A6
Cades La. Luton LU1 .......... 63 A6
Cadia Cl. Cad LU1 ............... 62 E4
Cadmore Ct. Ches EN8 ..... 148 D3
Cadmore La. Ches EN8 ..... 148 E2
Cadwell Ct. Hit SG4 ........... 22 A2
Cadwell La. Hit SG4 ........... 22 A2
Caernarvon Cl. Heml H HP2 ................. 124 D3
Caernarvon Cl. Stev SG2 .... 69 B7
Caernarvon Ct. Heml H HP2 ................. 124 D3
Caesars Rd. Whea AL4 ..... 108 E8
Cage Pond Rd. Shen WD7 156 F6
Cairn Way. Har HA7 ......... 176 F4
Caishowe Rd. Bor WD6 ... 170 B8
Caister Cl. Stev SG1 ........... 36 A1
Calbury Cl. St Alb AL1 ...... 128 B2
Caldbeck. Wa Aby EN9 .... 163 D5
Caldecot Ave. Gofs O EN7 147 F2
Caldecot Way. Hod EN10 . 134 F1
Caldecote Gdns. Bus WD2 168 E2
Caldecote La. Bus WD2 ... 168 F3
Caldecote Rd. Newn SG7 ... 12 E8
Calder Ave. Bro Pk AL9 .... 145 B5
Caldwell Rd. Sth Ox WD1 . 175 D6
Caleb Cl. Luton LU4 ........... 44 F2
Caledon Rd. Lon C AL2 .... 142 D5
Caledonian Ct. Watf WD1 167 B7
California. Bal SG7 ............ 12 F1
California La. Bus WD2 ..... 168 D1
Callanders The. Bus WD2 168 E1
Callisto Ct. Heml H HP2 ... 124 F6
Callowland Pl. Watf WD2 154 B1
Calnwood Rd. Dun LU4 ...... 44 C3
Calton Ave. Hert SG14 ..... 112 F7
Calton Ct. Hert SG14 ........ 112 F6
Calton House. Hert SG14 . 112 F6
Calverley Cl. Bis St CM23 ... 76 E4
Calvert Rd. Barn EN5 ....... 171 D7
Calverton Rd. Luton LU3 ..... 44 F6
Cam Ctr. Hit SG4 ................ 22 A3
Cam Sq. Hit SG4 ................. 22 A3
Camberley Pl. Harp AL5 ... 107 D6
Camborne Dr. Heml H HP2 ................. 124 E7
Cambrian Way. Heml H HP2 ................. 124 F6
Cambridge Cl. Ches EN8 .. 148 C2
Cambridge Cotts. Thun SG11 ..................... 72 E2
Cambridge Cres. Knee SG8 . 2 A8
Cambridge Dr. Pot B EN6 158 E8
Cambridge Rd. Bar SG8 ....... 9 A3
Cambridge Rd. Bar SG8 ..... 17 F7
Cambridge Rd. Bark SG8 ... 17 D5
Cambridge Rd. Harl CM20 118 C6
Cambridge Rd. Hit SG4 ...... 35 B8
Cambridge Rd. Saw CM21 . 97 E4
Cambridge Rd. St Alb AL1 128 B2
Cambridge Rd. Sta M CM24 .................. 59 E8
Cambridge Rd. Stand SG11 55 C2
Cambridge Rd. Watf WD1 167 C5
Cambridge St. Luton LU1 .... 63 F5
Cambridge Terr. Berk HP4 122 D4
Cameron Ct. Ware SG12 .... 93 D2 8
Cameron Dr. Ches EN8 ..... 162 D5
Camfield. Wel G C AL7 ..... 110 F2
Camford Way. Luton LU3 ... 44 B8
Camlet Way. St Alb AL3 .... 127 B4
Camp Jun Mix Inf Sch. St Alb ............................ 128 B2
Camp Rd. St Alb AL1 ........ 128 B2
Camp View Rd. St Alb AL1 128 B2
Campana Ct. Barn EN5 .... 171 D6
Campania Gr. Luton LU3 .... 45 A8
Campbell Cl. Hit SG4 ......... 35 B8
Campers Ave. Letw SG6 ..... 22 E5
Campers Rd. Letw SG6 ...... 22 E5
Campers Wlk. Letw SG6 .... 22 E5
Campfield Rd. Hert SG14 . 113 B5
Campfield Rd. St Alb AL1 . 128 A3
Campfield Way. Letw SG6 . 22 D5
Campine Cl. Ches EN8 ..... 148 D3
Campion Cl. Watf WD2 .... 154 A6
Campion Ct. Stev SG1 ........ 50 C8
Campion Rd. Heml H HP1 123 E2
Campion Way. Royst SG8 ... 7 E5
Campions Ct. Berk HP4 .... 122 B3
Campions The. Bor WD6 .. 157 A1
Campions The. Sta M CM24 .................. 59 E8
Campkin Mead. Stev SG2 ... 51 D3
Camps Hill Jun Mix Inf Sch. Stev ............................... 51 B6
Campus Five. Letw ............ 23 C7
Campus The. Wel G C AL8 110 D7
Canada La. Ches EN10 ..... 148 E6
Canadas The. Ches EN10 . 148 E6
Canberra Cl. Knee SG8 ........ 2 B5
Canberra Cl. St Alb AL3 ... 127 F7
Canberra Gdns. Luton LU3 . 45 B6
Candlefield Cl. Heml H HP3 ................ 139 A8
Candlefield Rd. Heml H HP3 ................ 139 A8
Candlefield Wlk. Heml H HP3 ................ 139 A8
Caneland Ct. Wa Aby EN9 163 F5
Canfield. Bis St CM23 ........ 76 E8
Cangelis Cl. Heml H HP1 .. 124 A1
Canham Cl. Kim SG4 .......... 66 D1
Cannix Cl. Stev SG2 ........... 51 A2
Cannon House. Hit SG4 ...... 34 F6 1
Cannon La. Luton LU2 ........ 46 B5
Cannon Rd. Watf WD1 ..... 167 C4
Cannon St. St Alb AL3 ...... 127 D4
Cannons Cl. Bis St CM23 .... 59 A1
Cannons Cl. Gu M SG8 ......... 1 F5
Cannons Ct. Stand SG11 .... 55 D3
Cannons Mead. Sta M CM24 .................. 59 D7
Cannons Meadow. Tewin AL6 ...................... 90 E2
Cannons Mill La. Bis St CM23 .................. 59 A1
Canon Brook Golf Club. Harl ............................. 117 A1
Canons Cl. Radl WD7 ....... 156 B4
Canons Field. Welw AL6 .... 89 E8
Canons Field. Whea AL6 .... 87 D1
Canons Gate. Harl CM20 . 117 A1
Canons Rd. Ware SG12 ..... 93 C2
Canonsfield Ct. Welw AL6 . 89 E7
Canonsfield Rd. Welw AL6 . 89 E8
Canopus Way. Mo Pk HA6 175 A6
Cantelowes House. Barn EN5 ..................... 171 D4
Canterbury Cl. Luton LU3 ... 44 F4
Canterbury Cl. Norwd HA6 174 F4
Canterbury Ct. St Alb AL1 127 F4
Canterbury House. Bor WD6 ...................... 170 A7
Canterbury Rd. Bor WD6 . 170 A7
Canterbury Rd. Watf WD1 167 B7
Canterbury Way. Cro Gr WD3 ................. 166 C6
Canterbury Way. Stev SG1 36 F2
Cape Rd. St Alb AL1 ......... 128 B3
Capel Ct. Alb SG11 ............ 57 E2
Capel House. Sth Ox WD1 175 D6
Capel Manor Prim Sch. Enf ............................... 162 B4
Capel Rd. Enf EN1 ............ 162 B3
Capel Rd. Watf WD1 ........ 167 E3
Capell Ave. Chor WD3 ..... 164 C4
Capell Rd. Chor WD3 ....... 164 D4
Capell Way. Chor WD3 .... 164 D4
Capella Rd. Mo Pk HA6 .... 174 F6
Capelvere Wlk. Watf WD1 166 E8
Caponfield. Wel G C AL7 .. 111 B4
Cappell La. Sta Ab SG12 .. 115 D5
Capron Rd. Luton LU4 ....... 44 E4
Captains Wlk. Berk HP4 .. 122 D3
Caractacus Cottage View. Watf WD1 ................... 167 A3
Caractacus Gn. Watf WD1 166 F3
Caravan La. Ric WD3 ....... 165 E2
Carbone Hill. Cuf EN6,SG13 .............. 146 D5
Carde Cl. Hert SG14 ......... 112 F7
Cardiff Cl. Stev SG2 ........... 69 B7
Cardiff Gr. Luton LU1 ......... 63 D7
Cardiff Pl. Knee SG8 ............ 2 A8
Cardiff Rd. Luton LU1 ........ 63 D7
Cardiff Rd. Watf WD1 ....... 167 B4
Cardigan Ct. Luton LU1 ...... 63 D7
Cardigan St. Luton LU1 ...... 63 D7
Cardinal Ave. Bor WD6 ..... 170 B5
Cardinal Cl. Ham St EN7 .. 147 F5
Cardinal Ct. Bor WD6 ...... 170 B6
Cardinal Gr. St Alb AL3 .... 127 B1
Cardinal Newman Sch. Luton ............................... 31 C1
Cardy Rd. Heml H HP1 .... 124 B3
Carew Rd. Norwd HA6 ..... 174 F4
Careys Croft. Berk HP4 .... 122 A7
Carisbrook Rd. Chis AL2 .. 141 B5
Carisbrooke Ave. Watf WD2 .................... 167 D8
Carisbrooke Rd. Harp AL5 . 86 C2
Carisbrooke Rd. Luton LU4 44 E1
Carleton Rd. Ches EN8 ..... 148 E4
Carleton Rise. Welw AL6 ... 89 C6
Carlisle Ave. St Alb AL3 ... 127 D4
Carlton Bank. Harp AL5 ..... 86 B1 3
Carlton Cl. Bor WD6 ........ 170 D5
Carlton Cl. Luton LU3 ......... 45 C2
Carlton Cres. Luton LU3 ..... 45 C2
Carlton Ct. Harp AL5 .......... 86 B1 1
Carlton Ct. Watf WD1 ...... 167 C3
Carlton Rd. Harp AL5 ......... 86 B2
Carman Ct. Tri HP23 .......... 99 F3
Carmelite Cl. Har HA3 ...... 176 C2
Carmelite Rd. Dun LU4 ...... 44 A3
Carmelite Rd. Har HA3 .... 176 C1
Carmelite Way. Har HA3 . 176 C1
Carmelite Wlk. Har HA3 .. 176 C2
Carmen Ct. Bor WD6 ....... 156 F1
Carnaby Rd. Hod EN10 .... 134 E3
Carnarvon Rd. Barn EN5 .. 171 E6
Carnegie Dr. St Alb AL3 ... 127 D7
Carnegie Gdns. Luton LU3 . 45 A8
Caro La. Heml H HP3 ....... 125 B1
Carol Cl. Luton LU3 ........... 45 B4
Caroline Pl. Watf WD1 ..... 167 E3
Caroon Dr. Sar WD3 ........ 152 B3
Carpenders Ave. Sth Ox WD1 ................. 175 E8
Carpenders Cl. Harp AL5 .... 85 D4
Carpenders Park Sta. Sth Ox ............................ 175 D7
Carpenter Way. Pot B EN6 159 D6
Carpenters Rd. Enf EN1 .... 162 C3
Carpenters The. Bis St CM23 .................. 76 B5
Carpenters Wood Dr. Chor WD3 .................... 164 B5
Carrigans. Bis St CM23 ...... 76 E8
Carrington Ave. Bor WD6 170 C4
Carrington Cl. Barn EN5 .. 171 A4
Carrington Cl. Bor WD6 ... 170 C4
Carrington Pl. Tri HP23 ... 100 C5
Carrington Sq. Stan HA3 .. 176 C3
Carsdale Cl. Luton LU3 ...... 45 A6
Cart Path. Watf WD2 ....... 154 C6
Carteret Rd. Luton LU2 ...... 46 C1
Carterhatch La. Enf EN1 ... 161 F1
Carters Cl. Arl SG15 ........... 11 A7
Carters Cl. Ast SG2 ............ 51 D4
Carters La. Hit SG5 ............ 34 A6
Carters Leys. Bis St CM23 .. 76 D8
Carters Way. Arl SG15 ...... 11 A7
Carters Wlk. Arl SG15 ....... 11 A7
Cartersfield Rd. Wa Aby EN9 ................. 163 C5
Cartwright Rd. Royst SG8 .... 7 D5
Cartwright Rd. Stev SG1 .... 37 C2
Carve Ley. Wel G C AL7 ... 111 B5
Carvers Croft. Welw SG3 ... 69 B2
Cashio La. Letw SG6 .......... 23 A8
Caslon Way. Letw SG6 ....... 11 F1
Cassandra Gate. Ches EN8 ...................... 148 F4

Cassio Coll. Watf .............. 154 A1
Cassio Rd. Watf WD1 ...... 167 B5
Cassiobridge Rd.
Watf WD1 .................... 166 E5
Cassiobridge Terr.
Cro Gr WD3 ................ 166 D4
Cassiobury Dr. Watf WD1 166 F7
Cassiobury Dr. Watf WD1 167 A6
Cassiobury Inf Sch. Watf . 166 E8
Cassiobury Park Ave.
Watf WD1 .................... 166 F6
Cassiobury Prim Sch. Watf166 E8
Castano Ct. Abb L WD5 .... 153 E8
Castellane Cl. Har HA7 .... 176 F3 1
Castile Ct. Ches EN8 ........ 163 A5
Castle Cl. Bus WD2 ........ 168 B3
Castle Cl. Hod EN11 ......... 115 C1
Castle Croft Rd. Luton LU1 63 A6
Castle Gate Way.
Berk HP4 ...................... 122 C6
Castle Hill Ave. Berk HP4 122 C5
Castle Hill. Berk HP4 ....... 122 C6
Castle Hill Cl. Berk HP4 ... 122 C5
Castle Mead Gdns.
Hert SG14 .................... 113 C6
Castle Mead. Heml H HP1 124 B1
Castle Mews. Berk HP4 ... 122 D4
Castle Rd. Enf EN3 ........... 162 E1
Castle Rd. Hod EN11 ........ 115 C1
Castle Rd. St Alb AL1 ....... 128 B3
Castle Rise. Whea AL4 ..... 86 F2
Castle St. Berk HP4 ........ 122 C4
Castle St. Bis St CM23 ....... 76 F6
Castle St. Hert SG14 ........ 113 C5
Castle St. Luton LU1 .......... 63 E6
Castle St. Wing HP22 ........ 60 B3
Castle View. Bis St CM23 .. 77 A7 3
Castle Wlk. Sta M CM24 .... 59 E6
Castles Cl. Stot SG5 ........... 11 F8
Catalin Ct. Wa Aby EN9 ... 163 D6
Caterham Ct. Wa Aby EN9 163 F5
Catesby Gn. Luton LU3 ....... 31 A1
Catham Cl. St Alb AL1 ...... 128 B1
Cathedral Ct. St Alb AL3 .. 127 B1
Catherall Rd. Luton LU3 ..... 45 B6
Catherine Cl. Heml H HP2 125 B8
Catherine Rd. Enf EN3 ..... 162 E3
Catherine St. St Alb AL3 ... 127 D4
Catisfield Rd. Enf EN3 ...... 162 E2
Catkin Cl. Heml H HP1 ..... 124 B4
Catlin St. Heml H HP3 ...... 138 B8
Catsbrook Rd. Luton LU3 ... 45 B6
Catsdell Bottom.
Heml H HP3 ................ 139 B8
Catsey La. Bus WD2 ........ 168 C2
Catsey Wood. Bus WD2 ... 168 C2
Catterick Way. Bor WD6 .. 169 F8
Cattlegate Hill. Nort EN6 . 160 D7
Cattlegate Rd. Cre H EN2 161 A5
Cattlegate Rd. Nort EN6 .. 160 D6
Cattsdell. Heml H HP2 ..... 124 E5
Causeway Cl. Pot B EN6 .. 159 D8
Causeway House.
Abb L WD5 .................. 153 E8
Causeway The.
Bis St CM23 .................. 76 F7
Causeway The. Brag SG9 .. 42 D1
Causeway The. Bre P SG9 . 30 B1
Causeway The. Bun SG9 .... 40 F8
Causeway The. Fur P SG9 . 43 A4
Causeway The. Knee SG8 .... 2 A5
Causeway The. Pot B EN6 159 D8
Causeway The. Ther SG8 ... 15 F7
Cautherly La. Gt Am SG12 115 A5
Cavalier Cl. Luton LU3 ........ 45 A5
Cavalier Ct. Berk HP4 ...... 122 C4
Cavalier. Stev SG1 ............ 36 B1
Cavan Ct. Hat AL10 .......... 130 A4
Cavan Dr. St Alb AL3 ........ 127 D8
Cavan Rd. Red AL3 ........... 106 A6
Cavell Rd. Ham St EN7 ..... 148 A4
Cavell Wlk. Stev SG2 .......... 51 C5
Cavendish Cres. Bor WD6 170 A5
Cavendish Ct. Cro Gr WD3 166 D4
Cavendish Rd. Barn EN5 .. 171 C6
Cavendish Rd. Luton LU3 ... 45 B2
Cavendish Rd. Mark AL3 .... 83 D6
Cavendish Rd. St Alb AL1 . 127 F3
Cavendish Rd. Stev SG1 ..... 50 B5
Cavendish Sch The.
Heml H ........................ 124 B4
Cavendish Way. Hat AL10 129 F5
Cawkell Cl. Sta M CM24 ..... 59 D7
Cawley Hill Sch. Bor ........ 170 A8
Caxton Ct. Enf EN3 .......... 162 E4
Caxton Hill. Hert SG13 ..... 113 F6
Caxton Rd. Hod EN11 ....... 115 B2
Caxton Way. Mo Pk WD1 . 166 D2
Caxton Way. Stev SG1 ....... 50 B4
Cecil Cl. Bis St CM23 ......... 77 D7
Cecil Cres. Hat AL10 ........ 130 B7
Cecil Ct. Barn EN5 ........... 171 D6
Cecil Rd. Bric SG13 .......... 113 C3
Cecil Rd. Ches EN8 .......... 162 E7
Cecil Rd. Hod EN11 .......... 135 C8
Cecil Rd. Pot B EN6 .......... 158 B7
Cecil Rd. St Alb AL1 ......... 127 F3
Cecil St. Watf WD2 .......... 154 B1
Cedar Ave. Ches EN8 ....... 162 D6
Cedar Ave. Ick SG5 ............ 21 E4
Cedar Cl. Hert SG14 ......... 113 B6
Cedar Cl. Pot B EN6 ......... 145 A1
Cedar Cl. Saw CM21 .......... 97 E1
Cedar Cl. Ware SG12 ....... 114 D8
Cedar Cres. Royst SG8 ........ 7 B6
Cedar Ct. Bis St CM23 ....... 58 F1
Cedar Ct. St Alb AL4 ......... 128 D3
Cedar Dr. Pnr HA5 ........... 176 A4
Cedar Gn. Hod EN11 ........ 135 A5
Cedar Lawn Ave.
Barn EN5 ...................... 171 E4
Cedar Park Rd. Enf EN2 ... 161 C1
Cedar Pk. Bis St CM23 ....... 76 D4
Cedar Pl. Norwd HA6 ....... 174 C4
Cedar Rd. Berk HP4 ......... 122 E3
Cedar Rd. Enf EN2 ............ 161 C1
Cedar Rd. Hat AL10 .......... 130 A4
Cedar Rd. Watf WD1 ........ 167 D3
Cedar Way. Berk HP4 ....... 122 D3
Cedar Wlk. Heml H HP3 ... 124 D1
Cedar Wood Dr.
Watf WD2 .................... 154 B4
Cedars Ave. Ric WD3 ....... 165 C1
Cedars Cl. Bor WD6 ......... 170 B5
Cedars Cty Prim Sch. Har 176 C2
Cedars The. Harp AL5 ........ 86 B1
Cedars The. St Alb AL3 ..... 127 C5
Cedarwood Dr. St Alb AL4 128 D3
Celandine Dr. Luton LU3 .... 45 A8
Cell Barnes Cl. St Alb AL1 128 B1
Cell Barnes Hospl. St Alb . 128 C1
Cell Barnes La. St Alb AL1 128 B1
Cemetery Hill.
Heml H HP1 ................ 124 C2
Cemetery Rd. Bis St CM23 . 76 F6
Cemmaes Court Rd.
Heml H HP1 ................ 124 C3
Cemmaes Meadow.
Heml H HP1 ................ 124 C3
Central App. Letw SG6 ....... 22 F6
Central Ave. Ches EN8 ..... 162 E6
Central Ave. Henlw SG16 ... 10 B3
Central Ave. Whip LU6 ....... 81 E8
Central Dr. St Alb AL4 ....... 128 C4
Central Dr. Wel G C AL7 ... 110 F8
Central Rd. Harl CM20 ...... 118 A4
Central Way. Norwd HA6 .. 174 E3
Centre Way. Wa Aby EN9 . 163 C3
Centro. Heml H HP2 ......... 125 C5
Century Rd. Hod EN11 ..... 135 A7
Century Rd. Ware SG12 ..... 93 D2
Cervantes Ct. Norwd HA6 174 F3
Chace Ave. Pot B EN6 ...... 159 D7
Chace The. Stev SG2 ......... 50 F1
Chad La. Fla AL3 ............... 84 C4
Chadwell Ave. Ches EN8 .. 148 C3
Chadwell Cl. Luton LU2 ...... 45 F1
Chadwell Rd. Stev SG1 ...... 50 B4
Chadwell Rise. Ware SG12114 C8
Chadwell. Ware SG12 ...... 114 C8
Chaffinch La. Watf WD1 ... 166 F2
Chaffinches Gn.
Heml H HP3 ................ 139 A7
Chagney Cl. Letw SG6 ....... 22 E6
Chalet Cl. Berk HP4 ......... 121 F4
Chalfont Cl. Heml H HP2 .. 125 B8
Chalfont La. Chor WD3 .... 164 B4
Chalfont La. Map Cr WD3 172 D3
Chalfont Pl. St Alb AL1 ..... 127 E3
Chalfont Rd. Map Cr WD3 172 C7
Chalfont Way. Luton LU2 ... 46 D2
Chalfont Wlk. Pnr HA5 ..... 175 C1 4
Chalgrove. Wel G C AL7 ... 111 D7
Chalk Dale. Wel G C AL7 .. 111 B7
Chalk Dell Inf Sch. Hert ... 113 C4
Chalk Field. Letw ................ 23 C3
Chalk Hill. Gt Of LU2 .......... 47 A5
Chalk Hill. Watf WD1 ....... 167 E3
Chalk Hills. Bal ................... 23 F5
Chalkdell Fields.
St Alb AL4 .................... 128 A7
Chalkdell Hill. Heml H HP2 124 E3
Chalkdell Path. Hit SG5 ..... 34 D8 8
Chalkdown Cl. Luton LU2 ... 45 E6
Chalkdown. Stev SG2 ......... 51 D7
Chalks Ave. Saw CM21 ...... 97 D3
Challney Cl. Luton LU4 ....... 44 D2
Challney High Sch. Luton ... 44 D2
Chalmers Ct. Cro Gr WD3 165 F3
Chalton Rd. Luton LU4 ....... 44 C5
Chamberlaines. Harp AL5 .. 85 A5
Chambers La. Ick SG5 ........ 21 E4
Chambers' St. Hert SG14 . 113 C6
Chambersbury La.
Heml H HP3 ................ 139 A7
Chambersbury Prim Sch.
Heml H ........................ 139 B8
Champions Cl. Bor WD6 .. 157 B2
Champions Gn. Hod EN11 115 B1
Champions Way.
Hod EN11 .................... 115 A1
Chancellor's Sch. Bro Pk . 145 A6
Chancellors Rd. Stev SG1 .. 36 D1
Chancery Cl. St Alb AL4 ... 128 D8
Chandler's La. Sar WD3 .. 152 E2
Chandlers Rd. St Alb AL4 . 128 C6
Chandlers Way.
Hert SG14 .................... 113 A6
Chandos Cl. L Chal HP6 ... 150 C1
Chandos Rd. Bor WD6 ..... 170 A7
Chandos Rd. Luton LU4 ...... 44 F1
Chantry Cl. Bis St CM23 .... 76 E8
Chantry Cl. Enf EN2 .......... 161 C1
Chantry Cl. Kin L WD4 ...... 139 A2
Chantry Ct. Hat AL10 ....... 130 A4
Chantry Fst & Mid Sch. Har176 C2
Chantry La. Hat AL10 ....... 129 F4
Chantry La. Hat AL10 ....... 130 A4
Chantry La. L Wy SG4 ....... 36 A3
Chantry La. L Wym SG4 ..... 35 F2
Chantry La. Lon C AL2 ...... 142 D5
Chantry Pl. Har HA3 ........ 176 B2
Chantry Rd. Bis St CM23 .... 76 E8
Chantry Rd. Har HA3 ........ 176 B2
Chantry The. Bis St CM23 .. 76 F8
Chantry The. Harl CM20 .. 118 A2
Chaomans. Letw SG6 ......... 22 F3
Chapel Cl. L Gad HP4 ....... 102 D6
Chapel Cl. Luton LU2 ......... 45 C8
Chapel Cl. St Alb AL1 ....... 141 D8
Chapel Cotts. Heml H HP2 124 D4
Chapel Croft. Chipf WD4 .. 152 A8
Chapel Crofts. Nthch HP4 121 E6
Chapel End. Bun SG9 ......... 40 E7
Chapel End. Hod EN11 ..... 135 A5
Chapel End La. Wils HP23 . 99 C8
Chapel Hill. Sta M CM24 .... 59 E6
Chapel La. Hertng SG14 ... 112 B3
Chapel La. L Had SG11 ....... 75 A8
Chapel La. Lon M HP23 ...... 79 B4
Chapel Meadow. Tri HP23 100 B6
Chapel Pl. Stot SG5 ........... 11 F5
Chapel Rd. Bre Gr SG4 ....... 65 E8
Chapel Rd. Fla AL3 ............ 84 B2
Chapel Row. Hare UB9 .... 173 C2
Chapel Row. Hit SG5 .......... 34 F8 6
Chapel St. Berk HP4 ........ 122 D4
Chapel St. Heml H HP2 .... 124 D4
Chapel St. Hin SG7 .............. 3 D6
Chapel St. Luton LU1 ......... 63 E6
Chapel St. Tri HP23 ........... 99 F3
Chapel Viaduct. Luton LU1 . 63 E7
Chapelfields. Sta Ab SG12 115 D4
Chapman Rd. Stev SG1 ...... 36 B1
Chapmans End.
Stand SG11 .................... 55 D3
Chapmans Yd. Watf WD1 167 C5
Chappell Ct. Ton SG12 ....... 92 E7
Chapter House Rd.
Dun LU4 ........................ 44 A3
Chard Dr. Luton LU3 .......... 31 B1
Chardins Cl. Heml H HP1 . 123 F4
Charles St. Berk HP4 ....... 122 B4
Charles St. Heml H HP1 ... 124 C2
Charles St. Luton LU2 ........ 63 F8
Charles St. Tri HP23 ........ 100 A3
Charlesworth Cl.
Heml H HP3 ................ 124 D1 4
Charlock Way. Watf WD1 166 F3
Charlton Cl. Hod EN11 ..... 135 A6
Charlton Mead La.
Hod EN11 .................... 135 D5
Charlton Rd. Hit SG5 ......... 34 D5
Charlton Way. Hod EN11 . 135 A6
Charlwood Cl. Har HA3 .... 176 E4
Charlwood Rd. Dun LU4 ..... 44 B1
Charmbury Rise. Luton LU2 46 A4
Charmouth Ct. St Alb AL1 128 A6
Charmouth Rd. St Alb AL1 128 A5
Charndon Cl. Luton LU3 ..... 31 B1
Charnwood Rd. Enf EN1 ... 162 B3
Charter Pl. Watf WD1 ..... 167 C6
Chartley Ave. Har HA7 ..... 176 F4
Chartridge Cl. Barn EN5 .. 171 A4
Chartridge Cl. Bus WD2 ... 168 C3
Chartridge Way.
Heml H HP2 ................ 125 C3
Chartwell Cl. Wa Aby EN9 163 E6
Chartwell Ct. Barn EN5 .... 171 E5 8
Chartwell Dr. Luton LU2 .... 45 E3
Chartwell Rd. Norwd HA6 174 F4
Chasden Rd. Heml H HP1 123 F5
Chase Cl. Arl SG15 ............ 11 A8
Chase Farm Hospl. Enf .... 161 A1
Chase Hill Rd. Arl SG15 ..... 11 A7
Chase St. Luton LU1 .......... 63 E6
Chase The. Bis St CM23 .... 76 F6
Chase The. Gofs O EN7 .... 147 B3
Chase The. Gt Am SG12 ... 115 A6
Chase The. Heml H HP2 ... 124 E2
Chase The. Hert SG13 ..... 113 F6
Chase The. Radl WD7 ..... 155 F4
Chase The. Watf WD1 ...... 166 E5
Chase The. Welw AL6 ........ 89 F7
Chaseside Cl. Ched LU7 ..... 80 A7
Chaseways. Saw CM21 .... 118 C8
Chasten Hill. Letw SG6 ...... 22 D7
Chater Inf Sch. Watf ........ 167 A5
Chatsworth Cl.
Bis St CM23 .................. 76 C7
Chatsworth Cl. Bor WD6 .. 170 A6
Chatsworth Ct. St Alb AL1 127 F3
Chatsworth Ct. Stev SG2 ... 50 F1
Chatsworth Rd. Luton LU4 . 45 B1
Chatteris Cl. Luton LU4 ..... 44 D4
Chatterton. Letw SG6 ........ 23 C5
Chatton Cl. Luton LU2 ........ 46 E2
Chaucer Cl. Berk HP4 ....... 121 F5
Chaucer House. Barn EN5 171 D5
Chaucer Rd. Luton LU3 ...... 45 C2
Chaucer Rd. Royst SG8 ........ 7 C8
Chaucer Way. Hit SG4 ....... 35 C7
Chaucer Way. Hod EN11 . 115 A2
Chaucer Wlk. Heml H HP2 105 B1
Chaul End La. Luton LU4 ... 44 E1
Chaul End Rd. Cad LU1 ...... 62 D6
Chaul End Rd. Dun LU1 ...... 44 B1
Chaulden House Gdns.
Heml H HP1 ................ 123 F1
Chaulden Jun & Inf Schs.
Heml H ........................ 123 F2
Chaulden La. Heml H HP1 123 E1
Chaulden Terr.
Heml H HP1 ................ 123 F2
Chauncey House.
Watf WD1 .................... 166 E3
Chauncy Ave. Pot B EN6 .. 159 C6
Chauncy Cl. Ware SG12 ..... 93 D3
Chauncy Ct. Hert SG14 .... 113 D6 16
Chauncy Gdns. Bal SG7 ...... 13 B1
Chauncy House. Stev SG1 .. 50 E6 3
Chauncy Rd. Stev SG1 ....... 50 E6
Chauncy Sch The. Ware ..... 93 B2
Chaworth Gn. Luton LU4 .... 44 C5
Cheapside. Luton LU1 ........ 63 E7
Cheapside Sq. Luton LU1 ... 63 E7
Chedburgh. Wel G C AL7 . 111 D7
Cheddington Cty Combd Sch.
Ched ............................. 80 A7
Cheddington La.
Ched HP23 .................... 79 C5
Cheddington La.
Lon M HP23 ................... 79 C5
Cheddington Rd. Pit LU7 .... 80 C4
Cheffins Rd. Hod EN11 ..... 114 F1
Chells La. Stev SG2 ........... 51 D7
Chells Way. Stev SG2 ........ 51 B6
Chelmsford Rd.
Hert SG14 .................... 113 B5
Chelsing Rise.
Heml H HP2 ................ 125 C2
Chelsworth Cl. Luton LU2 .. 46 D1
Chelveston. Wel G C AL7 . 111 D7
Chelwood Ave. Hat AL10 . 130 A8
Chelwood Cl. Norwd HA6 . 174 C3
Chenduit Way. Stan HA7 . 176 F5
Cheney Rd. Luton LU4 ....... 44 C5
Chenies Ave. L Chal HP6 .. 150 D1
Chenies Ct. Heml H HP2 .. 125 B8
Chenies Gr. Bis St CM23 .... 76 D6
Chenies Rd. Chor WD3 ..... 164 E6
Chenies Way. Watf WD1 . 166 E2
Chennells Cl. Hit SG4 ........ 22 B2
Chennells. Hat AL10 ......... 129 F4
Chennies The. Harp AL5 .. 107 C7
Chepstow Cl. Stev SG1 ...... 51 B8
Chepstow. Harp AL5 .......... 85 F2
Chequer Ct. Luton LU1 ....... 63 F6
Chequer La. Red AL3 ....... 106 B4
Chequer St. Luton LU1 ....... 63 F6
Chequer St. St Alb AL1 .... 127 D3
Chequers. Bis St CM23 ...... 76 C8
Chequers Bridge Rd.
Stev SG1 ...................... 50 C6
Chequers Cl. Bun SG9 ........ 40 D8
Chequers Cl. Pit LU7 .......... 80 C4
Chequers Cl. Stand SG11 ... 55 D4
Chequers Cl. Stot SG5 ........ 12 A6
Chequers Cotts. Pres SG4 . 48 D6
Chequers Field.
Wel G C AL7 ................. 110 D3
Chequers. Hat AL9 ........... 130 D8
Chequers Hill. Fla AL3 ....... 84 C2
Chequers La. Abb L WD5 . 140 C1
Chequers La. Pit LU7 ......... 80 C5
Chequers La. Pres SG4 ...... 48 D7
Chequers. Wel G C AL7 ... 110 D3
Chequers Wlk.
Wa Aby EN9 ................ 163 F6
Cheriton Cl. St Alb AL4 ..... 128 D7
Cherry Bank. Heml H HP2 124 D5
Cherry Cl. Kneb SG3 .......... 68 F4
Cherry Croft Gdns.
Pnr HA5 ...................... 175 F3 2
Cherry Croft. Wel G C AL8 . 89 D2
Cherry Dr. Royst SG8 .......... 7 E7
Cherry Gdns. Bis St CM23 . 77 A8
Cherry Gdns. Saw CM21 .... 97 E4
Cherry Gdns. Tri HP23 ....... 99 F3
Cherry Hill. Chis AL2 ........ 141 A6
Cherry Hill. Har HA3 ........ 176 E4
Cherry Hill. Ric WD3 ........ 165 B6
Cherry Hollow.
Abb L WD5 .................. 153 F8
Cherry Orch. Heml H HP1 124 A5
Cherry Rd. Enf EN3 .......... 162 C1
Cherry Tree Ave.
Lon C AL2 .................... 142 D5
Cherry Tree Cl. Arl SG15 ... 11 A4
Cherry Tree Cl. Luton LU2 . 46 A1
Cherry Tree Gn.
Hert SG14 .................... 112 F7
Cherry Tree Jun Mix Inf Sch.
Watf ............................ 154 A3
Cherry Tree La. Chol HP23 120 A3
Cherry Tree La. Chor WD3 164 C1
Cherry Tree La.
Heml H HP2 ................ 125 C7
Cherry Tree La. Whea AL4 87 A2
Cherry Tree Rd.
Hod EN11 .................... 135 A7
Cherry Tree Rd.
Watf WD2 .................... 154 B3
Cherry Tree Rise.
Walk SG2 ...................... 38 B1
Cherry Trees. L Ston SG16 10 B3
Cherry Way. Hat AL10 ..... 130 A2
Cherry Wlk. Ric WD3 ....... 165 C7
Cherrydale. Watf WD1 ..... 166 F5
Chertsey Cl. Luton LU2 ..... 64 D8
Chertsey Rise. Stev SG2 .... 51 C4
Cherwell Cl. Cro Gr WD3 . 166 A4
Chesfield Cl. Bis St CM23 .. 76 F5
Chesford Rd. Luton LU2 ..... 46 C4
Chesham Ct. Norwd HA6 . 174 F4
Chesham Prep Sch.
Ash Gr ........................ 136 A4
Chesham Rd. Berk HP4 .... 122 C3
Chesham Rd. Bov HP3 ..... 136 E3
Chesham Rd. Wigg HP23 . 120 E7
Chesham Way. Watf WD1 166 F3
Cheshunt Bonneygrove
Inf Sch. Ches ................ 148 A1
Cheshunt Bonneygrove
Jun Sch. Ches ............... 148 A1
Cheshunt Cottage Hospl.
Ches ............................ 148 D2
Cheshunt Ctr The.
Ches EN8 ..................... 148 D3
Cheshunt Gram Sch. Ches 148 E1
Cheshunt Sch The. Ches .. 148 C1
Cheshunt Wash.
Ches EN8 ..................... 148 E4
Cheslyn Cl. Luton LU2 ....... 46 E2
Chess Cl. Lat HP5 ............ 150 D3
Chess Cl. Ric WD3 ........... 165 D5
Chess Hill. Ric WD3 ......... 165 D5
Chess La. Ric WD3 ........... 165 D5
Chess Vale Rise.
Cro Gr WD3 ................. 165 F3
Chess Way. Chor WD3 .... 165 A6
Chesswood Way. Pnr HA5 175 D1
Chester Ave. Luton LU4 ..... 44 E3
Chester Cl. Luton LU4 ....... 44 F2
Chester Cl. Pot B EN6 ...... 145 B2
Chester Pl. Norwd HA6 .... 174 E3
Chester Rd. Bor WD6 ....... 170 D6
Chester Rd. Norwd HA6 ... 174 F3
Chester Rd. Stev SG1 ......... 37 A1
Chester Rd. Watf WD1 ..... 167 A5
Chesterfield Flats.
Barn EN5 ..................... 171 D4
Chesterfield Rd. Barn EN5 171 D4
Chesterfield Rd. Enf EN3 . 162 E2
Chesterfield Sch. Enf ....... 162 E2
Chesterton Ave. Harp AL5 . 86 D1
Chestnut Ave. Henlw SG16 10 C3
Chestnut Ave. Luton LU3 ... 44 C8
Chestnut Ave. Norwd HA6 174 F2
Chestnut Ave. Ric WD3 .... 165 A4
Chestnut Ave. Ware SG12 . 93 F3
Chestnut Cl. Bis St CM23 ... 76 E6

Chestnut Cl. Dagn HP4 ... 81 C5
Chestnut Cl. Hun SG12 ... 95 D1
Chestnut Cl. Pot En HP4 .. 123 B6
Chestnut Ct. Hit SG5 ... 34 D8 4
Chestnut Dr. Berk HP4 ... 122 D3
Chestnut Dr. Har HA3 ... 176 F2
Chestnut Dr. St Alb AL4 ... 128 C5
Chestnut La. Barn N20 ... 171 E1
Chestnut La. Knee SG8 ... 2 B6
Chestnut Rd. Enf EN3 ... 162 E3
Chestnut Rise. Bus WD2 .. 168 B2
Chestnut Wlk. Royst SG8 ... 7 E6
Chestnut Wlk. Stev SG1 ... 36 D1
Chestnut Wlk. Watf WD2 . 154 A2
Chestnuts The. Cod SG4 ... 67 F2
Chestnuts The. Heml H HP3 ... 137 F7
Chestnuts The. Hert SG13 113 D5
Cheverells Cl. Mark AL3 ... 83 D4
Cheviot Cl. Bus WD2 ... 168 C3
Cheviot Cl. Luton LU3 ... 44 D7
Cheviot Rd. Luton LU3 ... 44 D7
Cheviots. Hat AL10 ... 130 A3
Cheviots. Heml H HP2 ... 124 F6
Cheyne Cl. Pit LU7 ... 80 D4
Cheyne Cl. Ware SG12 ... 93 D3
Cheynes Inf Sch. Luton ... 44 D8
Chicheley Gdns. Har HA3 . 176 C3
Chichester Way. Watf WD2 ... 154 E6
Chigwell Hurst Ct. Pnr HA5 ... 175 D1
Chilcott Rd. Watf WD2 ... 153 F3
Chilcourt. Royst SG8 ... 7 C6
Childbrook House. Watf WD1 ... 166 E3
Childs Ave. Hare UB9 ... 173 C1
Childwick Ct. Heml H HP3 139 B8
Chilham Cl. Heml H HP2 .. 124 E2
Chiltern Ave. Bus WD2 ... 168 C3
Chiltern Cl. Bor WD6 ... 169 F7
Chiltern Cl. Bus WD2 ... 168 B3
Chiltern Cl. Gofs O EN7 ... 147 B4
Chiltern Cl. Ware SG12 ... 93 D3
Chiltern Ct. St Alb AL4 ... 128 D7
Chiltern Dr. Ric WD3 ... 165 A2
Chiltern Gdns. Luton LU4 ... 44 F3
Chiltern Park Ave. Berk HP4 ... 122 A6
Chiltern Rd. Bal SG7 ... 23 F6
Chiltern Rd. Hit SG4 ... 35 A7
Chiltern Rd. St Alb AL4 ... 128 C7
Chiltern Rd. Wing HP22 ... 60 A3
Chiltern Rise. Luton LU1 ... 63 D6
Chiltern View. Letw SG6 ... 22 D5
Chiltern Way. Tri HP23 ... 100 C5
Chilterns. Hat AL10 ... 130 A2
Chilterns. Heml H HP2 ... 124 E5
Chilterns The. Hit SG4 ... 35 A6
Chilterns The. Ken Co LU6 . 82 F8
Chilton Ct. Harp AL5 ... 86 B1
Chilton Gn. Wel G C AL7 .. 111 C6
Chilvers Bank. Bal SG7 ... 23 E7
Chilwell Gdns. Sth Ox WD1 ... 175 C6
Chilworth Gate. Hod EN10 134 F1
Chinnery Cl. Enf EN1 ... 161 F1
Chinnery Hill. Bis St CM23 . 76 F5
Chipperfield Rd. Bov HP3 . 137 C3
Chipperfield Rd. Heml H HP3 ... 138 C7
Chipperfield Rd. Kin L WD4 ... 138 D2
Chipping Cl. Barn EN5 ... 171 E6
Chippingfield. Harl CM17 . 118 C3
Chirdland House. Watf WD1 ... 166 E3
Chishill Rd. Bar SG8 ... 9 A2
Chishill Rd. Gt Ch SG8 ... 9 F3
Chishill Windmill. Gt Ch ... 9 C2
Chiswell Ct. Watf WD2 ... 154 C1
Chiswellgreen La. Chis AL2 ... 140 E6
Chobham Ct. Luton LU1 ... 63 F6
Chobham St. Luton LU1 ... 63 F6
Chobham Wlk. Luton LU1 ... 63 E6 5
Cholesbury La. Chol HP23 120 B2
Chorleywood Bottom. Chor WD3 ... 164 D4
Chorleywood Cl. Ric WD3 165 D2
Chorleywood Coll. Chor ... 164 F5
Chorleywood Cty Prim Sch. Chor ... 164 C3
Chorleywood Rd. Ric WD3 165 C4
Chorleywood Sta. Chor ... 164 D5
Chouler Gdns. Stev SG1 ... 36 C2
Chowns The. Harp AL5 ... 107 A5
Christ Church C of E Inf Sch. Barn ... 171 D7
Christ Church CE Jun Mix Inf Sch. Chor ... 164 F5
Christ Church Jun Mix & Inf Sch. Ware ... 93 E1
Christ Church La. Barn EN5 ... 171 E7
Christchurch Cl. St Alb AL3 ... 127 D4
Christchurch Cres. Radl WD7 ... 156 A3
Christchurch Rd. Heml H HP2 ... 124 D4
Christchurch Rd. Tri HP23 . 99 F4
Christie Cl. Hod EN10 ... 134 F3
Christie Rd. Stev SG2 ... 51 D5
Christopher Ct. Heml H HP3 ... 138 D8
Christopher Pl. St Alb AL3 ... 127 D3 3
Christy's Yd. Hin SG7 ... 3 D6
Church Cl. Cod SG4 ... 67 F2
Church Cl. Cuf EN6 ... 146 E2
Church Cl. L Berk SG13 ... 132 C4
Church Cl. Norwd HA6 ... 174 F3
Church Cl. Radl WD7 ... 156 A3
Church Cl. Stu LU6 ... 82 B4
Church Cotts. Gt Gd HP1 . 103 D3
Church Cres. Saw CM21 ... 97 F2
Church Cres. St Alb AL3 ... 127 C4
Church Ct. Hod EN10 ... 135 A3
Church End. Arl SG15 ... 11 A8
Church End. Bar SG8 ... 9 A1
Church End. Brag SG11 ... 55 F7
Church End. Fla AL3 ... 84 C2
Church End. Mark AL3 ... 83 D6
Church End. Red AL3 ... 106 A4
Church End. Sand AL4 ... 108 C2
Church End. Walk SG2 ... 38 C2
Church Field Path. Ches EN8 ... 148 C2
Church Field. Ware SG12 .. 93 B3
Church Gn. Ben SG2 ... 52 C4
Church Gn. Gt Wy SG4 ... 35 E6
Church Gn. Harp AL5 ... 86 A1
Church Green Row. Harp AL5 ... 86 A1
Church Hill. Abb L WD5 ... 139 F4
Church Hill. Ched LU7 ... 80 A8
Church Hill. Hare UB9 ... 173 C1
Church Hill. Hert H SG13 . 114 C4
Church La. Arl SG15 ... 11 A7
Church La. Ashw SG7 ... 4 D4
Church La. Bark SG8 ... 17 C4
Church La. Berk HP4 ... 122 C4
Church La. Bis St CM22 ... 76 D3
Church La. Bov HP3 ... 137 B4
Church La. Ched LU7 ... 80 A8
Church La. Ches EN8 ... 148 C2
Church La. Col H AL4 ... 143 B8
Church La. Dan En SG12 ... 71 F8
Church La. Gra SG4 ... 36 C4
Church La. Gu M SG8 ... 1 F4
Church La. Gu M SG8 ... 1 F5
Church La. Har HA3 ... 176 F2
Church La. Hat AL9 ... 130 C5
Church La. Hod EN10 ... 134 C1
Church La. Kim SG4 ... 66 D1
Church La. Kin L WD4 ... 139 A2
Church La. Letw SG6 ... 12 C1
Church La. Mars HP23 ... 79 F1
Church La. Muc H SG10 ... 74 F3
Church La. Nort EN6 ... 146 A1
Church La. Pres SG4 ... 48 D6
Church La. Reed SG8 ... 16 E5
Church La. Ric WD3 ... 165 B1
Church La. Royst SG8 ... 7 D6
Church La. Sar WD3 ... 152 A2
Church La. Stap SG14 ... 92 A6
Church La. Stev SG1 ... 50 C7
Church La. Ther SG8 ... 15 F7
Church La. Wes SG4 ... 24 D1
Church Manor. Bis St CM23 ... 77 B8
Church Mead. Roy CM19 . 116 B1
Church Mead. Stu LU6 ... 82 B4
Church Meadow Cotts. Gt Gd HP1 ... 103 D3
Church Path. L Wym SG4 ... 35 F3
Church Rd. Cad LU1 ... 63 C2
Church Rd. Fla AL3 ... 84 C2
Church Rd. Gt Ha CM22 ... 77 D3
Church Rd. Heml H HP3 ... 125 C2
Church Rd. Hert SG14 ... 113 C7
Church Rd. Kin Wd SG4 ... 47 F3
Church Rd. L Berk SG13 ... 132 C4
Church Rd. L Gad HP4 ... 102 D8
Church Rd. Norwd HA6 ... 174 F3
Church Rd. Pit LU7 ... 80 E3
Church Rd. Pit LU7 ... 80 F5
Church Rd. Pot B EN6 ... 145 B1
Church Rd. Pot En HP4 ... 123 B6
Church Rd. Stot SG5 ... 11 F6
Church Rd. Str LU3 ... 31 A6
Church Rd. Stu LU6 ... 82 B4
Church Rd. Watf WD1 ... 167 B8
Church Rd. Wel G C AL8 .. 110 D6
Church Row Mews. Ware SG12 ... 93 D1 2
Church St. Bal SG7 ... 12 E1
Church St. Bis St CM23 ... 76 F7
Church St. Bov HP3 ... 137 B4
Church St. Bun SG9 ... 40 E8
Church St. Ess AL9 ... 131 E6
Church St. Gu M SG8 ... 1 F5
Church St. Hat AL9 ... 130 C5
Church St. Heml H HP2 ... 124 D5
Church St. Hert SG14 ... 113 D6
Church St. Luton LU1 ... 63 F8
Church St. Ric WD3 ... 165 E1
Church St. Saw CM21 ... 97 E2
Church St. Shil SG5 ... 19 F8
Church St. St Alb AL3 ... 127 D4
Church St. Wa Aby EN9 ... 163 C6
Church St. Ware SG12 ... 93 D1
Church St. Watf WD1 ... 167 C5
Church St. Welw AL6 ... 89 C5
Church St. Whea AL4 ... 108 D8
Church St. Wing HP22 ... 60 B2
Church Street Ind Est. Ware ... 93 D1
Church View. Hod EN10 ... 134 F3
Church View. Lon M HP23 . 79 A4
Church Wlk. Bus WD2 ... 168 A3
Church Wlk. Saw CM21 ... 97 F2
Church Yd. Hit SG5 ... 34 E7
Church Yd. Tri HP23 ... 100 A3
Churchfield. Bar SG8 ... 9 A1
Churchfield. Harl CM20 ... 118 B2
Churchfield. Harp AL5 ... 107 C8
Churchfield House. Wel G C AL8 ... 110 C6
Churchfield Rd. Tewin AL6 . 90 C1
Churchfields. Hert SG13 .. 113 D5
Churchfields. Hod EN10 ... 135 A3
Churchfields La. Hod EN10 ... 135 A3
Churchfields Rd. Watf WD2 ... 153 F3
Churchfields. Sta M CM24 . 59 F6
Churchfields. Stand SG11 .. 55 E2
Churchgate C of E Prim Sch. Harl ... 118 F3
Churchgate. Ches EN8 ... 148 B1
Churchgate. Hit SG5 ... 34 E7 7
Churchgate Rd. Ches EN8 148 B2
Churchgate St. Harl CM17 118 E3
Churchill Cres. Wel G AL9 144 C8
Churchill Rd. Luton LU4 ... 45 A1
Churchill Rd. St Alb AL1 ... 128 A4
Churchyard Wlk. Hit SG5 ... 34 E7 6
Cicero Dr. Luton LU3 ... 45 A8
Cillocks Cl. Hod EN11 ... 135 A7
Claggy Rd. Kim SG4 ... 66 B2
Claire Ct. Bus WD2 ... 168 D1
Claire Ct. Ches EN8 ... 162 D7
Clamp Hill. Stan HA7 ... 176 E5
Clapgate Rd. Bus WD2 ... 168 B3
Clare Cl. Bor WD6 ... 169 F3
Clare Cres. Bal SG7 ... 23 E6
Clare Ct. Enf EN3 ... 162 E4
Clare Ct. Norwd HA6 ... 174 E5
Clare Ct. St Alb AL1 ... 127 F2
Claremont. Bri Wd AL2 ... 155 A8
Claremont Cres. Cro Gr WD3 ... 166 C4
Claremont. Gofs O EN7 ... 147 F2
Claremont Rd. Had W EN4 159 D2
Claremont Rd. Har HA3 ... 176 E1
Claremont Rd. Luton LU4 ... 45 B1
Clarence Cl. Bus WD2 ... 168 F2
Clarence Rd. Berk HP4 ... 122 C4
Clarence Rd. Harp AL5 ... 86 A3
Clarence Rd. St Alb AL1 ... 128 A4
Clarence Rd. Sta M CM24 .. 59 E7
Clarendon Cl. Heml H HP2 124 E4 1
Clarendon Ct. Harp AL5 ... 86 B3 2
Clarendon Mews. Bor WD6 ... 170 A6
Clarendon Par. Ches EN8 148 D2
Clarendon Rd. Bor WD6 ... 170 A6
Clarendon Rd. Ches EN8 .. 148 D2
Clarendon Rd. Harp AL5 ... 86 B3
Clarendon Rd. Luton LU2 ... 45 E1
Clarendon Rd. Watf WD1 167 B6
Clarion Cl. Gt Of SG5 ... 33 C2
Clarion House. Gt Of SG5 .. 33 C2
Clark Rd. Royst SG8 ... 7 D7
Clarke Way. Watf WD2 ... 154 A4
Clarke's Rd. Hat AL10 ... 130 B7
Clarke's Spring. Ald HP23 100 F5
Clarkfield. Ric WD3 ... 165 B1
Clarks Cl. Ware SG12 ... 93 D3
Clarks Mead. Bus WD2 ... 168 D2
Claudian Pl. St Alb AL3 ... 127 A1
Claverhambury Rd. Lo Naz EN9 ... 149 F2
Claverley Gn. Luton LU2 ... 46 E2
Claverton Cl. Bov HP3 ... 137 A3
Clay Hall Rd. Ken Co LU6 ... 82 F7
Clay Hill. Enf EN2 ... 161 D2
Clay La. Bus WD2 ... 168 E2
Claybury. Bus WD2 ... 168 B2
Claybush Rd. Ashw SG7 ... 4 D3
Claycroft. Wel G C AL7 ... 111 B7
Claydown Way. Cad LU1 ... 63 B1
Claygate Ave. Harp AL5 ... 85 E2
Claymore Dr. Ick SG5 ... 21 F5
Claymore. Heml H HP2 ... 124 E7
Claymores. Stev SG1 ... 50 E6
Clayponds. Bis St CM23 ... 77 B7
Clayton Par. Ches EN8 ... 148 D1
Cleall Ave. Wa Aby EN9 ... 163 C5
Cleave The. Harp AL5 ... 86 D1
Clement Pl. Tri HP23 ... 100 A3
Clement Rd. Ches EN8 ... 148 E4
Clements End Rd. Fla LU6 .. 82 E2
Clements End Rd. Gt Ga LU6 ... 82 E2
Clements End Rd. Stu LU6 . 82 E2
Clements Rd. Chor WD3 .. 164 D4
Clements St. Ware SG12 ... 93 E1
Clevedon Rd. Luton LU2 ... 46 B2
Cleveland Cres. Bor WD6 170 C4
Cleveland Rd. Heml H HP2 125 B5
Cleveland Rd. Mark AL3 ... 83 E5
Cleveland Way. Heml H HP2 ... 125 B5
Cleves Rd. Heml H HP2 ... 125 B8
Cleviscroft. Stev SG1 ... 50 E4
Clewer Cres. Har HA3 ... 176 D2
Clifford Cres. Luton LU4 ... 44 D5
Clifford Ct. Bis St CM23 ... 77 A7 6
Clifton Cl. Ches EN8 ... 148 E2
Clifton Rd. Luton LU1 ... 63 B8
Clifton Rd. Watf WD1 ... 167 B4
Clifton St. St Alb AL1 ... 127 E4
Clifton Way. Bor WD6 ... 170 A8
Clifton Way. Ware SG12 ... 93 D3
Climb The. Ric WD3 ... 165 B3
Clinton Ave. Luton LU2 ... 45 F3
Clinton End. Heml H HP2 . 125 C3
Clitheroe Gdns. Sth Ox WD1 ... 175 D7
Clive Cl. Pot B EN6 ... 158 F8
Clive Ct. Luton LU2 ... 45 E1
Clive Par. Norwd HA6 ... 174 E3
Clive Way. Watf WD2 ... 167 C8
Cloister Garth. Berk HP4 . 122 C4
Cloister Garth. St Alb AL1 141 E7
Cloister Lawns. Letw SG6 .. 22 F4
Cloisters Rd. Dun LU4 ... 44 B3
Cloisters The. Bus WD2 ... 168 B3
Cloisters The. Ric WD3 ... 165 E2
Cloisters The. Wel G C AL8 ... 110 D6
Clonard Way. Pnr HA5 ... 176 A4
Close The. Bal SG7 ... 23 E7
Close The. Bro Pk AL9 ... 144 E5
Close The. Bus WD2 ... 168 A4
Close The. Cod SG4 ... 67 F1
Close The. Harp AL5 ... 85 D4
Close The. Hin SG7 ... 3 D6
Close The. Luton LU3 ... 45 A5
Close The. Mark AL3 ... 83 E5
Close The. Pot B EN6 ... 159 A7
Close The. Radl WD7 ... 155 F6
Close The. Ric WD3 ... 165 B1
Close The. Royst SG8 ... 7 F7
Close The. St Alb AL1 ... 141 C8
Close The. Wal SG9 ... 25 E6
Close The. Ware SG12 ... 93 E1
Closemead Cl. Norwd HA6 ... 174 C4
Clothall Rd. Bal SG7 ... 23 F8
Clothall Rd. Clo SG7 ... 24 C6
Clovelly Way. Stev SG1 ... 50 A7
Clover Ave. Bis St CM23 ... 76 B6
Clover Cl. Dun LU4 ... 44 A3
Clover Way. Heml H HP2 . 124 B4
Cloverfield. Wel G C AL7 ... 89 F1
Cloverland. Hat AL10 ... 129 F2
Clump The. Ric WD3 ... 165 B4
Clusterbolts. Stap SG14 ... 92 A7
Clutterbucks. Sar WD3 ... 152 A3
Clyde Rd. Lo Naz EN11 ... 135 D4
Clyde Sq. Heml H HP2 ... 124 F8
Clyde St. Hert SG13 ... 114 A6
Clydesdale Cl. Bor WD6 ... 170 D4
Clydesdale Ct. Dun LU4 ... 44 A3
Clydesdale Path. Bor WD6 ... 170 D4
Clydesdale Rd. Dun LU4 ... 44 A3
Clydesdale Rd. Royst SG8 ... 7 E6
Clydesdale Wlk. Ches EN10 ... 148 F6
Clyfton Cl. Hod EN10 ... 148 F8
Clyston Rd. Watf WD1 ... 166 F3
Coach Dr. Hit SG4 ... 34 F5
Coachman's La. Bal SG7 ... 23 D8
Coates Dell. Watf WD2 ... 154 E6
Coates Rd. Elst WD6 ... 169 D2
Coates Way Jun Mix Inf Sch. Watf ... 154 E6
Coates Way. Watf WD2 ... 154 E6
Cob Cl. Bor WD6 ... 170 C4
Cobb Gn. Watf WD2 ... 154 B7
Cobb Rd. Berk HP4 ... 121 F4
Cobbett Cl. Enf EN3 ... 162 C3
Cobbetts Ride. Tri HP23 ... 99 F3
Cobbins The. Wa Aby EN9 163 E6
Cobbins Way. Harl CM17 . 118 E4
Cobbinsbank. Wa Aby EN9 163 D6
Cobblers Wick. Wing HP22 60 B3
Cobden Hill. Radl WD7 ... 156 B2
Cobden St. Luton LU2 ... 45 F1
Cobham Rd. Ware SG12 ... 93 F2
Cobmead. Hat AL10 ... 130 B7
Cock Gr. Nthch HP23 ... 121 C4
Cock La. Clav CM11 ... 30 F3
Cock La. Hod EN11 ... 134 D4
Cockbush Ave. Hert SG13 114 B7
Cocker Rd. Enf EN1 ... 162 C3
Cockernhoe Sch. Gt Of ... 46 E3
Cockfosters Rd. Had W EN4 ... 159 E1
Cockrobin La. East CM20 . 117 A7
Codicote Dr. Watf WD2 ... 154 D5
Codicote Heights. Cod SG4 68 B1
Codicote House. Stev SG1 . 36 C1
Codicote Jun & Mix Inf Sch. Cod ... 67 E1
Codicote Rd. A St L AL6 ... 88 C3
Codicote Rd. Welw AL6 ... 89 B7
Codicote Rd. Whea AL4 ... 87 D1
Codicote Rd. Whit SG4 ... 66 F6
Codicote Row. Heml H HP2 ... 105 B1
Codmore Wood Rd. Lat HP5 ... 150 D6
Coerdale Ct. Enf EN3 ... 162 E2
Colborne House. Watf WD1 ... 166 E3
Colburn Ave. Pnr HA5 ... 175 E4
Colchester Rd. Norwd HA6 ... 175 A1
Cold Christmas La. Thun SG12 ... 93 E6
Coldham Gr. Enf EN3 ... 162 E2
Coldharbour La. Bus WD2 168 C4
Coldharbour La. Harp AL5 . 86 C4
Cole Green La. Hertng AL7 ... 111 D4
Cole Green La. Wel G C AL7 ... 111 B4
Cole Green Way. Hertng SG14 ... 113 A4
Cole Rd. Watf WD1 ... 167 B8
Colebrook Ave. Luton LU3 .. 44 C7
Coleman Green La. Sand AL4 ... 108 E4
Coleman Green La. Whea AL4 ... 109 A7
Coleman's La. Lo Naz EN9 149 E5
Colemans Rd. Bre Gr SG4 .. 47 D1
Coleridge Cl. Ham St EN7 147 F4
Coleridge Cl. Hit SG4 ... 35 B8
Coleridge Cres. Heml H HP2 ... 105 B1
Coleridge Ct. Harp AL5 ... 86 B1 4
Coles Gn. Bus WD2 ... 168 C1
Coles Hill. Heml H HP1 ... 124 A5
Colesdale. Cuf EN6 ... 146 E1
Colestrete Cl. Stev SG1 ... 51 A5
Colestrete. Stev SG1 ... 50 F5
Coleswood Rd. Harp AL5 . 107 C7
Colgrove. Wel G C AL8 ... 110 C5
Colin Rd. Luton LU2 ... 45 F2
Colindale Ave. St Alb AL1 . 127 F1
College Ave. Har HA3 ... 176 E2
College Cl. Bis St CM23 ... 76 D7
College Cl. Fla AL3 ... 84 B1
College Cl. Har HA3 ... 176 E3
College Cl. Ware SG12 ... 114 D8
College Ct. Ches EN8 ... 148 C1
College Hill Rd. Har HA3 .. 176 E3
College La. Hat AL10 ... 129 E4
College Lake Wildlife Ctr. Mars ... 100 C8
College Pl. St Alb AL3 ... 127 C3
College Rd. Abb L WD5 ... 154 A8
College Rd. Ast Cl HP22 ... 78 C1
College Rd. Ches EN8 ... 148 D1
College Rd. Har HA3 ... 176 E2

College Rd. Hert H SG13 114 D2
College Rd. Hod EN11 134 F8
College Rd. St Alb AL1 128 B2
College St. St Alb AL3 127 D3
College Way. Norwd HA6 174 D4
College Way. Wel G C AL8 110 D7
Collens Rd. Harp AL5 107 B5
Collenswood Rd. Stev SG2 51 B4
Collenswood Sch. Stev 51 C4
Collet Cl. Ches EN8 148 D3
Collet Gdns. Ches EN8 148 D3
Collett Rd. Heml H HP1 124 C3
Collett Rd. Ware SG12 93 D2
Collett Sch The. Heml H 124 B4
Colley Land. Chor WD3 164 D5
Collingdon Ct. Luton LU1 63 D8
Collingdon St. Luton LU1 63 D8
Collings Wells Cl. Cad LU1 62 E4
Collingtree. Luton LU2 46 B4
Collingwood Ct. Royst SG8 7 D7
Collingwood Dr. Lon C AL2 142 D6
Collins Cross. Bis St CM23 59 B1
Collison Cl. Hit SG4 22 C2
Collyer Rd. Lon C AL2 142 D4
Colmer Pl. Har HA3 176 D3
Colnbrook Cl. Lon C AL2 142 E4
Colnbrook Sch. Sth Ox 175 C7
Colne Ave. Ric WD3 173 A8
Colne Ave. Watf WD1 167 C3
Colne Bridge Ret Pk. Watf 167 D4
Colne Gdns. Lon C AL2 142 E4
Colne Lodge. Ric WD3 165 A1
Colne Mead. Ric WD3 173 A8
Colne Way Ct. Watf WD2 154 D3
Colne Way. Heml H HP2 124 F8
Colne Way. Watf WD2 154 E2
Colney Heath La. Coln H AL4 128 E2
Colonial Way. Watf WD2 167 D8
Colonnade The. Ches EN8 148 D3
Colonsay. Heml H HP3 125 C1
Colston Cres. Gofs O EN7 147 B4
Colt Hatch. Harl CM20 117 B1
Colts Cnr. Stev SG2 51 B4
Colts Croft. Gt Ch SG8 9 E2
Colts The. Bis St CM23 76 E4
Coltsfield. Sta M CM24 59 E8
Coltsfoot Dr. Royst SG8 7 E6
Coltsfoot Gn. Dun LU4 44 A5
Coltsfoot La. Dat SG3 90 D7
Coltsfoot Rd. Ware SG12 93 E3
Coltsfoot The. Heml H HP1 123 E2
Coltsfoot. Wel G C AL7 111 B4
Columbus Cl. Stev SG2 51 A7
Columbus Gdns. Norwd HA6 175 A2
Colvin Gdns. Enf EN8 162 D4
Colwell Rd. Stev SG2 51 C3
Colwell Rise. Luton LU2 46 E2
Colwyn Cl. Stev SG1 50 B7
Colyer Cl. Welw AL6 89 F3
Combe House. Watf WD1 166 E3
Combe Rd. Watf WD1 166 F3
Combe St. Heml H HP1 124 C3
Combewood. Watf WD2 154 C7
Comet Cl. Watf WD2 153 F5
Comet Rd. Hat AL10 129 F6
Comet Way. Hat AL10,AL9 129 E5
Commerce Way. Letw SG6 22 F6
Common Field. Wigg HP23 100 D1
Common Gate Rd. Chor WD3 164 E4
Common Gdns. Pot En HP4 123 B6
Common La. Ashw SG7 4 B6
Common La. Kim SG4 66 B1
Common La. Kin L WD4 138 F3
Common La. Radl WD7,WD2 155 E1
Common La. Whea AL5 86 D5
Common Rd. Chor WD3 164 D5
Common Rd. Ken Co LU6 82 F8
Common Rd. Stan HA7 176 D7
Common Rd. Stot SG5 11 F7
Common Rd. Stu LU6 82 B3
Common Rise. Hit SG4 22 A1
Common The. Chipf WD4 152 B8
Common The. Harp AL5 85 C4
Common The. Hat AL10 130 A6
Common The. Pot En HP4 123 A6
Common The. Stan HA7 176 F8
Common View. Letw SG6 23 B8
Common View Sq. Letw SG6 23 A8
Common Wharf. Ware SG12 93 E1
Commonfields. Harl CM20 117 E1
Commons La. Heml H HP2 124 E4
Commons The. Wel G C AL7 111 B3
Commonswood Jun Mix Inf Sch. Wel G C 111 B3
Commonwealth Institute of Parasitology. St Alb 128 D3
Compass Point. Nthch HP4 121 E6
Compton Ave. Luton LU4 44 D4
Compton Gdns. Chis AL2 141 B5
Compton Pl. Sth Ox WD1 175 E6
Comyne Rd. Watf WD2 153 F3
Comyns The. Bus WD2 168 C1
Concorde Dr. Heml H HP2 124 D3
Concorde St. Luton LU2 63 F8
Conduit La E. Hod EN11 135 B6
Conduit La. Gt Ho SG9 29 B1
Conduit La. Hod EN11 135 A6
Coney Cl. Hat AL10 130 B3
Coney Gree. Saw CM21 97 D3
Coneydale. Wel G C AL8 110 D8
Congreve Rd. Wa Aby EN9 163 E6
Conifer Cl. Gofs O EN7 147 F2
Conifer Cl. Stev SG2 51 D7
Conifer Ct. Bis St CM23 76 F8
Conifer Wlk. Stev SG2 51 C7
Conifers The. Watf WD2 154 C4
Coningesby Dr. Watf WD1 166 E7
Coningsby Bank. St Alb AL1 141 D7
Coningsby Cl. Wel G AL9 144 D7
Coningsby Ct. Radl WD7 156 A3
Coningsby Dr. Pot B EN6 159 D6
Coniston Cl. Heml H HP3 125 C2
Coniston Rd. Abb L WD4 139 A4
Coniston Rd. Kin L WD4 138 F3
Coniston Rd. Luton LU3 44 F5
Connaught Cl. Heml H HP2 125 A5
Connaught Gdns. Berk HP4 121 F7
Connaught Rd. Barn EN5 171 D3
Connaught Rd. Har HA3 176 F2
Connaught Rd. Harp AL5 86 B2
Connaught Rd. Luton LU4 44 F1
Connaught Rd. St Alb AL3 127 C6
Connemara Cl. Bor WD6 170 D3
Connop Rd. Enf EN3 162 D1
Conquerors Hill. Whea AL4 108 E8
Conquest Cl. Hit SG4 34 F5
Constable Ct. Luton LU4 45 A1
Constantine Cl. Stev SG1 36 F1
Constantine Pl. Bal SG7 13 B1
Convent Cl. Hit SG5 34 F8
Conway Gdns. Enf EN2 161 E1
Conway House. Bor WD6 170 C5
Conway Rd. Luton LU4 45 B1
Conyers. Harl CM20 117 C2
Cook Rd. Stev SG2 51 B7
Cook's Hole Rd. Enf EN2 161 C1
Cooks Mead. Bus WD2 168 B3
Cooks Spinney. Harl CM20 118 A2
Cooks Vennel. Heml H HP1 124 B5
Cooks Way. Hat AL10 130 B3
Coombe Gdns. Berk HP4 121 F5
Coombe Hill Rd. Ric WD3 165 A2
Coombe Rd. Bus WD2 168 D2
Coombe Rd. Kel SG8 6 A1
Coombelands Rd. Royst SG8 2 E1
Coombes Rd. Lon C AL2 142 C5
Coonwood Cotts. Wars SG12 94 E4
Cooper's Cl. Kim SG4 66 B1
Cooper's Hill. Kim SG4 87 B8
Coopers Cl. Ast SG2 51 D4
Coopers Cres. Bor WD6 170 C8
Coopers Green La. Hat AL4,AL8,AL10 109 D1
Coopers La. Nort EN6 145 E1
Coopers Lane Rd. Nort EN6 160 B6
Coopers Meadow. Red AL3 106 A6
Coopers Rd. Pot B EN6 145 C1
Coopers Wlk. Ches EN8 148 D3
Cooters End La. Harp AL5 85 F5
Copenhagen Cl. Luton LU3 44 D8
Copmans Wick. Chor WD3 164 D4
Coppens The. Stot SG5 12 A5
Copper Beech Cl. Heml H HP3 137 F8
Copper Beeches. Harp AL5 86 B1
Copper Beeches. Welw AL6 89 D7
Copper Ct. Saw CM21 97 E2
Copperfields. Royst SG8 7 C6
Copperfields. Wel G C AL7 111 C5
Coppermill La. Map Cr WD3,UB9 172 F3
Copperwood. Hert SG13 113 F6
Coppice Cl. Har HA7 176 F4
Coppice Cl. Hat AL10 129 F1
Coppice Mead. Stot SG5 11 E5
Coppice The. Heml H HP2 125 B4
Coppice The. Watf WD1 167 C3
Coppice The. Wigg HP23 100 C1
Coppings The. Hod EN11 115 A1
Coppins Cl. Berk HP4 121 F4
Coppins The. Har HA3 176 E4
Coppins The. Mark AL3 83 D5
Copse Cl. Norwd HA6 174 C1
Copse Hill. Welw AL6 90 A8
Copse The. Bis St CM23 77 C8
Copse The. Heml H HP1 123 E5
Copse The. Hert SG13 114 A6
Copse Way. Luton LU3 44 D8
Copse Wood Way. Norwd HA6 174 C2
Copsewood Rd. Watf WD2 167 B8
Copthall Cl. Gt Ha CM22 77 F4
Copthorne Ave. Hod EN10 134 F3
Copthorne Cl. Cro Gr WD3 165 F4
Copthorne. Luton LU2 46 D3
Copthorne Rd. Cro Gr WD3 165 F4
Coral Gdns. Heml H HP2 124 F3
Corals Mead. Wel G C AL7 110 D5
Coram Cl. Berk HP4 122 C3
Corbridge Dr. Luton LU2 46 E2
Corby Cl. Chis AL2 141 A6
Cordell Cl. Ches EN8 148 E3
Corder Cl. St Alb AL3 141 A8
Coreys Mill La. Stev SG1 36 C1
Corinium Gate. St Alb AL3 127 A1
Corinium Gdns. Luton LU3 45 A8
Corn Mead. Wel G C AL8 89 C1
Corncastle Rd. Luton LU1 63 D6
Corncrake Cl. Luton LU2 46 C5
Corncroft. Hat AL10 130 B7
Cornel Cl. Luton LU1 63 A7
Cornel Ct. Luton LU1 63 A7
Corner Cl. Letw SG6 22 E6
Corner Hall Ave. Heml H HP3 124 D1
Corner Hall. Heml H HP3 124 D1
Corner View. Wel G AL9 144 C7
Corner Wood. Mark AL3 83 D5
Cornerfield. Hat AL10 130 B8
Corners. Wel G C AL7 111 A7
Cornfield Cres. Nthch HP4 121 D7
Cornfield Rd. Bus WD2 168 B5
Cornfields. Heml H HP1 124 B2
Cornmill. Wa Aby EN9 163 C6
Cornwall Cl. Ches EN8 162 E6
Cornwall Cl. Pnr EN8 175 F3
Cornwall House. Bis St CM23 76 E4
Cornwall Rd. Harp AL5 86 B2
Cornwall Rd. Pnr HA5 175 F3
Cornwall Rd. St Alb AL1 127 E1
Coronation Ave. Royst SG8 7 C5
Coronation Rd. Bis St CM23 76 E5
Coronation Rd. Ware SG12 93 D2
Corringham Ct. St Alb AL1 127 F4
Corton Cl. Stev SG1 50 B8
Cory-Wright Way. Whea AL4 87 E1
Cosgrove Way. Luton LU1 44 D1
Cotefield. Dun LU4 44 C3
Cotesmore Rd. Heml H HP1 123 E2
Cotlandswick. Lon C AL2 142 C5
Cotney Croft. Stev SG2 51 D3
Cotsmoor. St Alb AL1 127 F3
Cotswold Ave. Bus WD2 168 C3
Cotswold Bsns Pk. Cad LU1 62 D2
Cotswold Cl. St Alb AL4 128 C8
Cotswold Gdns. Luton LU3 44 C7
Cotswold. Heml H HP2 124 E6
Cotswolds. Hat AL10 130 A3
Cottage Cl. Cro Gr WD3 165 F3
Cottage Cl. Watf WD1 166 F7
Cottered Rd. Cotrd SG9 26 F1
Cotterells. Heml H HP1 124 C2
Cotterells Hill. Heml H HP1 124 C3
Cotton Dr. Hert SG13 114 B7
Cotton Field. Hat AL10 130 B7
Cotton Rd. Pot B EN6 159 C8
Cottonmill Cres. St Alb AL1 127 D2
Coulser Cl. Heml H HP1 124 A6
Coulson Ct. Luton LU1 62 F8
Coulter Cl. Cuf EN6 146 D4
Council Rd. Bis St CM23 77 B7
Counters Cl. Heml H HP1 124 A3
Countess Anne Prim Sch. Hat 130 C6
Countess Cl. Hare UB9 173 C1
Couper House. Watf WD1 166 E3
Coursers Rd. Col H AL2,AL4 143 C6
Courtaulds. Chipf WD4 138 B1
Courtenay Ave. Har HA3 176 C2
Courtenay Gdns. Har HA3 176 C1
Courtfield Cl. Hod EN10 135 A3
Courtfields. Harp AL5 86 D1
Courtlands Cl. Watf WD2 153 E4
Courtlands Dr. Watf WD1 153 E3
Courtleigh Ave. Had W EN4 159 D1
Courtway The. Sth Ox WD1 175 E8
Courtyard Mews. Sac SG12 92 E4
Courtyard The. Coln H AL4 128 F3
Covent Garden Cl. Luton LU4 44 F3
Coventry Cl. Stev SG1 37 B1
Coverdale. Heml H HP2 124 E6
Coverdale. Luton LU4 44 B6
Covert Cl. Nthch HP4 121 D6
Covert Rd. Nthch HP4 121 D6
Covert The. Norwd HA6 174 C2
Cow La. Bus WD2 168 A3
Cow La. Tri HP23 100 D4
Cow La. Watf WD2 154 C3
Cowards La. Cod SG4 88 F8
Cowbridge. Hert SG14 113 C6
Cowdray Cl. Luton LU2 46 C3
Cowles. Ham St EN7 147 F4
Cowley Hill. Bor WD6 157 B1
Cowlins. Harl CM17 118 D4
Cowper Cres. Hert SG14 92 B1
Cowper Ct. Mark AL3 83 D5
Cowper Ct. Watf WD2 154 A2
Cowper Endowed Prim Sch. Tewin 90 E2
Cowper Rd. Berk HP4 122 B4
Cowper Rd. Harp AL5 86 C1
Cowper Rd. Heml H HP1 124 B2
Cowper Rd. Mark AL3 83 D5
Cowper Rd. Wel G C AL7 110 F4
Cowper Rise. Mark AL3 83 D5
Cowper St. Luton LU1 63 E5
Cowpers Way. Tewin AL6 90 D5
Cowridge Cres. Luton LU2 64 A8
Cowslip Cl. Royst SG8 7 F5
Cowslip Hill. Letw SG6 22 E7
Cowslips. Wel G C AL7 111 C5
Cox Cl. Shen WD7 156 F7
Cox's Way. Arl SG15 11 A6
Coxfield Cl. Heml H HP2 124 E2
Coyney Gn. Luton LU3 45 C1
Cozens La E. Hod EN10 134 F1
Cozens La W. Hod EN10 134 F1
Cozens Rd. Ware SG12 94 A2
Crab La. Radl WD2 155 B4
Crab Tree La. Pirt SG5 20 D4
Crab Tree Rd. Kneb SG3 68 F4
Crabb's La. Sto P SG9 43 F6
Crabbes Cl. Hit SG5 34 E7
Crabtree Cl. Bus WD2 168 B4
Crabtree Cl. Heml H HP3 124 D1
Crabtree Ct. Heml H HP3 124 E1
Crabtree Dell. Letw SG6 23 B3
Crabtree Inf Sch. Harp 86 C1
Crabtree La. Harp AL5 107 C8
Crabtree La. Heml H HP3 124 D1
Crabtree Prim Sch. Harp 86 C1
Crackley Meadow. Heml H HP2 125 B8
Cradock Rd. Dun LU4 44 B1
Cragg Ave. Radl WD7 155 F3
Cragside. Stev SG2 69 C7
Craig Mount. Radl WD7 156 B4
Craigavon Rd. Heml H HP2 124 F7
Craiglands. St Alb AL4 128 D7
Craigs Wlk. Ches EN8 148 D3
Craigweil Ave. Radl WD7 156 B4
Crakers Mead. Watf WD1 167 B6
Cranborne Ave. Hit SG5 34 D6
Cranborne Cl. Bric SG13 113 C3
Cranborne Cl. Pot B EN6 158 E8
Cranborne Cres. Pot B EN6 158 E8
Cranborne Ct. Enf EN3 162 D3
Cranborne Gdns. Wel G C AL7 110 F5
Cranborne Ind Est. Pot B 144 E1
Cranborne Par. Pot B EN6 158 D8
Cranborne Prim Sch. Pot B 158 F8
Cranborne Rd. Ches EN8 162 D7
Cranborne Rd. Hat AL10 130 B6
Cranborne Rd. Hod EN11 135 C7
Cranborne Rd. Pot B EN6 144 E1
Cranbourne Dr. Harp AL5 107 D6
Cranbourne Dr. Hod EN11 115 C2
Cranbourne Prim Sch The. Hod 115 B2
Cranbourne Rd. Norwd HA6 174 F1
Cranbourne. Stev SG1 36 B1
Cranbrook Cl. Ware SG12 93 D3
Cranbrook Dr. Coln H AL4 128 E3
Cranbrook Dr. Luton LU3 44 D8
Crane Mead. Ware SG12 114 E8
Cranefield Dr. Watf WD2 154 E6
Cranes Way. Bor WD6 170 C4
Cranfield Cres. Cuf EN6 146 E2
Cranford Ct. Harp AL5 86 C1
Cranleigh Cl. Ches EN7 148 A3
Cranleigh Gdns. Luton LU3 45 D3
Cranmer Cl. Pot B EN6 145 C1
Cranmer House. Kin L WD4 139 A2
Cranmore Ct. St Alb AL1 127 F4
Cranwell Gdns. Bis St CM23 59 C1
Cravells Rd. Harp AL5 107 C7
Crawford Rd. Hat AL10 130 A7
Crawley Cl. Cad LU1 63 C1
Crawley Dr. Heml H HP2 124 F7
Crawley Gn. Luton LU2 46 B1
Crawley Green Rd. Luton LU1,LU2 46 D1
Crawley Rd. Luton LU1 63 D8
Crawley's La. Wigg HP23 120 F7
Creamery Ct. Letw SG6 23 C3
Crecy Gdns. Red AL3 106 A6
Creighton Ave. St Alb AL1 141 D8
Crescent E. Had W EN4 159 C1
Crescent Rd. Bis St CM23 77 A6
Crescent Rd. Heml H HP2 124 D3
Crescent Rd. Luton LU2 63 F8
Crescent Rise. Luton LU2 63 F8
Crescent The. Abb L WD5 139 F1
Crescent The. Ard SG2 38 F2
Crescent The. Bri Wd AL2 141 A1
Crescent The. Cad LU1 62 E3
Crescent The. Cotrd SG9 39 D7
Crescent The. Cro Gr WD3 166 B3
Crescent The. Harl CM17 118 C6
Crescent The. Henlw SG16 10 C4
Crescent The. Hit SG5 21 D1
Crescent The. Letw SG6 23 A5
Crescent The. Mars HP23 80 A1
Crescent The. Pit LU7 80 C4
Crescent The. St Ipp SG4 35 A3
Crescent The. Watf WD1 167 C5
Crescent The. Welw AL6 89 C4
Crescent W. Had W EN4 159 C1
Cress End. Ric WD3 165 A1
Cresset Cl. Gt Am SG12 115 C3
Cresswick. Whit SG4 66 E7
Crest Dr. Enf EN3 162 C1
Crest Pk. Heml H HP2 125 C4
Crest The. Gofs O EN7 147 B4
Crest The. Luton LU3 45 B7
Crest The. Saw CM21 97 D2
Crest The. Ware SG12 93 D3
Crest The. Welw AL6 89 D8
Cresta Cl. Dun LU5 44 A2
1 Creswick Ct. Wel G C AL7 110 D5
Creswick Jun Mix Inf Sch. Wel G C 110 D3
Crew Curve. Berk HP4 121 F7
Crews Hill. Cer H EN2 160 F5
Crews Hill Sta. Cer H 160 F5
Crib St. Ware SG12 93 D2
Cricketer's Rd. Arl SG15 11 A4
Cricketers Cl. St Alb AL3 127 E4
Cricketfield La. Bis St CM23 76 E8
Cringle Ct. Pot B EN6 145 C1
Crispin Field. Pit LU7 80 C4
Croasdaile Rd. Sta M CM24 59 E8
Croasdale Cl. Sta M CM24 59 E8
Crocus Field. Barn EN5 171 F3
4 Croft Cl. Chipf WD4 138 A1
Croft Ct. Hit SG5 34 E7
Croft End Rd. Chipf WD4 138 A1
Croft Field. Chipf WD4 138 A1
Croft Field. Hat AL10 130 A5
Croft La. Chipf WD4 138 A1
Croft La. Letw SG6 12 B1
Croft Meadow. Chipf WD4 138 A1
Croft Meadows. Ched LU7 80 A7
Croft Rd. Luton LU2 46 B3
Croft Rd. Ware SG12 93 C2
Croft The. Barn EN5 171 E5
Croft The. Chis AL2 141 A6
Croft The. Hod EN10 148 E8
Croft The. Luton LU3 44 D8

Croft The. Wars SG12 ........ 94 E4
Croft The. Wel G C AL7 ..... 110 F3
Crofters End. Saw CM21 ..... 97 E3
Crofters Rd. Mo Pk HA6 ... 174 E6
Crofters. Saw CM21 ........... 97 E3
Crofts Path. Heml H HP3 . 125 B1
Crofts The. Heml H HP3 ... 125 B2
Crofts The. Stot SG5 .......... 11 F6
Croftwell. Harp AL5 ......... 107 F8
Cromer Cl. L Gad HP4 ...... 102 E4
Cromer Cl. L Gad HP4 ...... 102 E5
Cromer Rd. Watf WD2 ...... 154 C1
Cromer Way. Luton LU2 ..... 45 D7
Crompton Rd. Stev SG1 ..... 50 A6
Cromwell Ave. Ches EN7 . 148 B1
Cromwell Cl. Bis St CM23 .. 76 B7
Cromwell Cl. St Alb AL4 ... 128 D8
Cromwell Gn. Letw SG6 ..... 23 B8
Cromwell Hill. Luton LU2 ... 45 D1
Cromwell Rd. Bor WD6 .... 169 E8
Cromwell Rd. Ches EN7 ... 148 B3
Cromwell Rd. Hert SG13 ... 114 A7
Cromwell Rd. Letw SG6 ..... 23 B8
Cromwell Rd. Luton LU3 .... 45 D1
Cromwell Rd. Stev SG2 ...... 51 C5
Cromwell Rd. Ware SG12 .. 93 F2
Cromwell Way. Pirt SG5 .... 20 D4
Crooked Mile. Wa Aby EN9 ........ 163 C7
Crookhams. Wel G C AL7 ... 90 A1
Crop Comm. Hat AL10 ...... 130 B7
Crosby Cl. Luton LU4 .......... 45 A2
Cross La. Harp AL5 .......... 107 D5
Cross La. Hert SG14 ......... 113 B6
Cross Oak Rd. Berk HP4 .. 122 A4
Cross Rd. Ches EN8 ......... 162 E6
Cross Rd. Hert SG14 ........ 113 C7
Cross Rd. Watf WD1 ......... 167 E3
Cross St. Letw SG6 ........... 22 F7
Cross St. Luton LU2 ........... 63 E8
Cross St. St Alb AL3 ......... 127 D3 2
Cross St. Ware SG12 ......... 93 E1
Cross St. Watf WD1 .......... 167 C6
Cross Way. Harp AL5 ......... 86 C3
Cross Way The. Har HA3 . 176 E1
Cross Way The. Luton LU1 63 C5
Crossbrook. Hat AL10 ...... 129 E4
Crossbrook St. Ches EN8 . 148 D1
Crossbrook St. Ches EN8 . 162 D8
Crossett Gn. Heml H HP3 125 C1
Crossfell Rd. Heml H HP3 125 C2
Crossfield Cl. Berk HP4 ... 121 F4
Crossfield Rd. Hod EN11 .. 135 B8
Crossfields. St Alb AL3 .... 141 B8
Crossgates. Stev SG1 ........ 50 E5
Crosslands. Cad LU1 ......... 62 E3
Crossleys. Letw SG6 .......... 11 F2
Crossmead. Watf WD1 .... 167 B3
Crossoaks La. Ridge WD6 157 F5
Crossoaks La. Shen WD6 157 D5
Crosspath The. Radl WD7 156 A4
Crosspaths. Harp AL5 ........ 85 C4
Crossway. Pnr HA5 .......... 175 B1
Crossway. Wel G C AL8 ...... 89 C2
Crossways. Bar SG8 ........... 8 F1
Crossways. Berk HP4 ...... 121 F3
Crossways. Heml H HP3 .. 125 C3
Crouch Hall Gdns. Red AL3 ........ 106 A6
Crouch Hall La. Red AL3 .. 106 A6
Crouch La. Gofs O EN7 ..... 147 C4
Crouchfield. Heml H HP1 . 124 B2
Crouchfield. Hert SG14 ...... 92 C1
Crouchfield La. Hert SG14 . 92 E4
Crow Furlong. Hit SG5 ....... 34 D7
Crowborough Path. Sth Ox WD1 ......... 175 D6
Crowland Rd. Luton LU2 .... 46 C5
Crown Cl. Sheer CM22 ....... 98 C1
Crown La. Reed SG8 .......... 16 F5
Crown Lodge. Arl SG15 ...... 11 A4
Crown Rd. Bor WD6 ......... 170 B8
Crown Rise. Watf WD2 .... 154 D5
Crown St. Red AL3 .......... 106 B5
Crown Terr. Bis St CM23 .... 77 A7
Crownfield. Lo Naz EN10 . 135 A2
Croxdale Rd. Bor WD6 ..... 170 A7
Croxley Ctr. Watf ............ 166 D4
Croxley Green Sta. Cro Gr 166 D4
Croxley Sta. Cro Gr ......... 166 B3
Croxley View. Watf WD1 . 166 E3
Croxton Cl. Luton LU3 ........ 45 A7
Crozier Ave. Bis St CM23 ... 76 C8
Crusader Way. Watf WD1 166 F3
Cubbington Cl. Luton LU3 .. 45 A7
Cubitts Cl. Welw AL6 ........ 89 F3
Cublands. Hert SG13 ....... 114 B6
Cuckmans Dr. Chis AL2 .... 141 A6
Cuckoo's Nest. Luton LU2 .. 64 A7
Cuffley Ave. Watf WD2 .... 154 D5
Cuffley Cl. Luton LU3 .......... 44 F4
Cuffley Ct. Heml H HP2 .... 125 C8
Cuffley Hill. Gofs O EN7 ... 147 B2
Cuffley Jun Mix Inf Sch. Cuf ........ 146 F1
Cuffley Sta. Cuf ........ 146 F2
Cullera Cl. Norwd HA6 ..... 174 F4
Cullings Ct. Wa Aby EN9 .. 163 F6
Culver Rd. St Alb AL1 ....... 127 E5
Culverden Rd. Sth Ox WD1 ........ 175 B7
Culverhouse Rd. Luton LU3 45 C3
Culworth Cl. Cad LU1 ......... 62 E3
Cumberland Cl. Abb L WD5 ........ 139 E7
Cumberland Cl. Hert SG14 113 C8
Cumberland Ct. Hod EN11 135 A7
Cumberland Ct. St Alb AL3 ........ 127 E4
Cumberland Dr. Red AL3 . 106 B6
Cumberland St. Luton LU1 . 63 E6
Cumberlow Pl. Heml H HP2 ........ 125 C2
Cumcum Hill. Ess AL9 ...... 131 E2
Cundalls Rd. Ware SG12 .... 93 E2
Cunningham Ave. Enf EN3 162 E3
Cunningham Ave. St Alb AL1 ........ 127 F1
Cunningham Hill Inf Sch. St Alb ........ 128 A1
Cunningham Hill Jun Sch. St Alb ........ 128 A1
Cunningham Hill Rd. St Alb AL1 ........ 128 A1
Cunningham Rd. Ches EN8 148 E4
Cupid Green La. Gt Gd HP2 ........ 104 E3
Cupid Green La. Heml H HP2 ........ 105 A1
Curlew Cl. Berk HP4 ........ 122 C3
Curlew Cl. Letw SG6 .......... 11 E1
Curlew Rd. Luton LU2 ........ 46 C5
Currie St. Hert SG13 ........ 113 E6
Curteys. Harl CM17 ......... 118 D5
Curtis Cl. Ric WD3 .......... 165 A1
Curtis Rd. Heml H HP3 ..... 125 D2
Curtis Way. Berk HP4 ...... 122 D3
Curzon Rd. Luton LU3 ........ 45 C1
Cussans House. Watf WD1 ........ 166 E3
Cussons Cl. Ches EN7 ...... 148 A2
Cut Throat Ave. Whip LU6 . 81 E7
Cutenhoe Rd. Luton LU1 .... 63 E4
Cutforth Rd. Saw CM21 ..... 97 E3
Cuthbert Cl. Gofs O EN7 .. 147 F2
Cutlers Gn. Luton LU2 ....... 46 F2
Cutmore Dr. Coln H AL4 ... 129 B1
Cutts La. Kim SG4 ............. 66 D1
Cuttsfield Terr. Heml H HP1 ........ 123 F2
Cuttys La. Stev SG1 .......... 50 E5
Cwmbran Ct. Heml H HP2 124 F7
Cygnet Cl. Bor WD6 ......... 170 C8
Cygnet Cl. Norwd HA6 ..... 174 C4
Cygnet Ct. Bis St CM23 ...... 76 F6
Cylers Thicket. Welw AL6 .. 89 C6
Cypress Ave. Cre H EN2 .. 161 A4
Cypress Cl. Wa Aby EN9 .. 163 D5
Cypress Rd. Har HA3 ....... 176 D1
Cypress Wlk. Watf WD2 .. 154 B4
Cyrils Way. St Alb AL1 ..... 141 D8

Dacorum Coll of F Ed. Heml H ........ 124 C4
Dacorum Way. Heml H HP1 ........ 124 C3
Dacre Cres. Kim SG4 ......... 66 C1
Dacre Gdns. Bor WD6 ...... 170 D4
Dacre Gn. Royst SG8 ........... 7 F6
Dacre Rd. Hit SG5 .............. 35 A8
Dagger La. Elst WD6 ........ 169 B4
Daggs Dell Rd. Heml H HP1 ........ 123 E5
Dagnall Cty Fst Sch. Dagn . 81 C5
Dagnall Rd. Gt Gd HP1 ..... 103 C5
Dagnall Rd. Whip LU6 ........ 81 D8
Dagnalls. Letw SG6 ............ 22 F2
Dahlia Cl. Luton LU2 .......... 46 B4
Daintrees. Widf SG12 ........ 95 E4
Daintry Lodge. Norwd HA6 ........ 174 F3
Daisy Ct. Letw CM1 ........... 23 A8
Dalby Cl. Dun LU4 ............. 44 B3
Dale Ave. Kim AL4 ............. 87 B5
Dale Cl. Hit SG4 ................ 34 F4
Dale Cl. Pnr HA5 ............. 175 B2
Dale Ct. Saw CM21 ............ 97 D1
Dale Rd. Luton LU1 ............ 63 C7
Dale The. Letw SG6 ........... 22 E5
Dale The. Wa Aby EN9 ..... 163 E5
Dales Path. Bor WD6 ....... 170 D4
Dales Rd. Bor WD6 .......... 170 D4
Daleside Dr. Pot B EN6 .... 158 F6
Dalewood. Harp AL5 .......... 86 D1
Dalewood. Wel G C AL7 ... 111 D5
Dalkeith Rd. Harp AL5 ........ 86 C1
Dallow Jun & Inf Schs. Luton ........ 63 C8
Dallow Rd. Luton LU1 ......... 63 B8
Dalroad Ind Est. Luton ....... 63 B8
Dalton Gdns. Bis St CM23 .. 76 E3
Dalton St. St Alb AL3 ........ 127 D4
Dalton Way. Whit SG4 ....... 66 E7
Daltry Cl. Stev SG1 ........... 36 C2
Daltry Rd. Stev SG1 ........... 36 C2
Damask Cl. Wes SG4 ......... 37 B8
Damask Gn. Heml H HP1 . 123 E2
Damask Green Rd. Wes SG4 ........ 37 B8
Dame Alice Owen's Sch. Pot B ........ 158 E6
Dammersey Cl. Mark AL3 .. 83 F4
Dancers End La. Ast Cl HP23 ........ 99 C2
Dancers Hill Rd. Pot B EN5 ........ 158 E3
Dancote. Kneb SG3 ........... 68 F5
Dane Acres. Bis St CM23 .... 76 D8
Dane Bridge La. Muc H SG10 ........ 75 B2
Dane Cl. Harp AL5 ............. 86 C4
Dane Cl. Stot SG5 .............. 11 F8
Dane Ct. Hert SG13 .......... 113 E6
Dane End House. Stev SG1 36 C1
Dane End La. Wes SG4 ...... 37 E5
Dane End Rd. Thun SG11 ... 72 E3
Dane House. Bis St CM23 .. 76 D8
Dane O'Coys Rd. Bis St CM23 ........ 58 E1
Dane Pk. Bis St CM23 ........ 76 D8
Dane Rd. Luton LU3 .......... 45 C2
Dane St. Bis St CM23 ......... 77 A7
Danebridge Rd. Muc H SG10 ........ 75 B2
Danefield Rd. Pirt SG5 ...... 20 C4
Danemead. Hod EN11 ...... 115 A1
Danes The. Chis AL2 ........ 141 C3
Danesbury Hospl. Welw .... 89 C7
Danesbury La. Welw AL6 ... 89 D8
Danesbury Park Caravan Site. Welw ........ 89 D8
Danesbury Park Rd. Welw AL6 ........ 89 D8
Danesbury Pk. Hert SG14 113 D7
Danesgate. Stev SG1 ......... 50 D4
Danestrete. Stev SG1 ........ 50 D5
Daniells. Wel G C AL7 ...... 111 A7
Danvers Croft. Tri HP23 .. 100 C5
Danvers Dr. Luton LU3 ....... 31 C1
Danziger Way. Bor WD6 .. 170 C8
Darby Dr. Wa Aby EN9 .... 163 C6
Darby Dr. Welw AL6 .......... 68 E3
Darcy Cl. Ches EN8 ......... 162 E8
Dark La. Ches EN7 .......... 148 A1
Dark La. Harp AL5 ........... 107 D7
Dark La. San SG9 ............. 15 B1
Dark La. Wing HP22 .......... 60 C3
Darkes La. Pot B EN6 ....... 159 A8
Darley Rd. Bre Gr SG4 ....... 47 C2
Darnicle Hill. Ham St EN7 147 A6
Darr's La. Nthch HP4 ....... 121 D6
Darrington Rd. Bor WD6 .. 169 E8
Darwin Cl. Heml H HP2 .... 105 B1
Darwin Cl. St Alb AL3 ....... 127 E7
Darwin Gdns. Sth Ox WD1 175 C5
Darwin Rd. Stev SG2 ......... 51 B6
Dashes The. Harl CM20 .... 117 E1
Datchet Cl. Heml H HP2 ... 125 B8
Datchworth Turn. Heml H HP2 ........ 125 C3
Davenham Ave. Mo Pk HA6 ........ 174 F5
Daventer Dr. Har HA7 ...... 176 F3
Davies St. Hert SG13 ....... 113 E6
Davis Cres. Pirt SG5 .......... 20 D4
Davis Ct. St Alb AL1 ......... 127 E3
Davis' Row. Arl SG15 ......... 11 A4
Davison Cl. Ches EN8 ...... 148 D3
Davison Dr. Ches EN8 ...... 148 D3
Davys Cl. Whea AL4 ......... 108 E7
Dawes La. Sar WD3 ......... 151 F3
Dawley Ct. Heml H HP2 .... 125 A7
Dawley. Wel G C AL7 ......... 89 F1
Dawlish Cl. Stev SG2 ......... 69 C7
Dawlish Rd. Luton LU4 ....... 44 F3
Dawson Cl. Henlw SG16 .... 10 C5
Day's Cl. Royst SG8 ............ 7 C5
Dayemead. Wel G C AL7 .. 111 B3
Days Cl. Hat AL10 ........... 129 F5
Days Mead. Hat AL10 ...... 129 F5
De Haviland Cl. Hat AL10 . 129 F6
De Havilland Ct. Shen WD7 ........ 156 E7
De Havilland Way. Abb L WD5 ........ 153 F7
De Tany Ct. St Alb AL1 ..... 127 D2
De Vere Wlk. Watf WD1 .. 166 E7
Deacon Cl. St Alb AL1 ...... 141 D7
Deacons Cl. Bor WD6 ...... 170 A5
Deacons Cl. Pnr HA5 ........ 175 B1
Deacons Ct. Luton LU2 ....... 63 D8 8
Deacons Hill. Watf WD1 .. 167 C3
Deacon's Hill Rd. Bor WD6 ........ 170 A4
Deacons Hts. Bor WD6 .... 170 A3
Deacons Way. Hit SG5 ....... 21 D1
Deaconsfield Rd. Heml H HP3 ........ 138 E8
Dead Woman's La. Pres SG4 ........ 48 C7
Deadman's Ash La. Sar WD3 ........ 152 B3
Deakin Cl. Watf WD1 ....... 166 E2
Dean Ct. Watf WD2 ......... 154 D6
Dean Field. Bov HP3 ........ 137 A4
Dean Moore Cl. St Alb AL1 127 D2
Dean The. Wing HP22 ........ 60 B3
Dean's Gdns. St Alb AL4 .. 128 A7
Deans Cl. Abb L WD5 ....... 153 D7
Deans Cl. Tri HP23 .......... 100 A4
Deans Furlong. Tri HP23 . 100 A4
Deans Meadow. Dagn HP4 81 C5
Deanscroft. Kneb SG3 ........ 68 F5
Deansway. Heml H HP3 ... 138 F8
Deard's End La. Kneb SG3 . 68 F6
Deards Wood. Kneb SG3 ... 68 F5
Debenham Ct. Barn EN5 .. 171 C4
Debenham Rd. Ham St EN7 ........ 148 B4
Dee The. Heml H HP2 ...... 124 F8
Deep Denes. Luton LU2 ..... 46 A2
Deepdene. Pot B EN6 ....... 158 D8
Deeping Cl. Kneb SG3 ........ 68 F4
Deer Cl. Hert SG13 .......... 113 F6
Deerfield Cl. Ware SG12 .... 93 D2
Deerings The. Harp AL5 ... 107 A4
Deerswood Ave. Hat AL10 130 B3
Deeves Hall La. Ridge WD6 ........ 157 E6
Deimos Dr. Heml H HP2 .. 125 A6
Delahay Rise. Berk HP4 ... 122 B6
Delamare Rd. Ches EN8 ... 148 F2
Delamere Rd. Bor WD6 .... 170 B8
Delfcroft. Ware SG12 ........ 93 C2
Delfield Cl. Cad LU1 ........... 62 E4
Delius Cl. Elst WD6 .......... 169 C3
Dell Cl. Harp AL5 ............... 86 B3
Dell La. L Hal CM22 ........... 98 A8
Dell La. Saw CM22 ............. 98 A8
Dell Meadow. Heml H HP3 138 E7
Dell Rd. Enf EN3 .............. 162 C1
Dell Rd. Nthch HP4 ......... 121 D7
Dell Rd. Watf WD2 ........... 154 A2
Dell Rise. Chis AL2 .......... 141 B5
Dell Side. Watf WD2 ........ 154 A2
Dell Springs. Bun SG9 ........ 40 E8
Dell The. Bal ..................... 23 E6
Dell The. Bric SG13 .......... 113 C3
Dell The. Cad LU1 .............. 62 E3
Dell The. Luton LU2 ........... 46 F1
Dell The. Mark AL3 ............ 83 D5
Dell The. Mo Pk HA6 ........ 174 E8
Dell The. Pnr HA5 ............ 175 D1
Dell The. Radl WD7 .......... 156 A4
Dell The. Royst SG8 ............. 7 C5
Dell The. St Alb AL1 ......... 128 A4
Dell The. Stev SG1 ............. 50 E5
Dell The. Welw AL6 ............ 90 A4
Dellcot Cl. Luton LU2 ......... 46 B4
Dellcott Cl. Wel G C AL8 .. 110 C7
Dellcroft Way. Harp AL5 .. 107 A5
Dellcut Rd. Heml H HP2 ... 125 A5
Dellfield Ave. Berk HP4 .... 122 B6
Dellfield. Berk HP4 .......... 122 A6
Dellfield Cl. Radl WD7 ...... 155 F4
Dellfield Cl. Watf WD1 ..... 167 A7
Dellfield Ct. Harl CM17 .... 118 C4
Dellfield Ct. Luton LU2 ...... 46 D2
Dellfield Rd. Hat AL10 ...... 130 A5
Dellfield. St Alb AL1 ......... 127 F2
Dellfield. Thun SG12 .......... 93 D8
Dellmeadow. Abb L WD5 . 139 E1
Dellors Cl. Barn EN5 ........ 171 D4
Dells The. Bis St CM23 ...... 76 F7 4
Dells The. Heml H HP3 .... 125 B2
Dellsome La. Col H AL9 .... 143 F8
Dellsome La. Wel G AL9 .. 144 B8
Dellswood Cl. Hert SG13 . 113 E5
Dellwood Cl. Ric WD3 ...... 165 B1
Delmar Ave. Heml H HP2 . 125 D2
Delmer Ct. Bor WD6 ........ 156 F1
Delmerend La. Fla AL3 ....... 84 C1
Delphine Cl. Luton LU1 ....... 63 A6
Delta Gain. Sth Ox WD1 ... 175 D7
Demontfort Rise. Ware SG12 ........ 93 C3
Denbigh High Sch. Luton .... 45 B2
Denbigh High Sch. Luton .... 45 C2
Denbigh Rd. Luton LU3 ..... 45 B2
Denby. Letw SG6 ............... 23 B4
Dencora Way. Luton LU3 .... 44 B8
Dendridge Cl. Enf EN1 ..... 162 B2
Dene La. Ast SG2 .............. 51 E2
Dene Rd. Norwd HA6 ....... 174 D4
Denes The. Heml H HP3 .. 138 F7
Denewood Cl. Watf WD1 . 153 F2
Denham Cl. Heml H HP2 .. 125 A8
Denham Cl. Luton LU3 ....... 44 E8
Denham La. C St P SL9 .... 172 A2
Denham Way. Bor WD6 ... 170 C8
Denham Way (North Orbital Rd). Map Cr WD3 ........ 172 E4
Denham Way (North Orbital Rd). Ric WD3 ........ 164 E1
Denmark Cl. Luton LU3 ...... 44 E8
Denmark Rd. Watf WD1 .. 167 B7
Denny Ave. Wa Aby EN9 .. 163 D5
Denny Ct. Bis St CM23 ...... 59 B2
Denny Gate. Ches EN8 ..... 148 F4
Denny's La. Berk HP4 ...... 121 F3
Densley Cl. Wel G C AL8 .. 110 D8
Denton Cl. Barn EN5 ........ 171 C4
Denton Cl. Dun LU4 ........... 44 B4
Denton Rd. Stev SG1 ......... 50 E4
Dents Cl. Letw SG6 ........... 23 C3
Derby Ave. Har HA3 ......... 176 D2
Derby House. Pnr HA5 ..... 175 D1
Derby Rd. Dun LU4 ............ 44 C2
Derby Rd. Lo Naz EN11 .... 135 D4
Derby Rd. Watf WD1 ....... 167 C5
Derby Way. Stev SG1 ........ 51 B8
Derwent Ave. Luton LU3 .... 45 B7
Derwent Ave. Pnr HA5 ..... 175 E4
Derwent Lower Sch. Henlw 10 C4
Derwent Rd. Harp AL5 ....... 85 C4
Derwent Rd. Heml H HP3 125 C2
Derwent Rd. Henlw SG16 .. 10 B4
Derwent Rd. Luton LU2 ...... 64 A8
Desborough Cl. Hert SG14 . 92 C1
Desborough Dr. Tewin AL6 90 D5
Desborough Rd. Hit SG4 .... 35 C8
Desmond Rd. Watf WD2 .. 153 F3
Deva Cl. St Alb AL3 ......... 127 A1
Devereux Dr. Watf WD1 .. 153 E1
Devoils La. Bis St CM23 .... 76 F7
Devon Ct. St Alb AL1 ...... 127 E2
Devon Rd. Luton LU2 .......... 64 B8
Devon Rd. Watf WD1 ....... 167 D8
Devonshire Cl. Stev SG2 .... 69 A8
Devonshire Rd. Harp AL5 .. 86 B1
Devonshire Rd. Pnr HA5 .. 175 F2
Dewars Cl. Welw AL6 ....... 89 C6
Dewes Green Rd. Clav CM23 ........ 30 F1
Dewgrass Gr. Enf EN8 ..... 162 D4
Dewhurst Rd. Ches EN8 ... 148 C2
Dewhurst St Mary Jun Mix Inf Sch. Ches ........ 148 C2
Dewpond Cl. Stev SG1 ....... 50 C8
Dewsbury Rd. Luton LU3 .. 45 C6
Dexter Cl. Luton LU3 ......... 31 B1
Dexter Rd. Barn EN5 ........ 171 D3
Dexter Rd. Hare UB9 ....... 173 C1
Diamond Rd. Watf WD2 ... 154 A1
Dickens Cl. St Alb AL3 ...... 127 D4
Dickens Ct. Heml H HP2 .. 105 B1
Dicker Mill. Hert SG13 .... 113 D7
Dicker Mill Ind Pk. Hert ... 113 E7
Dicket Mead. Welw AL6 ..... 89 C5
Dickins Cl. Ham St EN7 .... 148 A5
Dickinson Ave. Cro Gr WD3 ........ 166 A3
Dickinson Sq. Cro Gr WD3 166 A3
Dickson. Ham St EN7 ....... 147 F4
Dig Dag Hill. Ham St EN7 . 147 F4
Digswell Cl. Bor WD6 ...... 157 A1
Digswell Hill. Welw AL6 .... 89 B2
Digswell House Mews. Wel G C AL8 ........ 89 D2
Digswell La. Wel G C AL7 .. 89 F2
Digswell Park Rd. Wel G C AL8 ........ 89 D3
Digswell Park Rd. Wel G C AL8 ........ 89 E3
Digswell Rd. Wel G C AL8 .. 89 E1
Digswell Rise. Wel G C AL8 ........ 110 E8
Dimmocks La. Sar WD3 ... 152 B3
Dimsdale Cres. Bis St CM23 ........ 77 B6
Dimsdale St. Hert SG14 ... 113 C6
Dinant Link Rd. Hod EN11 135 B7

Dingle Cl. Edg EN5 ........... 170 F3
Dinmore. Bov HP3 ............ 136 F3
Ditchfield Rd. Hod EN11 .. 115 A1
Ditchling Cl. Luton LU2 ....... 46 C3
Ditchmore La. Stev SG1 ..... 50 D6
Ditton Gn. Gt Of LU2 .......... 46 E3
Divine Saviour RC Jun Mix
Inf Sch. Abb L ............... 153 D7
Divot Pl. Hert SG13 .......... 114 B7
Dixies Cl. Ashw SG7 ............. 4 D3
Dixon Pl. Bun SG9 ............... 40 E7
Dixons Hill Cl. Wel G AL9 . 144 B6
Dixons Hill Rd. Wel G AL9 144 C7
Dobb's Weir Rd.
Lo Naz EN11,CM19 ...... 135 D4
Docklands. Pirt SG5 ........... 20 D4
Doctor's Commons Rd.
Berk HP4 ...................... 122 B4
Dodds La. Fla HP2 ............ 104 E1
Dodwood. Wel G C AL7 ...... 111 B5
Dog Kennel La. Hat AL10 . 130 A6
Dog Kennel La. Royst SG8 ... 7 D6
Doggetts Way. St Alb AL1 127 C1
Dognell Gn. Wel G C AL8 . 110 B7
Dolesbury Dr. Welw AL6 .... 89 E8
Dollis Brook Wlk.
Barn EN5 ...................... 171 E3
Dollis Valley Way.
Barn EN5 ...................... 171 F3
Dolphin Ct. Har HA3 ......... 176 E1
Dolphin Sq. Tri HP23 ........ 100 A3
Dolphin Way. Bis St CM23 . 77 A8
Dolphin Yd. Hert SG14 ..... 113 D6 2
Dolphin Yd. St Alb AL1 ...... 127 D3
Dolphin Yd. Ware SG12 ..... 93 D1 6
Doncaster Cl. Stev SG1 ...... 51 C8
Doncaster Gn.
Sth Ox WD1 ................. 175 C5
Donkey La. Tri HP23 .......... 99 E2
Donne Cl. Royst SG8 ............ 7 C8
Dorant House. St Alb AL3 127 D7
Dorchester Ave.
Hod EN11 ..................... 135 A8
Dorchester Ct.
Cro Gr WD3 ................. 166 D4
Dorchester Ct. Watf WD3 167 E3
Dordans Rd. Luton LU4 ...... 44 F4
Dorel Cl. Luton LU2 ........... 45 F2
Dormans Cl. Norwd HA6 .. 174 D3
Dormer Cl. Barn EN5 ....... 171 D4
Dormie Cl. St Alb AL3 ....... 127 C5
Dorrien's Croft. Berk HP4 121 F7
Dorrington Cl. Luton LU3 .... 45 C1
Dorrofield Cl. Cro Gr WD3 166 D4
Dorset Cl. Berk HP4 ......... 121 F5
Dorset Ct. Luton LU1 .......... 63 F6
Douglas Ave. Watf WD2 .. 154 E2
Douglas Dr. Stev SG1 ......... 51 A8
Douglas House. Ches EN8 148 D3
Douglas Rd. Harp AL5 ........ 85 F2
Douglas Rd. Luton LU4 ....... 45 A2
Douglas Way.
Wel G C AL7 ................. 111 C6
Dove Cl. Bis St CM23 ......... 76 E3
Dove Cl. Sta M CM24 ......... 59 E8
Dove Ct. Hat AL10 ............ 130 A3
Dove House La.
Ken Co LU6 ................... 82 D8
Dove La. Pot B EN6 .......... 159 C5
Dove Pk. Chor WD3 .......... 164 C4
Dove Pk. Pnr HA5 ............ 176 A3
Dovedale Cl. Hare UB9 .... 173 C1
Dovedale. Luton LU2 .......... 45 E6
Dovedale. Stev SG2 ........... 51 B4
Dovedale. Ware SG12 ........ 93 C3
Dovehouse Croft.
Harl CM20 .................... 118 A2
Dovehouse Hill. Luton LU2 . 46 B1
Dover Cl. Luton LU3 ........... 45 A3
Dover Way. Cro Gr WD3 .. 166 C5
Doverfield. Gofs O EN7 .... 147 C2
Dower Ct. Hit SG4 ............. 34 F5 1
Dowland House. Enf EN1 . 161 F1
Dowling Ct. Heml H HP3 .. 138 D8
Down Edge. Red AL3 ........ 105 F5
Down Green La.
Whea AL4 .................... 108 B7
Downalong. Bus WD2 ...... 168 D1
Downedge. St Alb AL3 ...... 127 B4
Downer Dr. Sar WD3 ....... 152 A3
Downes Rd. St Alb AL4 .... 128 B7
Downfield Cl.
Hert H SG13 ................. 114 C4
Downfield Jun Mix Inf Sch.
Ches ............................ 162 E8
Downfield Rd. Ches EN8 .. 162 E8
Downfield Rd.
Hert H SG13 ................. 114 C5
Downfields. Wel G C AL8 . 110 B4
Downhall Ley. Bun SG9 ...... 40 E7
Downings Wood.
Map Cr WD3 ................ 172 D5
Downlands. Bal SG7 ........... 13 A1
Downlands. Luton LU3 ....... 44 C7
Downlands. Royst SG8 ......... 7 C6
Downlands. Stev SG2 ......... 51 D7
Downlands. Wa Aby EN9 . 163 E5
Downs Rd. Luton LU1 ........ 63 C7
Downs The. Hat AL10 ....... 130 A3
Downs View. Luton LU4 ..... 44 D4
Downsfield. Hat AL10 ...... 130 B2
Downside. Heml H HP2 .... 124 E4
Downside Inf Sch. Luton ... 44 E1
Downside Jun Sch. Luton .. 44 E1
Downsway Ct. Royst SG8 ..... 7 C6
Downton Ct. Luton LU3 ...... 63 D8 3
Downview. Dun LU4 ........... 44 B2
Dowry Wlk. Watf WD1 ...... 153 F1
Drakes Cl. Ches EN8 ........ 148 D3
Drakes Dr. Norwd HA6 .... 174 B2
Drakes Dr. St Alb AL1 ...... 128 C1
Drakes Dr. St Alb AL1 ...... 142 B8
Drakes Dr. Stev SG2 .......... 51 B7
Drakes Way. Hat AL10 ..... 130 B3
Drapers Mews. Luton LU3 . 45 C1
Drapers Way. Stev SG1 ..... 50 C7
Drayson Cl. Wa Aby EN9 .. 163 E7
Drayton Ave. Pot B EN6 ... 158 E7
Drayton Rd. Bor WD6 ...... 170 A5
Drayton Rd. Dun LU4 ......... 44 A3
Driftway. Reed SG8 ............ 16 E4
Driftway The. Heml H HP2 124 F3
Driftwood Ave. Chis AL2 .. 141 B5
Drive The. Barn EN5 ........ 171 E6
Drive The. Gofs O EN7 .... 147 B3
Drive The. Ham St EN8 .... 148 B3
Drive The. Harl CM20 ...... 117 E1
Drive The. Harp AL5 ........... 86 A1
Drive The. Hert SG14 ...... 113 C8
Drive The. Hod EN11 ....... 135 A8
Drive The. Kim AL4 ........... 87 B7
Drive The. Lon C AL2 ....... 142 A5
Drive The. Norwd HA6 ..... 174 E2
Drive The. Pot B EN6 ....... 158 F7
Drive The. Radl WD7 ....... 156 A5
Drive The. Ric WD3 ......... 165 C3
Drive The. Saw CM21 ......... 97 E2
Drive The. St Alb AL4 ...... 128 C1
Drive The. Watf WD1 ....... 153 E2
Drive The. Welw AL6 .......... 69 A1
Driver's End La. Cod SG4 ... 68 A4
Driveway The. Cuf EN6 .... 146 E3
Driveway The.
Heml H HP1 .................. 124 B1
Dromey Gdns. Har HA3 ... 176 F3
Drop La. Bri Wd AL2 ........ 155 C7
Drovers Way. Bis St CM23 76 C5
Drovers Way. Hat AL10 .... 130 B8
Drovers Way. St Alb AL3 . 127 D3
Drovewood Cl. Chor WD3 164 B4
Drummond Dr. Har HA7 ... 176 F3
Drummond Ride. Tri HP23 100 A5
Drummonds The. Dun LU4 . 44 C2
Drury La. Hun SG12 ........... 95 E1
Drycroft. Wel G C AL7 ...... 110 E2
Dryden Cres. Stev SG2 ....... 51 C8
Dryden Rd. Har HA3 ........ 176 F2
Drysdale Cl. Norwd HA6 .. 174 E3
Dubbs Knoll Rd. Gu M SG8 ... 1 F5
Dubrae Cl. St Alb AL3 ...... 127 A1
Duchess Cl. Bis St CM23 ... 76 C7
Duchy Rd. Had W EN4 ..... 159 D1
Duck La. Ben SG2 .............. 52 E4
Duck's Hill Rd.
Norwd HA6 ................... 174 B2
Ducketts La. Muc H SG10 .. 75 D1
Ducketts Mead. Roy CM19 116 B1
Ducketts Wood. Thun SG12 93 E7
Duckling La. Saw CM21 ..... 97 E2
Duckmore La. Tri HP23 ...... 99 E2
Dudley Ave. Ches EN8 ..... 162 D7
Dudley Hill Cl. Welw AL6 ... 89 E8
Dudley St. Luton LU2 .......... 63 E8
Dudswell La. Nthch HP4 .. 121 D7
Dugdale Ct. Hit SG5 ........... 21 C1
Dugdale Hill La. Pot B EN6 158 E7
Dugdales. Cro Gr WD3 .... 166 A5
Duke St. Hod EN11 .......... 135 A7
Duke St. Luton LU2 ........... 63 E8
Duke St. Watf WD1 .......... 167 C6
Duke's La. Hit SG5 ............ 34 F8
Dukes Ave. Whip LU6 ........ 81 E8
Dukes Ride. Bis St CM23 ... 76 C8
Dukes Way. Berk HP4 ...... 122 A6
Dulwich Way. Cro Gr WD3 166 A4
Dumbarton Ave. Ches EN8 162 D5
Dumfries Cl. Sth Ox WD1 . 175 A7
Dumfries St. Luton LU1 ...... 63 D6
Duncan Cl. Wel G C AL7 ... 110 E5
Duncan Way. Bus WD2 ..... 167 F7
Duncombe Cl. Hert SG14 . 113 C8
Duncombe Cl. Luton LU3 .... 45 C6
Duncombe Rd. Hert SG14 113 C8
Duncombe Rd. Nthch HP4 121 E6
Dundale Inf Sch. Tri ........ 100 A5
Dundale Jun Sch. Tri ........ 100 A5
Dundale Rd. Tri HP23 ...... 100 A4
Dunhams La. Letw SG6 ...... 23 C6
Dunkirks Mews.
Hert SG13 .................... 113 D4
Dunlin. Letw SG6 ............... 11 E1
Dunlin Rd. Heml H HP2 .... 124 E8
Dunmow Ct. Luton LU3 ...... 45 D2
Dunmow Rd. Bis St CM23 .. 77 C7
Dunmow Rd. Gt Ha CM22 .. 77 F7
Dunn Cl. Stev SG1 ............. 50 E3
Dunnock Cl. Bor WD6 ...... 170 A5
Dunny La. Chipf WD4 ...... 151 F7
Dunsby Rd. Luton LU3 ....... 45 A6
Dunsley Pl. Tri HP23 ....... 100 B3
Dunsmore Cl. Bus WD2 ... 168 D3
Dunsmore Rd. Luton LU1 ... 63 C6
Dunsmore Way. Bus WD2 168 D3
Dunstable Cl. Luton LU4 .... 45 A1
Dunstable Ct. Luton LU4 .... 44 F2
Dunstable Pl. Luton LU1 .... 63 D7
Dunstable Rd. Cad LU1 ...... 62 C3
Dunstable Rd. Dagn HP4 ... 81 C7
Dunstable Rd. Dun LU4 ...... 44 B2
Dunstable Rd. Luton LU4 ... 45 B1
Dunstable Rd. Red AL3 .... 106 A7
Dunstable Rd. Stu LU6 ....... 82 B6
Dunstable Rd. Whip LU6 .... 81 C7
Dunstable Rd. Whip LU6 .... 82 B6
Dunstable Road Jun &
Inf Sch. Luton ................ 63 C8
Dunster Cl. Barn EN5 ....... 171 D5
Dunster Cl. Hare UB9 ...... 173 B2
Dunster Rd. Heml H HP2 . 105 B1
Dunsters Mead.
Wel G C AL7 ................. 111 B4
Dunston Hill. Tri HP23 ..... 100 A4
Durban Rd E. Watf WD1 .. 167 A5
Durban Rd W. Watf WD1 . 167 A5
Durbar Rd. Luton LU4 ........ 45 B1
Durham Cl. Gt Am SG12 ... 115 B5
Durham Cl. Saw CM21 ....... 97 C1
Durham Rd. Bor WD6 ...... 170 D6
Durham Rd. Luton LU2 ....... 64 A7
Durham Rd. Stev SG1 ......... 37 A1
Durler Gdns. Luton LU1 ..... 63 D5
Durrant Ct. Har HA3 ........ 176 E2
Durrants Dr. Cro Gr WD3 166 C5
Durrants Hill Rd.
Heml H HP3 ................. 138 D8
Durrants La. Berk HP4 ..... 121 F5
Durrants Rd. Berk HP4 .... 121 F5
Dury Rd. Barn EN5 .......... 171 F7
Duxford Cl. Luton LU3 ........ 45 B7
Duxons Turn. Heml H HP2 125 B4
Dwight Rd. Mo Pk WD1 ... 166 D2
Dyes La. Lan SG1 ............... 49 F3
Dyke La. Whea AL4 .......... 108 E7
Dylan Cl. Elst WD6 .......... 169 D2
Dymoke Gn. St Alb AL4 ... 128 A7
Dymokes Way. Hod EN11 115 A1
Dyrham La. Pot B EN5 ..... 158 A3
Dyson Ct. Watf WD1 ........ 167 C5
Dysons Cl. Ches EN8 ....... 162 D6

Eagle Cl. Dun LU4 ............. 44 A4
Eagle Ct. Bal SG13 ............ 12 E1
Eagle Ct. Hert SG13 ......... 114 B7
Eagle Way. Hat AL10 ....... 130 A3
Ealing Cl. Bor WD6 .......... 170 D8
Earl St. Watf WD1 ........... 167 C6
Earls Cl. Bis St CM23 ........ 76 D6
Earls Hill Gdns. Royst SG8 ... 7 C6
Earls La. Ridge WD6 ........ 157 F6
Earls Meade. Luton LU2 ..... 45 D1
Earlsmead. Letw SG6 ......... 22 F3
Easington Rd.
Dan En SG12 .................. 71 E7
Easingwold Gdns.
Luton LU1 ...................... 62 F8
Easneye (Coll). Sta Ab ..... 115 C7
East Burrowfield.
Wel G C AL7 ................. 110 D4
East Cl. Chis AL2 ............. 141 B6
East Cl. Hit SG4 ................. 22 B1
East Cl. Stev SG1 .............. 50 F5
East Comm. Harp AL5 ...... 107 C7
East Comm. Red AL3 ....... 106 A4
East Dr. Coln H AL4 ......... 128 F4
East Dr. Lon C AL2 .......... 142 B5
East Dr. Mo Pk WD1 ....... 174 E8
East Dr. Saw CM21 ............ 97 E1
East Dr. Watf WD2 .......... 154 B3
East End Way. Pnr HA5 ... 175 F1
East Flint. Heml H HP1 .... 123 F4
East Gate. Harl CM20 ...... 117 D1
East Gn. Heml H HP3 ....... 139 A6
East Herts Coll of F Ed Annexe.
Ches ............................ 162 D8
East Herts Coll of F Ed.
Ches ............................ 148 F6
East Herts Hospl. Hert ..... 114 A7
East Hill. Luton LU3 ........... 45 B6
East La. Abb L WD5 ......... 140 A2
East La. Whea AL4 ............ 87 D1
East Lodge La. Had W EN2 160 E4
East Mead. Wel G C AL7 .. 111 B3
East Mimms. Heml H HP2 124 E4 4
East Mount. Whea AL4 ...... 87 D1
East Pk. Harl CM17 .......... 118 C3
East Pk. Saw CM21 ............ 97 E1
East Rd. Bis St CM23 ......... 77 B7
East Rd. Enf EN3 ............. 162 C1
East Rd. Harl CM20 ......... 118 B4
East Reach. Stev SG2 ......... 51 A2
East Ridgeway. Cuf EN6 .. 146 E3
East Riding. Tewin AL6 ...... 90 D5
East St. Heml H HP2 ........ 124 D3
East St. Lily LU2 ................ 32 D2
East St. Ware SG12 ........... 93 D1
East View. Barn EN5 ........ 171 F6
East View. Ess AL9 .......... 131 F6
East View. St Ipp SG4 ........ 35 C2
East Way. Wa Aby EN9 .... 163 D3
East Wlk. Harl CM20 ........ 117 D1
Eastbourne Ave. Stev SG1 . 50 A6
Eastbrook Inf Sch. Heml H 125 A8
Eastbrook Mix Inf Sch.
Heml H ........................ 125 A8
Eastbrook Rd.
Wa Aby EN9 ................ 163 E6
Eastbrook Way.
Heml H HP2 ................. 124 E3
Eastbury Ave. Mo Pk HA6 174 F5
Eastbury Cl. Mo Pk HA6 ... 174 E5
Eastbury Ct. St Alb AL1 .... 127 F4
Eastbury Farm Jun Mix &
Inf Sch. Mo Pk ............. 174 F6
Eastbury Pl. Mo Pk HA6 ... 174 F5
Eastbury Rd. Norwd HA6 . 174 E4
Eastbury Rd. Watf WD1 ... 167 C3
Eastcheap. Letw SG6 ......... 22 F6
Eastcote Dr. Harp AL5 ..... 107 D6
Eastcott Cl. Luton LU2 ........ 46 D1
Eastern Ave. Ches EN8 .... 162 F6
Eastern Ave. Henlw SG16 .. 10 C3
Eastern Way. Letw SG6 ...... 12 A1
Eastfield Ave. Watf WD2 . 167 D8
Eastfield Cl. Luton LU2 ....... 46 C4
Eastfield Ct. St Alb AL4 .... 128 D6
Eastfield Prim Sch. Enf .... 162 D1
Eastfield Rd. Ches EN8 ..... 162 F7
Eastfield Rd. Enf EN3 ...... 162 D1
Eastfield Rd. Royst SG8 ....... 7 E6
Eastgate. Stev SG1 ............ 50 D5
Eastglade. Mo Pk HA6 ...... 174 F5
Easthall House. Stev SG1 .. 36 C1
Eastham Cl. Barn EN5 ...... 171 F4
Eastholm Gn. Letw SG6 ..... 23 A8
Eastholm. Letw SG6 ........... 23 A8
Eastlea Ave. Watf WD2 ... 154 E2
Eastman Way.
Heml H HP2 ................. 125 A6
Eastmoor Ct. Harp AL5 .... 107 C6
Eastmoor Pk. Harp AL5 .... 107 C6
Eastnor. Bov HP3 ............ 137 A3
Easton Gdns. Bor WD6 ..... 170 E5
Eastor. Wel G C AL7 .......... 90 A1
Eastwick Cres. Ric WD3 .. 172 F8
Eastwick Hall La.
East CM20 .................... 117 A5
Eastwick Rd. East CM20 .. 117 B4
Eastwick Rd. East CM20 .. 117 C4
Eastwick Rd. East CM20 .. 117 E6
Eastwick Row.
Heml H HP2 ................. 125 A2
Eastwood Ct. Heml H HP2 125 A4
Eaton Gate. Norwd HA6 ... 174 C4
Eaton Green Ct. Luton LU2 64 C8
Eaton Green Rd. Luton LU2 64 C8
Eaton Pl. Luton LU2 ........... 46 D1
Eaton Rd. Heml H HP2 ..... 125 B6
Eaton Rd. St Alb AL1 ........ 128 B3
Eaton Valley Rd. Luton LU2 64 B8
Ebberns Rd. Heml H HP3 . 138 E8
Ebenezer St. Luton LU1 ...... 63 D6
Ebury App. Ric WD3 ........ 165 D1
Ebury Cl. Norwd HA6 ...... 174 C5
Ebury Rd. Ric WD3 .......... 165 D1
Ebury Rd. Watf WD1 ........ 167 C6
Echo Hill. Royst SG8 ............ 7 C5
Eddy St. Berk HP4 ............ 122 A5
Edenhall Cl. Heml H HP2 .. 125 D2
Edens Cl. Bis St CM23 ....... 77 B7
Edens Mount. Saw CM21 ... 97 F4
Edgars Ct. Wel G C AL7 ... 110 E5
Edgbaston Dr. Shen WD7 156 E7
Edgcott Cl. Luton LU3 ......... 31 B1
Edgecote Cl. Cad LU1 ......... 62 E3
Edgehill Gdns. Luton LU3 ... 44 C8
Edgewood Dr. Luton LU2 ... 46 C6
Edgeworth Cl. Stev SG2 ..... 51 C1
Edgware Way. Stan HA8 .. 169 D1
Edgwarebury La.
Stan WD6,HA8 ............. 169 F1
Edinburgh Ave. Ric WD3 .. 165 A2
Edinburgh Cres. Ches EN8 162 E6
Edinburgh Pl. Harl CM20 . 118 A4
Edinburgh Way.
Harl CM20 .................... 117 E3
Edison Rd. Stev SG2 ........... 51 B6
Edkins Cl. Luton LU2 .......... 45 E5
Edlyn Cl. Berk HP4 ........... 121 F5
Edmonds Dr. Ast SG2 ......... 51 D4
Edmund Beaufort Dr.
St Alb AL3 .................... 127 E5
Edmunds Rd. Hert SG14 .. 112 F7
Edna Daniels Sch The.
St Alb .......................... 128 C1
Edridge Cl. Bus WD2 ........ 168 C4
Edulf Rd. Bor WD6 ........... 170 B8
Edward Amey Cl.
Watf WD2 .................... 154 C3
Edward Cl. Abb L WD5 ..... 153 F7
Edward Cl. St Alb AL1 ...... 127 F2
Edward Ct. Heml H HP3 ... 138 D7
Edward Ct. Wa Aby EN9 .. 163 F6
Edward St. Luton LU2 ........ 45 F1
Edwards House. Stev SG1 . 50 E6 5
Edwick Ct. Ches EN8 ........ 148 D2
Edwin Ware Ct. Pnr HA5 .. 175 C1 2
Edwinstree Sch. Bun .......... 40 D8
Edwyn Cl. Barn EN5 ......... 171 D3
Egdon Dr. Luton LU2 .......... 45 D6
Egerton Rd. Berk HP4 ...... 122 B6
Egerton-Rothesay Sch.
Berk ............................ 121 E4
Eight Acres. Tri HP23 ...... 100 A4
Eighth Ave. Luton LU3 ........ 44 D7
Eisenberg Cl. Bal SG7 ........ 13 B1
Elaine Gdns. Cad LU1 ......... 63 A1
Elbow La. Hert H SG13 ..... 134 B7
Elbow La. Stev SG2 ............ 51 B1
Eldefield. Letw SG6 ............ 22 D7
Elder Ct. Bus WD2 ........... 176 E8
Elder Rd. Ware SG12 ......... 93 F3
Elder Way. Stev SG1 .......... 50 E3
Elderbeck Cl. Ches EN7 .... 148 A2
Elderberry Cl. Luton LU2 .... 46 B4
Elderberry Dr. Hit SG4 ....... 35 A4
Elderberry Way.
Watf WD2 .................... 154 B4
Elderfield. Harl CM17 ...... 118 D3
Eldon Ave. Bor WD6 ........ 170 B7
Eldon Rd. Dun LU4 ............. 44 C1
Eldon Rd. Lo Naz EN11 ..... 135 D4
Eleanor Ave. St Alb AL3 ... 127 D5
Eleanor Cross Rd.
Ches EN8 ..................... 162 F5
Eleanor Gdns. Barn EN5 .. 171 D4
Eleanor Rd. Ches EN8 ...... 162 E6
Eleanor Rd. Hert SG14 ..... 113 C7
Eleanor Way. Ches EN8 ... 162 F5
Elfrida Rd. Watf WD1 ...... 167 C4
Elgar Cl. Elst WD6 ........... 169 D2
Elgar Path. Luton LU2 ........ 63 E8 1
Elgin Dr. Norwd HA6 ....... 174 E3
Elgin House. Hit SG4 ......... 35 A6
Elgin Rd. Ches EN8 .......... 148 C1
Elgin Rd. Hod EN10 ......... 148 F8
Elgood Ave. Norwd HA6 ... 175 A3
Eliot Rd. Royst SG8 .............. 7 D8
Eliot Rd. Stev SG2 .............. 51 C6
Elizabeth Cl. Barn EN5 .... 171 D6
Elizabeth Cl. Lo Naz EN9 .. 149 D8
Elizabeth Cl. Wel G C AL7 111 C6
Elizabeth Ct. St Alb AL4 .... 128 D6
Elizabeth Ct. Watf WD1 .... 153 F1
Elizabeth Dr. Tri HP23 ..... 100 B6
Elizabeth House.
Wel G C AL7 ................. 111 C6
Elizabeth Rd. Bis St CM23 .. 76 E5
Elizabeth St. Luton LU1 ...... 63 D6
Elizabeth Way.
Harl CM19, CM20 ......... 117 B2
Ella Ct. Luton LU2 .............. 45 F1
Ellen Cl. Heml H HP2 ....... 124 F4
Ellenborough Cl.
Bis St CM23 .................... 76 D5
Ellenbrook Cres. Hat AL10 129 D5
Ellenbrook La. Hat AL10 .. 129 D4
Ellenhall Cl. Luton LU3 ....... 45 C1
Ellerdine Cl. Luton LU3 ....... 45 B4
Ellesborough Cl.
Sth Ox WD1 ................. 175 C5
Ellesfield. Welw AL6 .......... 89 B5
Ellesmere Gr. Barn EN5 ... 171 F4

Ellesmere Rd. Berk HP4 .. 122 D4
Ellice. Letw SG6 ... 23 B4
Ellingham Cl. Heml H HP2 125 A5
Ellingham Rd. Heml H HP2 ... 124 F4
Elliott Cl. Wel G C AL7 ... 110 D3
Ellis Ave. Stev SG1 ... 50 E8
Elliswick Rd. Harp AL5 ... 86 B2
Ellwood Gdns. Watf WD2 154 C5
Elm Ave. Cad LU1 ... 62 E3
Elm Ave. Watf WD1 ... 167 E2
Elm Cl. Wa Aby EN9 ... 163 D5
Elm Dr. Ches EN8 ... 148 E3
Elm Dr. Hat AL10 ... 130 A4
Elm Dr. St Alb AL4 ... 128 C3
Elm Gdns. Enf EN2 ... 161 D1
Elm Gdns. Wel G C AL8 ... 110 B6
Elm Gn. Heml H HP1 ... 123 E5
Elm Gr. Berk HP4 ... 122 C4
Elm Gr. Bis St CM23 ... 77 B7
Elm Gr. Watf WD2 ... 154 A2
Elm Hatch. Pnr HA5 ... 175 F3
Elm Park Rd. Pnr HA5 ... 175 D1
Elm Pk. Bal SG7 ... 23 F8
Elm Rd. Barn EN5 ... 171 F5
Elm Rd. Bis St CM23 ... 76 F8
Elm Terr. Har HA3 ... 176 D2
Elm Tree Wlk. Chor WD3 . 164 F5
Elm Tree Wlk. Tri HP23 ... 100 A5
Elm Way. Ric WD3 ... 165 B1
Elm Wlk. Radl WD7 ... 155 F3
Elm Wlk. Royst SG8 ... 7 F7
Elm Wlk. Stev SG2 ... 51 B3
Elmbank Ave. Barn EN5 ... 171 C5
Elmbridge. Harl CM17 ... 118 F3
Elmbrook Dr. Bis St CM23 . 76 E3
Elmcote Way. Cro Gr WD3 165 F3
Elmfield Cl. Pot B EN6 ... 158 E6
Elmfield Ct. Luton LU2 ... 46 A1
Elmfield Rd. Pot B EN6 ... 158 E6
Elmhurst Cl. Bis St CM23 ... 76 E7
Elmhurst. Hod EN10 ... 135 A4
Elmhurst Rd. Enf EN3 ... 162 C2
Elmoor Ave. Welw AL6 ... 89 B5
Elmoor Cl. Welw AL6 ... 89 B4
Elmore Rd. Enf EN3 ... 162 D1
Elmore Rd. Luton LU2 ... 46 A1
Elmroyd Ave. Pot B EN6 ... 158 F6
Elmroyd Cl. Pot B EN6 ... 158 F6
Elms Cl. L Wym SG4 ... 35 E3
Elms Rd. Har HA3 ... 176 E3
Elms Rd. Ware SG12 ... 94 A2
Elms The. Cod SG4 ... 67 F2
Elms The. Hert SG13 ... 114 A6
Elmscroft Gdns. Pot B EN6 ... 158 F7
Elmside. Ken Co LU6 ... 82 E8
Elmside Wlk. Hit SG5 ... 34 E7
Elmtree Ave. Gt Of LU2 ... 46 E3
Elmwood Ave. Bal SG7 ... 23 F7
Elmwood Ave. Bor WD6 ... 170 B5
Elmwood Cres. Luton LU2 .. 45 E3
Elmwood Ct. Bal SG7 ... 23 F8
Elmwood. Saw CM21 ... 97 F1
Elmwood. Wel G C AL8 ... 110 B5
Elsinge Rd. Enf EN1 ... 162 C3
Elstree Hill N. Elst WD6 ... 169 D4
Elstree Hill S. Elst WD6 ... 169 D2
Elstree Pk. Bor WD6 ... 170 D3
Elstree Rd. Bus WD2 ... 168 E2
Elstree Rd. Elst WD6 ... 169 A3
Elstree Rd. Heml H HP2 ... 105 A1
Elstree Sta. Bor ... 170 A5
Elstree Way. Bor WD6 ... 170 C7
Elstree Way. Bor WD6 ... 170 E6
Elton Ave. Barn EN5 ... 171 F4
Elton Ct. Hert SG14 ... 113 C7
Elton Rd. Hert SG14 ... 113 C7
Elton Way. Bus WD2 ... 168 B7
Elvaston Ct. Barn EN5 ... 171 C4
Elveden Cl. Luton LU2 ... 45 E6
Elvington Gdns. Luton LU3 . 31 B1
Ely Cl. Hat AL10 ... 129 F6
Ely Cl. Stev SG1 ... 37 B2
Ely Gdns. Bor WD6 ... 170 D4
Ely Rd. St Alb AL1 ... 128 B2
Ely Way. Luton LU4 ... 44 D4
Embleton Rd. Sth Ox WD1 175 A7
Emerald Ct. Bor WD6 ... 156 F1
Emerald Rd. Dun LU4 ... 44 A2
Emerton Ct. Nthch HP4 ... 121 E7
Emerton Garth. Nthch HP4 ... 121 E7
Emma Rothschild Ct. Tri HP23 ... 100 A5
Emma's Cres. Gt Am SG12 115 B4
Emmanuel Lodge. Ches EN8 ... 148 C1
Emmanuel Rd. Norwd HA6 ... 174 F3
Emmer Gn. Luton LU2 ... 46 F2
Emperor Cl. Nthch HP4 ... 121 F7
Emperors Gate. Stev SG2 .. 51 D8
Empire Ctr. Watf ... 167 C8
Empress Rd. Luton LU3 ... 44 E4
Endeavour Rd. Ches EN8 . 148 E4
Enderby Rd. Luton LU3 ... 45 C6
Enderley Cl. Har HA3 ... 176 E2
Enderley Rd. Har HA3 ... 176 E2
Endersby Rd. Barn EN5 ... 171 C4
Endymion Ct. Hat AL10 ... 130 C6
Endymion Rd. Hat AL10 ... 130 C6
Enfield Chase Lower Sch. Enf ... 161 E1
Enfield Lock Sta. Enf ... 162 E2
Englefield. Luton LU2 ... 45 F3
Englehurst. Harp AL5 ... 86 D1
Enid Cl. Bri Wd AL2 ... 154 F8
Enjakes Cl. Stev SG2 ... 69 B7
Ennerdale Cl. St Alb AL1 .. 128 B1
Ennis Cl. Harp AL5 ... 107 D6
Ennismore Cl. Letw SG6 ... 23 C3
Ennismore Gn. Luton LU2 .. 46 F1
Enslow Cl. Cad LU1 ... 62 E3
Enterprise Ctr. Luton ... 63 F8
Enterprise Ctr The. Stev ... 50 B8
Enterprise Way. Luton LU3 45 B8
Epping Gn. Heml H HP2 ... 125 B8
Epping House Sch. L Berk 132 C2
Epping Way. Luton LU3 ... 44 C8
Epsom Ct. Ric WD3 ... 165 B1
Ereswell Rd. Luton LU3 ... 45 A7
Erin Cl. Luton LU4 ... 45 A2
Erin Ct. Luton LU4 ... 45 A2
Ermine Cl. Ches EN7 ... 162 B8
Ermine Cl. Royst SG8 ... 7 D8
Ermine Cl. St Alb AL3 ... 127 A2
Ermine Ct. Bun SG9 ... 40 E8
Ermine Point Bsns Pk. Ware ... 93 B3
Ermine St. Thun SG12 ... 93 D7
Escarpment Ave. Whip LU6 81 D8
Escot Way. Barn EN5 ... 171 C4
Esdaile La. Hod EN11 ... 135 A5
Eskdale Ct. Heml H HP2 ... 124 E6
Eskdale. Lon C AL2 ... 142 F4
Eskdale. Luton LU4 ... 44 C5
Essendon Gdns. Wel G C AL7 ... 110 F6
Essendon Hill. Ess AL9 ... 131 E6
Essendon Jun Mix Inf Sch. Ess ... 131 F6
Essex Cl. Luton LU1 ... 63 F6
Essex Ct. Luton LU1 ... 63 E6
Essex La. Abb L WD4 ... 153 D6
Essex Mead. Heml H HP2 105 A1
Essex Rd. Bor WD6 ... 170 A6
Essex Rd. Hod EN11 ... 135 B7
Essex Rd. Hod EN11 ... 135 C6
Essex Rd. Stev SG1 ... 50 B8
Essex Rd. Watf WD1 ... 167 B7
Essex St. St Alb AL1 ... 127 E4
Estcourt Rd. Watf WD1 ... 167 C6
Ethelred Cl. Wel G C AL7 . 110 F5
Etna Rd. St Alb AL3 ... 127 D4
Etonbury Sch. Arl ... 11 C7
Europa Rd. Heml H HP2 ... 124 F6
Euston Ave. Watf WD1 ... 166 F4
Evan's Cl. Cro Gr WD3 ... 166 A4
Evans Ave. Watf WD2 ... 153 F4
Evans Gr. St Alb AL4 ... 128 C7
Evedon Cl. Luton LU3 ... 44 F6
Evelyn Dr. Pnr HA5 ... 175 D3
Evelyn Rd. Dun LU5 ... 44 A2
Everard Cl. St Alb AL1 ... 127 D1
Everest Cl. Arl SG15 ... 11 B5
Everest Way. Heml H HP2 125 A3
Everett Cl. Bus WD2 ... 168 E1
Everett Cl. Radl WD7 ... 156 A5
Evergreen Cl. Welw SG3 ... 69 A2
Evergreen Rd. Ware SG12 . 93 F3
Evergreen Way. Luton LU3 45 A8
Everlasting La. St Alb AL3 127 C5
Eversley Lodge. Hod EN11 135 A6
Evron Pl. Hert SG14 ... 113 D6
Exchange Rd. Stev SG1 ... 50 F5
Exchange Rd. Watf WD1 .. 167 B5
Executive Park Ind Est. St Alb ... 128 B3
Exeter Cl. Stev SG1 ... 37 B2
Exeter Cl. Watf WD1 ... 167 C7
Explorer Dr. Watf WD1 ... 166 F3
Exton Ave. Luton LU2 ... 46 A1
Eynsford Ct. Hit SG4 ... 34 F6
Eywood Rd. St Alb AL1 ... 127 C1
Faggots Cl. Radl WD7 ... 156 C4
Fair Cl. Bus WD2 ... 168 B2
Fair Oak Dr. Luton LU2 ... 45 F3
Fair View. Pot B EN6 ... 145 B2
Fairacre Ct. Norwd HA6 ... 174 E3
Fairacre. Heml H HP3 ... 138 F7
Fairacres Cl. Pot B EN6 ... 158 F6
Fairburn Cl. Bor WD6 ... 170 A8
Faircross Way. St Alb AL1 128 A5
Fairfax Ave. Luton LU3 ... 44 D7
Fairfax Rd. Hert SG13 ... 113 F7
Fairfield Ave. Sth Ox WD1 175 D7
Fairfield. Bun SG9 ... 40 F6
Fairfield Cl. Harp AL5 ... 86 D1
Fairfield Cl. Hat AL10 ... 130 C8
Fairfield Cl. Radl WD7 ... 155 E2
Fairfield Dr. Ches EN10 ... 148 F7
Fairfield Hospl. Stot ... 11 C3
Fairfield Prim Sch. Radl ... 155 E3
Fairfield Rd. Hod EN11 ... 135 A8
Fairfield Way. Hit SG4 ... 35 D8
Fairfield Wlk. Ches EN8 ... 148 E3
Fairfields Prim Sch. Ham St ... 148 A4
Fairfolds. Watf WD2 ... 154 E4
Fairford Ave. Luton LU2 ... 45 E4
Fairgreen Rd. Cad LU1 ... 62 F3
Fairhaven Cres. Sth Ox WD1 ... 175 A7
Fairhaven. Pk St AL2 ... 141 D4
Fairhill. Heml H HP3 ... 138 F7
Fairlands Inf Sch. Stev ... 50 D6
Fairlands Jun Sch. Stev ... 50 D6
Fairlands Way. Stev SG1 ... 51 A7
Fairlawns. Pnr WD1 ... 175 D1
Fairlawns. Watf WD1 ... 153 F1
Fairley Way. Ches EN7 ... 148 B3
Fairmead Ave. Harp AL5 ... 107 C8
Fairseat Cl. Bus WD2 ... 176 E8
Fairthorn Cl. Tri HP23 ... 99 E3
Fairview Dr. Watf WD1 ... 153 E3
Fairview Rd. Stev SG1 ... 50 B7
Fairway Ave. Bor WD6 ... 170 B7
Fairway. Bis St CM23 ... 77 C6
Fairway Cl. Chis AL2 ... 141 C4
Fairway Cl. Harp AL5 ... 107 A5
Fairway. Heml H HP3 ... 138 F7
Fairway House. Bor WD6 170 B6
Fairway. Saw CM21 ... 97 F2
3 Fairway The. Abb L WD5 . 153 D7
Fairway The. Mo Pk HA6 . 174 E6
Fairway. Ware SG12 ... 114 C8
Fairways. Ches EN8 ... 148 D5
Faithfield. Watf WD2 ... 167 E3
Falcon Cl. Hat AL10 ... 130 A3
Falcon Cl. Norwd HA6 ... 174 E3
Falcon Cl. Saw CM21 ... 97 C1
Falcon Cl. Stev SG2 ... 51 D2
4 Falcon Ct. Ware SG12 ... 93 C3
Falcon Ridge. Berk HP4 ... 122 C3
Falcon Way. Watf WD2 ... 154 E5
Falcon Way. Wel G C AL7 110 E8
Falconer Rd. Bus WD2 ... 168 A3
Falconer St. Bis St CM23 ... 76 C5
Falconers Field. Harp AL5 . 85 E3
Falconers Pk. Saw CM21 ... 97 D1
Falconers Rd. Luton LU2 ... 64 C1
Falkirk Gdns. Sth Ox WD1 175 D5
Falkland Rd. Barn EN5 ... 171 E7
Fallow Rise. Hert SG13 ... 113 F6
Fallowfield Cl. Hare UB9 .. 173 C2
Fallowfield. Luton LU3 ... 45 C4
Fallowfield. Stev SG2 ... 51 C3
Fallowfield. Wel G C AL7 ... 89 F1
Fallowfield Wlk. Heml H HP1 ... 124 A6
Fallows Gn. Harp AL5 ... 86 B3
Falstaff Gdns. St Alb AL1 . 141 C8
Falstone Gn. Luton LU2 ... 46 E1
Fanhams Hall Rd. Ware SG12 ... 93 F3
Fanhams Rd. Ware SG12 ... 93 E2
Fanshaw Ct. Hert SG14 ... 113 C7
Fanshawe Cres. Ware SG12 ... 93 C2
Fanshawe St. Hert SG14 .. 113 B7
Fanshaws La. Bric SG13 .. 133 C5
Fantail La. Tri HP23 ... 99 F4
Far End. Hat AL10 ... 130 B2
4 Faraday Cl. Watf WD1 ... 166 D3
Faraday Rd. Stev SG2 ... 51 B6
Faringdon Rd. Dun LU4 ... 44 C3
Faringford Cl. Pot B EN6 .. 159 D8
Farland Rd. Heml H HP2 .. 125 B3
Farley Ct. Luton LU1 ... 63 C5
Farley Farm Rd. Luton LU1 63 B5
Farley Hill. Luton LU1 ... 63 C5
Farley Jun Sch. Luton ... 63 C6
Farley Lodge. Luton LU1 ... 63 D5
Farm Ave. Harp AL5 ... 85 D4
Farm Cl. Barn EN5 ... 171 C4
Farm Cl. Bor WD6 ... 156 E1
Farm Cl. Ches EN8 ... 148 C1
Farm Cl. Cuf EN6 ... 146 E4
Farm Cl. Hert SG14 ... 113 A6
Farm Cl. Letw SG6 ... 12 A1
Farm Cl. Roy CM19 ... 116 B1
Farm Cl. Stev SG1 ... 50 E4
Farm Cl. Wel G C AL8 ... 110 C6
Farm Gn. Luton LU1 ... 63 C5
Farm Hill Rd. Wa Aby EN9 163 D6
Farm La. Ric WD3 ... 165 C6
Farm La. Stand SG11 ... 73 A8
Farm Pl. Berk HP4 ... 121 F5
Farm Rd. L Chal WD3 ... 164 A5
Farm Rd. Norwd HA6 ... 174 C5
Farm Rd. Nwml E LU1 ... 85 B7
Farm Rd. St Alb AL1 ... 128 B4
Farm Way. Bus WD2 ... 168 B5
Farm Way. Mo Pk HA6 ... 174 F6
Farmbrook. Luton LU2 ... 45 D7
Farmers Cl. Watf WD2 ... 154 B6
Farmhouse Cl. Ches EN10 148 F6
Farmhouse La. Heml H HP2 ... 125 A5
Farmstead Rd. Har HA3 ... 176 D1
Farnham C of E Prim Sch. Far ... 58 D6
Farnham Cl. Bov HP3 ... 137 A3
Farnham Cl. Saw CM21 ... 97 C1
Farnham Rd. Bis St CM23 ... 58 F3
Farquhar St. Hert SG14 ... 113 C7
Farr's La. Nwml E LU2 ... 65 A1
Farraline Rd. Watf WD1 .. 167 B5
Farrant Way. Bor WD6 ... 169 E8
Farrer Top. Mark AL3 ... 83 E5
Farriday Cl. St Alb AL3 ... 127 E7
Farriers Cl. Bal SG7 ... 12 E1
Farriers Cl. Cod SG4 ... 67 F1
Farriers End. Ches EN10 . 148 F5
Farriers. Gt Am SG12 ... 115 A6
Farriers Way. Bor WD6 ... 170 D4
Farringford Cl. Chis AL2 ... 141 B5
Farrow Cl. Luton LU3 ... 31 C1
Farthing Dr. Letw SG6 ... 23 C3
Farthings The. Heml H HP1 ... 124 B3
Faulkner Ct. St Alb AL1 ... 127 E5
Faverolle Gn. Ches EN8 ... 148 D3
Faversham Cl. Tri HP23 ... 100 A4
Fawbert & Barnard's Jun Mix & Inf Sch. Harl ... 118 C3
Fawbert & Bernard Inf Sch The. Saw ... 97 E2
Fawcett Rd. Stev SG2 ... 51 B7
Fawkon Wlk. Hod EN11 ... 135 A6
Fawn Ct. Hat AL9 ... 130 C7
Fay Gn. Abb L WD5 ... 153 D6
Fayerfield. Pot B EN6 ... 159 D8
2 Fayland Cotts. Gt Ho SG9 .. 41 E7
Feacey Down. Heml H HP1 ... 124 B5
Fearney Mead. Ric WD3 .. 165 A1
Fearnhill Sch. Letw ... 22 C5
Fearnley Rd. Wel G C AL8 110 C5
Fearnley St. Watf WD1 ... 167 B5
Feather Dell. Hat AL10 ... 130 A5
Featherbed La. Heml H HP3 ... 138 B7
Featherston Rd. Stev SG2 .. 51 C3
Featherstone Gdns. Bor WD6 ... 170 C5
Federal Way. Watf WD2 .. 167 C8
Felbrigg Cl. Luton LU2 ... 46 F2
Felden Cl. Watf WD2 ... 154 D5
Felden Dr. Heml H HP3 ... 138 A7
Felden La. Heml H HP3 ... 138 A7
Feldon Cl. Pnr HA5 ... 175 E3
Felix Ave. Luton LU2 ... 46 A2
Fellowes La. Col H AL4 ... 143 E8
Fellowes Way. Stev SG2 ... 51 A2
Fells Cl. Hit SG5 ... 34 F8
Felmersham Ct. Luton LU1 63 B7
Felmersham Rd. Luton LU1 63 A7
Felmongers. Harl CM20 ... 118 B2
Felstead Cl. Luton LU2 ... 45 F3
Felstead Rd. Ches EN8 ... 162 E7
Felstead Way. Luton LU2 ... 45 F3
Felton Cl. Bor WD6 ... 156 E1
Felton Cl. Ches EN10 ... 148 F6
Felton Cl. Luton LU2 ... 46 D1
Fen End. Stot SG5 ... 11 F8
Fennycroft Rd. Heml H HP1 ... 124 A6
Fensom's Alley. Heml H HP2 ... 124 D4
Fensom's Cl. Heml H HP2 124 D4
Fenwick Cl. Luton LU3 ... 45 B5
Fermor Cres. Luton LU2 ... 46 C1
Fern Cl. Hod EN10 ... 148 F8
Fern Dells. Hat AL10 ... 129 F4
Fern Dr. Heml H HP3 ... 124 E2
Fern Gr. Wel G C AL8 ... 89 D2
Fern Way. Watf WD2 ... 154 B4
Ferndale. Muc H SG10 ... 74 F2
Ferndale Rd. Enf EN3 ... 162 E2
Ferndale Rd. Luton LU1 ... 63 B7
Ferndene. Bri Wd AL2 ... 154 F8
Ferndown Cl. Pnr HA5 ... 175 E3
Ferndown. Pnr HA6 ... 175 A1
Ferndown Rd. Sth Ox WD1 ... 175 C6
Fernecroft. St Alb AL1 ... 141 D8
Fernheath. Luton LU3 ... 31 A1
Fernhills. Abb L WD4 ... 153 D6
Fernleigh Ct. Har HA2 ... 176 B1
Fernleys. St Alb AL4 ... 128 C5
Ferns Cl. Enf EN3 ... 162 E3
Fernville La. Heml H HP2 . 124 D3
Ferny Hill. Had W EN4 ... 159 F1
Ferrars Cl. Dun LU4 ... 44 B1
Ferrars Inf Sch. Dun ... 44 B3
Ferrars Jun Sch. Dun ... 44 B3
Ferrers La. Whea ... 108 B5
Ferrier Rd. Stev SG2 ... 51 C6
Ferryhills Cl. Sth Ox WD1 175 C7
Feryngs Cl. Harl CM17 ... 118 D4
Fesants Croft. Harl CM20 118 B3
Fetherstone Cl. Pot B EN6 159 D7
Fiddle Bridge La. Hat AL10 ... 129 F6
Fiddlebridge Ind Ctr. Hat . 129 F6
Fidler Pl. Bus WD2 ... 168 B3
Field Cl. Harp AL5 ... 107 D7
Field Cl. St Alb AL4 ... 128 A7
Field Cres. Royst SG8 ... 7 F7
Field End Cl. Luton LU2 ... 46 C4
Field End Cl. Watf WD1 ... 167 E2
Field End Cl. Wigg HP23 ... 100 D1
Field Fare Gn. Dun LU4 ... 44 A5
Field House Ct. Harp AL5 ... 86 A2
Field Inf Sch. Watf ... 167 C4
Field La. Letw SG6 ... 22 F4
Field Rd. Heml H HP2 ... 125 A3
Field Rd. Watf WD1 ... 167 E3
Field View. Barn EN5 ... 171 B5
Field View Rd. Pot B EN6 . 159 A6
Field View Rise. Bri Wd AL2 ... 140 E2
Field Way. Bov HP3 ... 137 A4
Field Way. Hod EN11 ... 115 C2
Field Way. Ric WD3 ... 165 B1
Field's Ct. Pot B EN6 ... 159 D6
Fielder Ctr (Univ of Herts). Hat ... 129 D8
Fieldfare. Letw SG6 ... 11 E1
Fieldfare. Stev SG2 ... 51 D3
Fieldfares. Lon C AL2 ... 142 D4
Fieldgate House. Stev SG1 50 F5
Fieldgate Rd. Luton LU4 ... 44 D2
Fieldings Rd. Ches EN8 ... 148 F3
Fields End La. Heml H HP1 ... 123 E5
Fields End. Tri HP23 ... 100 A6
Fieldway. Berk HP4 ... 122 E2
Fieldway. Gt Am SG12 ... 115 B4
Fieldway. Wigg HP23 ... 100 D1
Fifth Ave. Letw SG6 ... 23 C6
Fifth Ave. Watf WD2 ... 154 D4
Fifth Ave.Harl CM20 ... 117 D2
Figtree Hill. Heml H HP2 .. 124 D4
Filey Cl. Stev SG1 ... 50 A7
Filmer Rd. Luton LU4 ... 44 E4
Finch Cl. Dun LU4 ... 44 A4
Finch Cl. Hat AL10 ... 130 A3
Finch La. Bus WD2 ... 168 A5
Finch Rd. Berk HP4 ... 122 A4
Finchdale. Heml H HP1 ... 124 A3
Finche's End. Walk SG2 ... 52 B8
Finches The. Hert SG13 ... 114 B6
Finches The. Hit SG4 ... 35 A7
Finley Rd. Harp AL5 ... 86 D3
Finsbury Ct. Ches EN8 ... 162 E5
Finsbury Rd. Luton LU4 ... 44 D5
Finucane Rise. Bus WD2 .. 176 C8
Finway Ct. Watf WD1 ... 166 F4
Finway. Luton LU1 ... 63 A8
Finway Rd. Heml H HP2 ... 125 B7
Fir Cl. Stev SG2 ... 50 F1
Fir Tree Cl. Heml H HP3 ... 125 B2
Fir Tree Ct. Bor WD6 ... 169 F5
Fir Tree Hill. Sar WD3 ... 153 A2
Firbank Dr. Watf WD1 ... 167 E2
Firbank Rd. St Alb AL3 ... 127 F7
Firbank Trad Est. Luton ... 63 A8
Fire Station Alley. Barn EN5 ... 171 E7
Firecrest. Letw SG6 ... 11 E1
Firlands. Bis St CM23 ... 76 E6
Firlands House. Bis St CM23 ... 76 E6
Firs Cl. Hat AL10 ... 130 B4
Firs Cl. Hit SG5 ... 34 D8
Firs Dr. Kim AL4 ... 87 C5
Firs Jun Sch The. Bis St ... 76 E6
Firs La. Pot B EN6 ... 159 B6

Firs The. Ham St EN7 ....... 147 E4
Firs The. Harp AL5 ............. 86 D2
Firs The. St Alb AL1 ......... 142 B7
Firs The. Wel G C AL8 ........ 89 C2
Firs The. Wigg HP23 ........ 100 D1
Firs Wlk. Norwd HA6 ....... 174 D4
Firs Wlk. Tewin AL6 ........... 90 E5
Firs Wood Cl. Nort EN6 .... 159 F7
First Ave. Watf WD2 ........ 154 D4
First Ave. Harl CM20 ........ 117 E2
Firway Cl. Welw AL6 .......... 89 F7
Firway. Welw AL6 ............... 89 F7
Firwood Ave. Coln H AL4 . 128 E3
Fish Farm St. Red AL3 ..... 106 B5
Fish Hill. Royst SG8 ............. 7 D6
Fish St. Red AL3 ............... 106 B5
Fisher Cl. Kin L WD4 ........ 139 A2
Fisher Rd. Har HA3 .......... 176 F1
Fisher's Green Rd.
Stev SG1 ........................ 50 B8
Fisher's Ind Est. Watf ...... 167 C4
Fishers Cl. Ches EN8 ....... 163 A5
Fishers Cl. Stand SG11 ...... 55 D3
Fishers Gn. Stev SG1 ......... 36 A1
Fishers Mead. Stand SG11 55 D3
Fishery Cotts.
Heml H HP1 .................. 124 A1
Fishery Rd. Heml H HP1 .. 124 A1
Fishponds Rd. Hit SG5 ...... 34 E8
Fishpool St. St Alb AL3 ...... 127 C3
Fitzjohn Ave. Barn EN5 .... 171 F5
Fitzroy Ave. Luton LU3 ....... 45 B3
Fitzwarin Cl. Luton LU3 ...... 44 E8
Fitzwilliam Ct. Harl CM17 118 E4
Five Acres Ave.
Bri Wd AL2 .................... 140 F2
Five Acres. Kin L WD4 ..... 138 F2
Five Acres. Lon C AL2 ....... 142 D6
Five Acres. Sta M CM24 ..... 59 E8
Five Oaks. Cad LU1 ............ 62 F4
Five Oaks. Hat AL10 ......... 130 B2
Five Oaks Sch. Cad ............ 62 F3
Five Oaks Sch. Hat ............ 130 A3
Five Springs Ct. Luton LU3 . 44 E6
Five Springs. Luton LU3 ..... 44 E6
Five Springs Sch. Luton ..... 44 F7
Flags The. Heml H HP2 .... 125 B3
Flagstaff Rd. Wa Aby EN9 163 B6
Flamstead End Inf Sch.
Ham St ......................... 148 A4
Flamstead End Jun Sch.
Ham St ......................... 148 A4
Flamstead End Rd.
Ches EN8 ...................... 148 B3
Flamstead Jun Mix Inf Sch.
Fla .................................. 84 B1
Flamsteadbury La.
Red AL3 ........................ 106 A4
Flash La. Cre H EN2 ........ 161 C3
Flatfield Rd. Heml H HP3 . 125 A1
Flaunden Bottom.
Flau HP5 ...................... 150 E4
Flaunden Bottom. Lat HP5 150 E4
Flaunden Hill. Flau HP3 ..... 151 A6
Flaunden La. Bov HP3 ...... 137 D3
Flavian Cl. St Alb AL3 ...... 126 F1
Flax Mews. Mark AL3 ........ 83 E5
Flecker Cl. Stan HA7 ........ 176 F5
Fleet The. Royst SG8 ........... 7 C6
Fleetville Inf Sch. St Alb ... 128 B3
Fleetville Jun Mix Sch.
St Alb ........................... 128 A3
Fleetwood Cres. Stev SG1 . 50 B7
Fleetwood. Letw SG6 ......... 23 B4
Fleetwood Way.
Sth Ox WD1 ................. 175 C6
Fleming Cl. Ham St EN7 ... 148 A5
Fleming Cres. Hert SG14 . 113 A6
Fletcher Way.
Heml H HP2 ................. 124 D6
Flete House. Watf WD1 ... 166 E3
Flexley Wood.
Wel G C AL7 .................... 90 A1
Flinders Cl. St Alb AL1 ..... 128 A1
Flinders Cl. Stev SG2 ......... 51 D5
Flint Cl. Luton LU3 ............. 44 E7
Flint Copse. Red AL3 ........ 106 C6
Flint Rd. Letw SG6 ............. 23 C8
Flint Way. St Alb AL3 ....... 127 C7
Flora Gr. St Alb AL1 ......... 127 F2
Floral Dr. Lon C AL2 ......... 142 D5
Florence Ave. Luton LU3 .... 44 D6
Florence Cl. Watf WD2 ..... 154 A4
Florence St. Hit SG5 .......... 34 F8
Florence Wlk. Bis St CM23 76 F8
Flowers Ind Est. Luton ....... 63 E6 6
Flowers Way. Luton LU1 .... 63 E7
Flowton Gr. Harp AL5 ...... 107 A7
Fold Croft. Harl CM20 ...... 117 A1
Foldingshott. Dat SG3 ........ 69 D3
Follett Dr. Abb L WD5 ....... 153 F8
Folly Ave. St Alb AL3 ........ 127 D4
Folly Cl. Hit SG4 ............... 35 A5
Folly Cl. Radl WD7 ........... 155 F3
Folly Fields. Whea AL4 ...... 87 B2
Folly La. Cad LU1 ............... 62 E4
Folly La. St Alb AL3 .......... 127 C4
Folly Pathway. Radl WD7 155 F3
Folly The. Bun SG9 ............. 40 D7
Folly The. Hert SG14 ........ 113 D6
Folly View. Gt Am SG12 .... 115 B4
Fontmell Cl. St Alb AL3 .... 127 E5
Fontwell Cl. Har HA3 ....... 176 E3
Football Cl. Bal SG7 .......... 12 E1
Forbes Ave. Pot B EN6 ..... 159 D7
Ford Cl. Bus WD2 ............. 168 C5
Ford Hill. L Had SG11 ......... 75 B8
Ford St. Brag SG11 ............ 55 E6
Fordham Cl. Ashw SG7 ........ 4 D4
Fordham Rd. Royst SG8 ....... 7 E5
Fordwich Cl. Hert SG14 ... 113 A6
Fordwich Hill. Hert SG14 . 113 A6
Fordwich Rd. Wel G C AL8 110 C5
Fordwich Rise. Hert SG14 113 A6
Fore St. Harl CM17 ........... 118 C4
Fore St. Hat AL9 .............. 130 C6
Fore St. Hert SG14 ........... 113 D6
Fore St. Wes SG4 .............. 24 B1
Forebury Ave. Saw CM21 .. 97 F2
Forebury Cres. Saw CM21 . 97 F2
Forebury The. Saw CM21 .. 97 F2
Forefield. Chis AL2 ........... 141 A4
Forelands Pl. Saw CM21 .... 97 E2
Forest Ave. Heml H HP3 .. 124 D1 5
Forest Rd. Ches EN8 ........ 148 D2
Forest Rd. Enf EN3 .......... 162 E3
Forest Rd. Watf WD2 ....... 154 B6
Forest Row. Stev SG2 ........ 50 F1
Forest Wlk. Bus WD2 ....... 167 F8
Foresters Cl. Ham St EN7 147 E4
Foresthall Rd. Sta M CM24 59 E4
Forge Cl. Chipf WD4 ........ 152 A8
Forge Cl. Hit SG5 .............. 34 F8 5
Forge Cotts. Ess AL9 ........ 131 E6
Forge End. Chis AL2 ......... 141 A5
Forge La. Norwd HA6 ....... 174 E3
Forge La. Welw AL6 .......... 89 C5
Forres Cl. Hod EN11 ........ 135 A8
Forres Jun Mix & Inf Sch.
Hod .............................. 115 B1
Forrest Cres. Luton LU2 .... 46 A3
Forresters Dr. Wel G C AL7111 C5
Fortnums Acre. Har HA7 . 176 F4
Fortuna Cl. Stev SG1 .......... 51 C8
Fortune La. Elst WD6 ....... 169 D3
Forty Hill C of E Sch. Enf .. 162 A2
Forty Hill. Enf EN2 ........... 161 F1
Fosman Cl. Hit SG5 ........... 34 D8 7
Foster Cl. Stev SG1 ............ 36 D1
Foster Dr. Hit SG4 ............. 35 A5
Foster Rd. Heml H HP1 .... 124 B1
Foston Cl. Luton LU3 ......... 44 F6
Fotherley Rd. Ric WD3 ..... 172 F8
Foulds Jun Mix Inf Sch.
Barn ............................. 171 D6
Founceley Ave.
Dan En SG12 .................. 71 F8
Fountain Pl. Wa Aby EN9 . 163 C5
Fountains Rd. Luton LU3 .... 45 D3
Four Acres. Stev SG1 ......... 50 D7
Four Acres. Wel G C AL7 . 110 F4
Four Acres The.
Sheer CM21 .................... 98 A2
Four Limes. Whea AL4 ..... 108 D8
Four Swannes Jun Mix
Inf Sch. Ches ................ 162 E6
Four Tubs The. Bus WD2 . 168 D2
Fouracres. Letw SG6 ......... 23 A3
Fouracres Dr.
Heml H HP3 .................. 124 F1
Fouracres Wlk.
Heml H HP3 .................. 124 F1
Fourth Ave. Harl CM20 .... 117 C1
Fourth Ave. Letw SG6 ........ 23 C7
Fourth Ave. Luton LU3 ....... 44 D7
Fourth Ave. Watf WD2 ..... 154 D4
Fourways Market.
Wel G AL9 ..................... 144 C7
Fovant Cl. Harp AL5 ........ 107 C6
Fovant. Stev SG1 ............... 36 B1
Fowley Cl. Ches EN8 ........ 162 F5
Fowlmere Rd. Gt Ch SG8 ..... 9 F8
Fox Cl. Bus WD2 .............. 168 B5
Fox Cl. Elst WD6 .............. 169 D3
Fox Cl. Wigg HP23 .......... 100 D1
Fox Cnr. Gu M SG8 .............. 1 F5
Fox La. Ther SG8 ............... 15 F7
Fox Rd. Stev SG1 .............. 50 E4
Fox Rd. Wigg HP23 .......... 100 C2
Fox's La. Bro Pk AL9 ........ 144 F7
Foxbury Cl. Luton LU2 ........ 45 D6
Foxcroft. St Alb AL1 ......... 128 A1
Foxdell Inf Sch. Luton ........ 63 A8
Foxdell Jun Sch. Luton ....... 62 E8
Foxdell. Norwd HA6 ......... 174 D4
Foxdells. Hertng SG14 ...... 112 C3
Foxdells La. Bis St CM23 ... 58 F2
Foxes Cl. Hert SG13 ......... 114 B6
Foxes Dr. Ches EN7 ......... 148 A2
Foxfield Cl. Norwd HA6 .... 174 F4
Foxfield. Stev SG2 ............. 51 C3
Foxglove Bank. Royst SG8 ... 7 F5
Foxglove Cl. Bis St CM23 ... 76 C6
Foxglove Cl. Hat AL10 ...... 130 B4
Foxglove Way. Welw AL6 .. 89 E8
Foxgloves The.
Heml H HP1 .................. 123 E2
Foxgrove Path.
Sth Ox WD1 .................. 175 D5
Foxhill. Gu M SG8 ................ 1 F5
Foxhill. Luton LU2 ............. 45 E5
Foxhill Rd. Gu M SG8 .......... 1 F5
Foxhill. Watf WD2 ............ 154 A3
Foxholes Ave. Hert SG13 . 113 F6
Foxhollows. Hat AL10 ....... 130 B7
Foxlands Cl. Watf WD2 .... 154 A5
Foxley Dr. Bis St CM23 ...... 77 B8
Foxley Gr. Welw AL6 .......... 89 F4
Foxleys. Sth Ox WD1 ....... 175 E7
Foxton Rd. Hod EN11 ...... 135 A6
Foxtree House. Watf WD2 154 E3
Frampton Rd. Pot B EN6 .. 145 C1
Frampton St. Hert SG14 .. 113 D6
Francis Ave. St Alb AL3 .... 127 D6
Francis Bacon Sch. St Alb 142 B8
Francis Cl. Hit SG4 ............ 35 A5
Francis Cl. Stot SG5 ........... 11 E6
Francis Combe Sch. Watf 154 C7
Francis Rd. Hin SG7 ............. 3 C6
Francis Rd. Ware SG12 ..... 93 D2
Francis Rd. Watf WD1 ...... 167 B5
Francis St. Luton LU1 ......... 63 D8
Frank Martin Ct.
Ches EN7 ..................... 148 B1
Frankland Cl. Cro Gr WD3 166 A2
Frankland Rd. Cro Gr WD3 166 B3
Franklin Ave. Ches EN7 .... 148 B1
Franklin Cl. Coln H AL4 ... 129 E1
Franklin Cl. Heml H HP3 .. 138 E8
Franklin Cl. Pirt SG5 .......... 20 D4
Franklin Gdns. Hit SG4 ....... 22 B1
Franklin Rd. Watf WD1 ..... 167 B7
Franklin's Rd. Stev SG1 ..... 50 C8
Franks Cl. Henlw SG16 ...... 10 B5
Franshams Dr. Bus WD2 . 176 D8
Fraser Rd. Ches EN8 ........ 148 E3
Fred Millard Ct. Stev SG1 .. 50 E5
Frederick St. Luton LU2 ..... 45 E1
Frederick St Pas.
Luton LU2 ...................... 45 E1
Freeman Ave. Luton LU3 .... 45 B8
Freemans Cl. Hit SG5 ......... 21 D1
Freewaters Cl. Ick SG5 ...... 21 E4
Freman Dr. Bun SG9 .......... 40 D8
French Horn La. Hat AL10 130 B6
French Row. St Alb AL3 ... 127 D3 4
French's Cl. Gt Am SG12 .. 115 B4
Frensham Dr. Hit SG4 ........ 22 C2
Frensham. Ham St EN7 .... 148 A4
Freshwater Cl. Luton LU3 .. 44 F7
Freshwaters. Harl CM20 . 117 E1
Fretherne Rd.
Wel G C AL8 ................. 110 D6
Friars Cl. Luton LU1 ........... 63 B5
Friars Field. Nthch HP4 .... 121 E7
Friars Rd. Brag SG11 ......... 56 A7
Friars Rd. Wes SG4 ........... 24 B1
Friars Way. Bus WD2 ....... 167 F8
Friars Way. Kin L WD4 .... 139 A1
Friars Way. Luton LU1 ....... 63 B5
Friars Wlk. Tri HP23 ........ 100 A4
Friars Wood. Bis St CM23 . 77 C8
Friarscroft. Hod EN10 ...... 135 A3
Friday Furlong. Hit SG5 ..... 34 C8
Friedberg Ave.
Bis St CM23 ................... 76 D4
Friendless La. Fla AL3 ....... 83 E3
Friends Ave. Ches EN8 .... 162 D7
Friesian Cl. Dun LU4 ......... 44 A3
Frimley Rd. Heml H HP1 .. 123 E4
Fringewood Cl.
Norwd HA6 ................... 174 B2
Frinton Cl. Sth Ox WD1 .... 175 B8
Friston Gn. Luton LU2 ....... 46 D1
Frithsden Copse.
Pot En HP4 .................. 122 F8
Frithwood Ave.
Norwd HA6 ................... 174 F4
Frithwood Prim Sch.
Norwd ......................... 174 F4
Frobisher Dr. Stev SG2 ...... 51 B7
Frobisher Rd. St Alb AL1 .. 128 C1
Frobisher Way. Hat AL10 129 D8
Froghall La. Walk SG2 ....... 38 B1
Frogmoor Ct. Ric WD3 ..... 173 D8
Frogmoor La. Ric WD3 ..... 173 D8
Frogmore Hill. Ast SG14 .... 70 B7
Frogmore House. Stev SG1 36 C1
Frogmore. Pk St AL2 ........ 141 E4
Frogmore Rd.
Heml H HP3 .................. 138 D8
Frogmore St. Tri HP23 ..... 100 A3
Frogs Hall La.
Dan En SG11 ................... 53 F3
Frome Cl. Luton LU4 .......... 44 E4
Frome Sq. Heml H HP2 .... 125 A8
Front St. Cad LU1 .............. 63 C1
Front The. Pot En HP4 ..... 123 B7
Frowick Cl. Wel G AL9 ..... 144 B8
Frowyke Cres. Ridge EN6 158 A7
Fry Rd. Stev SG2 ................ 51 C5
Fryth Mead. St Alb AL3 .... 127 B4
Fulbeck Way. Har HA2 ..... 176 C1
Fulbourne Cl. Luton LU4 .... 44 E2
Fulford Gr. Sth Ox WD1 ... 175 B8
Fuller Ct. Bis St CM23 ........ 77 A7 1
Fuller Gdns. Watf WD2 .... 154 B2
Fuller Rd. Watf WD2 ........ 154 B2
Fuller Way. Cro Gr WD3 .. 166 A4
Fullers Ct. Letw SG6 .......... 22 E7
Fulling Mill La. Welw AL6 ... 89 B6
Fulmar Cres. Heml H HP1 124 A3
Fulmore Cl. Harp AL5 ......... 86 D4
Fulton Cl. Stev SG1 ............ 50 C5
Fulton Cres. Bis St CM23 ... 77 C8
Fulton Ct. Bor WD6 .......... 156 F1
Furham Field. Pnr HA5 .... 176 A3
Furlay Cl. Letw SG6 ............ 22 D7
Furlong Way.
Gt Am SG12 .................. 115 A7
Furlongs. Heml H HP1 ..... 124 A4
Furneux Pelham Jun Mix
Inf Sch. Fur P ................. 43 A4
Furrowfield. Hat AL10 ...... 130 B7
Furrows The. Luton LU3 .... 45 B7
Furse Ave. St Alb AL4 ...... 128 A7
Furtherfield. Abb L WD5 .. 153 E7
Furtherground.
Heml H HP2 .................. 124 E2 1
Furze Cl. Luton LU2 ........... 45 D7
Furze Cl. Sth Ox WD1 ....... 175 C5
Furze Gr. Royst SG8 ............. 7 E5
Furze Rd. Heml H HP1 ..... 123 E2
Furze View. Chor WD3 ..... 164 C4
Furzebushes La. Chis AL2 140 F6
Furzedown Ct. Harp AL5 .... 86 B1 10
Furzedown. Stev SG2 ......... 51 B4
Furzefield. Ches EN8 ........ 148 B3
Furzefield Ct. Pot B EN6 .. 158 E8
Furzefield Ctr The. Pot B . 158 D8
Furzefield Rd. Wel G C AL7110 E4
Furzehill Mid Sch. Bor ...... 170 A5
Furzehill Par. Bor WD6 .... 170 A6
Furzehill Rd. Bor WD6 ...... 170 B5
Furzen Cres. Hat AL10 ..... 129 F2

Gable Cl. Abb L WD5 ........ 153 E7
Gable Cl. Pnr HA5 ............ 176 A3
Gables Ave. Bor WD6 ....... 169 F6
Gables The. Saw CM21 ...... 97 E2
Gaddesden Cres.
Watf WD2 ..................... 154 E5
Gaddesden Gr.
Wel G C AL7 ................. 111 B6
Gaddesden La. Gt Gd AL3 105 C4
Gaddesden Row CP Sch.
Gt Gd ........................... 104 B6
Gaddesden Row.
Gt Gd HP2 .................... 104 C6
Gade Ave. Watf WD1 ....... 166 E5
Gade Bank. Cro Gr WD1 .. 166 D5
Gade Cl. Heml H HP1 ....... 124 B6
Gade Cl. Watf WD1 .......... 166 E5
Gade Side. Watf WD1 ...... 153 E4
Gade Valley Cl. Kin L WD4 139 A3
Gade Valley Cotts.
Gt Gd HP1 .................... 103 D4
Gade Valley Jun Mix Inf Sch.
Heml H ......................... 124 B4
Gade View Gdns.
Abb L WD4 ................... 153 C7
Gade View Rd.
Heml H HP3 .................. 138 D7
Gadebridge Ct.
Heml H HP1 .................. 124 C4
Gadebridge La.
Heml H HP1 .................. 124 B5
Gadebridge La.
Heml H HP1 .................. 124 C5
Gadebridge Rd.
Heml H HP1 .................. 124 B4
Gadeview. Heml H HP1 .... 124 C3
Gadswell Cl. Watf WD2 ... 154 E3
Gage Cl. Royst SG8 ............. 7 D7
Gainsborough Ave.
St Alb AL1 ..................... 127 F4
Gainsford Cres. Hit SG4 ..... 22 C2
Gainswood. Wel G C AL7 . 110 E5
Gall End La. Sta M CM24 ... 59 F7
Galleria The. Hat ............ 129 F5
Galley Gn. Hod SG13 ........ 115 A2
Galley Hill. Heml H HP1 ... 124 B6
Galley La. Barn EN5 ........ 171 B7
Galley La. Bor EN5 .......... 171 B7
Galleyhill Rd. Wa Aby EN9 163 E8
Galliard Cl. Luton LU3 ........ 45 B4
Galloway Cl. Bis St CM23 ... 76 F8
Galloway Cl. Ches EN10 ... 148 F5
Galloway Rd. Bis St CM23 . 58 F1
Gallows Hill. Abb L WD4 .. 153 C7
Gallows Hill La.
Abb L WD5 ................... 153 D8
Galston Rd. Luton LU3 ....... 44 D8
Gammons La.
Watf WD1,WD2 ............ 154 A2
Gamnel Terr. Tri HP23 ..... 100 B7
Ganders Ash. Watf WD2 . 154 A6
Gandhi Ct. Watf WD2 ...... 167 D7 1
Gangies Hill. H Wy CM21 ... 97 A4
Gant Ct. Wa Aby EN9 ...... 163 F5
Ganton Wlk. Sth Ox WD1 . 175 E6
Ganymede Pl.
Heml H HP2 .................. 124 F6
Gaping La. Hit SG5 ............ 34 D7
Garden Ave. Hat AL10 ..... 130 A2
Garden Cl. Barn EN5 ........ 171 C5
Garden Cl. Harp AL5 ........ 107 A5
Garden Cl. Royst SG8 ........... 7 E7
Garden Cl. St Alb AL1 ....... 128 B4
Garden Cl. Watf WD1 ....... 166 F7
Garden Cl. Welw SG3 ........ 69 B2
Garden Ct. Whea AL4 ........ 87 D1
Garden Field. Ast SG2 ........ 51 E2
Garden Field La. Berk HP4 122 F2
Garden Fields Jun Mix
Inf Sch. St Alb ............. 127 D6
Garden La. Royst SG8 .......... 7 D5
Garden Rd. Abb L WD5 .... 153 E8
Garden Rd. Bun SG9 .......... 40 E8
Garden Rd. Welw SG3 ....... 69 B2
Garden Row. Hit SG5 ........ 34 F8 6
Garden Terr. Sac SG12 ...... 92 E4
Garden Terrace Rd.
Harl CM17 .................... 118 C4
Garden Wlk. Royst SG8 ....... 7 E7
Garden Wlk. Stev SG1 ....... 50 E5
Gardenia Ave. Luton LU3 ... 45 A4
Gardens The. Bal SG7 ........ 23 E8
Gardens The. Bro Pk AL9 . 144 E4
Gardens The. Henlw SG16 . 10 D8
Gardens The. Stot SG5 ........ 11 E6
Gardens The. Watf WD1 .. 166 F7
Gardiners La. Ashw SG7 ...... 4 D4
Gareth Ct. Bor WD6 ......... 156 F1
Garfield Ct. Luton LU2 ...... 46 D3 3
Garfield St. Watf WD2 ...... 154 B1
Garland Cl. Heml H HP2 ... 124 D4
Garland Rd. Ware SG12 ..... 93 E1
Garnault Rd. Enf EN1 ....... 161 F1
Garner Dr. Ches EN10 ...... 148 E5
Garnett Cl. Watf WD2 ...... 154 D3
Garnett Dr. Bri Wd AL2 .... 140 F2
Garrard Way. Whea AL4 . 108 D8
Garratts Rd. Bus WD2 ..... 168 C2
Garretts Mead. Luton LU2 . 46 B3
Garrison Ct. Hit SG4 ......... 34 F7 2
Garrowsfield. Barn EN5 ... 171 F4
Garsmouth Way.
Watf WD2 ..................... 154 D3
Garston Cres. Watf WD2 . 154 C5
Garston Dr. Watf WD2 ..... 154 C5
Garston Inf Sch. Watf ...... 154 D4
Garston La. Watf WD2 ..... 154 D5
Garston Manor Medical
Rehab Ctr. Abb L .......... 154 C8
Garston Manor Sch. Watf 154 C7
Garston Park Par.
Watf WD2 ..................... 154 D5
Garston Sta. Watf ........... 154 D4
Garth Rd. Letw SG6 .......... 22 E3
Garth The. Abb L WD5 ..... 153 D6
Garthland Dr. Barn EN5 ... 171 C4
Gartlet Rd. Watf WD1 ...... 167 C6
Gas La. Bark SG8 .............. 17 C3
Gascoyne Cecil Prim Sch.
Hat .............................. 130 A7
Gascoyne Cl. Pot B EN6 ... 158 A7
Gascoyne Way.
Hert SG13,SG14 ........... 113 D5
Gate Cl. Bor WD6 ............ 170 C8
Gate Cotts. Chor WD3 ..... 164 D5
Gate End. Norwd HA6 ...... 175 A3

Gatecroft. Heml H HP3 ... 124 F1
Gatecroft. Heml H HP3 ... 139 A8
Gatehill Gdns. Luton LU3 ... 31 B1
Gatehill Rd. Norwd HA6 ... 175 A3
Gates Way. Stev SG1 ... 50 C6
Gatesbury Way. Stand SG11 ... 55 D3
Gatesdene Cl. L Gad HP4 . 102 C8
Gateshead Rd. Bor WD6 ... 170 A8
Gateway Cl. Norwd HA6 .. 174 C4
Gatwick Cl. Bis St CM23 ... 59 B1
Gauldie Way. Stand SG11 .. 55 D2
Gaumont App. Watf WD1 167 B6
Gaunts Way. Letw SG6 ... 12 A2
Gaveston Dr. Berk HP4 ... 122 B6
Gayland Ave. Luton LU2 ... 64 B8
Gayton Cl. Luton LU3 ... 45 B4
Gaywood Ave. Ches EN8 .. 148 D1
Gazelda Ind Est. Watf ... 167 D4
Geddes Rd. Bus WD2 ... 168 C5
Geddings Rd. Hod EN11 ... 135 B6
Generals Wlk The. Enf EN3 ... 162 E2
Gentle Ct. Bal SG7 ... 23 E8
Gentlemens Field. Ware SG12 ... 93 B3
George Gn. L Hal CM22 ... 77 B1
George La. Royst SG8 ... 7 D6
George Leighton Ct. Stev SG2 ... 51 B4
George St. Berk HP4 ... 122 D4
George St. Heml H HP2 ... 124 D4
George St. Hert SG14 ... 113 C6
George St. Luton LU1 ... 63 E7
George St. Mark AL3 ... 83 E5
George St. St Alb AL3 ... 127 D3
George St W. Luton LU1 ... 63 E7
George St. Watf WD1 ... 167 C5
George Street Sch. Heml H ... 124 D4
George V Ave. Pnr HA5 ... 175 F1
George V Way. Sar WD3 . 152 B3
George's Wood Rd. Bro Pk AL9 ... 145 B5
Georges Mead. Elst WD6 169 E3
Georgewood Rd. Heml H HP3 ... 139 A7
Georgina Ct. Arl SG15 ... 11 A3
Gerard Ave. Bis St CM23 ... 76 E4
Gernon Rd. Letw SG6 ... 22 F5
Gernon Wlk. Letw SG6 ... 22 F5
Gew's Cnr. Ches EN8 ... 148 D2
Gew's Corner Prim Sch. Ches ... 148 E2
Ghlbert Way. Berk HP4 ... 122 A4
Giant Tree Hill. Bus WD2 . 168 D1
Gibbons Cl. Bor WD6 ... 169 E8
Gibbons Cl. Sand AL4 ... 108 C1
Gibbons Way. Kneb SG3 ... 68 F5
Gibbs Cl. Ches EN8 ... 148 D2
Gibbs Couch. Sth Ox WD1 175 D7
Gibbs Field. Bis St CM23 ... 76 D5
Gibraltar Lodge. Harp AL5 . 86 D3
Gibson Cl. Hit SG4 ... 35 B7
Gidian Ct. Pk St AL2 ... 141 D4
Gifford's La. Dan E SG11 ... 54 A2
Gilbert Rd. Hare UB9 ... 173 D1
Gilbert St. Enf EN3 ... 162 C2
Gilbert's Hill. St Le HP23 . 119 E3
Gilbey Ave. Bis St CM23 ... 77 B6
Gilbey Cres. Sta M CM24 ... 59 E8
Gilden Cl. Harl CM17 ... 118 E4
Gilden Way. Harl CM17 ... 118 D4
Gilder Cl. Luton LU3 ... 45 A8
Gilderdale. Luton LU4 ... 44 B6
Gilders. Saw CM21 ... 97 D2
Giles Cl. Sand AL4 ... 108 C1
Giles Inf Sch The. Stev ... 37 A1
Giles Jun Sch The. Stev ... 37 A1
Gillam St. Luton ... 63 E8
Gillan Gn. Bus WD2 ... 176 C8
Gillian Ave. St Alb AL1 ... 141 C7
Gilliat's Gn. Chor WD3 ... 164 D5
Gilliflower House. Hod EN11 ... 135 A5
Gillings Ct. Barn EN5 ... 171 E5
Gillison Cl. Letw SG6 ... 23 B5
Gills Hill. Radl WD7 ... 115 F4
Gills Hill Inf Sch. Radl ... 155 F4
Gills Hill La. Radl WD7 ... 155 F3
Gills Hollow. Radl WD7 ... 155 F3
Gilmour Cl. Enf EN2 ... 162 A4
Gilpin Gn. Harp AL5 ... 86 C1
Gilpin Rd. Ware SG12 ... 114 E8
Gilpin's Gallop. Gt Am SG12 ... 115 B4
Gilpin's Ride. Berk HP4 ... 122 E5
Gilsland. Wa Aby EN9 ... 163 E4
Ginns Rd. Sto P SG9 ... 43 D6
Gippeswyck Cl. Pnr HA5 .. 175 D2
Gipsy La. Bis St CM23 ... 59 C4
Gipsy La. Kneb SG3 ... 68 E4
Gipsy La. Luton LU1 ... 64 A6
Gipsy La. Sta M CM23 ... 59 C4
Girdle Rd. Hit SG4 ... 22 A2
Girons Cl. Hit SG4 ... 35 B7
Girtin Rd. Bus WD2 ... 168 C5
Girton Ct. Ches EN8 ... 148 E1
Girton Way. Cro Gr WD3 . 166 C4
Glade The. Bal SG7 ... 23 E7
Glade The. Letw SG6 ... 22 F3
Glade The. Wel G C AL8 ... 110 C8
Glades The. Heml H HP1 . 123 E4
Gladeside. St Alb AL4 ... 128 D6
Gladeway The. Wa Aby EN9 ... 163 D6
Gladsmuir Rd. Barn EN5 .. 171 E7
Gladstone Ave. Luton LU1 .. 63 C7
Gladstone Ct. Stev SG2 ... 69 A8
Gladstone Pl. Barn EN5 ... 171 D5
Gladstone Rd. Dan En SG12 ... 71 F8
Gladstone Rd. Hod EN11 . 135 B7
Gladstone Rd. Ware SG12 . 93 C2
Gladstone Rd. Watf WD1 . 167 C6
Glamis Cl. Ches EN7 ... 148 A2
Glamis Cl. Heml H HP2 ... 105 B1
Glean Wlk. Hat AL10 ... 130 A2
Gleave Cl. St Alb AL1 ... 128 B4
Glebe Ave. Arl SG15 ... 11 A7
Glebe Cl. Ess AL9 ... 131 F6
Glebe Cl. Heml H HP3 ... 138 E7
Glebe Cl. Hert SG14 ... 113 D8
Glebe Cl. Pit LU7 ... 80 D5
Glebe Cl. Wat St SG14 ... 70 D3
Glebe Cotts. Ess AL9 ... 131 F6
Glebe Ct. Bis St CM23 ... 77 B8
Glebe Ct. Hat AL10 ... 130 C6
Glebe Ct. Wat St SG14 ... 70 E3
Glebe House. Ess AL9 ... 131 F6
Glebe La. Barn EN5 ... 171 A3
Glebe Rd. Hert SG14 ... 113 D8
Glebe Rd. Letw SG6 ... 23 B8
Glebe Rd. Welw AL6 ... 89 B5
Glebe The. Kin L WD4 ... 139 A2
Glebe The. Stev SG2 ... 51 B6
Glebe The. Watf WD2 ... 154 D6
Glebelands. Harl CM20 ... 117 F3
Gleed Ave. Bus WD2 ... 176 D8
Glemsford Cl. Luton LU4 ... 44 B6
Glemsford Dr. Harp AL5 ... 86 D2
Glen Chess. Ric ... 165 C6
Glen Faba Rd. Lo Naz CM19 ... 135 F6
Glen The. Cad LU1 ... 62 E3
Glen The. Heml H HP2 ... 124 F8
Glen The. Heml H HP2 ... 125 A8
Glen The. Norwd HA6 ... 174 D3
Glen Way. Watf WD1 ... 153 E1
Glenblower Ct. St Alb AL4 128 D3
Glencoe Rd. Bus WD2 ... 168 A3
Glencourse Gn. Sth Ox WD1 ... 175 D6
Glendale. Heml H HP1 ... 124 B3
Glendale Wlk. Ches EN8 .. 148 E1
Gleneagles Cl. Sth Ox WD1 ... 175 D6
Gleneagles Dr. Luton LU2 .. 45 E6
Glenester Cl. Hod EN11 ... 115 B1
Glenferrie Rd. St Alb AL1 . 128 A3
Glenfield Ct. Hert SG14 ... 112 F7
Glenfield Rd. Luton LU3 ... 45 C6
Glengall Pl. St Alb AL1 ... 141 E8
Glenhaven Ave. Bor WD6 170 A6
Glenlyn Ave. St Alb AL1 ... 128 B2
Glenmire Terr. Sta Ab SG12 ... 115 D4
Glenmore Gdns. Abb L WD5 ... 154 A7
Glenshee Cl. Norwd HA6 . 174 C4
Glenview Gdns. Heml H HP1 ... 124 B3
Glenview Rd. Heml H HP1 124 B3
Glenville Ave. Enf EN2 ... 161 D1
Glenwood Cl. Stev SG2 ... 51 C2
Glenwood. Hod EN10 ... 134 F4
Glenwood. Wel G C AL7 ... 111 D5
Glevum Cl. St Alb AL3 ... 126 F1
Globe Cl. Harp AL5 ... 86 B1
Globe Cres. Far CM23 ... 58 D6
Globe Ct. Hert SG14 ... 113 C8
Gloucester Ave. Ches EN8 162 E6
Gloucester Cl. Stev SG1 ... 36 D1
Gloucester Rd. Enf EN2 ... 161 C1
Gloucester Rd. Luton LU1 .. 63 F6
Glover Cl. Ham St EN7 ... 147 F4
Glovers Cl. Hert SG13 ... 113 C4
Glynde The. Stev SG2 ... 69 B8
Goat La. Enf EN1 ... 161 F1
Gobions Way. Bro Pk EN6 145 B3
Goblins Gn. Wel G C AL7 .. 110 D5
Goddard End. Stev SG2 ... 69 C8
Goddards Cl. L Berk SG13 132 C4
Gode Tower. Heml H HP3 138 F6
Godfrey Cl. Stev SG2 ... 51 B3
Godfreys Cl. Luton LU1 ... 63 B6
Godfreys Ct. Luton LU1 ... 63 B6
Godfries Cl. Tewin AL6 ... 90 E3
Godsafe. Harl CM17 ... 118 E4
Godwin Cl. Wa Aby EN9 ... 163 C1
Goff's La. Gofs O EN7 ... 147 E2
Goff's Oak Ave. Gofs O EN7 ... 147 C3
Goffs Cres. Gofs O EN7 ... 147 C2
Goffs La. Ches EN7 ... 148 A2
Goffs Oak Jun Mix Inf Sch. Gofs O ... 147 B3
Goffs Sch. Ches ... 148 A2
Gold Crest Cl. Dun LU4 ... 44 A5
Golda Cl. Barn EN5 ... 171 D3
Goldcrest Way. Bus WD2 168 C1
Goldcroft. Heml H HP3 ... 125 A1
Golden Dell. Wel G C AL7 110 F2
Goldfield Inf Sch. Tri ... 99 F3
Goldfield Rd. Tri HP23 ... 99 F3
Goldfinch Way. Bor WD6 . 170 A5
Goldings. Bis St CM23 ... 77 B8
Goldings Cres. Hat AL10 .. 130 B6
Goldings House. Hat AL10 130 B6
Goldings La. Stap SG14 ... 92 A2
Goldington Cl. Hod EN11 . 114 F1
Goldon. Letw SG6 ... 23 C4
Goldstone Cl. Ware SG12 .. 93 D2
Golf Cl. Bus WD2 ... 167 D6
Golf Club Rd. Bro Pk AL9 . 145 A6
Golf Ride. Cre H EN2 ... 161 A4
Gombards. St Alb AL3 ... 127 D4
Gomer Cl. Cod SG4 ... 67 E2
Gonville Ave. Cro Gr WD3 166 B3
Gonville Cres. Stev SG2 ... 51 C2
Goodey Meade. Ben SG2 ... 52 F2
Goodliffe Pk. Bis St ... 59 B2
Goodrich Cl. Watf WD2 ... 154 A4
Goodwin Ct. Ches EN8 ... 148 E3
Goodwin House. Watf WD1 ... 166 E3
Goodwin Stile. Bis St CM23 ... 76 D5
Goodwins Mead. Ched LU7 80 A7
Goodwood Ave. Enf EN3 .. 162 C2
Goodwood Ave. Watf WD2 ... 153 E3
Goodwood Cl. Hod EN11 .. 135 A7
Goodwood Par. Watf WD1 ... 153 E3
Goodwood Path. Bor WD6 170 A7
Goodwood Rd. Royst SG8 ... 7 F6
Goodyers Ave. Radl WD7 . 155 F5
Goose Acre. Bot HP5 ... 136 A1
Goose Acre. Ched LU7 ... 80 A7
Goose La. Hat H CM22 ... 98 E7
Gooseacre. Wel G C AL7 .. 110 F4
Gooseberry Hill. Luton LU3 ... 45 B7
Goosecroft. Heml H HP1 .. 123 F4
Goral Mead. Ric WD3 ... 165 D1
Gordian Way. Stev SG2 ... 37 C1
Gordon Ave. Har HA7 ... 176 F4
Gordon Cl. St Alb AL1 ... 128 B2
Gordon House. St Alb AL1 128 B2
Gordon Rd. Ches EN8 ... 163 A5
Gordon St. Luton LU1 ... 63 D7
Gordon Way. Barn EN5 ... 171 F5
Gore La. Stand SG11 ... 73 D3
Gorelands La. C St P HP8 172 A7
Gorham Dr. St Alb AL1 ... 141 E8
Gorle Cl. Watf WD2 ... 154 A4
Gorleston Cl. Stev SG1 ... 36 A1
Gorse Cl. Hat AL10 ... 129 F2
Gorse Cnr. St Alb AL3 ... 127 D5
Gorselands. Harp AL5 ... 107 C7
Gorst Cl. Letw SG6 ... 22 E5
Gosford House. Watf WD1 ... 166 E3
Gosforth La. Sth Ox WD1 . 175 B7
Gosforth Path. Sth Ox WD1 ... 175 A7
Goshawk Cl. Dun LU4 ... 44 A4
Goslett Ct. Bus WD2 ... 168 A4
Gosling Ave. Gt Of SG5 ... 33 C2
Gosling Sports Pk. Wel G C ... 110 C4
Gosmore Ley Cl. Hit SG4 ... 34 F3
Gosmore Rd. Hit SG4 ... 34 F5
Gosmore. Stev SG1 ... 36 C2
Gossamers The. Watf WD2 ... 154 E4
Gosselin Rd. Hert SG14 ... 113 C8
Gossoms Ryde. Berk HP4 122 A5
Gothic Mede Lower Sch. Arl ... 11 A5
Gothic Way. Arl SG15 ... 11 B5
Gould Cl. Wel G AL9 ... 144 B7
Government Row. Enf EN3 ... 163 A2
Gower Field. Pot B EN6 ... 158 A7
Gower Rd. Royst SG8 ... 7 C7
Gowers The. Harl CM20 .. 118 B2
Grace Cl. Bor WD6 ... 170 D8
Grace Gdns. Bis St CM23 ... 76 F4
Grace Way. Stev SG1 ... 50 E7
Graces Maltings. Tri HP23 ... 100 A3
Graemesdyke Rd. Berk HP4 ... 122 A3
Graham Ave. Hod EN10 ... 134 E2
Graham Cl. St Alb AL1 ... 127 D1
Graham Gdns. Luton LU3 ... 45 C4
Graham Rd. Har HA3 ... 176 E1
Grailands. Bis St CM23 ... 76 D8
Grammar School Wlk. Hit SG5 ... 34 E7
Grampian Way. Luton LU3 . 44 C8
Granaries The. Wa Aby EN9 ... 163 E5
Granary Cl. Whea AL4 ... 108 D8
Granary Ct. Saw CM21 ... 97 E2
Granary La. Harp AL5 ... 86 C1
Granary The. Roy CM19 ... 116 B1
Granby Ave. Harp AL5 ... 86 D2
Granby Rd. Luton LU4 ... 44 E2
Granby Rd. Stev SG1 ... 36 C2
Grandfield Ave. Watf WD1 ... 167 A8
Grange Ave. Barn N20 ... 171 E2
Grange Ave. Luton LU4 ... 44 D5
Grange Bottom. Royst SG8 .. 7 E5
Grange Cl. Heml H HP2 ... 125 A2
Grange Cl. Hert SG14 ... 113 B6
Grange Cl. Hit SG4 ... 35 A4
Grange Cl. Mark AL3 ... 83 D6
Grange Court Rd. Harp AL5 ... 107 C6
Grange Ct. Hert SG14 ... 113 C7
Grange Ct. Wa Aby EN9 ... 163 C5
Grange Dr. Stot SG5 ... 11 F5
Grange Gdns. Ware SG12 114 E8
Grange Hill. Welw AL6 ... 89 C6
Grange Jun Mix Sch The. Letw ... 12 A2
Grange La. Radl WD2 ... 168 D8
Grange Pk. Bis St CM23 ... 58 F1
Grange Rd. Bis St CM23 ... 77 A7
Grange Rd. Bor WD6 ... 169 F4
Grange Rd. Letw SG6 ... 22 F8
Grange Rd. Pit LU7 ... 80 D5
Grange Rd. Tri HP23 ... 100 C5
Grange Rd. Watf WD2 ... 167 F4
Grange Rd. Wils HP23 ... 79 D1
Grange Rise. Cod SG4 ... 67 F1
Grange St. St Alb AL3 ... 127 D4
Grange The. Abb L WD5 .. 153 E8
Grange The. Bis St CM23 ... 58 F1
Grange The. Hod EN11 ... 135 A5
Grange The. Ric WD3 ... 165 D2
Grange Wlk. Bis St CM23 .. 77 A7
Grangedale Cl. Norwd HA6 ... 174 E2
Grangeside. Bis St CM23 ... 59 A2
Grangewood Inf Sch. Ches ... 148 D1
Grangewood. Pot B EN6 .. 145 B1
Gransden Cl. Luton LU3 ... 45 A7
Grant Gdns. Harp AL5 ... 86 B2
Grantham Cl. Royst SG8 ... 7 B8
Grantham Gdns. Ware SG12 ... 93 E2
Grantham Gn. Bor WD6 ... 170 C4
Grantham Rd. Luton LU4 ... 45 B1
Granville Ct. St Alb AL1 ... 127 F3
Granville Dene. Bov HP3 .. 137 A4
Granville Gdns. Hod EN11 115 A2
Granville Rd. Barn EN5 ... 171 D6
Granville Rd. Hit SG4 ... 22 C1
Granville Rd. Luton LU1 ... 63 B8
Granville Rd. St Alb AL1 ... 127 F3
Granville Rd. Watf WD1 ... 167 C5
Grasmere Ave. Harp AL5 ... 86 C1
Grasmere Ave. Luton LU3 ... 45 B7
Grasmere Cl. Heml H HP3 125 B1
Grasmere Cl. Watf WD2 .. 154 B7
Grasmere Rd. Luton LU3 ... 45 C7
Grasmere Rd. St Alb AL1 . 128 B1
Grasmere Rd. Ware SG12 . 93 E3
Grass Meadows. Stev SG2 51 D7
Grass Warren. Tewin AL6 . 90 E1
Grassington Cl. Bri Wd AL2 ... 141 A1
Grassy Cl. Heml H HP1 ... 124 A4
Grave Inf Sch The. Harp .. 107 D7
Grave Jun Sch The. Harp . 107 D7
Gravel Dr. Ast Cl HP23 ... 99 B3
Gravel La. Heml H HP1 ... 124 A3
Gravel Path. Berk HP4 ... 122 E5
Gravel Path. Heml H HP1 124 A3
Graveley Ave. Bor WD6 ... 170 C4
Graveley Cl. Stev SG1 ... 36 C2
Graveley Dell. Wel G C AL7 ... 111 B5
Graveley La. Gt Wy SG4 ... 36 B5
Graveley Rd. Gra SG4 ... 36 B3
Graveley Rd. Gt Wy SG4 ... 35 F6
Gravelhill Terr. Heml H HP1 ... 124 A2
Gravelly La. Brag SG11 ... 55 F8
Gravely Ct. Heml H HP2 ... 125 C2
Gray's La. Hit SG5 ... 34 D7
Grayling Ct. Nthch HP4 ... 121 F6
Graylings The. Abb L WD5 ... 153 D6
Grays Cl. Royst SG8 ... 7 C8
Grays Ct. Bis St CM23 ... 76 E8
Graysfield. Wel G C AL7 ... 111 A3
Grazings The. Heml H HP2 ... 124 F5
Greasy Cl. Abb L WD5 ... 153 F8
Great Braitch La. Hat AL10 ... 109 F1
Great Break. Wel G C AL7 111 B5
Great Brookmead Sch. Bor ... 156 F1
Great Cambridge Rd. Ches EN8 ... 148 D4
Great Cambridge Rd. Enf EN1 ... 162 C6
Great Conduit. Wel G C AL7 ... 111 C7
Great Dell. Wel G C AL8 ... 89 D1
Great Elms Rd. Heml H HP3 ... 138 F7
Great Gaddesden Prim Sch. Gt Gd ... 103 D3
Great Ganett. Wel G C AL7 ... 111 C4
Great Gn. Pirt SG5 ... 20 D4
Great Gr. Bus WD2 ... 168 B5
Great Hadham Golf Club. Muc H ... 75 D4
Great Hadham Rd. Bis St CM23 ... 76 C6
Great Heart. Heml H HP2 124 E5
Great Heath. Hat AL10 ... 130 B8
Great Innings N. Wat St SG14 ... 70 D4
Great Innings S. Wat St SG14 ... 70 D3
Great Lawne. Dat SG3 ... 69 D2
Great Ley. Wel G C AL7 ... 110 E4
Great Meadow. Lo Naz EN10 ... 135 A1
Great Molewood. Hert SG14 ... 92 B1
Great North Rd. Barn EN5 171 E6
Great North Rd. Bro Pk AL9,EN6 ... 145 B5
Great North Rd.Hat AL8 ... 110 A4
Great North Rd. Hat AL9 .. 130 C5
Great North Rd. Newn SG7 12 D4
Great North Rd. Stot SG5 ... 3 A2
Great North Rd. Wel G C AL8 ... 110 A7
Great North Rd. Welw AL6 89 E7
Great Palmers. Heml H HP2 ... 124 F8
Great Pk. Kin L WD4 ... 139 A1
Great Plumtree. Harl CM20 ... 117 F2
Great Rd. Heml H HP2 ... 124 F4
Great Slades. Pot B EN6 .. 158 F6
Great Sturgess Rd. Heml H HP1 ... 123 F3
Great Whites Rd. Heml H HP3 ... 124 F1
Great Wood Ctry Pk. Cuf . 146 B5
Greatfield Cl. Harp AL5 ... 85 C4
Greatham Rd. Watf WD2 . 167 D6
Green Acres. Lily LU2 ... 32 D2
Green Acres. Stev SG2 ... 51 C1
Green Acres. Wel G C AL7 110 F3
Green Bushes. Luton LU4 .. 44 D6
Green Cl. Bro Pk AL9 ... 144 E5
Green Cl. Ches EN8 ... 162 E8
Green Cl. Luton LU4 ... 44 C5
Green Cl. Stev SG2 ... 50 F2
Green Croft. Hat AL10 ... 130 A8
Green Ct. Luton LU4 ... 44 B5
Green Dell Way. Heml H HP3 ... 125 C3
Green Drift. Royst SG8 ... 7 C7
Green Edge. Watf WD2 ... 154 A4
Green End Gdns. Heml H HP1 ... 124 A2

Green End La. Heml H HP1 ................ 123 F3
Green End Rd. Heml H HP1 ................ 124 A2
Green End. Welw AL6 ........ 89 B4
Green Hill Cl. Brag SG11 ... 55 F7
Green La. Ashw SG7 ............ 4 E5
Green La. Bov HP3 ........... 137 A3
Green La. Brag SG11 ......... 55 F7
Green La. Cro Gr WD3 ..... 165 F4
Green La. Heml H HP2 ..... 125 D4
Green La. Hit SG4 ............. 22 B1
Green La. Ken Co LU6 ........ 82 E8
Green La. Lat HP5 ............ 150 C6
Green La. Letw SG6 ........... 23 C8
Green La. Lo Naz EN10 .... 149 B8
Green La. Luton LU2 .......... 46 C4
Green La. Mark AL3 .......... 83 F5
Green La. Norwd HA6 ...... 174 E3
Green La. Pit LU7 ............... 80 E5
Green La. St Alb AL1 ........ 142 A7
Green La. St Alb AL3 ........ 127 D7
Green La. Watf WD1 ........ 167 C2
Green La. Wel G C AL7 .... 111 D5
Green Lane Cl. Harp AL5 . 107 E8
Green Lanes. Hat AL10 .... 109 F2
Green Lanes Sch. Hat ...... 109 F1
Green Leys Cotts. Stand SG11 .................... 55 F1
Green Meadow. Pot B EN6 ..................... 145 A1
Green Oaks. Luton LU2 ....... 45 F3
Green Path. Ast Cl HP22 .... 99 D4
Green St. Chor WD3 ........ 164 C6
Green St. Royst SG8 ............ 7 D8
Green St. Shen WD7 ........ 157 A3
Green St. Stev SG1 ........... 50 C7
Green The. Bis St CM23 ...... 76 F4
Green The. Ched LU7 ......... 80 A7
Green The. Ches EN8 ....... 148 C3
Green The. Cod SG4 ........... 67 F1
Green The. Kim SG4 ........... 65 C3
Green The. Kim SG4 ........... 66 D1
Green The. Kneb SG3 ......... 68 C5
Green The. Luton LU4 ........ 44 C5
Green The. Newn SG7 ....... 12 E7
Green The. Pit LU7 ............. 80 D4
Green The. Royst SG8 .......... 7 D6
Green The. Sar WD3 ........ 152 A3
Green The. Stot SG5 .......... 11 F7
Green The. Ware SG12 ...... 93 D3
Green The. Wel G C AL7 .. 111 A4
Green The. Welw AL6 ......... 89 B5
Green Vale. Wel G C AL7 . 111 A5
Green View Cl. Bov HP3 .. 137 A2
Green Way Gdns. Har HA3 ...................... 176 E1
Green Way The. Har HA3 176 E2
Greenacre Cl. Barn EN5 .. 158 F1
Greenacres. Bus WD2 ..... 176 D8
Greenacres. Heml H HP2 . 125 D2
Greenacres. Pit LU7 ........... 80 C4
Greenall Cl. Ches EN8 ...... 148 E1
Greenbank. Ches EN8 ...... 148 B3
Greenbank Rd. Watf WD1 153 D3
Greenbury Cl. Bar SG8 ......... 8 F1
Greenbury Cl. Chor WD3 . 164 C5
Greencoates. Hert SG13 .. 113 E5
Greene Field Rd. Berk HP4 ...................... 122 C4
Greene Wlk. Berk HP4 ..... 122 D3
Greenfield Ave. Ick SG5 ...... 21 D4
Greenfield Ave. Sth Ox WD1 ................ 175 E8
Greenfield. Hat AL9 ......... 130 D8
Greenfield La. Ick SG5 ....... 21 E4
Greenfield Rd. Stev SG1 .... 50 E7
Greenfield. Royst SG8 .......... 7 B7
Greenfield St. Wa Aby EN9 ................ 163 C5
Greenfield. Wel G C AL8 .... 89 D1
Greenfields. Cuf EN6 ....... 146 E1
Greenfields Jun Mix Inf Sch. Sth Ox ............................ 175 C5
Greenfields. Sta M CM24 ... 59 E7
Greengate. Luton LU3 ........ 44 C8
Greenheys Cl. Norwd HA6 174 E2
Greenhill Ave. Luton LU2 .... 45 E3
Greenhill Cres. Watf WD1 166 E3
Greenhill Ct. Heml H HP1 124 B2
Greenhill Pk. Bis St CM23 .. 76 D5
Greenhills Cl. Ric WD3 ..... 165 B4
Greenhills. Ware SG12 ...... 93 C3
Greenland Rd. Barn EN5 .. 171 C3
Greenlands. Bor NW7 ...... 170 D3
Greenlane Ind Est. Letw .... 23 C7
Greenriggs. Luton LU2 ....... 46 F2
Greenside. Bor WD6 ........ 157 A1
Greenside Sch. Stev ........... 51 B2
Greensleeves Cl. St Alb AL4 .................... 128 C2
Greenstead. Saw CM21 ..... 97 E1
Greensward. Bus WD2 .... 168 B3
Greenway. Berk HP4 ....... 122 A4
Greenway. Bis St CM23 ..... 77 C6
Greenway Cty Prim Sch. Berk ............................... 121 F4
Greenway. Harp AL5 ........ 107 E8
Greenway. Heml H HP2 ... 125 B3
Greenway. Letw SG6 ........ 23 A2
Greenway. Pnr HA5 ......... 175 B1
Greenway The. Enf EN3 ... 162 D4
Greenway The. Pot B EN6 159 A6
Greenway The. Ric WD3 .. 165 A2
Greenway The. Tri HP23 .... 99 F5
Greenway. Walk SG2 ......... 52 B8
Greenways. Abb L WD5 .... 153 E7
Greenways. Bun SG9 ......... 40 D8
Greenways. Gofs O EN7 .. 147 B2
Greenways. Hert SG14 .... 113 B6
Greenways. Luton LU2 ....... 46 B5
Greenways. Stev SG1 ........ 50 E6
Greenwood Ave. Ches EN7 .................... 162 B8
Greenwood Cl. Ches EN7 . 162 B8
Greenwood Dr. Watf WD2 154 B5
Greenwood Park L Ctr. Chis ............................... 141 B6
Greenyard. Wa Aby EN9 .. 163 C6
Greer Rd. Har HA3 .......... 176 C2
Gregories Cl. Luton LU3 ..... 45 D1
Gregory Ave. Pot B EN6 ... 159 C6
Gregson Cl. Bor WD6 ...... 170 C8
Grenadier Cl. St Alb AL4 .. 128 C2
Grenadine Cl. Ham St EN7 ................. 147 F4
Grenadine Way. Tri HP23 100 A5
Greneway Sch The. Royst .... 7 E7
Grenville Ave. Hod EN10 .. 134 F2
Grenville Cl. Ches EN8 ..... 162 D7
Grenville Ct. Chor WD3 ..... 164 C5
Gresford Cl. St Alb AL4 .... 128 D3
Gresham Cl. Luton LU2 ...... 64 D8
Gresham Ct. Berk HP4 ..... 122 B3
Gresley Cl. Wel G C AL8 ... 110 E8
Gresley Ct. Enf EN1 .......... 162 C4
Gresley Ct. Pot B EN6 ...... 145 C1
Gresley Way. Stev SG2 ...... 51 D5
Greville Cl. Wel G AL9 ...... 144 C7
Grey House The. Watf WD1 .................... 167 A7
Greycaine Rd. Watf WD2 . 154 D2
Greydells Rd. Stev SG1 ...... 50 E6
Greyfriars La. Harp AL5 .... 107 A7
Greyfriars. Ware SG12 ...... 93 B3
Greyhound La. Pot B EN6 . 158 A6
Greystoke Cl. Berk HP4 ... 122 A3
Griffiths Way. St Alb AL1 . 127 C1
Grimaldi Ave. Luton LU3 .... 45 A3
Grimsdyke Cres. Barn EN5 ...................... 171 C6
Grimsdyke Fst & Mid Sch. Pnr ................................ 175 F4
Grimsdyke Lodge. St Alb AL1 .................... 128 A3
Grimsdyke Rd. Pnr HA5 ... 175 E3
Grimsdyke Rd. Wigg HP23 100 D1
Grimston Rd. St Alb AL1 .. 127 F2
Grimstone Rd. L Wym SG4 35 E4
Grimthorpe Cl. St Alb AL3 127 D6
Grindcobbe Cl. St Alb AL1 141 D8
Grinstead La. L Hal CM22 .. 98 C6
Groom Rd. Ches EN10 ..... 148 F5
Grooms Cotts. Bot HP5 .... 136 B1
Groomsby Dr. Pit LU7 ........ 80 E5
Grosvenor Ave. Abb L WD4 ................... 139 C3
Grosvenor Cl. Bis St CM23 76 D4
Grosvenor Ct. Cro Gr WD3 ................. 166 D4
Grosvenor House. Bis St CM23 .................. 77 B8
Grosvenor Rd. Bal SG7 ...... 12 F1
Grosvenor Rd. Bor WD6 .. 170 B6
Grosvenor Rd. Hod EN10 . 134 F3
Grosvenor Rd. Luton LU3 ... 45 B5
Grosvenor Rd. Mo Pk HA6 174 F5
Grosvenor Rd. St Alb AL1 127 E2
Grosvenor Rd W. Bal SG7 .. 12 F1
Grosvenor Rd. Watf WD1 167 C6
Grosvenor Terr. Heml H HP1 ................. 124 A2
Grotto The. Ware SG12 ... 114 D8
Ground La. Hat AL10 ........ 130 B7
Grove Ave. Harp AL5 ....... 107 D7
Grove Cotts. Bus WD2 ..... 168 A3
Grove Cres. Cro Gr WD3 . 166 A5
Grove Ct. Barn EN5 .......... 171 F6
Grove Ct. Wa Aby EN9 ..... 163 B6
Grove End. Luton LU1 ........ 63 B5
Grove Farm Pk. Mo Pk HA6 .................. 174 D5
Grove Gdns. Enf EN3 ....... 162 D1
Grove Gdns. Tri HP23 ...... 100 B5
Grove Hall Rd. Watf WD2 167 E5
Grove Hill. Sta M CM24 ...... 59 E7
Grove House. Bus WD2 ... 167 F3
Grove House. Ches EN7 ... 148 B1
Grove La. Ash Gr HP5 ...... 136 B5
Grove Lea. Hat AL10 ....... 130 A2
Grove Mead. Hat AL10 ..... 129 F5
Grove Meadow. Wel G C AL7 ................ 111 C6
Grove Mill La. Sar WD1 ... 153 C1
Grove Park Rd. Cad LU1 .... 63 B3
Grove Path. Ches EN7 ...... 162 A8
Grove Pk. Tri HP23 .......... 100 C5
Grove Pl. Bis St CM23 ........ 76 F7
Grove Pl. Wel G AL9 ........ 144 C7
Grove Rd. Bor WD6 .......... 170 A8
Grove Rd. Cad LU1 ............ 63 B2
Grove Rd. Harp AL5 ......... 107 D7
Grove Rd. Heml H HP1 ..... 124 A1
Grove Rd. Hit SG4,SG5 ....... 21 F1
Grove Rd. Luton LU1 ......... 63 D7
Grove Rd. Norwd HA6 ...... 174 D5
Grove Rd. Ric WD3 .......... 173 A8
Grove Rd. St Alb AL1 ........ 127 D2
Grove Rd. Stev SG1 ........... 50 D7
Grove Rd. Tri HP23 .......... 100 C5
Grove Rd W. Enf EN3 ....... 162 C2
Grove Rd. Ware SG12 ........ 93 F2
Grove Road Inf Sch. Tri ... 100 C5
Grove Road Jun Sch. Tri .. 100 C5
Grove The. Bro Pk AL9 ..... 145 A4
Grove The. Gt Ha CM22 ..... 77 F4
Grove The. L Had SG11 ...... 75 E7
Grove The. Lat HP5 .......... 150 D3
Grove The. Luton LU1 ........ 63 B5
Grove The. Pot B EN6 ....... 159 C7
Grove The. Radl WD7 ....... 156 A5
Grove The. Tri HP23 ........ 100 C5
Grove Way. Chor WD3 ..... 164 B4
Grove Wlk. Hert SG14 ..... 113 C8
Grovebury Gdns. Chis AL2 141 C4
Grovedale Cl. Ches EN7 ... 147 F1
Groveland Way. Stot SG5 .. 12 A5
Grovelands Ave. Hit SG4 .... 22 C2
Grovelands. Chis AL2 ....... 141 B4
Grovelands. Heml H AL2 .. 125 C5
Grover Cl. Heml H HP2 .... 124 D4
Grover Rd. Watf WD1 ..... 167 D3
Grovewood Cl. Chor WD3 164 C4
Grubbs La. Hat AL9 .......... 145 C8
Grubs La. Hat AL9 ........... 131 A1
Guardian Ind Est. Luton ..... 63 C8
Guernsey Cl. Dun LU4 ........ 44 A3
Guernsey House. Enf EN3 162 D1
Guessens Ct. Wel G C AL8 110 C6
Guessens Gr. Wel G C AL8 ................. 110 C6
Guessens Rd. Wel G C AL8 ................. 110 C6
Guessens Wlk. Wel G C AL8 ................. 110 C7
Guilden Morden Sch. Gu M .. 1 F5
Guildford Rd. St Alb AL1 .. 128 B2
Guildford St. Luton LU1 ..... 63 E7
Guilfords The. Harl CM17 118 D5
Guinevere Gdns. Ches EN8 .................... 162 E8
Gulland Cl. Bus WD2 ........ 168 C4
Gullbrook. Heml H HP1 .... 124 A3
Gullet Wood Rd. Watf WD2 .................. 154 A4
Gulphs The. Hert SG13 .... 113 D5
Gun La. Kneb SG3 ............. 68 F4
Gun Meadow Ave. Kneb SG3 ...................... 69 A4
Gun Rd. Kneb SG3 ............. 69 A4
Gun Road Gdns. Kneb SG3 . 68 F4
Gunnels Wood Ind Est. Stev .............................. 50 D3
Gunnels Wood Rd. Stev SG1 ......................... 50 B5
Gurney Court Rd. St Alb AL1 .................... 127 F5
Gurney's La. Hol SG5 ......... 21 B7
Gwent Cl. Watf WD2 ........ 154 D5
Gwynfa Cl. Welw AL6 ......... 89 D7
Gwynne Cl. Tri HP23 ........ 100 A5
Gwynns Wlk. Hert SG13 ... 113 E6
Gyfford Wlk. Ches EN7 ..... 162 B8
Gypsy Cl. Gt Am SG12 ..... 114 F4
Gypsy La. Abb L WD4 ....... 153 D5
Gypsy La. Gt Am SG12 ..... 114 F4
Gypsy La. Hat AL7 ........... 110 F1

Haberdashers' Aske's Sch The. Radl .............. 169 B6
Hackforth Cl. Barn EN5 .... 171 B4
Hackney Cl. Bor WD6 ....... 170 D4
Haddon Cl. Bor WD6 ........ 170 A6
Haddon Cl. Heml H HP3 ... 125 A2
Haddon Cl. Stev SG2 ......... 69 C7
Haddon Ct. Harp AL5 ......... 86 B1
Haddon Rd. Chor WD3 ..... 164 C4
Haddon Rd. Luton LU2 ....... 63 F8
Hadham Rd. Bis St CM23 ... 76 D8
Hadham Rd. L Had SG11 .... 57 F1
Hadham Rd. Stand SG11 .... 55 F1
Hadleigh Ct. Hod EN10 .... 134 F1
Hadleigh Ct. Whea AL5 .... 107 E6
Hadleigh. Letw SG6 ........... 23 B4
Hadley Bourne (St Martha's Convent Sch). Barn ......... 171 F8
Hadley Cl. Bor WD6 ........ 169 F3
Hadley Ct. Luton LU3 ......... 45 D1 3
Hadley Gn. Barn EN5 ....... 171 F7
Hadley Gn W. Barn EN5 ... 171 F7
Hadley Gr. Barn EN5 ....... 171 E7
Hadley Green Rd. Barn EN5 ..................... 171 F7
Hadley Highstone. Barn EN5 ..................... 171 F8
Hadley Rd. Had W EN2,EN4 ........... 160 D1
Hadley Ridge. Barn EN5 ... 171 F6
Hadley Wood Jun Mix Inf Sch. Had W ........... 159 C1
Hadlow Down Cl. Luton LU3 ....................... 45 A5
Hadrain Cl. St Alb AL3 ...... 127 A1
Hadrian Way. Letw SG7 ...... 23 D7
Hadrians Wlk. Stev SG1 ..... 51 C8
Hadwell Cl. Stev SG2 ......... 51 A3
Hagdell Rd. Luton LU1 ....... 63 C5
Hagden La. Watf WD1 ...... 167 A4
Haggerston Rd. Bor WD6 156 E1
Hagsdell Rd. Hert SG13 ... 113 D5
Haig Cl. St Alb AL1 .......... 128 B2
Haig House. St Alb AL1 ..... 128 B2
Hailey Ave. Hod EN11 ..... 115 A2
Hailey Hall Sch. Hod ........ 114 F2
Hailey La. Hert H SG13 .... 114 E2
Hailey La. Hod SG13 ........ 114 E2
Haileybury Coll. Hert H .... 114 D2
Haines Way. Watf WD2 ... 154 A5
Haldens House. Wel G C AL7 .................... 89 F1 3
Haldens. Wel G C AL7 ........ 89 F1
Hale La. St Le HP22 ......... 119 A3
Hale Rd. Hert SG13 .......... 113 D5
Hales Meadow. Harp AL5 .. 86 A2
Hales Park Cl. Heml H HP2 ................. 125 C4
Hales Pk. Heml H HP2 ..... 125 C4
Haleswood Rd. Heml H HP2 ................. 125 B4
Half Acres. Bis St CM23 ..... 76 F8
Half Moon Meadow. Heml H HP2 ................. 125 C8
Half Moon La. Cad LU1 ...... 63 C1
Half Moon Mews. St Alb AL1 .................... 127 D3 5
Halfacre La. Gt Ho SG9 ...... 29 A1
Halfhide La. Ches EN8 ...... 148 D5
Halfhides. Wa Aby EN9 .... 163 D6
Halfway Ave. Luton LU4 ..... 44 D1
Halifax Rd. Chor WD3 ...... 164 C2
Halifax Way. Wel G C AL7 111 E6
Hall Cl. Ric WD3 .............. 165 A1
Hall Cotts. Gt Ho SG9 ........ 29 A1
Hall Dr. Hare UB9 ........... 173 C2
Hall Gdns. Col H AL4 ........ 143 D8
Hall Gr. Wel G C AL7 ........ 111 B4
Hall Heath Cl. St Alb AL1 .. 128 B5
Hall La. Gt Ch SG8 ............... 9 F2
Hall La. Gt Ho SG9 ............. 29 A1
Hall La. Kim SG4 ............... 87 C8
Hall La. Welw SG3 ............. 69 A2
Hall Mead. Letw SG6 ......... 22 D6
Hall Park Gate. Berk HP4 122 E3
Hall Park Hill. Berk HP4 ... 122 E3
Hall Pk. Berk HP4 ............ 122 E3
Hall Place Cl. St Alb AL1 ... 127 E4
Hall Place Gdns. St Alb AL1 .................... 127 E4
Hall Rd. Heml H HP2 ........ 125 B5
Hallam Cl. Watf WD1 ....... 167 C7
Hallam Gdns. Pnr HA5 ..... 175 E3
Halland Way. Norwd HA6 174 D4
Halleys Ridge. Hert SG14 113 A5
Halling Hill. Harl CM20 ..... 117 F2
Hallingbury Cl. L Hal CM22 77 B1
Hallingbury Rd. Bis St CM23 .................. 77 B4
Hallingbury Rd. Gt Ha CM22 .................. 77 B4
Hallingbury Rd. L Hal CM21 .................... 98 A4
Hallmores. Hod EN10 ...... 135 A4
Hallowell Rd. Norwd HA6 174 E3
Hallowes Cres. Sth Ox WD1 ................. 175 A7
Halls Cl. Welw AL6 ............ 89 C4
Hallside Rd. Enf EN1 ........ 161 F1
Hallwicks Rd. Luton LU2 .... 46 B3
Hallworth Dr. Stot SG5 ...... 11 E6
Hallworth House. Stot SG5 11 E6
Halsey Dr. Hit SG4 ............ 35 B7
Halsey Pk. Lon C AL2 ...... 142 F4
Halsey Pl. Watf WD2 ....... 154 B1
Halsey Rd. Watf WD1 ...... 167 B6
Halstead Hill. Gofs O EN7 147 E1
Halter Cl. Bor WD6 .......... 170 D4
Haltside. Hat AL10 .......... 129 E4
Halwick Cl. Heml H HP1 ... 124 B1
Halyard Cl. Luton LU3 ........ 45 B6
Halyard High Sch. Dun ....... 44 A3
Hamberlins La. Nthch HP4 121 C7
Hamble Ct. Watf WD1 ..... 167 A5
Hambridge Way. Pirt SG5 .. 20 D4
Hambro Cl. Nwml E LU2 .... 85 F7
Hamburgh Ct. Ches EN8 ... 148 D3
Hamels Dr. Hert SG13 ..... 114 B7
Hamer Cl. Bov HP3 .......... 137 A3
Hamilton Ave. Hod EN11 .. 135 A8
Hamilton Cl. Bri Wd AL2 ... 155 A8
Hamilton Cl. Ridge EN6 .... 158 A6
Hamilton Ct. Hat AL10 ..... 130 B3 3
Hamilton Mead. Bov HP3 . 137 A4
Hamilton Rd. Abb L WD4 . 153 C6
Hamilton Rd. Berk HP4 ... 122 B4
Hamilton Rd. St Alb AL1 ... 128 A4
Hamilton Rd. Sth Ox WD1 175 B7
Hamilton St. Watf WD1 ... 167 C4
Hamlet The. Pot En HP4 .. 123 A7
Hammarskjold Rd. Harl CM20 ................... 117 D2
Hammer La. Heml H HP2 . 124 F4
Hammers Gate. Chis AL2 . 141 A5
Hammond Cl. Ham St EN7 147 F5
Hammond Cl. Stev SG1 ...... 50 D6
Hammond Ct. Cad LU1 ....... 63 C1
Hammond Jun Mix Inf Sch The. Heml H ............................ 124 F6
Hammonds La. Sand AL4 . 109 B3
Hammondstreet Rd. Ham St EN7 ................. 147 D5
Hammondswick. Harp AL5 106 F4
Hamonte. Letw SG6 ........... 23 C4
Hampden Cl. Letw SG6 ...... 23 B8
Hampden Cres. Ches EN7 162 B8
Hampden Hill Cl. Ware SG12 .................... 93 F2
Hampden Hill. Ware SG12 . 93 F2
Hampden. Kim SG4 ........... 66 C1
Hampden Pl. Lon C AL2 ... 141 E2
Hampden Rd. Har HA3 ..... 176 C1
Hampden Rd. Hit SG4 ........ 22 C1
Hampden Way. Watf WD1 153 E3
Hampermill La. Watf WD1 167 A1
Hampton Cl. Stev SG2 ........ 69 C7
Hampton Gdns. Saw CM21 ................. 118 C7
Hampton Rd. Luton LU4 ..... 63 B8
Hamstel Rd. Harl CM20 ..... 117 C1
Hanaper Dr. Bar SG8 .......... 8 F2
Hanbury Cl. Ches EN8 ...... 148 E2
Hanbury Cl. Ware SG12 ..... 93 D1
Hanbury Cotts. Ess AL9 .... 131 E6
Hanbury Dr. Thun SG12 ..... 93 C6
Hanbury Mews. Thun SG12 93 C5
Hancock Ct. Bor WD6 ...... 170 C8
Hancock Dr. Luton LU2 ...... 45 E5
Hancroft Rd. Heml H HP3 124 F1
Hand La. Saw CM21 ........... 97 C1
Handa Cl. Heml H HP3 .... 139 B8
Handcross Rd. Luton LU2 .. 46 D2
Handside Cl. Wel G C AL8 110 C6
Handside Gn. Wel G C AL8 ................. 110 C7
Handside La. Wel G C AL8 110 C6
Handsworth Cl. Sth Ox WD1 ................. 175 A7
Hangar Ruding. Sth Ox WD1 ................. 175 F7
Hanger Cl. Heml H HP1 ... 124 B2
Hanger's Wood Sch. Sth Ox .......................... 175 B7
Hangmans La. Welw AL6 ... 89 F8
Hanover Cl. Stev SG2 ......... 50 F1
Hanover Ct. Cro Gr WD3 . 166 A4
Hanover Ct. Luton LU4 ...... 44 D5
Hanover Gdns. Abb L WD5 ................... 139 F1
Hanover Gn. Heml H HP1 124 A1
Hanover Wlk. Hat AL10 ... 129 F2
Hanscombe End Rd. Shil SG5 ........................ 19 D7
Hanselin Cl. Stan HA7 ...... 176 F5

Hanswick Cl. Luton LU2 ..... 46 B2
Hanworth Cl. Luton LU2 ..... 45 D7
Hanyards End. Cuf EN6 ..... 146 E3
Hanyards La. Cuf EN6 ..... 146 D3
Happy Valley Ind Pk. Kin L 139 B2
Harbell Cl. Hert SG13 ..... 114 B6
Harborne Cl. Sth Ox WD1 175 C5
Harbury Dell. Luton LU3 .... 45 B7
Harcourt Rd. Bus WD2 .... 168 C4
Harcourt Rd. Tri HP23 ..... 100 C4
Harcourt St. Luton LU1 ..... 63 E5
Harding Cl. Luton LU3 ..... 44 E7
Harding Cl. Red AL3 ..... 106 B5
Harding Cl. Watf WD2 ..... 154 C6
Harding Par. Harp AL5 ..... 86 B1
Hardings. Wel G C AL7 .... 111 C7
Hardingstone Ct. Ches EN8 ..... 162 F5
Hardwick Cl. Stev SG2 ..... 69 C7
Hardwick Gn. Luton LU3 .... 45 B7
Hardwick Pl. Lon C AL2 .... 142 D4
Hardy Cl. Barn EN5 ..... 171 E4
Hardy Cl. Hit SG4 ..... 35 C7
Hardy Dr. Royst SG8 ..... 7 D8
Hardy Rd. Heml H HP2 ..... 124 F4
Hare Cres. Watf WD2 ..... 154 A7
Hare La. Hat AL10 ..... 130 B3
Hare Street Rd. Bun SG9 ... 41 C8
Harebell. Wel G C AL7 ..... 110 E3
Harebreaks The. Watf WD2 ..... 154 A2
Harefield Ct. Luton LU1 ..... 62 F8
Harefield. Harl CM20 ..... 118 A1
Harefield Hospl. Hare ..... 173 C3
Harefield Inf Sch. Hare .... 173 C2
Harefield Jun Sch. Hare .. 173 C2
Harefield Pl. St Alb AL4 ... 128 D6
Harefield Rd. Luton LU1 ..... 62 F8
Harefield Rd. Ric WD3 .... 173 D7
Harefield. Stev SG2 ..... 51 C3
Harepark Cl. Heml H HP1 123 F4
Harewood Rd. Sth Ox WD1 ..... 175 B7
Harewood. Ric WD3 ..... 165 C4
Harford Dr. Watf WD1 ..... 166 E8
Harforde Ct. Hert ..... 114 A6
Hargrave Cl. Sta M CM24 .. 59 E8
Hargreaves Ave. Ches EN7 ..... 162 B8
Hargreaves Cl. Ches EN7 162 B8
Hargreaves Rd. Royst SG8 .. 7 D5
Harkett Cl. Har HA3 ..... 176 F1
Harkness. Ches EN8 ..... 148 B2
Harkness Ct. Hit SG4 ..... 22 B1
Harkness Way. Hit SG4 ..... 22 C2
Harlequin The. Watf WD1 167 C5
Harlesden Rd. St Alb AL1 . 128 A3
Harlestone Cl. Luton LU3 ... 31 A1
Harley Ct. St Alb AL4 ..... 128 D7
Harlings The. Hert H SG13 ..... 114 C2
Harlow Coll. Harl ..... 117 E1
Harlow Ct. Heml H HP2 ... 125 A7
Harlow Mill Sta. Harl ..... 118 C5
Harlow Rd. Roy CM19 ..... 116 C1
Harlow Rd. Saw CM21 ..... 118 C8
Harlow Sport Ctr. Harl ..... 117 D2
Harlow The Spinney Cty Jun & Inf Sch. Harl ..... 118 A1
Harlow Town Sta. Harl ..... 117 D3
Harlowbury Cty Prim Sch. Harl ..... 118 D4
Harlton Ct. Wa Aby EN9 ... 163 F5
Harmer Dell. Welw AL6 ..... 89 F4
Harmer Green La. Welw AL6 ..... 90 B5
Harmony Cl. Hat AL10 ..... 130 A7
Harmsworth Way. Barn N20 ..... 171 F1
Harness Way. St Alb AL4 . 128 D6
Harold Cres. Wa Aby EN9 163 C7
Harpenden Central Sta. Harp ..... 86 B1
Harpenden Hospl. Harp ..... 86 A4
Harpenden La. Red AL3 ... 106 B6
Harpenden Memorial Hospl. Harp ..... 86 B2
Harpenden Rd. Whea AL4 108 B8
Harpenden Rise. Harp AL5 85 F3
Harper Ct. Stev SG1 ..... 50 F5
Harper La. Lon C WD7,AL2 ..... 156 B8
Harperbury Hospl. Lon C . 156 C8
Harps Hill. Mark AL3 ..... 83 E5
Harpsfield Broadway. Hat AL10 ..... 129 F6
Harptree Way. St Alb AL1 128 A5
Harriet Way. Bus WD2 ... 168 D2
Harrington Cl. Bis St CM23 77 A7
Harrington Ct. Hert H SG13 ..... 114 C3
Harris La. Gt Of SG5 ..... 33 D2
Harris La. Shen WD7 ..... 157 A6
Harris Rd. Watf WD2 ..... 154 A4
Harris's La. Ware SG12 ..... 93 C1
Harrison Cl. Hit SG4 ..... 34 F7
Harrison Cl. Norwd HA6 . 174 C4
Harrison Wlk. Ches EN8 .. 148 D1
Harrisons. Birhr CM23 ..... 59 D2
Harrogate Rd. Sth Ox WD1 ..... 175 C7
Harrow Coll of F Ed. Pnr .. 176 A3
Harrow Ct. Stev SG1 ..... 50 E5
Harrow View. Har HA2 .... 176 C1
Harrow Way. Sth Ox WD1 ..... 175 E6
Harrow Weald Pk. Stan HA3 ..... 176 D4
Harrow Weald Sixth Form Coll. Stan ..... 176 E4
Harrow Yd. Tri HP23 ..... 100 A3
Harrowden Ct. Luton LU2 .. 64 C8
Harrowden Rd. Luton LU2 . 64 C8
Harrowdene. Stev SG2 ..... 51 C4
Harry Scott Ct. Luton LU4 .. 44 C6
Hart Hill Dr. Luton LU2 ..... 63 F8
Hart Hill Jun & Inf Sch. Luton ..... 63 F8
Hart Hill La. Luton LU2 ..... 63 F8
Hart La. Luton LU2 ..... 46 A1
Hart Lodge. Barn EN5 ..... 171 E6
Hart Rd. Harl CM17 ..... 118 C6
Hart Rd. St Alb AL1 ..... 127 D2
Hart Wlk. Luton LU2 ..... 46 A1
Hartfield Ave. Bor WD6 .... 170 A4
Hartfield Cl. Bor WD6 ..... 170 A4
Hartfield Ct. Ware SG12 .... 93 D2
Hartforde Rd. Bor WD6 ... 170 B8
Harthall La. Abb L WD4,WD5 ..... 139 D4
Hartham La. Hert SG14 ... 113 D6
Hartland Rd. Ches EN8 .... 148 D1
Hartley Rd. Luton LU2 ..... 63 F8
Hartmoor Mews. Enf EN3 162 D2
Harts Cl. Bus WD2 ..... 168 A8
Hartsbourne Ave. Bus WD2 ..... 176 D8
Hartsbourne Cl. Bus WD2 176 D8
Hartsbourne Country Club. Bus ..... 176 C8
Hartsbourne Jun Mix Inf Sch. Bus ..... 176 D8
Hartsbourne Rd. Bus WD2 ..... 176 D8
Hartsbourne Way. Heml H HP2 ..... 125 C2
Hartsfield Jun Mix Inf Sch. Bal ..... 12 F1
Hartsfield Rd. Luton LU2 .... 46 B2
Hartspring La. Bus WD2 .. 168 A8
Hartswood Gn. Bus WD2 . 176 D8
Hartwell Gdns. Harp AL5 .... 85 E1
Hartwood. Luton LU2 ..... 63 F8
Harvest Cl. Dun LU4 ..... 44 A3
Harvest Ct. St Alb AL4 ..... 128 D7
Harvest Ct. Welw AL6 ..... 89 E7
Harvest End. Watf WD2 .. 154 D3
Harvest Mead. Hat AL10 .. 130 B7
Harvest Rd. Bus WD2 ..... 168 B5
Harvey Rd. Cro Gr WD3 .... 166 A3
Harvey Rd. Lon C AL2 ..... 142 C5
Harvey Rd. Stev SG2 ..... 51 B6
Harvey Road Jun Mid Inf Sch. Cro Gr ..... 166 A3
Harvey's Hill. Luton LU2 .... 45 F5
Harveyfields. Wa Aby EN9 163 C5
Harveys Cotts. L Had SG11 75 F8
Harwood Cl. Tewin AL6 ..... 90 E2
Harwood Cl. Wel G C AL8 .. 89 E2
Harwood Hill Jun Mix Inf Sch. Wel G C ..... 89 E2
Harwood Hill. Wel G C AL8 89 E1
Harwoods Rd. Watf WD1 167 A5
Hasedines Rd. Heml H HP1 ..... 124 A4
Haseldine Meadows. Hat AL10 ..... 129 F4
Haseldine Rd. Lon C AL2 .. 142 D5
Haselfoot. Letw SG6 ..... 22 E6
Hasketon Dr. Luton LU4 ..... 44 B6
Haslemere. Bis St CM23 .... 77 A4
Haslemere Ind Est. Wel G C ..... 110 F7
Haslewood Ave. Hod EN11 ..... 135 A6
Haslewood Jun Sch. Hod . 135 A6
Haslingden Cl. Harp AL5 .... 85 D3
Hassobury Waterside Sch. Far ..... 58 F7
Haste Hill Golf Course. Norwd ..... 174 E1
Hastings Cl. Stev SG1 ..... 50 A8
Hastings St. Luton LU1 ..... 63 D6
Hastings Way. Cro Gr WD3 ..... 166 C5
Hastings Way. Watf WD2 167 E5
Hastoe La. Tri HP23 ..... 100 A2
Hatch End High Sch. Har . 176 B2
Hatch End Sta. Pnr ..... 176 A3
Hatch Gn. L Hal CM22 ..... 98 B8
Hatch La. Wes SG4 ..... 24 A3
Hatching Green Cl. Harp AL5 ..... 107 A6
Hatfield Aerodrome. Hat . 129 D6
Hatfield Ave. Hat AL10 ..... 129 E8
Hatfield Bsns Ctr. Hat ..... 129 E8
Hatfield Cres. Heml H HP2 ..... 124 F7
Hatfield Rd. Coln H AL4 ... 128 C3
Hatfield Rd. Ess SG14 ..... 111 E1
Hatfield Rd. Hertng SG14 112 B4
Hatfield Rd. Pot B EN6 ..... 159 C8
Hatfield Rd. St Alb AL1,AL4 ..... 128 C3
Hatfield Rd. Watf WD2 .... 167 B8
Hatfield Sch. Wel Gr ..... 130 B1
Hatfield Sta. Hat ..... 130 C6
Hatfield Tunnel. Hat AL10 129 F6
Hathaway Cl. Dun LU4 ..... 44 B2
Hathaway Ct. Coln H AL4 . 128 E3
Hatherleigh Gdns. Pot B EN6 ..... 159 D7
Hatters La. Watf WD1 ..... 166 D3
Hatters Way. Luton LU1,LU4 ..... 63 B8
Hatton Rd. Ches EN8 ..... 148 D2
Havelock Rd. Kin L WD4 .. 138 F3
Havelock Rd. Luton LU2 ..... 45 E1
Havelock Rise. Luton LU2 .. 45 E1
Haven Cl. Hat AL10 ..... 129 F6
Havenfield. Chipf WD4 ..... 152 B8
Havercroft Cl. St Alb AL3 . 127 C1
Haverdale. Luton LU4 ..... 44 C4
Havers Inf Sch The. Bis St . 76 E5
Havers La. Bis St CM23 ..... 76 F5
Havers Par. Bis St CM23 .... 76 F5
Haward Rd. Hod EN11 ..... 135 C8
Hawbush Cl. Welw AL6 ..... 89 B4
Hawbush Rise. Welw AL6 .. 89 B5
Hawes Cl. Norwd HA6 ..... 174 F3
Hawes La. Wa Aby EN9 .. 163 C1
Haweswater Dr. Watf WD2 ..... 154 C6
Hawfield Gdns. Pk St AL2 141 D5
Hawkesworth Cl. Norwd HA6 ..... 174 E3
Hawkfield. Letw SG6 ..... 22 E8
Hawkfields. Luton LU2 ..... 45 E6
Hawkins Cl. Bor WD6 ..... 170 C7
Hawkins Hall La. Dat SG3 .. 69 E2
Hawkshead Ct. Ches EN8 162 F5
Hawkshead La. Bro Pk AL9 ..... 144 D3
Hawkshead Rd. Pot B EN6 145 B2
Hawkshill Dr. Heml H HP3 137 F8
Hawkshill. St Alb AL1 ..... 128 A2
Hawksmead Cl. Enf EN3 .. 162 D3
Hawksmoor. Shen WD7 ... 157 A6
Hawkwell Dr. Tri HP23 .... 100 C4
Hawridge & Cholesbury C of E Combd Sch. Chol 120 E2
Hawridge La. Chol HP5 .... 120 F1
Hawridge Vale. Chol HP5 120 F1
Hawsley Rd. Harp AL5 ..... 107 A4
Hawthorn Ave. Luton LU2 .. 46 B4
Hawthorn Cl. Abb L WD5 . 154 A7
Hawthorn Cl. Harp AL5 .... 107 D7
Hawthorn Cl. Hert SG14 .. 113 A7
Hawthorn Cl. Hit SG5 ..... 34 E6
Hawthorn Cl. Royst SG8 ..... 7 F7
Hawthorn Cl. Watf WD1 .. 153 F1
Hawthorn Cres. Cad LU1 ... 62 E3
Hawthorn Gr. Enf EN2 ..... 161 D1
Hawthorn Hill. Letw SG6 ... 22 F7
Hawthorn La. Heml H HP1 ..... 123 F4
Hawthorn Rd. Hod EN11 .. 135 B8
Hawthorn Rise. Bis St CM23 ..... 76 F3
Hawthorn Way. Chis AL2 . 141 A7
Hawthorn Way. Royst SG8 .. 7 F7
Hawthorne Ave. Ches EN7 ..... 162 B8
Hawthorne Cl. Ches EN7 . 162 B8
Hawthorne Ct. Pnr HA6 ... 175 A1
Hawthorne Rd. Radl WD7 156 A5
Hawthornes. Hat AL10 ..... 129 F3
Hawthorns The. Berk HP4 122 A5
Hawthorns The. Heml H HP3 ..... 137 F7
Hawthorns The. Map Cr WD3 ..... 172 D5
Hawthorns The. Stev SG1 .. 51 A4
Hawthorns The. Ware SG12 ..... 93 C3
Hawthorns. Wel G C AL8 . 110 D8
Hawtrees. Radl WD7 ..... 155 F4
Hay Cl. Bor WD6 ..... 170 C7
Hay La. Harp AL5 ..... 86 A1
Haybourn Mead. Heml H HP1 ..... 124 B2
Haycroft. Bis St CM23 ..... 77 C7
Haycroft Rd. Stev SG1 ..... 50 E7
Haydock Rd. Royst SG8 ..... 7 F6
Haydon Hill House. Bus WD2 ..... 167 F2
Haydon Rd. Watf WD1 ..... 167 E3
Hayes Cl. Luton LU2 ..... 46 C5
Hayes Wlk. Ches EN10 ..... 148 F6
Hayfield Cl. Bus WD2 ..... 168 B5
Hayfield. Stev SG2 ..... 51 D7
Haygarth. Kneb SG3 ..... 69 A4
Hayhurst Rd. Dun LU4 ..... 44 B1
Hayley Bell Gdns. Bis St CM23 ..... 76 F3
Hayley Comm. Stev SG2 .... 51 C3
Hayling Dr. Luton LU2 ..... 46 D3
Hayling Rd. Sth Ox WD1 .. 175 B8
Haymeads La. Bis St CM23 77 C6
Haymeads. Wel G C AL8 .... 89 E1
Haymoor. Letw SG6 ..... 22 E7
Haynes Cl. Wel G C AL7 ... 111 A5
Haynes Mead. Berk HP4 .. 122 A6
Haysman Cl. Letw SG6 ..... 23 B7
Hayton Cl. Luton LU3 ..... 31 B2
Haywood Cl. Pnr HA5 ..... 175 D1
Haywood Ct. Wa Aby EN9 163 F5
Haywood La. Ther SG8 ..... 16 A6
Haywood Pk. Chor WD3 .. 164 F4
Haywoods Dr. Heml H HP3 ..... 137 F8
Haywoods La. Royst SG8 ..... 7 E7
Hazel Cl. Ham St EN7 ..... 147 E5
Hazel Cl. Welw AL6 ..... 89 E3
Hazel Ct. Hit SG4 ..... 35 A7
Hazel Gdns. Sheer CM21 ... 97 F1
Hazel Gr. Hat AL10 ..... 129 F2
Hazel Gr. Stot SG5 ..... 11 E5
Hazel Gr. Watf WD2 ..... 154 B4
Hazel Gr. Wel G C AL7 ..... 111 C7
Hazel Mead. Barn EN5 ..... 171 B4
Hazel Rd. Berk HP4 ..... 122 D3
Hazel Rd. Chis AL2 ..... 141 B3
Hazel Tree Rd. Watf WD2 154 B3
Hazelbury Ave. Abb L WD5 ..... 153 C7
Hazelbury Cres. Luton LU1 63 C8
Hazelcroft. Pnr HA5 ..... 176 B4
Hazeldell Link. Heml H HP1 ..... 123 E2
Hazeldell Rd. Heml H HP1 123 F2
Hazeldell. Wat St SG14 ..... 70 D3
Hazeldene. Ches EN8 ..... 162 E7
Hazelend Rd. Bis St CM23 . 59 B4
Hazelgrove Prim Sch. Hat 129 F2
Hazelmere Rd. St Alb AL4 128 C6
Hazelmere Rd. Stev SG2 .... 69 A8
Hazels The. Tewin AL6 ..... 90 E2
Hazelwood Cl. Hit SG5 ..... 34 F8
Hazelwood Cl. Luton LU2 ... 46 B4
Hazelwood Dr. Pnr HA5 ... 175 B1
Hazelwood Dr. St Alb AL4 128 C4
Hazelwood Inf Sch. Abb L 153 E8
Hazelwood La. Abb L WD5 153 D7
Hazelwood Rd. Cro Gr WD3 ..... 166 C3
Hazely. Tri HP23 ..... 100 C4
Heacham Cl. Dun LU4 ..... 44 B4
Headingley Cl. Ham St EN7 ..... 147 F5
Headingley Cl. Shen WD7 156 E7
Headingley Cl. Stev SG1 .... 50 E8
Headstone La. Har HA2,HA3 ..... 176 B2
Headstone Lane Sta. Har . 176 B2
Healey Rd. Watf WD1 ..... 166 F3
Health Farm La. St Alb AL3 ..... 127 E5
Healy Ct. Barn EN5 ..... 171 D3
Heath Ave. Royst SG8 ..... 7 C6
Heath Ave. St Alb AL3 ..... 127 D5
Heath Brow. Heml H HP1 124 C1
Heath Cl. Harp AL5 ..... 107 C7
Heath Cl. Heml H HP1 ..... 124 C2
Heath Cl. Luton LU1 ..... 63 B6
Heath Cl. Pot B EN6 ..... 145 B1
Heath Dr. Pot B EN6 ..... 145 A1
Heath Dr. Ware SG12 ..... 93 D3
Heath Farm Ct. Sar WD1 . 153 D2
Heath Hall. Bal ..... 23 F7
Heath Hill. Cod SG4 ..... 67 D1
Heath La. Cod SG4 ..... 67 E1
Heath La. Heml H HP1 ..... 124 C2
Heath La. Hert H SG13 .... 114 C2
Heath Lodge. Bus WD2 .... 168 D1
Heath Mount Sch. Wat St .. 71 B2
Heath Rd. Bre Gr SG4 ..... 47 D1
Heath Rd. Pot B EN6 ..... 145 B1
Heath Rd. St Alb AL1 ..... 127 E5
Heath Rd. Watf WD1 ..... 167 E2
Heath Rd. Welw AL6 ..... 68 F1
Heath Row. Bis St CM23 .... 59 B1
Heath The. Bre Gr SG4 ..... 47 D2
Heath The. Radl WD7 ..... 156 A6
Heathbourne Rd. Stan WD2,HA7 ..... 168 F1
Heathbrow Rd. Welw AL6 .. 89 F8
Heathcote Ave. Hat AL10 . 130 A7
Heathcote Sch. Stev ..... 51 A2
Heather Cl. Abb L WD5 .... 154 A7
Heather Cl. Bis St CM23 .... 76 D6
Heather Rd. Wel G C AL8 . 110 C4
Heather Rise. Bus WD2 ... 167 F7
Heather Way. Har HA7 .... 176 F4
Heather Way. Heml H HP2 ..... 124 D4
Heather Way. Pot B EN6 . 158 F7
Heathermere. Letw SG6 ..... 11 F1
Heathfield Cl. Cad LU1 ..... 62 F4
Heathfield Cl. Pot B EN6 .. 145 B1
Heathfield Ct. St Alb AL1 . 127 E4
Heathfield Lower Sch. Cad 62 E4
Heathfield Rd. Hit SG5 ..... 21 F1
Heathfield Rd. Luton LU3 ... 45 C4
Heathfield Rd. Watf WD2 167 F5
Heathfield. Royst SG8 ..... 7 B6
Heathgate. Hert H SG13 .. 114 B2
Heathlands Dr. St Alb AL3 127 E5
Heathlands Sch. St Alb .... 127 E6
Heathlands. Welw AL6 ..... 68 F1
Heathside Cl. Mo Pk HA6 . 174 D5
Heathside. Col H AL4 ..... 143 B8
Heathside Rd. Mo Pk HA6 174 D6
Heathside. St Alb AL3 ..... 127 E5
Heathview. Harp AL5 ..... 107 B8
Heaton Ct. Ches EN8 ..... 148 D2
Heaton Dell. Luton LU2 ..... 46 E1
Heay Fields. Wel G C AL7 111 C7
Hebden Cl. Dun LU4 ..... 44 B4
Hedge Row. Heml H HP1 . 124 A5
Hedgebrooms. Wel G C AL7 ..... 111 C7
Hedgerows. Saw CM21 ..... 97 F2
Hedgerows The. Stev SG2 . 51 D8
Hedges Cl. Hat AL10 ..... 130 B6
Hedgeside. Pot En HP4 .... 123 A7
Hedgeside Rd. Norwd HA6 ..... 174 C5
Hedley Rd. St Alb AL1 ..... 128 B3
Hedley Rise. Luton LU2 ..... 46 F2
Hedworth Ave. Ches EN8 . 162 D6
Heights The. Heml H HP2 124 F6
Heights The. Luton LU3 ..... 44 E5
Helena Cl. Had W EN4 ..... 159 D1
Helena Pl. Heml H HP2 .... 124 D5
Helens Gate. Ches EN8 .... 148 F5
Hellards Rd. Stev SG1 ..... 50 D7
Hellebore Ct. Stev SG1 ..... 51 B8
Helmsley Cl. Luton LU4 ..... 44 C5
Helston Cl. Pnr HA5 ..... 175 F3
Helston Gr. Heml H HP2 .. 124 D8
Helston Pl. Abb L WD5 ..... 153 F7
Hemel Hempstead General Hospl. Heml H ..... 124 D3
Hemel Hempstead Rd. Heml H HP3 ..... 125 E1
Hemel Hempstead Rd. Red AL3 ..... 105 E2
Hemel Hempstead Rd. St Alb AL3 ..... 126 D1
Hemel Hempstead Rd. Stu HP4 ..... 81 E1
Hemel Hempstead Sch. Heml H ..... 124 C2
Hemel Hempstead Sta. Heml H ..... 138 A8
Hemingford Dr. Luton LU2 . 45 D6
Hemingford Rd. Watf WD1 ..... 153 E3
Hemming Way. Watf WD2 154 A4
Hemmings The. Berk HP4 121 F3
Hemp La. Wigg HP23 ..... 100 F1
Hempstall. Wel G C AL7 ... 111 B4
Hempstead La. Pot En HP4 ..... 123 C6
Hempstead Rd. Abb L WD4 ..... 139 A3
Hempstead Rd. Bov HP3 .. 137 B5
Hempstead Rd. Watf WD1 ..... 153 E2
Henbury Way. Sth Ox WD1 ..... 175 D7

Henderson Cl. St Alb AL3 . 127 C7
Henderson Pl. Abb L WD5 139 F4
Hendon Wood La.
Edge NW1 .................... 171 A1
Henge Way. Luton LU3 ...... 44 E7
Henry Cl. Enf EN2 ............. 161 E1
Henry St. Heml H HP3 ..... 138 D7
Henry St. Tri HP23 ........... 100 A3
Henrys Grant. St Alb AL1 . 127 E2
Hensley Cl. Hit SG4 ........... 35 B6
Hensley Cl. Welw AL6 ........ 89 C6
Henstead Pl. Luton LU2 ..... 46 D1 1
Herald Cl. Bis St CM23 ....... 76 D6
Herbert St. Heml H HP2 .. 124 D4
Hereford Rd. Dun LU4 ........ 44 A3
Hereward Cl.
Wa Aby EN9 ................. 163 C7
Herga Ct. Watf WD1 ........ 167 A7
Heritage Cl. St Alb AL3 .... 127 D3
Herkomer Cl. Bus WD2 .... 168 B3
Herkomer Rd. Bus WD2 ... 168 A3
Herm House. Enf EN3 ...... 162 D1
Hermitage Ct. Pot B EN6 . 159 C6
Hermitage Rd. Hit SG5 ....... 34 F7
Herne Ct. Bus WD2 .......... 168 C2
Herne Rd. Bus WD2 ......... 168 B3
Herne Rd. Stev SG1 .......... 36 B1
Herneshaw. Hat AL10 ...... 129 F3
Herns La. Wel G C AL7 ..... 111 B8
Herns Way. Wel G C AL7 . 111 A7
Heron Cl. Ric WD3 ........... 173 D8
Heron Cl. Saw CM21 .......... 97 D1
Heron Ct. Bis St CM23 ....... 77 A7
Heron Dr. Gt Am SG12 ..... 115 C3
Heron Dr. Luton LU2 .......... 45 E6
Heron Trad Est. Luton ....... 44 C7
Heron Way. Hat AL10 ...... 130 A3
Heron Wlk. Mo Pk HA6 ..... 174 E6
Heronfield. Pot B EN6 ...... 145 C1
Herongate Rd. Ches EN8 . 148 E4
Herons Elm. Nthch HP4 ... 121 E7
Herons Way. St Alb AL1 ... 142 B8
Herons Wood. Harl CM20 117 B2
Heronsgate Rd.
Chor WD3 .................... 164 B3
Heronslea. Watf WD2 ...... 154 C3
Heronswood Pl.
Wel G C AL7 ................. 111 A5
Heronswood Rd.
Wel G C AL7 ................. 111 A5
Heronswood. Wa Aby EN9 163 E5
Hertford County Hospl.
Hert ............................. 113 B6
Hertford East Sta. Hert .... 113 D6
Hertford Heath Cty Prim Sch.
Hert H .......................... 114 C4
Hertford Mews.
Pot B EN6 ..................... 159 C8
Hertford North Sta. Hert . 113 B6
Hertford Rd. Enf EN3 ....... 162 D3
Hertford Rd. Ess AL9 ....... 111 B1
Hertford Rd. Gt Am SG12 . 114 F4
Hertford Rd. Hat AL9 ....... 111 B1
Hertford Rd. Hat AL9 ....... 130 E8
Hertford Rd. Hod EN11 .... 134 E8
Hertford Rd. Stev SG2 ....... 68 F8
Hertford Rd. Stev SG2 ....... 69 B7
Hertford Rd. Tewin AL6 ..... 90 F2
Hertford Rd. Welw AL6 ..... 89 D3
Hertfordshire Bsns Ctr.
Lon C ........................... 142 D5
Hertfordshire Coll of
Building. St Alb ............ 127 E3
Hertfordshire & Essex
High Sch. Bis St ............ 77 B7
Hertfordshire Golf &
Country Clubs The. Hod 134 C3
Hertingfordbury Rd.
Hert SG14 ..................... 113 B5
Hertingfordbury Rd.
Hertng SG14 ................ 112 F4
Hertingfordbury Sch.
Hertng .......................... 112 C4
Hertswood Ct. Barn EN5 .. 171 E5 1
Hester House. Harl CM20 117 C2
Heswall Ct. Luton LU1 ........ 63 F6
Heswell Gn. Sth Ox WD1 . 175 A7
Hetchleys. Heml H HP1 .... 124 A6
Hewitt Cl. Whea AL4 ........ 108 D7
Hewlett Rd. Luton LU3 ...... 44 E5
Hexton Jun Mix Inf Sch.
Hex ................................ 19 A1
Hexton Rd. Gt Of SG5 ........ 33 E8
Hexton Rd. Lily LU2 ........... 32 C4
Heybridge Ct. Hert SG14 . 112 F7
Heydon Rd. Gt Ch SG8 ......... 9 E3
Heydons Cl. St Alb AL3 .... 127 D5
Heyford Rd. Radl WD7 ..... 155 F2
Heyford Way. Hat AL10 ... 130 C7
Heysham Dr. Sth Ox WD1 175 D5
Heywood Dr. Luton LU2 ..... 45 F2
Hibbert Ave. Watf WD2 ... 154 D1
Hibbert Rd. Har HA3 ........ 176 F1
Hibbert St. Luton LU1 ........ 63 E6
Hickling Cl. Luton LU2 ........ 46 D1
Hickling Way. Harp AL5 ..... 86 C3
Hickman Ct. Luton LU3 ...... 44 D8
Hicks Rd. Mark AL3 ........... 83 F6
Hidalgo Ct. Heml H HP2 ... 124 F6
Hideaway The.
Abb L WD5 ................... 153 F8
Hides The. Harl CM20 ...... 117 D1
High Acres. Abb L WD5 .... 153 D7
High Ash Rd. Whea AL4 ... 108 C7
High Ave. Letw SG6 ........... 22 E4
High Beech Rd. Luton LU3 . 44 D7
High Beeches Sch. Harp .... 86 D1
High Canons. Shen WD6 .. 157 D2
High Cl. Ric WD3 .............. 165 C4
High Cross. Radl WD2 ..... 155 D2
High Dane. Hit SG4 ............ 22 A2
High Dells. Hat AL10 ........ 129 F4
High Elms Cl. Norwd HA6 174 D4
High Elms. Harp AL5 ........ 107 A6
High Elms La.
Abb L WD2,WD5 .......... 154 C8
High Elms La. Ben SG14 .... 70 E8
High Elms La. Ben SG2 ...... 52 F1
High Firs Cres. Harp AL5 . 107 D8
High Firs. Radl WD7 ........ 156 A4
High Gr. Wel G C AL8 ....... 110 C7
High House Est.
Harl CM17 .................... 118 F4
High La. Sta M CM24 ......... 59 F8
High Mead. Luton LU3 ....... 45 A3
High Meads. Whea AL4 .... 108 C8
High Oak Rd. Ware SG12 ... 93 E3
High Oaks. Enf EN2 .......... 160 F1
High Oaks Rd.
Wel G C AL8 ................. 110 B7
High Oaks. St Alb AL3 ...... 127 D7
High Pastures.
Sheer CM22 .................. 98 D1
High Plash. Stev SG1 ......... 50 E5
High Point. Luton LU1 ........ 63 D6
High Rd. Bus WD2 ........... 168 D1
High Rd. Ess AL9 .............. 131 E5
High Rd. Har HA3 ............ 176 E3
High Rd. Hod EN10 .......... 134 F4
High Rd. Shil SG5 .............. 19 E8
High Rd. Stap SG14 ........... 92 A2
High Rd. Watf WD2 .......... 153 F5
High Rd. Watf WD2 .......... 154 A7
High Ridge. Cuf EN6 ........ 146 E4
High Ridge. Harp AL5 ........ 85 E3
High Ridge. Luton LU2 ....... 46 C1
High Ridge Rd.
Heml H HP3 .................. 138 D7
High Road Broxbourne.
Hod EN10 ..................... 134 F1
High Road Turnford.
Ches EN8 ..................... 148 E6
High Road Wormley.
Ches EN8 ..................... 148 F8
High Road Wormley.
Hod EN8 ....................... 148 F8
High St. Abb L WD5 ......... 139 F1
High St. Abb L WD5 ......... 139 F4
High St. Arl SG15 .............. 11 A5
High St. Ashw SG7 ............. 4 D4
High St. Bal SG7 ............... 23 F8
High St. Bar SG8 ................. 8 F2
High St. Bark SG8 .............. 17 C3
High St. Barn EN5 ........... 171 F5
High St. Berk HP4 ........... 122 B4
High St. Bis St CM23 ......... 76 F7
High St. Bov HP3 ............ 137 A4
High St. Bun SG9 .............. 40 E8
High St. Bus WD2 ............ 168 A3
High St. Ched LU7 ............. 80 A7
High St. Ches EN8 ........... 148 D2
High St. Ches EN8 ........... 162 D7
High St. Ches EN8 ........... 162 E5
High St. Cod SG4 ............... 67 F1
High St. Coln H AL4 ......... 129 B1
High St. Elst WD6 ............ 169 D3
High St. Fla AL3 ................ 84 B2
High St. Gra SG4 ............... 36 C4
High St. Gt Am SG12 ....... 115 C4
High St. Gt Of SG5 ............. 33 C3
High St. Gu M SG8 .............. 1 F4
High St. Har HA3 ............. 176 E1
High St. Hare UB9 ........... 173 C1
High St. Harl CM17 .......... 118 D4
High St. Harp AL5 .............. 86 A1
High St. Heml H HP1,HP3 124 D4
High St. Hin SG7 ................. 3 D6
High St. Hit SG4 ................ 34 F3
High St. Hit SG5 ................ 34 E7
High St. Hod EN11 .......... 135 A5
High St. Hun SG12 ............. 95 D1
High St. Kim SG4 ............... 66 C1
High St. Kin L WD4 .......... 139 A2
High St. Lon C AL2 .......... 142 D5
High St. Luton LU4 ............ 44 C4
High St. Mark AL3 ............. 83 E5
High St. Muc H SG10 ......... 74 F3
High St. Norwd HA6 ........ 174 F2
High St. Nthch HP4 ......... 121 E6
High St. Nthch HP4 ......... 121 E7
High St. Pirt SG5 ............... 20 D4
High St. Pit LU7 ................. 80 E5
High St. Pot B EN6 .......... 159 C7
High St. Red AL3 ............. 106 B5
High St. Reed SG8 ............. 16 E5
High St. Ric WD3 ............. 165 E1
High St. Roy CM19 .......... 116 B1
High St. Royst SG8 .............. 7 D6
High St. Sand AL4 ........... 108 C2
High St. St Alb AL3 .......... 127 D3
High St. Stand SG11 .......... 55 D3
High St. Stand SG11 .......... 55 F1
High St. Stev SG1 .............. 50 C7
High St. Stot SG5 ............... 11 F6
High St. Tri HP23 ............ 100 A3
High St. Walk SG2 ............. 38 B1
High St. Ware SG12 ........... 93 D1
High St. Wat St SG14 ......... 70 E3
High St. Watf WD1 .......... 167 B6
High St. Watf WD1 .......... 167 C5
High St. Welw AL6 ............. 89 C5
High St. Whea AL4 ............. 87 D1
High St. Whit SG4 .............. 66 F7
High St. Widf SG12 ............ 95 E5
High Street Gn.
Heml H HP2 .................. 125 A5
High Town Rd. Luton LU2 .. 45 F1
High View. Birhr CM23 ....... 59 D3
High View. Chor WD3 ...... 165 A5
High View Ct. Har HA3 ..... 176 E3
High View. Hat AL10 ........ 130 A2
High View. Hit SG5 ............ 34 D7
High View. Mark AL3 ......... 83 E4
High View. Watf WD1 ...... 166 F3
High Wickfield.
Wel G C AL7 ................. 111 C5
High Wood Cl. Luton LU1 ... 63 A7
High Wood Rd. Hod EN11 114 F1
High Wych Jun Mix Inf Sch.
H Wy .............................. 97 A1
High Wych La. H Wy CM21 97 A2
High Wych Rd.
H Wy CM21 ................. 117 F7
High Wych Rd. Saw CM21 . 97 B1
High Wych Way.
Heml H HP2 .................. 105 A1
Higham Dr. Luton LU2 ........ 46 D1
Highbanks Rd. Pnr HA5 ... 176 B4
Highbarns. Heml H HP3 ... 139 A6
Highbridge St.
Wa Aby EN9 ................. 163 B6
Highbury Ave. Hod EN11 . 135 B8
Highbury House (North Herts
Rural Music Sch). Hit ...... 35 A7
Highbury Inf Sch. Hit ......... 34 F6
Highbury Rd. Hit SG4 ........ 35 A7
Highbury Rd. Luton LU3 ..... 45 C1
Highbush Rd. Stot SG5 ....... 11 E5
Highclere Ct. St Alb AL1 ... 127 E4
Highclere Dr. Heml H HP3 139 B7
Highcroft Rd. Heml H HP3 138 B6
Highcroft. Stev SG2 ........... 50 F1 2
Highfield Ave. Bis St CM23 77 C6
Highfield Ave. Harp AL5 ... 107 D8
Highfield. Bus WD2 .......... 176 E8
Highfield Cl. Norwd HA6 .. 174 E2
Highfield Cres.
Norwd HA6 .................. 174 E2
Highfield Ct. Stev SG1 ........ 50 F7
Highfield Dr. Hod EN10 .... 134 E2
Highfield. Kin L WD4 ........ 138 E3
Highfield La. Coln H AL1 .. 142 E8
Highfield La. Heml H HP2 124 F5
Highfield. Letw SG6 ........... 22 E4
Highfield Oval. Harp AL5 ... 86 A4
Highfield Rd. Berk HP4 .... 122 D4
Highfield Rd. Ham St EN7 147 E5
Highfield Rd. Hert SG13 ... 113 D4
Highfield Rd. Luton LU4 ..... 45 B1
Highfield Rd. Norwd HA6 . 174 E2
Highfield Rd. Sand AL4 .... 108 B1
Highfield Rd. Tri HP23 ....... 99 E3
Highfield Rd. Watf WD2 ... 167 E4
Highfield Rd. Wigg HP23 . 100 D1
Highfield. Saw CM21 .......... 97 E3
Highfield Sch The. Letw ..... 22 D3
Highfield Way. Ric WD3 ... 165 B3
Highfields Cl. Dun LU5 ...... 44 A2
Highfields. Cuf EN6 .......... 146 E3
Highfields. Radl WD7 ....... 155 F4
Highfiled Way. Pot B EN6 159 B7
Highgate Gr. Saw CM21 .... 97 D2
Highgrove Ct. Ches EN8 ... 162 D5
Highland Dr. Bus WD2 ..... 168 C2
Highland Dr. Heml H HP3 125 B3
Highland Rd. Bis St CM23 .. 76 F3
Highland Rd. Lo Naz EN9 . 135 E1
Highland Rd. Norwd HA6 . 175 A1
Highlands. Hat AL9 .......... 130 C8
Highlands. Royst SG8 .......... 7 E6
Highlands The. Pot B EN6 145 C1
Highlands The. Ric WD3 .. 165 B2
Highlands. Watf WD1 ...... 167 C1
Highmead. Sta M CM24 ..... 59 E8
Highmill. Ware SG12 .......... 93 D3
Highmoor. Harp AL5 .......... 86 A4
Highover Cl. Luton LU2 ...... 46 B1
Highover Prim Sch. Hit ...... 22 B1
Highover Rd. Letw SG6 ...... 22 D5
Highover Way. Hit SG4 ...... 22 B1
Highview Cl. Pot B EN6 ..... 159 C6
Highview Gdns.
Pot B EN6 ..................... 159 C6
Highview Gdns.
St Alb AL4 ..................... 128 C8
Highway The. Har HA7 .... 176 F2
Highwick Sch. Stev ............ 50 F7
Highwood Ave. Bus WD2 . 167 F8
Highwood Jun Mix Inf Sch.
Bus ............................... 167 E8
Highwoodhall La.
Heml H WD4,WD5 ....... 139 C7
Hilbury. Hat AL10 ............ 129 F4
Hilfield La. Radl WD2 ....... 168 D6
Hilfield La S. Bus WD2 ..... 168 F3
Hill Cl. Barn EN5 ............. 171 C4
Hill Cl. Harp AL5 ............... 86 C4
Hill Cl. Luton LU3 .............. 45 C7
Hill Comm. Heml H HP3 ... 139 A8
Hill Crest. Pot B EN6 ........ 159 C5
Hill Crest. Whit SG4 .......... 66 E6
Hill Croft Cl. Luton LU4 ...... 44 C6
Hill Ct. Berk HP4 ............. 122 D5
Hill Dyke Rd. Whea AL4 ... 108 E7
Hill End Hospl. St Alb ....... 128 D2
Hill End La. St Alb AL4,AL1 128 C2
Hill End Rd. Hare UB9 ...... 173 C3
Hill Farm Ave. Abb L WD2 154 A6
Hill Farm Cl. Abb L WD2 .. 154 A6
Hill Farm La. A St L AL6 ..... 88 C5
Hill Farm La. Red AL3 ...... 106 C1
Hill House Ave. Har HA7 .. 176 F3
Hill House. Hert SG13 ..... 113 C5
Hill Ley. Hat AL10 ............ 129 F5
Hill Leys. Cuf EN6 ............ 146 E3
Hill Mead. Berk HP4 ........ 122 A3
Hill Rd. Cod SG4 ................ 67 E1
Hill Rd. Norwd HA6 ......... 174 D4
Hill Rise. Cuf EN6 ............ 146 E3
Hill Rise. Luton LU3 ........... 44 D7
Hill Rise. Pot B EN6 ......... 159 C5
Hill Rise. Ric WD3 ........... 165 B2
Hill Side. Ched LU7 ............ 79 F7
Hill St. St Alb AL3 ............ 127 C3
Hill The. Harl CM17 ......... 118 C4
Hill The. Whea AL4 .......... 108 D8
Hill Top. Bal ..................... 23 E7
Hill Tree Cl. Saw CM21 ...... 97 D1
Hill View. Berk HP4 ......... 122 A6
Hill View. Buck SG9 ........... 27 D8
Hill View. Whit SG4 ........... 66 E6
Hillary Cl. Luton LU3 ........ 44 D7
Hillary Cres. Luton LU1 ..... 63 C6
Hillary Rd. Heml H HP2 ..... 125 A4
Hillary Rise. Arl SG15 ........ 11 B5
Hillborough Rd. Luton LU1 . 63 D6
Hillbrow. Letw SG6 ............ 22 D5
Hillcrest Ave. Luton LU2 .... 45 C8
Hillcrest. Bal SG7 .............. 23 F7
Hillcrest. Hat AL10 .......... 130 A5
Hillcrest Rd. Shen WD7 .... 157 A6
Hillcrest. St Alb AL3 ........ 127 B1
Hillcrest. Stev SG1 ............ 50 F5
Hillcroft Cres. Watf WD1 . 175 B8
Hilldown Rd. Heml H HP1 124 A5
Hillfield Ave. Hit SG4 ......... 22 A2
Hillfield Ct. Heml H HP2 ... 124 E3
Hillfield. Hat AL10 ........... 130 C8
Hillfield Rd. Heml H HP2 .. 124 D3
Hillgate. Hit SG4 ............... 22 A3
Hillhouse. Wa Aby EN9 .... 163 F6
Hilliard Rd. Norwd HA6 .... 174 F2
Hillingdon House
(St Nicholas Sch). Harl 118 F3
Hillingdon Rd.
Watf WD2 .................... 154 B5
Hillmead Jun Mix Inf Sch.
Bis St ............................. 59 C1
Hillmead. Stev SG1 ............ 51 A6
Hillrise Ave. Watf WD2 .... 154 D2
Hills La. Norwd HA6 ......... 174 E2
Hillsborough Gn.
Sth Ox WD1 ................. 175 A7
Hillshott. Letw SG6 ............ 23 A6
Hillshott Sch. Letw ............ 23 A6
Hillside Ave. Bis St CM23 ... 77 A7
Hillside Ave. Bor WD6 ..... 170 B5
Hillside Ave. Ches EN8 ..... 162 D8
Hillside Cl. Abb L WD5 ..... 153 E7
Hillside. Cod SG4 ............... 67 F1
Hillside Cotts. Wars SG12 . 94 F4
Hillside Cres. Ches EN8 ... 162 D8
Hillside Cres. Enf EN2 ...... 161 D1
Hillside Cres. Gt Am SG12 115 B4
Hillside Cres. Norwd HA6 175 A2
Hillside Cres. Watf WD1 .. 167 D3
Hillside Ct. Ches EN8 ....... 162 D8
Hillside Gdns. Barn EN5 ... 171 E5
Hillside Gdns. Berk HP4 ... 122 D3
Hillside Gdns. Norwd HA6 175 B2
Hillside. Hat AL10 ........... 130 A5
Hillside. Hod EN11 .......... 134 F7
Hillside House. Stev SG1 ... 50 F5
Hillside Jun Inf Sch.
Norwd ......................... 175 A3
Hillside La. Gt Am SG12 ... 115 A5
Hillside Mansions.
Barn EN5 ..................... 171 F5
Hillside Rd. Chor WD3 ..... 164 C4
Hillside Rd. Harp AL5 ......... 85 F3
Hillside Rd. Luton LU3 ....... 45 D1 4
Hillside Rd.
Norwd HA6,HA5 ........... 175 B3
Hillside Rd. Radl WD7 ..... 156 B4
Hillside Rd. St Alb AL1 .... 127 E4
Hillside Rd. Watf WD2 ..... 167 E4
Hillside Rise. Norwd HA6 . 175 A3
Hillside. Royst SG8 ............. 7 D5
Hillside Sch. Bor ............. 170 C5
Hillside. Stev SG1 ............. 50 F5
Hillside Terr. Hert SG13 ... 113 C4
Hillside. Ware SG12 ........ 114 D8
Hillside Way. Welw AL6 ..... 90 A8
Hillside. Wel G C AL7 ....... 111 B3
Hilltop Cl. Ham St EN7 .... 147 F5
Hilltop Cotts. Gt Of SG5 ..... 33 C3
Hilltop Ct. Luton LU1 ......... 63 C7
Hilltop Rd. Abb L WD4 ..... 139 D4
Hilltop Rd. Berk HP4 ....... 122 C3
Hilltop. Red AL3 ............. 105 F6
Hilltop Sch. Stev .............. 50 F7
Hillview Cl. Pnr HA5 ....... 175 F4
Hillview Cres. Luton LU2 ... 45 C8
Hillview Gdns. Ches EN8 .. 148 E4
Hillview Rd. Pnr HA5 ....... 175 F4
Hilly Fields. Wel G C AL7 . 111 C7
Hilmay Dr. Heml H HP1 ... 124 C2
Hilton Cl. Stev SG1 ........... 50 B7
Himalayan Way.
Watf WD1 .................... 166 F3
Hindhead Gn.
Sth Ox WD1 ................. 175 C5
Hine Way. Hit SG5 ............ 21 C1
Hinxworth Rd. Ashw SG7 ..... 4 B4
Hinxworth Rd. Hin SG7 ........ 3 C3
Hipkins. Bis St CM23 ......... 76 E4
Hitchens Cl. Heml H HP1 . 123 F4
Hitchin Boys' Sch. Hit ....... 34 E8
Hitchin Girls' Sch. Hit ....... 34 F7
Hitchin Hill. Hit SG4 ......... 34 F5
Hitchin Hospl. Hit ............ 34 D8
Hitchin Rd. Arl SG15 ......... 11 A2
Hitchin Rd. Gt Wy SG4 ...... 35 D6
Hitchin Rd. Henlw SG16 ..... 10 C6
Hitchin Rd. Hit SG4 .......... 34 F3
Hitchin Rd Ind Est. Luton ... 45 F1
Hitchin Rd. Kim SG4 .......... 66 D2
Hitchin Rd. Letw SG6 ........ 22 E3
Hitchin Rd. Luton LU2 ....... 46 A2
Hitchin Rd. Luton LU2 ....... 46 A4
Hitchin Rd. Luton LU2 ....... 46 B5
Hitchin Rd. Pirt SG5 .......... 20 E2
Hitchin Rd. Shil SG5 .......... 19 E1
Hitchin Rd. Stev SG1 ......... 36 B1
Hitchin Rd. Stot SG5 ......... 11 D4
Hitchin Rd. Wes SG4 ......... 24 B1
Hitchin St. Bal SG7 ........... 23 E8
Hitchin Sta. Hit ................ 35 B8
Hither Field. Ware SG12 .... 93 E3
Hitherbaulk. Wel G C AL7 110 E4
Hitherfield La. Harp AL5 .... 86 A2
Hitherway. Wel G C AL8 .... 89 D2
Hitherwell Dr. Har HA3 .... 176 D2
Hive Rd. Bus WD2 ........... 176 E8
Hobart Wlk. St Alb AL3 .... 127 F7
Hobbs Cl. Ches EN8 ......... 148 D2
Hobbs Cl. Coln H AL4 ...... 128 E2
Hobbs Cross Rd.
Harl CM17 .................... 118 F2
Hobbs Ct. Stev SG1 ........... 51 A8
Hobbs Hill Rd.
Heml H HP3 .................. 138 F8

Hobbs Hill Wood Jun Mix
Inf Sch. Heml H ........... 125 B1
Hobbs Way. Wel G C AL8 . 110 C5
Hobletts Inf Sch. Heml H . 125 A4
Hobletts Jun Mix Sch.
Heml H ........................ 125 A4
Hobletts Rd. Heml H HP2 . 124 F4
Hobsons Cl. Hod EN11 ..... 114 F1
Hobsons Wlk. Tri HP23 ...... 99 F5
Hobtoe Rd. Harl CM20 ..... 117 A1
Hockerill Ct. Bis St CM23 ... 77 A7
Hockerill Sch. Bis St ............ 77 B7
Hockerill St. Bis St CM23 ... 77 A7
Hockerill. Wat St SG14 ...... 70 E3
Hocklands. Wel G C AL7 .. 111 C7
Hockwell Ring. Luton LU4 ... 44 C4
Hoddesdon Bsns Ctr. Hod 135 A6
Hoddesdon Rd.
Gt Am SG12 ................ 115 C3
Hodges Way. Watf WD1 .. 167 A3
Hodings Rd. Harl CM20 .... 117 B2
Hodwell. Ashw SG7 ............. 4 D4
Hoe La. Enf EN1,EN3 ....... 162 B1
Hoe La. Lo Naz EN9 ......... 135 F1
Hoe La. Ware SG12 ......... 114 D7
Hoe The. Sth Ox WD1 ...... 175 D8
Hoecroft Ct. Enf EN3 ........ 162 C1
Hoecroft. Lo Naz EN9 ....... 135 F1
Hoestock Rd. Saw CM21 .... 97 D2
Hog Hall La. Dagn HP4 ...... 81 A5
Hog La. Chol HP5 ............. 121 D2
Hogarth Ct. Bus WD2 ...... 168 B2
Hogg End La. St Alb AL3 .. 126 C6
Hogg La. Elst WD6 ........... 169 A5
Hogsdell La. Hert H SG13 114 B4
Holbeck La. Ham St EN7 .. 147 F5
Holbein Gate. Mo Pk HA6 174 E5
Holborn Cl. St Alb AL4 ...... 128 D8
Holbrook Cl. Enf EN1 ........ 162 A1
Holcroft Rd. Harp AL5 ........ 86 D3
Holdbrook. Hit SG4 ............ 35 B7
Holdbrook Sch. Ches ........ 162 F5
Holden Cl. Hert SG13 ....... 113 E7
Holders La. Ast SG2 .......... 51 E5
Holdings The. Hat AL9 ...... 130 D7
Holecroft. Wa Aby EN9 .... 163 E5
Holford Way. Luton LU3 ..... 31 B1
Holgate Dr. Dun LU4 .......... 44 B3
Holkham Cl. Dun LU4 ......... 44 A4
Holland Ct. Luton LU3 ........ 45 C2
Holland Gdns. Watf WD2 . 154 C4
Holland Rd. Luton LU3 ....... 45 B2
Holland's Croft. Hun SG12 . 95 D1
Holliday St. Berk HP4 ....... 122 D4
Hollier Ct. Hat AL10 ......... 130 B6
Holliers Way. Hat AL10 .... 130 A5
Hollies Cl. Royst SG8 ........... 7 E6
Hollies The. Bov HP3 ....... 137 A2
Hollies The. Chor WD3 .... 164 C2
Hollies The. St Alb AL3 .... 127 C5
Hollies The. Watf WD1 ..... 166 F5
Hollies The. Wigg HP23 ... 100 D1
Hollies Way. Pot B EN6 .... 159 C8
Hollow La. Hit SG4 ............ 34 F7
Holloway La. Chen WD3 .. 151 C2
Holloway The. Ast Cl HP22 99 C4
Holloways La. Wel G AL9 . 144 D7
Holly Cl. Hat AL10 ............ 129 F4
Holly Copse. Stev SG1 ....... 50 F4
Holly Croft. Hert SG14 ..... 113 A7
Holly Dell. Hert SG13 ....... 113 C4
Holly Dr. Berk HP4 ........... 122 D3
Holly Dr. Pot B EN6 .......... 159 B6
Holly Farm Cl. Cad LU1 ...... 62 E3
Holly Gr. Pnr HA5 ............. 175 E2
Holly Grove Rd.
Bram SG14 ..................... 91 C3
Holly Hedges La. Bov HP3 151 C8
Holly La. Whea AL5 ............ 86 E6
Holly Leys. Stev SG2 .......... 69 C8
Holly Rd. Enf EN3 ............ 162 D3
Holly Rd. Welw SG3 ........... 69 B1
Holly Shaws. Stev SG2 ....... 51 B1
Holly St. Luton LU1 ............. 63 E6
Holly Street Trad Est.
Luton ............................. 63 E6
Holly Tree Ct.
Heml H HP2 ................. 125 B3
Holly Wlk. Harp AL5 ........... 86 D1
Holly Wlk. Wel G C AL8 ...... 89 C2
Hollybush Ave. Chis AL2 .. 141 A7
Hollybush Cl. Har HA3 ..... 176 E2
Hollybush Cl. Pot En HP4 . 123 D7
Hollybush Cl. Watf WD1 .. 167 C2
Hollybush Cl. Welw AL6 ..... 89 E8
Hollybush Hill. Gt Of LU2 ... 32 F1
Hollybush House.
Wel G C AL7 ................ 110 E4
Hollybush Jun Mix Inf Sch.
Hert ............................. 113 A6
Hollybush La. Dat SG3 ....... 69 C3
Hollybush La. Fla AL3 ........ 84 B3
Hollybush La. Harp AL5 ..... 86 A3
Hollybush La. Heml H HP1 123 F4
Hollybush La.
Wel G C AL7 ................. 110 E3
Hollybush La. Whit SG4 ..... 66 B8
Hollybush Rd. Luton LU2 ... 46 C1
Hollybush Way. Ches EN7 148 A3
Hollycross Rd.
Sta Ab SG12 ................ 115 B7
Hollyfield Cl. Tri HP23 ...... 100 C5
Hollyfield. Hat AL10 ......... 130 A2
Hollyfield. Tri HP23 ......... 100 C5
Hollyfields. Ches EN10 ..... 148 E5
Hollygrove. Bus WD2 ....... 168 D2
Hollytree Cl. Bot HP5 ....... 150 B8
Hollytree House.
Watf WD1 ................... 153 E3
Hollywood Ct. Bor WD6 ... 170 A5
Holmbrook Ave. Luton LU3 45 C5
Holmbury Cl. Bus WD2 .... 176 E8
Holmdale Cl. Bor WD6 ..... 169 F7
Holmdale. Letw SG6 .......... 23 B5
Holme Cl. Ches EN8 ......... 162 E8
Holme Cl. Hat AL10 .......... 129 F8
Holme Lea. Watf WD2 ..... 154 C5
Holme Pk. Bor WD6 ......... 169 F7
Holme Rd. Hat AL10 ......... 129 F8
Holme Way. Har HA7 ....... 176 F4
Holmes Ct. St Alb AL3 ...... 127 E4
Holmesdale. Enf EN8 ....... 162 D4
Holmfield Cl. Luton LU1 ..... 63 D5
Holmscroft Rd. Luton LU3 .. 44 F6
Holmshill La. Ridge WD6 . 157 F2
Holmshill Sec Sch. Bor ... 170 C7
Holmside Rise.
Sth Ox WD1 ................. 175 B7
Holmwood Rd. Enf EN3 .... 162 D3
Holroyd Cres. Bal SG7 ....... 23 F7
Holt Cl. Bor WD6 ............. 169 F5
Holt The. Heml H HP2 ...... 124 E2
Holt The. Wel G C AL7 ..... 111 D5
Holts Meadow. Red AL3 ... 106 B6
Holtsmere Cl. Luton LU2 ... 46 D1
Holtsmere Cl. Watf WD2 . 154 C4
Holtsmere End Inf Sch.
Heml H ........................ 125 B8
Holtsmere End Jun Sch.
Heml H ........................ 125 B8
Holwell Hyde La.
Wel G C AL7 ................ 111 C3
Holwell Hyde.
Wel G C AL7 ................ 111 C4
Holwell Jun & Inf Sch.
Wel G C ....................... 110 F5
Holwell La. Ess AL9 ......... 131 E8
Holwell Rd. Hol SG5 .......... 21 B7
Holwell Rd. Pirt SG5 .......... 20 E6
Holwell Rd. Wel G C AL7 .. 110 E5
Holwell. Stev SG1 .............. 36 C2
Holy Cross Hill. Bric EN7 . 148 A8
Holy Family RC Prim Sch The.
Wel G C ......................... 90 A1
Holy Rood RC Inf Sch.
Watf ............................ 153 D3
Holy Rood RC Jun Mix Sch.
Watf ............................ 153 D3
Holy Trinity C of E Jun Mix
Inf Sch. Ches ............... 162 D7
Holy Trinity C of E Prim Sch.
Norwd ......................... 174 C4
Holyfield Rd. Wa Aby EN9 149 D2
Holyrood Cres. St Alb AL1 141 D7
Holyrood Ct. Watf WD1 ... 167 B5
Holywell Cl. Whip LU6 ........ 82 C6
Holywell Ct. Luton LU3 ...... 45 B4
Holywell Cty Inf Sch.
Watf ............................ 166 F3
Holywell Hill. St Alb AL1 .. 127 D2
Holywell Jun Sch. Watf .... 166 F3
Holywell Rd. Watf WD1 ... 167 A4
Holywell Rd. Whip LU6 ...... 82 B7
Home Cl. Ches EN10 ....... 148 F7
Home Cl. Luton LU4 .......... 44 C4
Home Cl. Stot SG5 ............ 11 F6
Home Ct. Luton LU4 .......... 44 C4
Home Farm Ind Pk. Sta Ab 115 F5
Home Farm Rd.
Nthch HP4 ................... 121 D7
Home Farm Rd. Ric WD3 . 174 A6
Home Field. Barn EN5 ...... 171 F4
Home Ley. Wel G C AL7 ... 110 E6
Home Meadow.
Wel G C AL7 ................ 110 F6
Home Park Ind Est. Kin L . 139 B1
Home Pastures.
Sheer CM22 ................... 98 F3
Home Way. Ric WD3 ........ 164 F1
Homedale Dr. Luton LU4 .... 44 D2
Homedell House. Harp AL5 85 E3
Homefield. Bov HP3 ......... 137 B3
Homefield. Hin SG7 ............. 3 D6
Homefield La. Lan SG4 ....... 49 F2
Homefield. Pot En HP4 .... 123 B7
Homefield Rd. Bus WD2 .. 168 A4
Homefield Rd. Chor WD3 . 164 D5
Homefield Rd.
Heml H HP2 ................. 125 A2
Homefield Rd. Radl WD7 . 155 F2
Homefield Rd. Radl WD7 . 156 A2
Homefield Rd. Ware SG12 . 93 E2
Homeleigh Ct. Ches EN8 .. 148 B1
Homeleigh St. Ches EN8 .. 148 B1
Homerfield. Wel G C AL8 . 110 C7
Homerswood Jun & Inf Sch.
Wel G C ......................... 89 D2
Homerswood La. Welw AL6 89 A2
Homerton Rd. Luton LU3 ... 45 A6
Homestead Cl. Chis AL2 ... 141 C4
Homestead Ct.
Wel G C AL7 ................ 110 F4
Homestead La.
Wel G C AL7 ................ 110 F4
Homestead Moat.
Stev SG1 ........................ 50 E4
Homestead Rd. Hat AL10 . 130 B8
Homestead Rd. Ric WD3 .. 165 D2
Homestead Way.
Luton LU1 ...................... 63 C5
Homewood Ave. Cuf EN6 . 146 E4
Homewood La. Cuf EN6 ... 146 C4
Homewood Rd. St Alb AL1 128 B5
Homewood Sch. Chis ....... 141 B3
Honey Brook.
Wa Aby EN9 ................ 163 E6
Honey La. Bun SG9 ........... 40 E8
Honey La. Clav CM11 ......... 30 F3
Honey La. Hert SG14 ....... 113 D6
Honey La. Wa Aby EN9 .... 163 E5
Honeybourne.
Bis St CM23 ................... 76 E4
Honeycroft. Wel G C AL8 . 110 C5
Honeycross Rd.
Heml H HP1 ................. 123 E2
Honeygate. Luton LU2 ....... 45 E4
Honeymead. Welw AL6 ...... 89 F3
Honeymeade. Saw CM21 . 118 C7
Honeysuckle Cl.
Hert SG13 .................... 114 A6
Honeysuckle Gdns.
Hat AL10 ..................... 130 B4
Honeyway. Royst SG8 .......... 7 E6
Honeywood Cl. Pot B EN6 159 D6
Honilands Inf Sch. Enf ..... 162 B3
Honilands Jun Sch. Enf .... 162 B3
Honours Mead. Bov HP3 ... 137 A4
Hoo Cotts. Gt Of SG5 ........ 33 D1
Hoo Farm Cotts. Gt Of SG5 33 D1
Hoo St. Luton LU1 ............. 63 E5
Hoo The. Harl CM17 ........ 118 C5
Hook Gate. Enf EN1 ......... 162 B3
Hook La. Nort EN6 .......... 159 F7
Hook La. Nort EN6 .......... 160 A8
Hookers Ct. Luton LU4 ....... 44 C5
Hoops La. Ther SG8 ........... 15 F6
Hope Gn. Watf WD2 ........ 154 A6
Hopewell Rd. Bal SG7 ....... 23 D8
Hopground Cl. St Alb AL1 . 128 A1
Hopkins Cres. Sand AL4 ... 108 B1
Hoppit Rd. Wa Aby EN9 ... 163 B6
Hopton Rd. Stev SG1 ......... 50 A8
Horace Brightman Cl.
Luton LU3 ...................... 45 A8
Horace Gay Gdns.
Letw SG6 ........................ 22 E6
Horbeam Cl. Bor WD6 ..... 170 A8
Hordle Gdns. St Alb AL1 .. 127 F2
Hormead C of E Prim Sch.
Gt Ho ............................. 41 F8
Horn Hill. Whit SG4 ........... 66 E6
Hornbeam Cl. Hert SG14 . 113 B7
Hornbeam Ct. Gt Wy SG4 .. 35 E5
Hornbeam La. Ess AL9 ..... 131 E2
Hornbeam Spring.
Kneb SG3 ....................... 68 F4
Hornbeam Way.
Gofs O EN7 .................. 147 F2
Hornbeams Ave. Enf EN1 . 162 C4
Hornbeams. Bri Wd AL2 .. 140 F1
Hornbeams The.
Harl CM20 .................... 117 B2
Hornbeams The. Stev SG2 . 51 B4
Hornbeams. Wel G C AL7 111 B5
Hornets The. Watf WD1 .. 167 B5
Hornhill Rd. Map Cr WD3 172 D5
Horns Cl. Hert SG13 ........ 113 C4
Horns Mill Rd. Hert SG13 113 C3
Horns Rd. Hert SG13 ....... 113 C5
Hornsby Cl. Luton LU2 ...... 46 C1
Hornsfield. Wel G C AL7 .. 111 C7
Horrocks Cl. Ware SG12 .... 93 D3
Horse Hill. Bot HP3 .......... 150 D7
Horsecroft Rd.
Heml H HP1 ................. 124 A1
Horselers. Heml H HP3 .... 139 A8
Horsemans Dr. Chis AL2 .. 141 B6
Horseshoe Ct.
Sta Ab SG12 ................ 115 D4
Horseshoe Hill. Gt Ho SG9 . 42 A8
Horseshoe La. Barn N20 .. 171 D1
Horseshoe La. Gt Ho SG9 .. 42 A8
Horseshoe La. Watf WD2 154 C7
Horseshoe The.
Heml H HP3 ................. 125 C1
Horseshoes Cl. Ched LU7 .. 80 A7
Horsham Cl. Luton LU2 ...... 46 D2
Horsleys. Map Cr WD3 .... 172 D5
Horton Gdns. Heml H HP2 105 A1
Horwood Ct. Watf WD2 ... 154 E2
Hospital Rd. Arl SG15 ........ 11 A4
Housden Cl. Whea AL4 .... 108 E7
House La. Arl SG15 ............ 11 A7
House La. Sand AL4 ......... 108 C1
House La. St Alb AL4 ....... 128 D7
Housewood End.
Heml H HP1 ................. 124 B6
Housman Ave. Royst SG8 .... 2 C1
How Field. Harp AL5 .......... 85 E3
How Wood. Chis AL2 ....... 141 B3
How Wood Jun Mix Inf Sch.
Chis ............................. 141 C4
How Wood Sta. Chis ........ 141 C3
Howard Agne Cl. Bov HP3 137 A4
Howard Cl. Bus WD2 ....... 168 E2
Howard Cl. Luton LU3 ....... 45 A4
Howard Cl. St Alb AL1 ...... 128 C1
Howard Cl. Wa Aby EN9 .. 163 D5
Howard Cl. Watf WD2 ..... 154 A2
Howard Ct. Letw ................ 23 B4
Howard Ctr The.
Wel G C AL8 ................ 110 D6
Howard Dr. Bor WD6 ....... 170 D5
Howard Dr. Letw SG6 ........ 23 B3
Howard Gate. Letw SG6 .... 23 B4
Howard Way. Barn EN5 ... 171 D4
Howard Way. Harl CM20 . 117 F2
Howards Cl. Pnr HA5 ....... 175 B1
Howards Dr. Heml H HP1 124 A5
Howards Wood. Letw SG6 . 23 B3
Howardsgate.
Wel G C AL8 ................ 110 D6
Howe Cl. Shen WD7 ......... 156 E7
Howe Dell. Hat AL10 ........ 130 B5
Howe Dell Jun Mix Inf Sch.
Hat ............................... 130 B5
Howe Rd. Heml H HP3 ..... 125 A1
Howell Hill Cl. Men LU7 ..... 61 D5
Howfield Gn. Hod EN11 ... 115 A1
Howicks Gn. Wel G C AL7 111 A3
Howland Garth.
St Alb AL1 .................... 141 C7
Howlands House.
Wel G C AL7 ................ 111 A3
Howlands. Wel G C AL7 ... 111 B3
Howton Pl. Bus WD2 ....... 168 D1
Hoylake Ct. Luton LU1 ....... 63 F5
Hoylake Gdns.
Sth Ox WD1 ................. 175 D6
Hubbards Rd. Chor WD3 . 164 D4
Huckleberry Cl. Luton LU3 . 45 A8
Hudnall La. L Gad HP4 ..... 102 E7
Hudson Cl. St Alb AL1 ..... 141 D8
Hudson Cl. Watf WD2 ..... 153 F3
Hudson Rd. Stev SG2 ......... 51 B7
Huggins La. Wel G AL9 .... 144 C8
Hugh Villas. Bis St CM23 ... 77 A5
Hugh's Tower. Harl CM20 117 D1
Hughenden Rd. St Alb AL4 128 C6
Hull La. Brag SG11 ............ 55 E7
Humberstone Cl. Luton LU4 44 E2
Humberstone Rd.
Luton LU4 ...................... 44 E2
Humphrey Talbot Ave.
Whip LU6 ....................... 81 F7
Hunsdon Jun Mix Inf Sch.
Hun ................................ 95 D1
Hunsdon Rd. Sta Ab SG12 115 E5
Hunsdon Rd. Widf SG12 .... 95 E3
Hunsdon. Wel G C AL7 .... 111 D6
Hunston Cl. Luton LU4 ....... 44 B5
Hunt Cl. St Alb AL4 .......... 128 D6
Hunter Cl. Bor WD6 ......... 170 C4
Hunter Cl. Pot B EN6 ....... 159 B6
Hunter Wlk. Bor WD6 ...... 170 D4
Hunter's La. Abb L WD2 .. 153 F6
Huntercrombe Gdns.
Sth Ox WD1 ................. 175 C5
Hunters Cl. Bov HP3 ........ 137 A2
Hunters Cl. Stev SG2 ......... 51 D7
Hunters Cl. Stot SG5 .......... 11 E6
Hunters Cl. Tri HP23 ........ 100 B5
Hunters Gate. Watf WD2 . 154 A6
Hunters Oak. Heml H HP2 125 B8
Hunters Pk. Berk HP4 ...... 122 E5
Hunters Reach.
Gofs O EN7 .................. 147 F2
Hunters Ride. Bri Wd AL2 155 A8
Hunters Way. Royst SG8 ..... 7 E6
Hunters Way.
Wel G C AL7 ................ 110 F3
Hunting Gate.
Heml H HP2 ................. 124 E7
Hunting Gate. Hit SG4 ........ 22 A3
Huntingdon Cl. Ches EN10 148 E7
Huntingdon Rd. Stev SG1 ... 50 B8
Hunton Bridge Hill.
Abb L WD4 .................. 153 C6
Hunts Cl. Luton LU1 .......... 63 C6
Huntsmans Cl. Dagn HP4 ... 81 C5
Huntsmill Rd. Heml H HP1 123 E2
Hurlock Way. Luton LU4 .... 44 C5
Hurricane Way.
Abb L WD5 .................. 154 A7
Hurst Cl. Bal SG7 ............... 13 A1
Hurst Cl. Wel G C AL7 ...... 111 C5
Hurst Dr. Ches EN8 .......... 162 D5
Hurst Drive Prim Sch.
Ches ............................ 162 D5
Hurst Pl. Norwd HA6 ....... 174 B2
Hurst Way. Luton LU3 ........ 44 F5
Hurstlings. Wel G C AL7 ... 111 B5
Hutton Cl. Hert SG14 ....... 113 A6
Hutton La. Har HA3 ......... 176 D3
Hutton Wlk. Har HA3 ....... 176 C3
Hyatt Ind Est. Stev ............. 50 A5
Hyburn Cl. Bri Wd AL2 ..... 140 F1
Hyburn Cl. Heml H HP3 .... 125 B2
Hyde Ave. Pot B EN6 ........ 159 B6
Hyde Ave. Stot SG5 ............ 11 E5
Hyde Cl. Barn EN5 ........... 171 F6
Hyde Cl. Harp AL5 ............. 86 B4
Hyde Gn E. Stev SG2 ......... 51 B3
Hyde Gn N. Stev SG2 ......... 51 B3
Hyde Gn S. Stev SG2 ......... 51 B3
Hyde La. Abb L WD4,WD5 139 C4
Hyde La. Bov HP3 ............ 137 A3
Hyde La. Kim LU2 ............... 65 C2
Hyde La. Pk St AL2 .......... 141 D3
Hyde Mead House.
Lo Naz EN9 .................. 149 E8
Hyde Mead. Lo Naz EN9 ... 149 E8
Hyde Meadows. Bov HP3 . 137 A4
Hyde Rd. Cad LU1 .............. 62 F4
Hyde Rd. Watf WD1 ......... 167 A7
Hyde Sch The. Wel G C .... 111 C5
Hyde The. Stev SG2 ........... 51 C3
Hyde The. Ware SG12 ....... 93 B2
Hyde Valley. Wel G C AL7 110 F4
Hyde View Rd. Harp AL5 .... 86 B4
Hyde Way. Wel G C AL7 ... 110 E6
Hydean Way. Stev SG2 ...... 51 B3
Hyperion Ct. Heml H HP2 124 F6
Hyver Hill. Edg NW7 ........ 170 D2

Ibberson Way. Hit SG4 ...... 35 A7
Ickleford Bury. Ick SG5 ...... 21 E4
Ickleford Jun Mix Inf Sch.
Ick ................................. 21 E4
Ickleford Rd. Hit SG5 ......... 34 F8
Ickley Cl. Luton LU4 ........... 44 B5
Icknield Cl. Ick SG5 ........... 21 E4
Icknield Cl. St Alb AL3 ...... 126 F1
Icknield Gn. Letw SG6 ....... 22 E6
Icknield Gn. Tri HP23 ....... 100 A6
Icknield High Sch. Luton .... 45 C5
Icknield Inf Sch. Letw ........ 22 D6
Icknield Inf Sch. Luton ....... 45 B5
Icknield Jun Sch. Luton ..... 45 B5
Icknield Rd. Luton LU3 ....... 44 F4
Icknield Walk Fst Sch.
Royst ............................... 7 E7
Icknield Way. Bal SG7 ....... 12 E1
Icknield Way. Dagn HP4 .... 81 A8
Icknield Way E. Bal SG7 .... 12 F1
Icknield Way. Letw SG6 ..... 22 E6
Icknield Way. Luton LU3 .... 45 B7
Icknield Way. Tri HP23 ...... 99 E4
Icknield Wlk. Royst SG8 ...... 7 F7
Idenbury Ct. Luton LU1 ...... 63 C7
Ilex Ct. Berk HP4 ............. 122 B4
Ilford Cl. Luton LU2 ........... 46 D3
Ilkley Rd. Sth Ox WD1 ..... 175 D5
Imberfield. Dun LU4 .......... 44 C3
Imperial Way. Watf WD2 167 C8
Indells. Hat AL10 ............. 129 F4
Ingelheim Ct. Stev SG1 ...... 50 D7
Ingersoll Rd. Enf EN3 ....... 162 C1
Inglefield. Pot B EN6 ....... 145 A1
Ingles. Wel G C AL8 ........... 89 E2
Ingleside Dr. Stev SG1 ...... 36 B1
Inkerman Rd. St Alb AL1 .. 127 E2

Inkerman St. Luton LU1 63 D7
Inn's Cl. Stev SG1 50 D6
Innes Ct. Heml H HP3 138 D8
Inskip Cres. Stev SG1 50 E5
Iredale View. Bal SG7 13 A1
Irene Stebbings House. St Alb AL4 128 C4
Iron Dr. Hert SG13 114 B7
Irving Cl. Bis St CM23 76 D4
Irving Cres. Ched LU7 80 A8
Isabelle Cl. Gofs O EN7 147 C2
Isenburg Way. Heml H HP2 124 D8
Isherwood Cl. Royst SG8 7 C8
Islington Way. Stev SG1 36 F2
Italstyle Bldg The. Harl CM17 118 C6
Iveagh Cl. Norwd HA6 174 B2
Iveagh Ct. Heml H HP2 124 D4
Ivel Ct. Letw SG6 23 C4
Ivel Rd. Stev SG1 50 C7
Ivel Way. Bal SG7 24 A6
Ivel Way. Stot SG5 11 F8
Ives Rd. Hert SG14 113 B7
Ivinghoe Cl. St Alb AL4 128 C8
Ivinghoe Cl. Watf WD2 154 D4
Ivinghoe Rd. Bus WD2 168 D2
Ivinghoe Rd. Ric WD3 165 A2
Ivory Ct. Heml H HP3 138 E8
Ivy House La. Berk HP4 122 E4
Ivy Lea. Ric WD3 165 A1
Ivy Rd. Luton LU1 63 C8
Ivy Terr. Hod EN11 135 C8
Ivybridge. Hod EN10 135 A4

Jackdaw Cl. Stev SG2 51 D4
Jackdaws. Wel G C AL7 111 C6
Jackets La. Norwd HA6 174 B3
Jacketts Field. Abb L WD5 153 F8
Jackman's Pl. Letw SG6 23 B5
Jacks La. Hare UB9 173 A1
Jackson Sq. Bis St CM23 76 F7
Jackson St. Bal SG7 12 E1
Jackson's La. Reed SG8 16 E5
Jacksons Dr. Ches EN7 148 A3
James Bedford Cl. Pnr HA5 175 C1
James Cl. Watf WD2 167 E4
James Ct. Dun LU4 44 B2
James Ct. Luton LU1 63 E6 9
James Marshall Commercial Ctr. Harp 86 A1
James Way. Stev SG1 50 C7
Jameson Ct. St Alb AL1 127 F4
Jameson Rd. Harp AL5 86 B3
Jane Cl. Heml H HP2 125 B8
Jarden. Letw SG6 23 C4
Jarman Cl. Heml H HP3 124 E1
Jarman Way. Heml H HP2 124 F2
Jarman Way. Royst SG8 7 B7
Jarvis Cl. Barn EN5 171 D4
Jarvis Cleys. Ham St EN7 147 F5
Jasmin Way. Heml H HP1 123 E4
Jasmine Dr. Hert SG13 114 A6
Jasmine Gdns. Hat AL10 130 A7
Jasons Hill. Bot HP5 136 B2
Jasper Cl. Enf EN3 162 C1
Jay Cl. Letw SG6 22 E8
Jaywood. Luton LU2 46 C6
Jeans Way. Dun LU5 44 A1
Jeffrey Cl. Royst SG8 7 C8
Jeffries Rd. Ware SG12 93 E1
Jellicoe Gdns. Har HA7 176 F4
Jellicoe Rd. Watf WD1 167 A3
Jenkins Ave. Bri Wd AL2 140 E1
Jenkins La. Gt Ha CM22 77 C5
Jenkins La. St Le HP23 119 E3
Jenning Wood. Welw AL6 89 F7
Jennings Cl. Stev SG1 50 E3
Jennings Rd. St Alb AL1 128 A4
Jennings Way. Barn EN5 171 C6
Jennings Way. Heml H HP3 124 E1
Jenningsbury Ct. Hert SG13 114 A4
Jepps La. Royst SG8 7 D6
Jerome Dr. St Alb AL3 127 A1
Jersey Cl. Hod EN11 135 A7
Jersey House. Enf EN3 162 D1
Jersey La. St Alb AL4 128 B5
Jersey La. St Alb AL4 128 C8
Jersey Rd. Dun LU4 44 A3
Jervis Ave. Enf EN3 162 E4
Jervis Rd. Bis St CM23 76 F6
Jessop Rd. Stev SG1 37 A1
Jeve Cl. Bal SG7 13 A1
Jillifer Rd. Dun LU4 44 A2
Jim Desormeaux Bglws. Harl CM20 117 E2
Jinnings The. Wel G C AL7 111 B3
Jocelyns. Harl CM17 118 C4
Jocketts Hill. Heml H HP1 123 F3
Jocketts Rd. Heml H HP1 123 F2
Joel St. Norwd HA6 175 A1
John Barker Pl. Hit SG5 21 C1
John Ct. Hod EN11 115 A1
John Dyde Training Coll The. Bis St 77 A6
John Eliot Cl. Lo Naz EN9 135 E2
John F Kennedy Sch. Heml H 123 F4
John Henry Newman RC Sch The. Stev 36 B1
John Lamb Ct. Har HA3 176 E2
John Penrose Sch. Hare 173 D2
John Rand Sch. Hol 21 B7
John St. Luton LU1 63 E7
John St. Royst SG8 7 D6
John Tate Rd. Hert SG13 113 F6
John Warner Sch The. Hod 115 B1
Johnby Cl. Enf EN3 162 E2
Johns La. Chol HP5 121 E1
Johns Rd. Bis St CM23 59 A1
Johnson Ct. Heml H HP3 124 E1
Joiner's Close. Bot HP5 136 B1
Joint The. Reed SG8 16 E6
Jones Rd. Gofs O EN7 147 B1
Jonquil Cl. Wel G C AL7 111 B4
Jordan Cl. Watf WD2 153 F4
Jordan's Way. Bri Wd AL2 140 F1
Jordans Way. Ric WD3 165 A1
Jordans. Wel G C AL7 111 C7
Jowitt House. Stev SG1 50 E6 1
Joyce Ct. Wa Aby EN9 163 D5
Jubilee Ave. Lon C AL2 142 D5
Jubilee Ave. Ware SG12 93 F2
Jubilee Cl. Pnr HA5 175 C1
Jubilee Cotts. Asp SG9 40 D5
Jubilee Cres. Arl SG15 11 A2
Jubilee Ct. Harp AL5 86 C3
Jubilee Ct. Hat AL10 130 B8
Jubilee Ct. Wa Aby EN9 163 F6
Jubilee Memorial Ave. Stev SG1 50 D8
Jubilee Rd. Letw SG6 23 D7
Jubilee Rd. Stev SG1 50 B6
Jubilee Rd. Watf WD2 154 A1
Jubilee St. Luton LU2 45 F1
Jubilee Trade Ctr. Letw 23 D7
Judge St. Watf WD2 154 B1
Judge's Hill. Nort EN6 145 F2
Julia Gate. Stev SG2 51 C8
Julian's Ct. Stev SG1 50 C8
Julian's Rd. Stev SG1 50 B8
Julius Gdns. Luton LU3 44 F7
Juniper Ave. Bri Wd AL2 155 A8
Juniper Cl. Barn EN5 171 D4
Juniper Cl. Ches EN10 148 F6
Juniper Cl. Luton LU4 44 E2
Juniper Ct. Har HA3 176 F2
Juniper Gate. Ric WD3 173 D8
Juniper Gdns. Welw AL6 89 E7
Juniper Gn. Heml H HP1 123 E3
Juniper Gr. Watf WD1 154 A1
Jupiter Dr. Heml H HP2 124 F5
Jupiter Drive Jun Mix Inf Sch. Heml H 124 F5
Juxon Cl. Har HA3 176 B2

Kardwell Cl. Hit SG4 35 A6
Katescroft. Wel G C AL7 110 E2
Katherine Cl. Heml H HP3 138 E8
Katrine Sq. Heml H HP2 124 E7
Keats Cl. Heml H HP2 105 B1
Keats Cl. Royst SG8 7 C8
Keats Cl. Stev SG2 51 C7
Keats Way. Hit SG4 35 C7
Keble Terr. Abb L WD5 153 F7
Kecksy's. Saw CM21 97 F4
Keeble Cl. Luton LU2 46 E1
Keele Cl. Watf WD1 167 C7
Keepers Cl. Ched LU7 80 A7
Keepers Cl. Luton LU2 46 C2
Keiths Rd. Heml H HP3 125 A2
Keiths Wood. Kneb SG3 68 F5
Kelbys. Wel G C AL7 111 C7
Keller Cl. Stev SG2 51 B4
Kelling Cl. Luton LU2 45 C8
Kelly Cl. Bor WD6 170 D7
Kelman Cl. Ches EN8 162 D8
Kelmscott Cl. Watf WD1 167 A4
Kelmscott Cres. Watf WD1 167 A4
Kelshall St. Kel SG8 15 E5
Kelshall. Watf WD2 154 E3
Kelvin Cl. Luton LU1 63 E6
Kelvin Cres. Har HA3 176 E3
Kemble Cl. Pot B EN6 159 D6
Kemp Pl. Bus WD2 168 A3
Kempe Cl. St Alb AL1 141 C7
Kempe Rd. Enf EN1 162 C3
Kemprow. Radl WD2 155 D3
Kemps Dr. Norwd HA6 174 F3
Kempsey Cl. Luton LU2 46 D2
Ken Davies Ct. St Alb AL3 127 F7
Kendal Cl. Luton LU3 44 D7
Kendale. Heml H HP3 125 B2
Kendale Rd. Dun LU4 44 B2
Kendale Rd. Hit SG4 34 F6 5
Kendall Cl. Wel G C AL7 110 F2
Kendall Ct. Bor WD6 170 C8
Kendals Cl. Radl WD7 155 E3
Kenerne Dr. Barn EN5 171 E4
Kenford Cl. Watf WD2 154 B7
Kenilworth Cl. Bor WD6 170 C6
Kenilworth Cl. Heml H HP2 124 E2
Kenilworth Cl. Stev SG2 69 C7
Kenilworth Cres. Enf EN1 161 E1
Kenilworth Ct. Watf WD1 167 A8
Kenilworth Dr. Bor WD6 170 D6
Kenilworth Dr. Cro Gr WD3 166 B5
Kenilworth Gdns. Sth Ox WD1 175 C5
Kenilworth Prim Sch. Bor 170 D6
Kenilworth Rd. Luton LU1 63 C8
Kennedy Ave. Hod EN11 134 F6
Kennedy Cl. Ches EN8 148 E3
Kennedy Cl. Pnr HA5 175 F4
Kennedy Rd. Dan En SG12 71 E7
Kennelwood La. Hat AL10 130 B6
Kenneth Rd. Luton LU2 46 A1
Kenning Rd. Hod EN11 135 B8
Kennington Rd. Luton LU3 45 B3
Kensington Ave. Watf WD1 166 F5
Kensworth Rd. Stu LU6 82 D4
Kensworth Vol Con Lower Sch. Ken Co 82 F8
Kent Cl. Bor WD6 157 D1
Kent Cres. Bis St CM23 76 E4
Kent Pl. Hit SG5 34 D8
Kent Rd. Luton LU1 62 F8
Kent's La. Stand SG11 55 E2
Kentish La. Hat AL9 145 C7
Kenton Gdns. St Alb AL1 127 F2
Kenton La. Har HA3 176 F3
Kents Ave. Heml H HP3 138 D7
Kenwood Dr. Ric WD3 172 F8
Kenworth Cl. Ches EN8 162 D6
Kerdistone Cl. Pot B EN6 145 B1
Kernow Ct. Luton LU2 46 A1
Kerr Cl. Kneb SG3 68 F5
Kerri Cl. Barn EN5 171 C5
Kerril Croft. Harl CM20 117 A1
Kershaw Cl. Luton LU3 45 A8
Kershaw's Hill. Hit SG4 34 F6
Kessingland Ave. Stev SG1 36 A1
Keston Mews. Watf WD1 167 B7
Kestrel Cl. Berk HP4 122 C3
Kestrel Cl. Stev SG2 51 D2
Kestrel Cl. Watf WD2 154 E5
Kestrel Ct. Ware SG12 93 C3 4
Kestrel Gdns. Bis St CM23 76 C6
Kestrel Gn. Hat AL10 130 A4
Kestrel Way. Dun LU4 44 A5
Kestrel Way. Wel G C AL7 110 F8
Kestrel Wlk. Letw SG6 23 B3
Kestrels The. Bri Wd AL2 154 F8
Keswick Cl. St Alb AL1 128 B1
Keswick Dr. Enf EN3 162 C3
Kettering Rd. Enf EN3 162 D2
Kettle Green Rd. Muc H SG10 74 E2
Ketton Cl. Luton LU2 64 A7
Ketton Ct. Luton LU2 64 A7
Kewferry Dr. Norwd HA6 174 C5
Kewferry Rd. Norwd HA6 174 C5
Keyfield Terr. St Alb AL1 127 D2
Keymer Cl. Luton LU2 46 C3
Keynton Cl. Hert SG14 112 F7
Keysers Rd. Lo Naz EN10 135 A1
Kibes La. Ware SG12 93 E1
Kidner Cl. Luton LU2 45 E5
Kilbride Ct. Heml H HP2 124 F7
Kilby Cl. Watf WD2 154 D4
Kildonan Cl. Watf WD1 166 F8
Kilfillan Gdns. Berk HP4 122 A4
Kilfillan Pk. Berk HP4 122 A4
Killigrew Inf Sch. Chis 141 B6
Killigrew Jun Mix Sch. Chis 141 B6
Kilmarnock Dr. Luton LU2 45 E5
Kilmarnock Rd. Sth Ox WD1 175 D6
Kiln Ave. L Chal HP6 150 C1
Kiln Ground. Heml H HP3 125 A1
Kiln House Cl. Ware SG12 93 E2
Kiln House Yd. Royst SG8 7 C6
Kiln La. Bot HP5 150 B8
Kiln Way. Norwd HA6 174 E4
Kilncroft. Heml H HP3 125 B1
Kilnfield. Wel G C AL7 89 F1
Kilsmore La. Ches EN8 148 D2
Kilvinton Dr. Enf EN2 161 D1
Kilworth Cl. Wel G C AL7 111 B4
Kimberley Cl. Bis St CM23 77 A5
Kimberley. Letw SG6 11 F2
Kimberley Rd. St Alb AL3 127 D4
Kimble Cl. Watf WD1 166 E2
Kimble Cres. Bus WD2 168 C2
Kimblewick. Sth Ox WD1 167 E1
Kimbolton Cres. Stev SG2 69 A7
Kimbolton Gn. Bor WD6 170 C5
Kimps Way. Heml H HP3 139 A8
Kimpton Bottom. Kim SG4 86 E7
Kimpton Cl. Heml H HP2 125 B8
Kimpton Cty Prim Sch. Kim 66 C1
Kimpton La. Luton LU2 64 D7
Kimpton Pl. Watf WD2 154 D5
Kimpton Rd. A St P AL6 89 A6
Kimpton Rd. Cod SG4 67 B1
Kimpton Rd. Kim AL4 87 C7
Kimpton Rd. Kim SG4 65 E2
Kimpton Rd. Kim SG4 67 B1
Kimpton Rd. Luton LU1,LU2 64 B6
Kimptons Cl. Pot B EN6 158 D7
Kimptons Mead. Pot B EN6 158 D7
Kinderscout. Heml H HP3 125 A1
Kindersley Cl. Welw AL6 89 C6
Kindersley Way. Abb L WD5 153 D8
King Arthur Ct. Ches EN8 162 E8
King Charles Rd. Shen WD7 156 E7
King Croft Rd. Harp AL5 107 D7
King Edward Rd. Ches EN8 162 E6
King Edward Rd. Shen WD7 156 F6
King Edward Rd. Watf WD1 167 E3
King Edward St. Heml H HP3 138 D7
King Edward's Rd. Ware SG12 93 E2
King George Ave. Bus WD2 168 B3
King George Cl. Stev SG1 50 E6
King George Rd. Wa Aby EN9 163 C5
King George Rd. Ware SG12 93 E2
King George's Way. Whit SG4 66 E6
King Georges Ave. Watf WD1 166 E5
King Georges Cl. Hit SG5 21 D1
King Harold Sch. Wa Aby 163 E6
King Harry La. St Alb AL3 127 B1
King Harry St. Heml H HP2 124 D2
King Henry's Mews. Enf EN3 163 A2
King James Ave. Cuf EN6 146 E2
King James Way. Royst SG8 7 D6
King St. Bis St CM23 76 F7
King St. Luton LU1 63 E7
King St. Mark AL3 83 E5
King St. Tri HP23 100 A3
King St. Watf WD1 167 C5
King Street Mews. Bis St CM23 76 F7 1
King's Cotts. Bis St CM23 77 A6
King's La. Chipf WD4 152 B8
King's Mews. Heml H HP2 124 D4 3
King's Rd. Ches EN8 162 E5
King's Rd. Hert SG13 114 A7
King's Rd. Hit SG5 34 F8
King's Rd. Lon C AL2 142 C5
King's Rd. St Alb AL3 127 C3
King's Walden Rd. Gt Of SG5 33 D2
King's Wlk. Royst SG8 7 D5
Kingfisher Cl. Gt Am SG12 115 C3
Kingfisher Cl. Har HA3 176 F3
Kingfisher Cl. Norwd HA6 174 B2
Kingfisher Cl. Whea AL4 87 D1
Kingfisher Lure. Kin L WD4 139 B2
Kingfisher Lure. Ric WD3 165 B5
Kingfisher Rise. Stev SG2 51 D2
Kingfisher Way. Bis St CM23 77 A7
Kingham Rd. Wars SG12 94 E5
Kinghamway. Luton LU2 45 E1
Kings Ave. Heml H HP3 138 F7
Kings Ave. Watf WD1 167 A5
Kings Cl. Chipf WD4 152 B8
Kings Cl. Norwd HA6 174 F4
Kings Cl. Watf WD1 167 C5
Kings Ct. Berk HP4 122 C5
Kings Ct. Bis St CM23 77 A8
Kings Farm Rd. Chor WD3 164 D3
Kings Field Cotts. Abb L WD5 153 F8
Kings Hedges. Hit SG5 34 C8
Kings Langley Jun Sch. Kin L 138 F3
Kings Langley Sch. Kin L 138 E3
Kings Langley Sta. Kin L 139 B1
Kings Meadow. Kin L WD4 139 A3
Kings Oak. Cro Gr WD3 166 A5
Kings Park Ind Est. Kin L 139 B2
Kings Rd. Barn EN5 171 C6
Kings Rd. Berk HP4 122 B3
Kings Walden Rise. Stev SG2 51 C8
Kingsbridge Rd. Bis St CM23 77 A8
Kingsbury Ave. St Alb AL3 127 C4
Kingsbury Water Mill Mus. St Alb 127 B4
Kingscroft. Wel G C AL7 111 B7
Kingsdale House. Welw AL6 89 B3
Kingsdale Rd. Berk HP4 122 A3
Kingsdown Ave. Luton LU2 45 D5
Kingsdown. Hit SG4 35 B6
Kingsfield Ct. Watf WD1 167 D2
Kingsfield Dr. Enf EN3 162 D4
Kingsfield. Hod EN11 135 A8
Kingsfield Rd. Dan En SG12 71 E8
Kingsfield Rd. Watf WD1 167 D3
Kingsfield Way. Enf EN3 162 D4
Kingsgate. St Alb AL3 127 B1
Kingshill Ave. St Alb AL4 128 B6
Kingshill Ct. Barn EN5 171 E5 6
Kingshill Inf Sch. Ware 93 D3
Kingshill Way. Berk HP4 122 B2
Kingshott Sch. Hit 35 B5
Kingsland Ct. Luton LU1 63 F6
Kingsland Rd. Heml H HP1 124 A1
Kingsland Rd. Luton LU1 63 F6
Kingsland Way. Ashw SG7 4 D4
Kingsley Ave. Bor WD6 169 F7
Kingsley Ave. Ches EN8 148 C2
Kingsley Ct. Wel G C AL7 110 F2
Kingsley Rd. Luton LU3 45 A5
Kingsley Wlk. Tri HP23 100 A4
Kingsmead. Ches EN8 148 D3
Kingsmead. Cuf EN6 146 E3
Kingsmead Nursery Sch. Hert 114 A7
Kingsmead Rd. Bis St CM23 77 A8
Kingsmead. Saw CM21 97 E1
Kingsmead. St Alb AL4 128 D6
Kingsmill Ct. Hat AL10 130 B3 1
Kingston Pl. Har HA3 176 F3
Kingston Rd. Luton LU2 45 F1
Kingston Vale. Royst SG8 7 E5
Kingsway. Cuf EN6 146 E1
Kingsway Gdns. Stot SG5 11 E7
Kingsway Ind Est. Luton 63 A8
Kingsway Inf Sch. Watf 154 A5
Kingsway Jun Sch. Watf 154 A5
Kingsway. Luton LU1,LU4 45 A1
Kingsway North Orbital Rd. Watf WD2 154 B5
Kingsway. Royst SG8 7 C8
Kingsway. Stot SG5 11 F7
Kingsway. Ware SG12 93 D3
Kingswell Ride. Cuf EN6 146 E1
Kingswood Ave. Hit SG4 35 D8
Kingswood Rd. Watf WD2 154 B5
Kingwell Rd. Had W EN4 159 D1
Kinross Cres. Luton LU3 44 D8
Kinsbourne Cl. Harp AL5 85 C4
Kinsbourne Cres. Harp AL5 85 D4
Kinsbourne Green La. Harp AL5 85 B3
Kipling Cl. Hit SG4 35 C7
Kipling Gr. Heml H HP2 105 B1
Kipling Pl. Stan HA7 176 F4
Kipling Rd. Royst SG8 2 E1
Kipling The. Luton LU3 45 B6
Kipling Way. Harp AL5 86 B1
Kirby Cl. Norwd HA6 174 F4
Kirby Dr. Luton LU3 45 A8
Kirkcaldy Gn. Sth Ox WD1 175 C7 1
Kirkdale Ct. Luton LU1 63 E6 3
Kirkdale Rd. Harp AL5 86 A2
Kirklands. Wel G C AL8 89 D2

Kirkwick Ave. Harp AL5 ..... 86 A1
Kit's La. Wal SG7 .............. 25 C8
Kitchener Cl. St Alb AL1 ... 128 B2
Kitching La. St Ipp SG4 ...... 49 F5
Kitching La. Stev SG1 ......... 50 A5
Kite Field. Nthch HP4 ........ 121 E7
Kite Way. Letw SG6 ........... 22 E8
Kitsbury Rd. Berk HP4 ...... 122 B4
Kitsbury Terr. Berk HP4 .. 122 B4
Kitson Way. Harl CM20 .... 117 C1
Kitswell Rd. Radl WD7 ..... 156 A6
Kitswell Way. Radl WD7 .. 155 F6
Kitt's End Rd. Pot B EN5 ... 158 E2
Knap Cl. Letw SG6 ............ 23 D8
Knebworth Ct. Bis St CM23 76 D6
Knebworth Ctry Pk. Kneb ... 68 C7
Knebworth Jun & Mix Inf Sch. Kneb ................ 69 A5
Knebworth Path. Bor WD6 ...................... 170 D5
Knebworth Sta. Kneb ......... 68 F5
Kneesworth House Hospl. Knee ................................ 2 C5
Kneesworth Rd. Melb SG8 ... 2 F8
Kneesworth St. Royst SG8 ... 7 C6
Knella Gn. Wel G C AL7 .... 111 A6
Knella Road Workshops. Wel G C ....................... 111 A6
Knight St. Saw CM21 ........ 97 E2
Knight's Ct. Saw CM21 ...... 97 E2
Knights Cl. Bis St CM23 ..... 76 C8
Knights Cl. Bun SG9 ........... 40 E6
Knights Ct. Bus WD2 ........ 168 D1
Knights Ct. Stand SG11 ...... 55 F1
Knights Field. Luton LU2 .... 45 D1
Knights Orch. Heml H HP1 ................ 123 F5
Knights Orch. St Alb AL3 .. 127 C3
Knights Templar Sch The. Bal ........................................ 23 E8
Knights Templars Gn. Stev SG2 ........................ 51 C8
Knightsbridge Way. Heml H HP2 ................ 124 E4
Knightsfield. Wel G C AL8 .. 89 D2
Knoll Cres. Norwd HA6 ..... 174 F2
Knoll Gn. Heml H HP2 ...... 124 E5
Knoll Rise. Luton LU2 ......... 45 E4
Knoll The. Hert SG13 ....... 114 B7
Knolles Cres. Wel G AL9 .. 144 B7
Knolls Cl. Wing HP22 ......... 60 B3
Knowl Piece. Hit SG4 ......... 22 A3
Knowl Pk. Elst WD6 ......... 169 E4
Knowl Way. Bor WD6 ....... 169 F4
Knowle Dr. Harp AL5 ....... 107 D7
Knowle. Stev SG1 .............. 36 B1
Knowle The. Hod EN11 .... 135 A5
Knutsford Ave. Watf WD2 154 D1
Knutsford Jun Mix Inf Sch. Watf ............................. 154 D1
Koh-I-Noor Ave. Bus WD2 168 A3
Kristiansand Way. Letw SG6 ......................... 23 C8
Kymswell Rd. Stev SG2 ...... 51 C3
Kynance Cl. Luton LU2 ....... 46 A2
Kynaston Cl. Har HA3 ...... 176 D3
Kynaston Wood. Har HA3 176 D3
Kyrkeby. Letw SG6 ............. 23 C4
Kytes Dr. Watf WD2 ........ 154 D6

Laburnum Cl. Ches EN8 ... 162 D8
Laburnum Cl. Luton LU3 .... 45 C7
Laburnum Gr. Chis AL2 .... 141 B6
Laburnum Gr. Luton LU3 .... 45 B7
Laburnum Rd. Hod EN11 .. 135 B8
Lachbury Cl. Luton LU1 ...... 63 A6
Lackmore Rd. Enf EN1 ...... 162 C4
Lacre Way. Letw SG6 ......... 23 C7
Ladbrooke Cl. Pot B EN6 .. 159 A7
Ladbrooke Dr. Pot B EN6 . 159 A7
Ladbrooks Prim Sch. Pot B 159 B7
Ladies Gr. St Alb AL3 ....... 127 C5
Lady Gr. Wel G C AL7 ...... 110 E2
Lady Spencer's Gr. St Alb AL1 .................... 127 C2
Lady Zia Wernher Sch The. Luton ................................ 46 B3
Lady's Cl. Watf WD1 ........ 167 C5
Ladyhill. Luton LU4 ............ 44 B6
Ladymeadow. Kin L HP3 .. 138 D4
Ladyshot. Harl CM20 ....... 118 A1
Ladysmith Rd. Har HA3 ..... 176 E1
Ladysmith Rd. Pit LU7 ........ 80 E5
Ladysmith Rd. St Alb AL3 . 127 D4
Ladywalk. Map Cr WD3 ... 172 E6
Ladywell Prospect. Sheer CM21 ................... 98 A1
Ladywood Cl. Ric WD3 ...... 165 C6
Ladywood Rd. Hert SG14 . 112 F6
Laidon Sq. Heml H HP2 .... 124 D7
Lake Dr. Bus WD2 ............ 176 D8
Lake Rd. Lo Naz EN9 ........ 135 E2
Lake The. Bus WD2 .......... 168 D1
Lake View. Pot B EN6 ...... 159 C6
Lake Villas. Fur P SG9 ........ 43 B4
Lakeland Cl. Stan HA3 ..... 176 D4
Lakeside. Bor WD6 .......... 170 A4
Lakeside Pl. Lon C AL2 .... 142 D4
Lakeside Rd. Ches EN8 .... 148 C3
Lakeside Sch. Wel G C ..... 110 B4
Lakeside. Tri HP23 ........... 100 A5
Lalleford Rd. Luton LU2 ..... 46 D1
Lamb Cl. Hat AL10 ............ 130 B4
Lamb Cl. Watf WD2 ......... 154 C5
Lamb Ct. Whea AL4 .......... 108 E7
Lamb La. Red AL3 ............ 106 B5
Lamb Meadow. Arl SG15 ... 11 A3
Lambert Ct. Watf WD2 .... 167 D5
Lambourn Chase. Radl WD7 ....................... 155 F3
Lambourn Gdns. Harp AL5 ........................ 85 F3
Lambs Cl. Cuf EN6 ............ 146 F2
Lambs Cl. Dun LU5 ............ 44 A1
Lambs Gdns. Widf SG12 .... 95 D4
Lambton Ave. Ches EN8 ... 162 D6
Lamer La. Whea AL4 .......... 87 D3
Lamers Rd. Luton LU2 ........ 46 B2
Lammas Mead. Hit SG5 ..... 21 E2
Lammas Path. Stev SG2 ..... 51 B4
Lammas Rd. Ched LU7 ....... 80 A7
Lammas Rd. Wat St SG14 .. 70 D4
Lammas Rd. Watf WD1 ... 167 C4
Lammas Way. Letw SG6 ..... 22 F8
Lammasmead. Hod EN10 . 148 F8
Lamorna Cl. Luton LU3 ...... 44 F6
Lamorna Cl. Radl WD7 ..... 156 B5
Lampits. Hod EN11 .......... 135 B6
Lamsey Rd. Heml H HP3 .. 124 D1
Lancaster Ave. Had W EN4 ................. 159 D1
Lancaster Ave. Hit SG5 ...... 34 E8
Lancaster Ave. Luton LU2 .. 45 C8
Lancaster Cl. Stev SG1 ...... 36 E2
Lancaster Dr. Bov HP3 ..... 136 F4
Lancaster Rd. Hit SG5 ........ 34 E8
Lancaster Rd. St Alb AL1 . 127 F5
Lancaster Way. Abb L WD5 .................. 153 F8
Lancaster Way. Bis St CM23 .................. 76 C8
Lancaster Way. Wel G C AL6 ................... 89 C3
Lancing Rd. Luton LU2 ....... 46 D3
Lancing Way. Cro Gr WD3 166 B4
Landau Way. Ches EN10 .. 148 F5
Landford Cl. Ric WD3 ....... 173 E8
Landmead Rd. Ches EN8 .. 148 E2
Lands' End. Elst WD6 ....... 169 D3
Lane End. Berk HP4 ......... 121 F4
Lane End. Hat AL10 .......... 129 F2
Lane Gdns. Bus WD2 ....... 168 E2
Lanefield Wlk. Wel G C AL8 ................ 110 C6
Lanercost Cl. Welw AL6 ..... 90 A7
Langbridge Cl. Hit SG4 ...... 35 A4
Langdale Ave. Harp AL5 ..... 86 D2
Langdale Ct. Heml H HP2 124 E6
Langdale Gdns. Enf EN3 ... 162 D4
Langdon St. Tri HP23 ....... 100 A3
Langfield Cl. Lo Naz EN9 .. 135 E1
Langford Dr. Luton LU2 ..... 46 A3
Langham Cl. Luton LU2 ..... 45 D7
Langham Cl. St Alb AL4 .... 128 D8
Langholme. Bus WD2 ....... 168 C1
Langland Ct. Norwd HA6 . 174 D3
Langland Dr. Pnr HA5 ...... 175 E3
Langley Ave. Heml H HP3 138 F8
Langley Cres. Kin L WD4 . 139 A1
Langley Cres. St Alb AL3 .. 127 C5
Langley Gr. Sand AL4 ....... 108 C2
Langley Hill Cl. Kin L WD4 139 A2
Langley Hill. Kin L WD4 .... 138 F2
Langley La. Abb L WD5 .... 153 F7
Langley La. Lan SG4 .. ....... 49 E2
Langley Lodge La. Kin L WD4 .................... 153 A8
Langley Rd. Abb L WD5 .... 153 F8
Langley Rd. Chipf WD4 .... 138 B1
Langley Rd. Watf WD1 ..... 167 A8
Langley Row. Barn EN5 .... 171 F8
Langley St. Luton LU1 ........ 63 E6
Langley Warf. Abb L ........ 139 A4
Langley Way. Watf WD1 .. 166 F8
Langleybury La. Abb L WD4 ................... 153 B4
Langleybury Sch. Abb L .... 153 B5
Langmead Dr. Bus WD2 .. 168 D1
Langthorne Ave. Stev SG1 . 50 E6
Langton Gr. Norwd HA6 ... 174 C5
Langton House. Hod EN11 134 F6
Langton Rd. Har HA3 ....... 176 C3
Langton Rd. Hod EN11 ..... 134 F6
Langwood Gdns. Watf WD1 .................... 167 A8
Lankester Rd. Royst SG8 ..... 7 C5
Lannock Hill. Wes SG4 ....... 23 E1
Lannock Jun Mix Inf Sch. Letw ................................. 23 C4
Lannock. Letw SG6 ............ 23 D4
Lanrick Copse. Berk HP4 . 122 E5
Lansdowne Cl. Watf WD2 154 D4
Lansdowne Ct. Hod EN10 135 A3
Lansdowne Rd. Luton LU3 . 45 D1
Lanterns La. Stev SG2 ....... 51 D5
Lanthony Ct. Arl SG15 ........ 11 A4
Laporte Way. Luton LU4 .... 44 F1
Laporte Way. Luton LU4 .... 45 A1
Lapwing Cl. Heml H HP2 .. 124 E6
Lapwing Dell. Letw SG6 ..... 23 B3
Lapwing Rd. Dun LU4 ........ 44 A4
Lapwing Rise. Stev SG2 ..... 51 D3
Larch Ave. Bri Wd AL2 ..... 140 E1
Larch Ave. Hit SG4 ............ 35 A4
Larch Cl. Ham St EN7 ....... 147 E4
Larch La. Welw AL6 ........... 89 F8
Larch Rise. Berk HP4 ....... 122 A5
Larches Ave. Enf EN1 ....... 162 C4
Larches The. Luton LU2 ..... 45 D1
Larches The. Norwd HA6 . 174 C4
Larches The. Nthch HP4 .. 121 D5
Larches The. St Alb AL4 ... 128 D7
Larches The. Ware SG12 ... 93 C4
Larches The. Watf WD2 .. 167 E4
Larchwood. Bis St CM23 .... 76 D5
Lark Rise. Hat AL10 ......... 130 A3
Larke Way. Luton LU4 ........ 44 C5
Larken Cl. Bus WD2 ......... 168 C1
Larken Dr. Bus WD2 ........ 168 C1
Larkens Cl. Stand SG11 ..... 55 D3
Larkins Cl. Bal SG7 ............ 12 F1
Larkinson. Stev SG1 .......... 50 C7
Larks Ridge. Chis AL2 ...... 141 A4
Larksfield. Ware SG12 ....... 93 E3
Larkspur Cl. Bis St CM23 ... 76 D6
Larkspur Cl. Heml H HP1 . 123 E4
Larkspur Gdns. Luton LU4 . 44 F2
Larksway. Bis St CM23 ..... 76 C6
Larkswood Rise. St Alb AL4 ................... 128 C8
Larmans Rd. Enf EN3 ....... 162 D3
Larsen Dr. Wa Aby EN9 ..... 163 D5
Larwood Gr. Stev SG1 ...... 51 A8
Latchmore Bank. L Hal CM22 ..................... 77 B1
Latchmore Cl. Hit SG4 ....... 34 F5
Latimer Cl. Heml H HP2 ... 125 B8
Latimer Cl. Pnr HA5 ........ 175 C2
Latimer Cl. Watf WD1 ..... 166 E2
Latimer Ct. Ches EN8 ....... 162 F5
Latimer Gdns. Pnr HA5 .... 175 C2
Latimer Gdns. Wel G C AL7 ................ 111 B6
Latimer Rd. L Chal HP6 .... 150 C2
Latimer Rd. Luton LU1 ....... 63 E6
Latium Cl. St Alb AL1 ....... 127 D2
Lattimore Rd. St Alb AL1 .. 127 E3
Lattimore Rd. Whea AL4 .. 108 C8
2 Latton Hall Cl. Harl CM20 118 A1
Lauderdale Rd. Abb L WD4 .................. 153 C6
Laughton Ct. Bor WD6 ..... 170 D7
Laundry La. Lo Naz EN9 ... 149 E6
Launton Cl. Luton LU3 ........ 31 B1
Laurance Haines Inf & Jun Sch The. Watf ....... 167 A3
Laureate Way. Heml H HP1 ................ 124 B5
Laurel Ave. Pot B EN6 ...... 158 F7
Laurel Cl. Heml H HP2 ...... 124 F4
Laurel Fields. Pot B EN6 .. 158 F8
Laurel Mews. Bal SG7 ........ 12 F1
Laurel Pk. Har HA3 .......... 176 F3
Laurel Rd. St Alb AL1 ....... 127 F3
Laurel Way. Ick SG5 .......... 21 E3
Laureldene. Muc H SG10 ... 74 F1
Laurels Cl. St Alb AL3 ...... 141 B8
Laurels The. Ham St EN7 . 147 E5
Laurels The. Pot En HP4 .. 123 C6
Laurino Pl. Bus WD2 ........ 176 C8
Lavender Cl. Ham St EN7 . 147 F4
Lavender Cl. Luton LU2 ...... 45 E7
Lavender Ct. Bal SG7 .......... 12 E1
Lavender Gdns. Enf EN2 .. 161 B1
Lavender Gdns. Har HA3 . 176 E4
Lavender Rd. Enf EN2 ...... 161 D1
Lavender Sch. Enf ........... 161 E1
Lavender Wlk. Hit SG5 ...... 34 D7
Lavender Wlk. Heml H HP2 ................. 124 D5
Lavinia Ave. Watf WD2 ..... 154 D5
Lavrock La. Cro Gr WD3 .. 165 F2
Law Hall La. Whit SG4 ....... 66 A8
Lawford Ave. Chor WD3 .. 164 C3
Lawford Cl. Chor WD3 ..... 164 C3
Lawford Cl. Luton LU1 ........ 63 C7
Lawn Ave. Kim SG4 ............ 66 C1
Lawn Gdns. Luton LU1 ....... 63 D6
Lawn La. Heml H HP3 ...... 138 D8
Lawn The. Harl CM20 ...... 118 B3
Lawn Vale. Pnr HA5 ......... 175 E1
Lawns Cl. Gt Of SG5 .......... 33 C2
Lawns Ct. Royst SG8 ............ 7 D5
Lawns Dr The. Hod EN10 . 134 F2
Lawns The. Har HA5 ........ 176 B3
Lawns The. Heml H HP1 ... 123 E4
Lawns The. St Alb AL3 ..... 127 C4
Lawns The. Stev SG2 ......... 51 D4
Lawns The. Wel G C AL8 .... 89 D1
Lawrance Gdns. Ches EN8 148 D3
Lawrance Rd. St Alb AL3 .. 127 C7
Lawrence Ave. Gt Am SG12 ................. 115 C3
Lawrence Ave. Letw SG6 ... 23 A4
Lawrence Ave. Saw CM21 . 97 E4
Lawrence Ave. Stev SG1 ... 50 E7
Lawrence Cl. Hert SG14 .. 112 E7
Lawrence End Rd. Bre Gr LU2 ..................... 65 D4
Lawrence Moorings. Sheer CM21 ................... 97 F1
Lawrie Ct. Har HA3 .......... 176 F3
Laxton Cl. Luton LU2 .......... 46 E1
Laxton Gdns. Bal SG7 ........ 24 A7
Lay Brook. St Alb AL4 ...... 128 A7
Layard Rd. Enf EN1 .......... 161 F1
Layham Dr. Luton LU2 ....... 46 D1
Layhill. Heml H HP2 ........ 124 D5
Layston Fst Sch. Bun .......... 40 F8
Layston Meadow. Bun SG9 40 F6
Layston Pk. Royst SG8 ......... 7 D5
Lea Bank Ct. Luton LU3 ..... 44 E6
Lea Bank. Luton LU3 ........ 44 E6
Lea Bushes. Watf WD2 .... 154 E4
Lea Cl. Bis St CM23 ........... 59 B1
Lea Cl. Bus WD2 ............. 168 B4
Lea Farm Jun Mix Sch. Watf ............................ 154 D4
Lea Gr. Bis St CM23 ........... 59 B1
Lea Manor High Sch. Luton 44 F8
Lea Manor Recn Ctr. Luton 44 F8
Lea Mount. Gofs O EN7 .... 147 E3
Lea Rd. Ches EN8 ............. 163 A5
Lea Rd. Harp AL5 ............... 86 B3
Lea Rd. Hod EN11 ............ 135 C8
Lea Rd. Luton LU1 .............. 63 F7
Lea Rd. Watf WD2 ........... 154 B1
Lea Wlk. Harp AL5 ............. 86 C4
Leacroft. Harp AL5 ............. 86 D3
Leaders Cl. Wing HP22 ...... 60 B3
Leaf Cl. Norwd HA6 .......... 174 D3
Leafield. Luton LU3 ........... 44 F4
Leaford Cres. Watf WD2 . 153 F2
Leaford Ct. Watf WD2 ..... 153 F3
Leaforis Rd. Ches EN7 ..... 148 A3
Leafy La. Ast Cl HP23 ......... 99 E1
Leagrave High St. Dun LU4 ......................... 44 B3
Leagrave Inf Sch. Luton ..... 44 C4
Leagrave Jun Mix Sch. Luton ............................. 44 C4
Leagrave Rd. Luton LU3,LU4 ................ 45 B2
Leagrave Sta. Luton ........... 44 E5
Leahoe Gdns. Hert SG13 . 113 C5
Lealands High Sch. Luton .. 44 C8
Leamington Rd. Luton LU3 . 45 A7
Leander Gdns. Watf WD2 154 B2
Leas The. Bal SG7 .............. 23 E7
Leas The. Bus WD2 .......... 167 F7
Leas The. Heml H HP3 ..... 139 A7
Leaside Ct. Harp AL5 ......... 86 C3
Leaside. Heml H HP2 ....... 125 C2
Leaside Wlk. Ware SG12 .... 93 D1 5
Leat Cl. Saw CM21 ............ 97 F3
Leathersellers Cl. Barn EN5 ...................... 171 E6
Leathwaite Cl. Luton LU3 .... 44 F6
Leaves Spring. Stev SG2 ... 51 A2
Leavesden Green Inf Sch. Watf ............................ 154 A5
Leavesden Green Jun Mix Sch. Watf ............. 154 A5
Leavesden Hospl. Abb L ... 154 A8
Leavesden Rd. Watf WD2 154 B1
Leaview. Wa Aby EN9 ...... 163 B6
Lebanon Cl. Watf WD1 .... 153 D3
Lectern La. St Alb AL1 ...... 141 E7
Leda Ave. Enf EN3 ........... 162 D1
Ledgemore La. Gt Gd HP2 103 F5
Ledwell Rd. Cad LU1 .......... 62 F3
Lee Cl. Gt Am SG12 .......... 115 C4
Lee Cl. Hert SG13 ............ 113 C4
Lee Farm Cl. Bot HP5 ....... 136 A1
Lee Road Ind Pk. Ches ..... 163 A5
Leeches Way. Ched LU7 .... 80 A7
Leecroft Rd. Barn EN5 ..... 171 E5
Leefe Way. Cuf EN6 ......... 146 D3
Leeming Rd. Bor WD6 ...... 169 F8
Lees Ave. Norwd HA6 ...... 174 F2
Leeside. Barn EN5 ........... 171 E3
Leeside. Pot B EN6 .......... 159 D7
Leete Pl. Royst SG8 ............. 7 D7
Leggatts Campus The. Watf ............................. 154 A3
Leggatts Cl. Watf WD2 .... 153 F3
Leggatts Rise. Watf WD2 154 A4
Leggatts Way. Watf WD2 154 A3
Leggatts Wood Ave. Watf WD2 .................... 154 B3
Leggett Gr. Stev SG1 ......... 50 E8
Leggfield Terr. Heml H HP1 ................. 123 F3
Leghorn Cres. Dun LU4 ...... 44 A3
Legions Way. Bis St CM23 . 77 A8
Leicester Rd. Luton LU4 ..... 44 E1
Leigh Comm. Wel G C AL7 110 F4
Leigh Ct. Bor WD6 ........... 170 D7
Leigh Rodd. Sth Ox WD1 .. 175 F7
Leighton Buzzard Rd. Gt Gd HP1 .................... 103 E2
Leighton Buzzard Rd. Heml H HP1 ................. 124 C5
Leighton Ct. Ches LU6 ...... 148 D2
Leighton Rd. Har HA3 ...... 176 D1
Leighton Rd. Wing HP22 .... 60 C3
Lemon Field Dr. Watf WD2 .................... 154 E6
Lemsford Ct. Bor WD6 ..... 170 C5
Lemsford La. Wel G C AL8 110 B4
Lemsford Rd. Hat AL10 .... 130 A6
Lemsford Rd. St Alb AL1 .. 127 F4
Lemsford Springs (Nature Reserve). Hat . 110 A5
Lemsford Village. Hat AL8 ........................ 109 F5
Lennon Ct. Luton LU1 ......... 63 D7
Lennox Gn. Luton LU2 ........ 46 F2
Lensbury Cl. Ches EN8 ..... 148 E3
Leonard's Cl. Welw AL6 ..... 89 E8
Lesbury Cl. Luton LU2 ....... 46 E1
Leslie Cl. Stev SG2 ............. 51 C2
Letchfield. Bot HP5 .......... 150 B8
Letchmore Cl. Stev SG1 ..... 50 D6
Letchmore Rd. Radl WD7 . 156 A3
Letchmore Rd. Stev SG1 ... 50 D7
Letchmore Road Inf Sch. Stev ............................... 50 D7
Letchworth Bsns & Ret Pk. Letw .............................. 23 C6
Letchworth Cl. Sth Ox WD1 ................. 175 D5
Letchworth Gate. Letw SG6 ........................ 23 B4
Letchworth La. Letw SG6 ... 22 F3
Letchworth Rd. Bal SG7 .... 23 D7
Letchworth Rd. Letw SG6 .. 23 D7
Letchworth Rd. Luton LU3 . 45 A4
Letter Box Row. Hit SG4 .... 34 F3
Leven Cl. Ches EN8 ......... 162 D6
Leven Cl. Sth Ox WD1 ...... 175 D5
Leven Dr. Ches EN8 ........ 162 D6
Leven Way. Heml H HP2 .. 124 D7
Levenage La. Widf SG12 .... 95 E3
Leventhorpe Sch The. Saw 97 E4
Leveret Cl. Watf WD2 ...... 154 A5
Leverstock Green Jun Mix Inf Sch. Heml H ........... 125 D2
Leverstock Green Rd. Heml H HP2,HP3 .......... 125 B3
Leverstock Green Rd. Heml H HP2,HP3 .......... 125 C2
Leverstock Green Way. Heml H HP2,HP3 .......... 125 C3
Leverton Cty Prim & Inf Sch The. Wa Aby .......... 163 F5
Leverton Way. Wa Aby EN9 .................. 163 C6
Lewes Way. Cro Gr WD3 . 166 C5
Lewis Cl. Hare UB9 .......... 173 C1
Lewsey Park Ct. Dun LU4 .. 44 A4
Lewsey Rd. Dun LU4 ......... 44 B2
Lexington Cl. Bor WD6 ..... 169 F6
Lexington Ct. Pot B EN6 ... 158 D8
Lexington Way. Barn EN5 171 D5
Ley House. Wel G C AL7 ... 111 C6
Ley Park Inf Sch. Hod ...... 134 F1
Ley Park Jun Sch. Hod ..... 134 F1
Ley Wlk. Wel G C AL7 ...... 111 C6
Leyburne Cl. Men LU7 ........ 61 C8
Leyburne Rd. Luton LU3 ..... 45 B6
Leycroft Way. Harp AL5 ... 107 E7

Leyden House (Adult Training Ctr). Stev 50 D2
Leyden Rd. Stev SG1 .......... 50 D2
Leygreen Cl. Luton LU2 ....... 64 A8
Leyhill Dr. Luton LU1 .......... 63 B4
Leyland Ave. St Alb AL1 ... 127 D1
Leyland Cl. Ches EN8 ....... 148 C2
Leys Ave. Letw SG6 ............ 22 F6
Leys Cl. Hare UB9 ........... 173 D2
Leys Rd. Heml H HP3 ....... 124 F1
Leys The. St Alb AL4 ......... 128 D6
Leys The. Tri HP23 .......... 100 B4
Leysdown. Wel G C AL7 ... 111 D6
Leyton Gn. Harp AL5 ......... 86 A1
Leyton Rd. Harp AL5 .......... 86 A1
Library Rd. Luton LU1 ......... 63 E7
Lichfield Rd. Norwd HA6 .. 175 A1
Lichfield Way. Hod EN10 . 134 F1
Liddel Cl. Luton LU3 ........... 45 B3
Lidgate Cl. Luton LU4 ......... 44 B6
Lighthorne Rise. Luton LU3 45 A7
Lilac Ave. Enf EN1 ........... 162 C3
Lilac Cl. Ches EN7 ........... 162 B8
Lilac Gr. Luton LU3 ............ 44 C8
Lilac Rd. Hod EN11 .......... 135 B8
Lilac Way. Harp AL5 ......... 107 D6
Lilley Bottom. Bre Gr SG5 .. 47 C5
Lilley Bottom. Gt Of SG4 .... 47 C5
Lilley Bottom Rd. Bre Gr SG4 ..................... 48 B1
Lilley Bottom Rd. Whit SG4 48 B1
Lilley CE Jun Mix Inf Sch. Lily ................................. 32 D2
Lilleyhoo La. Lily LU2 .......... 32 F2
Lilliard Cl. Hod EN11 ........ 115 B2
Limberlost The. Welw AL6 . 89 B7
Limbrick Rd. Harp AL5 ..... 107 C6
Limbury Rd. Luton LU3 ........ 44 F4
Lime Ave. Dun LU4 ............ 44 C3
Lime Ave. Kim AL4 ............. 87 B7
Lime Cl. Ast SG2 ................. 51 D4
Lime Cl. Ware SG12 ........... 93 E2
Lime Cl. Watf WD1 ........... 167 D2
Lime Gr. Barn N20 ........... 171 F1
Lime Gr. Royst SG8 .............. 7 E8
Lime Tree Pl. St Alb AL1 .. 127 E2
Lime Tree Wlk. Bus WD2 . 176 E8
Lime Tree Wlk. Enf EN2 ... 161 C1
Lime Tree Wlk. Ric WD3 .. 165 B4
Lime Walk Prim Sch. Heml H ......................... 124 F1
Lime Wlk. Heml H HP3 ..... 124 F1
Limedene Cl. Pnr HA5 ...... 175 D2
Limekiln La. Bal SG7 .......... 23 F7
Limekiln La. Sta M CM24 ... 59 C5
Limes Cres. Bis St CM23 .... 77 A7
Limes Ct. Hod EN11 ......... 135 A6
Limes Rd. Ches EN8 ......... 162 E7
Limes The. Arl SG15 ........... 11 A8
Limes The. Hit SG5 ........... 34 D6
Limes The. St Alb AL1 ...... 127 E5
Limes The. Wel G C AL7 ... 111 A4
Limetree Ave. Nwml E LU1 85 A7
Limetree Ct. Pnr HA5 ....... 176 A3
Linacres. Luton LU4 .......... 44 D4
Linbridge Way. Luton LU2 .. 46 E2
Linces Way. Wel G C AL7 . 111 B4
Lincoln Cl. Bis St CM23 ...... 76 D5
Lincoln Cl. Wel G C AL7 .... 111 D6
Lincoln Ct. Berk HP4 ........ 122 B4
Lincoln Ct. Bor WD6 ......... 170 D4
Lincoln Dr. Cro Gr WD3 .... 166 B6
Lincoln Dr. Sth Ox WD1 .... 175 C7
Lincoln Hill. Ans SG9 .......... 29 A5
Lincoln Mews. St Alb AL3 . 127 C2
Lincoln Rd. Luton LU4 ........ 45 B1
Lincoln Rd. Stev SG1 .......... 37 B2
Lincoln Way. Cro Gr WD3 166 B5
Lincoln's Cl. St Alb AL4 .... 128 D8
Lincot La. Whit SG4 ............ 67 C7
Lindbergh. Wel G C AL7 .... 111 C6
Linden Cl. Ches EN7 ......... 148 B1
Linden Cres. St Alb AL4 .... 128 C3
Linden Ct. Harp AL5 ......... 107 B8
Linden Ct. Luton LU2 .......... 63 F8
Linden Glade. Heml H HP1 ................ 124 A2
Linden Lea. Watf WD2 ..... 154 A6
Linden Rd. Luton LU4 ......... 44 E4
Linden Rd. Red AL3 .......... 106 A6
Lindencroft. Letw SG6 ........ 12 A1
Lindens The. Bis St CM23 .. 76 F6
Lindens The. Hat AL10 ..... 129 F6
Lindens The. Heml H HP3 137 F8
Lindens The. Stev SG1 ....... 50 E4
Lindley Cl. Harp AL5 .......... 86 A4
Lindley Ct. Harp AL5 .......... 86 A4
Lindlings. Heml H HP1 ..... 123 E2
Lindsay Ave. Hit SG4 .......... 35 B5
Lindsay Cl. Royst SG8 .......... 2 C1
Lindsay Pl. Ches EN7 ....... 148 B1
Lindsey Cl. Bis St CM23 .... 58 F1
Lindsey Rd. Bis St CM23 .... 58 F1
Lindsey Rd. Luton LU2 ....... 46 D1
Lindum Pl. St Alb AL3 ....... 127 A1
Lingfield Cl. Norwd HA6 .. 174 E3
Lingfield Rd. Royst SG8 ....... 7 E6
Lingfield Rd. Stev SG1 ........ 37 C1
Lingholm Way. Barn EN5 . 171 D4
Lingmoor Dr. Watf WD2 .. 154 C6
Linington Ave. Bot HP5 ..... 136 A1
Link Cl. Hat AL10 ............. 130 B5
Link Dr. Hat AL10 ............. 130 B5
Link Rd. Bis St CM23 .......... 76 F8
Link Rd. Bus WD2 ............ 167 D7
Link Rd. Welw AL6 ............. 89 F8
Link The. Letw SG6 ............ 12 A1
Link Way. Bis St CM23 ....... 76 E6
Link Wlk. Hat AL10 ........... 130 B6
Linkfield. Wel G C AL7 ...... 110 E2
Links Ave. Hert SG13 ....... 114 B7
Links Bsns Ctr The. Bis St .. 77 C7
Links Dr. Bor WD6 ........... 169 F5
Links Dr. Radl WD7 .......... 155 F6
Links The. Ches EN8 ........ 148 D5
Links The. Wel G C AL8 .... 110 B6
Links View. St Alb AL3 ...... 127 C5
Links Way. Cro Gr WD3 .... 166 C5
Links Way. Luton LU2 ........ 45 D8
Linksway. Norwd HA6 ....... 174 C2
Linkway. Pnr HA5 ............ 175 D2
Linkways E. Stev SG1 ......... 50 F5
Linkways W. Stev SG1 ........ 50 F5
Linnet Cl. Bus WD2 .......... 168 C1
Linnet Cl. Dun LU4 ............ 44 A4
Linnet Cl. Letw SG6 ............ 22 E8
Linnet Wlk. Hat AL10 ....... 130 A3
Linsey Cl. Heml H HP3 ...... 139 A7
Linster Gr. Bor WD6 ......... 170 C4
Linten Cl. Hit SG4 .............. 35 C6
Linton Ave. Bor WD6 ........ 169 F7
Lintott Cl. Stev SG1 ........... 50 D6
Linwood Rd. Harp AL5 ..... 107 C7
Linwood Rd. Ware SG12 .... 93 F3
Linwood. Saw CM21 ........... 97 E2
Lion Ct. Bor WD6 ............. 170 C8
Lion Yd. Kim SG4 .............. 66 D1
Liphook Rd. Sth Ox WD1 .. 175 D6
Lippitts Hill. Luton LU2 ...... 45 E5
Lismore. Heml H HP3 ....... 125 C1
Lismore. Stev SG2 ............. 51 C1
Lister Ave. Hit SG4 ............ 34 F5
Lister Cl. Stev SG1 ............ 36 C2
Lister Hospl. Stev ............... 36 B2
Liston Cl. Luton LU4 .......... 44 B5
Little Acre. St Alb AL3 ...... 127 D6
Little Acres. Ware SG12 .. 114 D8
Little Berries. Luton LU3 .... 44 E7
Little Bridge Rd. Berk HP4 122 D4
Little Burrow. Wel G C AL7 ................ 110 D4
Little Bushey La. Bus WD2 ...................... 168 C5
Little Catherells. Heml H HP1 ................ 123 F5
Little Chishill Rd. Gt Ch SG8 ....................... 18 C8
Little Church Rd. Luton LU2 46 B3
Little Dell. Wel G C AL8 .... 110 D8
Little Furze Jun Mix Inf Sch. Sth Ox ........................... 175 B7
Little Gaddesden C of E Sch. L Gad ............................ 102 C8
Little Ganett. Wel G C AL7 111 C4
Little Gr. Bus WD2 ........... 168 B5
Little Graylings. Abb L WD5 ................... 153 E6
Little Green Cty Prim Sch. Cro Gr ......................... 166 B6
Little Green La. Cro Gr WD3 ................ 166 B6
Little Green La. Sar WD3 . 166 B6
Little Hadham Cty Prim Sch. L Had ............................... 57 C2
Little Hallingbury CE Prim Sch. L Hal .................... 98 C8
Little Hardings. Wel G C AL7 ................ 111 C7
Little Hayes. Kin L WD4 ... 139 A2
Little Heath La. Berk HP4 123 B4
Little Heath La. Pot En HP4 .................... 123 B4
Little Heath Prim Sch. Pot B ............................ 145 C1
Little Heath. Sheer CM22 .. 98 F3
Little Heath Spinney. St Alb AL3 ................... 127 E5
Little Henleys. Hun SG12 ... 95 D1
Little Hill. Chor WD3 ........ 164 C3
Little Hoo. Tri HP23 .......... 99 F4
Little How Croft. Abb L WD5 ................... 153 C8
Little Hyde. Stev SG2 ........ 51 B4
Little La. Harp AL5 ........... 107 C6
Little La. Pirt SG5 ............... 20 D5
Little Lake. Wel G C AL7 .. 111 B3
Little Larkins. Barn EN5 ... 171 E3
Little Ley. Wel G C AL7 .... 110 E3
Little Martins. Bus WD2 .. 168 B4
Little Mead. Hat AL10 ....... 130 B8
Little Mimms. Heml H HP2 124 E4 2
Little Mollards. Wing HP22 60 A3
Little Moss La. Pnr HA5 ... 175 E1
Little Mundells. Wel G C AL7 ................ 110 F8
Little Mundem Jun Mix & Inf Sch. Dan En ............. 71 E8
Little Orchard Cl. Abb L WD5 ................... 153 D7
Little Orchard Cl. Pnr HA5 175 E1
Little Oxhey La. Sth Ox WD1 ................ 175 E6
Little Parndon Cty Jun & Inf Schs. Harl .... 117 B1
Little Piper's Cl. Gofs O EN7 ................. 147 B2
Little Pk. Bov HP3 ........... 137 A3
Little Potters. Bus WD2 ... 168 E2
Little Rd. Heml H HP2 ...... 124 F4
Little Reddings Sch. Bus .. 168 B4
Little Ridge. Wel G C AL7 . 111 A6
Little Rivers. Wel G C AL7 111 A7
Little Thistle. Wel G C AL7 111 C4
Little Tring Rd. Tri HP23 .... 99 F6
Little Twye Rd. Chol HP23 120 A3
Little Twye Rd. St Le HP23 .................. 119 F3
Little Wade. Wel G C AL7 110 F3 1
Little Widbury La. Ware SG12 ................... 93 F1
Little Widbury. Ware SG12 93 F1
Little Windmill Hill. Chipf WD4 .................... 151 F7
Little Wlk. Harl CM20 ....... 117 D1
Little Wood Croft. Luton LU3 ...................... 44 E7
Little Youngs. Wel G C AL8 ................ 110 C6
Littlebrook Gdns. Ches EN8 ...................... 148 D1
Littlecote Pl. Pnr HA5 ...... 175 E2
Littlefield Rd. Luton LU2 ..... 46 B2
Littlegreen La. Cad LU1 ..... 62 E3
Liverpool Rd. Luton LU1 ..... 63 D7
Liverpool Rd. St Alb AL1 ... 127 E3
Liverpool Rd. Watf WD1 ... 167 B4
Livingstone Ct. Barn EN5 .. 171 E7
Livingstone Link. Stev SG2 . 51 B8
Livingstone Wlk. Heml H HP2 ................. 124 F7
Lloyd Way. Kim SG4 ........... 66 C1
Loates La. Watf WD1 ....... 167 C6
Loates Pasture. Sta M CM24 .................. 59 D8
Local Board Rd. Watf WD1 .................. 167 D4
Locarno Ave. Luton LU4 ..... 44 C6
Lochinvar House Sch. Pot B ........................... 145 B1
Lochnell Rd. Berk HP4 ..... 121 F6
Lock View. Saw CM21 ........ 97 F2
Lockers Park La. Heml H HP1 ................ 124 B3
Locket Rd. Har HA3 .......... 176 F1
Lockley Cres. Hat AL10 .... 130 B7
Lockleys Dr. Welw AL6 ...... 89 C5
Lodge Ave. Bor WD6 ........ 169 F4
Lodge Cl. Hert SG14 ........ 113 C8
Lodge Cres. Ches EN8 ..... 162 D5
Lodge Ct. Abb L HA0 ........ 154 A7
Lodge Ct. Ick SG5 ............. 21 E3
Lodge Dr. Hat AL9 ........... 130 D8
Lodge Dr. Ric WD3 .......... 165 C5
Lodge End. Cro Gr WD3 ... 166 D5
Lodge End. Radl WD7 ...... 156 B5
Lodge Farm Inf & Jun Sch. Stev ............................... 51 C7
Lodge Field. Wel G C AL7 ... 89 E1
Lodge Gdns. Harp AL5 ...... 86 A2
Lodge La. Wa Aby EN9 .... 163 D4
Lodge Way. Stev SG2 ......... 51 A1
Loftus Cl. Dun LU4 ............ 44 B3
Logans. Barn EN5 ............ 171 D6
Lombardy Cl. Heml H HP2 125 D2
Lombardy Dr. Berk HP4 ... 122 D3
Lombardy Way. Bor WD6 169 E7
Lomond Rd. Heml H HP2 .. 124 D7
London Bible Coll. Norwd 174 D4
London Colney Jun Mix Inf Sch. Lon C ................. 142 D6
London Luton Airport. Luton ............................ 64 E7
London Rd. Ast Cl HP22 ..... 99 A4
London Rd. Bal SG7 ........... 23 F6
London Rd. Bar SG8 ............. 8 F1
London Rd. Bark SG8,SG9 .. 17 D1
London Rd. Berk HP4 ....... 122 E3
London Rd. Bis St CM23 ..... 77 A4
London Rd. Bun SG9 .......... 40 F6
London Rd. Bus WD2 ....... 167 F3
London Rd. Harl CM17 ..... 118 C2
London Rd. Heml H HP1,HP3 .......... 124 A1
London Rd. Hert SG13 ..... 113 E5
London Rd. Hert H SG13 .. 114 B3
London Rd. Hit SG4 ........... 34 F5
London Rd. Kneb SG3 ........ 69 A3
London Rd. Lan SG4 ........... 49 D5
London Rd. Luton LU1 ........ 63 E4
London Rd. Mark AL3 ........ 83 F5
London Rd. Nwml E LU1 .... 84 F7
London Rd. Ric WD3 ....... 173 E8
London Rd. Royst SG8 .......... 7 D5
London Rd. Saw CM21 ....... 97 E2
London Rd. Shen WD7 ..... 157 A5
London Rd. Stev SG1,SG2 .. 50 D3
London Rd. Tri HP23 ....... 100 C3
London Rd. Ware SG12 .... 114 E7
London Rd. Welw AL6 ........ 69 A3
London Rd. Welw AL6 ........ 89 C4
London Row. Arl SG15 ........ 11 A3
Londrina Ct. Berk HP4 ..... 122 D4
Londrina Terr. Berk HP4 .. 122 D4
Long Acre. Harl CM17 ...... 118 B4
Long Arrotts. Heml H HP1 124 B5
Long Barn Cl. Watf WD2 .. 154 A7
Long Buftlers. Harp AL5 .. 107 F8
Long Chaulden. Heml H HP1 ................ 123 E3
Long Cl. Luton LU2 ........... 46 C3
Long Croft Dr. Ches EN8 .. 163 A5
Long Croft Rd. Luton LU1 ... 63 A7
Long Croft Rd. Map Cr WD3 ............... 172 D5
Long Croft. Sta M CM22 ..... 59 D8
Long Croft. Watf WD1 ..... 167 B2
Long Cutt. Red AL3 .......... 106 A6
Long Elmes. Har HA3 ....... 176 C2
Long Elms. Abb L WD5 ..... 153 D6
Long Elms Cl. Abb L WD5 . 153 D6
Long Fallow. Chis AL2 ...... 141 A4
Long Hyde. Stev SG2 .......... 51 B4
Long John. Heml H HP3 ... 124 F1
Long La. Ast SG2 ................ 51 E5
Long La. Bov HP3 ............ 150 F8
Long La. Chor WD3 .......... 164 D2
Long La. Ric WD3 ............ 172 F8
Long La. Whit SG4 ............ 66 A7
Long Leaves. Stev SG2 ....... 51 A2
Long Ley. Ched LU7 ........... 80 A7
Long Ley. Harl CM20 ........ 117 F1
Long Ley. Wel G C AL7 ..... 111 C6
Long Marston Jun Mix Inf Sch. Lon M .................... 79 B4
Long Marston Rd. Mars HP23 ..................... 79 F2
Long Meadow. Bis St CM23 76 D6
Long Meadow. Mark AL3 ... 83 F5
Long Mimms. Heml H HP2 124 E4 3
Long Moor. Ches EN8 ...... 148 E2
Long Ridge. Ast SG2 .......... 51 D1
Long Spring. St Alb AL3 ... 127 F7
Long View. Berk HP4 ....... 122 A6
Longacres. St Alb AL4 ...... 128 D3
Longbridge Cl. Tri HP23 ... 100 A6
Longcliffe Path. Sth Ox WD1 ................ 175 A7
Longcroft Ave. Harp AL5 .... 85 F1
Longcroft Gn. Wel G C AL8 110 D5
Longcroft La. Bov HP3 ..... 137 D5
Longcroft La. Wel G C AL8 110 D5
Longcroft Rd. Stev SG1 ...... 50 E7
Longcrofts. Wa Aby EN9 .. 163 E5
Longdean Pk. Heml H HP3 139 A7
Longdean Sch. Heml H .... 139 B8
Longfield Ave. Enf EN3 ..... 162 C1
Longfield Ct. Letw SG6 ....... 22 D7
Longfield Dr. Luton LU4 ..... 44 D1
Longfield Gdns. Tri HP23 ... 99 E3
Longfield. Heml H HP3 ..... 125 B1
Longfield La. Ham St EN7 148 A4
Longfield Rd. Harp AL5 .... 107 C7
Longfield Rd. Tri HP23 ....... 99 F3
Longfield Sch. Stev ........... 50 B8
Longfields. Stev SG2 ......... 51 C1
Longlands Cl. Ches EN8 ... 162 D7
Longlands. Heml H HP2 ... 125 A3
Longlands Prim Sch. Ches 148 F6
Longlands Rd. Wel G C AL7 ................ 110 F5
Longleigh. Letw SG6 .......... 11 F1
Longley Terrace Ind Pk. Luton ............................ 63 E6 8
Longmans. Brag SG11 ....... 55 F7
Longmead. Bun SG9 .......... 40 D7
Longmead. Hat AL10 ....... 130 B8
Longmead Jun & Inf Sch. Stev ............................... 51 B1
Longmead. Letw SG6 ......... 22 E7
Longmead. Welw SG3 ........ 69 A2
Longmeadow Dr. Ick SG5 .. 21 F5
Longmore Cl. Map Cr WD3 ............... 172 F6
Longmore Gdns. Wel G C AL7 ................ 110 F6
Longspring. Watf WD2 .... 154 B2
Longwood Rd. Hert SG14 . 112 F8
Loning The. Enf EN3 ........ 162 C1
Lonsdale Cl. Luton LU3 ...... 45 B5
Lonsdale Cl. Pnr HA5 ....... 175 E2
Lonsdale Ct. Stev SG1 ........ 50 F7
Lonsdale. Heml H HP2 ..... 124 E6
Lonsdale Rd. Stev SG1 ...... 50 F7
Lonsdale Sch. Stev ............ 50 F7
Loom La. Radl WD7 .......... 156 A2
Loom Pl. Radl WD7 .......... 156 A3
Loop Rd. Wa Aby EN9 ...... 163 B7
Lorane Ct. Watf WD1 ....... 167 A7
Lord Mead La. A St L AL6 ... 88 C7
Lord St. Hod EN11 ........... 134 D6
Lord St. Watf WD1 ........... 167 C6
Lords Ave. Bis St CM23 ...... 76 B7
Lords Cl. Shen WD7 ......... 156 E7
Lords Meadow. Red AL3 .. 106 A5
Lords Wood. Wel G C AL7 111 C6
Lordship Ctr. Letw SG6 ...... 23 A3
Lordship Farm Jun Mix Inf Sch. Letw .................. 23 A3
Lordship La. Letw SG6 ....... 23 B4
Lordship Rd. Ches EN7 .... 148 B1
Loreto Coll. St Alb ............ 127 E3
Loring Rd. Berk HP4 ........ 122 C3
Lorne Rd. Har HA3 ........... 176 F1
Lorraine Pk. Har HA3 ....... 176 E3
Lorrimer Cl. Luton LU2 ....... 45 E6
Lothair Rd. Luton LU2 ........ 46 A4
Loudwater Dr. Ric WD3 ... 165 C5
Loudwater House. Ric WD3 ....................... 165 C5
Loudwater Hts. Ric WD3 . 165 C6
Loudwater La. Ric WD3 ... 165 C4
Loudwater Ridge. Ric WD3 ....................... 165 C5
Louisa Cotts. Tri HP23 ..... 100 A3
Louise Wlk. Bov HP3 ....... 137 A3
Louvain Way. Watf WD2 .. 154 B7
Lovatts. Cro Gr WD3 ........ 166 A5
Love La. Abb L WD5 ........ 139 F1
Love La. Ashw SG7 .............. 4 A4
Love La. Kin L WD4 ......... 138 E3
Love La. Pnr HA5 ............ 175 E1
Lovel Cl. Heml H HP1 ....... 124 A3
Lovell Cl. Hit SG4 .............. 35 A6
Lovell Rd. Enf EN1 .......... 162 B3
Low Hill Rd. Lo Naz CM19 135 F6
Low Rd. Ess AL9 .............. 131 F8
Lowbell La. Lon C AL2 ...... 142 E4
Lower Adeyfield Rd. Heml H HP2 ................ 124 D4
Lower Barn. Heml H HP3 . 138 F8
Lower Bourne Gdns. Ware SG12 .................... 93 C3
Lower Clabdens. Ware SG12 .................... 93 F1
Lower Dagnall St. St Alb AL3 .................... 127 C3
Lower Emms. Heml H HP2 125 C8
Lower End. Wing HP22 ...... 60 B2
Lower Gower Rd. Royst SG8 7 D8
Lower Harpenden Rd. Luton LU1 ........................ 64 C3
Lower Harpenden Rd. Nwml E LU2 .................... 64 C3
Lower Hatfield Rd. Bay SG13 ..................... 112 F1
Lower High St. Watf WD1 167 D4
Lower Ickfield Way. Ast Cl HP22 ..................... 99 C7
Lower Icknield Way. Mars HP23 ...................... 80 A1
Lower Icknield Way. Wils HP23 ....................... 99 C7
Lower Innings. Hit SG5 ...... 34 D8
Lower Island Way. Wa Aby EN9 ................. 163 B4
Lower King St. Royst SG8 .... 7 D6
Lower Kings Rd. Berk HP4 122 C5
Lower Luton Rd. Harp AL5 . 86 C3
Lower Luton Rd. Whea AL4 86 C3
Lower Mardley Hill. Welw AL6 ......................... 89 F8
Lower Meadow. Ches EN8 148 D4

Lower Paddock Rd. Watf WD1 ... 167 E3
Lower Park Cres. Bis St CM23 ... 76 F5
Lower Paxton Rd. St Alb AL1 ... 127 E2
Lower Plantation. Ric WD3 ... 165 C6
Lower Rd. Bre Gr SG4 ... 47 F1
Lower Rd. Chor WD3 ... 164 D5
Lower Rd. Gt Am SG12 ... 114 F6
Lower Rd. Heml H HP3 ... 139 A5
Lower Rd. L Hal CM22 ... 98 C7
Lower Sales. Heml H HP1 ... 123 F2
Lower Sean. Stev SG2 ... 51 A3
Lower St. Sta M CM24 ... 59 E7
Lower Tail. Sth Ox WD1 ... 175 E7
Lower Tub. Bus WD2 ... 168 D2
Lower Yott. Heml H HP2 ... 124 F2
Lowerfield. Wel G C AL7 ... 111 A5
Lowestoft Rd. Watf WD2 ... 167 B8
Loweswater Cl. Watf WD2 ... 154 C6
Lowfield La. Hod EN11 ... 135 A6
Lowfield. Saw CM21 ... 97 E1
Lowgate La. Dan En SG12 ... 72 A4
Lowgate La. Thun SG11 ... 72 C5
Lowlands. Hat AL9 ... 130 C8
Lowson Gr. Watf WD1 ... 167 E2
Lowswood Cl. Norwd HA6 ... 174 C2
Lowther Cl. Bor WD6 ... 169 F4
Loxley Rd. Berk HP4 ... 121 F6
Lucan Rd. Barn EN5 ... 171 E6
Lucas Ct. Wa Aby EN9 ... 163 F6
Lucas Gdns. Luton LU3 ... 45 B8
Lucas La. Ashw SG7 ... 4 E4
Lucas La. Hit SG5 ... 34 D7
Lucerne Way. Luton LU3 ... 45 C4
Lucks Hill. Heml H HP1 ... 123 E3
Ludgate. Tri HP23 ... 99 F4
Ludlow Ave. Luton LU1 ... 63 E4
Ludlow Mead. Sth Ox WD1 ... 175 B7
Ludlow Way. Cro Gr WD3 ... 166 C5
Ludwick Cl. Wel G C AL7 ... 110 F4
Ludwick Gn. Wel G C AL7 ... 110 F5
Ludwick Way. Wel G C AL7 ... 110 F5
Lukes La. Lon M HP23 ... 79 D3
Lukes Lea. Mars HP23 ... 80 A1
Lullington Cl. Luton LU2 ... 46 C3
Lullington Garth. Bor WD6 ... 170 B4
Lulworth Ave. Gofs O EN7 ... 147 B2
Lumbards. Wel G C AL7 ... 90 A1
Lumen Rd. Royst SG8 ... 7 D7
Lundin Wlk. Sth Ox WD1 ... 175 D6
Luton Coll of Higher Ed. Luton ... 63 F7
Luton Dr The. Nwml E LU1 ... 64 B3
Luton & Dunstable Hospl. Dun ... 44 C2
Luton & Dunstable Hospl (Faringdon Wing). Dun ... 44 C3
Luton Hoo. Nwml E ... 64 A2
Luton Ind Coll. Luton ... 63 E7
Luton La. Red AL3 ... 106 A8
Luton Maternity Hospl. Dun ... 44 C2
Luton Rd. Cad LU1 ... 63 A4
Luton Rd. Dun LU5 ... 44 A1
Luton Rd. Gt Of LU2 ... 46 E3
Luton Rd. Gt Of SG5 ... 33 B2
Luton Rd. Harp AL5 ... 85 E4
Luton Rd. Kim SG4 ... 66 B2
Luton Rd. Luton LU4 ... 44 A7
Luton Rd. Mark AL3 ... 83 E7
Luton Rd. Str LU3 ... 31 A6
Luton Regional Sports Ctr. Luton ... 46 A4
Luton Sta. Luton ... 63 E8
Luton Town Football Gnd. Luton ... 63 C8
Luton VIth Form Coll. Luton ... 45 E4
Luton White Hill. Gt Of SG5 ... 33 B2
Luxembourg Cl. Luton LU3 ... 44 D8
Luynes Rise. Bun SG9 ... 40 E6
Lybury La. Red AL3 ... 105 F7
Lycaste Cl. St Alb AL1 ... 128 A2
Lych Gate. Watf WD2 ... 154 D6
Lydia Ct. Wel G AL9 ... 144 C7
Lydia Mews. Wel G AL9 ... 144 C7
Lye Hill. Bre Gr SG4 ... 65 D7
Lye La. Bri Wd AL2 ... 141 A2
Lye La. Chis AL2 ... 141 A2
Lygean Ave. Ware SG12 ... 93 E1
Lygetun Dr. Luton LU3 ... 44 F7
Lygrave. Stev SG2 ... 69 C8
Lyle's Row. Hit SG4 ... 34 F6
Lyles La. Wel G C AL8 ... 110 E8
Lymans Rd. Arl SG15 ... 11 A6
Lyme Ave. Nthch HP4 ... 121 D7
Lymington Ct. Watf WD2 ... 154 A5
Lymington Rd. Stev SG1 ... 50 B8
Lynbury Ct. Watf WD1 ... 167 A6
Lynch Hill. Ken Co LU6 ... 83 A8
Lynch The. Hod EN11 ... 135 B6
Lyndale Sch. St Alb ... 127 E4
Lyndale. Stev SG1 ... 50 E4
Lyndhurst Ave. Pnr HA5 ... 175 B2
Lyndhurst Cl. Harp AL5 ... 86 C2
Lyndhurst Cty Sec Sch. Bor ... 169 F8
Lyndhurst Dr. Harp AL5 ... 86 C2
Lyndhurst Gdns. Pnr HA5 ... 175 B2
Lyndhurst Rd. Luton LU1 ... 63 C7
Lyndon Ave. Pnr HA5 ... 175 E4
Lyndon Mead. Sand AL4 ... 108 C2
Lyne Way. Heml H HP1 ... 123 F5
Lyneham Rd. Luton LU2 ... 46 C1
Lynn Cl. Har HA3 ... 176 D1
Lynsey Cl. Red AL3 ... 106 A6
Lynton Ave. Arl SG15 ... 11 A5
Lynton Ave. St Alb AL1 ... 128 C2
Lynton Ct. Bis St CM23 ... 76 E4
Lynwood Ave. Luton LU2 ... 46 A3
Lynwood Dr. Norwd HA6 ... 174 F2
Lynwood Hts. Ric WD3 ... 165 C4
Lyon Way. Coln H AL4 ... 129 A3
Lyrical Way. Heml H HP1 ... 124 B5
Lys Hill Gdns. Hert SG14 ... 113 B8
Lysander Cl. Bov HP3 ... 137 A4
Lysander Way. Abb L WD5 ... 154 A7
Lysander Way. Wel G C AL7 ... 111 D7
Lytham Ave. Sth Ox WD1 ... 175 D5
Lytton Ave. Enf EN3 ... 162 E1
Lytton Ave. Letw SG6 ... 22 F5
Lytton Fields. Kneb SG3 ... 68 F5
Lytton Gdns. Wel G C AL8 ... 110 D6
Lytton Rd. Pnr HA5 ... 175 E3
Lytton Way. Stev SG1 ... 50 C6
Lyttons Way. Hod EN11 ... 115 A1

Mabbutt Cl. Bri Wd AL2 ... 140 E1
Mabey's Wlk. H Wy CM21 ... 97 B1
Macaulay Rd. Dun LU4 ... 44 A2
Macdonnell Gdns. Watf WD2 ... 153 F4
Macer's La. Ches EN10 ... 148 F7
Mackenzie Sq. Stev SG2 ... 51 B3
Mackerel Hall. Royst SG8 ... 7 B6
Maddles. Letw SG6 ... 23 D4
Maddox Rd. Harl CM20 ... 117 E1
Maddox Rd. Heml H HP2 ... 125 B3
Made Field. Stev SG1,SG2 ... 50 F5
Madgeways Cl. Gt Am SG12 ... 114 F5
Madgeways La. Gt Am SG12 ... 114 F5
Magellan Cl. Stev SG2 ... 51 D5
Magna Cl. Harp AL5 ... 107 D6
Magnaville Rd. Bis St CM23 ... 76 E4
Magnaville Rd. Bus WD2 ... 168 F2
Magnolia Ave. Abb L WD5 ... 154 A7
Magnolia Cl. Hert SG13 ... 114 A6
Magnolia Cl. Pk St AL2 ... 141 D5
Magpie Cl. Enf EN1 ... 162 A1
Magpie Cres. Stev SG2 ... 51 D4
Magpie Hall Rd. Stan WD2 ... 176 E8
Magpie Wlk. Hat AL10 ... 130 A3 2
Magpies The. Luton LU2 ... 45 E6
Maiden St. Wes SG4 ... 24 C1
Maidenhall CP Jun & Inf Sch. Luton ... 45 A2
Maidenhall Rd. Luton LU4 ... 45 A2
Maidenhead St. Hert SG14 ... 113 D6 3
Maidenhead Yd. Hert SG14 ... 113 D6
Main Ave. Mo Pk HA6 ... 174 C7
Main Par. Chor WD3 ... 164 C5
Main Rd. Bram SG14 ... 91 D3
Main Rd N. Dagn HP4 ... 81 A6
Main Rd S. Dagn HP4 ... 81 D4
Maitland Rd. Sta M CM24 ... 59 E6
Malborough Rd. Watf WD1 ... 167 B5
Malden Rd. Bor WD6 ... 170 A6
Malden Rd. Watf WD1 ... 167 B7
Maldon Ct. Harp AL5 ... 86 B2
Malham Cl. Luton LU4 ... 44 F2
Malins Cl. Barn EN5 ... 171 C4
Mall The. Chis AL2 ... 141 C4
Mallard Gdns. Luton LU3 ... 45 A5
Mallard Rd. Royst SG8 ... 7 C6
Mallard Rd. Stev SG2 ... 51 D2
Mallard Way. Norwd HA6 ... 174 C3
Mallard Way. Watf WD2 ... 154 E3
Mallion Ct. Wa Aby EN9 ... 163 F6
Mallories. Harl CM20 ... 117 F2
Mallow Wlk. Gofs O ... 147 D3
Mallow Wlk. Royst SG8 ... 7 E5
Malm Cl. Ric WD3 ... 173 D8
Malmes Croft. Heml H HP3 ... 125 C1
Malmsdale. Wel G C AL8 ... 89 D2
Maltby Dr. Enf EN1 ... 162 B1
Malthouse Ct. St Alb AL1 ... 127 D2
Malthouse Gn. Luton LU2 ... 46 F1
Malthouse La. Stot SG5 ... 12 A7
Malthouse Pl. Radl WD7 ... 156 A5
Malthouse The. Hert SG14 ... 113 D6 13
Malting Cotts. Asp SG9 ... 40 D5
Malting La. Ald HP23 ... 101 D5
Malting La. Brag SG11 ... 55 E7
Malting La. Dagn HP4 ... 81 C5
Malting La. Muc H SG10 ... 74 F2
Malting Mead. Hat AL10 ... 130 C6
Maltings Cl. Bal SG7 ... 13 B1
Maltings Cl. Royst SG8 ... 7 C7
Maltings Ct. Ware SG12 ... 114 D8
Maltings Dr. Whea AL4 ... 108 C8
Maltings Ind Est The. Sta Ab ... 115 D4
Maltings La. Gt Ch SG8 ... 9 E2
Maltings The. Abb L WD4 ... 153 C5
Maltings The. Heml H HP2 ... 124 D4
Maltings The. Letw SG6 ... 12 C1
Maltings The. St Alb AL1 ... 127 D3
Maltings The. Walk SG2 ... 52 B8
Malus Cl. Heml H HP2 ... 125 A4
Malvern Cl. St Alb AL4 ... 128 C7
Malvern Rd. Enf EN3 ... 162 E2
Malvern Rd. Luton LU1 ... 63 B7
Malvern Way. Cro Gr WD3 ... 166 B4
Malvern Way. Heml H HP2 ... 124 F6
Malvern Way Inf Sch. Cro Gr ... 166 C4
Malzeard Ct. Luton LU3 ... 45 D1 2
Malzeard Rd. Luton LU3 ... 45 D1
Manan Cl. Heml H HP3 ... 125 C1
Manchester Cl. Stev SG1 ... 36 F3
Manchester St. Luton LU1 ... 63 E7
Mancroft Rd. Cad LU1 ... 62 E2
Mandela Ave. Harl CM20 ... 117 E2
Mandela Pl. Watf WD2 ... 167 D7 4
Mandelyns. Nthch HP4 ... 121 E7
Mandeville Cl. Hert SG13 ... 113 C3
Mandeville Cl. Hod EN10 ... 134 F3
Mandeville Cl. Watf WD1 ... 153 F1
Mandeville Dr. St Alb AL1 ... 141 D8
Mandeville Jun Mix Inf Sch. Saw ... 97 D3
Mandeville Prim Sch. St Alb ... 141 D8
Mandeville Rd. Enf EN3 ... 162 E3
Mandeville Rd. Hert SG13 ... 113 C3
Mandeville Rd. Pot B EN6 ... 159 C7
Mandeville Rise. Wel G C AL8 ... 110 D8
Mandeville. Stev SG2 ... 69 C8
Mangrove Dr. Hert SG13 ... 113 E4
Mangrove La. Bric SG13 ... 113 E2
Mangrove La. Bric SG13 ... 133 F7
Mangrove Rd. Gt Of LU2 ... 46 E4
Mangrove Rd. Hert SG13 ... 113 E5
Mangrove Rd. Luton LU2 ... 46 C2
Manland Ave. Harp AL5 ... 86 C2
Manland Way. Harp AL5 ... 86 C3
Manley Rd. Heml H HP2 ... 124 E4
Manly Dixon Dr. Enf EN3 ... 162 E2
Mannicotts. Wel G C AL8 ... 110 B6
Manning Ct. Watf WD1 ... 167 D3
Manor Ave. Heml H HP3 ... 138 D8
Manor Cl. Barn EN5 ... 171 E5
Manor Cl. Berk HP4 ... 122 C4
Manor Cl. Hat AL10 ... 129 F8
Manor Cl. Hert SG14 ... 113 D8
Manor Cl. Ick SG5 ... 21 E3
Manor Cl. Letw SG6 ... 22 F3
Manor Cotts. Chor WD3 ... 164 B3
Manor Cotts. Norwd HA6 ... 174 F2
Manor Cres. Hit SG4 ... 35 B6
Manor Ct. Cad LU1 ... 62 F4
Manor Ct. Ches EN8 ... 162 D8
Manor Ct. Enf EN1 ... 162 B3
Manor Ct. Pot B EN6 ... 158 F7
Manor Ct. Wa Aby EN9 ... 163 D6
Manor Dr. Chis AL2 ... 141 A4
Manor Farm Cl. Dun LU4 ... 44 C3
Manor Farm La. Men LU7 ... 61 C8
Manor Farm Rd. Enf EN1 ... 162 B4
Manor Fields Jun, Mid & Inf Sch. Bis St ... 76 D5
Manor House Dr. Norwd HA6 ... 174 B3
Manor House Gdns. Abb L WD5 ... 153 D8
Manor Links. Bis St CM23 ... 77 C7
Manor Lodge Sch. Shen ... 143 C1
Manor Par. Hat AL10 ... 129 F8
Manor Pound Rd. Ched LU7 ... 80 A7
Manor Rd. Barn EN5 ... 171 E5
Manor Rd. Bis St CM23 ... 77 A7
Manor Rd. Cad LU1 ... 62 E3
Manor Rd. Ched LU7 ... 79 F7
Manor Rd. Harl CM17 ... 118 C5
Manor Rd. Hat AL10 ... 129 F8
Manor Rd. Hod EN11 ... 135 A7
Manor Rd. Lon C AL2 ... 142 C5
Manor Rd. Luton LU1 ... 63 F6
Manor Rd. Pot B EN6 ... 159 A8
Manor Rd. St Alb AL1 ... 127 E4
Manor Rd. Sta M CM24 ... 59 E5
Manor Rd. Tri HP23 ... 100 A4
Manor Rd. Wa Aby EN9 ... 163 D6
Manor Rd. Watf WD1 ... 167 B8
Manor Rd. Whea AL4 ... 86 F2
Manor St. Berk HP4 ... 122 D4
Manor View. Stev SG2 ... 51 B1
Manor Way. Bor WD6 ... 170 C6
Manor Way. Ches EN8 ... 148 E1
Manor Way. Cro Gr WD3 ... 166 B5
Manor Way. Letw SG6 ... 22 F3
Manor Way. Pot B EN6 ... 145 A1
Manorcroft Par. Ches EN8 ... 148 E1
Manorside. Barn EN5 ... 171 E5
Manorville Rd. Heml H HP3 ... 138 C7
Mansard Cl. Tri HP23 ... 100 A3
Manscroft Rd. Heml H HP1 ... 124 B5
Mansdale Rd. Red AL3 ... 105 F4
Mansfield Ct. Hert SG14 ... 113 C8
Mansfield Gdns. Hert SG14 ... 113 C8
Mansfield. H Wy CM21 ... 97 A1
Mansfield Rd. Bal SG7 ... 23 E8
Mansfield Rd. Luton LU4 ... 45 B1
Mansion Dr. Tri HP23 ... 100 B3
Manston Cl. Ches EN8 ... 148 C1
Manston Dr. Bis St CM23 ... 59 B1
Manton Dr. Luton LU2 ... 45 D3
Manton Rd. Hit SG4 ... 35 B6
Manx Cl. Luton LU4 ... 45 A2
Maple Ave. Bis St CM23 ... 76 D8
Maple Ave. St Alb AL3 ... 127 C7
Maple Cl. Bis St CM23 ... 76 D8
Maple Cl. Bus WD2 ... 167 E7
Maple Cl. Hat AL10 ... 130 A4
Maple Cotts. Harp AL5 ... 107 B5
Maple Cross Jun Mix Inf Sch. Map Cr ... 172 E5
Maple Ct. Pnr HA5 ... 175 C1 5
Maple Ct. Sta Ab SG19 ... 115 D4
Maple Ct. Watf WD2 ... 154 D3
Maple Flats. Harp AL5 ... 86 A3
Maple Gn. Heml H HP1 ... 123 E5
Maple Gr. Bis St CM23 ... 76 D8
Maple Gr. Watf WD1 ... 167 A8
Maple Gr. Wel G C AL7 ... 89 F1
Maple Leaf Cl. Abb L WD5 ... 154 A7
Maple Lodge Cl. Map Cr WD3 ... 172 E6
Maple Rd E. Luton LU4 ... 63 B8
Maple Rd. Harp AL5 ... 85 F1
Maple Rd W. Luton LU4 ... 63 B8
Maple River Ind Est. Harl ... 118 B6
Maple Sch. St Alb ... 127 E4
Maple Spring. Bis St CM23 ... 76 D8
Maple Way. Ken Co LU6 ... 82 E8
Maple Way. Royst SG8 ... 7 E8
Maplecroft La. Lo Naz EN9 ... 135 E2
Maplefield. Chis AL2 ... 141 C2
Maples Ct. Hit SG5 ... 34 E7 1
Maples The. Hit SG4 ... 34 F5
Mapleton Cres. Enf EN3 ... 162 C1
Maplewood. Ware SG12 ... 93 C3
Maran Ave. Welw AL6 ... 89 C4
Marbury Pl. Luton LU3 ... 44 F4
Marchmont Green. Heml H HP2 ... 124 D5
Marcus Cl. Stev SG1 ... 51 C8
Mardley Ave. Welw AL6 ... 90 A8
Mardley Dell. Welw AL6 ... 68 F1
Mardley Hts. Welw AL6 ... 69 A1
Mardley Wood. Welw AL6 ... 68 F1
Mardleybury Ct. Welw SG3 ... 69 A1
Mardleybury Rd. Welw SG3 ... 69 B1
Mardyke Rd. Harl CM20 ... 118 A2
Marford Rd. Hat AL4 ... 109 D6
Marford Rd. Whea AL4 ... 108 E8
Margaret Ave. St Alb AL3 ... 127 D5
Margaret Cl. Abb L WD5 ... 153 F7
Margaret Cl. Pot B EN6 ... 159 C6
Margaret Cl. Wa Aby EN9 ... 163 D6
Margaret Wix Inf Sch. St Alb ... 127 C7
Margaret Wix Jun Sch. St Alb ... 127 C7
Margeholes. Sth Ox WD1 ... 175 E8
Margery Wood. Wel G C AL7 ... 90 A1
Margherita Pl. Wa Aby EN9 ... 163 F5
Marian Gdns. Watf WD2 ... 154 B6
Maricas Ave. Har HA3 ... 176 D2
Marigold Pl. Harl CM17 ... 118 B4
Marina Gdns. Ches EN8 ... 148 C1
Mariner Way. Heml H HP2 ... 125 A2 2
Marion Cl. Bus WD2 ... 167 F8
Marion Wlk. Heml H HP2 ... 124 F8 4
Mark Hall Comp Sch. Harl ... 118 C3
Mark Hall Moors. Harl CM20 ... 118 B3
Mark Rd. Heml H HP2 ... 125 B5
Markab Rd. Mo Pk HA6 ... 175 A5 3
Markeston Gn. Sth Ox WD1 ... 175 D6
Market Hill. Bun SG9 ... 40 E7
Market Hill. Royst SG8 ... 7 D6
Market House. Harl CM20 ... 117 D1
Market Oak La. Heml H HP3 ... 139 A7
Market Pl. Hat AL10 ... 130 B7
Market Pl. Hert SG14 ... 113 D6 6
Market Pl. Hit SG5 ... 34 E7
Market Pl. St Alb AL3 ... 127 D3
Market Pl. Stev SG1 ... 50 D5
Market Pl. Watf WD1 ... 167 C5
Market Sq. Bis St CM23 ... 76 F7
Market Sq. Luton LU1 ... 63 B6
Market Sq. Stev SG1 ... 50 D5
Market St. Bis St CM23 ... 76 F7
Market St. Harl CM17 ... 118 C4
Market St. Hert SG14 ... 113 D6
Market St. Watf WD1 ... 167 B5
Markfield Cl. Luton LU3 ... 45 C6
Markham Rd. Luton LU3 ... 45 C8
Markyate Jun Mix Inf Sch. Mark ... 83 D6
Markyate Rd. Cad LU1 ... 63 B1
Marlands. Saw CM21 ... 97 E4
Marlborough Cl. Bis St CM23 ... 76 F5
Marlborough Cl. Welw AL6 ... 89 F8
Marlborough Cl. Wes SG4 ... 37 B8
Marlborough Gate. St Alb AL1 ... 127 E3
Marlborough Rd. Luton LU3 ... 45 D1
Marlborough Rd. St Alb AL1 ... 127 E3
Marlborough Rd. Stev SG2 ... 51 C5
Marlborough Rise. Heml H HP2 ... 124 E6
Marlborough Sch. St Alb ... 141 C8
Marle Gdns. Wa Aby EN9 ... 163 C7
Marley Rd. Wel G C AL7 ... 111 A4
Marlin Cl. Berk HP4 ... 121 F5
Marlin Copse. Berk HP4 ... 122 A3
Marlin Hill. Tri HP23 ... 120 A8
Marlin Sq. Abb L WD5 ... 153 F8
Marlins Cl. Chor WD3 ... 164 E7
Marlins Meadow. Watf WD1 ... 166 D3
Marlins The. Mo Pk HA6 ... 174 F5
Marlins Turn. Heml H HP1 ... 124 B6
Marlowe Cl. Stev SG2 ... 51 C8
Marlowes. Heml H HP1 ... 124 D3
Marmet Ave. Letw SG6 ... 22 E5
Marnham Rise. Heml H HP1 ... 124 A5
Marquis Cl. Bis St CM23 ... 76 B7
Marquis Cl. Harp AL5 ... 86 D2
Marquis La. Harp AL5 ... 86 D2
Marrilyne Ave. Enf EN3 ... 162 F1
Marriott Rd. Barn EN5 ... 171 D6
Marriott Rd. Luton LU3 ... 45 B6
Marriotts Way. Heml H HP3 ... 124 D1
Marryat Rd. Enf EN1 ... 162 B4
Marschefield. Stot SG5 ... 11 E6
Marsden Cl. Wel G C AL8 ... 110 B4
Marsden Gn. Wel G C AL8 ... 110 B4
Marsden Rd. Wel G C AL8 ... 110 C5
Marsh Cl. Ches EN8 ... 162 F6
Marsh Hill. Lo Naz EN9 ... 149 E4
Marsh La. Harl CM17 ... 118 E5
Marsh La. Sta Ab SG12 ... 115 D4
Marsh La. Ware SG12 ... 114 E8
Marsh Rd. Luton LU3 ... 44 F4
Marshal's Dr. St Alb AL1 ... 128 A6
Marshall Ave. St Alb AL3 ... 127 F6

Marshall Rd. Luton LU2 ....... 46 C2
Marshall's La. Thun SG11 ... 72 C2
Marshalls Heath La.
 Whea AL4 ...................... 87 A4
Marshalls Way. Whea AL4 86 F2
Marshalswick La.
 St Alb AL1 ..................... 128 B6
Marshbarns. Bis St CM23 .. 76 C8
Marshcroft Dr. Ches EN8 . 148 F1
Marshcroft La. Tri HP23 .. 100 D6
Marshe Cl. Pot B EN6 ...... 159 D7
Marshgate Dr. Hert SG13 113 E7
Marshgate. Stev SG1 ......... 50 D5
Marshmoor Cres. Hat AL9 130 D1
Marshmoor La. Wel G AL9 144 D8
Marsom Gr. Luton LU3 ....... 45 B8
Marston Cl. Heml H HP3 .. 125 A2
Marston Ct. Lon M HP23 .... 79 B4
Marston Gdns. Luton LU2 ... 45 D4
Marston Rd. Hod EN11 ..... 135 B7
Marsworth Ave. Pnr HA5 . 175 D2
Marsworth C of E Prim Sch.
 Mars ............................. 80 A2
Marsworth Rd. Watt WD1 166 E2
Marsworth Rd. Pit LU7 ...... 80 D4
Marten Dr. Hert SG13 ...... 114 B6
Marten Gate. St Alb AL4 .. 128 A7
Martham Ct. Harp AL5 ...... 86 C3
Marthorne Cres. Har HA3 176 D1
Martian Ave. Heml H HP2 124 F6
Martin Cl. Hat AL10 ......... 130 A3
Martindale Prim Sch.
 Heml H ......................... 123 F4
Martindale Rd.
 Heml H HP1 .................. 123 F4
Martindales The.
 Luton LU2 ...................... 63 F7
Martinfield Bsns Ctr.
 Wel G C ........................ 110 F7
Martinfield. Wel G C AL7 . 110 F7
Martingale Rd. Royst SG8 ... 7 E6
Martins Cl. Radl WD7 ...... 155 E3
Martins Dr. Ches EN8 ..... 148 E3
Martins Way. Stev SG1 ...... 36 E1
Martins Wlk. Bor WD6 .... 170 A5
Martins Wood Jun Mix Inf
 Sch. Stev ....................... 37 B1
Martlesham. Wel G C AL7 111 C6
Martyr Cl. St Alb AL1 ...... 141 D7
Marwood Cl. Kin L WD4 .. 138 F2
Mary Brash Ct. Luton LU2 .. 46 C3
Mary Exton Jun Mix Inf Sch.
 Hit ................................ 35 C7
Mary McArthur Pl.
 Sta M CM24 ................... 59 E8
Mary Park Gdns.
 Bis St CM23 .................. 76 F4
Mary Proud Ct. Welw AL6 . 89 E7
Maryland. Hat AL10 ........ 129 F5
Marymead Ct. Stev SG2 ..... 69 A8
Marymead Dr. Stev SG2 .... 69 A8
Marymead Ind Est. Stev .... 69 A8
Maryport Rd. Luton LU4 ... 45 A2
Masefield Ave. Bor WD6 . 170 B4
Masefield Ave. Stan HA7 . 176 F5
Masefield Ct. Harp AL5 ..... 86 B4
Masefield La. Knee .......... 35 C7
Masefield Rd. Harp AL5 ..... 86 B4
Mason Cl. Bor WD6 ........ 170 D7
Mason Way. Wa Aby EN9 163 F6
Masons Ct. Bis St CM23 ... 76 E7
Masons Rd. Enf EN1 ........ 162 C3
Masons Rd. Heml H HP2 .. 124 A6
Masters Cl. Luton LU1 ....... 63 B5
Matching La. Bis St CM23 .. 76 D8
Mathams Dr. Bis St CM23 .. 76 D5
Matlock Cres. Dun LU4 ..... 44 C1
Matlock Cres.
 Sth Ox WD1 ................... 175 C7
Matthew Gate. Hit SG4 ..... 35 A5
Mattocke Rd. Hit SG5 ...... 21 C1
Maud Jane's Cl. Pit LU7 .... 80 E5
Maude Cres. Watt WD2 ... 154 B1
Maulden Cl. Luton LU2 ...... 46 C1
Maxted Cl. Heml H HP2 .. 125 C6
Maxted Cnr. Heml H ........ 125 B6
Maxted Rd. Heml H HP2 .. 125 C6
Maxwell Cl. Ric WD3 ...... 173 A8
Maxwell Rd. Bor WD6 .... 170 B6
Maxwell Rd. Norwd HA6 .. 174 E3
Maxwell Rd. St Alb AL1 .. 128 B2
Maxwell Rd. Stev SG1 ...... 50 B5
Maxwell Rise. Watf WD1 . 167 E2
May Cl. St Alb AL3 .......... 127 E6
May St. Gt Ch SG8 ............. 9 E2
May St. Luton LU1 ............ 63 E5
Maybury Ave. Ches EN8 .. 148 B3
Maycock Gr. Norwd HA6 .. 174 F4

Maycroft. Letw SG6 ......... 12 A1
Maycroft. Pnr HA5 .......... 175 B1
Maycroft Rd. Ham St EN7 147 E5
Maydencroft La.
 St Ipp SG4 ..................... 34 E3
Maydwell Lodge.
 Bor WD6 ....................... 169 F7
Mayes Cl. Bis St CM23 ..... 77 D8
Mayfair Cl. St Alb AL4 .... 128 C8
Mayfare. Cro Gr WD3 ..... 166 D4
Mayfield Cl. Heml H HP2 .. 124 D3
Mayfield Cl. Harp AL5 ....... 85 E3
Mayfield Cl. Shes CM23 148 E4
Mayfield Pk. Bis St CM23 .. 76 D3
Mayfield Rd. Luton LU2 ..... 46 B4
Mayfield. Wel G C AL8 ...... 89 C2
Mayflower Ave.
 Heml H HP2 .................. 124 D3
Mayflower Cl. Cod SG4 .... 67 F1
Mayflower Cl.
 Hertng SG14 ................. 112 E4
Mayflower Cl. Lo Naz EN9 135 E1
Mayflower Gdns.
 Bis St CM23 .................. 76 C6
Mayflower Rd. Chis AL2 .. 141 A4
Mayflower Rd. Barn EN5 .. 171 E3
Maylands Ave.
 Heml H HP2 .................. 125 B5
Maylands Ct. Heml H ...... 125 B4
Maylands Rd. Sth Ox WD1 175 C6
Maylin Cl. Hit SG4 ............ 35 C8
Maylins Dr. Saw CM21 ..... 97 D2
Maynard Ct. Wa Aby EN9 163 F5
Maynard Dr. St Alb AL1 .. 128 A1
Maynard Pl. Cuf EN6 ...... 146 E2
Maynard Rd. Heml H HP2 124 D2
Mayne Ave. Luton LU4 ..... 44 C4
Mayne Ave. St Alb AL3 ... 127 A2
Mayo Cl. Ches EN8 ......... 148 C3
Mays La. Barn EN5 ......... 171 D3
Mayshades Cl. Welw SG3 .. 69 A2
Maythorne Cl. Watf WD1 . 166 E5
Maytree Cres. Watf WD2 153 F3
Maytree La. Har HA7 ...... 176 F3
Maytrees. Hit SG4 ............. 35 A6
Maytrees. Radl WD7 ....... 156 A2
Maze Green Rd.
 Bis St CM23 .................... 76 D7
Mazoe Cl. Bis St CM23 ..... 76 F5
Mazoe Rd. Bis St CM23 .... 76 F5
Mc Gredy. Ches EN8 ....... 148 B2
Mc Kenzie Rd. Hod EN10 . 135 A3
McAdam Cl. Hod EN11 .... 135 A8
McDonald Ct. Hat AL10 ... 130 A3
McKellar Cl. Bus WD2 ... 176 C8
Mead Business Ctr. Hert . 113 E7
Mead Cl. Har HA3 ........... 176 D2
Mead Cl. Stev SG1 ............ 50 F6
Mead Ct. Wa Aby EN9 .... 163 B5
Mead Ct. Sta M CM24 ...... 59 D7
Mead La. Harp AL10 ....... 130 B8
Mead La. Hert SG13 ........ 113 E7
Mead Park Ind Est. Harl ... 117 F4
Mead Pl. Ric WD3 ........... 165 B1
Mead Rd. Shen WD7 ...... 157 A6
Mead The. Ches EN8 ...... 148 C2
Mead The. Hit SG5 ........... 21 F2
Mead The. Lo Naz EN9 ... 135 E2
Mead The. Sth Ox WD1 .. 175 E7
Mead View. Sto P SG9 ...... 43 E6
Mead Way. Bus WD2 ...... 167 E2
Meadgate Rd. Lo Naz EN9 135 C3
Meadow Cl. Barn EN5 .... 171 F3
Meadow Cl. Berk HP4 ..... 122 A2
Meadow Cl. Bri Wd AL2 .. 141 A2
Meadow Cl. Dat SG3 ......... 69 F1
Meadow Cl. Enf EN3 ...... 162 E1
Meadow Cl. Lon C AL2 .... 142 C8
Meadow Cl. St Alb AL4 ... 128 C6
Meadow Cl. Tri HP23 ...... 100 A4
Meadow Cl. Wel G AL9 ... 144 D7
Meadow Croft. Cad LU1 .... 62 F4
Meadow Dell. Hat AL10 ... 129 F5
Meadow Gn. Wel G C AL8 110 C6
Meadow La. Pit LU7 ......... 80 E3
Meadow Rd. Berk HP4 .... 122 B6
Meadow Rd. Bor WD6 .... 170 B7
Meadow Rd. Bus WD2 .... 168 B4
Meadow Rd. Heml H HP3 139 A7
Meadow Rd. Luton LU3 .... 45 B8
Meadow Rd. Watf WD2 ... 154 B5
Meadow Road Cl.
 Berk HP4 ....................... 122 A6
Meadow The.
 Hert H SG13 .................. 114 E2
Meadow The.
 Wel G C AL7 ................. 111 C6
Meadow View. Bun SG9 .... 40 D6
Meadow Way. Abb L WD5 139 F4
Meadow Way. Cad LU1 ..... 62 E4

Meadow Way. Cod SG4 .... 67 E1
Meadow Way. Gt SG5 ..... 33 C3
Meadow Way. Hit SG5 ...... 34 D6
Meadow Way. Kin L WD4 139 A1
Meadow Way. Letw SG6 ... 22 F5
Meadow Way. Pot B EN6 . 159 A5
Meadow Way. Ric WD3 ... 165 C2
Meadow Way. Sheer CM21 98 A1
Meadow Way. Stev SG1 .... 50 F5
Meadow Way. Stot SG5 .... 11 F6
Meadow Way The.
 Har HA3 ........................ 176 E2
Meadow Way. Ther SG8 .... 16 A6
Meadow Wlk. Harp AL5 ... 107 C8
Meadow Wlk. Stand SG11 . 55 E2
Meadow Wood Sch. Bus .. 168 C4
Meadowbank. Hat SG4 ...... 22 E1
Meadowbank. Kin L WD4 . 139 A1
Meadowbanks. Barn EN5 . 171 A4
Meadowbrook. Tri HP23 .. 100 B6
Meadowcroft. Bus WD2 .. 168 B3
Meadowcroft. Nthch HP4 121 D7
Meadowcroft. St Alb AL1 . 142 A8
Meadowcroft.
 Sta M CM24 ................... 59 E7
Meadowcross.
 Wa Aby EN9 ................. 163 E5
Meadowlands. Bis St CM23 59 A2
Meadows The. Bis St CM23 76 D4
Meadows The. Bre Gr SG4 47 E1
Meadows The. Sheer CM21 98 A2
Meadowsweet Cl.
 Bis St CM23 .................... 76 C6
Meads Jun Mix & Inf
 Sch The. Luton ............... 45 A8
Meads La. Whea AL4 ........ 87 D1
Meads The. Berk HP4 ..... 121 F6
Meads The. Bri Wd AL2 .. 140 F2
Meads The. Letw SG6 ..... 22 E6
Meads The. Luton LU3 ..... 45 A3
Meads The. Sta M CM24 ... 59 F6
Meadview Rd. Ware SG12 114 D8
Meadway. Barn EN5 ....... 171 F5
Meadway. Berk HP4 ....... 122 E5
Meadway. Cu Pnr HA5 ... 176 B4
Meadway. Col H AL4 ...... 143 D8
Meadway. Enf EN3 ......... 162 D3
Meadway. Harp AL5 ....... 107 E8
Meadway. Hod EN11 ...... 135 A4
Meadway. Kneb SG3 ........ 68 F4
Meadway The. Cuf EN6 .. 146 F2
Meadway. Wel G C AL7 .. 110 F4
Meautys. St Alb AL2 ........ 127 A1
Medalls Link. Stev SG2 ..... 51 A3
Medalls Path. Stev SG2 .... 51 A3
Medcalf Rd. Enf EN3 ....... 162 F2
Medina Rd. Luton LU4 ..... 45 A1
Medlows. Harp AL5 ........... 85 E2
Medow Mead. Radl WD7 . 155 F6
Medway Cl. Watf WD2 ... 154 C5
Medway Rd. Heml H HP2 . 124 F8
Medwick Mews.
 Heml H HP2 .................. 125 B8
Mees Cl. Luton LU3 .......... 31 A1
Meeting Alley. Watf WD1 167 C5
Meeting House La. Bal SG7 12 E1
Megg La. Chipf WD4 ....... 138 B1
Melbourn Cl. Stot SG5 ...... 11 F5
Melbourn Ct. St Alb AL3 . 127 F7
Melbourn St. Royst SG8 ..... 7 D7
Melbourne Cl. St Alb AL3 . 127 F7
Melbourne Ct.
 Wel G C AL8 ................. 110 B5
Melbourne Rd. Bus WD2 . 168 B3
Melford Cl. Luton LU2 ...... 46 D1
Melings The. Heml H HP2 125 B8
Melne Rd. Stev SG2 .......... 69 B8
Melrose Ave. Bor WD6 ... 170 A4
Melrose Ave. Pot B EN6 . 159 B7
Melrose Pl. Watf WD1 .... 153 F1
Melson Sq. Luton LU1 ...... 63 E7
Melson St. Luton LU1 ....... 63 E7
Melsted Rd. Heml H HP1 . 124 B3
Melwood Rd. Luton LU2 ... 46 C1
Memorial Rd. Luton LU3 ... 44 F4
Mendip Cl. St Alb AL4 .... 128 C8
Mendip Rd. Bus WD2 ..... 168 C3
Mendip Way. Heml H HP2 124 E6
Mendlesham.
 Wel G C AL7 ................. 111 C6
Mentley La E. Stand SG11 . 55 D4
Mentley La. Gt Mu SG11 ... 54 E4
Mentley La. Stand SG11 ... 54 E4
Mentley La W. Stand SG11 55 D4
Mentmore Park. Men ....... 61 D3
Mentmore Rd. Ched LU7 ... 79 F8
Mentmore Rd. St Alb AL1 . 127 E3
Mentmore Sch. St Alb .... 127 D6

Mentmore View. Tri HP23 . 99 F5
Mepham Cres. Har HA3 .. 176 C3
Mepham Gdns. Har HA3 .. 176 C3
Mercer Pl. Pnr HA5 ........ 175 C1
Mercers Ave. Bis St CM23 . 76 C4
Mercers. Heml H HP2 .... 124 E8
Mercers Row. St Alb AL1 . 127 C1
Merchant Dr. Hert SG13 .. 113 F7
Merchant Taylors' Sch.
 Mo Pk ........................... 166 E1
Merchants Wlk. Bal SG7 ... 13 B1
Mercia Rd. Bal SG7 .......... 24 A8
Mercury Wlk. Heml H HP2 124 F6
Mereden Ct. St Alb AL1 ... 141 C8
Meredith Cl. Pnr HA5 ..... 175 D3
Meredith Rd. Stev SG1 ..... 51 A8
Merefield. Saw CM21 ....... 97 E1
Meriden House. Barn EN5 171 E5
Merenden Inf & Jun Mix Sch.
 Watt ............................. 154 D3
Meriden Way. Watf WD2 . 154 E2
Meridian Sch The. Royst ..... 7 E7
Meridian Way.
 Gt Am SG12 .................. 115 B5
Merle Ave. Hare UB9 ..... 173 C1
Merlin Ctr The. Coln H ... 128 F3
Merling Croft. Nthch HP4 121 E7
Merritt Wlk. Wel G AL7 ... 144 B8
Merrow Dr. Heml H HP1 .. 123 E4
Merrows Cl. Norwd HA6 . 174 C4
Merry Hill Jun Sch. Bus .. 168 B2
Merry Hill Mount.
 Bus WD2 ....................... 168 B1
Merry Hill Rd. Bus WD2 .. 168 B1
Merryfield Cl. Bor WD6 ... 169 F7
Merryfields. Coln H AL4 .. 128 E3
Mersey Pl. Heml H HP2 .. 124 F8
Mersey Pl. Luton LU1 ...... 63 D7
Merton Rd. Enf EN2 ....... 161 D1
Merton Rd. Watf WD1 .... 167 B5
Meryfield Sch. Bor ........ 169 F8
Metro Ctr. St Alb .......... 127 F7
Metropolitan Station App.
 Watf WD1 ...................... 166 F5
Meux Cl. Ches EN7 ........ 162 A8
Mews The. Harp AL5 ........ 86 B1
Mews The. Letw SG6 ...... 12 C1
Mews The. Saw CM21 ...... 97 E3
Mews The. St Alb AL1 .... 128 B2
Mews The. Sta M CM24 ... 59 F7
Meyer Gn. Enf EN1 ........ 162 A1
Meyrick Ave. Luton LU1 ... 63 C6
Mezen Cl. Norwd HA6 .... 174 D5
Michaels Rd. Bis St CM23 . 59 A2
Micklefield Rd.
 Heml H HP2 .................. 125 C3
Micklefield Way. Bor WD6 156 E1
Micklem Dr. Heml H HP1 . 123 F4
Micklem Sch The. Heml H . 124 A4
Midcot Way. Berk HP4 ... 121 F6
Middle Drift. Royst SG8 ..... 7 E6
Middle Furlong. Bus WD2 168 B5
Middle La. Bov HP3 ........ 137 A1
Middle Ope. Watf WD2 ... 154 B2
Middle Rd. Berk HP4 ...... 122 B6
Middle Rd. Wa Aby EN9 .. 163 B7
Middle Row. Bis St CM23 . 76 F6
Middle Row. Stev SG1 ...... 50 F7
Middle St. Lo Naz EN9 ... 149 F8
Middle Way. The. Har HA3 176 F1
Middle Way. Watf WD2 ... 154 B2
Middlefield Ave. Hod EN11 135 A8
Middlefield Cl. Hod EN11 . 135 A8
Middlefield Cl. St Alb AL4 . 128 C6
Middlefield. Letw SG6 ...... 11 F1
Middlefield. Hat AL10 ..... 130 A6
Middlefield Rd. Hod EN11 135 A8
Middlefield. Wel G C AL7 . 110 E3
Middlefields. Letw SG6 ..... 11 F1
Middlehill. Heml H HP1 ... 123 E3
Middleknights Hill.
 Heml H HP1 .................. 124 A6
Middlesborough Cl.
 Stev SG1 ........................ 36 F2
Middleton Mid Sch. Ware . 114 D7
Middleton Rd. Luton LU2 ... 46 D4
Middleton Rd. Ric WD3 ... 165 A1
Midhurst Gdns. Luton LU3 . 45 C4
Midhurst. Letw SG6 ......... 22 F8
Midland Cotts. Hit SG5 ..... 22 A1
Midland Rd. Heml H HP2 . 124 E6
Midland Rd. Luton LU2 .... 63 E8
Midway. St Alb AL3 ........ 141 B8
Milbourne St. Watf WD1 . 167 A7
Milburn Cl. Luton LU3 ...... 31 B1
Mildmay Rd. Stev SG1 ...... 37 B1
Mildred Ave. Bor WD6 ... 170 A5
Mildred Ave. Watf WD1 .. 167 A5
Mile Cl. Wa Aby EN9 ...... 163 E6
Mile House Cl. St Alb AL1 . 142 A8
Mile House La. St Alb AL1 141 F8

Milestone Cl. Ast SG2 ...... 51 D4
Milestone Rd. Hit SG5 ..... 21 D2
Milestone Rd. Kneb SG3 ... 69 A5
Milford Cl. St Alb AL4 ..... 128 D7
Milford Hill. Harp AL5 ...... 86 D3
Milksey La. Gra SG4 ........ 36 C5
Mill Bridge. Barn EN5 .... 171 F3
Mill Bridge. Hert SG14 ... 113 C6
Mill Cl. Hat AL8 ............. 110 A5
Mill Cl. Heml H HP1 ....... 124 B7
Mill Cl. Heml H HP3 ....... 139 A6
Mill Cl. Stot SG5 .............. 12 A6
Mill Cl. Ware SG12 .......... 93 D1
Mill Cl. Wing HP22 ........... 60 A3
Mill Cnr. Barn EN5 ......... 171 F8
Mill End. Stand SG11 ....... 55 F2
Mill Farm Cl. Pnr HA5 .... 175 C1
Mill Field. Harl CM17 ..... 118 C4
Mill Gdns. Tri HP23 ....... 100 A4
Mill Green. La. Hat AL9 .. 110 E1
Mill Green Rd.
 Wel G C AL7 ................. 110 E5
Mill Hatch. Harl CM20 .... 118 A4
Mill Hill. Far CM23 .......... 58 E5
Mill Hill. Royst SG8 ........... 7 E4
Mill Hill. Sta M CM24 ...... 59 E6
Mill La. Alb SG11 ............. 57 C6
Mill La. Arl SG15 ............. 10 F4
Mill La. Ches EN8 .......... 148 E3
Mill La. Fla AL3 ............... 84 A1
Mill La. Harl CM17 ......... 118 E4
Mill La. Hex SG5 ............. 19 B3
Mill La. Hit SG4 ................ 34 F3
Mill La. Hod EN10 .......... 135 A2
Mill La. Kin L WD4 ......... 139 A2
Mill La. Mee SG9 ............. 30 A5
Mill La. Saw CM21 ........... 97 F3
Mill La. Sheer CM22 ........ 98 F3
Mill La. Stot SG5 .............. 12 A6
Mill La. Ther SG8 ............. 15 F8
Mill La. Wat St SG12,SG14 71 A6
Mill La. Welw AL6 ............ 89 C5
Mill La. Wing HP22 .......... 60 A2
Mill Lane Cl. Hod EN10 .. 134 F2
Mill Mead Sch. Hert ...... 113 C6
Mill Race. Sta Ab SG12 .. 115 D4
Mill Rd. Hert SG14 ........ 113 C6
Mill Rd. Royst SG8 ............ 7 D7
Mill Rd. St Ipp SG4 .......... 35 A3
Mill Side. Sta M CM24 ..... 59 E6
Mill St. Ashw SG7 ............. 4 F5
Mill St. Berk HP4 ........... 122 C4
Mill St. Bis St CM23 ........ 77 A5
Mill St. Heml H HP3 ....... 138 D8
Mill St. Luton LU1 ............ 63 D8
Mill View Rd. Tri HP23 ...... 99 F4
Mill Way. Bus WD2 ........ 167 E8
Mill Way. Ric WD3 ......... 164 F1
Millacres. Ware SG12 ...... 93 E1
Milland Ct. Bor WD6 ...... 170 D8
Millard Way. Hit SG4 ....... 22 C1
Millbank. Heml H HP3 .... 138 D7
Millbridge Mews.
 Hert SG14 ..................... 113 C6
Millbrook Rd. Bus WD2 .. 167 F8
Millcrest Rd. Gofs O EN7 . 147 B3
Millcroft. Bis St CM23 ...... 59 A1
Miller Cl. Pnr HA5 .......... 175 C1
Millers La. Sta Ab SG12 . 115 D4
Millers Rise. St Alb AL1 .. 127 E2
Millers View. Muc H SG10 . 74 E1
Millers Yd. Hert SG14 .... 113 D6
Millfield. Berk HP4 ........ 122 D5
Millfield House. Watf ...... 166 D3
Millfield La. Cad LU1 ....... 62 C2
Millfield La. Hit SG4 ......... 34 F4
Millfield La. L Had SG11 .. 75 D8
Millfield La. Mark LU1 ...... 83 D8
Millfield Rd. Luton LU3 ..... 45 B3
Millfield Sch. Bun ........... 40 E7
Millfield. Thun SG12 ........ 43 E8
Millfield Way. Cad LU1 .... 62 D3
Millfield. Wel G C AL7 .... 111 C7
Millfield Wlk. Heml H HP3 139 A4
Millfields. Saw CM21 ....... 97 F3
Millfields. Sta M CM24 ..... 59 E6
Millhoo Ct. Wa Aby EN9 . 163 F5
Millhouse La. Abb L WD5 140 A4
Milliners Way. Luton LU1 .. 46 A6
Millside. Bis St ................ 77 A5
Millstream Cl. Hert SG14 . 113 B6
Millstream. Hit SG4 ........ 21 E1
Millthorne Cl. Cro Gr WD3 165 F4
Millwards. Hat AL10 ....... 130 B2
Millway. Bre Gr SG4 ........ 47 D2
Milman Cl. Letw SG6 ........ 22 D3
Milne Cl. Letw SG6 .......... 23 B3
Milne Field. Pnr HA5 ...... 176 A3
Milne Wlk. Watf WD2 ..... 154 B6
Milner Ct. Bus WD2 ....... 168 B3
Milner Pl. Luton LU2 ........ 63 F8

Mil - New 201

Milneway. Hare UB9 ........ 173 B2
Milton Ave. Barn EN5 ....... 171 F4
Milton Cl. Royst SG8 ........... 2 C1
Milton Ct. Ham St EN7 ...... 147 F5
Milton Ct. Harp AL5 ........... 86 B1 6
Milton Ct. Heml H HP2 ..... 105 B1
Milton Ct. Wa Aby EN9 ..... 163 C5
Milton Dene. Heml H HP2 125 B8
Milton Dr. Bor WD6 ........... 170 B4
Milton Rd. Harp AL5 .......... 86 B1
Milton Rd. Luton LU1 .......... 63 C6
Milton Rd. Ware SG12 ....... 93 D2
Milton St. Wa Aby EN9 ..... 163 C5
Milton St. Watf WD2 .......... 167 B8
Milton View. Hit SG4 .......... 35 C7
Milverton Gn. Luton LU3 .... 45 A7
Mimms Hall Rd. Pot B EN6 158 D7
Mimms La. Shen WD7 ...... 157 C6
Mimram Cl. Whit SG4 ........ 66 E7
Mimram Pl. Welw AL6 ....... 89 C5
Mimram Rd. Hert SG14 .... 113 B5
Mimram Rd. Welw AL6 ...... 89 C5
Mimram Wlk. Welw AL6 .... 89 C5
Minchen Rd. Harl CM20 ... 118 A1
Minehead Way. Stev SG1 .. 50 A7
Minerva Dr. Watf WD2 ....... 153 E3
Minims The. Hat AL10 ...... 130 A7
Minorca Way. Dun LU4 ...... 44 A3
Minsden Rd. Stev SG2 ....... 51 D3
Minster Cl. Hat AL10 ........ 130 A3
Minster House. Hat AL10 . 130 A3
Minster Rd. Royst SG8 ......... 7 C8
Minstrel Cl. Heml H HP1 .. 124 B4
Minstrel Ct. Har HA3 ....... 176 E1
Miss Joans Ride.
Whip LU6 ...................... 81 E7
Missden Dr. Heml H HP3 . 125 C1
Mistletoe Hill. Luton LU2 ... 64 C8
Mistley Rd. Harl CM20 ..... 118 A2
Miswell La. Tri HP23 ......... 99 F3
Mitchell Cl. Abb L WD5 .... 154 A7
Mitchell Cl. Bov HP3 ........ 136 F4
Mitchell Cl. St Alb AL1 ...... 141 D7
Mitchell Cl. Wel G C AL7 .. 111 C6
Mitre Ct. Hert SG14 ......... 113 D6 17
Mitre Gdns. Bis St CM23 .... 77 A4
Mixes Hill Ct. Luton LU2 .... 46 A4
Mixes Hill Rd. Luton LU2 .... 45 F4
Mixies The. Stot SG5 .......... 11 E6
Moakes The. Luton LU3 ..... 44 E7
Moat Cl. Bus WD2 ........... 168 B4
Moat La. Luton LU3 ........... 45 B4
Moat La. Wing HP22 .......... 60 B2
Moat The. Stand SG11 ....... 55 D3
Moatfield Rd. Bus WD2 .... 168 B4
Moatside. Ans SG9 ............ 29 B7
Moatview Ct. Bus WD2 .... 168 B4
Moatwood Gn.
Wel G C AL7 ................ 110 E5
Mobbsbury Way. Stev SG2 51 C7
Mobley Gn. Luton LU2 ....... 46 B3
Moffats Cl. Bro Pk AL9 .... 145 A5
Moffats La. Bro Pk AL9 .... 144 F5
Moira Cl. Luton LU3 ........... 44 D7
Moles La. Wyd SG9 ............ 28 A3
Molescroft. Harp AL5 ........ 85 D4
Molesworth. Hod EN11 .... 115 A2
Molewood Rd. Hert SG14 113 B7
Mollison Ave. Enf EN3 ...... 163 A3
Molteno Rd. Watf WD1 .... 167 A8
Momples Rd. Harl CM20 .. 118 B1
Monarch's Way. Ches EN8 162 E6
Monastery Cl. St Alb AL3 . 127 C3
Money Hill Par. Ric WD3 . 165 C1
Money Hill Rd. Ric WD3 ... 165 C1
Money Hole La.
Tewin AL7 .................... 111 E7
Moneyhill Ct. Ric WD3 ..... 165 B1
Monica Cl. Watf WD2 ...... 167 D7
Monklands. Letw SG6 ........ 22 D6
Monks Cl. Hod EN10 ........ 135 A3
Monks Cl. Letw SG6 .......... 22 C6
Monks Cl. Red AL3 ........... 106 B5
Monks Cl. St Alb AL1 ........ 127 E1
Monks Horton Way.
St Alb AL1 .................... 128 A4
Monks Rise. Wel G C AL8 .. 89 D2
Monks Row. Ware SG12 .... 93 D2 7
Monks View. Stev SG2 ...... 50 F2
Monks Walk Sch. Wel G C . 89 C3
Monks Wlk. Bun SG9 ......... 40 E7
Monksmead. Bor WD6 ..... 170 C5
Monksmead Sch. Bor ....... 170 C6
Monkswick Rd. Harl CM20 117 F1
Monkswood Ave.
Wa Aby EN9 ................ 163 D6
Monkswood Dr.
Bis St CM23 .................. 76 D6
Monkswood Gdns.
Bor WD6 ...................... 170 D5
Monkswood Ret Pk. Stev ... 50 E3
Monkswood Way.
Stev SG1 ........................ 50 E3
Monkswood. Wel G C AL8 .. 89 C2
Monmouth Rd. Watf WD1 167 B6
Monro Gdns. Har HA3 ...... 176 E3
Mons Ave. Bal SG7 ............ 23 F6
Mons Cl. Harp AL5 ........... 107 D6
Monson Rd. Hod EN10 ..... 134 F3
Montacute Rd. Bus WD2 .. 168 E2
Montague Ave. Luton LU4 .. 44 C6
Montague Rd. Berk HP4 .. 122 B4
Montayne Rd. Ches EN8 .. 162 D7
Montesole Ct. Pnr HA5 .... 175 C1 6
Montfitchet Wlk. Stev SG2 . 51 D7
Montgomerie Cl.
Berk HP4 ...................... 122 A6
Montgomery Ave.
Heml H HP2 ................. 125 A4
Montgomery Dr.
Ches EN8 ..................... 148 E3
Monton Cl. Luton LU3 ......... 44 F6
Montrose Ave. Luton LU3 .. 45 C3
Montrose Rd. Har HA3 ..... 176 F1
Moon La. Barn EN5 .......... 171 F6
Moor End Rd. Heml H HP1 124 C2
Moor Hall Rd. Harl CM17 . 118 F4
Moor La. Mo Pk WD3 ....... 174 A8
Moor La. Sar WD3 ........... 151 E3
Moor Lane Crossing.
Mo Pk WD1 ................. 166 C2
Moor Mill La. Lon C AL2 ... 141 E2
Moor Park (Golf Course).
Mo Pk ......................... 174 B8
Moor Park Rd.
Norwd HA6 ................. 174 D4
Moor Park Sta. Mo Pk ...... 174 D7
Moor St. Luton LU1 ........... 63 C8
Moor View. Watf WD1 ..... 167 A3
Moore Rd. Berk HP4 ........ 121 F6
Moorend. Wel G C AL7 ..... 111 A3
Moorfields. Gt Ho SG9 ....... 41 E8
Moorhead Cl. Hit SG5 ....... 34 D6
Moorhurst Ave.
Gofs O EN7 ................. 147 B2
Moorland Gdns. Luton LU2 63 D8
Moorland Rd. Harp AL5 ..... 86 B4
Moorland Rd. Heml H HP1 124 A1
Moorlands. Pk St AL2 ....... 141 E3
Moorlands Sch. Dun .......... 44 C3
Moorlands. Wel G C AL7 .. 111 A3
Moormead Hill. Hit SG5 .... 34 D6
Moors Ley. Walk SG2 ........ 38 B1
Moors The. Wel G C AL7 .. 111 A7
Moors Wlk. Wel G C AL7 . 111 C6
Moorside. Heml H HP3 .... 138 B8
Moorside. Wel G C AL7 .... 111 A3
Moortown Rd.
Sth Ox WD1 ................. 175 C6
Moorymead Cl.
Wat St SG14 .................. 70 D3
Morecambe Cl. Stev SG1 ... 50 B7
Morefields. Tri HP23 ........ 100 A6
Moremead. Wa Aby EN9 .. 163 D6
Moreton Ave. Harp AL5 ..... 85 F2
Moreton Cl. Ham St EN7 .. 148 B4
Moreton End Cl. Harp AL5 . 85 F2
Moreton End La. Harp AL5 . 85 F2
Moreton Pl. Harp AL5 ........ 85 F3
Moreton Rd. Luton LU2 ...... 46 A2
Morgan Cl. Norwd HA6 .... 174 F4
Morgan Cl. Stev SG1 ......... 36 D1
Morgan's Rd. Hert SG13 .. 113 D4
Morgan's Wlk. Hert SG13 113 D3
Morgans Cl. Hert SG13 .... 113 D4
Morgans Jun Mix Inf Sch.
Hert ............................ 113 D4
Morland Way. Ches EN8 .. 148 E3
Morley Gr. Harl CM20 ...... 117 C2
Morley Hill. Enf EN2 ......... 161 D1
Morningside. Ric WD3 ..... 165 C1
Mornington Rd. Radl WD7 156 B5
Mornington. Welw AL6 ...... 90 A4
Morpeth Ave. Bor WD6 ..... 156 F1
Morrell Cl. Luton LU3 ......... 45 A7
Morrell Ct. Wel G C .......... 110 F7
Morris Cl. Henlw SG16 ...... 10 C5
Morris Cl. Luton LU3 ......... 44 E8
Morris Ct. Wa Aby EN9 .... 163 F5
Morris Way. Lon C AL2 .... 142 D5
Morrison Ct. Barn EN5 ..... 171 E5 5
Morriston Cl. Sth Ox WD1 175 C5
Morse Cl. Hare UB9 ......... 173 C1
Mortain Dr. Berk HP4 ...... 121 F6
Mortimer Cl. Bus WD2 .... 168 B3
Mortimer Cl. Luton LU1 ...... 62 F7
Mortimer Gate. Ches EN8 148 F4
Mortimer Hill. Tri HP23 ... 100 B4
Mortimer Rd. Royst SG8 ...... 7 E7
Mortimer Rise. Tri HP23 .. 100 B4
Morton St. Royst SG8 .......... 7 D7
Morven Cl. Pot B EN6 ....... 159 C8
Moss Bury Inf & Jun Sch.
Stev ............................... 51 A7
Moss Cl. Pnr HA5 ............ 175 F1
Moss Cl. Ric WD3 ............ 173 D8
Moss Gn. Wel G C AL7 ..... 110 E4
Moss La. Pnr HA5 ............ 175 E1
Moss Rd. Watf WD2 ........ 154 B5
Moss Side. Bri Wd AL2 ..... 140 F1
Moss Way. Hit SG5 ........... 21 C1
Mossbank Ave. Luton LU2 . 64 C8
Mossendew Cl. Hare UB9 173 D2
Mostyn Rd. Bus WD2 ....... 168 C4
Mostyn Rd. Luton LU3 ........ 44 E4
Motor Vehicle Works.
Luton ............................. 64 B7
Mott St. Wa Aby EN9 ....... 163 D1
Motts Cl. Wat St SG14 ....... 70 D4
Moulton Rise. Luton LU2 .... 63 F8
Mount Cl. Heml H HP1 ...... 123 F3
Mount Dr. Pk St AL2 ......... 141 D6
Mount Dr. Sta M CM24 ...... 59 E5
Mount Garrison. Hit SG4 .... 34 F7
Mount Grace Rd. Luton LU2 46 C6
Mount Grace Rd.
Pot B EN6 ..................... 159 B8
Mount Grove Sch. Pot B ... 159 B8
Mount Pleasant Cl.
Hat AL9 ....................... 130 D8
Mount Pleasant.
Hare UB9 ..................... 173 A2
Mount Pleasant. Hit SG5 ... 34 D6
Mount Pleasant La.
Bri Wd AL2 .................. 140 E1
Mount Pleasant La.
Hat AL9 ....................... 130 C8
Mount Pleasant Lane Jun
Mix Inf Sch. Bri Wd ..... 140 E1
Mount Pleasant Rd.
Luton LU3 ...................... 44 E5
Mount Pleasant.
St Alb AL3 ................... 127 C3
Mount Rd. Hert SG14 ....... 113 A5
Mount Rd. Whea AL4 ......... 87 D1
Mount The. Bar SG8 ............ 8 F1
Mount The. Ham St EN7 ... 147 D5
Mount The. Luton LU3 ........ 63 D8 4
Mount The. Pot B EN6 ...... 145 B1
Mount The. Ric WD3 ........ 165 C3
Mount Vernon & The Radium
Inst Hospl. Norwd ....... 174 B4
Mount View. Enf EN2 ....... 160 F1
Mount View. Lon C AL2 .... 142 F4
Mount View. Ric WD3 ...... 165 B1
Mount Way. Wel G C AL7 . 110 F3
Mountbatten Cl.
St Alb AL1 ................... 142 B8
Mounteagle. Royst SG8 ....... 7 D5
Mountfield Rd.
Heml H HP2 ................. 124 E3
Mountfield Rd. Luton LU2 .. 45 E2
Mountfitchet High Sch The.
Sta M ............................. 59 F4
Mountfitchet Rd.
Sta M CM24 ................... 59 E5
Mountjoy. Hit SG4 ............. 22 C1
Mountside. Har HA7 ........ 176 F2
Mountsorrel. Hert SG13 .. 113 F6
Mountview. Norwd HA6 .... 174 F4
Mountview Rd.
Ham St EN7 .................. 147 E5
Mountway Cl.
Wel G C AL7 ................ 110 F3
Mountway. Pot B EN6 ...... 145 A1
Mowbray Cres. Stot SG5 ... 11 F7
Mowbray Gdns. Hit SG4 ..... 35 A5
Mowbray Rd. Harl CM20 .. 118 A3
Moxes Wood. Luton LU3 .... 44 E7
Moxon St. Barn EN5 ......... 171 F6
Mozart Ct. Stev SG1 ........... 50 C5
Muddy La. Letw SG6 .......... 22 F3
Muirfield Cl. Sth Ox WD1 . 175 C6
Muirfield Gn. Sth Ox WD1 175 C6
Muirfield. Luton LU2 .......... 45 E6
Muirfield Rd. Sth Ox WD1 175 B6
Muirhead Way. Kneb SG3 .. 68 F5
Mulberry Cl. Ches EN10 ... 148 F7
Mulberry Cl. Chis AL2 ....... 141 B3
Mulberry Cl. Luton LU1 ..... 63 B7
Mulberry Cl. Stot SG5 ....... 11 F5
Mulberry Cl. Tri HP23 ...... 100 A5
Mulberry Ct. Bis St CM23 .. 77 A5
Mulberry Gn. Harl CM17 .. 118 D4
Mulberry Way. Hit SG5 ...... 21 D2
Mullion Cl. Har HA3 ......... 176 B2
Mullion Cl. Luton LU2 ......... 46 B5
Mullion Wlk. Sth Ox WD1 . 175 D6
Mullway. Letw SG6 ............ 22 C6
Mundells Ct. Wel G C ...... 110 F8
Mundells. Ham St EN7 ..... 148 A4
Mundells. Wel G C AL7 ..... 111 A8
Munden Gr. Watf WD2 .... 154 D1
Munden Rd. Dan En SG12 .. 71 E7
Munden View. Watf WD2 154 D3
Mundesley Cl. Stev SG1 ..... 36 B1
Mundesly Cl. Sth Ox WD1 175 C6
Mungo-Park Cl. Bus WD2 176 C8
Munro Rd. Bus WD2 ........ 168 C4
Muntings The. Stev SG2 ..... 51 A3
Munts Meadow. Wes SG4 . 24 C1
Murchison Rd. Hod EN11 . 115 B1
Muriel Ave. Watf WD1 ..... 167 C4
Murray Cres. Pnr HA5 ..... 175 D2
Murray Rd. Berk HP4 ....... 122 C6
Murray Rd. Norwd HA6 .... 174 E3
Murrell La. Stot SG5 ......... 12 A5
Murton Ct. St Alb AL1 ...... 127 E4
Museum Ct. Tri HP23 ....... 100 A3
Musgrave Cl. Ham St EN7 147 F4
Musk Hill. Heml H HP1 .... 123 E2
Muskalls Cl. Ham St EN7 . 148 A4
Muskham Rd. Harl CM20 . 118 B3
Musleigh Manor.
Ware SG12 .................... 93 F1
Musley Hill. Ware SG12 ..... 93 E2
Musley Inf Sch. Ware ........ 93 E2
Musley La. Ware SG12 ...... 93 E2
Mussons Path. Luton LU2 .. 45 E1
Muswell Cl. Luton LU3 ....... 45 B6
Mutchetts Cl. Watf WD2 .. 154 E6
Mutford Croft. Luton LU2 ... 46 D1 5
Mutton La. Pot B EN6 ...... 158 E8
Myddelton Ave. Enf EN1 .. 161 E1
Myddleton Rd.
Ware SG12 ................... 114 D8
Myles Ct. Gofs O EN7 ...... 147 C2
Mylne Ct. Hod EN11 ......... 115 A1
Mymms Dr. Bro Pk AL9 ... 145 B4
Mymwood Sch. Bro Pk ..... 145 C4
Myrtle Cotts. Sar WD3 ..... 152 A3
Myrtle Gr. Enf EN2 .......... 161 D1
Myrtleside Cl. Norwd HA6 174 D3

Nails La. Bis St CM23 ......... 76 F7
Nairn Cl. Harp AL5 ........... 107 D6
Nairn Gn. Sth Ox WD1 ..... 175 A7
Nan Aires. Wing HP22 ........ 60 A3
Nancy Downs. Watf WD1 167 C2
Nap The. Kin L WD4 ......... 139 A2
Napier Cl. Lon C AL2 ........ 142 D6
Napier Ct. Ches EN8 ........ 148 B3
Napier Ct. Luton LU1 ......... 63 D7
Napier Dr. Watf WD2 ....... 167 E5
Napier Rd. Luton LU1 ........ 63 D7
Nappsbury Rd. Luton LU4 .. 44 D5
Napsbury Ave. Lon C AL2 . 142 C5
Napsbury La. St Alb AL1 .. 142 A7
Nascot Pl. Watf WD1 ....... 167 B7
Nascot Rd. Watf WD1 ....... 167 B7
Nascot St. Watf WD1 ....... 167 B7
Nascot Wood Inf Sch.
Watf ............................ 154 A1
Nascot Wood Jun Sch.
Watf ............................ 154 A1
Nascot Wood Rd.
Watf WD1 .................... 153 F1
Naseby Rd. Luton LU1 ........ 63 B7
Nash Cl. Bor WD6 ............ 169 F5
Nash Cl. Stev SG2 .............. 51 B6
Nash Cl. Wel G AL9 .......... 144 D8
Nash Gn. Heml H HP3 ...... 138 F6
Nash Gn. Heml H HP3 ...... 139 A6
Nash Mills C of E Sch.
Heml H ........................ 138 F6
Nash Mills La.
Heml H HP3 ................. 138 F5
Nash Rd. Royst SG8 ............ 7 D5
Nathaniel Wlk. Tri HP23 .. 100 A5
Nathans Cl. Welw AL6 ....... 89 C6
Nayland Cl. Luton LU2 ....... 46 E1 1
Nazeing New Rd.
Hod EN10 ..................... 135 B2
Nazeing New Rd.
Lo Naz EN10 ................ 135 B2
Nazeing Prim Sch. Lo Naz 149 E8
Nazeing Rd. Lo Naz EN9 ... 135 D1
Neal Cl. Norwd HA6 ......... 175 A2
Neal Ct. Hert SG14 ........... 113 C6
Neal Ct. Wa Aby EN9 ........ 163 F6
Neal St. Watf WD1 ........... 167 C4
Neaole Cl. Bor WD6 ......... 170 C8
Necton Rd. Whea AL4 ...... 108 E8
Needham Rd. Luton LU4 .... 44 B6
Nell Gwynn Cl. Shen WD7 156 E7
Nelson Ave. St Alb AL1 .... 142 B8
Nelson Rd. Bis St CM23 .... 77 A5
Nelson Rd. Dagn HP4 ......... 81 C5
Nelson St. Hert SG14 ....... 113 B7
Nene Rd. Henlw SG16 ........ 10 B4
Neptune Ct. Bor WD6 ...... 170 A6
Neptune Dr. Heml H HP2 . 124 E5
Neston Rd. Watf WD2 ..... 154 C2
Nether St. Widf SG12 ........ 95 E4
Netherby Cl. Tri HP23 ...... 100 C6
Nethercott Cl. Luton LU2 ... 46 C1
Netherfield La.
Sta Ab SG12 ................. 115 E3
Netherfield Rd. Harp AL5 . 107 B4
Netherhall Rd.
Lo Naz CM19 ................ 135 F5
Netherstones. Stot SG5 ...... 11 F7
Netherway. St Alb AL3 ..... 141 A8
Netley Dell. Letw SG6 ........ 23 B3
Netteswell Cross.
Harl CM20 .................... 117 E2
Netteswell Orch.
Harl CM20 .................... 117 D1
Netteswell Rd. Harl CM20 117 F3
Netteswell Tower.
Harl CM20 .................... 117 D1
Nettlecroft. Heml H HP1 .. 124 B2
Nettlecroft. Wel G C AL7 . 111 B7
Nettleden Rd. L Gad HP4 . 102 E4
Nettleden Rd. Pot En HP1 103 D1
Nettleden Rd. Pot En HP4 123 B8
Nevell's Gn. Letw SG6 ....... 22 F6
Nevells Rd. Letw SG6 ......... 22 F6
Nevill Gr. Watf WD2 ........ 167 B8
Neville Cl. Pot B EN6 ........ 158 F8
Neville Rd. Luton LU3 ......... 45 A5
Neville's Ct. Letw SG6 ........ 23 B7
New Barn La. L Hal CM22 .. 77 D1
New Barnes Ave.
St Alb AL1 .................... 142 A8
New Barns La. Muc H SG10 74 E4
New Bedford Rd.
Luton LU1,LU2,LU3 ........ 45 D3
New Briars Jun Mix Inf Sch.
Hat .............................. 130 A5
New Cl. Kneb SG3 ............. 68 F6
New Cotts. Bro Pk AL9 .... 144 D3
New Cotts. Ches EN8 ...... 162 C5
New Cotts. Mark AL3 ........ 83 E6
New Ct. Welw SG3 ............. 69 A2
New England Cl. Hit SG4 .... 34 F4
New England St.
St Alb AL3 ................... 127 C3
New Farm La. Norwd HA6 174 E2
New Ford Rd. Ches EN8 ... 162 F5
New Forge Pl. Red AL3 .... 106 B5
New Greens Ave.
St Alb AL3 ................... 127 D7
New House Pk. St Alb AL1 142 B7
New Inn Rd. Hin SG7 ........... 3 D5
New Kent Rd. St Alb AL1 .. 127 D3
New Mill Terr. Tri HP23 .... 100 B6
New Par. Chor WD3 ........ 164 C5
New Park Dr. Heml H HP2 125 B3
New Park La. Ast SG2 ........ 51 F2
New Park Rd. Hare UB9 .. 173 C2
New Park Rd.
New St SG13 ................ 146 D7
New Pl. Welw AL6 ............. 89 B4
New Rd. Berk HP4 .......... 122 D6
New Rd. Chipf WD4 ......... 137 F1
New Rd. Cro Gr WD3 ...... 166 A4
New Rd. Elst WD6 ........... 169 D3
New Rd. Gt Ch SG8 .............. 9 D6
New Rd. Harl CM17 ......... 118 D4
New Rd. Hat AL8 .............. 110 A3
New Rd. Henlw SG16 ......... 10 A8
New Rd. Hert SG14 .......... 113 D8
New Rd. Hod EN10 .......... 135 A4
New Rd. L Had SG11 .......... 75 A7
New Rd. Nthch HP4 ......... 121 F7
New Rd. Radl WD7 .......... 155 E2
New Rd. Radl WD7 .......... 168 E8
New Rd. Ridge EN6 .......... 158 A6
New Rd. Sar WD3 ............ 151 F1
New Rd. Shen WD7 .......... 157 A5
New Rd. Tri HP23 ............ 100 B6
New Rd. Ware SG12 .......... 93 D1
New Rd. Watf WD1 .......... 167 C5
New Rd. Welw AL6 ............ 89 F3
New Rd. Welw SG3 ............ 69 B3
New River Ave.
Gt Am SG12 ................. 115 B4
New River Cl. Hod EN11 .. 135 B7
New River Ct. Ches EN7 .. 162 B8
New River Trad Est. Ches 148 D5
New St. Berk HP4 ............ 122 D4
New St. Cad LU1 ............... 63 C1
New St. Ched LU7 ............. 79 F7
New St. Luton LU1 ............ 63 E6
New St. Saw CM21 ............ 97 E3
New St. Watf WD1 ........... 167 C5
New Town. Cod SG4 .......... 67 F1
New Town Rd. Luton LU1 ... 63 E6
New Town St. Luton LU1 ... 63 E6
New Wood. Wel G C AL7 . 111 C7
Newark Cl. Royst SG8 .......... 7 C8

Newark Gn. Bor WD6 ...... 170 D6
Newark Rd. Luton LU4 ....... 45 A2
Newberries Ave. Radl WD7 .................... 156 B4
Newberries Jun Mix Inf Sch. Radl ............................. 156 C4
Newbiggin Path. Sth Ox WD1 ................ 175 C6
Newbold Rd. Luton LU3 ..... 45 B7
Newbolt Rd. Stan HA7 ...... 176 F5
Newbolt. Royst SG8 ............ 7 D8
Newbury Ave. Enf EN3 ...... 162 F2
Newbury Cl. Bis St CM23 ... 76 E8
Newbury Cl. Luton LU4 ...... 44 E2
Newbury Cl. Stev SG1 ........ 36 D1
Newcastle Cl. Stev SG1 ..... 36 F2
Newcombe Rd. Luton LU1 .. 63 C7
Newcome Path. Shen WD7 .................... 157 A5
Newcome Rd. Shen WD7 . 157 A5
Newdigate Gn. Hare UB9 . 173 D2
Newdigate Rd E. Hare UB9 .................... 173 D2
Newdigate Rd. Hare UB9 . 173 C2
Newell La. Ard SG2 ........... 38 D7
Newell Rd. Heml H HP3 ... 138 E8
Newell Rise. Heml H HP3 138 E8
Newells Hedge. Pit LU7 ..... 80 D5
Newells. Letw SG6 ............ 23 D4
Newfield La. Heml H HP2 124 F3
Newfields. Wel G C AL8 ... 110 B5
Newford Cl. Heml H HP2 . 125 B4
Newgate Cl. St Alb AL4 .... 128 D6
Newgate St. New St SG13 ............... 146 D7
Newgate. Stev SG2 ........... 51 A4
Newgate Street Village. New St SG13 ............... 146 E6
Newgatestreet Rd. Gofs O EN7 .................. 147 B4
Newground Rd. Ald HP23 101 B3
Newhall Cl. Bov HP3 ....... 137 A4
Newhall Ct. Wa Aby EN9 .. 163 F6
Newhouse Cres. Watf WD2 ................... 154 B6
Newhouse Rd. Bov HP3 ... 137 A4
Newland Cl. Pnr HA5 ....... 175 F4
Newland Cl. St Alb AL1 .... 142 A8
Newlands Ave. Radl WD7 155 F5
Newlands Cl E. Hit SG4 ...... 34 F4
Newlands Cl W. Hit SG4 .... 34 F4
Newlands. Hat AL9 .......... 130 C7
Newlands La. Hit SG4 ........ 34 F4
Newlands. Letw SG6 .......... 23 A3
Newlands Pl. Barn EN5 .... 171 D4
Newlands Rd. Heml H HP1 ................. 123 E3
Newlands Rd. Luton LU1 .... 63 C3
Newlands Way. Pot B EN6 145 B1
Newlands Wlk. Watf WD2 154 D6
Newlyn Cl. Bri Wd AL2 ..... 140 E1
Newlyn Cl. Stev SG1 .......... 50 A6
Newlyn Rd. Barn EN5 ........ 171 F5
Newman Ave. Royst SG8 ...... 7 F6
Newmans Ct. Wat St SG14 70 D3
Newmans Dr. Harp AL5 ..... 85 F2
Newmarket Rd. Royst SG8 .. 7 E6
Newnham Cl. Luton LU2 .... 46 D1
Newnham Par. Ches EN8 . 148 D1
Newnham Rd. Newn SG7 ... 12 E6
Newnham Way. Ashw SG7 .. 4 B2
Newport Cl. Enf EN3 ........ 162 E2
Newport Mead. Sth Ox WD1 ................ 175 D6
Newports. Saw CM21 ........ 97 C1
Newquay Gdns. Sth Ox WD1 ................ 175 B8
Newstead. Hat AL10 ........ 129 F2
Newstead House. Hare UB9 .................... 173 C1
Newteswell Dr. Wa Aby EN9 ................ 163 D7
Newton Cl. Harp AL5 ....... 107 D6
Newton Cl. Hod EN11 ...... 115 B2
Newton Cres. Bor WD6 ... 170 C5
Newton Dr. Saw CM21 ....... 97 D1
Newton Rd. Har HA3 ........ 176 E1
Newton Rd. Stev SG2 ......... 51 B6
Newtondale. Luton LU4 ..... 44 C5
Newtons Way. Hit SG4 ...... 34 F6
Newtown Rd. Bis St CM23 . 76 F6
Niagara Cl. Ches EN8 ....... 148 D2
Nicholas Breakspear Sch Annexe. Coln H ............ 128 E2
Nicholas Breakspear Sch. Coln H .......................... 128 E2
Nicholas Cl. St Alb AL3 ..... 127 D7
Nicholas Cl. Watf WD2 .... 154 B2
Nicholas Hawksmoor Sch. Bor .............................. 170 C8
Nicholas La. Hert SG14 .... 113 D6
Nicholas Pl. Stev SG1 ........ 36 D1
Nicholas Rd. Bor WD6 ..... 169 F4
Nicholas Way. Heml H HP2 ................ 124 F5
Nicholas Way. Norwd HA6 174 C2
Nicholls Cl. Red AL3 ......... 105 F5
Nichols Cl. Luton LU2 ........ 46 C2
Nicola Cl. Har HA3 ........... 176 D1
Nicoll Way. Bor WD6 ....... 170 D5
Nicolson Dr. Bus WD2 ..... 176 C8
Nidderdale. Heml H HP2 .. 124 F6
Nightingale Ave. Knee SG8 .. 2 A5
Nightingale Cl. Luton LU2 .. 46 C6
Nightingale Cl. Radl WD7 155 F3
Nightingale Ct. Hert SG14 113 C6
Nightingale Ct. Hit SG5 ...... 35 A8
Nightingale Ct. Luton LU3 .. 63 C8
Nightingale Ct. Ric WD3 .. 165 C2
Nightingale La. St Alb AL1 142 C7
Nightingale Lodge. Berk HP4 ..................... 122 B4
Nightingale Pl. Ric WD3 ... 165 D2
Nightingale Rd. Bus WD2 168 A4
Nightingale Rd. Hit SG5 ..... 34 F8
Nightingale Rd. Ric WD3 . 165 C2
Nightingale Terr. Arl SG15 11 A3
Nightingale Way. Bal SG7 .. 23 F6
Nightingale Wlk. Heml H HP2 ................ 105 C1
Nightingale Wlk. Stev SG2 . 51 C5
Nightingales. Wa Aby EN9 163 E5
Nimmo Dr. Bus WD2 ........ 168 D2
Nine Acre La. Ess AL9 ...... 132 A1
Ninefields. Wa Aby EN9 ... 163 F6
Ninesprings Way. Hit SG4 . 35 B6
Ninian Rd. Heml H HP2 .... 124 E8
Ninning's La. Welw AL6 ..... 68 D2
Ninth Ave. Luton LU3 ........ 44 D7
Niton Cl. Barn EN5 .......... 171 D3
Niven Cl. Bor WD6 .......... 170 C8
Nobel Sch. Stev .................. 51 C7
Nobel Villas. Wa Aby EN9 163 D5
Nobles The. Bis St CM23 ... 76 D6
Nodes Dr. Stev SG2 ........... 51 A1
Noke La. Bri Wd AL2 ........ 140 E4
Noke Shot. Harp AL5 ......... 86 C4
Noke Side. Chis AL2 ......... 141 A4
Noke The. Stev SG2 ........... 69 B8
Nokes The. Heml H HP1 .. 124 A5
Nokeside. Stev SG2 ........... 69 B8
Nook The. Gt Am SG12 .... 115 C4
Norbury Ave. Watf WD1 .. 167 C7
Norfolk Ave. Watf WD2 ... 154 C1
Norfolk Ct. Barn EN5 ........ 171 E5 4
Norfolk Gdns. Bor WD6 ... 170 D5
Norfolk Rd. Bun SG9 .......... 40 E8
Norfolk Rd. Luton LU2 ....... 64 A7
Norfolk Rd. Ric WD3 ........ 165 E1
Norfolk Way. Bis St CM23 . 76 F5
Norman Ave. Bis St CM23 .. 76 D6
Norman Cl. Wa Aby EN9 .. 163 D6
Norman Cres. Pnr HA5 .... 175 C2
Norman Ct. Pot B EN6 ..... 145 C1
Norman Ct. Sta M CM24 .... 59 E7
Norman Ct. Stev SG1 ........ 36 F1
Norman Rd. Luton LU3 ....... 45 B2
Norman Rd. Welw AL6 ....... 89 B3
Norman's La. Royst SG8 ...... 7 D5
Norman's Way. Sta M CM24 .................. 59 E7
Normandy Ave. Barn EN5 171 F5
Normandy Dr. Berk HP4 .. 122 B6
Normandy Rd. St Alb AL3 . 127 D4
Normans Cl. Letw SG6 ....... 11 F1
Normans La. Welw AL6 ..... 68 E2
Normansfield Cl. Bus WD2 ..................... 168 B2
Norris Cl. Bis St CM23 ....... 77 C7
Norris Gr. Hod EN10 ........ 134 E3
Norris La. Hod EN11 ........ 135 A7
Norris Rd. Hod EN11 ....... 135 A6
Norris Rise. Hod EN11 ..... 134 F7
North App. Mo Pk HA6 .... 174 C8
North App. Watf WD2 ...... 154 A5
North Ave. Letw SG6 ......... 23 B8
North Ave. Shen WD7 ...... 156 E7
North Barn. Lo Naz EN10 . 135 B1
North Cl. Barn EN5 .......... 171 C4
North Cl. Chis AL2 ........... 141 B6
North Cl. Royst SG8 ............ 7 C7
North Comm. Red AL3 ...... 106 A5
North Common Rd. Red AL3 ....................... 106 A4
North Ct. Mark AL3 ........... 83 E5
North Dr. St Alb AL5 ........ 128 E5
North Dr. Thun SG11 ......... 72 E1
North Drift Way. Luton LU1 ....................... 63 B6
North Gate. Harl CM20 .... 117 C1
North Hertfordshire Coll (Hitchin Ctr). Hit ............ 35 B8
North Hertfordshire Coll (Lethchworth Ctr). Letw 22 F6
North Hertfordshire Coll ........ (Shephalbury Ctr). Stev . 51 A1
North Hertfordshire Coll (Stevenage Ctr). Stev .... 50 D4
North Hill. Chor WD3 ....... 164 E8
North Luton Ind Est. Luton 44 B7
North Orbital Rd. Bri Wd AL2 .................. 140 E2
North Orbital Rd. Chis AL2 141 B5
North Orbital Rd. Coln H AL4 .................. 129 C2
North Orbital Rd. Lon C .... 142 D6
North Orbital Rd. Pk St AL2 ..................... 141 E6
North Orbital Rd. Watf WD2 .................. 154 D7
North Orbital Trad Est. St Alb .......................... 142 A7
North Pl. Harl CM20 ......... 118 B5
North Pl. Hit SG5 .............. 21 D1
North Pl. Wa Aby EN9 ...... 163 B6
North Rd. Bal SG7 .............. 12 E2
North Rd. Berk HP4 ......... 122 B4
North Rd. Ches EN8 ......... 162 E6
North Rd. Chor WD3 ....... 164 D4
North Rd. Hert SG14 ....... 113 A7
North Rd. Hert SG14 ........ 113 C6
North Rd. Hod EN11 ......... 135 A7
North Rd. Stev SG1 ............ 36 C2
North Ride. Welw AL6 ....... 89 C6
North Riding. Bri Wd AL2 . 141 A1
North Road Ave. Hert SG14 .................... 113 A7
North Road Gdns. Hert SG14 .................... 113 B6
North St. Bis St CM23 ........ 76 F7
North St. Lo Naz EN9 ....... 135 E1
North St. Luton LU2 ........... 45 E1
North St. Luton LU2 ........... 63 E8
North Terr. Bis St CM23 .... 76 F8
North View Cotts. Widf SG12 ...................... 95 D4
North Western Ave. Abb L WD2 .................. 153 D4
North Western Ave. Stan WD6 .................... 169 B2
North Western Ave. Watf WD2 .................... 154 C3
Northaw C of E Jun Mix Inf Sch. Nort ................ 146 A1
Northaw Cl. Heml H HP2 . 125 B8
Northaw Pk. Nort EN6 ..... 159 F7
Northaw Rd E. Cuf EN6 .... 146 E1
Northaw Rd W. Nort EN6 . 160 C8
Northbridge Rd. Berk HP4 122 A6
Northbridge Way. Heml H HP1 ................ 124 A3
Northbrook Dr. Norwd HA6 ................. 174 E3
Northbrook Rd. Barn EN5 171 E3
Northchurch St Mary's CE Fst Sch. Nthch .............. 121 E6
Northcliffe Dr. Barn N20 .. 171 F1
Northcote. Pnr HA5 ......... 175 C1 1
Northcotts. Hat AL9 ......... 130 C6
Northcourt. Ric WD3 ........ 165 A1
Northdown Rd. Hat AL10 . 130 A2
Northend. Heml H HP3 .... 125 C1
Northern Ave. Henlw SG16 10 B3
Northern House. Hit .......... 35 B7
Northfield. Brag SG11 ........ 55 F7
Northfield Gdns. Watf WD2 ................... 154 C2
Northfield. Hat AL10 ........ 130 B8
Northfield Rd. Ashw SG7 ..... 1 C3
Northfield Rd. Bor WD6 ... 170 B8
Northfield Rd. Ches EN8 .. 162 E7
Northfield Rd. Harp AL5 ..... 86 C4
Northfield Rd. Saw CM21 .. 97 E4
Northfield Sch. Watf ........ 167 A8
Northfield. Stand SG11 ...... 55 E2
Northfields Inf Sch. Letw ... 11 F1
Northfields. Letw SG6 ........ 11 F1
Northgate End. Bis St CM23 .................. 76 F8
Northgate House. Ches EN8 ...................... 148 D2
Northgate Jun Mix Inf Sch. Bis St ............................. 76 E8
Northgate. Norwd HA6 .... 174 C3
Northgate Path. Bor WD6 169 F8
Northlands. Pot B EN6 ..... 159 D8
Northolt Ave. Bis St CM23 . 59 B1
Northridge Way. Heml H HP1 ................ 124 A3
Northside. Sand ............... 108 B1
Northumberland Ave. Enf EN1 ....................... 162 B1
Northview Rd. Luton LU2 ... 45 F2
Northway. Ric WD3 ......... 165 D2
Northway. Wel G C AL7 .... 89 F1 1
Northwell Dr. Luton LU3 .... 44 F7
Northwick Rd. Sth Ox WD1 ................ 175 C6
Northwood Cl. Ham St EN7 ................. 147 F4
Northwood Coll. Norwd ... 174 D3
Northwood Golf Course. Norwd ........................... 174 D2
Northwood Hills Cir. Norwd HA6 ................. 175 A2
Northwood Hills Sta. Pnr . 175 A1
Northwood, Pinner & District Hospl. Norwd .. 175 A2
Northwood Rd. Hare UB9 173 E3
Northwood Sch. Pnr ......... 175 B2
Northwood Sta. Norwd .... 174 E3
Northwood Way. Hare UB9 .................... 173 D2
Northwood Way. Norwd HA6 ................. 175 A3
Northwood. Wel G C AL7 . 111 D6
Norton Bury La. Letw SG7 . 12 C2
Norton Cl. Bor WD6 ......... 170 A8
Norton Cres. Bal SG7 ......... 23 E8
Norton Gn. Stev SG1 .......... 50 B3
Norton Green Rd. Stev SG1 50 C4
Norton Mill La. Newn SG7 . 12 D3
Norton Rd. Bal SG7 ............ 12 C2
Norton Rd. Letw SG6 ......... 12 A4
Norton Rd. Letw SG6 ......... 12 C2
Norton Rd. Luton LU3 ........ 44 F4
Norton Rd Prim Sch. Luton 44 F4
Norton Rd. Stev SG1 .......... 50 D4
Norton Rd. Stot SG5 .......... 12 A4
Norton Sch The. Letw ........ 23 A8
Norton Way N. Letw SG6 ... 23 A7
Norton Way S. Letw SG6 ... 23 A5
Nortonstreet La. Whit SG4 67 B7
Norvic Rd. Mars HP23 ....... 80 A1
Norwich Cl. Stev SG1 ......... 37 B1
Norwich Way. Cro Gr WD3 ................ 166 B5
Norwood Cl. Hert SG14 .... 112 F7
Nottingham Cl. Watf WD2 154 A6
Nottingham Rd. Chor WD3 164 C1
Novello Way. Bor WD6 .... 170 D8
Nugent's Pk. Pnr HA5 ...... 175 F2
Nugents Ct. Pnr HA5 ........ 175 E2
Nun's Cl. Hit SG5 ................ 34 E7
Nunfield. Chipf WD4 ........ 152 B8
Nunnery Cl. St Alb AL1 ..... 127 E1
Nunnery La. Luton LU3 ...... 45 B5
Nunnery Stables. St Alb AL1 .................... 127 D1
Nuns La. St Alb AL1 .......... 141 E8
Nunsbury Dr. Ches EN10 . 148 E6
Nup End Cl. Wing HP22 .... 60 B3
Nup End La. Wing HP22 ..... 60 B3
Nupton Dr. Barn EN5 ....... 171 C3
Nurseries Rd. Whea AL4 . 108 E7
Nursery Cl. Bis St CM23 .... 76 F6
Nursery Cl. Stev SG2 ......... 69 A8
Nursery Cotts. Stev SG1 .... 50 A6
Nursery Fields. Saw CM21 97 D2
Nursery Gdns. Tri HP23 ... 100 B4
Nursery Gdns. Ware SG12 93 E1
Nursery Gdns. Wel G C AL7 89 E1
Nursery Hill. Wel G C AL7 .. 89 E1
Nursery Par. Luton LU3 ..... 44 E5
Nursery Rd. Bis St CM23 ... 76 F6
Nursery Rd. Ches EN10 ... 148 F6
Nursery Rd. Hod EN11 ..... 115 B1
Nursery Rd. Lo Naz EN9 .. 135 D2
Nursery Rd. Luton LU3 ....... 44 F5
Nut Gr. Wel G C AL8 .......... 89 D1
Nut Slip. Bun SG9 ............... 40 E6
Nutcroft. Dat SG3 .............. 69 D2
Nutfield. Wel G C AL7 ........ 90 A1
Nutleigh Gr. Hit SG5 .......... 21 D1
Nuttfield Cl. Cro Gr WD3 . 166 B3
Nye Way. Bov HP3 ........... 137 A3
Nymans Cl. Luton LU2 ....... 46 D3

Oak Ave. Bri Wd AL2 ........ 141 A1
Oak Ave. Enf EN2 ............ 160 F1
Oak Cl. Heml H HP3 ......... 138 F7
Oak Cl. Wa Aby EN9 ......... 163 D5
Oak Ct. Norwd HA6 .......... 174 D4
Oak Dr. Berk HP4 ............ 122 D3
Oak Dr. Saw CM21 ........... 118 C8
Oak End. Bun SG9 .............. 40 D7
Oak Farm. Bor WD6 ......... 170 C4
Oak Glade. Norwd HA6 .... 174 B2
Oak Gn. Abb L WD5 ......... 153 E7
Oak Gr. Hat AL10 ............. 129 F5
Oak Gr. Hert SG13 ........... 113 E4
Oak Green Way. Abb L WD5 .................. 153 E7
Oak La. Chol HP23 ........... 120 B2
Oak La. Cuf EN6 .............. 146 F3
Oak La. Gra SG4 ................. 36 C4
Oak Piece Ct. Welw AL6 .... 89 E7
Oak Piece. Welw AL6 ......... 89 E7
Oak Rd. Luton LU4 ............. 63 C8
Oak Rd. Welw SG3 ............. 69 B1
Oak St. Bis St CM23 ........... 76 F6
Oak St. Heml H HP3 ......... 138 F7
Oak Tree Cl. Abb L WD5 .. 153 D7
Oak Tree Cl. Hat AL10 ..... 130 A6
Oak Tree Cl. Hert H SG13 114 C3
Oak Tree Ct. Elst WD6 ..... 169 D3
Oak Tree Ct. Welw AL6 ...... 89 E8
Oak Way. Harp AL5 .......... 107 A5
Oak Wood. Berk HP4 ....... 121 F3
Oakbank. Radl WD7 ......... 156 B3
Oakcroft Cl. Pnr HA5 ....... 175 B1
Oakdale Ave. Pnr HA6 ...... 175 A1
Oakdale Cl. Sth Ox WD1 .. 175 C6
Oakdale Rd. Sth Ox WD1 . 175 C6
Oakdale. Wel G C AL8 ........ 89 D1
Oakdene. Ches EN8 .......... 148 E1
Oakdene Cl. Pnr HA5 ....... 175 F3
Oakdene Rd. Heml H HP3 138 F7
Oakdene Rd. Watf WD2 ... 154 B3
Oakdene Way. St Alb AL4 128 C3
Oaken Gr. Wel G C AL7 .... 110 E3
Oakfield Ave. Hit SG4 ........ 35 B5
Oakfield Cl. Pot B EN6 ..... 158 F8
Oakfield Rd. Harp AL5 ...... 107 A5
Oakfield. Ric WD3 ............ 165 A2
Oakfields Ave. Kneb SG3 ... 69 A6
Oakfields Cl. Stev SG2 ....... 51 C1
Oakfields Rd. Kneb SG3 ..... 69 A6
Oakfields. Stev SG2 ........... 51 C1
Oakhill Ave. Pnr HA5 ........ 175 E1
Oakhill Cl. Map Cr WD3 ... 172 E6
Oakhill Dr. A St P AL6 ........ 89 A6
Oakhill. Letw SG6 ............... 23 D4
Oakhill Rd. Map Cr WD3 .. 172 D6
Oakhurst Ave. Harp AL5 .. 107 A5
Oakhurst Rd. Enf EN3 ...... 162 D3
Oakington. Wel G C AL7 ... 111 D6
Oakland's Coll. St Alb ...... 128 D1
Oaklands Ave. Bro Pk AL9 144 E4
Oaklands Ave. Watf WD1 167 B1
Oaklands Avenue Inf Sch. Watf ............................ 167 B1
Oaklands. Berk HP4 ........ 122 A4
Oaklands Cl. Bis St CM23 .. 59 B2
Oaklands Coll. Bor ........... 170 C7
Oaklands Coll. Hat ........... 130 A5
Oaklands Coll (Lemsford Lane Campus). Wel G C 110 B4
Oaklands Coll. Pot B ........ 159 B7
Oaklands Coll. Wel G C .... 110 D7
Oaklands Ct. Watf WD1 ... 167 A8
Oaklands Dr. Bis St CM23 .. 59 B2
Oaklands Gate. Norwd HA6 ................. 174 E4
Oaklands Gr. Ches EN10 .. 148 E7
Oaklands (Herts Coll of Agriculture & Horticulture). St Alb ..... 128 D3
Oaklands La. Barn EN5 .... 171 B5
Oaklands La. Coln H AL4 .. 128 F5
Oaklands Pk. Bis St CM23 .. 59 B2
Oaklands Rd. Barn EN7 ... 171 F2
Oaklands Rd. Ham St EN7 147 E5
Oaklands Rise. Welw AL6 .. 89 F7
Oaklands Sch. Welw .......... 89 E7
Oaklawn. Tri HP23 ........... 100 A3
Oaklea Cl. Welw AL6 .......... 89 E8
Oaklea. Welw AL6 .............. 89 E7
Oaklea Wood. Welw AL6 ... 89 E7
Oakleigh Dr. Cro Gr WD3 166 C3
Oakleigh Rd. Pnr HA5 ...... 175 F4
Oakley Cl. Luton LU4 ......... 44 D4
Oakley Ct. Royst SG8 ........... 7 D7
Oakley Rd. Harp AL5 ....... 107 D7
Oakley Rd. Luton LU4 ........ 44 E3
Oakmeade. Barn EN5 ....... 171 D5
Oakmeade. Pnr HA5 ........ 176 A4
Oakmere Ave. Pot B EN6 . 159 C6
Oakmere Cl. Pot B EN6 ... 159 D8
Oakmere La. Pot B EN6 ... 159 C7
Oakridge Ave. Radl WD7 . 155 F6
Oakridge. Bri Wd AL2 ...... 140 F2
Oakridge La. Radl WD2 ... 155 E5
Oakroyd Ave. Pot B EN6 .. 158 F6
Oakroyd Cl. Pot B EN6 .... 158 F6
Oaks Cl. Hit SG4 ................ 34 F5
Oaks Cl. Radl WD7 ........... 155 F4
Oaks Cross. Stev SG2 ......... 51 B1
Oaks Ret Pk. Harl ............ 117 F3
Oaks The. Berk HP4 ........ 122 A4
Oaks The. Cad LU1 ............. 63 C1
Oaks The. Watf WD1 ....... 167 C1

Oaktree Garth.
Wel G C AL7 ............... 110 E5
Oakview Cl. Dren EN7 ...... 148 B3
Oakway. Whip HP6 ............. 82 B7
Oakwell Cl. Stev SG2 ......... 69 D7
Oakwood Ave. Bor WD6 .. 170 B5
Oakwood Cl. Stev SG2 ......... 51 C2
Oakwood Dr. Luton LU3 ...... 44 C8
Oakwood Dr. St Alb AL4 .. 128 C4
Oakwood Est. Harl ........... 118 B4
Oakwood Prim Sch
(Jun Mix & Inf). St Alb . 128 C4
Oakwood Rd. Bri Wd AL2 . 140 F2
Oakwood Rd. Pnr HA5 ..... 175 B1
Oberon Cl. Bor WD6 ....... 170 C8
Occupation Rd. Watf WD1 167 B4
Octavia Ct. Watf WD2 ...... 167 C7
Oddy Hill. Tri HP23 ......... 100 C3
Oddy Hill. Wigg HP23 ..... 100 C2
Odessey Rd. Bor WD6 ..... 170 B8
Offa Rd. St Alb AL3 ........ 127 C3
Offas Way. Whea AL4 ...... 108 D8
Offley Endowed
Jun Mix Inf Sch. Gt Of .. 33 C3
Offley Hill. Gt Of SG5 ....... 33 C3
Offley Rd. Hit SG5 ........... 34 D6
Ogard Rd. Hod EN11 ...... 135 C8
Okeford Cl. Tri HP23 ......... 99 F4
Okeford Dr. Tri HP23 ......... 99 F4
Okeley La. Tri HP23 ......... 99 E3
Old Barn La. Cro Gr WD3 . 165 F4
Old Bedford Rd. Luton LU2 45 D6
Old Bedford Rd. Luton LU2 45 E4
Old Brewery Pl. Kans SG4 .. 66 D1
Old Chantry La. L Wym SG4 35 F2
Old Charlton Rd. Hit SG5 ... 34 E6
Old Church La. Thun SG12 . 93 E7
Old Common The.
Fur P SG9 .................. 43 B4
Old Cross. Hertf SG14 ..... 113 C6
Old Dean. Bov HP3 ......... 137 A4
Old Dr The. Wel G C AL8 . 110 B5
Old Farm. Pit LU7 ............. 80 D4
Old Fishery La.
Heml H HP1 ............... 123 F1
Old Fishery La.
Heml H HP1 ............... 137 F8
Old Fold Cl. Barn EN5 ..... 171 F8
Old Fold La. Barn EN5 ..... 171 F8
Old Fold Manor Golf Club.
Barn ......................... 171 E8
Old Fold View. Barn EN5 .. 171 C6
Old Forge Cl. Abb L WD5 . 154 A6
Old Forge Cl. Wel G C AL7 . 89 F2
Old Forge Rd. Enf EN1 .... 161 F1
Old French Horn La.
Hat AL10 .................. 130 B6
Old Gannon Cl. Mo Pk HA6 174 C5
Old Garden Ct. St Alb AL3 127 C3
Old Hale Way. Hit SG5 ...... 21 E2
Old Hall Cl. Pnr HA5 ...... 175 E2
Old Hall Dr. Pnr HA5 ...... 175 E2
Old Harpenden Rd.
St Alb AL3 ............... 127 E6
Old Herns La. Wel G C AL7 111 C8
Old Hertford Rd. Hat AL9 . 130 C7
Old Highway. Hod EN11 ... 135 C8
Old House Ct. Heml H HP2 124 F3
Old House La. Sar WD4 ... 152 F4
Old House Rd.
Heml H HP2 ............... 124 F3
Old Knebworth La.
Kneb SG2 .................. 68 D8
Old La. Kneb SG3 ............. 69 B5
Old Leys. Hat AL10 ......... 130 A2
Old London Rd. Hert SG13 113 E6
Old London Rd. St Alb AL1 127 E2
Old Maltings The.
Bis St CM23 ............... 77 A7
Old Maple. Fla HP2 ......... 104 F1
Old Mill Gdns. Berk HP4 .. 122 D4
Old Mill La. L Hal CM22 .... 98 B6
Old Mill Rd. Abb L WD4 ... 153 C5
Old Nazeing Rd. Hod EN10 135 B1
Old Nazeing Rd.
Lo Naz EN10 ............. 135 B1
Old North Rd. Knee SG8 ..... 2 B4
Old North Rd. Royst SG8 ..... 7 C8
Old Oak Cl. Arl SG15 ....... 11 A8
Old Oak Gdns. Nthch HP4 121 C7
Old Oak. St Alb AL1 ....... 141 E8
Old Oaks. Wa Aby EN9 .... 163 E7
Old Orch. Pk St AL2 ....... 141 D5
Old Orchard. Luton LU1 ... 63 D5
Old Orchard Mews.
Berk HP4 .................. 122 C3
Old Park Rd. Hit SG5 ........ 34 E7
Old Parkbury La.
Lon C AL2 ................ 141 F1
Old Rd. Harl CM17 ......... 118 D5
Old Rectory Cl. Harp AL5 ... 86 A2

Old Rectory Dr. Hat AL10 . 130 B5
Old Rectory Gdns.
Whea AL4 .................. 108 D8
Old Redding. Stan HA3 ... 176 C6
Old School Cl. Cod SG4 ..... 67 F1
Old School Gn. Ben SG2 ... 52 E5
Old School Orch.
Wat St SG14 ............... 70 E3
Old School The. Shil SG5 . 19 E8
Old School Wlk. Arl SG15 . 11 A4
Old School Wlk. Cad LU1 .. 63 C1
Old Shire La. C St P WD3 . 172 B6
Old Shire La. Chor WD3 ... 164 A2
Old Sopwell Gdns.
St Alb AL1 ............... 127 E1
Old Uxbridge Rd.
Map Cr WD3 ............. 172 E3
Old Vicarage Gdns.
Mark AL3 .................... 83 D6
Old Walled Garden The.
Stev SG1 ................... 36 C1
Old Watford Rd.
Bri Wd AL2 ............... 140 E2
Old Watling St. Fla AL3 ..... 84 B3
Old Wellbury. Hit SG4 ....... 33 D5
Old's App. Mo Pk WD1 ... 166 C1
Old's Cl. Mo Pk WD1 ...... 166 B1
Olden Mead. Letw SG6 .... 23 B3
Oldfield Cl. Ches EN8 ..... 148 E3
Oldfield Ct. St Alb AL1 .... 127 E3
Oldfield Dr. Ches EN8 ..... 148 E3
Oldfield Farm Rd.
Henlw SG16 .............. 10 C4
Oldfield Rd. Heml H HP1 . 123 E2
Oldfield Rd. Lon C AL2 ... 142 D6
Oldfield Rise. Whit SG4 ..... 66 E7
Oldhall Ct. Whit SG4 ....... 66 E7
Oldhall St. Hert SG14 .... 113 D6
Oldhouse Croft.
Harl CM20 ............... 117 E2
Oldings Cnr. Hat AL10 .... 110 B1
Oldpark Ride. Gofs O EN7 161 D7
Oldwood. Welw AL6 ......... 89 D7
Olive Taylor Ct.
Heml H HP3 ............... 124 F7
Oliver Cl. Heml H HP3 .... 138 E7
Oliver Cl. Pk St AL2 ....... 141 D4
Oliver Ct. Sac SG12 ......... 92 E4
Oliver Rd. Heml H HP3 ... 138 E7
Oliver Rise. Heml H HP3 . 138 E7
Oliver's La. Stot SG5 ...... 11 F7
Olivers Cl. Pot En HP4 ... 123 C7
Olivia Gdns. Hare UB9 ... 173 C2
Olleberrie La. Sar WD3 ... 151 D7
Olwen Mews. Pnr HA5 ... 175 D1
Olympus Rd. Henlw SG16 . 10 B4
Omega Ct. Ware SG12 ..... 93 D1
Omega Maltings.
Ware SG12 ................ 93 E1
On-The-Hill. Sth Ox WD1 . 175 E8
Onslow Cl. Hat AL10 ...... 130 B5
Onslow Rd. Luton LU4 .... 44 D5
Onslow St Audrey's Sch.
Hat ......................... 130 B5
Open Air Museum, Chor . 164 A1
Opening The. Cod SG4 ..... 88 F8
Openshaw Way. Letw SG6 23 A6
Oram Pl. Heml H HP3 .... 138 D8
Orbital Cres. Watf WD2 ... 153 F4
Orchard Ave. Berk HP4 .... 85 F1
Orchard Ave. Harp AL5 .... 85 F1
Orchard Ave. Watf WD2 . 154 B8
Orchard Cl. Bor WD6 ..... 169 F6
Orchard Cl. Bus WD2 ..... 168 D1
Orchard Cl. Chor WD3 .... 146 D5
Orchard Cl. Cuf EN6 ...... 146 E3
Orchard Cl. Heml H HP2 . 124 F5
Orchard Cl. Knee SG8 ....... 2 A5
Orchard Cl. L Berk SG13 . 132 C4
Orchard Cl. Letw SG6 ...... 22 F8
Orchard Cl. Radl WD7 .... 155 E3
Orchard Cl. St Alb AL1 ... 127 F2
Orchard Cl. St Ipp SG4 .... 34 F3
Orchard Cl. Sta Ab SG12 . 115 C4
Orchard Cl. Ware SG12 ... 93 D2
Orchard Cl. Watf WD1 .... 166 F7
Orchard Cl. Wing HP22 .... 60 B3
Orchard Cres. Stev SG1 ... 50 C7
Orchard Croft. Harl CM20 118 A2
Orchard Ct. Bov HP9 ..... 137 A4
Orchard Dr. Chis AL2 ..... 141 B5
Orchard Dr. Chor WD3 ... 164 D5
Orchard Dr. Watf WD1 ... 166 F8
Orchard Gdns.
Wa Aby EN9 ............. 163 C5
Orchard House La.
St Alb AL1 ............... 127 D2
Orchard Jun Mix Inf Sch.
Watf ........................ 153 F3
Orchard Lea. Saw CM21 .... 97 C1
Orchard Mead. Hat AL10 . 129 F5

Orchard On The Green The.
Cro Gr WD3 ............. 165 F4
Orchard Rd. Bal SG7 ....... 12 E1
Orchard Rd. Barn EN5 .... 171 F5
Orchard Rd. Bis St CM23 .. 59 B1
Orchard Rd. Hit SG4 ....... 22 B1
Orchard Rd. Royst SG8 ..... 7 B7
Orchard Rd. Stev SG1 ..... 50 C2
Orchard Rd. Tewin AL6 .... 90 C5
Orchard Rd. Welw AL6 .... 89 C5
Orchard Sq. Hod EN10 ... 148 F7
Orchard St. Heml H HP3 . 138 D8
Orchard St. St Alb AL1 ... 127 C2
Orchard The. Cod SG4 ..... 67 F1
Orchard The. Kin L WD4 . 139 A2
Orchard The. Ton SG12 .... 92 E7
Orchard The. Wel G C AL8 110 D8
Orchard Way. Bov HP3 .... 137 A4
Orchard Way. Bre Gr SG4 . 47 E1
Orchard Way. Bro Pk EN6 145 E2
Orchard Way. Gofs O EN7 147 B3
Orchard Way. Kneb SG3 ... 68 E5
Orchard Way. L Ston SG16 10 B3
Orchard Way. Letw SG6 .... 22 F8
Orchard Way. Luton LU4 ... 44 C7
Orchard Way. Pit LU7 ...... 80 E5
Orchard Way. Ric WD3 ... 165 A2
Orchard Way. Royst SG8 .... 7 C8
Orchards The. Saw CM21 .. 97 E3
Orchards The. Tri HP23 .... 99 F3
Ordelmere. Letw SG6 ...... 11 F1
Ordnance Rd. Enf EN3 .... 162 E2
Oregon Way. Luton LU3 ... 45 A8
Organ Hall Rd. Bor WD6 . 169 E8
Oriole Way. Bis St CM23 .. 76 C6
Orion Way. Mo Pk HA6 .. 175 A6
Orlando Cl. Hit SG4 ........ 35 A6
Ormesby Dr. Pot B EN6 .. 158 D7
Ormonde Rd. Mo Pk HA6 . 174 D6
Ormsby Cl. Luton LU1 ...... 63 E5
Ormskirk Rd. Sth Ox WD1 175 D5
Oronsay. Heml H HP3 .... 125 B1
Orphanage Rd. Watf WD1 167 C7
Orpington Cl. Dun LU4 .... 44 A3
Orton Cl. St Alb AL4 ...... 128 A7
Orwell Cl. Watf WD2 ...... 167 D7
Orwell View. Bal SG7 ...... 13 B1
Osborn Way. Wel G C AL8 110 D6
Osborne Cl. Luton LU1 .... 63 F6
Osborne Gdns. Pot B EN6 145 B1
Osborne Rd. Ches EN8 ... 148 E4
Osborne Rd. Hod EN10 ... 135 A4
Osborne Rd. Luton LU1 ... 63 F6
Osborne Rd. Pot B EN6 ... 145 B1
Osborne Rd. Watf WD2 .. 154 C1
Osborne Way. Wigg HP23 100 D1
Osbourne Ave. Kin L WD4 138 F3
Osmington Pl. Tri HP23 .... 99 F4
Osprey Gdns. Ware SG12 . 93 C3
Osprey House. Ware SG12 93 C3
Osprey Wlk. Dun LU4 ...... 44 A5
Oster St. St Alb AL3 ....... 127 C4
Osterley Cl. Stev SG2 ...... 69 C7
Oswald Rd. St Alb AL1 ... 127 C2
Otley Way. Sth Ox WD1 .. 175 C7
Otter Gdns. Hat AL10 .... 130 B4
Otterspool La. Bus WD2 . 154 E1
Otterspool Way. Bus WD2 154 F1
Ottoman Terr. Watf WD1 167 C6
Ottway Wlk. Welw AL6 .... 89 C5
Otways Cl. Pot B EN6 .... 159 B6
Oudle La. Muc H SG10 .... 74 F2
Oughton Cl. Hit SG5 ....... 34 C8
Oughton Head Way.
Hit .......................... 34 D8
Oughtonhead Inf Sch. Hit . 21 C1
Oughtonhead Jun Sch. Hit . 21 C1
Oughtonhead Jun Sch. Hit . 34 C8
Oughtonhead La. Hit SG5 . 34 D8
Oughtonhead Way. Hit SG5 34 D8
Oulton Cres. Pot B EN6 .. 158 D7
Oulton Rise. Harp AL5 ..... 86 D3
Oulton Way. Sth Ox WD1 . 175 F6
Oundle Ave. Bus WD2 .... 168 C3
Oundle Ct. Sac SG12 ...... 92 E4
Oundle Path. Stev SG2 .... 69 C8
Oundle The. Stev SG2 ..... 69 C8
Our Lady of Light Ind Day
Sch. Tri ..................... 99 F3
Our Lady's Jun Mix Inf Sch.
Wel G C ................... 110 E4
Our Lady's RC Jun Mix Inf
Sch. Hit .................... 21 E2
Ousden Cl. Ches EN8 .... 148 E1
Ousden Dr. Ches EN8 .... 148 E1
Ouse Cl. Bal SG7 ........... 13 A8
Oval The. Ches EN10 ..... 148 E7
Oval The. Henlw SG16 ..... 10 C3
Oval The. Stev SG1 ......... 51 A1
Overfield Rd. Luton LU2 ... 46 C1
Overstone Rd. Harp AL5 ... 86 C1

Overstone Rd. Luton LU4 .. 44 D1
Overstream. Ric WD3 .... 165 B5
Overtrees. Harp AL5 ....... 85 F3
Oving Cl. Luton LU2 ........ 46 D2
Owen Jones Cl.
Henlw SG16 .............. 10 C5
Owens Way. Cro Gr WD3 166 A5
Owles La. Bun SG9 ......... 41 A6
Ox La. Harp AL5 ............. 86 B3
Oxcroft. Bis St CM23 ....... 76 F3
Oxen Rd. Luton LU2 ........ 45 F1
Oxendon Dr. Hod EN11 ... 135 A5
Oxfield Cl. Berk HP4 ...... 122 B3
Oxford Ave. St Alb AL1 .. 128 C2
Oxford Cl. Ches EN8 ..... 148 D2
Oxford Cl. Knee SG8 ......... 2 A7
Oxford Rd. Bre Gr SG4 .... 47 E1
Oxford St. Watf WD1 ..... 167 B4
Oxhey Ave. Watf WD1 .... 167 D2
Oxhey Dr. Sth Ox WD1 .. 175 B7
Oxhey Dr. Sth Ox WD1 .. 175 B7
Oxhey La. Pnr HA5 ....... 176 A5
Oxhey La. Sth Ox WD1 .. 175 B7
Oxhey La. Watf WD1 .... 167 D2
Oxhey Rd. Watf WD1 .... 167 D2
Oxhey Ridge Cl.
Sth Ox HA6 ............... 175 B5
Oxhey Wood Jun Mix Inf
Schs. Sth Ox ............ 175 C7
Oxlease Dr. Hat AL10 .... 130 B4
Oxleys Rd. Stev SG2 ...... 51 B3
Oxleys Rd. Stev SG2 ...... 51 B3
Oxleys The. Harl CM17 .. 118 F4
Oxlip Cl. St Alb AL3 ...... 127 C4
Oysterfields. St Alb AL3 . 127 C4

Pacatian Way. Stev SG1 ... 51 C8
Packhorse Cl. St Alb AL4 . 128 C6
Packhorse La.
Shen WD7,AL2 ........... 157 D8
Paddick Cl. Hod EN11 .... 134 F7
Paddock Cl. Hun SG12 ..... 95 D1
Paddock Cl. Letw SG6 .... 23 A5
Paddock House.
Wel G C AL7 ............. 111 B6
Paddock Rd. Bun SG9 ..... 40 E8
Paddock The. Bis St CM23 . 76 D3
Paddock The. Hat AL10 .. 130 A6
Paddock The. Hit SG4 ..... 35 A5
Paddock The. Hod EN10 . 135 A3
Paddock Wood. Harp AL5 107 E7
Paddocks Cl. Stev SG2 ..... 51 B4
Paddocks The. Chor WD3 164 F5
Paddocks The. Cod SG4 ... 68 A1
Paddocks The.
Hert N SG13 ............. 114 B3
Paddocks The. Kim AL4 .... 87 B6
Paddocks The. Stev SG2 ... 51 B3
Paddocks The.
Wel G C AL7 ............. 111 B7
Page Cl. Bal SG7 ............. 23 F6
Page Hill. Ware SG12 ...... 93 C2
Page Rd. Hert SG13 ...... 114 A6
Pages Cl. Bis St CM23 .... 76 D5
Pages Croft. Berk HP4 ... 122 A6
Paget Cotts. Dan En SG12 . 71 F7
Paine's La. Pnr HA5 ...... 175 E1
Paines Orch. Ched LU7 .... 80 A8
Painters La. Enf EN3 ...... 162 F4
Palace Cl. Kin L WD4 ..... 139 A1
Palace Gdns. Royst SG8 .... 7 C6
Palfrey Cl. St Alb AL3 .... 127 D5
Pallas Rd. Heml H HP2 .. 124 F5
Palmer Ave. Bus WD2 .... 168 B4
Palmer Cl. Hert SG14 .... 113 C8
Palmer Cl. Sac SG12 ....... 92 E4
Palmer Gdns. Barn EN5 . 171 D4
Palmer Rd. Hert SG14 ... 113 D8
Palmers Gr. Lo Naz EN9 . 135 F1
Palmers La. Bis St CM23 .. 77 B7
Palmers Way. Ches EN8 . 148 E2
Palmerston.
Wel G C AL8 ............. 110 C6
Palmerston Cl. Stev SG2 .. 51 B7
Pamela Ave. Heml H HP3 138 B8
Pamela Gdns. Bis St CM23 76 F3
Pams La. Kim SG4 ........... 66 D1
Pancake La. Heml H HP2 . 125 D2
Pankhurst Cres. Stev SG2 . 51 C6
Pankhurst Pl. Watf WD2 . 167 C6
Panshanger Dr.
Wel G C AL7 ............. 111 C6
Panshanger Prim Sch.
Wel G C ................... 111 A7
Pantiles The. Bus WD2 .. 168 D1
Panxworth Rd.
Heml H HP3 ............. 124 D1
Paper Mill La. Stand SG11 . 55 E1
Paper Mill Rd. Hat AL10 . 130 C7
Parade The. Luton LU3 .... 44 C7
Parade The. Sth Ox WD1 . 175 D7

Parade The. Sth Ox WD1 . 175 E7
Parade The. Watf WD1 .. 167 B6
Paradise Cl. Ham St EN7 . 148 B3
Paradise. Heml H HP2 ... 124 D2
Paradise Rd. Wa Aby EN9 163 C5
Paradise Wildlife Park.
Bric ......................... 133 F2
Parishes Mead. Ast SG2 .. 51 D4
Park Ave. Bis St CM23 ..... 76 F3
Park Ave. Bus WD2 ...... 167 E7
Park Ave. Luton LU3 ....... 44 C7
Park Ave. N. Harp AL5 ..... 85 F1
Park Ave. Pot B EN6 ..... 159 D6
Park Ave. Radl WD7 ...... 156 B6
Park Ave. Ric WD3 ....... 165 A5
Park Ave. S. Harp AL5 ..... 85 F1
Park Ave. St Alb AL1 ..... 128 A4
Park Ave. Watf WD1 ..... 167 A5
Park Avenue Trad Est.
Luton ........................ 44 C7
Park Cl. Bal SG7 ............. 23 F7
Park Cl. Bro Pk AL9 ...... 145 A5
Park Cl. Bus WD2 ........ 167 D6
Park Cl. Har HA3 .......... 176 E2
Park Cl. Harl AL9 .......... 130 C6
Park Cl. Mark AL3 .......... 83 D5
Park Cl. Ric WD3 .......... 174 B6
Park Cl. Stev SG2 ........... 51 B1
Park Cres. Bal SG7 ......... 23 E7
Park Cres. Bor WD6 ...... 169 F6
Park Cres. Har HA3 ...... 176 E2
Park Ct. Hare UB9 ......... 173 B2
Park Ct. Harl CM20 ...... 117 D1
Park Ct. Letw SG6 .......... 23 A6
Park Dr. Bal SG7 ............. 23 E7
Park Dr. Pot B EN6 ...... 159 B8
Park Dr. Stan HA3 ........ 176 F4
Park Dr. Stand SG11 ....... 55 D3
Park Farm Cl. Henlw SG16 10 D8
Park Farm Ind Est. Bun .... 40 D8
Park Farm La. Nut SG8 ..... 18 C2
Park Gate. Hit SG4 .......... 34 F6
Park Gdns. Bal SG7 ......... 23 E7
Park Hill. Harl CM17 ...... 118 B3
Park Hill. Harp AL5 ......... 85 F2
Park Hill Rd. Heml H HP1 124 B3
Park House. Berk HP4 .... 122 B5
Park House. Wel G C AL8 110 D7
Park La. Bis St CM23 ...... 76 F4
Park La. Ches EN7 ........ 162 D6
Park La. Col H AL4 ....... 143 C8
Park La. Coln H AL4 ...... 129 C1
Park La. Ham St EN7 .... 148 A4
Park La. Hare UB9 ........ 173 B2
Park La. Harl CM20 ...... 117 D2
Park La. Heml H HP2 .... 124 D2
Park La. Hod EN10 ....... 134 F3
Park La. Kim SG4 ........... 66 C1
Park La. Kneb SG3 .......... 68 D5
Park La. Stand SG11 ....... 55 D3
Park Lane Paradise.
Ham St EN7 ............. 148 A6
Park Lodge. Watf WD2 .. 154 D5
Park Mansions.
Mo Pk HA6 ............... 174 C7
Park Mead. Harl CM20 .. 117 B1
Park Meadow. Hat AL9 .. 130 C6
Park Mews. Hat AL9 ..... 130 C6
Park Mount. Harp AL5 ..... 85 F3
Park Nook Gdns. Enf EN2 161 D2
Park Pl. Hare UB9 ......... 173 C2
Park Pl. Pk St AL2 ........ 141 D4
Park Rd. Barn EN5 ....... 171 F5
Park Rd. Bus WD2 ........ 168 A3
Park Rd. Ches EN8 ....... 162 D6
Park Rd. Enf EN3 .......... 162 E3
Park Rd. Heml H HP1 .... 124 C1
Park Rd. Hert SG13 ...... 113 E6
Park Rd. Hod EN11 ....... 135 A6
Park Rd. Nort EN6 ....... 146 A1
Park Rd. Ric WD3 ........ 165 E2
Park Rd. Sta M CM24 ..... 59 E6
Park Rd. Tri HP23 ......... 100 A3
Park Rd. Ware SG12 ....... 93 B2
Park Rd. Watf WD1 ...... 167 B8
Park Rise. Cl. Harp AL5 .... 85 E3
Park Rise. Han HA3 ...... 176 F2
Park Rise. Harp AL5 ........ 85 E3
Park Rise. Nthch HP4 .... 121 E6
Park Sq. Luton LU1 ......... 63 E7
Park St. Bal SG7 ............. 23 E8
Park St. Berk HP4 ........ 122 B5
Park St. Hat AL9 ........... 130 C6
Park St. Hit SG4 ............. 34 E6
Park St. Luton LU1 .......... 63 E7
Park St. Pk St AL2 ....... 141 D5
Park St. Tri HP23 .......... 100 A3

Park St W. Luton LU1 ......... 63 E7
Park Street La. Chis AL2 .. 141 C3
Park Street Sch. Pk St ..... 141 D4
Park Terr. Enf EN3 ........... 162 E1
Park The. Red AL3 ........... 106 B5
Park The. St Alb AL1 ........ 128 A5
Park Viaduct. Luton LU1 .... 63 E6
Park View Cl. Luton LU3 .... 44 D6
Park View Cl. St Alb AL1 .. 128 A2
Park View Ct. Berk HP4 .... 122 B4
Park View Dr. Mark AL3 ..... 83 D6
Park View. Hat AL9 .......... 130 C7
Park View. Hod EN11 ........ 135 A5
Park View. Pnr HA5 .......... 175 F2
Park View. Pot B EN6 ....... 159 C6
Park View Rd. Berk HP4 ... 122 B4
Park View Rd. Pnr HA5 ..... 175 B3
Park View. Stev SG2 .......... 51 B1
Park Way. Hit SG5 ............ 34 E6
Park Way. Ric WD3 .......... 165 C1
Parker Ave. Hert SG14 ..... 113 D8
Parker Cl. Letw SG6 .......... 22 E4
Parker St. Watf WD2 ....... 167 B8
Parker's Field. Stev SG2 ..... 51 C4
Parkfield Ave. Har HA2 ..... 176 C1
Parkfield. Chor WD3 ........ 164 F5
Parkfield Cres. Har HA2 .. 176 C1
Parkfield Cres. Kim SG4 ..... 66 D1
Parkfield House. Har HA2 176 B2
Parkfield. Letw SG6 ........... 23 D4
Parkfield Rd. Mark AL3 ...... 83 D5
Parkfields. Wel G C AL8 ... 110 D6
Parkgate Inf Sch. Watf ..... 154 C2
Parkgate Jun Sch. Watf ... 154 C2
Parkgate Rd. Watf WD2 .. 154 C2
Parkhurst Rd. Hert SG14 . 113 C7
Parkinson Cl. Whea AL4 .. 108 D8
Parkland Cl. Hod EN11 ..... 115 B1
Parkland Dr. Luton LU1 ..... 63 D5
Parklands Cl. Had W EN4 159 D1
Parklands Dr. St Alb AL3 . 127 A2
Parklands. Royst SG8 .......... 7 E6
Parklands. Wa Aby EN9 ... 163 D7
Parkmead. Luton LU1 ......... 63 F6
Parkside Ct. Ches EN7 ..... 148 B3
Parkside Dr. Watf WD1 ... 166 F7
Parkside Fst Sch. Bor ...... 156 F1
Parkside. Pot B EN6 ......... 159 C7
Parkside Rd. Mo Pk HA6 .. 174 F5
Parkside. Watf WD1 ......... 167 C3
Parkside. Welw AL6 .......... 89 C5
Parkside. Wyd SG9 ........... 27 D2
Parkview House. Watf WD1 .................. 167 D3
Parkway Cl. Wel G C AL8 . 110 C6
Parkway Ct. St Alb AL1 .... 142 B8
Parkway Gdns. Wel G C AL8 ................ 110 D5
Parkway Inf Sch. Wel G C 110 C5
Parkway. Saw CM21 ........... 97 E1
Parkway. Stev SG2 ............ 51 A1
Parkway. Wel G C AL8 ..... 110 C6
Parkwood Cl. Hod EN10 ... 134 F4
Parkwood Dr. Heml H HP1 123 F3
Parliament Sq. Hert SG14 113 D5
Parmiter's Sch. Abb L ...... 154 C8
Parndon Mill La. Harl CM20 .................... 117 B3
Parnel Rd. Ware SG12 ....... 93 F2
Parnell Cl. Abb L HA8 ....... 139 F1
Parr Cres. Heml H HP2 .... 125 B8
Parrott's La. Chol HP23 .... 120 A4
Parrotts Cl. Cro Gr WD3 .. 166 A4
Parrotts Field. Hod EN11 . 135 B7
Parson's Cl. Fla AL3 .......... 84 B1
Parsonage Cl. Abb L WD5 139 E1
Parsonage Cl. Tri HP23 .... 100 A4
Parsonage Farm. Ric WD3 165 C2
Parsonage Farm Trad Est. Sta M ............................ 59 F3
Parsonage Farm. Wing HP22 .................... 60 B3
Parsonage La. Alb SG11 .... 57 A6
Parsonage La. Bis St CM23 77 C8
Parsonage La. Sta M CM23 59 F4
Parsonage La. Wel G AL9 144 B8
Parsonage Pl. Tri HP23 .... 100 A3
Parsonage Rd. Ric WD3 ... 165 D2
Parsonage Rd. Wel G AL9 144 B8
Parsons Green Est. Stev .... 37 C2
Parthia Cl. Royst SG8 .......... 7 E6
Partridge Cl. Barn EN5 ..... 171 C3
Partridge Cl. Bus WD2 ..... 168 C1
Partridge Cl. Dun LU4 ........ 44 A5
Partridge Hill. Ashw SG7 ..... 4 C3
Partridge Rd. St Alb AL3 .. 127 D7
Parva Cl. Harp AL5 .......... 107 D6
Parvills. Wa Aby EN9 ...... 163 D7
Parys Rd. Luton LU3 .......... 45 B6
Pascal Way. Letw SG6 ....... 23 B8
Pasfield. Wa Aby EN9 ...... 163 D6
Passfield Cotts. Thun SG11 72 F1
Passingham Ave. Hit SG4 .. 35 A6
Paston Rd. Heml H HP2 ... 124 E5
Pasture Cl. Bus WD2 ....... 168 C2
Pasture La. Bre Gr SG4 ..... 65 E8
Pasture Rd. Letw SG6 ........ 22 E3
Pastures Ct. Dun LU4 ......... 44 A3
Pastures The. Barn N20 .. 171 F1
Pastures The. Chis AL2 .... 141 A7
Pastures The. Hat AL10 ... 130 B4
Pastures The. Heml H HP1 ................. 123 E4
Pastures The. Stev SG2 ..... 51 D8
Pastures The. Ware SG12 . 93 C3
Pastures The. Watf WD1 . 167 C2
Pastures The. Wel G C AL7 ................. 111 B4
Pastures Way. Dun LU4 ..... 44 A4
Paternoster Cl. Wa Aby EN9 ................. 163 F6
Paternoster Hill. Wa Aby EN9 ................. 163 F7
Pathway The. Radl WD7 .. 155 F3
Pathway The. Watf WD1 . 167 D1
Patmore Cl. Bis St CM23 .... 76 C8
Patmore Link Rd. Heml H HP2 ................. 125 C2
Patmore Rd. Wa Aby EN9 163 E5
Patricia Gdns. Bis St CM23 76 E5
Paul's Gn. Ches EN8 ........ 162 E6
Pauls La. Hod EN11 ......... 135 A6
Paxton Rd. Berk HP4 ....... 122 D4
Paxton Rd. St Alb AL1 ...... 127 E2
Payne End. San SG9 ........... 15 B1
Payne's Pk. Hit SG5 ........... 34 E7
Paynes Cl. Letw SG6 .......... 12 A1
Paynes La. Lo Naz EN9 ..... 149 C7
Paynesfield Rd. Bus WD2 168 F2
Pea La. Nthch HP4 ........... 121 D7
Peace Cl. Ches EN8 .......... 148 B2
Peace Gr. Welw AL6 .......... 90 A7
Peach Ct. Luton LU1 ........... 63 F6
Peacocks Cl. Berk HP4 ...... 121 F6
Peakes La. Ham St EN7 ... 147 F4
Peakes Pl. St Alb AL1 ....... 127 F3
Peakes Way. Ham St EN7 147 F4
Pear Tree Cl. L Ston SG16 . 10 B3
Pear Tree Dell. Letw SG6 .. 23 B3
Pear Tree Wlk. Ham St EN7 ................. 147 E5
Pearman Dr. Dan En SG12 . 71 E7
Pearsall Cl. Letw SG6 ........ 23 B5
Pearson Ave. Hert SG13 .. 113 C4
Pearson Cl. Hert SG13 ...... 113 C4
Peartree Cl. Heml H HP1 . 124 A4
Peartree Cl. Wel G C AL7 . 110 E6
Peartree Ct. Watf WD2 ... 154 D3
Peartree Ct. Wel G C AL7 110 E5
Peartree Farm. Wel G C AL7 ................ 110 E6
Peartree Jun Mix Inf Sch. Wel G C ........................ 110 E5
Peartree La. Wel G C AL7 110 E6
Peartree Rd. Heml H HP1 124 A4
Peartree Rd. Luton LU2 ..... 46 C4
Peartree Spring Inf Sch. Stev ................................ 51 B3
Peartree Spring Jun Sch. Stev ................................ 51 B3
Peartree Way. Stev SG2 ..... 51 A3
Peascroft Rd. Heml H HP3 125 B1
Peasecroft. Cotrd SG9 ....... 39 C7
Peasmead. Bun SG9 .......... 40 E6
Peck's Hill. Lo Naz EN9 .... 135 E2
Pedlars La. Ther SG8 ......... 15 E7
Pedley Hill. Stu LU6 ........... 82 C2
Peel Cres. Hert SG14 ....... 113 C8
Peel Pl. Luton LU1 ............. 63 D7
Peel St. Luton LU1 ............. 63 D7
Peerglow Ctr. Ware ......... 114 E8
Peg's La. Hert SG13 ......... 113 D5
Pegmire La. Radl WD2 ..... 168 C8
Pegs La. Widf SG12 ........... 95 D5
Pegsdon Cl. Luton LU3 ....... 45 B7
Pegsdon Way. Shil SG5 ..... 19 E1
Pelham Ct. Heml H HP2 ... 125 C3
Pelham Ct. Wel G C AL7 ... 111 C5
Pelham Rd. Brag SG11 ....... 55 F7
Pelhams The. Watf WD2 . 154 D4
Pelican Way. Letw SG6 ...... 11 F1
Pemberton Cl. St Alb AL1 . 141 D8
Pembridge Chase. Bov HP3 ........................... 137 A3
Pembridge La. Bric EN10 . 133 E2
Pembridge Rd. Bov HP3 ... 137 A3
Pembroke Ave. Enf EN1 ... 162 B1
Pembroke Ave. Luton LU4 . 44 F3
Pembroke Cl. Hod EN10 ... 148 E8
Pembroke Dr. Gofs O EN7 147 B2
Pembroke Rd. Bal SG7 ....... 23 F8
Pembroke Rd. Mo Pk HA6 174 C7
Pemsel Ct. Heml H HP3 ... 124 E1
Penda Cl. Luton LU3 .......... 44 F7
Pendennis Ct. Harp AL5 ... 107 D7
Pengelly Cl. Ches EN7 ...... 148 B1
Penhill Ct. Luton LU3 ......... 44 E6
Penhill. Luton LU3 ............. 44 E6
Penman Cl. Chis AL2 ........ 141 A4
Penn Cl. Chor WD3 ......... 164 D3
Penn House. Mo Pk HA6 .. 174 C7
Penn Pl. Ric WD3 ............ 165 D2
Penn Rd. Chis AL2 ........... 141 C4
Penn Rd. Ric WD3 ........... 165 A1
Penn Rd. Stev SG1 ............. 50 E4
Penn Way. Chor WD3 ...... 164 D3
Penn Way. Letw SG6 ......... 23 B3
Penne Cl. Radl WD7 ......... 156 A5
Pennine Ave. Luton LU3 ..... 44 D8
Pennington La. Sta M CM24 .................. 59 D8
Penningtons. Bis St CM23 . 76 D5
Penny Croft. Harp AL5 ..... 107 A4
Pennyfathers La. Welw AL6 ....................... 90 B4
Pennymead. Harl CM20 ... 118 A1
Penrose Ave. Sth Ox WD1 175 E8
Penrose Ct. Heml H HP2 .. 124 E7
Penscroft Gdns. Bor WD6 170 D5
Penshurst Cl. Harp AL5 ..... 85 D4
Penshurst. Harl CM17 ...... 118 B3
Penshurst Rd. Pot B EN6 . 159 D7
Pentland. Heml H HP2 ..... 124 F6
Pentland Rd. Bus WD2 ..... 168 C3
Pentley Cl. Wel G C AL8 ..... 89 D1
Penton Dr. Ches EN8 ....... 148 D2
Pentrich Ave. Enf EN1 ...... 162 A1
Penzance Cl. Hare UB9 .... 173 D1
Peplins Cl. Bro Pk AL9 ..... 144 E5
Peplins Way. Bro Pk AL9 . 144 E5
Pepper Ct. Bal SG7 ............ 23 F8
Pepper Hill. Gt Am SG12 .. 114 F4
Peppett's Gn. Chol HP5 ... 120 D1
Pepsal End Rd. Cad LU1 ..... 84 C7
Pepsal End Rd. Fla LU1 ...... 84 C7
Pepsal End. Stev SG2 ......... 69 B8
Pepys Cres. Barn EN5 ...... 171 C4
Pepys Way. Bal SG7 .......... 23 E8
Percheron Dr. Dun LU4 ...... 44 A3
Percheron Rd. Bor WD6 .. 170 D3
Percival Way. Luton LU2 .... 64 C7
Percy Rd. Watf WD1 ........ 167 B5
Peregrine Cl. Bis St CM23 . 76 D6
Peregrine Cl. Watf WD2 .. 154 E5
Peregrine House. Ware SG12 .................... 93 C3
Peregrine Rd. Dun LU4 ...... 44 A4
Perham Way. Lon C AL2 .. 142 D6
Perivale Gdns. Watf WD2 154 B5
Periwinkle Cl. Bark SG8 ..... 17 C5
Periwinkle La. Hit SG5 ....... 21 F1
Perowne Way. Stand SG11 55 E3
Perram Cl. Ches EN10 ...... 148 E5
Perriors Cl. Ham St EN7 .. 148 A4
Perry Dr. Royst SG8 ............. 7 E7
Perry Gn. Heml H HP2 ..... 105 A1
Perry Hill. Lo Naz EN9 ...... 149 F8
Perry Mead. Bus WD2 ...... 168 C3
Perrymead. Luton LU2 ....... 46 F2
Perrysfield Rd. Ches EN8 . 148 E5
Perrywood La. Wat St SG14 ................. 91 B7
Perrywood. Wel G C AL8 . 110 D8
Pescot Hill. Heml H HP1 .. 124 B5
Petard Cl. Dun LU4 ............ 44 A2
Peter Kirk Sch. Sta M ......... 59 E6
Peter's Pl. Nthch HP4 ...... 121 E6
Peterlee Ct. Heml H HP2 . 124 F7
Peters Ave. Lon C AL2 ..... 142 C5
Peters Way. Kneb SG3 ...... 68 F6
Peters Wood Hill. Ware SG12 ................. 114 E7
Petersfield. St Alb AL3 ..... 127 E7
Petunia Ct. Luton LU3 ........ 45 C1
Petworth Cl. Stev SG2 ........ 69 C7
Pevensey Cl. Luton LU2 ..... 46 D4
Pheasant Cl. Berk HP4 ..... 122 C3
Pheasant Cl. Tri HP23 ...... 100 B6
Pheasants Way. Ric WD3 165 B2
Phillimore Pl. Radl WD7 .. 155 E3
Phillipers. Watf WD2 ....... 154 E4
Phillips Ave. Royst SG8 ........ 7 C8
Phipps Hatch La. Enf EN2 161 C1
Phoenix Cl. Mo Pk HA6 .... 174 F6
Phoenix Ct. Enf EN3 ......... 162 C1
Phyllis Courtnage House. Heml H HP2 ................ 124 D5
Piccotts End. Heml H HP1 124 C6
Piccotts End La. Heml H HP2 ................. 124 D7
Piccotts End Rd. Heml H HP1 ................ 124 B7
Pick Hill. Wa Aby EN9 ...... 163 F7
Pickets Cl. Bus WD2 ........ 168 E1
Picketts. Wel G C AL8 ........ 89 D1
Pickford Hill. Harp AL5 ...... 86 D4
Pickford Rd. Fla AL3 ........... 83 C4
Pickford Rd. Mark AL3 ....... 83 C4
Picknage Cnr. Bar SG8 ......... 9 A2
Picknage Rd. Bar SG8 .......... 9 A2
Pie Cnr. Fla AL3 ................ 84 B1
Pie Garden. Fla AL3 ........... 84 C1
Pietley Hill. Fla AL3 ........... 84 A1
Pig La. Bis St CM22,CM23 . 77 A3
Pigeonwick. Harp AL5 ........ 86 B3
Piggotts La. Luton LU4 ....... 44 D4
Piggotts Way. Bis St CM23 .................. 76 E5
Piggottshill La. Harp AL5 . 107 D8
Pightle Cl. Royst SG8 ........... 7 D7
Pikes Cl. Luton LU1 ............ 63 E7
Pilgrim Cl. Chis AL2 .......... 141 C4
Pilgrim Cl. Watf WD2 ....... 154 D6
Pilgrims Row. West SG9 .... 40 F3
Pilgrims Way. Stev SG1 ..... 37 B2
Piltdown Rd. Sth Ox WD1 175 D6
Pin Green Jun Mix Inf Sch. Stev ............................... 50 F6
Pinchfield. Map Cr WD3 ... 172 D5
Pindar Rd. Hod EN11 ....... 135 C7
Pine Cl. Berk HP4 ............. 122 B4
Pine Cl. Ches EN8 ............ 148 D3
Pine Cl. Norwd HA6 ......... 174 E4
Pine Crest. Welw AL6 ........ 89 E8
Pine Gr. Barn N20 ............ 171 F1
Pine Gr. Bis St CM23 .......... 77 B6
Pine Gr. Bri Wd AL2 ......... 140 F1
Pine Gr. Bro Pk AL9 ......... 145 B6
Pine Gr. Bus WD2 ............ 167 F8
Pine Ridge. St Alb AL1 ..... 142 A8
Pine Tree Cl. Heml H HP2 124 D4
Pine Wlk. Nthch HP4 ........ 121 D7
Pinecroft Cres. Barn EN5 . 171 E5
Pinecroft. Heml H HP3 ..... 138 F7
Pinehall Hospl. Hit ............. 35 A7
Pinehurst Cl. Abb L WD5 . 153 E7
Pinelands. Bis St CM23 ...... 58 F1
Pineridge Ct. Barn EN5 .... 171 D5
Pines Ave. Enf EN1 ........... 162 B3
Pines Hill. Sta M CM24 ...... 59 D5
Pines Jun Mix Inf Sch The. Hert ............................ 114 B7
Pines The. Bor WD6 ......... 169 F7
Pines The. Heml H HP3 .... 137 F7
Pinetree House. Watf WD2 .................... 154 E3
Pinewood Ave. Pnr HA5 ... 176 B4
Pinewood Cl. Bor WD6 .... 170 D7
Pinewood Cl. Pnr HA5 ..... 176 B4
Pinewood Cl. St Alb AL4 ... 128 C3
Pinewood Dr. Pot B EN6 .. 158 F8
Pinewood Gdns. Heml H HP1 ................. 124 B3
Pinewood Sch. Ware ....... 114 D7
Pinewood. Wel G C AL7 ... 110 E4
Pinewoods. Stev SG2 ......... 50 F1
Pinfold Rd. Bus WD2 ........ 167 F7
Pinford Dell. Luton LU2 ...... 46 D1
Pinnacles. Wa Aby EN9 .... 163 E5
Pinnate Pl. Wel G C AL7 ... 110 E2
Pinner Gn. Pnr HA5 .......... 175 C1
Pinner Hill. Pnr HA5 ......... 175 B3
Pinner Hill Rd. Pnr HA5 .... 175 C1
Pinner Park Ave. Har HA2 176 C1
Pinner Park Gdns. Har HA2 ....................... 176 C1
Pinner Rd. Norwd HA6 ..... 175 A1
Pinner Rd. Pnr HA5 .......... 175 A1
Pinner Rd. Watf WD1 ...... 167 E2
Pinner Wood Fst & Mid Schs. Pnr ..................... 175 C2
Pinnocks Cl. Bal SG7 .......... 23 F7
Pinnocks La. Bal SG7 ......... 23 F8
Pinto Cl. Bor WD6 ........... 170 D3
Piper's Hill. Gt Gd HP1 ..... 103 D3
Pipers Ave. Harp AL5 ....... 107 D7
Pipers Cl. Red AL3 ........... 106 A6
Pipers La. Cad LU1 ............ 62 F1
Pipers La. Mark AL3 .......... 62 F1
Pipers La. Whea AL5 ........ 107 F7
Pippens. Wel G C AL8 ........ 89 E1
Pirton Cl. Heml H HP2 ...... 124 F4
Pirton Cl. Hit SG5 .............. 34 D6
Pirton Cl. St Alb AL4 ......... 128 C8
Pirton Hill Inf Sch. Luton ... 44 B6
Pirton Hill Jun Sch. Luton .. 44 B6
Pirton Jun Mix Inf Sch. Pirt 20 D4
Pirton Rd. Hit SG5 ............. 34 C6
Pirton Rd. Hol SG5 ............ 21 A7
Pirton Rd. Luton LU4 ......... 44 D5
Pishiobury Dr. Saw CM21 118 D8
Pishiobury Mews. Saw CM21 .................... 118 D7
Pitsfield. Wel G C AL8 ........ 89 D1
Pitstone Cl. St Alb AL4 ..... 128 C8
Pitt Ct. Stev SG2 ................. 51 B1
Pittman's Field. Harl CM20 .................... 117 F1
Pix Farm La. Heml H HP1 123 C2
Pix Rd. Letw SG6 ................ 23 A6
Pix Rd. Stot SG5 ................. 11 E5
Pixies Hill Cres. Heml H HP1 ................. 123 F2
Pixies Hill Jun Mix Inf Sch. Heml H ......................... 123 F2
Pixies Hill Rd. Heml H HP1 ................. 123 F2
Pixmore Ave. Letw SG6 ..... 23 B6
Pixmore Ind Est. Letw ....... 23 A6
Pixmore Jun Sch. Letw ...... 23 A5
Pixmore Way. Letw SG6 ..... 23 A5
Plaistow Way. Gt Ch SG8 ..... 9 E2
Plaiters Cl. Tri HP23 ........ 100 B4
Plaitford Cl. Ric WD3 ....... 173 E8
Plantaganet Pl. Wa Aby EN9 ................. 163 B6
Plantation Rd. Luton LU3 ... 44 D7
Plantation Wlk. Heml H HP1 ................. 124 A6
Plash Dr. Stev SG1 ............. 50 E5
Plashes Cl. Stand SG11 ..... 55 D2
Plashets. Sheer CM22 ....... 98 D1
Plaw Hatch Cl. Bis St CM23 77 C8
Playford Sq. Luton LU4 ...... 44 D5
Pleasance The. Harp AL5 .. 85 D4
Pleasant Mount. Hert H SG13 ................. 114 C4
Pleasant Pl. Map Cr WD3 172 E3
Pleasant Rd. Bis St CM23 .. 76 E8
Pleasant Rise. Hat AL9 .... 130 C8
Plewes Cl. Ken Co LU6 ....... 82 E8
Plough Hill. Cuf EN6 ......... 146 E2
Plough La. Hare UB9 ........ 173 C4
Plough La. Kin Wd SG4 ...... 48 A5
Plough La. Pot En HP4 ..... 123 B7
Plough La. Sar WD3 ......... 151 F6
Ploughmans End. Wel G C AL7 ................ 111 C5
Plover Cl. Berk HP4 ......... 122 C3
Plum Tree Rd. L Ston SG16 10 B2
Plummers La. Kim SG4 ...... 65 C2
Plumpton Cl. Luton LU2 ..... 46 D3
Plumpton Rd. Hod EN11 .... 135 C8
Pluto Rise. Heml H HP2 ... 124 F5
Plymouth Cl. Luton LU2 ..... 46 B1
Poets Cl. Heml H HP1 ...... 124 B4
Poets Gn. Dun LU4 ............. 44 A2
Polayn Garth. Wel G C AL8 ................ 110 C7
Polegate. Luton LU2 .......... 46 D2
Polehanger La. Heml H HP1 ................. 123 E5
Poles Hill. Sar HP5 ........... 151 E6
Poles La. Thun SG12 ......... 93 C6
Poles La. Ware SG12 ......... 93 C3
Police Row. Ther SG8 ........ 15 F7
Police Station La. Bus WD2 ...................... 168 B2
Pollard Gdns. Stev SG1 ...... 50 F8
Pollards Cl. Gofs O EN7 ... 147 C2
Pollards. Map Cr WD3 ...... 172 D5
Pollards Way. Pirt SG5 ...... 20 C4
Pollicott Cl. St Alb AL4 ..... 128 C8
Pollywick Rd. Wigg HP23 . 100 D1
Polzeath Cl. Luton LU2 ...... 64 C8
Pomeroy Cres. Watf WD2 154 B3
Pomeroy Gr. Luton LU2 ...... 45 E6
Pomfret Ave. Luton LU2 ..... 63 F8
Pond Cl. Hare UB9 ........... 173 C1
Pond Cl. Luton LU4 ............ 44 B5
Pond Cl. Stev SG1 .............. 50 C7
Pond Cl. Tri HP23 ............ 100 A4
Pond Croft. Hat AL10 ....... 129 F5
Pond Croft. Wel G C AL7 .. 110 E5
Pond Field. Wel G C AL7 .... 90 A1
Pond La. Bal SG7 ............... 23 E8
Pond Lodge. Cod SG4 ......... 67 F1
Pond Rd. Heml H HP3 ...... 139 A6
Pondcroft Rd. Kneb SG3 .... 69 A4
Pondfield Cres. St Alb AL4 128 B7
Pondside. Gra SG4 ............ 36 C4
Pondsmeade. Red AL3 ...... 106 B5
Pondwick Rd. Harp AL5 ..... 85 E2
Pondwicks Cl. St Alb AL1 . 127 C2
Pondwicks Rd. Luton LU1 ... 63 F7
Ponsbourne Park Cotts. New St SG13 ................ 146 F8
Ponsbourne St Mary's Jun Mix Inf Sch. New St ..... 146 E7
Pooleys La. Wel G AL9 ..... 144 C8
Pope Paul Prim Sch. Pot B 158 F6
Pope's Rd. Abb L WD5 ..... 153 E8

Popes La. Watf WD2 ... 154 B1
Popes Row. Ware SG12 ... 93 D3
Popis Gdns. Ware SG12 ... 93 E2
Poplar Ave. Hat AL4 ... 129 D5
Poplar Ave. Luton LU3 ... 45 C8
Poplar Cl. Hit SG4 ... 35 B6
Poplar Cl. Pnr HA5 ... 175 D2
Poplar Cl. Royst SG8 ... 7 E7
Poplar Cl. Thun SG11 ... 72 F2
Poplar Dr. Royst SG8 ... 7 E7
Poplar Rd. Ken Co LU6 ... 82 E8
Poplar Shaw. Wa Aby EN9 163 F6
Poplar View. Sac SG14 ... 92 E4
Poplars Cl. Hat AL10 ... 129 D5
Poplars Cl. Luton LU2 ... 46 B3
Poplars Cl. Watf WD2 ... 154 B7
Poplars The. Arl SG15 ... 11 A8
Poplars The. Gt Ha CM22 .. 77 F4
Poplars The. Ham St EN7 147 E5
Poplars The. Hare UB9 ... 173 C2
Poplars The. Heml H HP1 124 B2
Poplars The. Ick SG5 ... 21 F5
Poplars The. St Alb AL1 ... 142 B7
Poplars. Wel G C AL7 ... 111 B7
Popple Way. Stev SG1 ... 50 E6
Poppy Cl. Heml H HP1 ... 123 E4
Poppy Mead. Stev SG1 ... 50 F4
Poppyfields. Wel G C AL7 111 C5
Porlock Dr. Luton LU2 ... 46 C1
Port Hill. Hert SG14 ... 113 C7
Port La. L Hal CM22 ... 77 B2
Port Vale. Hert SG14 ... 113 C6
Porters Cl. Bun SG9 ... 40 E8
Porters Hill. Harp AL5 ... 86 C4
Porters Park Dr. Shen WD7 ... 156 E7
Porters Wood. St Alb AL3 127 F7
Portland Dr. Ches EN7 ... 162 A8
Portland Dr. Enf EN2 ... 161 E1
Portland Pl. Bis St CM23 ... 76 F7
Portland Pl. Hert H SG13 . 114 C4
Portland Rd. Bis St CM23 .. 76 F7
Portland Rd. Luton LU4 ... 45 A1
Portland St. St Alb AL3 ... 127 C4
Portman Cl. Hit SG5 ... 21 D2
Portman Cl. St Alb AL4 ... 128 C7
Portman House. St Alb AL3 ... 127 D6
Portmill La. Hit SG5 ... 34 F7
Post Office Rd. Harl CM20 117 D1
Post Office Row. Wes SG4 24 B1
Post Wood Rd. Ware SG12 ... 114 E7
Postfield. Wel G C AL7 ... 90 A1
Postwood Gn. Hert H SG13 ... 114 C3
Potash La. Lon M HP23 ... 79 A5
Potten End Hill. Heml H HP1 ... 123 E8
Potten End Jun Mix Inf Sch. Pot En ... 123 B6
Potter St. Bis St CM23 ... 76 F7
Potter St. Pnr HA5 ... 175 B2
Potter Street Hill. Norwd HA5 ... 175 B3
Potters Bar Sta. Pot B ... 158 F7
Potters Field. St Alb AL3 .. 127 E7
Potters Heights Cl. Pnr HA5 ... 175 B3
Potters La. Bor WD6 ... 170 C8
Potters La. Stev SG1 ... 50 B4
Potters Mews. Elst WD6 .. 169 D3
Potterscrouch La. St Alb AL2 ... 140 E7
Pottersheath Rd. Cod AL6 . 68 D1
Pottery Cl. Luton LU3 ... 44 F7
Potton Rd. Gu M SG8 ... 1 F6
Pouchen End La. Heml H HP1 ... 123 D3
Poulteney Rd. Sta M CM24 59 E8
Poultney Cl. Shen WD7 ... 156 F7
Pound Ave. Stev SG1 ... 50 D6
Pound Cl. Lo Naz EN9 ... 149 E8
Pound Cl. Sand AL4 ... 108 C2
Pound Field. Watf WD2 ... 153 F4
Pound Gn. Gu M SG8 ... 1 F5
Pound La. Shen WD7 ... 156 F6
Poundwell. Wel G C AL7 .. 111 A5
Powdermill La. Wa Aby EN9 ... 163 B6
Powdermill Way. Wa Aby EN9 ... 163 B6
Power Ct. Luton LU1 ... 63 F7
Powis Ct. Bus WD2 ... 168 D1
Powis Ct. Pot B EN6 ... 159 C5
Poynders Hill. Heml H HP2 ... 125 C3
Poynders Meadow. Cod SG4 ... 88 F8
Poynings Cl. Harp AL5 ... 107 F8
Poynters Rd. Dun LU5 ... 44 A2
Prae Cl. St Alb AL3 ... 127 B3
Prae Wood Sch. St Alb ... 127 A1
Praetorian Ct. St Alb AL1 . 141 C8
Prebendal Dr. Cad LU1 ... 63 B2
Precinct The. Hod EN10 ... 134 F3
Premier Ct. Enf EN3 ... 162 D1
Prescott Rd. Ches EN8 ... 148 E4
Presdales Dr. Ware SG12 114 E8
Presdales Sch. Ware ... 114 D7
President Way. Luton LU2 . 64 D8
Prestatyn Cl. Stev SG1 ... 50 B8
Preston Gdns. Enf EN3 ... 162 E2
Preston Gdns. Luton LU2 ... 45 F2
Preston Prim Sch. Pres ... 48 D6
Preston Rd. Pres SG4 ... 48 E7
Preston Rd. St Ipp SG4 ... 34 F1
Prestwick Cl. Luton LU2 ... 45 E5
Prestwick Dr. Bis St CM23 . 59 B1
Prestwick Rd. Sth Ox WD1 ... 175 D6
Pretoria Rd. Watf WD1 ... 167 A5
Pretty Cnr. Mo Pk HA6 ... 175 A5
Priestleys. Luton LU1 ... 63 A7
Primary Way. Arl SG15 ... 11 A4
Primett Rd. Stev SG1 ... 50 C7
Primley La. Sheer CM22 ... 98 C1
Primrose Cl. Arl SG15 ... 11 A4
Primrose Cl. Hat AL10 ... 130 B4
Primrose Cotts. Radl WD7 156 A4
Primrose Ct. Stev SG1 ... 50 D7
Primrose Dr. Hert SG13 ... 114 B6
Primrose Gdns. Bus WD2 168 B2
Primrose Hill. Abb L WD4 139 B3
Primrose Hill Rd. Stev SG1 50 D7
Primrose La. Arl SG15 ... 11 A4
Primrose Path. Ches EN7 162 A8
Primrose View. Royst SG8 ... 7 F5
Prince Andrew's Cl. Royst SG8 ... 7 D5
Prince Edward St. Berk HP4 ... 122 C4
Prince of Wales Sch. Enf . 162 F2
Prince Pk. Heml H HP1 ... 124 A2
Prince St. Watf WD1 ... 167 C6
Prince Way. Luton LU2 ... 64 D8
Prince's St. Stot SG5 ... 11 F7
Princes Ave. Enf EN3 ... 162 E4
Princes Ave. Watf WD1 ... 167 A5
Princes Cl. Berk HP4 ... 122 A6
Princes Ct. Bis St CM23 ... 76 C7
Princes Gate. Bis St CM23 . 76 C7
Princes Gate. Harl ... 117 E3
Princes Mews. Royst SG8 ... 7 C6
Princes St. Ware SG12 ... 93 D2
Princess Alexandra Hospl. Harl ... 117 B1
Princess Helena Coll. Pres 48 E6
Princess St. Luton LU1 ... 63 D7
Printers Way. Harl CM20 . 118 A5
Priors Cl. Hert H SG13 ... 114 B3
Priors Ct. Sheer CM21 ... 98 A2
Priors Hill. Pirt SG5 ... 20 C4
Priors Wood Rd. Hert H SG13 ... 114 C3
Priory Cl. Barn N20 ... 171 F2
Priory Cl. Ches EN8 ... 148 E7
Priory Cl. Hod EN11 ... 135 A5
Priory Cl. Royst SG8 ... 7 E6
Priory Cl. Stan HA7 ... 176 F7
Priory Ct. Berk HP4 ... 122 C4
Priory Ct. Bis St CM23 ... 76 F7
Priory Ct. Bus WD2 ... 168 C1
Priory Ct. Hert SG14 ... 113 C6 11
Priory Ct. Hit ... 34 F5
Priory Ct. St Alb AL1 ... 127 E2
Priory Dell. Stev SG1 ... 50 F5
Priory Dr. Sta M CM24 ... 59 E5
Priory Dr. Stan HA7 ... 176 F7
Priory End. Hit SG4 ... 34 F5
Priory Gate. Ches EN8 ... 148 F4
Priory Gdns. Berk HP4 ... 122 C4
Priory Gdns. Luton LU2 ... 45 D4
Priory La. Gt Wy SG4 ... 35 F4
Priory La. Royst SG8 ... 7 D6
Priory Orch. Fla AL3 ... 84 B2
Priory Rd. Harl CM17 ... 118 C5
Priory Sch The. Hit ... 21 E2
Priory St. Hert SG14 ... 113 D6
Priory St. Ware SG12 ... 93 C1
Priory View. Bus WD2 ... 168 E2
Priory View. L Wym SG4 ... 35 E4
Priory Way. Hit SG4 ... 34 F4
Priory Wharf. Hert SG14 . 113 C6 10
Priory Wlk. St Alb AL1 ... 141 E8
Proctor Way. Luton LU2 ... 64 C7
Proctors Way. Bis St CM23 77 A4
Progress Way. Luton LU4 .. 44 B7
Progression Ctr. Heml H .. 125 A6
Prospect La. Harp AL5 ... 107 A4
Prospect Pl. Welw AL6 ... 89 C5
Prospect Rd. Ches EN8 ... 148 C2
Prospect Rd. St Alb AL1 ... 127 D1
Protea Way. Letw SG6 ... 23 B6
Providence Gr. Stev SG1 ... 50 E8
Providence Way. Bal SG7 .. 23 F7
Provost Way. Luton LU2 ... 64 C8
Prowse Ave. Bus WD2 ... 176 C8
Pryor Cl. Abb L WD5 ... 153 F7
Pryor Rd. Bal SG7 ... 23 F6
Pryor Way. Letw SG6 ... 23 D5
Pryors Cl. Bis St CM23 ... 77 A6
Puddephat's La. Fla AL3 .. 104 D7
Pudding La. Bar SG8 ... 9 A1
Pudding La. Heml H HP1 .. 124 A5
Pudgell The. Gt Ch SG8 ... 9 E2
Pullar Memorial Jun Mix & Inf Sch. Thun ... 72 E2
Puller Rd. Barn EN5 ... 171 E7
Puller Rd. Heml H HP1 ... 124 A2
Pulleys Cl. Heml H HP1 ... 123 F4
Pulleys La. Heml H HP1 ... 123 F4
Pulter's Way. Hit SG4 ... 35 A6
Pump Hill. Bre P SG9 ... 30 A2
Punch Bowl La. Red AL3 .. 126 B8
Purbrock Ave. Watf WD2 . 154 C3
Purcell Cl. Dat AL6 ... 90 E6
Purcell Cl. Radl WD6 ... 169 D8
Purcell Ct. Stev SG1 ... 50 C8
Purkiss Rd. Bric SG13 ... 113 C3
Purley Ctr. Luton ... 44 E7
Purlings Rd. Bus WD2 ... 168 B4
Pursley Gdns. Bor WD6 ... 157 A1
Purway Cl. Luton LU3 ... 44 E8
Purwell La. Hit SG4 ... 35 C8
Purwell Sch (Jun Mix & Inf). Hit ... 35 D8
Putney Rd. Enf EN3 ... 162 D3
Puttenham Cl. Sth Ox WD1 ... 175 D8
Putteridge High Sch. Luton 46 C5
Putteridge Inf Sch. Luton ... 46 C5
Putteridge Prim Sch. Luton 46 C5
Putteridge Rd. Luton LU2 ... 46 C5
Putteridge Rec Ctr. Luton .. 46 C5
Putterills The. Harp AL5 ... 86 A1
Putters Croft. Heml H HP2 ... 124 F8
Puttocks Cl. Wel G AL9 ... 144 C8
Puttocks Dr. Wel G AL9 ... 144 C8
Pye Cnr. East CM20 ... 117 D5
Pyghtle Ct. Luton LU1 ... 63 A7
Pyghtle The. Bun SG9 ... 40 D7
Pyghtle The. Luton LU1 ... 63 A7
Pyms Cl. Letw SG6 ... 23 B8
Pynchbek. Bis St CM23 ... 76 E3
Pynchon Paddocks. L Hal CM22 ... 98 D7
Pytchley Cl. Luton LU2 ... 45 E5
Quadrangle The. Wel G C AL8 ... 110 C7
Quadrant The. Letw SG6 ... 22 F6
Quadrant The. Royst SG8 ... 7 C8
Quadrant The. St Alb AL4 128 B6
Quadrant The. Stev SG1 ... 50 D4
Quaker La. Wa Aby EN9 .. 163 C5
Quaker Rd. Ware SG12 ... 93 E3
Quakers La. Pot B EN6 ... 159 B8
Quantock Cl. Luton LU3 ... 45 B8
Quantock Cl. St Alb AL4 ... 128 C7
Quantock Rise. Luton LU3 .. 31 B1
Quantocks. Heml H HP2 .. 124 F6
Quartermass Cl. Heml H HP1 ... 124 A4
Quartermass Rd. Heml H HP1 ... 124 A4
Queen Anne's Cl. Stot SG5 11 F5
Queen Elizabeth Ct. Barn EN5 ... 171 F5
Queen Elizabeth II Hospl. Wel G C ... 111 A2
Queen Elizabeth's Boys Sch. Barn ... 171 D6
Queen Elizabeth's Girls Gram Sch. Barn ... 171 F5
Queen Hoo La. Tewin AL6 .. 90 F6
Queen Mary's Ave. Watf WD1 ... 166 E5
Queen St. Chipf WD4 ... 152 A7
Queen St. Hit SG4,SG5 ... 34 F7
Queen St. Pit LU7 ... 80 D4
Queen St. St Alb AL3 ... 127 C3
Queen St. Stot SG5 ... 12 A6
Queen St. Tri HP23 ... 100 A3
Queen Victoria Memorial Hospl. Welw ... 89 B4
Queen's Cl. Saw CM21 ... 97 F4
Queen's Ct. Asp SG9 ... 40 D5
Queen's Ct. Hert SG13 ... 113 D5
Queen's Ct. St Alb AL1 ... 128 B3
Queen's Dr. Ches EN8 ... 163 A5
Queen's Dr The. Ric WD3 165 A3
Queen's Pl. Watf WD1 ... 167 C6
Queen's Rd. Ches EN8 ... 162 E6
Queen's Rd. Harp AL5 ... 107 B7
Queen's Rd. Hert SG13 ... 113 D5
Queen's Rd. Watf WD1 ... 167 C6
Queen's Sq The. Heml H HP2 ... 124 F4
Queens Ave. Watf WD1 ... 166 F4
Queens Cl. Luton LU1 ... 63 F6
Queens Cl. Sta M CM24 ... 59 E8
Queens Cres. Bis St CM23 . 76 E5
Queens Cres. St Alb AL4 . 128 B6
Queens Dr. Abb L WD5 ... 153 F7
Queens Rd. Barn EN5 ... 171 D6
Queens Rd. Berk HP4 ... 122 A5
Queens Rd. Royst SG8 ... 7 D7
Queens Rd. Ware SG12 ... 93 F2
Queens Sch. Bus ... 167 F6
Queens Way. Ches EN8 ... 162 F5
Queens Way. Shen WD7 .. 156 E7
Queensgate Ctr. Harl ... 117 F4
Queenside Dr. Hit SG5 ... 34 D8
Queensway. Hat AL10 ... 130 B6
Queensway. Heml H HP1,HP2 ... 124 E4
Queensway. Royst SG8 ... 7 D7
Queensway. Stev SG1 ... 50 D5
Queenswood Cres. Watf WD2 ... 154 A6
Queenswood Dr. Hit SG4 ... 22 C1
Queenswood Sch. Bro Pk 145 D3
Quendell Wlk. Heml H HP2 ... 124 E3
Quendon Dr. Wa Aby EN9 163 D6
Quickbeams. Wel G C AL7 . 90 A1
Quickley La. Chor WD3 ... 164 C3
Quickley Rise. Chor WD3 . 164 C3
Quickly Brow. Chor WD3 . 164 B3
Quickmoor La. Sar WD4 .. 152 C6
Quickswood. Luton LU3 ... 45 A7
Quickwood Cl. Ric WD3 ... 165 A3
Quills. Letw SG6 ... 23 D4
Quilter Cl. Luton LU3 ... 44 F4
Quinces Croft. Heml H HP1 ... 124 A5
Quincey Rd. Ware SG12 ... 93 C4
Quinn Ct. Brag SG11 ... 55 F7
Quinn Way. Letw SG6 ... 23 C5
Quinta Dr. Barn EN5 ... 171 C4
Quinton Way. Wa Aby EN9 ... 163 C4
Raans Rd. L Chal HP6 ... 150 A1
Raban Cl. Stev SG2 ... 51 C1
Rabley Heath Rd. Cod AL6 . 68 B2
Radburn Sch (Jun Mix & Inf). Letw ... 23 C5
Radburn Way. Letw SG6 ... 23 C4
Radcliffe Rd. Hit SG5 ... 35 A8
Radlett La. Shen WD7 ... 156 E6
Radlett Nursery & Inf Sch. Radl ... 156 B3
Radlett Park Rd. Radl WD7 ... 156 A5
Radlett Rd. Lon C AL2 ... 141 E2
Radlett Rd. Radl WD2 ... 155 C1
Radlett Rd. Watf WD1,WD2 ... 167 D7
Radnor Ct. Har HA3 ... 176 F2
Radstone Pl. Luton LU2 ... 46 E1 3
Radwell La. Letw SG7 ... 12 C4
Raebarn Gdns. Barn EN5 . 171 B4
Raffin Cl. Dat SG3 ... 69 E3
Raffin Green La. Dat SG3 ... 69 F4
Raffin Pk. Dat SG3 ... 69 E3
Ragged Hall La. Chis AL2 . 140 E7
Raglan Ave. Ches EN8 ... 162 D5
Raglan Gdns. Watf WD1 .. 167 B1
Raglan House. Berk HP4 . 122 A4
Rags La. Ham St EN7 ... 147 E4
Railway Pl. Hert SG13 ... 113 E6
Railway Rd. Ches EN8 ... 162 F6
Railway St. Hert SG13,SG14 ... 113 D6
Railway Terr. Abb L WD4 . 139 A4
Rainbow Cl. Red AL3 ... 105 F6
Rainbow Ct. Watf WD1 ... 167 C3
Rainer Cl. Ches EN8 ... 148 D2
Rainsford Rd. Sta M CM24 . 59 E8
Raleigh Cres. Stev SG2 ... 51 B8
Raleigh Gr. Luton LU4 ... 44 D1
Rally The. Arl SG15 ... 11 A7
Ralph Sadleir Mid Sch. Stand ... 55 E3
Ralston Way. Sth Ox WD1 175 D8
Ram Gorse. Harl CM20 ... 117 B2
Ramblers Way. Wel G C AL7 ... 111 C5
Rambling Way. Pot En HP4 ... 123 C6
Ramerick Gdns. Arl SG15 .. 11 A2
Ramney Dr. Enf EN3 ... 162 E2
Ramparts The. St Alb AL3 127 B2
Ramridge Jun Sch. Luton ... 46 B2
Ramridge Rd. Luton LU2 ... 46 A2
Ramsay Cl. Hod EN10 ... 134 E2
Ramsbury Rd. St Alb AL1 . 127 E2
Ramsdell. Stev SG1 ... 50 F5
Ramsey Cl. Bro Pk AL9 ... 145 D4
Ramsey Cl. St Alb AL1 ... 128 A1
Ramsey Lodge Ct. St Alb AL1 ... 127 E4
Ramson Rise. Heml H HP1 123 E2
Rand's Cl. Hol SG5 ... 21 B7
Rand's Meadow. Hol SG5 ... 21 B7
Randalls Ride. Heml H HP2 ... 124 E5
Randals Hill. Stev SG2 ... 51 C3
Randon Cl. Har HA2 ... 176 B1
Ranelagh Rd. Heml H HP2 125 B3
Ranleigh Wlk. Harp AL5 ... 107 D6
Ranock Cl. Luton LU3 ... 44 D8
Ranskill Rd. Bor WD6 ... 170 A8
Ransom Cl. Hit SG4 ... 34 F4
Rant Meadow. Heml H HP3 ... 125 A1
Rant Meadow. Heml H HP3 ... 125 A2
Ranworth Ave. Hod EN11 115 B2
Ranworth Ave. Stev SG2 ... 69 C7
Ranworth Cl. Heml H HP3 124 D1 2
Raphael Cl. Shen WD7 ... 156 E7
Raphael Dr. Watf WD2 ... 167 D7
Rasehill Cl. Ric WD3 ... 165 C4
Rathlin. Heml H HP3 ... 139 B8
Ratty's La. Hod EN11 ... 135 D6
Raven Cl. Ric WD3 ... 165 D2
Raven Ct. Hat AL10 ... 130 A4
Ravenbank Rd. Luton LU2 .. 46 C5
Ravenfield Rd. Wel G C AL7 ... 110 F6
Ravenhill Way. Dun LU4 ... 44 B4
Ravens La. Berk HP4 ... 122 D4
Ravens Wharf. Berk HP4 . 122 D4
Ravenscroft. Harp AL5 ... 107 D6
Ravenscroft Pk. Barn EN5 171 D5
Ravenscroft Sch. Barn ... 171 F2
Ravenscroft. Watf WD2 ... 154 E4
Ravensdell. Heml H HP1 .. 123 F4
Ravensthorpe. Luton LU2 .. 46 B4
Ravenswood Pk. Norwd HA6 ... 175 A4
Rawdon Dr. Hod EN11 ... 135 A5
Ray's Hill. Chol HP5 ... 120 C2
Rayburn Rd. Heml H HP1 . 124 A5
Raydon Rd. Ches EN8 ... 162 D7
Rayfield. Wel G C AL8 ... 89 D1
Rayleigh House. Abb L WD5 ... 153 F7
Raymer Cl. St Alb AL1 ... 127 E4
Raymond Cl. Abb L WD5 .. 153 D7
Raymonds Cl. Wel G C AL7 110 E4
Raymonds Plain. Wel G C AL7 ... 110 E4
Raynham Cl. Bis St CM23 .. 77 C8
Raynham Rd. Bis St CM23 . 77 B8
Raynham St. Hert SG13 ... 113 E6
Raynham Way. Luton LU2 .. 46 D1
Raynsford Rd. Ware SG12 . 93 E1
Raynton Rd. Enf EN3 ... 162 D2
Readings The. Chor WD3 . 164 F6
Recreation Ground. Sta M CM24 ... 59 E6
Rectory Cl. Bis St CM23 ... 76 D3
Rectory Cl. Ess AL9 ... 131 F6
Rectory Cl. Hun SG12 ... 116 D8
Rectory Gdns. Hat AL10 ... 130 B5
Rectory La. Berk HP4 ... 122 C4
Rectory La. Far CM23 ... 58 D6
Rectory La. Kin L WD4 ... 139 A3
Rectory La. Lily LU2 ... 32 D2
Rectory La. Ric WD3 ... 165 D1
Rectory La. Shen WD7,AL2 ... 157 B7
Rectory La. Stev SG1 ... 36 D1
Rectory La. Wat St SG14 ... 70 D3
Rectory La. Welw SG3 ... 69 C2
Rectory Rd. Ric WD3 ... 165 D2
Rectory Rd. Wel G C AL8 ... 89 B1
Rectory Wood. Harl CM20 117 C1
Red House Cl. Ware SG12 114 E8
Red Lion Cotts. Gt Of SG5 33 D2
Red Lion Ct. Bis St CM23 ... 77 A7
Red Lion La. Heml H HP3 . 139 A5
Red Lion La. Sar WD3 ... 152 A4
Red Lodge. Bor WD6 ... 169 F6
Red Lodge Gdns. Berk HP4 ... 122 A3
Red Rails. Luton LU1 ... 63 C5

Red Rd. Bor WD6 ... 169 F6
Redan Rd. Ware SG12 ... 93 E3
Redbourn Ind Est. Red ... 106 B5
Redbourn Inf Sch. Red ... 106 A6
Redbourn Jun Sch. Red ... 106 A6
Redbourn La. Harp AL5 ... 106 E6
Redbourn Rd. Heml H HP2 125 A6
Redbourn Rd. Heml H HP2 125 B8
Redbourn Rd. St Alb AL3 .. 126 E7
Redbournbury La.
Red AL3 ... 106 D2
Redcar Dr. Stev SG1 ... 50 A6
Redding House.
Watf WD1 ... 166 E3
Redding La. Red AL3 ... 105 F8
Reddings Ave. Bus WD2 .. 168 B4
Reddings Cty Prim Sch The.
Heml H ... 125 A1
Reddings. Heml H HP3 ... 125 A1
Reddings The. Bor WD6 .. 169 F6
Reddings. Wel G C AL8 ... 110 C7
Redfern Ct. Luton LU1 ... 63 A6
Redferns Cl. Luton LU1 ... 63 A6
Redgrave Gdns. Luton LU3 44 F7
Redhall Cl. Hat AL10 ... 129 F1
Redhall Dr. Hat AL10 ... 129 F1
Redhall La. Coln H AL4 ... 129 E1
Redhall La. Sar WD3 ... 165 E8
Redheath Cl. Watf WD2 ... 153 F4
Redhill Rd. Hit SG5 ... 34 D8
Redhoods Way E.
Letw SG6 ... 22 E7
Redhoods Way W.
Letw SG6 ... 22 E6
Redlands Rd. Enf EN3 ... 162 E1
Redmire Cl. Luton LU4 ... 44 B6
Redricks La. Saw CM21 ... 118 B7
Redvers Cl. Bis St CM23 ... 59 A2
Redwell Ct. Ches EN8 ... 162 F5
Redwood Cl. Sth Ox WD1 175 D6
Redwood Dr.
Heml H HP3 ... 124 E1
Redwood Dr. Luton LU3 ... 44 C8
Redwood Rise. Bor WD6 . 157 B2
Redwood Way. Barn EN5 . 171 D4
Redwoods. Hert AL8 ... 113 C7
Redwoods. Wel G C AL8 ... 89 D3
Reed Cl. Lon C AL2 ... 142 E4
Reed Jun Mix Inf Sch.
Reed ... 16 E5
Reed Pl. Harp AL5 ... 85 F3 1
Reedham Cl. Bri Wd AL2 .. 141 A2
Reedings Jun Sch. Saw ... 97 E3
Reedings Way. Saw CM21 . 97 F4
Reeds Cres. Watf WD1 ... 167 C7
Reeds The. Wel G C AL7 .. 110 D5
Reedsdale. Luton LU2 ... 46 F2
Reeves Ave. Luton LU3 ... 45 B4
Reeves Pightle. Gt Ch SG8 ... 9 F3
Regal Cl. Stand SG11 ... 55 E2
Regal Ct. Hit SG5 ... 34 F8 4
Regal Way. Watf WD2 ... 154 C1
Regency Cl. Bis St CM23 ... 76 E7
Regency Heights.
Heml H HP2 ... 124 D3
Regent Cl. Kin L WD4 ... 139 A3
Regent Cl. St Alb AL4 ... 128 C7
Regent Cl. Wel G C AL7 ... 110 E5
Regent Ct. Stot SG5 ... 11 F7
Regent Gate. Ches EN8 ... 162 E5
Regent St. Luton LU1 ... 63 E7
Regent St. Stot SG5 ... 11 F7
Regent St. Watf WD2 ... 154 B1
Regents Cl. Radl WD7 ... 156 A5
Regina Cl. Barn EN5 ... 171 D6
Reginald Rd. Norwd HA6 . 174 F3
Reginald St. Luton LU2 ... 45 E1
Rendlesham Ave.
Radl WD7 ... 155 F2
Rendlesham Cl.
Ware SG12 ... 93 B2
Rendlesham Rd. Enf EN2 . 161 B1
Rendlesham Way.
Chor WD3 ... 164 C3
Rennison Cl. Ham St EN7 . 147 F4
Renshaw Cl. Luton LU2 ... 46 E2
Repton Cl. Luton LU3 ... 44 F6
Repton Gn. St Alb AL3 ... 127 D6
Repton Way. Cro Gr WD3 166 A4
Reson Way. Heml H HP1 . 124 B2
Reston Cl. Bor WD6 ... 157 B1
Retford Cl. Bor WD6 ... 157 A1
Retreat The. Abb L WD5 .. 153 C8
Revels Cl. Hert SG14 ... 113 D8
Revels Rd. Hert SG14 ... 113 D8
Reynard Copse.
Bis St CM23 ... 58 F1
Reynard Way. Hert SG13 . 114 B6
Reynard's Way.
Bri Wd AL2 ... 140 F2
Reynards Rd. Welw AL6 ... 89 C7
Reynolds Cl. Heml H HP1 . 124 A4
Reynolds Cres. Sand AL4 . 128 B8
Reynolds. Letw SG6 ... 11 F1
Rhee Spring. Bal SG7 ... 13 B1
Rhodes Ave. Bis St CM23 ... 76 F5
Rhodes Memorial Mus &
Commonwealth
Ctr. Bis St ... 77 A6
Rhodes Way. Watf WD2 .. 167 D8
Rib Cl. Stand SG11 ... 55 E2
Rib Vale. Hert SG14 ... 92 D1
Ribbledale. Lon C AL2 ... 142 F4
Ribblesdale. Heml H HP2 . 124 E6
Ribocon Way. Luton LU4 ... 44 B7
Ribston Cl. Shen WD7 ... 156 D6
Rice Cl. Heml H HP2 ... 124 F4
Richard Ct. Barn EN5 ... 171 E6
Richard Hale Sch. Hert ... 113 D5
Richard Stagg Cl.
St Alb AL1 ... 128 C1
Richard Whittington Jun
Mix Inf Sch. Bis St ... 76 E4
Richards Cl. Bus WD2 ... 168 D2
Richards Cl. Luton LU1 ... 63 B6
Richards Ct. Luton LU1 ... 63 B6
Richardson Cl. Lon C AL2 . 142 E4
Richardson Pl. Coln H AL4 129 B1
Richfield Rd. Bus WD2 ... 168 C2
Richmond Cl. Bis St CM23 .. 76 C7
Richmond Cl. Ches EN8 ... 148 C2
Richmond Cl. Ware SG12 ... 93 B3
Richmond Ct. Hat AL10 ... 130 B3 4
Richmond Ct. Hod EN10 ... 134 F3
Richmond Ct. Luton LU2 ... 45 F1
Richmond Ct. Pot B EN6 ... 159 C8
Richmond Dr. Watf WD1 . 166 E7
Richmond Gdns. Har HA3 176 F3
Richmond Gn. Abb L WD5 139 F4
Richmond Hill. Luton LU2 ... 45 F2
Richmond Hill Sch. Luton ... 45 E2
Richmond Rd. Pot B EN6 .. 159 C8
Richmond Way.
Cro Gr WD3 ... 166 C5
Richmond Wlk. St Alb AL4 128 D7
Rickfield Cl. Hat AL10 ... 130 A3
Rickmansworth La.
C St P SL9 ... 172 A5
Rickmansworth Park Jun
Mix Inf Sch. Ric ... 165 E2
Rickmansworth Rd.
Chor WD3 ... 164 F5
Rickmansworth Rd.
Cro Gr WD1 ... 166 E5
Rickmansworth Rd.
Hare UB9 ... 173 D3
Rickmansworth Rd.
Norwd HA6 ... 174 D3
Rickmansworth Rd.
Pnr HA5 ... 175 C1
Rickmansworth Rd.
Watf WD1 ... 166 E5
Rickmansworth Rd.
Watf WD1 ... 167 B6
Rickmansworth Sch.
Cro Gr ... 165 F3
Rickmansworth Sta. Ric ... 165 D2
Rickyard Cl. Luton LU2 ... 46 B3
Rickyard Meadow.
Red AL3 ... 106 A5
Rickyard The. Ashw SG7 ... 4 D4
Rickyard The. Letw SG7 ... 12 C1
Riddell Gdns. Bal SG7 ... 23 F8
Riddy Hill Cl. Hit SG4 ... 35 A6
Riddy La. Hit SG4 ... 35 A6
Riddy La. Luton LU3 ... 45 C5
Riddy The. Cod SG4 ... 88 F8
Ridge Ave. Harp AL5 ... 85 E4
Ridge Ave. Letw SG6 ... 23 A6
Ridge Ct. Luton LU2 ... 46 A1
Ridge La. Watf WD1 ... 153 F2
Ridge Lea. Heml H HP1 ... 123 F2
Ridge Rd. Letw SG6 ... 23 A6
Ridge St. Watf WD2 ... 154 B1
Ridge The. Barn EN5 ... 171 F4
Ridge The. Letw SG6 ... 23 A6
Ridge The. Norwd HA6 ... 174 F3
Ridge View. Tri HP23 ... 100 C5
Ridge Way. Ric WD3 ... 165 B2
Ridgedown. Red AL3 ... 106 A5
Ridgefield. Watf WD1 ... 153 E2
Ridgehurst Ave.
Watf WD2 ... 153 F5
Ridgeview Cl. Barn EN5 ... 171 D3
Ridgeway. Berk HP4 ... 121 F4
Ridgeway Cl. Heml H HP3 138 F5
Ridgeway Ct. Pnr HA5 ... 176 A3
Ridgeway. Harp AL5 ... 85 E4
Ridgeway. Ken Co LU6 ... 82 E8
Ridgeway. L Had SG11 ... 57 B1
Ridgeway. Stev SG1 ... 50 F5
Ridgeway The. Cod SG4 ... 67 F1
Ridgeway The. Cuf EN6 ... 146 A4
Ridgeway The.
Had W EN2,EN4 ... 160 D3
Ridgeway The. Hert SG14 112 F7
Ridgeway The. Hit SG5 ... 34 D6
Ridgeway The. Radl WD7 155 F2
Ridgeway The. St Alb AL4 128 C7
Ridgeway The. Ware SG12 93 C3
Ridgeway The. Watf WD1 153 E2
Ridgeway. Wel G C AL7 ... 111 B6
Ridgewood Dr. Harp AL5 ... 85 E4
Ridgewood Gdns.
Harp AL5 ... 85 E4
Ridgmont Rd. St Alb AL1 .. 127 E2
Ridgway Rd. Luton LU2 ... 45 F1
Ridings The. Bis St CM23 ... 76 D4
Ridings The. Hert SG14 ... 113 A5
Ridings The. Lat HP5 ... 150 D3
Ridings The. Luton LU3 ... 45 C1
Ridings The. Mark AL3 ... 83 E6
Ridings The. Stev SG2 ... 51 B3
Ridler Rd. Enf EN1 ... 161 E1
Ridlins End. Stev SG2 ... 51 C2
Rigery La. Stand SG11 ... 72 F6
Riley Rd. Enf EN3 ... 162 C1
Ringshall Dr. L Gad HP4 .. 102 C8
Ringshall Rd. Dagn HP4 ... 81 B3
Ringtale Pl. Bal SG7 ... 13 B1
Ringway Rd. Chis AL2 ... 141 C4
Ringwood Rd. Luton LU2 ... 45 D6
Ripley Rd. Dun LU4 ... 44 C1
Ripley Rd. Enf EN2 ... 161 C1
Ripley Way. Ches EN7 ... 148 B1
Ripley Way. Heml H HP1 . 123 E4
Ripon Rd. Stev SG1 ... 37 A2
Ripon Way. Bor WD6 ... 170 D4
Ripon Way. St Alb AL4 ... 128 D7
Rise Cotts. Hun SG12 ... 95 D2
Rise The. Bal SG7 ... 23 E7
Rise The. Bor WD6 ... 169 F4
Rise The. Pk St AL2 ... 141 D6
Risedale Cl. Heml H HP3 . 138 E8
Risedale Hill. Heml H HP3 138 E8
Risedale Rd. Heml H HP3 138 E8
Rising Hill Cl. Norwd HA6 174 C4
Risingholme Cl. Bus WD2 168 B2
Risingholme Cl. Har HA3 . 176 E2
Risingholme Rd. Har HA3 176 E1
Ritcroft Cl. Heml H HP3 ... 125 B2
Ritcroft Dr. Heml H HP3 .. 125 B2
Ritcroft St. Heml H HP3 ... 125 B2
Ritz Ct. Pot B EN6 ... 159 A8
Rivenhall End.
Wel G C AL7 ... 111 C6
River Ave. Hod EN11 ... 135 B7
River Cl. Ches EN8 ... 163 A5
River Ct. Ick SG5 ... 21 F4
River Ct. Sac SG14 ... 92 E4
River Gn. Bun SG9 ... 40 E8
River Hill. Fla AL3 ... 84 B2
River Mead. Hit SG5 ... 21 C2
River Meads. Gt Am SG12 115 C4
River Park Ind Est. Berk .. 122 A5
River Pk. Heml H HP1 ... 124 A1
River St. Ware SG12 ... 93 E1
River View. Wel G C AL7 ... 89 F2
River Way. Harl CM20 ... 118 A5
River Way. Harl CM20 ... 118 C6
River Way. Luton LU3 ... 44 E5
Riverfield La. Saw CM21 ... 97 E3
Riverford Cl. Harp AL5 ... 86 B4
Rivermill Adult Education Ctr.
Harl ... 117 C2
Rivermill Ct. Royst SG8 ... 7 C7
Rivermill. Harl CM20 ... 117 C2
Rivers Hospl The. Saw ... 97 C1
Riversend Rd.
Heml H HP3 ... 138 C8
Rivershill. Wat St SG14 ... 70 E3
Riverside Ave.
Lo Naz EN10 ... 135 A1
Riverside. Bis St CM23 ... 76 F7
Riverside. Bun SG9 ... 40 E7
Riverside Cl. Kin L WD4 ... 139 B2
Riverside Cl. St Alb AL1 ... 127 E1
Riverside Cotts.
Gt Am SG12 ... 115 C4
Riverside Ct. Saw CM17 .. 118 C6
Riverside Ct. St Alb AL1 ... 127 E1
Riverside Dr. Ric WD3 ... 165 D1
Riverside Gdns. Berk HP4 122 A5
Riverside Mews.
Ware SG12 ... 93 D1 7
Riverside Path. Ches EN8 148 C2
Riverside Rd. Luton LU3 ... 45 A5
Riverside Rd. St Alb AL1 .. 127 E2
Riverside Rd. Watf WD1 .. 167 B3
Riverside. Welw AL6 ... 89 B5
Riverside Wlk. Bis St CM23 76 F7
Riversmead. Hod EN11 ... 135 A5
Riversmeet. Hert SG14 ... 113 B5
Rivett Cl. Bal SG7 ... 13 A1
Roan Wlk. Royst SG8 ... 7 E6
Roaring Meg Ret &
Leisure Pk. Stev ... 50 D3
Robbery Bottom La.
Welw AL6 ... 90 A8
Robbs Cl. Heml H HP1 ... 124 A5
Robe End. Heml H HP1 ... 123 F5
Robert Allen Ct. Luton LU1 63 E6 1
Robert Ave. St Alb AL1 ... 141 C7
Robert Cl. Pot B EN6 ... 158 E6
Robert Humbert House.
Letw SG6 ... 23 A5
Robert Saunders Ct.
Letw SG6 ... 22 E4
Robert Tebbutt Ct. Hit SG5 34 E6
Robert Wallace Cl.
Bis St CM23 ... 58 F1
Roberts La. C St P SL9 ... 172 B5
Roberts Rd. Watf WD1 ... 167 C4
Roberts Way. Hat AL10 ... 129 F3
Roberts Wood Dr.
C St P SL9 ... 172 A5
Robertson Cl. Ches EN10 . 148 E5
Robeson Way. Bor WD6 .. 170 C8
Robin Cl. Gt Am SG12 ... 115 C3
Robin Hill. Berk HP4 ... 122 C3
Robin Hood Dr. Bus WD2 . 167 F8
Robin Hood Dr. Har HA3 .. 176 F3
Robin Hood La. Hat AL10 . 130 A6
Robin Hood Meadow.
Heml H HP2 ... 124 F8
Robin Mead. Wel G C AL7 .. 90 A1
Robin Way. Cuf EN6 ... 146 E3
Robina Cl. Norwd HA6 ... 174 F2
Robins Nest Hill.
L Berk SG13 ... 132 C6
Robins Rd. Heml H HP3 ... 125 A1
Robins Way. Hat AL10 ... 129 F2
Robinsfield. Heml H HP1 . 124 A3
Robinson Ave. Gofs O EN7 147 B3
Robinson Cl. Bis St CM23 .. 76 F5
Robinson Cres. Bus WD2 . 168 C1
Robinsway. Wa Aby EN9 .. 163 E5
Robinswood. Luton LU2 ... 45 E5
Robsons Cl. Ches EN8 ... 148 C2
Rochdale Ct. Luton LU1 ... 63 E6 2
Rochester Ave. Luton LU2 . 46 C4
Rochester Dr. Watf WD2 . 154 C4
Rochester Way.
Cro Gr WD3 ... 166 B5
Rochester Way. Royst SG8 .. 7 D8
Rochford Ave.
Wa Aby EN9 ... 163 D5
Rochford Cl. Ches EN10 ... 148 E5
Rochford Dr. Luton LU2 ... 46 E2
Rochford Rd. Bis St CM23 .. 59 C1
Rock Rd. Royst SG8 ... 7 C8
Rockfield Ave. Ware SG12 . 93 D3
Rockingham Way.
Stev SG1 ... 50 E4
Rockleigh. Hert SG14 ... 113 C6
Rockley Rd. Luton LU1 ... 63 A7
Rockliffe Ave. Kin L WD4 . 139 A1
Rockways. Edg EN5 ... 170 F3
Rodeheath. Luton LU4 ... 44 D3
Roden Cl. Harl CM17 ... 118 F4
Rodgers Cl. Elst WD6 ... 169 D3
Rodings The. Barn EN5 ... 171 E5
Rodney Ave. St Alb AL1 ... 128 A1
Rodney Cres. Hod EN11 ... 135 A8
Roe Cl. Stot SG5 ... 11 E5
Roe End La. Mark AL3 ... 83 B4
Roe Green Cl. Hat AL10 ... 129 F4
Roe Green Ctr. Hat AL10 . 129 F4
Roe Green La. Hat AL10 .. 129 F5
Roe Hill Cl. Hat AL10 ... 129 F4
Roebuck Cl. Luton LU1 ... 63 B6
Roebuck Ct. Stev SG2 ... 50 F1 1
Roebuck Gate. Stev SG2 ... 50 F1
Roebuck Jun Mix & Inf Sch.
Stev ... 50 F2
Roebuck Ret Pk. Stev ... 50 E2
Roedean Ave. Enf EN3 ... 162 C1
Roedean Cl. Luton LU2 ... 46 D3
Roefields Cl. Heml H HP3 138 A7
Roehyde Way. Hat AL10 .. 129 E2
Roestock Gdns.
Coln H AL4 ... 129 E1
Roestock La. Coln H AL4 .. 129 E1
Rofant Rd. Norwd HA6 ... 174 E4
Rogate Rd. Luton LU2 ... 46 C5
Roger de Clare Fst Sch.
Stand ... 55 E2
Rogers Ruff. Norwd HA6 . 174 C2
Rokewood Mews.
Ware SG12 ... 93 D2 3
Roland St. St Alb AL1 ... 128 B2
Rolleston Cl. Ware SG12 ... 93 C3
Rollswood Rd. Welw AL6 ... 89 B8
Rollswood. Wel G C AL7 .. 110 E3
Rollys La. Ashw SG7 ... 4 D4
Roman Gdns. Abb L WD4 . 139 B1
Roman La. Bal SG7 ... 24 A8
Roman Rd. Luton LU3,LU4 . 44 E3
Roman St. Hod EN11 ... 135 A7
Roman Vale. Harl CM17 ... 118 C5
Roman Way Fst Sch. Royst .. 7 C8
Roman Way. Mark AL3 ... 83 E6
Roman Way. Stand SG11 ... 55 D3
Roman Way. Welw AL6 ... 89 C6
Romans Rise. Saw CM21 ... 97 D2
Romany Cl. Letw SG6 ... 22 C6
Romeland. Elst WD6 ... 169 D3
Romeland Hill. St Alb AL3 127 C3
Romeland. St Alb AL3 ... 127 C3
Romeland. Wa Aby EN9 ... 163 C6
Romilly Dr. Sth Ox WD1 ... 175 F6
Rondini Ave. Luton LU3 ... 45 B3
Rook Tree Cl. Stot SG5 ... 12 A6
Rook Tree La. Stot SG5 ... 12 A6
Rookery Dr. Luton LU2 ... 45 E6
Rookery The. Hat AL9 ... 144 D8
Rookery The. Sta M CM24 . 59 E8
Rookery The. West SG9 ... 40 F3
Rookery Yd. Stev SG1 ... 50 C7
Rookes Cl. Letw SG6 ... 23 B3
Rooks Cl. Wel G C AL8 ... 110 D5
Rooks Hill. Ric WD3 ... 165 D5
Rooks Hill. Wel G C AL8 ... 110 C5
Rooks Nest La. Ther SG8 ... 16 A5
Rookwood Dr. Stev SG2 ... 51 B1
Rosary Ct. Pot B EN6 ... 145 B1
Rose Acre. Red AL3 ... 105 F6
Rose Cl. Hat AL10 ... 130 A8
Rose Cotts. Wyd SG9 ... 28 A3
Rose Ct. Ham St LU6 ... 148 A4
Rose Ct. St Alb AL4 ... 128 C5
Rose Gdns. Watf WD1 ... 167 A4
Rose La. Ess AL9 ... 131 C5
Rose La. Whea AL4 ... 87 C2
Rose Lawn. Bus WD2 ... 168 C1
Rose Mead. Pot B EN6 ... 145 C1
Rose Meadow. Gt Ho SG11 41 E4
Rose Vale. Hod EN11 ... 135 A6
Rose Wlk. Royst SG8 ... 7 C7
Rose Wlk. St Alb AL4 ... 128 C5
Rose Wlk The. Radl WD7 . 156 B3
Rose Wood Cl. Luton LU2 ... 45 F3
Roseacre Gdns.
Wel G C AL7 ... 111 D6
Roseacres. Saw CM21 ... 97 D3
Rosebank. Wa Aby EN9 ... 163 E6
Roseberry Ct. Watf WD1 . 167 A8
Rosebery Ave. Harp AL5 ... 85 F1
Rosebery. Bis St CM23 ... 77 C6
Rosebery Mews. Men LU7 . 61 D4
Rosebery Rd. Bus WD2 ... 168 B2
Rosebery Way. Tri HP23 . 100 B5
Rosebriar Wlk. Watf WD2 153 F3
Rosecroft Ave. St Alb AL4 128 C1
Rosecroft Ct. Norwd HA6 174 C4
Rosecroft Dr. Watf WD1 .. 153 E3
Rosecroft La. Welw AL6 ... 90 A8
Rosecroft Sch. Stot ... 11 F6
Rosedale Ave. Gofs O EN7 147 F2
Rosedale Cl. Bri Wd AL2 .. 140 E1
Rosedale Cl. Luton LU3 ... 44 C7
Rosedale Way. Ches EN7 148 A3
Rosedale. Wel G C AL7 ... 89 F2
Roseheath. Heml H HP1 .. 123 E4
Rosehill. Berk HP4 ... 122 B4
Rosehill Cl. Hod EN11 ... 134 F6
Rosehill Ct. Heml H HP1 .. 124 A1
Rosehill Gdns. Abb L WD5 153 C7
Rosehill Hospl. Hit ... 22 D2
Roselands Ave. Hod EN11 114 F1
Roselands Jun Mix Inf Sch.
Hod ... 114 F1
Rosemary Cl. Harl CM17 .. 118 C4
Rosemont Cl. Letw SG6 ... 22 E6
Rosewood Ct. Heml H HP1 123 E4
Rosewood Dr. Cre H EN2 . 161 A4
Roslyn Cl. Hod EN10 ... 134 E2
Ross Cl. Luton LU1 ... 63 B6
Ross Cl. Stan HA3 ... 176 C3
Ross Cres. Watf WD2 ... 154 A4
Ross Ct. Stev SG2 ... 51 B7
Ross Way. Mo Pk HA6 ... 174 F6
Rossfold Rd. Luton LU3 ... 44 D8
Rossgate. Heml H HP1 ... 124 A5
Rossgate Sch. Heml H ... 124 A5
Rossington Ave. Bor WD6 156 E1
Rossiter Fields. Barn EN5 171 F3
Rosslyn Cres. Luton LU3 ... 45 C5
Rosslyn Rd. Watf WD1 ... 167 B6
Rossway. Cad LU1 ... 63 B1
Rossway Dr. Bus WD2 ... 168 D4
Rossway La. Wigg HP4 ... 121 A7

Roswell Cl. Ches EN8 ... 148 E1
Rothamsted Ave. Harp AL5 86 A1
Rothamsted Ct. Harp AL5 .. 86 A1
Rothamsted Experimental Sta. Harp ... 107 A8
Rother Cl. Watf WD2 ... 154 C5
Rother Field. Luton LU2 ... 46 D3
Rotheram Ave. Luton LU1 .. 63 B5
Rotherfield Rd. Enf EN3 ... 162 D2
Rothesay Ct. Berk HP4 ... 122 A4
Rothesay Rd. Luton LU1 ... 63 D7
Roughdown Ave. Heml H HP3 ... 138 A8
Roughdown Rd. Heml H HP3 ... 138 B8
Roughdown Villas Rd. Heml H HP3 ... 138 A8
Roughs The. Mo Pk HA6 .. 174 E7
Roughwood Cl. Watf WD1 153 E1
Round Diamond Jun Mix Inf Sch. Stev ... 51 B8
Roundabout La. Welw AL6 . 89 F8
Roundcroft. Ham St EN7 .. 147 F5
Roundfield Ave. Harp AL5 .. 86 D3
Roundhaye. Stand SG11 ... 55 D3
Roundhedge Way. Enf EN2 ... 160 F1
Roundhills. Wa Aby EN9 .. 163 E4
Roundings The. Hert H SG13 ... 114 C2
Roundmoor Dr. Ches EN8 148 E2
Roundway The. Watf WD1 166 F2
Roundwood Cl. Hit SG4 ... 22 C2
Roundwood Cl. Welw AL6 .. 89 D8
Roundwood Dr. Wel G C AL8 ... 110 C7
Roundwood Gdns. Harp AL5 ... 85 E2
Roundwood. Kin L HP3 ... 138 E4
Roundwood La. Harp AL5 .. 85 D3
Roundwood Park Sch & Roundwood Jun Mix Inf Sch. Harp ... 85 E2
Roundwood Pk. Harp AL5 .. 85 E3
Rounton Rd. Wa Aby EN9 163 E6
Rousebarn La. Sar WD3 .. 166 C7
Rowan Cl. Bri Wd AL2 ... 155 A8
Rowan Cl. Coln H AL4 ... 128 E3
Rowan Cl. Har HA7 ... 176 F4
Rowan Cl. Luton LU1 ... 63 B7
Rowan Cl. Wes SG4 ... 37 B8
Rowan Cres. Letw SG6 ... 22 E7
Rowan Cres. Stev SG1 ... 50 E7
Rowan Dr. Ches EN10 ... 148 F6
Rowan Gr. Hit SG4 ... 35 A4
Rowan Way. Harp AL5 ... 107 C8
Rowan Wlk. Hat AL10 ... 130 A2 2
Rowans Jun Mix Inf Sch The. Wel G C ... 90 A1
Rowans The. Bal SG7 ... 23 E7
Rowans The. Heml H HP1 124 A3
Rowans The. Hod EN10 ... 134 F4
Rowans. Wel G C AL7 ... 90 A1
Rowcroft. Heml H HP1 ... 123 E2
Rowelfield. Luton LU2 ... 46 C1
Rowington Cl. Luton LU2 ... 46 E2
Rowland Pl. Norwd HA6 .. 174 E3
Rowland Rd. Stev SG1 ... 50 F4
Rowland Way. Letw SG6 ... 22 F6
Rowlands Ave. Pnr HA5 ... 176 B4
Rowlands Cl. Ches EN8 ... 148 D1
Rowlands Ct. Ches EN8 ... 148 D1
Rowlatt Dr. St Alb AL3 ... 127 A1
Rowley Cl. Watf WD1 ... 167 E3
Rowley Gdns. Ches EN8 ... 148 D3
Rowley Green Rd. Barn EN5 ... 171 A4
Rowley La. Bor WD6 ... 170 D7
Rowley La. Edg EN5 ... 170 F5
Rowley's Rd. Hert SG13 ... 113 F7
Rowney Gdns. Saw CM21 118 C8
Rowney La. Dan En SG12 ... 72 B5
Rowney Wood. Saw CM21 . 97 C1
Rows The. Harl CM20 ... 117 D1
Roy Rd. Norwd HA6 ... 174 F3
Royal Ave. Ches EN8 ... 162 E6
Royal Caledonian Schs. Bus ... 168 A7
Royal Ct. Heml H HP3 ... 138 E8
Royal Masonic Sch. Ric ... 165 D4
Royal National Orthopaedic Hospl. Stan ... 169 B1
Royal Oak Cl. Buck SG9 ... 27 D5
Royal Oak Gdns. Bis St CM23 ... 76 F6
Royal Oak La. Pirt SG5 ... 20 D4
Royal Rd. St Alb AL1 ... 128 B3
Royal Veterinary Coll. Bro Pk ... 144 D3
Royce Cl. Hod EN10 ... 134 F2
Roydon Cl. Dun LU4 ... 44 A4
Roydon Ct. Heml H HP2 ... 105 A1
Roydon Lodge Chalet Est. Roy ... 116 C1
Roydon Mill Leisure Pk. Roy ... 116 A1
Roydon Rd. Roy CM19 ... 116 E1
Roydon Rd. Sta Ab SG12 .. 115 E4
Royse Gr. Royst SG8 ... 7 D4
Royslo Mid Sch. Royst ... 7 D8
Royston Cl. Hert SG14 ... 113 B6
Royston Gr. Pnr HA5 ... 176 A4
Royston Hospl. Royst ... 7 D4
Royston Park Rd. Pnr HA5 176 A5
Royston Rd. Bal SG7 ... 13 C2
Royston Rd. Bar SG8 ... 8 F3
Royston Rd. Bark SG8 ... 17 C5
Royston Rd. Clo SG7 ... 13 C2
Royston Rd. St Alb AL1 ... 128 B2
Royston Sta. Royst ... 7 C7
Rucklers La. Kin L WD4 ... 138 C4
Ruckles Cl. Stev SG1 ... 50 E5
Rudd Cl. Stev SG2 ... 51 B3
Rudham Gr. Letw SG6 ... 23 C3
Rudolf Steiner Sch The. Kin L ... 138 E2
Rudolph Rd. Bus WD2 ... 168 A3
Rudyard Cl. Luton LU4 ... 44 D3
Rue de St Lawrence. Wa Aby EN9 ... 163 C5
Rueley Dell Rd. Lily LU2 ... 32 D2
Rugby Way. Cro Gr WD3 . 166 B4
Ruins The. Red AL3 ... 106 B5
Rumballs Cl. Heml H HP3 139 A8
Rumballs Rd. Heml H HP3 139 A8
Rumbold Rd. Hod EN11 ... 135 C8
Rumsley. Ham St EN7 ... 148 A4
Runcie Cl. St Alb AL4 ... 128 A7
Runcorn Cres. Heml H HP2 ... 124 F7
Rundells. Letw SG6 ... 23 D4
Runfold Ave. Luton LU3 ... 45 A5
Runham Cl. Dun LU4 ... 44 A4
Runham Rd. Heml H HP3 . 124 E1
Runley Rd. Luton LU1 ... 62 F7
Runnalow. Letw SG6 ... 22 F7
Runsley. Wel G C AL7 ... 90 A1
Ruscombe Dr. Chis AL2 ... 141 C5
Rush Cl. Gt Am SG12 ... 115 C4
Rushall Gn. Luton LU2 ... 46 E2
Rushby Mead. Letw SG6 ... 23 A5
Rushby Pl. Letw SG6 ... 23 A5
Rushby Wlk. Letw SG6 ... 23 A6
Rushden Rd. San SG9 ... 26 A8
Rushen Dr. Hert H SG13 .. 114 C3
Rushendon Furlong. Pit LU7 ... 80 E5
Rushes Ct. Bis St CM23 ... 77 A5
Rushfield. Pot B EN6 ... 158 E6
Rushfield Rd. Ware SG12 .. 93 F3
Rushfield. Saw CM21 ... 97 E2
Rushleigh Ave. Ches EN8 . 148 D1
Rushleigh Gn. Bis St CM23 76 D4
Rushmere La. Ash Gr HP5 136 B3
Rushmoor Cl. Ric WD3 ... 173 D8
Rushmore Cl. Cad LU1 ... 62 E5
Rushton Ave. Watf WD2 .. 154 A4
Rushton Ct. Ches EN8 ... 148 D2
Ruskin Ave. Wa Aby EN9 . 163 E5
Ruskin Cl. Ham St EN7 ... 147 E5
Ruskin La. Hit SG4 ... 35 C7
Rusper Gn. Luton LU2 ... 46 D3
Russell Ave. St Alb AL3 ... 127 D3
Russell Cl. Ken Co LU6 ... 82 E8
Russell Cl. Stev SG2 ... 51 B2
Russell Cres. Watf WD2 .. 153 F4
Russell Ct. Bri Wd AL2 ... 141 A1
Russell Cty Prim Sch. Chor 164 B5
Russell La. Watf WD1 ... 153 D3
Russell Pl. Heml H HP3 ... 138 B8
Russell Rd. Enf EN1 ... 161 F1
Russell Rd. Mo Pk HA6 ... 174 C6
Russell Rise. Luton LU1 ... 63 D6
Russell St. Hert SG14 ... 113 C6
Russell St. Luton LU1 ... 63 D6
Russell Way. Mo Pk HA6 . 174 C5
Russell's Ride. Ches EN8 . 162 E8
Russellcroft Rd. Wel G C AL8 ... 110 C7
Russet Cl. Ham St EN7 ... 147 E5
Russet Dr. St Alb AL4 ... 128 D2
Russett House. Wel G C AL7 ... 111 D6
Russett Wood. Wel G C AL7 ... 111 D5
Rutherford Cl. Bor WD6 ... 170 C7
Rutherford Cl. Stev SG1 ... 50 B6
Rutherford Way. Bus WD2 168 E1
Ruthin Cl. Luton LU1 ... 63 D5
Ruthven Ave. Ches EN8 ... 162 D6
Rutland Cres. Luton LU2 ... 64 A7
Rutland Pl. Bus WD2 ... 168 D1
Rutts The. Bus WD2 ... 168 D1
Ryall Cl. Bri Wd AL2 ... 140 E2
Rydal Ct. Watf WD2 ... 154 B7
Rydal Mount. Pot B EN6 ... 158 E6
Rydal Way. Luton LU3 ... 44 F5
Ryde Sch The. Hat ... 130 C8
Ryde The. Hat AL9 ... 130 C8
Ryder Ave. Ick SG5 ... 21 D3
Ryder Cl. Bov HP3 ... 137 A4
Ryder Cl. Bus WD2 ... 168 B3
Ryder Cl. Hert SG13 ... 114 B7
Ryder Way. Ick SG5 ... 21 D3
Ryders Ave. Coln H AL4 ... 129 E3
Rye Cl. Harp AL5 ... 86 B4
Rye Gdns. Bal SG7 ... 13 B1
Rye Hill. Harp AL5 ... 86 B4
Rye House Sta. Hod ... 135 C8
Rye Rd. Hod EN11 ... 135 C8
Rye Rd. Sta Ab EN11 ... 115 D1
Rye St. Bis St CM23 ... 58 F1
Ryecroft Cl. Heml H HP2 .. 125 C2
Ryecroft Cres. Barn EN5 .. 171 B4
Ryecroft Ct. Coln H AL4 ... 128 F3
Ryecroft. Hat AL10 ... 129 F3
Ryecroft. Stev SG1 ... 50 E7
Ryecroft Way. Luton LU2 ... 46 A4
Ryefeld Cl. Hod EN11 ... 115 B2
Ryefield Cres. Pnr HA6 ... 175 A1
Ryefield. Luton LU3 ... 31 A1
Ryelands Heath. Luton LU2 46 F2
Ryelands. Wel G C AL7 ... 110 F3
Ryley Cl. Henlw SG16 ... 10 B5
Ryman Ct. Chor WD3 ... 164 C3
Rymill Cl. Bov HP3 ... 137 A3
Ryton Cl. Luton LU1 ... 63 B6

Saberton Cl. Red AL3 ... 105 F4
Sabine House. Abb L WD5 153 F7
Sacombe Gn. Luton LU3 ... 31 B1
Sacombe Green Rd. Sac SG12 ... 71 E4
Sacombe Pound. Sac SG12 71 E3
Sacombe Rd. Heml H HP1 123 F5
Sacombe Rd. Hert SG14 ... 92 C1
Sacombe Rd. Stap SG14 ... 92 B4
Sacombs Ash La. H Wy SG10 ... 96 E7
Sacred Heart High Sch. Har ... 176 E1
Sacred Heart Inf Sch. Luton ... 46 A3
Sacred Heart Jun Sch. Luton ... 46 A3
Sacred Heart Jun Sch. St Alb ... 127 B1
Sacred Heart RC Jun Mix Inf Sch. Ware ... 93 D1
Sacred Heart RC Prim Sch The. Bus ... 167 F3
Saddlers Cl. Bal SG7 ... 23 E8
Saddlers Cl. Bor WD6 ... 170 D3
Saddlers Cl. Pnr HA5 ... 176 A4
Saddlers Path. Bor WD6 ... 170 D4
Saddlers Pl. Royst SG8 ... 7 C7
Saddlers Wlk. Kin L WD4 . 139 A2
Sadleir Rd. St Alb AL1 ... 127 E1
Sadlers Way. Hert SG14 .. 113 A6
Sadlier Rd. Stand SG11 ... 55 E2
Saffron Cl. Arl SG15 ... 11 A7
Saffron Cl. Hod EN11 ... 134 F7
Saffron Cl. Luton LU2 ... 45 E6
Saffron Green Prim Sch. Bor ... 170 E5
Saffron Hill. Letw SG6 ... 22 E6
Saffron La. Heml H HP1 ... 124 B4
Saffron Meadow. Stand SG11 ... 55 E2
Saffron St. Royst SG8 ... 7 F5
Sainfoin End. Heml H HP2 125 A5
SS Alban & Stephen Jun Mix Sch. St Alb ... 128 A3
SS Alban & Stephen Sch. St Alb ... 127 F2
St Adrian's RC Prim Sch. St Alb ... 141 C8
St Agnells Ct. Heml H HP2 125 A7
St Agnells La. Heml H HP2 125 A8
St Alban's Cath. St Alb ... 127 D3
St Alban's Sch. St Alb ... 127 C3
St Albans Catholic Prim Sch. Harl ... 117 F2
St Albans City Hospl Mid Herts Wing. St Alb 127 C4
St Albans City Hospl. St Alb ... 127 C5
St Albans City Sta. St Alb . 127 F3
St Albans Coll. St Alb ... 127 E3
St Albans Dr. Stev SG1 ... 36 E1
St Albans Girls' Sch. St Alb ... 127 E7
St Albans High Sch. St Alb 127 E4
St Albans Hill. Heml H HP3 ... 124 F1
St Albans La. Abb L WD5 . 140 A5
St Albans Link. Stev SG1 ... 36 E1
St Albans Music Sch. St Alb ... 127 D6
St Albans Rd. Barn EN5 ... 171 E7
St Albans Rd. Cod SG4 ... 88 F7
St Albans Rd E. Hat AL10 . 130 B6
St Albans Rd. Harp AL5 ... 107 B6
St Albans Rd. Heml H HP2,HP3 ... 124 E2
St Albans Rd. Pot B EN5 .. 158 C3
St Albans Rd. Red AL3 ... 106 C3
St Albans Rd. Ridge AL2,WD6 ... 157 F8
St Albans Rd. Sand AL4 ... 108 B1
St Albans Rd. St Alb AL4 .. 128 A8
St Albans Rd W. Hat AL4 . 129 D5
St Albans Rd. Watf WD1,WD2 ... 167 B7
St Albans Rd. Watf WD2 .. 154 C5
St Albert the Great RC Prim Sch. Heml H ... 125 A2
St Alders Ct. Luton LU3 ... 45 B3
St Andrew St. Hert SG14 . 113 C6
St Andrew's Ave. Harp AL5 ... 85 F1
St Andrew's CE Prim Sch. Hit ... 35 A7
St Andrew's Cl. Cad LU1 ... 63 B1
St Andrew's House. Harl CM20 ... 117 F2
St Andrew's Pl. Hit SG4 ... 34 F6 2
St Andrew's Rd. Heml H HP3 ... 138 D7
St Andrews C of E Jun Mix Inf Sch. Muc H ... 74 F2
St Andrews Dr. Stev SG1 ... 36 F2
St Andrews Jun Mix & Inf Sch. Sta Ab ... 115 D4
St Andrews Mews. Hert SG14 ... 113 C6 1
St Andrews Rd. Sth Ox WD1 ... 175 D7
St Andrews Terr. Sth Ox WD1 ... 175 C5
St Andrews Wlk. Cad LU1 .. 63 C1
St Ann's Rd. Luton LU1 ... 63 F7
St Anna Rd. Barn EN5 ... 171 D4
St Anne's Cl. Ches EN7 ... 148 A3
St Anne's Pk. Hod EN10 ... 135 A4
St Anne's Rd. Hit SG5 ... 34 F8
St Anne's Rd. Lon C AL2 ... 142 D4
St Annes Cl. Sth Ox WD1 . 175 C6
St Anthony's RC Prim Sch. Watf ... 166 E4
St Anthonys Ave. Heml H HP3 ... 125 B1
St Audreys Cl. Hat AL10 ... 130 B2
St Audreys Gn. Wel G C AL7 ... 110 F5
St Augusta Ct. St Alb AL3 . 127 D5
St Augustine Ave. Luton LU3 ... 45 C3
St Augustine Cl. Hit SG5 ... 34 F8 1
St Augustine's RC Jun Mix Inf Sch. Hod ... 135 B5
St Augustines Cl. Hod EN10 ... 134 F3
St Augustines Dr. Hod EN10 ... 134 F3
St Barnabas Ct. Har HA3 . 176 C2
St Barnabas Ct. Heml H HP2 ... 125 A3
St Bartholomew's Prim Sch. Wigg ... 100 D1
St Bernadette's RC Prim Sch. Lon C ... 142 D4
St Bernard's Cl. Luton LU3 45 C3
St Bernard's Rd. St Alb AL3 ... 127 E4
St Brelades Pl. St Alb AL4 128 D7
St Catharine's Rd. Hod EN10 ... 135 A4
St Catherine of Siena RC Jun Mix Inf Sch. Watf .. 154 D6
St Catherines Ave. Luton LU3 ... 45 B3
St Catherines Ct. Bis St CM23 ... 76 E7
St Christopher Sch. Letw ... 22 F3
St Clement Danes Sch. Chor ... 164 D7
St Clement's C of E Jun Mix Sch. Ches ... 148 E4
St Columba's Coll. St Alb . 127 C1
St Cross Ct. Hod EN11 ... 135 A4
St Cross RC Sch. Hod ... 135 A4
St Cuthbert Mayne RC Jun Mix Sch. Heml H ... 124 B4
St Cuthberts Gdns. Pnr HA5 ... 175 F3 1
St Cuthberts Rd. Hod EN11 ... 115 C1
St David's Cl. Heml H HP2 125 D2
St David's Dr. Hod EN10 .. 134 F4
St Davids Cl. Stev SG1 ... 36 F2
St Dominics RC Jun Mix Inf Sch. Harp ... 107 B8
St Dunstan's Rd. Hun SG12 ... 116 D8
St Edmund's Coll. Stand ... 73 A8
St Edmund's Way. Harl CM17 ... 118 C4
St Edmunds. Berk HP4 ... 122 C3
St Edward's Coll. Barn ... 171 B1
St Elizabeth's Sch & Home. Muc H ... 96 C6
St Elmo Ct. Hit SG4 ... 34 F5
St Ethelbert Ave. Luton LU3 45 C4
St Etheldreda's Dr. Hat AL10 ... 130 C5
St Evroul Ct. Ware SG12 ... 93 D2 5
St Faiths Cl. Hit SG4 ... 22 B1
St Francis Cl. Pot B EN6 ... 159 C5
St Francis Cl. Watf WD1 .. 167 B1
St Francis' Coll. Letw ... 22 E4
St Francis Sch. Bun ... 40 F6
St George's C of E Inf Sch. Enf ... 162 D3
St George's Dr. Sth Ox WD1 ... 175 E6
St George's Rd. Enf EN1 .. 161 F1
St George's Rd. Heml H HP3 ... 138 C7
St George's Rd. Watf WD2 ... 154 B2
St George's Sch. Harp ... 86 B2
St George's Way. Stev SG1 50 D5
St Georges Sq. Luton LU1 .. 63 E7
St Giles' Ave. Pot B EN6 ... 158 B7
St Giles' C of E Jun Mix Inf Sch. Pot B ... 158 A7
St Giles Rd. Cod SG4 ... 67 F2
St Helen's Cl. Whea AL4 .. 108 D8
St Helen's Sch. Norwd ... 174 E4
St Helens C of E Prim Sch. Whea ... 108 D8
St Heliers Rd. St Alb AL4 . 128 B8
St Hilda's Sch. Bus ... 168 B2
St Ignatius Coll Upper Sch. Enf ... 162 B2
St Ippollitts CE Sch. St Ipp 35 B3
St Ives Cl. Luton LU3 ... 45 B3
St Ives Cl. Welw AL6 ... 89 F3
St James Ctr. Harl ... 118 A4
St James Rd. Harp AL5 ... 86 B4
St James' Rd. Luton LU3 ... 45 B3
St James Rd. Watf WD1 .. 167 B4
St James Way. Bis St CM23 ... 76 B5
St James's Ct. Harp AL5 ... 86 B3 1
St James's Rd. Gofs O EN7 ... 147 D3
St John Cl. Luton LU1 ... 63 B5
St John Fisher RC Jun Mix Inf Sch. St Alb ... 128 C6
St John the Baptist C of E Sch. Gt Am ... 115 A5
St John's Ave. Harl CM17 118 D4
St John's CE Prim Sch. Cre H ... 161 B2
St John's Cl. Pot B EN6 ... 159 C6
St John's Cres. Sta M CM24 ... 59 E7
St John's Ct. Harp AL5 ... 107 C7
St John's Ct. Hert SG13 ... 113 D6 18
St John's La. Sta M CM24 .. 59 E7
St John's RC Jun Mix & Inf Sch. Bal ... 23 F7
St John's RC Jun Mix Inf Sch. Ric ... 165 B1
St John's Rd. Arl SG15 ... 11 A4
St John's Rd. Harp AL5 ... 107 C7
St John's Rd. Heml H HP1 124 B1
St John's Rd. Hit SG4 ... 34 F6
St John's Rd. Sta M CM24 . 59 E7
St John's Rd. Watf WD1 .. 167 B7
St John's Sch. Hat ... 109 F5
St John's Sch (Jun Mix Inf). Wel G C ... 89 F2
St John's St. Hert SG13 ... 113 D6
St John's Terr. Enf EN2 ... 161 D2
St John's Well Ct. Berk HP4 ... 122 B5
St John's Well La. Berk HP4 ... 122 B5
St Johns Cl. Welw AL6 ... 89 C6

St Johns Ct. Luton LU1 63 B5
St Johns Ct. St Alb AL1 128 B5
St Johns. Stand SG11 55 E3
St Johns Wlk. Harl CM17 118 C4
St Joseph's Cl. Luton LU3 45 A4
St Joseph's Inf Sch. Luton 45 A4
St Joseph's Jun Sch. Luton 45 A4
St Joseph's RC Jun Mix Inf Sch. Bis St 76 E6
St Joseph's RC Jun Mix & Inf Sch. Ches 162 E7
St Joseph's RC Jun Mix Inf Sch. Sth Ox 175 C7
St Joseph's RC Sch. Hert 113 A7
St Joseph's Rd. Ches EN8 162 E6
St Joseph's Sch. Hertng 113 A4
St Joseph's Wlk. Harp AL5 107 A8
St Julian's Rd. St Alb AL1 127 D1
St Katharines Cl. Ick SG5 21 D3
St Katherine's Way. Berk HP4 121 F7
St Laurence Dr. Hod EN10 148 F8
St Lawrence C of E Jun Sch. Wa Aby 163 F6
St Lawrence Cl. Abb L HP3 139 E1
St Lawrence Cl. Bov HP3 137 A4
St Lawrence Way. Bri Wd AL2 140 F1
St Lawrences Ave. Luton LU3 45 C3
St Leonard's Ct. Sand AL4 108 C1
St Leonard's Rd. Hert SG14 113 D8
St Leonards Cl. Hert SG14 113 E8
St Leonards Cl. Watf WD2 167 E5
St Leonards Cres. Sand AL4 108 C1
St Leonards Rd. Lo Naz EN9 149 D6
St Luke's Ave. Enf EN2 161 D1
St Luke's Cl. Luton LU4 44 E2
St Luke's Sch. Red 106 A6
St Margaret Clitheroe RC Prim Sch. Stev 50 F2
St Margaret of Scotland Inf Sch. Luton 63 B5
St Margaret of Scotland Jun Sch. Luton 63 B5
St Margaret's Cl. Berk HP4 122 D3
St Margaret's Lower Sch. Bus 168 B1
St Margaret's Rd. Hod EN11 115 B2
St Margaret's Sch. Bus 168 A2
St Margarets Ave. Luton LU3 45 B3
St Margarets Cl. Str LU3 31 A6
St Margarets Sta. Gt Am 115 C4
St Margarets. Stev SG2 50 F2
St Margarets Way. Heml H HP2 125 D3
St Margaretsbury House. Gt Am SG12 115 B4
St Mark's Cl. Hit SG5 21 D1
St Marks Cl. Coln H AL4 129 B1
St Martha's Convent Sch. Barn 171 E5
St Martin de Parres RC Inf Sch. Dun 44 A4
St Martin de Parres RC Jun Sch. Dun 44 A4
St Martin's Ave. Luton LU2 45 F2
St Martin's Rd. Kneb SG3 69 A5
St Martin's Sch. Norwd 174 D5
St Martins Cl. Harp AL5 86 C4
St Martins Cl. Sth Ox WD1 175 C6
St Mary's Ave. Mo Pk HA6 174 E5
St Mary's Ave. Nthch UB2 121 D6
St Mary's Ave. Stot SG5 11 F6
St Mary's C of E Jun Mix Inf Sch. Wel G 144 B8
St Mary's C of E Prim Sch. Sta M 59 E7
St Mary's C of E Sch. Ric 173 D7
St Mary's Catholic Prim Sch. Royst 7 D7
St Mary's Catholic Sch. Bis St 76 E7
St Mary's Cl. Letw SG6 22 F2
St Mary's Cl. Pirt SG5 20 D4
St Mary's Cl. Red AL3 106 A4
St Mary's Ct. Heml H HP2 124 D4 4
St Mary's Ct. Pot B EN6 159 B7
St Mary's Ct. Welw AL6 89 C4
St Mary's Ctyd. Ware SG12 93 D1 3
St Mary's Dr. Sta M CM24 59 F5
St Mary's High Sch. Ches 148 B1
St Mary's Inf Sch. Bal 23 E6
St Mary's Jun Mix Inf Sch. Ast 51 E2
St Mary's Jun Mix Inf Sch. Welw 89 B4
St Mary's Jun Sch. Bal 23 E6
St Mary's (Kingshill) Jun Mix Inf Sch. Ware 93 D3
St Mary's La. Hertng SG14 112 F3
St Mary's Lower Sch. Stot 12 A6
St Mary's Park Convent Sch. Royst 7 D6
St Mary's Rd. Ches EN8 148 C2
St Mary's Rd. Heml H HP2 124 D4
St Mary's Rd. Luton LU1 63 F7
St Mary's Rd. Stand SG11 55 D2
St Mary's Rd. Watf WD1 167 B5
St Mary's Rise. Bre Gr SG4 47 D1
St Mary's Way. Bal SG7 23 E6
St Marys Cl. Ast SG2 51 E2
St Marys Rd. Welw AL6 89 C5
St Marys Wlk. St Alb AL4 128 B7
St Mathews Cl. Luton LU2 63 E8
St Matthew's Jun Sch. Luton 63 F8
St Matthews Cl. Watf WD1 167 D3
St Meryl Jun Mix Inf Sch. Sth Ox 175 E7
St Michael's Cl. Harl CM20 117 E1
St Michael's Cres. Luton LU3 45 D3
St Michael's Jun Mix & Inf Sch. St Alb 127 B3
St Michael's Mount. Hit SG4 35 A8
St Michael's Prim Sch. Bis St 76 F7
St Michael's Rd. Hod CM7 135 A3
St Michael's Sch. Watf 154 D7
St Michael's St. St Alb AL3 127 B3
St Michaels Ave. Heml H HP3 125 B1
St Michaels Cl. Harp AL5 107 D7
St Michaels Dr. Watf WD2 154 B6
St Michaels Rd. Hit SG4 35 B7
St Michaels View. Hat AL10 130 B7
St Michaels Way. Pot B EN6 145 B1
St Micheals Ct. Stev SG1 51 B8
St Mildreds Ave. Luton LU3 45 C3
St Monicas Ave. Luton LU3 45 B3
St Neots Cl. Bor WD6 157 A1
St Nicholas Ave. Harp AL5 86 A1
St Nicholas CE Jun Mix Inf Sch. Letw 12 C1
St Nicholas Cl. Elst WD6 169 D3
St Nicholas Ct. Harp AL5 85 F3 2
St Nicholas House Sch. Heml H 139 B6
St Nicholas Mount. Heml H HP1 123 F3
St Nicholas Prim Sch. Elst 169 D3
St Ninian's Ct. Luton LU2 63 D8 7
St Olam's Cl. Luton LU3 45 B6
St Olives. Stot SG5 11 E6
St Paul's Jun Mix Inf Sch. Chipf 152 A8
St Paul's Rd. Heml H HP2 124 E4
St Paul's Rd. Luton LU1 63 E5
St Paul's Walden Jun Mix & Inf Sch. Whit 66 D7
St Pauls (C of E) Sch. Abb L 153 C5
St Pauls Catholic Prim Sch. Ham St 148 B4
St Pauls Ct. Stev SG2 50 F1 3
St Pauls Inf Sch. Hod 135 B5
St Pauls Pl. St Alb AL1 128 A3
St Pauls Way. Wa Aby EN9 163 D6
St Pauls Way. Watf WD2 167 C7
St Peter's Ave. Arl SG15 11 A7
St Peter's C of E Prim Sch. Ric 165 B1
St Peter's Cl. Barn EN5 171 B4
St Peter's Cl. Bus WD2 168 D1
St Peter's Cl. Ric WD3 165 B1
St Peter's Cl. St Alb AL1 127 D4
St Peter's Cty Prim Sch. St Alb 127 E2
St Peter's Prim Sch. St Alb 127 E2
St Peter's Rd. St Alb AL1 127 E4
St Peter's St. St Alb AL1 127 D4
St Peters Cl. Hat AL10 130 A6
St Peters Hill. Tri HP23 100 A4
St Peters Rd. Luton LU1 63 B7
St Peters Way. Chor WD3 164 B5
St Philip Howard RC Prim Sch. Hat 130 B5
St Raphaels Ct. St Alb AL1 127 E4
St Ronans Cl. Had W EN4 159 D1
St Rose's Inf Sch. Heml H 124 A1
St Saviours's Cres. Luton LU1 63 D6
St Stephen's Ave. St Alb AL3 141 B8
St Stephen's Cl. St Alb AL3 141 B8
St Stephen's Hill. St Alb AL1 127 C1
St Stephen's Hospl. Barn 171 D4
St Stephen's Rd. Enf EN3 162 D2
St Stephens Rd. Barn EN5 171 D4
St Teresa's Sch. Bor 170 B7
St Thomas' Dr. Pnr HA5 175 E2
St Thomas More Prim Sch. Berk 122 A4
St Thomas More Prim Sch. Letw 22 D4
St Thomas of Canterbury RC Jun Mix Inf Sch. Stand 55 C3
St Thomas Pl. Whea AL4 108 D8
St Thomas's Rd. Luton LU2 46 A4
St Vincent de Paul Jun Mix Inf Sch. Stev 51 A6
St Vincent Dr. St Alb AL1 128 A1
St Vincent's Way. Pot B EN6 159 C6
St Winifreds Ave. Luton LU3 45 C3
St Yon Ct. Coln H AL4 128 E3
Sale Dr. Bal SG7 13 A1
Salisbury Ave. 85 F1
Salisbury Ave. St Alb AL1 128 B4
Salisbury Cl. Bis St CM23 76 F5
Salisbury Cl. Pot B EN6 159 C7
Salisbury Cres. Ches EN8 162 D7
Salisbury Gdns. Wel G C AL7 110 F5
Salisbury House. St Alb AL3 127 C2
Salisbury Inf Sch. Hat 130 B7
Salisbury Rd. Bal SG7 12 F1
Salisbury Rd. Barn EN5 171 E6
Salisbury Rd. Enf EN3 162 F2
Salisbury Rd. Harp AL5 86 D3
Salisbury Rd. Hod EN11 135 C8
Salisbury Rd. Luton LU1 63 D6
Salisbury Rd. Stev SG1 37 A2
Salisbury Rd. Watf WD2 154 C1
Salisbury Rd. Wel G C AL7 111 A5
Salisbury Sq. Hat AL9 130 C6
Salisbury Sq. Hert SG14 113 D6 7
Sally Deards La. Cod AL6 68 B3
Salmon Cl. Wel G C AL7 90 A1
Salmons Cl. Ware SG12 93 D4
Saltdean Cl. Luton LU2 46 D4
Salter's Cl. Berk HP4 121 F6
Salters Gdns. Watf WD1 167 A8
Saltfield Cres. Luton LU4 44 C4
Salusbury La. Gt Of SG5 33 C2
Salvatarian RC Coll (Boys Gram). Har 176 E1
Salwey Cres. Hod EN10 134 F3
Samian Gate. St Alb AL3 126 F1
Sampson Ave. Barn EN5 171 D4
Samuel Lucas Jun Mix Inf Sch. Hit 34 D7
Sancroft Rd. Har HA3 176 F1
Sanctuary Cl. Hare UB9 173 C3
Sandalls Spring. Heml H HP1 123 F5
Sandalwood Cl. Luton LU3 45 B7
Sanday Cl. Heml H HP3 125 B1
Sandbrook La. Wils HP23 79 C1
Sandell Cl. Luton LU2 45 F2
Sanderling Cl. Letw SG6 22 E8
Sanders Cl. Heml H HP3 138 F7
Sanders Cl. Lon C AL2 142 D4
Sanders Rd. Heml H HP3 139 A7
Sandfield Rd. St Alb AL1 128 A3
Sandgate Rd. Luton LU4 44 D2
Sandhurst Ct. Harp AL5 107 D6
Sandifield. Hat AL10 130 B2
Sandle Rd. Bis St CM23 77 A7
Sandmere Cl. Heml H HP2 125 A2
Sandon Cl. Tri HP23 99 F4
Sandon Jun Mix Inf Sch. San 15 C1
Sandon Rd. Ches EN8 148 C1
Sandover Cl. Hit SG4 35 B6
Sandown Rd. Stev SG1 37 C1
Sandown Rd. Watf WD2 154 C1
Sandpit Hill Cotts. Chol HP23 120 B3
Sandpit La. St Alb AL1,AL4 128 C5
Sandpit Rd. Wel G C AL7 110 E4
Sandridge Cl. Heml H HP2 105 A1
Sandridge Ct. St Alb AL4 128 D7
Sandridge Jun Mix Inf Sch. Sand 108 D1
Sandridge Rd. St Alb AL1,AL3 127 F5
Sandridgebury La. Sand AL3 108 A2
Sandridgebury La. St Alb AL3 127 E8
Sandringham Cres. St Alb AL4 128 C8
Sandringham Rd. Pot B EN6 145 B1
Sandringham Rd. Watf WD2 154 C2
Sandringham Sch. St Alb 128 B7
Sandringham Way. Ches EN8 162 D5
Sandy Cl. Hert SG14 113 B6
Sandy Gr. Hit SG4 34 F6
Sandy La. Bus WD2 168 C6
Sandy La. Mo Pk HA6 175 A5
Sandy Lodge Ct. Norwd HA6 174 E5
Sandy Lodge Golf Course. Mo Pk 174 E8
Sandy Lodge La. Mo Pk HA6 174 E8
Sandy Lodge. Mo Pk HA6 174 E8
Sandy Lodge Rd. Mo Pk WD3 174 C8
Sandy Lodge Way. Norwd HA6 174 E4
Sandycroft Rd. L Chal HP6 150 C1
Sanfoin Rd. Dun LU4 44 A4
Sanfoine Cl. Hit SG4 35 C8
Santers La. Pot B EN6 158 E6
Santingfield N. Luton LU1 63 B6
Santingfield S. Luton LU1 63 B6
Sanville Gdns. Gt Am 115 C4
Sappers Cl. Saw CM21 97 F2
Saracen Est. Heml H 125 B5
Saracens Head. Heml H HP2 125 A4
Sark House. Enf EN3 162 D1
Sarratt Ave. Heml H HP2 125 A8
Sarratt Jun Mix Inf Sch. Sar 152 A3
Sarratt La. Ric WD3 165 C6
Sarratt La. Sar WD3 165 D8
Sarratt Rd. Sar WD3 165 C8
Sarum Pl. Heml H HP2 124 E7
Sarum Rd. Luton LU3 44 F4
Saturn Way. Heml H HP2 124 F6
Sauncey Ave. Harp AL5 86 B3
Sauncey Wood La. Whea AL5 86 E6
Sauncey Wood. Whea AL5 86 E4
Saunders Cl. Ches SG6 148 D4
Saunders Cl. Letw SG6 23 C7
Savoy Cl. Hare UB9 173 D1
Sawbridgeworth Rd. L Hal CM22 98 B6
Sawbridgeworth Rd. Sheer CM22 98 D3
Sawbridgeworth Sta. L Hal 98 A3
Sawells. Hod EN10 134 F2
Sawtry Cl. Luton LU3 45 A6
Sawtry Way. Bor WD6 157 A1
Sawyers La. Pot B EN6 158 D5
Sawyers Way. Heml H HP2 124 F3
Sax House. Letw SG6 11 E1
Saxon Ave. Stot SG5 11 F8
Saxon Cl. Harp AL5 86 C4
Saxon Cl. Letw SG6 11 F1
Saxon Ct. Bor WD6 169 E8
Saxon Rd. Luton LU3 45 C2
Saxon Rd. Welw AL6 89 B3
Saxon Rd. Whea AL4 108 D7
Saxon Way. Bal SG7 13 B1
Saxon Way. Wa Aby EN9 163 C6
Saxtead Cl. Luton LU2 46 D1
Sayer Way. Kneb SG3 68 F4
Sayers Gdns. Berk HP4 122 A6
Sayes Gdns. Saw CM21 97 F2
Sayesbury Ave. Saw CM21 97 E3
Sayesbury Rd. Saw CM21 97 E2
Saywell Rd. Luton LU2 46 B1
Scammel Way. Watf WD1 166 F3
Scarborough Ave. Stev SG1 50 B7
Scatterdells La. Chipf WD4 138 A2
Scholar's Hill. Wars SG12 95 A4
Scholars Ct. Col H AL4 143 C8
Scholars Wlk. Hat AL10 130 A2 4
School Cl. Stev SG2 51 B3
School Gdns. Pot En HP4 123 B6
School La. Ard SG2 38 F3
School La. Ast SG2 51 E2
School La. Bar SG8 9 A1
School La. Bri Wd AL2 155 A7
School La. Bus WD2 168 B2
School La. Ess AL9 131 F6
School La. Gt Of SG5 33 C3
School La. Harl CM20 117 E2
School La. Hat AL10 130 C6
School La. Luton LU4 44 D4
School La. Pres SG4 48 E5
School La. Tewin AL6 90 E2
School La. Wat St SG14 70 E3
School La. Welw AL6 89 B4
School La. Wes SG4 24 C1
School Mead. Abb L WD5 153 D7
School Rd. Pot B EN6 145 C1
School Row. Heml H HP1 123 F2
School Wlk. Letw SG6 23 B6
Schoolfields. Letw SG6 23 C5
Schubert Rd. Elst WD6 169 D3
Scot Gr. Pnr HA5 175 D3
Scotfield Ct. Luton LU2 46 D3 4
Scots Hill Cl. Cro Gr WD3 165 F3
Scots Hill. Cro Gr WD3 165 F3
Scotscraig. Radl WD7 155 F4
Scott Ave. Gt Am SG12 115 B4
Scott Cl. Royst SG8 2 D1
Scott Rd. Bis St CM23 76 E6
Scott Rd. Stev SG2 51 B6
Scott's Rd. Ware SG12 114 D8
Scotts Cl. Ware SG12 114 D8
Scotts View. Wel G C AL8 110 C5
Scottswood Cl. Bus WD2 167 E7
Scottswood Rd. Bus WD2 167 E7
Scriveners Cl. Heml H HP2 124 E3
Scrubbits Sq. Radl WD7 156 A4
Scrubbitts Park Rd. Radl WD7 156 A4
Seabrook. Dun LU4 44 B3
Seabrook Rd. Abb L WD5 139 D4
Seacroft Gdns. Sth Ox WD1 175 D7
Seaford Cl. Luton LU2 46 C3
Seaforth Dr. Ches EN8 162 D5
Seaman Cl. Pk St AL2 141 D6
Searches La. Bri Wd WD5 140 C3
Seaton Rd. Heml H HP3 124 E1
Seaton Rd. Lon C AL2 142 D5
Seaton Rd. Luton LU4 44 F3
Sebright Rd. Barn EN5 171 E6
Sebright Rd. Heml H HP1 124 A1
Sebright Rd. Mark AL3 83 E5
Secker Cres. Har HA3 176 C2
Second Ave. Letw SG6 23 C6
Second Ave. Watf WD2 154 D4
Sedbury Cl. Luton LU3 45 A6
Sedge Gn. Lo Naz EN9 135 E3
Sedgwick Rd. Luton LU4 44 B7
Seebohm Cl. Hit SG5 21 C1
Seeleys. Harl CM17 118 C3
Sefton Ave. Har HA3 176 D2
Sefton Cl. St Alb AL1 127 F4
Sefton Rd. Stev SG1 37 B1
Selbourne Rd. Luton LU4 45 A2
Selby Ave. St Alb AL3 127 D3
Selden Hill. Heml H HP2 124 D2
Sele Rd. Hert SG14 113 B6
Sele Sch The. Hert 112 F6
Selina Cl. Luton LU3 44 C7
Sellers Cl. Bor WD6 170 C8
Sells Rd. Ware SG12 93 F2
Sellwood Dr. Barn EN5 171 D4
Selsey Dr. Luton LU2 46 D5
Selwyn Ave. Hat AL10 129 E4
Selwyn Cres. Hat AL10 129 E5
Selwyn Dr. Hat AL10 129 E5
Sempill Rd. Heml H HP3 124 E1
Sentis Ct. Norwd HA6 174 F4
Sequoia Cl. Bus WD2 168 D1
Sequoia Pk. Pnr HA5 176 B4
Serby Ave. Royst SG8 7 D8
Sergehill La. Abb L WD5 140 A5
Service Rd The. Pot B EN6 159 A7
Seven Acres. Mo Pk HA6 175 A4
Sevenoaks Ct. Norwd HA6 174 C3
Severalls The. Luton LU2 46 B3
Severn Dr. Enf EN1 162 A1
Severn Way. Watf WD2 154 C5
Severnmead. Heml H HP2 124 E6
Severnvale. Lon C AL2 142 F4
Sewardstone Rd. Wa Aby EN9 163 D3
Sewardstone St. Wa Aby EN9 163 C5
Sewardstone Way. Wa Aby EN9 163 C3
Sewell Cl. Coln H AL4 128 E3
Sewell Harris Cl. Harl CM20 117 F1
Sewells. Wel G C AL8 89 E2
Seymour Ave. Luton LU1 63 F5

Seymour Cl. Pnr HA5 ....... 175 F2
Seymour Cres. Heml H HP2 ................. 124 E3
Seymour Ct. Nthch HP4 ... 121 E6
Seymour Mews. Saw CM21 .................... 118 E7
Seymour Rd. Luton LU1 ..... 63 F5
Seymour Rd. Nthch HP4 .. 121 E6
Seymour Rd. St Alb AL3 .. 127 E6
Shackledell. Stev SG2 ........ 50 F2
Shacklegate La. Whit SG4 . 66 E5
Shackleton Spring. Stev SG2 ........................ 51 A3
Shackleton Way. Abb L WD5 ................... 154 A7
Shackleton Way. Wel G C AL7 ................ 111 D6
Shady Bush Cl. Bus WD2 . 168 C2
Shady La. Watf WD1 ........ 167 B7
Shaftenhoe End Rd. Bar SG8 ............................ 9 A1
Shaftesbury Ct. Stev SG1 ... 50 E4
Shaftesbury Ind Est. Letw . 23 B7
Shaftesbury Quay. Hert SG14 ................... 113 D6 9
Shaftesbury Rd. Luton LU4 45 B1
Shaftesbury Rd. Watf WD1 .................... 167 C6
Shaftesbury Sch. Har ....... 176 B2
Shaftesbury Way. Abb L WD4 ................... 139 C3
Shaftesbury Way. Royst SG8 ........................ 7 E5
Shakespeare Ct. Hod EN11 .................... 115 B2
Shakespeare Ind Est. Watf ............................ 154 A1
Shakespeare Rd. Dun LU4 . 44 B2
Shakespeare Rd. Harp AL5 ........................ 86 B1
Shakespeare. Royst SG8 ..... 7 D8
Shakespeare St. Watf WD2 .................... 154 B1
Shalcross Dr. Ches EN8 ... 148 F1
Shallcross Cres. Hat AL10 130 A2 6
Shangani Rd. Bis St CM23 . 76 F5
Shanklin Cl. Gofs O EN7 ... 147 F2
Shanklin Cl. Luton LU3 ....... 45 A7
Shanklin Gdns. Sth Ox WD1 ................. 175 C6
Shantock Hall La. Bov HP3 136 E1
Shantock La. Bov HP3 ...... 136 E1
Sharmans Cl. Welw AL6 ..... 89 F4
Sharose Ct. Mark AL3 ........ 83 E5
Sharpcroft. Heml H HP2 .. 124 D5 1
Sharpenhoe Rd. Str LU3 ..... 31 A5
Sharpes La. Heml H HP1 . 123 B1
Sharples Gn. Luton LU3 ..... 45 B8
Shaw Cl. Bus WD2 .......... 176 E8
Shaw Cl. Ches EN8 ........... 148 C3
Shaws The. Wel G C AL7 . 111 C5
Sheares Hoppit. Hun SG12 95 D2
Shearwater Cl. Stev SG2 ... 51 D4
Sheepcot Dr. Watf WD2 .. 154 C5
Sheepcot La. Watf WD2 .. 154 B6
Sheepcot La. Watf WD2 .. 154 C5
Sheepcote La. Whea AL4 ... 87 F1
Sheepcote Rd. Heml H HP2 ................. 124 F3
Sheepcote. Wel G C AL7 .. 111 A3
Sheepcroft Hill. Stev SG2 ... 51 D3
Sheephouse Rd. Heml H HP3 ................. 124 F1
Sheering CE Sch. Sheer ..... 98 D1
Sheering Dr. Harl CM17 ... 118 E4
Sheering Lower Rd. Sheer CM21,CM17 ....... 118 F7
Sheering Mill La. Saw CM21 ...................... 97 F2
Sheering Mill La. Sheer CM21 ................... 98 A1
Sheering Rd. Harl CM17 .. 118 E4
Sheering Rd. Harl CM17 .. 118 F5
Sheethanger La. Heml H HP3 ................. 138 A7
Shefton Rise. Norwd HA6 175 A3
Sheldon Cl. Ham St EN7 ... 147 E5
Shelford Rd. Barn EN5 ..... 171 C3
Shelley Cl. Hit SG4 ............. 35 C7
Shelley Cl. Mo Pk HA6 ...... 174 F5
Shelley Cl. Royst SG8 ........... 2 D1
Shelley Ct. Harp AL5 .......... 86 B1 8
Shelley Ct. Wa Aby EN9 ... 163 F6
Shelley Rd. Dun LU4 .......... 44 B2
Shelton Way. Luton LU2 .... 46 A3
Shendish Edge. Heml H HP3 ................. 138 F6
Shenley Ct. Heml H HP2 .. 125 B8
Shenley Fst Sch. Shen ...... 156 F5
Shenley Hill. Radl WD7 .... 156 B4
Shenley Hospl. Shen ........ 156 E6
Shenley La. Lon C AL2 ...... 142 C4
Shenley Rd. Bor WD6 ...... 170 B6
Shenley Rd. Heml H HP2 .. 105 B1
Shenley Rd. Radl WD7 ..... 156 C4
Shenleybury Cotts. Shen WD7 ................... 156 E8
Shenleybury. Shen WD7,AL2 ............. 156 E8
Shenlybury Villas. Shen AL2 ...................... 156 E8
Shenstone Hill. Berk HP4 122 E5
Shenval House. Harl ........ 118 A4
Sheperd Jun Mix Inf Sch. Ric ................................ 165 A1
Shephall Gn. Stev SG2 ....... 51 B2
Shephall View. Stev SG1 ... 51 A5
Shephall Way. Stev SG2 .... 51 C3
Shepherd Cl. Royst SG8 ....... 7 E5
Shepherd Inf Sch. Ric ...... 165 A1
Shepherd's La. Chor WD3 164 E2
Shepherd's Row. Red AL3 106 B5
Shepherds Ct. Hert SG14 ... 92 C1
Shepherds Gn. Heml H HP1 ................. 123 E2
Shepherds La. Stev SG1 .... 50 A6
Shepherds Mead. Hit SG5 .. 21 F2
Shepherds Rd. Watf WD1 166 F5
Shepherds Way. Bro Pk AL9 ................... 145 D4
Shepherds Way. Harp AL5 . 85 D4
Shepherds Way. Ric WD3 165 B2
Shepherds Wlk. Bus WD2 176 D8
Shepley Mews. Enf EN3 ... 163 A2
Sheppard Cl. Enf EN1 ....... 162 B1
Sheppards Cl. St Alb AL3 . 127 E6
Shepperton Cl. Bor WD6 .. 170 D8
Sheppey's La. Abb L WD5 139 E3
Sheraton Cl. Bor WD6 ...... 169 F4
Sheraton House. Chor WD3 ................... 164 C5
Sherborne Ave. Luton LU2 . 45 D6
Sherborne Way. Cro Gr WD3 ................. 166 B5
Sherbourne Cl. Heml H HP2 ................. 124 E2
Sherd Cl. Luton LU3 ........... 44 F7
Sheredes Cty Prim Sch. Hod ............................. 134 F4
Sheredes Dr. Hod EN11 ... 134 F4
Sheredes Sch. Hod .......... 134 F5
Sherfield Ave. Ric WD3 .... 173 E8
Sheridan Cl. Heml H HP1 . 124 B2
Sheridan Cl. Heml H HP1 . 124 D4
Sheridan Rd. Luton LU3 ..... 45 C2
Sheridan Rd. Watf WD1 ... 167 D2
Sheriff Way. Watf WD2 ... 154 A5
Sheringham Ave. Stev SG1 36 B1
Sheringham Cl. Luton LU2 . 45 C7
Sherington Ave. Pnr HA5 . 176 A3
Sherland Ct. Radl WD7 .... 156 A4
Shernbroke Rd. Wa Aby EN9 ................. 163 F5
Sherrardspark Rd. Wel G C AL8 ................. 110 D8
Sherrardswood Sch. Wel G C ............................ 110 D8
Sherrardswood Sch. Welw 89 D4
Sherwood Ave. Pot B EN6 158 E7
Sherwood Ave. St Alb AL4 128 B6
Sherwood House. Abb L HA2 ................... 153 F8
Sherwood. Letw SG6 ......... 22 F8
Sherwood Pl. Heml H HP2 ................. 124 F7 1
Sherwood Rd. Luton LU4 ... 45 A2
Sherwoods Rd. Watf WD1 167 E2
Sherwoods Rise. Harp AL5 ...................... 107 D8
Shetland Cl. Bor WD6 ...... 170 D3
Shillington Rd. Pirt SG5 ..... 20 B5
Shillitoe Ave. Pot B EN6 ... 158 E7
Shingle Cl. Luton LU3 ........ 45 A8
Shire Cl. Ches EN10 ......... 148 F5
Shire La. C St P WD3 ....... 172 C4
Shire La. Chor WD3 ......... 164 C4
Shire La. Map Cr WD3 ..... 172 B5
Shire La. Tri HP23 ............ 120 B4
Shiremeade. Bor WD6 ...... 169 F4
Shires The. Luton LU2 ........ 45 D1 5
Shires The. Royst SG8 ......... 7 E6
Shirley Cl. Ches EN8 ........ 148 C2
Shirley Cl. Hod EN10 ....... 148 F7
Shirley Cl. Stev SG2 .......... 51 C8
Shirley Rd. Abb L WD5 ..... 153 F7
Shirley Rd. Luton LU1 ......... 63 C8
Shirley Rd. St Alb AL1 ...... 127 F2
Shooters Dr. Lo Naz EN9 . 135 E1
Shootersway. Berk HP4 ... 121 E4
Shootersway La. Berk HP4 ...................... 121 F4
Shootersway. Nthch HP23 121 C5
Shootersway Pk. Berk HP4 ...................... 121 F3
Shoplands. Wel G C AL8 .... 89 D2
Shoreham Cl. Stev SG1 ...... 50 A8
Short La. Ast SG2 .............. 51 E4
Short La. Bri Wd AL2 ....... 140 E2
Shortcroft. Bis St CM23 ..... 77 D7
Shortlands Gn. Wel G C AL7 ................ 110 F5
Shortlands Pl. Bis St CM23 76 F8
Shortmead Dr. Ches EN8 . 162 E8
Shothanger Way. Heml H HP3 ................. 137 D6
Shott La. Letw SG6 ............ 23 A5
Shott Lower. Ham St EN7 147 F5
Shottfield Cl. Sand AL4 .... 108 D2
Shrub Hill Rd. Heml H HP1 123 F2
Shrubbery Gr. Royst SG8 ..... 7 D4
Shrubbery The. Heml H HP1 ................. 123 E4
Shrublands Ave. Berk HP4 122 A4
Shrublands. Bro Pk AL9 ... 145 B5
Shrublands Rd. Berk HP4 122 A5
Shrublands The. Pot B EN6 ..................... 158 E6
Shugars Gn. Tri HP23 ...... 100 B5
Sibley Ave. Harp AL5 ....... 107 E7
Sibley Cl. Luton LU2 .......... 46 B3
Sibthorpe Rd. Wel G AL9 . 144 D7
Siccut Rd. L Wym SG4 ........ 35 E4
Sicklefield Cl. Ham St EN7 147 F5
Siddons Rd. Stev SG2 ........ 51 C6
Sidford Cl. Heml H HP1 .... 123 F3
Sidings The. Hat AL10 ..... 129 E4
Sidings The. Heml H HP2 . 124 D3
Sidmouth Cl. Sth Ox WD1 175 B8
Sidney Terr. Bis St CM23 ... 76 F6
Silam Rd. Stev SG1 ............ 50 E5
Silecroft Rd. Luton LU2 ...... 64 B8
Silk Mill Ct. Watf WD1 ..... 167 B2
Silk Mill Rd. Watf WD1 .... 167 B2
Silk Mill Way. Tri HP23 .... 100 A5
Silkin Ct. Stev SG2 ............ 51 D3
Silver Cl. Har HA3 ........... 176 D3
Silver Dell. Watf WD2 ...... 153 F4
Silver Hill. Shen WD6 ....... 157 B3
Silver St. Ans SG9 ............. 29 A5
Silver St. Ashw SG7 ............. 4 D4
Silver St. Gofs O EN7 ....... 147 D1
Silver St. Gu M SG8 .............. 1 F4
Silver St. Luton LU1 ........... 63 E7
Silver St. Sta M CM24 ........ 59 D6
Silver St. Wa Aby EN9 ...... 163 C6
Silver Trees. Bri Wd AL2 . 140 F1
Silverbirch Ave. Stot SG5 ... 11 F8
Silverdale Rd. Watf WD2 . 167 E4
Silverfield. Hod EN10 ....... 134 F1
Silverthorn Dr. Heml H HP3 ................. 139 B7
Silverwood Cl. Norwd HA6 174 C2
Simmonds Rise. Heml H HP3 ................. 124 D1
Simon Balle Sch. Hert ...... 113 E5
Simon Dean. Bov HP3 ...... 137 A4
Simpson Dr. Bal SG7 .......... 23 F8
Simpsons Ct. Bal SG7 ......... 23 F8
Sinderby Cl. Bor WD6 ...... 169 E8
Sinfield Cl. Stev SG1 .......... 51 A5
Singlets La. Fla AL3 ............ 84 C2
Sir Frederic Osborn Sch The. Wel G C ......... 111 B7
Sir Herbert Janes Village The. Luton LU4 ... 44 D4
Sir James Altham Pool. Sth Ox .......................... 175 E5
Sir John Lawes Sch. Harp .. 86 B3
Sir John Newsom Sch The. Wel G C ......... 110 E3
Sir Peter's Way. Whip LU6 81 E6
Sirita Cl. Har HA3 ............ 176 D1
Sirus Rd. Mo Pk HA6 ........ 175 A5
Sish Cl. Stev SG1 ............... 50 D6
Sish La. Stev SG1 ............... 50 D6
Siskin Cl. Bor WD6 ........... 170 A5
Siskin Cl. Watf WD2 ......... 167 E5
Sisson Cl. Stev SG2 ............ 51 C2
Sitwell Gr. Stan HA7 ........ 176 F5
Six Acres. Heml H HP3 ..... 139 A8
Six Hills Way. Stev SG1,SG2 ................. 50 C4
Sixth Ave. Letw SG6 ........... 23 C6
Sixth Ave. Watf WD2 ....... 154 D4
Skegness Rd. Stev SG1 ...... 50 A8
Skegsbury La. Kim SG4 ...... 65 F1
Skelton Cl. Luton LU3 ......... 31 B1
Skidmore Way. Ric WD3 .. 165 E1
Skimpans Cl. Wel G AL9 ... 144 D7
Skimpot Rd. Dun LU5 ........ 44 A1
Skipton Cl. Stev SG2 .......... 68 F8
Skua Cl. Dun LU4 ................ 44 A5
Skylark Cnr. Stev SG2 ........ 51 D3
Skys Wood Rd. St Alb AL4 128 B7
Skyswood Prim Sch (Jun Mix & Inf). St Alb . 128 C6
Slade Ct. Radl WD7 .......... 156 A4
Slaughter Ctts. Ric WD3 165 E2
Sleaford Gn. Sth Ox WD1 . 175 D7
Sleapcross Gdns. Coln H AL4 .................... 129 C2
Sleaps Hyde. Stev SG2 ....... 51 C1
Sleapshyde La. Coln H AL4 .................... 129 C2
Sleddale. Heml H HP2 ...... 124 E6
Sleets End. Heml H HP1 .. 124 B5
Slimmons Dr. St Alb AL4 .. 128 A7
Slip End Lower Sch. Cad .... 63 B1
Slip La. Cod SG3 ................. 68 C4
Slipe La. Ches EN10 .......... 148 F7
Slipe The. Ched LU7 ........... 80 A7
Sloan Ct. Stev SG1 ............. 50 F6
Sloansway. Wel G C AL7 .... 90 A1
Slype The. Whea AL4 ......... 87 B5
Small Acre. Heml H HP1 .. 123 F3
Smallcroft. Wel G C AL7 ... 111 B7
Smallford La. Coln H AL4 . 129 B2
Smallwood Cl. Whea AL4 . 108 E7
Smarts Gn. Ham St EN7 ... 147 F5
Smeaton Cl. Wa Aby EN9 . 163 E7
Smith St. Watf WD1 ......... 167 C5
Smithfield. Heml H HP2 ... 124 D5
Smith's End La. Bar SG8 .... 17 F8
Smiths La. Ham St EN7 .... 147 D5
Smiths Lane Mall. Luton LU1 ....................... 63 E7
Smiths Sq. Luton LU1 ......... 63 E7
Smithy The. L Had SG11 .... 57 B2
Smug Oak Bsns Ctr. Bri Wd .......................... 141 B1
Smug Oak La. Bri Wd AL2 141 D1
Snailswell La. Ick SG5 ....... 21 E5
Snatchup. Red AL3 ........... 106 A5
Snells Mead. Bun SG9 ........ 40 F7
Snipe The. Wes SG4 .......... 24 B1
Snowford Cl. Luton LU3 ..... 45 A7
Snowley Par. Bis St CM23 .. 59 B1
Soham Rd. Enf EN3 .......... 162 F2
Solar Ct. Watf WD1 ......... 166 F4
Solesbridge Cl. Chor WD3 164 F6
Solesbridge Ct. Chor WD3 164 F6
Solesbridge La. Chor WD3 165 B7
Solesbridge La. Sar WD3 . 165 B7
Sollershott E. Letw SG6 ..... 22 F4
Sollershott Hall. Letw SG6 . 22 F4
Sollershott W. Letw SG6 .... 22 E4
Solomon's Hill. Ric WD3 .. 165 D2
Solway. Heml H HP2 ........ 124 F5
Solway Rd N. Luton LU3 ..... 45 A4
Solway Rd S. Luton LU3 ..... 45 A3
Somerby Cl. Hod EN10 ..... 135 A2
Someries Inf Sch. Luton .... 46 C3
Someries Jun Sch. Luton ... 46 C3
Someries Rd. Harp AL5 ...... 86 C4
Someries Rd. Heml H HP1 123 F5
Somers Rd. Wel G AL9 ..... 144 C7
Somers Sq. Wel G AL9 ..... 144 C8
Somers Way. Bus WD2 ..... 168 C2
Somersby Cl. Luton LU1 ..... 63 E5
Somerset Ave. Luton LU2 .. 46 A1
Somerset Rd. Enf EN3 ...... 163 A1
Somersham. Wel G C AL7 111 D6
Sonia Cl. Watf WD1 ......... 167 C2
Soothouse Spring. St Alb AL3 .................... 127 F7
Sopers Rd. Cuf EN6 .......... 146 F2
Sopwell La. St Alb AL1 ..... 127 D2
Sorrel Cl. Luton LU3 .......... 45 B8
Sorrel Cl. Royst SG8 ............ 7 F5
Sorrel Garth. Hit SG4 ......... 35 A6
Sotheron Rd. Watf WD1 .. 167 C6
Souberie Ave. Letw SG6 .... 22 F5
Souldern St. Watf WD1 ... 167 B4
South App. Mo Pk HA6 ..... 174 D7
South Bank Rd. Nthch HP4 121 F6
South Block. Sheer CM21 .. 97 F2
South Cl. Bal SG7 .............. 23 F7
South Cl. Barn EN5 .......... 171 F6
South Cl. Chis AL2 ........... 141 B6
South Cl. Pnr HA5 ............ 175 D2
South Cl. Royst SG8 ............. 7 B7
South Cottage Dr. Chor WD3 ................... 164 F4
South Dr. Cuf EN6 ............ 146 E1
South Dr. St Alb AL4 ........ 128 E4
South Drift Way. Luton LU1 63 B5
South Gardens Gdns. Chor WD3 ................... 164 F4
South Hill Cl. Hit SG4 ......... 35 A6
South Hill Jun Mix Inf Sch. Heml H ......................... 124 C2
South Hill Rd. Heml H HP1 124 C3
South Ley Ct. Wel G C AL7 110 E3
South Ley. Wel G C AL7 ... 110 E3
South Par. Wa Aby EN9 ... 163 C6
South Park Ave. Chor WD3 .................... 164 F4
South Park Gdns. Berk HP4 ...................... 122 B5
South Pl. Harl CM20 ......... 118 A4
South Pl. Hit SG5 ................ 34 D8
South Rd. Bal SG7 .............. 24 A7
South Rd. Bis St CM23 ....... 77 A5
South Rd. Chor WD3 ........ 164 C4
South Rd. Harl CM20 ....... 118 A4
South Rd. Luton LU1 .......... 63 E6
South Rd. Stand SG11 ........ 55 D2
South Riding. Bri Wd AL2 . 141 A1
South St. Bis St CM23 ....... 76 F6
South St. Hert SG14 ......... 113 D6
South St. Sta Ab SG12 ..... 115 C4
South Street Commercial Ctr. Bis St CM23 ............ 76 F6
South View. Letw SG6 ........ 22 F5
South View Rd. Pnr HA5 .. 175 B4
South Way. Abb L WD5 .... 153 E6
South Way. Hat AL10 ....... 130 B2
South Way. Wa Aby EN9 .. 163 C3
South Weald Dr. Wa Aby EN9 ................. 163 D6
Southacre Way. Pnr HA5 . 175 C2
Southall Cl. Ware SG12 ..... 93 D2
Southbrook Dr. Ches EN8 148 D3
Southbrook. Saw CM21 ..... 97 E1
Southdown Ct. Hat AL10 .. 130 A2
Southdown House. Harp AL5 ...................... 107 C7
Southdown Ind Est. Harp 107 C8
Southdown Rd. Harp AL5 . 107 B8
Southdown Rd. Hat AL10 . 130 A2
Southend Cl. Stev SG1 ....... 50 D7
Southern Ave. Henlw SG16 10 C3
Southern Rise. Nwml E LU2 ................... 85 F7
Southern Terr. Hod EN11 115 B1
Southern Way. Letw SG6 ... 22 E8
Southern Way. Stu LU6 ...... 82 C4
Southernwood Cl. Heml H HP2 ................. 125 A4
Southfield Ave. Watf WD2 154 C1
Southfield. Barn EN5 ........ 171 D3
Southfield. Brag SG11 ........ 55 F7
Southfield Rd. Ches EN8 .. 162 E7
Southfield Rd. Hod EN11 .. 135 A7
Southfield Way. St Alb AL4 .................... 128 D6
Southfield. Wel G C AL7 ... 110 D4
Southfields. Letw SG6 ........ 11 F1
Southfields. Stand SG11 .... 55 E2
Southgate House. Ches EN8 ........................ 148 D1
Southgate Rd. Pot B EN6 . 159 C6
Southgate. Stev SG1 .......... 50 D4
Southmead Cres. Ches EN8 ..................... 148 F1
Southmill Rd. Bis St CM23 . 77 A5
Southmill Trad Ctr. Bis St .. 77 A6
Southsea Ave. Watf WD1 167 A5
Southsea Rd. Stev SG1 ...... 50 B8
Southside. Wyd SG9 .......... 28 A3
Southview Cl. Ham St EN7 147 E5
Southview Rd. Harp AL5 .... 86 D3
Southwark Cl. Stev SG1 ..... 37 B2
Southwold Rd. Watf WD2 154 C2
Sovereign Ct. Watf WD1 .. 167 A5
Sovereign Gate. Watf WD1 .................... 166 F5
Sowerby Ave. Luton LU2 .... 46 C3
Sparhawke. Letw SG6 ........ 12 A1
Sparrow Cl. Dun LU4 .......... 44 A4
Sparrows Herne. Bus WD2 ......................... 168 C2
Sparrows Way. Bus WD2 168 C1
Sparrowswick Ride. St Alb AL3 .................... 127 C8
Spayne Cl. Luton LU3 ......... 45 B8
Spear Cl. Luton LU3 ........... 44 E6
Speedwell Cl. Luton LU3 .... 45 A8
Speke Cl. Stev SG2 ............. 51 D5
Spellbrook Jun Mix Inf Sch. Saw ................................ 97 F7
Spellbrook La E. Saw CM22 97 F8
Spellbrook La W. Saw CM23 ...................... 97 E7
Spellbrooke. Hit SG5 .......... 34 D8 5
Spencer Ave. Ham St EN7 147 E5
Spencer Cl. Sta M CM24 .... 59 E6
Spencer Gate. St Alb AL1 . 127 E5
Spencer Jun Sch. St Alb ... 127 E6
Spencer Mews. St Alb AL1 127 E4
Spencer Pl. Sand AL4 ....... 108 C2
Spencer Rd. Har HA3 ....... 176 E1

Spencer Rd. Luton LU3 ...... 45 C2
Spencer St. Hert SG13 ..... 113 E7
Spencer St. St Alb AL3 ..... 127 D3
Spencer Way.
Heml H HP1 ... 124 A6
Spencer Wlk. Ric WD3 ..... 165 C4
Spenser Cl. Royst SG8 ... 2 D1
Spenser Rd. Harp AL5 ... 86 C1
Sperberry Hill. St Ipp SG4 . 35 B2
Sphere Ind Est The. St Alb 128 A2
Spicer St. St Alb AL3 ... 127 C3
Spicersfield. Ham St EN7 . 148 A4
Spindle Berry Cl. Welw AL6 90 A7
Spinney Ct. Saw CM21 ... 97 E2
Spinney La. Welw AL6 ... 68 E3
Spinney Rd. Luton LU3 ... 44 D7
Spinney St. Hert SG13 ... 114 A6
Spinney The. Bal SG7 ... 23 E7
Spinney The. Berk HP4 ... 121 F3
Spinney The. Harp AL5 ... 85 E3
Spinney The. Hert SG13 ... 113 F6
Spinney The. Hod EN10 ... 134 F4
Spinney The. Pot B EN6 ... 159 D8
Spinney The. Sta M CM24 .. 59 E6
Spinney The. Stev SG2 ... 51 D7
Spinney The. Watf WD1 ... 167 A8
Spinney The. Wel G C AL7 110 E5
Spinneys Dr. St Alb AL3 ... 127 B1
Spires The. Barn EN5 ... 171 E6
Spittlesea Rd. Luton LU2 ... 64 C6
Spooners Dr. Chis AL2 ... 141 C4
Spratts La. Ken Co LU6 ... 82 F8
Spreckley Cl. Henlw SG16 . 10 B5
Spring Cl. Barn EN5 ... 171 D4
Spring Cl. Bor WD6 ... 170 A8
Spring Cl. Hare UB9 ... 173 D2
Spring Cl. Lat HP5 ... 150 D3
Spring Cotts. Ches EN10 .. 148 E7
Spring Court Rd. Enf EN2 . 161 A1
Spring Crofts. Bus WD2 ... 168 A4
Spring Dr. Stev SG2 ... 69 B8
Spring Field Rd.
Berk HP4 ... 122 A6
Spring Gdns. Watf WD2 ... 154 C3
Spring Glen. Hat AL10 ... 129 F4
Spring Hills. Harl CM20 ... 117 B1
Spring Hills Tower.
Harl CM20 ... 117 B1
Spring La. Cotrd SG9 ... 39 C5
Spring La. Heml H HP1 ... 124 A4
Spring Pl. Luton LU1 ... 63 D6
Spring Rd. Harp AL5 ... 85 A4
Spring Rd. Letw SG6 ... 22 E5
Spring View Rd.
Ware SG12 ... 114 C8
Spring Way. Heml H HP2 . 125 C5
Spring Wlk. Hod EN10 ... 134 C2
Springfield. Bus WD2 ... 168 D1
Springfield Cl.
Cro Gr WD3 ... 166 B4
Springfield Cl. Nort EN6 ... 159 E8
Springfield Cres.
Whea AL5 ... 86 B5
Springfield Ct. Bis St CM23 76 E8
Springfield Ct. Ric WD3 ... 165 B1
Springfield Rd. Ches EN8 . 162 E7
Springfield Rd. Coln H AL4 129 B3
Springfield Rd.
Heml H HP2 ... 124 F4
Springfield Rd. Luton LU3 .. 45 C6
Springfield Rd. St Alb AL1 128 A2
Springfield Rd. Watf WD2 154 B6
Springfields. Hod EN10 ... 134 F4
Springfields House.
Wel G C AL8 ... 110 C4
Springfields. Wa Aby EN9 163 E5
Springfields. Wel G C AL8 110 B4
Springhall Ct. Saw CM21 ... 97 E2
Springhall La. Saw CM21 ... 97 E1
Springhall Rd. Saw CM21 .. 97 E2
Springhead. Ashw SG7 ... 4 D4
Springle La. Hod SG13 ... 114 F2
Springmead Jun & Mix
Inf Sch. Wel G C ... 111 C7
Springs The. Ches EN10 .. 148 E6
Springs The. Hert SG13 ... 113 F7
Springshott. Letw SG6 ... 22 E5
Springwell Ave. Ric WD3 . 173 A8
Springwell La. Hare WD3 173 A6
Springwood Cl. Hare UB9 173 D2
Springwood. Ham St EN7 . 148 A5
Springwood Wlk.
St Alb AL4 ... 128 D6
Spruce Way. Chis AL2 ... 141 B4
Spur Cl. Abb L WD5 ... 153 D6
Spur The. Ches EN8 ... 148 D3
Spur The. Stev SG1 ... 50 E4
Spurcroft. Luton LU3 ... 31 C1
Spurrs Cl. Hit SG4 ... 35 B7
Square The. Brag SG11 ... 55 F7
Square The. Buck SG9 ... 27 D5
Square The. Heml H HP1 . 124 C3
Square The. Muc H SG10 ... 74 F3
Square The. Red AL3 ... 105 F6
Square The. Saw CM21 ... 97 E2
Square The. Watf WD2 ... 154 B2
Squires Cl. Bis St CM23 ... 76 C8
Squires Ride. Fla HP2 ... 104 F1
Squirrel Chase.
Heml H HP1 ... 123 E4
Squirrels Cl. Bis St CM23 ... 76 F8
Squirrels The. Bus WD2 ... 168 D3
Squirrels The. Hert SG13 . 114 B6
Squirrels The.
Wel G C AL7 ... 111 C5
Stable Ct. St Alb AL1 ... 127 E5
Stacey Ct. Bis St CM23 ... 76 F6
Stackfield. Harl CM20 ... 118 A3
Stacklands. Wel G C AL8 . 110 B4
Staddles. L Hal CM22 ... 98 B8
Stafford Cl. Ches EN8 ... 148 B2
Stafford Dr. Hod EN10 ... 135 A3
Stafford Rd. Har HA3 ... 176 C3
Staffords. Harl CM17 ... 118 E4
Stag Green Ave. Hat AL9 . 130 C7
Stag La. Berk HP4 ... 122 B5
Stag La. Chor WD3 ... 164 C3
Stagg Hill. Had W EN4 ... 159 E3
Stainer Rd. Bor WD6 ... 156 D1
Stainer Rd. Radl WD6 ... 169 D8
Stains Cl. Ches EN8 ... 148 F3
Stake Piece Rd. Royst SG8 .. 7 C5
Stakers Ct. Harp AL5 ... 86 B1
Stamford Ave. Royst SG8 ... 7 D7
Stamford Cl. Har HA3 ... 176 E3
Stamford Cl. Pot B EN6 ... 159 D7
Stamford Ct. Royst SG8 ... 7 D7
Stamford Rd. Watf WD1 .. 167 B7
Stamford Yd. Royst SG8 ... 7 C6
Stanborough Ave.
Bor WD6 ... 157 B1
Stanborough Cl.
Wel G C AL8 ... 110 C5
Stanborough Gn.
Wel G C AL8 ... 110 C4
Stanborough La.
Wel G C AL8 ... 110 C4
Stanborough Prim Sch.
Watf ... 154 C4
Stanborough Rd.
Wel G C AL8 ... 110 C4
Stanborough Sch. Wel G C 110 B4
Stanborough Sec Sch.
Watf ... 154 B4
Stanbury Ave. Watf WD1 . 153 E2
Standard Rd. Enf EN3 ... 162 E2
Standfield. Abb L WD5 ... 139 E1
Standhill Cl. Hit SG4 ... 34 F6
Standhill Rd. Hit SG4 ... 34 F6
Standon Ct. Stand SG11 ... 55 F1
Standon Hill. Stand SG11 ... 55 D2
Standon Rd. Brag SG11 ... 56 E3
Standring Rise.
Heml H HP3 ... 138 B8
Stane Field. Letw SG6 ... 23 B3
Stane St. Bal SG7 ... 13 A1
Stanelow Cres. Stand SG11 55 D2
Stanford Rd. Luton LU2 ... 46 A1
Stangate Cres. Edg WD6 . 170 E4
Stanhope Ave. Har HA3 ... 176 D2
Stanhope Rd. Barn EN5 ... 171 D3
Stanhope Rd. Ches EN8 ... 162 E6
Stanhope Rd. St Alb AL1 .. 127 F3
Stanier Rise. Berk HP4 ... 121 F7
Stanley Ave. Chis AL2 ... 141 A6
Stanley Dr. Hat AL10 ... 130 B3
Stanley Gdns. Bor WD6 ... 169 E8
Stanley Gdns. Tri HP23 ... 99 F3
Stanley Rd. Hert SG13 ... 113 E5
Stanley Rd. Norwd HA6 ... 175 A2
Stanley Rd. Stev SG2 ... 51 B7
Stanley Rd. Str LU3 ... 31 A5
Stanley Rd. Watf WD1 ... 167 C5
Stanley St. Luton LU1 ... 63 D6
Stanmore Cres. Luton LU3 . 44 F4
Stanmore Rd. Stev SG1 ... 50 D7
Stanmore Rd. Watf WD2 . 167 B8
Stanmount Rd. Chis AL2 .. 141 A6
Stannington Path.
Bor WD6 ... 170 A8
Stanstead Dr. Hod EN11 .. 135 B8
Stanstead Rd. Hert SG13 . 114 A6
Stanstead Rd.
Hert H SG13 ... 114 D5
Stanstead Rd. Hod EN11 ... 115 B1
Stansted Hill. Muc H SG10 . 75 A1
Stansted Mountfitchet Sta.
Sta M ... 59 E6
Stansted Rd. Birhr CM23 ... 59 B3
Stansted Rd.
Bis St CM22,CM23 ... 59 B3
Stanton Cl. St Alb AL4 ... 128 D7
Stanton Rd. Dun LU4 ... 44 C1
Staplefield Cl. Pnr HA5 ... 175 E3
Stapleford Jun Mix Inf Sch.
Stap ... 92 A6
Stapleford Rd. Luton LU2 ... 46 C4
Stapleford. Wel G C AL7 .. 111 D6
Stapleton Cl. Pot B EN6 ... 159 D8
Stapleton Rd. Bor WD6 ... 157 A2
Stapley Rd. St Alb AL3 ... 127 D4
Staplyton Rd. Barn EN5 ... 171 E6
Star Holme Ct. Ware SG12 93 E1
Star St. Ware SG12 ... 93 E1
Starling La. Cuf EN6 ... 146 F3
Startpoint. Luton LU1 ... 63 C7
Statham Cl. Luton LU3 ... 31 B1
Station App. Ches EN8 ... 162 E5
Station App. Chor WD3 ... 164 D5
Station App. Harp AL5 ... 86 B1
Station App. Hit SG4 ... 35 A8
Station App. Kneb SG3 ... 68 F5
Station App. Norwd HA6 .. 174 E3
Station App. Radl WD7 ... 156 A4
Station App. Sth Ox WD1 . 175 D7
Station Cl. Bro Pk AL9 ... 144 E5
Station Cl. Pot B EN6 ... 158 F8
Station Footpath.
Abb L WD4 ... 139 B1
Station Mews. Pot B EN6 . 159 A8
Station Par. Letw SG6 ... 22 F6
Station Pl. Letw SG6 ... 22 F6
Station Rd. Abb L WD4 ... 139 B1
Station Rd. Ald HP23 ... 101 B5
Station Rd. Arl SG15 ... 11 A4
Station Rd. Ashw SG7 ... 5 B3
Station Rd. Bal SG7 ... 12 F1
Station Rd. Berk HP4 ... 122 D4
Station Rd. Bis St CM23 ... 77 A7
Station Rd. Bor WD6 ... 170 A5
Station Rd. Brag SG11 ... 55 E5
Station Rd. Bri Wd AL2 ... 155 A8
Station Rd. Bro Pk AL9 ... 144 D6
Station Rd. Bun SG9 ... 40 E7
Station Rd. Ched LU7 ... 79 F8
Station Rd. Ches EN8 ... 163 A5
Station Rd. Coln H AL4 ... 129 B3
Station Rd. Cuf EN6 ... 146 F2
Station Rd. Gt Am SG12 ... 115 C4
Station Rd. Harl CM17 ... 118 C4
Station Rd. Harp AL5 ... 86 C2
Station Rd. Heml H HP1 ... 124 C1
Station Rd. Hertng SG14 .. 112 B3
Station Rd. Hod EN10 ... 135 A3
Station Rd. Kneb SG3 ... 68 F5
Station Rd. Kneb SG3 ... 69 A5
Station Rd. L Ston SG16 ... 10 A4
Station Rd. Letw SG6 ... 22 F6
Station Rd. Lon M HP23 ... 79 B4
Station Rd. Luton LU1 ... 63 E8
Station Rd. Luton LU4 ... 44 E5
Station Rd. Muc H SG10 ... 74 E1
Station Rd. Odsey SG7 ... 5 B3
Station Rd. Odsey SG7 ... 5 C5
Station Rd. Pit LU7 ... 80 E5
Station Rd. Radl WD7 ... 156 A4
Station Rd. Ric WD3 ... 165 D2
Station Rd. Saw CM21 ... 97 F3
Station Rd. Sta M CM24 ... 59 E6
Station Rd. Stand SG11 ... 55 E2
Station Rd. Ste Mo SG8 ... 5 C5
Station Rd. Tri HP23 ... 100 D4
Station Rd. Ware SG12 ... 93 E1
Station Rd. Wat St SG14 ... 70 D3
Station Rd. Watf WD1 ... 167 B7
Station Rd. Wel G AL9 ... 144 D6
Station Rd. Welw AL6 ... 89 E3
Station Rd. Whea AL4 ... 87 D1
Station Terr. Hit SG4 ... 35 A8
Station Terr. Pk St AL2 ... 141 D5
Station Way. Letw SG6 ... 22 E6
Staveley Rd. Dun LU4 ... 44 C1
Steeplands. Bus WD2 ... 168 B2
Steeple View. Bis St CM23 76 F8
Stephall Green Inf Sch.
Stev ... 51 B2
Stephall Manor Sch. Stev ... 51 A1
Stephens Cl. Luton LU2 ... 46 A3
Stephens Way. Red AL3 ... 105 F5
Stephenson Cl. Royst SG8 ... 7 B7
Stephenson Way.
Bus WD2 ... 167 D7
Stephenson Way.
Watf WD2 ... 167 D7
Stepnells. Mars HP23 ... 80 A1
Sterling Ave. Ches EN8 ... 162 D5
Sterling Rd. Enf EN2 ... 161 D1
Stevenage Cres. Bor WD6 169 E7
Stevenage Rd. Hit SG4 ... 34 F5
Stevenage Rd. Kneb SG3 ... 68 F7
Stevenage Rd. L Wym SG4 35 E2
Stevenage Rd. L Wym SG4 35 E3
Stevenage Rd. St Ipp SG4 .. 35 C2
Stevenage Rd. Walk SG2 ... 51 E8
Stevenage Rise.
Heml H HP2 ... 124 F7
Stevenage Sta. Stev ... 50 C5
Stevens Gn. Bus WD2 ... 168 C1
Steward Cl. Ches EN8 ... 148 E1
Stewart Cl. Abb L WD5 ... 154 A7
Stewart Rd. Harp AL5 ... 86 B2
Stewarts The. Bis St CM23 76 E6
Stirling Cl. Stev SG2 ... 69 D7
Stirling Cnr. Bor EN5 ... 170 D3
Stirling House. Bor WD6 .. 170 C5
Stirling Way. Bor WD6 ... 170 D4
Stirling Way. Wel G C AL7 111 E6
Stobarts Cl. Kneb SG3 ... 68 F6
Stock Bank. Bark SG8 ... 8 D1
Stockbreach Cl. Hat AL10 130 A6
Stockbreach Rd. Hat AL10 130 A6
Stockens Dell. Kneb SG3 ... 68 F4
Stockens Gn. Kneb SG3 ... 68 F4
Stockers Farm Rd.
Ric WD3 ... 173 D8
Stockfield Ave. Hod EN11 135 B8
Stockholm Way. Luton LU3 44 E8
Stocking Hill. Cotrd SG9 ... 39 B8
Stocking La. Nut SG8 ... 18 C1
Stockings La. L Berk SG13 132 D6
Stockingstone Rd.
Luton LU2 ... 45 E2
Stockport Rd. Chor WD3 .. 164 C2
Stocks Meadow.
Heml H HP2 ... 125 A4
Stocks Rd. Ald HP23 ... 101 D7
Stockwell Cl. Ches EN7 ... 148 B3
Stockwell La. Ches EN7 ... 148 B3
Stockwood Cres.
Luton LU1 ... 63 D6
Stockwood Ct. Luton LU1 ... 63 D6
Stockwood High Sch. Luton 63 F5
Stoffold House. Stot SG5 ... 11 F6
Stone Cross. Harl CM20 .. 117 D1
Stonecroft. Kneb SG3 ... 68 F5
Stonecross Rd. Hat AL10 . 130 B7
Stonecross. St Alb AL1 ... 127 E4
Stonehill Jun Mix Inf Sch.
Letw ... 11 E1
Stonehills. Wel G C AL8 ... 110 D7
Stonelea Rd. Heml H HP3 138 F8
Stoneleigh Ave. Enf EN1 .. 162 B1
Stoneleigh Cl. Ches EN8 .. 162 D6
Stoneleigh Cl. Luton LU3 ... 45 B7
Stoneleigh Dr. Hod EN11 . 115 B1
Stoneleigh. Saw CM21 ... 97 D3
Stoneley. Letw SG6 ... 11 F1
Stonemead. Wel G C AL8 .. 89 D3
Stonesdale. Luton LU4 ... 44 C4
Stoneways Cl. Luton LU4 ... 44 C6
Stoney Comm. Sta M CM24 59 E5
Stoney Common Rd.
Sta M CM24 ... 59 D5
Stoney Croft. Ald HP23 ... 101 C5
Stoney La. Bov HP3 ... 137 C5
Stoney La. Chipf HP3 ... 137 F1
Stoney Pl. Sta M CM24 ... 59 E5
Stoneycroft. Heml H HP1 . 124 A3
Stoneycroft. Wel G C AL7 111 A7
Stoneyfield Dr.
Sta M CM24 ... 59 E6
Stoneygate Rd. Luton LU4 . 44 D3
Stonnells Cl. Letw SG6 ... 22 F8
Stony Croft. Stev SG1 ... 50 E6
Stony Hills. Sac SG14 ... 92 C7
Stony La. Chen HP6 ... 150 E1
Stony La. Gt Of SG4 ... 47 C4
Stonyshotts. Wa Aby EN9 163 E6
Stookslade. Wing HP22 ... 60 A3
Stopsley High Sch &
Community Coll. Luton ... 45 F4
Stopsley Inf Sch. Luton ... 46 A4
Stopsley Jun Sch. Luton ... 46 A4
Stopsley Way. Luton LU2 ... 46 A3
Storehouse La. Hit SG4 ... 34 F6
Storey Ct. Bus WD2 ... 168 B4
Storey St. Heml H HP3 ... 138 D7
Stormont Rd. Hit SG5 ... 21 F1
Stormont Sch. Pot B ... 159 D8
Stornoway. Heml H HP3 .. 125 B1
Stort Lodge. Bis St CM23 ... 76 D8
Stort Mill. Harl CM20 ... 118 B6
Stort Rd. Bis St CM23 ... 76 F6
Stort Valley Ind Pk. Bis St . 59 B2
Stortford Hall Ind Pk.
Bis St ... 77 B7
Stortford Hall Pk.
Bis St CM23 ... 77 B8
Stortford Hall Rd.
Bis St CM23 ... 77 B8
Stortford Rd. Hod EN11 ... 135 C7
Stortford Rd. L Had SG11 .. 57 C2
Stortford Rd. Sheer CM22 . 98 F3
Stortford Rd. Stand SG11 ... 55 F2
Stotfold House. Stot SG5 ... 11 F6
Stotfold Rd. Arl SG15 ... 11 B7
Stotfold Rd. Letw SG6 ... 22 C4
Stotfold Rd. Newn SG7 ... 3 C1
Stow The. Harl CM20 ... 117 F2
Stox Mead. Har HA3 ... 176 D2
Strafford Cl. Pot B EN6 ... 159 A7
Strafford Ct. Kneb SG3 ... 69 A5
Strafford Gate. Pot B EN6. 159 A7
Strafford Gate. Pot B EN6 159 A7
Strafford Rd. Barn EN5 ... 171 E6
Straits The. Wa Aby EN9 . 163 B7
Strangers Way. Luton LU4 . 44 C4
Strangeways. Watf WD1 . 153 E3
Stratfield Dr. Hod EN10 ... 134 E4
Stratfield Rd. Bor WD6 ... 170 A7
Stratford Lodge.
Watf WD1 ... 167 B8
Stratford Rd. Luton LU4 ... 45 B1
Stratford Rd. Watf WD1 .. 167 A7
Stratford Way.
Bri Wd AL2 ... 140 F2
Stratford Way.
Heml H HP3 ... 138 B8
Stratford Way. Watf WD1 167 A7
Strathmore Ave. Hit SG5 ... 21 F1
Strathmore Ave. Luton LU1 63 F5
Strathmore Inf &
Nursery Sch. Hit ... 21 E2
Strathmore Rd. Whit SG4 .. 66 E6
Strathmore Wlk. Luton LU1 63 F6
Stratton Ave. Enf EN2 ... 161 D2
Stratton Gdns. Luton LU2 .. 45 D4
Straw Plait Way. Arl SG15 . 10 F4
Strawberry Field.
Hat AL10 ... 130 A2 8
Strawberry Field.
Luton LU3 ... 44 E7
Strawberry Fields.
Ware SG12 ... 93 B2
Strawfields. Wel G C AL7 . 111 B7
Strawmead. Hat AL10 ... 130 B7
Strawplaiters Cl.
Welw SG3 ... 69 A2
Strayfield Rd. Cre H EN2 .. 161 B2
Stream Woods Jun Mix
Inf Sch. Hat ... 130 B4
Street The. Brag SG11 ... 55 F7
Street The. Chipf WD4 ... 152 A8
Street The. Dan En SG11 ... 53 F3
Street The. Fur P SG9 ... 43 A4
Street The. Sheer CM22 ... 98 E1
Street The. Wal SG7 ... 25 C8
Stretton Way. Bor WD6 ... 156 E1
Stringers La. Ast SG2 ... 51 E2
Stripling Way. Watf WD1 167 A3
Stroma Cl. Heml H HP3 ... 125 C1
Stronsay. Heml H HP3 ... 125 C1
Stuart Ct. Elst WD6 ... 169 D3
Stuart Dr. Hit SG4 ... 35 B7
Stuart Dr. Royst SG8 ... 7 D8
Stuart Pl. Luton LU1 ... 63 D7
Stuart Rd. Welw AL6 ... 89 B3
Stuart St. Luton LU1 ... 63 D7
Stuart Way. Ches EN7 ... 162 B8
Stuarts Cl. Heml H HP3 ... 124 D1 3
Stud Gn. Watf WD2 ... 154 B7
Studham Cty Prim Sch. Stu 82 B4
Studham La. Dagn HP4 ... 81 D4
Studham La. Whip HP4 ... 82 A7
Studio Way. Bor WD6 ... 170 C8
Studios The. Bus WD2 ... 168 A3
Studlands Rise Fst Sch.
Royst ... 7 E5
Studlands Rise. Royst SG8 .. 7 E6
Studley Rd. Luton LU3 ... 45 D1
Sturgeon's Rd. Hit SG4 ... 22 B2
Sturlas Way. Ches EN8 ... 162 D6
Stylemans La. Bis St CM23 77 B5
Styles Cl. Luton LU2 ... 46 C2
Such Cl. Letw SG6 ... 23 B7
Sudbury Rd. Luton LU4 ... 44 B6
Suffolk Cl. Bor WD6 ... 170 D4
Suffolk Cl. Dun LU4 ... 44 A3
Suffolk Cl. Lon C AL2 ... 142 C6
Suffolk Rd. Pot B EN6 ... 158 E7
Suffolk Rd. Royst SG8 ... 7 E6
Sugar La. Heml H HP1 ... 123 B1
Sulgrave Cres. Tri HP23 .. 100 C5
Sullivan Cres. Hare UB9 .. 173 D1
Sullivan Way. Elst WD6 ... 169 C3
Summer Ct. Heml H HP2 .. 124 D5
Summer Dale.
Wel G C AL8 ... 89 D1
Summer Gr. Elst WD6 ... 169 D3
Summer Hill. Bor WD6 ... 170 A4
Summer St. Cad LU1 ... 63 C1
Summer Wlk. Mark AL3 ... 83 E5

Summercroft Inf Sch. Bis St 77 C8
Summercroft Jun Sch. Bis St 77 C8
Summerfield Cl. Lon C AL2 142 C5
Summerfield. Hat AL10 130 A2
Summerfield Rd. Luton LU1 62 F8
Summerfield Rd. Watf WD2 154 A4
Summerhouse La. Hare UB9 173 A3
Summerhouse La. Radl WD2 168 C8
Summerhouse Way. Abb L WD5 139 F1
Summers Rd. Luton LU2 46 C1
Summers Way. Lon C AL2 142 E4
Summersland Rd. St Alb AL4 128 C7
Summerswood La. Ridge WD6 157 E4
Summerswood Prim Sch. Bor 170 B5
Summit Rd. Pot B EN6 144 E1
Sumpter Yd. St Alb AL1 127 D2
Sun Hill. Royst SG8 7 C5
Sun La. Harp AL5 86 A2
Sun Sq. Heml H HP1 124 D4 2
Sun St. Bal SG7 23 E8
Sun St. Hit SG5 34 E6
Sun St. Sheer CM21 97 F1
Sun St. Wa Aby EN9 163 C6
Sunbury Ct. Barn EN5 171 E5 2
Sunderland Ave. St Alb AL1 128 A4
Sundew Rd. Heml H HP1 123 E2
Sundon Park Jun Sch. Luton 44 C8
Sundon Park Rd. Luton LU3 44 C7
Sunmead Rd. Heml H HP2 124 D5
Sunningdale. Bis St CM23 76 E6
Sunningdale. Luton LU2 45 F3
Sunningdale Mews. Wel G C AL7 89 F2
Sunny Bank. Ched LU7 79 F7
Sunny Hill. Bun SG9 40 F7
Sunnybank Rd. Pot B EN6 159 A6
Sunnydell. Chis AL2 141 B5
Sunnyfield. Hat AL9 130 D8
Sunnyhill Rd. Heml H HP1 124 B3
Sunnyhill Rd. Map Cr WD3 172 D4
Sunnyside. Lo Naz EN9 135 F1
Sunnyside Rd. Hit SG4 35 A5
Sunnyside. Sta M CM24 59 E6
Sunridge Ave. Luton LU2 45 E2
Sunrise Cres. Heml H HP3 138 F8
Sunset Dr. Luton LU2 45 F3
Sunset View. Barn EN5 171 E7
Surrey Pl. Tri HP23 100 A3
Surrey St. Luton LU1 63 E6
Surrey Street Prim Sch. Luton 63 E6
Sursham Ct. Mark AL3 83 E5
Sussex Cl. Hod EN11 135 A7
Sussex Pl. Luton LU2 46 D2
Sussex Rd. Watf WD2 154 A1
Sutcliffe Cl. Bus WD2 168 C5
Sutcliffe Cl. Stev SG1 51 A8
Sutherland Ave. Cuf EN6 146 D3
Sutherland Cl. Barn EN5 171 E5
Sutherland Ct. Wel G C AL7 110 F7
Sutherland Pl. Luton LU1 63 D5
Sutherland Way. Cuf EN6 146 E3
Sutton Acres. L Hal CM22 98 D7
Sutton Cl. Hod EN10 134 E4
Sutton Cl. Tri HP23 100 B6
Sutton Cres. Barn EN5 171 D4
Sutton Gdns. Luton LU3 44 D6
Sutton Path. Bor WD6 170 A6
Sutton Rd. St Alb AL1 128 B3
Sutton Rd. Watf WD1 167 C6
Swallow Cl. Bus WD2 168 C1
Swallow Cl. Dun LU4 44 A4
Swallow Cl. Ric WD3 165 C2
Swallow Ct. Hert SG14 113 C6
Swallow Ct. Wel G C AL7 110 F6
Swallow End. Wel G C AL7 110 F6
Swallow Gdns. Hat AL10 130 A3
Swallow Oaks. Abb L WD5 153 F7
Swallowdale La. Heml H HP2 125 B6
Swallowfields. Wel G C AL7 110 F6
Swallows. Harl CM17 118 C4
Swallows The. Wel G C AL7 89 F2
Swan & Pike Rd. Enf EN3 163 A1
Swan Ct. Bis St CM23 76 F6
Swan La. Gu M SG8 1 F4
Swan Mead. Dun LU4 44 B4
Swan St. Ashw SG7 4 D4
Swanells Wood. Stu LU6 82 C4
Swanfield Rd. Ches EN8 162 E6
Swangley's La. Kneb SG3 69 B4
Swanhill. Wel G C AL7 90 A1
Swanland Rd. Pot B EN6 144 B3
Swanland Rd. Wel G EN6 144 B3
Swanley Bar La. Bro Pk EN6 145 B3
Swanley Cres. Bro Pk EN6 145 B2
Swanley Ct. Watf WD2 154 C2
Swans Cl. Coln H AL4 128 E2
Swans Ct. Ches EN8 162 E5
Swanstand. Letw SG6 23 D4
Swanston Grange. Dun LU4 44 B2
Swanston Path. Sth Ox WD1 175 C7
Swasedale Rd. Luton LU3 45 A6
Sweet Briar. Wel G C AL7 111 A5
Sweetbriar Cl. Heml H HP1 124 A6
Sweyns Mead. Stev SG2 51 C7
Swift Cl. Gt Am SG12 115 C3
Swift Cl. Letw SG6 22 E8
Swift Cl. Royst SG8 2 D1
Swiftfields. Wel G C AL7 111 A7
Swifts Green Cl. Luton LU2 46 B5
Swifts Green Rd. Luton LU2 46 B5
Swinburne Ave. Hit SG5 21 C1
Swinburne Cl. Royst SG8 2 D1
Swing Gate La. Berk HP4 122 D2
Swing Gate Sch. Berk 122 D3
Swingate. Stev SG1 50 D5
Swinnell Cl. Knee SG8 2 B5
Swiss Ave. Watf WD1 166 E6
Swiss Cl. Watf WD1 166 E6
Sworders Yd. Bis St CM23 76 F7 2
Sycamore Ave. Hat AL10 130 A4
Sycamore Cl. Bus WD2 167 E7
Sycamore Cl. Ham St EN7 147 F4
Sycamore Cl. Hit SG4 35 A4
Sycamore Cl. Watf WD2 154 B4
Sycamore Dr. Pk St AL2 141 D4
Sycamore Dr. Tri HP23 100 B4
Sycamore Rd. Cro Gr WD3 166 D4
Sycamore Rise. Berk HP4 122 D3
Sycamores The. Bis St CM23 77 B6
Sycamores The. Heml H HP3 137 F8
Sycamores The. Radl WD7 156 B5
Sycamores The. St Alb AL1 127 D2
Sydney Rd. Watf WD1 166 F4
Sylam Cl. Luton LU3 44 E7
Sylvan Cl. Heml H HP3 125 A2
Sylvan Way. Wel G C AL7 111 C5
Sylvandale. Wel G C AL7 111 C5
Sylvia Ave. Pnr HA5 175 F4
Symonds Green La. Stev SG1 50 A6
Symonds Green Rd. Stev SG1 50 A7
Symonds Rd. Hit SG5 34 D8

Tabbs Cl. Letw SG6 23 B7
Tacitus Cl. Stev SG1 51 C8
Takeley Cl. Wa Aby EN9 163 D6
Talbot Ave. Watf WD1 167 E2
Talbot Ct. Heml H HP3 124 D1
Talbot Rd. Har HA3 176 F1
Talbot Rd. Hat AL10 130 A8
Talbot Rd. Luton LU2 45 F2
Talbot Rd. Ric WD3 165 E1
Talbot St. Hert SG13 113 E6
Talbot St. Hit SG5 34 C8
Talbot Way. Letw SG6 12 B1
Tall Trees. Hit SG4 35 A4
Tall Trees. Royst SG8 7 E6
Tallack Cl. Har HA3 176 E3
Tallents Cres. Harp AL5 86 D3
Tallents Farm (Research Farm). Kim 86 F8
Tallis Way. Bor WD6 169 E8
Tamar Gn. Heml H HP2 124 F8
Tamarisk Cl. St Alb AL3 127 D7
Tameton Cl. Luton LU2 46 F2
Tamworth Rd. Hert SG13 113 F7
Tancred Rd. Luton LU2 46 A4
Tanfield Cl. Ham St EN7 148 A4
Tanfield Gn. Luton LU2 46 E1
Tanglewood Cl. Stan HA7 176 E8
Tanglewood. Welw AL6 90 A7
Tanners Cl. St Alb AL3 127 C4
Tanners Cres. Hert SG13 113 C4
Tanners Hill. Abb L WD5 154 A8
Tanners Way. Hun SG12 116 C8
Tanners Wood Cl. Abb L WD5 153 E7
Tanners Wood Ct. Abb L WD5 153 E7
Tanners Wood Jun Mix Inf Sch. Abb L 153 E7
Tanners Wood La. Abb L WD5 153 E7
Tannery Cl. Royst SG8 7 C6
Tannery Drift. Royst SG8 7 C6
Tannery Drift Sch. Royst 7 C6
Tannery The. Bun SG9 40 E7
Tannery Yd. Whit SG4 66 F6
Tannsfield Dr. Heml H HP2 124 F5 1
Tannsmore Cl. Heml H HP2 124 F5 2
Tansycroft. Wel G C AL7 111 B7
Tanworth Cl. Norwd HA6 174 C4
Tanworth Gdns. Pnr HA5 175 C1
Tany's Dell Cty Prim Sch. Harl 118 A3
Tany's Dell. Harl CM20 118 A3
Tanyard La. Cod SG4 88 B8
Tapster St. Barn EN5 171 F6
Taransay. Heml H HP3 125 B1
Tarpan Way. Ches EN10 148 F6
Tarrant Dr. Harp AL5 107 D7
Tarrant. Stev SG1 36 B1
Tasmin Cl. Norwd HA6 174 F2
Tassell Hall. Red AL3 105 F6
Tatlers La. Ast SG2 51 E4
Tatsfield Ave. Lo Naz EN9 149 D8
Tattershall Dr. Heml H HP2 105 B1
Tattle Hill. Bram SG14 91 E2
Tattlers Hill. Wing HP22 60 B3
Tauber Cl. Bor WD6 169 F5
Taunton Rd. Luton LU2 46 B1
Taverners. Heml H HP2 124 E5
Taverners Way. Hod EN11 135 A6
Tavistock Ave. St Alb AL1 141 D8
Tavistock Cl. Pot B EN6 159 D8
Tavistock Cl. St Alb AL1 141 D8
Tavistock Cres. Luton LU1 63 E5
Tavistock Rd. Watf WD2 167 D8
Tavistock St. Luton LU1 63 E6
Taylor Cl. St Alb AL4 128 A8
Taylor St. Luton LU2 63 F8
Taylor Trad Est. Hert 114 B7
Taylor's Hill. Hit SG4 34 F6
Taylor's La. Barn EN5 171 F8
Taylor's Rd. Stot SG5 3 A1
Taylor's Rd. Stot SG5 11 F8
Taylors Ave. Hod EN11 135 A5
Taywood Cl. Stev SG2 51 B2
Teal Dr. Norwd HA6 174 C3
Teal House. Watf WD2 154 E3
Teasdale Cl. Royst SG8 2 D1
Teasel Cl. Royst SG8 7 E5
Tedder Ave. Henlw SG16 10 C5
Tedder Rd. Heml H HP2 125 A4
Tee Side. Hert SG13 114 B7
Teesdale. Heml H HP2 124 E6
Teesdale. Luton LU4 44 C5
Telford Ave. Stev SG2 51 B6
Telford Cl. Watf WD2 154 D4
Telford Ct. Hat AL10 129 F3
Telford Ct. St Alb AL1 127 E2
Telford Rd. Lon C AL2 142 C4
Telford Way. Luton LU1 63 D8
Telmere Ind Est. Luton 63 E6 11
Telscombe Way. Luton LU2 46 C3
Temperance St. St Alb AL3 127 C3
Tempest Ave. Pot B EN6 159 D7
Templar Ave. Bal SG7 23 F6
Templars Dr. Stan HA3 176 D4
Templars La. Pres SG4 48 D6
Temple Bank. Harl CM20 118 B5
Temple Cl. Ches EN7 162 A8
Temple Cl. Luton LU2 45 E5
Temple Cl. Pres SG5 34 B4
Temple Cl. Watf WD1 166 F7
Temple Ct. Bal SG7 23 F6
Temple Ct. Hert SG14 92 D1
Temple Ct. Pot B EN6 158 D8
Temple Fields. Hert SG14 92 D1
Temple Gdns. Letw SG6 23 C8
Temple Gdns. Mo Pk WD3 174 B6
Temple La. Ton SG12 92 F8
Temple Mead. Heml H HP2 124 D5
Temple Mead. Roy CM19 116 B1
Temple View. St Alb AL3 127 C5
Templefields Ent Ctr. Harl 118 A3
Templepan La. Sar WD3 152 E2
Templewood Sch. Wel G C 110 D8
Templewood. Wel G C AL8 89 D1
Tempsford Ave. Bor WD6 170 D5
Tempsford. Wel G C AL7 111 D6
Temsford Cl. Har HA2 176 C1
Tenby Dr. Luton LU4 44 F3
Tene The. Bal SG7 23 F8
Tennand Cl. Ham St EN7 147 F5
Tennison Ave. Bor WD6 170 B4
Tennyson Ave. Hit SG4 35 C7
Tennyson Ave. Wa Aby EN9 163 E5
Tennyson Cl. Royst SG8 2 E1
Tennyson Rd. Chis AL2 141 B5
Tennyson Rd. Harp AL5 86 A2
Tennyson Rd. Luton LU1 63 E5
Tennyson Road Prim Sch. Luton 63 E5
Tenterfield House. Welw AL6 89 C4
Tenth Ave. Luton LU3 44 C7
Tenzing Rd. Luton LU1 63 C6
Tenzing Rd. Heml H HP2 125 A3
Teresa Gdns. Ches EN8 162 D5
Terminus St. Harl CM20 117 D1
Terrace Gdns. Watf WD1 167 B7
Terrace The. Ess AL9 131 E6
Terrace The. Red AL3 106 A5
Terrace The. Tri HP23 100 A3
Tethys Rd. Heml H HP2 124 F6
Tewin Cl. St Alb AL4 128 C7
Tewin Cl. Tewin AL6 90 C5
Tewin Ct. Wel G C AL7 110 F7
Tewin Hill. Tewin AL6 90 F5
Tewin Rd. Heml H HP2 125 C3
Tewin Rd. Wel G C AL7 110 F7
Tewin Water Sch. Tewin 90 B2
Thackeray Cl. Royst SG8 2 D1
Thames Ave. Heml H HP2 124 F8
Thames Ct. Luton LU3 45 B3
Thamesdale. Lon C AL2 142 F4
Thatchers Croft. Heml H HP2 124 E7
Thatchers End. Hit SG4 35 D8
Thaxted Cl. Luton LU2 46 F2
Thaxted Way. Wa Aby EN9 163 D6
Thaynesfield. Pot B EN6 159 D8
Theabald's Grove Sta. Ches 162 D7
Thelby Cl. Luton LU3 44 F6
Thele Ave. Sta Ab SG12 115 D4
Thelusson Ct. Radl WD7 156 A3
Theobald Cres. Har HA3 176 C2
Theobald St. Bor WD6 169 F7
Theobald St. Radl WD7 156 D2
Theobald's La. Ches EN8 162 B7
Theobald's La. Ches EN8 162 C7
Theobald's Rd. Cuf EN6 146 F1
Theobalds Cl. Cuf EN6 146 F1
Theobalds Park Coll. Ches 162 A6
Theobalds Park Rd. Cre H EN2 161 B3
Therfield Fst Sch. Ther 15 F7
Therfield Rd. St Alb AL3 127 D6
Thetford Gdns. Luton LU2 45 E6
Thieves' La. Hert SG14 112 F7
Third Ave. Letw SG6 23 C7
Third Ave. Luton LU3 44 D7
Third Ave. Watf WD2 154 D4
Thirlestane. St Alb AL1 127 F4
Thirlestone Rd. Luton LU4 44 D1
Thirlmere Dr. St Alb AL1 128 B1
Thirlmere Gdns. Norwd HA6 174 C4
Thirsk Rd. Bor WD6 157 A1
Thirston Path. Bor WD6 170 A7
Thistle Cl. Heml H HP1 123 E2
Thistle Gr. Wel G C AL7 111 C3
Thistle Rd. Luton LU1 63 F7
Thistlecroft. Heml H HP1 124 B2
Thistles The. Heml H HP1 124 B4
Thistley La. St Ipp SG4 34 F1
Thomas Alleyne Sch The. Stev 50 C8
Thomas Ct. Berk HP4 121 F5
Thomas Heskin Ct. Bis St CM23 77 A7 5
Thomas Rochford Way. Ches EN8 148 F4
Thomas Tallis Cty Inf Sch The. Wa Aby 163 F6
Thomas Watson Cottage Homes The. Barn EN5 171 E4
Thompson Way. Ric WD3 165 A1
Thompsons Cl. Harp AL5 86 A1
Thorley Ctr The. Bis St 76 D4
Thorley High. Bis St CM23 76 F2
Thorley Hill. Bis St CM23 76 F5
Thorley Hill Prim Sch. Bis St 76 F4
Thorley La. Bis St CM23 76 C4
Thorley Park Rd. Bis St CM23 76 F4
Thorn Ave. Bus WD2 168 C1
Thorn Gr. Bis St CM23 77 B6
Thorn Tree Dr. Tri HP23 99 F4
Thornage Cl. Luton LU2 45 D7
Thornbera Cl. Bis St CM23 76 F4
Thornbera Gdns. Bis St CM23 76 F4
Thornbera Rd. Bis St CM23 76 F4
Thornbury Cl. Hod EN11 115 B2
Thornbury Cl. Stev SG2 69 A8
Thornbury Gdns. Bor WD6 170 C5
Thornbury. Harp AL5 86 D1
Thorncroft. Heml H HP3 125 B1
Thorndyke Ct. Pnr HA5 175 F3
Thorne Grove Jun Mix Inf Sch. Bis St 77 B6
Thornfield Rd. Bis St CM23 76 E8
Thornhill Rd. Luton LU4 44 F2
Thornhill Rd. Mo Pk HA6 174 C6
Thornton Gr. Pnr HA5 176 A4
Thornton Rd. Barn EN5 171 E6
Thornton Rd. Pot B EN6 145 C1
Thornton St. Hert SG14 113 D6
Thornton St. St Alb AL3 127 C4
Thorntondale. Luton LU4 44 C5
Thorpe Cres. Watf WD1 167 C2
Thorpe Rd. St Alb AL1 127 D2
Thorpefield Cl. St Alb AL4 128 D6
Thrales Cl. Luton LU3 44 E7
Three Cherrytrees La. Heml H HP2 125 B7
Three Close La. Berk HP4 122 C4
Three Corners. Heml H HP3 125 A1
Three Crosses. Pirt SG5 20 D4
Three Houses La. Kneb SG4 67 D5
Three Stiles. Ben SG2 52 E4
Thremhall Ave. Birhr CM23 77 F8
Thricknells Cl. Luton LU3 44 E7
Thrift Farm La. Bor WD6 170 C7
Thristers Cl. Letw SG6 23 B3
Throcking La. Cotrd SG9 27 C1
Thrums. Watf WD2 154 B2
Thrush Ave. Hat AL10 130 A3
Thrush Gn. Ric WD3 165 C2
Thrush La. Cuf EN6 146 F3
Thumbswood Inf Sch. Wel G C 111 A5
Thumbswood. Wel G C AL7 111 A3
Thumpers. Heml H HP2 124 E5
Thunder Hall. Ware SG12 93 D2 1
Thundercourt. Ware SG12 93 D2
Thundridge Cl. Wel G C AL7 111 B5
Thurgood Rd. Hod EN11 135 A8
Thurlow Cl. Stev SG1 36 D2
Thurnall Ave. Royst SG8 7 D5
Thurnall Cl. Bal SG7 23 F8
Tibbles Cl. Watf WD2 154 E4
Tibbs Hill Rd. Abb L WD5 139 F1
Tiberius Rd. Luton LU3 44 F6
Tichborne. Map Cr WD3 172 D5
Tile Kiln Cl. Heml H HP3 125 B2
Tile Kiln Cres. Heml H HP3 125 B2
Tile Kiln La. Heml H HP3 125 B2
Tilecroft. Wel G C AL8 89 D1
Tilehouse Cl. Bor WD6 169 F6
Tilehouse La. Map Cr UB9 172 E2
Tilehouse St. Hit SG5 34 E6
Tilgate. Luton LU2 46 D3
Tillers Link. Stev SG2 51 A2
Tillotson Rd. Har HA3 176 B3
Tilsworth Wlk. St Alb AL4 128 C8
Timber Orch. Stap SG14 92 A2
Timber Ridge. Ric WD3 165 D5
Timbercroft. Wel G C AL7 89 F1
Timbers Ct. Harp AL5 85 F2
Times Cl. Hit SG5 21 D2
Timplings Row. Heml H HP1 124 B5
Timworth Cl. Luton LU2 46 D1
Tingeys Cl. Red AL3 106 A5
Tinkers La. Wigg HP23 121 A6
Tinsley Cl. Luton LU1 63 B5
Tintagel Cl. Heml H HP2 124 D8
Tintagel Cl. Luton LU3 45 B4
Tintern Cl. Harp AL5 85 C4
Tintern Cl. Stev SG2 69 A7
Tinwell Mews. Bor WD6 170 D4
Tippendell La. Chis AL2 141 C5
Tippet Ct. Stev SG1 50 D3
Titan Ct. Luton LU4 44 F1
Titan Rd. Heml H HP2 124 F6
Titchfield Rd. Enf EN3 162 E2
Tithe Barn Cl. St Alb AL1 141 C8

Tithe Cl. Cod SG4 67 F1
Titian Ave. Bus WD2 168 E2
Titmus Cl. Stev SG1 50 E6
Tiverton Ct. Whea AL5 107 E6
Tiverton Rd. Nort EN6 159 E8
Toddington Rd. Luton LU4 44 C6
Toland Cl. Dun LU4 44 C1
Tolcarne Dr. Pnr HA5 175 A1
Tollgate Cl. Chor WD3 164 F5
Tollgate Rd. Col H AL4 143 E7
Tollgate Rd. Enf EN3 162 D4
Tollgate Rd. Wel G AL4 144 A6
Tollpit End. Heml H HP1 124 A6
Tolmers Ave. Cuf EN6 146 E3
Tolmers Gdns. Cuf EN6 146 F2
Tolmers Mews.
New St SG13 146 E6
Tolmers Rd. Cuf EN6 146 E3
Tolpits Cl. Watf WD1 166 F4
Tolpits La. Watf WD1 166 E2
Tom's Hill. Sar WD3 152 E3
Tom's La.
Abb L WD4,WD5 139 D3
Tomkins Cl. Bor WD6 169 E8
Toms Croft. Heml H HP2 124 E2
Toms Field. Hat AL10 129 E4
Toms Hill Rd. Ald HP23 101 D5
Tonwell Jun Mix Inf Sch.
Ton 92 E7
Tooke Cl. Pnr HA5 175 E2
Toorack Rd. Har HA3 176 D1
Tooveys Mill Cl.
Kin L WD4 139 A2
Topstreet Way. Harp AL5 107 C8
Torquay Cres. Stev SG1 50 B7
Torquay Dr. Luton LU4 44 D4
Torridge Wlk.
Heml H HP2 124 F8 2
Torrington Dr. Pot B EN6 159 D7
Torrington Rd. Berk HP4 122 B4
Tortoiseshell Way.
Berk HP4 121 F6
Torwood Cl. Berk HP4 121 F4
Torworth Rd. Bor WD6 157 A1
Tot La. Birhr CM23 59 D4
Totteridge Comm.
Barn N20 171 D1
Totteridge Pk. Barn N20 171 C1
Totteridge Rd. Enf EN3 162 D2
Totteridge Village.
Barn N20 171 F1
Totton Mews. Red AL3 106 B5
Totts La. Walk SG2 38 C1
Toulmin Dr. St Alb AL3 127 C7
Tovey Ave. Hod EN11 135 A8
Tovey Cl. Lo Naz EN9 149 F8
Tovey Cl. Lon C AL2 142 D5
Tower Cl. Berk HP4 122 A3
Tower Cl. Knee SG8 2 A5
Tower Cl. L Wym SG4 35 F3
Tower Ct. Luton LU2 46 A1 2
Tower Ctr. Hod 135 A7
Tower Hill.
Chipf HP3,WD4 137 F1
Tower Hill La. Sand AL4 108 F4
Tower Hill. Muc H SG10 74 F2
Tower Rd. Cod SG4 67 F2
Tower Rd. Luton LU2 64 A8
Tower Rd. Ware SG12 93 F2
Tower Sch. Ware 93 E3
Tower St. Hert SG14 113 C8
Tower Way. Luton LU2 64 A8
Towers Rd. Heml H HP2 124 E4
Towers Rd. Pnr HA5 175 E2
Towers Rd. Stev SG1 50 D4
Towers The. Stev SG1 50 D4
Town Ctr. Hat AL10 130 A6
Town Farm. Ched LU7 80 A7
Town Farm Cres.
Stand SG11 55 F2
Town Farm. Whea AL4 108 D8
Town Fields. Hat AL10 130 A6
Town La. Ben SG2 52 E4
Town Mead Rd.
Wa Aby EN9 163 C5
Town Sq. Stev SG1 50 D5
Towne Rd. Royst SG8 7 D5
Townfield. Ric WD3 165 C2
Townley. Letw SG6 23 D4
Townsend Ave. St Alb AL1 127 E4
Townsend C of E Sch.
St Alb 127 C8
Townsend Cl. Bark SG8 17 C3
Townsend Cl. Harp AL5 85 F1
Townsend Dr. St Alb AL3 127 D5
Townsend. Heml H HP2 124 D5
Townsend La. Harp AL5 85 E1
Townsend Rd. Harp AL5 86 A2
Townsend Way.
Norwd HA6 175 A3
Townshend St. Hert SG13 113 E6
Townsley Cl. Luton LU1 63 E6
Tracey Ct. Luton LU1 63 E6 10
Trafalgar Ave. Hod EN10 134 F2
Trafford Cl. Shen WD7 156 E7
Trafford Cl. Stev SG1 36 E1
Traherne Cl. Hit SG4 34 F5 2
Trajan Gate. Walk SG2 37 D1
Trapstyle Rd. Hert SG12 93 A2
Travellers Cl. Wel G AL9 144 C8
Travellers La.
Hat AL9,AL10 130 B2
Travellers La. Wel Gr AL9 130 C1
Treacle La. Rus SG9 25 F3
Treacy Cl. Bus WD2 176 C8
Trebellan Dr. Heml H HP2 124 F4
Tree Cl. Heml H HP3 125 B1
Tree Ct. Elst WD6 169 D3
Treehanger Cl. Tri HP23 100 B4
Treetops Cl. Norwd HA6 174 D5
Trefoil Cl. Dun LU4 44 A4
Trefusis Wlk. Watf WD1 166 E8
Tregelles Rd. Hod EN11 135 A8
Tremaine Gr. Heml H HP2 124 E7
Trent Cl. Shen WD7 156 E7
Trent Cl. Stev SG1 50 E8
Trent Rd. Luton LU3 45 B4
Tresco Rd. Berk HP4 121 F5
Trescott Cl. Luton LU2 46 E2
Tresilion Sq. Heml H HP2 125 A8
Treslian Sq. Heml H HP2 124 F8 1
Trevalga Way.
Heml H HP2 124 E7
Trevellance Way.
Watf WD2 154 D6
Trevelyan Way. Berk HP4 122 B6
Trevero Ct. Ches EN8 162 E6
Trevor Cl. Har HA3 176 F3
Trevor Rd. Hit SG4 35 A8 2
Trevose Way.
Sth Ox WD1 175 C7
Trewenna Dr. Pot B EN6 159 D7
Triangle The. Hit SG4 34 F6
Trident Ave. Hat AL10 129 E6
Trident Ind Est. Hod 135 C7
Trident Rd. Watf WD2 153 F5
Triggs Way. Gt Of LU2 46 E3
Trimley Cl. Luton LU4 44 B5
Trinder Rd. Barn EN5 171 C4
Tring Ford Rd. Wils HP23 100 A7
Tring Hill. Ast Cl HP23 99 C3
Tring Rd. Lon M HP23 79 C3
Tring Rd. Nthch HP4 121 D7
Tring Rd. Wing HP22 60 C1
Tring Sch. Tri 100 B4
Tring Sta. Ald 101 A5
Trinity Cl. Bis St CM23 76 F6
Trinity Cl. Norwd HA6 174 E4
Trinity Ct. Hert SG14 113 C8
Trinity Gr. Hert SG14 113 C8
Trinity Hall Cl. Watf WD2 167 C6
Trinity La. Ches EN8 162 E7 2
Trinity Mews. Heml H HP2 125 D2
Trinity Pl. Stev SG1 50 D6
Trinity Rd. Hert H SG13 114 C3
Trinity Rd. Luton LU3 45 B4
Trinity Rd. Stev SG1 50 C6
Trinity Rd. Stot SG5 11 F7
Trinity Rd. Ware SG12 93 E2
Trinity St. Bis St CM23 76 F6
Trinity Way. Bis St CM23 76 F6
Trinity Wlk. Hert H SG13 114 C3
Tristram Rd. Hit SG4 22 B2
Triton Way. Heml H HP2 124 F5
Trojan Terr. Saw CM21 97 E3
Troon Gdns. Luton LU2 45 E6
Trooper Rd. Ald HP23 101 C5
Trotter's Gap.
Sta Ab SG12 115 E4
Trotters Bottom.
Pot B EN5 158 B2
Trotts Hill Jun & Inf Sch.
Stev 36 F1
Trout Rise. Ric WD3 165 B6
Troutstream Way.
Ric WD3 165 B5
Trouvere Pk. Heml H HP1 124 B5
Trowbridge Gdns.
Luton LU2 45 E3
Trowley Bottom. Fla AL3 105 B8
Trowley Hill Rd. Fla AL3 84 B1
Trowley Rise. Abb L WD5 153 F8
Truemans Rd. Hit SG5 21 D2
Trumper Rd. Stev SG1 36 F1
Trumpington Dr.
St Alb AL1 141 D8
Trundlers Way. Bus WD2 168 E1
Truro Gdns. Luton LU3 45 C5
Trust Rd. Ches EN8 162 E5
Tucker St. Watf WD1 167 C4
Tucker's Row. Bis St CM23 76 F6
Tudor Ave. Ches EN7 162 B8
Tudor Ave. Watf WD2 154 D2
Tudor Cl. Ches EN7 162 B8
Tudor Cl. Hat AL10 129 F2
Tudor Cl. Hun SG12 116 D8
Tudor Cl. Stev SG1 36 C1
Tudor Cres. Enf EN2 161 C1
Tudor Ct. Bor WD6 169 E7
Tudor Ct. Hit SG5 34 D6
Tudor Ct. Knee SG8 2 B4
Tudor Ct. Ric WD3 165 A1
Tudor Ct. Saw CM21 97 E3
Tudor Dr. Watf WD2 154 D2
Tudor Jun Mix Inf Sch.
Heml H 124 E1
Tudor Manor Gdns.
Watf WD2 154 D7
Tudor Par. Ric WD3 165 A2
Tudor Rd. Har HA3 176 D1
Tudor Rd. Luton LU3 45 B2
Tudor Rd. Pnr HA5 175 C1
Tudor Rd. St Alb AL3 127 E7
Tudor Rd. Welw AL6 89 B3
Tudor Rd. Whea AL4 108 E8
Tudor Rise. Hod EN10 134 E2
Tudor Way. Hert SG14 113 A7
Tudor Way. Ric WD3 165 A2
Tudor Way. Wa Aby EN9 163 D6
Tudor Wlk. Watf WD2 154 D2
Tuffnells Way. Harp AL5 85 D4
Tunfield Rd. Hod EN11 115 B1
Tunnel Wood Cl.
Watf WD1 153 F2
Tunnel Wood Rd.
Watf WD1 153 F2
Tunnmeade. Harl CM20 118 A1
Turf La. Gra SG4 36 B4
Turkey St. Enf EN1,EN3 162 C2
Turkey Street Sta. Enf 162 C2
Turmore Dale.
Wel G C AL8 110 C5
Turn Braemar.
Heml H HP2 105 B1
Turnberry Ct. Sth Ox WD1 175 C7
Turnberry Dr. Bri Wd AL2 140 E1
Turner Cl. Stev SG1 36 C2
Turner Rd. Bus WD2 168 C5
Turners Cl. Bram SG14 91 C4
Turners Cl. Harp AL5 86 C4
Turners Ct. Ches EN8 162 D8
Turners Hill. Ches EN8 148 D1
Turners Hill. Heml H HP2 124 E2
Turners Orch. Chor WD3 164 D4
Turners Rd N. Luton LU2 46 A2
Turners Rd S. Luton LU2 46 A2
Turnford Sch. Ches 148 E3
Turnford Villas.
Ches EN10 148 F5
Turnpike Dr. Luton LU3 31 C1
Turnpike Gn. Heml H HP2 124 F7
Turnpike La. Ick SG5 21 E3
Turnstones The.
Watf WD2 154 E3
Turpin's Ride. Royst SG8 7 D5
Turpin's Rise. Stev SG2 50 F1
Turpin's Way. Bal SG7 23 F7
Turpins Chase. Welw AL6 89 F7
Turpins Cl. Hert SG14 112 F6
Turpins Ride. Welw AL6 89 F7
Tuxford Cl. Bor WD6 156 E1
Tweed Cl. Berk HP4 122 B5
Twelve Acres.
Wel G C AL7 110 E4
Twelve Leys. Wing HP22 60 B3
Twickenham Gdns.
Har HA3 176 E3
Twigden Ct. Luton LU3 44 E5
Twinwoods. Stev SG1 50 F4
Twist The. Wigg HP23 100 D2
Twitchell The. Bal SG7 23 F8
Two Acres. Wel G C AL7 110 F3
Two Beeches.
Heml H HP2 124 F8
Two Dells La. Ash Gr HP5 136 A4
Two Oaks Dr. Welw AL6 90 C6
Two Waters Jun Mix
Inf Sch. Heml H 138 D6
Two Waters Rd.
Heml H HP3 124 C1
Two Waters Rd.
Heml H HP3 138 D8
Twyford Bsns Ctr The.
Bis St 77 A5
Twyford Bury La.
Bis St CM22 77 A4
Twyford Cl. Bis St CM23 77 A5
Twyford Dr. Luton LU2 46 D1
Twyford Gdns. Bis St CM23 76 F4
Twyford Rd. Bis St CM23 77 A5
Twyford Rd. St Alb AL4 128 D7
Tye End. Stev SG2 69 B8
Tyfield Cl. Ches EN8 148 C1
Tylers Cl. Kin L WD4 138 F3
Tylers Cswy. New St SG13 132 C1
Tylers. Harp AL5 86 D1
Tylers Hill Rd. Bot HP5 150 A8
Tylers Mead. Luton LU2 45 E5
Tylers Way. Radl WD2 168 E4
Tylers Wood. Welw AL6 90 C6
Tylersfield. Abb L WD5 154 A8
Tynedale. Lon C AL2 142 F4
Tynemouth Dr. Enf EN1 162 A1
Typleden Cl. Heml H HP2 124 D5
Tysoe Ave. Enf EN3 162 F2
Tythe Rd. Luton LU4 44 C6
Tyttenhanger Gn.
Coln H AL1 142 E8

Uckfield Rd. Enf EN3 162 D2
Ufford Cl. Har HA3 176 B3
Ufford Rd. Har HA3 176 B3
Ullswater Rd. Heml H HP3 125 C1
Underacres Cl.
Heml H HP2 125 A4
Underhill Inf Sch. Barn 171 E4
Underhill Jun Sch. Barn 171 E4
Underwood Rd. Stev SG1 36 C2
Union Gn. Heml H HP2 124 D4
Union St. Barn EN5 171 E6
Union St. Luton LU1 63 E6
Union Terr. Bun SG9 40 E7
United States International
University Sch. Bus 167 F5
Unity Rd. Enf EN3 162 D2
University Cl. Bus WD2 168 A5
University of Hertfordshire.
Hat 129 F3
University of Herts (Hertford
Campus). Hert 113 E4
Unwin Cl. Letw SG6 22 E4
Unwin Pl. Stev SG2 51 C3
Unwin Rd. Stev SG2 51 C3
Updale Cl. Pot B EN6 158 E6
Upland Dr. Bro Pk AL9 145 B6
Uplands Ave. Hit SG4 35 B6
Uplands. Brag SG11 55 F6
Uplands. Cro Gr WD3 165 F3
Uplands. Luton LU3 44 D8
Uplands. Stev SG2 51 D7
Uplands The. Bri Wd AL2 140 E1
Uplands The. Harp AL5 107 A4
Uplands. Ware SG12 93 F2
Uplands. Wel G C AL8 89 C2
Upper Ashlyns Rd.
Berk HP4 122 B3
Upper Barn. Heml H HP3 138 F8
Upper Clabdens.
Ware SG12 93 F2
Upper Culver Rd.
St Alb AL1 127 F5
Upper Dagnall St.
St Alb AL3 127 D3
Upper George St.
Luton LU1 63 D7
Upper Gn. Tewin AL6 90 D3
Upper Green Rd.
Tewin AL6 90 E2
Upper Hall Pk. Berk HP4 122 E2
Upper Heath Rd.
St Alb AL1 127 F5
Upper Highway.
Abb L WD5 153 D6
Upper Hill Rise. Ric WD3 165 B3
Upper Hitch. Sth Ox WD1 167 E1
Upper Icknield Way.
Ald LU7 80 E1
Upper Icknield Way.
Ast Cl HP22 99 A3
Upper Icknield Way.
Tri HP23 100 D8
Upper King St. Royst SG8 7 D6
Upper Lattimore Rd.
St Alb AL1 127 E3
Upper Marlborough Rd.
St Alb AL1 127 E3
Upper Marsh La.
Hod EN11 135 A5
Upper Maylins. Letw SG6 23 C3
Upper Paddock Rd.
Watf WD1 167 E3
Upper Pk. Harl CM20 117 B1
Upper Sales. Heml H HP1 123 F2
Upper Sean. Stev SG2 51 A3
Upper Shot. Wel G C AL7 111 A7
Upper Shott. Ham St EN7 147 F5
Upper Station Rd.
Radl WD7 156 A4
Upper Tail. Sth Ox WD1 175 E7
Upper Tilehouse St.
Hit SG5 34 E7
Upperfield Rd.
Wel G C AL7 110 F5
Upperstone Cl. Stot SG5 11 F6
Upshire Rd. Wa Aby EN9 163 F7
Upton Ave. St Alb AL3 127 D4
Upton Cl. Luton LU2 45 D6
Upton Cl. Pk St AL2 141 D6
Upton Lodge Cl. Bus WD2 168 C2
Upton Rd. Watf WD1 167 B6
Upwell Rd. Luton LU2 46 B2
Uranus Rd. Heml H HP2 124 F5
Urban Rd. Bis St CM23 77 B7
Uxbridge Rd. Ric WD3 173 A8
Uxbridge Road (Harrow
Weald). Stan HA3 176 D3
Uxbridge Road (Hatch End).
Pnr HA5 175 F3
Uxbridge Road (Pinner).
Pnr HA5 175 D2
Uxbridge Road (Stanmore).
Stan HA7 176 F4

Vadis Cl. Luton LU3 44 E7
Vale Ave. Bor WD6 170 B4
Vale Cl. Harp AL5 85 D4
Vale Ct. Whea AL4 108 D7
Vale Rd. Watf WD2 167 E4
Valence Dr. Ches EN7 148 A3
Valency Cl. Mo Pk HA6 174 F6
Valerian Way. Stev SG2 51 D8
Valerie Cl. St Alb AL1 128 B3
Valeside. Hert SG14 113 A5
Vallans Cl. Ware SG12 93 D3
Vallansgate. Stev SG2 51 B1
Valley Cl. Hert SG13 113 D5
Valley Cl. Pnr HA5 175 B1
Valley Cl. Stu LU6 82 B4
Valley Cl. Wa Aby EN9 163 C7
Valley Cl. Ware SG12 93 B2
Valley Cl. Whip LU6 81 E7
Valley Gn. Heml H HP2 105 B1
Valley Gn The.
Wel G C AL8 110 C7
Valley La. Fla AL3 83 E1
Valley Rd. Berk HP4 121 F6
Valley Rd. Cod SG4 67 F1
Valley Rd. Letw SG6 22 D7
Valley Rd. Ric WD3 165 B3
Valley Rd. St Alb AL3 127 F7
Valley Rd. Stu LU6 82 B4
Valley Rd. Wel G C AL8 110 B6
Valley Rise. Royst SG8 7 E6
Valley Rise. Watf WD2 154 B6
Valley Rise. Whea AL4 86 F2
Valley Sch The. Stev 50 F2
Valley The. Whit SG4 66 E7
Valley View. Barn EN5 171 E3
Valley View. Gofs O EN7 147 C3
Valley Way. Stev SG2 51 A3
Valley Wlk. Cro Gr WD3 166 C4
Valleyside. Heml H HP1 123 F3
Vanda Cres. St Alb AL1 127 F2
Vantorts Cl. Saw CM21 97 E2
Vantorts Rd. Saw CM21 97 E2
Vardon Rd. Stev SG1 50 F8
Varna Cl. Luton LU3 45 A3
Varney Cl. Ham St EN7 148 A4
Varney Cl. Heml H HP1 123 F3
Varney Rd. Heml H HP1 123 F3
Vaughan Mead. Red AL3 106 A4
Vaughan Rd. Harp AL5 86 B1
Vaughan Rd. Stot SG5 11 E7
Vauxhall Rd. Heml H HP2 125 B3
Vauxhall Rd. Luton LU1 64 B5
Vauxhall Way. Luton LU2 46 B2
Vega Cres. Mo Pk HA6 175 A5 1
Vega Rd. Bus WD2 168 C2
Velizy Ave. Harl CM20 117 D1
Venetia Rd. Luton LU2 46 A4
Ventnor Gdns. Luton LU3 45 A7
Ventura Pk. Lon C AL2 141 F2
Venus Hill. Bov HP3 151 A8
Ver Rd. Red AL3 106 C6
Ver Rd. St Alb AL3 127 C3
Vera Ct. Watf WD1 167 D2
Vera La. Welw AL6 90 B4
Verdure Cl. Bri Wd WD2 154 E7
Verity Way. Stev SG1 51 B8
Veritys. Hat AL10 130 A5
Verney Cl. Berk HP4 121 F5
Verney Cl. Tri HP23 100 C5
Vernon Ave. Enf EN3 162 E3
Vernon Ct. Bis St CM23 76 E4
Vernon Dr. Hare UB9 173 C2
Vernon Rd. Luton LU1 63 C8
Vernon Rd. Watf WD2 167 E4
Vernon's Cl. St Alb AL1 127 E2
Veronica House.
Wel G C AL7 111 B4
Verulam Cl. Wel G C AL7 110 F6
Verulam Gdns. Luton LU3 44 F7

Verulam Golf Course. St Alb .... 127 F1
Verulam Rd. Hit SG5 .... 34 F8
Verulam Rd. St Alb AL3 .... 127 C4
Verulam Sch. St Alb .... 128 A4
Verwood Rd. Har HA2 .... 176 C1
Vespers Cl. Dun LU4 .... 44 A2
Vesta Ave. St Alb AL1 .... 141 C8
Veysey Cl. Heml H HP1 .... 124 B1
Viaduct Rd. Ware SG12 .... 114 E8
Viaduct Way. Wel G C AL7 . 89 F2
Vian Ave. Enf EN3 .... 162 E4
Vicarage Cl. Arl SG15 .... 11 A8
Vicarage Cl. Bis St CM23 .... 76 F7 3
Vicarage Cl. Heml H HP1 . 124 C2
Vicarage Cl. Nort EN6 .... 145 F1
Vicarage Cl. Shil SG5 .... 19 F8
Vicarage Cl. St Alb AL1 .... 141 C8
Vicarage Cl. Stand SG11 .... 55 E2
Vicarage Cswy. Hert H SG13 .... 114 B4
Vicarage Gdns. Fla AL3 .... 84 B1
Vicarage Gdns. Mars HP23 80 A2
Vicarage Gdns. Pot En HP4 .... 123 B7
Vicarage La. Bov HP3 .... 137 B4
Vicarage La. Kin L WD4 .... 138 F2
Vicarage La. Pit LU7 .... 80 F5
Vicarage La. Stap SG14 .... 92 B2
Vicarage Rd. Bun SG9 .... 40 E8
Vicarage Rd. Mars HP23 .... 80 A2
Vicarage Rd. Pit LU7 .... 80 D3
Vicarage Rd. Pot En HP4 . 123 A7
Vicarage Rd. Ware SG12 .... 93 E1
Vicarage Rd. Watf WD1 .... 167 A4
Vicarage Rd. Wigg HP23 . 100 D1
Vicarage Road Prec. Watf WD1 .... 167 B5
Vicarage St. Luton LU1 .... 63 F7
Vicarage Wood. Harl CM20 .... 118 A1
Vicerons Pl. Bis St CM23 .... 76 D4
Victoria C of E Sch. Berk .. 122 C4
Victoria Cl. Ric WD3 .... 165 D2
Victoria Cl. Stev SG1 .... 50 D7
Victoria Cres. Royst SG8 .... 7 D7
Victoria Dr. Stot SG5 .... 12 A5
Victoria La. Barn EN5 .... 171 F5
Victoria Pl. Heml H HP2 ... 124 D3
Victoria Rd. Berk HP4 .... 122 C4
Victoria Rd. Bus WD2 .... 168 B1
Victoria Rd. Harp AL5 .... 86 B1
Victoria Rd. Wa Aby EN9 . 163 C5
Victoria Rd. Watf WD2 .... 154 B1
Victoria St. Luton LU1 .... 63 E6
Victoria St. St Alb AL1 .... 127 E3
Victoria Way. Hit SG5 .... 34 D8
Victors Way. Barn EN5 .... 171 F6
Victory Rd. Berk HP4 .... 122 A5
View Point. Stev SG1 .... 50 A5
View Rd. Pot B EN6 .... 159 C7
Vigors Croft. Hat AL10 .... 129 F4
Villa Ct. Luton LU2 .... 63 D8 6
Villa Rd. Luton LU2 .... 63 D8
Village Ct. St Alb AL4 .... 128 D7
Village St. Lan SG4 .... 49 F1
Villiers Cres. St Alb AL4 ... 128 D6
Villiers Rd. Watf WD1 .... 167 E3
Villiers St. Hert SG13 .... 113 E6
Villiers-Sur-Marne Ave. Bis St CM23 .... 76 D4
Vincent Cl. Ches EN8 .... 148 E3
Vincent Ct. Norwd HA6 .... 174 F2
Vincent. Letw SG6 .... 23 C4
Vincent Rd. Luton LU4 .... 44 D5
Vincenzo Cl. Wel G AL9 .... 144 C8
Vine Cl. Wel G C AL8 .... 110 E8
Vine Gr. East CM20 .... 117 E5
Vines The. Stot SG5 .... 11 E6
Vineyard The. Ware SG12 . 94 A2
Vineyard The. Wel G C AL8 .... 110 E8
Vineyards Rd. Cuf EN6 .... 146 B2
Vineyards Rd. Nort EN6 ... 146 B2
Vinters Ave. Stev SG1 .... 50 F5
Violet Ave. Enf EN2 .... 161 D1
Violet Way. Ric WD3 .... 165 C5
Violets La. Fur P SG9 .... 43 B5
Virgil Dr. Hod EN10 .... 148 F8
Virginia Cl. Luton LU2 .... 45 F3
Viscount Cl. Luton LU3 .... 45 A5
Vivian Cl. Watf WD1 .... 167 A1
Vivian Gdns. Watf WD1 .... 167 A1
Vixen Dr. Hert SG13 .... 114 A6
Vyse Cl. Barn EN5 .... 171 C5

Wacketts. Ham St EN7 .... 148 A4
Waddesdon Cl. Luton LU2 .. 46 D2
Waddington Rd. St Alb AL3 .... 127 D3 1
Wade The. Wel G C AL7 ... 111 A3
Wades The. Hat AL10 .... 130 A2
Wadesmill Rd. Ton SG14 ... 92 D3
Wadesmill Rd. Ware SG12 93 D2
Wadham Rd. Abb L WD5 . 153 F8
Wadhurst Ave. Luton LU3 .. 45 C4
Wadley Cl. Heml H HP2 ... 124 F2 1
Wadnall Way. Welw SG3 ... 68 F3
Waggon Rd. Had W EN4 .. 159 E2
Waggoners Yd. Ware SG12 .... 93 D2 4
Wagon Rd. Pot B EN4 .... 159 B2
Wagon Way. Ric WD3 .... 165 C6
Wain Cl. Pot B EN6 .... 145 B2
Wakefield Wlk. Ches EN8 162 E8
Walcot Ave. Luton LU2 .... 46 B1
Waldeck Rd. Luton LU1,LU3 .... 63 C8
Waldegrave Pk. Harp AL5 . 86 D1
Walden End. Stev SG1 .... 50 E4
Walden Pl. Wel G C AL8 ... 110 D8
Walden Rd. Wel G C AL8 . 110 D8
Waleran Cl. Stan HA7 .... 176 F4
Waleys Cl. Luton LU3 .... 44 E8
Walfords Cl. Harl CM17 ... 118 C3
Walk The. Pot B EN6 .... 159 B7
Walkern Jun Mix Inf Sch. Walk .... 52 B8
Walkern Rd. Ben SG2 .... 52 A3
Walkern Rd. Ben SG2 .... 52 D5
Walkern Rd. Stev SG1 .... 50 D8
Walkern Rd. Wat St SG14 .. 70 D5
Walkers Cl. Harp AL5 .... 107 C7
Walkers' Ct. Bal SG7 .... 23 F8
Walkers Rd. Harp AL5 .... 107 B7
Wall Hall Coll. Radl .... 155 B3
Wallace Way. Hit SG4 .... 22 A2
Waller Ave. Luton LU3,LU4 44 F2
Waller Dr. Norwd HA6 .... 175 A2
Waller Street Mall. Luton LU1 .... 63 E7
Waller's Cl. Gt Ch SG8 .... 9 F2
Wallers Way. Hod EN11 ... 115 B1
Wallingford Wlk. St Alb AL1 .... 141 D8
Wallington Rd. Bal SG7 .... 13 D1
Wallington Rd. Clo SG7 .... 13 D1
Walnut Ave. Bal SG7 .... 24 A7
Walnut Cl. Chis AL2 .... 141 B4
Walnut Cl. Hit SG4 .... 35 A6
Walnut Cl. Luton LU2 .... 46 B4
Walnut Cl. Muc H SG10 .... 74 F2
Walnut Cl. Stot SG5 .... 11 F6
Walnut Cotts. Saw CM21 ... 97 E3
Walnut Ct. Wel G C AL7 ... 110 E3
Walnut Ct. Whea AL4 .... 108 D8
Walnut Dr. Bis St CM23 .... 76 D3
Walnut Gn. Bus WD2 .... 167 F7
Walnut Gr. Heml H HP2 ... 124 D3
Walnut Gr. Wel G C AL7 .. 110 E3
Walnut House. Wel G C AL7 .... 110 F3
Walnut Tree Ave. Saw CM21 .... 97 E4
Walnut Tree Cl. Ast SG2 .... 51 D4
Walnut Tree Cl. Ches EN8 162 D8
Walnut Tree Cl. Hod EN11 135 A6
Walnut Tree Cres. Saw CM21 .... 97 E3
Walnut Tree La. Far CM23 . 58 E4
Walnut Tree Rd. Pirt SG5 .. 20 D3
Walnut Tree Wlk. Gt Am SG12 .... 114 E6
Walnut Way. Ick SG5 .... 21 E4
Walpole Cl. Pnr HA5 .... 176 A4
Walpole Ct. Stev SG2 .... 69 C7
Walsh Cl. Hit SG5 .... 34 D7
Walsham Cl. Stev SG2 .... 69 C7
Walshford Way. Bor WD6 157 A1
Walsingham Cl. Hat AL10 129 F6
Walsingham Cl. Luton LU2 . 45 D7
Walsingham Way. Lon C AL2 .... 142 C4
Walsworth Rd. Hit SG4 .... 35 A8
Waltham Cross Sta. Ches 162 F5
Waltham Gdns. Enf EN3 ... 162 C2
Waltham Holy Cross Cty Jun & Inf Sch. Wa Aby 163 D6
Waltham Rd. Hit SG4 .... 34 F6 6
Waltham Rd. Lo Naz EN9 . 149 F5
Walton Gdns. Wa Aby EN9 .... 163 B6
Walton Rd. Hod EN11 .... 135 C8
Walton Rd. Ware SG12 .... 114 D8
Walton Rd. Watf WD2 .... 167 E5
Walton St. St Alb AL1 .... 127 F5
Walverns Cl. Watf WD1 ... 167 C3
Wandon Cl. Luton LU2 .... 46 C4
Wannions Cl. Bot HP5 .... 136 A1
Wansford Pk. Bor WD6 ... 170 E5
Warburton Cl. Stan HA3 .. 176 D4
Ward Cl. Ham St EN7 .... 148 A4
Ward Cl. Ware SG12 .... 93 C2
Ward Cres. Bis St CM23 .... 76 E6
Ward Freman Sch. Bun .... 40 D8
Warden Hill Cl. Luton LU2 .. 45 C8
Warden Hill Gdns. Luton LU2 .... 45 C8
Warden Hill Inf Sch. Luton 45 C7
Warden Hill Jun Sch. Luton 45 C7
Warden Hill Rd. Luton LU2 45 C8
Wardown Cres. Luton LU2 . 45 E2
Wardown Ct. Luton LU3 .... 45 D2
Wardown House (Luton Mus & Art Gall). Luton ... 45 D2
Ware Coll. Ware .... 114 D8
Ware Park Rd. Hert SG14 113 E8
Ware Rd. Gt Am SG13 .... 115 A2
Ware Rd. Hert SG13,SG14 113 F7
Ware Rd. Hod EN11 .... 115 A2
Ware Rd. Sac SG12 .... 71 C3
Ware Rd. Ton SG12 .... 92 F6
Ware Rd. Wat St SG12,SG14 .... 71 C3
Ware Rd. Widf SG12 .... 95 D4
Ware St Catherine's Jun Mix & Inf Sch. Ware .... 93 B2
Ware Sta. Ware .... 114 D8
Wareham's La. Hert SG14 113 C5
Warenford Way. Bor WD6 170 A8
Wareside CE Prim Sch. Wars .... 94 E3
Wareside Cl. Wel G C AL7 111 B5
Wareside. Heml H HP2 .... 105 A1
Warham Rd. Har HA3 .... 176 F1
Warmark Rd. Heml H HP1 123 E5
Warminster Cl. Luton LU2 . 46 F1
Warneford Pl. Watf WD1 167 E3
Warner Rd. Ware SG12 .... 114 D8
Warners Ave. Hod EN11 .. 134 F4
Warners Cl. Stev SG2 .... 51 C3
Warners End Rd. Heml H HP1 .... 124 B4
Warren Cl. Hat AL10 .... 130 B8
Warren Cl. Letw SG6 .... 22 D7
Warren Dale. Wel G C AL8 89 D1
Warren Dell Sch. Sth Ox .. 175 C7
Warren Dr The. Nwml E LU1 .... 64 C1
Warren Gn. Hat AL10 .... 130 B8
Warren Gr. Bor WD6 .... 170 D5
Warren La. Clo SG7 .... 24 D7
Warren La. Cotrd SG9 .... 39 B6
Warren La. Stan HA7 .... 176 F8
Warren Park Rd. Hert SG14 .... 113 D7
Warren Pl. Hert SG14 .... 113 D6 14
Warren Rd. Bus WD2 .... 168 D1
Warren Rd. Luton LU1 .... 62 F8
Warren Rd. St Alb AL1 .... 141 C7
Warren Terr. Hert SG14 .. 113 D8
Warren The. Harp AL5 .... 107 A6
Warren The. Radl WD7 .... 156 B6
Warren The. Royst SG8 .... 7 D5
Warren Way. Welw AL6 .... 89 E4
Warrenfield Cl. Ches EN7 162 A8
Warrengate La. Pot B EN6 158 C8
Warrengate Rd. Wel G AL9 .... 144 C4
Warrensgreen La. Wes SG4 .... 37 D5
Warton Gn. Luton LU2 .... 46 E2
Warwick Ave. Cuf EN6 .... 146 D4
Warwick Cl. Bus WD2 .... 168 E2
Warwick Cl. Cuf EN6 .... 146 D4
Warwick Cl. Hert SG13 .... 113 C4
Warwick Ct. Luton LU4 .... 63 B8
Warwick Dr. Ches EN8 .... 148 D3
Warwick Rd. Bis St CM23 .. 77 B6
Warwick Rd. Bor WD6 .... 170 D6
Warwick Rd E. Luton LU4 .. 63 B8
Warwick Rd. Enf EN3 .... 162 F2
Warwick Rd. St Alb AL1 ... 127 F5
Warwick Rd. Stev SG2 .... 51 C6
Warwick Rd W. Luton LU4 . 63 B8
Warwick Way. Cro Gr WD3 .... 166 C5
Wash La. Pot B EN6 .... 158 C4
Wash La. Pot B EN6 .... 158 C5
Wash The. Fur P SG9 .... 43 D5
Wash The. Hert SG14 .... 113 D6
Washington Ave. Heml H HP2 .... 124 E8
Watchlytes Jun Mix & Inf Sch. Wel G C .... 111 C6
Watchlytes. Wel G C AL7 . 111 C6
Watchmead. Wel G C AL7 111 A6
Water End Rd. Pot En HP4 123 C7
Water La. Abb L WD4 .... 139 B2
Water La. Berk HP4 .... 122 C4
Water La. Bis St CM23 .... 76 F8
Water La. Bov HP3 .... 137 B1
Water La. Hert SG14 .... 113 C5
Water La. Hit SG5 .... 21 F1
Water La. Sta M CM24 .... 59 E6
Water La. Watf WD1 .... 167 D5
Waterbeach. Wel G C AL7 111 D6
Watercress Cl. Ast SG2 .... 51 D5
Waterdale. Hert SG13 .... 113 C4
Waterdell La. St Ipp SG4 ... 35 A2
Waterend La. A St P AL6 ... 88 E1
Waterend La. Red AL3 .... 106 B5
Waterfield. Wel G C AL7 .. 111 B7
Waterfields Way. Watf WD1 .... 167 D5
Waterford Comm. Stap SG14 .... 92 B2
Waterford Gn. Wel G C AL7 .... 111 B6
Watergate The. Sth Ox WD1 .... 175 D8
Waterhouse Gate. St Alb AL1 .... 127 D3
Waterhouse St. Heml H HP1 .... 124 C2
Waterhouse The. Heml H HP1 .... 124 C3
Waterloo La. Hol SG5 .... 21 A6
Waterlow Mews. L Wym SG4 .... 35 E3
Waterman Cl. Watf WD1 . 167 B3
Watermark Way. Hert SG13 .... 113 F6
Watermead Rd. Luton LU3 44 F6
Watermill Ind Est. Bun .... 40 E6
Watermill La. Hert SG14 .. 113 D8
Waterside. Berk HP4 .... 122 D4
Waterside Cl. Kin L UB5 .. 139 B2
Waterside. Kin L WD4 .... 139 A2
Waterside. Lon C AL2 .... 142 E4
Waterside Pl. Sheer CM21 98 A2
Waterside. Sta M CM24 .... 59 E6
Waterside. Wel G C AL7 .... 90 B1
Waterslade Gn. Luton LU3 . 45 B6
Watersplash Ct. Lon C AL2 .... 142 F4
Watery La. Harp AL3 .... 84 E3
Watery La. Hat AL10 .... 129 E4
Watery La. Mars HP23 .... 79 F1
Watford Arches Ret Pk. Watf .... 167 D4
Watford By-Pass. Stan WD6 .... 169 C2
Watford Central Prim Sch. Watf .... 167 C5
Watford Coll. Watf .... 167 D6
Watford County Ct. Watf . 167 C5
Watford Enterprise Ctr. Watf .... 166 E3
Watford Field Jun Mix & Inf Sch. Watf .... 167 C4
Watford Fields Rd. Watf WD1 .... 167 C4
Watford Football Gd. Watf 167 B4
Watford General Hospl (Shrodells Wing). Watf 167 B4
Watford Gram Sch. Watf . 166 F5
Watford Gram Sch for Girls. Watf .... 167 B5
Watford Heath. Watf WD1 167 D2
Watford High Street Sta. Watf .... 167 C5
Watford Junction Sta. Watf .... 167 C7
Watford North Sta. Watf . 154 C2
Watford Rd. Abb L WD4 .... 153 C6
Watford Rd. Chis AL2 .... 141 A6
Watford Rd. Cro Gr WD3 . 166 B3
Watford Rd. Elst WD6 .... 169 C3
Watford Rd. Kin L WD4 .... 139 A1
Watford Rd. Mo Pk HA6 .. 175 A4
Watford Rd. Radl WD7 .... 155 F4
Watford Rd. St Alb AL2 .... 141 A6
Watford Sch of Art & Design. Watf .... 154 B1
Watford Sch of Music. Watf .... 154 A1
Watford Sta. Watf .... 166 F6
Watford Stadium Sta. Watf .... 167 A3
Watling Cl. Heml H HP2 .. 124 E6 1
Watling Ct. Elst WD6 .... 169 D3
Watling Knoll. Radl WD7 . 155 F6
Watling St. Pk St AL2 .... 141 D6
Watling St. St Alb AL1 .... 141 C8
Watling View Sch. St Alb . 141 D7
Watling View. St Alb AL1 . 141 C8
Watlington Rd. Harl CM17 118 D4
Watson Ave. St Alb AL3 ... 127 F6
Watson's Wlk. St Alb AL1 127 E2
Watton at Stone Prim Sch. Wat St .... 70 D3
Watton at Stone Sta. Wat St .... 70 D3
Watton House. Wat St SG14 .... 70 F3
Watton Rd. Kneb SG3 .... 69 A5
Watton Rd. Ware SG12 .... 93 C2
Watton Rd. Wat St SG3 .... 70 B2
Watts Cl. L Had SG11 .... 57 C2
Waulud Inf Sch. Luton .... 44 E7
Waulud Jun Sch. Luton .... 44 E7
Wauluds Bank Dr. Luton LU3 .... 44 E7
Wavell Cl. Ches EN8 .... 148 E4
Wavell House. St Alb AL1 128 A2
Waveney. Heml H HP2 .... 124 F8
Waveney Rd. Harp AL5 .... 86 C3
Waverley Cl. Stev SG2 .... 69 A8
Waverley Gdns. Norwd HA6 .... 175 A2
Waverley Rd. St Alb AL3 .. 127 D5
Waxwell Cl. Pnr HA5 .... 175 D1
Waxwell La. Pnr HA5 .... 175 D1
Wayre St. Harl CM17 .... 118 C4
Wayre The. Harl CM17 .... 118 C4
Waysbrook. Letw SG6 .... 23 B5
Wayside Ave. Bus WD2 .... 168 D3
Wayside. Chipf WD4 .... 138 B1
Wayside. Pot B EN6 .... 159 D7
Wayside. Shen WD7 .... 156 D6
Wayside The. Heml H HP3 .... 125 C2
Waysmeet. Letw SG6 .... 23 B4
Waytemore Rd. Bis St CM23 .... 76 E6
Weald Coll (Annexe). Har 176 E2
Weald Fst Sch. Har .... 176 F3
Weald La. Har HA3 .... 176 D2
Weald Mid Sch. Har .... 176 F3
Weald Rise. Har HA3 .... 176 F2
Wealdwood Gdns. Pnr HA5 .... 176 B4
Weall Gn. Watf WD2 .... 154 B7
Weardale Ct. Barn EN5 .... 171 C4
Weatherby Rd. Luton LU4 .. 44 D2
Weavers Rd. Tri HP23 .... 99 E4
Weavers Way. Bal SG7 .... 24 A8
Webb Cl. Letw SG6 .... 23 C5
Webb Rise. Stev SG1 .... 50 F7
Webber Cl. Elst WD6 .... 169 D3
Wedgewood Cl. Norwd HA6 .... 174 C4
Wedgewood Pk. Stev SG1 . 37 C2
Wedgwood Ct. Stev SG1 ... 37 C2
Wedgwood Way. Stev SG1 37 B2
Wedmore Rd. Hit SG4 .... 35 A6
Wedon Way. Byg SG7 .... 13 C4
Weedon Cl. Henlw SG16 .... 10 C5
Weighton Rd. Har HA3 .... 176 D2
Welbeck Cl. Bor WD6 .... 170 A6
Welbeck Rise. Harp AL5 .. 107 D6
Welbury Ave. Luton LU3 .... 45 C7
Welch Pl. Pnr HA5 .... 175 C2
Welclose St. St Alb AL3 .... 127 C3
Welcote Dr. Norwd HA6 .. 174 D4
Weldon Cl. Luton LU2 .... 46 E1
Welham Cl. Wel G AL9 .... 144 C7
Welham Ct. Wel G AL9 .... 144 C7
Welham Green Sta. Wel G 144 D8
Welham Manor. Wel G AL9 .... 144 C7
Well App. Barn EN5 .... 171 C4
Well Croft. Heml H HP1 .... 124 B4
Well End Rd. Bor WD6 .... 157 D1
Well Garth. Wel G C AL7 .. 110 E5
Well Gn. Bram SG14 .... 91 C4
Well La. Harl CM19 .... 117 A1
Well La. Men LU7 .... 61 B8
Well Rd. Barn EN5 .... 171 C4
Well Rd. Nort EN6 .... 145 E2
Well-Row. Bay SG13 .... 132 F6
Wellands. Hat AL10 .... 130 A7
Wellbrook Mews. Tri HP23 .... 100 B4
Wellcroft Cl. Wel G C AL7 111 A4
Wellcroft. Pit HP1 .... 80 F5
Wellcroft Rd. Wel G C AL7 111 A4
Wellen Rise. Heml H HP3 138 E8
Wellers Gr. Ches EN7 .... 148 A3
Wellesley Ave. Mo Pk HA6 174 F5
Wellesley Cres. Pot B EN6 158 E6
Wellfield Ave. Luton LU3 .... 44 C8
Wellfield Cl. Hat AL10 .... 130 A6
Wellfield Ct. Stev SG1 .... 37 B1
Wellfield Rd. Hat AL10 .... 130 A7
Wellfield Wood Jun Mix Sch. Stev .... 37 A2
Wellgate Rd. Luton LU4 .... 44 D2
Wellhouse Cl. Luton LU1 .... 63 A7
Wellhouse La. Barn EN5 .. 171 D5
Wellingham Ave. Hit SG5 ... 21 D1

Wellington Ave. Pnr HA5 . 175 F2
Wellington Dr. Wel G C AL7 ... 111 C6
Wellington Pl. Knee SG8 ... 2 B5
Wellington Rd. Lon C AL2 142 D5
Wellington Rd. Pnr HA5 ... 175 F2
Wellington Rd. St Alb AL1 128 B2
Wellington Rd. Stev SG2 ... 51 C5
Wellington Rd. Watf WD1 167 B7
Wellington St. Hert SG14 . 113 B7
Wellington St. Luton LU1 ... 63 D7
Wells Cl. Harp AL5 ... 85 E4
Wells Cl. St Alb AL3 ... 127 C4
Wells Yd. Ware SG12 ... 93 D1 8
Wells Yd. Watf WD1 ... 167 B6
Wellside Cl. Barn EN5 ... 171 C5
Wellstones. Watf WD1 ... 167 B5
Wellswood Cl. Heml H HP2 ... 125 B4
Welsummer Way. Ches EN8 ... 148 D3
Weltmore Rd. Luton LU3 ... 44 F6
Welwyn By Pass Rd. Welw AL6 ... 89 C5
Welwyn Ct. Heml H HP2 .. 124 F7
Welwyn Garden City Sta. Wel G C ... 110 D6
Welwyn North Sta. Welw .. 89 F3
Welwyn Rd. Hert SG14 ... 112 F7
Wendover Cl. Harp AL5 ... 86 D1
Wendover Cl. St Alb AL4 .. 128 C8
Wendover Ct. Welw AL6 ... 89 C5
Wendover Dr. Welw AL6 ... 89 C5
Wendover Way. Bus WD2 168 C3
Wendover Way. Luton LU2 45 F3
Wengeo La. Ware SG12 ... 93 B2
Wenham Ct. Walk SG2 ... 52 B8
Wenlock Jun Sch. Luton ... 64 B8
Wenlock St. Luton LU2 ... 63 E8
Wensley Cl. Harp AL5 ... 107 D6
Wensley Dale. Luton LU2 ... 45 E1
Wensleydale. Heml H HP2 124 F6
Wensum Way. Ric WD3 ... 165 D1
Wentbridge Path. Bor WD6 ... 157 A1
Wentworth Ave. Bor WD6 169 F4
Wentworth Ave. Luton LU4 44 C6
Wentworth Cl. Pot B EN6 . 159 A8
Wentworth Cl. Watf WD1 153 F1
Wentworth Cotts. Hod EN10 ... 134 E1
Wentworth Ct. Barn EN5 . 171 E6
Wentworth Dr. Bis St CM23 ... 76 D6
Wentworth Rd. Barn EN5 171 D6
Wentworth Rd. Hert SG13 113 C3
Wenwell Cl. Ast Cl HP22 ... 99 A3
Wesley Cl. Arl SG15 ... 11 A4
Wesley Cl. Gofs O EN7 ... 147 C3
Wesley Rd. Mark AL3 ... 83 E5
Wessex Ct. Barn EN5 ... 171 D5
Wessex Dr. Pnr HA5 ... 175 E3
West Alley. Hit SG5 ... 34 E7 3
West Ave. Bal SG7 ... 23 E8
West Ave. Chis AL2 ... 141 B6
West Burrowfield. Wel G C AL7 ... 110 D4
West Chantry. Har HA3 ... 176 B2
West Cl. Barn EN5 ... 171 B4
West Cl. Hit SG4 ... 22 B1
West Cl. Hod EN11 ... 135 A8
West Cl. Stev SG1 ... 50 F5
West Comm. Harp AL5 ... 107 B6
West Comm. Red AL3 ... 106 A4
West Common Cl. Harp AL5 ... 107 B5
West Common Gr. Harp AL5 ... 107 B5
West Common Way. Harp AL5 ... 107 A5
West Ct. Saw CM21 ... 97 E3
West Dene. Gt Gd HP2 ... 104 A8
West Dr. Arl SG15 ... 11 B4
West Dr. Stan HA3 ... 176 D4
West Dr. Watf WD2 ... 154 B3
West Drive Gdns. Stan HA3 ... 176 D4
West End. Ashw SG7 ... 4 C3
West End La. Barn EN5 ... 171 D5
West End La. Ess AL9 ... 131 D6
West End Rd. Bric EN7 ... 147 F8
West End Rd. Ched LU7 ... 79 F7
West Herts Coll Watford Campus. Watf ... 167 A6
West Herts Golf Course. Sar ... 166 C7
West Hill. Hit SG5 ... 34 D7
West Hill Rd. Hod EN11 ... 134 F8
West Hill Rd. Luton LU1 ... 63 E5
West Hyde La. C St P SL9 172 A4
West La. Gt Of SG5 ... 33 C2
West La. Pirt SG5 ... 20 D5
West Lieth. Tri HP23 ... 99 F1
West Mead. Wel G C AL7 111 B3
West Passage. Tri HP23 .. 100 A3
West Rd. Berk HP4 ... 122 A5
West Rd. Bis St CM23 ... 76 E6
West Rd. H Wy CM21 ... 97 C3
West Rd. Harl CM20 ... 118 A4
West Rd. Saw CM21 ... 97 C3
West Rd. Sta M CM24 ... 59 E6
West Reach. Stev SG2 ... 50 F2
West Riding. Bri Wd AL2 . 140 F1
West Riding. Tewin AL6 ... 90 D5
West Side. Ches EN10 ... 148 E6
West St. Hert SG13 ... 113 C5
West St. Lily LU2 ... 32 D1
West St. Ware SG12 ... 93 D1
West St. Watf WD1 ... 167 B7
West Valley Rd. Heml H HP3 ... 138 D7
West View Gdns. Elst WD6 ... 169 D3
West View. Hat AL10 ... 130 A7
West View. Letw SG6 ... 22 E5
West View Rd. St Alb AL3 127 D4
West Watford Sta. Watf .. 166 F4
West Way. Harp AL5 ... 86 C2
West Way. Ric WD3 ... 165 B1
West Way. Wa Aby EN9 .. 163 B2
West Ways. Norwd HA6 .. 175 A1
Westall Cl. Hert SG13 ... 113 C5
Westall Mews. Hert SG13 113 C5
Westbourne Mews. St Alb AL1 ... 127 D3
Westbourne Rd. Luton LU4 45 B1
Westbrook Cl. Ste Mo SG8 .. 5 B8
Westbrook Hay (Sch). Heml H ... 137 D7
Westbury Cl. Hit SG5 ... 34 D8
Westbury Gdns. Luton LU2 45 E3
Westbury Pl. Letw SG6 ... 22 E5
Westbury Prim Sch. Letw .. 22 E5
Westbury Rd. Mo Pk HA6 174 E7
Westbury Rd. Watf WD1 . 167 B4
Westbush Cl. Hod EN11 ... 114 F1
Westcott. Wel G C AL7 ... 111 D7
Westcroft Cl. Enf EN3 ... 162 C1
Westcroft Ct. Hod EN10 .. 135 A4
Westell Cl. Bal SG7 ... 24 A8
Westerdale. Heml H HP2 . 124 E6
Westerdale. Luton LU4 ... 44 B4
Western Ave. Henlw SG16 10 B3
Western Cl. Letw SG6 ... 11 E1
Western House Hospl. Ware ... 93 E2
Western Rd. Lo Naz EN9 .. 135 E1
Western Rd. Luton LU1 ... 63 D6
Western Rd. Tri HP23 ... 99 F3
Western Terr. Hod EN11 .. 115 B1
Western Way. Letw SG6 ... 11 F1
Westfield Ave. Harp AL5 ... 86 A3
Westfield Ave. Watf WD2 154 D1
Westfield Cl. Bis St CM23 .. 76 E8
Westfield Cl. Ches EN8 ... 162 F8
Westfield Cl. Hit SG5 ... 34 D7
Westfield Ct. St Alb AL4 ... 128 D6
Westfield Cty Prim Sch. Berk ... 121 F5
Westfield Cty Prim Sch. Hod ... 134 F7
Westfield Dr. Harp AL5 ... 86 B4
Westfield. Hat AL9 ... 144 F8
Westfield La. Hit SG5 ... 34 D7
Westfield Pk. Pnr HA5 ... 175 F3
Westfield Pl. Harp AL5 ... 86 B4
Westfield Rd. Bis St CM23 . 76 E8
Westfield Rd. Harp AL5 ... 86 B4
Westfield Rd. Hert SG14 .. 113 C8
Westfield Rd. Hod EN11 .. 134 F7
Westfield Rd. Nthch HP4 . 121 E6
Westfield Sch. Watf ... 166 F3
Westfield. Wel G C AL7 ... 111 A7
Westfield Wlk. Ches EN8 . 162 F8
Westfields. St Alb AL3 ... 141 A8
Westgate. Stev SG1 ... 50 D5
Westholm. Letw SG6 ... 23 A8
Westholme. Letw SG6 ... 22 F8
Westland Dr. Bro Pk AL9 . 144 E4
Westland Rd. Watf WD1 .. 167 B7
Westlea Ave. Watf WD2 .. 154 E2
Westlea Cl. Hod EN10 ... 148 F8
Westlea Rd. Hod EN10 ... 148 F8
Westlecote Gdns. Luton LU2 ... 45 D4
Westly Wood. Wel G C AL7 ... 111 A7
Westmeade Cl. Ches EN8 148 B2
Westmill La. Ick SG5 ... 21 C3
Westmill Rd. Hit SG5 ... 21 D1
Westmill Rd. Thun SG12 ... 93 A3
Westminster Ct. St Alb AL1 ... 127 C1
Westmorland Ave. Luton LU3 ... 44 F5
Weston Ave. Royst SG8 ... 7 C7
Weston Cl. Pot B EN6 ... 158 F7
Weston Jun Mix Inf Sch. Wes ... 24 C1
Weston Rd. Stev SG1 ... 36 E1
Weston Way. Bal SG7 ... 23 E7
Westray. Heml H HP3 ... 125 C1
Westridge Cl. Heml H HP1 ... 123 F3
Westview Ct. Elst WD6 ... 169 D3
Westview Rise. Heml H HP2 ... 124 D4
Westway. Luton LU2 ... 46 C4
Westwick Cl. Heml H HP2 125 D2
Westwick Pl. Watf WD2 .. 154 C5
Westwick Row. Heml H HP2 ... 125 E2
Westwood Ave. Hit SG4 ... 35 A6
Westwood Cl. Pot B EN6 . 145 A1
Wetherby Cl. Stev SG1 ... 51 C8
Wetherby Rd. Bor WD6 ... 169 E8
Wetherby Rd. Enf EN2 ... 161 C1
Wetherfield. Sta M CM24 .. 59 D7
Wetherly Cl. Harl CM17 ... 118 F4
Wetherne Link. Luton LU4 . 44 C5
Wexham Cl. Luton LU3 ... 44 E8
Weybourne Cl. Harp AL5 ... 86 D2
Weybourne Dr. Luton LU2 . 45 C7
Weymouth St. Heml H HP3 ... 138 D7
Weyver Ct. St Alb AL1 ... 127 E4
Whaley Rd. Pot B EN6 ... 159 C6
Wharf La. Nthch HP4 ... 121 C8
Wharf La. Ric WD3 ... 165 E1
Wharf Rd. Bis St CM23 ... 76 F6
Wharf Rd. Heml H HP1 ... 124 B1
Wharf Rd. Hod EN10 ... 148 F8
Wharf Row. Ast Cl HP22 ... 99 B4
Wharfdale. Luton LU4 ... 44 C5
Wharfedale. Heml H HP2 124 E6
Wheat Cl. St Alb AL4 ... 128 A7
Wheat Croft. Bis St CM23 .. 76 E4
Wheat Hill. Letw SG6 ... 22 F8
Wheatbarn. Wel G C AL7 . 111 B7
Wheatcotes. Welw SG3 ... 69 C1
Wheatcroft. Ches EN7 ... 148 B3
Wheatcroft Jun Mix Inf Sch. Hert ... 114 A7
Wheatfield Ave. Harp AL5 107 A5
Wheatfield Cres. Royst SG8 ... 7 E6
Wheatfield. Hat AL10 ... 130 B6
Wheatfield. Heml H HP2 .. 124 D5
Wheatfield Rd. Harp AL5 . 107 A4
Wheatfields. Harl CM17 .. 118 C6
Wheatfields Inf Sch. St Alb ... 128 B7
Wheatfields Jun Mix Sch. St Alb ... 128 B7
Wheathampstead Rd. Harp AL5 ... 107 E8
Wheathampstead Rd. Whea AL4 ... 108 A8
Wheathampstead Sch. Whea ... 108 C7
Wheatlands. Stev SG2 ... 51 C7
Wheatley Cl. Saw CM21 ... 97 C1
Wheatley Cl. Wel G C AL7 111 A4
Wheatley Rd. Wel G C AL7 ... 111 A4
Wheatleys. St Alb AL4 ... 128 C5
Wheatlock Mead. Red AL3 106 A5
Wheatsheaf Dr. Ware SG12 ... 93 B3
Wheatsheaf Rd. Hun SG12 95 D1
Wheelers Cl. Lo Naz EN9 . 135 F1
Wheelers La. Heml H HP3 124 E1
Wheelright Cl. Bus WD2 .. 168 B3
Whempstead La. Wat St SG12 ... 71 B6
Whempstead Rd. Wat St SG12 ... 71 B7
Whetstone Cl. Welw AL6 ... 89 E8
Whinbush Gr. Hit SG5 ... 34 F8
Whinbush Rd. Hit SG5 ... 34 F8
Whippendell Hill. Chipf WD4 ... 138 C1
Whippendell Rd. Watf WD1 ... 166 F4
Whipperley Ct. Luton LU1 .. 63 C5
Whipperley Inf Sch. Luton . 63 A6
Whipperley Ring. Luton LU1 ... 63 A6
Whipperley Way. Luton LU1 ... 63 B5
Whipsnade Park Golf Course. Whip ... 81 E5
Whipsnade Wildlife Animal Pk. Whip ... 81 F7
Whisper Wood. Ric WD3 . 165 B6
Whisperwood Cl. Har HA3 176 E3
Whit Hern Ct. Ches EN8 ... 148 C1
Whitby Rd. Luton LU3 ... 45 C1
White Bear. Sta M CM24 ... 59 E8
White Craig Cl. Pnr HA5 .. 176 A5
White Crofts. Stot SG5 ... 11 F6
White Gate Gdns. Har HA3 176 F3
White Hart Cl. Bun SG9 ... 40 E8
White Hart Dr. Heml H HP2 ... 124 F2
White Hart Rd. Heml H HP2 ... 125 A2
White Hart St. Heml H HP11 ... 138 D7
White Hedge Dr. St Alb AL3 ... 127 C5
White Hill. Ash Gr HP5 ... 136 C7
White Hill. Fla AL3 ... 105 B8
White Hill. Heml H HP1 ... 123 F2
White Hill. Ric WD3 ... 174 A4
White Hill. Walk SG2 ... 38 C2
White Hill. Welw AL6 ... 89 A3
White Horse La. Lon C AL2 ... 142 E5
White Horse La. Welw AL6 90 C7
White House The. Ches EN8 ... 148 B2
White La. St Ipp SG4 ... 49 C7
White Orchards. Barn N20 171 F1
White Post Field. Saw CM21 ... 97 D2
White Shack La. Sar WD3 152 F2
White Stubbs La. Bric EN10 ... 133 C2
White Stubbs La. New St SG13 ... 133 C2
White Way The. Stev SG2 .. 51 C7
Whitebarns. Fur P SG9 ... 43 A5
Whitebarns La. Fur P SG9 . 43 A6
Whitebeam Cl. Ham St EN7 ... 147 E5
Whitebeams. Chis AL2 ... 141 C3
Whitebeams. Hat AL10 ... 130 A2
Whitebroom Rd. Heml H HP1 ... 123 E5
Whitechurch Cl. Luton LU2 46 D2
Whitechurch Gdns. Letw SG6 ... 23 C3
Whitecroft Rd. Luton LU2 .. 64 A8
Whitecroft. St Alb AL1 ... 142 B8
Whitefield Ave. Luton LU3 . 44 C7
Whitefield House. Hat AL10 ... 130 C7
Whitefield Inf Sch. Luton ... 44 E8
Whitefield Jun Sch. Luton .. 44 E8
Whitefields Rd. Ches EN8 148 C3
Whitefriars Ave. Har HA3 176 E1
Whitefriars Centre Coll. ... 176 D1
Whitefriars Dr. Har HA3 .. 176 E1
Whitefriars Fst & Mid Sch. Har ... 176 E1
Whitefriars Trad Est. Har 176 D1
Whitegale Cl. Hit SG4 ... 35 A6
Whitegates Cl. Cro Gr WD3 ... 166 A5
Whitehall Cl. Lo Naz EN9 . 135 E1
Whitehall Coll. Bis St ... 58 E1
Whitehall Jun Sch. Hit ... 35 A5
Whitehall La. Bis St CM23 .. 58 F1
Whitehall Rd. Bis St CM23 . 58 E1
Whitehall Village. Bis St CM23 ... 58 E1
Whitehands Cl. Hod EN11 134 F6
Whitehart Cross. Bov HP3 136 F3
Whitehicks. Letw SG6 ... 12 A1
Whitehill Ave. Luton LU1 ... 63 D5
Whitehill. Berk HP4 ... 122 D5
Whitehill Cotts. Welw AL6 . 89 A3
Whitehill Ct. Berk HP4 ... 122 D5
Whitehill Rd. Hit SG4 ... 35 A6
Whitehorse Ct. Bark SG8 ... 17 D4
Whitehorse St. Bal SG7 ... 23 F8
Whitehorse Vale. Luton LU3 ... 31 A1
Whitehouse Ave. Bor WD6 170 B5
Whitehouse La. Bri Wd EN2 ... 140 C4
Whitehurst Ave. Hit SG5 ... 21 F1
Whitelands Ave. Chor WD3 ... 164 C5
Whiteleaf Rd. Heml H HP3 138 C8
Whiteley Cl. Dan En SG12 .. 71 E7
Whiteley La. Buck SG9 ... 27 C8
Whitesmead Rd. Stev SG1 . 50 E7
Whitestone Wlk. Heml H HP1 ... 124 A6
Whitethorn La. Letw SG6 ... 23 A4
Whitethorn Way. Luton LU1 ... 63 A6
Whitethorn. Wel G C AL7 . 111 B5
Whitewaites. Harl CM20 . 117 E1
Whiteway. Letw SG6 ... 23 C4
Whitewaybottom La. Kim SG4 ... 66 A3
Whitewebbs La. Enf EN2 . 161 F4
Whitewebbs Pk. Cre H ... 161 D4
Whitewebbs Rd. Cre H EN2 ... 161 C4
Whitewood Rd. Berk HP4 122 A4
Whitfield Way. Ric WD3 .. 164 F1
Whitings Cl. Harp AL5 ... 86 D4
Whitings Hill Jun Mix & Inf Sch. Barn ... 171 C4
Whitings Rd. Barn EN5 ... 171 C4
Whitlars Dr. Kin L WD4 ... 138 F3
Whitley Cl. Abb L WD5 ... 154 A7
Whitley Ct. Hod HP21 ... 135 B8
Whitley Gn. Luton LU2 ... 46 D2
Whitley Rd. Hod EN11 ... 135 B8
Whitmores Wood. Heml H HP2 ... 125 B4
Whitney Dr. Stev SG1 ... 36 C1
Whittingham Cl. Luton LU2 46 F1
Whittingstall Rd. Hod EN11 ... 135 B8
Whittington La. Stev SG1 ... 50 E4
Whittington Way. Bis St CM23 ... 76 F3
Whittle Cl. Henlw SG16 ... 10 B4
Whittlesea Cl. Har HA3 ... 176 C3
Whittlesea Path. Har HA3 176 C2
Whittlesea Rd. Har HA3 .. 176 C2
Whittlesea Sch. Har ... 176 C3
Whitwell Cl. Luton LU3 ... 45 B8
Whitwell Rd. Watf WD2 ... 154 D4
Whitworth Jones Ave. Henlw SG16 ... 10 C5
Whitworth Rd. Stev SG1 ... 37 B3
Whomerley Rd. Stev SG1 ... 50 E4
Whydale Rd. Royst SG8 ... 7 E5
Whytingham Rd. Tri HP23 100 C4
Wick Ave. Whea AL4 ... 108 D8
Wick Hill. Ken Co LU6 ... 82 F8
Wick Rd. Wigg HP23 ... 120 D8
Wick The. Hert SG14 ... 92 C1
Wicken Fields. Ware SG12 93 C3
Wickets The. Luton LU2 ... 45 E1
Wickfield Cl. Welw SG3 ... 69 A2
Wickham Cl. Hare UB9 ... 173 D2
Wickham Rd. Har HA3 ... 176 D1
Wickham Way. Stand SG11 55 E3
Wickhams Wharf. Ware SG12 ... 93 E1
Wicklands Rd. Hun SG12 . 116 D8
Wickmere Cl. Luton LU2 ... 45 C7
Wickstead Ave. Luton LU4 . 44 E4
Wickwood Ct. St Alb AL1 . 128 B5
Widbury Gdns. Ware SG12 93 F1
Widbury Hill. Ware SG12 ... 93 F1
Widford Jun Mix & Inf Sch. Widf ... 95 D4
Widford Rd. Hun SG12 ... 95 D2
Widford Rd. Muc H SG10 ... 95 F7
Widford Rd. Wel G C AL7 . 111 B6
Widford Terr. Heml H HP2 105 A1
Widgeon Way. Watf WD2 154 E2
Widmore Dr. Heml H HP2 125 A5
Wieland Rd. Norwd HA6 .. 175 A3
Wiggenhall Rd. Watf WD1 167 C4
Wiggington Bottom. Wigg HP23 ... 120 E8
Wigmore La. Luton LU2 ... 46 D3
Wigmore Park Ctr. Luton ... 46 E1
Wigmore Prim Sch. Luton .. 46 E2
Wigmores N. Wel G C AL8 110 D7
Wigram Way. Stev SG2 ... 51 B3
Wilbury Cl. Letw SG6 ... 22 C7
Wilbury Hills Rd. Letw SG6 22 C7
Wilbury Jun Mix Sch. Letw 22 D6
Wilbury Lodge. Barn EN5 . 171 D5
Wilbury Rd. Letw SG6 ... 22 E8
Wilbury Way. Hit SG4 ... 22 A3
Wilcot Ave. Watf WD1 ... 167 E2
Wilcox Cl. Bor WD6 ... 170 C8
Wild Cherry Dr. Luton LU1 . 63 D5
Wild March Ct. Enf EN8 ... 162 E2
Wild Oaks Cl. Norwd HA6 174 F4
Wilderness The. Berk HP4 122 C4
Wildwood Ave. Bri Wd AL2 ... 140 F1
Wildwood La. Stev SG1 ... 50 E3
Wildwood. Norwd HA6 ... 174 D4
Wilford Cl. Norwd HA6 ... 174 D3
Wilga Rd. Welw AL6 ... 89 B5
Wilkin's Green La. Coln H AL4 ... 129 C4
Wilkins Gr. Wel G C AL8 .. 110 D5

Willenhall Cl. Luton LU3 ..... 45 A7
William Austin Sch. Luton .. 45 C4
William Covell Cl. Enf EN2 160 F1
William Ct. Heml H HP3 ... 138 D7
William Pl. Stev SG2 ......... 51 A3
William Ransom Sch The
(Jun Mix & Inf). Hit ........ 35 B7
William St. Berk HP4 ....... 122 D4
William St. Luton LU2 ....... 45 E1
William St. Mark AL3 ........ 83 E5
William St. Watf WD2 ...... 167 D6
Williams Way. Radl WD7 . 156 C4
Williamson St. Luton LU1 ... 63 E7
Williamson Way. Ric WD3 165 A1
Willian Church Rd.
Letw SG6 ....................... 23 A2
Willian Rd. Gt Wy SG4 ....... 35 F7
Willian Rd. Hit SG4,SG6 ..... 22 D1
Willian Way. Bal SG7 ......... 23 E6
Willian Way. Letw SG6 ....... 23 A3
Willingale Cl. Wa Aby EN9 163 D7
Williton Rd. Luton LU2 ....... 46 C2
Willoughby Cl. Hod EN10 . 134 E2
Willoughby Rd. Harp AL5 ... 86 B4
Willoughby Way. Hit SG4 ... 35 A6
Willow Cl. Bis St CM23 ...... 76 E8
Willow Cl. Gt Ho SG9 ......... 42 A8
Willow Cl. Ham St EN7 ..... 147 E5
Willow Cl. Reed SG8 .......... 16 D5
Willow Cnr. Bay SG13 ...... 132 F5
Willow Cres. St Alb AL4 ... 128 C3
Willow Ct. Har HA3 .......... 176 F2
Willow Ct. Luton LU3 ......... 44 E5
Willow Dean. Pnr HA5 ..... 175 D1
Willow Dene. Bus WD2 ..... 168 E2
Willow Dr. Barn EN5 ........ 171 E5
Willow Edge. Kin L WD4 .. 139 A2
Willow End. Norwd HA6 .. 175 A4
Willow Gn. Bor WD6 ........ 170 D4
Willow Gr. Wel G C AL8 ..... 89 D3
Willow La. Hit SG5 ............ 34 D6
Willow La. Watf WD1 ...... 167 A4
Willow Mead. Saw CM21 ... 97 E2
Willow Springs.
Bis St CM23 .................. 76 D8
Willow Way. Chis AL2 ...... 141 A4
Willow Way. Harp AL5 ...... 86 C4
Willow Way. Hat AL10 ...... 129 F2
Willow Way. Heml H HP1 124 B5
Willow Way. Luton LU3 ...... 44 E5
Willow Way. Pot B EN6 .... 159 B6
Willow Way. Radl WD7 .... 155 E3
Willow Wlk. Welw AL6 ....... 89 C8
Willowby Ct. Lon C AL2 .... 142 D5
Willowdene. Ches EN8 ..... 148 E4
Willowfield Sch. Cad .......... 62 F4
Willowgate Trad Est. Luton 44 B8
Willowmead. Hert SG14 .. 113 B5
Willows Cl. Pnr HA5 ........ 175 C1
Willows Link. Stev SG2 ...... 69 A8
Willows The. Bun SG9 ....... 40 D8
Willows The. Heml H HP2 125 B5
Willows The. Hit SG4 ........ 35 A5
Willows The. Ric WD3 ...... 173 A8
Willows The. St Alb AL1 ... 142 B7
Willows The. Stev SG2 ....... 51 A1
Willows The. Watf WD1 .. 167 B2
Willowside. Lon C AL2 ..... 142 E4
Willowside Way. Royst SG8 7 C8
Wilsden Ave. Luton LU1 ..... 63 C6
Wilshere Ave. St Alb AL1 . 127 C1
Wilshere Cres. Hit SG4 ...... 35 C8
Wilshere Rd. Welw AL6 ..... 89 A5
Wilshere-Dacre Sch
(Jun Mix). Hit ................. 34 E8
Wilsmere Dr. Har HA3 ..... 176 E3
Wilson Cl. Stev SG1 .......... 36 D1
Wilsons La. Ashw SG7 ......... 4 C4
Wilstone Dr. St Alb AL4 ... 128 C8
Wilton Cl. Bis St CM23 ....... 77 B7
Wilton Cres. Hert SG13 ... 113 C4
Wilton Rd. Hit SG5 ............ 21 E1
Wilton Way. Hert SG13 .... 113 C4
Wiltshire Rd. Stev SG2 ....... 51 A4
Wimborne Cl. Saw CM21 ... 97 D2
Wimborne Gr. Watf WD1 153 E2
Wimborne Rd. Luton LU1 ... 63 B8
Wimple Rd. Dun LU4 ......... 44 A2
Winch Cl. Cod SG4 ............ 88 F8
Winch St. Luton LU2 ......... 45 F1
Winchdells. Heml H HP3 .. 139 A8
Winches Farm Dr.
St Alb AL4 .................... 128 D3
Winchester Cl. Bis St CM23 76 D4
Winchester Cl. Stev SG1 .... 37 B2
Winchester House.
St Alb AL3 ..................... 127 C2
Winchester Rd. Norwd HA6174 F1
Winchester Way.
Cro Gr WD3 ................. 166 B4
Winchfield Way. Ric WD3 165 C2
Windermere Ave.
St Alb AL1 .................... 128 B1
Windermere Cl.
Chor WD3 .................... 164 D4
Windermere Cl.
Heml H HP3 ................. 125 C2
Windermere Cres.
Luton LU3 ....................... 44 F5
Windermere Jun Mix
Inf Sch. St Alb .............. 128 B1
Windhill. Bis St CM23 ........ 76 E7
Windhill Old Rd.
Bis St CM23 .................. 76 E7
Windhill. Wel G C AL7 ...... 111 A7
Winding Hill. Muc H SG10 .. 75 A4
Winding Shot.
Heml H HP1 .................. 124 A4
Winding Shott. Bram SG14 91 C4
Windmill Ave. St Alb AL4 . 128 C7
Windmill Cl. Bark SG8 ........ 17 C5
Windmill Cl. Pit LU7 .......... 80 F5
Windmill Cl. Wa Aby EN9 . 163 E5
Windmill Dr. Cro Gr WD3 165 F3
Windmill Field.
Ware SG12 .................. 114 D8
Windmill Fields.
Harl CM17 .................... 118 F4
Windmill Hill. Bun SG9 ....... 40 F6
Windmill Hill. Chipf WD4 . 151 F7
Windmill Hill. Hit SG4 ........ 34 F7
Windmill La. Bus WD2 ...... 168 E1
Windmill La. Ches EN8 ..... 148 E1
Windmill La. Edg EN5 ....... 170 F3
Windmill Rd. Bre Gr SG4 ... 47 D2
Windmill Rd. Heml H HP2 124 F2
Windmill Rd. Luton LU1 ..... 63 F6
Windmill Rd. Mark AL3 ...... 84 B6
Windmill St. Bus WD2 ...... 168 E1
Windmill Way. Muc H SG10 74 E1
Windmill Way. Tri HP23 ..... 99 F4
Windmills. Dan En SG12 .... 71 E8
Windmore Ave. Pot B EN6 158 C8
Windridge Cl. St Alb AL3 .. 127 A1
Winds End Cl. Heml H HP2 125 A5
Windsor Cl. Bor WD6 ....... 170 A8
Windsor Cl. Bov HP3 ....... 137 A3
Windsor Cl. Ches EN7 ...... 148 A1
Windsor Cl. Heml H HP3 .. 124 E2
Windsor Cl. Norwd HA6 .. 175 A1
Windsor Cl. Stev SG2 ......... 69 B7
Windsor Cl. Welw AL6 ....... 89 B3
Windsor Ct. Kin L WD4 .... 139 B2
Windsor Ct. St Alb AL1 .... 128 A2
Windsor Gdns. Bis St CM23 76 C7
Windsor Rd. Barn EN5 ..... 171 E3
Windsor Rd. Enf EN3 ....... 162 D3
Windsor Rd. Har HA3 ...... 176 D2
Windsor Rd. Royst SG8 ........ 7 F6
Windsor Rd. Watf WD2 .... 154 C1
Windsor Rd. Welw AL6 ...... 89 B3
Windsor St. Luton LU1 ....... 63 D6
Windsor Way. Ric WD3 .... 165 A1
Windsor Wlk. Luton LU1 .... 63 D6
Windsor Wood.
Wa Aby EN9 ................. 163 E6
Windward Cl. Enf EN3 ...... 162 D4
Windy Rise. Dan En SG12 .. 71 F7
Winford Dr. Hod EN10 ..... 134 F1
Wingate Gdns. Welw AL6 .. 89 B5
Wingate Rd. Luton LU4 ...... 44 F2
Wingate Way. St Alb AL1 . 128 A2
Wingrave C of E Combd
Sch. Wing ...................... 60 A3
Wingrave Rd. Tri HP23 .... 100 B6
Wingrave Rd. Wils HP23 ... 79 D1
Winifred House (Conv Hospl
for Children). Edg ........ 170 F3
Winifred Rd. Heml H HP3 138 D7
Winkfield Cl. Dun LU4 ....... 44 B1
Winnington Rd. Enf EN3 ... 162 C2
Winsdon Rd. Luton LU1 ..... 63 D6
Winslow Cl. Luton LU3 ....... 45 C4
Winslow Rd. Wing HP22 .... 60 B3
Winston Cl. Har HA3 ....... 176 F4
Winston Cl. Hit SG5 .......... 34 D7
Winston Ct. Har HA3 ....... 176 B3
Winston Gdns. Berk HP4 . 121 F4
Winston Way. Pot B EN6 . 159 A6
Winstre Rd. Bor WD6 ...... 170 A8
Winters La. Walk SG2 ........ 38 C1
Winterscroft Rd.
Hod EN11 ..................... 134 F7
Winton App. Cro Gr WD3 . 166 C4
Winton Cl. Letw SG6 .......... 23 D8
Winton Cl. Luton LU2 ....... 45 D6
Winton Cres. Cro Gr WD3 166 B4
Winton Dr. Ches EN8 ....... 148 E2
Winton Dr. Cro Gr WD3 ... 166 C4
Winton Rd. Ware SG12 ...... 93 F1
Wisden Rd. Stev SG1 ......... 36 F1
Wiseman Cl. Luton LU2 ...... 45 E7
Wisemans Gdns.
Saw CM21 ...................... 97 C1
Wistlea Cres. Coln H AL4 . 129 B1
Wistow Rd. Luton LU3 ....... 45 A6
Witchford. Wel G C AL7 ... 111 D6
Withy Cl. Luton LU4 ........... 44 B4
Withy Pl. Chis AL2 ............ 141 C3
Witney Cl. Pnr HA5 ......... 175 F4
Witsend. Bric SG13 ......... 113 E1
Witter Ave. Ick SG5 ........... 21 E4
Wiveton Cl. Luton LU2 ....... 45 D7
Woburn Ave. Bis St CM23 .. 76 C7
Woburn Cl. Bus WD2 ....... 168 C3
Woburn Cl. Stev SG2 ......... 69 C7
Woburn Ct. Luton LU4 ....... 44 D5
Wodecroft Rd. Luton LU3 ... 45 B6
Wodson Park Sports & L Ctr.
Ware ............................ 93 D4
Wolfsburg Ct. Luton LU4 .... 44 C5
Wolsey Ave. Gofs O EN7 .. 147 F2
Wolsey House. Kin L WD4 139 A2
Wolsey Mansions.
Mo Pk HA6 ................... 174 C7
Wolsey Rd. Heml H HP2 .. 124 D2
Wolsey Rd. Mo Pk HA6 .... 174 D7
Wolston Cl. Luton LU1 ....... 63 C7
Wolves Mere. Welw SG3 .... 69 A2
Wolvescroft. Welw SG3 ..... 69 A2
Wood Cl. Hat AL10 ........... 130 B5
Wood Comm. Hat AL10 .... 130 B8
Wood Cres. Heml H HP3 .. 124 E1
Wood Dr. Stev SG2 ............ 51 B2
Wood End. Chis AL2 ......... 141 C3
Wood End Cl. Heml H HP2 125 C4
Wood End Hill. Harp AL5 .... 85 D4
Wood End Inf Sch. Harp .... 85 D3
Wood End Jun Mix Sch.
Harp ............................... 85 D3
Wood End La. Fla AL3 ...... 104 E8
Wood End Rd. Harp AL5 .... 85 D3
Wood Farm Rd.
Heml H HP2 ................. 124 E2
Wood Green Cl. Luton LU2 46 B5
Wood Green Rd. Luton LU2 46 C5
Wood Green Way.
Ches EN8 ..................... 162 E8
Wood La. Heml H HP2 ..... 124 D2
Wood La. Mee SG9 ........... 30 A6
Wood Lane End.
Heml H HP2 ................. 125 B4
Wood St. Barn EN5 .......... 171 D5
Wood St. Luton LU1 ........... 63 F6
Wood Vale. Hat AL10 ....... 130 B5
Wood View. Cuf EN6 ........ 146 E4
Wood View. Heml H HP1 . 124 B5
Woodacre Dr. Welw AL6 .... 90 A8
Woodbine Gr. Enf EN2 ..... 161 D1
Woodbridge Cl. Luton LU4 . 44 E4
Woodbrook Gdns.
Wa Aby EN9 ................. 163 E6
Woodbury Hill. Luton LU2 .. 45 E2
Woodcock Hill. Ric WD3 .. 173 E4
Woodcock Hill. Sand AL4 . 108 E1
Woodcock Rd. Luton LU1 ... 63 A7
Woodcock Rd. Stev SG2 ..... 51 D2
Woodcote Cl. Ches EN8 ... 148 C1
Woodcote House. Hit SG4 . 34 F7 1
Woodcroft Ave.
Sta Ab SG12 ................. 115 E4
Woodcroft. Hit SG5 ........... 34 E6
Woodfall Ave. Barn EN5 .. 171 F4
Woodfield Ave.
Mo Pk HA6 ................... 174 E6
Woodfield Cl. Sta M CM24 . 59 E6
Woodfield Dr. Heml H HP3 125 D1
Woodfield Gdns.
Heml H HP3 ................. 125 D1
Woodfield La. Hat AL9 ..... 145 E8
Woodfield Rd. Radl WD7 . 156 A3
Woodfield Rd. Stev SG1 ..... 36 C1
Woodfield Rd.
Wel G C AL7 ................. 110 F6
Woodfield Rise. Bus WD2 168 D2
Woodfield Sch. Heml H .... 125 C1
Woodfield Terr.
Sta M CM24 .................. 59 E6
Woodfield Way.
St Alb AL4 .................... 128 C6
Woodfields. Sta M CM24 ... 59 E6
Woodfields. Watf WD1 .... 167 C5
Woodford Cres. Pnr HA5 . 175 B1
Woodford Rd. Watf WD1 . 167 C7
Woodforde Cl. Ashw SG7 .... 4 E4
Woodgate Cres.
Norwd HA6 .................. 175 A4
Woodgate. Watf WD2 ...... 154 B6
Woodgrange Ct.
Hod EN11 ..................... 135 A5
Woodhall Ave. Pnr HA5 ... 175 E2
Woodhall Cl. Hert SG14 .. 113 C8
Woodhall Ct. Wel G C AL7 110 E5
Woodhall Dr. Pnr HA5 ..... 175 E2
Woodhall Gate. Pnr HA5 .. 175 D2
Woodhall Gr. Bis St CM23 . 76 D6
Woodhall Jun Mix & Inf
Schs. Sth Ox ................ 175 E6
Woodhall La. Heml H HP2 124 E4
Woodhall La. Shen WD7 .. 156 F4
Woodhall La. Sth Ox WD1 175 E6
Woodhall La. Wel G C AL7 110 E4
Woodham Way.
Gt Am SG12 ................. 115 C4
Woodhouse Eaves.
Mo Pk HA6 ................... 175 A5
Woodhurst Ave.
Watf WD2 .................... 154 D4
Woodhurst. Letw SG6 ........ 22 F8
Woodland Ave.
Heml H HP1 ................. 124 B2
Woodland Ave. Luton LU3 .. 45 B2
Woodland Cl. Heml H HP1 124 B2
Woodland Cl. Tri HP23 ...... 99 F2
Woodland Dr. St Alb AL4 . 128 C4
Woodland Dr. Watf WD1 . 166 F8
Woodland La. Chor WD3 . 164 D6
Woodland Mount.
Hert SG13 .................... 113 F6
Woodland Pl. Heml H HP1 124 B2
Woodland Rd.
Hert H SG13 ................. 114 C3
Woodland Rd.
Map Cr WD3 ................ 172 D5
Woodland Rise.
Wel G C AL8 ................. 110 C8
Woodland Rise. Whip LU6 . 82 B7
Woodland Way. Bal SG7 .... 23 F6
Woodland Way.
Gofs O EN7 .................. 147 B3
Woodland Way. Stev SG2 .. 51 A1
Woodland Way. Welw AL6 90 A7
Woodlands Ave. Berk HP4 122 D3
Woodlands. Bis St CM23 .... 77 C8
Woodlands. Bro Pk AL9 ... 145 B4
Woodlands. Chis AL2 ....... 141 C4
Woodlands Cl. Bor WD6 .. 170 B5
Woodlands Cl. Hod EN11 . 135 A5
Woodlands Dr. Abb L WD4 139 C3
Woodlands Dr. Har HA7 .. 176 F4
Woodlands Dr. Hod EN11 135 A4
Woodlands. Harp AL5 ........ 85 E3
Woodlands Meade.
Wes SG4 ........................ 37 B8
Woodlands. Radl WD7 ..... 156 A5
Woodlands Rd.
Abb L WD4 .................. 139 A4
Woodlands Rd. Enf EN2 ... 161 D1
Woodlands Rd. Hert SG13 113 F6
Woodlands Rd. Thun SG12 93 D6
Woodlands Rd. Watf WD2 167 E4
Woodlands. Royst SG8 ........ 7 E6
Woodlands Sch. Bor ........ 170 A8
Woodlea. Chis AL2 ........... 141 A6
Woodlea Gr. Norwd HA6 . 174 C4
Woodley Rd. Ware SG12 ... 93 F2
Woodleys. Harl CM20 ..... 118 A1
Woodman Rd.
Heml H HP3 ................. 124 E1 2
Woodmere Ave. Bus WD2 154 E1
Woodmere. Luton LU3 ....... 31 A1
Woodmill Mews.
Hod EN11 ..................... 135 B8
Woodpecker Cl. Bus WD2 168 C1
Woodpecker Cl. Har HA3 . 176 F2
Woodpecker Cl. Hat AL10 129 F2
Woodridge Way.
Norwd HA6 .................. 174 E4
Woodridings Ave. Pnr HA5 175 F2
Woodridings Cl. Pnr HA5 . 175 F3
Woods Ave. Hat AL10 ...... 130 B4
Woods Pl. Tri HP22 .......... 100 A3
Woods The. Radl WD7 ..... 156 B5
Woods The. Sth Ox HA6 ... 175 A5
Woodshots Meadow.
Watf WD1 .................... 166 D4
Woodside. Bis St CM23 ..... 77 D8
Woodside. Bor WD6 ........ 169 F5
Woodside. Ches EN7 ....... 162 A8
Woodside Farm & Wild
Fowl Park. Mark ............ 84 A8
Woodside. Hert SG13 ... 114 C2
Woodside House.
Wel G C AL8 ................. 110 C7
Woodside Ind Pk. Letw ...... 23 B7
Woodside Jun Mix Inf Sch.
Gofs O .......................... 147 B2
Woodside La. Hat AL9 ..... 131 A1
Woodside Pl. Hat AL9 ...... 131 B2
Woodside Rd. Abb L WD5 154 B8
Woodside Rd. Bri Wd AL2 140 F2
Woodside Rd. Cad LU1 ...... 63 B3
Woodside Rd. Welw AL6 ... 89 F3
Woodside. Watf WD2 ...... 154 A3
Woodstock Cl.
Hert H SG13 ................. 114 B4
Woodstock Rd. Bus WD2 . 168 F2
Woodstock Rd. Hod EN10 134 E4
Woodstock Rd N.
St Alb AL1 .................... 128 B4
Woodstock Rd S.
St Alb AL1 .................... 128 B3
Woodstock. Welw SG3 ...... 68 F3
Woodville Court Mews.
Watf WD1 .................... 167 A7
Woodville Ct. Watf WD1 .. 167 A7
Woodville Pl. Hert SG14 .. 113 B8
Woodward Gdns. Har HA7 176 F3
Woodwaye. Watf WD1 .... 167 C2
Woodwicks. Map Cr WD3 172 D5
Woolenwick Prim Schs.
Stev ................................ 50 B6
Woolgrove Ct. Hit SG4 ....... 22 B1
Woolgrove Rd. Hit SG4 ...... 22 B1
Woolgrove Sch. Letw ......... 23 D5
Woollam Cres. St Alb AL3 127 C7
Woollams. Red AL3 .......... 106 A4
Woollard St. Wa Aby EN9 163 C5
Woolmans Cl. Hod EN10 .. 134 F1
Woolmer Cl. Bor WD6 ..... 157 A1
Woolmer Dr. Heml H HP2 125 C3
Woolmer Green C of E Sch.
Welw ............................. 69 A1
Woolmers La.
Hertng SG14 ................ 112 B2
Woolners Way. Stev SG1 ... 50 C6
Woolsgrove Ct. Royst SG8 ... 7 E5
Woolston Ave. Letw SG6 ... 23 A4
Wootton Cl. Luton LU3 ....... 45 B7
Wootton Dr. Heml H HP2 . 124 F8
Worboys Ct. Gu M SG8 ........ 1 F5
Worcester Rd. Hat AL10 .. 129 F6
Worcesters Ave. Enf EN1 162 A1
Worcesters Prim Sch. Enf 161 F1
Wordsworth Cl. Royst SG8 .. 2 D1
Wordsworth Rd. Dun LU4 .. 44 A2
Wordsworth Rd. Harp AL5 . 86 A3
Works Rd. Letw SG6 .......... 23 C7
Worley Rd. St Alb AL3 ...... 127 D4
Wormley Lodge Cl.
Hod EN10 ..................... 148 F8
Wormley Prim Sch. Hod ... 148 E8
Worsted La. Gt Ho SG9 ...... 41 E7
Wortham Rd. Royst SG8 ...... 7 E4
Wortham Way. Stev SG2 ... 51 B3
Wraglins The. Bis St CM23 77 B5
Wratten Cl. Hit SG5 ........... 34 E6
Wratten Rd E. Hit SG5 ....... 34 E6
Wratten Rd W. Hit SG5 ...... 34 E6
Wrayfields. Stot SG5 ......... 12 B8
Wren Cl. Kim SG4 .............. 66 B1
Wren Cl. Luton LU2 ............ 46 C6
Wren Cl. Stev SG2 ............. 51 B6
Wren Cres. Bus WD2 ....... 168 C1
Wren Wood. Wel G C AL7 111 B7
Wrenbrook Rd.
Bis St CM23 .................. 76 F6
Wrensfield. Heml H HP1 .. 124 B3
Wrestlers Cl. Hat AL10 .... 130 C7
Wrexham Terr. Royst SG8 ... 7 D7
Wright Cl. Whea AL4 ....... 108 E7
Wright's Bldgs. Watf WD1 167 B7
Wrights Green La.
L Hal CM22 .................... 98 D7
Wrights Meadow.
Walk SG2 ....................... 52 B8
Wrights Orch. Ast SG2 ....... 51 E2
Wrotham Park. Pot B ....... 158 E3
Wrotham Rd. Barn EN5 ... 171 E7
Wroxham Ave.
Heml H HP3 ................. 124 D1
Wroxham Gdns.
Cre H EN2 .................... 161 B4
Wroxham Gdns.
Pot B EN6 .................... 158 D8
Wroxham Jun Mix Inf Sch.
Pot B ........................... 158 D8
Wroxham Way. Harp AL5 ... 86 C3
Wulfrath Way. Ware SG12 93 C3
Wulwards Cl. Luton LU1 .... 63 B6
Wulwards Ct. Luton LU1 .... 63 B6
Wyatt Cl. Bus WD2 .......... 168 E2
Wyatt Cl. Ick SG5 .............. 21 D4
Wyatt's Cl. Chor WD3 ...... 165 A6
Wyatt's Rd. Chor WD3 ..... 165 A6
Wyburn Ave. Barn EN5 .... 171 F6
Wych Elm. Harl CM20 ...... 117 C1
Wych Elm La. Welw AL6 .... 68 F2
Wych Elms. Chis AL2 ....... 141 B3
Wychdell. Stev SG2 ........... 69 C8
Wychford Dr. Saw CM21 ... 97 C1
Wychwood Ave. Luton LU2 45 E3

Wychwood Way.
　Norwd HA6 .................. 174 F3
Wycklond Cl. Stot SG5 ....... 11 E6
Wycliffe Cl. Luton LU3 ........ 45 C6
Wycliffe Ct. Abb L WD5 .... 153 E7
Wycombe Way. Luton LU3 . 45 C8
Wycombe Way.
　St Alb AL4 .................... 128 B6
Wyddial Gn. Wel G C AL7 . 111 B6
Wyddial Rd. Bun SG9 ........ 40 E8
Wyedale. Lon C AL2 ........ 142 F4
Wykeham Rise.
　Barn N20 ...................... 171 E1
Wyken Cl. Luton LU3 .......... 45 A7
Wyldwood Cl. Harl CM17 . 118 C6
Wyllyotts Cl. Pot B EN6 .... 158 F7

Wyllyotts Pl. Pot B EN6 .... 158 F7
Wylo Dr. Edge EN5 ............ 171 A3
Wymondley Cl. Hit SG4 ...... 35 A7
Wymondley Jun Mix Inf
　Sch. L Wym ..................... 35 E4
Wymondley Rd. Hit SG4 ..... 35 B6
Wymondley Rd. Letw SG4 .. 23 A1
Wynchgate. Har HA3 ....... 176 E3
Wynchlands Cres.
　St Alb AL4 .................... 128 D3
Wynd Arcade The.
　Letw SG6 ......................... 22 F6
Wyndham Rd. Dun LU4 ...... 44 C2
Wyndhams End.
　Wel G C AL7 .................. 110 F2
Wynlie Gdns. Pnr HA5 ..... 175 B1
Wynn Cl. Bal SG7 ............. 13 A1
Wyrley Dell. Letw SG6 ....... 23 A3
Wyton. Wel G C AL7 ........ 111 D6

Wyvern Cl. Luton LU4 ........ 44 E3

Yardley Ave. Pit LU7 .......... 80 D4
Yardley Ct. Harp AL5 ........ 86 B1　7
Yardley. Letw SG6 ............. 23 C4
Yarmouth Rd. Stev SG1 ...... 50 A7
Yarmouth Rd. Watf WD2 . 154 C1
Yately Cl. Luton LU2 .......... 45 D7
Yeatman House.
　Watf WD2 .................... 154 B3
Yeats Cl. Royst SG8 ............. 2 D1
Yeomanry Dr. Bal SG7 ....... 13 A1
Yeomans Ave. Harp AL5 .... 85 D3
Yeomans Cl. Bis St CM23 ... 76 D6
Yeomans Dr. Ast SG2 ........ 51 E8
Yeomans Ride.
　Heml H HP2 ................. 105 A1
Yeovil Rd. Luton LU2 ......... 46 B2
Yew Cl. Ham St EN7 ........ 147 E4

Yew Gr. Wel G C AL7 ....... 111 C5
Yew Tree Cl. Bot HP5 ........ 136 A1
Yew Tree Cl. Pit LU7 .......... 80 E5
Yew Tree Ct. Bov HP3 ...... 137 B3
Yew Tree Ct.
　Heml H HP1 ................. 124 A1
Yew Tree Pl. Bis St CM23 .. 76 F8
Yew Wlk. Hod EN11 ......... 135 A5
Yewlands. Hod EN11 ........ 135 A5
Yewlands. Saw CM21 ........ 97 F1
Yews Ave. Enf EN1 ........... 162 B3
Yewtree End. Chis AL2 ..... 141 B4
York Cl. Kin L WD4 .......... 139 A2
York Cres. Bor WD6 ......... 170 D7
York House. St Alb AL3 .... 127 C2
York Mead Jun Mix Inf
　Sch. Cro Gr .................. 166 A4
York Rd. Ches EN8 ........... 162 E6
York Rd. Hit SG5 ............... 34 E8

York Rd. Norwd HA6 ....... 175 A1
York Rd. St Alb AL1 .......... 127 F4
York Rd. Stev SG1 ............. 36 F1
York Rd. Watf WD1 ......... 167 C4
York St. Luton LU2 ............ 63 F8
York Terr. Enf EN2 ........... 161 C1
York Way. Heml H HP2 .... 124 E2
York Way. Royst SG8 .......... 7 B8
York Way. Watf WD2 ...... 154 E3
York Way. Wel G C AL6 ..... 89 C3
Yorke Rd. Cro Gr WD3 .... 166 A3
Youngfield Rd.
　Heml H HP1 ................. 123 F4
Youngs Rise. Wel G C AL8 110 C6
Youngsbury La.
　Thun SG12 ..................... 93 E8
Yule Cl. Bri Wd AL2 ........ 140 F1

Zambesi Rd. Bis St CM23 ... 77 A5